D0364398

PAID
22 NOV 2010

WITHDRAWN
FROM STOCK

30109 0 17011746

Ordnance Survey

STREET ATLAS Surrey

Contents

III Key to map symbols

IV-V Key to map pages

VI-VII Route planning

VIII Administrative and post code boundaries

1 Street maps

219 Extra-large-scale maps of town centres

- 219 Dorking
- 219 Epsom
- 220 Guildford
- 220 Kingston upon Thames
- 221 Leatherhead
- 221 Woking

222 Index of hospitals, industrial estates, railway stations, schools, shopping centres, street names and universities

PHILIP'S

First colour edition published 1996
Second colour edition published 2000 by

Ordnance Survey®	and	George Philip Ltd, a division of
Romsey Road		Octopus Publishing Group Ltd
Maybush		2-4 Heron Quays
Southampton		London
SO16 4GU		E14 4JP

ISBN 0-540-07794-1 (hardback)
ISBN 0-540-07795-X (spiral)

To the best of the Publishers' knowledge, the information in this atlas was correct at the time of going to press. No responsibility can be accepted for any errors or their consequences.

The representation in this atlas of a road, track or path is no evidence of the existence of a right of way.

The mapping between pages 1 and 221 (inclusive) in this atlas is derived from Ordnance Survey® OSCAR® and Land-Line® data and Landranger® mapping.

Ordnance Survey, OSCAR, Land-line and Landranger are registered trade marks of Ordnance Survey, the national mapping agency of Great Britain.

Printed and bound in Spain by Cayfosa

Digital Data

The exceptionally high-quality mapping found in this book is available as digital data in TIFF format, which is easily convertible to other bit-mapped (raster) image formats. The data can be provided as pages or, in some regions, as larger extracts of up to 200 sq km. The larger extracts can also be supplied on paper.

The index is also available in digital form as a standard database table. It contains all the details found in the printed index together with the National Grid reference for the map square in which each entry is named.

For further information and to discuss your requirements, please contact Philip's on 0171 531 8440 or george.philip@philips-maps.co.uk

Key to map symbols

22a	**Motorway** (with junction number)
	Primary route (dual carriageway and single)
	A road (dual carriageway and single)
	B road (dual carriageway and single)
	Minor road (dual carriageway and single)
	Other minor road (dual carriageway and single)
	Road under construction
	Pedestrianised area
DY7	**Postcode boundaries**
	County and Unitary Authority boundaries
	Railway
	Tramway, miniature railway
	Rural track, private road or narrow road in urban area
	Gate or obstruction to traffic (restrictions may not apply at all times or to all vehicles)
	Path, bridleway, byway open to all traffic, road used as a public path
	The representation in this atlas of a road, track or path is no evidence of the existence right of way
126 / 94	**Adjoining page indicators**
164	**The map area within the pink band is shown at a larger scale on the page indicated by the red block and arrow**

■ The dark grey border on the inside edge of some pages indicates that the mapping does not continue onto the adjacent page

■ The small numbers around the edges of the maps identify the 1 kilometre National Grid lines

Walsall	**Railway station**
	London Underground station
	Croydon Tramlink
	Private railway station
	Bus, coach station
	Ambulance station
	Coastguard station
	Fire station
	Police station
	Accident and Emergency entrance to hospital
H	**Hospital**
+	**Places of worship**
i	**Information Centre** (open all year)
P P&R	**Parking, Park and Ride**
PO	**Post Office**
Prim Sch	**Important buildings, schools, colleges, universities and hospitals**
River Medway	**Water name**
	Stream
	River or canal (minor and major)
	Water
	Tidal water
	Woods
	Houses
House	**Non-Roman antiquity**
VILLA	**Roman antiquity**

Acad	**Academy**	Ent	**Enterprise**	LC	**Level Crossing**	Obsy	**Observatory**	Sch	**School**
Crem	**Crematorium**	Ex H	**Exhibition Hall**	Liby	**Library**	Pal	**Royal Palace**	Sh Ctr	**Shopping Centre**
Cemy	**Cemetery**	Ind Est	**Industrial Estate**	Mkt	**Market**	PH	**Public House**	TH	**Town Hall/House**
C Ctr	**Civic Centre**	Inst	**Institute**	Meml	**Memorial**	Recn Gd	**Recreation Ground**	Trad Est	**Trading Estate**
CH	**Club House**	Ct	**Law Court**	Mon	**Monument**	Resr	**Reservoir**	Univ	**University**
Coll	**College**	L Ctr	**Leisure Centre**	Mus	**Museum**	Ret Pk	**Retail Park**	YH	**Youth Hostel**

The scale of the maps is 5.52 cm to 1 km ($3\frac{1}{2}$ inches to 1 mile)

0 — 1/4 — 1/2 — 3/4 — 1 mile
0 — 250 m — 500 m — 750 m — 1 kilometre

The scale of the maps on pages numbered in red is 11.04 cm to 1 km (7 inches to 1 mile)

0 — 220 yards — 440 yards — 660 yards — 1/2 mile
0 — 125 m — 250 m — 375 m — 1/2 kilometre

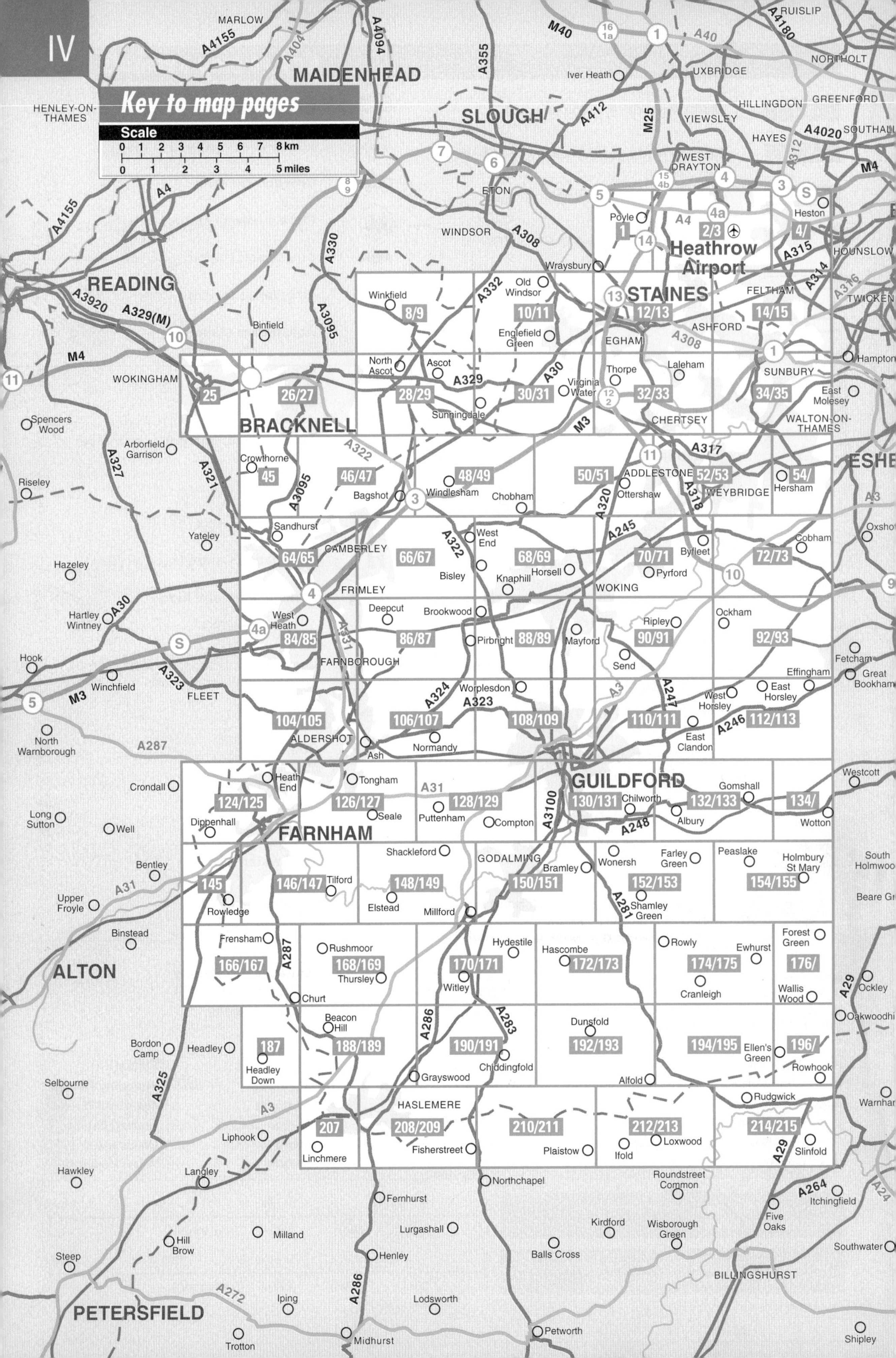

IV
Key to map pages
Scale
0 1 2 3 4 5 6 7 8 km
0 1 2 3 4 5 miles
MARLOW
A4155
A404
A4094
MAIDENHEAD
A355
M40
RUISLIP
A4180
A40
NORTHOLT
Iver Heath
UXBRIDGE
HILLINGDON
GREENFORD
HENLEY-ON-THAMES
SLOUGH
A412
M25
YIEWSLEY
HAYES
A4020
SOUTHALL
A312
WEST DRAYTON
M4
ETON
Poyle
A4
Heston
WINDSOR
A308
Heathrow Airport
HOUNSLOW
A315
A314
A316
TWICKENHAM
A4155
A4
A330
READING
A3920
A329(M)
A3095
Binfield
Winkfield
Old Windsor
Wraysbury
STAINES
FELTHAM
ASHFORD
EGHAM
Englefield Green
A332
M4
WOKINGHAM
North Ascot
Ascot
A329
A30
Virginia Water
Thorpe
Laleham
SUNBURY
Hampton
East Molesey
WALTON-ON-THAMES
Spencers Wood
BRACKNELL
Sunningdale
M3
CHERTSEY
Arborfield Garrison
A327
A321
Crowthorne
A322
A317
ADDLESTONE
WEYBRIDGE
Hersham
ESHER
Riseley
A3095
Bagshot
Windlesham
Chobham
Ottershaw
A320
A318
A3
Yateley
Sandhurst
CAMBERLEY
West End
A245
Byfleet
Cobham
Oxshott
Hazeley
Bisley
Knaphill
Horsell
Pyrford
WOKING
FRIMLEY
Hartley Wintney
A30
West Heath
Deepcut
Brookwood
Ripley
Ockham
A331
Pirbright
Mayford
Send
Fetcham
Great Bookham
Hook
FARNBOROUGH
Effingham
East Horsley
West Horsley
A247
A323
Winchfield
FLEET
Worplesdon
A324
A323
A3
M3
North Warnborough
A287
ALDERSHOT
Ash
Normandy
East Clandon
A246
Heath End
Tongham
Crondall
A31
GUILDFORD
Gomshall
Westcott
Dippenhall
Seale
Puttenham
Compton
A3100
Chilworth
Albury
Wotton
A248
Long Sutton
Well
FARNHAM
Bentley
Shackleford
GODALMING
Bramley
Wonersh
Farley Green
Peaslake
Holmbury St Mary
South Holmwood
A31
Upper Froyle
Rowledge
Tilford
Elstead
Millford
Shamley Green
A281
Beare Green
Binstead
Frensham
A287
Rushmoor
Thursley
Hydestile
Hascombe
Rowly
Ewhurst
Forest Green
ALTON
Witley
Cranleigh
Wallis Wood
A29
Ockley
Churt
A286
A283
Oakwoodhill
Bordon Camp
Headley
Headley Down
Beacon Hill
Dunsfold
Ellen's Green
Rowhook
Chiddingfold
Selbourne
A325
Grayswood
Alfold
A3
Rudgwick
Warnham
HASLEMERE
Liphook
Linchmere
Fisherstreet
Plaistow
Ifold
Loxwood
Slinfold
A29
Hawkley
Langley
Northchapel
Roundstreet Common
A264
Itchingfield
A24
Fernhurst
Five Oaks
Hill Brow
Milland
Lurgashall
Kirdford
Wisborough Green
Steep
Henley
Balls Cross
Southwater
BILLINGSHURST
A272
A286
PETERSFIELD
Iping
Lodsworth
Trotton
Midhurst
Petworth
Shipley
1
2/3
4/
8/9
10/11
12/13
14/15
25
26/27
28/29
30/31
32/33
34/35
45
46/47
48/49
50/51
52/53
54/
64/65
66/67
68/69
70/71
72/73
84/85
86/87
88/89
90/91
92/93
104/105
106/107
108/109
110/111
112/113
124/125
126/127
128/129
130/131
132/133
134/
145
146/147
148/149
150/151
152/153
154/155
166/167
168/169
170/171
172/173
174/175
176/
187
188/189
190/191
192/193
194/195
196/
207
208/209
210/211
212/213
214/215

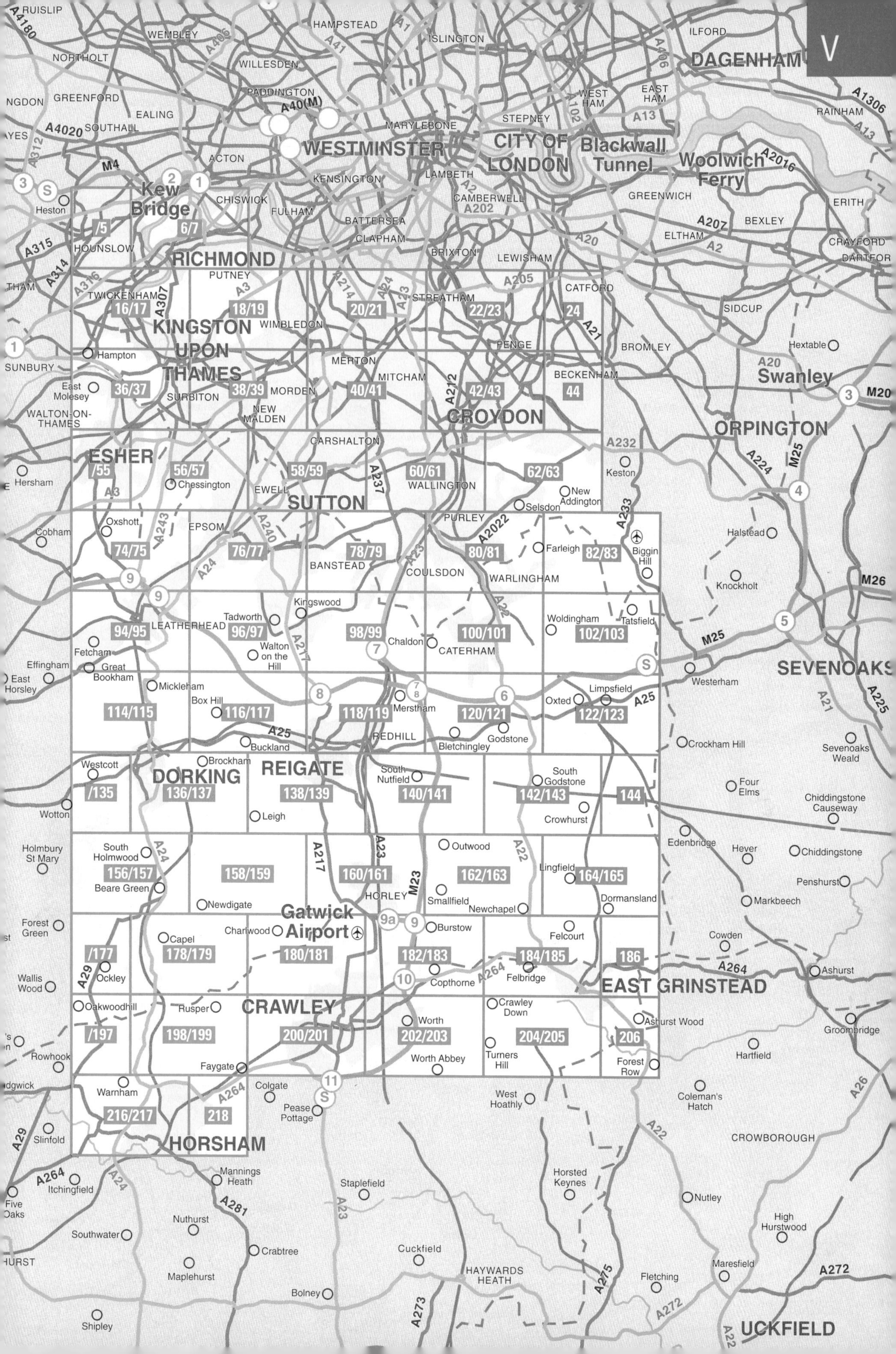
RUISLIP
A4180
WEMBLEY
HAMPSTEAD
A1
ISLINGTON
ILFORD
A406
DAGENHAM
NORTHOLT
A41
WILLESDEN
A406
NGDON
GREENFORD
PADDINGTON
WEST HAM
EAST HAM
A1306
RAINHAM
EALING
A40(M)
A102
A13
A4020
SOUTHALL
MARYLEBONE
STEPNEY
A13
YES
A312
WESTMINSTER
CITY OF LONDON
Blackwall Tunnel
Woolwich Ferry
A2016
M4
ACTON
3
S
2
1
Kew Bridge
KENSINGTON
LAMBETH
A2
Heston
CHISWICK
CAMBERWELL
GREENWICH
ERITH
FULHAM
A202
/5
6/7
BATTERSEA
A207
BEXLEY
A315
ELTHAM
HOUNSLOW
CLAPHAM
A20
A2
CRAYFORD
DARTFORD
RICHMOND
BRIXTON
LEWISHAM
A314
THAM
PUTNEY
A316
A3
A214
A24
A23
A205
CATFORD
TWICKENHAM
A307
STREATHAM
16/17
18/19
20/21
22/23
24
SIDCUP
KINGSTON UPON THAMES
WIMBLEDON
A21
1
PENGE
BROMLEY
Hextable
Hampton
MERTON
SUNBURY
A20
Swanley
MITCHAM
BECKENHAM
A212
East Molesey
36/37
38/39
MORDEN
40/41
42/43
44
3
M20
SURBITON
NEW MALDEN
WALTON-ON-THAMES
CROYDON
ORPINGTON
CARSHALTON
A232
M25
A224
ESHER
/55
56/57
58/59
60/61
62/63
Keston
A237
Hersham
Chessington
WALLINGTON
New Addington
A3
EWELL
SUTTON
Selsdon
4
A233
Oxshott
PURLEY
A243
EPSOM
A240
A2022
Halstead
Cobham
Biggin Hill
74/75
76/77
78/79
A23
80/81
Farleigh
82/83
A24
BANSTEAD
COULSDON
9
WARLINGHAM
Knockholt
M26
9
Kingswood
A22
LEATHERHEAD
Tadworth
Woldingham
Tatsfield
94/95
96/97
98/99
100/101
102/103
5
7
Chaldon
CATERHAM
A217
M25
Fetcham
Walton on the Hill
Effingham
Great Bookham
S
East Horsley
Westerham
SEVENOAKS
Mickleham
8
7 8
6
Limpsfield
Box Hill
Merstham
Oxted
A25
A21
A225
114/115
116/117
118/119
120/121
122/123
A25
REDHILL
Godstone
Sevenoaks Weald
Buckland
Bletchingley
Crockham Hill
Westcott
Brockham
REIGATE
South Nutfield
South Godstone
DORKING
Four Elms
/135
136/137
138/139
140/141
142/143
144
Chiddingstone Causeway
Wotton
Leigh
Crowhurst
Edenbridge
Holmbury St Mary
South Holmwood
A24
A217
A23
Outwood
A22
Hever
Chiddingstone
156/157
158/159
160/161
162/163
Lingfield
164/165
M23
Penshurst
Beare Green
HORLEY
Smallfield
Markbeech
Newdigate
Newchapel
Dormansland
Forest Green
Gatwick Airport
9a
9
Burstow
Charlwood
Capel
Felcourt
Cowden
/177
178/179
180/181
182/183
184/185
186
A264
A29
Ockley
10
Copthorne
A264
Felbridge
EAST GRINSTEAD
Ashurst
Wallis Wood
Oakwoodhill
Rusper
CRAWLEY
Crawley Down
Worth
Ashurst Wood
Groombridge
/197
198/199
200/201
202/203
204/205
206
Rowhook
Turners Hill
Hartfield
Faygate
Worth Abbey
Forest Row
dgwick
11
Warnham
Colgate
A264
S
West Hoathly
Coleman's Hatch
A26
Pease Pottage
216/217
218
A22
A29
Slinfold
HORSHAM
CROWBOROUGH
Mannings Heath
A264
Itchingfield
A24
Staplefield
Horsted Keynes
Nutley
Five Oaks
A281
A23
Nuthurst
High Hurstwood
Southwater
HURST
Crabtree
Cuckfield
Maresfield
A272
Maplehurst
HAYWARDS HEATH
A275
Fletching
Bolney
A273
A272
Shipley
A22
UCKFIELD

Route planning
Scale
0 1 2 3 4 5 6 7 8 km
0 1 2 3 4 5 miles
MARLOW
Medmenham
Cookham Dean
Cookham
Burnham Beeches
Hedsor
Fulmer
Denham
Ickenham
NORTHOLT
Aston
Remenham Hill
Hurley
Cookham Rise
Farnham Common
Stoke Poges
Iver Heath
UXBRIDGE
HILLINGDON
GREENFORD
Taplow
Burnham
Farnham Royal
Iver
Cowley
YIEWSLEY
Yeading
HAYES
SOUTHALL
Bray
SLOUGH
WEST DRAYTON
Norwood Green
Dorney
Upton
Langley
Sipson
Cranford
Heston
Boveney
ETON
Colnbrook
Longford
Holyport
Fifield
Oakley Green
WINDSOR
Datchet
Poyle
London Heathrow Airport
Hatton
HOUNSLOW
ISLEWORTH
Paley Street
Horton
Wraysbury
Stanwell
East Bedfont
Hawthorn Hill
Old Windsor
Windsor Forest
GREAT PARK
Hythe End
STAINES
FELTHAM
TWICKENHAM
Twyford
Sonning
Caversham
Shiplake
Ruscombe
Hare Hatch
Waltham St Lawrence
White Waltham
Sheriock Row
Whistley Green
Woodley
Hurst
Winkfield
Warfield
Cranbourne
Winkfield Row
Woodside
Englefield Green
EGHAM
ASHFORD
Hanworth
Binfield
Newell Green
North Ascot
SUNBURY
Winnersh
Sindlesham
BRACKNELL
Ascot
Sunningdale
Virginia Water
Thorpe
Laleham
Littleton
Hampton
Bushy Park
East Molesey
Thames Ditton
Arborfield
Easthampstead
Sunninghill
Lyne
Shepperton
WALTON-ON-THAMES
Shinfield
Arborfield Cross
Barkham
WOKINGHAM
CHERTSEY
Spencers Wood
Farley Hill
Arborfield Garrison
Caesar's Camp
Windlesham
Common
ADDLESTONE
WEYBRIDGE
ESHER
Swallowfield
Wick Hill
Surrey Hill
Bagshot
Ottershaw
Hersham
Finchampstead
Crowthorne
Burrowhill
Esher Common
Riseley
Eversley
CAMBERLEY
Royal Military Academy
Lightwater
Chobham
Woodham
Whiteley Village
Bramshill Plantn
Yateley
Sandhurst
Bagshot Heath
West End
Byfleet
Cobham
Oxshott
Bramshill
Eversley Cross
Frogmore
Blackwater
Donkey Town
Horsell
Pyrford
Stoke D'Abernon
Hazeley
Bisley
Chobham Ridges
Wisley
Hartfordbridge
Hawley
Fox Lane
FRIMLEY
Knaphill
WOKING
Hartley Wintney
Minley Manor
West Heath
Deepcut
Brookwood
West Green
Phoenix Green
Cove
Mytchett
Pirbright
Mayford
Ripley
Ockham
Effingham Junc
Send
Fetcham
Winchfield
FLEET
FARNBOROUGH
Henley Park
West Horsley
East Horsley
Great Bookham
Dogmersfield
Church Crookham
Worplesdon
Pitch Place
North Warnborough
Crookham Village
Fairlands
Wood Street
Stoughton
Burpham
West Clandon
Effingham
Odiham
ALDERSHOT
Normandy
East Clandon
Westhumble
Long Valley
Heath End
Ash
Flexford
Onslow Village
GUILDFORD
DORKING
Mill Lane
Ewshot
Crondall
Hale
Tongham
Hog's Back
Gomshall
Westcott
Long Sutton
FARNHAM
Puttenham
Shalford
Albury
Shere
Abinger Hammer
Wotton
South Warnborough
Well
Dippenhall
Runfold
Seale
Compton
Chilworth
Sutton Abinger
Blackheath
Farncombe
Wonersh
Bramley
Farley Green
Peaslake
Abinger Common
Holmbury St Mary
South Holmwood
Bentley
Shackleford
Peper Harow
Shamley Green
Hurt Wood
Coldharbour
Lower Froyle
Waverley Abbey
Leith Hill
Upper Froyle
Rowledge
Tilford
Elstead
GODALMING
Thorncombe Street
Millbridge
Bucks Horn Oak
Milford
Busbridge
Blacknest
Spreakley
Wheelerstreet
Rowly
Forest Green
Jayes Park
Frensham
Rushmoor
Thursley
Hydestile
Ewhurst
Ockley
Binsted
Wheatley
Witley
Hascombe
Cranleigh
Walliswood
ALTON
Wyck
Kingsley
East Worldham
Churt
Brook
Hambledon
Oakwoodhill
Sleaford
Bowlhead Green
Loxhill
West Worldham
Lindford
Gibbet Hill
Hawton
Upper Farringdon
Bordon Camp
Headley
Hindhead
Chiddingfold
Dunsfold
Ellen's Green
Oakhanger
Whitehill
Standford
Grayshott
Grayswood
Selborne
Rudgwick
Rowhook
Blackmoor
BORDON
Shottermill
HASLEMERE
Alfold
Tisman's Common
Warnham
Bramshott
Bucks Green
Longmoor Camp
Liphook
Camelsdale
Ifold
Slinfold
Broadbridge Heath
Empshott
Greatham
Linchmere
Kingsley Green
Fisherstreet
Plaistow
Loxwood
LOW WEALD
Hawkley
Liss Forest
Langley
Roundstreet Common
Itchingfield
Northchapel
Fernhurst
Five Oaks
Barns Green
Christ's Hospital
Liss
East Liss
Rake
Milland
Lurgashall
Kirdford
Newpound Common
Southwater
Steep
Sheet
Hill Brow
Henley
Lickfold
Balls Cross
Wisborough Green
BILLINGSHURST
Brooks Green
Stroud
Rogate
Coneyhurst
Chithurst
Iping
Woolbeding
Easebourne
Lodsworth
Coolham
Shipley
PETERSFIELD
Trotton
Stedham
Midhurst
Upperton
Petworth House
Petworth
North Heath
Gay Street
Nursted
East
Nyewood
West
Tillington
Selham
Byworth
Broomer's Corner

LONDON
HAMPSTEAD
STOKE NEWINGTON
HACKNEY
ILFORD
WEMBLEY
CAMDEN TOWN
ISLINGTON
BARKING
DAGENHAM
NORTHOLT
WILLESDEN
Harlesden
FINSBURY
BETHNAL GREEN
Forest Gate
STRATFORD
EAST HAM
Hornchurch
GREENFORD
PADDINGTON
MARYLEBONE
SHOREDITCH
BOW
WEST HAM
Beckton
Creekmouth
RAINHAM
EALING
Holborn
CITY OF LONDON
STEPNEY
London (City Airport)
SOUTHALL
ACTON
Hyde Park
POPLAR
Blackwall Tunnel
Woolwich Ferry
WOOLWICH
Thamesmead
Wennington
Norwood Green
HAMMERSMITH
BRENTFORD
WESTMINSTER
KENSINGTON
CHELSEA
LAMBETH
BERMONDSEY
Isle of Dogs
Belvedere
Kew Bridge
CHISWICK
FULHAM
Charlton
Plumstead
ERITH
Heston
BARNES
BATTERSEA
CAMBERWELL
DEPTFORD
Blackheath
GREENWICH
Kidbrooke
Welling
Slade Green
Kew
HOUNSLOW
Mortlake
CLAPHAM
Hatton
ISLEWORTH
RICHMOND
PUTNEY
BRIXTON
LEWISHAM
Hither Green
ELTHAM
Bexleyheath
CRAYFORD
BEXLEY
DARTFORD
FELTHAM
TWICKENHAM
Richmond Park
Roehampton
Wimbledon Park
WANDSWORTH
Upper Tooting
STREATHAM
Dulwich
Sydenham
CATFORD
New Eltham
SIDCUP
Coldblow
North Cray
Wilmington
Hanworth
TEDDINGTON
WIMBLEDON
West Norwood
Crystal Palace
Mottingham
Grove Park
Foots Cray
Hawley
KINGSTON UPON THAMES
Bushy Park
Hampton
MERTON
PENGE
CHISLEHURST
Hextable
East Molesey
Hampton Court
SURBITON
MORDEN
MITCHAM
BECKENHAM
Eden Park
BROMLEY
St Paul's Cray
Swanley
WALTON-ON-THAMES
Thames Ditton
NEW MALDEN
South Norwood
Bickley
Petts Wood
St Mary Cray
Crockenhill
Farningham
Long Ditton
Tolworth
Worcester Park
CARSHALTON
Beddington
West Wickham
Hayes
Bromley Common
ORPINGTON
ESHER
Hook
Chessington
WALLINGTON
CROYDON
Keston
Farnborough
Chelsfield
Lullingstone Castle
Eynsford
Hersham
Cheam
Green Street Green
Esher Common
Claygate
EWELL
SUTTON
New Addington
Well Hill
Whiteley Village
PURLEY
Leaves Green
Pratt's Bottom
Badgers Mount
Cobham
Oxshott
EPSOM
Selsdon
Downe
Halstead
Shoreham
Woodmansterne
Sanderstead
Farleigh
Biggin Hill Airport
Stoke D'Abernon
Epsom Downs Station
BANSTEAD
Kenley
COULSDON
WARLINGHAM
Biggin Hill
Cudham
Knockholt
Knockholt Pound
Otford
Kemsing
Tattenham Corner
Ashtead
Burgh Heath
Whyteleafe
Tatsfield
Chevening
Dunton Green
Seal
LEATHERHEAD
Tadworth
Kingswood
Chipstead
Woldingham
Fetcham
Chaldon
Riverhead
Headley
Walton on the Hill
CATERHAM
Brasted
Sundridge
SEVENOAKS
Great Bookham
Westerham
Mickleham
Merstham
Godstone
Brasted Chart
Effingham
The Hermitage
Limpsfield
Whitley Row
Westhumble
Buckland
REDHILL
Oxted
Hurst Green
Crockham Hill
Ide Hill
Sevenoaks Weald
Nutfield
Bletchingley
Tandridge
Toy's Hill
DORKING
Brockham
Betchworth
REIGATE
South Nutfield
Godstone Sta
South Godstone
Marlpit Hill
Four Elms
Bough Beech Resr
Westcott
Crowhurst
Chiddingstone Causeway
Leigh
Wotton
North Holmwood
Salfords
Blindley Heath
Edenbridge
Bough Beech
Penshurst Sta
Sutton Abinger
Abinger Common
Holmbury St Mary
South Holmwood
Anstiebury
Norwood Hill
Outwood
Horne
Lingfield
Marsh Green
Hever
Chiddingstone
Penshurst Place
Penshurst
Coldharbour
Leith Hill
Holmwood Sta
Beare Green
Parkgate
HORLEY
Smallfield
Newchapel
Dormansland
Markbeech
Newdigate
Hookwood
Burstow
Felcourt
Cowden Sta
Forest Green
Jayes Park
Charlwood
London (Gatwick) Airport
Cowden
Fordcombe
Capel
Copthorne
Ockley
Felbridge
Blackham
Ashurst
Walliswood
EAST GRINSTEAD
Langton Green
Oakwoodhill
Crawley Down
Pound Hill
Three Bridges
Sunnyside
Ashurst Wood
Ifield
Rusper
Kingsfold
Lambs Green
Worth
Turners Hill
Saint Hill
Forest Row
Hartfield
Withyham
CRAWLEY
Faygate
Rowhook
Broadfield
Selsfield Common
Weir Wood Resr
Upper Hartfield
Coleman's Hatch
Worth Abbey
West Hoathly
Sharpthorne
Friar's Gate
Warnham
Roffey
Colgate
Pease Pottage
Slinfold
Broadbridge Heath
HORSHAM
ST LEONARD'S FOREST
Wych Cross
Highbrook
CROWBOROUGH
ASHDOWN FOREST
Itchingfield
Handcross
Balcombe
Ardingly
Horsted Keynes
Chelwood Gate
Mannings Heath
Staplefield
Ardingly Resr
Five Oaks
Barns Green
Christ's Hospital
Slaugham
Danehill
Nutley
Southwater
Lower Beeding
Nuthurst
Whitemans Green
Fairwarp
High Hurstwood
Warninglid
Copsale
Brooks Green
Crabtree
Cuckfield
Lindfield
HAYWARDS HEATH
Coneyhurst
Maplehurst
Fletching
Maresfield
Hadlow Down
Bolney
Ansty
Scayne's Hill
Sheffield Park Sta
Buxted
Shipley
Cowfold
Newick
UCKFIELD
Littleworth
Wivelsfield
Blackboys
Possingworth
M25
M23
M26
M20
M4
A40(M)
A23
A22
A24
A25
A21
A20
A2
A3
A264
A272
A217
A13
A205
A232

Major administrative and Postcode boundaries

- County and unitary authority boundaries
- District boundaries
- Postcode boundaries
- Area covered by this atlas

1 Hammersmith and Fulham
2 Royal Borough of Kensington and Chelsea
3 City of Westminster
4 County of the City of London
5 Wandsworth
6 Kingston upon Thames

Scale: 0 – 5 – 10 – 15 km; 0 – 5 – 10 miles

2
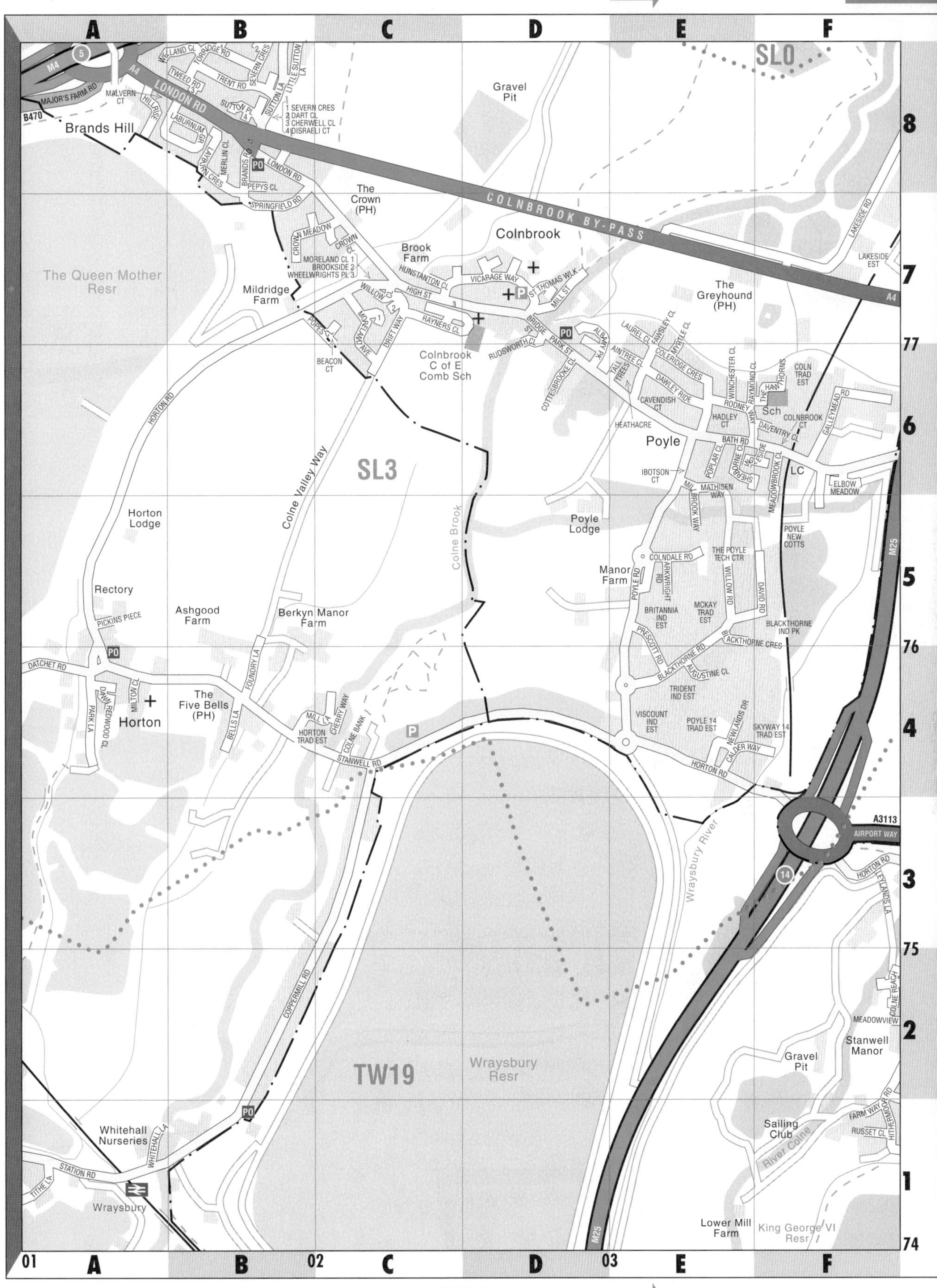
A
B
C
D
E
F
8
7
77
6
5
76
4
3
75
2
1
74
01
02
03
SL0
M4
5
B470
MAJOR'S FARM RD
MALVERN CT
Brands Hill
HILLRISE
WELLAND CL
TORRIDGE RD
TWEED RD
TRENT RD
SEVERN CRES
LITTLE SUTTON LA
SUTTON PL
SUTTON LA
A4
LONDON RD
1 SEVERN CRES
2 DART CL
3 CHERWELL CL
4 DISRAELI CT
LABURNUM GR
MERLIN CL
LAYBURN CRES
BRANDS RD
PO
LONDON RD
PEPYS CL
SPRINGFIELD RD
Gravel Pit
The Crown (PH)
COLNBROOK BY-PASS
Colnbrook
CROWN MEADOW
CROWN CL
MORELAND CL 1
BROOKSIDE 2
WHEELWRIGHTS PL 3
Brook Farm
HUNSTANTON CL
HIGH ST
VICARAGE WAY
ST THOMAS WLK
MILL ST
The Queen Mother Resr
Mildridge Farm
WILLOW CL
POPES CL
MORLAND AVE
DRIFT WAY
RAYNERS CL
BEACON CT
Colnbrook C of E Comb Sch
BRIDGE ST
PARK ST
RUDSWORTH CL
ALBANY PK
TALL TREES
AINTREE CL
COTTESBROOKE CL
LAUREL CL
FAWSLEY CL
MYRTLE CL
COLERIDGE CRES
DAWLEY RIDE
CAVENDISH CT
HEATHACRE
The Greyhound (PH)
LAKESIDE RD
LAKESIDE EST
WINCHESTER CL
RAYMOND CL
THE HAWTHORNS
COLN TRAD EST
Sch
RODNEY WAY
HADLEY CT
DAVENTRY CL
COLNBROOK CT
GALLEYMEAD RD
BATH RD
Poyle
POPLAR CL
SHERBORNE CL
HOLLY SIDE
MEADOWBROOK CL
LC
ELBOW MEADOW
IBOTSON CT
MATHISEN WAY
MILLBROOK WAY
HORTON RD
SL3
Colne Valley Way
Colne Brook
Poyle Lodge
POYLE NEW COTTS
M25
Horton Lodge
COLNDALE RD
THE POYLE TECH CTR
ARKWRIGHT RD
WILLOW RD
DAVID RD
Manor Farm
POYLE RD
Rectory
Ashgood Farm
Berkyn Manor Farm
BRITANNIA IND EST
MCKAY TRAD EST
BLACKTHORNE IND PK
PICKINS PIECE
BLACKTHORNE CRES
PRESCOTT RD
BLACKTHORNE RD
AUGUSTINE CL
DATCHET RD
FOUNDRY LA
MILTON CL
DAWN REDWOOD CL
PARK LA
Horton
The Five Bells (PH)
BELLS LA
MILL LA
CHERRY WAY
HORTON TRAD EST
COLNE BANK
P
TRIDENT IND EST
VISCOUNT IND EST
POYLE 14 TRAD EST
NEWLANDS DR
SKYWAY 14 TRAD EST
CALDER WAY
STANWELL RD
HORTON RD
A3113
AIRPORT WAY
Wraysbury River
14
HORTON RD
LEYLANDS LA
COPPERMILL RD
COLNE REACH
MEADOWVIEW
Stanwell Manor
Gravel Pit
TW19
Wraysbury Resr
Sailing Club
FARM WAY
HITHERMOOR RD
RUSSET CL
River Colne
Whitehall Nurseries
WHITEHALL LA
STATION RD
TITHE LA
Wraysbury
Lower Mill Farm
King George VI Resr
12
2

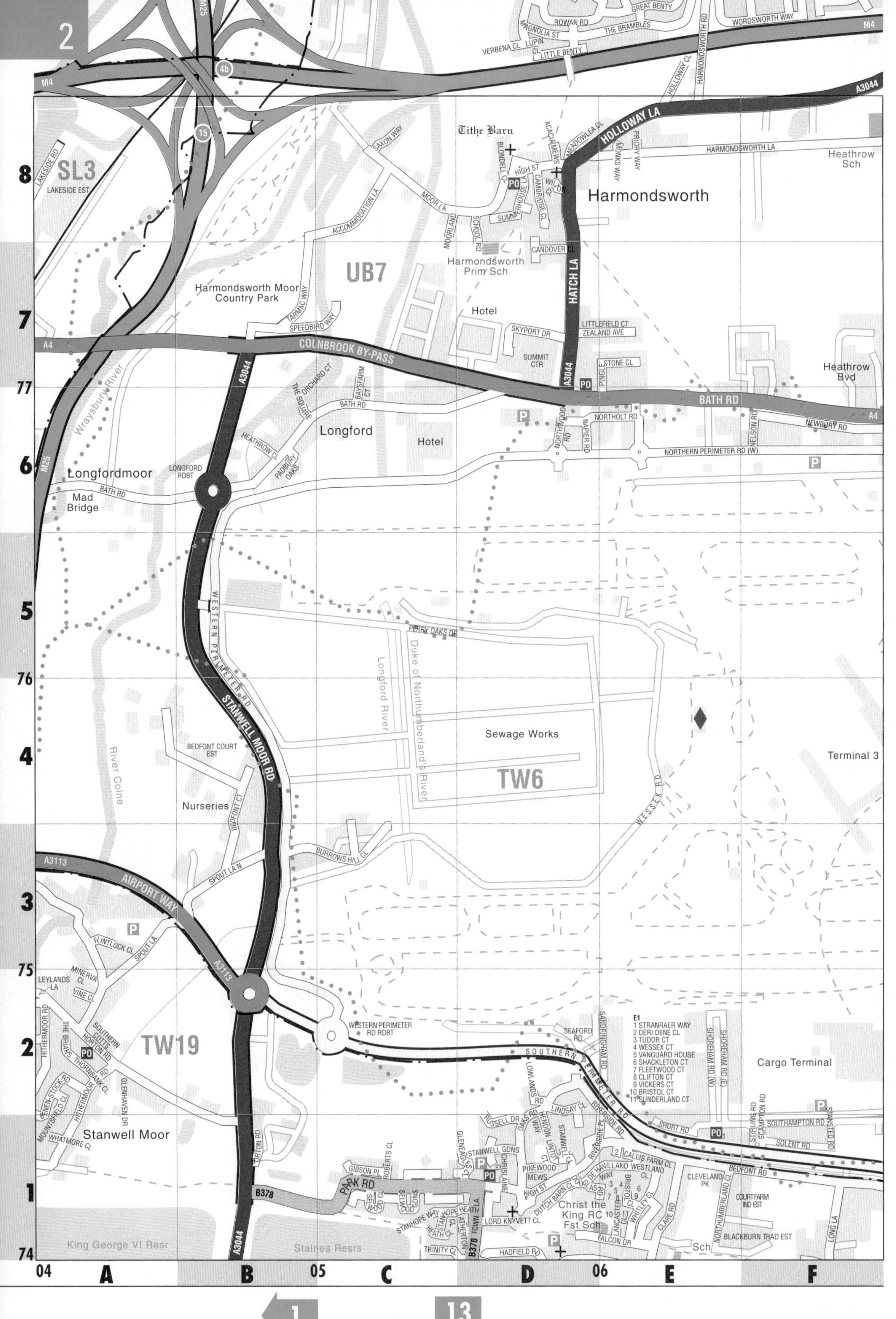

M25
M4
A3044
A4
A3113
B378
SL3
UB7
TW6
TW19
Harmondsworth
Harmondsworth Moor Country Park
Harmondsworth Prim Sch
Tithe Barn
Hotel
SUMMIT CTR
Heathrow Sch
Heathrow Bvd
Longford
Longfordmoor
Mad Bridge
LONGFORD RDBT
Wraysbury River
River Colne
Longford River
Duke of Northumberland's River
Sewage Works
Terminal 3
Cargo Terminal
Nurseries
BEDFONT COURT EST
Stanwell Moor
Christ the King RC Fst Sch
Sch
King George VI Resr
Staines Resrs
CLEVELAND PK
COURTFARM IND EST
BLACKBURN TRAD EST
LAKESIDE EST
LAKESIDE RD
HOLLOWAY LA
HATCH LA
HARMONDSWORTH LA
HARMONDSWORTH RD
HOLLOWAY CL
WORDSWORTH WAY
GREAT BENTY
ROWAN RD
THE BRAMBLES
MAGNOLIA ST
LUPIN CL
VERBENA CL
LITTLE BENTY
SAXON WAY
MOOR LA
BLONDELL CL
HIGH ST
SUMMERHOUSE LA
CAMBRIDGE CL
ACACIA MEWS
MEADOWLEA CL
MONKS WAY
PRIORY WAY
WILTON CL
MOORLAND
SCHOOL RD
CANDOVER CL
ACCOMMODATION LA
TARMAC WAY
SPEEDBIRD WAY
SKYPORT DR
LITTLEFIELD CT
ZEALAND AVE
STONE CL
PINGLE
COLNBROOK BY-PASS
BATH RD
NORTHOLT RD
NORTHWOOD RD
NAPIER RD
NELSON RD
NEWBURY RD
NORTHERN PERIMETER RD (W)
THE ORCHARD CT
THE SQUARE
BAYSFARM CT
HEATHROW CL
PADBURY OAKS
WESTERN PERIMETER RD
STANWELL MOOR RD
PERRY OAKS DR
WESSEX RD
BEDFONT CT
BURROWS HILL CL
SPOUT LA N
AIRPORT WAY
LINTLOCK CL
SPOUT LA
LEYLANDS LA
MINERVA CL
VINE CL
HITHERMOOR RD
THE BRIARS
SOUTHERN COTTS
HORTON RD
THORNBANK CL
GLENHAVEN DR
BENENSTOCK RD
MOUNTSFIELD CL
WHATMORE CL
WESTERN PERIMETER RD RDBT
SEAFORD RD
SANDRINGHAM RD
SOUTHERN PERIMETER RD
LOWLANDS RD
OAKS RD
HENDON WAY
LINTOTT CT
LINDSAY CL
STANWELL CL
RIVERSIDE PL
RIVERSIDE RD
RUSSELL DR
SHORT RD
SHOREHAM RD (W)
SHOREHAM RD (E)
STIRLING RD
SCAMPTON RD
SOUTHAMPTON RD
STANSTED RD
SOLENT RD
BEDFONT RD
CALLIS FARM CL
DE HAVILLAND WAY
WESTLAND CL
BRISTOL CL
WHITLEY CL
LANCASTER CL
CLARE RD
NORTHUMBERLAND CL
LONG LA
E1
1 STRANRAER WAY
2 DERI DENE CL
3 TUDOR CT
4 WESSEX CT
5 VANGUARD HOUSE
6 SHACKLETON CT
7 FLEETWOOD CT
8 CLIFTON CT
9 VICKERS CT
10 BRISTOL CT
11 SUNDERLAND CT
HORTON RD
GIBSON PL
ROBERTS CL
PARK RD
SELWOOD CL
SELWOOD GDNS
GLENEAGLES CL
STANWELL GDNS
CHRISLAINE CL
PINEWOOD MEWS
HIGH ST
DUTCH BARN CL
STANHOPE WAY
STANHOPE HEATH
HEATH CL
ATHERTON PL
TOWN LA
LORD KNYVETT CL
FALCON DR
HADFIELD RD
TRINITY CL
PO
P
4b
15
8
7
77
6
5
76
4
3
75
2
1
74
04
05
06
A
B
C
D
E
F

1
13

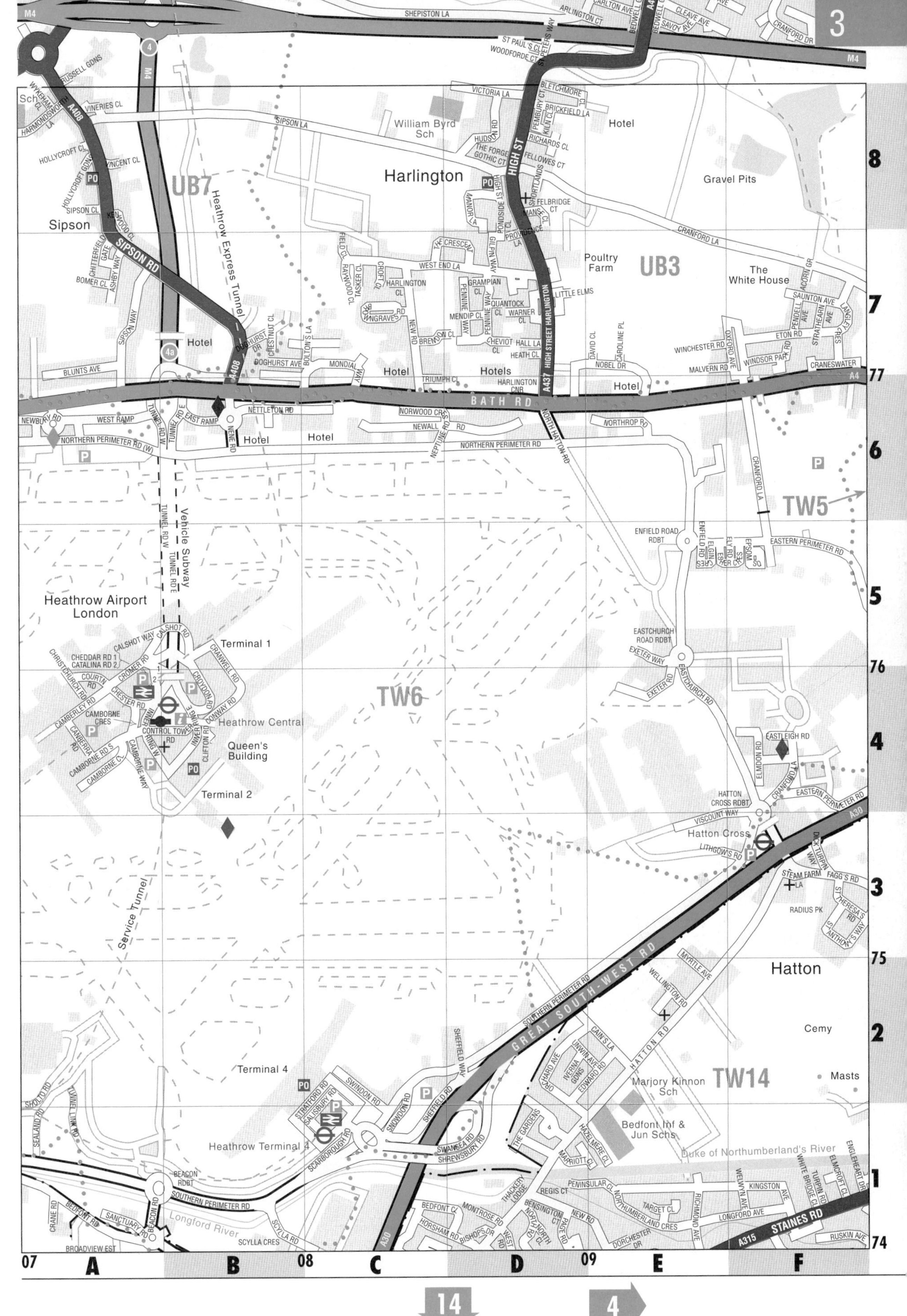

M4
SHEPISTON LA
ARLINGTON CT
CARLTON AVE
BEDWELL GDNS
A437
CROYDE AVE
CLEAVE AVE
SAVOY AVE
CRANFORD DR
ST PAUL'S CL
WOODFORDE CT
ST PETERS WAY
RUSSELL GDNS
WYKEHAM CL
HARMONDSWORTH LA
VINERIES CL
Sch
A408
HOLLYCROFT CL
HOLLYCROFT GDNS
VINCENT CL
PO
SIPSON CL
KENWOOD CL
Sipson
SIPSON RD
CHITTERFIELD GATE
ASHBY WAY
BOMER CL
SIPSON WAY
BLUNTS AVE
UB7
Heathrow Express Tunnel
Hotel
4a
4
VICTORIA LA
SIPSON LA
William Byrd Sch
Harlington
BLETCHMORE CL
BRICKFIELD LA
KILN CL
PEMBURY CT
HUDSON RD
RICHARDS CL
THE FORGE
GOTHIC CT
FELLOWES CT
HIGH ST
Hotel
Gravel Pits
MANOR LA
PONDSIDE CL
HIGH ST
SHORTLANDS
FELBRIDGE CT
MANSE CL
PROVIDENCE LA
CRANFORD LA
THE CRESCENT
GILPIN WAY
WEST END LA
FIELD CL
RAYWOOD CL
TASKER CL
CROFT CL
HARLINGTON CL
Poultry Farm
UB3
The White House
GRAMPIAN CL
PENNINE WAY
MENDIP CL
QUANTOCK CL
WARNER CL
LITTLE ELMS
HIGH STREET HARLINGTON
BROWNGRAVES RD
NEW RD
BRENDON CL
HEVIOT CL
HALL LA
HEATH CL
DOGHURST DR
CHESTNUT CL
DOGHURST AVE
BOLTON'S LA
MONDIAL WAY
DAVID CL
CAROLINE PL
NOBEL DR
WINCHESTER RD
OXFORD AVE
SAUNTON AVE
PENDELL AVE
STRATHEARN AVE
LANGLEY CRES
ACORN GR
ETON RD
WINDSOR PARK RD
MALVERN RD
CRANESWATER
Hotel
Hotels
TRIUMPH CL
HARLINGTON CNR
Hotel
A4
BATH RD
NETTLETON RD
NORWOOD CRES
NEWALL RD
NEPTUNE RD
NORTH HATTON RD
NORTHROP RD
NEWBURY RD
WEST RAMP
EAST RAMP
TUNNEL RD W
TUNNEL RD E
NENE RD
Hotel
Hotel
NORTHERN PERIMETER RD (W)
NORTHERN PERIMETER RD
P
CRANFORD LA
TW5
Vehicle Subway
ENFIELD ROAD RDBT
ENFIELD RD
ELGIN CRES
ESHER CRES
ELY RD
EPSOM SQ
EASTERN PERIMETER RD
Heathrow Airport London
EASTCHURCH ROAD RDBT
EXETER WAY
EXETER RD
EASTCHURCH RD
CALSHOT WAY
CALSHOT RD
Terminal 1
CHEDDAR RD
CATALINA RD
CHRISTCHURCH RD
CROMER RD
COURTNEY RD
CRANWELL RD
CROYDON RD
CHESTER RD
CONWAY RD
CAMBERLEY RD
CAMBORNE CRES
CANBERRA RD
CAMBORNE RD S
CAMBORNE CL
CAMBORNE WAY
CONTROL TOWER RD
INNER RING W
INNER RING E
CLIFTON RD
Heathrow Central
Queen's Building
TW6
Terminal 2
EASTLEIGH RD
ELMDON RD
CRANFORD LA
HATTON CROSS RDBT
EASTERN PERIMETER RD
VISCOUNT WAY
Hatton Cross
LITHGOW'S RD
A30
DICK TURPIN WAY
STEAM FARM LA
FAGG'S RD
ST THERESA'S RD
ST ANTHONY'S WAY
RADIUS PK
Service Tunnel
GREAT SOUTH-WEST RD
SOUTHERN PERIMETER RD
MYRTLE AVE
WELLINGTON RD
Hatton
Cemy
Masts
SHEFFIELD WAY
CAIN'S LA
UNWIN AVE
IVERNA GDNS
EDWARD RD
ORCHARD AVE
HATTON RD
Marjory Kinnon Sch
TW14
Terminal 4
PO
STRATFORD RD
SALISBURY RD
SWINDON RD
SNOWDON RD
SHEFFIELD RD
SCARBOROUGH RD
SWANSEA RD
SHREWSBURY RD
Heathrow Terminal 4
THE GARDENS
HAZELMERE CL
MARRIOTT CL
Bedfont Inf & Jun Schs
Duke of Northumberland's River
ENGLEHEART DR
ELMCROFT CL
TURPIN RD
WHITE BRIDGE CL
SHOLTO RD
SEALAND RD
TUNNEL LINK RD
BEACON RDBT
BEACON RD
SOUTHERN PERIMETER RD
CRANE RD
BEDFONT RD
SANCTUARY RD
BROADVIEW EST
Longford River
SCYLLA RD
SCYLLA CRES
BEDFONT CL
HORSHAM RD
MONTROSE RD
BISHOPS DR
WEST RD
THACKERY LODGE
BENSINGTON CT
NORTH CL
PAGE RD
NEW RD
REGIS CT
PENINSULAR CL
NORTHUMBERLAND CRES
TARGET CL
DORCHESTER DR
RICHMOND AVE
WELWYN AVE
KINGSTON AVE
LONGFORD AVE
A315
STAINES RD
RUSKIN AVE
8
7
77
6
5
76
4
3
75
2
1
74
07
A
B
08
C
D
09
E
F

14
4

3

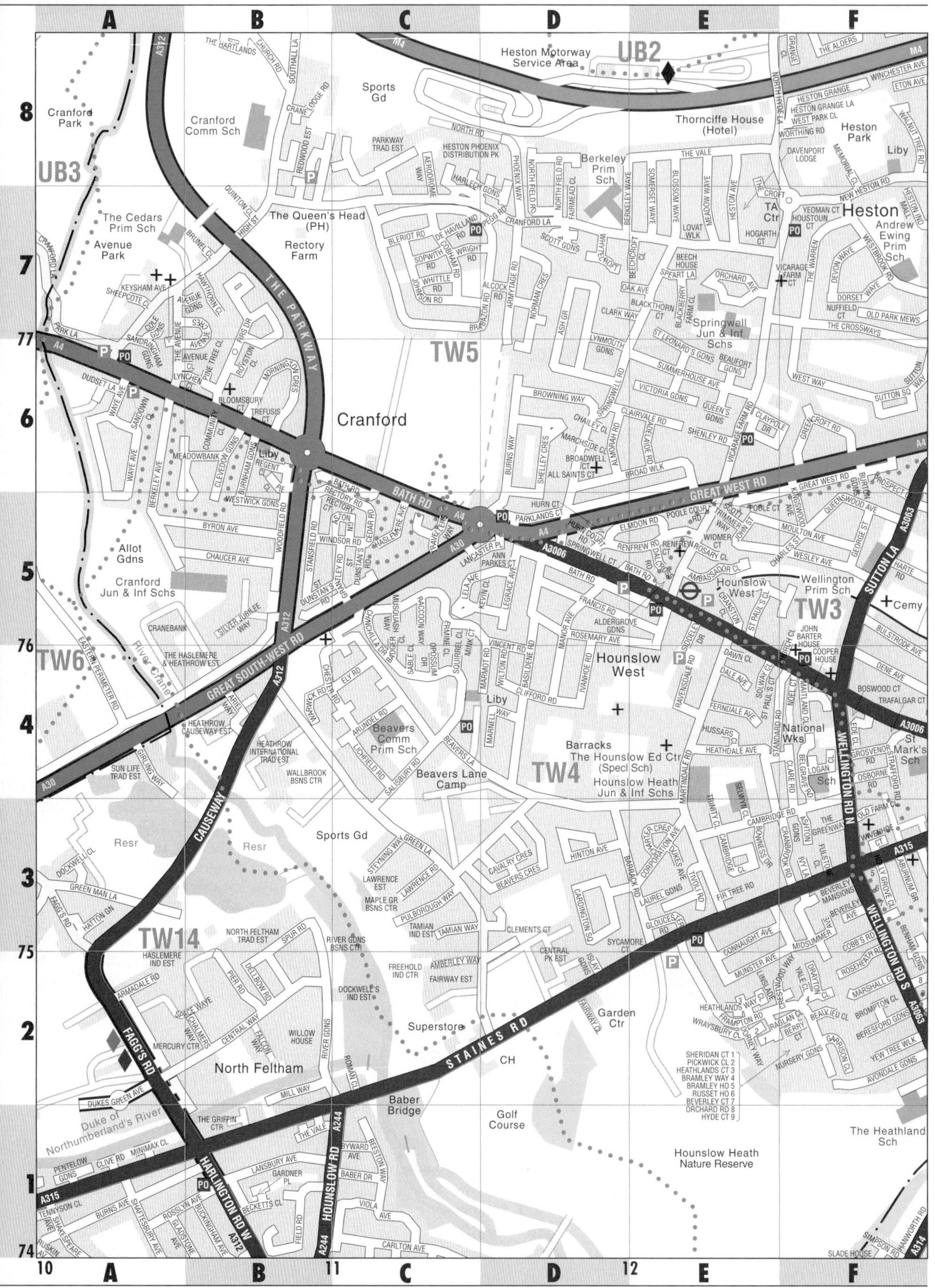

Heston Motorway Service Area
UB2
M4
Sports Gd
Cranford Park
Cranford Comm Sch
UB3
Thorncliffe House (Hotel)
Heston Park
Liby
Berkeley Prim Sch
The Queen's Head (PH)
Rectory Farm
The Cedars Prim Sch
Avenue Park
Heston
Andrew Ewing Prim Sch
TA Ctr
Springwell Jun & Inf Schs
TW5
Cranford
THE PARKWAY
BATH RD
GREAT WEST RD
A4
A30
A312
A3006
A3063
A315
A244
A314
Allot Gdns
Cranford Jun & Inf Schs
Hounslow West
Wellington Prim Sch
TW3
Cemy
TW6
GREAT SOUTH-WEST RD
River Crane
Hounslow West
Beavers Comm Prim Sch
Beavers Lane Camp
Barracks
The Hounslow Ed Ctr (Specl Sch)
Hounslow Heath Jun & Inf Schs
TW4
National Wks
St Mark's Sch
Sch
CAUSEWAY
Resr
Resr
Sports Gd
TW14
North Feltham
Superstore
STAINES RD
Garden Ctr
CH
Golf Course
Baber Bridge
Duke of Northumberland's River
HOUNSLOW RD
HARLINGTON RD W
FAGG'S RD
WELLINGTON RD N
WELLINGTON RD S
SUTTON LA
Hounslow Heath Nature Reserve
The Heathland Sch
SHERIDAN CT 1
PICKWICK CL 2
HEATHLANDS CT 3
BRAMLEY WAY 4
BRAMLEY HO 5
RUSSET HO 6
BEVERLEY CT 7
ORCHARD RD 8
HYDE CT 9

3

15

6

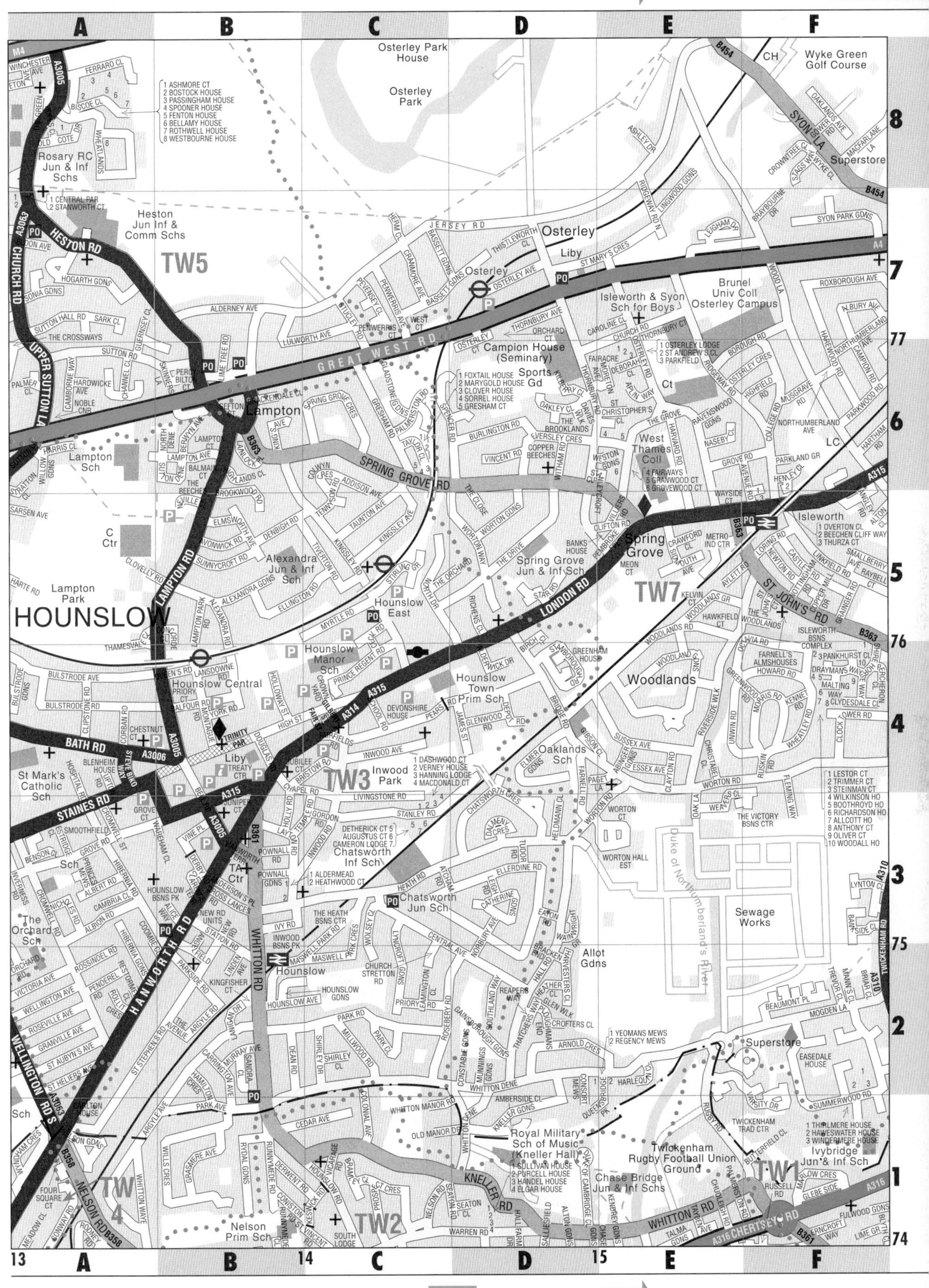
A
B
C
D
E
F
Osterley Park House
Osterley Park
Wyke Green Golf Course
Superstore
Rosary RC Jun & Inf Schs
Heston Jun Inf & Comm Schs
TW5
HESTON RD
CHURCH RD
UPPER SUTTON LA
JERSEY RD
Osterley
Liby
Brunel Univ Coll Osterley Campus
Isleworth & Syon Sch for Boys
GREAT WEST RD
Campion House (Seminary)
Sports Gd
Lampton
Lampton Sch
SPRING GROVE RD
West Thames Coll
Isleworth
Spring Grove
TW7
Spring Grove Jun & Inf Sch
Alexandra Jun & Inf Sch
Lampton Park
HOUNSLOW
LAMPTON RD
Hounslow East
LONDON RD
ST JOHN'S RD
Hounslow Manor Sch
Hounslow Central
Hounslow Town Prim Sch
Woodlands
BATH RD
STAINES RD
St Mark's Catholic Sch
TW3
Inwood Park
Oaklands Sch
Chatsworth Inf Sch
Chatsworth Jun Sch
Sewage Works
Duke of Northumberland's River
HANWORTH RD
WHITTON RD
Hounslow
Allot Gdns
The Orchard Sch
WELLINGTON RD S
Superstore
Royal Military Sch of Music (Kneller Hall)
Twickenham Rugby Football Union Ground
Chase Bridge Jun & Inf Schs
Ivybridge Jun & Inf Sch
TW1
TW2
TW4
Nelson Prim Sch
KNELLER RD
WHITTON RD
CHERTSEY RD
NELSON RD
8
7
6
5
4
3
2
1
77
76
75
74
13
14
15

16

6

5

D8
1 BROCKSHOT CL
2 WESTBURY PL
3 BROOK LA N
4 BROOK LA BNS CTR
5 BREAMAR CT
6 BROOK CT
7 CLIFDEN HOUSE
8 CEDAR CT
9 CRANBROOK CT
10 ALEXANDRA RD
11 BERKELEY HOUSE
12 WATERMANS CT

E8
1 FERRY SQ
2 WATERMANS CT
3 WILKES RD
4 ALBANY PAR
5 CHARLTON HOUSE
6 ALBANY HOUSE
7 ALMA HOUSE
8 GRIFFIN CT
9 CRESSAGE HOUSE
10 TUNSTALL WLK
11 TRIMMER WLK
12 RUNNING HORSE YD
13 MISSION SQ
14 DISTILLERY WLK
15 COATES WLK
16 PERRAN WLK

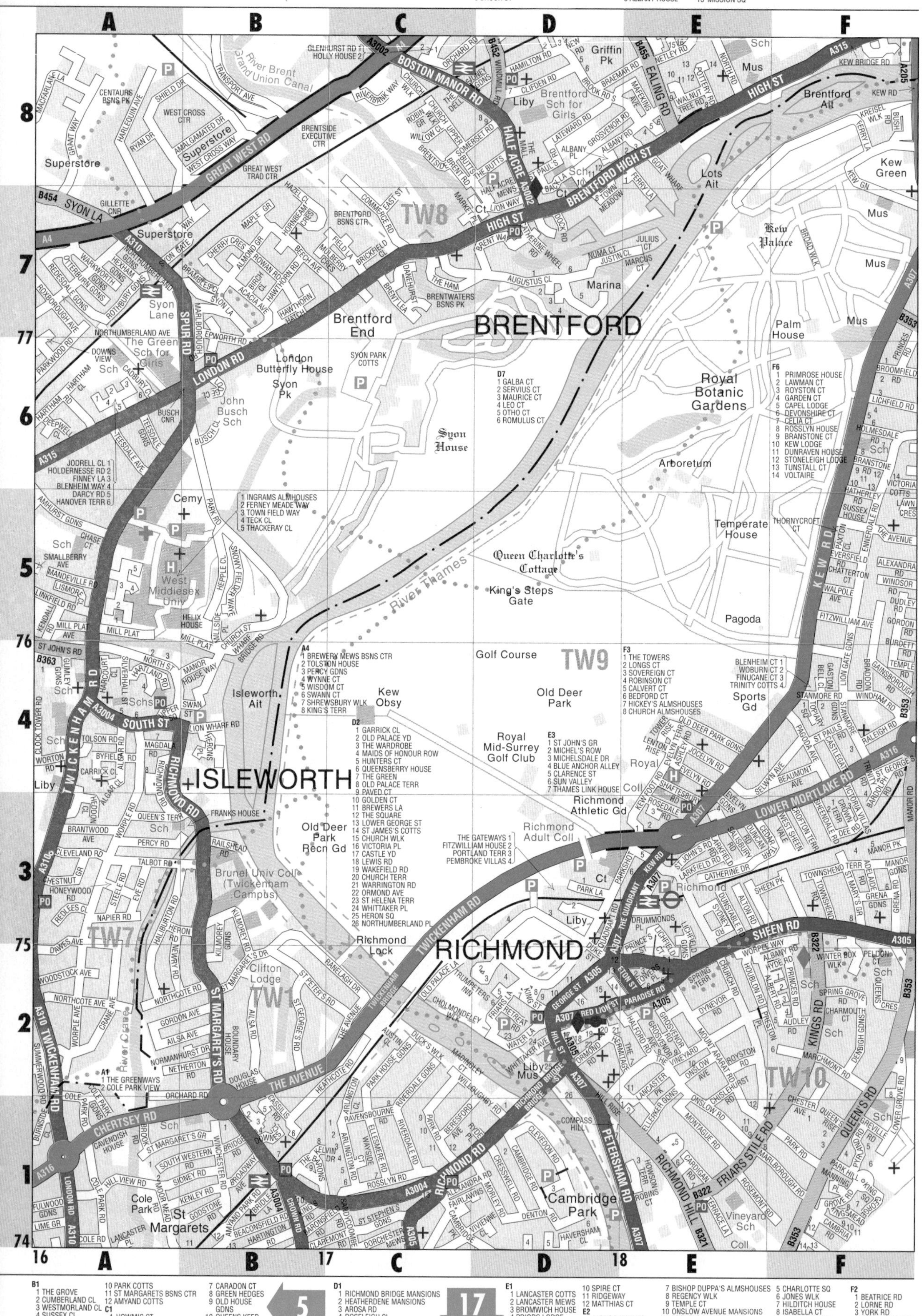

B1
1 THE GROVE
2 CUMBERLAND CL
3 WESTMORLAND CL
4 SUSSEX CL
5 NORFOLK CL
6 NICOL CL
7 OLD LODGE PL
8 KELVIN CT
9 ST MARGARET'S CT
10 PARK COTTS
11 ST MARGARETS BSNS CTR
12 AMYAND COTTS

C1
1 HOWMIC CT
2 SEFTON LODGE
3 RAVENSBOURNE
4 ARLINGTON CT
5 GEORGINA CT
6 TREVELYAN HOUSE
7 CARADON CT
8 GREEN HEDGES
9 OLD HOUSE GDNS
10 QUEENS KEEP
11 BERESFORD CT
12 LANGHAM CT
13 POPLAR CT

5

D1
1 RICHMOND BRIDGE MANSIONS
2 HEATHERDENE MANSIONS
3 AROSA RD
4 ROSELEIGH CL
5 BEAULIEU CL
6 RICHMOND MANSIONS
7 MALLARD CT

17

E1
1 LANCASTER COTTS
2 LANCASTER MEWS
3 BROMWICH HOUSE
4 PRIORS LODGE
5 RICHMOND HILL CT
6 GLENMORE HOUSE
7 HILLBROW
8 HEATHSHOT
9 FRIARS STILE PLACE
10 SPIRE CT
11 RIDGEWAY
12 MATTHIAS CT

E2
1 LICHFIELD TERR
2 UNION CT
3 CARRINGTON LODGE
4 WILTON CT
5 EGERTON CT
6 BEVERLEY LODGE
7 BISHOP DUPPA'S ALMSHOUSES
8 REGENCY WLK
9 TEMPLE CT
10 ONSLOW AVENUE MANSIONS
11 MICHELS ALMSHOUSES

F1
1 CHESTER CL
2 GROSVENOR CT
3 QUEEN'S CT
4 RUSSELL WLK
5 CHARLOTTE SQ
6 JONES WLK
7 HILDITCH HOUSE
8 ISABELLA CT
9 DAMER HOUSE
10 ELIOT HOUSE
11 FITZHERBERT HOUSE
12 REYNOLDS PL
13 CHISHOLM RD
14 HOBART PL

F2
1 BEATRICE RD
2 LORNE RD
3 YORK RD
4 CONNAUGHT RD
5 ALBANY TERR
6 KINGSWOOD CT
7 SELWYN CT
8 BROADHURST CL
9 GROVE RD

A6
1 CLARENDON CT
2 QUINTOCK HOUSE
3 BROOME CT
4 LONSDALE MEWS
5 ELIZABETH COTTS
6 SANDWAYS
7 VICTORIA COTTS
8 NORTH AVE
9 GROVEWOOD
10 HAMILTON HOUSE
11 MELVIN CT

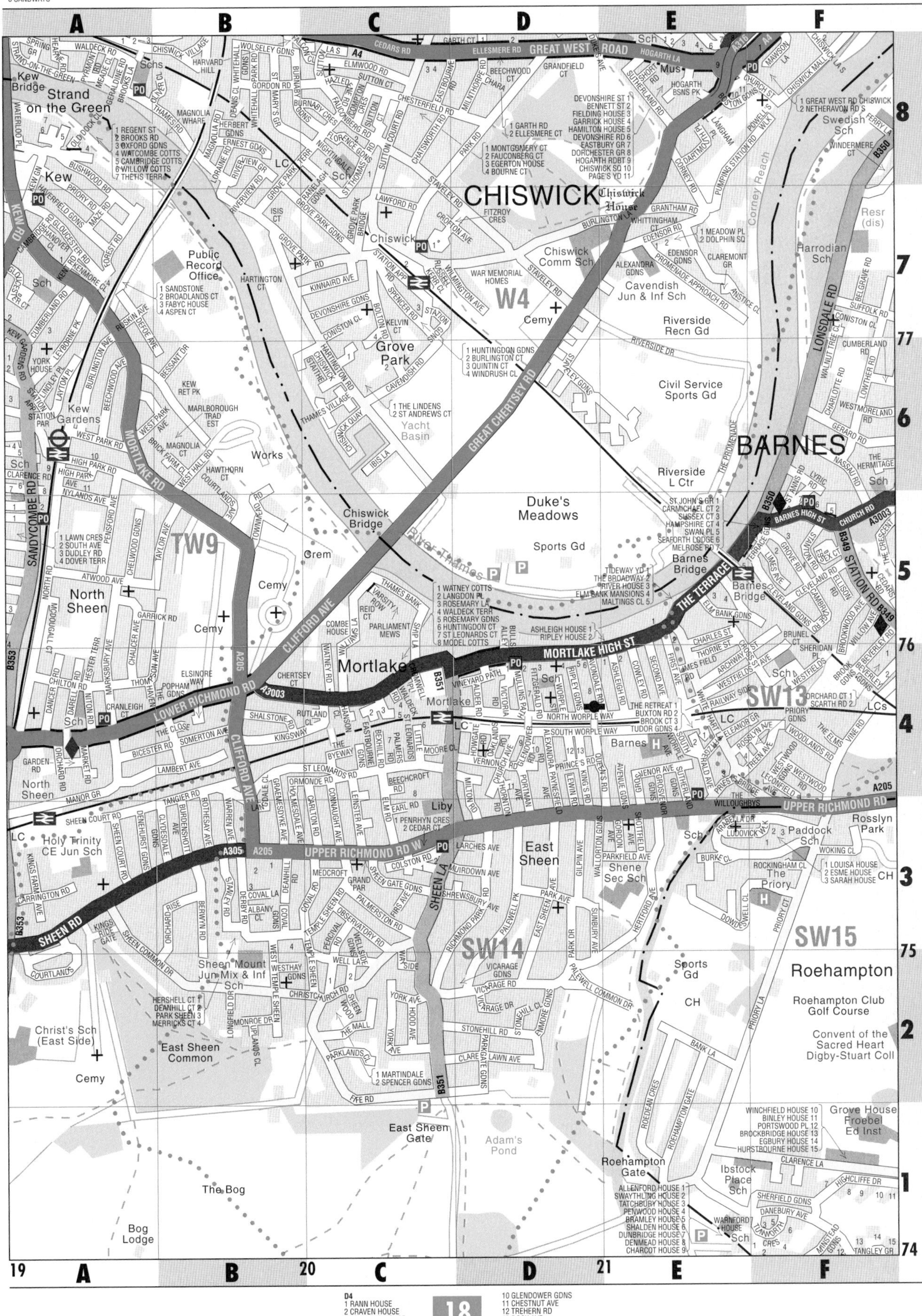

A B C D E F

8 7 77 6 5 76 4 3 75 2 1 74

Kew Bridge
Strand on the Green
Kew
Public Record Office
Kew Gardens
CHISWICK
Chiswick House
W4
Grove Park
Chiswick Comm Sch
Cavendish Jun & Inf Sch
Riverside Recn Gd
Civil Service Sports Gd
Harrodian Sch
Swedish Sch
BARNES
Riverside L Ctr
Duke's Meadows
Sports Gd
River Thames
Chiswick Bridge
Barnes Bridge
TW9
North Sheen
Mortlake
SW13
SW14
East Sheen
Shene Sec Sch
Holy Trinity CE Jun Sch
Sheen Mount Jun Mix & Inf Sch
East Sheen Common
Christ's Sch (East Side)
East Sheen Gate
Adam's Pond
The Bog
Bog Lodge
Roehampton Gate
Ibstock Place Sch
SW15
Roehampton
Roehampton Club Golf Course
Convent of the Sacred Heart Digby-Stuart Coll
Grove House Froebel Ed Inst
Rosslyn Park
The Priory

GREAT WEST ROAD
GREAT CHERTSEY RD
MORTLAKE HIGH ST
LOWER RICHMOND RD
UPPER RICHMOND RD W
UPPER RICHMOND RD
SHEEN RD
CLIFFORD AVE
MORTLAKE RD
KEW RD
SHEEN LA
THE TERRACE
STATION RD
LONSDALE RD

19 A B 20 C D 21 E F

D4
1 RANN HOUSE
2 CRAVEN HOUSE
3 JOHN DEE HOUSE
4 KINDELL HOUSE
5 MONTGOMERY HOUSE
6 AVONDALE HOUSE
7 ADDINGTON CT
8 DOVECOTE GDNS
9 FIRMSTON HOUSE
10 GLENDOWER GDNS
11 CHESTNUT AVE
12 TREHERN RD
13 ROCK AVE

18

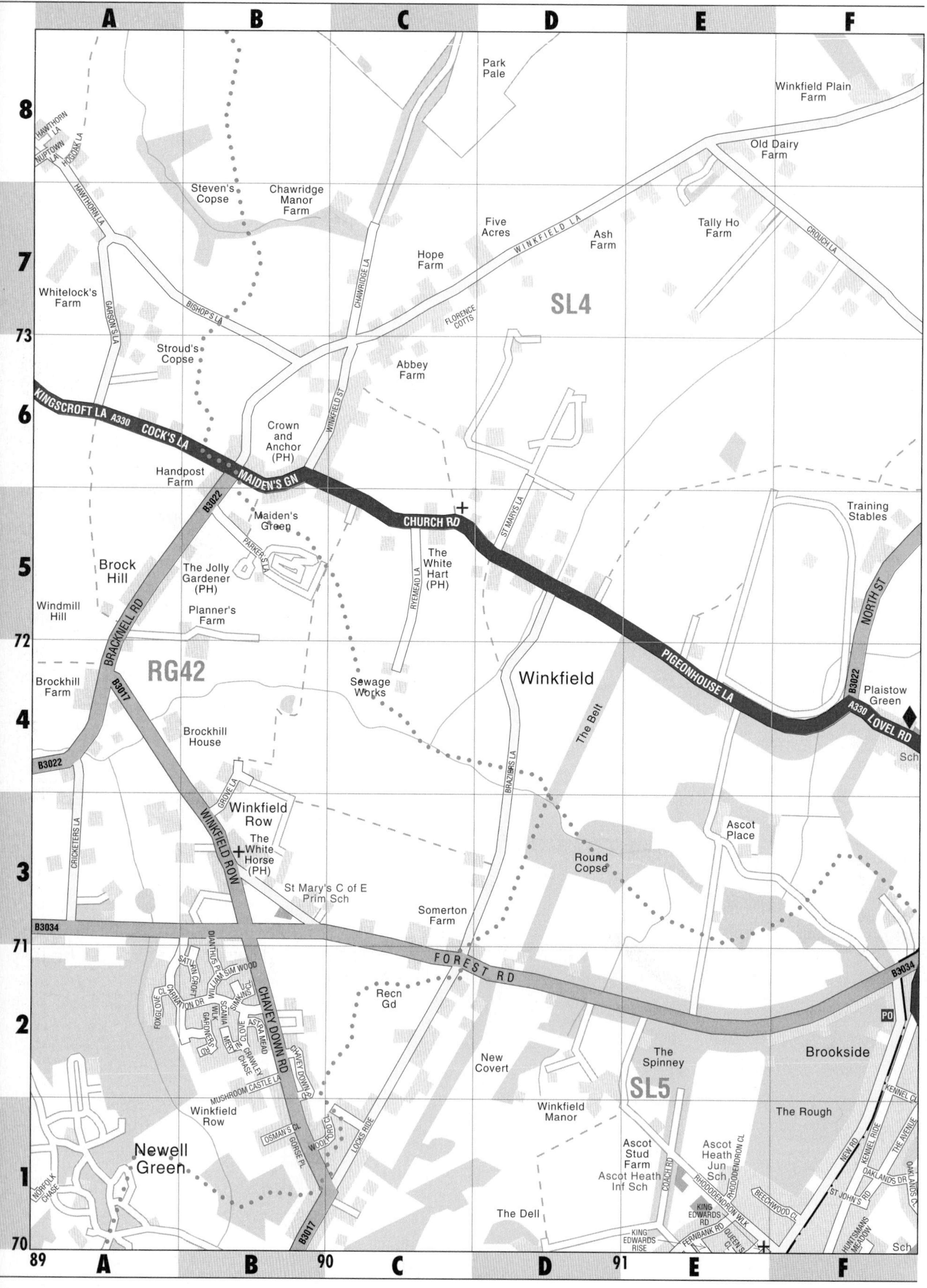
A
B
C
D
E
F
Park Pale
Winkfield Plain Farm
Old Dairy Farm
Steven's Copse
Chawridge Manor Farm
Five Acres
Ash Farm
Tally Ho Farm
Hope Farm
Whitelock's Farm
SL4
Stroud's Copse
Abbey Farm
Crown and Anchor (PH)
Handpost Farm
Maiden's Green
Training Stables
Brock Hill
The Jolly Gardener (PH)
The White Hart (PH)
Windmill Hill
Planner's Farm
Winkfield
RG42
Brockhill Farm
Sewage Works
Plaistow Green
Brockhill House
Winkfield Row
The White Horse (PH)
Ascot Place
Round Copse
St Mary's C of E Prim Sch
Somerton Farm
Recn Gd
The Spinney
Brookside
New Covert
SL5
The Rough
Winkfield Row
Winkfield Manor
Newell Green
Ascot Stud Farm
Ascot Heath Inf Sch
Ascot Heath Jun Sch
The Dell
KINGSCROFT LA
A330
COCK'S LA
MAIDEN'S GN
CHURCH RD
PIGEONHOUSE LA
LOVEL RD
NORTH ST
B3022
BRACKNELL RD
B3017
WINKFIELD ROW
CHAVEY DOWN RD
B3034
FOREST RD
WINKFIELD LA
CHAWRIDGE LA
WINKFIELD ST
BISHOP'S LA
GARSON'S LA
HAWTHORN LA
NUPTOWN LA
HOGOAK LA
CROUCH LA
FLORENCE COTTS
ST MARYS LA
RYEMEAD LA
PARKER'S LA
The Belt
BRAZIERS LA
GROVE LA
CRICKETERS LA
MUSHROOM CASTLE LA
OSMAN'S CL
GORSE PL
WOODFORD CL
LOCKS RIDE
NORFOLK CHASE
COACH RD
RHODODENDRON WLK
RHODODENDRON CL
KING EDWARDS RD
KING EDWARDS RISE
FERNBANK RD
BEECHWOOD CL
NEW RD
KENNEL RIDE
KENNEL CL
THE AVENUE
OAKLANDS DR
ST JOHN'S RD
HUNTSMANS MEADOW
PO
Sch
89
90
91
70
71
72
73
1
2
3
4
5
6
7
8

28

10

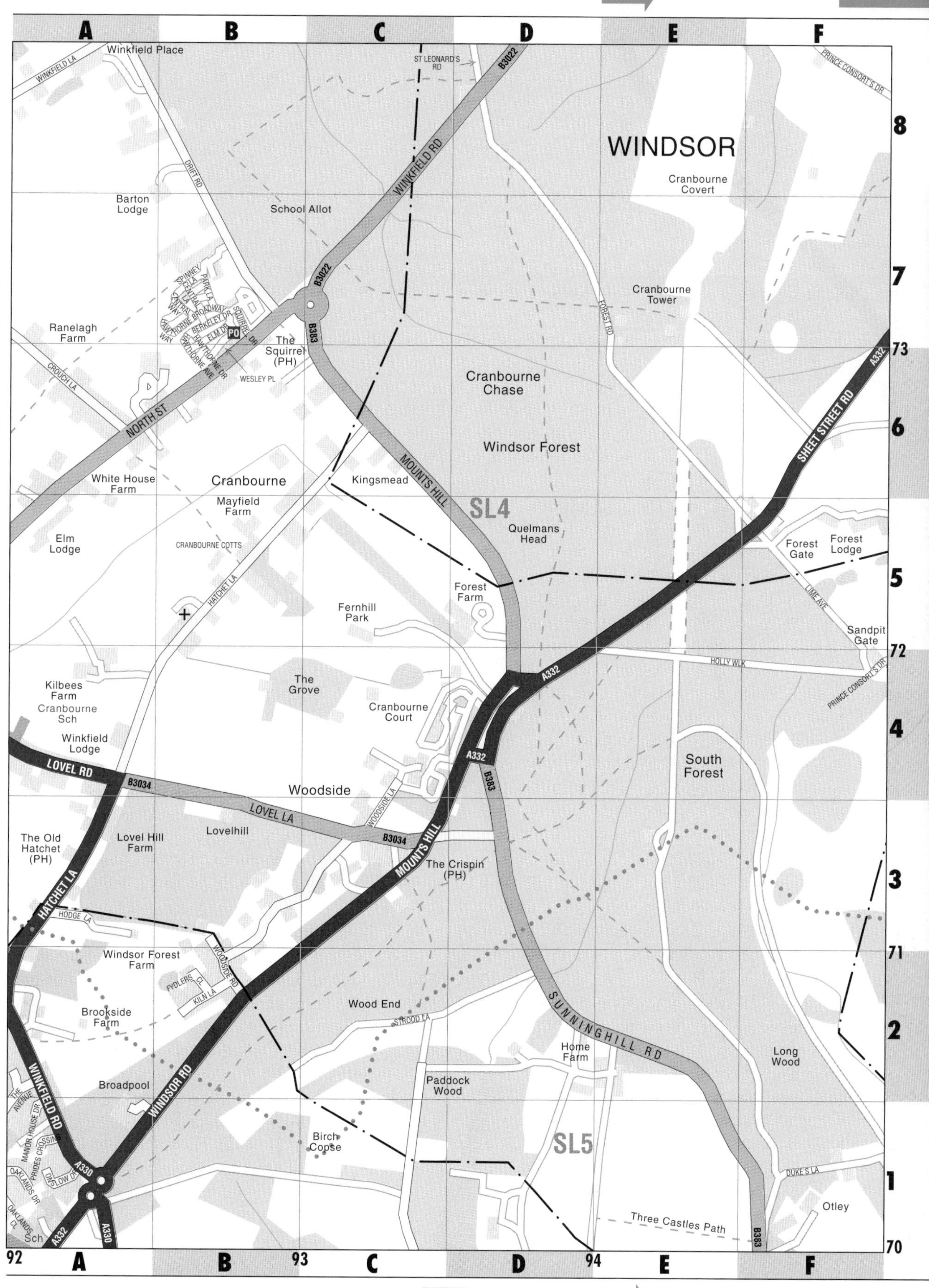
A
B
C
D
E
F
8
7
73
6
5
72
4
3
71
2
1
70
92
93
94
WINDSOR
Winkfield Place
WINKFIELD LA
ST LEONARD'S RD
B3022
PRINCE CONSORT'S DR
WINKFIELD RD
DRIFT RD
Cranbourne Covert
Barton Lodge
School Allot
Cranbourne Tower
Ranelagh Farm
PO
The Squirrel (PH)
B383
FOREST RD
WESLEY PL
CROUCH LA
NORTH ST
Cranbourne Chase
A332
SHEET STREET RD
Windsor Forest
White House Farm
Cranbourne
Kingsmead
MOUNTS HILL
SL4
Mayfield Farm
Quelmans Head
Forest Gate
Forest Lodge
Elm Lodge
CRANBOURNE COTTS
HATCHET LA
Forest Farm
Fernhill Park
LIME AVE
Sandpit Gate
HOLLY WLK
The Grove
Kilbees Farm
Cranbourne Sch
Cranbourne Court
A332
PRINCE CONSORT'S DR
Winkfield Lodge
LOVEL RD
B3034
A332
South Forest
Woodside
B383
WOODSIDE LA
LOVEL LA
The Old Hatchet (PH)
Lovel Hill Farm
Lovelhill
B3034
MOUNTS HILL
The Crispin (PH)
HATCHET LA
HODGE LA
Windsor Forest Farm
WOODSIDE RD
FYDLERS CL
KILN LA
Wood End
SUNNINGHILL RD
Brookside Farm
STROOD LA
Home Farm
Long Wood
Paddock Wood
WINKFIELD RD
Broadpool
WINDSOR RD
THE AVENUE
MANOR HOUSE DR
PRIDES CROSSING
Birch Copse
SL5
A330
DUKE'S LA
OAKLANDS DR
Otley
OAKLANDS CL
Three Castles Path
Sch
A332
A330
B383

9

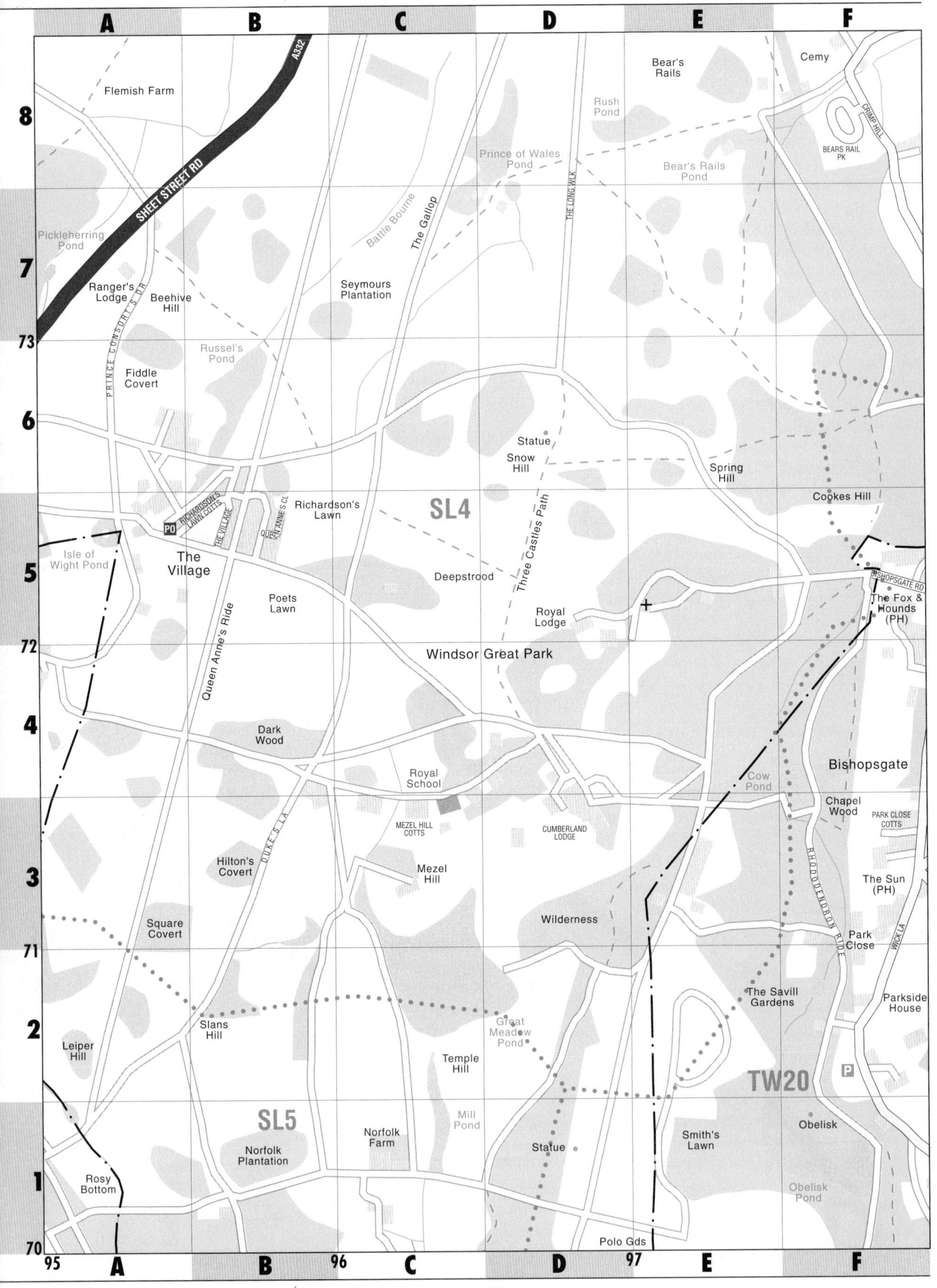
A
B
C
D
E
F
8
7
73
6
5
72
4
3
71
2
1
70
95
96
97
Flemish Farm
A332
SHEET STREET RD
Pickleherring Pond
Ranger's Lodge
Beehive Hill
PRINCE CONSORT'S DR
Russel's Pond
Fiddle Covert
Battle Bourne
The Gallop
Seymours Plantation
Prince of Wales Pond
THE LONG WLK
Rush Pond
Bear's Rails
Bear's Rails Pond
Cemy
CRIMP HILL
BEARS RAIL PK
Statue
Snow Hill
Spring Hill
Cookes Hill
PO
RICHARDSON'S LAWN COTTS
THE VILLAGE
QUEEN ANNE'S CL
Richardson's Lawn
SL4
Three Castles Path
Isle of Wight Pond
The Village
Deepstrood
BISHOPSGATE RD
The Fox & Hounds (PH)
Poets Lawn
Royal Lodge
Queen Anne's Ride
Windsor Great Park
Dark Wood
Royal School
Bishopsgate
Cow Pond
Chapel Wood
PARK CLOSE COTTS
MEZEL HILL COTTS
CUMBERLAND LODGE
Hilton's Covert
DUKE'S LA
Mezel Hill
The Sun (PH)
RHODODENDRON RIDE
Square Covert
Wilderness
Park Close
WICK LA
The Savill Gardens
Parkside House
Slans Hill
Great Meadow Pond
Leiper Hill
Temple Hill
P
TW20
SL5
Mill Pond
Norfolk Farm
Obelisk
Norfolk Plantation
Statue
Smith's Lawn
Rosy Bottom
Obelisk Pond
Polo Gds

9
30

12

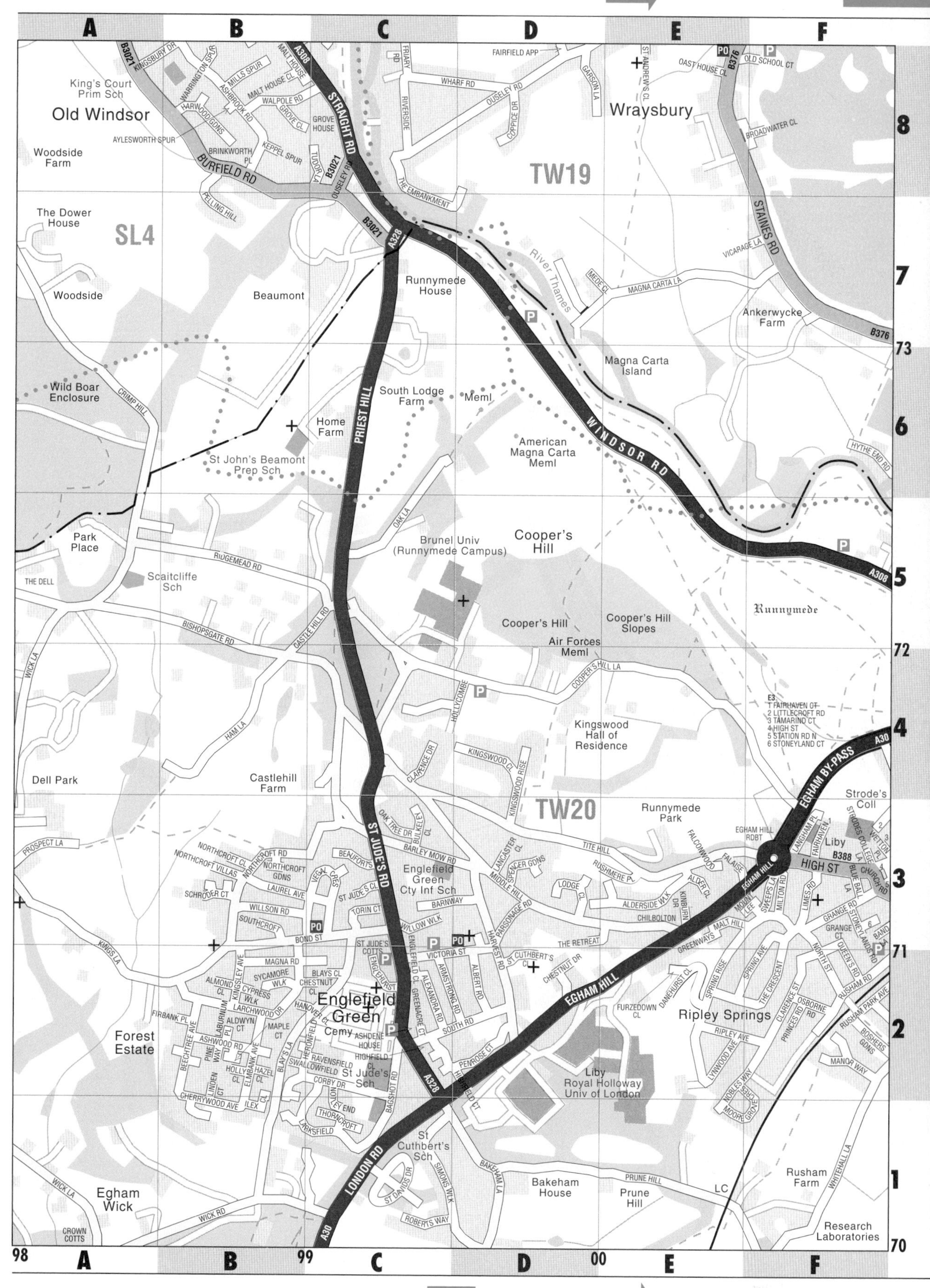

A B C D E F
8 7 73 6 5 72 4 3 71 2 1 70
98 99 00
Old Windsor
King's Court Prim Sch
Woodside Farm
The Dower House
SL4
Woodside
Beaumont
Wild Boar Enclosure
Home Farm
St John's Beamont Prep Sch
Park Place
Scaitcliffe Sch
THE DELL
Dell Park
Castlehill Farm
Forest Estate
Egham Wick
CROWN COTTS
Wraysbury
TW19
River Thames
Runnymede House
South Lodge Farm
Meml
American Magna Carta Meml
Magna Carta Island
Ankerwycke Farm
Brunel Univ (Runnymede Campus)
Cooper's Hill
Cooper's Hill Air Forces Meml
Cooper's Hill Slopes
Runnymede
Kingswood Hall of Residence
TW20
Runnymede Park
Englefield Green Cty Inf Sch
Englefield Green
Cemy
St Jude's Sch
St Cuthbert's Sch
Liby Royal Holloway Univ of London
Ripley Springs
Strode's Coll
Liby
EGHAM HILL RDBT
Bakeham House
Prune Hill
Rusham Farm
Research Laboratories
LC
E3
1 FAIRHAVEN CT
2 LITTLECROFT RD
3 TAMARIND CT
4 HIGH ST
5 STATION RD N
6 STONEYLAND CT
STRAIGHT RD
PRIEST HILL
ST JUDE'S RD
WINDSOR RD
EGHAM BY-PASS
EGHAM HILL
LONDON RD
HIGH ST
STAINES RD
BURFIELD RD
A308 A328 A30 B3021 B376 B388

31

12

11
1

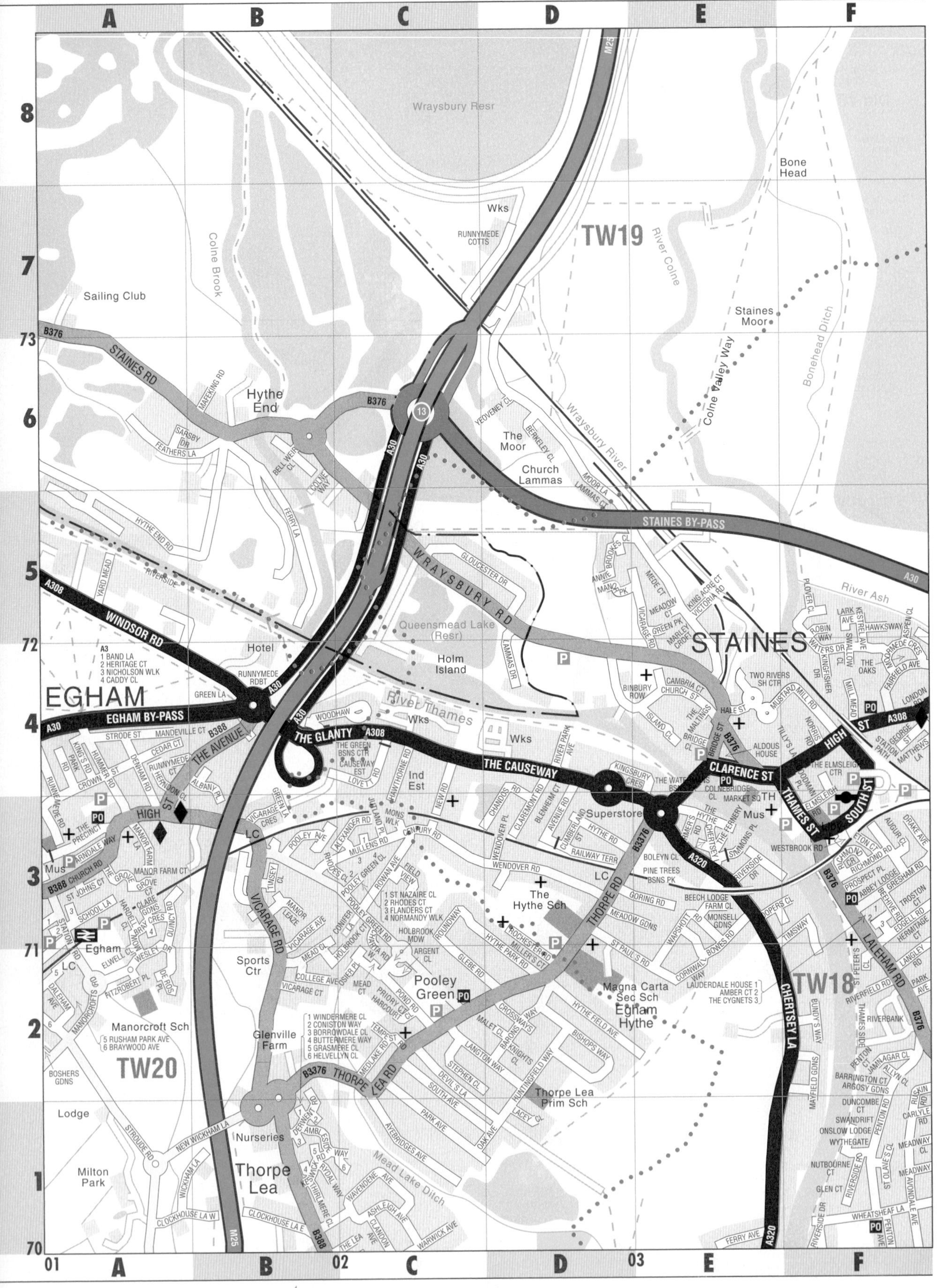
Wraysbury Resr
TW19
STAINES
EGHAM
TW20
TW18
Hythe End
Staines Moor
Bone Head
Sailing Club
The Moor
Church Lammas
Queensmead Lake (Resr)
Holm Island
River Thames
River Colne
Colne Brook
Colne Valley Way
Bonehead Ditch
Wraysbury River
River Ash
STAINES BY-PASS
STAINES RD
WINDSOR RD
EGHAM BY-PASS
THE GLANTY
THE CAUSEWAY
CLARENCE ST
THAMES ST
HIGH ST
WRAYSBURY RD
VICARAGE RD
THORPE RD
THORPE LEA RD
CHERTSEY LA
LALEHAM RD
SOUTH ST
Superstore
The Hythe Sch
Magna Carta Sec Sch
Egham Hythe
Pooley Green
Thorpe Lea
Thorpe Lea Prim Sch
Manorcroft Sch
Glenville Farm
Nurseries
Milton Park
Lodge
Sports Ctr
Mead Lake Ditch
Two Rivers Sh Ctr
Runnymede Rdbt
Hotel
Ind Est
Wks
Mus
TH
Lib
Egham

11
32

A B C D E F

St Mary's C of E Sch
St Anne's Prim Sch
Recn Gd
West Bedfont
CAMGATE EST
Liby
Town Farm Cty Prim Sch
Cemy
HAWTHORNE CT 1
TOWN FARM WAY 2
EVERGREEN CT 3
ANDOVER CT 4
1 LANCASTER CT
2 TENSING CT
3 HILLARY CT
4 LIVINGSTONE CT
5 CHICHESTER CT
King George VI Resr
Stanwell
TW19
STANWELL MOOR RD
A3044
TOWN LA
B378
Staines Resrs
Cemy
Ashford
LONDON RD
A30
The Ashford High Sch
St David's Jun Sch
Hengrove Farm
Recn Gd
Shortwood Cty Inf Sch
Cemy
Birch Green
A308
Shortwood Pond
Shortwood Common
Ashford Park Cty Prim Sch
Ashford
Clarendon Cty Prim Sch
TW15
Spelthorne Coll
Liby
Sports Centre
HM Remand Ctr
STANWELL RD
CHURCH RD
Staines
STAINES BY-PASS
Staines Reservoirs Aqueduct
River Ash
TW18
Knowle Green
L Ctr
Sch
Cts
Kingscroft Cty Jun Sch
Our Lady of the Rosary RC Sch
Sweep's Ditch
The Matthew Arnold Sch
KINGSTON RD
FORDBRIDGE RD
CH
ASHFORD
Ashford Manor Golf Club
LALEHAM RD
STAINES RD
B376
ASHFORD RD
B377
Works
Buckland Cty Jun & Inf Sch
Queen Mary Resr
River Ash

8 7 73 6 5 72 4 3 71 2 1 70

04 A B 05 C D 06 E F

33
14

13
3

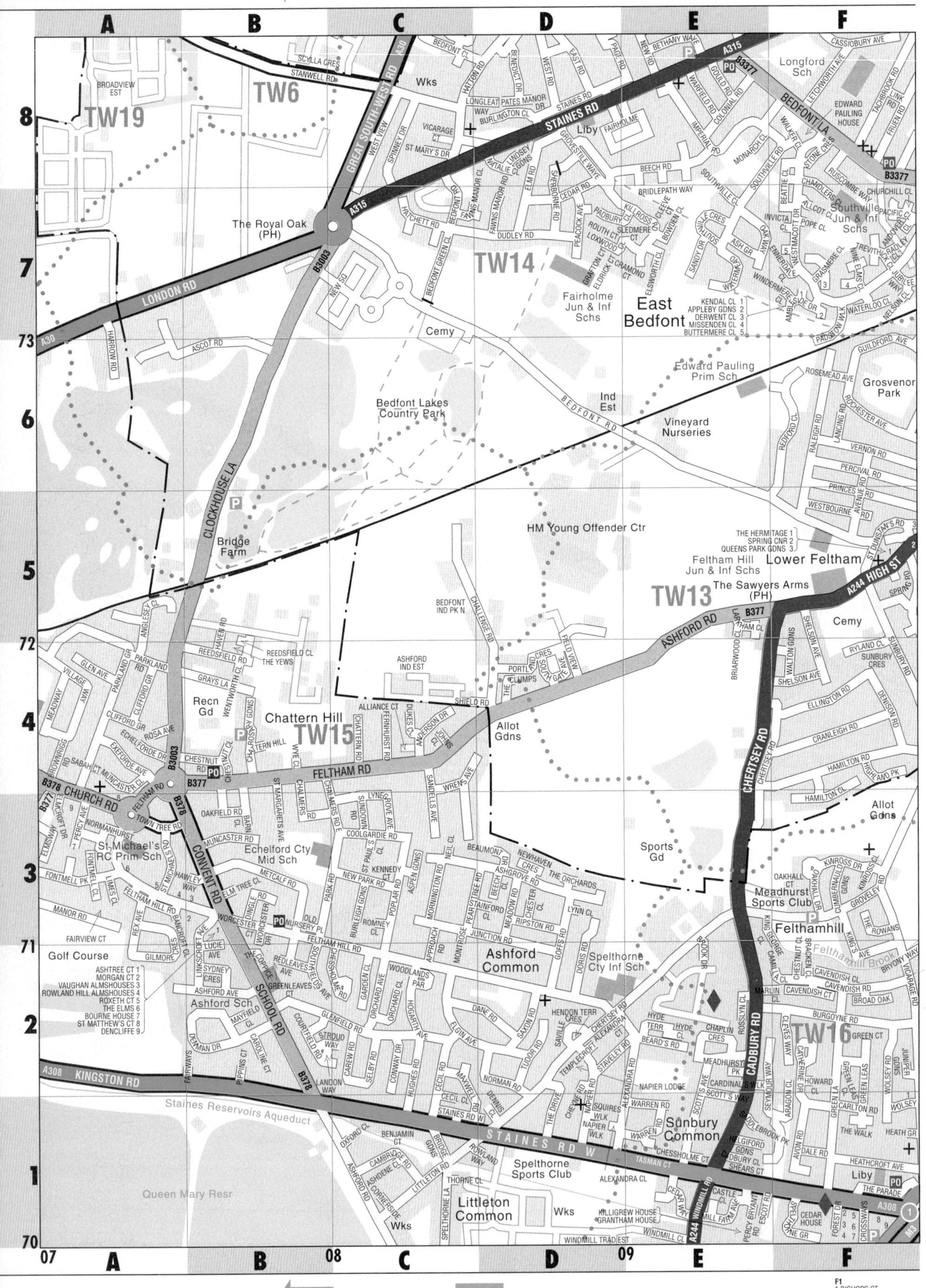

13
34

F1
1 BISHOPS CT
2 ASH LODGE
3 LIME LODGE
4 OAK LODGE
5 ELM CT
6 WILLOW LODGE
7 SYCAMORE LODGE
8 PRISCILLA HOUSE
9 SUNBURY CROSS CTR

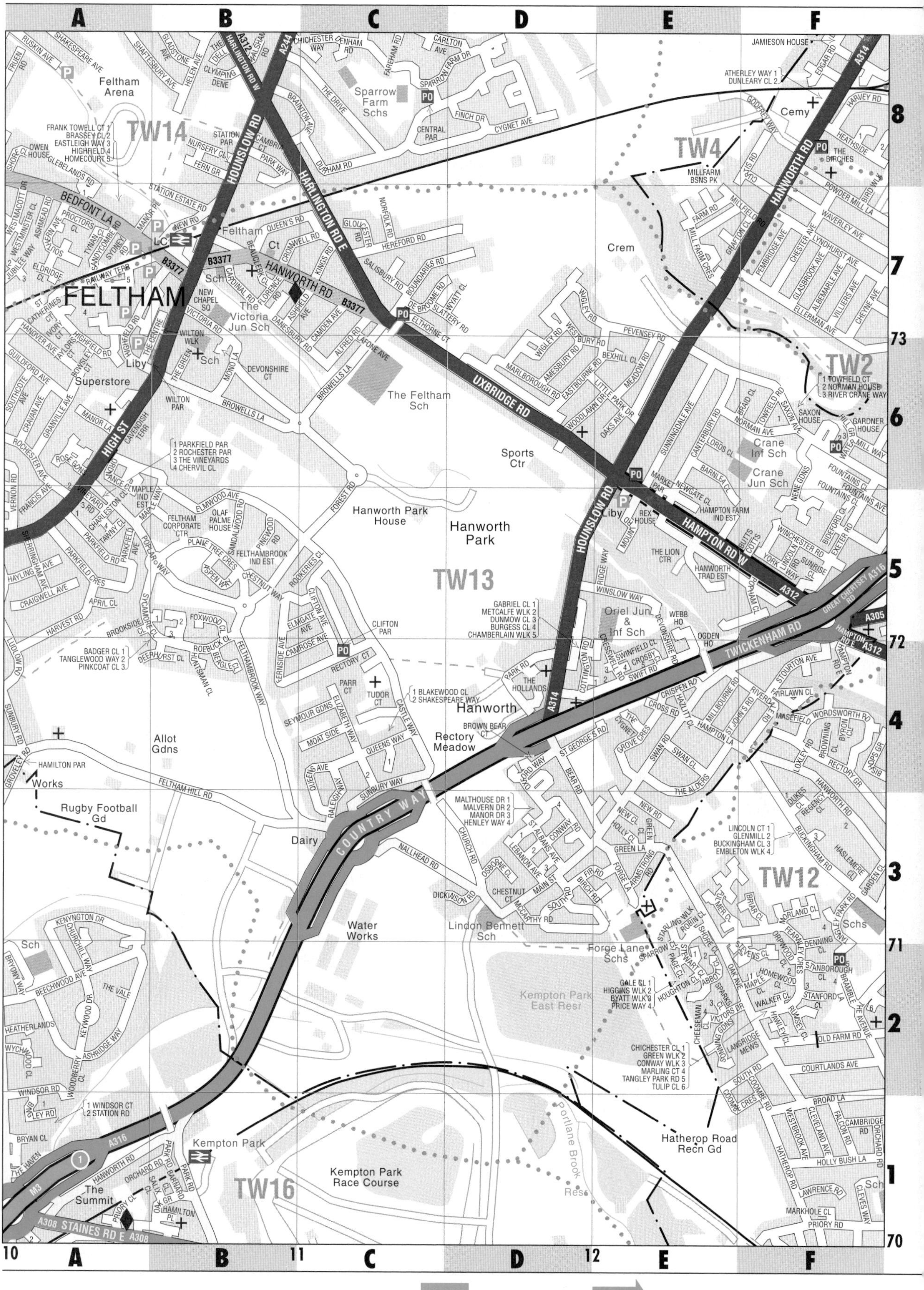

A B C D E F

FELTHAM

Feltham Arena

TW14

TW4

TW2

TW13

TW12

TW16

Sparrow Farm Schs

The Feltham Sch

Hanworth Park House

Hanworth Park

Sports Ctr

Crem

Cemy

Hanworth

Rectory Meadow

Allot Gdns

Works

Rugby Football Gd

Dairy

Water Works

Lindon Bennett Sch

Forge Lane Schs

Kempton Park East Resr

Kempton Park

Kempton Park Race Course

Hatherop Road Recn Gd

The Summit

Superstore

Crane Inf Sch

Crane Jun Sch

Oriel Jun & Inf Sch

The Victoria Jun Sch

FRANK TOWELL CT 1
BRASSEY CL 2
EASTLEIGH WAY 3
HIGHFIELD 4
HOMECOURT 5

1 PARKFIELD PAR
2 ROCHESTER PAR
3 THE VINEYARDS
4 CHERVIL CL

BADGER CL 1
TANGLEWOOD WAY 2
PINKCOAT CL 3

1 BLAKEWOOD CL
2 SHAKESPEARE WAY

GABRIEL CL 1
METCALFE WLK 2
DUNMOW CL 3
BURGESS CL 4
CHAMBERLAIN WLK 5

MALTHOUSE DR 1
MALVERN DR 2
MANOR DR 3
HENLEY WAY 4

ATHERLEY WAY 1
DUNLEARY CL 2

1 TOWFIELD CT
2 NORMAN HOUSE
3 RIVER CRANE WAY

LINCOLN CT 1
GLENMILL 2
BUCKINGHAM CL 3
EMBLETON WLK 4

GALE CL 1
HIGGINS WLK 2
BYATT WLK 3
PRICE WAY 4

CHICHESTER CL 1
GREEN WLK 2
CONWAY WLK 3
MARLING CT 4
TANGLEY PARK RD 5
TULIP CL 6

1 WINDSOR CT
2 STATION RD

10 11 12

70 71 72 73

35

16

15
5

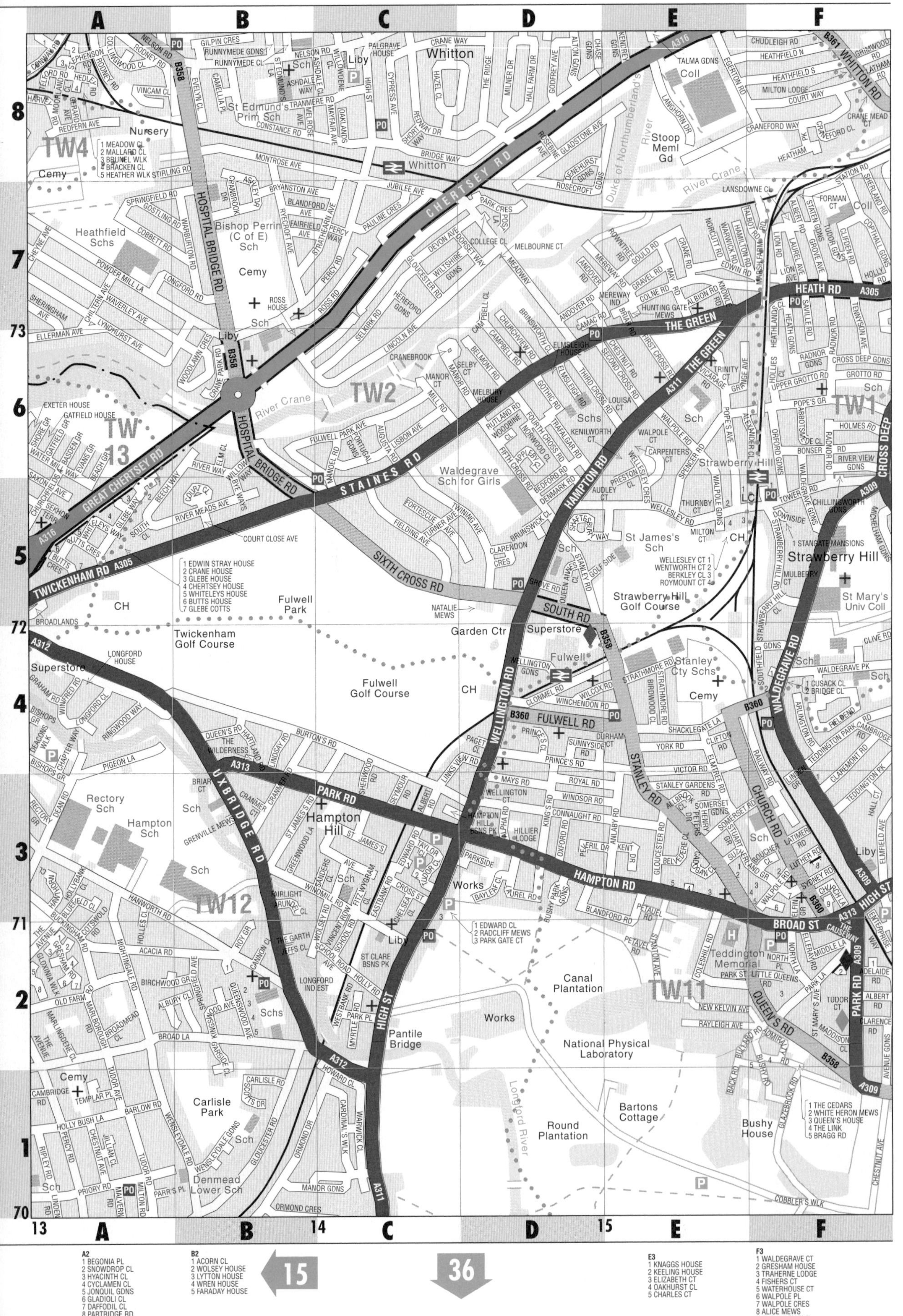

A2
1 BEGONIA PL
2 SNOWDROP CL
3 HYACINTH CL
4 CYCLAMEN CL
5 JONQUIL GDNS
6 GLADIOLI CL
7 DAFFODIL CL
8 PARTRIDGE RD

B2
1 ACORN CL
2 WOLSEY HOUSE
3 LYTTON HOUSE
4 WREN HOUSE
5 FARADAY HOUSE

15
36

E3
1 KNAGGS HOUSE
2 KEELING HOUSE
3 ELIZABETH CT
4 OAKHURST CL
5 CHARLES CT

F3
1 WALDEGRAVE CT
2 GRESHAM HOUSE
3 TRAHERNE LODGE
4 FISHERS CT
5 WATERHOUSE CT
6 WALPOLE PL
7 WALPOLE CRES
8 ALICE MEWS
9 BYCHURCH END

A7
1 KATHARINE RD
2 GARFIELD RD
3 ARRAGON RD
4 FLOOD LA
5 JOHN WESLEY CT
6 KING STREET PAR
7 THAMES EYOT

A8
1 GRIMWOOD RD
2 PERRYN CT
3 IVYBRIDGE CL
4 BROOK HOUSE
5 LATHAM CL
6 MARCH RD
7 BERKLEY CT
8 COLE COURT LODGE
9 CHELTENHAM AVE
10 RAILWAY APP

B8
1 HARTINGTON RD
2 MELTON CT
3 AMYAND PARK GDNS
4 CROWN CT
5 BURRELL HOUSE
6 OWEN HOUSE
7 BRENTFORD HOUSE
8 LEESON HOUSE
9 WESTBOURNE HOUSE
10 ORLEANS CT
11 LEBANON CT

6
18

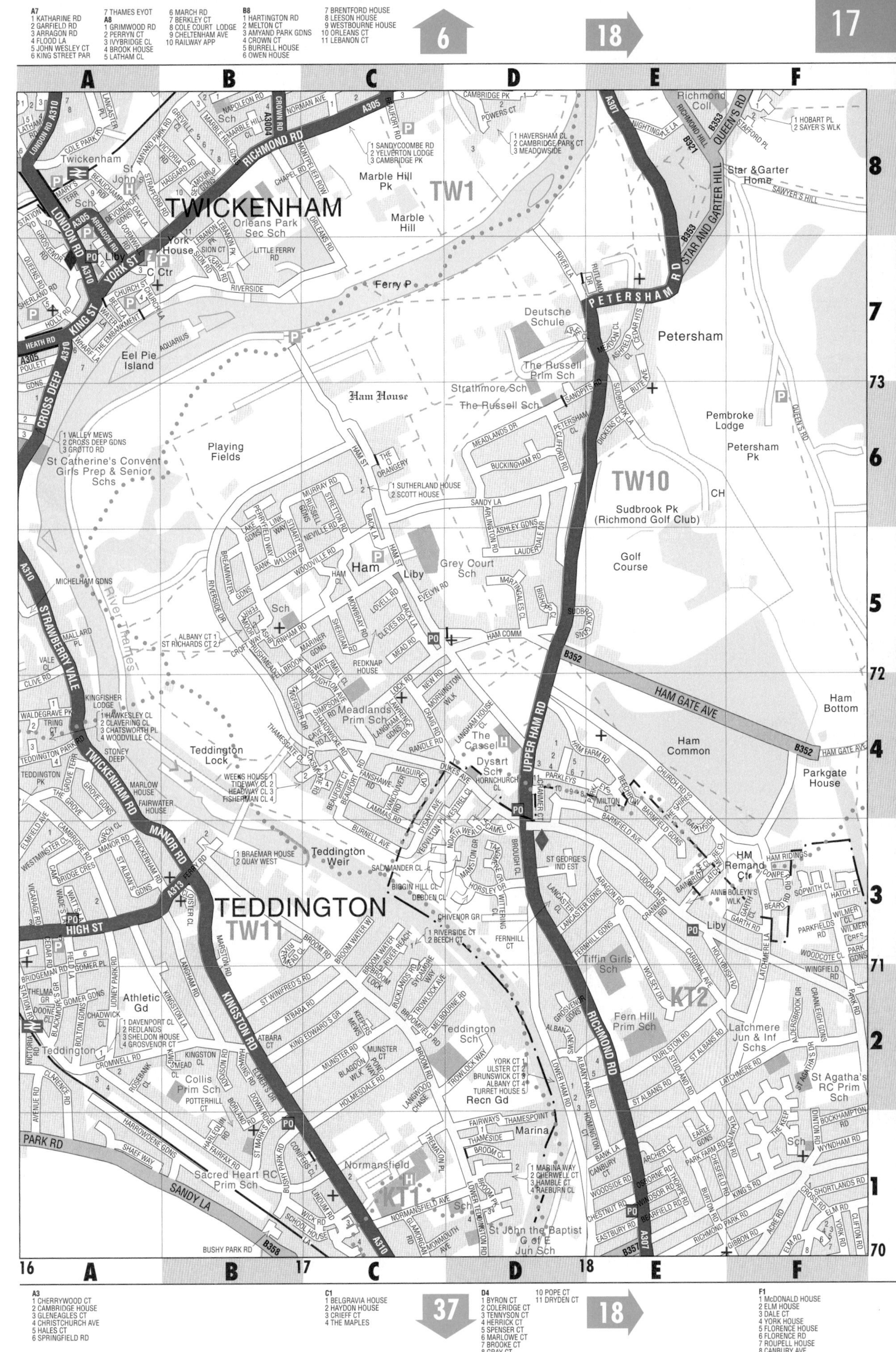

A3
1 CHERRYWOOD CT
2 CAMBRIDGE HOUSE
3 GLENEAGLES CT
4 CHRISTCHURCH AVE
5 HALES CT
6 SPRINGFIELD RD

C1
1 BELGRAVIA HOUSE
2 HAYDON HOUSE
3 CRIEFF CT
4 THE MAPLES

37

D4
1 BYRON CT
2 COLERIDGE CT
3 TENNYSON CT
4 HERRICK CT
5 SPENSER CT
6 MARLOWE CT
7 BROOKE CT
8 GRAY CT
9 SHELIEY CT
10 POPE CT
11 DRYDEN CT

18

F1
1 McDONALD HOUSE
2 ELM HOUSE
3 DALE CT
4 YORK HOUSE
5 FLORENCE HOUSE
6 FLORENCE RD
7 ROUPELL HOUSE
8 CANBURY AVE

17
7

19 A B 20 C D 21 E F

A1
1 QUEEN'S CT
2 ST GEORGES RD
3 PARK ROAD HOUSE
4 DAGMAR RD
5 TAPPING CL
6 ARTHUR RD
7 BOROUGH RD
8 BELVEDERE CT
9 BRAYWICK CT
10 DEAN CT
11 ROWAN CT
12 RICHMOND CT
13 SUNNINGDALE CT
14 HAWKER CT
15 CROMWELL CT
16 KINGS CT

B1
1 BRAMLEY HOUSE
2 ABINGER HOUSE
3 THURSLEY HOUSE
4 RIDGE HOUSE
5 THE CLONE
6 MOUNT CT
7 HILLSIDE CT
8 HILL CT
9 ROYAL CT
10 LAKESIDE
11 HIGH ASHTON

17
38

20

A8
1 WOODCOTT HOUSE
2 LYNDHURST HOUSE
3 WHEATLEY HOUSE
4 NEPEAN ST
5 ALLBROOK HOUSE
6 BORDON WLK
7 CHILCOMBE HOUSE
8 VICARAGE CT
9 SHAWFORD CT
10 EASTLEIGH WLK
11 KINGS CT

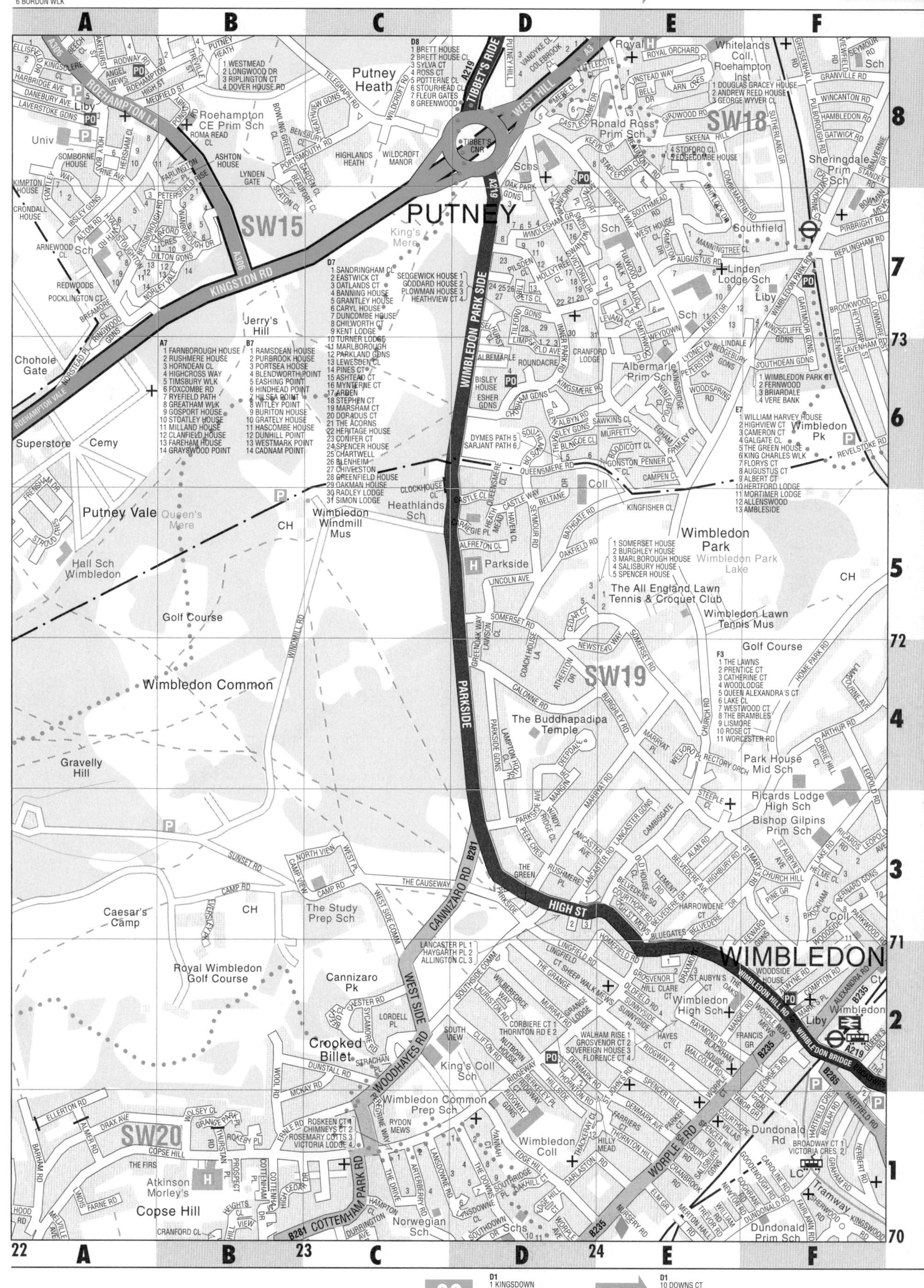

39

D1
1 KINGSDOWN
2 WIMBLEDON CL
3 BERYL HARDING HOUSE
4 UPTON CT
5 LANHERNE HOUSE
6 CUMBERLAND CL
7 THAXTED PL
8 RATHBONE HOUSE
9 PRINCESS CT

20

D1
10 DOWNS CT
11 RAVENSCAR LODGE
12 SAVONA CL

19

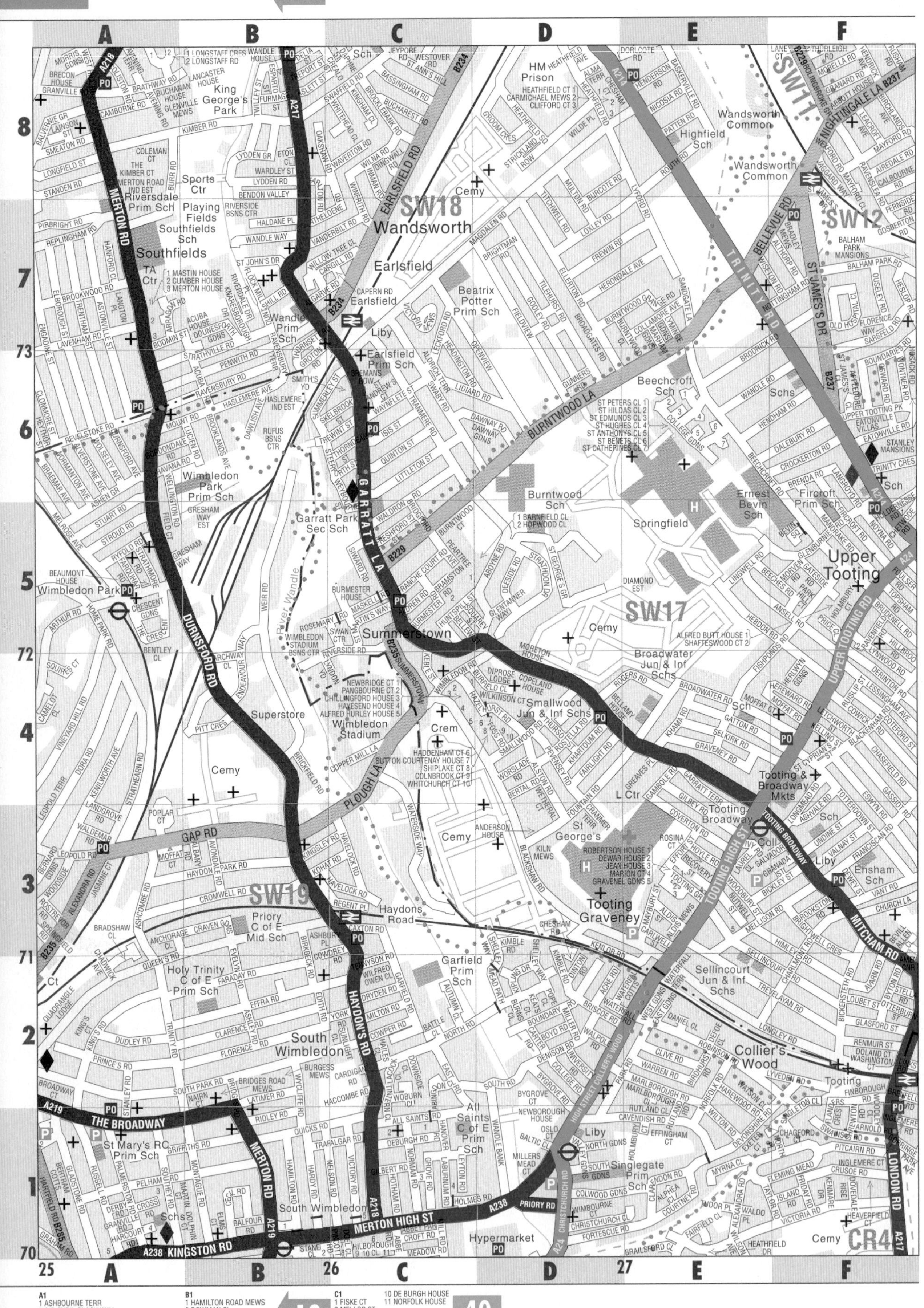

A1
1 ASHBOURNE TERR
2 SIR CYRIL BLACK WAY
3 DOWNING HOUSE
4 PALMERSTON GR
5 GLADSTONE CT

B1
1 HAMILTON ROAD MEWS
2 DOWMAN CL

C1
1 FISKE CT
2 MELLOR CT
3 OLIVE RD
4 ALLERTON HOUSE
5 VICTORY ROAD MEWS
6 WILL MILES CT
7 VANGUARD HOUSE
8 MYCHELL HOUSE
9 MERTON PL
10 DE BURGH HOUSE
11 NORFOLK HOUSE

19

40

D8
1 RILEY HOUSE
2 BENNETT HOUSE
3 WHITE HOUSE
4 RODGERS HOUSE
5 DUMPHREYS HOUSE
6 HOMAN HOUSE
7 PRENDERGAST HOUSE
8 HUTCHINS HOUSE
9 WHITELEY HOUSE
10 TRESIDDER HOUSE
11 PRIMROSE CT
12 ANGUS HOUSE
13 CURRIE HOUSE

E8
1 PICTON HOUSE
2 RIGG HOUSE
3 WATSON HOUSE
4 MACARTHUR HOUSE
5 SANDON HOUSE
6 THOROLD HOUSE
7 PEARCE HOUSE
8 MUDIE HOUSE
9 MILLER HOUSE
10 LYCETT HOUSE
11 LAFONE HOUSE
12 LUCRAFT HOUSE
13 FREEMAN HOUSE
14 NEW PARK PAR
15 ARGYLL CT
16 DUMBARTON CT
17 KINTYRE CT
18 COTTON HOUSE
19 CROSSMAN HOUSES
20 CAMEFORD CT
21 PARSONS HOUSE
22 BRINDLEY HOUSE
23 ARKWRIGHT HOUSE
24 PERRY HOUSE
25 BRUNEL HOUSE
26 NEW PARK CT
27 TANHURST HOUSE

F8
1 HYPERION HOUSE
2 SOMERS RD
3 ARCHBISHOP'S PL
4 LEANDER RD
5 WITLEY HOUSE
6 OUTWOOD HOUSE
7 DUNSFOLD HOUSE
8 DEEPDENE LODGE
9 WARNHAM HOUSE
10 ALBURY LODGE
11 TILFORD HOUSE
12 ELSTEAD HOUSE
13 THURSLEY HOUSE
14 BROCKHAM HOUSE
15 CAPEL LODGE
16 LEITH HOUSE
17 FAIRVIEW HOUSE
18 WEYMOUTH CT
19 ASCALON CT

22

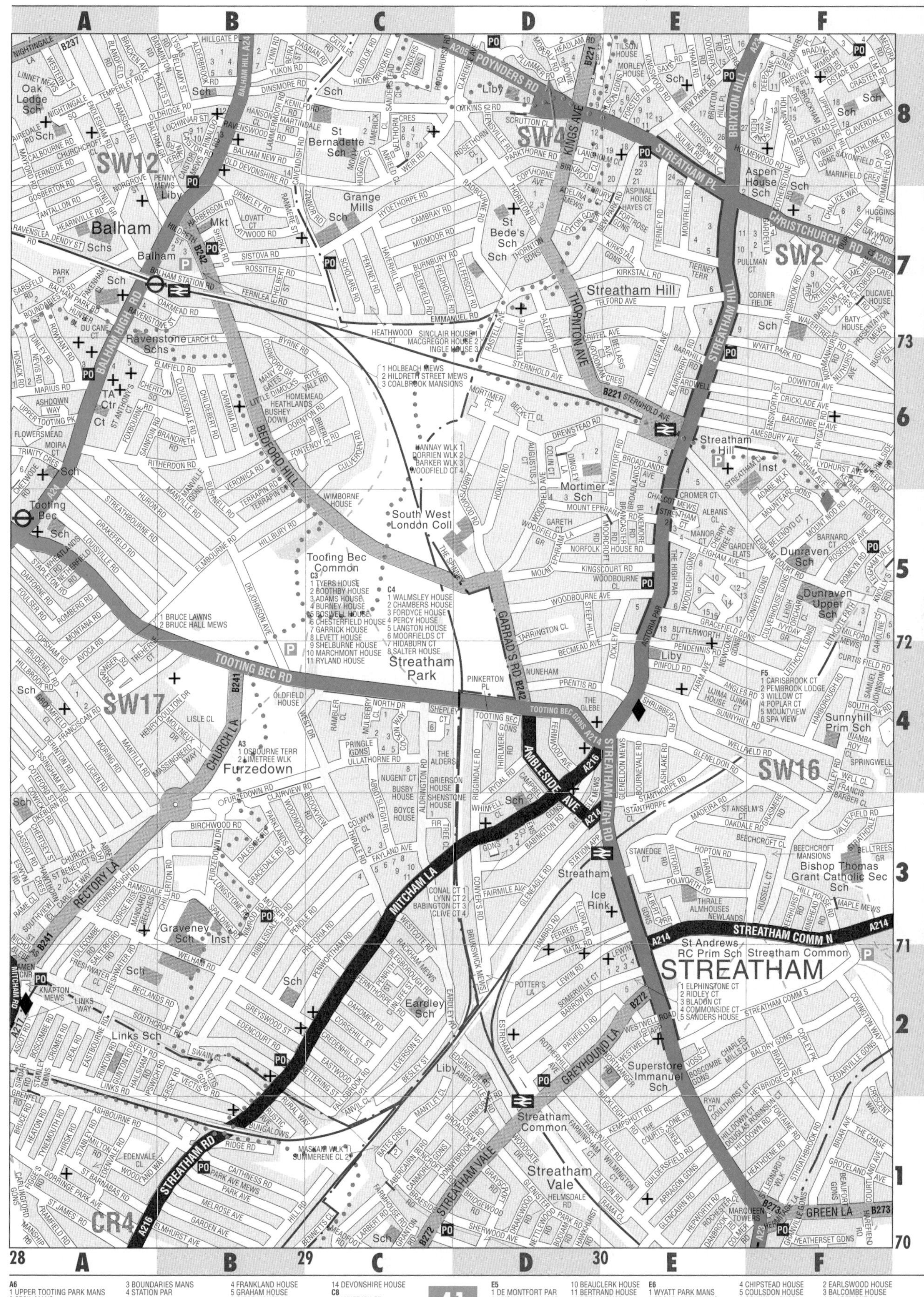

A6
1 UPPER TOOTING PARK MANS
2 CECIL MANS
3 MARIUS MANS
4 THE BOULEVARD
5 ELMFIELD MANS
6 HOLDERNESSE RD

A7
1 HESLOP CT
2 ST JAMES'S TERR
3 BOUNDARIES MANS
4 STATION PAR

A8
1 ST ANTHONY'S CT
2 HOLLIES WAY
3 ENDLESHAM CT

B8
1 MEYER HOUSE
2 FARADAY HOUSE
3 HALES HOUSE
4 FRANKLAND HOUSE
5 GRAHAM HOUSE
6 GIBBS HOUSE
7 DALTON HOUSE
8 ANSLIE WLK
9 ROKEBY HOUSE
10 CAISTER HOUSE
11 IVANHOE HOUSE
12 CATHERINE BAIRD CT
13 MARMION HOUSE
14 DEVONSHIRE HOUSE

C8
1 LIMERICK CT
2 HOMEWOODS
3 JEWELL HOUSE
4 GLANVILLE HOUSE
5 DAN BRYANT HOUSE
6 OLDING HOUSE
7 QUENNEL HOUSE
8 WEIR HOUSE
9 WEST HOUSE
10 NEVILLE CT

41

E5
1 DE MONTFORT PAR
2 LEIGHAM HALL PAR
3 LEIGHAM HALL
4 ENDSLEIGH MANS
5 JOHN KIRK HOUSE
6 RAEBARN CT
7 WAVEL CT
8 HOMELEIGH CT
9 HOWLAND HOUSE
10 BEAUCLERK HOUSE
11 BERTRAND HOUSE
12 DREW HOUSE
13 DOWES HOUSE
14 DUNTON HOUSE
15 RAYNALD HOUSE
16 SACKVILLE HOUSE
17 THURLOW HOUSE
18 ASTORIA MANS

E6
1 WYATT PARK MANS
2 BROADLANDS MANS
3 STONEHILL'S MANS
4 STREATLEIGH PAR
5 DORCHESTER CT

E7
1 BEAUMONT HOUSE
2 CHRISTCHURCH HOUSE
3 STAPLEFIELD CL
4 CHIPSTEAD HOUSE
5 COULSDON HOUSE
6 CONWAY HOUSE
7 TELFORD AVE MANS
8 TELFORD PAR MANS
9 WAVERTREE CT
10 HARTSWOOD HOUSE
11 WRAY HOUSE

F7
1 CHARLWOOD HOUSE
2 EARLSWOOD HOUSE
3 BALCOMBE HOUSE
4 CLAREMONT CL
5 HOLBROOK HOUSE
6 GWYNNE HOUSE
7 KYNASTON HOUSE
8 TILLMAN HOUSE
9 REGENT LODGE
10 HAZELMERE CT
11 DYKES CT

A3
1 BELLTREES GR
2 ASH CT
3 ALDER CT
4 BEECH CT
5 ACACIA CT
6 BLACKTHORN CT
7 CYPRESS CT
8 HAWTHORN CT
9 HAZEL CT
10 SYCAMORE CT
11 MAPLE CT
12 LABURNAM CT
13 FERN LODGE

21

A4
1 JAMES BOSWELL
2 ST ALBANS HOUSE
3 SUFFOLK CT
4 ROCKHAMPTON CL
5 DELPHIAN CT

A7
1 VALENS HOUSE
2 LOVEDAY HOUSE
3 STRODE HOUSE
4 ETHELWORTH CT
5 HARBIN HOUSE
6 BROOKS HOUSE
7 GODOLPHIN HOUSE
8 SHEPPARD HOUSE
9 McCORMICK HOUSE
10 TAYLOR HOUSE
11 SAUNDERS HOUSE
12 TALCOTT PATH
13 DERRICK HOUSE
14 WILLIAMS HOUSE
15 BALDWIN HOUSE
16 BERKELEY CT
17 CHURSTON CL
18 NEIL WATES CRES
19 BURNELL HOUSE
20 PORTLAND HOUSE

A8
1 ELLACOMBE HOUSE
2 BOOTH HOUSE
3 HATHERSLEY HOUSE
4 BRERETON HOUSE
5 HOLDSWORTH HOUSE
6 DEARMER HOUSE
7 CHERRY CL
8 GREENLEAF CL
9 LONGFORD WLK
10 SCARLETTE MANOR WLK
11 CHANDLERS WAY
12 UPGROVE MANOR WAY
13 ROPERS WLK
14 TEBBS HOUSE
15 BELL HOUSE
16 WORTHINGTON HOUSE
17 COURIER HOUSE
18 MACKIE HOUSE
19 HAMERS HOUSE
20 KELYWAY HOUSE

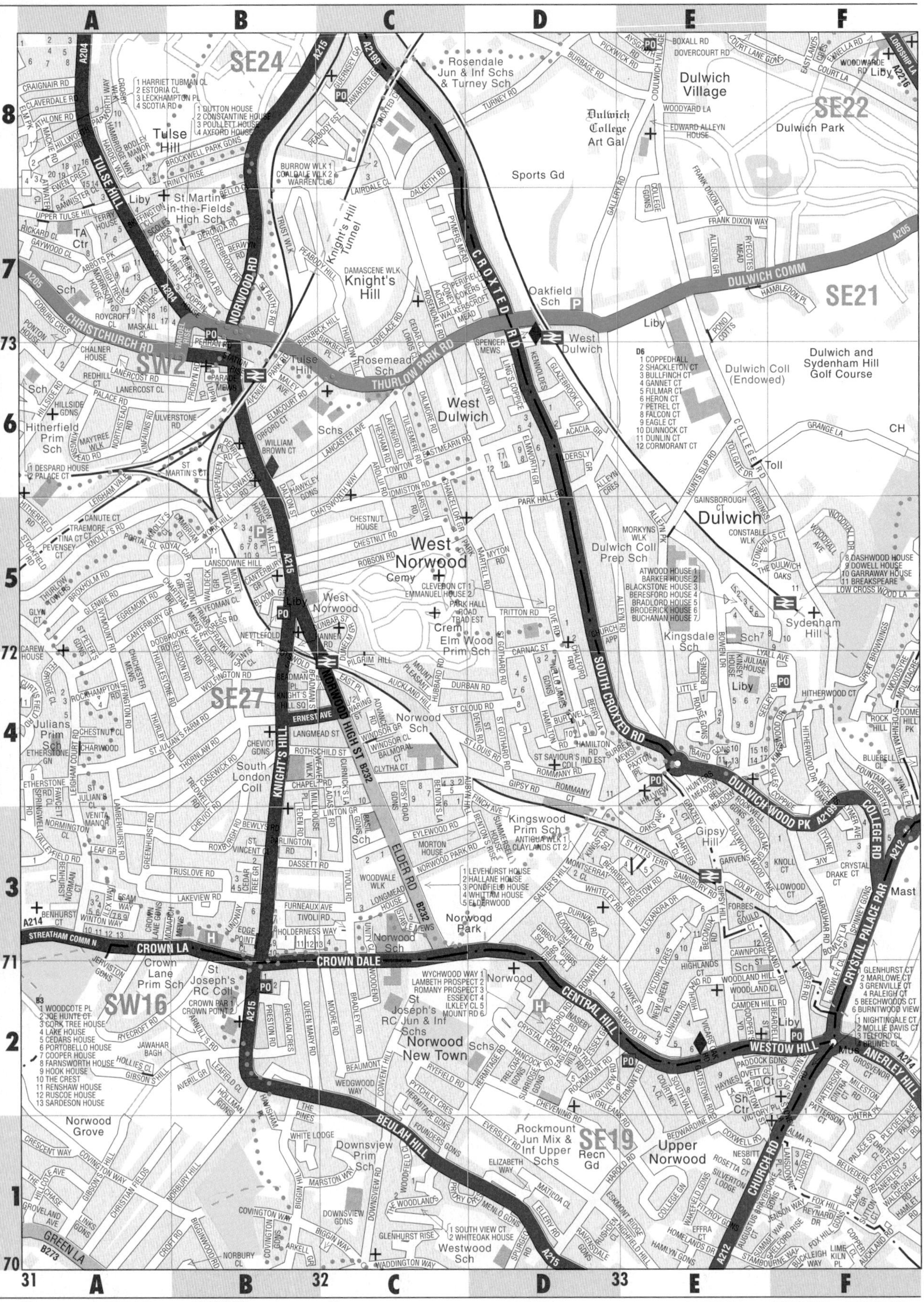

B5
1 THANET HOUSE
2 CHAPMAN HOUSE
3 BEAUFOY HOUSE
4 EASTON HOUSE
5 ROBERTS HOUSE
6 LLOYD CT
7 KERSHAW HOUSE
8 WAKELING HOUSE
9 EDRIDGE HOUSE
10 JESTON HOUSE
11 LANSDOWNE WOOD CL

C4
1 MOORE HOUSE
2 CHAUCER HOUSE
3 BUSHELL HOUSE
4 BLIGH HOUSE
5 HOBBS RD
6 HOGARTH HOUSE
7 GOODBEHERE HOUSE
8 ASTLEY HOUSE
9 ELDER GDNS
10 ELDERBERRY GR
11 THE PAVEMENT
12 DUNKIRK ST

D4
1 JOSEF PERRIN HOUSE
2 JEAN HUMBERT HOUSE
3 CHARLES STAUNTON HOUSE
4 VIOLETTE SZABO HOUSE

21

D4
5 LILIAN ROLFE HOUSE
6 ODETTE HOUSE
7 ROBERT GERARD HOUSE
8 ST BERNARDS CL
9 CHAMPNESS CL
10 PENNINGTON CL
11 QUEENSWOOD CT

42

E2
1 NORTHWOOD WAY

E2
1 NORTHWOOD WAY
2 HIGH LIMES
3 VALLEY PROSPECT
4 PLANE TREE WLK
5 CITY PROSPECT
6 BANKSIDE WAY
7 ROCHDALE
8 BARRINGTON WLK
9 GATESTONE CT
10 CHILDS LA
11 CARBERRY RD

E3
1 OAKDENE
2 THORSDEN WAY
3 OAKFIELD GDNS
4 GEORGETOWN CL
5 BRIDGETOWN CL
6 MOUNTBATTEN CL
7 BRABOURNE CL
8 ALEXANDRA WLK
9 COMPTON CT
10 BATTENBERG WLK
11 BURMA TERR
12 WISEMAN CT

E4
1 LINLEY CT
2 MELLOR HOUSE
3 WHITFIELD CT
4 MICHAELSON HOUSE
5 HOLBERRY HOUSE
6 HOVENDEN HOUSE
7 HUNTLEY HOUSE
8 TELFEI HOUSE
9 MARKHAM HOUSE
10 OLDHAM HOUSE
11 PARNALL HOUSE
12 PIERSON HOUSE
13 ROPER HOUSE
14 ROUNDELL HOUSE
15 SAWYER HOUSE
16 RANSFORD HOUSE
17 CARMICHAEL HOUSE

F1
1 HETLEY GDNS
2 HIGHLAND LODGE
3 MASON CT
4 KENDALL CT
5 HIGH VIEW

C7
1 HARLECH CT
2 ANGELA CT
3 WESTWOOD CT
4 NEW BELMONT HOUSE
5 PEARCEFIELD AVE
6 WALDRAM PL
7 HORNIMAN GRANGE

D5
1 STANDLAKE POINT
2 RADCOT POINT
3 NEWBRIDGE POINT
4 NORTHMOOR
5 KELMSCOTT
6 RADNOR CT
7 HEATHWOOD POINT
8 ASHLEIGH POINT
9 DEEPDENE POINT
10 ROSEMOUNT POINT
11 WOODFIELD HOUSE
12 CLAIRVILLE POINT
13 TREVENNA HOUSE
14 HYNDEWOOD

24

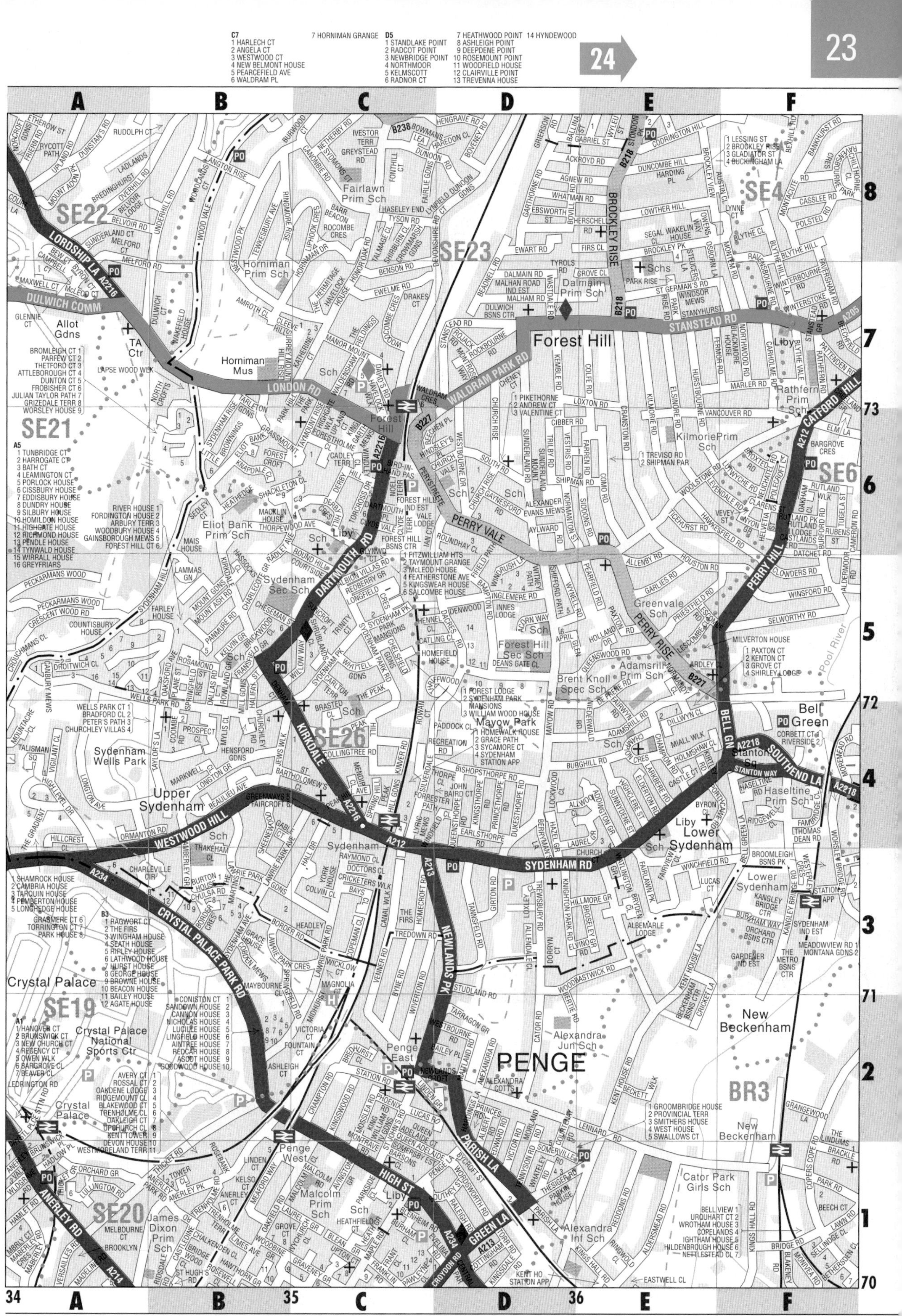

C1
1 WATERMEN'S SQ
2 ST JOHN'S COTTS
3 GLADSTONE MEWS
4 BIRLING HOUSE
5 SURREY TOWER
6 MIDDLESEX HOUSE
7 ADISHAM HOUSE
8 BETHESDA CT
9 OSPRINGE CL
10 GOUDHURST HOUSE
11 WALMER HOUSE
12 STROOD HOUSE
13 GREATSTONE HOUSE
14 JOHN BAIRD HOUSE

43

24

23

B8
1 SILVERMERE RD
2 BROOKDALE RD
3 SCROOBY ST

E8
1 BEAUMONT TERR
2 LITTLEBOURNE
3 VERDANT CT

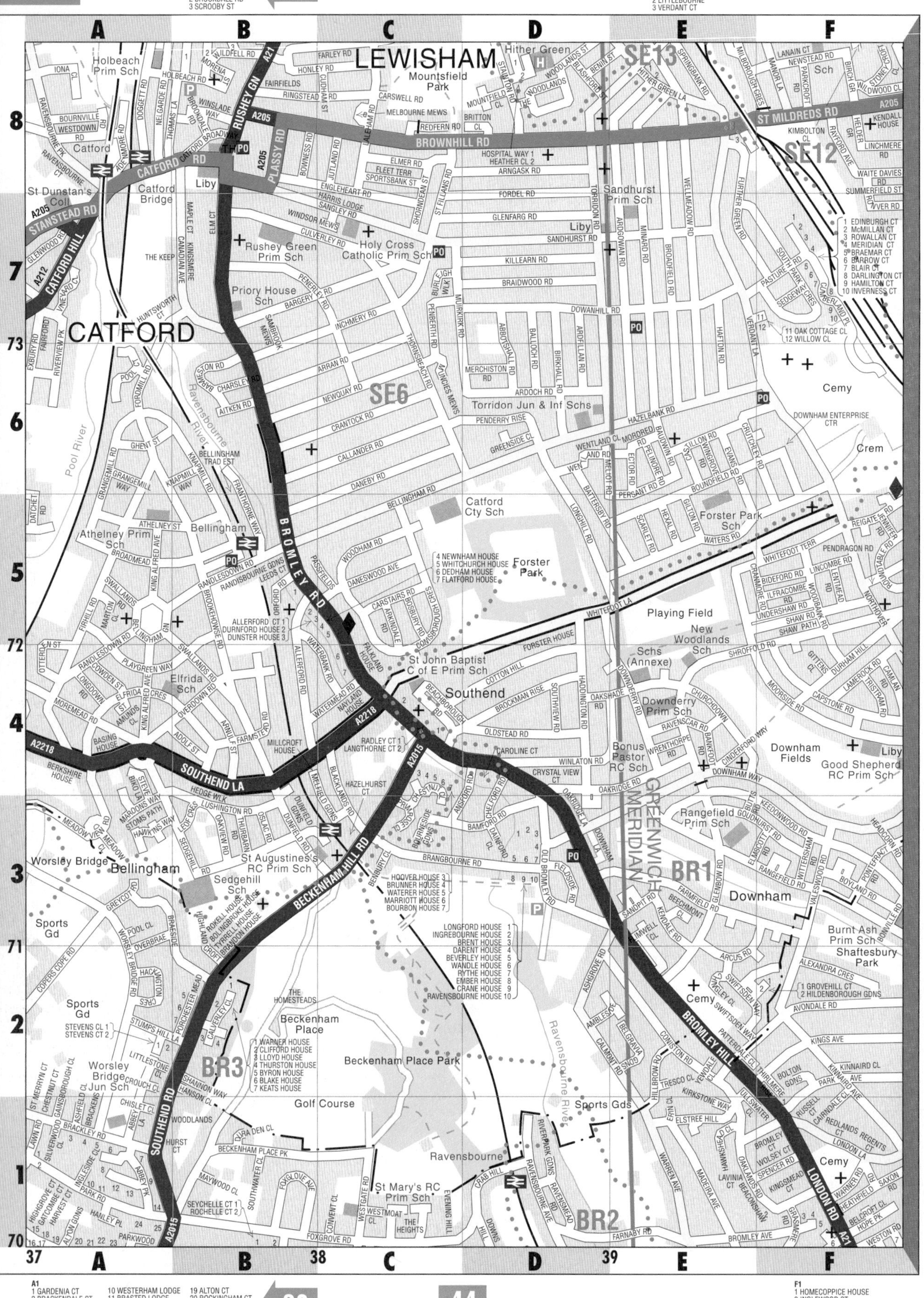

A1
1 GARDENIA CT
2 BRACKENDALE CT
3 DANIEL CT
4 MOLINER CT
5 CHARTWELL LODGE
6 RANDMORE CT
7 DOVER HOUSE
8 LUCERNE CT
9 MALLING HOUSE
10 WESTERHAM LODGE
11 BRASTED LODGE
12 MILTON HOUSE
13 BRADSOLE HOUSE
14 SANDGATE HOUSE
15 ADELAIDE CT
16 NETTLESTEAD CL
17 COPERS COPE RD
18 WARREN CT
19 ALTON CT
20 ROCKINGHAM CT
21 CAMELLIA CT
22 SINCLAIR CT
23 REGENTS CT
24 MINSHULL PL
25 SOUTH PARK CT

23

44

F1
1 HOMECOPPICE HOUSE
2 INGLEWOOD CT
3 MAVERY CT
4 GLEN CT
5 CAWSTON CT
6 HIGHLAND RD
7 MOORELAND RD

26

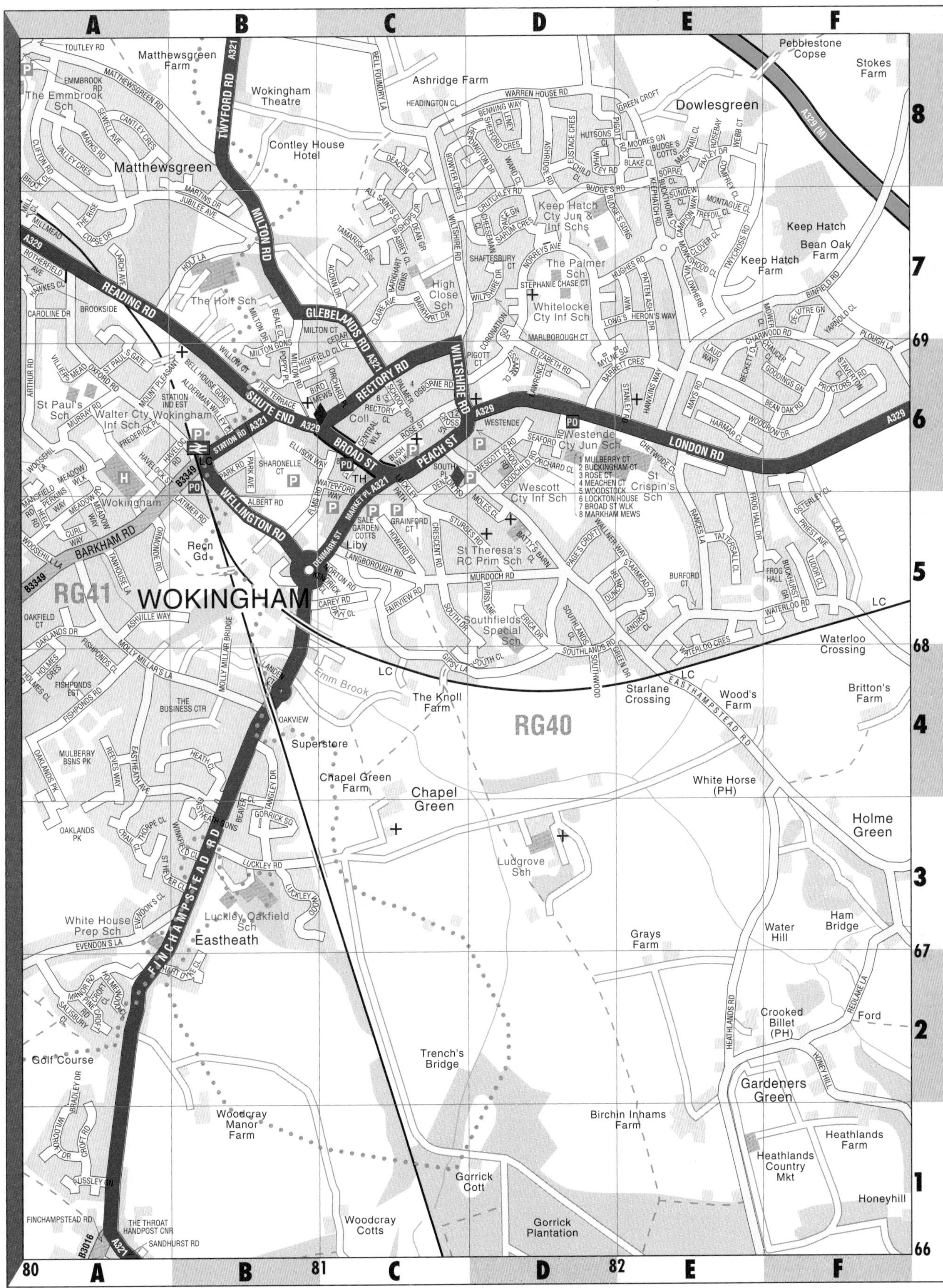

WOKINGHAM
RG41
RG40
Matthewsgreen
Matthewsgreen Farm
The Emmbrook Sch
Wokingham Theatre
Contley House Hotel
Ashridge Farm
Dowlesgreen
Pebblestone Copse
Stokes Farm
Keep Hatch
Bean Oak Farm
Keep Hatch Farm
Keep Hatch Cty Jun & Inf Schs
The Palmer Sch
Whitelocke Cty Inf Sch
High Close Sch
The Holt Sch
St Paul's Sch
Walter Cty Inf Sch
Westende Cty Jun Sch
St Crispin's Sch
Wescott Cty Inf Sch
St Theresa's RC Prim Sch
Southfields Special Sch
Recn Gd
Waterloo Crossing
Starlane Crossing
The Knoll Farm
Wood's Farm
Britton's Farm
Superstore
Chapel Green Farm
Chapel Green
White Horse (PH)
Holme Green
Ludgrove Sch
Luckley Oakfield Sch
Eastheath
White House Prep Sch
Grays Farm
Water Hill
Ham Bridge
Crooked Billet (PH)
Ford
Golf Course
Trench's Bridge
Gardeners Green
Woodcray Manor Farm
Birchin Inhams Farm
Heathlands Farm
Heathlands Country Mkt
Gorrick Cott
Honeyhill
Woodcray Cotts
Gorrick Plantation
Emm Brook
READING RD
LONDON RD
MILTON RD
TWYFORD RD
WELLINGTON RD
FINCHAMPSTEAD RD
BARKHAM RD
EASTHAMPSTEAD RD
A329
A321
A329(M)
B3349
B3016
1 MULBERRY CT
2 BUCKINGHAM CT
3 ROSE CT
4 MEACHEN CT
5 WOODSTOCK
6 LOCKTON HOUSE
7 BROAD ST WLK
8 MARKHAM MEWS
A
B
C
D
E
F
8
7
6
5
4
3
2
1
69
68
67
66
80
81
82

26

25

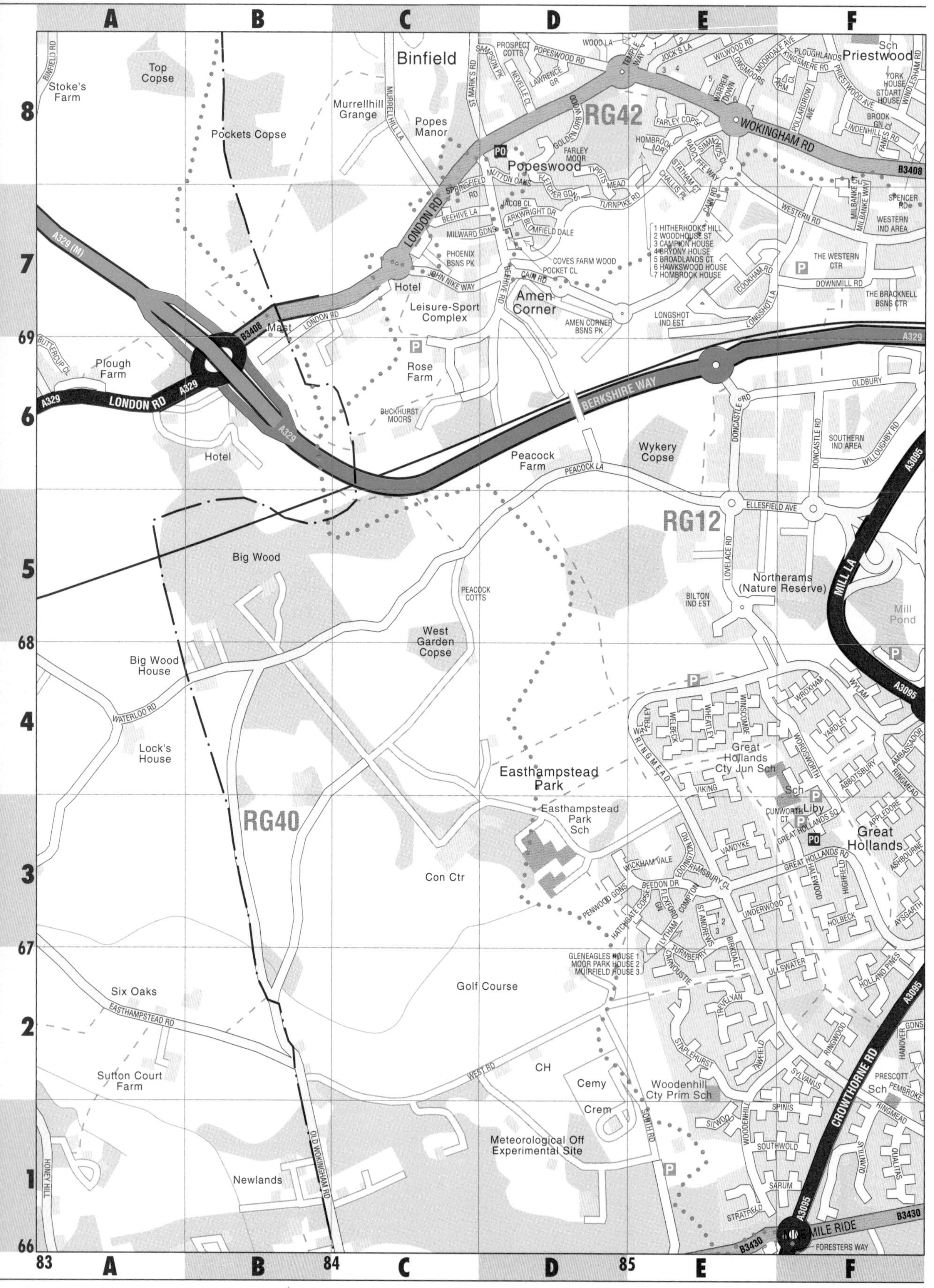

Binfield
Priestwood
Popeswood
Amen Corner
RG42
RG12
RG40
Top Copse
Stoke's Farm
Pockets Copse
Murrellhill Grange
Popes Manor
Plough Farm
Hotel
Mast
Leisure-Sport Complex
Rose Farm
Buckhurst Moors
Peacock Farm
Wykery Copse
Big Wood
Big Wood House
West Garden Copse
Lock's House
Easthampstead Park
Easthampstead Park Sch
Con Ctr
Golf Course
Six Oaks
Sutton Court Farm
CH
Cemy
Crem
Meteorological Off Experimental Site
Newlands
Woodenhill Cty Prim Sch
Great Hollands
Great Hollands Cty Jun Sch
Northerams (Nature Reserve)
Mill Pond
Bilton Ind Est
Western Ind Area
The Western Ctr
The Bracknell Bsns Ctr
Southern Ind Area
Longshot Ind Est
Amen Corner Bsns Pk
Phoenix Bsns Pk
Liby
Sch
A329(M)
A329
B3408
A3095
B3430
London Rd
Wokingham Rd
Berkshire Way
Mill La
Crowthorne Rd
Nine Mile Ride
Peacock La
Ellesfield Ave
Waterloo Rd
Easthampstead Rd
West Rd
Old Wokingham Rd
South Rd
Ringmead
1 Hitherhooks Hill
2 Woodhouse St
3 Campion House
4 Bryony House
5 Broadlands Ct
6 Hawkswood House
7 Hombrook House
Gleneagles House 1
Moor Park House 2
Muirfield House 3
A B C D E F
8 7 69 6 5 68 4 3 67 2 1 66
83 84 85

25
45

A8
1 PRIESTWOOD SQ
2 SALTIRE GDNS
3 WINDLEBROOK GN
4 APPLETREE PL
5 PORTMAN CL

B8
1 HART CL
2 BIRCHETTS CL
3 ASHRIDGE GN

C8
1 LYNWOOD CHASE
2 DENE CL
3 LAKESIDE
4 EDMONDS CT

28

F5
1 THE WILLOWS
2 CEDARS
3 MAPEL CT
4 GREENWOOD
5 LARCHWOOD
6 THE FIRS
7 CHARLBURY CL
8 HOLTON HEATH
9 BLOXWORTH CL

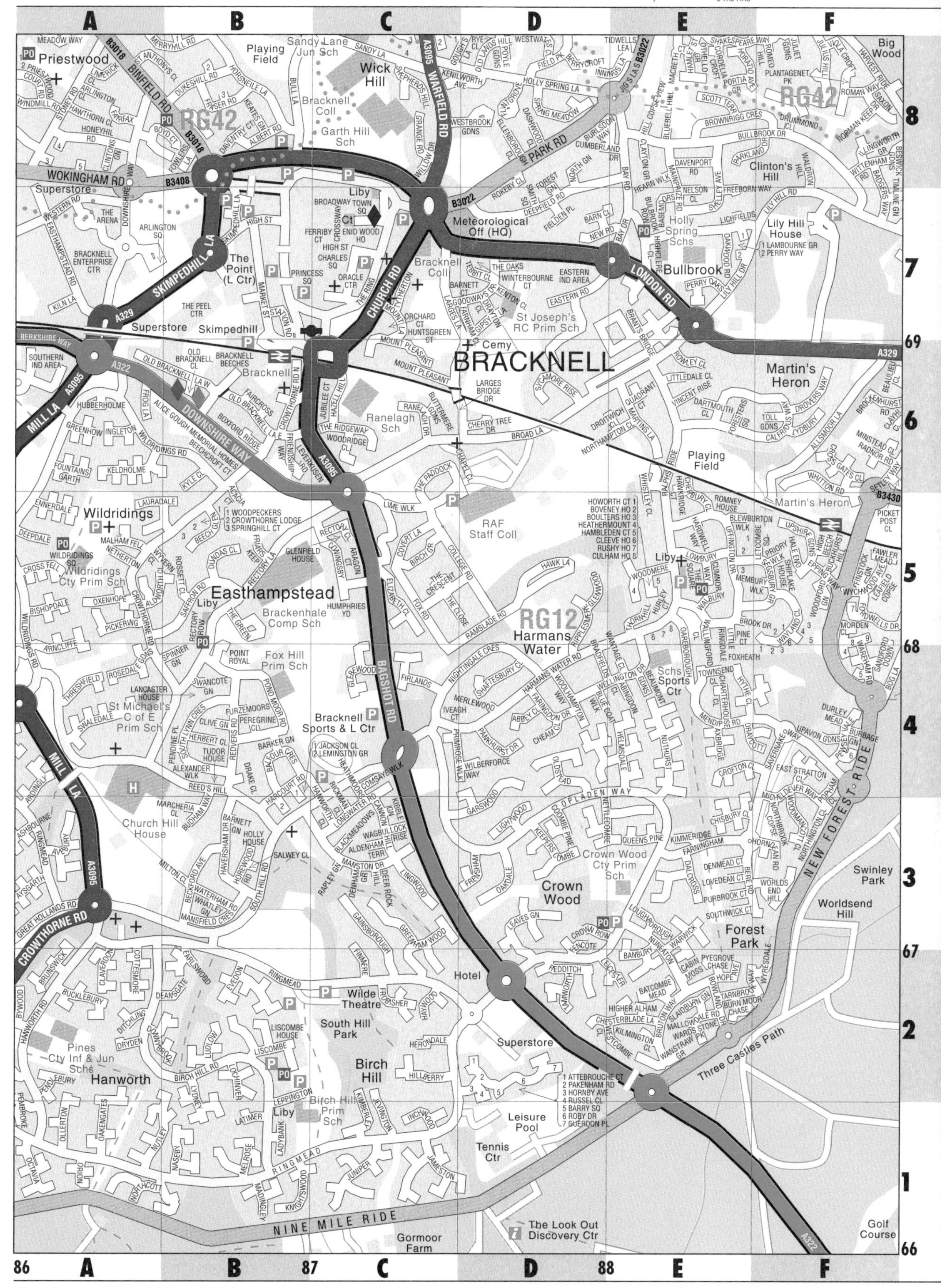

46

28

F4
1 MULBERRY CT
2 ROWAN
3 LINDEN
4 LYTCHET MINSTER CL
5 STOKEFORD CL
6 FROXFIELD DOWN

27
8

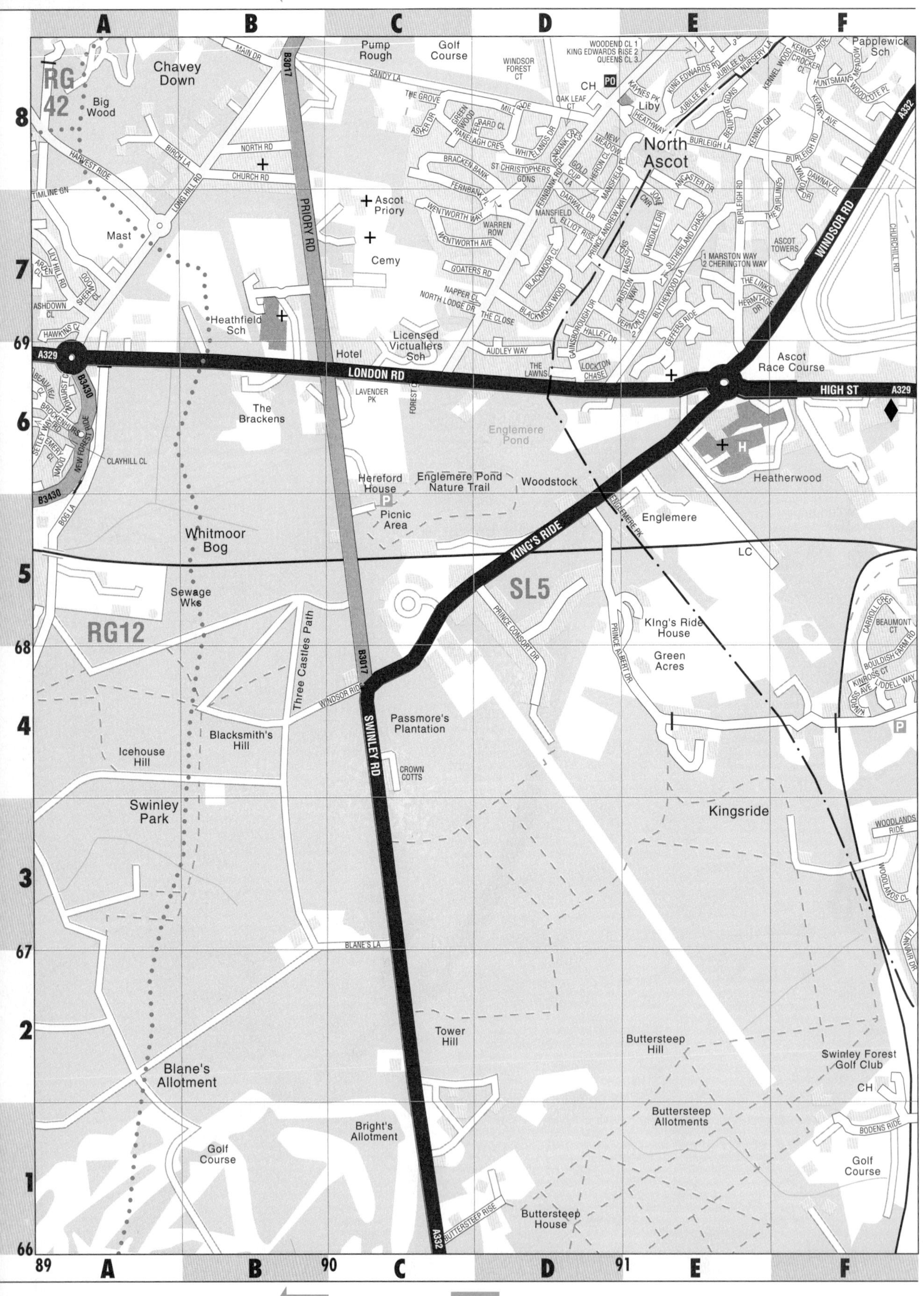
Chavey Down
Big Wood
Pump Rough
Golf Course
North Ascot
Ascot Priory
Cemy
Heathfield Sch
Licensed Victuallers Sch
Hotel
LONDON RD
HIGH ST
Ascot Race Course
The Brackens
Englemere Pond
Heatherwood
Hereford House
Englemere Pond Nature Trail
Woodstock
Picnic Area
Englemere
Whitmoor Bog
KING'S RIDE
SL5
RG12
Sewage Wks
King's Ride House
Green Acres
PRIORY RD
SWINLEY RD
Three Castles Path
Passmore's Plantation
Blacksmith's Hill
Icehouse Hill
Swinley Park
Kingsride
Tower Hill
Buttersteep Hill
Swinley Forest Golf Club
Blane's Allotment
Buttersteep Allotments
Bright's Allotment
Golf Course
Buttersteep House
WINDSOR RD
A329
A332
B3017
B3430

27
47

9
30

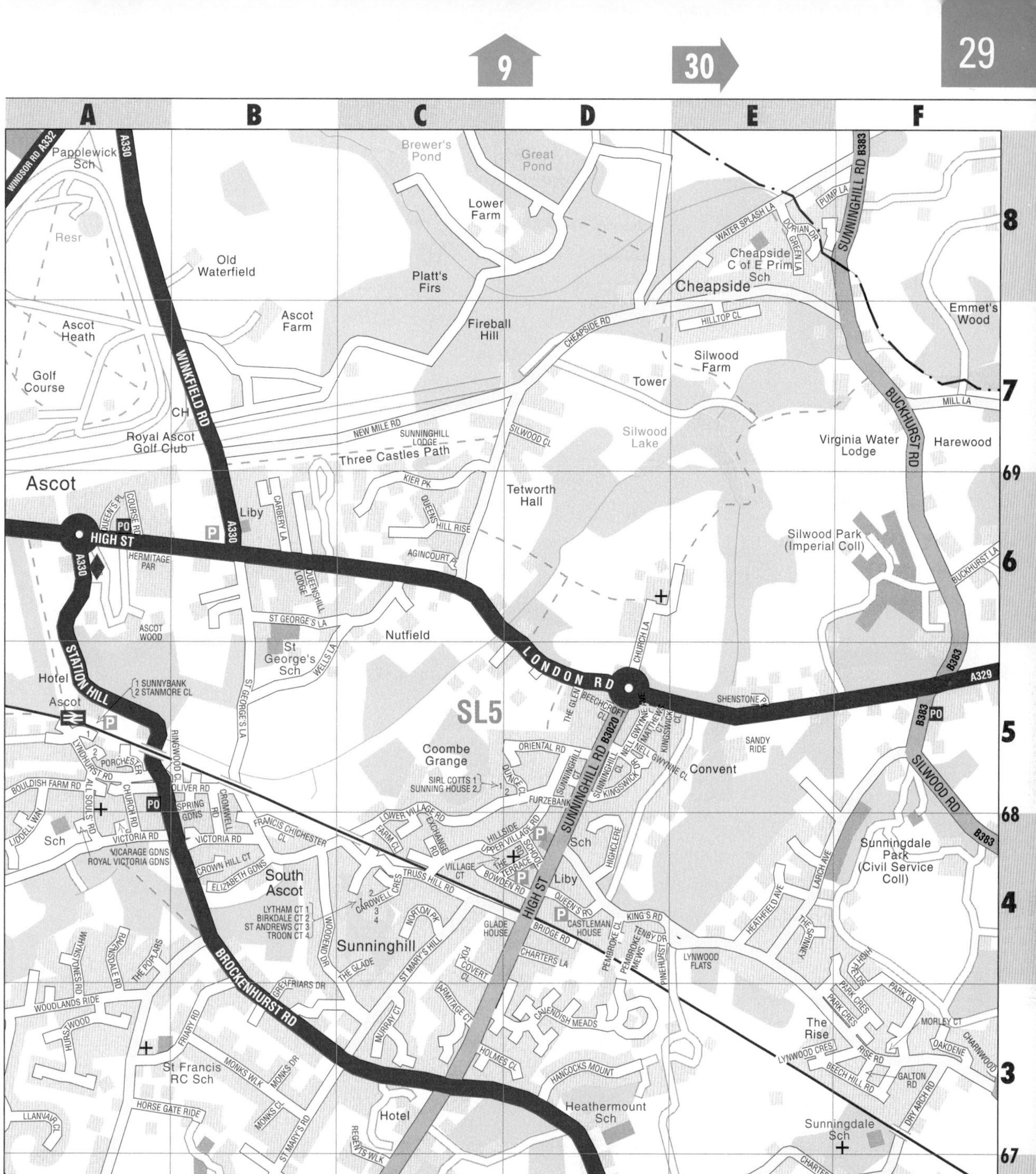
Ascot
Sunninghill
South Ascot
Cheapside
SL5
GU20
Silwood Park (Imperial Coll)
Sunningdale Park (Civil Service Coll)
Royal Ascot Golf Club
Old Windsor Bog
Broadlands
Charters Sch
Heathermount Sch
St Mary's Sch
St Francis RC Sch
Stubbington House Sch
Sunningdale Sch
Hurst Lodge Sch
Coombe Grange
Tetworth Hall
Virginia Water Lodge
Harewood
Emmet's Wood
King's Beeches
The Rise
HIGH ST
LONDON RD
WINKFIELD RD
STATION HILL
BROCKENHURST RD
BAGSHOT RD
DEVENISH RD
BUCKHURST RD
SILWOOD RD
SUNNINGHILL RD
CHEAPSIDE RD
NEW MILE RD
Three Castles Path

48
30

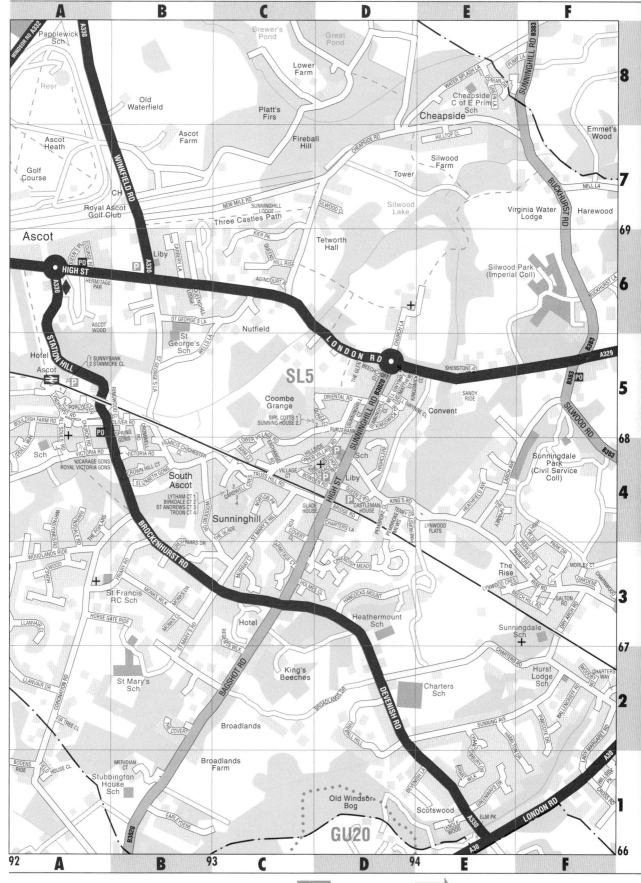

29
10

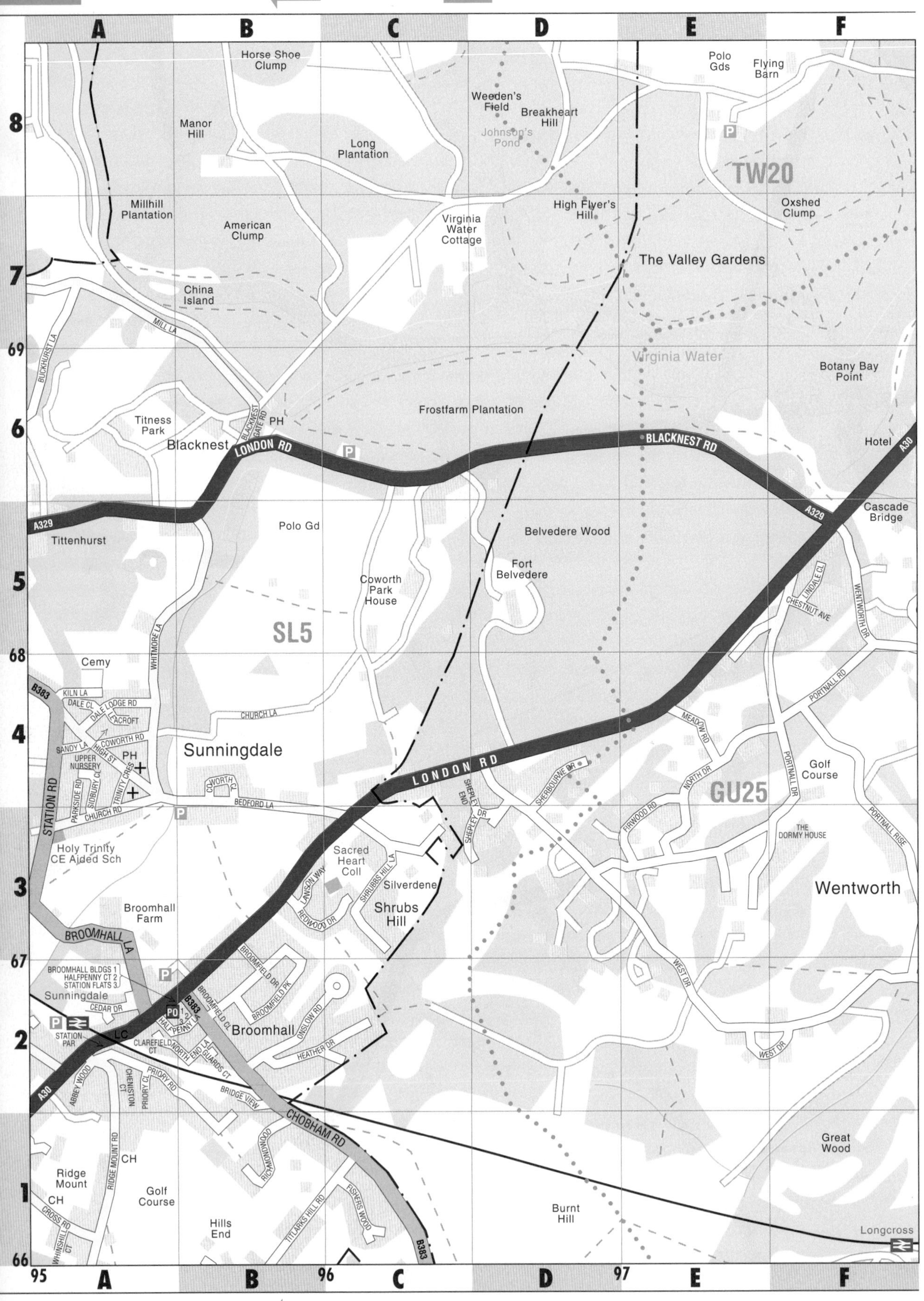
Horse Shoe Clump
Manor Hill
Long Plantation
Weeden's Field
Breakheart Hill
Johnson's Pond
Polo Gds
Flying Barn
TW20
Millhill Plantation
American Clump
Virginia Water Cottage
High Flyer's Hill
Oxshed Clump
The Valley Gardens
China Island
MILL LA
BUCKHURST LA
Virginia Water
Botany Bay Point
Titness Park
BLACKNEST GATE RD
PH
Frostfarm Plantation
Blacknest
LONDON RD
BLACKNEST RD
Hotel
A30
A329
Cascade Bridge
Tittenhurst
Polo Gd
Belvedere Wood
Fort Belvedere
Coworth Park House
SL5
LINDALE CL
CHESTNUT AVE
WENTWORTH DR
Cemy
WHITMORE LA
B383
KILN LA
DALE CL
DALE LODGE RD
LEACROFT
CHURCH LA
MEADOW RD
PORTNALL RD
Sunningdale
SANDY LA
COWORTH RD
HIGH ST
UPPER NURSERY
SIDBURY CL
TRINITY CRES
COWORTH CL
LONDON RD
SHERLEY END
SHERLEY DR
SHERBOURNE DR
NORTH DR
PORTNALL DR
Golf Course
GU25
STATION RD
PARKSIDE RD
CHURCH RD
BEDFORD LA
FIRWOOD RD
THE DORMY HOUSE
PORTNALL RISE
Holy Trinity CE Aided Sch
Sacred Heart Coll
SHRUBS HILL LA
LANSDOWN WAY
Silverdene
Shrubs Hill
Wentworth
Broomhall Farm
REDWOOD DR
BROOMHALL LA
BROOMFIELD DR
BROOMHALL BLDGS 1
HALFPENNY CT 2
STATION FLATS 3
Sunningdale
BROOMFIELD PK
WEST DR
CEDAR DR
ONSLOW RD
STATION PAR
LC
BROOMFIELD CL
Broomhall
HEATHER DR
CLAREFIELD CT
NORTH END LA
GUARDS CT
WEST DR
ABBEY WOOD
CHENISTON CT
PRIORY CL
PRIORY RD
BRIDGE VIEW
CHOBHAM RD
RICHMONDWOOD
Great Wood
RIDGE MOUNT RD
CH
Ridge Mount
CH
Golf Course
CROSS RD
WHINSHILL CT
Hills End
TITLARKS HILL RD
FISHERS WOOD
B383
Burnt Hill
Longcross
A B C D E F
8 7 69 6 5 68 4 3 67 2 1 66
95 96 97

29
49

11
32

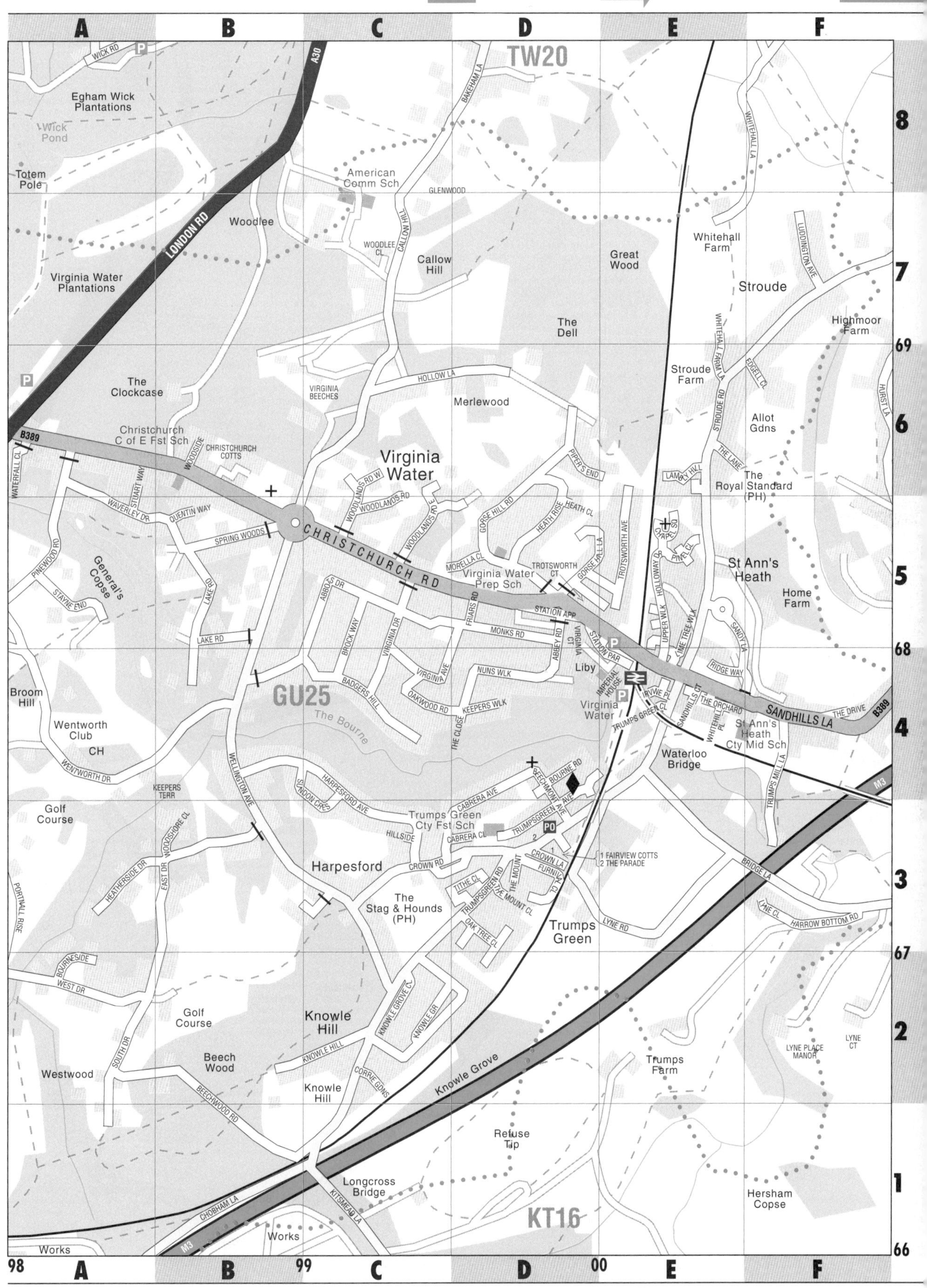
A
B
C
D
E
F
TW20
8
7
69
6
5
68
4
3
67
2
1
66
98
99
00
Egham Wick Plantations
Wick Pond
Totem Pole
Woodlee
LONDON RD
A30
Virginia Water Plantations
American Comm Sch
Callow Hill
Great Wood
The Dell
Whitehall Farm
Stroude
Highmoor Farm
Stroude Farm
Allot Gdns
The Clockcase
Christchurch C of E Fst Sch
CHRISTCHURCH COTTS
Merlewood
Virginia Water
The Royal Standard (PH)
CHRISTCHURCH RD
St Ann's Heath
Home Farm
General's Copse
Virginia Water Prep Sch
Broom Hill
Wentworth Club
CH
GU25
The Bourne
Liby
Virginia Water
Waterloo Bridge
St Ann's Heath Cty Mid Sch
SANDHILLS LA
B389
Golf Course
Trumps Green Cty Fst Sch
Harpesford
The Stag & Hounds (PH)
Trumps Green
1 FAIRVIEW COTTS
2 THE PARADE
Golf Course
Knowle Hill
Beech Wood
Westwood
Knowle Hill
Knowle Grove
Trumps Farm
LYNE PLACE MANOR
LYNE CT
Refuse Tip
Longcross Bridge
KT16
Hersham Copse
Works
Works
M3

50
32

31
12

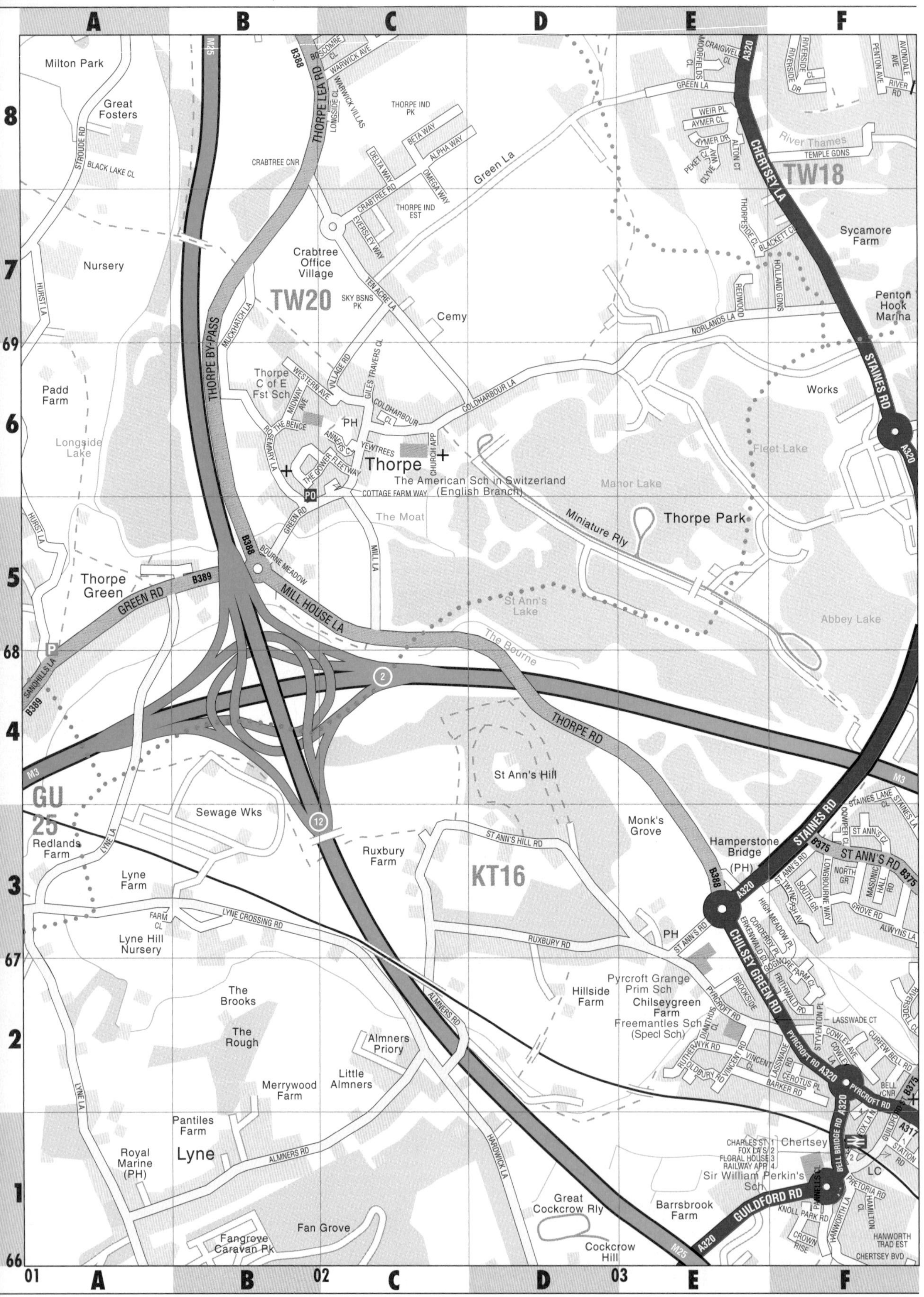
A
B
C
D
E
F
Milton Park
Great Fosters
Nursery
Padd Farm
Longside Lake
Thorpe Green
TW20
Crabtree Office Village
Thorpe
The American Sch in Switzerland (English Branch)
The Moat
Cemy
Thorpe Park
Manor Lake
Miniature Rly
St Ann's Lake
The Bourne
Abbey Lake
Fleet Lake
Works
Penton Hook Marina
Sycamore Farm
TW18
River Thames
St Ann's Hill
Sewage Wks
Redlands Farm
Lyne Farm
Lyne Hill Nursery
Ruxbury Farm
KT16
Monk's Grove
Hamperstone Bridge (PH)
The Brooks
The Rough
Merrywood Farm
Almners Priory
Little Almners
Pantiles Farm
Royal Marine (PH)
Lyne
Fan Grove
Fangrove Caravan Pk
Great Cockcrow Rly
Cockcrow Hill
Barrsbrook Farm
Hillside Farm
Pyrcroft Grange Prim Sch
Chilseygreen Farm
Freemantles Sch (Specl Sch)
Chertsey
Sir William Perkin's Sch
GU 25
THORPE BY-PASS
THORPE LEA RD
GREEN RD
MILL HOUSE LA
THORPE RD
CHERTSEY LA
STAINES RD
CHILSEY GREEN RD
GUILDFORD RD
ST ANN'S RD
Green La
CHARLES ST 1
FOX LA S 2
FLORAL HOUSE 3
RAILWAY APP 4
01
02
03
66
67
68
69
1
2
3
4
5
6
7
8

31
51

A B C D E F

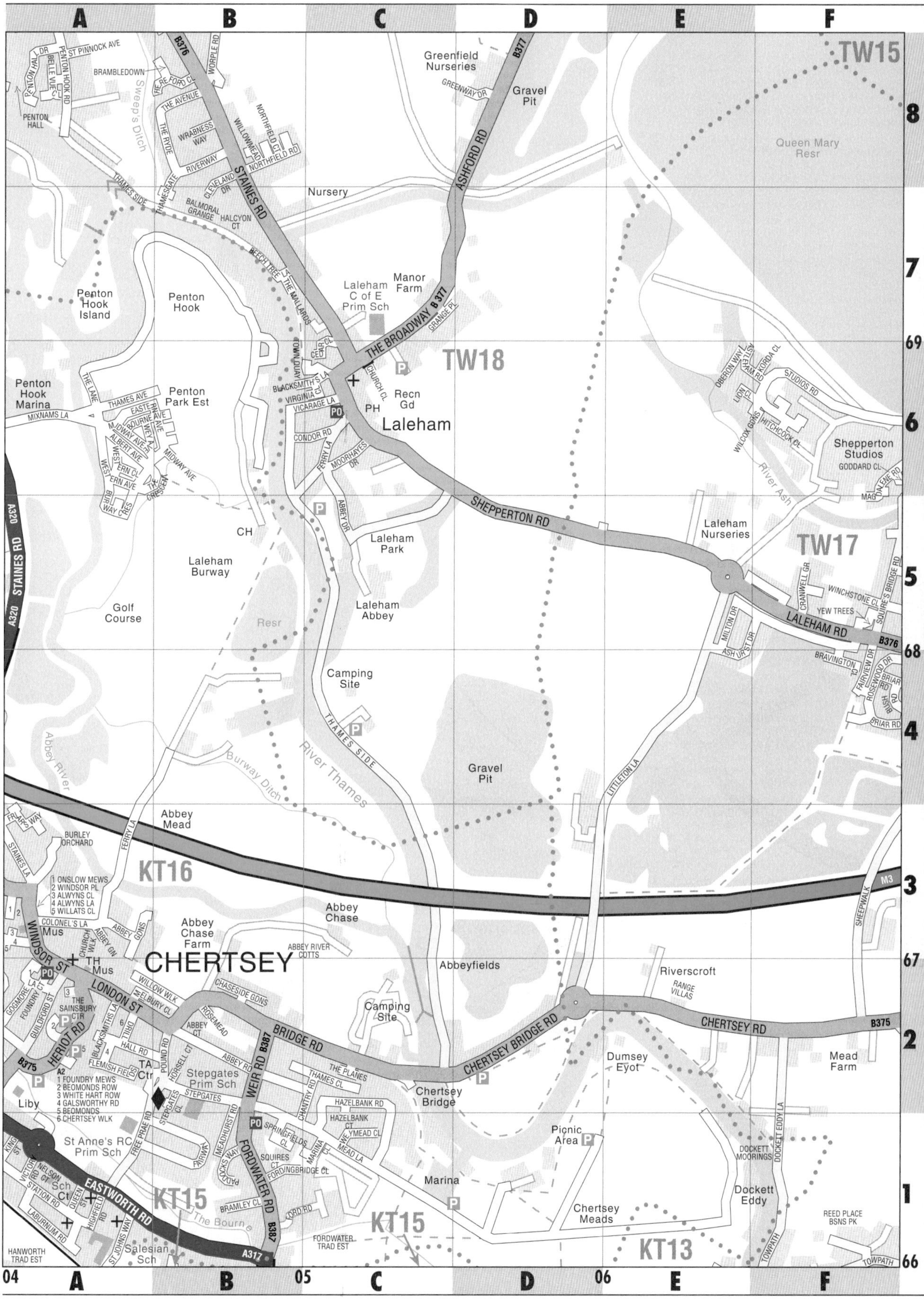

TW15
8
Greenfield Nurseries
Gravel Pit
Queen Mary Resr
ST PINNOCK AVE
BRAMBLEDOWN
PENTON HALL
Sweep's Ditch
THE AVENUE
WRABNESS WAY
THE RYDE
RIVERWAY
THAMESGATE
CLEVELAND DR
NORTHFIELD RD
WILLOWMEAD
STAINES RD
ASHFORD RD
B376
B377
GREENWAY DR
Nursery
THAMES SIDE
BALMORAL GRANGE
HALCYON CT
BEECH TREE
THE MALLARDS
7
Penton Hook Island
Penton Hook
Laleham C of E Prim Sch
Manor Farm
THE BROADWAY B377
GRANGE PL
69
TW18
Penton Hook Marina
THE LANE
THAMES AVE
Penton Park Est
MIXNAMS LA
BLACKSMITHS LA
VIRGINIA CL
VICARAGE LA
CHURCH CL
PO
PH
Recn Gd
Laleham
6
CONDOR RD
FERRY LA
MOORHAYES DR
MIDWAY AVE
ALBERT AVE
ABBEY DR
SHEPPERTON RD
CH
Laleham Park
Laleham Burway
Golf Course
Resr
Laleham Abbey
A320 STAINES RD
5
OBERON WAY
KORDA CL
STUDIOS RD
LION CL
WILCOX GDNS
HITCHCOCK CL
Shepperton Studios
GODDARD CL
River Ash
Laleham Nurseries
TW17
CRANWELL GR
WINCHSTONE CL
SQUIRE'S BRIDGE RD
YEW TREES
LALEHAM RD
B376
MILTON DR
ASHURST DR
BRAVINGTON CL
FAIRVIEW DR
ROSEWOOD DR
BRIAR RD
68
Camping Site
THAMES SIDE
4
Abbey River
Burway Ditch
River Thames
Gravel Pit
LITTLETON LA
Abbey Mead
FERRY LA
BURLEY ORCHARD
STAINES LA
KT16
1 ONSLOW MEWS
2 WINDSOR PL
3 ALWYNS CL
4 ALWYNS LA
5 WILLATS CL
3
M3
SHEEPWALK
COLONEL'S LA
Mus
Abbey Chase
Abbey Chase Farm
ABBEY RIVER COTTS
WINDSOR ST
TH Mus
CHERTSEY
Abbeyfields
Riverscroft
RANGE VILLAS
67
LONDON ST
WILLOW WLK
CHASESIDE GDNS
THE SAINSBURY CTR
GUILDFORD ST
Camping Site
HERIOT RD
BRIDGE RD
CHERTSEY BRIDGE RD
CHERTSEY RD
B375
2
WEIR RD B387
Dumsey Eyot
Mead Farm
A2
1 FOUNDRY MEWS
2 BEOMONDS ROW
3 WHITE HART ROW
4 GALSWORTHY RD
5 BEOMONDS
6 CHERTSEY WLK
TA Ctr
Stepgates Prim Sch
STEPGATES
THE PLANES
Chertsey Bridge
HAZELBANK RD
Liby
St Anne's RC Prim Sch
Picnic Area
DOCKETT MOORINGS
DOCKETT EDDY LA
FORDWATER RD
Marina
Dockett Eddy
1
EASTWORTH RD
KT15
Sch
Ct
The Bourne
Chertsey Meads
REED PLACE BSNS PK
KT15
KT13
HANWORTH TRAD EST
Salesian Sch
A317
FORDWATER TRAD EST
TOWPATH
66

04 A B 05 C D 06 E F

33
14

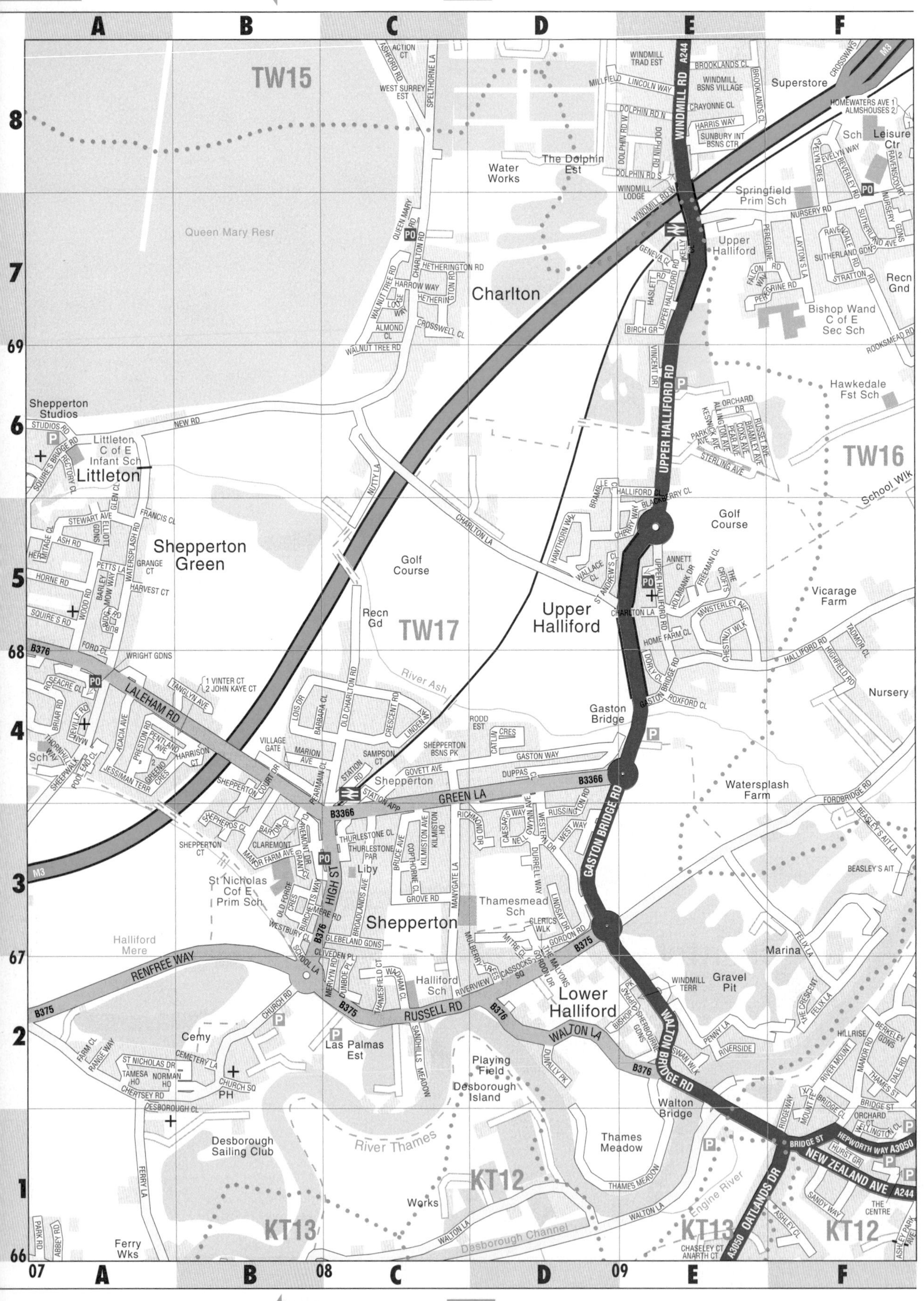
A
B
C
D
E
F
8
7
69
6
5
68
4
3
67
2
1
66
07
08
09
TW15
TW16
TW17
KT12
KT13
Queen Mary Resr
Superstore
Windmill Trad Est
Brooklands Cl
Windmill Bsns Village
Crayonne Cl
Harris Way
Sunbury Int Bsns Ctr
Lincoln Way
Millfield
Dolphin Rd N
Dolphin Rd W
Dolphin Rd S
Dolphin Rd
Windmill Rd
A244
Windmill Lodge
Windmill Rd W
The Dolphin Est
Water Works
Action Ct
Ashford Rd
West Surrey Est
Spelthorne La
Queen Mary Ave
Charlton Rd
Hetherington Rd
Harrow Way
Lodge Way
Walnut Tree Rd
Almond Cl
Crosswell Cl
Charlton
Crossways
M3
Homewaters Ave 1 Almshouses 2
Sch
Leisure Ctr
Evelyn Cres
Evelyn Way
Beverley Rd
Ravenscourt
Springfield Prim Sch
Nursery Rd
Nursery Gdns
Sutherland Ave
Sutherland Gdns
Ravensdale Rd
Upper Halliford
Peregrine Rd
Falcon Way
Layton's La
Stratton Rd
Recn Gnd
Bishop Wand C of E Sec Sch
Rooksmead Rd
Geneva Cl
Haslett Rd
Kelly Cl
Upper Halliford Rd
Birch Gr
Vincent Dr
Hawkedale Fst Sch
Orchard Dr
Allington Ave
Keswick Ave
Park Ave
Bramley Ave
Coxs Ave
Pear Ave
Russet Ave
Sterling Ave
School Wlk
Shepperton Studios
Studios Rd
Squire's Bridge Rd
Rectory Cl
New Rd
Littleton C of E Infant Sch
Littleton
Nutty La
Charlton La
Bramble Cl
Halliford Cl
Blackberry Cl
Cherry Way
Hawthorn Way
Wallace Cl
St Andrew's Cl
Golf Course
Annett Cl
Freeman Cl
The Crofts
Holmbank Dr
Stewart Ave
Ash Rd
Elliott Gdns
Glen Cl
Francis Cl
Hermitage Cl
Horne Rd
Waterssplash Rd
Grange Ct
Harvest Ct
Shepperton Green
Petts La
Barley Mow Way
Bugle Rd
Squire's Rd
Wood Rd
Ford Cl
Recn Gd
Upper Halliford
Charlton La
Westerley Cl
Chestnut Wlk
Home Farm Cl
Dorly Cl
Gaston Bridge Rd
Roxford Cl
Halliford Rd
Highfield Rd
Tadmor Cl
Vicarage Farm
Nursery
B376
Laleham Rd
Wright Gdns
1 Vinter Ct
2 John Kaye Ct
Tanglyn Ave
Seacre Cl
Briar Rd
Mandeville Rd
Thornhill Way
Sheepwalk
Poole End Cl
Acacia Ave
Preston Rd
Pentland Ave
Greenock Cres
Harrison Ct
Jessiman Terr
Village Gate
Marion Ave
Lois Dr
Barbara Cl
Old Charlton Rd
Crescent Rd
Linden Way
River Ash
Rodd Est
Catlin Cres
Gaston Bridge
Shepperton Bsns Pk
Sampson Ct
Gaston Way
Govett Ave
Duppas Cl
Station Rd
Shepperton
B3366
Station App
Green La
Shepperton Court Dr
Pearmain Cl
Watersplash Farm
Fordbridge Rd
Beasley's Ait La
Beasley's Ait
Shepherds Cl
Barton Cl
Claremont
Manor Farm Ave
Grant Cl
Claremont Dr
Shepperton Ct
High St
Thurlestone Cl
Thurlestone Par
Liby
Bruce Ave
Copthorne Cl
Kilmiston Ave
Kilmiston Ho
Richmond Dr
Caesar's Way
Nell
Manygate La
Western Dr
Durrell Way
Russington Rd
West Way
St Nicholas C of E Prim Sch
Old Forge Cres
Burchetts Way
Broadlands Ave
Grove Rd
Thamesmead Sch
Lindsay Dr
Clerics Wlk
Gordon Rd
Westbury Cl
Elmer Rd
Glebeland Gdns
Mulberry Cl
Mitre Cl
Halliford Mere
Renfree Way
School La
Cliveden Pl
Mervyn Rd
Dunboe Pl
Thamesfield Ct
Wyndham Cl
Halliford Sch
Riverview
Cassocks Sq
The Malyons
Gordon Rd
B375
Lower Halliford
Windmill Terr
Gravel Pit
Marina
Felix La
The Crescent
Felix La
Church Rd
Russell Rd
Bishop's Gr
Sherbourne Gdns
Walton Bridge Rd
Penny La
Riverside
Hillrise
Berkeley Gdns
Manor Rd
River Mount
Dale Rd
Thames St
Cemy
Farm Cl
Range Way
St Nicholas Dr
Tamesa Ho
Norman Ho
Cemetery La
Church Sq
Chertsey Rd
PH
Las Palmas Est
Sandhills Meadow
Walton La
Dunally Pk
Swan Wlk
Playing Field
Desborough Island
Walton Bridge
Ridgeway
Mount Pl
Bridge Cl
Bridge St
Orchard Ct
Wellington Cl
Hepworth Way A3050
New Zealand Ave
A244
Hurst Gr
Desborough Cl
Ferry La
Desborough Sailing Club
River Thames
Thames Meadow
Engine River
Sandy Way
The Centre
Ashley Park Ave
Works
Oatlands Dr
A3050
Ashley Cl
Park Rd
Abbey Rd
Ferry Wks
Desborough Channel
Chaseley Ct
Anarth Ct
PO
P

33
53

15
36

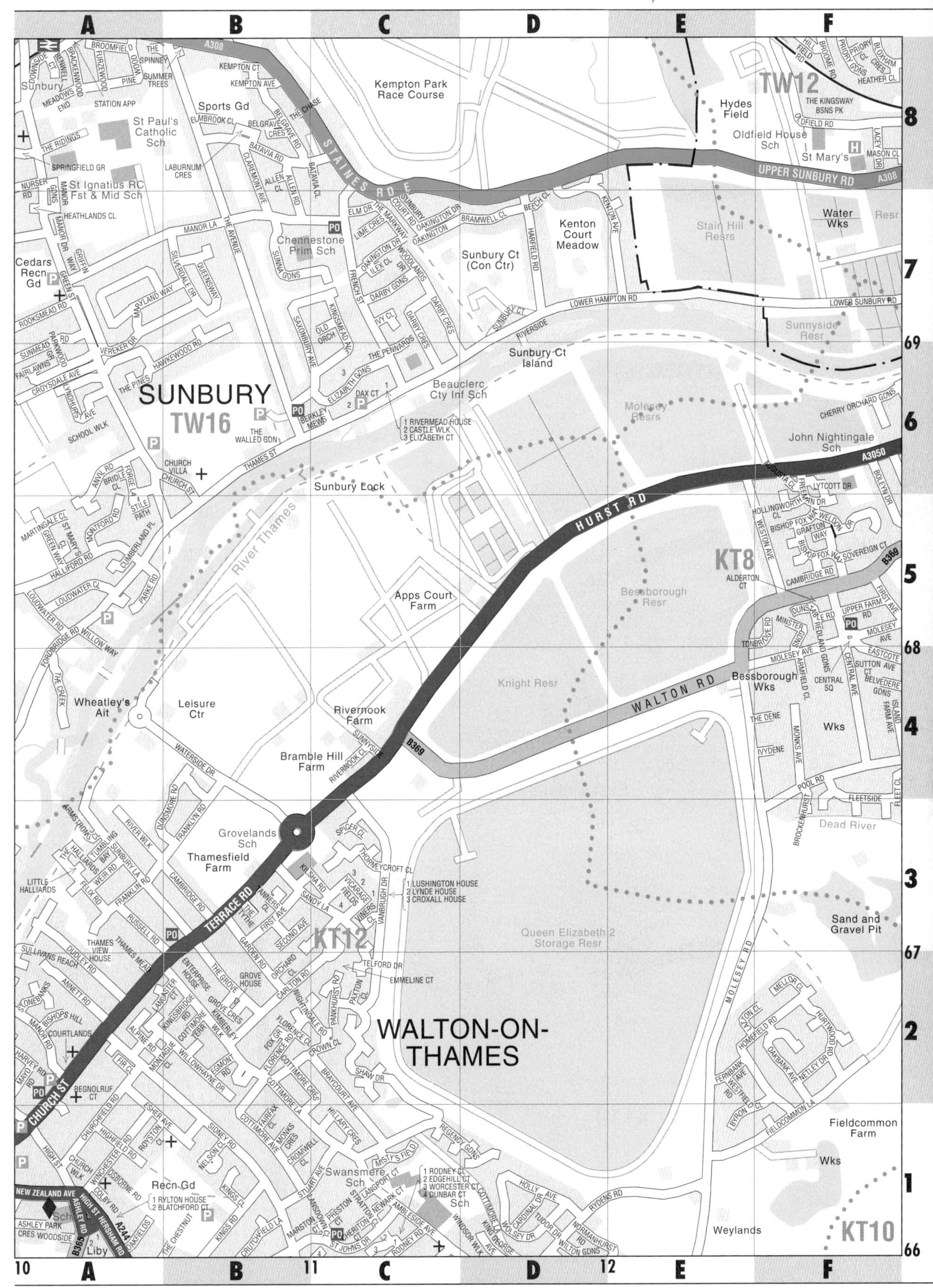
A
B
C
D
E
F
SUNBURY
TW16
TW12
KT8
KT12
KT10
WALTON-ON-
THAMES
Kempton Park
Race Course
Sports Gd
St Paul's
Catholic
Sch
St Ignatius RC
Fst & Mid Sch
Hydes
Field
Oldfield House
Sch
St Mary's
UPPER SUNBURY RD
STAINES RD E
Stain Hill
Resrs
Water
Wks
Resr
Kenton
Court
Meadow
Sunbury Ct
(Con Ctr)
Chennestone
Prim Sch
Cedars
Recn
Gd
Sunnyside
Resr
LOWER HAMPTON RD
LOWER SUNBURY RD
Sunbury Ct
Island
Beauclerc
Cty Inf Sch
Molesey
Resrs
John Nightingale
Sch
Sunbury Lock
River Thames
HURST RD
Apps Court
Farm
Bessborough
Resr
Knight Resr
WALTON RD
Bessborough
Wks
Wks
Wheatley's
Ait
Leisure
Ctr
Rivernook
Farm
Bramble Hill
Farm
Grovelands
Sch
Thamesfield
Farm
TERRACE RD
Dead River
Sand and
Gravel Pit
Queen Elizabeth 2
Storage Resr
MOLESEY RD
Fieldcommon
Farm
Wks
Weylands
Swansmere
Sch
Recn Gd
CHURCH ST
Liby
1 LUSHINGTON HOUSE
2 LYNDE HOUSE
3 CROXALL HOUSE
1 RIVERMEAD HOUSE
2 CASTLE WLK
3 ELIZABETH CT
1 RODNEY CL
2 EDGEHILL CT
3 WORCESTER CT
4 DUNBAR CT
1 RYLTON HOUSE
2 BLATCHFORD CT
8
7
69
6
5
68
4
3
67
2
1
66
10
11
12

54
36

A8
1 BLOXHAM CRES
2 SHERBOURNE CT
3 SOMERSET CT
4 TUDOR RD
5 JUBILEE HOUSE
6 RUSHBURY CT
7 HEMMING CL
8 RYEDALE CT
9 NORMAN CT

35
16

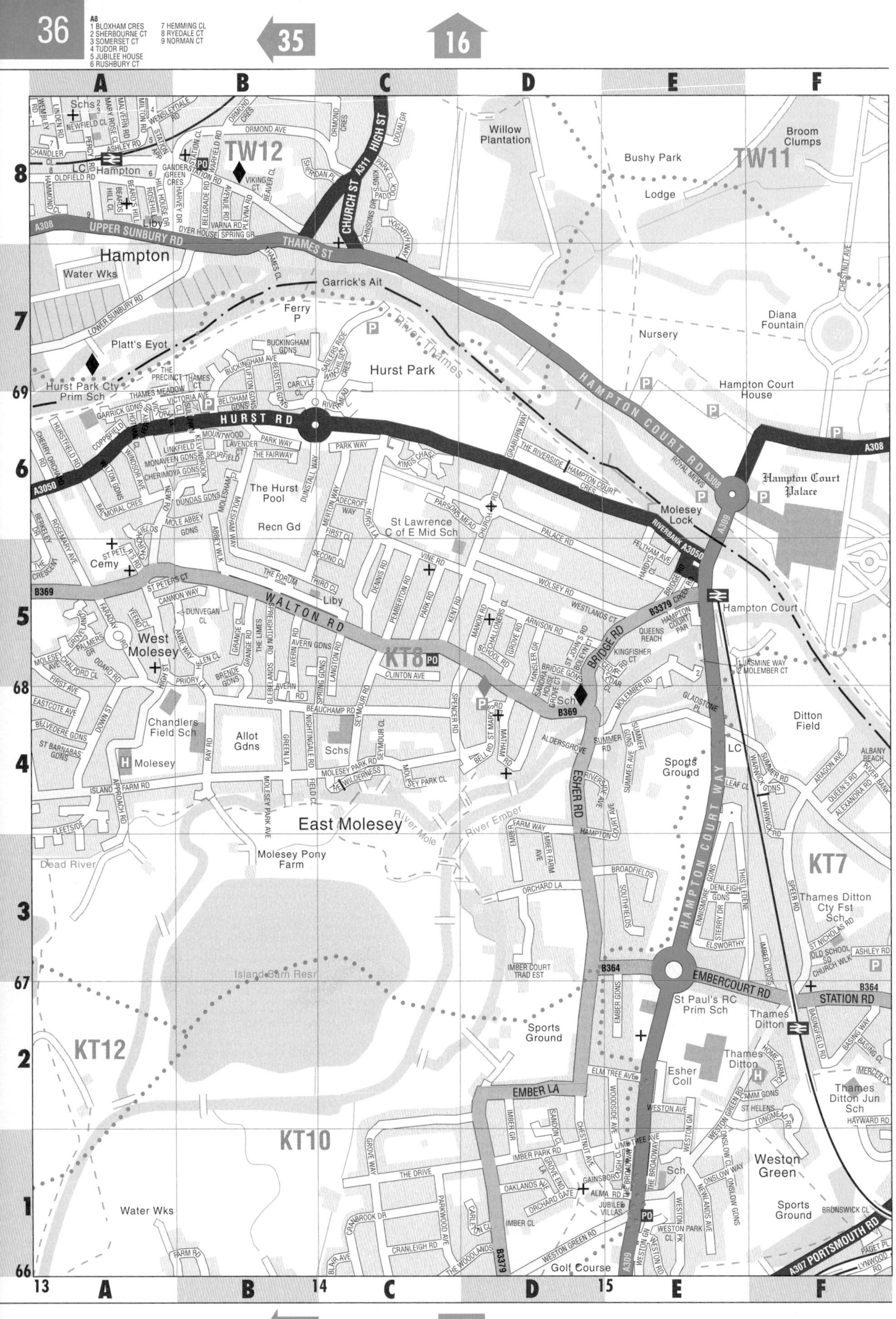

E5
1 MARQUIS CT
2 GARRICK HOUSE

E6
1 COLLEGE RDBT
2 EDINBURGH CT
3 WESTON CT
4 GREBE TERR
5 HERON CT
6 AGAR HOUSE
7 ST JAMES' CT
8 GROVE CT
9 SPRINGFIELD CT
10 COLLEGE WLK

E7
1 CLEAVE'S ALMSHOUSES
2 THE PARADE
3 DROVERS CT
4 GOUGH HOUSE
5 EDEN WLK
6 ALDERMAN JUDGE MALL
7 LADY BOOTH RD
8 CAVERSHAM HOUSE
9 LITTLEFIELD CL
10 THE BENTALL SH CT
11 ADAMS WL
12 THE KINGFISHER SPORTS CTR

17

E8
1 REGENTS PL
2 WALTER ST
3 CANBURY BSNS PK
4 SIGRIST SQ
5 ASHWAY CTR
6 WARWICK HOUSE

38

F7
1 VICARAGE HOUSE
2 RAYLEIGH CT
3 SCHOOL PAS
4 CHIPPENHAM
5 CAMM GDNS

F8
1 ONSLOW HOUSE
2 DOWLER CT

KINGSTON UPON THAMES

SURBITON

A2
1 RALEIGH HOUSE
2 LEICESTER HOUSE
3 GRESHAM HOUSE

D2
1 NAPIER CT
2 DARLINGTON HOUSE
3 CHARMINSTER CT
4 MULBERRY CT
5 LEANDER CT
6 CLINTON HOUSE
7 HOLLINGWORTH CT
8 GLOUCESTER CT
9 PALMERSTON CT
10 REDWOOD CT
11 HURSLEY CT
12 WESTMORLAND CT
13 LAWSON CT
14 ALEXANDER CT
15 WINTON CT
16 SYDENHAM HOUSE
17 CAROLINE CT
18 ELLSWOOD CT
19 MASEFIELD CT

E1
1 ASH TREE CL
2 THE SHRUBBERY
3 MALVERN CT
4 GATE HOUSE

E3
1 STATION APP
2 SOUTH BANK LODGE
3 BRAMSHOTT CT
4 PANDORA CT
5 WELLINGTON CT
6 GLENBUCK CT
7 LEIGHTON HOUSE
8 OAKHILL CT
9 DOWNS VIEW LODGE
10 OSBORNE CT

56

E4
1 EFFINGHAM LODGE
2 MAPLE HOUSE
3 CHANNON CT
4 FALCONHURST
5 FERNDOWN
6 VICEROY LODGE
7 FRENSHAM HOUSE
8 KINGSLEY HOUSE
9 RANNOCH CT

38

10 STRATTON CT
11 MORAY HOUSE
12 DULVERTON CT
13 WESTERHAM
14 HILL CT
15 ASSHETON-BENNETT HOUSE
16 HATFIELD HOUSE
17 OXFORD CT
18 PENNINGTON LODGE
19 AUSTIN HOUSE
20 WENTWORTH CT
21 THE PRIORY
22 THE SHERATON

F3
1 PERCY CT
2 HOLMWOOD
3 MIDDLE GREEN CL

F4
1 WOODLEIGH
2 HIGHCROFT
3 CAERNARVON CT
4 REGENCY CT

A8
1 THE FARTHINGS
2 BRAE CT
3 PRINCETON MEWS
4 STATION APP

A7
1 WIMPOLE CL
2 CONNINGTON
3 GRANTCHESTER
4 FULBOURN
5 CAMBRIDGE GROVE RD

37

A7
6 OAKINGTON
7 GRAVELEY
8 IMPINGTON
9 SHELFORD
10 DUXFORD

18

E5
1 KINGSTON LODGE
2 FAIRHOLME
3 MARSHALL HOUSE
4 NORTON HOUSE
5 MARTIN HOUSE

E4
1 MERRYWEATHER CT
2 ROEBUCK CT
3 SABLE CT

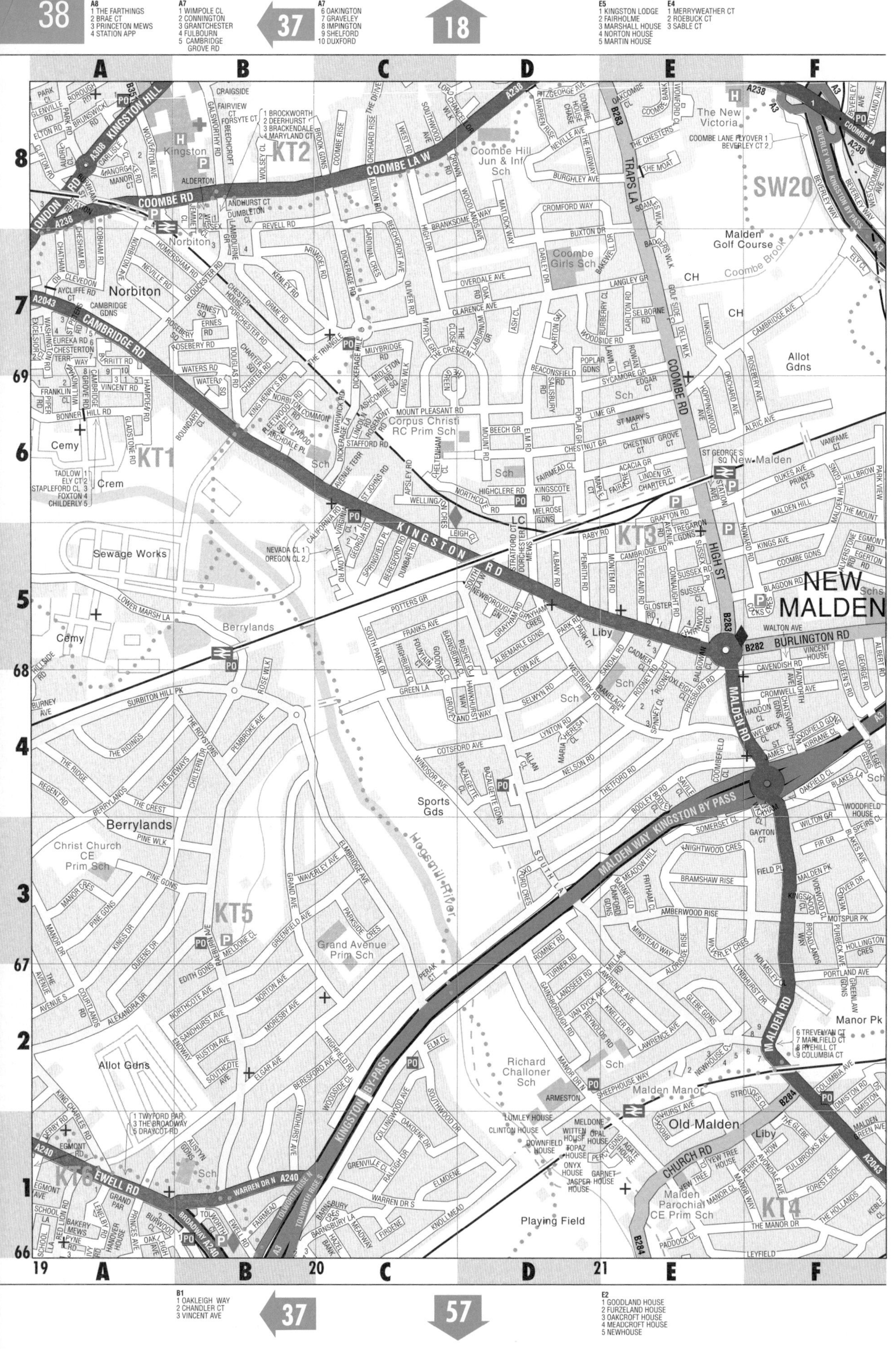

B1
1 OAKLEIGH WAY
2 CHANDLER CT
3 VINCENT AVE

37

57

E2
1 GOODLAND HOUSE
2 FURZELAND HOUSE
3 OAKCROFT HOUSE
4 MEADCROFT HOUSE
5 NEWHOUSE

19
40

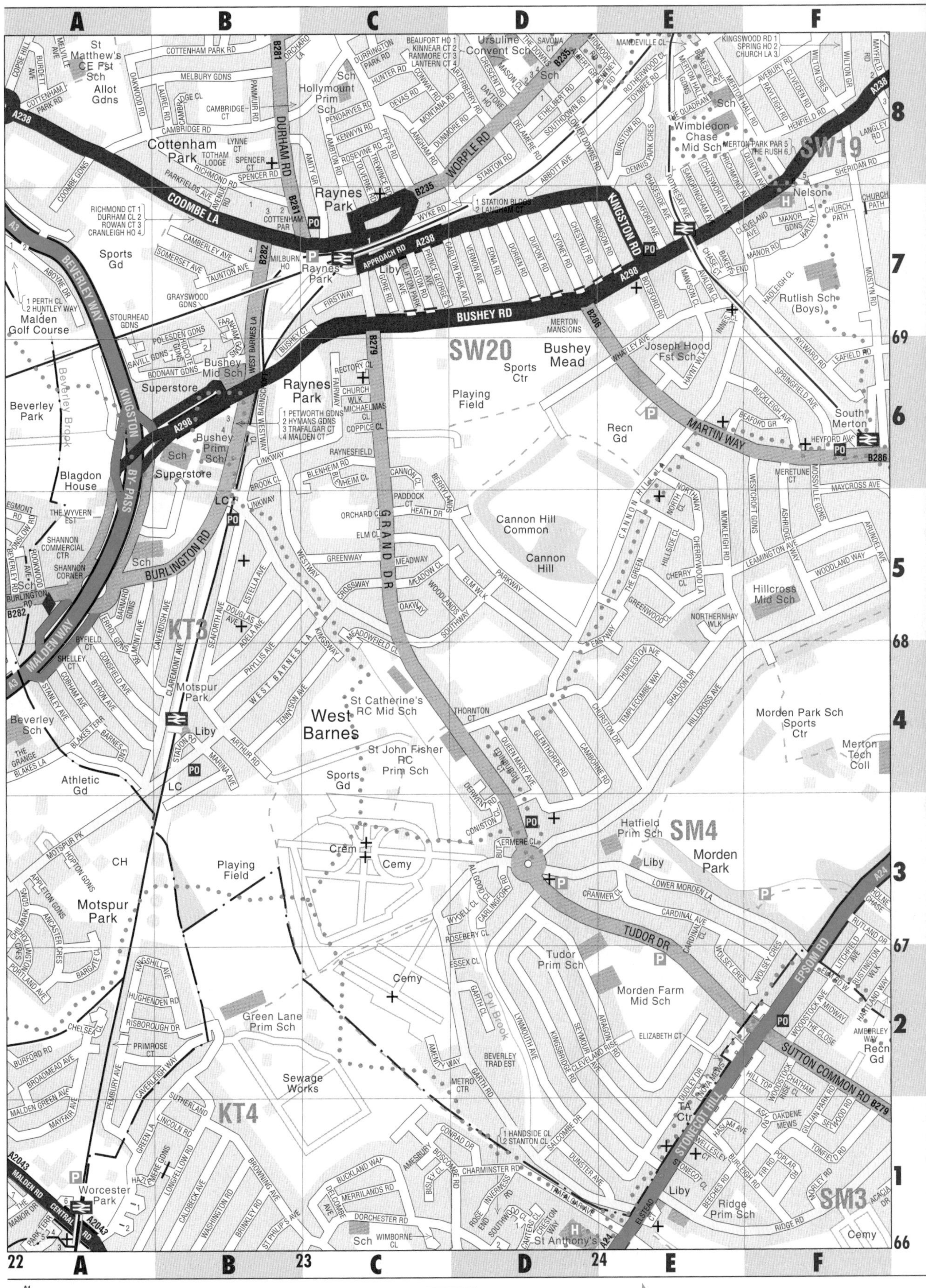

A1
1 BROOKSIDE CRES
2 BEVERLEY GDNS
3 PURDEY CT
4 THE AVENUE
5 BRIARWOOD CT
6 STATION APP
7 DOWNFIELD

58
40

A
B
C
D
E
F
8
7
69
6
5
68
4
3
67
2
1
66
25
26
27
MERTON
Merton Park
SW19
Morden Hall Park
Morden Hall
Morden
Merton Abbey Prim Sch
Harland Fst Sch
Haslemere Fst Sch
Liberty Mid Sch
Bond Fst Sch
Benedict Fst & Prim Schs
Phipps Bridge
Belgrave Wlk
Cricket Green Sch
Melrose Sch
MITCHAM
The Canons L Ctr
SS Peter & Paul's RC Prim Sch
Ravensbury Park
River Wandle
CR4
Mitcham
Wilson
Cranmer Mid Sch
Morden Park Sch Sports Ctr
Morden South
St Ann's Sch
Abbotsbury Fst Sch
Merton Tech Coll
Phoenix Coll
Playing Fields
SM4
MORDEN
Recn Gd
Moreton Green Fst Sch
Watermeads & Garth High Schs
Poulter Park
Haig Homes
St Helier
Malmesbury Schs
Green Wrythe Prim Sch
Glastonbury Prim Sch
Tweeddale Schs
Wandle Valley Sch
Glenthorne High Sch
Rosehill
SM3
SM1
SM5
Allot Gdns
MERANTUM WAY
MORDEN RD
MORDEN HALL RD
CENTRAL RD
ST HELIER AVE
BISHOPSFORD RD
WESTERN RD
LONDON RD
MARTIN WAY
CROWN LA
DORSET RD
GREEN LA
REIGATE AVE
ROSE HILL
WRYTHE LA
SUTTON COMMON RD
CRICKET GN
MADEIRA RD
CRANMER RD
Tramway

21
42

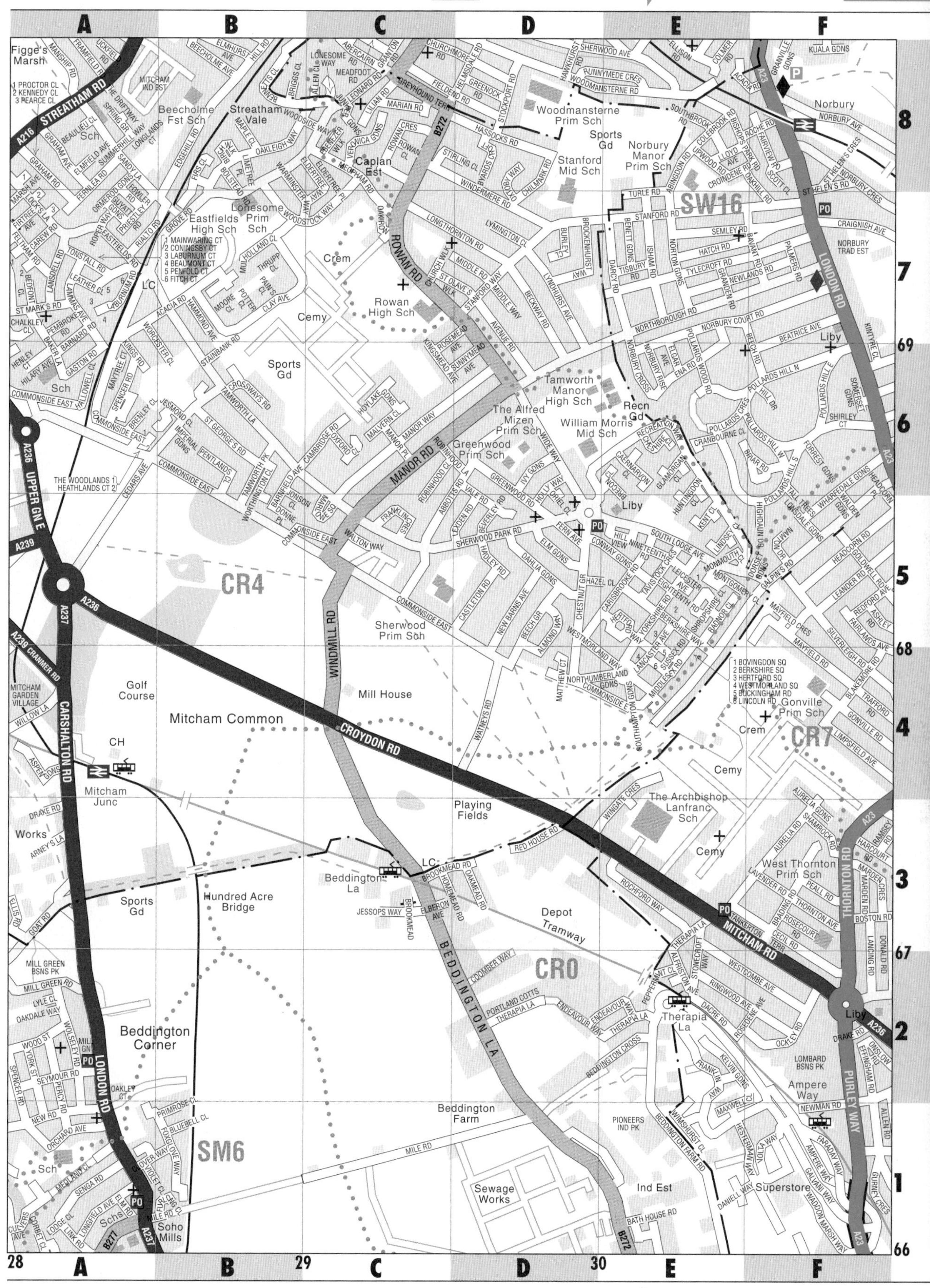
A
B
C
D
E
F
8
7
69
6
5
68
4
3
67
2
1
66
28
29
30
Figge's Marsh
STREATHAM RD
A216
Mitcham Ind Est
Beecholme Fst Sch
Streatham Vale
Sch
Caplan Est
Woodmansterne Prim Sch
Sports Gd
Norbury Manor Prim Sch
Stanford Mid Sch
Norbury
SW16
LONDON RD
Norbury Trad Est
Eastfields High Sch
Lonesome Prim Sch
Crem
Rowan High Sch
Cemy
LC
ROWAN RD
B272
Sports Gd
Tamworth Manor High Sch
The Alfred Mizen Prim Sch
William Morris Mid Sch
Recn Gd
Greenwood Prim Sch
Liby
PO
MANOR RD
UPPER GN E
A236
A239
A237
CR4
WINDMILL RD
Sherwood Prim Sch
Golf Course
Mill House
Mitcham Common
CROYDON RD
CH
Mitcham Junc
Playing Fields
Gonville Prim Sch
Crem
CR7
Cemy
The Archbishop Lanfranc Sch
Cemy
West Thornton Prim Sch
THORNTON RD
A23
Works
Beddington La
Hundred Acre Bridge
Sports Gd
Depot
Tramway
MITCHAM RD
CR0
CARSHALTON RD
BEDDINGTON LA
Therapia La
Beddington Corner
LONDON RD
Lombard Bsns Pk
Ampere Way
PURLEY WAY
Beddington Farm
Pioneers Ind Pk
SM6
MILE RD
Sewage Works
Ind Est
Superstore
Sch
Schs
Soho Mills
B277
Mill Green Bsns Pk

60
42

41
22

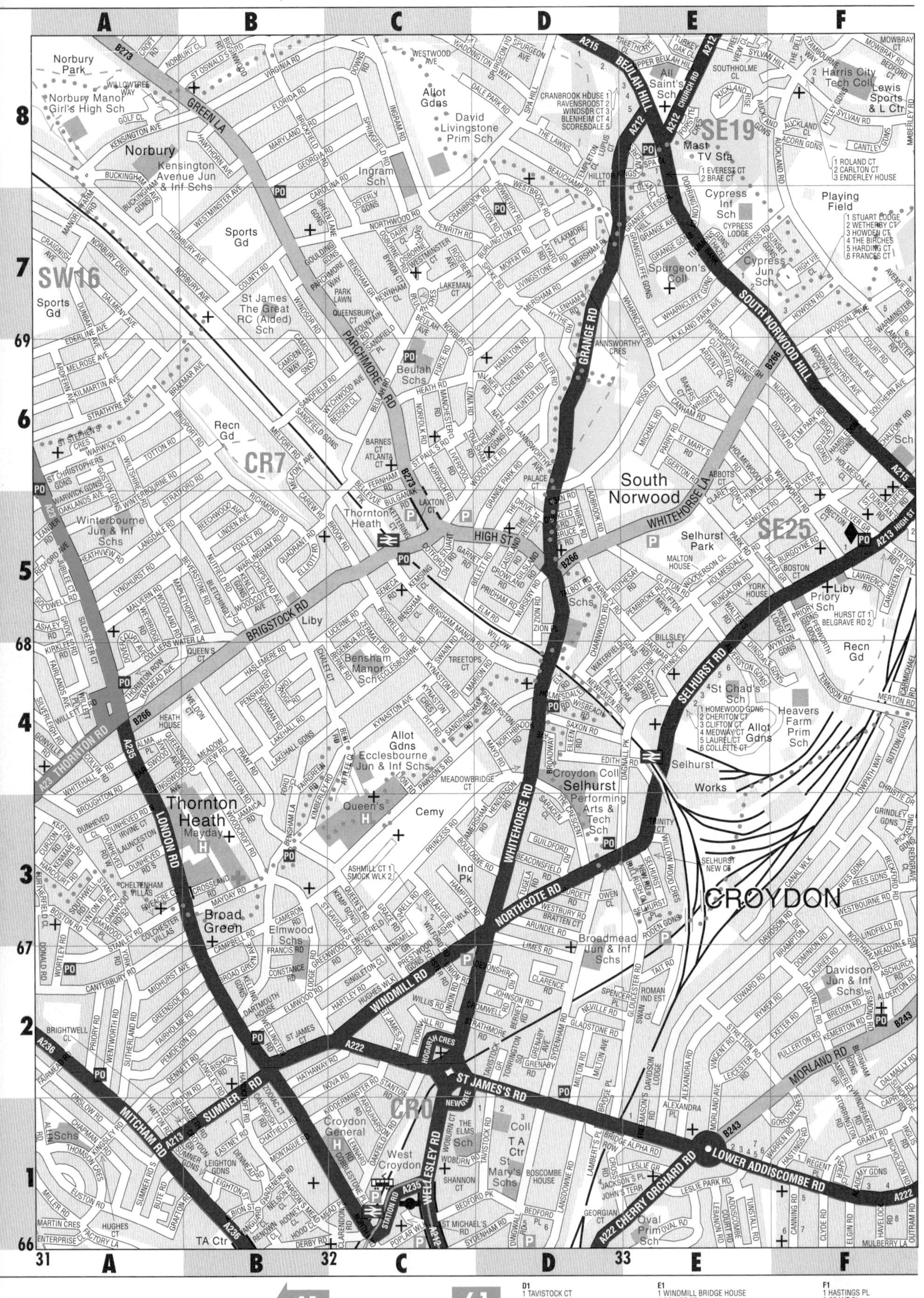

D1
1 TAVISTOCK CT
2 CHARTWELL CL
3 SPEAKER'S CT
4 CUMBERLAND CT
5 VICEROY CT
6 ORIEL CT

E1
1 WINDMILL BRIDGE HOUSE
2 SQUIRE CT
3 HOUSTON CT
4 ST JAMES'S LODGE
5 KENDAL HOUSE
6 WARREN CT
7 KENDAL CT

F1
1 HASTINGS PL
2 GRANT PL
3 CLIVE HOUSE
4 HAVELOCK HOUSE
5 BELLMORE CT
6 HEREFORD CT
7 CHEQUERS CT
8 HAVELOCK HALL

41
61

A B C D E F

8 7 69 6 5 68 4 3 67 2 1 66

A1
1 FARLEYCROFT
2 EDGECUMBE CT
3 WESSON HOUSE
4 SULLIVAN CT
5 KENLEY HOUSE
6 CHRISTOPHER CT
7 JAYSON CT

34 A B 35 C D 36 E F

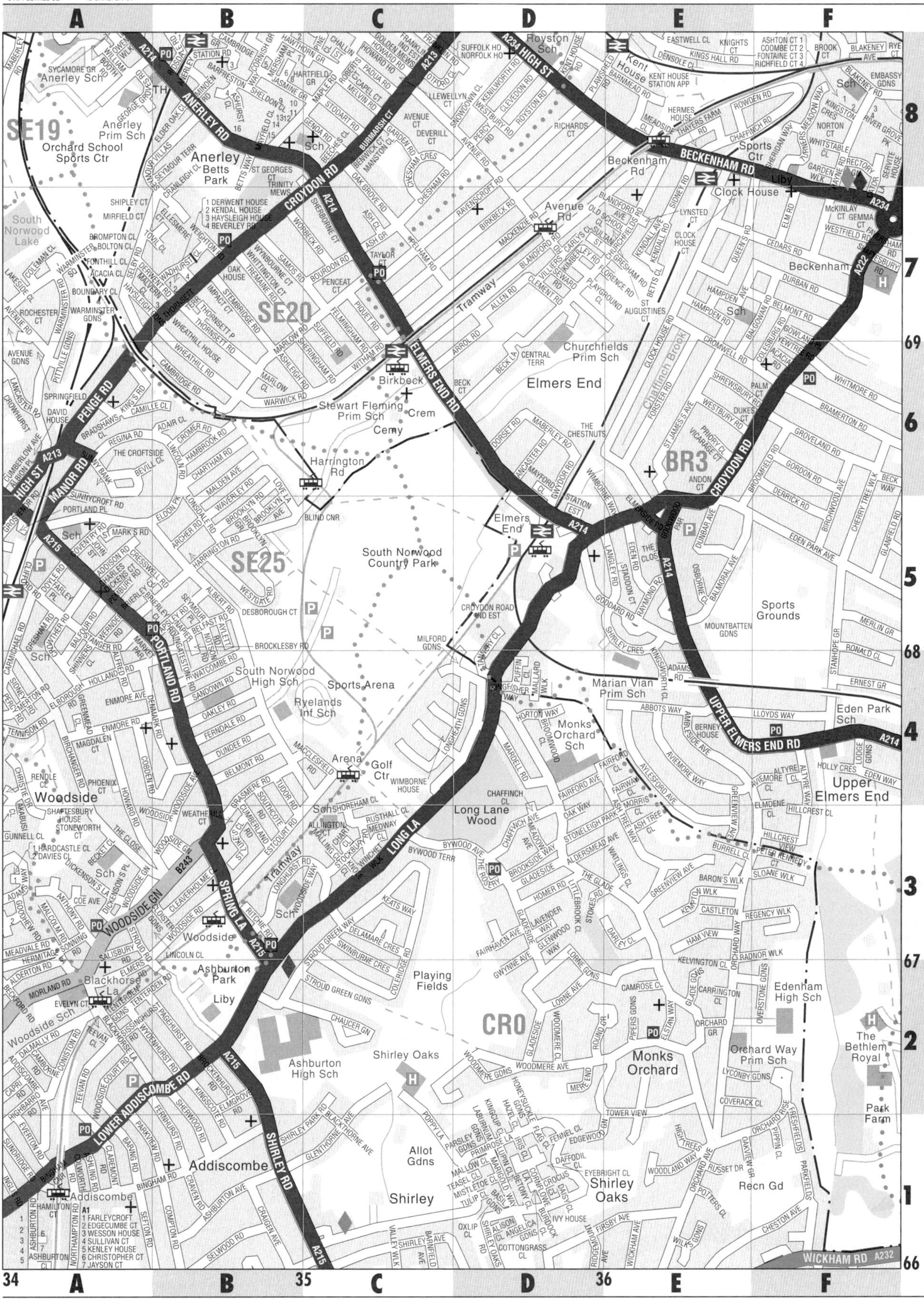

62 44

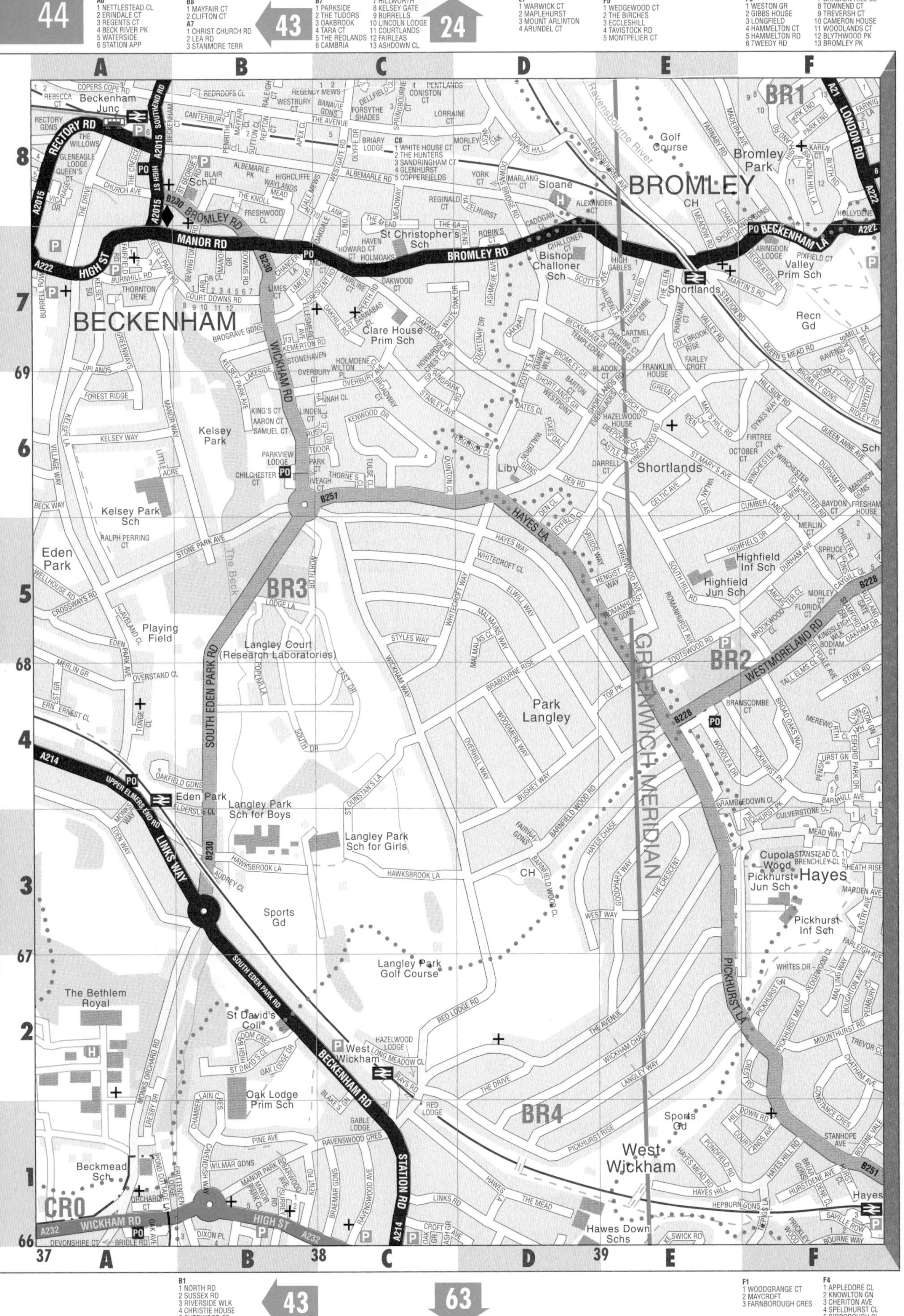
A8
1 NETTLESTEAD CL
2 ERINDALE CT
3 REGENTS CT
4 BECK RIVER PK
5 WATERSIDE
6 STATION APP
B8
1 MAYFAIR CT
2 CLIFTON CT
A7
1 CHRIST CHURCH RD
2 LEA RD
3 STANMORE TERR
43
B7
1 PARKSIDE
2 THE TUDORS
3 OAKBROOK
4 TARA CT
5 THE REDLANDS
6 CAMBRIA
7 HILLWORTH
8 KELSEY GATE
9 BURRELLS
10 LINCOLN LODGE
11 COURTLANDS
12 FAIRLEAS
13 ASHDOWN CL
24
E7
1 WARWICK CT
2 MAPLEHURST
3 MOUNT ARLINTON
4 ARUNDEL CT
F5
1 WEDGEWOOD CT
2 THE BIRCHES
3 ECCLESHILL
4 TAVISTOCK RD
5 MONTPELIER CT
F8
1 WESTON GR
2 GIBBS HOUSE
3 LONGFIELD
4 HAMMELTON CT
5 HAMMELTON RD
6 TWEEDY RD
7 BRACKEN HILL CL
8 TOWNEND CT
9 TREVERSH CT
10 CAMERON HOUSE
11 WOODLANDS CT
12 BLYTHWOOD PK
13 BROMLEY PK
A
B
C
D
E
F
8
7
69
6
5
68
4
3
67
2
1
66
37
38
39
BECKENHAM
BROMLEY
BR1
BR2
BR3
BR4
CR0
Beckenham Junc
Shortlands
Eden Park
West Wickham
Hayes
Park Langley
Kelsey Park
Kelsey Park Sch
Langley Court (Research Laboratories)
Langley Park Sch for Boys
Langley Park Sch for Girls
Langley Park Golf Course
The Bethlem Royal
St David's Coll
Oak Lodge Prim Sch
Beckmead Sch
Hawes Down Schs
Highfield Inf Sch
Highfield Jun Sch
Pickhurst Jun Sch
Pickhurst Inf Sch
Cupola Wood
Bishop Challoner Sch
St Christopher's Sch
Clare House Prim Sch
Valley Prim Sch
Bromley Park
Golf Course
Ravensbourne River
Recn Gd
Sports Gd
Playing Field
GREENWICH MERIDIAN
RECTORY RD
HIGH ST
MANOR RD
BROMLEY RD
BECKENHAM LA
LONDON RD
WICKHAM RD
SOUTH EDEN PARK RD
HAYES LA
WESTMORELAND RD
PICKHURST LA
LINKS WAY
BECKENHAM RD
STATION RD
UPPER ELMERS END RD
WICKHAM RD
A21
A222
A2015
A214
A232
B230
B251
B228
B1
1 NORTH RD
2 SUSSEX RD
3 RIVERSIDE WLK
4 CHRISTIE HOUSE
5 SHERWOOD CT
43
63
F1
1 WOODGRANGE CT
2 MAYCROFT
3 FARNBOROUGH CRES
F4
1 APPLEDORE CL
2 KNOWLTON GN
3 CHERITON AVE
4 SPELDHURST CL
5 BIDBOROUGH CL
6 PENSHURST WLK

A B C D E F

RG40
B3430
NINE MILE RIDE
Pine Wood
HONEY HILL
B3430
PALMER CL
POLYANTHUS WAY
LUPIN RIDE
ST MICHAELS COTTS
TELFORD AVE
BRUNEL DR
LANCHESTER DR
Clay Hill
A3095
Hut Hill
RG12
8

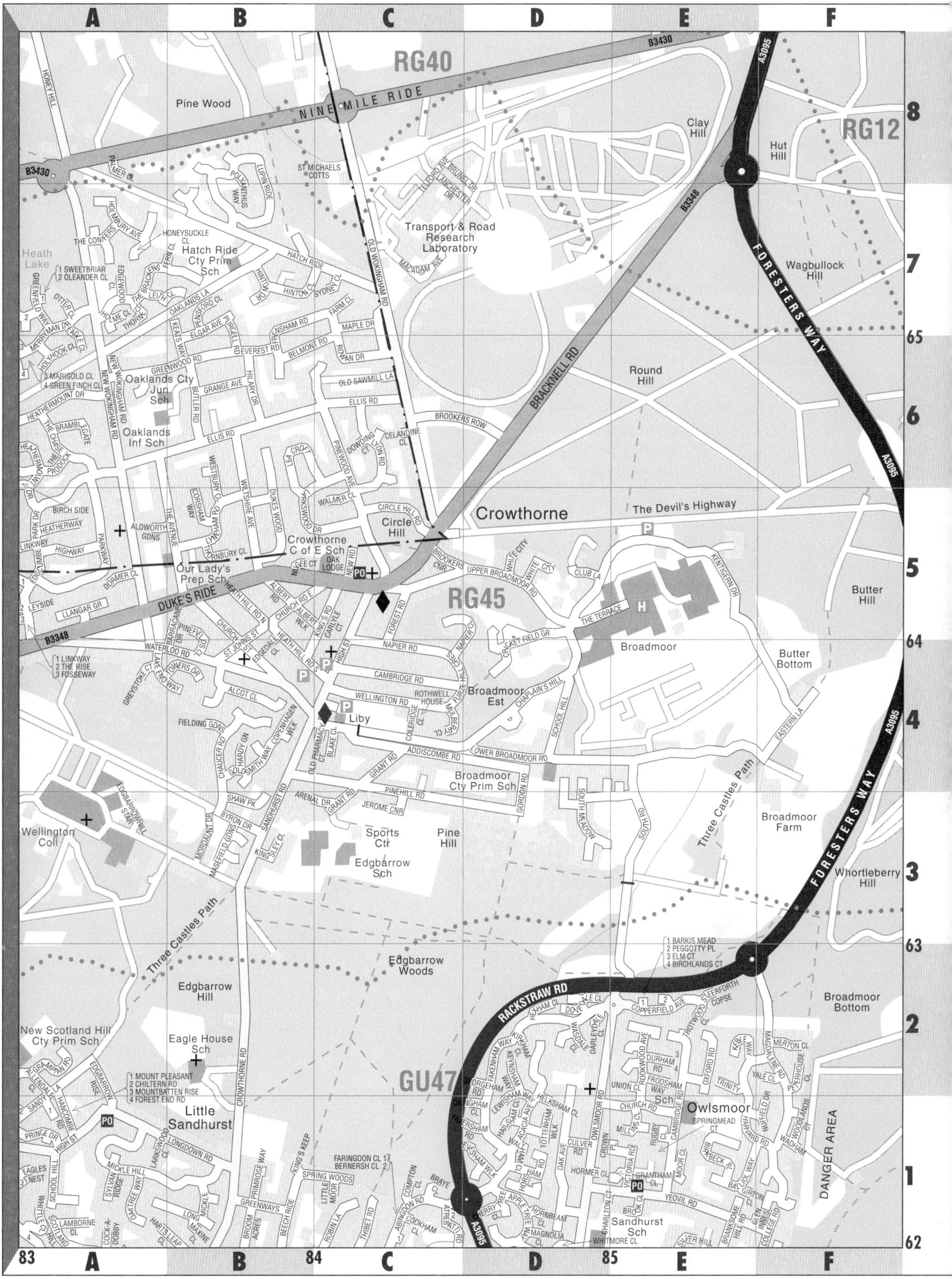

Heath Lake
THE CONIFERS
HOLMBURY AVE
HONEYSUCKLE CL
Hatch Ride Cty Prim Sch
HATCH RIDE
1 SWEETBRIAR
2 OLEANDER CL
EDGEWOOD CL
THE BRACKENS
FERN CL
LEITH CL
HINTON DR
HINTON CL
SYDNEY CL
OLD WOKINGHAM RD
Transport & Road Research Laboratory
MACADAM AVE
B3348
FORESTERS WAY
Wagbullock Hill
7

GREENFIELD WAY
OTTER CL
MERRYMAN DR
EAGLE CL
HOLYHOOK CL
OAKLANDS LA
KEATS WAY
PENSFORD CL
ELGAR AVE
PURCELL RD
FRENSHAM RD
FARM CL
MAPLE DR
BELMONT RD
ROWAN DR
EVEREST RD
GREENWOOD RD
3 MARIGOLD CL
4 GREEN FINCH CL
NEW WOKINGHAM RD
Oaklands Cty Jun Sch
GRANGE AVE
HILARY DR
OLD SAWMILL LA
BRACKNELL RD
Round Hill
65

HEATHERMOUNT DR
THE CHASE
BRAMBLEGATE
THE PADDOCK
Oaklands Inf Sch
BUTLER RD
ELLIS RD
ELLIS RD
BROOKERS ROW
DOWDING CT
LYON RD
CELANDINE CL
PINEWOOD AVE
LEA CROFT
WESTBURY CL
WILTSHIRE AVE
DUKES WOOD
CORSHAM WAY
LATHAM RD
6

BIRCH SIDE
HEATHERWAY
PARKWAY
LINKWAY
HIGHWAY
ALDWORTH GDNS
THE AVENUE
THORNBURY CL
WALMER CL
CIRCLE HILL RD
Circle Hill
Crowthorne
The Devil's Highway
Crowthorne C of E Sch
OAK LODGE
NEW RD
Our Lady's Prep Sch
DORMER CL
BROOKERS CNR
UPPER BROADMOOR RD
WHITE CITY
CLUB LA
KENTIGERN DR
Butter Hill
5

LEYSIDE
LLANGAR GR
DUKE'S RIDE
B3348
HEATH HILL RD N
ALBERT RD
CHURCH RD E
ALBERT WLK
KING'S RD
CARLYLE CT
FOREST RD
RG45
THE TERRACE
Broadmoor
CRICKET FIELD GR
NAPIER CL
NAPIER RD
Butter Bottom
64

1 LINKWAY
2 THE RISE
3 FOSSEWAY
WATERLOO RD
BARRACANE DR
PINEFIELDS
CHURCH ST
ST JOHNS ST
EDGEDALE CL
HEATH HILL RD S
HIGH ST
CAMBRIDGE RD
WELLINGTON RD
ROTHWELL HOUSE
FURZE HILL CRES
Broadmoor Est
CHAPLAIN'S HILL
GREYSTOKE CT
LAKE END WAY
TOWERS DR
ALCOT CL
FIELDING GDNS
COPENHAGEN WLK
Liby
BLAKE CL
COLERIDGE CL
MULBERRY CL
SCHOOL HILL
EASTERN LA
4

CHAUCER RD
HARDY GN
GOLDSMITH WAY
OLD PHARMACY CT
GRANT RD
ADDISCOMBE RD
LOWER BROADMOOR RD
Broadmoor Cty Prim Sch
GORDON RD
EDGBARROW RISE
SHAW PK
SANDHURST RD
ARENAL DR
GRANT RD
PINEHILL RD
JEROME CNR
SOUTH MEADOW
SOUTH RD
Three Castles Path
Broadmoor Farm
Wellington Coll
BYRON DR
MORDAUNT DR
MASEFIELD GDNS
KINGSLEY CL
Sports Ctr
Pine Hill
Edgbarrow Sch
Whortleberry Hill
3

Three Castles Path
Edgbarrow Woods
1 BARKIS MEAD
2 PEGGOTTY PL
3 ELM CT
4 BIRCHLANDS CT
63

Edgbarrow Hill
RACKSTRAW RD
COPPERFIELD AVE
SEEFORTH COPSE
Broadmoor Bottom
New Scotland Hill Cty Prim Sch
Eagle House Sch
TROTWOOD CL
MERTON CL
2

GRAMPIAN RD
EDGBARROW RISE
1 MOUNT PLEASANT
2 CHILTERN RD
3 MOUNTBATTEN RISE
4 FOREST END RD
CROWTHORNE RD
GU47
GEORGEHAM RD
FAKENHAM WAY
KIRKHAM CL
KEYNSHAM WAY
DARLEYDALE CL
WASDALE CL
ROOKWOOD AVE
DURHAM RD
OXFORD RD
TRINITY
YALE CL
PEVERHOUSE CL
Little Sandhurst
PO
HANCOMBE RD
SANDY LA
PRINCE DR
HIGH ST
LONGDOWN RD
LARKSWOOD CL
OKINGHAM CL
LEWISHAM WAY
HELKSHAM CL
UNION CL
FRODSHAM WAY
Sch
Owlsmoor
SPRINGMEAD CT
HARVARD RD
WOODLANDS CL
DANGER AREA
FAVERSHAM RD
HAILSHAM CL
ACACIA AVE
TOTTENHAM WLK
OWLSMOOR RD
CHURCH RD
MILLINS CL
RUGBY CL
CAMBRIDGE RD
WADHAM
EAGLES NEST
SCHOOL HILL
SYLVAN RIDGE
MICKLE HILL
OAKTREE WAY
PRIMROSE WAY
KING'S KEEP
FARINGDON CL 1
BERNERSH CL 2
SPRING WOODS
COMPTON CL
BRAYE CL
EVESHAM WLK
HORSHAM RD
OAK AVE
CULVER RD
CROWN PL
HORMER CL
VICTORIA RD
GRANTHAM CL
MOOR CL
GIRTON CL
1

LAMBORNE CL
SCOTLAND HILL
COCK-A-DOBBY
HARTS LEAP CL
LONG MAXINE CL
GREENWAYS
BROOM ACRES
BEECH RIDE
LITTLE MOOR
ROBIN LA
THIBET RD
ABINGDON RD
COOKHAM CL
ATREBATTI RD
A3095
CHERRY TREE CL
APPLE TREE WAY
HORNBEAM CL
MAGNOLIA CL
CHARLTON CT
YEOVIL RD
Sandhurst Sch
WHITMORE CL
SILVER HILL
BRANKSOME HILL RD
GLEN INNES
COLLEGE RD
62

83 A B 84 C D 85 E F

64
46

45
27

A
B
C
D
E
F
8
7
65
6
5
64
4
3
63
2
1
62
86
87
88
Gormoor Farm
Penny Hill
A322
Gravel Hill
Caesar's Camp
Pudding Hill
Mill Pond
RG12
New England Hill
Wickham Bushes
Roman Star or Upper Star Post
The Devil's Highway
DANGER AREA
FORESTERS WAY
A3095
Windsor Ride
GU19
Lower Star Post
RG45
Wishmoor Cross
Poppy Hills
Deer Rock Hill
GU15
Paschal Wood
GU47
Wishmoor Bottom
Olddean Common
Saddleback Hill
The Devil's Pound
WINDSOR RIDE
MATTHEWS RD
KING'S RIDE
QUEEN ELIZABETH RD
DUKE OF CORNWALL AVE
HIGHVIEW CRES
WIMBLEDON RD
WIMBLEDON CL
BRACKNELL CL
BERKSHIRE RD
P
Sch

45
65

A B C D E F

CH
Thornhill Allotment
SL5
A332
SWINLEY RD
Winklands Allotment
Fern Hill
8
A322
RG 12
Dukeshill Allotment
Red Cottage
Broom Covert
Picnic Area
Golf Course
GU20
7
Rapley Farm
Fan Covert
HOLLYBUSH RIDE
65
DUKES COVERT
BRACKNELL RD
6
Longacres Nursery
Cuckoo Pen
Rapley Lake
Lake Cottage
The Orangery
Laundry Cottage
DUKE'S HILL
HALLGROVE BOTTOM
A30
Bagshot Park
5
Hall Grove Farm
Cobblers Hole
The Cricketers (Hotel)
Surrey Hill
Bagshot Park
GROVE END
64
Freemantle Cottage
GU19
Lutine Farm
Windle Brook
Queen's Wood
4
LORY RIDGE
ANDERSON PL
Bagshot
1 FAULKNER PL
2 HEWLETT PL
3 GLOUCESTER GDNS
4 CHEWTER CL
STATION RD
Ford
VICARAGE RD
TALBOT PL
HART DENE CL
FREEMANTLE RD
GLOUCESTER RD
Bagshot Heath
TANNERS YD
HALF MOON ST
B3029
BRIDGE RD
WARDLE CL
PARKERS CT
Park Lodge
PARK VIEW
PARK ST
HIGH ST
KEPPLE PL
Gloucester Br
OLIVIA
BELL PL
NEW RD
THE SQUARE
GUILDFORD RD
Bagshot
Liby
PO
P
PROVIDENCE HOUSE
3
Nurseries
CONNAUGHT RD
CHURCH RD
WAVERLEY RD
MEADE CT
NEW RD
SWIFT LA
WELLESLEY CL
ST ANNES GLADE
MILL CL
CEDAR CL
HEATH RD
GREEN FARM RD
HIGGS LA
MILL FIELD
HAMILTON CL
MANOR WAY
PINEWOOD GDNS
COLLEGE RIDE
HEYWOOD DR
LONDON RD
ST MARY'S GDNS
BAGSHOT GN
63
SCHOOL LA
BROOK RD
GREEN LA
REGENT CT
YAVERLAND DR
LOWER MILL FIELD
CHANTRY RD
Bagshot Cty Inf Sch
ELIZABETH AVE
GUILDFORD RD
LAMBOURNE DR
CHAPEL LA
BROOM SQUARES
CHAPEL LA
STABLE CROFT
WAGGONERS HOLLOW
Connaught Cty JunSch
A322
WESTON GR
Mast
JENKINS' HILL
KEMP CT
BUTLER RD
M3
2
Hotel
Golf Course
P
SUFFOLK CL
SEBASTOPOL
HORSE DR
WHITMOOR RD
GU15
Penny Hill
SHEPHERDS CHASE
SHIRE CL
Pine Ridge Cty Inf Sch
WEBB CL
PRINCES CT
SURRIDGE CT
LARD CT
HOULTON CT
3
HODGES CL
HAWKSWORTH DR
ALBERT RD
VICTORIA CT
Nurseries
LUPIN CL
BRACKNELL RD
ESHER RD
MITCHAM RD
MAULTWAY N
Hammond's Pond
1
WALLINGTON RD
SURBITON RD
KINGSTON RD
SUTTON RD
CARSHALTON RD
SOUTHWICK
ARTHUR CL
Lightwater Country Park
GU18
Sports Ctr
Coll
WYCHWOOD PL
A30
M3
62

89 A B 90 C D 91 E F

47
29

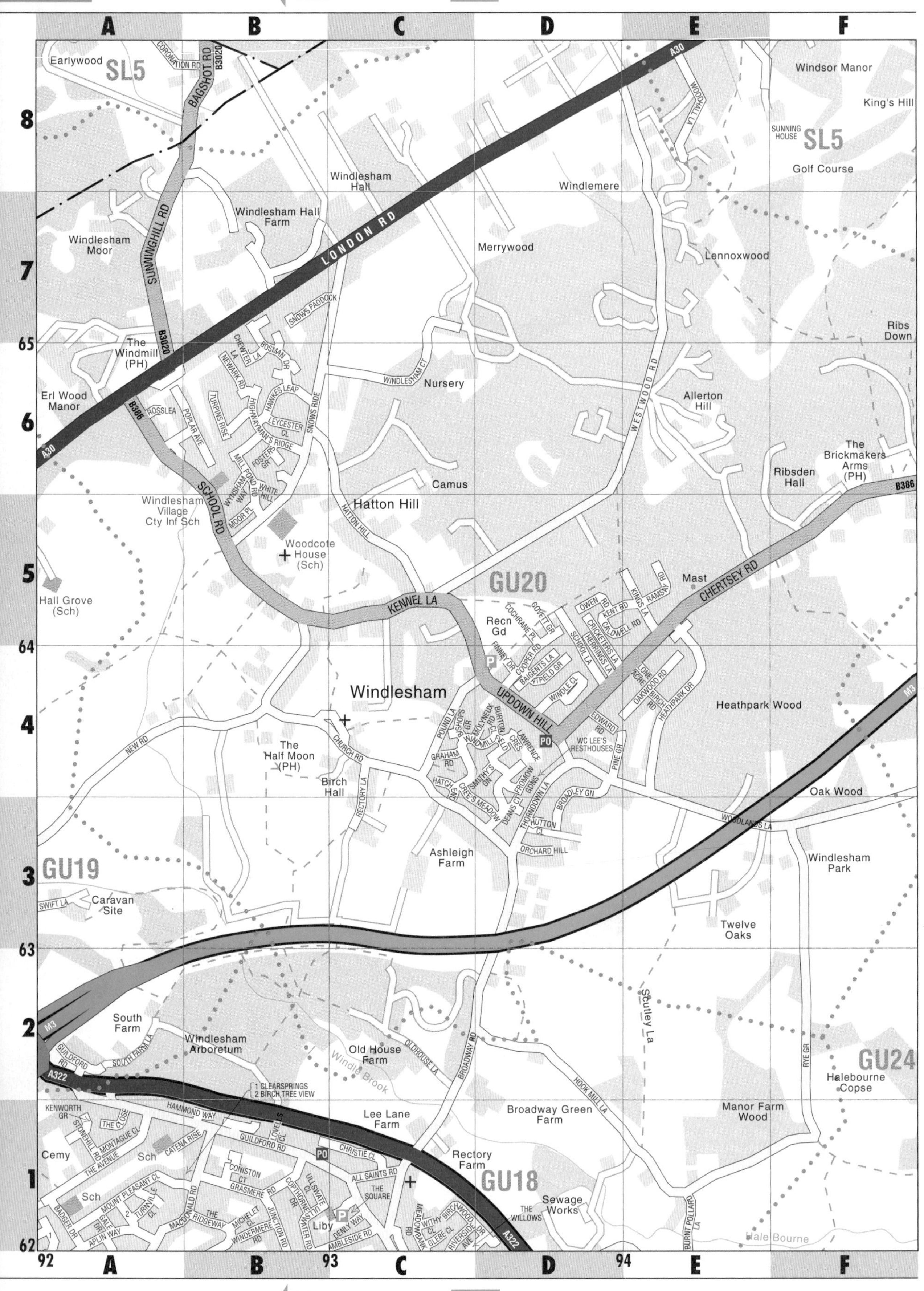
Earlywood
SL5
Windsor Manor
King's Hill
SUNNING HOUSE
SL5
Golf Course
Windlesham Hall
Windlemere
Windlesham Hall Farm
LONDON RD
Windlesham Moor
Merrywood
Lennoxwood
SUNNINGHILL RD
BAGSHOT RD
The Windmill (PH)
Ribs Down
Nursery
Erl Wood Manor
Allerton Hill
WESTWOOD RD
The Brickmakers Arms (PH)
Ribsden Hall
Camus
Windlesham Village Cty Inf Sch
Hatton Hill
SCHOOL RD
Woodcote House (Sch)
Hall Grove (Sch)
GU20
Mast
CHERTSEY RD
KENNEL LA
Recn Gd
Windlesham
UPDOWN HILL
Heathpark Wood
The Half Moon (PH)
Birch Hall
WC LEE'S RESTHOUSES
Oak Wood
WOODLANDS LA
Ashleigh Farm
Windlesham Park
GU19
Caravan Site
Twelve Oaks
South Farm
Windlesham Arboretum
Old House Farm
Windle Brook
Scutley La
GU24
Halebourne Copse
Lee Lane Farm
Broadway Green Farm
Manor Farm Wood
Cemy
Sch
Rectory Farm
GU18
Sewage Works
Liby
Hale Bourne
A30
B386
B3020
M3
A322

47
67

30
50

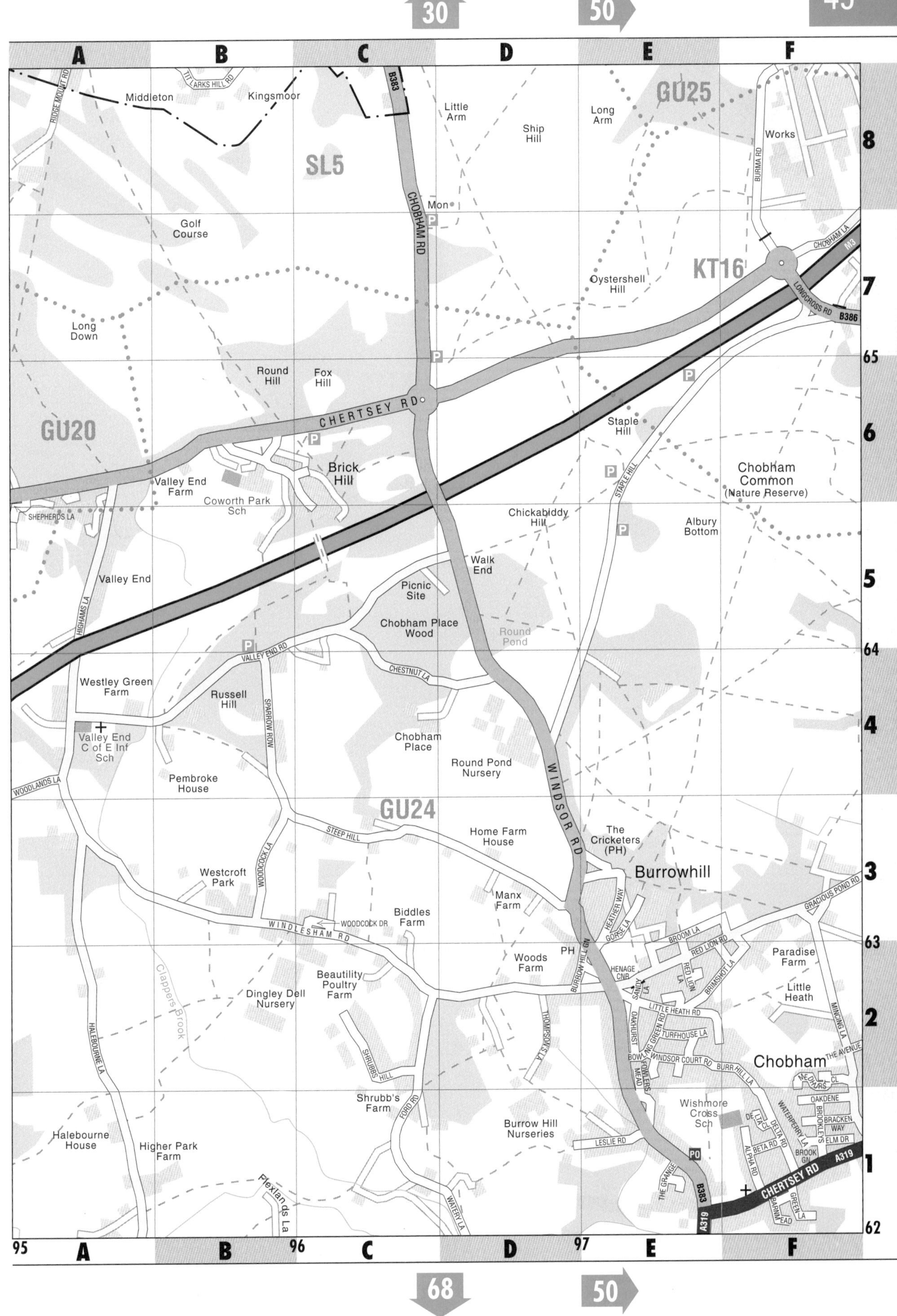
A
B
C
D
E
F
Middleton
Kingsmoor
SL5
GU25
Little Arm
Ship Hill
Long Arm
Works
Golf Course
Mon
CHOBHAM RD
KT16
Oystershell Hill
Long Down
Round Hill
Fox Hill
CHERTSEY RD
GU20
Staple Hill
Brick Hill
Chobham Common (Nature Reserve)
Valley End Farm
Coworth Park Sch
Chickabiddy Hill
Albury Bottom
Valley End
Walk End
Picnic Site
Chobham Place Wood
Round Pond
Westley Green Farm
Russell Hill
Valley End C of E Inf Sch
Chobham Place
Round Pond Nursery
Pembroke House
GU24
Home Farm House
The Cricketers (PH)
Burrowhill
Westcroft Park
Manx Farm
Biddles Farm
WINDLESHAM RD
Woods Farm
Paradise Farm
Beautility Poultry Farm
Dingley Dell Nursery
Little Heath
Chobham
Clappers Brook
Shrubb's Farm
Wishmore Cross Sch
Burrow Hill Nurseries
Halebourne House
Higher Park Farm
Flexlands La
WINDSOR RD
CHERTSEY RD
95
96
97
62
1
2
63
3
4
64
5
6
65
7
8

68
50

49
31

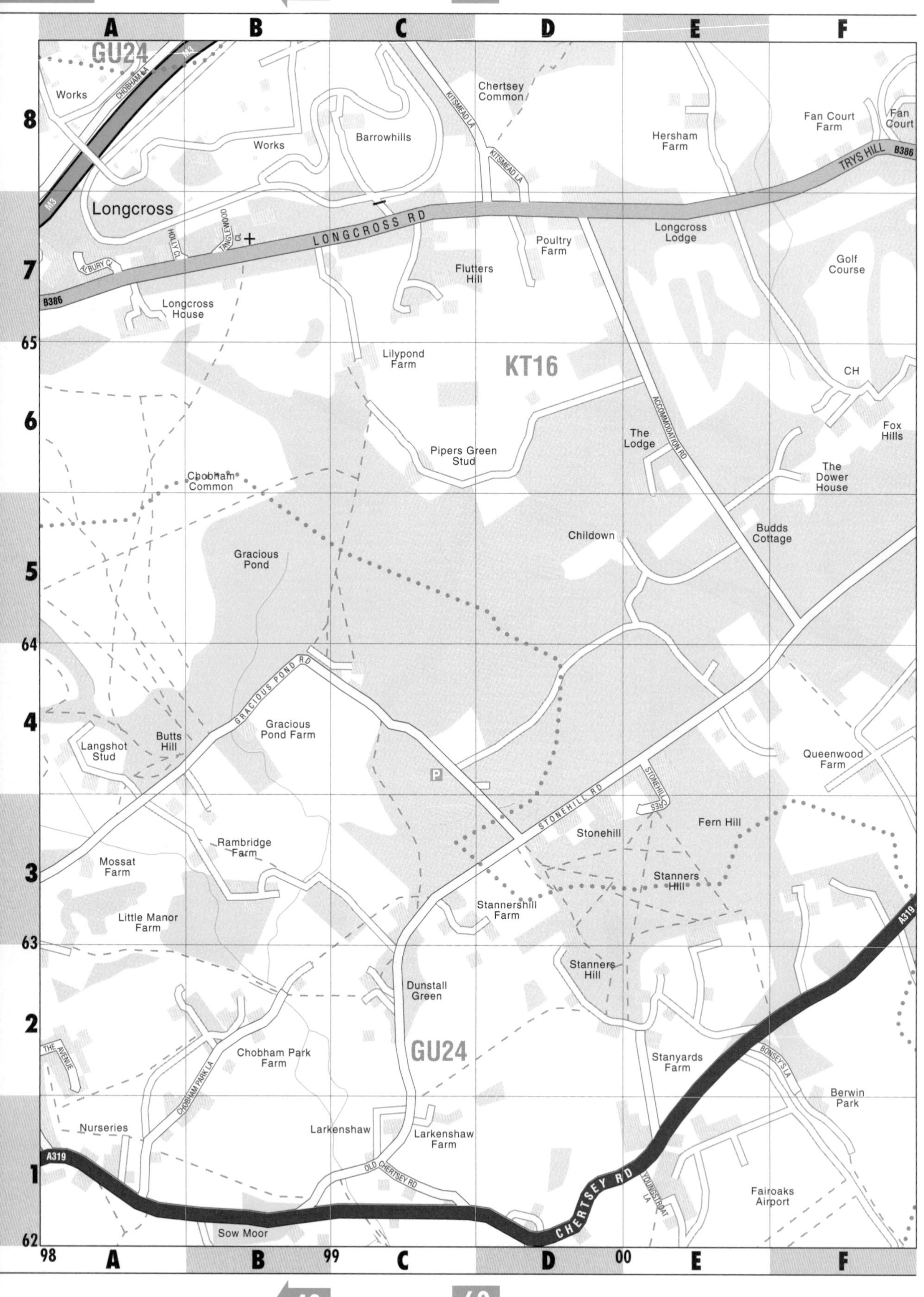
A
B
C
D
E
F
GU24
Works
CHOBHAM LA
M3
Chertsey Common
KITSMEAD LA
Barrowhills
Works
Hersham Farm
Fan Court Farm
Fan Court
TRYS HILL
B386
Longcross
HOLLY CL
TANGLEWOOD CL
LONGCROSS RD
Poultry Farm
Longcross Lodge
Flutters Hill
Golf Course
ALBURY CL
B386
Longcross House
Lilypond Farm
KT16
CH
ACCOMMODATION RD
The Lodge
Fox Hills
Pipers Green Stud
The Dower House
Chobham Common
Budds Cottage
Childown
Gracious Pond
GRACIOUS POND RD
Gracious Pond Farm
Langshot Stud
Butts Hill
Queenwood Farm
P
STONEHILL RD
STONEHILL CRES
Fern Hill
Stonehill
Rambridge Farm
Mossat Farm
Stanners Hill
Stannershill Farm
Little Manor Farm
Stanners Hill
Dunstall Green
GU24
THE AVENUE
Chobham Park Farm
Stanyards Farm
BONSEY'S LA
Berwin Park
CHOBHAM PARK LA
A319
Nurseries
Larkenshaw
Larkenshaw Farm
A319
OLD CHERTSEY RD
CHERTSEY RD
YOUNGSTROAT LA
Fairoaks Airport
Sow Moor
8
7
65
6
5
64
4
3
63
2
1
62
98
99
00

49
69

32
52

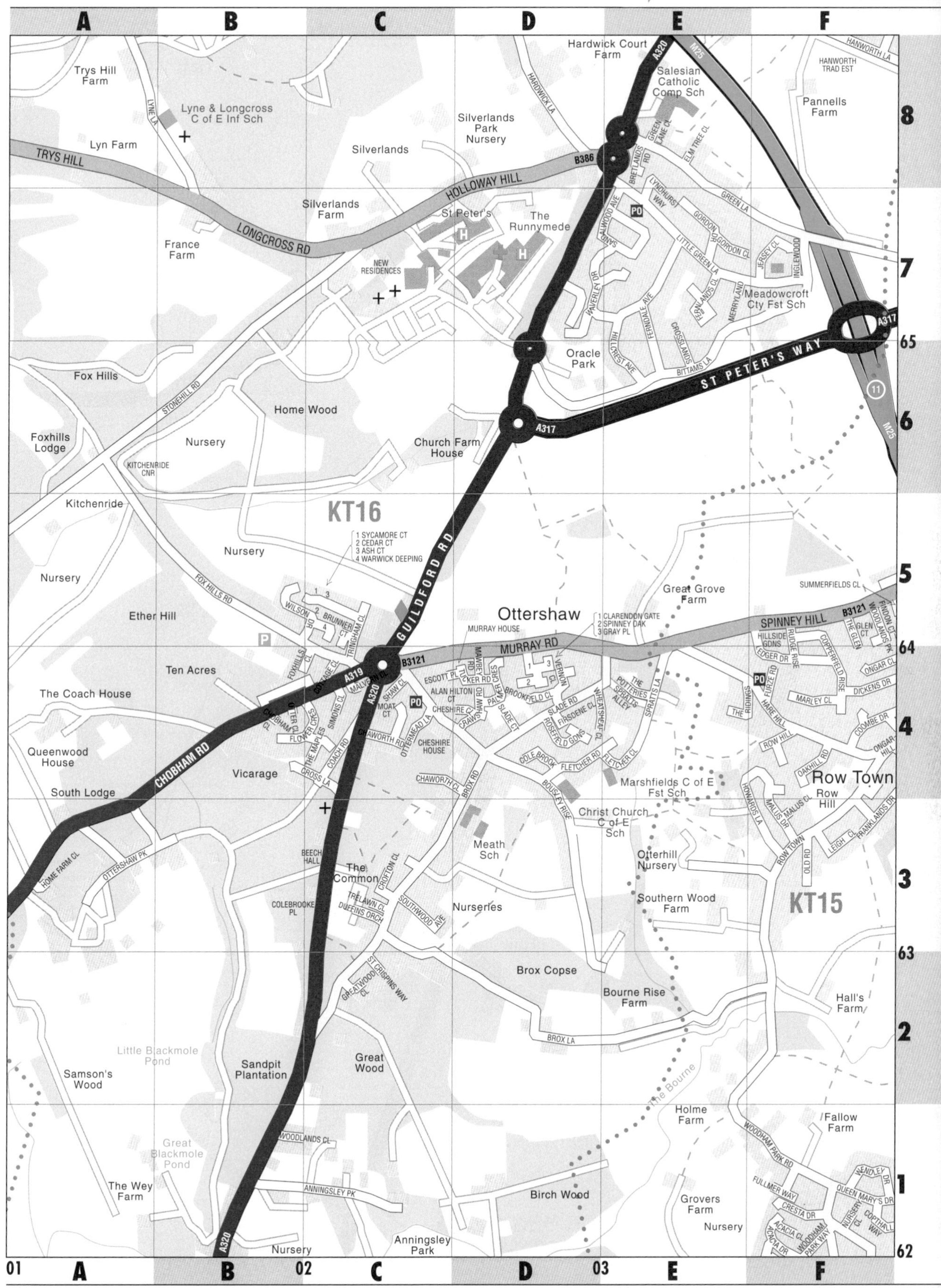
A
B
C
D
E
F
8
7
65
6
5
64
4
3
63
2
1
62
01
02
03
Trys Hill Farm
Lyne & Longcross C of E Inf Sch
Lyn Farm
TRYS HILL
LONGCROSS RD
HOLLOWAY HILL
B386
France Farm
Silverlands
Silverlands Farm
Silverlands Park Nursery
Hardwick Court Farm
HARDWICK LA
Salesian Catholic Comp Sch
M25
A320
HANWORTH LA
HANWORTH TRAD EST
Pannells Farm
St Peter's
The Runnymede
NEW RESIDENCES
Meadowcroft Cty Fst Sch
ST PETER'S WAY
A317
Oracle Park
Fox Hills
Foxhills Lodge
STONEHILL RD
Home Wood
Nursery
Church Farm House
KITCHENRIDE CNR
Kitchenride
KT16
1 SYCAMORE CT
2 CEDAR CT
3 ASH CT
4 WARWICK DEEPING
GUILDFORD RD
FOX HILLS RD
Ether Hill
Great Grove Farm
SUMMERFIELDS CL
Ottershaw
1 CLARENDON GATE
2 SPINNEY OAK
3 GRAY PL
MURRAY HOUSE
SPINNEY HILL
B3121
MURRAY RD
Ten Acres
The Coach House
A319
Queenwood House
CHOBHAM RD
Vicarage
South Lodge
CHESHIRE HOUSE
Marshfields C of E Fst Sch
Christ Church C of E Sch
Row Town
Row Hill
Meath Sch
Otterhill Nursery
Southern Wood Farm
KT15
HOME FARM CL
OTTERSHAW PK
BEECH HALL
The Common
COLEBROOKE PL
Nurseries
Brox Copse
Bourne Rise Farm
Hall's Farm
BROX LA
Little Blackmole Pond
Samson's Wood
Sandpit Plantation
Great Wood
The Bourne
Holme Farm
Fallow Farm
Great Blackmole Pond
WOODLANDS CL
The Wey Farm
ANNINGSLEY PK
Birch Wood
Grovers Farm
Nursery
Anningsley Park

70
52

51
33

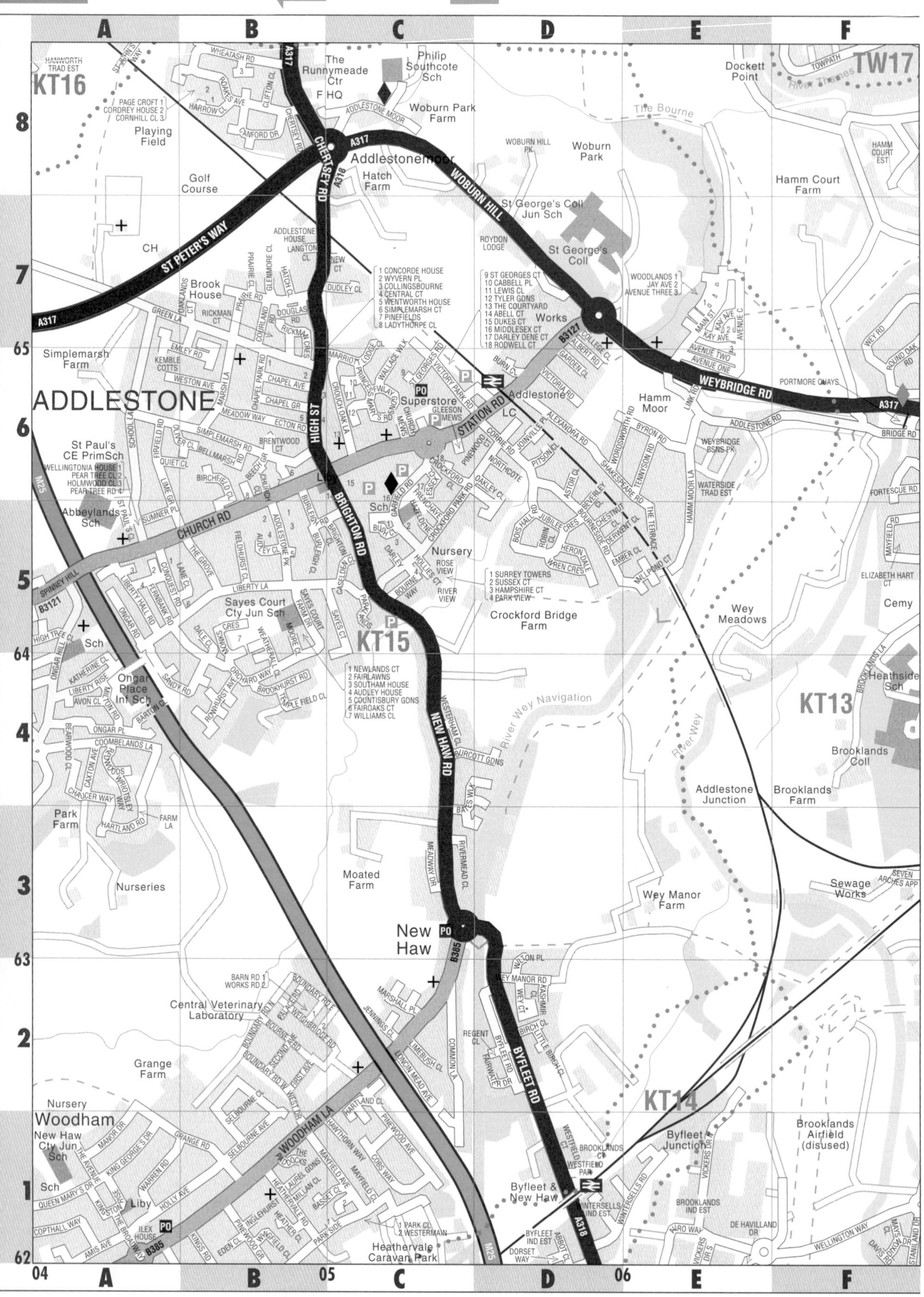
A
B
C
D
E
F
8
7
65
6
5
64
4
3
63
2
1
62
04
05
06
KT16
TW17
KT15
KT13
KT14
HANWORTH TRAD EST
WHEATASH RD
ROAKES AVE
HARROW CL
CLIFTON CL
CANFORD DR
CHERTSEY RD
PAGE CROFT 1
CORDREY HOUSE 2
CORNHILL CL 3
Playing Field
Golf Course
CH
The Runnymeade Ctr
F HQ
Philip Southcote Sch
ADDLESTONE MOOR
Woburn Park Farm
A317
A318
Addlestonemoor
Hatch Farm
WOBURN HILL
WOBURN HILL PK
Woburn Park
St George's Coll Jun Sch
ROYDON LODGE
St George's Coll
Dockett Point
TOWPATH
River Thames
The Bourne
HAMM COURT EST
Hamm Court Farm
ST PETER'S WAY
ADDLESTONE HOUSE
LANGTON CL
NEW CT
DUDLEY CL
Brook House
1 CONCORDE HOUSE
2 WYVERN PL
3 COLLINGSBOURNE
4 CENTRAL CT
5 WENTWORTH HOUSE
6 SIMPLEMARSH CT
7 PINEFIELDS
8 LADYTHORPE CL
9 ST GEORGES CT
10 CABBELL PL
11 LEWIS CL
12 TYLER GDNS
13 THE COURTYARD
14 ABELL CT
15 DUKES CT
16 MIDDLESEX CT
17 DARLEY DENE CT
18 RODWELL CT
Works
WOODLANDS 1
JAY AVE 2
AVENUE THREE 3
MAIN ST
KAY AVE
AVENUE C
AVENUE TWO
AVENUE ONE
WEY RD
ROUND OAK RD
GREEN LA
RICKMAN CT
DOUGLAS RD
RICKMAN CRES
Simplemarsh Farm
EMLEY RD
KEMBLE COTTS
WESTON AVE
CHAPEL PARK RD
CHAPEL AVE
CHAPEL GR
MEADOW WAY
ECTON RD
ADDLESTONE
SIMPLEMARSH RD
BELLMARSH RD
QUIET CL
HIGH ST
Superstore
PO
GLEESON MEWS
STATION RD
VICTORY PARK RD
Addlestone
LC
B3127
COLLEGE CL
ALBERT RD
GARDEN CL
VICTORIA RD
WEYBRIDGE RD
PORTMORE QUAYS
Hamm Moor
BYRON RD
ADDLESTONE RD
BRIDGE RD
WEYBRIDGE BSNS PK
WATERSIDE TRAD EST
St Paul's CE PrimSch
WELLINGTONIA HOUSE 1
PEAR TREE CL 2
HOLMWOOD CL 3
PEAR TREE RD 4
Liby
BRIGHTON RD
Sch
CHURCH RD
Abbeylands Sch
SPINNEY HILL
B3121
M25
Nursery
ROSE VIEW
RIVER VIEW
1 SURREY TOWERS
2 SUSSEX CT
3 HAMPSHIRE CT
4 PARK VIEW
Crockford Bridge Farm
Wey Meadows
Cemy
ELIZABETH HART CT
FORTESCUE RD
MAYFIELD RD
LIBERTY LA
Sayes Court Cty Jun Sch
HIGH TREE CL
Ongar Place Inf Sch
1 NEWLANDS CT
2 FAIRLAWNS
3 SOUTHAM HOUSE
4 AUDLEY HOUSE
5 COUNTISBURY GDNS
6 FAIROAKS CT
7 WILLIAMS CL
NEW HAW RD
River Wey Navigation
River Wey
Heathside Sch
Brooklands Coll
BROOKLANDS LA
Addlestone Junction
Brooklands Farm
Park Farm
Nurseries
Moated Farm
Wey Manor Farm
Sewage Works
SEVEN ARCHES APP
New Haw
B385
BARN RD 1
WORKS RD 2
Central Veterinary Laboratory
Grange Farm
Nursery
Woodham
New Haw Cty Jun Sch
Sch
WOODHAM LA
BYFLEET RD
Brooklands Airfield (disused)
Byfleet Junction
BROOKLANDS CT
WESTFIELD PAR
Byfleet & New Haw
WINTERSELLS IND EST
BROOKLANDS IND EST
DE HAVILLAND DR
WELLINGTON WAY
BYFLEET IND EST
DORSET WAY
ILEX HOUSE
1 PARK CL
2 WESTERMAIN
Heathervale Caravan Park

51
71

B6
1 ALEXANDRA LODGE
2 BRIDGE CT
3 ALBANY CT

B7
1 BROADWATER HOUSE
2 DENMARK CT
3 TUDOR WLK
4 GATE CT
5 AGNES SCOTT CT
6 CATHERINE HOWARD CT

C5
1 ST MICHAELS CT
2 PINE CT
3 PINE GROVE MEWS
4 ANGAS CT

D4
1 WILLERTON LODGE
2 HOLMESDALE
3 EASTWOOD
4 HURST LODGE
5 SUMMERLEIGH
6 BURCOTE

D6
1 DOVEHOUSE GN
2 STAFFORD SQ
3 HUNGERFORD SQ

D7
1 GROSVENOR PL
2 GLENLION CT
3 VILLAGE CL
4 ST MARY'S
5 CULVERDEN TERR
6 THE LAURELS

34
54

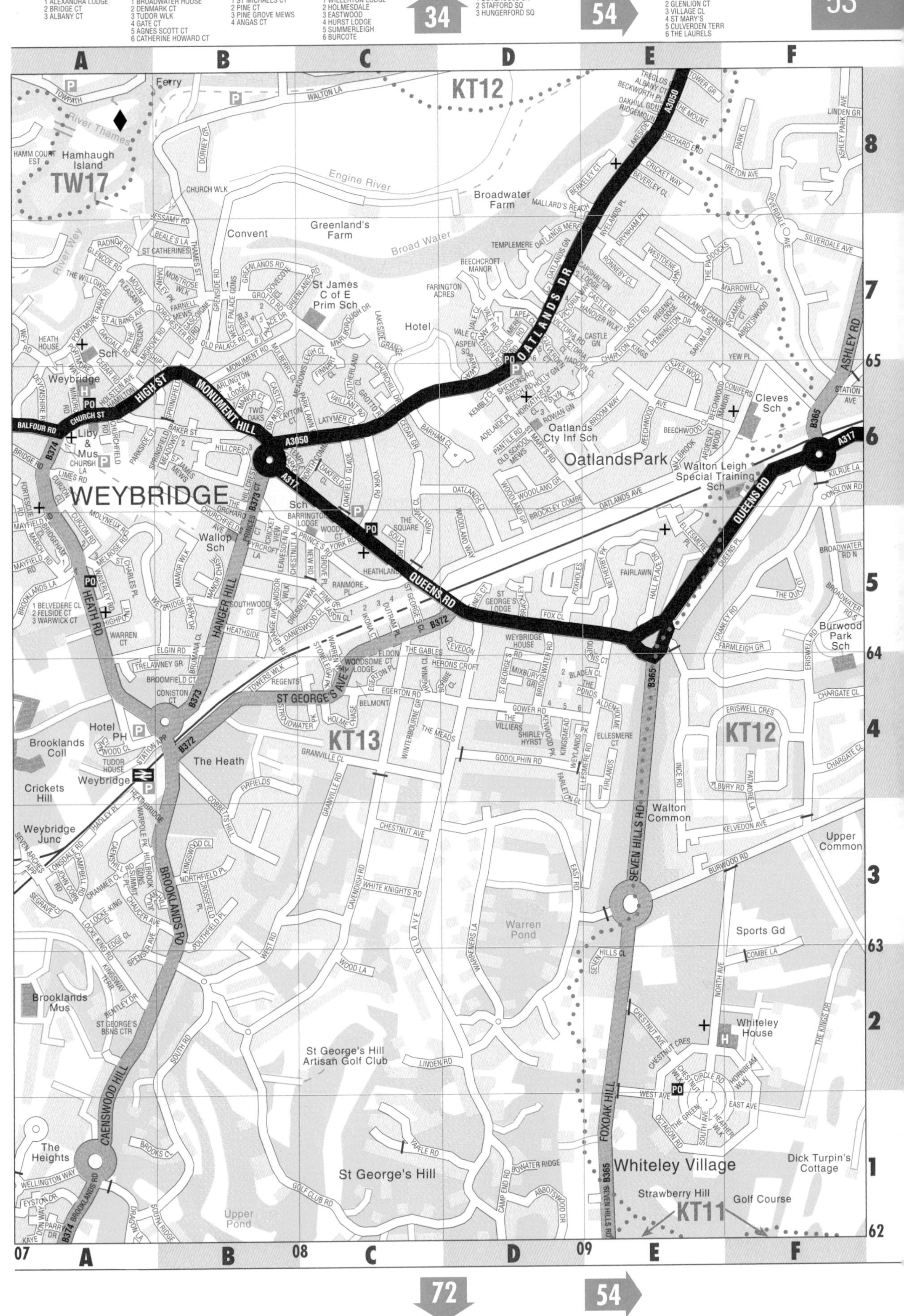

72
54

53
35

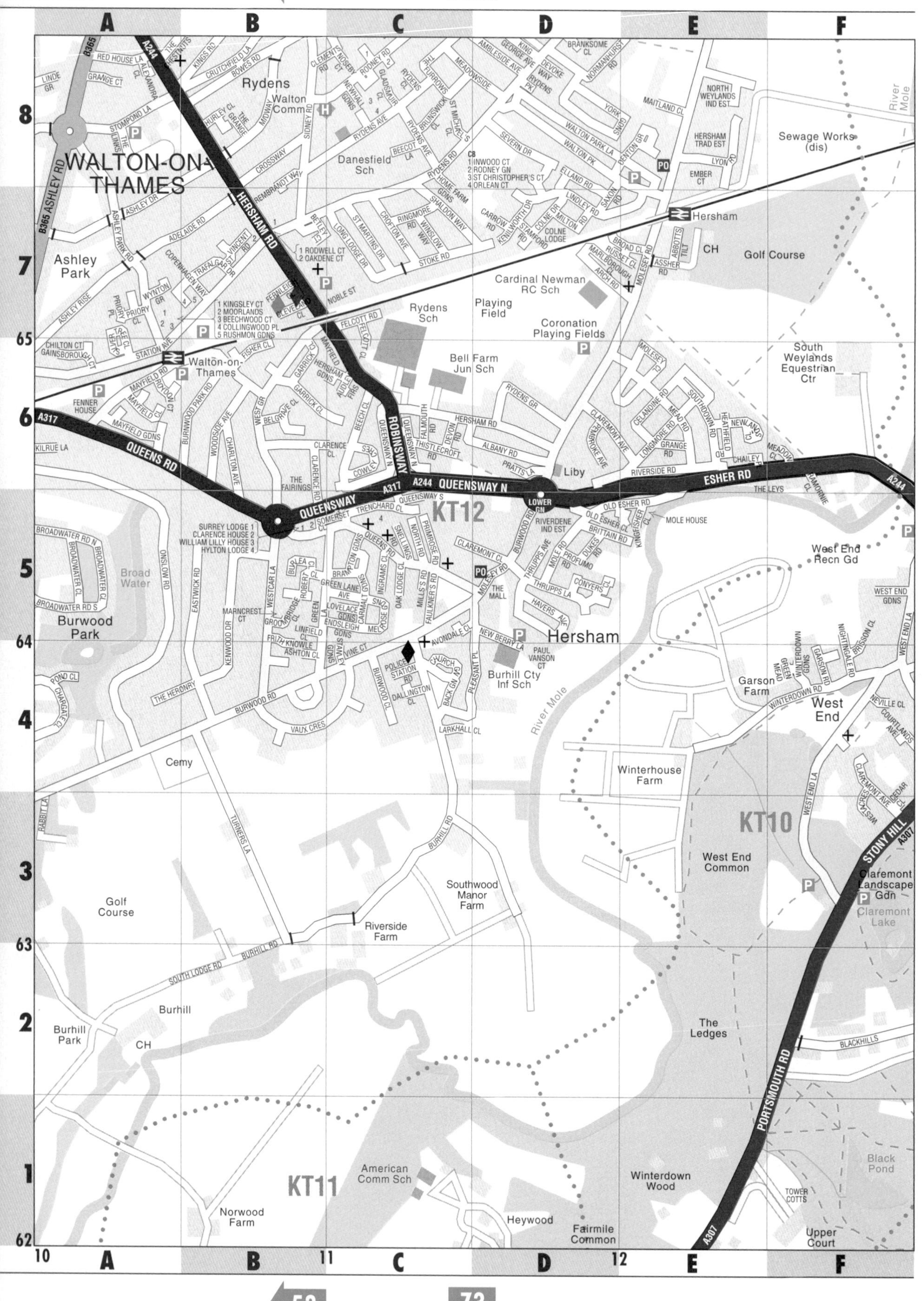
A
B
C
D
E
F
8
7
65
6
5
64
4
3
63
2
1
62
10
11
12
WALTON-ON-THAMES
Rydens
Walton Comm
Danesfield Sch
Ashley Park
Walton-on-Thames
Rydens Sch
Playing Field
Cardinal Newman RC Sch
Coronation Playing Fields
Bell Farm Jun Sch
Hersham
CH
Golf Course
Sewage Works (dis)
River Mole
NORTH WEYLANDS IND EST
HERSHAM TRAD EST
South Weylands Equestrian Ctr
Liby
KT12
QUEENS RD
QUEENSWAY
QUEENSWAY N
ESHER RD
HERSHAM RD
ROBINSWAY
A244
A317
B365
B365 ASHLEY RD
Broad Water
Burwood Park
Hersham
Burhill Cty Inf Sch
West End Recn Gd
Garson Farm
West End
Winterhouse Farm
KT10
West End Common
Claremont Landscape Gdn
Claremont Lake
STONY HILL
A307
Cemy
Golf Course
Southwood Manor Farm
Riverside Farm
Burhill
Burhill Park
CH
The Ledges
PORTSMOUTH RD
Black Pond
Winterdown Wood
Tower Cotts
Upper Court
American Comm Sch
KT11
Norwood Farm
Heywood
Fairmile Common
BURHILL RD
SOUTH LODGE RD
TURNERS LA
BURWOOD RD
WINTERDOWN RD
WEST END LA
BLACKHILLS
MOLE HOUSE
LOWER GN
FENNER HOUSE
1 RODWELL CT
2 OAKDENE CT
1 KINGSLEY CT
2 MOORLANDS
3 BEECHWOOD CT
4 COLLINGWOOD PL
5 RUSHMON GDNS
C8
1 INWOOD CT
2 RODNEY GN
3 ST CHRISTOPHER'S CT
4 ORLEAN CT
SURREY LODGE 1
CLARENCE HOUSE 2
WILLIAM LILLY HOUSE 3
HYLTON LODGE 4

36
56

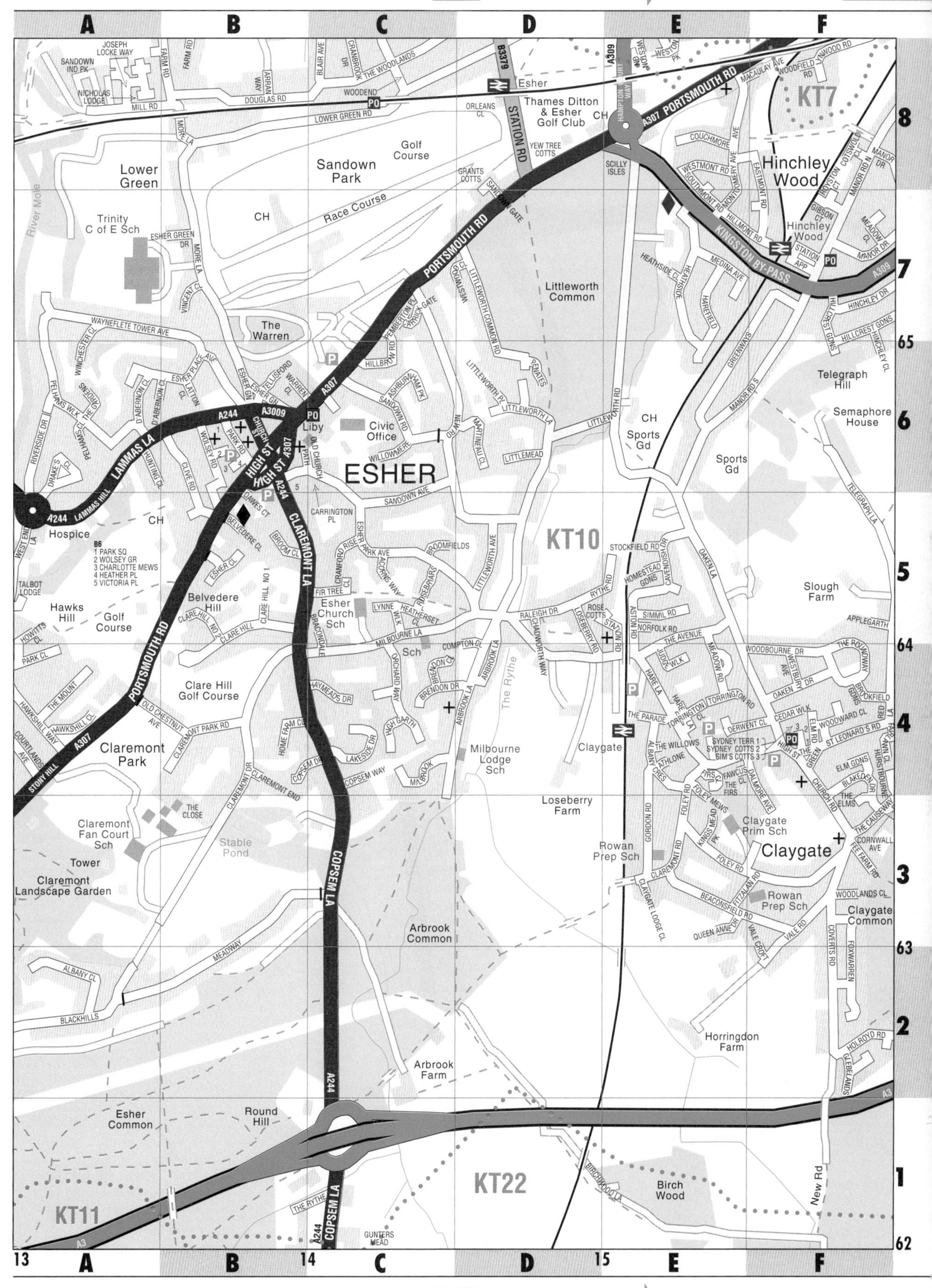
ESHER
Lower Green
Sandown Park
Golf Course
Race Course
Thames Ditton & Esher Golf Club
Trinity C of E Sch
The Warren
Littleworth Common
Hinchley Wood
Telegraph Hill
Semaphore House
Sports Gd
Civic Office
Liby
Hospice
Hawks Hill
Golf Course
Belvedere Hill
Esher Church Sch
Clare Hill Golf Course
Claremont Park
Claremont Fan Court Sch
Tower
Claremont Landscape Garden
Stable Pond
Milbourne Lodge Sch
Loseberry Farm
Claygate
Claygate Prim Sch
Rowan Prep Sch
Slough Farm
Claygate Common
Arbrook Common
Arbrook Farm
Horringdon Farm
Esher Common
Round Hill
Birch Wood
KT7
KT10
KT11
KT22
PORTSMOUTH RD
KINGSTON BY-PASS
COPSEM LA
CLAREMONT LA
HIGH ST
LAMMAS LA
STATION RD
B6
1 PARK SQ
2 WOLSEY GR
3 CHARLOTTE MEWS
4 HEATHER PL
5 VICTORIA PL

74
56

55
37

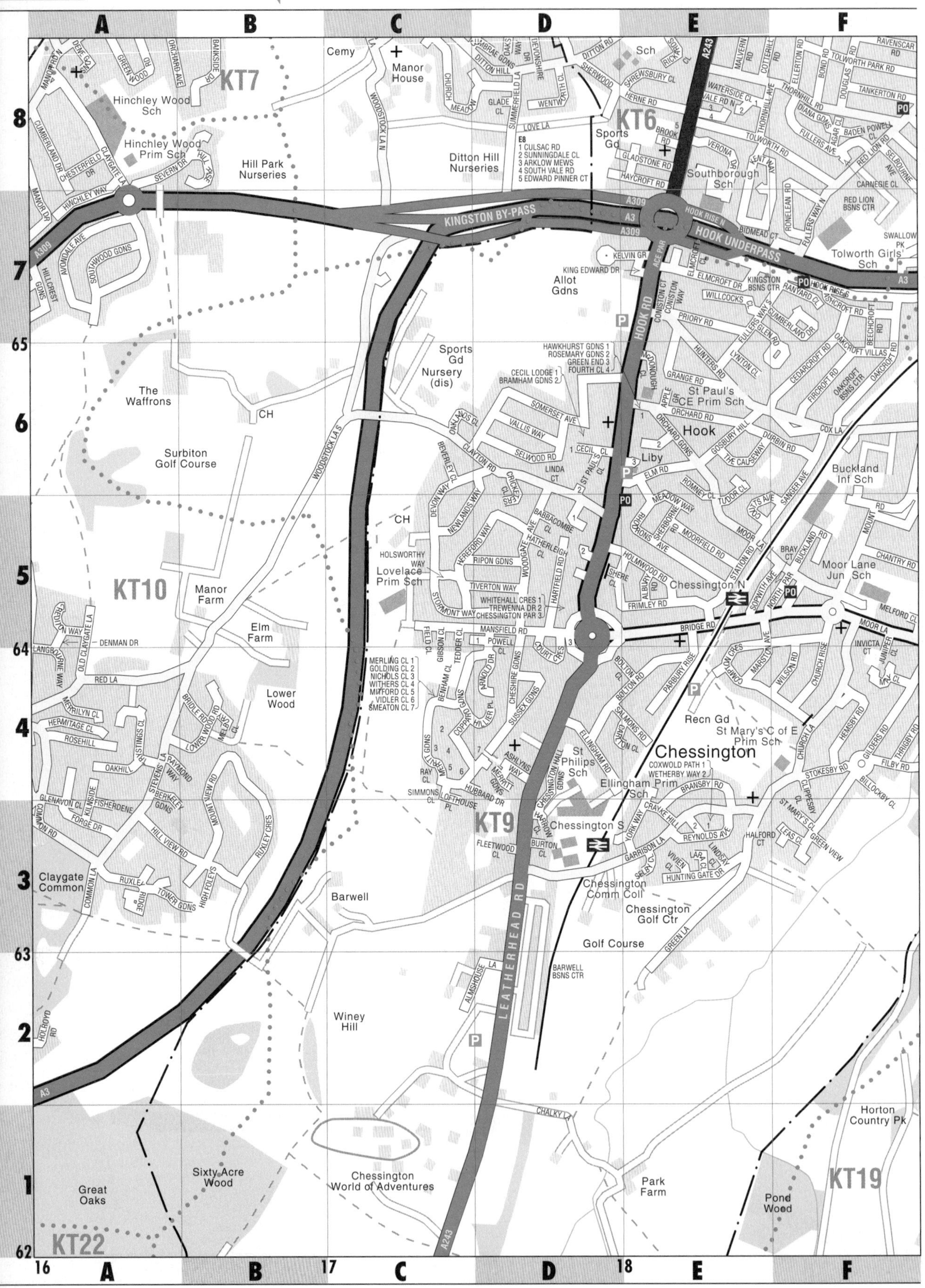
A
B
C
D
E
F
8
7
65
6
5
64
4
3
63
2
1
62
16
17
18
KT7
KT6
KT10
KT9
KT19
KT22
Hinchley Wood Sch
Hinchley Wood Prim Sch
Hill Park Nurseries
Cemy
Manor House
Ditton Hill Nurseries
Sports Gd
Southborough Sch
Tolworth Girls' Sch
KINGSTON BY-PASS
HOOK UNDERPASS
HOOK RD
A3
A309
A243
Allot Gdns
The Waffrons
Surbiton Golf Course
Sports Gd Nursery (dis)
St Paul's CE Prim Sch
Hook
Liby
Buckland Inf Sch
Moor Lane Jun Sch
Lovelace Prim Sch
Manor Farm
Elm Farm
Lower Wood
Chessington N
Chessington
Recn Gd
St Mary's C of E Prim Sch
St Philips Sch
Ellingham Prim Sch
Chessington S
Claygate Common
Barwell
Chessington Comm Coll
Chessington Golf Ctr
Golf Course
Winey Hill
LEATHERHEAD RD
Horton Country Pk
Chessington World of Adventures
Park Farm
Pond Wood
Great Oaks
Sixty Acre Wood
E8
1 CULSAC RD
2 SUNNINGDALE CL
3 ARKLOW MEWS
4 SOUTH VALE RD
5 EDWARD PINNER CT
HAWKHURST GDNS 1
ROSEMARY GDNS 2
GREEN END 3
FOURTH CL 4
CECIL LODGE 1
BRAMHAM GDNS 2
WHITEHALL CRES 1
TREWENNA DR 2
CHESSINGTON PAR 3
MERLING CL 1
GOLDING CL 2
NICHOLS CL 3
WITHERS CL 4
MITFORD CL 5
VIDLER CL 6
SMEATON CL 7
COXWOLD PATH 1
WETHERBY WAY 2

55
75

38
58

A B C D E F

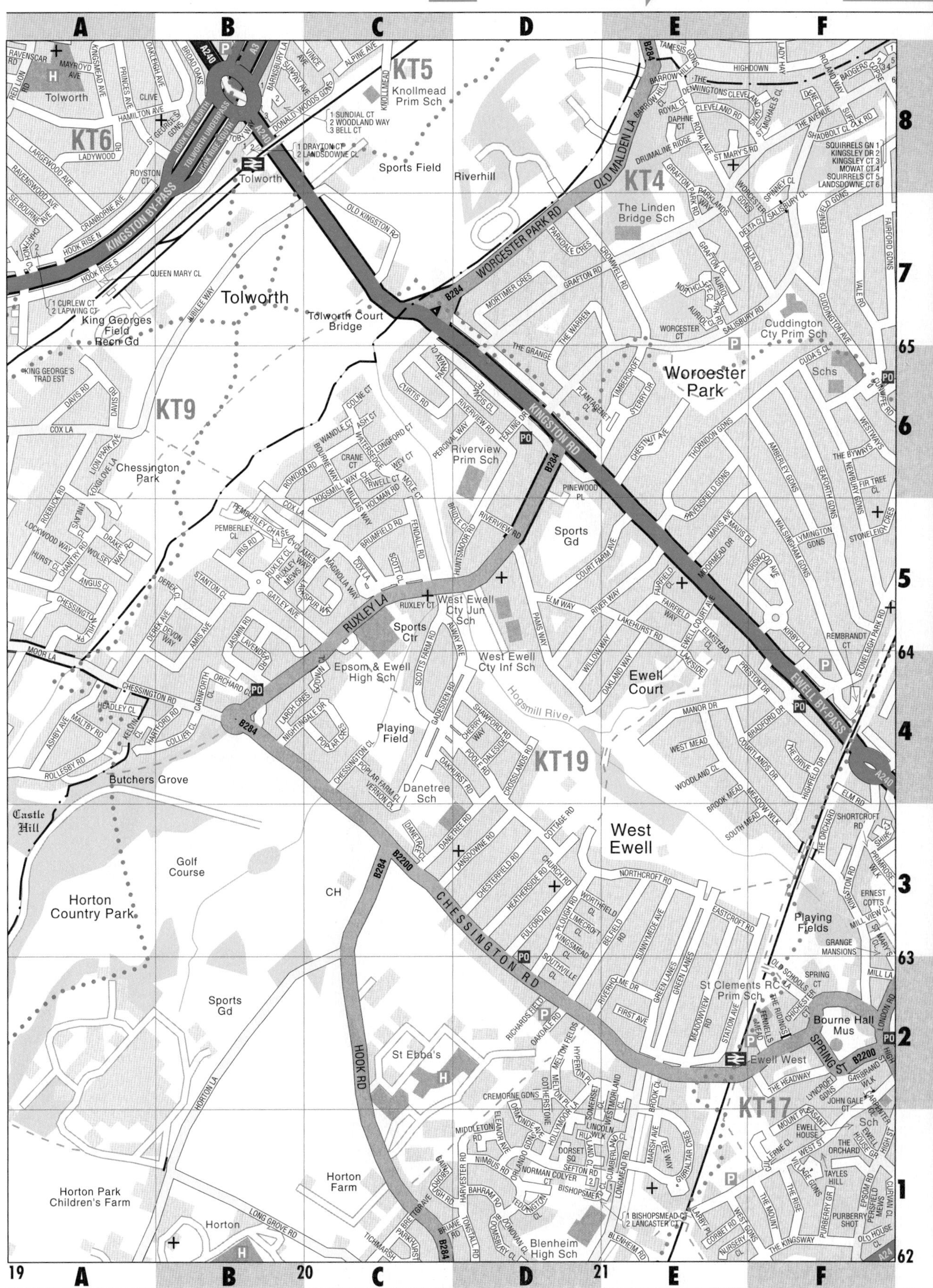

A B C D E F

76
58

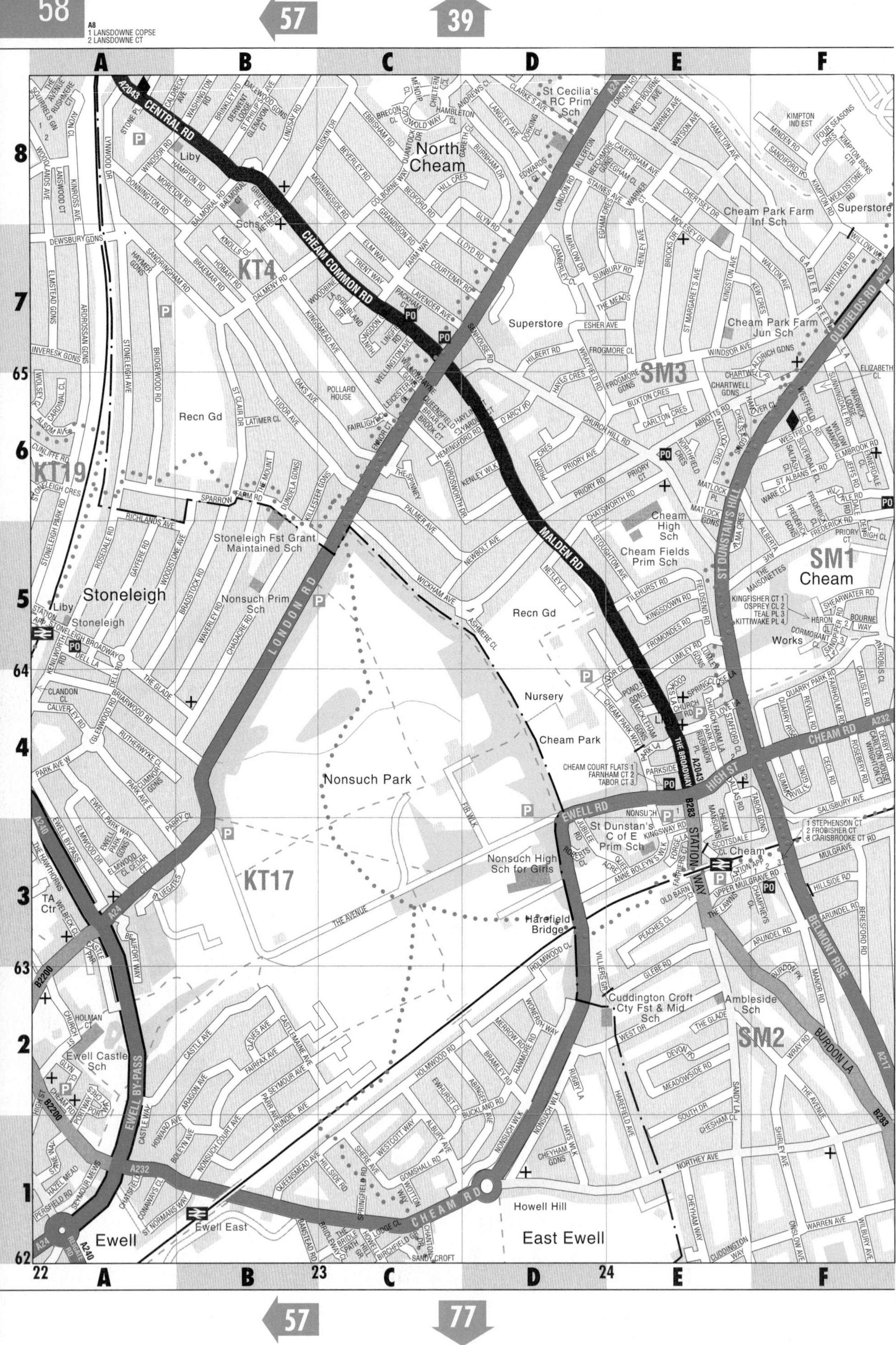
North Cheam
KT4
St Cecilia's RC Prim Sch
Cheam Park Farm Inf Sch
Cheam Park Farm Jun Sch
Superstore
SM3
KT19
Stoneleigh
Stoneleigh Fst Grant Maintained Sch
Nonsuch Prim Sch
Recn Gd
Pollard House
Cheam High Sch
Cheam Fields Prim Sch
SM1
Cheam
Works
Nursery
Cheam Park
Nonsuch Park
KT17
St Dunstan's C of E Prim Sch
Nonsuch High Sch for Girls
Harefield Bridge
Cuddington Croft Cty Fst & Mid Sch
Ambleside Sch
SM2
Ewell Castle Sch
Ewell East
Ewell
Howell Hill
East Ewell
TA Ctr
CENTRAL RD
CHEAM COMMON RD
LONDON RD
MALDEN RD
EWELL RD
HIGH ST
CHEAM RD
STATION WAY
ST DUNSTAN'S HILL
OLDFIELDS RD
BELMONT RISE
BURDON LA
EWELL BY-PASS
THE AVENUE
KINGFISHER CT 1
OSPREY CL 2
TEAL PL 3
KITTIWAKE PL 4
CHEAM COURT FLATS 1
FARNHAM CT 2
TABOR CT 3
1 STEPHENSON CT
2 FROBISHER CT
3 CARISBROOKE CT
A B C D E F
8 7 6 5 4 3 2 1
65 64 63 62
22 23 24

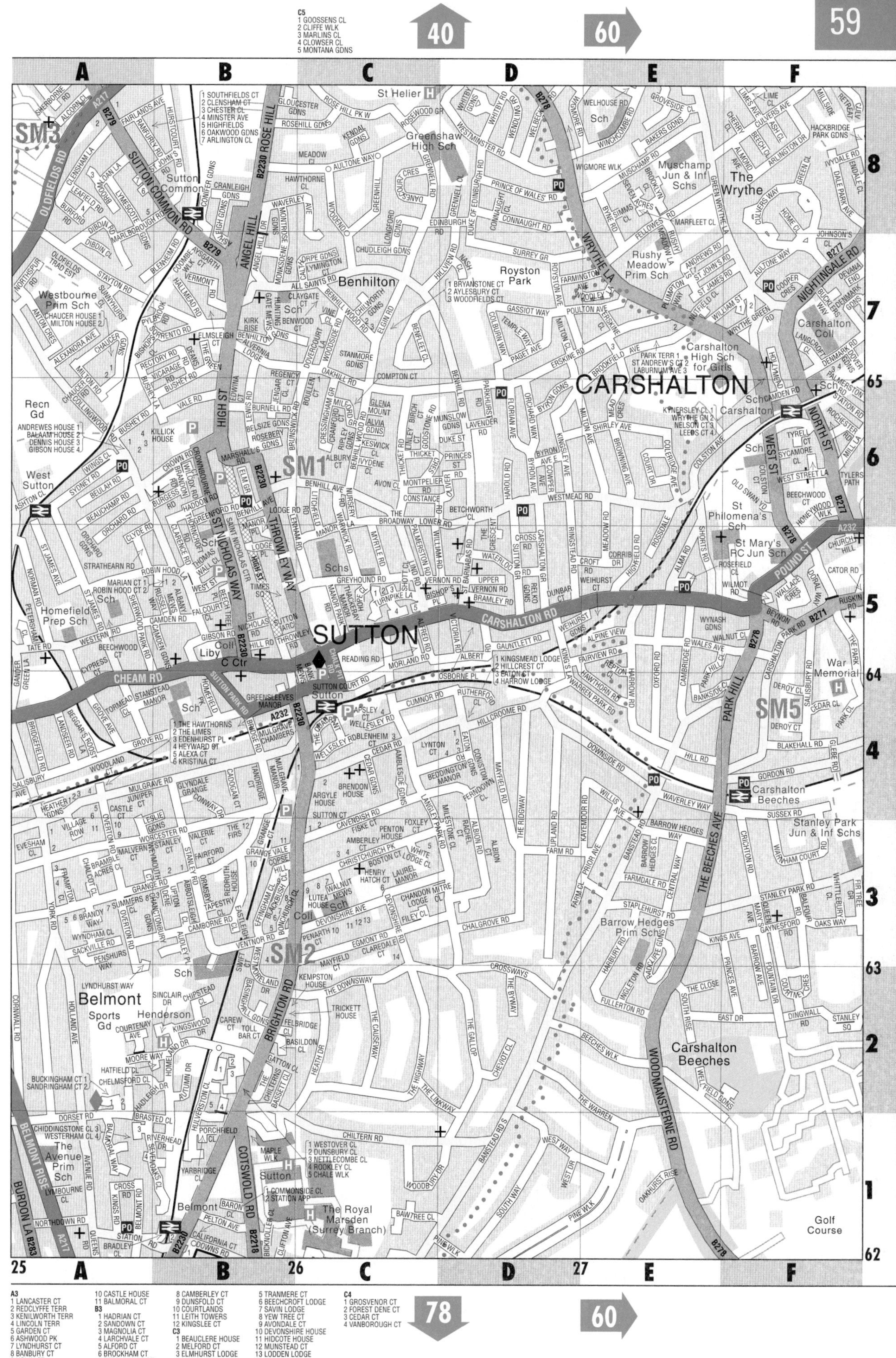

A3
1 LANCASTER CT
2 REDCLYFFE TERR
3 KENILWORTH TERR
4 LINCOLN TERR
5 GARDEN CT
6 ASHWOOD PK
7 LYNDHURST CT
8 BANBURY CT
9 HOLLY CT
10 CASTLE HOUSE
11 BALMORAL CT

B3
1 HADRIAN CT
2 SANDOWN CT
3 MAGNOLIA CT
4 LARCHVALE CT
5 ALFORD CT
6 BROCKHAM CT
7 BERRYLANDS CT
8 CAMBERLEY CT
9 DUNSFOLD CT
10 COURTLANDS
11 LEITH TOWERS
12 KINGSLEE CT

C3
1 BEAUCLERE HOUSE
2 MELFORD CT
3 ELMHURST LODGE
4 MANSARD MANOR
5 TRANMERE CT
6 BEECHCROFT LODGE
7 SAVIN LODGE
8 YEW TREE CT
9 AVONDALE CT
10 DEVONSHIRE HOUSE
11 HIDCOTE HOUSE
12 MUNSTEAD CT
13 LODDEN CT
14 STEETLEY CT

C4
1 GROSVENOR CT
2 FOREST DENE CT
3 CEDAR CT
4 VANBOROUGH CT

B6
1 LORAINE HOUSE
2 HARCOURT LODGE
3 CONISTON CT
4 ALCESTER CT
5 FRIARS CT
6 CAMPBELL HOUSE
7 BRODIE HOUSE
8 LESLEY CT
9 BIRCH CT
10 AIRBORNE HOUSE

59
41

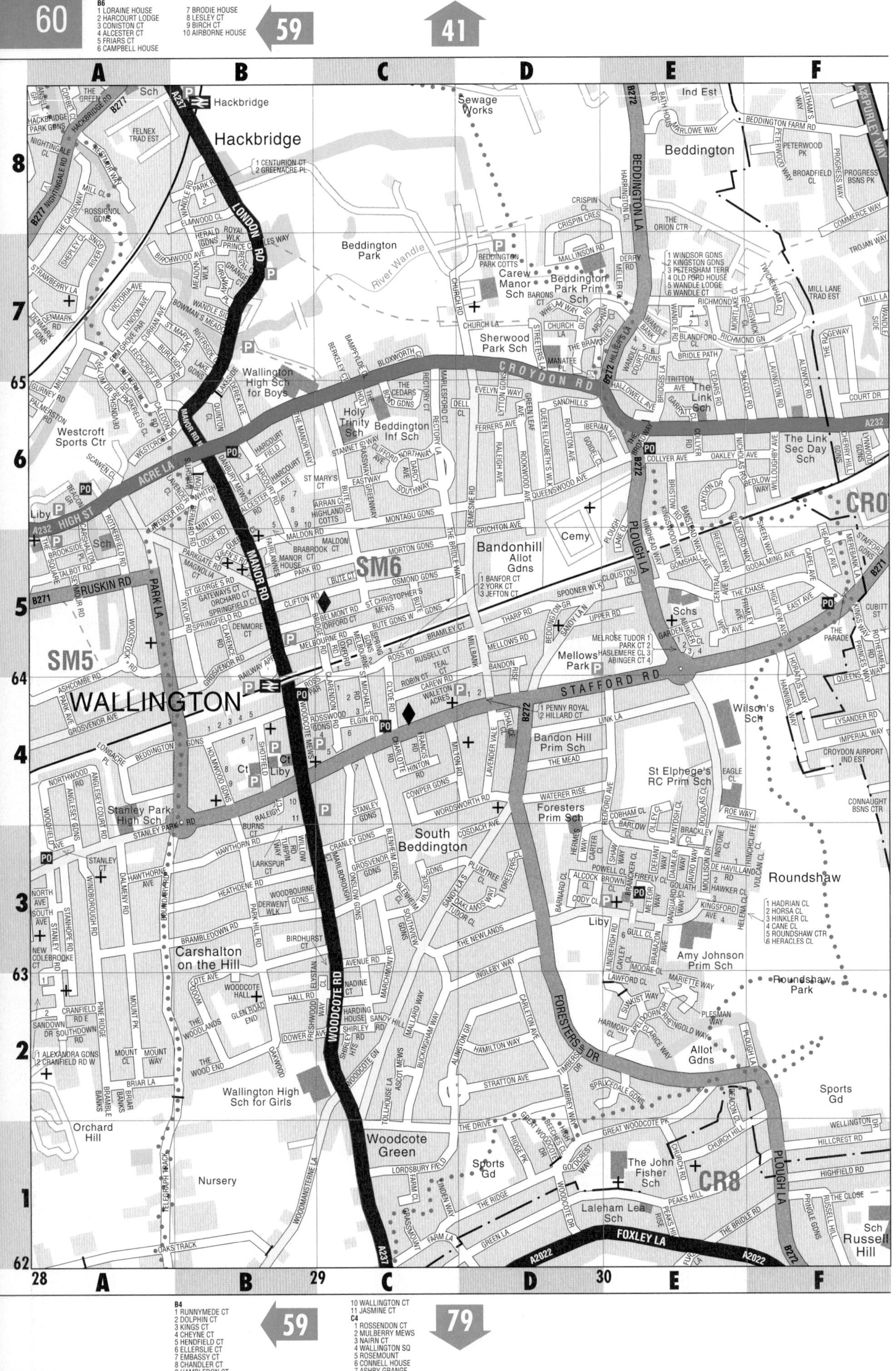

B4
1 RUNNYMEDE CT
2 DOLPHIN CT
3 KINGS CT
4 CHEYNE CT
5 HENDFIELD CT
6 ELLERSLIE CT
7 EMBASSY CT
8 CHANDLER CT
9 HAMBLEDON CT
10 WALLINGTON CT
11 JASMINE CT

C4
1 ROSSENDON CT
2 MULBERRY MEWS
3 NAIRN CT
4 WALLINGTON SQ
5 ROSEMOUNT
6 CONNELL HOUSE
7 ASHBY GRANGE

59
79

A B C D E F

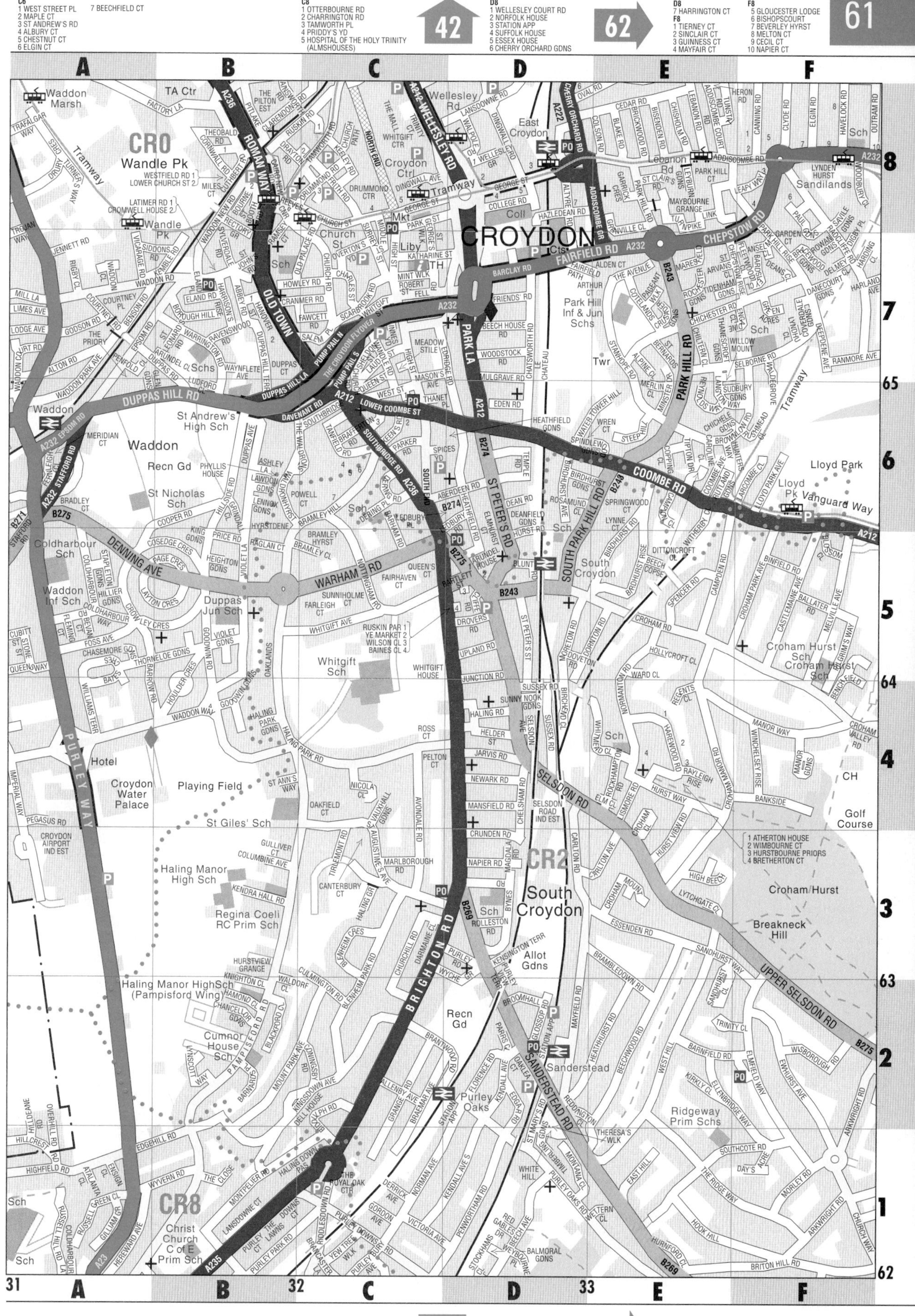

31 A B 32 C D 33 E F

43

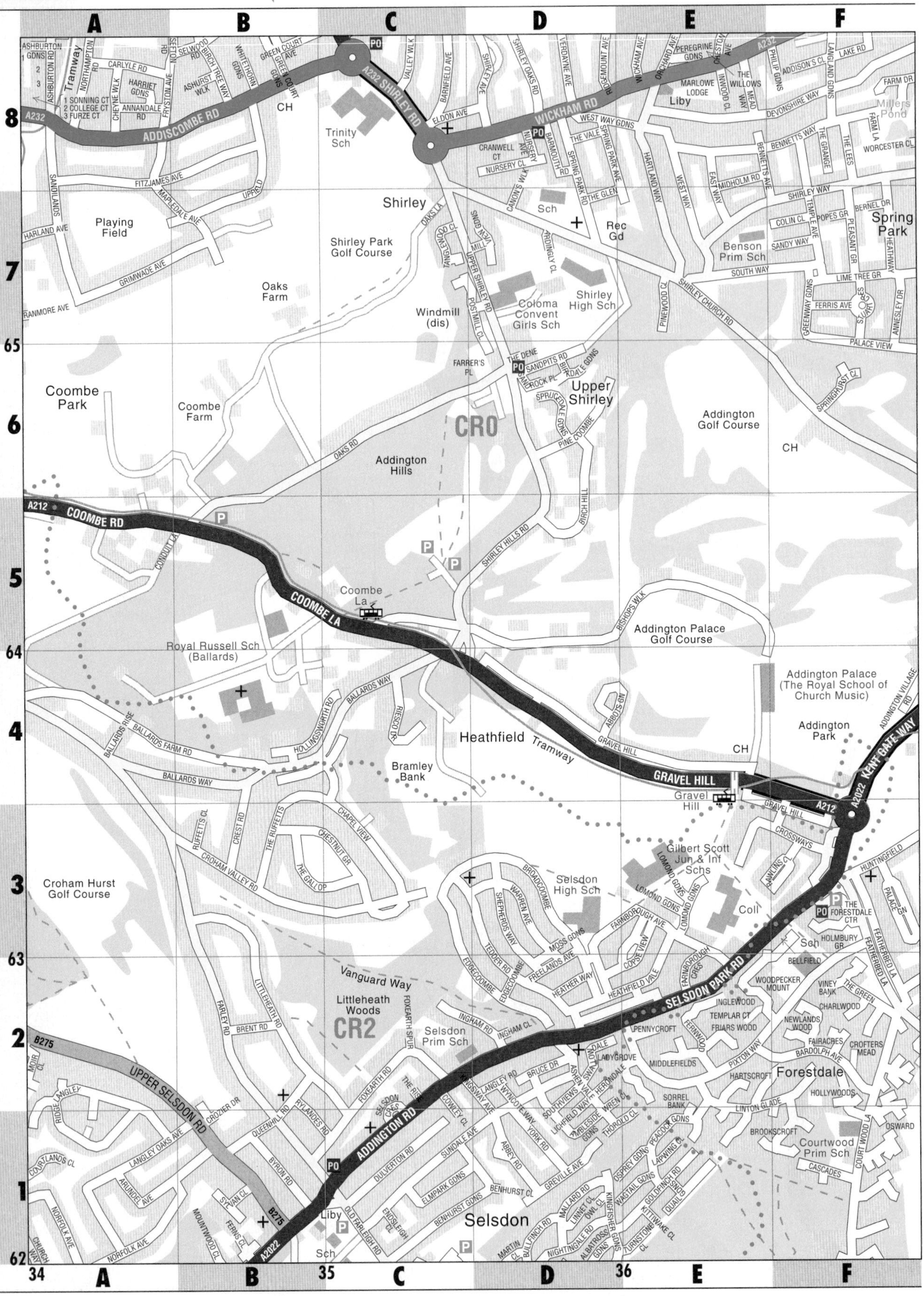

A B C D E F

8 7 65 6 5 64 4 3 63 2 1 62

Ashburton Gdns, Tramway, Northampton Rd, Carlyle Rd, Harriet Gdns, Cheyne Wlk, Annandale Rd, Ashburton Rd, 1 Sonning Ct, 2 College Ct, 3 Furze Ct, Fryston Ave, Selwood Rd, Sefton Rd, Ashurst Wlk, Birch Tree Way, Whitethorn Gdns, Green Court Ave, Green Court Gdns, CH, A232, Addiscombe Rd, Fitzjames Ave, Mapledale Ave, Upfield, Sandilands, Playing Field, Harland Ave, Grimwade Ave, Ranmore Ave, Oaks Farm

Trinity Sch, A232 Shirley Rd, Valley Wlk, Barnfield Ave, Shirley Ave, Eldon Ave, Shirley, Shirley Park Golf Course, Oaks La, Tanglewood Cl, Mill Lane, Upper Shirley Rd, Windmill (dis), Postmill Cl, Coloma Convent Girls Sch, Shirley High Sch

Shirley Oaks Rd, Verdayne Ave, Ridgemount Ave, Wickham Ave, Orchard Ave, Peregrine Gdns, Cheston Ave, A232, Wickham Rd, Cranwell Ct, Nursery Cl, Nursery Ave, Barmouth Rd, The Vale, Spring Park Ave, Spring Park Rd, The Glen, West Way Gdns, Canon's Wlk, Sch, Ardingly Cl, Rec Gd, Hartland Way, West Way, Pinewood Cl, Shirley Church Rd

Marlowe Lodge, The Willows, Inwood Cl, Mead Way, Liby, Philip Gdns, Addison's Cl, Langland Gdns, Lake Rd, Devonshire Way, Farm Dr, Millers Pond, Farm La, Bennetts Way, The Grange, The Lees, Worcester Cl, East Way, Midholm Rd, Bennetts Ave, Shirley Way, Colin Cl, Temple Ave, Popes Gr, Bernel Dr, Spring Park, Benson Prim Sch, Sandy Way, Pleasant Gr, Heathway, South Way, Lime Tree Gr, Greenway Gdns, Ferris Ave, St John's Cres, Annesley Dr, Palace View

Coombe Park, Coombe Farm, Farrer's Pl, The Dene, Sandpits Rd, Rock Pl, Birdhurst Gdns, Sprucedale Gdns, Upper Shirley, CR0, Pine Coombe, Oaks Rd, Addington Hills, Addington Golf Course, CH, Springhurst Cl, Birch Hill, Shirley Hills Rd

A212, Coombe Rd, Conduit La, Coombe La, Coombe La, Bishops Wlk, Addington Palace Golf Course, Royal Russell Sch (Ballards), Addington Palace (The Royal School of Church Music), Addington Village Rd, Ballards Way, Riesco Dr, Abbots Gn, Addington Park, Kent Gate Way, A2022, Ballards Rise, Ballards Farm Rd, Hollingsworth Rd, Heathfield, Tramway, Gravel Hill, CH, Bramley Bank, Ballards Way, Gravel Hill, A212

Ruffetts Cl, Crest Rd, The Ruffetts, Chestnut Gr, Chapel View, Croham Valley Rd, The Gallop, Croham Hurst Golf Course, Broadcoombe, Warren Ave, Shepherds Way, Selsdon High Sch, Gilbert Scott Jun & Inf Schs, Lomond Gdns, Crossways, Rawlins Cl, Huntingfield, Palace Gn, The Forestdale Ctr, Coll, Moss Gdns, Farnborough Ave, Copse View, Tedder Rd, Edgecoombe, Freelands Ave, Heather Way, Heathfield Vale, Farnborough Cres, Selsdon Park Rd, Holmbury Gr, Bellfield, Featherbed La, Woodpecker Mount, Viney Bank, The Green, Vanguard Way

Littleheath Rd, Farley Rd, Brent Rd, Littleheath Woods, CR2, Foxearth Spur, Selsdon Prim Sch, Ingham Rd, Ingham Cl, Inglewood, Templar Ct, Friars Wood, Pennycroft, Fernwood, Charlwood, Newlands Wood, Fairacres, Crofters Mead, Bardolph Ave, Middlefields, Pixton Way, Hartscroft, Forestdale, Ladygrove, Swan Dale, Ashen Vale

B275, Upper Selsdon Rd, Moir Cl, Ridge Langley, Crozier Dr, Queenhill Rd, Rylandes Rd, Foxearth Rd, The Rise, Selsdon Cres, Kingsway Ave, Cowley Cl, Langley Rd, Bruce Dr, Wyncote Way, Southviews, Lichfield Way, Heronsdale, Ambleside Gdns, Wren Cl, Thorold Cl, Sorrel Bank, Linton Glade, Hollywoods, Oswald, Brookscroft, Courtwood Prim Sch, Court Wood La, Cascades

Courtlands Cl, Langley Oaks Ave, Arundel Ave, Byron Rd, A2022, Addington Rd, Dulverton Rd, Sundale Ave, York Rd, Abbey Rd, Greville Ave, Peacock Gdns, Lapwing Cl, Osprey Gdns, Wagtail Gdns, Goldfinch Rd, Quail Gdns, Sylvan Cl, Norfolk Ave, Mountwood Cl, Ferns Cl, Church Way, Norfolk Ave, Liby, Sch, Old Farleigh Rd, Endsleigh Cl, Elmpark Gdns, Benhurst Gdns, Benhurst Cl, Selsdon, Martin Cres, Bullfinch Rd, Mallard Rd, Linnet Cl, Owl Cl, Nightingale Rd, Albatross Gdns, Kingfisher Gdns, Turnstone Cl, Kittiwake Cl

34 A B 35 C D 36 E F

61

81

44

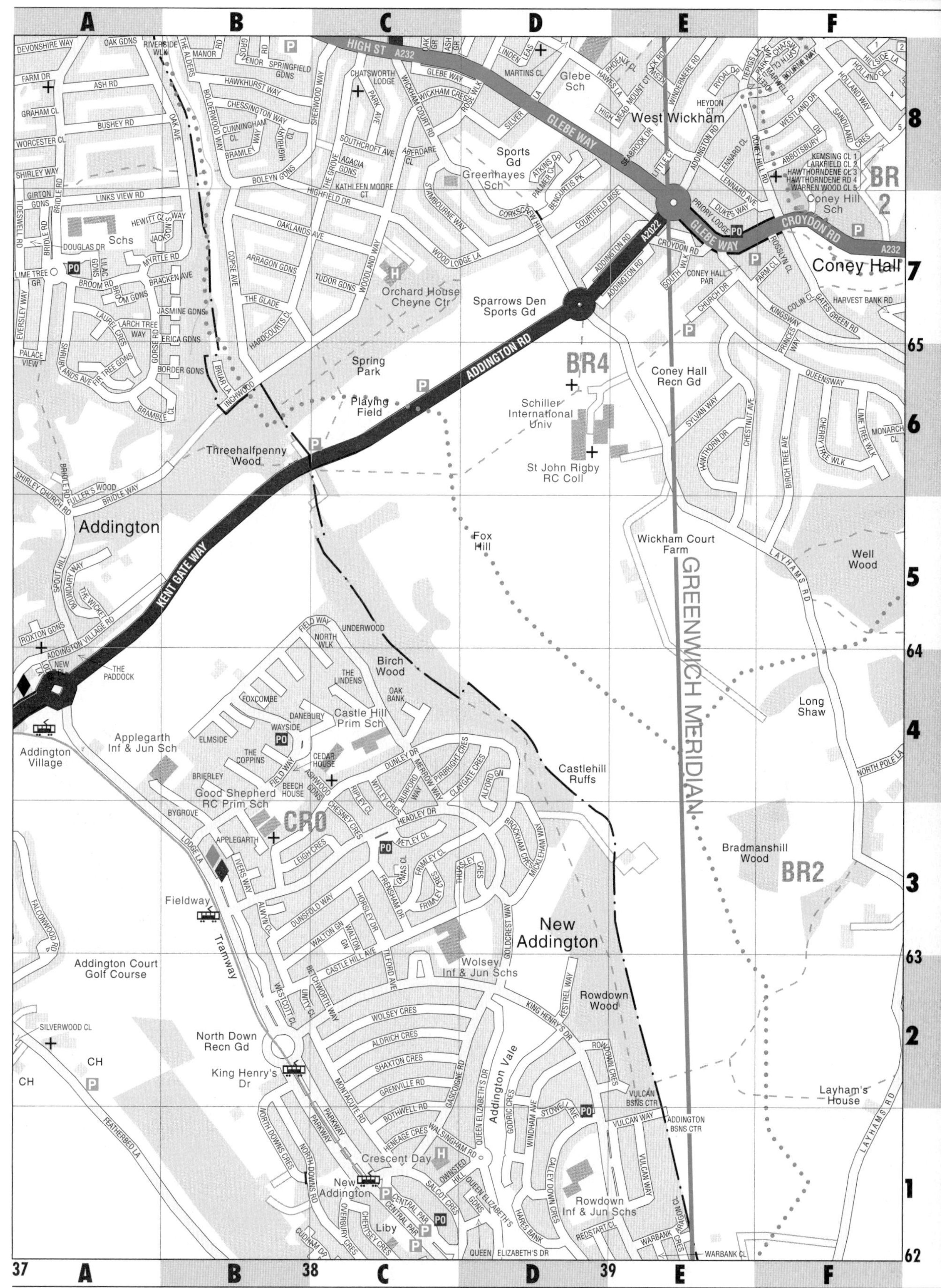
A
B
C
D
E
F
HIGH ST
A232
GLEBE WAY
West Wickham
Glebe Sch
Sports Gd
Greenhayes Sch
Coney Hill Sch
CROYDON RD
Coney Hall
BR 2
BR4
A2022
Orchard House Cheyne Ctr
Sparrows Den Sports Gd
ADDINGTON RD
Spring Park
Playing Field
Coney Hall Recn Gd
Schiller International Univ
St John Rigby RC Coll
Threehalfpenny Wood
Addington
KENT GATE WAY
Fox Hill
Wickham Court Farm
GREENWICH MERIDIAN
Well Wood
Birch Wood
Castle Hill Prim Sch
Long Shaw
Applegarth Inf & Jun Sch
Addington Village
Castlehill Ruffs
Good Shepherd RC Prim Sch
CR0
Bradmanshill Wood
BR2
Fieldway
Tramway
New Addington
Addington Court Golf Course
Wolsey Inf & Jun Schs
Rowdown Wood
North Down Recn Gd
King Henry's Dr
Addington Vale
Layham's House
LAYHAMS RD
Crescent Day
New Addington
Liby
Rowdown Inf & Jun Schs
ADDINGTON BSNS CTR
DEVONSHIRE WAY
OAK GDNS
FARM DR
ASH RD
GRAHAM CL
BUSHEY RD
WORCESTER CL
SHIRLEY WAY
LINKS VIEW RD
Schs
DOUGLAS DR
LIME TREE GR
BROOM RD
EVERSLEY WAY
PALACE VIEW
SHIRLEY CHURCH RD
FULLER'S WOOD
BRIDLE WAY
SPOUT HILL
ROXTON GDNS
ADDINGTON VILLAGE RD
THE PADDOCK
SILVERWOOD CL
FEATHERBED LA
FALCONWOOD RD
CH
ELMSIDE
FOXCOMBE
DANEBURY
WAYSIDE
THE COPPINS
BRIERLEY
BYGROVE
APPLEGARTH
LODGE LA
FIELD WAY
UNDERWOOD
NORTH WLK
THE LINDENS
OAK BANK
DUNLEY DR
HEADLEY DR
GOLDCREST WAY
KING HENRY'S DR
WOLSEY CRES
ALDRICH CRES
SHAXTON CRES
GRENVILLE RD
BOTHWELL RD
HENEAGE CRES
PARKWAY
NORTH DOWNS CRES
NORTH DOWNS RD
CENTRAL PAR
QUEEN ELIZABETH'S DR
WARBANK CL
VULCAN WAY
VULCAN BSNS CTR
KESTREL WAY
ROWDOWN CRES
STOWELL AVE
WINDHAM AVE
GODRIC CRES
CALLEY DOWN CRES
HARES BANK
REDSTART CL
WARBANK CRES
CASTLE HILL AVE
TILFORD AVE
WESTCOTT CL
BETCHWORTH WAY
DUNSFOLD WAY
WALTON GN
HORSLEY DR
FRENSHAM DR
QUEENSWAY
KINGSWAY
PRINCES WAY
SYLVAN WAY
HAWTHORN DR
CHESTNUT AVE
BIRCH TREE AVE
CHERRY TREE WLK
LIME TREE WLK
MONARCH CL
NORTH POLE LA
HARVEST BANK RD
GATES GREEN RD
COLIN CL
ROSSLYN CL
FARM CL
CHURCH DR
CONEY HALL PAR
SOUTH WLK
CROYDON RD
ADDINGTON RD
COURTFIELD RISE
CORKSCREW HILL
WOOD LODGE LA
STAMBOURNE WAY
KEMSING CL 1
LARKFIELD CL 2
HAWTHORNDENE CL 3
HAWTHORNDENE RD 4
WARREN WOOD CL 5
37
38
39
62
63
64
65
1
2
3
4
5
6
7
8

82

45

D8
1 MULBERRY CL
2 MAY CL
3 SHRIVENHAM CL
4 CENTURION CL
5 CHAFFINCH CL
6 TARBAT CT
7 ROCKFIELD WAY
8 BALINTORE CT

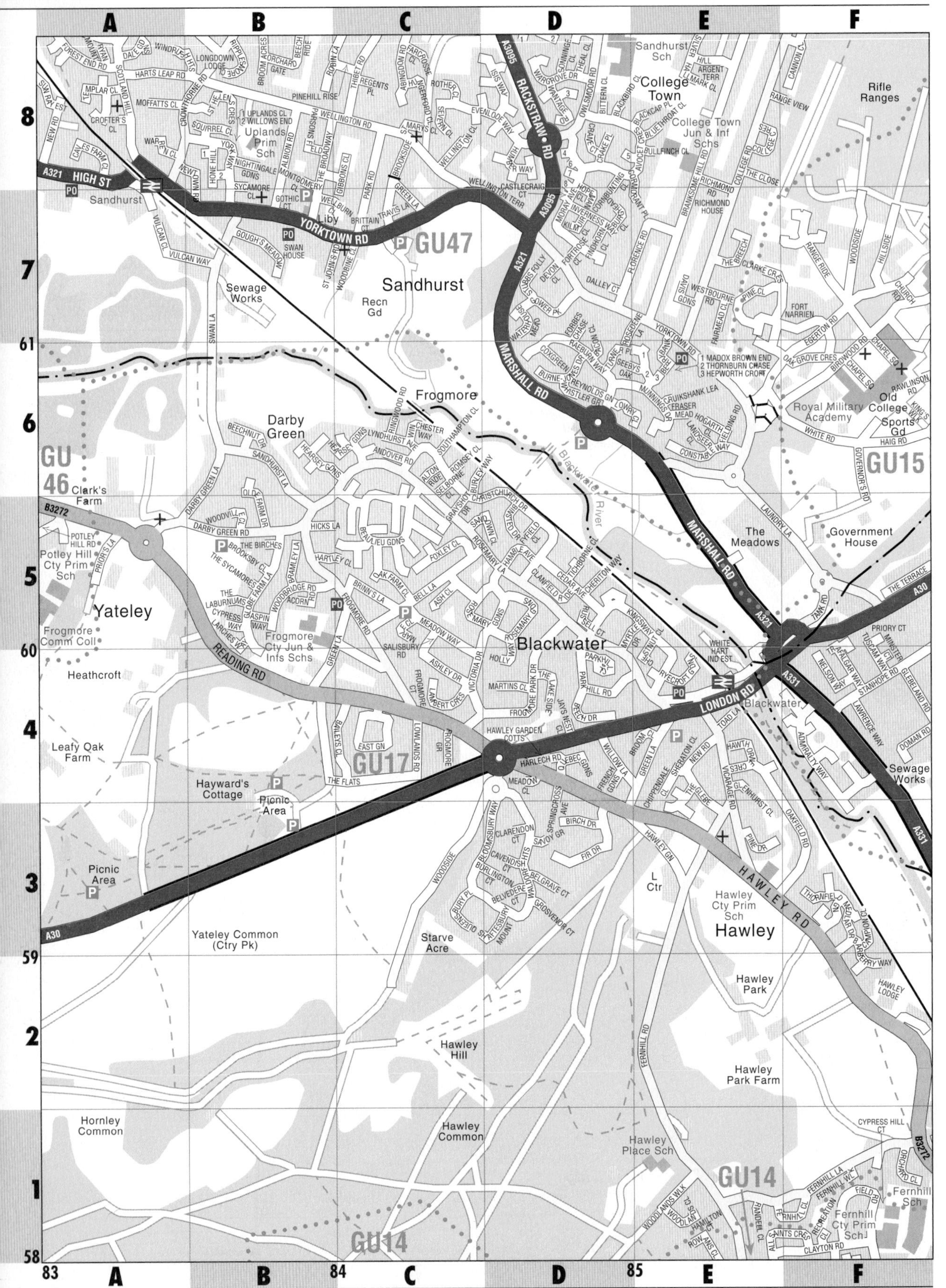

84

46
66

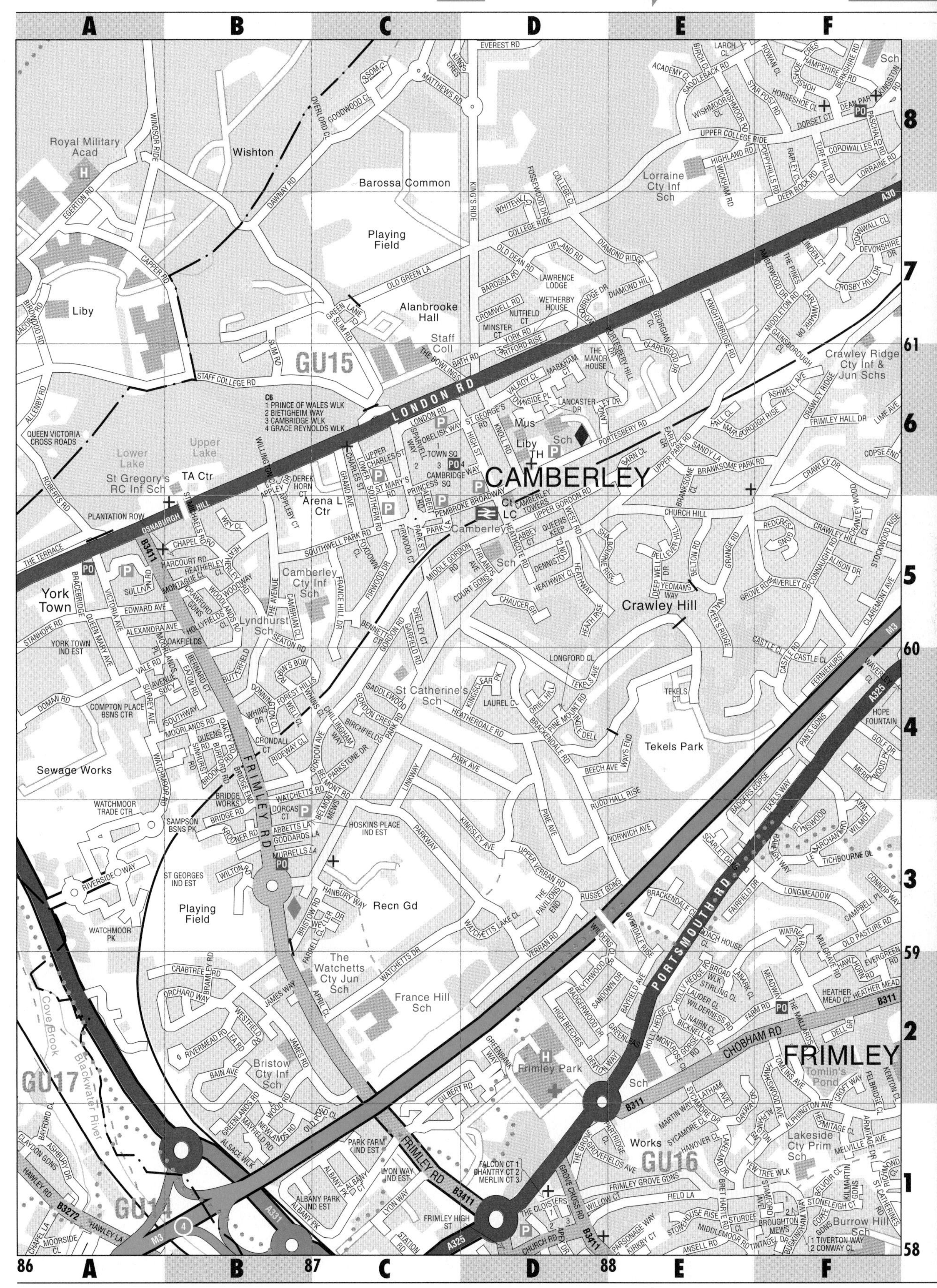
A
B
C
D
E
F
8
7
61
6
5
60
4
3
59
2
1
58
86
87
88
Royal Military Acad
Wishton
Barossa Common
Playing Field
Alanbrooke Hall
Staff Coll
Liby
GU15
Lorraine Cty Inf Sch
Crawley Ridge Cty Inf & Jun Schs
LONDON RD
A30
C6
1 PRINCE OF WALES WLK
2 BIETIGHEIM WAY
3 CAMBRIDGE WLK
4 GRACE REYNOLDS WLK
Upper Lake
Lower Lake
St Gregory's RC Inf Sch
TA Ctr
Arena L Ctr
Mus
Sch
TH
CAMBERLEY
Ct
LC
Camberley
York Town
Camberley Cty Inf Sch
Lyndhurst Sch
Crawley Hill
St Catherine's Sch
Tekels Park
Sewage Works
FRIMLEY RD
B3411
Recn Gd
Playing Field
The Watchetts Cty Jun Sch
France Hill Sch
PORTSMOUTH RD
M3
A325
A331
B3272
B311
CHOBHAM RD
FRIMLEY
Tomlin's Pond
Frimley Park
Bristow Cty Inf Sch
GU17
GU14
GU16
Works
Lakeside Cty Prim Sch
Burrow Hill Sch
Cove Brook
Blackwater River
FALCON CT 1
CHANTRY CT 2
MERLIN CT 3
1 TIVERTON WAY
2 CONWAY CL

85
66

65
47

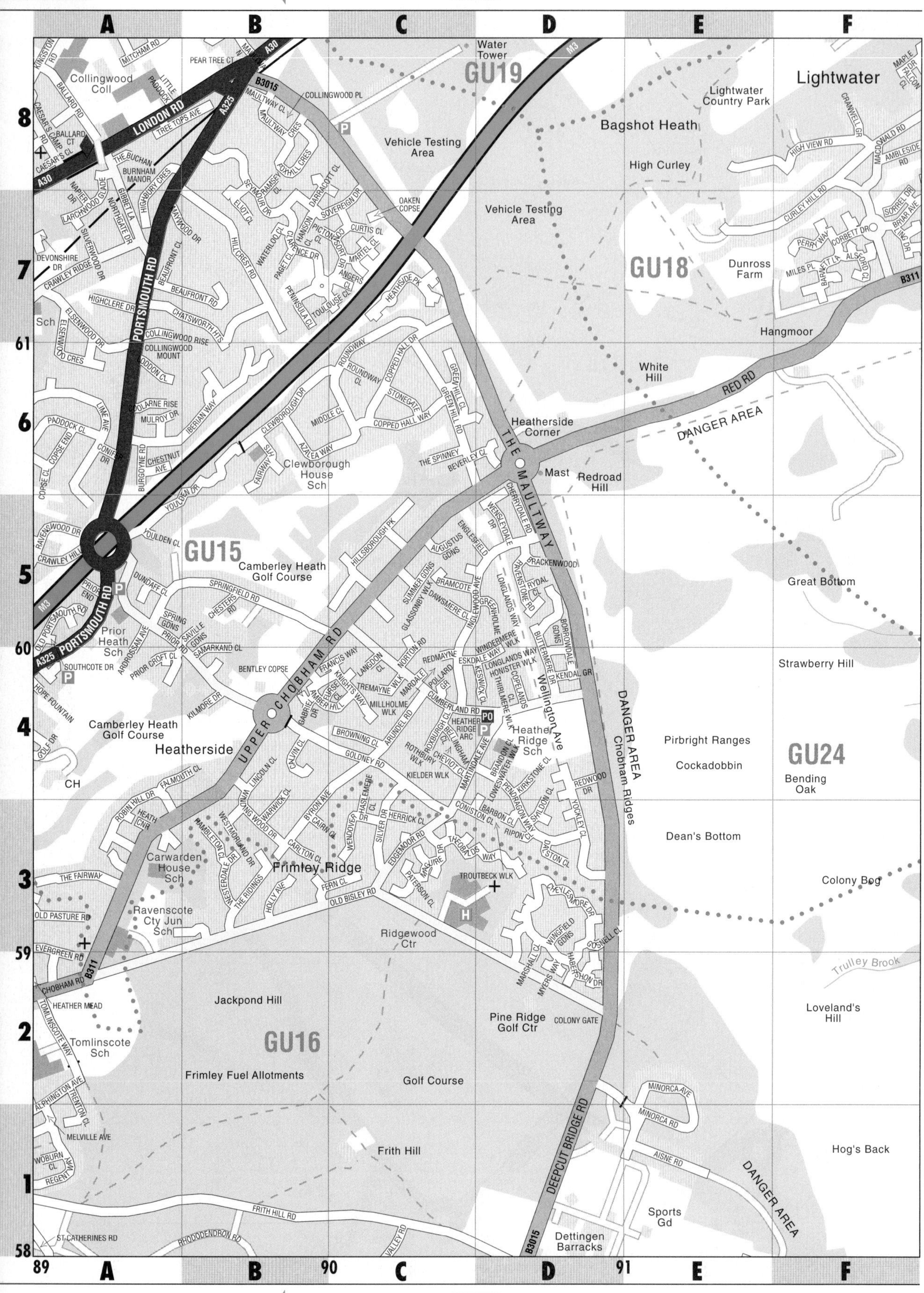
A
B
C
D
E
F
8
7
61
6
5
60
4
3
59
2
1
58
89
90
91
Collingwood Coll
Lightwater
Lightwater Country Park
Bagshot Heath
High Curley
Water Tower
GU19
Vehicle Testing Area
Vehicle Testing Area
GU18
Dunross Farm
Hangmoor
White Hill
LONDON RD
A30
A325
M3
B3015
B311
PORTSMOUTH RD
RED RD
DANGER AREA
Heatherside Corner
Mast
Redroad Hill
THE MAULTWAY
Clewborough House Sch
GU15
Camberley Heath Golf Course
Great Bottom
Strawberry Hill
Prior Heath Sch
UPPER CHOBHAM RD
Wellington Ave
Heather Ridge Sch
DANGER AREA
Chobham Ridges
Pirbright Ranges
Cockadobbin
GU24
Bending Oak
Camberley Heath Golf Course
Heatherside
CH
Dean's Bottom
Carwarden House Sch
Frimley Ridge
Colony Bog
Ravenscote Cty Jun Sch
Ridgewood Ctr
Trulley Brook
Jackpond Hill
Pine Ridge Golf Ctr
COLONY GATE
Loveland's Hill
GU16
Tomlinscote Sch
Frimley Fuel Allotments
Golf Course
DEEPCUT BRIDGE RD
MINORCA AVE
MINORCA RD
AISNE RD
Frith Hill
Hog's Back
DANGER AREA
FRITH HILL RD
Sports Gd
Dettingen Barracks
ST CATHERINES RD
RHODODENDRON RD
VALLEY RD
A
B
C
D
E
F

65
86

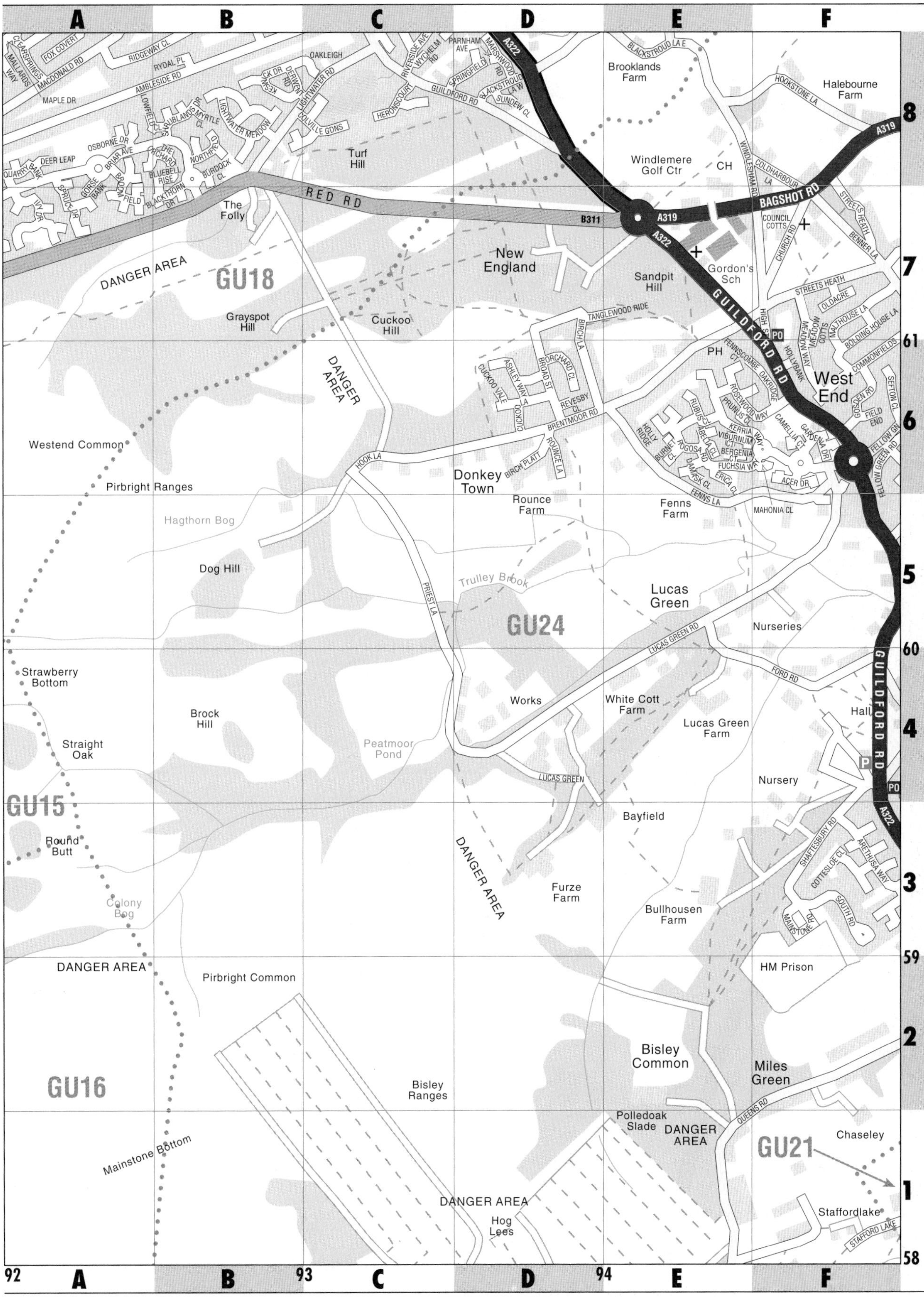

A B C D E F

8
7
61
6
5
60
4
3
59
2
1
58

Brooklands Farm
Halebourne Farm
Turf Hill
Windlemere Golf Ctr
CH
RED RD
BAGSHOT RD
B311
A319
A322
The Folly
New England
Sandpit Hill
Gordon's Sch
COUNCIL COTTS
DANGER AREA
GU18
Grayspot Hill
Cuckoo Hill
GUILDFORD RD
PO
PH
West End
Westend Common
Pirbright Ranges
Donkey Town
Rounce Farm
Fenns Farm
Hagthorn Bog
Dog Hill
Trulley Brook
Lucas Green
GU24
Nurseries
Strawberry Bottom
Works
White Cott Farm
Lucas Green Farm
Brock Hill
Straight Oak
Peatmoor Pond
Hall
P
Nursery
GU15
Round Butt
Bayfield
Colony Bog
Furze Farm
Bullhousen Farm
DANGER AREA
HM Prison
Pirbright Common
Bisley Common
Miles Green
GU16
Bisley Ranges
Polledoak Slade
DANGER AREA
Chaseley
GU21
Mainstone Bottom
DANGER AREA
Hog Lees
Staffordlake

92 A B 93 C D 94 E F

67
49

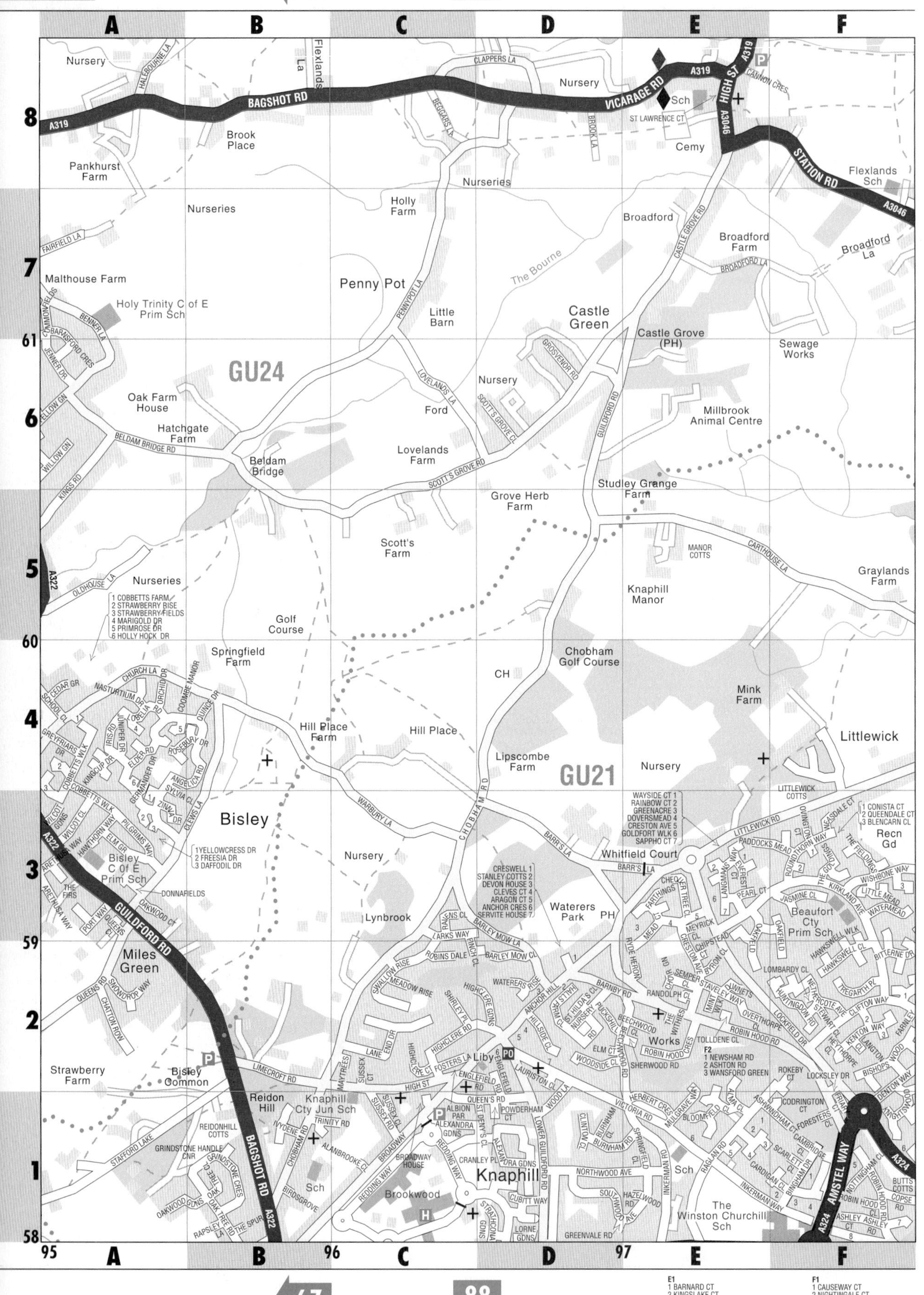

67
88

E1
1 BARNARD CT
2 KINGSLAKE CT
3 WILLIAM RUSSELL CT
4 SAYER CT
5 ROBERTSON CT
6 WELLINGTON TERR

F1
1 CAUSEWAY CT
2 NIGHTINGALE CT
3 MOYNE CT
4 GUINNESS CT
5 NOTTINGHAM CT
6 CRANFIELD CT
7 CAPSTANS WHARF
8 BARRACK PATH

50
70
A
B
C
D
E
F
8
7
61
6
5
60
4
3
59
2
1
58
98
99
00
Emmett's Mill
Nursery
Mill Bourne
Fairoaks Airport
KT16
Willow Farm
GU24
Sunfield Farm
Nursery
Highfield
The Bourne
Scotchers Farm
Bonseys Cottages
Milford Green
Mimbridge
SANDPIT HALL RD
PHILPOT LA
MOUNT RD
Wapshott Farm
Danewell Gutter
STATION RD
White Lodge Farm
Heather Farm
Cox Hill
Coxhill Green
Border Farm
Mim Bridge
Horsell Common
Deep Pool Farm
Garden Ctr
CHOBHAM RD
The Woking Nuffield
A245
SHORE'S RD
COMMON CL
LITTLEWICK RD
HORSELL COMMON RD
CHEAPSIDE
Wesbury Farm
CARTHOUSE LA
GU21
Woking High Sch
KETTLEWELL HILL
Parley Brook Farm
Horsell Birch
HORSELL BIRCH
Horsell C of E Jun Sch
Horsell
St Andrew's Sch
Cable House Sch
CHOBHAM RD
221
Goldsworth Park Trad Est
Sythwood Cty Prim Sch
Horsell Village Cty Inf
WISHBONE WAY
Goldsworth Park
VICTORIA WAY
A3046
A320
A324
Goldsworth Park Ctr
LOCKFIELD DR
Basingstoke Canal
Sch
Goldsworth Road Ind Est
WOKING
GUILDFORD RD
Woking
GU22
Woking Comm
The Peacocks Sh Ctr
Wolsey Pl Sh Ctr
Mkt
Liby
89
70
A1
1 HALLEY'S CT
2 WENDRON CL
3 HELFORD WLK
4 BUTTS COTTS
5 LOWTHORPE
6 GOLDSWORTH ORCH
7 WOODLANDS CT
B1
1 SELBY WLK
2 WATERSIDE WAY
3 HELMSDALE
4 ALLOWAY CL
5 MILLCOMBE CL
E1
1 WAVERLEY CT
2 MONTGOMERY RD
3 THE ROWANS
4 LAMPETER CL
5 EBBAGE CT
6 EVERLANDS CL
7 HOMEBEECH HOUSE
8 HOMEWORTH HOUSE
9 CARMEL CL
10 THORSDEN CT
11 PARK GATE CT
12 ELMCROFT
13 HILLMOUNT
14 SOUTHVIEW CT
15 HILL VIEW CT
F1
1 RADSTONE CT
2 WILDBANK CT
3 BEECHVALE
4 PARK PL
5 WESTVIEW
6 HIGHDENE
7 MEADSIDE
8 PINEHURST
9 FIRCROFT CT
F2
1 CHOBHAM RD
2 CHRISTCHURCH WAY
3 TOWN SQ
4 WOLSEY WLK
5 MERCIA WLK
6 CHAPEL ST
7 CHURCH PATH
8 ADDISON RD
9 GROSVENOR PL

69
51

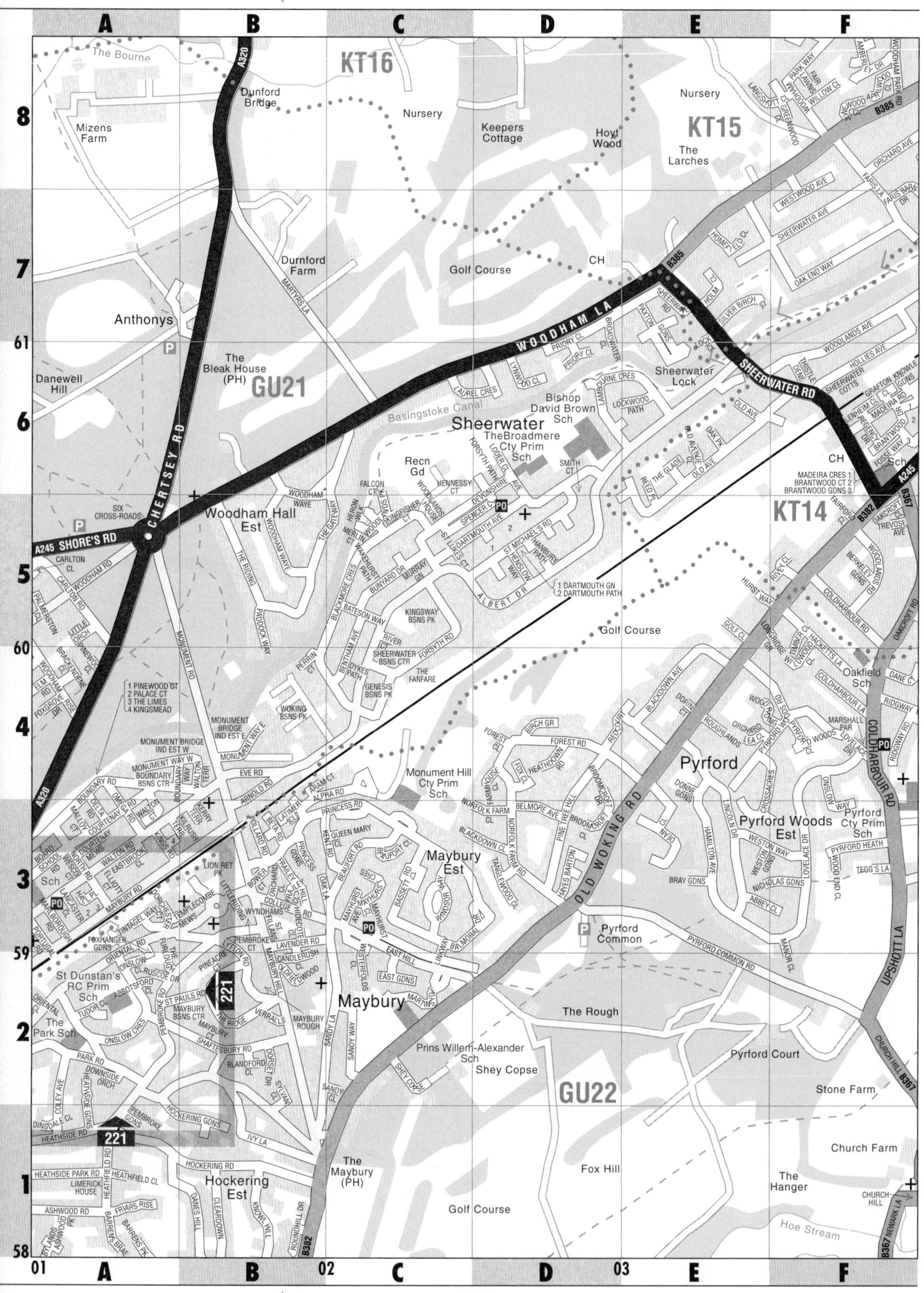
A
B
C
D
E
F
8
7
61
6
5
60
4
3
59
2
1
58
01
02
03
The Bourne
A320
Dunford Bridge
KT16
Nursery
Keepers Cottage
Hoyt Wood
KT15
The Larches
Mizens Farm
B385
Durnford Farm
Golf Course
CH
Anthonys
WOODHAM LA
SHEERWATER RD
Danewell Hill
The Bleak House (PH)
GU21
Basingstoke Canal
Sheerwater
Sheerwater Lock
Bishop David Brown Sch
TheBroadmere Cty Prim Sch
Recn Gd
CHERTSEY RD
SIX CROSS-ROADS
A245 SHORE'S RD
Woodham Hall Est
KT14
A245
B367
B382
MARTYRS LA
MONUMENT RD
THE RIDING
PADDOCK WAY
WOODHAM WAYE
KINGSWAY BSNS PK
SHEERWATER BSNS CTR
GENESIS BSNS PK
WOKING BSNS PK
THE FANFARE
1 DARTMOUTH GN
2 DARTMOUTH PATH
1 PINEWOOD CT
2 PALACE CT
3 THE LIMES
4 KINGSMEAD
MONUMENT BRIDGE IND EST E
MONUMENT BRIDGE IND EST W
BOUNDARY BSNS CTR
Monument Hill Cty Prim Sch
Maybury Est
Pyrford
Pyrford Woods Est
Pyrford Cty Prim Sch
Oakfield Sch
MADEIRA CRES 1
BRANTWOOD CT 2
BRANTWOOD GDNS 3
OLD WOKING RD
COLDHARBOUR RD
UPSHOTT LA
Pyrford Common
PYRFORD COMMON RD
St Dunstan's RC Prim Sch
The Park Sch
Maybury
MAYBURY BSNS CTR
MAYBURY ROUGH
LION RET PK
221
The Rough
Pyrford Court
Prins Willem-Alexander Sch
Shey Copse
GU22
Stone Farm
Church Farm
Fox Hill
The Hanger
The Maybury (PH)
Hockering Est
Golf Course
Hoe Stream
CHURCH HILL
B367 NEWARK LA
CHURCH HILL B367
LIMERICK HOUSE
HEATHSIDE RD
HOCKERING RD
HOCKERING GDNS
ROUNDHILL DR

69
90

52
72

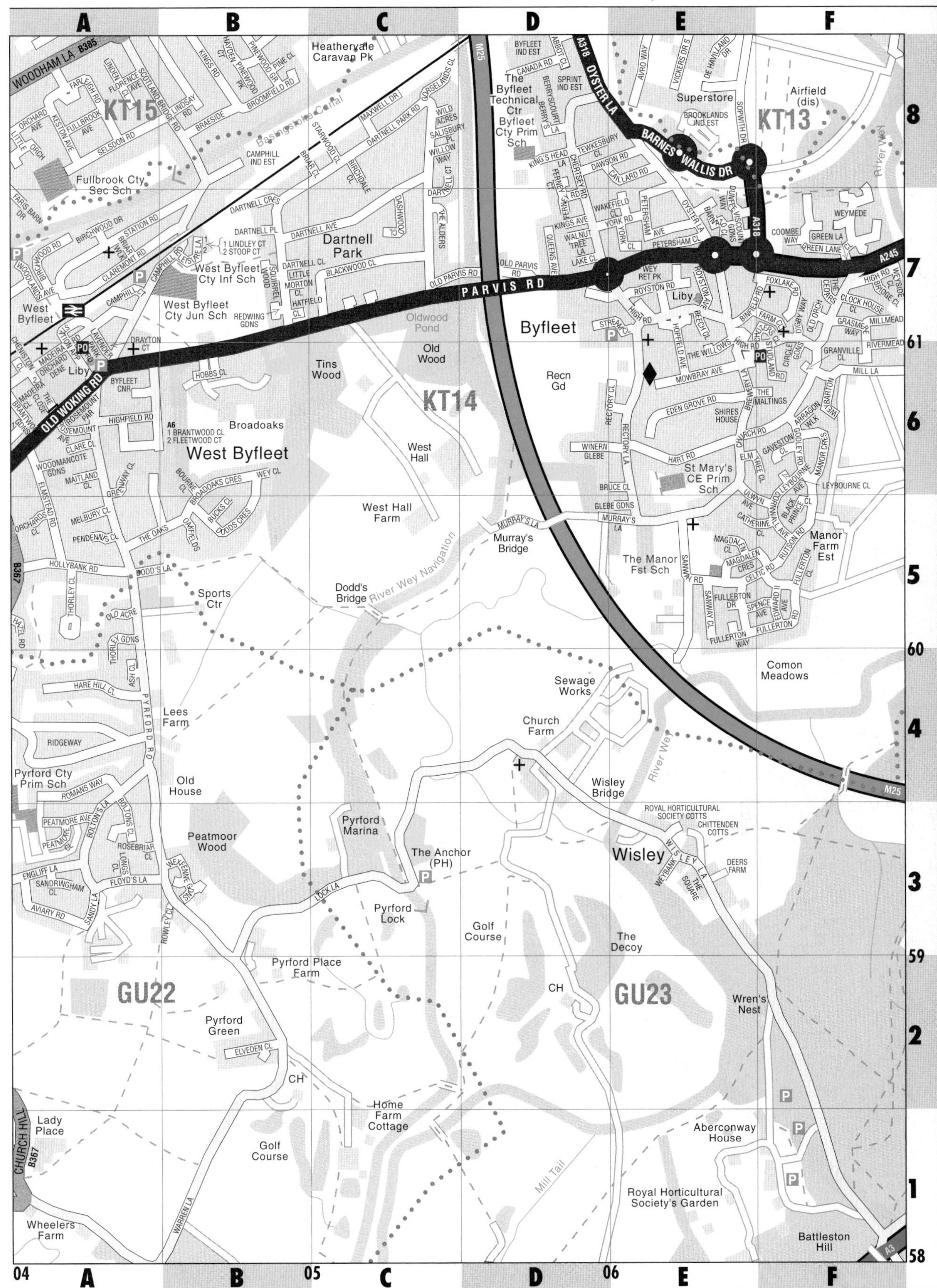
A
B
C
D
E
F
8
7
61
6
5
60
4
3
59
2
1
58
04
05
06
KT15
KT13
KT14
GU22
GU23
WOODHAM LA
B385
Heathervale Caravan Pk
Basingstoke Canal
Fullbrook Cty Sec Sch
CAMPHILL IND EST
West Byfleet Cty Inf Sch
West Byfleet Cty Jun Sch
West Byfleet
Liby
OLD WOKING RD
Dartnell Park
DARTNELL AVE
PARVIS RD
OLD PARVIS RD
M25
Oldwood Pond
Old Wood
Tins Wood
Broadoaks
West Byfleet
West Hall
West Hall Farm
BYFLEET IND EST
The Byfleet Technical Ctr
Byfleet Cty Prim Sch
SPRINT IND EST
A318
OYSTER LA
BARNES WALLIS DR
Superstore
BROOKLANDS IND EST
Airfield (dis)
River Wey
A245
Byfleet
Recn Gd
St Mary's CE Prim Sch
Murray's Bridge
The Manor Fst Sch
Manor Farm Est
HIGH RD
HART RD
RECTORY LA
MOWBRAY AVE
EDEN GROVE RD
SHIRES HOUSE
THE MALTINGS
LEYBOURNE CL
MILL LA
Dodd's Bridge
River Wey Navigation
Sports Ctr
B367
HOLLYBANK RD
DODD'S LA
Comon Meadows
Sewage Works
Church Farm
Lees Farm
PYRFORD RD
RIDGEWAY
Pyrford Cty Prim Sch
Old House
Peatmoor Wood
Pyrford Marina
The Anchor (PH)
Wisley Bridge
ROYAL HORTICULTURAL SOCIETY COTTS
CHITTENDEN COTTS
Wisley
WISLEY LA
DEERS FARM
LOCK LA
Pyrford Lock
Golf Course
The Decoy
Pyrford Place Farm
CH
Wren's Nest
Pyrford Green
ELVEDEN CL
ROWLEY CL
Lady Place
CHURCH HILL
Home Farm Cottage
Golf Course
Mill Tail
Aberconway House
Royal Horticultural Society's Garden
Wheelers Farm
WARREN LA
Battleston Hill
A3

91
72

71 53

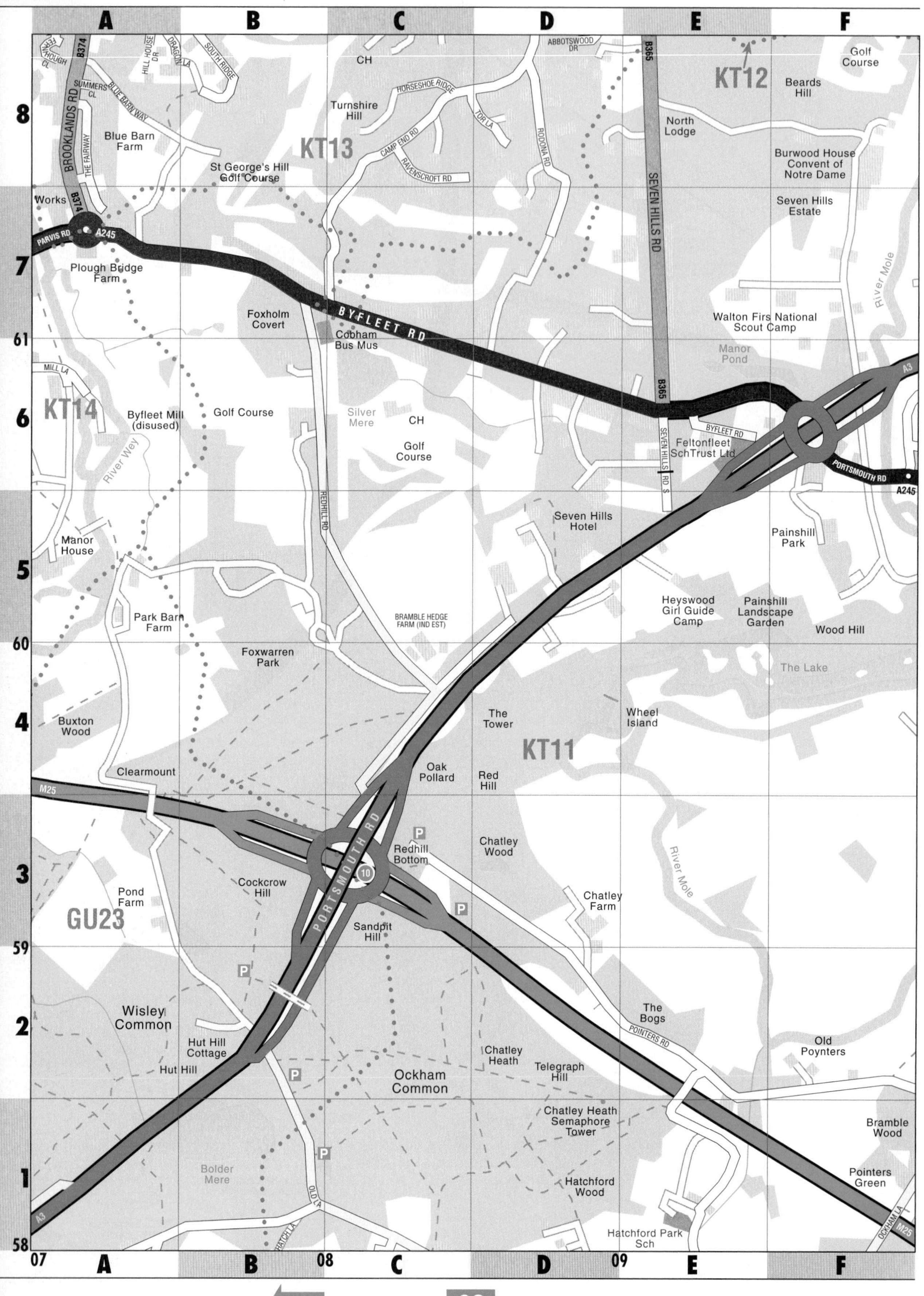
A B C D E F
8 7 61 6 5 60 4 3 59 2 1 58
07 08 09
KT12
KT13
KT14
KT11
GU23
Golf Course
Beards Hill
CH
Turnshire Hill
HORSESHOE RIDGE
CAMP END RD
RAVENSCROFT RD
TOR LA
RODONA RD
ABBOTSWOOD DR
B365
SEVEN HILLS RD
North Lodge
Burwood House Convent of Notre Dame
Seven Hills Estate
BROOKLANDS RD
B374
SUMMERS CL
BLUE BARN WAY
THE FAIRWAY
HILL HOUSE DR
DRAGON LA
SOUTH RIDGE
Blue Barn Farm
St George's Hill Golf Course
Works
PARVIS RD
A245
Plough Bridge Farm
BYFLEET RD
Foxholm Covert
Cobham Bus Mus
River Mole
Walton Firs National Scout Camp
Manor Pond
MILL LA
Byfleet Mill (disused)
Golf Course
Silver Mere
CH
Golf Course
A3
BYFLEET RD
Feltonfleet SchTrust Ltd
SEVEN HILLS RD S
PORTSMOUTH RD
River Wey
REDHILL RD
Seven Hills Hotel
Painshill Park
Manor House
Park Barn Farm
BRAMBLE HEDGE FARM (IND EST)
Heyswood Girl Guide Camp
Painshill Landscape Garden
Wood Hill
Foxwarren Park
The Lake
Buxton Wood
The Tower
Wheel Island
Clearmount
Oak Pollard
Red Hill
M25
PORTSMOUTH RD
P
Redhill Bottom
Chatley Wood
10
Cockcrow Hill
Pond Farm
Sandpit Hill
Chatley Farm
River Mole
Wisley Common
The Bogs
POINTERS RD
Hut Hill Cottage
Hut Hill
Chatley Heath
Telegraph Hill
Ockham Common
Old Poynters
Chatley Heath Semaphore Tower
Bramble Wood
Bolder Mere
OLD LA
Hatchford Wood
Pointers Green
OCKHAM LA
Hatchford Park Sch
HATCH LA

71 92

54
74

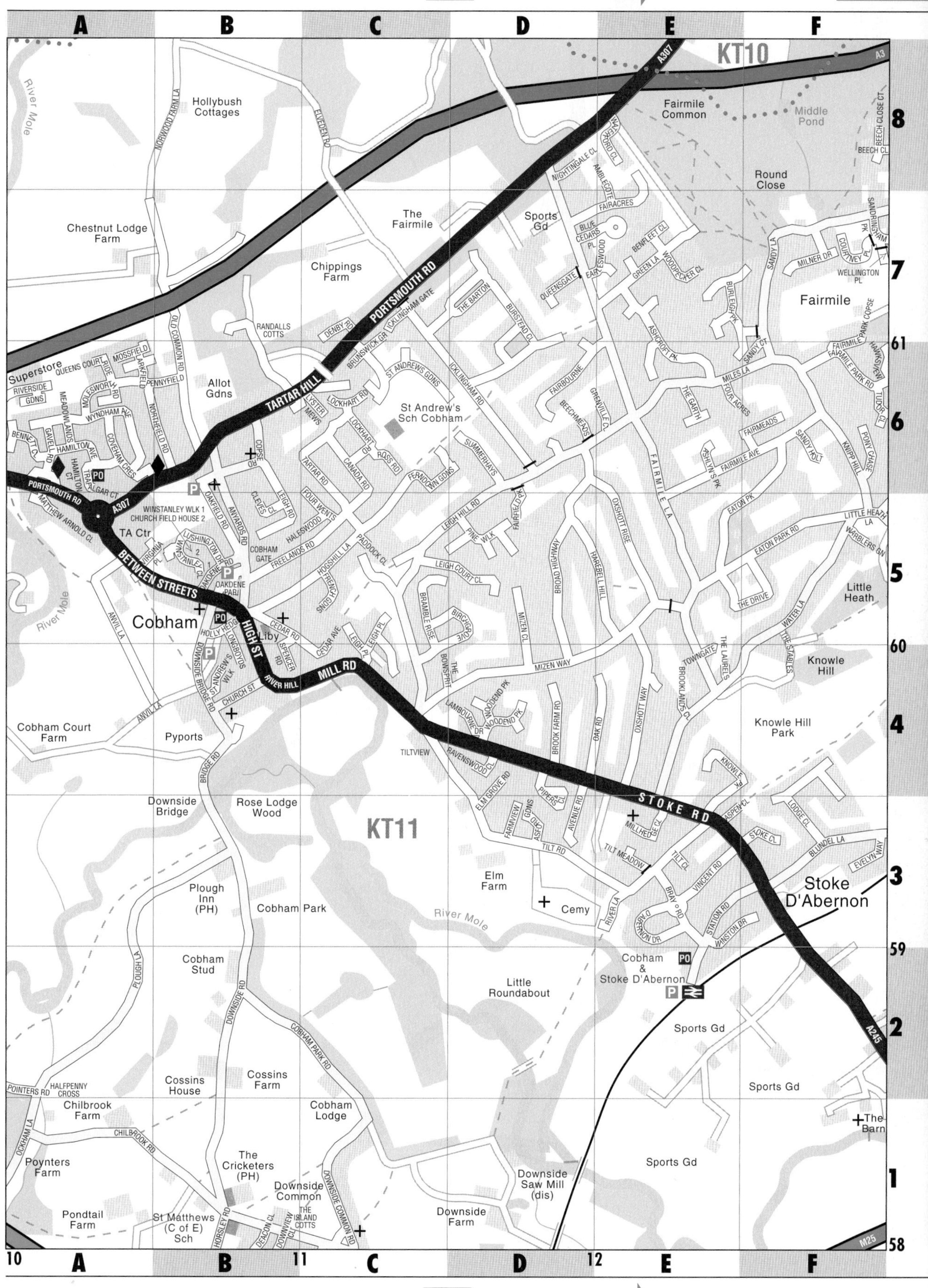
A
B
C
D
E
F
KT10
KT11
Cobham
Stoke D'Abernon
Fairmile
Fairmile Common
Middle Pond
Round Close
Hollybush Cottages
Chestnut Lodge Farm
The Fairmile
Chippings Farm
Sports Gd
Allot Gdns
St Andrew's Sch Cobham
Superstore
Little Heath
Knowle Hill
Knowle Hill Park
Cobham Court Farm
Pyports
Downside Bridge
Rose Lodge Wood
Plough Inn (PH)
Cobham Park
Elm Farm
Cemy
Cobham Stud
Little Roundabout
Cobham & Stoke D'Abernon
Cossins House
Cossins Farm
Chilbrook Farm
Cobham Lodge
Poynters Farm
The Cricketers (PH)
Downside Common
Downside Saw Mill (dis)
Downside Farm
Pondtail Farm
St Matthews (C of E) Sch
The Barn
River Mole
PORTSMOUTH RD
TARTAR HILL
BETWEEN STREETS
HIGH ST
RIVER HILL
MILL RD
STOKE RD
A307
A3
A245
M25
TA Ctr
Liby
8
7
61
6
5
60
4
3
59
2
1
58
10
11
12

93
74

73
55

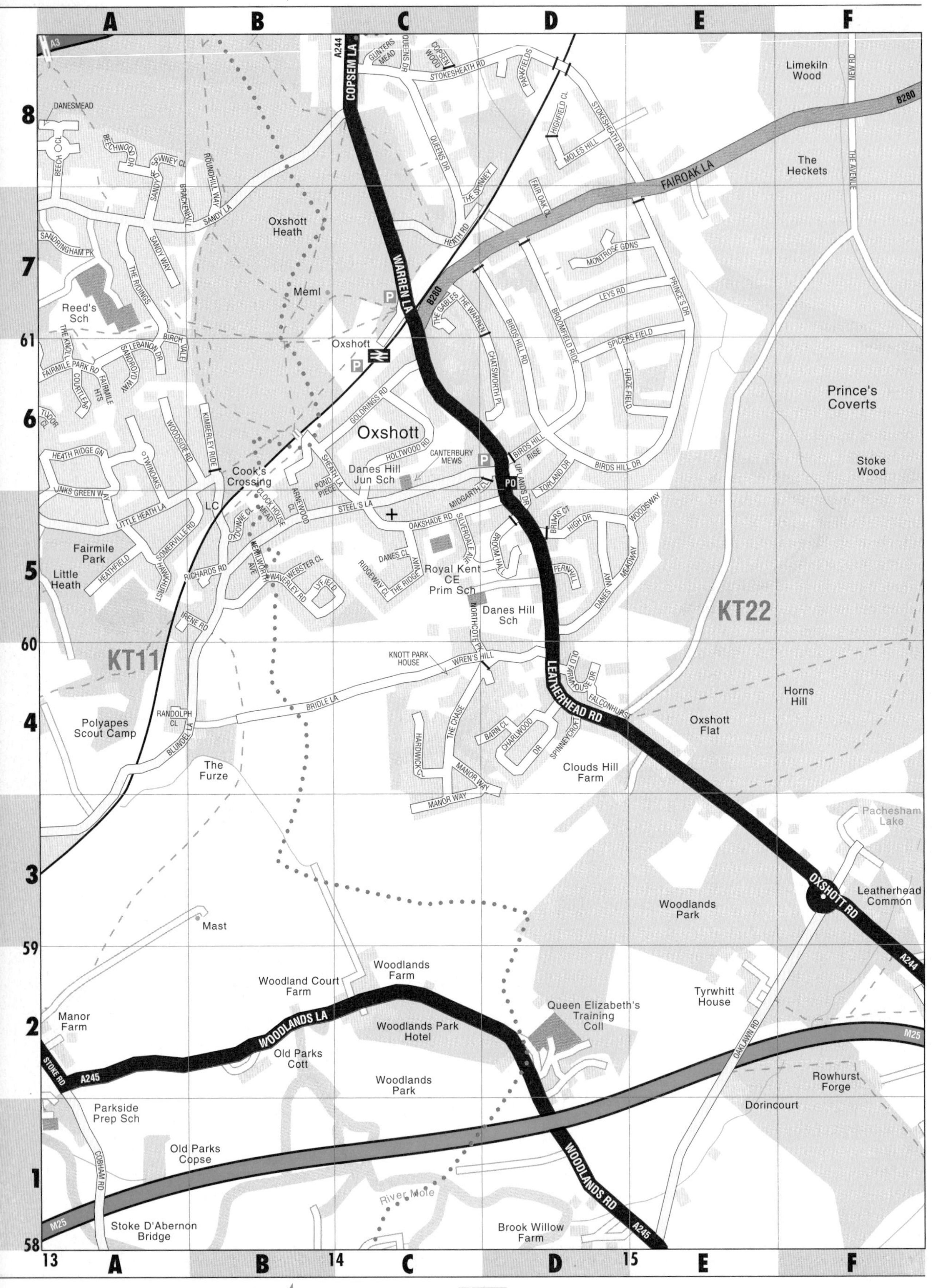

Oxshott
Oxshott Heath
Meml
Reed's Sch
Cook's Crossing
Danes Hill Jun Sch
Royal Kent CE Prim Sch
Danes Hill Sch
Fairmile Park
Little Heath
KT11
KT22
Polyapes Scout Camp
The Furze
Mast
Limekiln Wood
The Heckets
Prince's Coverts
Stoke Wood
Horns Hill
Oxshott Flat
Clouds Hill Farm
Pachesham Lake
Leatherhead Common
Woodlands Park
Tyrwhitt House
Queen Elizabeth's Training Coll
Woodlands Farm
Woodland Court Farm
Woodlands Park Hotel
Old Parks Cott
Manor Farm
Parkside Prep Sch
Old Parks Copse
Stoke D'Abernon Bridge
Brook Willow Farm
Rowhurst Forge
Dorincourt
River Mole
COPSEM LA
WARREN LA
LEATHERHEAD RD
OXSHOTT RD
WOODLANDS LA
WOODLANDS RD
FAIROAK LA
STOKE RD
COBHAM RD
OAKLAWN RD
BRIDLE LA
STEEL'S LA
BIRDS HILL RD
STOKESHEATH RD
QUEENS DR
PRINCE'S DR
BLUNDEL LA
SANDY LA
M25
A244
A245
B280
A3

73
94

56
76

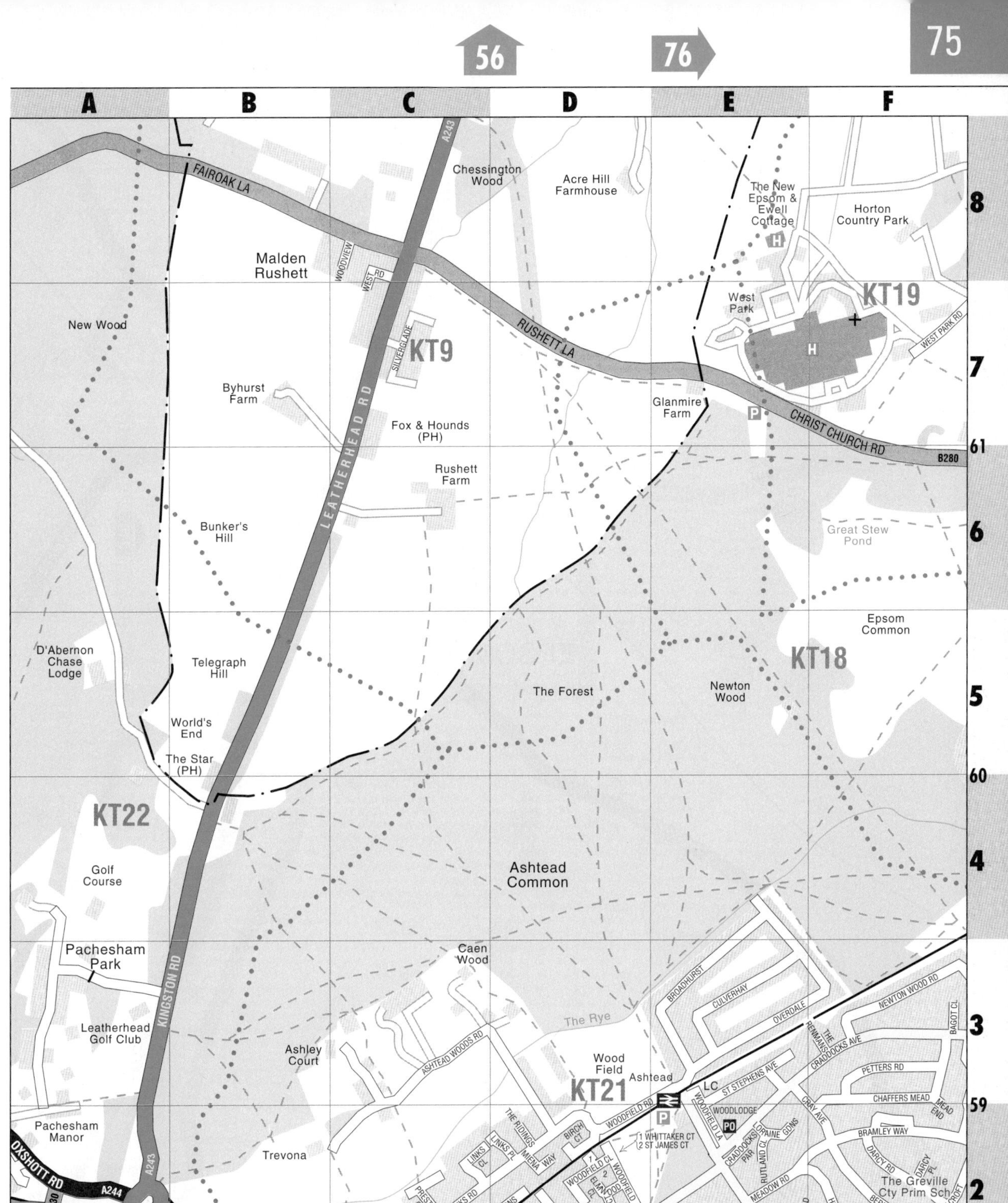
A
B
C
D
E
F
8
7
61
6
5
60
4
3
59
2
1
58
16
17
18
FAIROAK LA
Chessington Wood
Acre Hill Farmhouse
The New Epsom & Ewell Cottage
Horton Country Park
Malden Rushett
WOODVIEW
WEST RD
KT19
West Park
New Wood
RUSHETT LA
SILVERGLADE
KT9
WEST PARK RD
Byhurst Farm
LEATHERHEAD RD
Glanmire Farm
CHRIST CHURCH RD
Fox & Hounds (PH)
B280
Rushett Farm
Bunker's Hill
Great Stew Pond
Epsom Common
D'Abernon Chase Lodge
Telegraph Hill
KT18
The Forest
Newton Wood
World's End
The Star (PH)
KT22
Golf Course
Ashtead Common
Pachesham Park
Caen Wood
BROADHURST
CULVERHAY
OVERDALE
NEWTON WOOD RD
Leatherhead Golf Club
KINGSTON RD
The Rye
Ashley Court
ASHTEAD WOODS RD
Wood Field
Ashtead
KT21
LC
ST STEPHENS AVE
THE REMNANTS
CRADDOCKS AVE
BAGOT CL
PETTERS RD
CHAFFERS MEAD
MEAD END
Pachesham Manor
WOODFIELD RD
WOODLODGE
WOODFIELD LA
THE RIDINGS
CRADDOCKS PAR
LORAINE GDNS
CRAY AVE
BRAMLEY WAY
OXSHOTT RD
A244
A243
1 WHITTAKER CT
2 ST JAMES CT
Trevona
LINKS PL
LINKS CL
MIENA WAY
BIRCH CT
RUTLAND CL
MEADOW RD
DARCY RD
DARCY PL
The Greville Cty Prim Sch
BERRY MEADE
STONNY CROFT
PRESTON GR
LINKS RD
WOODFIELD CL
ELM CL
ELMWOOD
WALTER'S MEAD
HILLSIDE RD
B2430
WARWICK GDNS
TAYLOR RD
READ RD
BALQUHAIN CL
Barnett Wood Cty Inf Sch
MOAT CT
CLAVERTON
FAIRHOLME CRES
BUSHY SHAW
BROOKERS CL
BROOKERS HOUSE
CHURCH RD
Recn Gd
Liby
BROADMEAD
APRIL CL
CRISPIN CL
9
TEAZLEWOOD PK
RYEBRIDGE CL
KINGSTON RD
WOODBRIDGE GR
THE CHASE
GREEN LA
Lower Ashtead
RICHBELL CL
THE MARLD
BURNSIDE
WISHFORD CT
CORFE CL
FLORAL CT
ROSEDALE RD
BARNETT WOOD LA
MULBERRY CT
GLEBE RD
OAKFIELD RD
Ashtead
CROFTON
WESTFIELD
BOWYERS CL
A24
RYE BROOK RD
WOODBRIDGE AVE
OAKHILL CL
OAKHILL RD
GREVILLE PARK AVE
POUND CT
EPSOM RD
KINGSBROOK
SANDES PL
CLARE WOOD
CAEN WOOD RD
PADDOCKS
PADDOCKS WAY
GREVILLE PARK RD
GREVILLE CT
THE STREET
BERKELEY CT
PARK'S LA
BROOK WAY
FAIRWAY
West Hill Sch
REGENT PK
APERDELE
CLARE CRES
MERTON WALK
M25
WEST FARM AVE
ASTON CL
THE MURREYS
Murreys Court
AGATES LA
THE BYWAYS
SKINNERS LA
GLADSTONE RD
VIRGINIA CT
OLDFIELD GDNS
PARK RD
GAYTON CL
LIME TREE CT
ALBERT RD
GAYWOOD RD
PURCELL'S CL
HOWARD CL
GROVE RD
Sch
DENE RD
RYELANDS CT
MERTON WAY

95
76

75
57

D6
1 KING'S SHADE WLK
2 SPREAD EAGLE WLK
3 ASHURST
4 MEADSIDE
5 ASHLEY CT
6 MISTLEY CT
7 STUART LODGE
8 SWAIL HOUSE

E6
1 HOMEWATER HOUSE
2 THE KIRKGATE
3 FIRE STATION FLATS
4 BADGERS CT
5 BADGERS LODGE
6 CHURCH CL
7 GROVE HOUSE
8 DENEWOOD
9 FAIRBRIAR CT

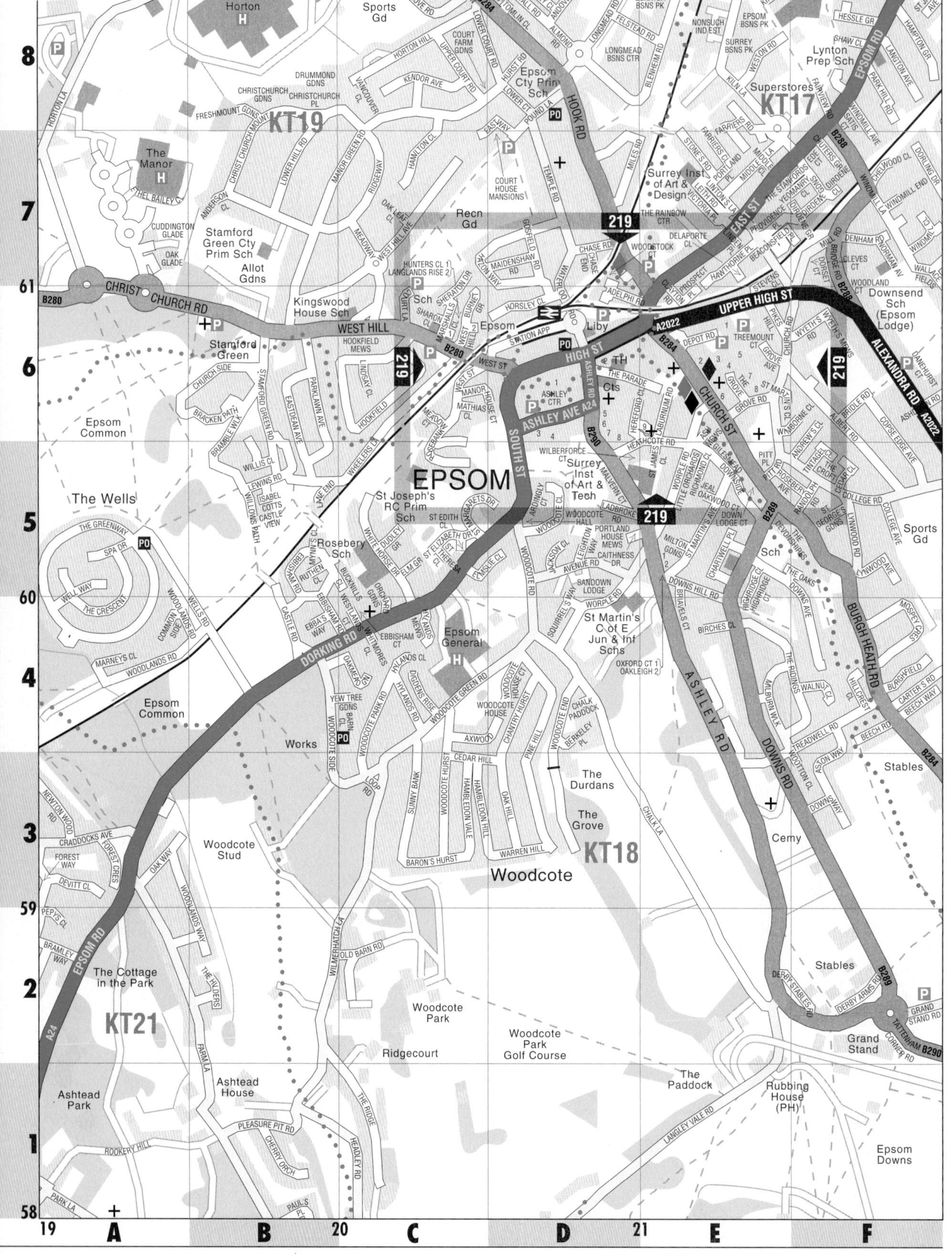

75
96

58
78

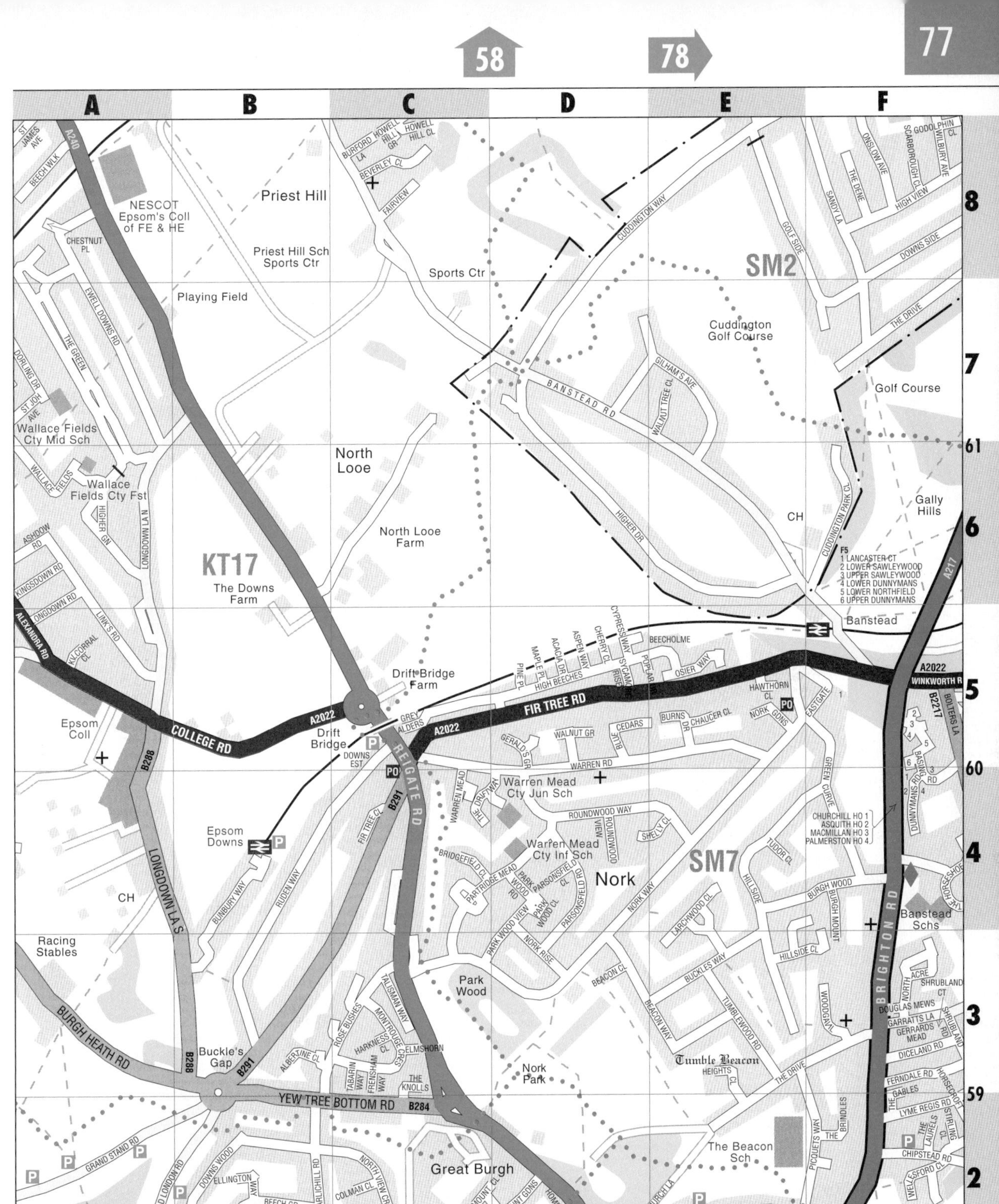
A
B
C
D
E
F
Priest Hill
NESCOT
Epsom's Coll of FE & HE
Priest Hill Sch Sports Ctr
Playing Field
Sports Ctr
SM2
Cuddington Golf Course
Golf Course
CUDDINGTON WAY
BANSTEAD RD
HIGHER DR
GILHAM'S AVE
WALNUT TREE CL
North Looe
North Looe Farm
Wallace Fields Cty Mid Sch
Wallace Fields Cty Fst
KT17
The Downs Farm
Gally Hills
CH
F5
1 LANCASTER CT
2 LOWER SAWLEYWOOD
3 UPPER SAWLEYWOOD
4 LOWER DUNNYMANS
5 LOWER NORTHFIELD
6 UPPER DUNNYMANS
Banstead
Drift Bridge Farm
Drift Bridge
Epsom Coll
COLLEGE RD
A2022
FIR TREE RD
WINKWORTH RD
REIGATE RD
Warren Mead Cty Jun Sch
Warren Mead Cty Inf Sch
Epsom Downs
Nork
SM7
CHURCHILL HO 1
ASQUITH HO 2
MACMILLAN HO 3
PALMERSTON HO 4
Banstead Schs
BRIGHTON RD
Racing Stables
LONGDOWN LA S
Park Wood
Tumble Beacon
BURGH HEATH RD
Buckle's Gap
Nork Park
YEW TREE BOTTOM RD
Great Burgh
The Beacon Sch
KT18
TATTENHAM WAY
Shawley Cty Prim Sch
TATTENHAM CORNER RD
TATTENHAM CRES
Liby
Tattenham Corner
GREAT TATTENHAMS
Superstore
KT20
Canons Wood
8
7
61
6
5
60
4
3
59
2
1
58
22
23
24

97
78

77
59

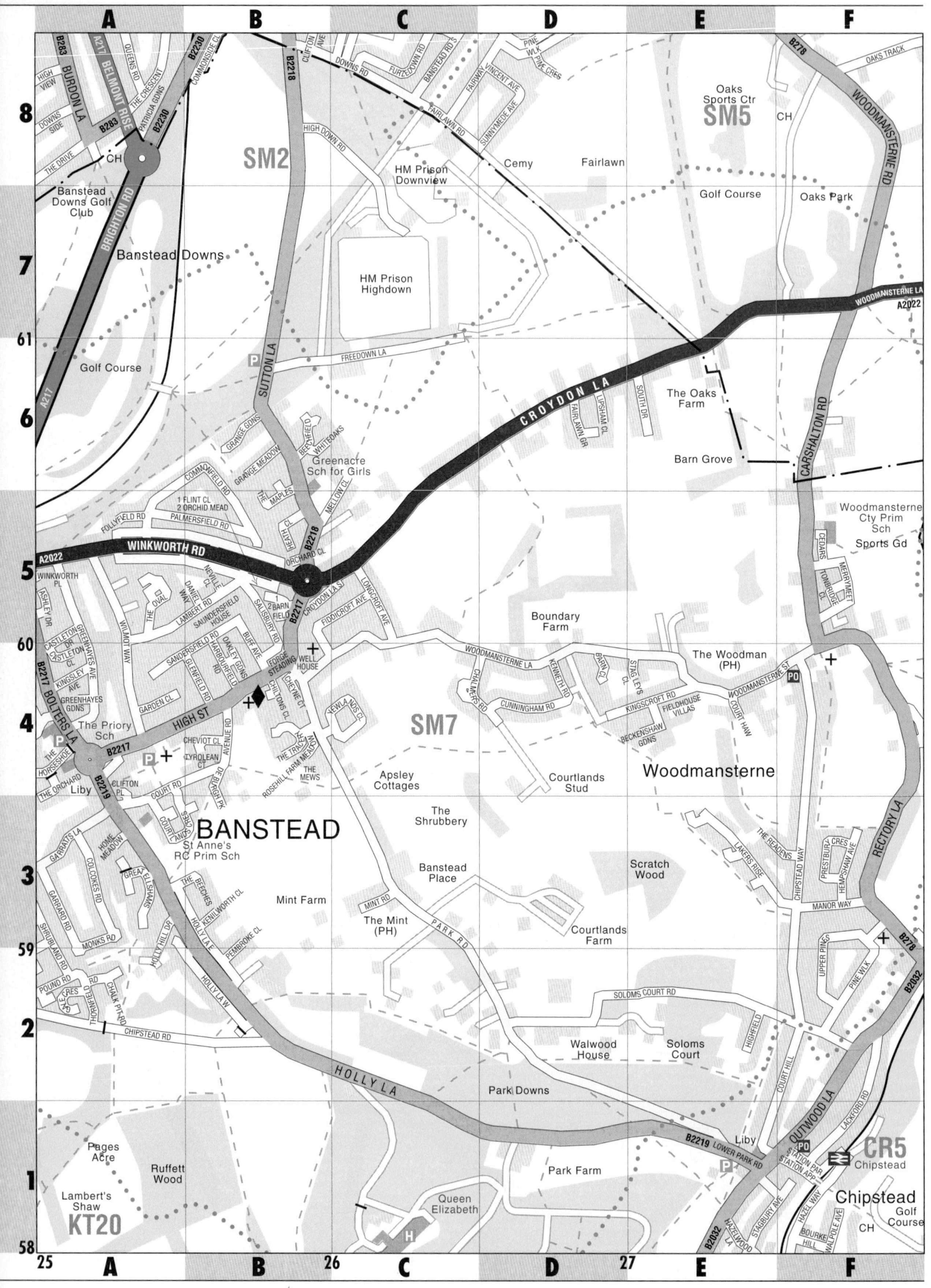
A
B
C
D
E
F
8
7
61
6
5
60
4
3
59
2
1
58
25
26
27
SM2
SM5
SM7
KT20
CR5
BANSTEAD
Woodmansterne
Chipstead
Oaks Sports Ctr
CH
Fairlawn
Cemy
HM Prison Downview
HM Prison Highdown
Golf Course
Oaks Park
Banstead Downs Golf Club
Banstead Downs
Golf Course
The Oaks Farm
Barn Grove
Greenacre Sch for Girls
Woodmansterne Cty Prim Sch
Sports Gd
Boundary Farm
The Woodman (PH)
The Priory Sch
Liby
Apsley Cottages
Courtlands Stud
The Shrubbery
Banstead Place
St Anne's RC Prim Sch
Mint Farm
The Mint (PH)
Scratch Wood
Courtlands Farm
Walwood House
Soloms Court
Park Downs
Park Farm
Queen Elizabeth
Pages Acre
Ruffett Wood
Lambert's Shaw
Chipstead Golf Course
BRIGHTON RD
BURDON LA
BELMONT RISE
SUTTON LA
CROYDON LA
WINKWORTH RD
WOODMANSTERNE RD
WOODMANSTERNE LA
CARSHALTON RD
RECTORY LA
HIGH ST
BOLTERS LA
HOLLY LA
LOWER PARK RD
OUTWOOD LA
PARK RD
CHIPSTEAD RD
SOLOMS COURT RD
FREEDOWN LA
HIGH DOWN RD
DOWNS RD
FAIRLAWN RD
OAKS TRACK
A217
A2022
B2217
B2218
B2219
B2230
B283
B278
B2032

77
98

60
80

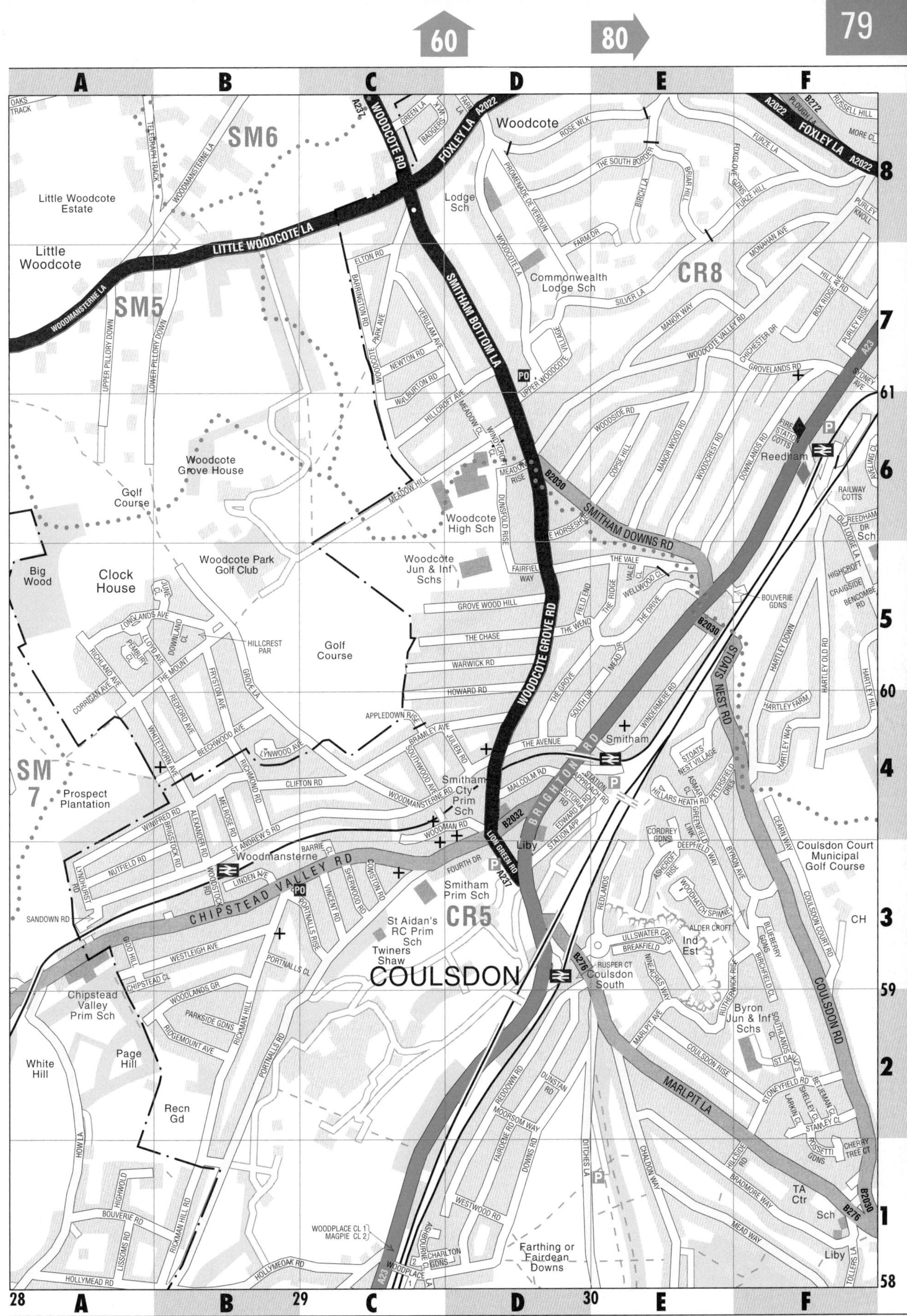
SM6
Woodcote
Little Woodcote Estate
Little Woodcote
SM5
Lodge Sch
Commonwealth Lodge Sch
CR8
Woodcote Grove House
Golf Course
Big Wood
Clock House
Woodcote Park Golf Club
Woodcote High Sch
Woodcote Jun & Inf Schs
Golf Course
Reedham
SM 7
Prospect Plantation
Smitham
Smitham Cty Prim Sch
Woodmansterne
Smitham Prim Sch
St Aidan's RC Prim Sch
CR5
Twiners Shaw
COULSDON
Coulsdon South
Ind Est
Coulsdon Court Municipal Golf Course
Chipstead Valley Prim Sch
White Hill
Page Hill
Recn Gd
Byron Jun & Inf Schs
TA Ctr
Farthing or Fairdean Downs
Liby
Sch
CH
WOODCOTE RD
FOXLEY LA
LITTLE WOODCOTE LA
WOODMANSTERNE LA
SMITHAM BOTTOM LA
WOODCOTE GROVE RD
SMITHAM DOWNS RD
CHIPSTEAD VALLEY RD
BRIGHTON RD
STOATS NEST RD
MARLPIT LA
COULSDON RD
LION GREEN RD
A23
A237
A2022
B2030
B2032
B276
B272
28
29
30
A
B
C
D
E
F
1
2
3
4
5
6
7
8
58
59
60
61

99
80

A8
1 BOURNE CT
2 PURLEY PAR
3 RUSSELL PAR
4 RUSSELL HILL PAR
5 KIMBERLEY PL
6 THE EXCHANGE

A7
1 BYRNE CT
2 ADAMS CT
3 LIDDELL CT

B7
1 LISTER CT
2 NICHOLASS CT
3 GODSTONE MOUNT

79
61

79
100

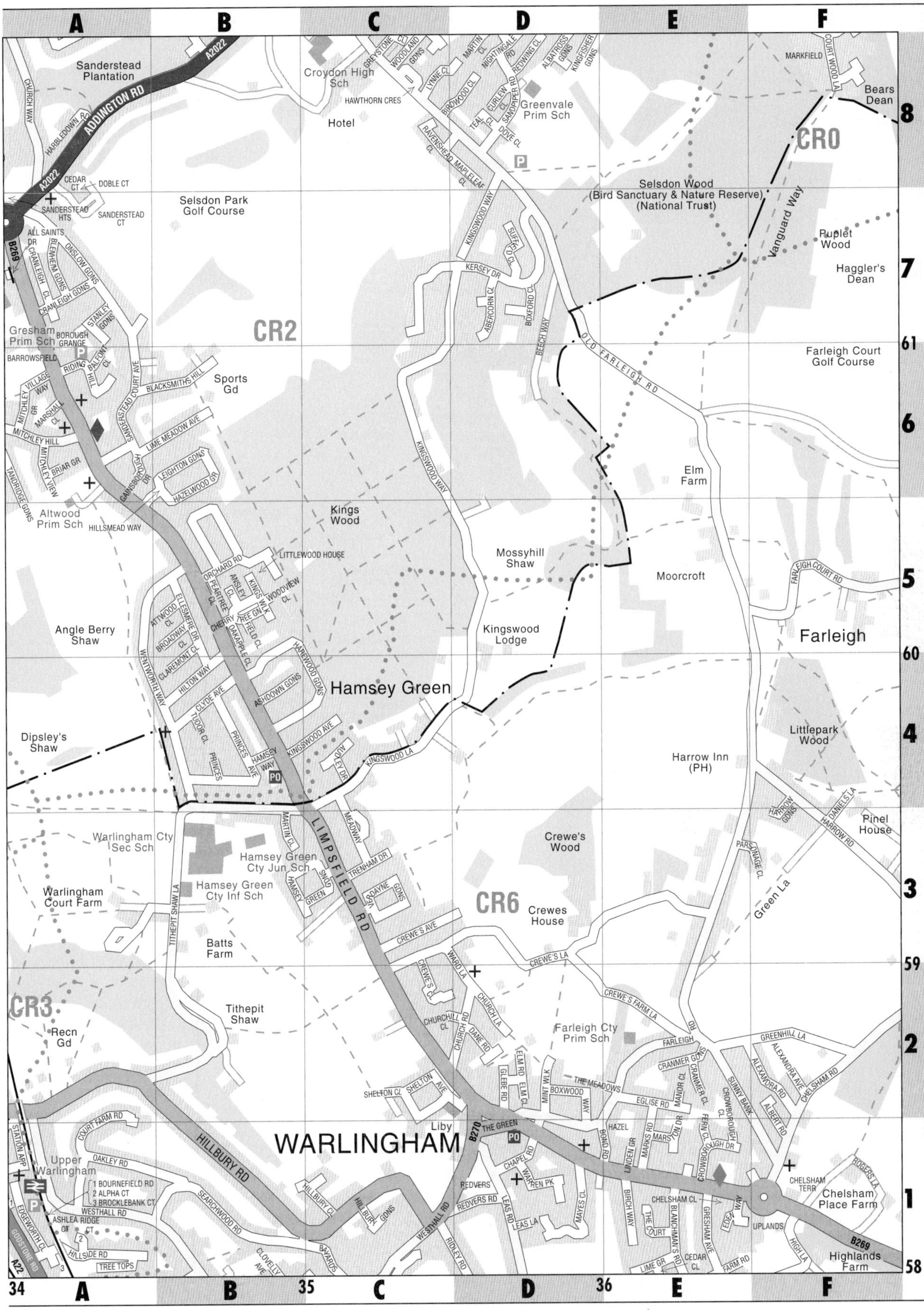

A B C D E F

Sanderstead Plantation
ADDINGTON RD
A2022
CHURCH WAY
HARBLEDOWN RD
Croydon High Sch
GREYSTONE CL
WOODLAND GDNS
LYNNE CL
MARTIN CL
NIGHTINGALE RD
REDWING CL
ALBATROSS GDNS
KINGFISHER GDNS
MARKFIELD
COURT WOOD LA
Bears Dean
8
HAWTHORN CRES
BIRDWOOD CL
CURLEW CL
SANDPIPER RD
TEAL CL
Greenvale Prim Sch
DOVE CL
Hotel
RAVENSHEAD CL
MAPLELEAF CL
CR0
CEDAR CT
DOBLE CT
SANDERSTEAD HTS
SANDERSTEAD CT
Selsdon Park Golf Course
Selsdon Wood (Bird Sanctuary & Nature Reserve) (National Trust)
KINGSWOOD WAY
SUFFOLK CL
Vanguard Way
Puplet Wood
ALL SAINTS DR
B269
BLENHEIM GDNS
ONSLOW GDNS
CRANLEIGH CL
CRANLEIGH GDNS
KERSEY DR
Haggler's Dean
7
STANLEY GDNS
ABERCORN CL
BOXFORD CL
BEECH WAY
Gresham Prim Sch
BOROUGH GRANGE
CR2
OLD FARLEIGH RD
61
Farleigh Court Golf Course
BARROWSFIELD
RIDING HILL
BALFONT CL
VILLAGE WAY
MITCHLEY GR
MARSHALL CL
SANDERSTEAD COURT AVE
BLACKSMITHS HILL
Sports Gd
MITCHLEY HILL
MITCHLEY VIEW
LIME MEADOW AVE
6
BRIAR GR
TANDRIDGE GDNS
GAINSBOROUGH DR
LEIGHTON GDNS
HAZELWOOD GR
Elm Farm
Altwood Prim Sch
HILLSMEAD WAY
Kings Wood
LITTLEWOOD HOUSE
Mossyhill Shaw
ORCHARD RD
ANSLEY CL
KINGS WLK
WOODVIEW CL
PEARTREE CL
Moorcroft
FARLEIGH COURT RD
5
ATTWOOD CL
ELLESMERE DR
CHERRY TREE GN
BROADWAY CL
CLAREMONT CL
OAKAPPLE CL
FIELD CL
Angle Berry Shaw
Kingswood Lodge
Farleigh
WENTWORTH WAY
HILTON WAY
HARDWOOD GDNS
ASHDOWN GDNS
60
Hamsey Green
CLYDE AVE
TUDOR CL
PRINCES AVE
Dipsley's Shaw
KINGSWOOD AVE
HAMSEY WAY
AUDLEY DR
KINGSWOOD LA
Littlepark Wood
4
Harrow Inn (PH)
PO
MEADWAY
HARROW GDNS
DANIELS LA
HARROW RD
Pinel House
MARTIN CL
Warlingham Cty Sec Sch
Hamsey Green Cty Jun Sch
LIMPSFIELD RD
Crewe's Wood
TRENHAM DR
PARSONAGE CL
Warlingham Court Farm
Hamsey Green Cty Inf Sch
HAMSEY GREEN GDNS
VERDAYNE GDNS
CR6
Crewes House
Green La
3
TITHEPIT SHAW LA
Batts Farm
CREWE'S AVE
WARD LA
CREWE'S LA
CREWE'S CL
59
CR3
Tithepit Shaw
CHURCH LA
CREWE'S FARM LA
Recn Gd
CHURCHILL RD
CHURCH RD
DANE RD
Farleigh Cty Prim Sch
FARLEIGH RD
GREENHILL LA
2
ALEXANDRA AVE
ALEXANDRA RD
CHELSHAM RD
CRANMER GDNS
CRANMER CL
MANOR CL
ELM RD
GLEBE RD
ELM CL
MINT WLK
THE MEADOWS
BOXWOOD WAY
SUNNY BANK
EGLISE RD
FERN CL
CROWBOROUGH CL
SHELTON CL
SHELTON AVE
COURT FARM RD
STATION APP
HILLBURY RD
Liby
B270
THE GREEN
PO
HAZEL
BOND RD
LINDEN GR
MARKS RD
MARSTON DR
CROWBOROUGH DR
ALBERT RD
WARLINGHAM
Upper Warlingham
OAKLEY RD
1 BOURNEFIELD RD
2 ALPHA CT
3 BROCKLEBANK CT
WESTHALL RD
SEARCHWOOD RD
HILLBURY CL
HILLBURY GDNS
REDVERS
REDVERS RD
CHAPEL RD
WARREN PK
MAYES CL
BIRCH WAY
CHELSHAM CL
BLANCHMAN'S RD
GRESHAM AVE
EDEN WAY
ROGERS LA
CHELSHAM TERR
Chelsham Place Farm
1
ASHLEA RIDGE CT
EDGEWORTH CL
HILLSIDE RD
TREE TOPS
CLOVELLY AVE
BAYARDS
WESTHALL RD
RIDLEY RD
LEAS RD
LEAS LA
THE COURT
LIME GR
CEDAR CL
FARM RD
UPLANDS
HIGH LA
B269
Highlands Farm
GODSTONE RD
A22
58

34 A B 35 C D 36 E F

81
63

A
B
C
D
E
F
Addington Court Golf Course
Bears Wood
Frith Wood
Farleigh Dean
Dumpsy Derry
Frylands Wood
Crab Wood
CR0
Recn Gd
Kennels
BR2
Fairchildes Prim Sch
Addington High Sch
CH
Farleigh Court Golf Course
Limekiln Shaw
Coldblow Shaw
Chapel Hill
Fairchildes Farm
The White Bear (PH)
Fickleshole Farm
Fickleshole
GREENWICH MERIDIAN
Farleigh Court
Little Farleigh Green Farm
Greatpark Wood
The Gripes
Five Acre Shaw
Greathill Shaw
CR6
Midgley Shaws
Honeyoak Wood
Holt Wood
Warlingham Park Sch
Holt Wood
Bull Inn (PH)
Ledgers Farm
Henley Wood
Chelsham
Henley Wood
Owls Wood
Broom Lodge Farm
Chelsham Court
Chelsham Court Farm
Mast
Cony Crook
White Bank
FARLEIGH DEAN CRES
CUDHAM DR
OVERBURY CRES
CHERTS CRES
CLEVES CRES
ST EDWARDS CL
LEVERET CL
CALLEY DOWN CRES
REDSTART CL
ARNHEM DR
WARBANK CRES
VALENTYNE CL
HUTCHINSON'S RD
MATTHEW'S GDNS
MILNE PK W
MILNE PK E
UVEDALE CL
UVEDALE CRES
LEIGH CT
CATOR CL
CATOR CRES
KING HENRY'S DR
FRYLANDS CT
THORPE CL
FLORA GDNS
KENNEL WOOD CRES
HOMESTEAD WAY
THISTLEWOOD CRES
WALSH CRES
COMPORT GN
CORBETT CL
FAIRCHILDES AVE
FEATHERBED LA
LAYHAMS RD
SHEEPBARN LA
FAIRCHILDES COTTS
PARK RD
BLACKMAN'S LA
SKID HILL LA
FARLEIGH COURT RD
HIGH HILL RD
SCOTSHALL LA
FAIRCHILDES RD
CHURCH LA
HARROW RD
CHELSHAM COMMON RD
CHELSHAM RD
HESIERS RD
HESIERS HILL
LEDGERS RD
WASHPOND LA
BEECH FARM RD
CHELSHAM COURT RD
BEDLESTEAD LA
LIMPSFIELD RD
B269
8
7
61
6
5
60
4
3
59
2
1
58
37
38
39

81
102

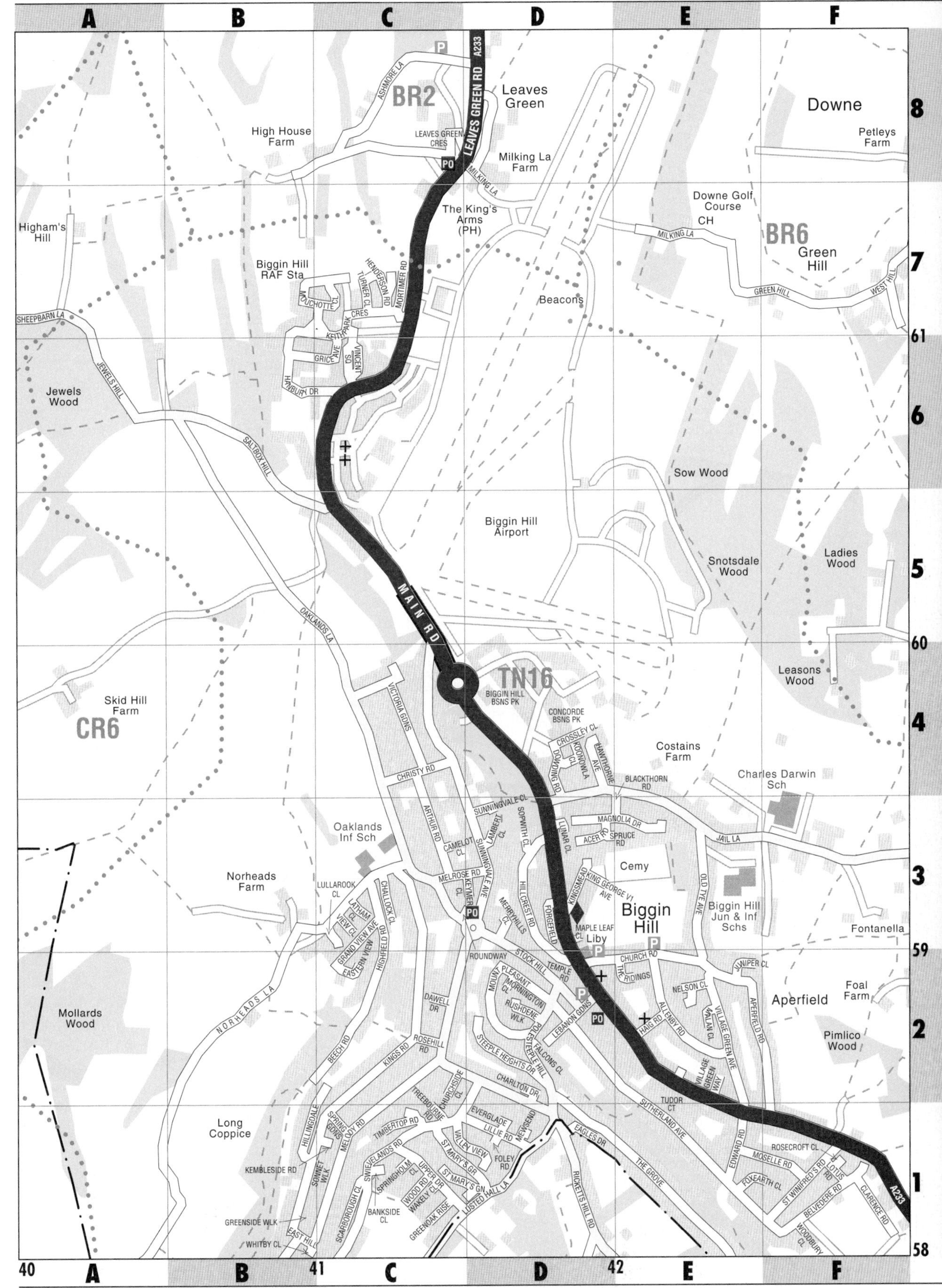

BR2
Leaves Green
LEAVES GREEN RD
A233
High House Farm
Downe
Petleys Farm
Milking La Farm
The King's Arms (PH)
Downe Golf Course
CH
Higham's Hill
BR6
Green Hill
Biggin Hill RAF Sta
Beacons
Jewels Wood
Sow Wood
Biggin Hill Airport
Snotsdale Wood
Ladies Wood
MAIN RD
TN16
BIGGIN HILL BSNS PK
Leasons Wood
Skid Hill Farm
CR6
CONCORDE BSNS PK
Costains Farm
Charles Darwin Sch
Oaklands Inf Sch
Norheads Farm
Cemy
Biggin Hill
Biggin Hill Jun & Inf Schs
Fontanella
Liby
Aperfield
Foal Farm
Mollards Wood
Pimlico Wood
Long Coppice

64

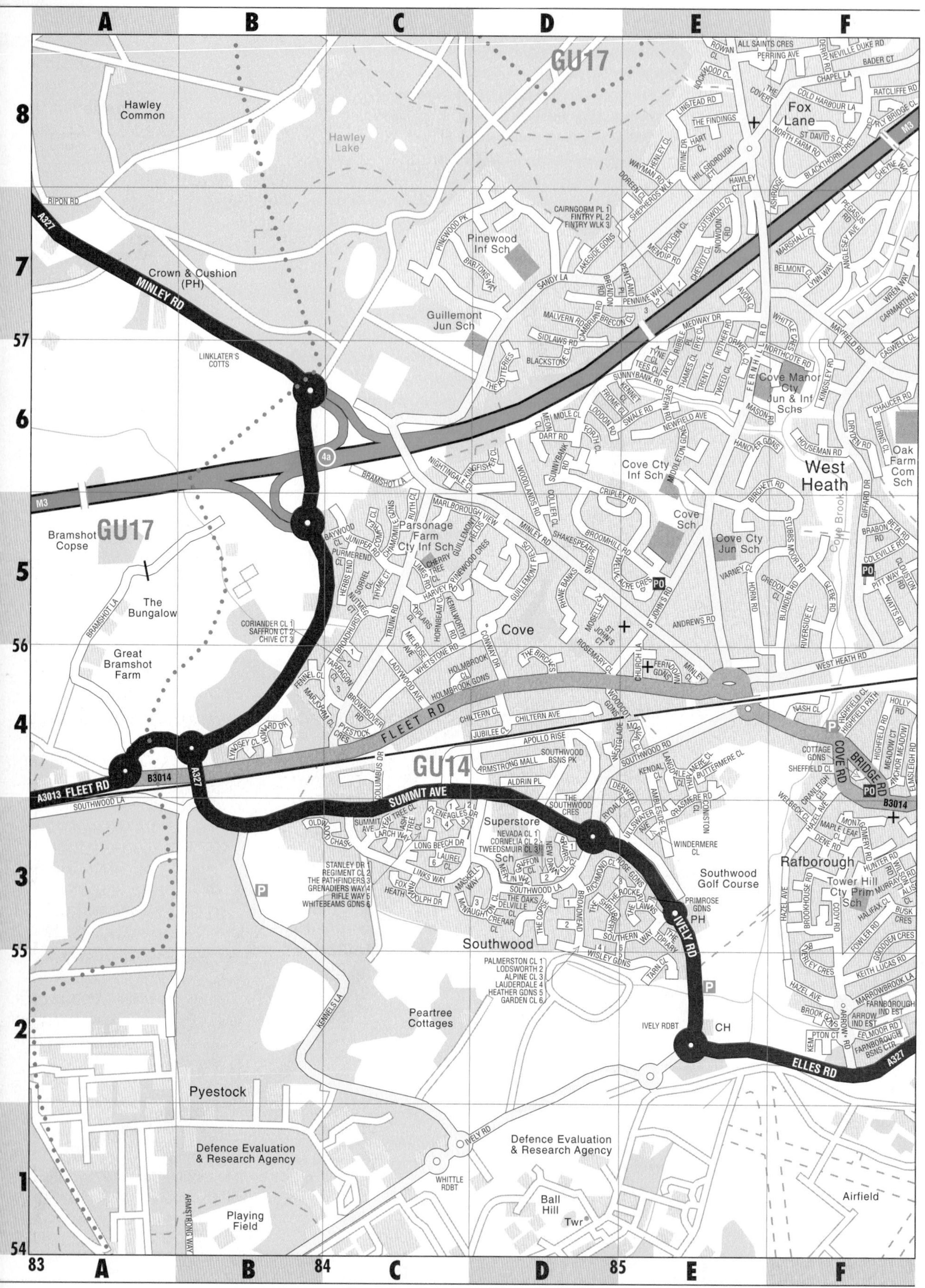

A
B
C
D
E
F
8
7
57
6
5
56
4
3
55
2
1
54
83
84
85
GU17
GU17
GU14
Hawley Common
Hawley Lake
RIPON RD
A327
MINLEY RD
Crown & Cushion (PH)
LINKLATER'S COTTS
M3
4a
Bramshot Copse
The Bungalow
Great Bramshot Farm
BRAMSHOT LA
CORIANDER CL 1
SAFFRON CT 2
CHIVE CT 3
A3013 FLEET RD
B3014
SOUTHWOOD LA
FLEET RD
SUMMIT AVE
Pinewood Inf Sch
Guillemont Jun Sch
SANDY LA
Parsonage Farm Cty Inf Sch
Cove
Cove Cty Inf Sch
Cove Sch
Cove Cty Jun Sch
Cove Manor Cty Jun & Inf Schs
West Heath
Oak Farm Com Sch
Fox Lane
Cove Brook
MINLEY RD
FERNHILL RD
WEST HEATH RD
CHILTERN AVE
APOLLO RISE
SOUTHWOOD BSNS PK
ARMSTRONG MALL
ALDRIN PL
Superstore
NEVADA CL 1
CORNELIA CL 2
TWEEDSMUIR CL 3
Sch
STANLEY DR 1
REGIMENT CL 2
THE PATHFINDERS 3
GRENADIERS WAY 4
RIFLE WAY 5
WHITEBEAMS GDNS 6
Southwood
Southwood Golf Course
PRIMROSE GDNS
PH
IVELY RD
PALMERSTON CL 1
LODSWORTH 2
ALPINE CL 3
LAUDERDALE 4
HEATHER GDNS 5
GARDEN CL 6
Peartree Cottages
IVELY RDBT
CH
ELLES RD
A327
COVE RD
BRIDGE RD
B3014
Rafborough
Tower Hill Cty Prim Sch
FARNBOROUGH BSNS CTR
Pyestock
KENNELS LA
Defence Evaluation & Research Agency
Defence Evaluation & Research Agency
WHITTLE RDBT
IVELY RD
Playing Field
ARMSTRONG WAY
Ball Hill
Twr
Airfield
CAIRNGORM PL 1
FINTRY PL 2
FINTRY WLK 3

104

A6
1 SAUNTON GDNS
2 LISKEARD DR
A7
1 HEDDON WLK
2 LYDFORD CL

B7
1 WOODSIDE
2 HIGHGROVE

65
86

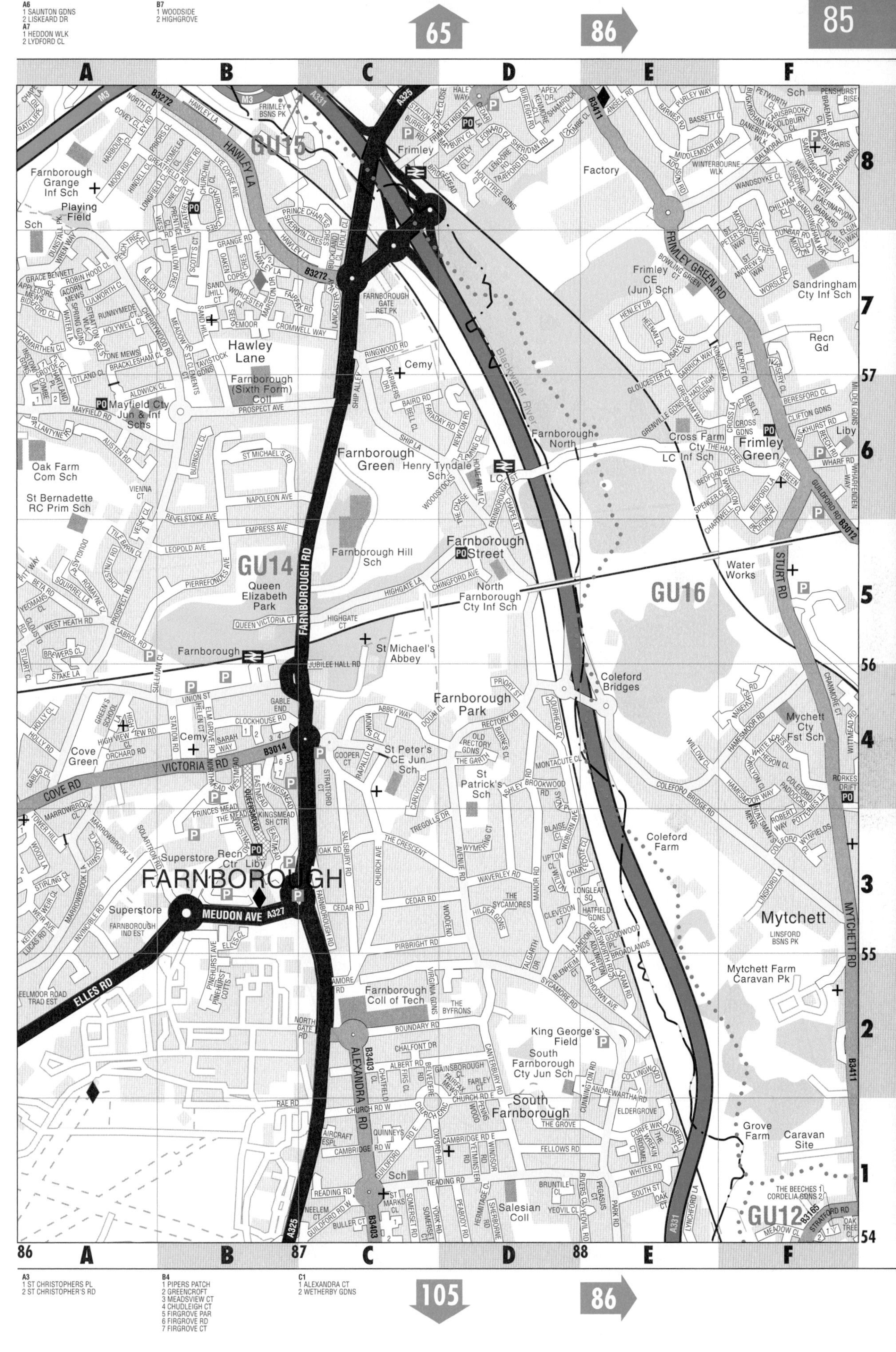

105
86

A3
1 ST CHRISTOPHERS PL
2 ST CHRISTOPHER'S RD

B4
1 PIPERS PATCH
2 GREENCROFT
3 MEADSVIEW CT
4 CHUDLEIGH CT
5 FIRGROVE PAR
6 FIRGROVE RD
7 FIRGROVE CT

C1
1 ALEXANDRA CT
2 WETHERBY GDNS

85
66

Loen
The Grange
Blackdown Hill
Dettingen Barracks
Alma Barracks
Mainstone Hill
Blackdown Prim Sch
Royal Logistic Corps Mus
Pirbright Ranges
DANGER AREA
St Cross
Richmond Hill
The Princess Royal Barracks
Sports Gd
Devil's Pound
Blackdown Barracks
Deepcut
Old Windmill Hill
Porridgepot Hill
Wharfenden Lake
Basingstoke Canal
Frimhurst Farm
GU16
Lodge Hill
Cheswycks Sch
Gapemouth Plantation
Hodge Bottom
The Old Mill
Deepcut Place
Four Winds
Rangelands
Longdown Hill
GU24
Stoney Castle Ranges
DANGER AREA
Tunnel Hill
Emperor's Hill
Potters (PH)
Mytchett Place
GU12
Mytchett Gate
Pirbright Common
Hangman's Hill
Bridge Hill
Ash Ranges
Mytchett Lake
Keogh Barracks
Spur Hill
Scragley Hill
Playing Field
DANGER AREA
Play Hill
VALLEY RD
BLACKDOWN RD
DEEPCUT BRIDGE RD
B3015
FRITH HILL RD
NEWFOUNDLAND RD
LAKE RD
BRUNSWICK RD
GUILDFORD RD
B3012
GAPEMOUTH RD
OLD GUILDFORD RD
MYTCHETT PLACE RD
MYTCHETT LAKE RD
B3411
1 ESSEX CL
2 WALMER CL
3 BANBURY CL
4 RADCLIFFE CL
A B C D E F
8 7 57 6 5 56 4 3 55 2 1 54
89 90 91

85
106

67
88

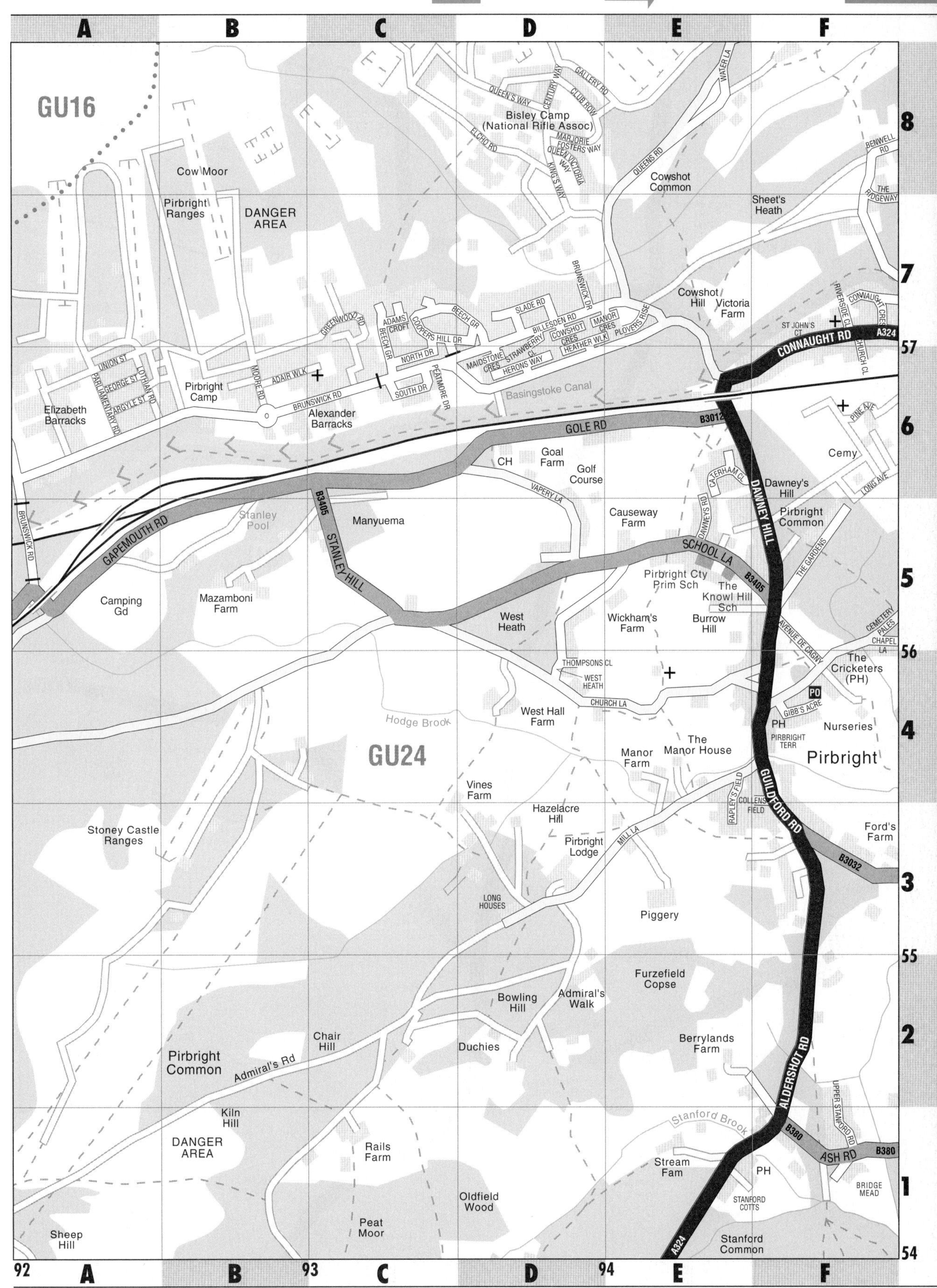
A
B
C
D
E
F
GU16
Cow Moor
Pirbright Ranges
DANGER AREA
Bisley Camp (National Rifle Assoc)
QUEEN'S WAY
CENTURY WAY
GALLERY RD
CLUB ROW
ELCHO RD
MARJORIE FOSTERS WAY
QUEEN VICTORIA WAY
KING'S WAY
QUEENS RD
Cowshot Common
WATER LA
BENWELL RD
THE RIDGEWAY
Sheet's Heath
BRUNSWICK DR
Cowshot Hill
Victoria Farm
RIVERSIDE CL
CONNAUGHT CRES
ST JOHN'S CT
CHURCH CL
CONNAUGHT RD
A324
GREENWOOD RD
ADAMS CROFT
BEECH GR
COOPERS HILL DR
SLADE RD
BILLESDEN RD
COWSHOT CRES
MANOR CRES
PLOVERS RISE
NORTH DR
MAIDSTONE CRES
STRAWBERRY CL
HERONS WAY
HEATHER WLK
UNION ST
GEORGE ST
LOTHIAN RD
PARLIAMENTARY RD
ARGYLE ST
Pirbright Camp
MOORE RD
ADAIR WLK
SOUTH DR
PEATMORE DR
BRUNSWICK RD
Alexander Barracks
Elizabeth Barracks
Basingstoke Canal
PINE AVE
GOLE RD
B3012
Cemy
CH
Goal Farm
Golf Course
VAPERY LA
CATERHAM CL
Dawney's Hill
DAWNEY HILL
LONG AVE
BRUNSWICK RD
GAPEMOUTH RD
Stanley Pool
B3405
Manyuema
STANLEY HILL
Causeway Farm
Pirbright Common
DAWNEYS RD
SCHOOL LA
THE GARDENS
Pirbright Cty Prim Sch
The Knowl Hill Sch
B3405
Camping Gd
Mazamboni Farm
West Heath
Wickham's Farm
Burrow Hill
AVENUE DE CAGNY
CEMETERY PALES
CHAPEL LA
THOMPSONS CL
WEST HEATH
The Cricketers (PH)
PO
CHURCH LA
GIBB'S ACRE
West Hall Farm
Hodge Brook
PH
PIRBRIGHT TERR
Nurseries
GU24
The Manor House
Manor Farm
Pirbright
Vines Farm
RAPLEY'S FIELD
COLLENS FIELD
GUILDFORD RD
Hazelacre Hill
Stoney Castle Ranges
Pirbright Lodge
MILL LA
Ford's Farm
B3032
LONG HOUSES
Piggery
Furzefield Copse
Bowling Hill
Admiral's Walk
Chair Hill
Duchies
Berrylands Farm
ALDERSHOT RD
Pirbright Common
Admiral's Rd
Kiln Hill
Stanford Brook
B380
UPPER STANFORD RD
ASH RD
B380
DANGER AREA
Rails Farm
Stream Fam
PH
BRIDGE MEAD
STANFORD COTTS
Oldfield Wood
Peat Moor
Sheep Hill
Stanford Common
A324
8
7
57
6
5
56
4
3
55
2
1
54
92
93
94

107
88

87
68

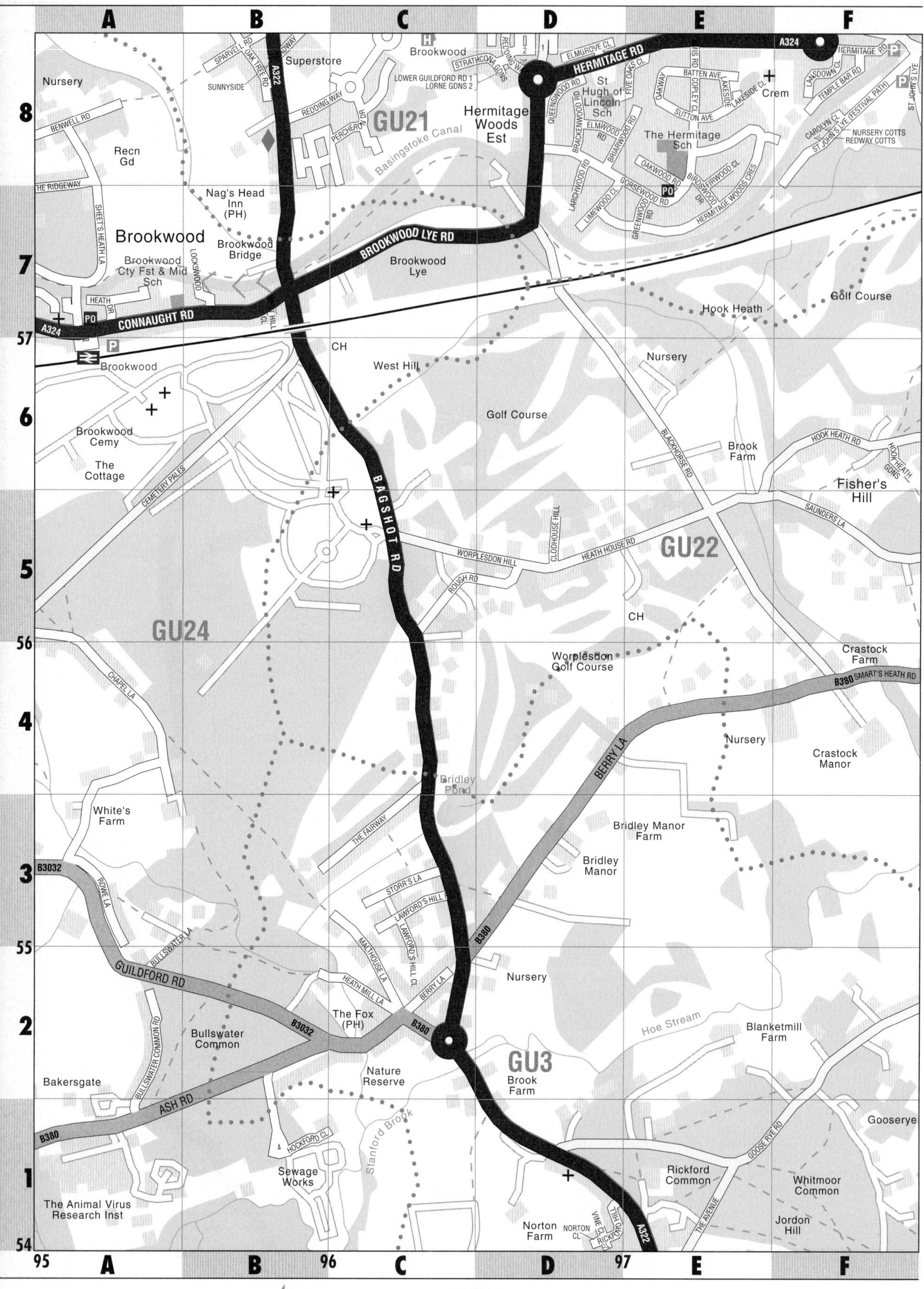
Brookwood
Superstore
Nursery
Recn Gd
GU21
Basingstoke Canal
Hermitage Woods Est
St Hugh of Lincoln Sch
The Hermitage Sch
Crem
Nag's Head Inn (PH)
Brookwood Bridge
Brookwood Cty Fst & Mid Sch
Brookwood Lye
BROOKWOOD LYE RD
CONNAUGHT RD
HERMITAGE RD
Hook Heath
Golf Course
West Hill
Nursery
Brookwood Cemy
The Cottage
BAGSHOT RD
Brook Farm
Fisher's Hill
GU22
GU24
WORPLESDON HILL
HEATH HOUSE RD
Worplesdon Golf Course
Crastock Farm
Crastock Manor
Bridley Pond
White's Farm
Bridley Manor Farm
Bridley Manor
BERRY LA
GUILDFORD RD
Bullswater Common
The Fox (PH)
Nature Reserve
GU3
Brook Farm
Blanketmill Farm
Hoe Stream
Bakersgate
ASH RD
Sewage Works
Stanford Brook
Rickford Common
Whitmoor Common
Gooserye
Jordon Hill
Norton Farm
The Animal Virus Research Inst

87
108

A B C D E F

1 ST JOHNS CT 5
2 RAEBURN CT 6
1 ST JOHNS MEWS
2 WOODEND CL
3 SCYLLA PL
4 APOLLO PL
1 EFFINGHAM CT
2 WOODLANDS CT
3 CRAIGMORE TOWER
TAMERTON SQ 1
BROOKLYN CT 2
WOOTTON GRANGE 3
HANOVER CT 4
MIDHOPE GDNS 5
WHITEGATES 1
GABLES CT 2
NEW FOREST COTTS 3

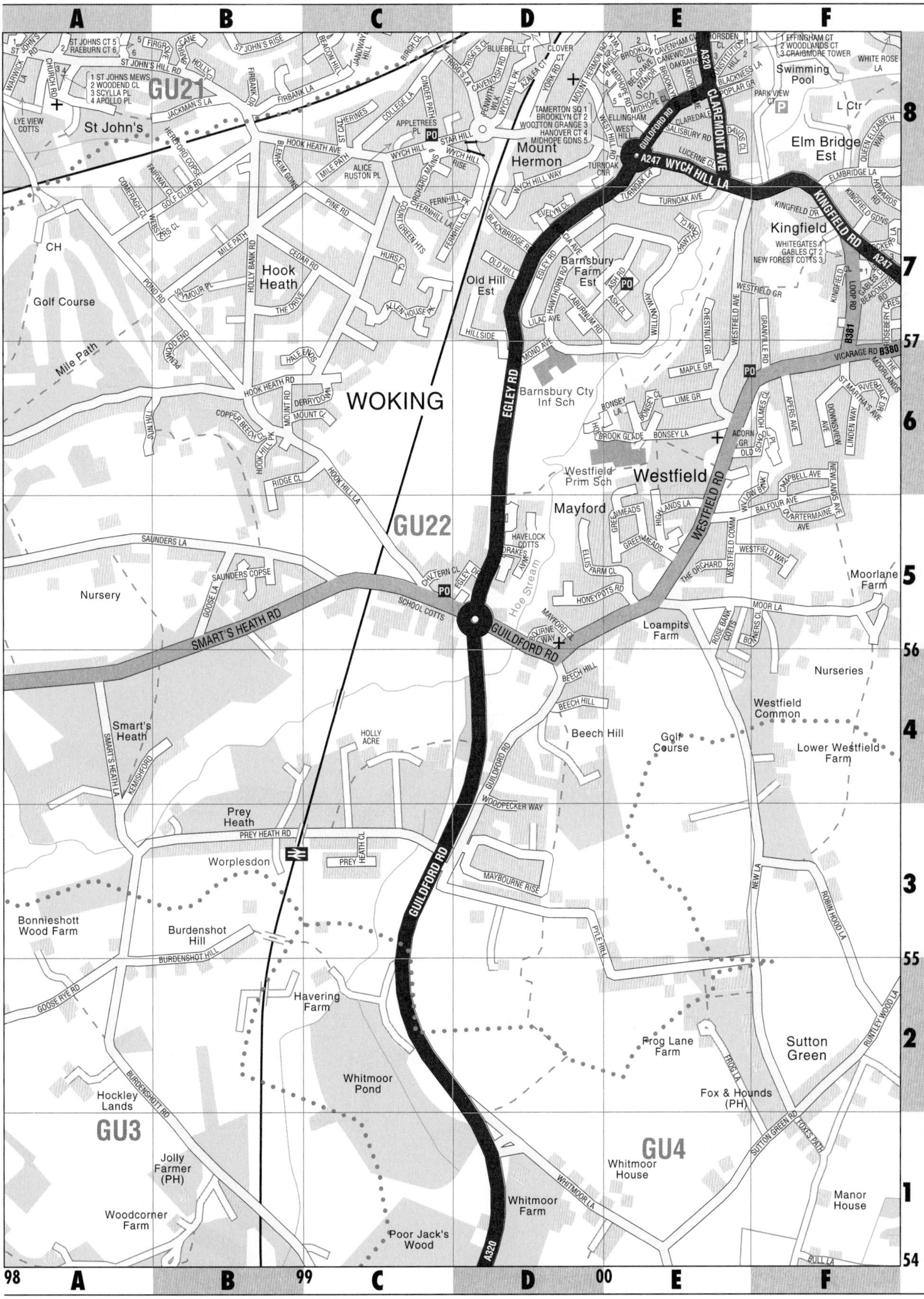

GU21
St John's
LYE VIEW COTTS
ST JOHN'S HILL RD
JACKMAN'S LA
FIRBANK LA
ST JOHN'S RISE
BEACON HILL
JANOWAY HILL
BIRCH CL
BLUEBELL CT
CLOVER CT
CAVENDISH RD
AZALEA CT
YORK RD
MOUNT HERMON RD
HOOK HEATH AVE
COLLEGE LA
CINDER PATH
APPLETREES PL
ALICE RUSTON PL
WYCH HILL
WYCH HILL RISE
STAR HILL
Mount Hermon
WYCH HILL WAY
ELLINGHAM
WEST HILL
TURNOAK CNR
A247 WYCH HILL LA
CLAREMONT AVE
A320
Sch
Swimming Pool
PARK VIEW CT
L Ctr
Elm Bridge Est
ELMBRIDGE LA
KINGFIELD RD
A247
Kingfield
KINGFIELD DR
GOLF CLUB RD
FAIRWAY CL
COMERAGH CL
MILE PATH
PINE RD
COURT GREEN HTS
FERNHILL CL
FERNHILL PK
BLACKBRIDGE RD
TURNOAK AVE
EVELYN CL
CH
Golf Course
Hook Heath
HOLLY BANK RD
CEDAR RD
THE DRIVE
HURST CL
ALLEN HOUSE PK
Old Hill Est
OLD HILL
HILLSIDE
Barnsbury Farm Est
EGLEY RD
ASH RD
ASH CL
LILAC AVE
LABURNUM RD
WILLOW WAY
CHESTNUT GR
WESTFIELD AVE
GRANVILLE RD
WESTFIELD GR
LOOP RD
B381
VICARAGE RD B380
Mile Path
PONDWOOD END
POND RD
SEYMOUR PL
HALEEENDS
HOOK HEATH RD
DERRYDOWN
MOUNT CL
MOUNT RD
WOKING
Barnsbury Cty Inf Sch
MAPLE GR
LIME GR
BONSEY LA
BONSEY CL
BROOK GLADE
ACORN GR
OLD SCH PL
HOLMES CL
APERS AVE
DOWNSVIEW AVE
LINDEN WAY
ST MARTHA'S AVE
COPPER BEECH CL
HOOK HILL PK
RIDGE CL
HOOK HILL LA
Westfield Prim Sch
Westfield
WESTFIELD RD
Mayford
GREENMEADS
HIGHLANDS LA
WILLOW BANK
CAMPBELL AVE
BALFOUR AVE
QUARTERMAINE AVE
NEWLANDS AVE
GU22
SAUNDERS LA
SAUNDERS COPSE
GOOSE LA
HAVELOCK COTTS
DRAKES WAY
Hoe Stream
ELLIS FARM CL
HONEYPOTS RD
THE ORCHARD
WESTFIELD COMM
WESTFIELD WAY
Moorlane Farm
Nursery
CHILTERN CL
SCHOOL COTTS
SMART'S HEATH RD
GUILDFORD RD
MAYFORD CL
BOURNE WAY
Loampits Farm
MOOR LA
ROSE BANK COTTS
BONNERS CL
Nurseries
BEECH HILL
Beech Hill
Golf Course
Westfield Common
Lower Westfield Farm
Smart's Heath
SMART'S HEATH LA
KEMISHFORD
HOLLY ACRE
WOODPECKER WAY
Prey Heath
PREY HEATH RD
PREY HEATH CL
Worplesdon
MAYBOURNE RISE
NEW LA
ROBIN HOOD LA
Bonnieshott Wood Farm
Burdenshot Hill
BURDENSHOT HILL
PYLE HILL
GOOSE RYE RD
Havering Farm
Frog Lane Farm
FROG LA
Sutton Green
RUNTLEY WOOD LA
Whitmoor Pond
Hockley Lands
BURDENSHOTT RD
Fox & Hounds (PH)
SUTTON GREEN RD
FOXES PATH
GU3
GU4
Whitmoor House
Jolly Farmer (PH)
WHITMOOR LA
Whitmoor Farm
Manor House
Woodcorner Farm
Poor Jack's Wood
BULL LA

8 57 7 6 5 56 4 3 55 2 1 54

98 A B 99 C D 00 E F

89
70

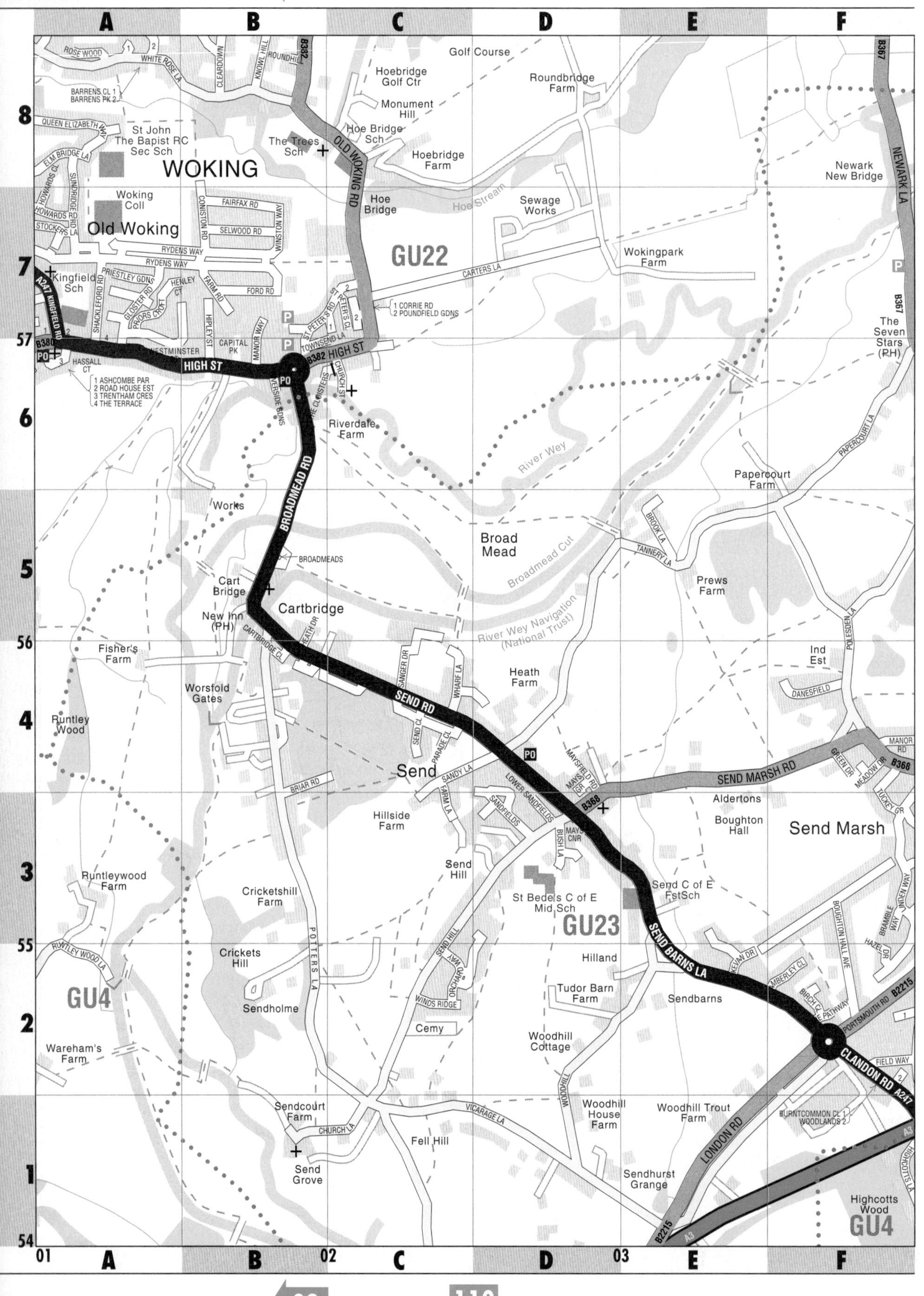
WOKING
Old Woking
GU22
GU23
GU4
Send
Send Marsh
Cartbridge
HIGH ST
BROADMEAD RD
SEND RD
SEND BARNS LA
CLANDON RD
OLD WOKING RD
SEND MARSH RD
NEWARK LA
LONDON RD
KINGFIELD RD
Golf Course
Hoebridge Golf Ctr
Monument Hill
Hoe Bridge Sch
The Trees Sch
Hoebridge Farm
Roundbridge Farm
Newark New Bridge
Sewage Works
Hoe Stream
Hoe Bridge
St John The Bapist RC Sec Sch
Woking Coll
Kingfield Sch
Wokingpark Farm
The Seven Stars (PH)
Riverdale Farm
River Wey
Papercourt Farm
Works
Broad Mead
Broadmead Cut
Prews Farm
Cart Bridge
New Inn (PH)
River Wey Navigation (National Trust)
Fisher's Farm
Heath Farm
Ind Est
Worsfold Gates
Runtley Wood
Hillside Farm
Aldertons
Boughton Hall
Send Hill
Runtleywood Farm
Cricketshill Farm
St Bede's C of E Mid Sch
Send C of E FstSch
Crickets Hill
Hilland
Tudor Barn Farm
Sendbarns
Sendholme
Cemy
Wareham's Farm
Woodhill Cottage
Sendcourt Farm
Woodhill House Farm
Woodhill Trout Farm
Fell Hill
Send Grove
Sendhurst Grange
Highcotts Wood

89
110

71
92

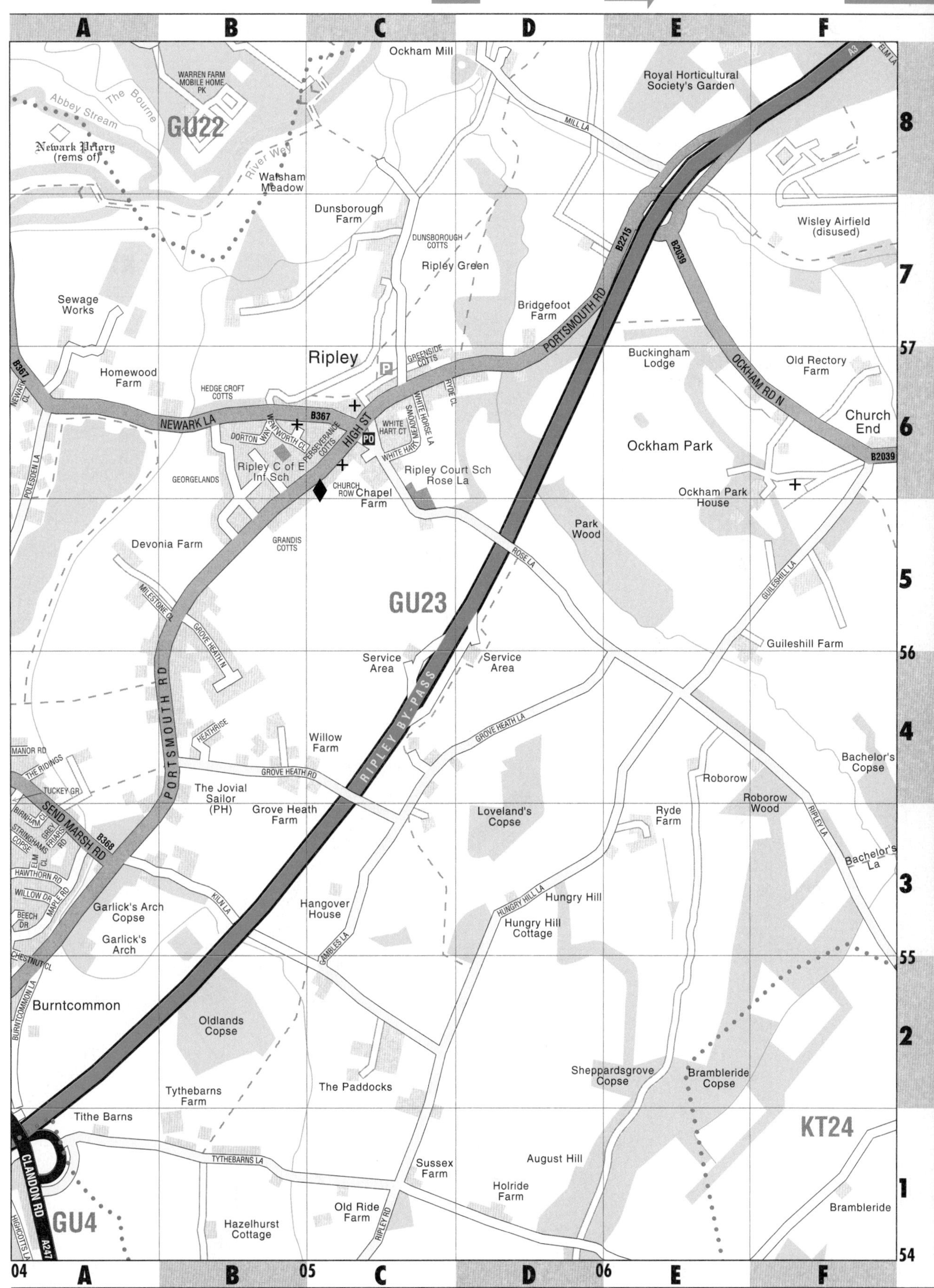
Ockham Mill
Royal Horticultural Society's Garden
WARREN FARM MOBILE HOME PK
GU22
Abbey Stream
The Bourne
Newark Priory (rems of)
River Wey
Walsham Meadow
Dunsborough Farm
DUNSBOROUGH COTTS
Ripley Green
MILL LA
Wisley Airfield (disused)
Sewage Works
Bridgefoot Farm
PORTSMOUTH RD
B2215
B2039
A3
ELM LA
Ripley
Homewood Farm
GREENSIDE COTTS
Buckingham Lodge
OCKHAM RD N
Old Rectory Farm
Church End
B367
NEWARK CL
HEDGE CROFT COTTS
NEWARK LA
DORTON WAY
WENTWORTH CL
PERSEVERANCE COTTS
HIGH ST
WHITE HART CT
MEADOWS
WHITE HORSE LA
RYDE CL
WHITE HART
Ockham Park
B2039
POLESDEN LA
GEORGELANDS
Ripley C of E Inf Sch
CHURCH ROW
Chapel Farm
Ripley Court Sch Rose La
Ockham Park House
Park Wood
Devonia Farm
GRANDIS COTTS
ROSE LA
GU23
MILESTONE CL
GROVE HEATH N
GUILESHILL LA
Guileshill Farm
Service Area
Service Area
PORTSMOUTH RD
RIPLEY BY-PASS
GROVE HEATH LA
HEATHRISE
Willow Farm
MANOR RD
THE RIDINGS
TUCKEY GR
GROVE HEATH RD
Bachelor's Copse
Roborow
Roborow Wood
The Jovial Sailor (PH)
Grove Heath Farm
Loveland's Copse
Ryde Farm
SEND MARSH RD
B368
BIRNHAM CL
GREY FRIARS RD
STRINGHAMS COPSE
ELM CL
RIPLEY LA
Bachelor's La
HAWTHORN RD
WILLOW DR
MAPLE RD
BEECH DR
KILN LA
Hangover House
HUNGRY HILL LA
Hungry Hill
Hungry Hill Cottage
Garlick's Arch Copse
Garlick's Arch
GAMBLES LA
CHESTNUT CL
Burntcommon
BURNTCOMMON LA
Oldlands Copse
Tythebarns Farm
The Paddocks
Sheppardsgrove Copse
Brambleride Copse
Tithe Barns
KT24
CLANDON RD
TYTHEBARNS LA
Sussex Farm
August Hill
Holride Farm
GU4
Hazelhurst Cottage
Old Ride Farm
RIPLEY RD
Brambleride
HIGHCOTTS LA
A247
A B C D E F
8 7 57 6 5 56 4 3 55 2 1 54
04 05 06

111
92

91
72

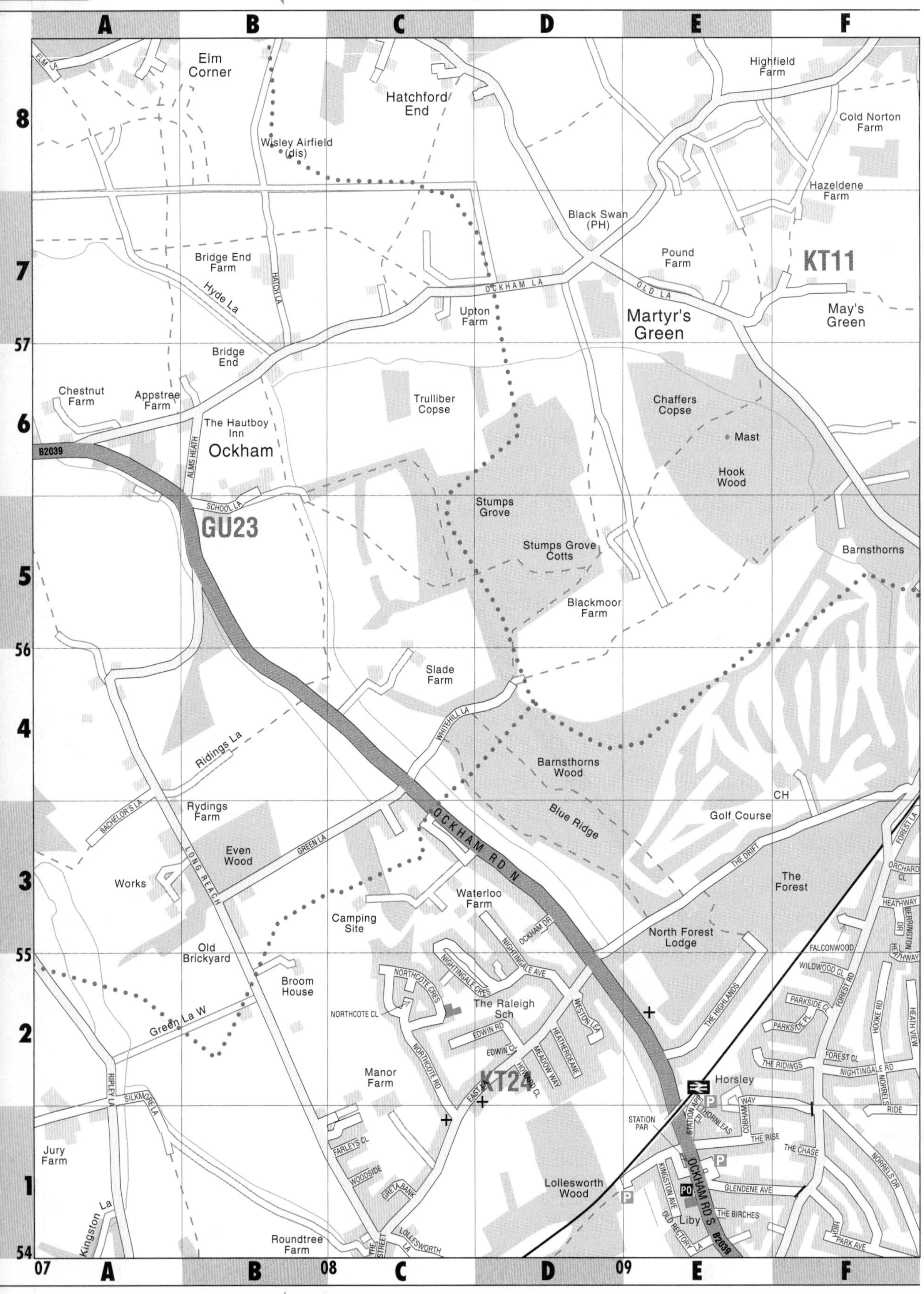
Elm Corner
Hatchford End
Wisley Airfield (dis)
Highfield Farm
Cold Norton Farm
Hazeldene Farm
Black Swan (PH)
Pound Farm
KT11
Bridge End Farm
Hyde La
Ockham La
Old La
Upton Farm
Martyr's Green
May's Green
Bridge End
Chestnut Farm
Appstree Farm
Trulliber Copse
Chaffers Copse
Mast
The Hautboy Inn
Ockham
B2039
Hook Wood
Alms Heath
School La
GU23
Stumps Grove
Stumps Grove Cotts
Barnsthorns
Blackmoor Farm
Slade Farm
Whitehill La
Ridings La
Barnsthorns Wood
CH
Bachelor's La
Rydings Farm
Blue Ridge
Golf Course
Ockham Rd N
Even Wood
Green La
The Drift
The Forest
Forest La
Works
Long Reach
Waterloo Farm
Orchard Cl
Camping Site
Ockham Dr
Heathway
Berrington Dr
North Forest Lodge
Old Brickyard
Nightingale Ave
Nightingale Cres
Falconwood
Broom House
Northcote Cres
Wildwood Cl
Green La W
The Raleigh Sch
Weston Lea
The Highlands
Parkside Cl
Forest Rd
Hooke Rd
Heath View
Northcote Cl
Edwin Rd
Parkside Pl
Edwin Cl
Heatherdeane
Meadow Way
Howard Cl
Northcote Rd
The Ridings
Forest Cl
Nightingale Rd
Manor Farm
KT24
Horsley
Norrels Ride
Ripley La
Silkmore La
East La
Station Par
Station App
Thornleas Pl
Cobham Way
The Rise
The Chase
Farleys Cl
Jury Farm
Woodside
Greta Bank
Ockham Rd S
Glendene Ave
Norrels Dr
Lollesworth Wood
Kingston Ave
PO
Old Rectory La
The Birches
Liby
Kingston La
Roundtree Farm
The Street
Lollesworth La
High Park Ave
A
B
C
D
E
F
8
7
57
6
5
56
4
3
55
2
1
54
07
08
09

91
112

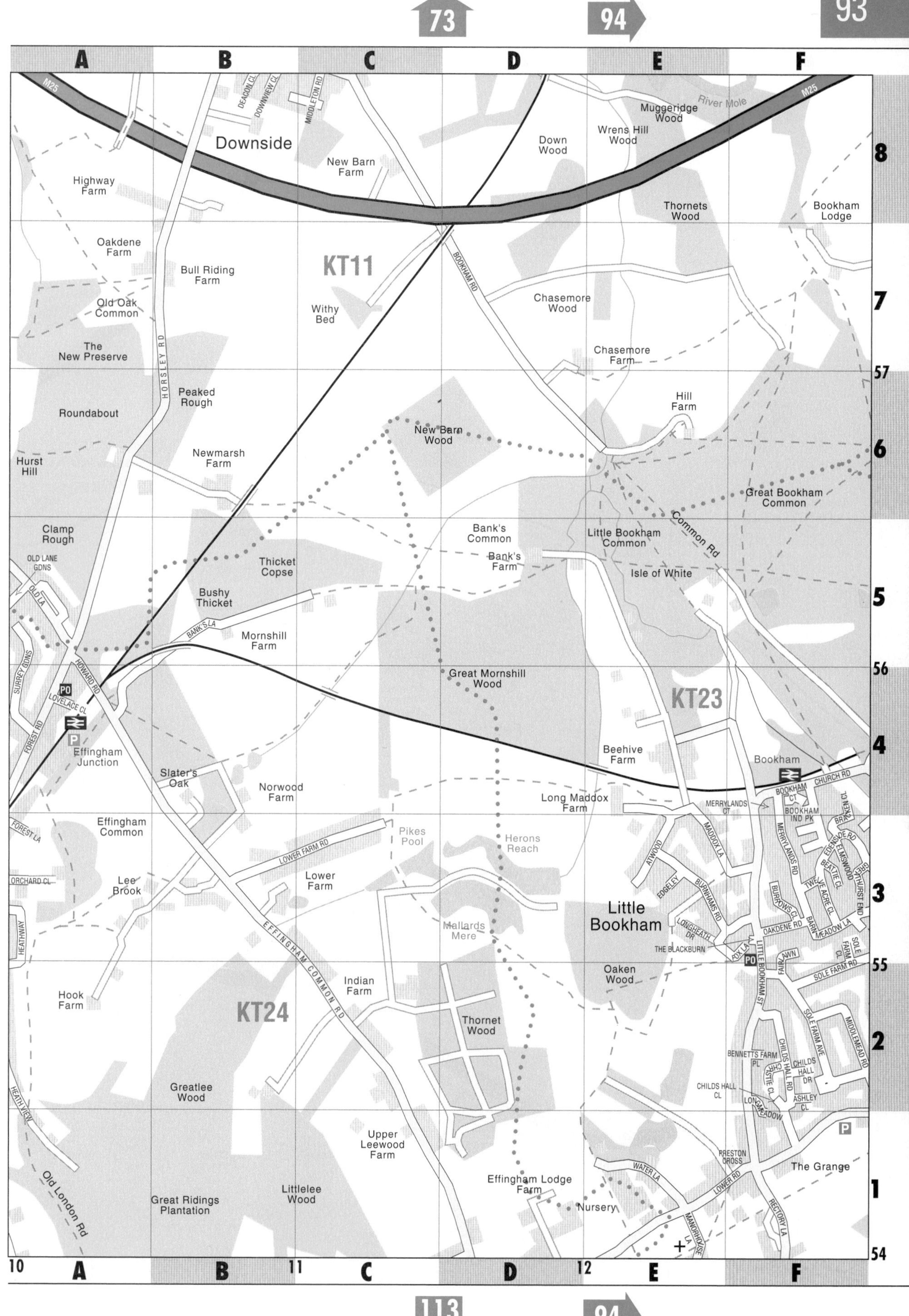

73
94
A
B
C
D
E
F
8
7
57
6
5
56
4
3
55
2
1
54
10
11
12
M25
Downside
DEACON CL
DOWNVIEW CL
MIDDLETON RD
New Barn Farm
Highway Farm
Down Wood
Wrens Hill Wood
Muggeridge Wood
River Mole
Thornets Wood
Bookham Lodge
Oakdene Farm
Bull Riding Farm
KT11
BOOKHAM RD
Withy Bed
Old Oak Common
The New Preserve
Chasemore Wood
Chasemore Farm
HORSLEY RD
Peaked Rough
Roundabout
Hill Farm
New Barn Wood
Newmarsh Farm
Hurst Hill
Great Bookham Common
Clamp Rough
Bank's Common
Little Bookham Common
Common Rd
OLD LANE GDNS
OLD LA
Thicket Copse
Bank's Farm
Isle of White
Bushy Thicket
BANK'S LA
Mornshill Farm
SURREY GDNS
HOWARD RD
LOVELACE CL
PO
P
Great Mornshill Wood
KT23
FOREST RD
Effingham Junction
Beehive Farm
Bookham
Slater's Oak
Norwood Farm
Long Maddox Farm
CHURCH RD
BOOKHAM CT
MERRYLANDS CT
BOOKHAM IND PK
Effingham Common
FOREST LA
Pikes Pool
Herons Reach
LOWER FARM RD
ATWOOD
MADDOX LA
MERRYLANDS RD
EDENSIDE RD
ELMSWOOD
BEATTIE CL
Lee Brook
ORCHARD CL
Lower Farm
EDGELEY
BURNHAMS RD
BURROWS CL
TWELVE ACRE CL
Little Bookham
Mallards Mere
LONGHEATH DR
BARN MEADOW LA
OAKDENE RD
THE BLACKBURN
FOX LA
LITTLE BOOKHAM ST
FAIRLAWN
SOLE FARM CL
SOLE FARM RD
HEATHWAY
EFFINGHAM COMMON RD
Indian Farm
Oaken Wood
Hook Farm
KT24
SOLE FARM AVE
MIDDLEMEAD RD
Thornet Wood
BENNETTS FARM PL
CHILDS HALL RD
CHRISTIE CL
CHILDS HALL DR
CHILDS HALL CL
LONG MEADOW
ASHLEY CL
Greatlee Wood
HEATH VIEW
Upper Leewood Farm
PRESTON CROSS
The Grange
Effingham Lodge Farm
WATER LA
LOWER RD
RECTORY LA
Old London Rd
Great Ridings Plantation
Littlelee Wood
Nursery
MANORHOUSE LA
113
94

93
74

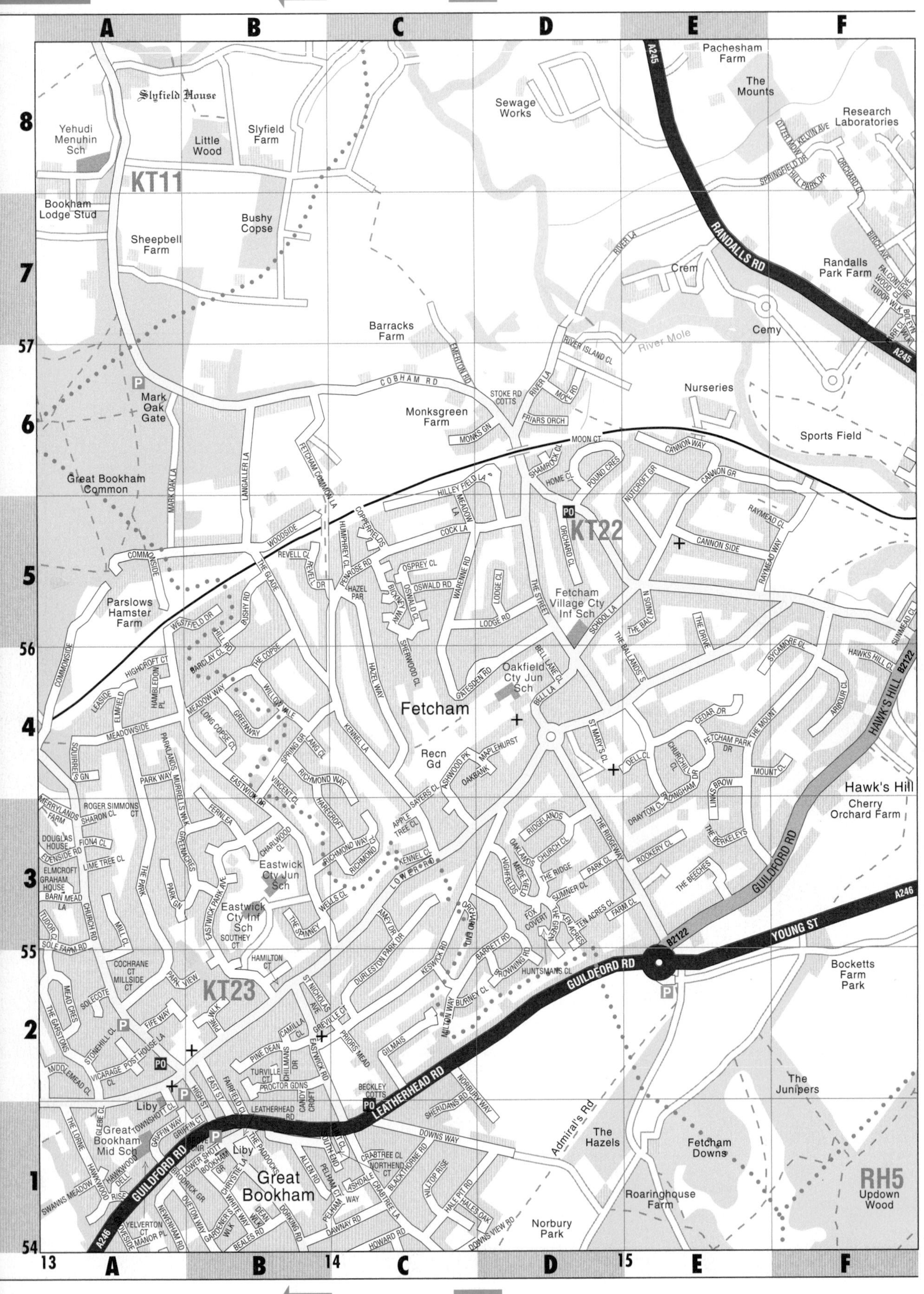
Fetcham
Great Bookham
KT11
KT22
KT23
RH5
Slyfield House
Little Wood
Slyfield Farm
Yehudi Menuhin Sch
Bookham Lodge Stud
Bushy Copse
Sheepbell Farm
Barracks Farm
Sewage Works
Pachesham Farm
The Mounts
Research Laboratories
Randalls Park Farm
Crem
Cemy
River Mole
Nurseries
Sports Field
Monksgreen Farm
Mark Oak Gate
Great Bookham Common
Parslows Hamster Farm
Fetcham Village Cty Inf Sch
Oakfield Cty Jun Sch
Recn Gd
Eastwick Cty Jun Sch
Eastwick Cty Inf Sch
Hawk's Hill
Cherry Orchard Farm
Bocketts Farm Park
The Junipers
The Hazels
Fetcham Downs
Roaringhouse Farm
Norbury Park
Updown Wood
Great Bookham Mid Sch
Liby
RANDALLS RD
GUILDFORD RD
LEATHERHEAD RD
YOUNG ST
HAWK'S HILL
COBHAM RD
A245
A246
B2122

93
114

75
96

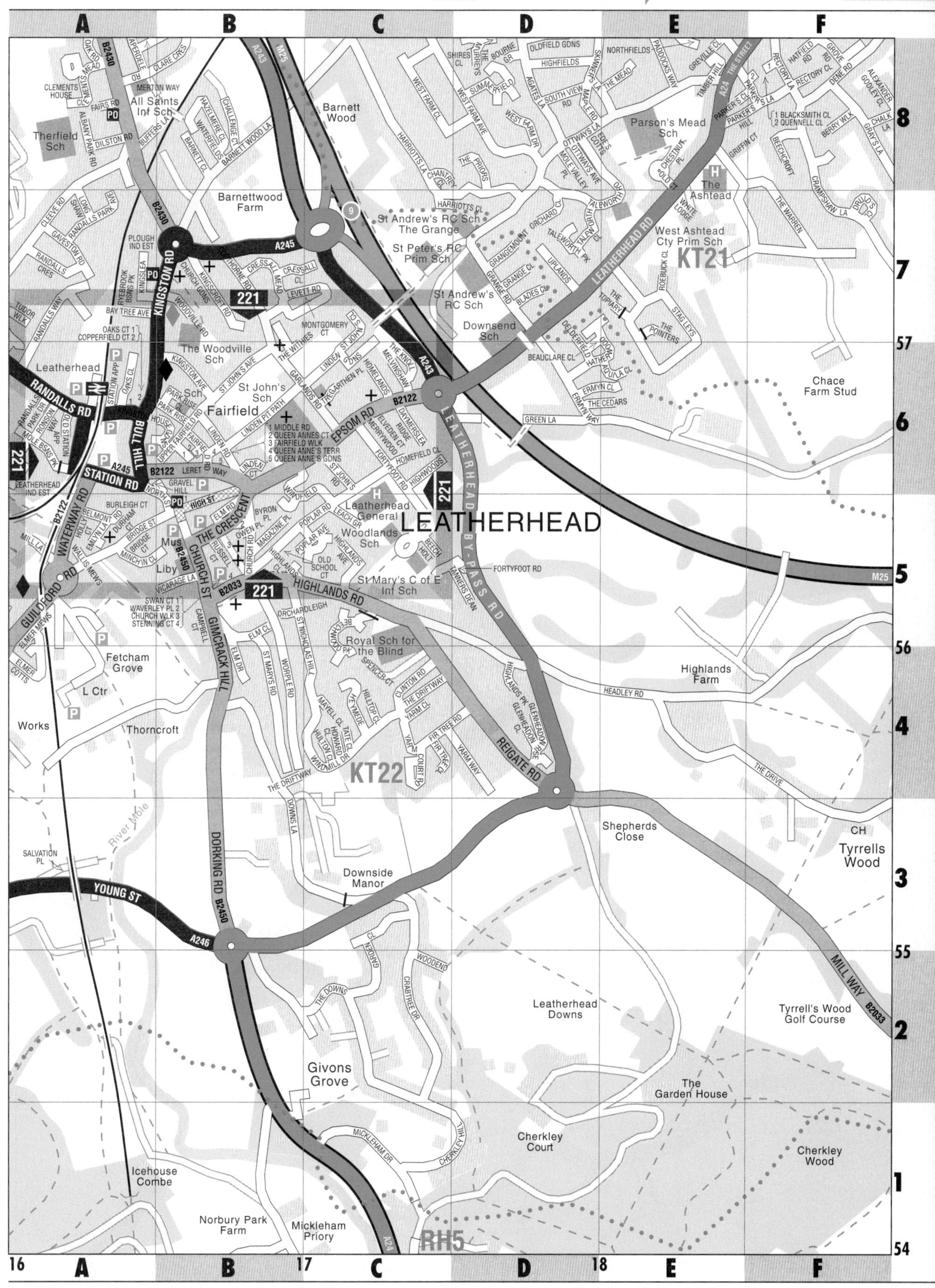
LEATHERHEAD
KT21
KT22
RH5
Barnett Wood
Barnettwood Farm
Therfield Sch
All Saints Inf Sch
Leatherhead
The Woodville Sch
St John's Sch
Fairfield
Leatherhead General
Woodlands Sch
St Mary's C of E Inf Sch
Royal Sch for the Blind
St Andrew's RC Sch The Grange
St Peter's RC Prim Sch
St Andrew's RC Sch
Downsend Sch
Parson's Mead Sch
The Ashtead
West Ashtead Cty Prim Sch
Chace Farm Stud
Highlands Farm
Fetcham Grove
L Ctr
Works
Thorncroft
Shepherds Close
Tyrrells Wood
Downside Manor
Leatherhead Downs
Tyrrell's Wood Golf Course
Givons Grove
The Garden House
Cherkley Court
Cherkley Wood
Icehouse Combe
Norbury Park Farm
Mickleham Priory
River Mole
LEATHERHEAD BY-PASS RD
REIGATE RD
HIGHLANDS RD
HEADLEY RD
MILL WAY
YOUNG ST
DORKING RD
GIMCRACK HILL
CHURCH ST
THE CRESCENT
STATION RD
RANDALLS RD
KINGSTON RD
BULL HILL
EPSOM RD
LEATHERHEAD RD
WATERWAY RD
GUILDFORD RD
M25
A24
A243
A245
A246
B2430
B2122
B2033
B2450
221

95
76

A
B
C
D
E
F
Langley Bottom Wood
City of London Freemen's Sch
KT21
Ashtead Park
Epsom Downs Cty Inf Sch
Langley Vale
Langley Vale Farm
The Warren
Larch Field
Tudor Croft
Walton Downs
Thirty Acres Barn
Nohome Farm
Gilletts Cotts
Downs View
Downs View Wood
Addlestead Wood
Round Wood
Addlestead Farm
Fourfield Close
Little Hurst Wood
Hurst Farm
KT18
Twistwood
Hambleton Wood
Headley Court
Edes Barn Cotts
KT20
Headley Park
KT22
Hook Wood
Great Hurst Wood
Court Farm
Sandhill Wood
Oyster Hill
Nower Wood
The Cock Horse (PH)
Costal Wood
Headley
Walton Park Wood
Nature Reserve
Heath Farm
Manor House
Heath House
RH5
M25
B2033
MILL WAY
LEECH LA
CHALK LA
PARK LA
OAKEN COPPICE
RALLIWOOD RD
GRAY'S LA
CRAMPSHAW LA
FARM LA
HEADLEY RD
CHALK PIT RD
DOWNS RD
LANGLEY VALE RD
SHEPHERDS WLK
PEBBLE LA
WALTON RD
SHEEP WLK
HURST LA
HURST RD
EBBISHAM LA
ROSEBERRY RD
GROSVENOR RD
BEACONSFIELD RD
HARDING RD
MILLERS COPSE
SADDLERS WAY
STRAND CL
MANNAMEAD
SPENCER CL
TILLEY LA
DALE VIEW
CUNLIFFE CL
FARRIERS
HOOKWOOD COTTS
HURST CL
CLAY LA
THE DRIVE
SLOUGH LA
Langley La
TUMBER ST
CHURCH LA
BROOME CL
CRABTREE LA
LODGEBOTTOM RD
HOWARD CL
Love La
8
7
57
6
5
56
4
3
55
2
1
54
19
20
21

95
116

77
98

A B C D E F

8 7 57 6 5 56 4 3 55 2 1 54

Race Course
KT18
Walton Downs
South Tadworth Farm
Burgh Heath
Merland Rise Cty Prim Sch
Sports Ctr
Pit Wood Mast
EPSOM DOWNS METRO CTR
Canons Farm Cottages
Canons Farm
Ambrose Cottages
BROOMFIELD COTTS
GARDENFIELDS
MEMORY COTTS
PH
Garden Farm
Kingswood
KINGSWOOD PK
The Childrens Trust (Tadworth Court)
THE WALLED GARDEN
Tadworth Cty Prim Sch
Tadworth
Chinthurst Sch
KT20
Kingswood Warren
Walton Mill (dis)
Kingswood Court
Walton on the Hill
Ebbisham Farm
Mere Pond
Blue Ball (PH)
Walton Manor
Castle House
Hogden Bottom
The Gallops
Banstead Heath
Holly Lodge (Mobile Home Pk)
CH
The Red Lodge
Golf Course
Recn Gd
The Gallops

EPSOM LA N
B290
A240 REIGATE RD
A217
BRIGHTON RD
ASHURST RD
STATION APP
TADWORTH ST
B2220
B2032
BONSOR DR
WATERHOUSE LA
MILL RD
NEW RD
MERE RD
WALTON ST
DORKING RD
CHEQUERS LA
SHELVERS WAY
THE WARREN
CHIPSTEAD LA
BEECHEN LA
GREEN LA
READS REST LA
COPT HILL LA
CANONS LA
OATLANDS RD
EGMONT WAY
MAYBURY CL
BALLARDS GN
THE PARADE
DUNCAN RD
SOMERFIELD CL
KINGSWOOD RD
DOWNS WAY
DOWNSWAY CL
WHITE BEAM WAY
MOTTS HILL LA
EBBISHAM LA
HURST RD
SANDLANDS GR
SANDLANDS RD
WITHYBED CNR
TADWORTH CL
HEATHLANDS
HEATHER CL
WOODLAND WAY
GLEN CL
BEARS DEN
BEECH DR
HAMILTON PL
WARREN DR
EYHURST CL
EYHURST SPUR
SANDY LA
MILLFIELD LA
WARREN LODGE DR
VICARAGE CL
WALNUT DR
HEMLOCK CL
ACORN GR
GROVE SHAW
SILVER CL
BIRCH GR
2ND AVE
4TH AVE
6TH AVE
8TH AVE
10TH AVE
12TH AVE
14TH AVE
16TH AVE
1ST AVE
3RD AVE
5TH AVE
7TH AVE
9TH AVE
11TH AVE
13TH AVE
15TH AVE
THE MOUNT
JOSEPHINE AVE
ORCHARD WAY
SMITHY CL
SMITHY LA
BRIER LEA
THE BARNYARD
QUEENS CL
THE THOROUGHFARE
CHEQUERS CT
SCHOOL LA
BREECH LA
CHEQUERS CL
EGMONT PARK RD
HOWARD CL
NURSERY RD
NURSERY CL
DEANS LA
HOLMCROFT
GREENWAYS
RUSSELL CL
HEATH DR
WONFORD CL
HURST DR
LOVE LA
NYEFIELD PK
MEADOW WLK
CHUCK'S LA
OLD RECTORY CL
POND FARM CL
DUFFIELD RD
DEANS CL
THE WAPLINGS
MEADE CT
HEDGE CNR
1 HEATHWOOD
2 CHRISTOPHER CT
HEATHSIDE CT
RUSSETS
KILLASSER CT
COOMBE CT
AVENUE CT
HIGH ST
TOWER RD
CHAPEL RD
STOKES RIDINGS
THE AVENUE
LOTHIAN WOOD
AVENUE CL
SPINDLEWOODS
MILSTEAD CL
MEON CL
BEECHDENE
KINGSDENE
DOWNS VIEW
WILLOWBANK GDNS
CORNER FARM CL
KINGS CT
CROSS RD
LYWOOD CL
OAKLANDS WAY
THE LYE
EPSOM LA S
TADORNE RD
THE HORNBEAM
MERE CL
WATTS MEAD
WATT'S LA
HARENDON
MABBOTTS
WESSELS
TRITONS
STEWART
COFFETS
HUDSONS
MORTON
SAXONS
PROSSERS
WILSONS
HARPURS
DELVES
HEATHCOTE
KIPINGS
RADOLPH
BAYEUX
RUSSELLS
SHELVERS SPUR
SHELVERS GN
SHELVERS HILL
HILL VIEW CL
CHANDLERS
THE DELL
FAIRACRES
BIDHAMS CRES
THE RISE
THURNHAM WAY
FLEETWOOD CL
LINDEN CL
COPLEY WAY
VERNON WALK
PRESTON LA
HOMEFIELD GDNS
MICHELHAM GDNS
CHEAM CL
WATERMEAD
WATERFIELD
ASHCOMBE TERR
OATFIELD RD
PIT WOOD GN
MERLAND GN
MERLAND CL
LONGFIELD CRES
BROADFIELD CL
GUDDINGTON CL
HAWES RD
HATCH GDNS
MORDEN CL
MERTON GDNS
MEREFIELD GDNS
MARBLES WAY
CHETWODE RD
BROAD WLK
LONG WLK
MERLAND RISE
CHAPEL GR
CHAPEL WAY
ST LEONARDS RD
ELM GDNS
HEADLEY DR
HEADLEY GR
HEWERS WAY
TULYAR CL
STAITHS WAY
MORNSTON CL
LORDSGROVE CL
WHITEGATE WAY
CAMPION DR
MALLOW CL
BRIER RD
1 ROWAN MEAD
2 HENBIT CL
DERBY CL
TATTENHAM GR
THE SPINNEY
OAKS WAY
ROYAL DR
THE GREEN
COPLEIGH DR
OAKDENE
ALCOCKS CL
ALCOCKS LA
SUMMERLAY CL
CEDAR WLK
THE RIDINGS
FURZE GR
FURZE HILL
BALLANTYNE DR
HILL LA
ST MONICA'S RD
DORIC DR

22 23 24

A B C D E F

117
98

97
78

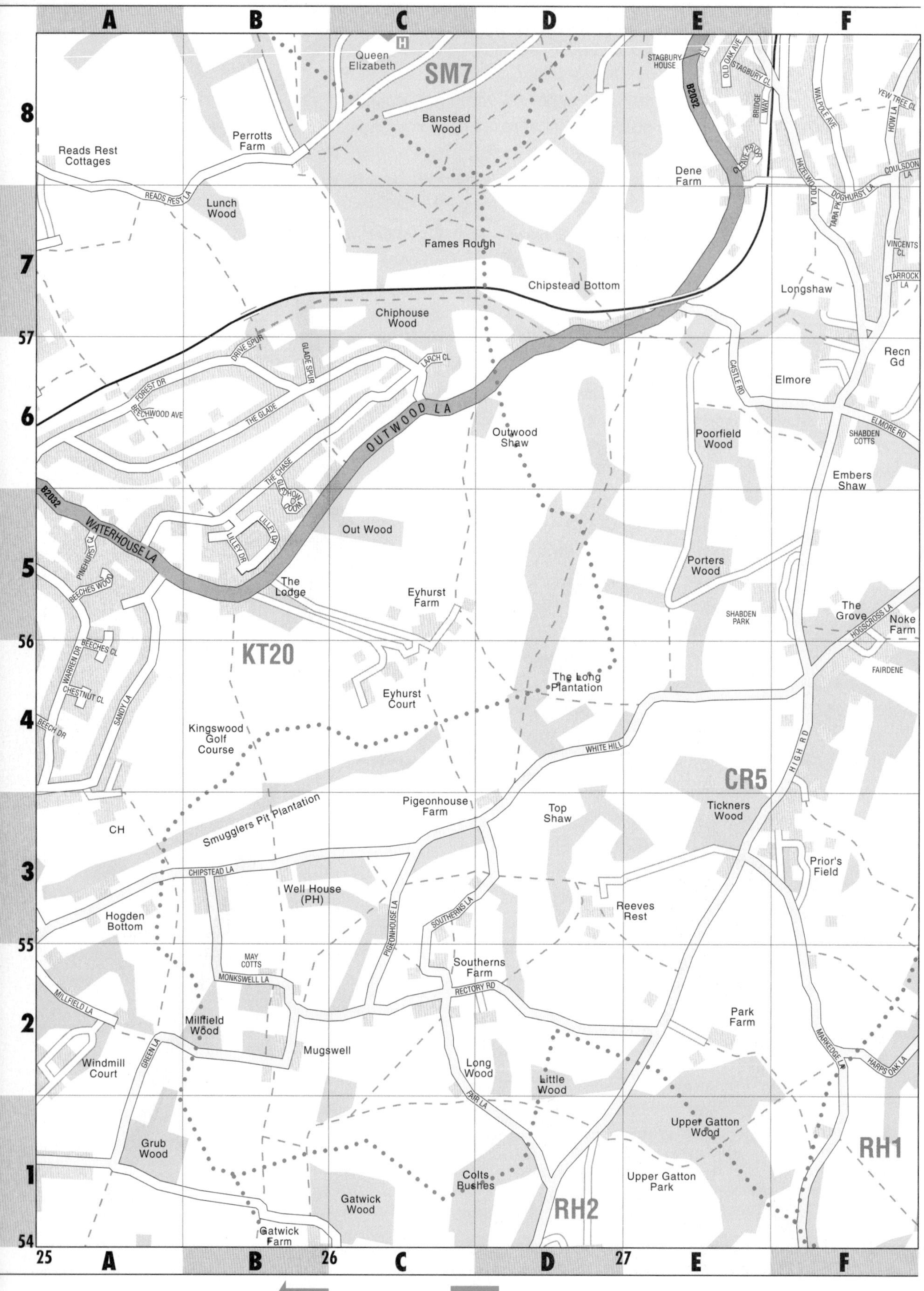
A
B
C
D
E
F
8
7
57
6
5
56
4
3
55
2
1
54
25
26
27
Queen Elizabeth
SM7
Banstead Wood
Perrotts Farm
Reads Rest Cottages
READS REST LA
Lunch Wood
Fames Rough
Chipstead Bottom
STAGBURY HOUSE
B2032
OLD OAK AVE
STAGBURY CL
BRIDGE WAY
Dene Farm
WALPOLE AVE
YEW TREE CL
HOW LA
HAZELWOOD LA
COULSDON LA
DOGHURST LA
TAPA PK
VINCENTS CL
STARROCK LA
Longshaw
Chiphouse Wood
DRIVE SPUR
GLADE SPUR
LARCH CL
FOREST DR
BEECHWOOD AVE
THE GLADE
OUTWOOD LA
CASTLE RD
Recn Gd
Elmore
ELMORE RD
SHABDEN COTTS
Outwood Shaw
Poorfield Wood
Embers Shaw
THE CHASE
GLENHOW COOMB
LILLEY DR
WATERHOUSE LA
Out Wood
Porters Wood
PINEHURST CL
BEECHES WOOD
The Lodge
Eyhurst Farm
SHABDEN PARK
The Grove
HOGSCROSS LA
Noke Farm
BEECHES CL
WARREN DR
KT20
The Long Plantation
FAIRDENE
CHESTNUT CL
Eyhurst Court
SANDY LA
BEECH DR
Kingswood Golf Course
WHITE HILL
HIGH RD
CR5
Pigeonhouse Farm
Top Shaw
Tickners Wood
CH
Smugglers Pit Plantation
Prior's Field
CHIPSTEAD LA
Well House (PH)
Reeves Rest
Hogden Bottom
SOUTHERNS LA
PIGEONHOUSE LA
MAY COTTS
Southerns Farm
MONKSWELL LA
RECTORY RD
MILLFIELD LA
Millfield Wood
Park Farm
Mugswell
MARKEDGE LA
HARPS OAK LA
Windmill Court
GREEN LA
Long Wood
Little Wood
FAIR LA
Upper Gatton Wood
RH1
Grub Wood
Colts Bushes
Upper Gatton Park
Gatwick Wood
RH2
Gatwick Farm

97
118

A B C D E F

Hooley Farm
WOODFIELD HILL
STARROCK RD
LAVENDER CL
WOODFIELD CL
PETWORTH
A23
WOODPLACE CL
THE NETHERLANDS
WILHELMINA AVE
CHALDON WAY
TOLLERS LA
8
COULSDON LA
GRASSFIELD CL
Farthing or Fairdean Downs
Starrock Wood
STARROCK LA
DRIVE RD
Tollers Farm
CURLING CL
ELLIS CL
ELLIS RD
WOODPLACE LA
Drive Rd
JUTLAND GDNS
THE ADMIRAL'S WLK
GOODENOUGH WAY
WESTON CL
7
Woodplace Farm
Star Shaw
Three Cornered Shaw
PRETTY LA
57
Happy Valley
BRIGHTON RD
CR5
DUTCHES LA
Devilsden Wood
Boxers Wood
Petershole Shaw
6
MAPLE WAY
BELL CRES
ROWAN GR
PARK LA
CLOVER HILL
ST MARGARET'S RD
Netherne House
PO
ELMORE RD
Court Lodge
STAR LA
Hooley
Forge Bridge
The Gullet
Figgs Wood
HOGSCROSS LA
LANE DR
CHURCH LANE AVE
CHURCH
CHURCH LA
5
NETHERNE LA
Netherne Wood
BROAD WLK
GARDEN WLK
56
Grasscuts Shaw
Lord's Wood
4
A23
Coldroast Shaw
Dean Farm
Court Farm
CHURCH LA
CR3
Road under construction
Furzefield Wood
GLEBE RD
Alderstead Heath
3
Harps Wood
Sparticles Wood
DEAN LA
55
ROOK LA
B2031
ALDERSTEAD LA
LONDON RD N
7
M23
Tollsworth Cottages
2
HARPS OAK LA
Harps Oak
RH1
Alderstead Farm
Tollsworth Manor
Boorsgreen Farm
Tollsworth Manor Farm
BEECH RD
B2031
SHEPHERD'S HILL
PILGRIMS' LA
PH
1
CHURCH HILL
North Downs Way
Furzefield Shaw
Marling Glen Wood
JOLLIFFE RD
Church Hill
A23
M23
54

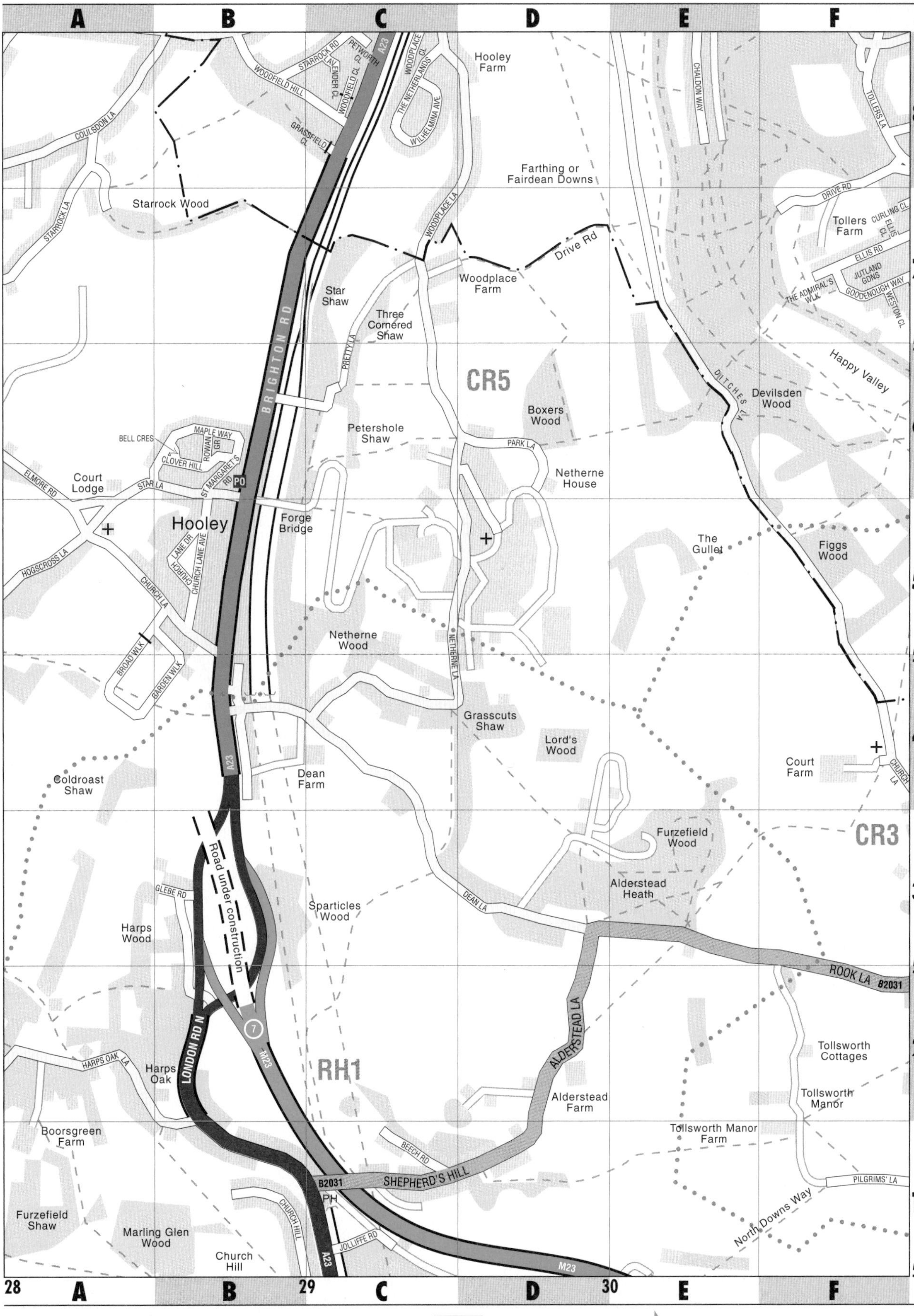

28 A B 29 C D 30 E F

99
80

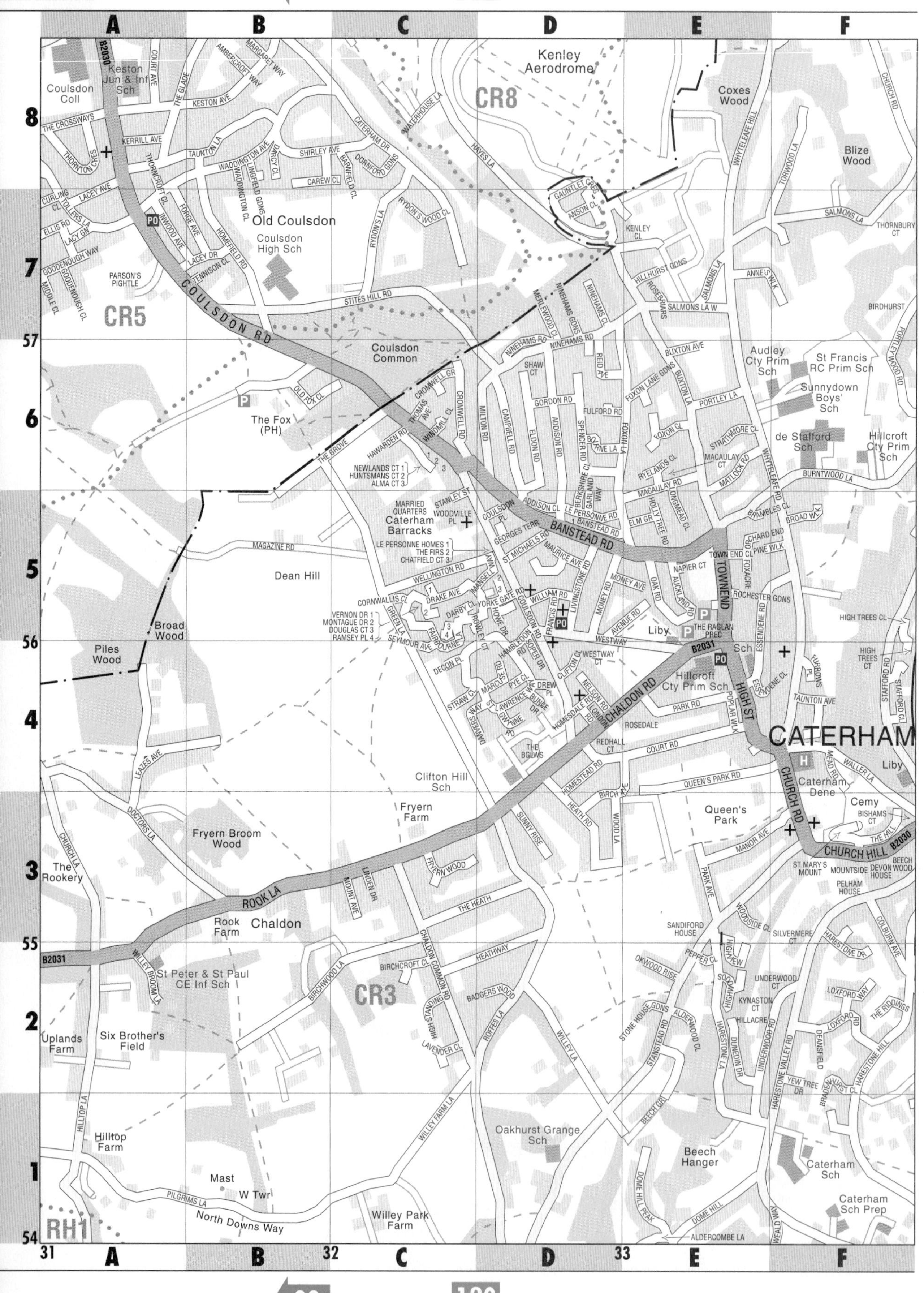
A
B
C
D
E
F
8
7
57
6
5
56
4
3
55
2
1
54
31
32
33
Kenley Aerodrome
CR8
Coxes Wood
Blize Wood
Coulsdon Coll
Keston Jun & Inf Sch
B2030
COURT AVE
THE GLADE
AMBERCROFT WAY
MARGARET WAY
KESTON AVE
THE CROSSWAYS
KERRILL AVE
THORNTON CRES
TAUNTON LA
WADDINGTON AVE
WADDINGTON CL
LINGFIELD GDNS
DARCY CL
SHIRLEY AVE
CAREW CL
BARNFIELD CL
DORNFORD GDNS
CATERHAM DR
WATERHOUSE LA
HAYES LA
GAUNTLET CRES
ANSON CL
KENLEY CL
WHYTELEAFE HILL
TORWOOD LA
CHURCH RD
SALMONS LA
THORNBURY CT
CURLING CL
TOLLERS LA
LACEY AVE
ELLIS RD
LACY GN
GOODENOUGH WAY
GOODENOUGH CL
MIDDLE CL
THORNCROFT CL
P0
INWOOD AVE
FORGE AVE
HOMEFIELD RD
LACEY DR
TENNISON CL
Old Coulsdon
Coulsdon High Sch
RYDON'S LA
RYDON'S WOOD CL
PARSON'S PIGHTLE
CR5
COULSDON RD
STITES HILL RD
MERLEWOOD CL
NINEHAMS GDNS
NINEHAMS CL
HILLHURST GDNS
ROSEBRIARS
SALMONS LA W
ANNES WLK
BIRDHURST
PORTLEY WOOD RD
Coulsdon Common
NINEHAMS RD
SHAW CT
REID AVE
BUXTON AVE
Audley Cty Prim Sch
St Francis RC Prim Sch
Sunnydown Boys' Sch
OLD FOX CL
CROMWELL GR
THOMAS AVE
WINDMILL CL
CROMWELL RD
MILTON RD
CAMPBELL RD
GORDON RD
EDDON RD
ADDISON RD
FULFORD RD
SPENCER RD
FOXON LANE GDNS
FOXON LA
BUXTON LA
PORTLEY LA
The Fox (PH)
HAWARDEN RD
THE GROVE
BOVRINE LA
FOXON CL
STRATHMORE CL
de Stafford Sch
Hillcroft Cty Prim Sch
NEWLANDS CT 1
HUNTSMANS CT 2
ALMA CT 3
BERKSHIRE CL
GARLAND WAY
RYELANDS CL
MACAULAY CT
MATLOCK RD
WHYTELEAFE RD
BURNTWOOD LA
MARRIED QUARTERS
STANLEY ST
WOODVILLE PL
Caterham Barracks
COULSDON CT
ADDISON CL
LE PERSONNE RD
1 BANSTEAD RD
MACAULAY RD
ELM GR
HOLLY TREE RD
LONGMEAD CL
BRAMBLES CL
BROAD WLK
MAGAZINE RD
LE PERSONNE HOMES 1
THE FIRS 2
CHATFIELD CT 3
GEORGES TERR
BANSTEAD RD
ST MICHAELS RD
MAURICE AVE
CHARD END
TOWN END CL
PINE WLK
Dean Hill
WELLINGTON RD
LIVINGSTONE RD
NAPIER CT
TOWNEND
FOXACRE
CORNWALLIS CL
DRAKE AVE
MANSELL WAY
MONEY AVE
OAK RD
AUCKLAND RD
ROCHESTER GDNS
VERNON DR 1
MONTAGUE DR 2
DOUGLAS CT 3
RAMSEY PL 4
GREEN LA
DARBY CL
YORKE GATE RD
HOWE DR
WILLIAM RD
FRANCIS RD
AVENUE RD
MONEY RD
ESSENDENE RD
HIGH TREES CL
Broad Wood
FAIRBOURNE
ROWLEY CT
HAMBLEDON RD
COULSDON RD
Liby
THE RAGLAN PREC
SEYMOUR AVE
WESTWAY
Piles Wood
DECON PL
GUE CT
MARCUS CT
PYE CL
DREW PL
LAWRENCE WAY
BUNCE DR
SOPER DR
CLIFTON CL
WESTWAY CT
B2031
Sch
HIGH TREES CT
Hillcroft Cty Prim Sch
ESSENDENE CL
FURROWS PL
STAFFORD RD
STAFFORD CL
STRAW CL
DAMMERS WAY
GWYNNE AVE
NELSON RD
LONDON RD
HOMESDALE RD
CHALDON RD
PARK RD
POPLAR WLK
HIGH ST
TAUNTON AVE
CATERHAM
LEAZES AVE
ROSEDALE
THE BGLWS
REDHALL CT
COURT RD
H
MEAD RD
WALLER LA
Liby
Clifton Hill Sch
HOMESTEAD RD
QUEEN'S PARK RD
Caterham Dene
CHURCH RD
Fryern Farm
BIRCH AVE
Cemy
BISHAMS CT
DOCTORS LA
HEATH RD
WOOD LA
Queen's Park
CHURCH LA
Fryern Broom Wood
SUNNY RISE
MANOR AVE
THE HILL
B2030
CHURCH HILL
The Rookery
FRYERN WOOD
PARK AVE
ST MARY'S MOUNT
MOUNTSIDE
DEVON HOUSE
BEECH WOOD
ROOK LA
LINDEN DR
MOUNT AVE
THE HEATH
PELHAM HOUSE
Rook Farm
Chaldon
SANDIFORD HOUSE
WOODSIDE CL
SILVERMERE CT
COLBURN AVE
HARESTONE DR
B2031
WILLEY BROOM LA
CHALDON COMMON RD
HEATHWAY
BIRCHCROFT CL
PEPPER CL
HIGH VIEW
OKWOOD RISE
UNDERWOOD CT
St Peter & St Paul CE Inf Sch
BIRCHWOOD LA
CR3
HIGH STANDING
BADGERS WOOD
ROFFES LA
SOLOMONS
HIGHWAY
KYNASTON CT
LOXFORD WAY
THE RIDDINGS
LOXFORD RD
HILLACRE
Uplands Farm
Six Brother's Field
LAVENDER CL
STONE HOUSE GDNS
ALDERWOOD CL
STANSTEAD RD
HARESTONE LA
DUNEDIN DR
UNDERWOOD RD
HARESTONE VALLEY RD
DEANSFIELD
HARESTONE HILL
WILLEY LA
YEW TREE DR
BRADENHURST CL
HILLTOP LA
WILLEY FARM LA
BEECH GR
Hilltop Farm
Oakhurst Grange Sch
Beech Hanger
Caterham Sch
Mast
W Twr
PILGRIMS LA
North Downs Way
Willey Park Farm
DOME HILL PEAK
DOME HILL
ALDERCOMBE LA
WEALD WAY
Caterham Sch Prep
RH1

99
120

81

A B C D E F

8
7
57
6
5
56
4
3
55
2
1
54

34 35 36

CR6
CR3
RH9

Whyteleafe South
LC
THE MOUNT
CONEYBURY CL
PADDOCK WLK
WESTHALL RD
WEST VIEW RD
SOUTHVIEW RD
ALTAMONT
KOORINGA
SUCCOMBS PL
WELL FARM RD
JOHNS WLK
WHITEGATES
COURT BUSHES RD
WHYTEACRE
GREENACRE
SUCCOMBS HILL
GLADESIDE CT
LANDSCAPE RD
NARROW LA
DORIN CT
BADGERS LA
WATERFIELD
OLD WESTHALL CL
WESTHALL PK
BROADLANDS DR
HUNTSMANS CL
HOMEFIELD RD
HIGH PINES
OVERHILL
BURFIELD DR
ASHWOOD
BUTTERFLY WLK
RIDLEY RD
TANDRIDGE RD
TYDCOMBE RD
LEAS RD
BEECHWOOD LA
LARCH CL
CEDAR CL
BLANCHMANS RD
FARM RD
PLANTATION LA
Halliloo Plantation
HIGH LA
Golf Course
BUTLERS DENE RD
BUG HILL
Halliloo Farm
SLINES NEW RD
Dukes Hill House
DUKES HILL
LUNGHURST RD
SALMONS LA
THE AVENUE
GODSTONE RD
A22
PORTLEY WOOD RD
Manor Park
Cloisters
P
STUART RD
Viaduct Lodge
Scoldhill Plantation
BEULAH WLK
HILLTOP WLK
PARK LEY RD
CAMP RD
Woldingham Garden Village
B2208
PO
WOLDINGHAM RD
Marden Lodge Cty Prim Sch
Birchwood Farm
Burntwood Hill
BURNTWOOD LA
BURNTWOOD CL
PORTLEY WOOD RD
GREENHILL AVE
Birchwood
LONG HILL
Stony Hill
STAFFORD RD
MILNER RD
MILNER APP
MILNER CL
Recn Gd
AVONDALE HIGH
TILLINGDOWN HILL
WALTHAM RD
HIGHFIELD RD
BEECHWOOD GDNS
GAIST AVE
1 ROGERS CL
2 EVERARD LA
ABBOTS WLK
TANDRIDGE CT
CROYDON RD
VALLEY CT
Woldingham
STATION RD
SOUTHDOWN RD
PARK VIEW RD
HIGH DR
STABLE CT
BEECHWOOD RD
ELGIN CRES
FARNINGHAM CRES
CATERHAM BY-PASS
The Bushes
Church Road Farm
Woodlea Cty Prim Sch
CROFT RD
TRENHOLME CT
KNOWLE LODGE
FARNINGHAM RD
COMMONWEALTH RD
Worlds End
Park Shaw
CHURCH RD
Marden Park Farm
COLIN RD
MOUNT PLEASANT RD
Caterham
STAFFORD RD
STATION AV
Mus
CRESCENT RD
TIMBER HILL RD
TIMBER HILL
CHURCH WLK
Tillingdown Farm
Marden Hillboxes Farm
Little Church Wood
HARESTONE HILL
EOTHEN CL
CLAREVILLE RD
THE CLARS
DEERSWOOD CL
TILLINGDOWN LA
FERN TOWERS
TUPWOOD CT
RUSSETT CT
ELIZABETH HOUSE
COLLIERS
ROSENEATH CT
GREENWOOD GDNS
ASPREY GR
LONGSDON WAY
Rookery
GRANGE RD
ST KATHARINES RD
WHITE KNOBS WAY
B2030
Great Church Wood
Carr's Croft
MARKVILLE GDNS
MARKFIELD RD
Woldingham Sch
Marden Park
ALEXANDERS WLK
St John's CE (VA) Inf Sch
St John's CE Jun Sch
Paddock Barn
WOOLHAMS
THE COPSE
TUPWOOD LA
NEWSTEAD HOUSE
NEWSTEAD RISE
LISKEARD LODGE
Paddock Wood
Paddock Barn
Stubbs Copse
HARESTONE HILL
The Chalet

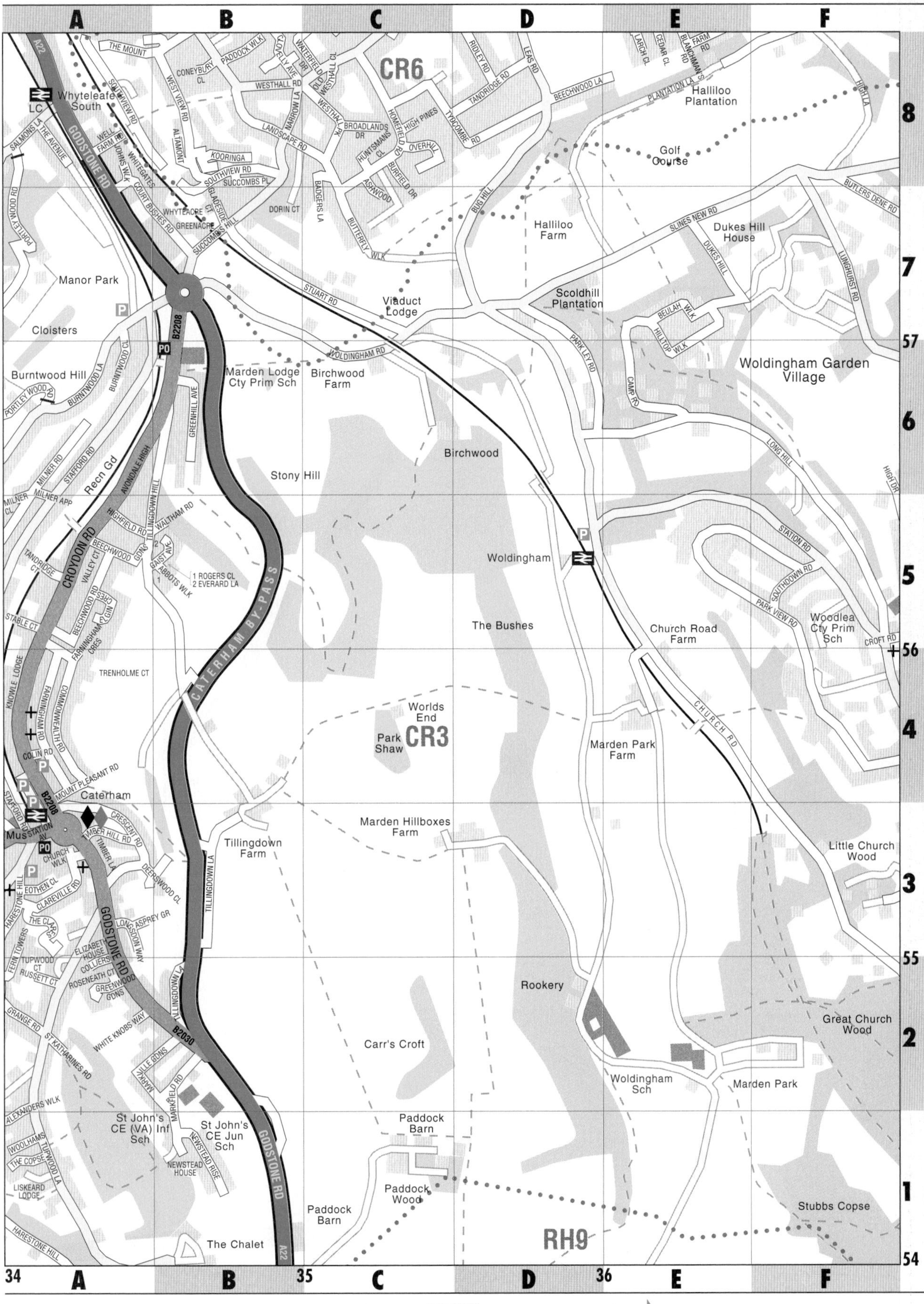

121

102

101
82

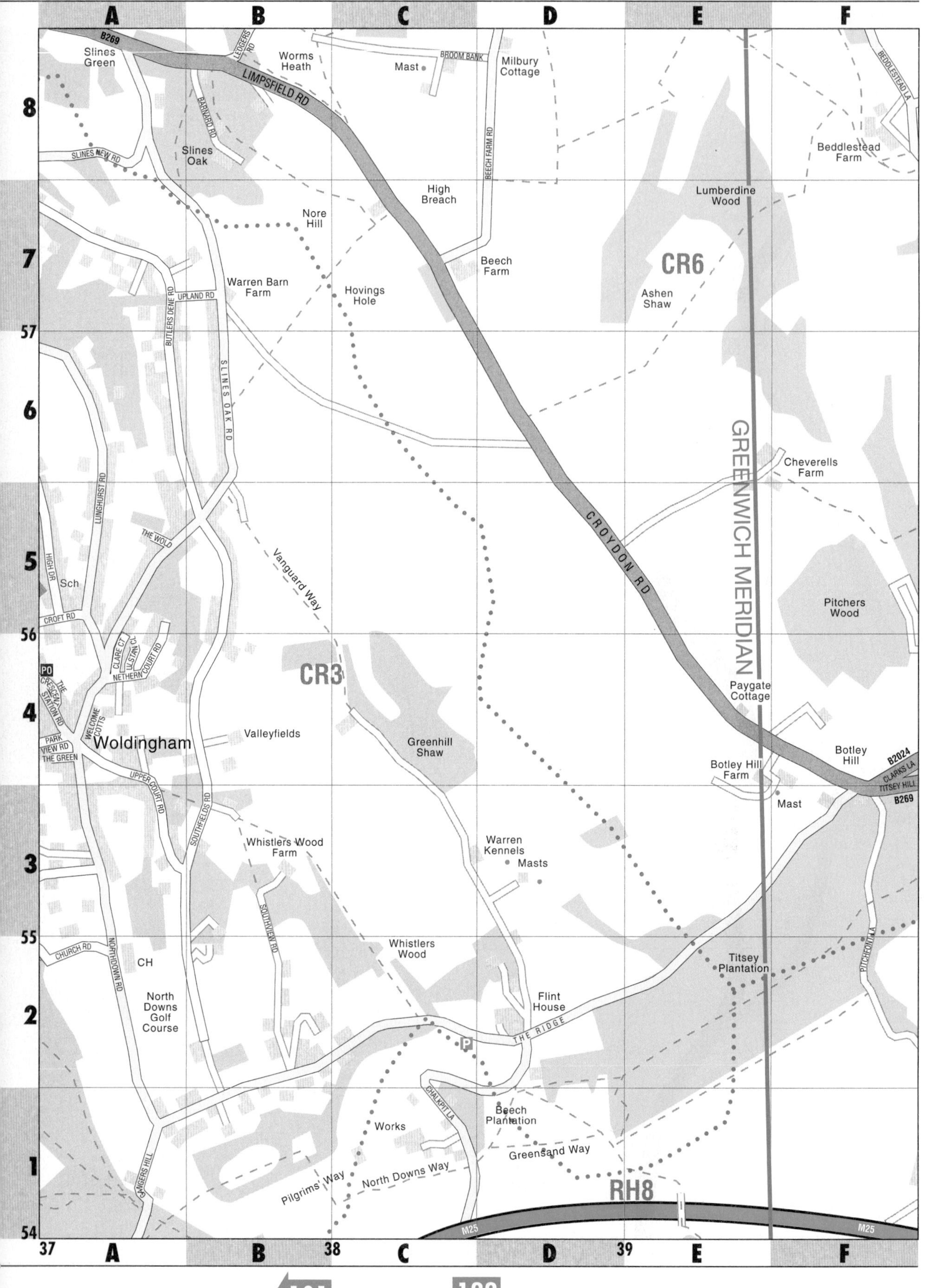

101
122

83

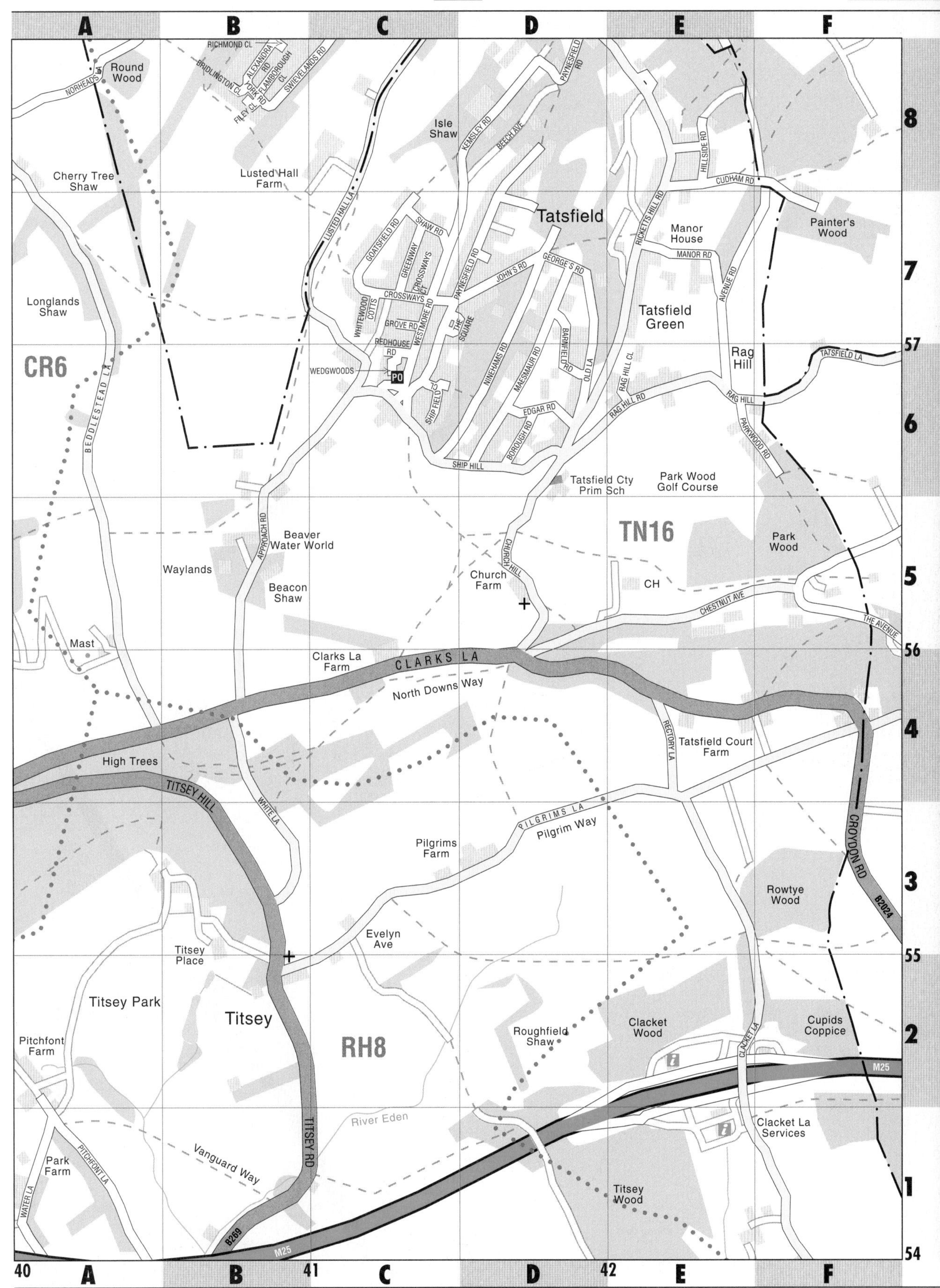
Round Wood
Cherry Tree Shaw
Lusted Hall Farm
Isle Shaw
Tatsfield
Longlands Shaw
Manor House
Painter's Wood
Tatsfield Green
Rag Hill
CR6
Tatsfield Cty Prim Sch
Park Wood Golf Course
TN16
Beaver Water World
Waylands
Beacon Shaw
Church Farm
Park Wood
CH
Mast
Clarks La Farm
CLARKS LA
North Downs Way
Tatsfield Court Farm
High Trees
TITSEY HILL
Pilgrims Farm
PILGRIMS LA
Pilgrim Way
CROYDON RD
Rowtye Wood
Evelyn Ave
Titsey Place
Titsey Park
Titsey
RH8
Roughfield Shaw
Clacket Wood
Cupids Coppice
Pitchfont Farm
River Eden
Vanguard Way
Clacket La Services
Park Farm
Titsey Wood
TITSEY RD
M25
B269
B2024

123

84

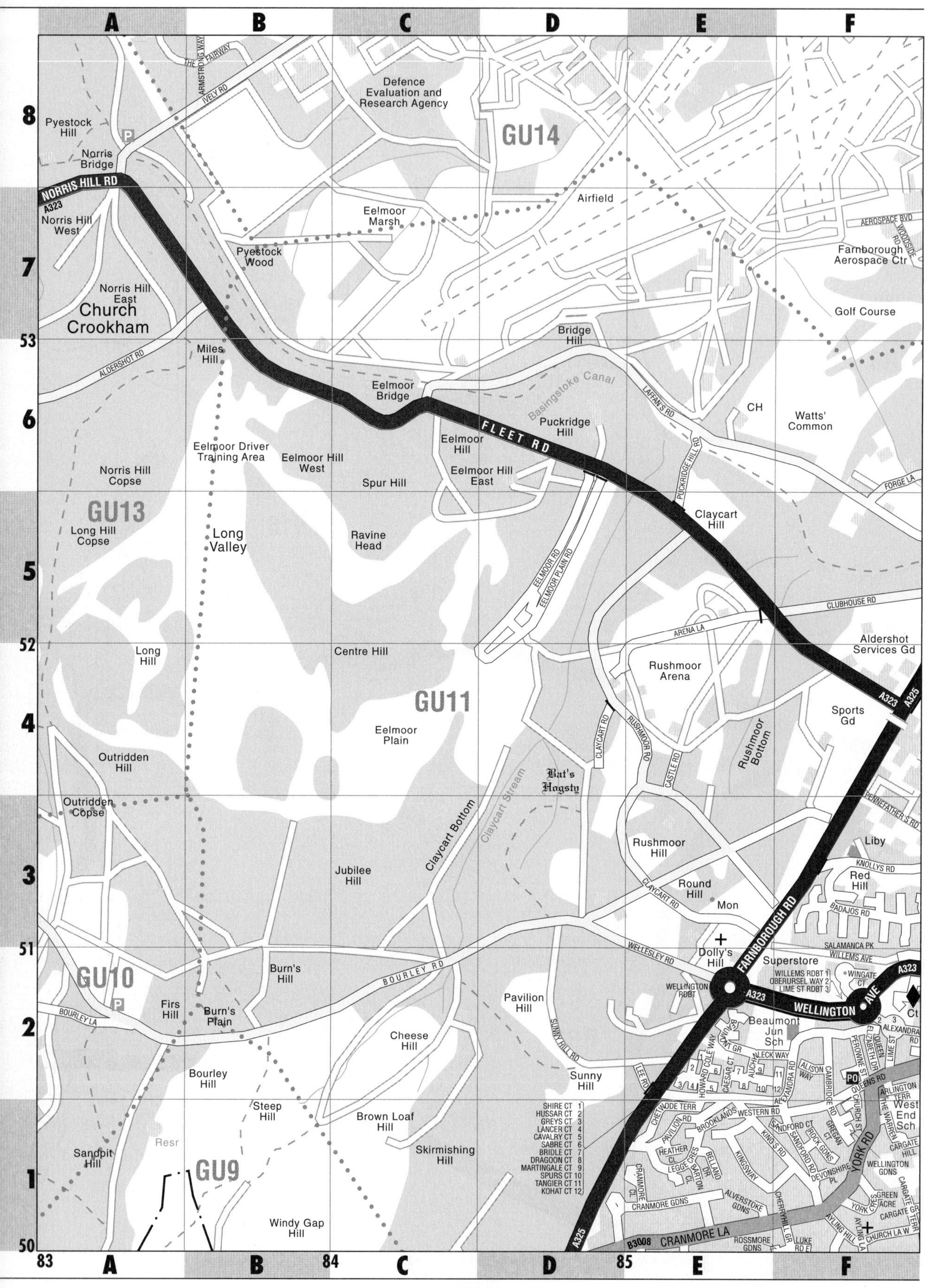
A
B
C
D
E
F
8
7
53
6
5
52
4
3
51
2
1
50
83
84
85
Pyestock Hill
Norris Bridge
NORRIS HILL RD
A323
Norris Hill West
Norris Hill East
Church Crookham
ALDERSHOT RD
ARMSTRONG WAY
THE FAIRWAY
IVELY RD
Defence Evaluation and Research Agency
GU14
Airfield
Eelmoor Marsh
Pyestock Wood
Miles Hill
Eelmoor Bridge
Bridge Hill
Basingstoke Canal
LAFFAN'S RD
AEROSPACE BVD
WOODSIDE RD
Farnborough Aerospace Ctr
Golf Course
CH
Watts' Common
FLEET RD
Puckridge Hill
Eelmoor Hill
Eelmoor Hill East
Eelmoor Driver Training Area
Eelmoor Hill West
Spur Hill
Norris Hill Copse
GU13
Long Hill Copse
Long Valley
Ravine Head
PUCKRIDGE HILL RD
Claycart Hill
FORGE LA
EELMOOR RD
EELMOOR PLAIN RD
CLUBHOUSE RD
ARENA LA
Long Hill
Centre Hill
Rushmoor Arena
Aldershot Services Gd
GU11
Eelmoor Plain
CLAYCART RD
RUSHMOOR RD
CASTLE RD
Rushmoor Bottom
Sports Gd
A325
Outridden Hill
Outridden Copse
Bat's Hogsty
Claycart Stream
Claycart Bottom
PENNEFATHER'S RD
Liby
Rushmoor Hill
KNOLLYS RD
Red Hill
Jubilee Hill
Round Hill
Mon
BADAJOS RD
FARNBOROUGH RD
SALAMANCA PK
WILLEMS AVE
WELLESLEY RD
Dolly's Hill
Superstore
GU10
Burn's Hill
BOURLEY RD
WILLEMS RDBT 1
OBERURSEL WAY 2
LIME ST RDBT 3
WINGATE CT
WELLINGTON RDBT
WELLINGTON AVE
Ct
Firs Hill
Burn's Plain
BOURLEY LA
Pavilion Hill
Beaumont Jun Sch
ALEXANDRA RD
Cheese Hill
SUNNY HILL RD
Bourley Hill
LEE RD
Sunny Hill
PO
West End Sch
SHIRE CT 1
HUSSAR CT 2
GREYS CT 3
LANCER CT 4
CAVALRY CT 5
SABRE CT 6
BRIDLE CT 7
DRAGOON CT 8
MARTINGALE CT 9
SPURS CT 10
TANGIER CT 11
KOHAT CT 12
Steep Hill
Brown Loaf Hill
Skirmishing Hill
WESTERN RD
BROOKLANDS
KINGSWAY
YORK RD
WELLINGTON GDNS
Sandpit Hill
Resr
GU9
CRANMORE CL
CRANMORE GDNS
ALVERSTOKE GDNS
CHERRYHILL GR
GREEN ACRE
CARGATE GR
CARGATE TERR
Windy Gap Hill
B3008
CRANMORE LA
ROSSMORE GDNS
LUKE RD E
AYLING HILL
CHURCH LA W

125

85
106

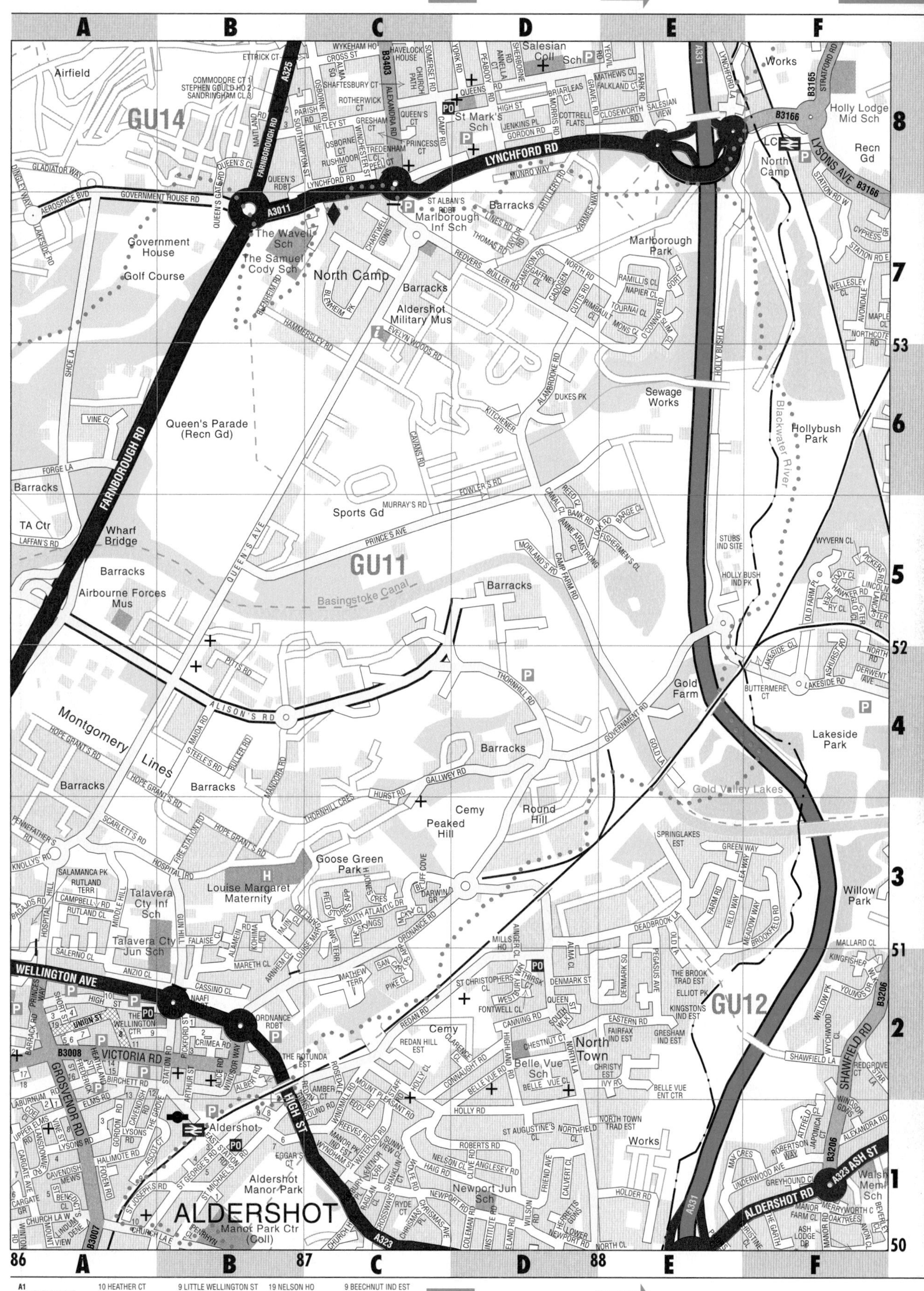

86
A
B
87
C
D
88
E
F

A1
1 LABURNUM PAS
2 LABURNUM CL
3 WOLSELEY RD
4 CULLENS MEWS
5 CHASEWATER CT
6 BURLINGTON CT
7 SALES CT
8 PARK HO
9 HEREFORD HO
10 HEATHER CT

A2
1 UPPER UNION ST
2 EDWARD ST
3 NELSON ST
4 LOWER NELSON ST
5 UPPER UNION TERR
6 CROSS ST
7 UNION TERR
8 WELLINGTON ST
9 LITTLE WELLINGTON ST
10 COURT RD
11 THE ARCADE
12 STRATFIELD HO
13 PHOENIX CT
14 FIR TREE ALLEY
15 MOUNTBATTEN CT
16 SEFTON HO
17 WILLIAM FARTHING CL
18 HIGH VIEW LODGE
19 NELSON HO

B1
1 MANOR WLK
2 BOULTERS RD
3 WELLESLEY GATE
4 ST DAVIDS CT
5 HERALD CT
6 ST GEORGE'S RD E
7 CHERRY LODGE
8 BEECHNUT RD
9 BEECHNUT IND EST

B2
1 ARTILLERY RD
2 SEBASTOPOL RD
3 WALPOLE HO

126
106

105
86

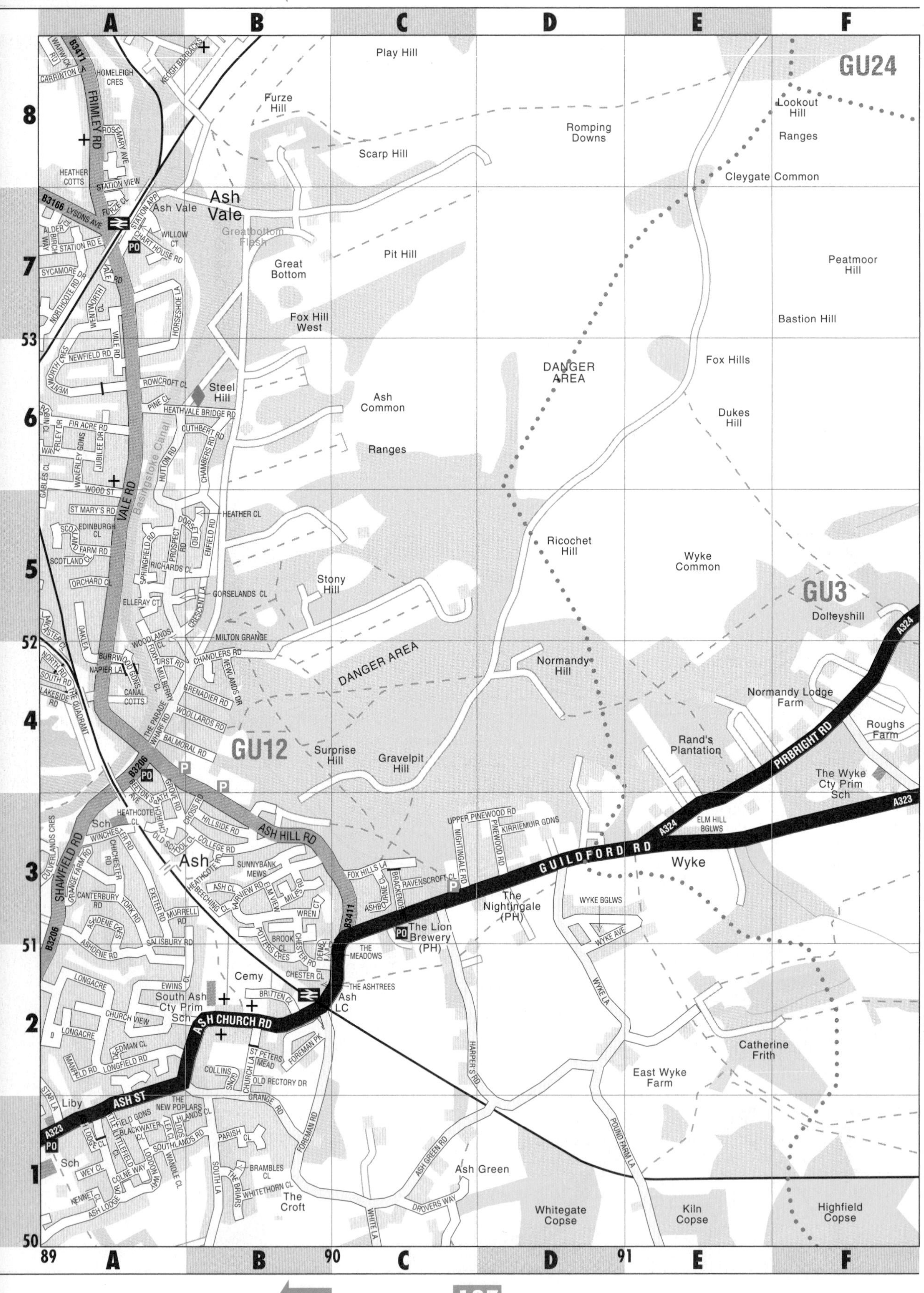

105
127

A B C D E F

Foxholes Bottom
Long Hill
Peatmoor Pond
HENLEY GATE
Stream House
Stanford Brook
ALDERSHOT RD A324
Cobbetthill Common
Mast
8
Rifle Range
GU24
Henleypark Pond
Longhill Bottom
Standinghill Wood
Mast
7
Leapingbar Copse
Slyfield Wood
Park Farm
53
Whitepatch Hill
Works
The Glen
PIRBRIGHT RD
Clasford Bridge
DANGER AREA
Vine Farm
Henleypark Farm
Henley Park
Island Copse
Clasford Common
6
Whitepatch Bottom
A323
Kiln Copse
Grassypiece Copse
ALDERSHOT RD
Whipley Manor
Withybed Copse
5
Nursery
Longerend Farm
52
Hunts Hill Farm
HUNTS HILL RD
Nursery
Anchor Copse
Caravan Park
FROG GROVE LA
Normandy Common
Duke of Normandy (PH)
SANDY LA
4
Sandpit Farm
Picnic Site
GUILDFORD RD
WELLS LA
Fair View Farm
Willey Green
MARINERS DR
PO
North Wyke Farm
Manor Fruit Farm
BAILES LA
Bales Farm
Normandy
GU3
WALDEN COTTS
3
Walden's Copse
Ashfield Lodge Farm
Russellplace Farm
Nursery
51
BAILES LA
GLAZIERS LA
Claygate Farm
Strawberry Farm
Westwood Place
WESTWOOD LA
Passenger's Farm
2
Pussey's Copse
Claygate Copse
Backside Common
Chy
Wanborough
Bushy Hill
SZABO CRES
THE PADDOCKS
1
BEECH LA
ORCHARD WAY
ORCHARD CL
CHRISTMASPIE AVE
CULL'S RD
The Folly
LAURELDENE
WILLOW DR
Flexford
WEST FLEXFORD LA
FLEXFORD RD
Wanborough Youth House
PO
50

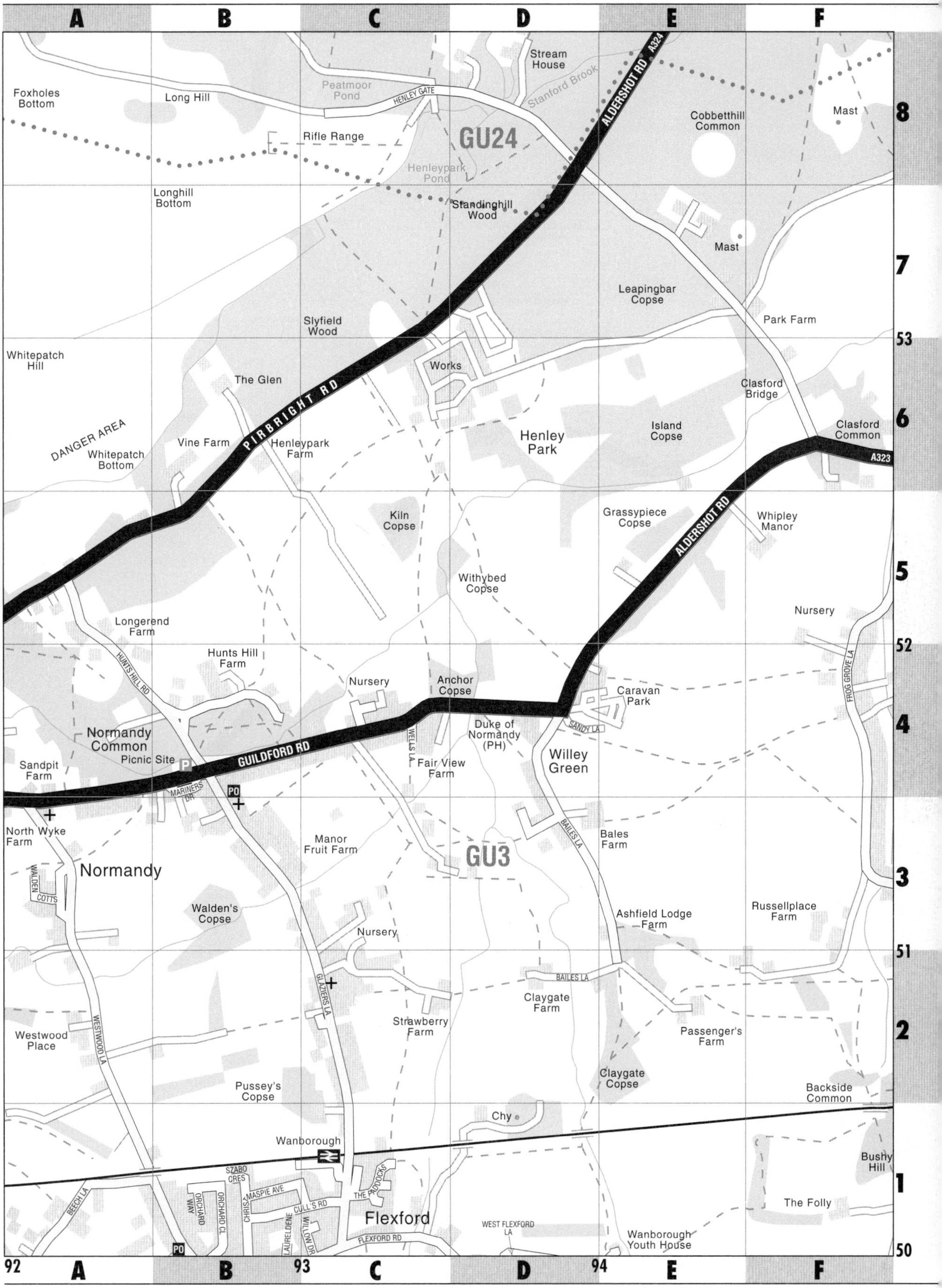

92 A B 93 C D 94 E F

107
88

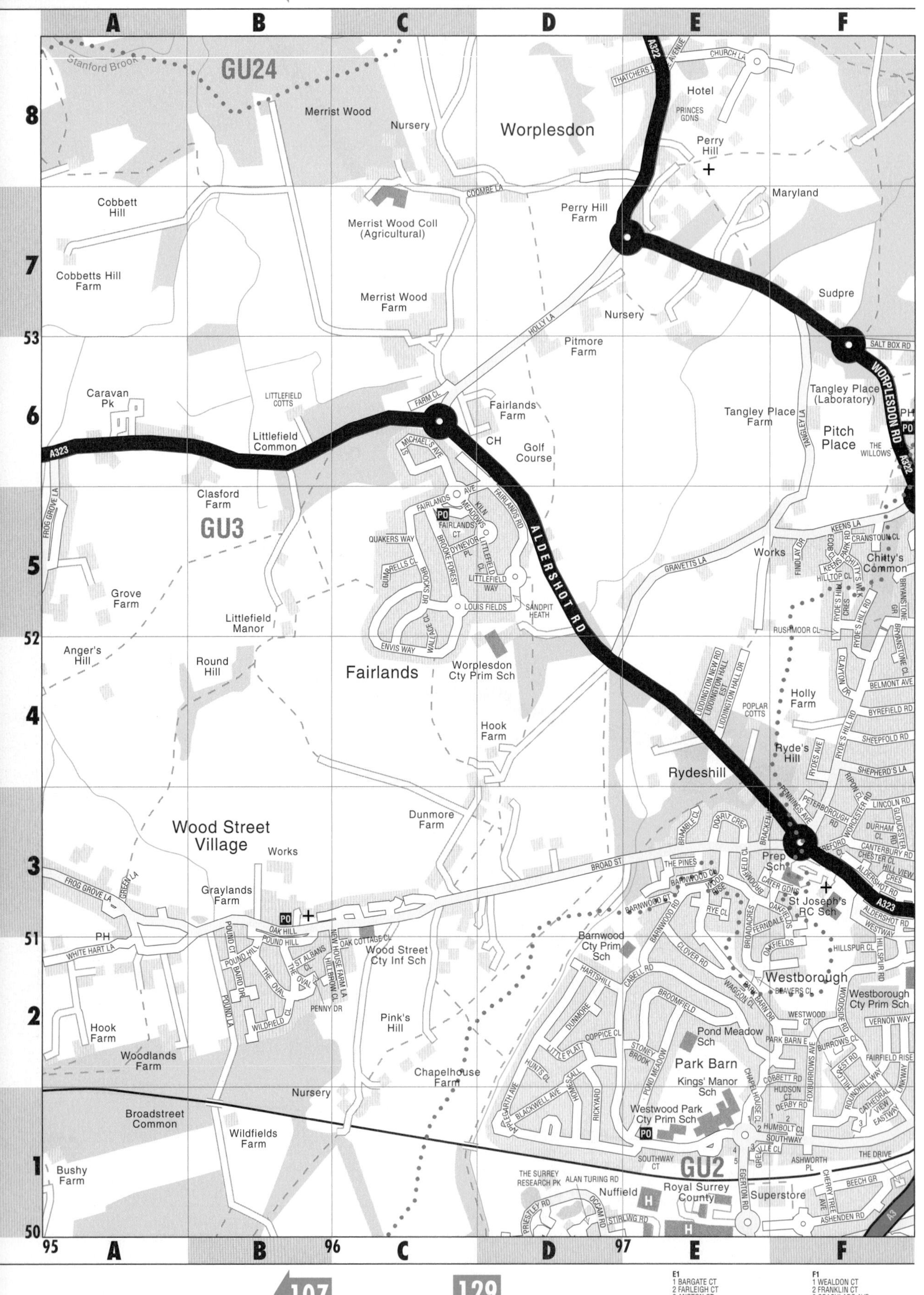

107
129

E1
1 BARGATE CT
2 FARLEIGH CT
3 ANSTON CT
4 PURBECK CT
5 EGERTON CT

F1
1 WEALDON CT
2 FRANKLIN CT
3 COACHLADS AVE

A B C D E F

8
Whitmoor Common
Burdenshott Rd
The Old Cottage
A320 Guildford Rd
Cox's Farm
Sutton Park House
Ladygrove Farm
Bull La
Blanchards Hill

7
GU3
Mount Pleasant
Nursery
Jacobswell
Britten's Pond
GU4
Burpham Court Farm Park
Burpham Court Farm
Sutherland Ave
Tynley Gr
Holly Lea
Clay La
Stringer's Ave
Oak Tree Cl
Grangefields Rd
Treebys Ave
Fernhythe Rd
Douglas Cl
Barnett Row
Brookside
Jacobs Well Rd
White House La

53
Salt Box Rd
Range
Stringer's Common
GUILDFORD
1 Weydown La
2 Cinnamon Gdns
3 Hamilton Pl
4 Hamilton Cl
Brittens Cl
Lyons Dr
Cumberland Ave
Hamilton Dr
Montgomerie Dr
Escombe Dr
Mansel Cl
Regan Cl
Burden Way
Oregano Way
Coriander Cres
5 Oakwood
6 Tamarind Cl
7 Caraway Pl

6
Juniper Cl
Yew Tree Dr
Lilac Cl
Opus Park
Ennis Way
North Moors
Westfield Rd
Slyfield Ind Est
Foundation Units
Rivett-Drake Rd
Henderson Ave
Knox Rd
Anderson Ave
Grange Rd
Whatley Rd
Tyrwhitt Ave
Carlton Cl
Tylehost
Gwynne Vaughan Ave
Johnston Gr
Johnston Wlk
Saffron Platt
Tarragon Dr
Angelica Rd
Robin Way
Spring Ct
Dayspring
Deeprose Cl
Willow Way
Downsview Ct
Bellfield Ct
Palm Gr
Clockhouse Ct
Hazel Ct
Oak Tree Dr
Woking Rd
The Moorfield Ctr
Moorfield Rd
Slyfield
Woodlands Rd
Enterprise Est

5
1 Tarragon Ct
2 Reeve Ct
3 Cardamom Cl
4 Regalfield Cl
5 Marjoram Cl
6 Rosemary Cres
Little St
Grange Cl
Waltham Ave
Lime Gr
Hazel Ave
Mayree Cl
Almond Cl
Whitemore Rd
Slyfield Gn
Slyfield Ct
Old Farm Rd
The Stables
Lock Rd
Marigold Ct
A3

52
Worplesdon Rd
Bryanstone Ave
White Ct
Thorn
Mandeville Cl
Whitfield Cl
Harts Gdns
1 John Russell Cl
2 Whitfield Cl
Kirkfield
Thorpes Cl
Somertons Cl
Belmont Ave
Byrefield Rd
Sheepfold Rd
Fairbourne Way
Giffard Way
Sch
Blackberry Cl
Rowan Cl
1 Russell Ct
2 Ramin Ct
Stoke Hill Cty Prim Sch
Kaye Ct
Fir Tree Rd
Farm Cl
Waterside Rd
Works
Hanson Cl
Turner Cl
Banks Way
Gatley Dr

4
Stoughton
Stoughton Inf Sch
3 King George's Lodge
4 Nugent Ct
North Rd
Badger Cl
Heron Cl
Bishop Reindorp CE Sch
Bellfields
Larch Ave
Laburnum Cl
Cypress Rd
Cedar Way
Woking Rd
Christie Cl
Weyfield Prim Sch
1 Parsons Green Ct
2 Parsons Gn
Abbotswood Cl
Abbotswood
Shepherd's La
Galvins Cl
Queen's Dr
Barrack Rd
Franks Rd
Martin Rd
New Cross Rd
Regent Ct
Berberis Cl 1
Catalpa Cl 2
Forsythia Pl 3
Cemy
Birch Gr
Medlar Cl
Hornbeam Rd
School Cl
Bellfields Rd
Mangles Rd
Stoke Lock
Swan La
Westward Ho
Northway
Scott Cl
Fentum Rd
Emmanuel Cl
Belvedere Cl
Manor Gdns
Manor Lodge
Stoughton Rd
Baden Rd
South Rd
Percy Rd

3
GU2
Recn Gd
Woodbridge Hill
Woodbridge Hill Gdns
Wendy Cres
Tenniel Cl
Ardmore Way
Francis Ct
Manor Rd
Ardmore Ave
Ardmore House
Manor Cres
Weyside Rd
Weyside Gdns
Weyview Cl
Riverwood Ct
Waterside Mews
Riverside
Maple Gr
GU1
River Wey Navigation (National Trust)
River Wey
Abbotswood

Aldershot Rd
PO
The Crescent
Firsway
Grantley Gdns
Bridgehill Cl
Wood Ct
Woodbridge Hill
Heather Cl
Parkhurst Rd
Caxton Gdns
Weston Rd
Deerbarn Rd
A323
A322
L Ctr

51
Grantley Rd
Beckingham Rd
Southway
Ladymead Retail Ctr
Europa Park Rd
Ladymead
Parkway
A25
Burchatt's Farm Cottages
Braganza Ct 1
St Mildred's Rd 2

2
Midleton Rd
A25
Midleton Industrial Estate Rd
Woodbridge Rd
A322
Springside Ct
Stocton Cl
Angle Ct
Joseph's Rd
Hamilton Gordon Ct
Lido Rd
Stocton Rd
Guildford Coll of F Ed & H Ed
Stoke Park
Newlands Flats 3
Eversleigh Flats 4
London Rd
A3100
Lindfield Gdns
Avonmore Ave
Buckingham Cl
Cathedral Hill Ind Est
Guildford Ind Est
Ash Gr
Deacon Field
Guildford Business Park
Park Rd
Woodbridge Meadows
Woodbridge Park Est
Pound Field

D1
1 Regal Ct
2 Kings's Rd
3 Nettles Terr
4 Drummond Ct
5 Stoke Park Ct
6 Stoke Hosp (Almhouses)
7 Artillery Rd
8 Stoke Fields
9 Finch Rd

Univ of Surrey
Recreation Rd
Linden Rd
Chestnut Ave
Sycamore Rd
Acacia Rd
Stoke Rd
Margaret Rd
Tormead Rd

1
Walnut Tree Pk
Walnut Tree Cl
Gardner Rd
Markenfield Rd
St Saviour's Pl 1
Dapdune Ct 2
Wharf Rd
Dapdune Rd
Drummond Rd
Park Rd
Queen's Rd
Onslow Rd
Coll
Nightingale Rd
Berkley Ct
Avington Cl
Park Chase
Home Farm
Sch
London Road
Ennismore Ave
Glebe Ct
Mathon Ct
Cross Lanes
Hilgay Cl
Watford Cl
Cranley Rd
Aldersey Rd
Tormead Sch
Riverside Bsns Ctr
William Rd
George Rd
Artillery Ter
Stoke Gr
Eagle Rd
Falcon Rd
Springfield Rd
Foxenden Rd
Victoria Rd
Sutton Lodge
Hilgay Ct
Maori Rd
Sch
Stag Hill
Guildford Cath
The Chase
A320
A322
220

50
98 A B 99 C D 00 E F

109
90

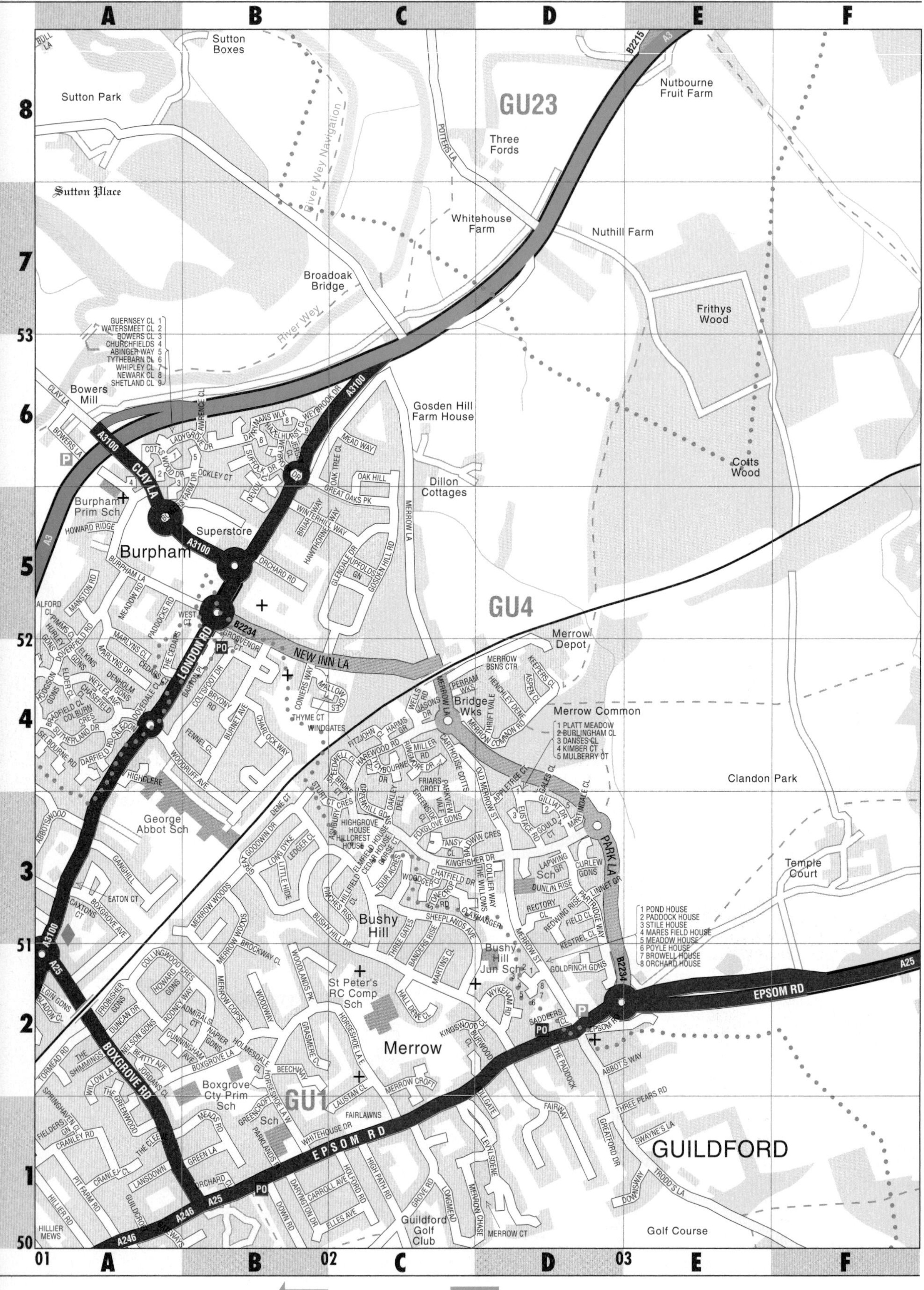

109
131

91
112

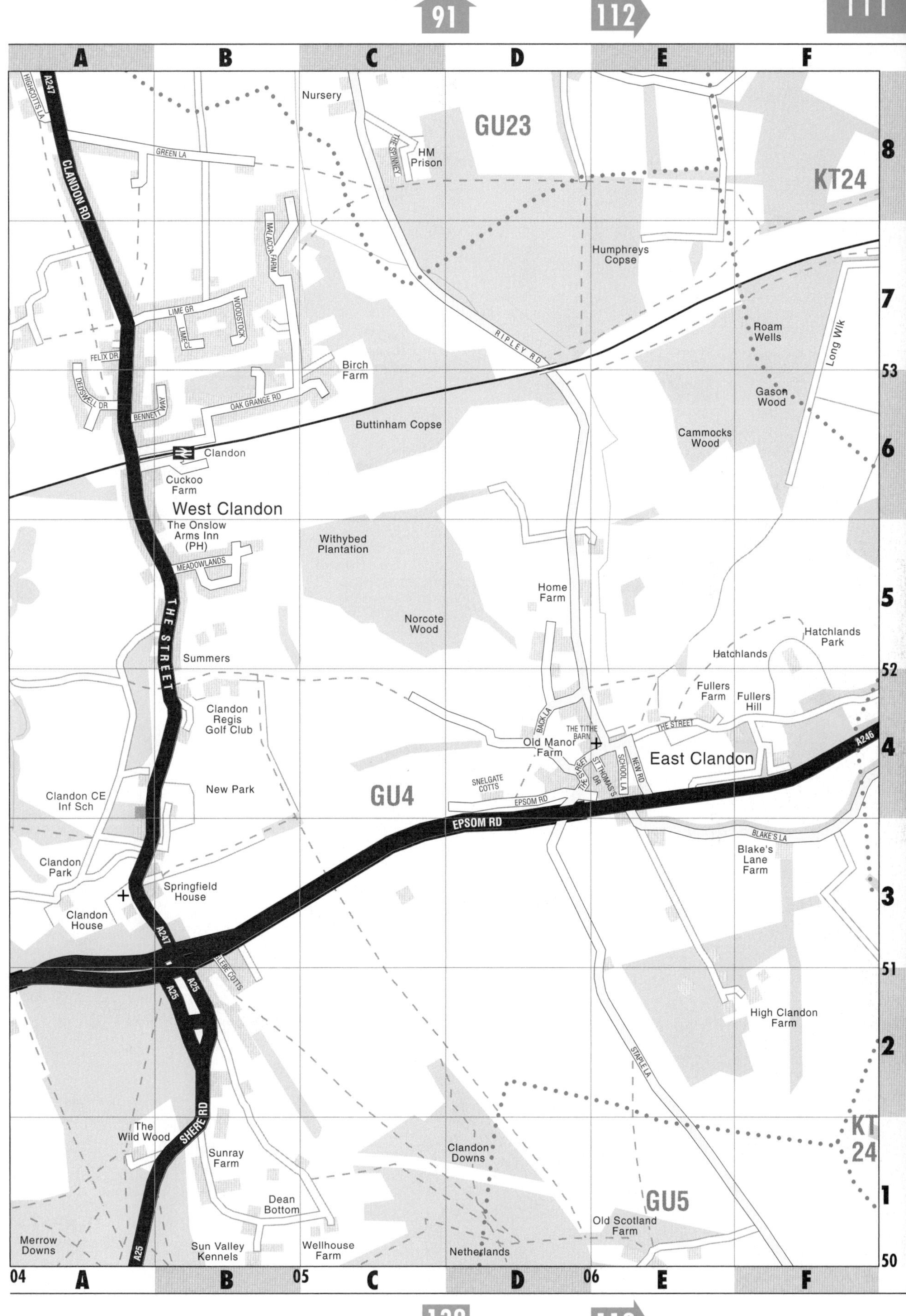

132
112

111
92

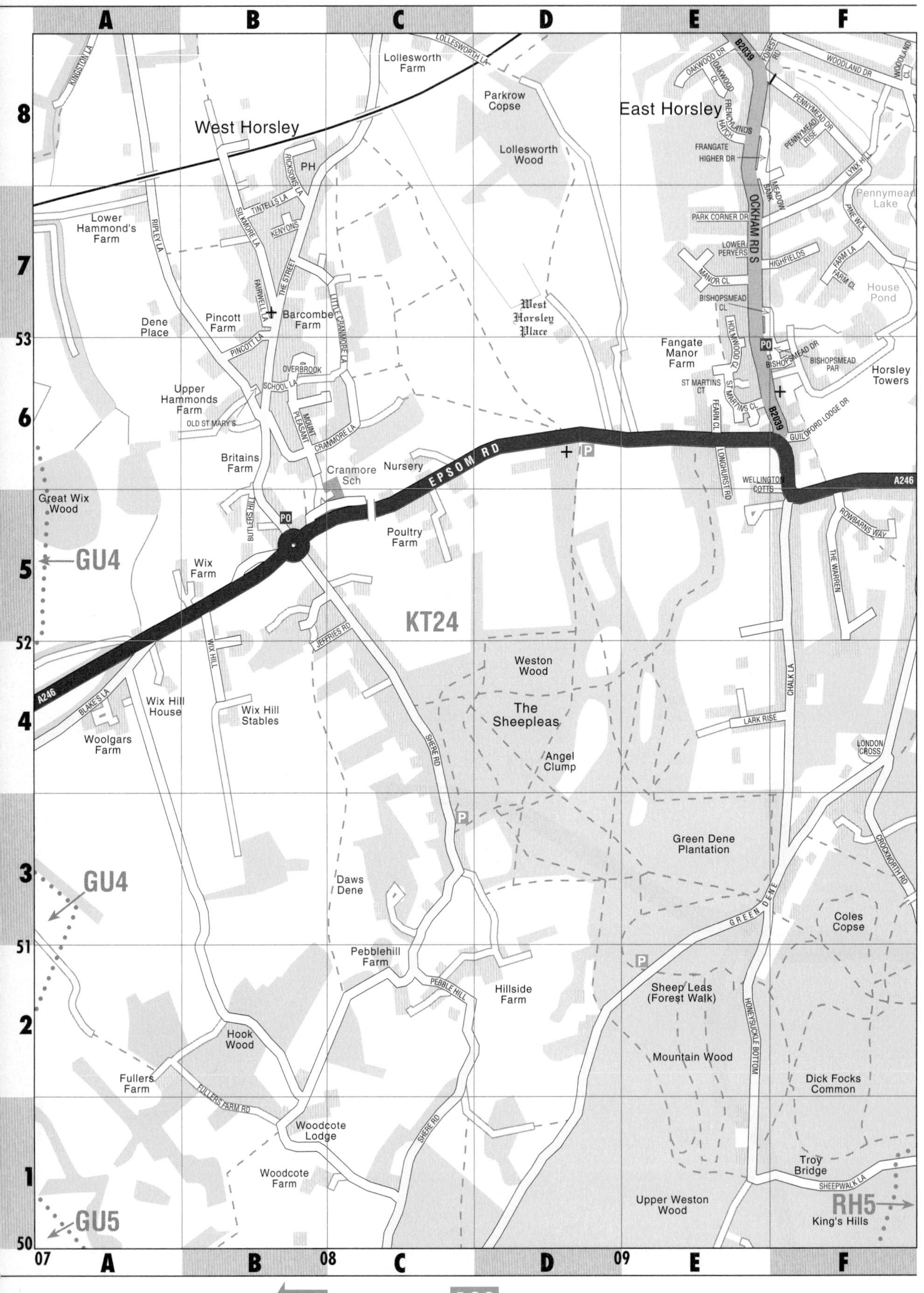

111
133

93
114

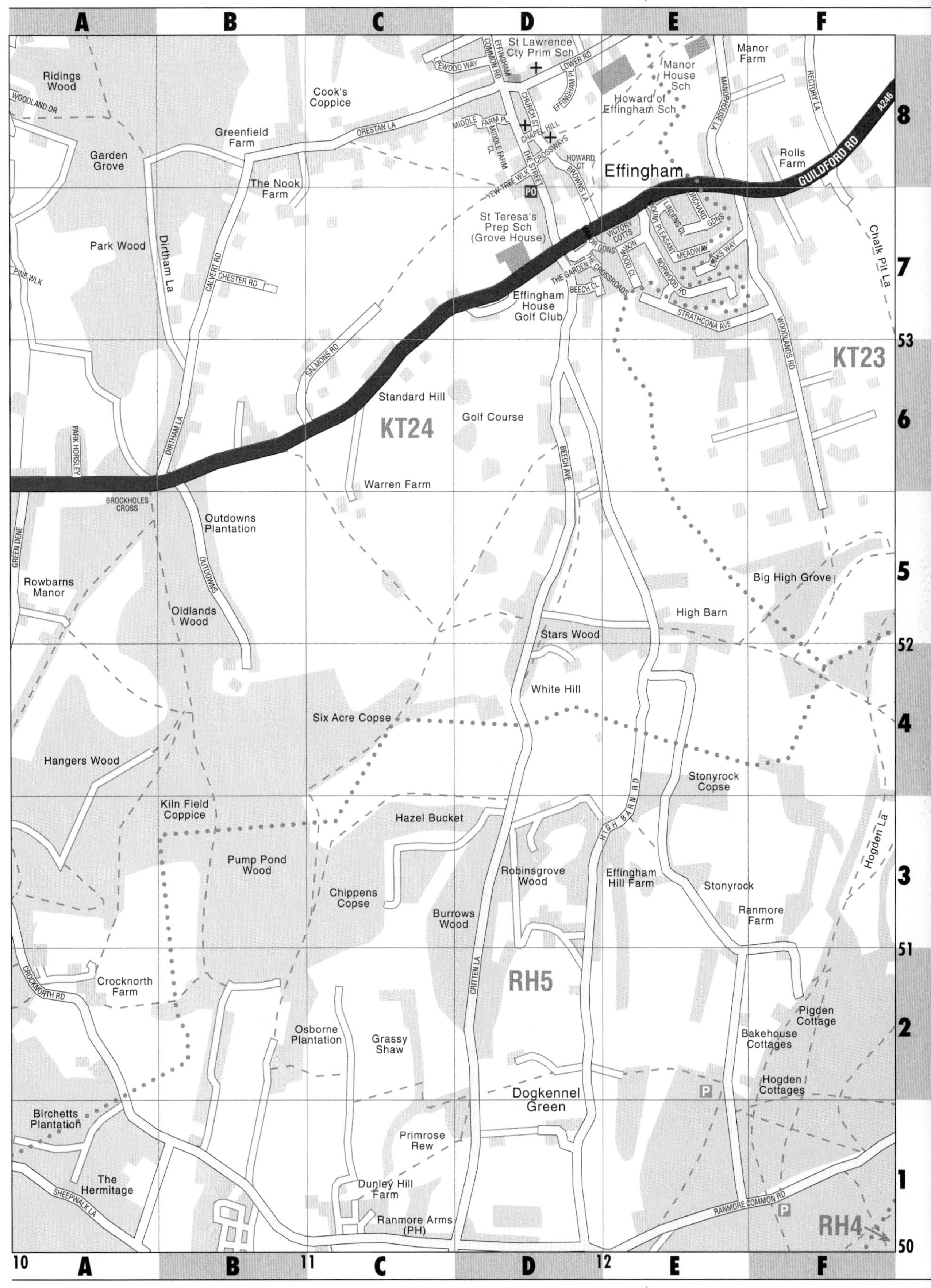

134
114

113
94

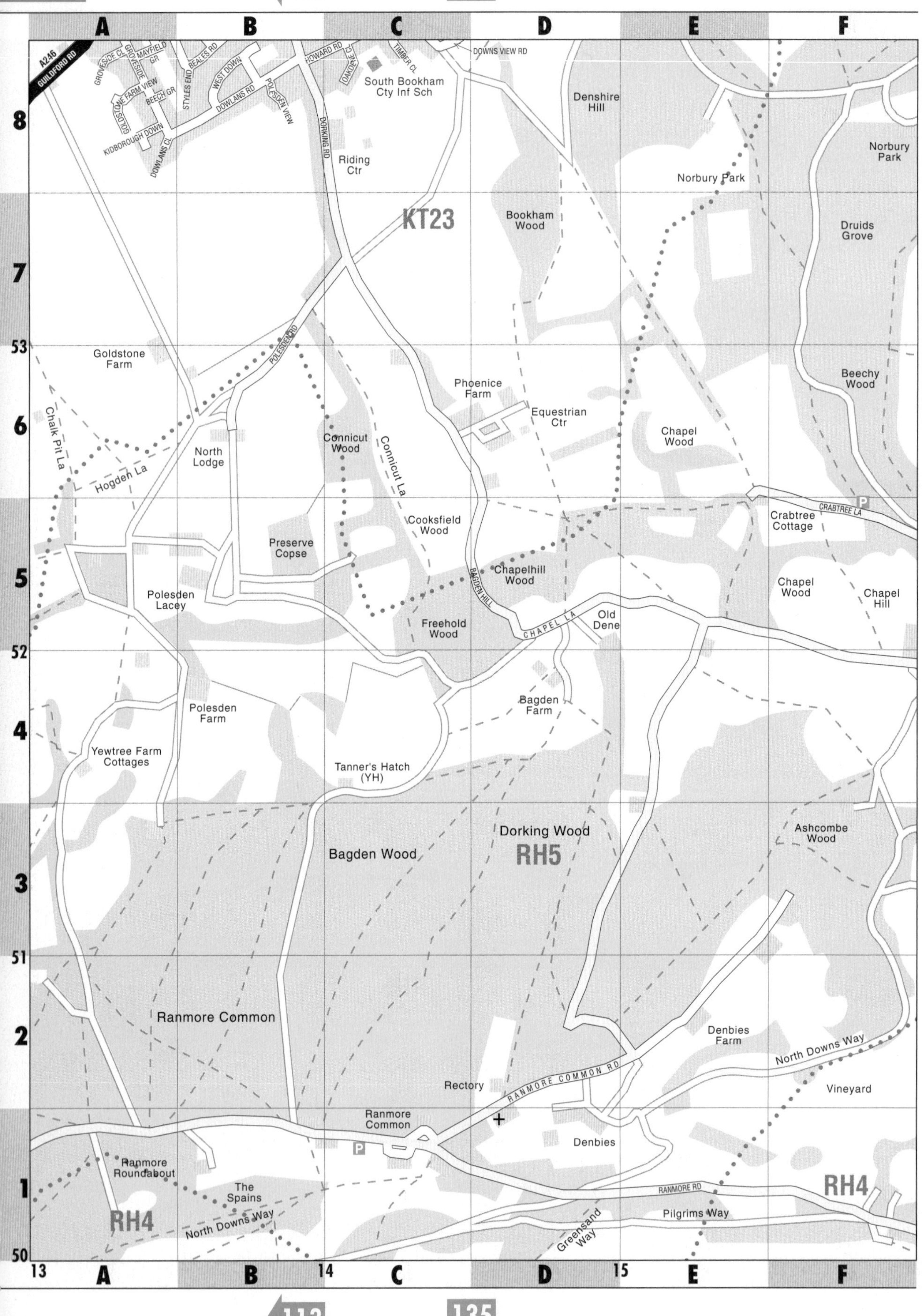

113
135

95
116

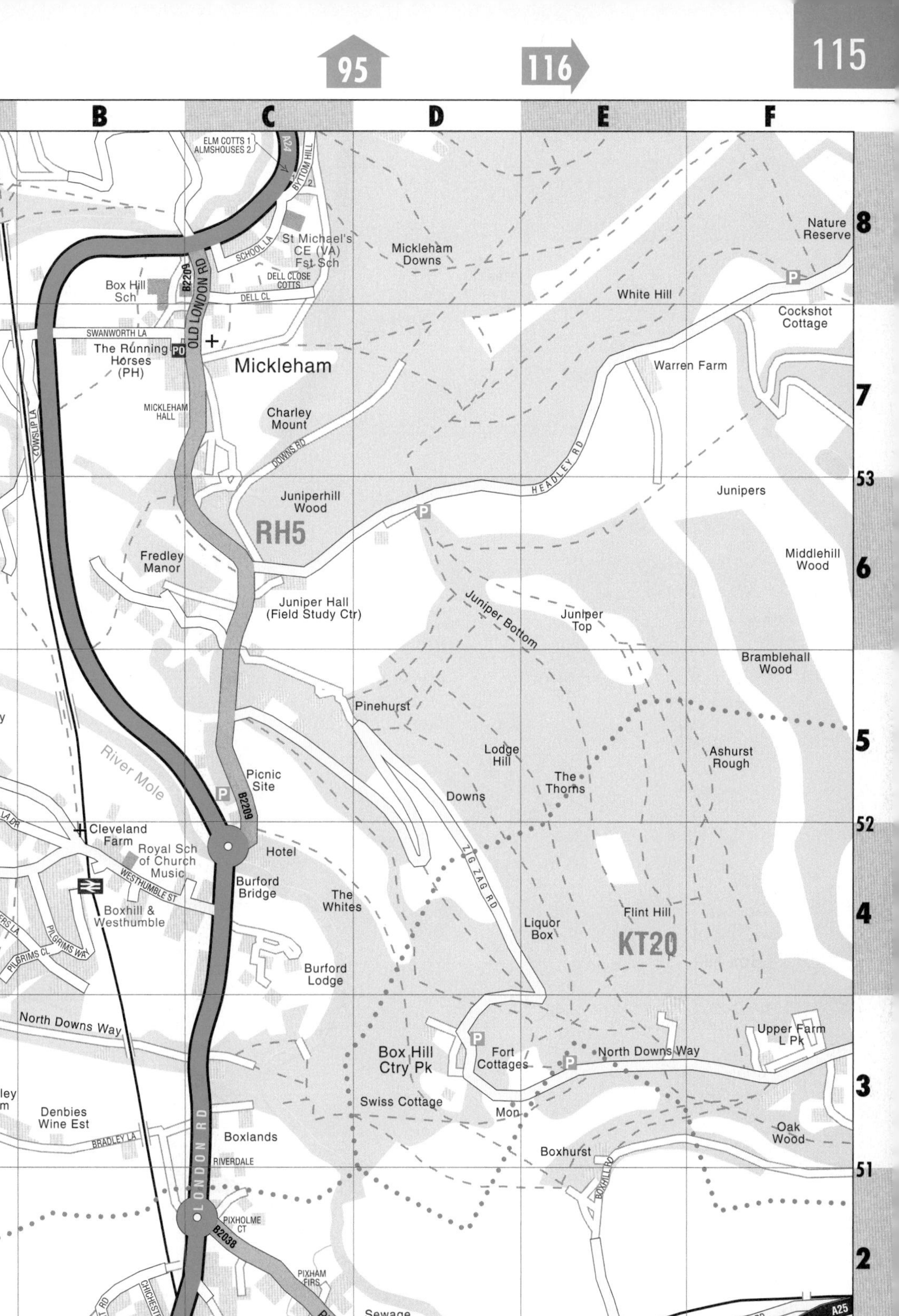

136
116

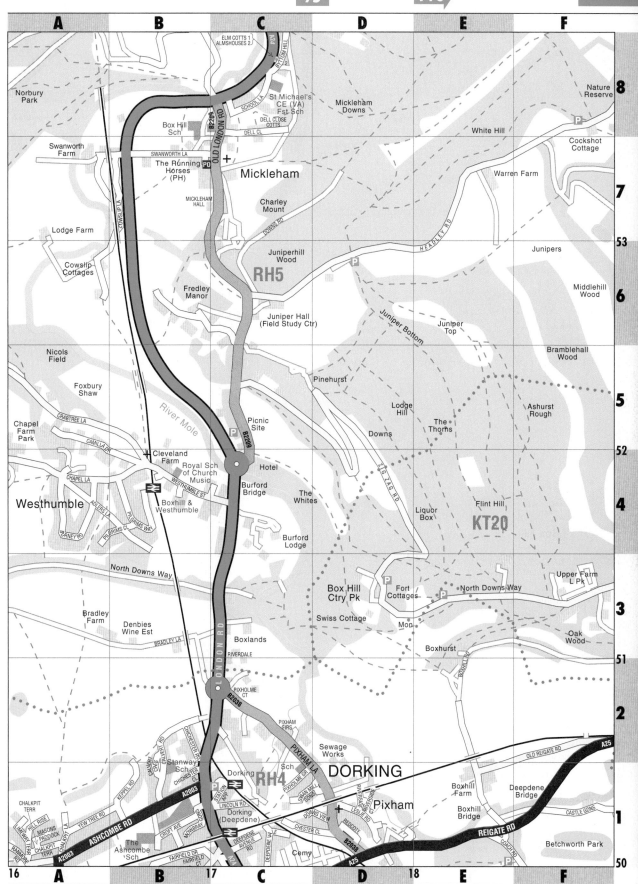

115
96

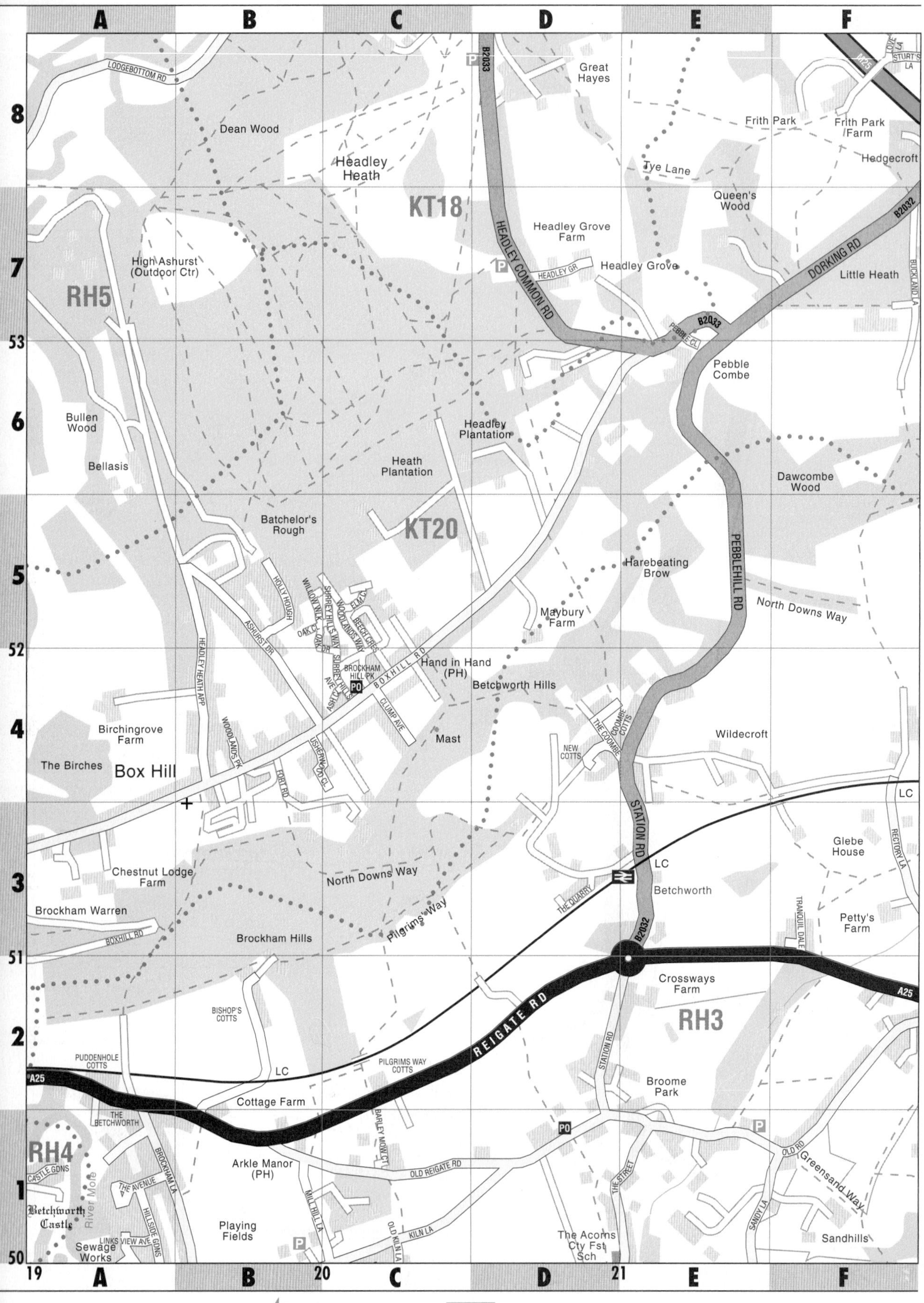

115
137

97
118

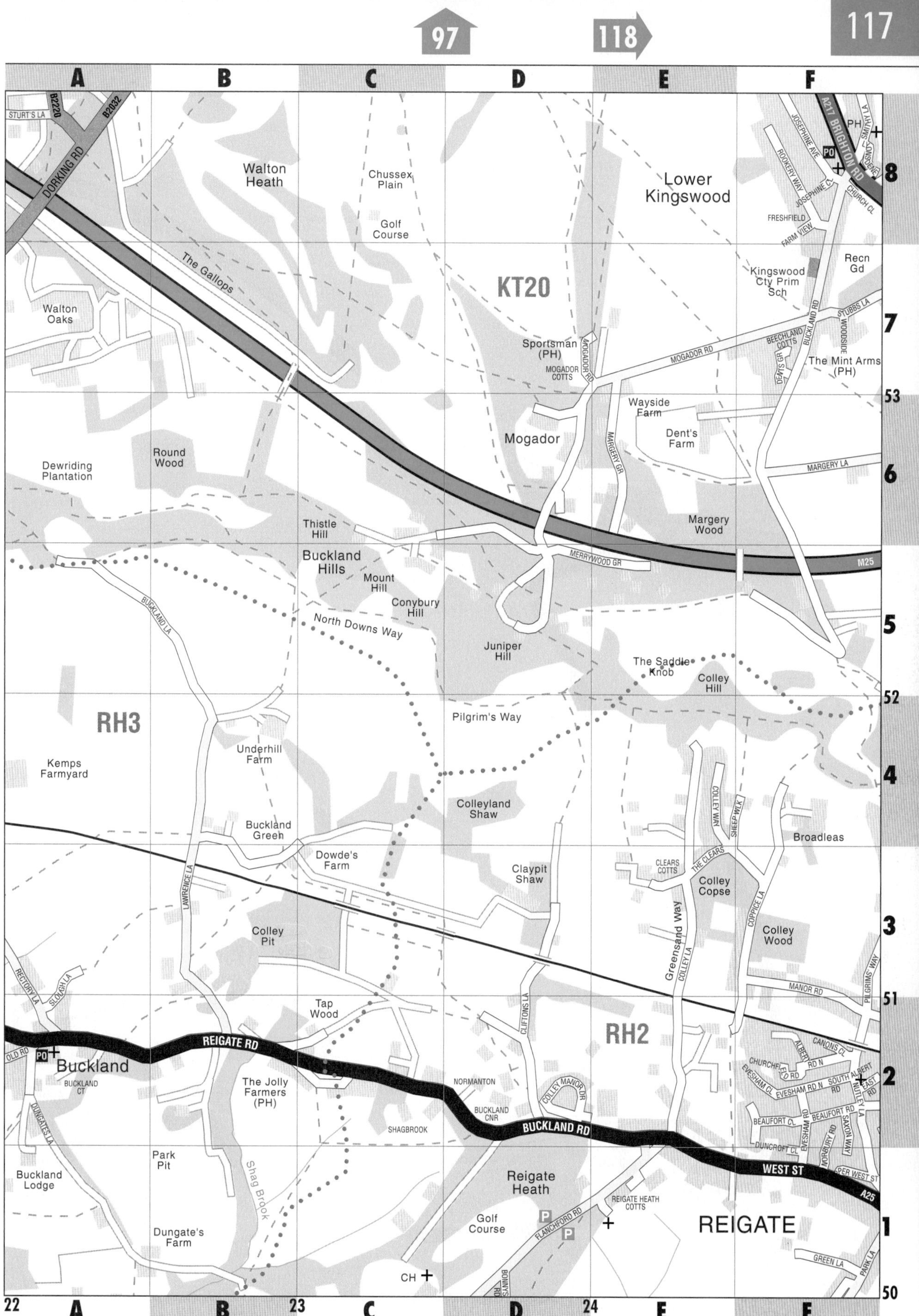

138
118

117
98

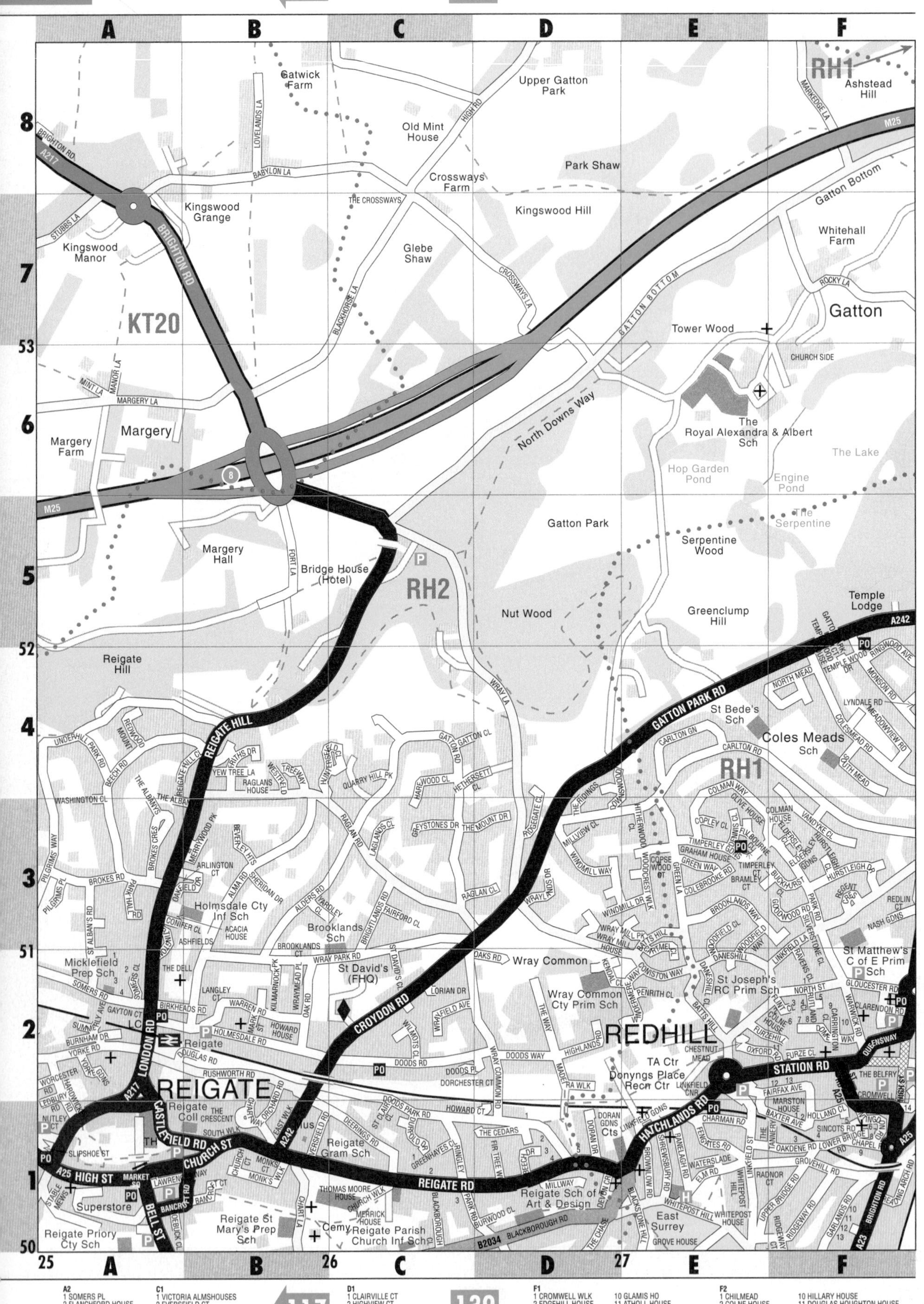

A2
1 SOMERS PL
2 FLANCHFORD HOUSE
3 CLAYHALL HOUSE
4 LITTLETON HOUSE

C1
1 VICTORIA ALMSHOUSES
2 EVERSFIELD CT
3 HILLBROW

117

D1
1 CLAIRVILLE CT
2 HIGHVIEW CT
3 TREEVIEW CT
4 HARLOW CT
5 WRAYMILL CT

139

F1
1 CROMWELL WLK
2 EDGEHILL HOUSE
3 MORRISS CT
4 OBSERVATORY WLK
5 WAVENEY HOUSE
6 GROVE HOUSE
7 ELY HOUSE
8 MAPLE HO
9 CHRISTCHURCH HTS
10 GLAMIS HO
11 ATHOLL HOUSE
12 DUNVEGAN HOUSE
13 STIRLING HOUSE
14 MARKETFIELD RD

F2
1 CHILMEAD
2 COLNE HOUSE
3 TAVY HOUSE
4 ROTHER HOUSE
5 WANDLE HOUSE
6 KENNET HOUSE
7 ORWELL HOUSE
8 WINDRUSH HOUSE
9 AVON HOUSE
10 HILLARY HOUSE
11 DOUGLAS HOUGHTON HOUSE
12 SQUIRRELS GN
13 CHILWORTH CT

99
120

A B C D E F

Ockley Hill
Bedlams Bank
North Downs Way
ROCKSHAW RD
Heronswood Mere
M23
M25
A23
LONDON RD N
GATTON BOTTOM
CHURCH HILL
Merstham
North Downs Way
Golf Course
RH2
CH
Home Farm
GRANGE CT
GRANGE CL
GRANGE DR
HIGH ST
STATION RD
SCHOOL HILL
HANOVER CL
1 BROADMEAD
2 STATION RD
BROOK RD
Recn Gd
WOOD ST
LAXTON GDNS
RADSTOCK WAY
HUDDLESTON CRES
CHESTERTON DR
Furzefield Cty Prim Sch
DELABOLE RD
DUNDREY CRES
CHILMARK GDNS
BOLSOVER GR
MANSFIELD DR
MALMSTONE AVE
PORTLAND DR
GREENSAND CL
The Bushetts
ROCKY LA
BUSHETTS GR
BRAMBLEWOOD
SOUTH CLOSE GN
LONDON RD S
ROOKWOOD CL
Sch
DOWNSIDE CT
STACEY CT
ALBURY PL
BLETCHINGLEY CL
Liby
SERPENTINE GN
WORSTED GN
BLETCHINGLEY RD
SUTTON GDNS
TAYNTON DR
WELDON WAY
St Nicholas Specl Sch
SUNSTONE GR
Woodfield Sch
MANOR RD
ALBERT RD
ENDSLEIGH RD
ALBURY RD
SOUTHCOTE RD
East Lodge Farm
WELLS PL
THE CROSSWAYS
DEANS RD
DEVON RD
South Merstham
BATTLEBRIDGE LA
ORPIN RD
MELTON RD
NUTFIELD RD
BOURNE RD
Sewage Works
Temple Wood
A242
GATTON PARK RD
FAIRHAVEN RD
1 VALORNUS
2 BATTLEBRIDGE HOUSE
Sand Pit
WYECLIFFE GDNS
ASH CL
CHILBERTON DR
RH1
GATTON POINT
East Surrey Coll
ELMWOOD RD
RINGWOOD AVE
HOLCON CT
CLAREMONT RD
LYNDALE RD
RANMORE CL
WESTWAY GDNS
ORMSIDE WAY
MILL LA
LC
TOWERS WAY
Country Park
Mercers Farm
HOLMETHORPE IND EST
MONSON RD
ALPINE RD
COLLEGE CRES
FRENCHES RD
METHORPE AVE
MALLARD CL
SPARROWS MEAD
OSBORNE RD
GORDON RD
ROBIN GDNS
KINGFISHER DR
Holmethorpe
Hall Lands Cottage
Nutfield Marsh
NUTFIELD MARSH RD
LONDON RD
BUDGEN DR
LAKESIDE
CYGNETS CL
THE FRENCHES
ABBOTTS RISE
WIGGIE LA
The Moors
CHILMEAD LA
PEYTON'S COTTS
Chilmead Farm
LYNWOOD RD
PARKLANDS
LADBROKE RD
KEATS AVE
WORDSWORTH MEAD
CORMONGERS LA
NUTFIELD CT
The Warwick Sch
ST ANNES DR
ST ANNES RISE
LADBROKE GR
PRINCESS WAY
CHURCH HILL
Nutfield
Redhill
GREENSAND RD
NOKE DR
CLYDE CL
CAVENDISH GDNS
CAXTON RISE
CAVENDISH RD
A25
PARKWOOD RD
PARK WORKS RD
SHORTACRE
Doods Brow Sch
BLACKLANDS MEADOW
HIGH ST
REDSTONE HILL
CROSSLAND RD
HILLFIELD CL
HILLFIELD RD
FENTON CL
FENTON RD
OAKWOOD CL
REDSTONE PK
Works
Cemy
Patteson Court
NUTFIELD RD
Fox Hole
Holmesdale Park
Furze Hill
Nutfield Priory (Hotel)
Priory Farm
SANDY LA
MID ST
FULLERS WOOD LA
Stockers Hill
REDSTONE MANOR
RURAL WAY
CHART CHASE
Allot Gdns

8
53
7
6
5
52
4
3
51
2
1
50

28 A B 29 C D 30 E F

A2
1 PRINCESS HOUSE
2 LADBROKE COTTS
3 QUEENS CT
4 DIAMOND CT
5 ST ANNES WAY
6 CLEEVES CT
7 ST ANNES MOUNT
8 NIGHTINGALE CT
9 GABLE CT
10 HATHAWAY CT
11 BOLEYN CT
12 TUDOR CT
13 LENNOX CT
14 BRONTE CT
15 OAKLEY CT
16 STUART CT
17 CLYDE CT
18 LANCELOT HO
19 GIUNEVERE HO
20 GALAHAD HO
21 KNIGHTS PL
22 WARWICK QUADRANT

A3
1 ALTON HOUSE
2 SWALE HOUSE
3 BOVEY HOUSE
4 FRENCHES CT
5 PENRYN HOUSE
6 NASH DR
7 LADBROKE CT
8 PEBWORTH CT
9 BARFIELD CT

A4
1 RINGWOOD LODGE
2 DOWNS CT
3 LYNDALE CT
4 VICTORIA ALMSHOUSES
5 SPEEDWELL HOUSE
6 CAMPION HOUSE

140
120

119
100

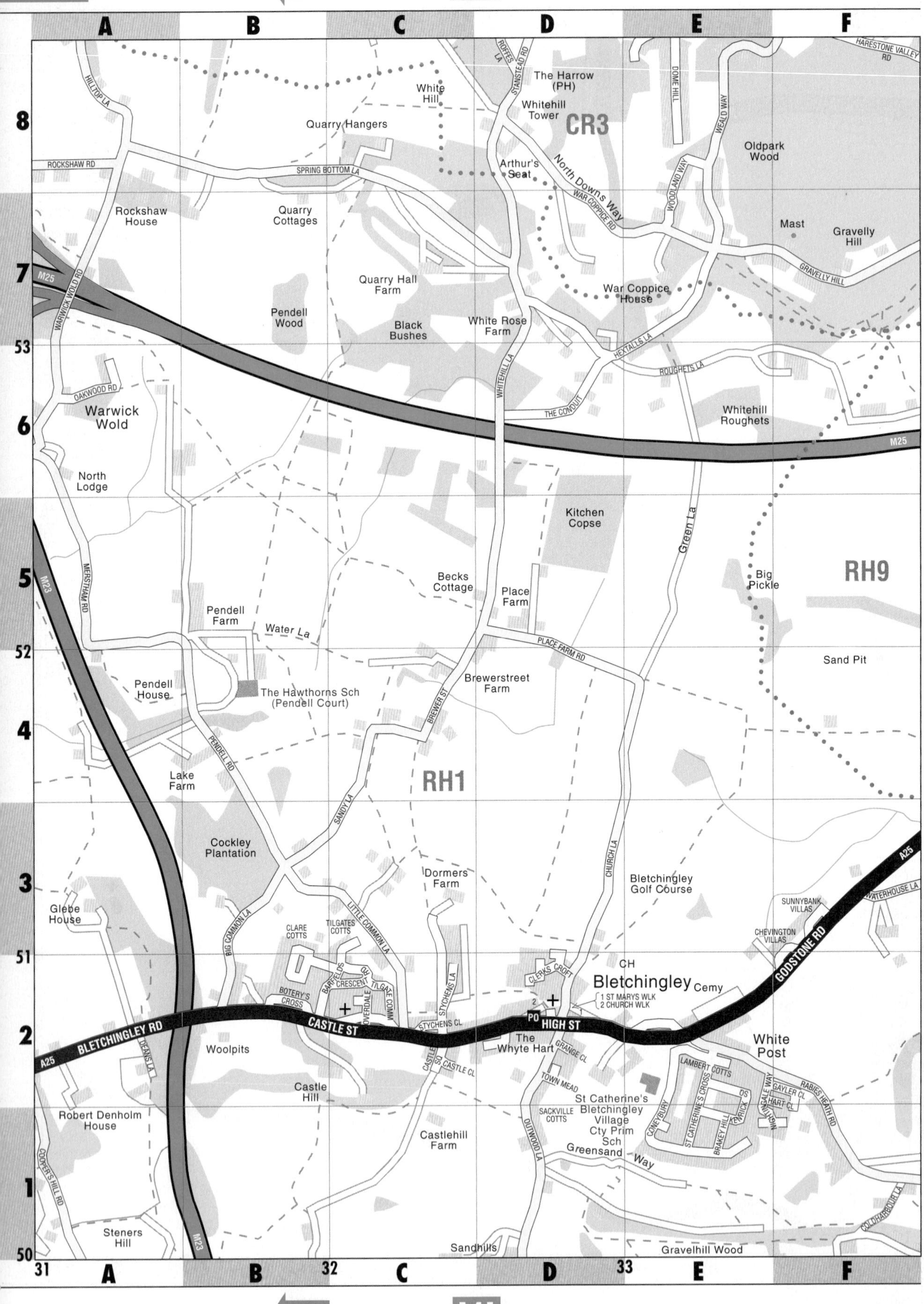

119
141

101
122

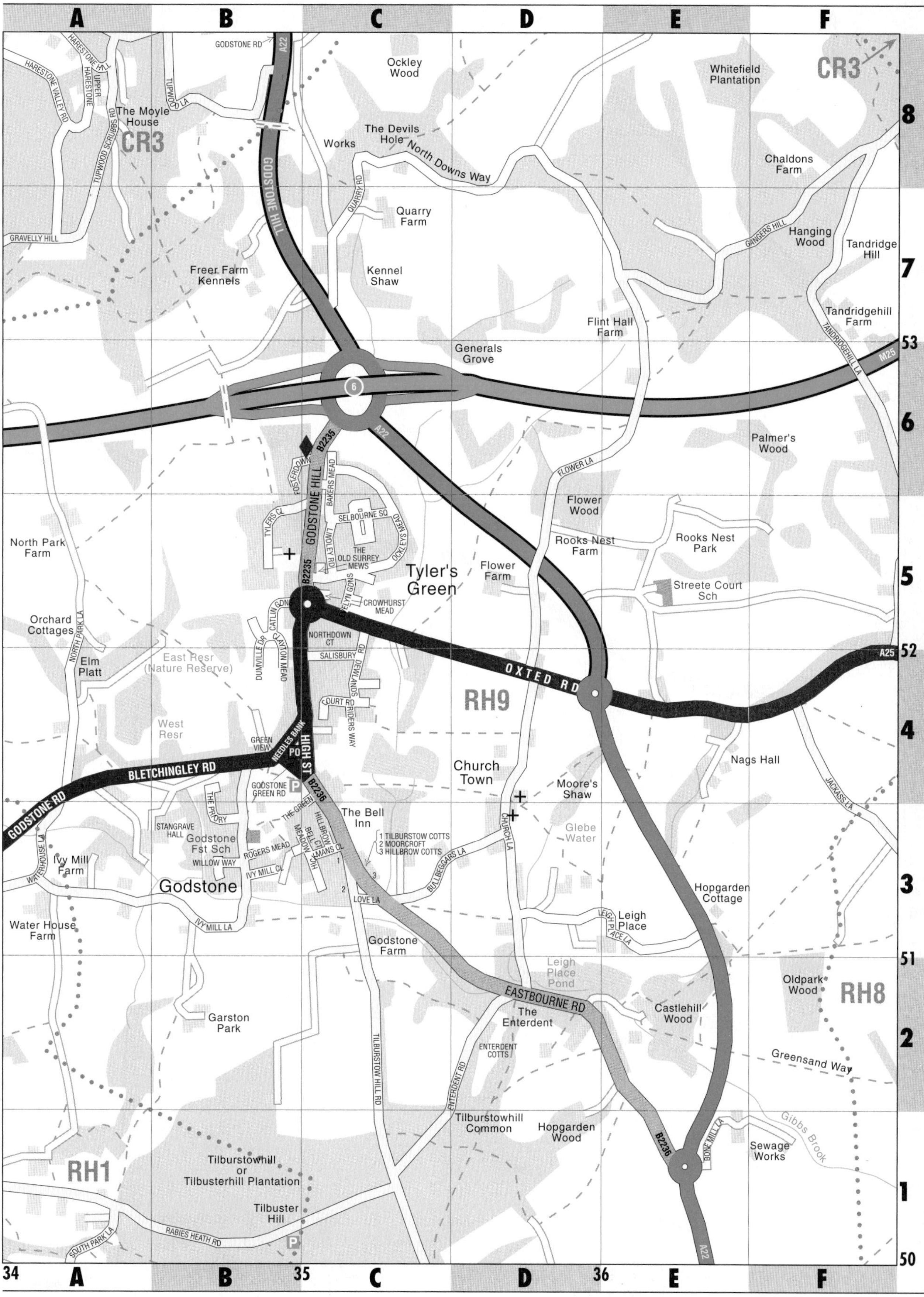

A B C D E F

Ockley Wood
Whitefield Plantation
CR3
The Moyle House
CR3
Works
The Devils Hole
North Downs Way
Chaldons Farm
Quarry Farm
Hanging Wood
Tandridge Hill
Freer Farm Kennels
Kennel Shaw
Tandridgehill Farm
Flint Hall Farm
Generals Grove
Palmer's Wood
Flower Wood
North Park Farm
Rooks Nest Farm
Rooks Nest Park
Tyler's Green
Flower Farm
Streete Court Sch
Orchard Cottages
Elm Platt
East Resr (Nature Reserve)
RH9
West Resr
Nags Hall
Church Town
Moore's Shaw
The Bell Inn
Glebe Water
Ivy Mill Farm
Godstone Fst Sch
Godstone
Hopgarden Cottage
Water House Farm
Leigh Place
Godstone Farm
Leigh Place Pond
Oldpark Wood
RH8
Garston Park
The Enterdent
Castlehill Wood
Greensand Way
Tilburstowhill Common
Hopgarden Wood
Sewage Works
Gibbs Brook
Tilburstowhill or Tilbusterhill Plantation
RH1
Tilbuster Hill

GODSTONE RD
HARESTONE HILL
HARESTONE VALLEY RD
UPPER HARESTONE
TUPWOOD LA
TUPWOOD SCRUBBS RD
GRAVELLY HILL
GODSTONE HILL
QUARRY RD
GANGERS HILL
TANDRIDGEHILL LA
M25
A22
B2235
FOSTERDOWN
BAKERS MEAD
SELBOURNE SQ
TYLERS CL
LINDLEY RD
OCKLEYS MEAD
THE OLD SURREY MEWS
FLOWER LA
EVELYN GDNS
CROWHURST MEAD
CATLIN GDNS
NORTHDOWN CT
SALISBURY RD
DUMVILLE DR
CLAYTON MEAD
DEWLANDS
OXTED RD
A25
COURT RD
RIDERS WAY
NORTH PARK LA
GREEN VIEW
NEEDLES BANK
HIGH ST
PO
BLETCHINGLEY RD
GODSTONE GREEN RD
B2236
THE PRIORY
THE GREEN
STANGRAVE HALL
HILLBROW
BELL CT
MEADOW
HICKMANS CL
1 TILBURSTOW COTTS
2 MOORCROFT
3 HILLBROW COTTS
CHURCH LA
JACKASS LA
ROGERS MEAD
WILLOW WAY
IVY MILL CL
BULLBEGGARS LA
WATERHOUSE LA
GODSTONE RD
LOVE LA
LEIGH PLACE LA
IVY MILL LA
EASTBOURNE RD
ENTERDENT COTTS
ENTERDENT RD
TILBURSTOW HILL RD
BONE MILL LA
RABIES HEATH RD
SOUTH PARK LA

8 7 53 6 5 52 4 3 51 2 1 50
34 35 36

142
122

121
102

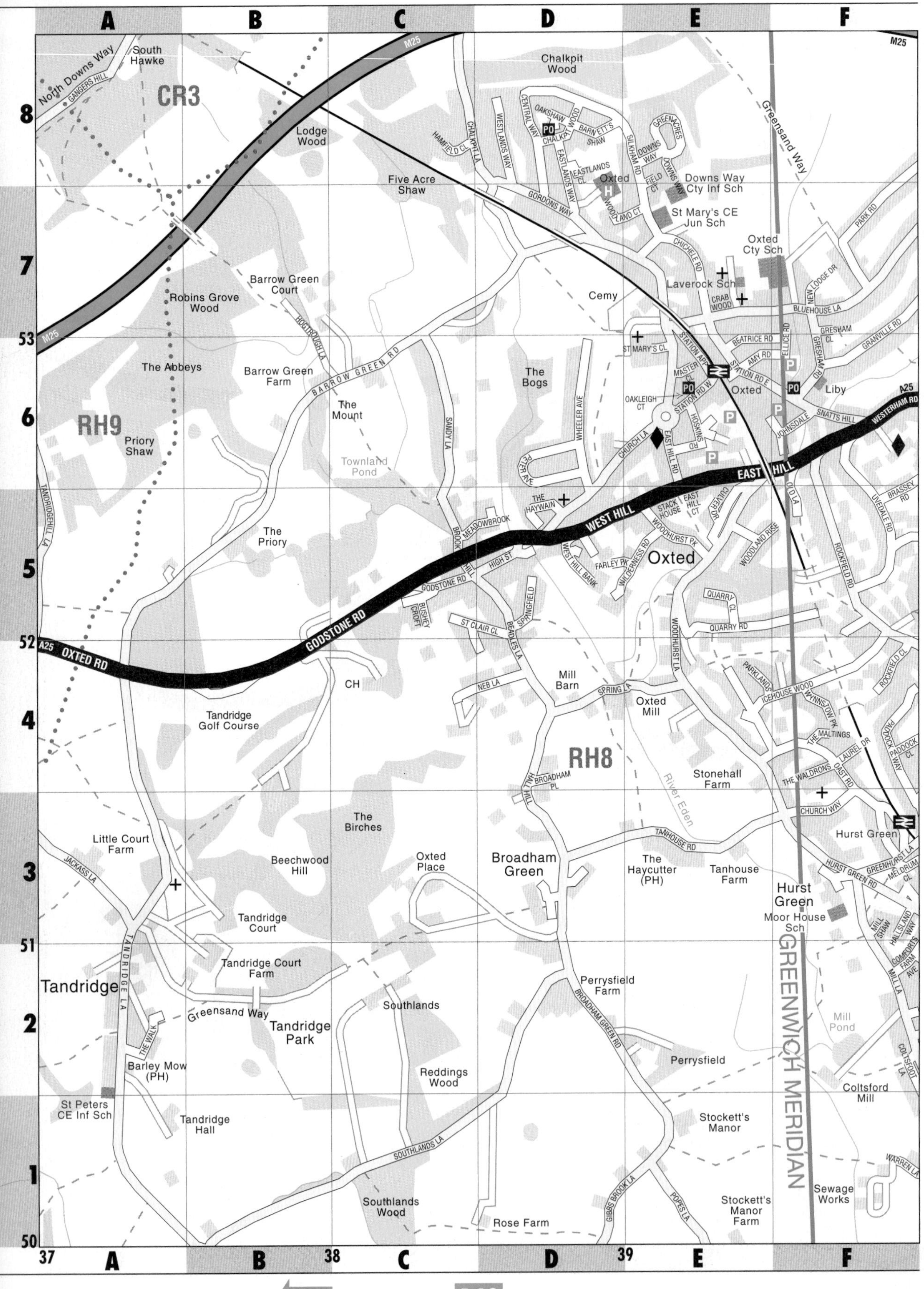

121
143

103

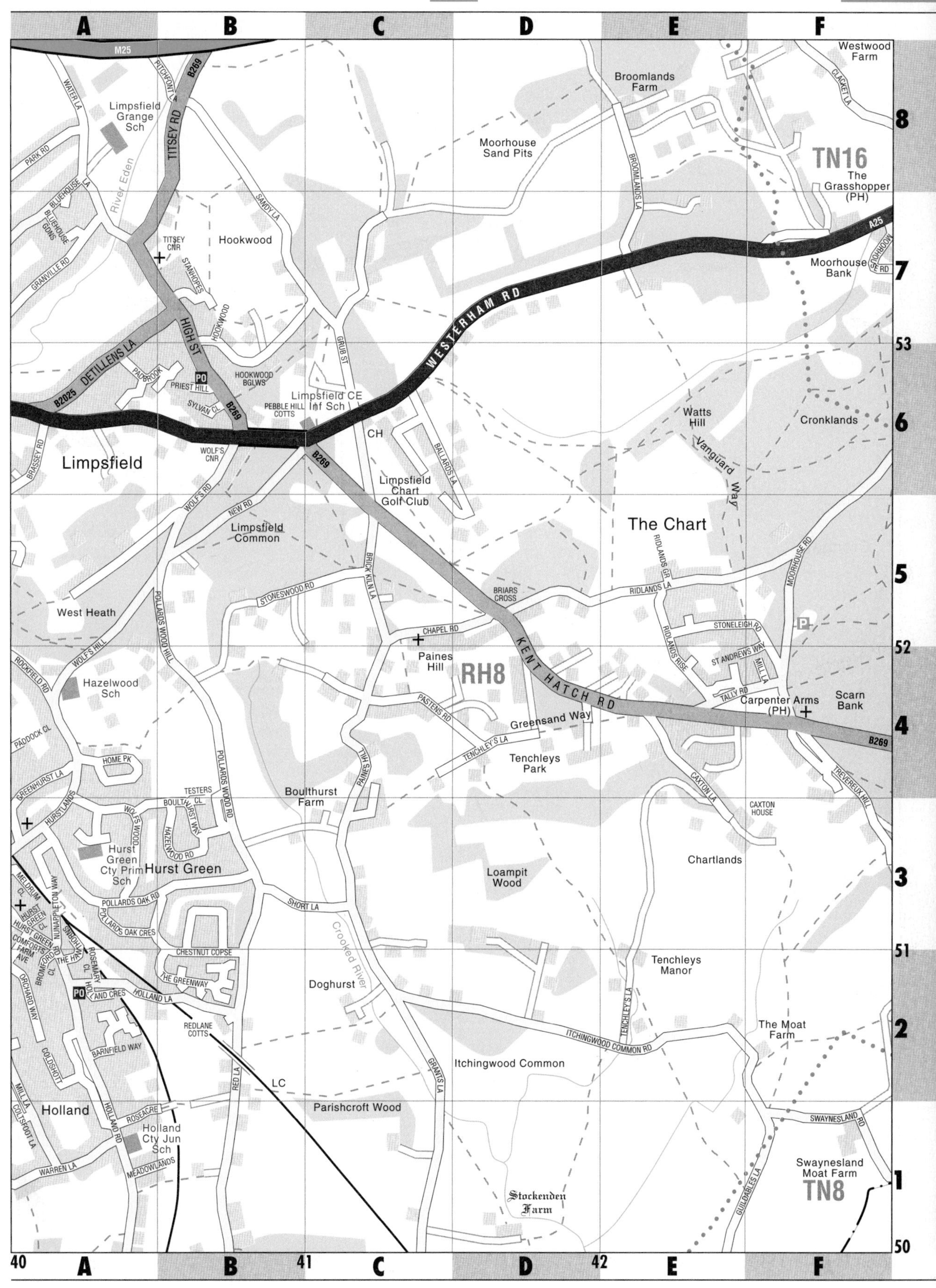

Westwood Farm
Broomlands Farm
Limpsfield Grange Sch
Moorhouse Sand Pits
TN16
The Grasshopper (PH)
Hookwood
Moorhouse Bank
WESTERHAM RD
Limpsfield CE Inf Sch
Watts Hill
Cronklands
Limpsfield
Vanguard Way
Limpsfield Chart Golf Club
The Chart
Limpsfield Common
West Heath
Paines Hill
RH8
KENT HATCH RD
Hazelwood Sch
Carpenter Arms (PH)
Scarn Bank
Greensand Way
Tenchleys Park
Boulthurst Farm
Hurst Green Cty Prim Sch
Hurst Green
Loampit Wood
Chartlands
Tenchleys Manor
Doghurst
Crooked River
The Moat Farm
Itchingwood Common
Parishcroft Wood
Holland
Holland Cty Jun Sch
Swaynesland Moat Farm
TN8
Stockenden Farm

144

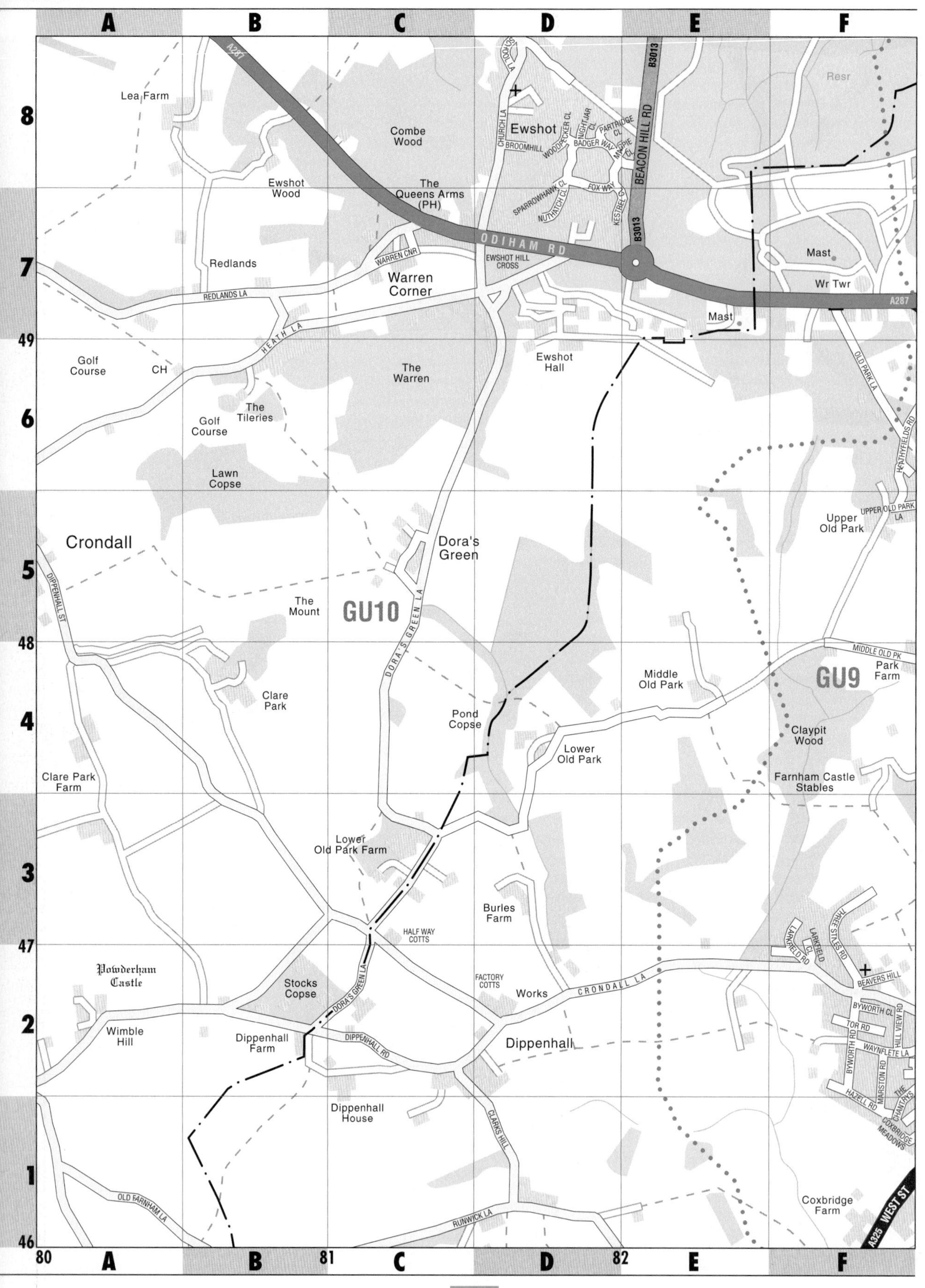
A
B
C
D
E
F
8
7
49
6
5
48
4
3
47
2
1
46
80
81
82
Lea Farm
A287
Combe Wood
SCHOOL LA
Ewshot
CHURCH LA
BROOMHILL
WOODPECKER CL
NIGHTJAR CL
PARTRIDGE CL
BADGER WAY
MAGPIE CL
BEACON HILL RD
B3013
Resr
Ewshot Wood
The Queens Arms (PH)
SPARROWHAWK CL
NUTHATCH CL
FOX WAY
KESTREL CL
ODIHAM RD
Redlands
WARREN CNR
EWSHOT HILL CROSS
Warren Corner
Mast
Wr Twr
REDLANDS LA
HEATH LA
Golf Course
CH
The Warren
Ewshot Hall
OLD PARK LA
Golf Course
The Tileries
Lawn Copse
HEATHYFIELDS RD
Upper Old Park
UPPER OLD PARK LA
Crondall
Dora's Green
DIPPENHALL ST
The Mount
GU10
DORA'S GREEN LA
MIDDLE OLD PK
Park Farm
GU9
Middle Old Park
Clare Park
Pond Copse
Claypit Wood
Lower Old Park
Clare Park Farm
Farnham Castle Stables
Lower Old Park Farm
Burles Farm
HALF WAY COTTS
LARKFIELD RD
LARKFIELD CL
THREE STILES RD
Powderham Castle
FACTORY COTTS
Works
CRONDALL LA
BEAVERS HILL
Stocks Copse
BYWORTH CL
HILL VIEW RD
Wimble Hill
Dippenhall Farm
DIPPENHALL RD
Dippenhall
TOR RD
BYWORTH RD
WAYNFLETE LA
MARSTON RD
HAZELL RD
THE CHANTRYS
COXBRIDGE MEADOWS
Dippenhall House
CLARKS HILL
OLD FARNHAM LA
RUNWICK LA
Coxbridge Farm
A325 WEST ST

145

104
126

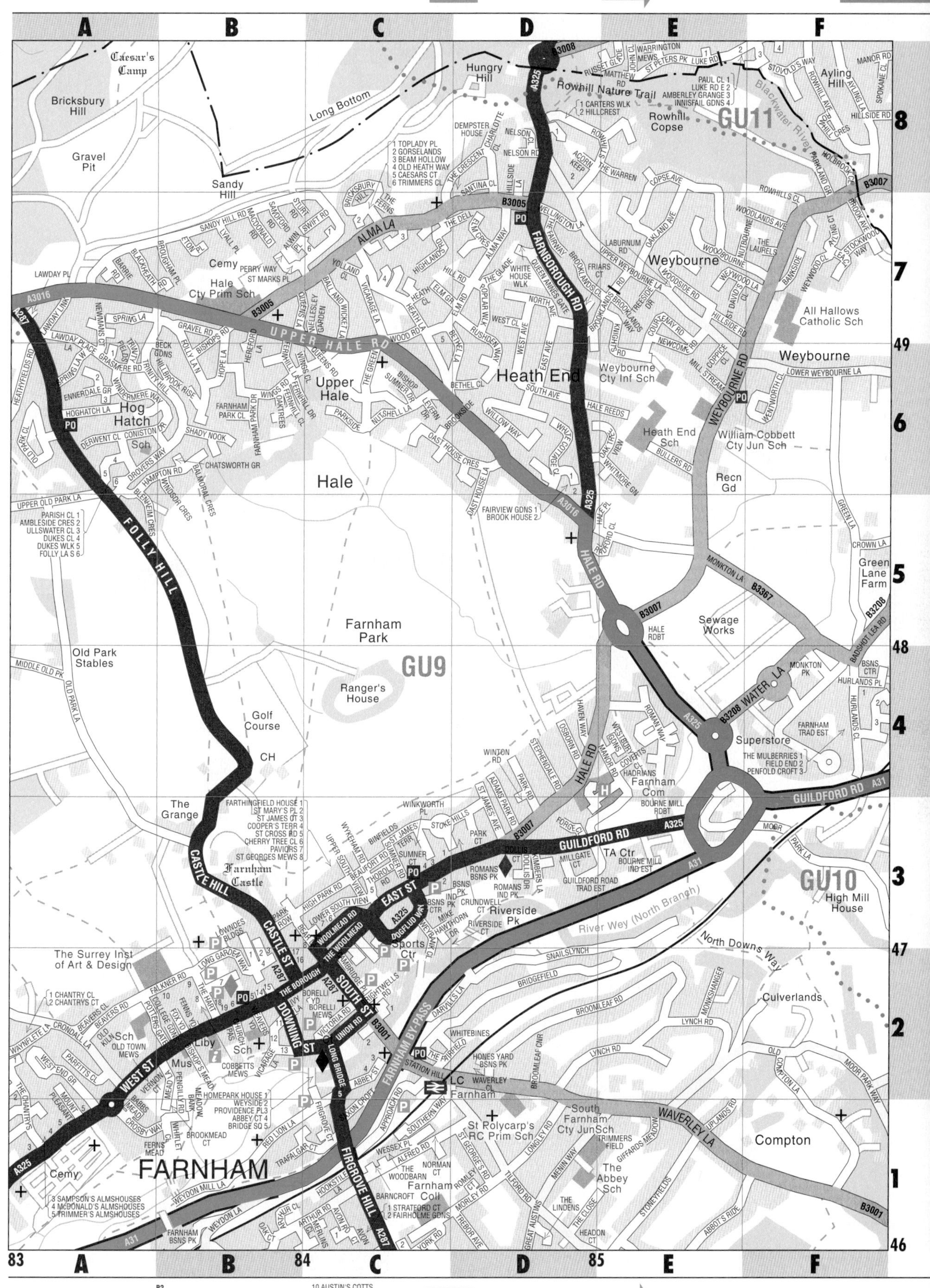

B2
1 LONG GARDEN WLK W
2 LONG GARDEN WLK E
3 LONG GARDEN MEWS
4 LONG GARDEN WLK
5 LION AND LAMB YD
6 ARUNDELL PL
7 LION AND LAMB WAY
8 WESTMEAD
9 LOVETT HOUSE
10 AUSTIN'S COTTS
11 UPPER CHURCH LA
12 MIDDLE CHURCH LA
13 LOWER CHURCH LA
14 HARTS YD
15 OLD KILN COURT YD
16 THE MEWS
17 ST GEORGES YD
18 TIMBER PL
19 CRAVEN HOUSE

146
126

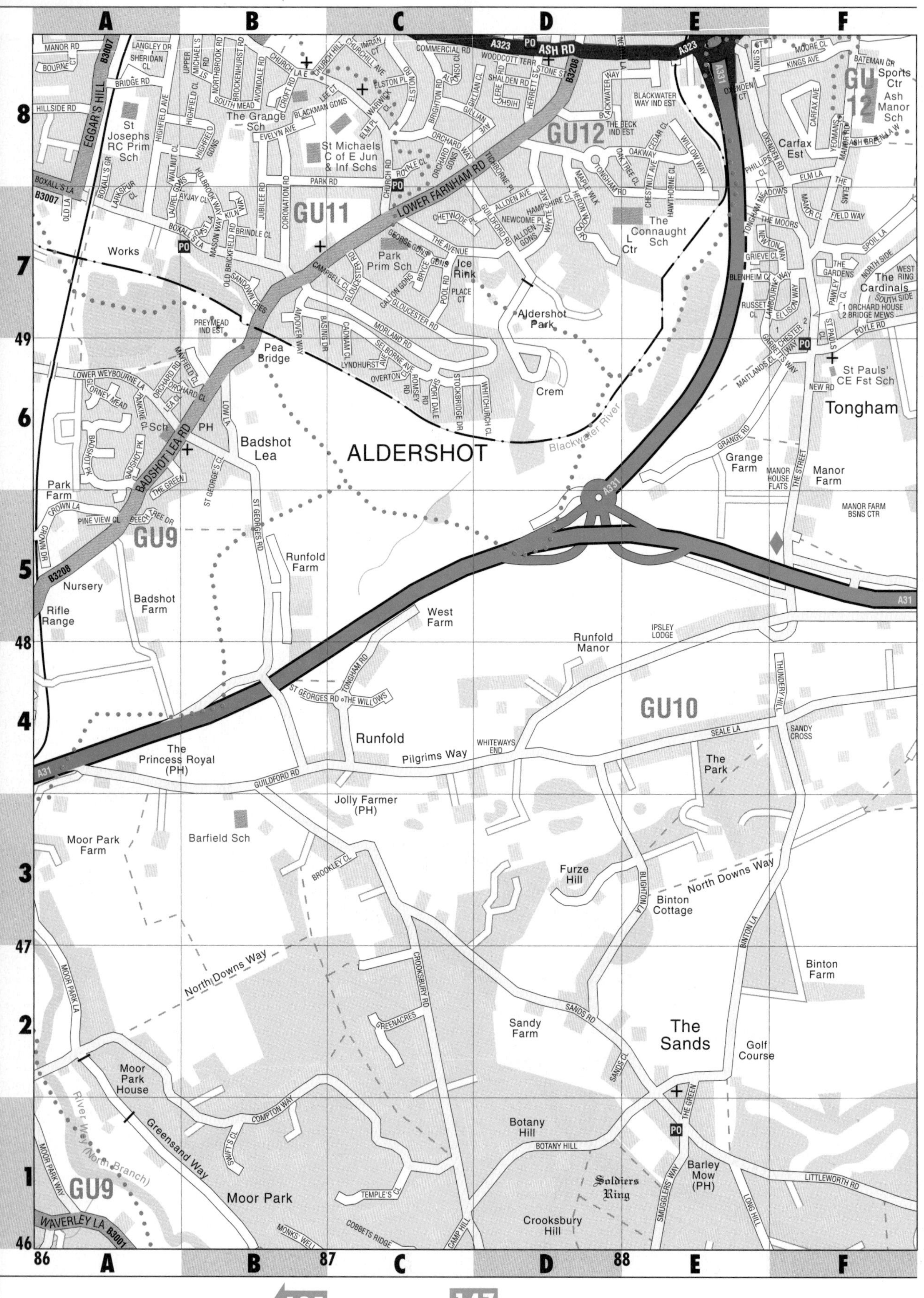
A
B
C
D
E
F
8
7
49
6
5
48
4
3
47
2
1
46
86
87
88
ALDERSHOT
GU11
GU12
GU9
GU10
Tongham
Badshot Lea
Runfold
The Sands
Moor Park
A31
A331
A323
B3208
B3007
LOWER FARNHAM RD
ASH RD
Works
Pea Bridge
Aldershot Park
Crem
Blackwater River
Runfold Farm
Badshot Farm
West Farm
Runfold Manor
Pilgrims Way
North Downs Way
Greensand Way
Furze Hill
Binton Cottage
Binton Farm
Sandy Farm
Golf Course
Botany Hill
Crooksbury Hill
Soldiers Ring
Barley Mow (PH)
Moor Park House
Moor Park Farm
Barfield Sch
Jolly Farmer (PH)
The Princess Royal (PH)
Nursery
Rifle Range
Park Farm
Grange Farm
Manor Farm
The Park
St Pauls' CE Fst Sch
The Connaught Sch
St Michaels C of E Jun & Inf Schs
St Josephs RC Prim Sch
The Grange Sch
Park Prim Sch
Ice Rink
Sports Ctr
Ash Manor Sch
Carfax Est
The Cardinals

106
128

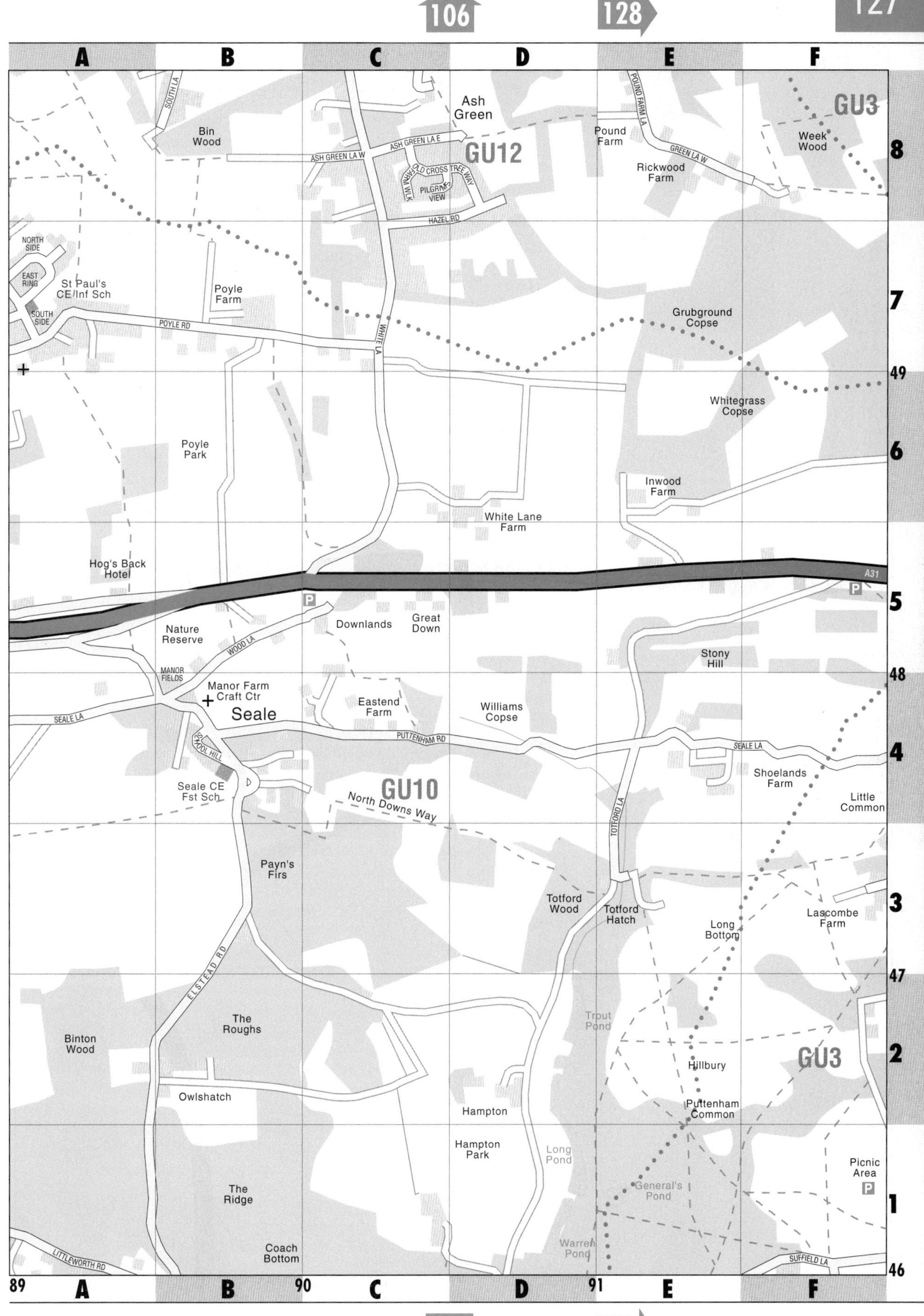
Ash Green
GU12
Bin Wood
Pound Farm
Rickwood Farm
Week Wood
GU3
ASH GREEN LA W
ASH GREEN LA E
OLD CROSS TREE WAY
PILGRIMS VIEW
FARM WLK
HAZEL RD
GREEN LA W
POUND FARM LA
SOUTH LA
NORTH SIDE
EAST RING
SOUTH SIDE
St Paul's CE Inf Sch
Poyle Farm
POYLE RD
WHITE LA
Grubground Copse
Whitegrass Copse
Poyle Park
Inwood Farm
White Lane Farm
Hog's Back Hotel
A31
Nature Reserve
Downlands
Great Down
Stony Hill
WOOD LA
MANOR FIELDS
Manor Farm Craft Ctr
Seale
Eastend Farm
Williams Copse
SEALE LA
PUTTENHAM RD
SCHOOL HILL
Shoelands Farm
Little Common
Seale CE Fst Sch
GU10
North Downs Way
TOTFORD LA
Payn's Firs
Totford Wood
Totford Hatch
Long Bottom
Lascombe Farm
ELSTEAD RD
The Roughs
Binton Wood
Trout Pond
Hillbury
GU3
Owlshatch
Hampton
Puttenham Common
Hampton Park
Long Pond
Picnic Area
General's Pond
The Ridge
Coach Bottom
Warren Pond
LITTLEWORTH RD
SUFFIELD LA
A B C D E F
8 7 49 6 5 48 4 3 47 2 1 46
89 90 91

148
128

127
107

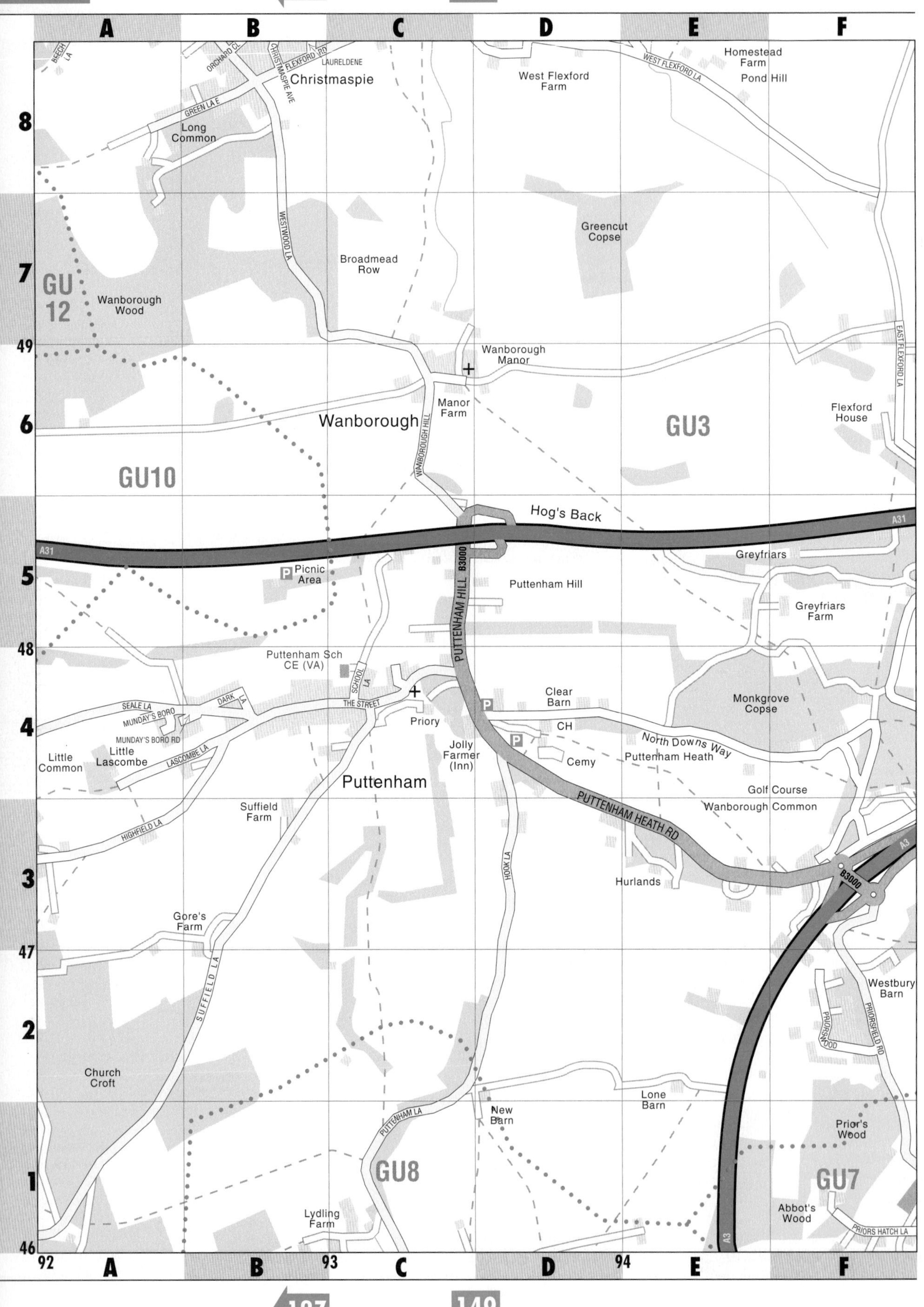

127
149

108
130 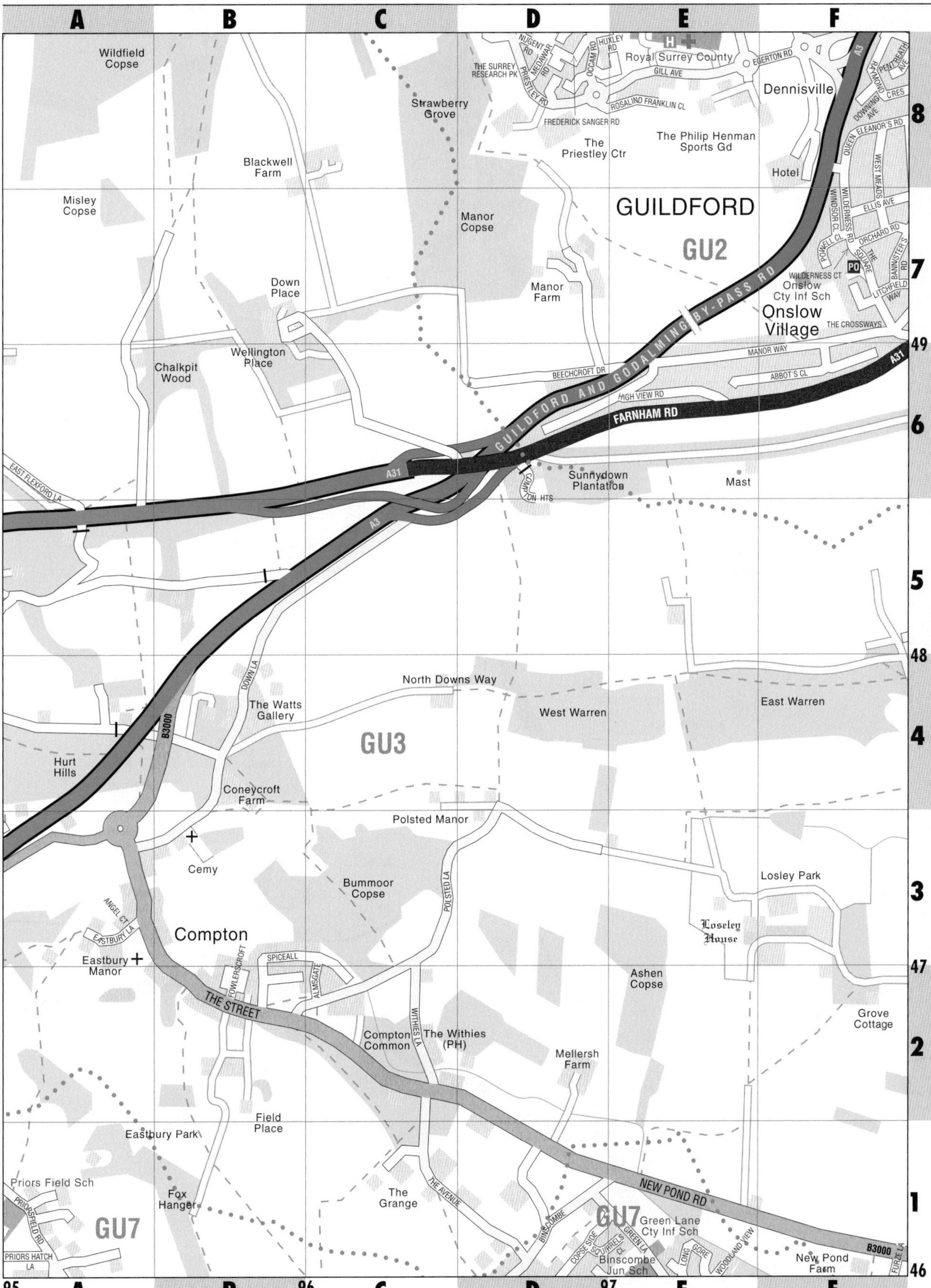
150
130

A B C D E F

Wildfield Copse
Misley Copse
Blackwell Farm
Strawberry Grove
Manor Copse
Down Place
Wellington Place
Chalkpit Wood
Manor Farm
The Surrey Research Pk
Royal Surrey County
Dennisville
The Priestley Ctr
The Philip Henman Sports Gd
Hotel
GUILDFORD
GU2
Onslow Cty Inf Sch
Onslow Village
GUILDFORD AND GODALMING BY-PASS RD
FARNHAM RD
A31
A3
Sunnydown Plantation
Mast
North Downs Way
The Watts Gallery
GU3
West Warren
East Warren
Hurt Hills
Coneycroft Farm
Polsted Manor
Cemy
Bummoor Copse
Losley Park
Loseley House
Compton
Eastbury Manor
Ashen Copse
Grove Cottage
Compton Common
The Withies (PH)
Mellersh Farm
THE STREET
Field Place
Eastbury Park
Priors Field Sch
Fox Hanger
GU7
The Grange
NEW POND RD
Green Lane Cty Inf Sch
Binscombe Jun Sch
New Pond Farm
B3000

95 96 97
46 47 48 49
1 2 3 4 5 6 7 8

129
109

C8
1 MANGLES CT
2 BAYLISS CT
3 BEDFORD HO
4 FRIARY HO
5 THE FRIARY
6 THE MALL

F8
1 FRESHBOROUGH CT
2 TELFORD CT
3 SHELDON CT
4 BEECH CT
5 GRAYLANDS CT
6 EDGEBOROUGH CT
7 COMPTON CT
8 GROSVENOR HO
9 ST LUKE'S SQ
10 KNIGHTSBRIDGE HO
11 CADOGAN HO
12 ALEXANDRA LODGE
13 LYNNE CT
14 CHESHAM MEWS

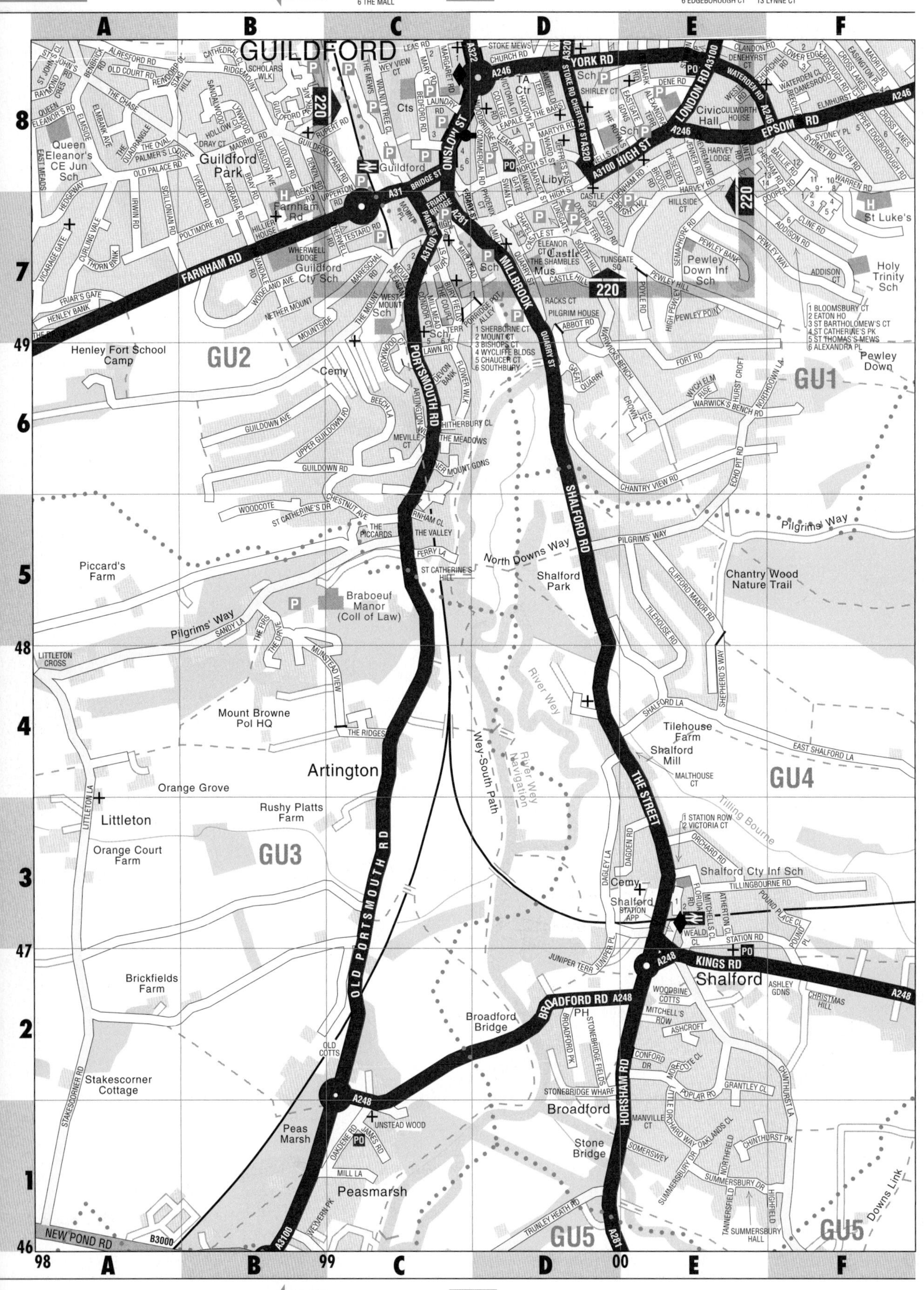

129
151

110
132

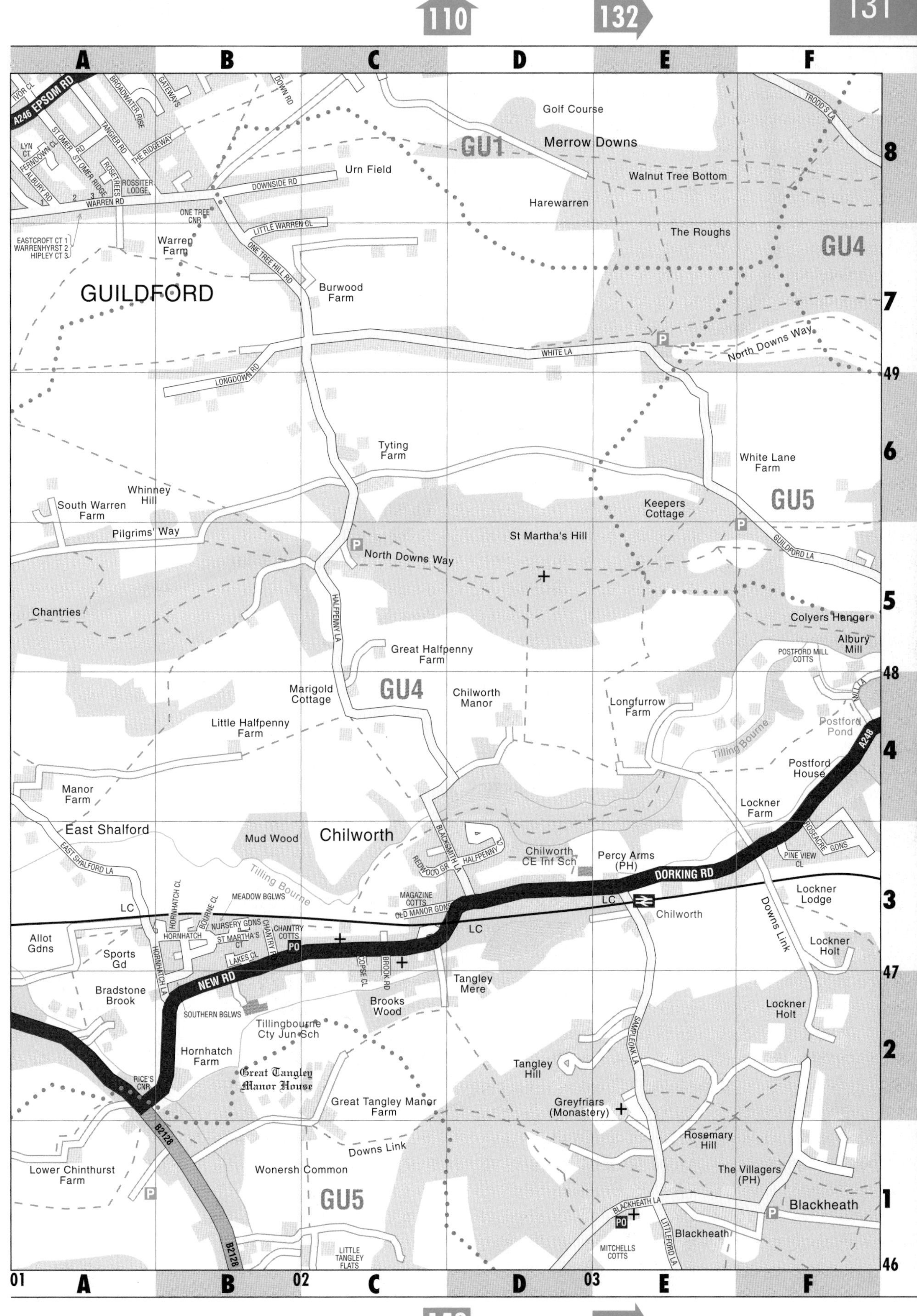

152
132

131
111

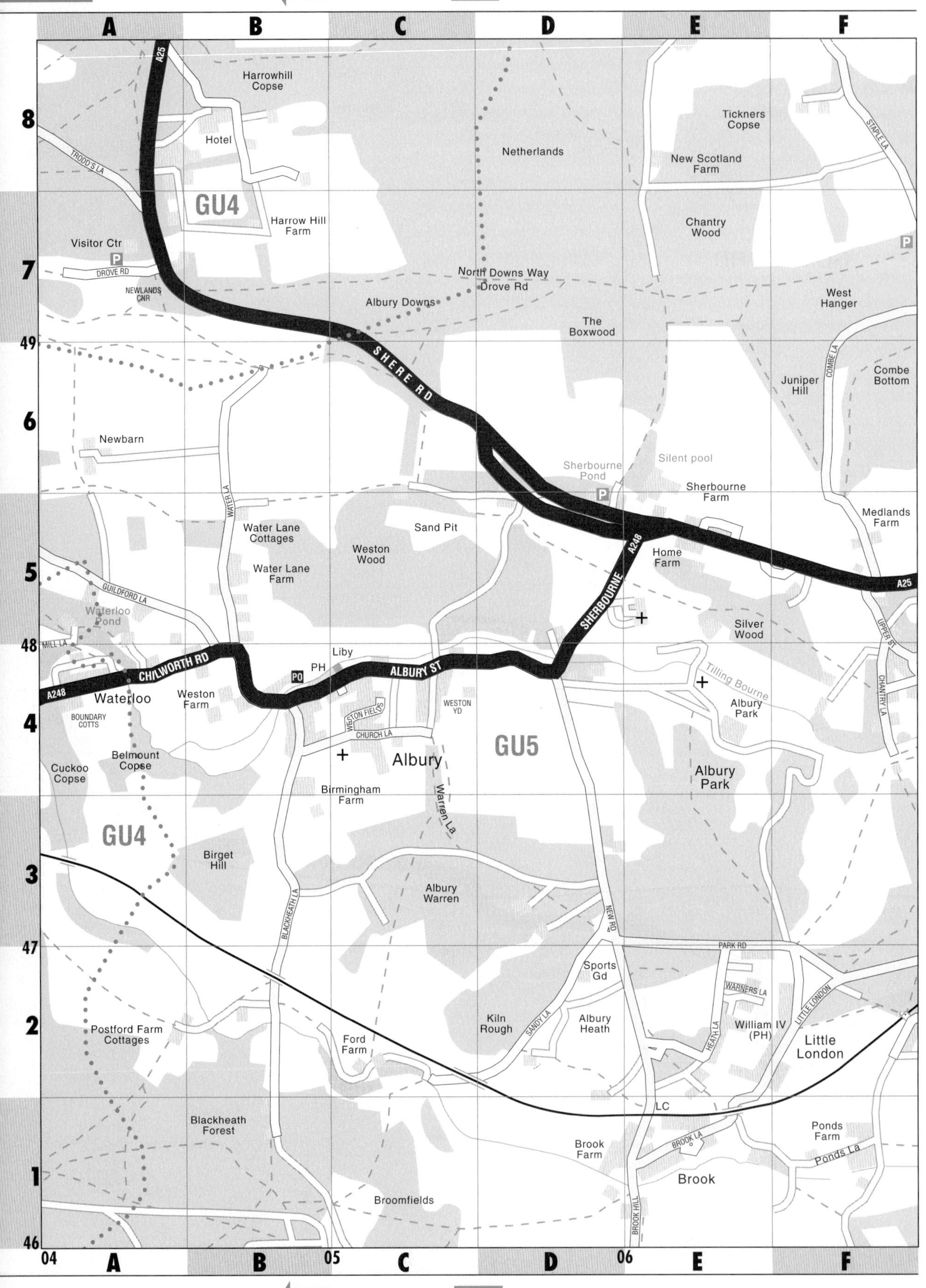

131
153

A B C D E F

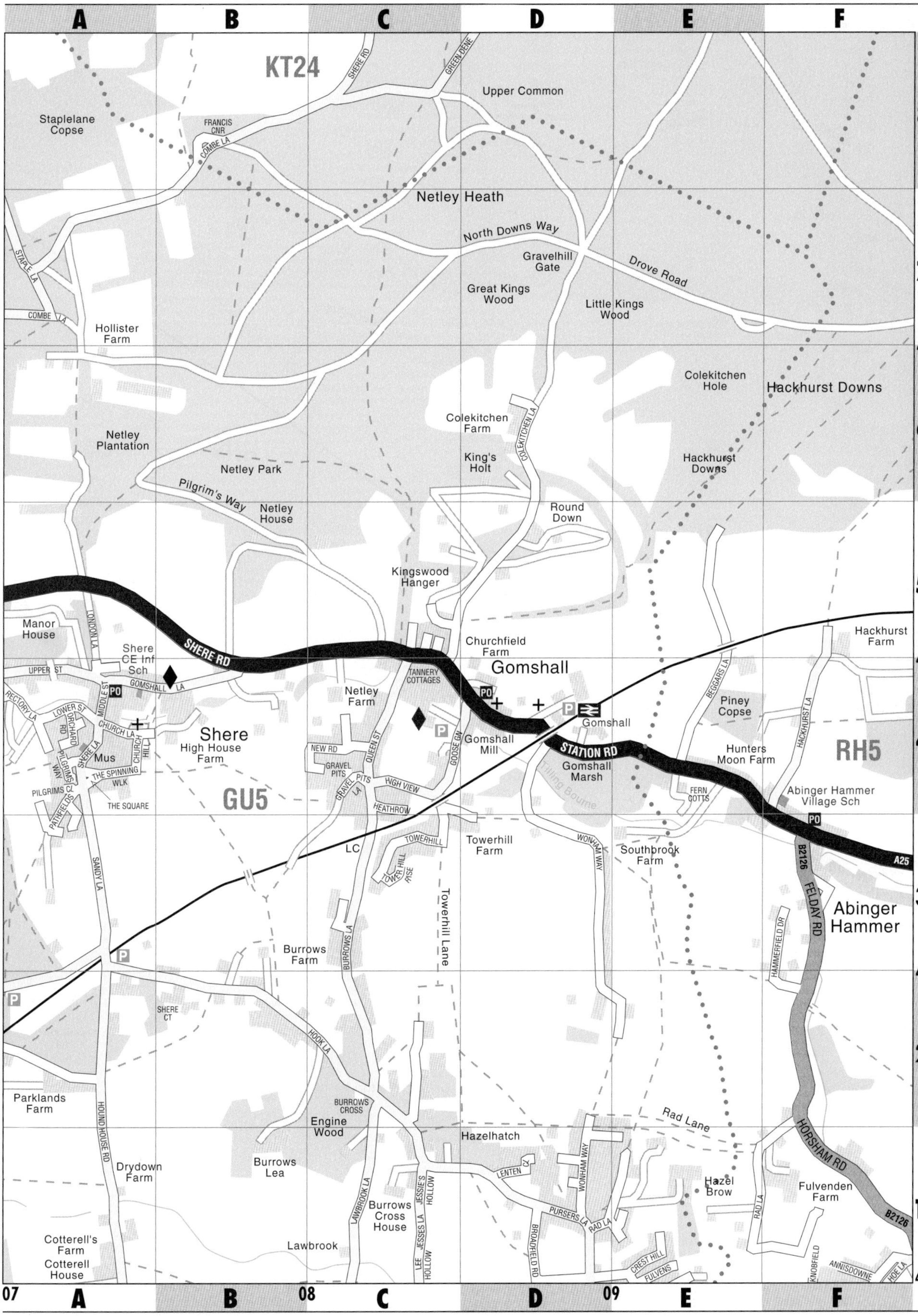

8
7
49
6
5
48
4
3
47
2
1
46

KT24
Staplelane Copse
FRANCIS CNR
COMBE LA
SHERE RD
GREEN DENE
Upper Common
Netley Heath
North Downs Way
Gravelhill Gate
Drove Road
STAPLE LA
COMBE LA
Hollister Farm
Great Kings Wood
Little Kings Wood
Colekitchen Hole
Hackhurst Downs
Netley Plantation
Colekitchen Farm
COLEKITCHEN LA
King's Holt
Netley Park
Hackhurst Downs
Pilgrim's Way
Netley House
Round Down
Kingswood Hanger
Manor House
LONDON LA
SHERE RD
Churchfield Farm
Hackhurst Farm
Shere CE Inf Sch
Gomshall
UPPER ST
GOMSHALL LA
PO
TANNERY COTTAGES
Netley Farm
PO
BEGGARS LA
Piney Copse
RECTORY LA
LOWER ST
MIDDLE ST
ORCHARD RD
CHURCH LA
Shere
High House Farm
Gomshall
P
STATION RD
PILGRIMS WAY
SHERE LA
Mus
CHURCH HILL
NEW RD
GRAVEL PITS
QUEEN ST
GOOSE GN
Gomshall Mill
Gomshall Marsh
Hunters Moon Farm
HACKHURST LA
RH5
THE SPINNING WLK
PILGRIMS CL
PATHFIELDS
THE SQUARE
GU5
GRAVEL PITS LA
HIGH VIEW
HEATHROW
Tilling Bourne
FERN COTTS
Abinger Hammer Village Sch
PO
TOWERHILL
Towerhill Farm
WONHAM WAY
Southbrook Farm
A25
B2126
SANDY LA
LC
TOWER HILL RISE
Towerhill Lane
FELDAY RD
Abinger Hammer
HAMMERFIELD DR
Burrows Farm
BURROWS LA
P
P
SHERE CT
HOOK LA
Parklands Farm
BURROWS CROSS
Engine Wood
Rad Lane
HORSHAM RD
Hazelhatch
HOUND HOUSE RD
Drydown Farm
Burrows Lea
LAWBROOK LA
JESSIE'S HOLLOW
LENTEN CL
WONHAM WAY
Hazel Brow
Fulvenden Farm
Burrows Cross House
JESSIES LA
PURSERS LA
RAD LA
RAD LA
B2126
Cotterell's Farm
Lawbrook
BROADFIELD RD
CREST HILL
KNOBFIELD
ANNISDOWNE
HOE LA
Cotterell House
LEE HOLLOW
FULVENS

07 A B 08 C D 09 E F

133
113

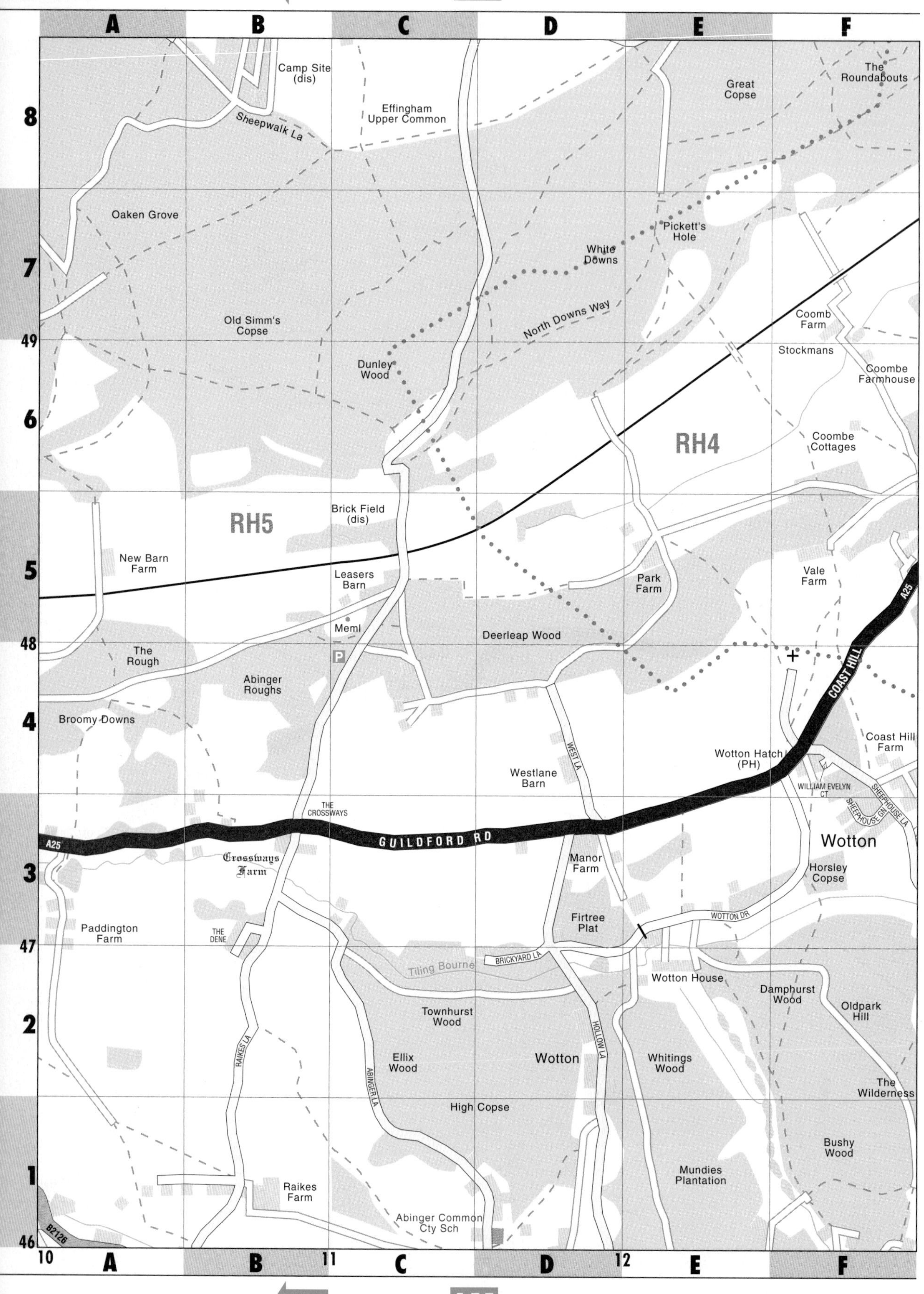

133
155

114
136

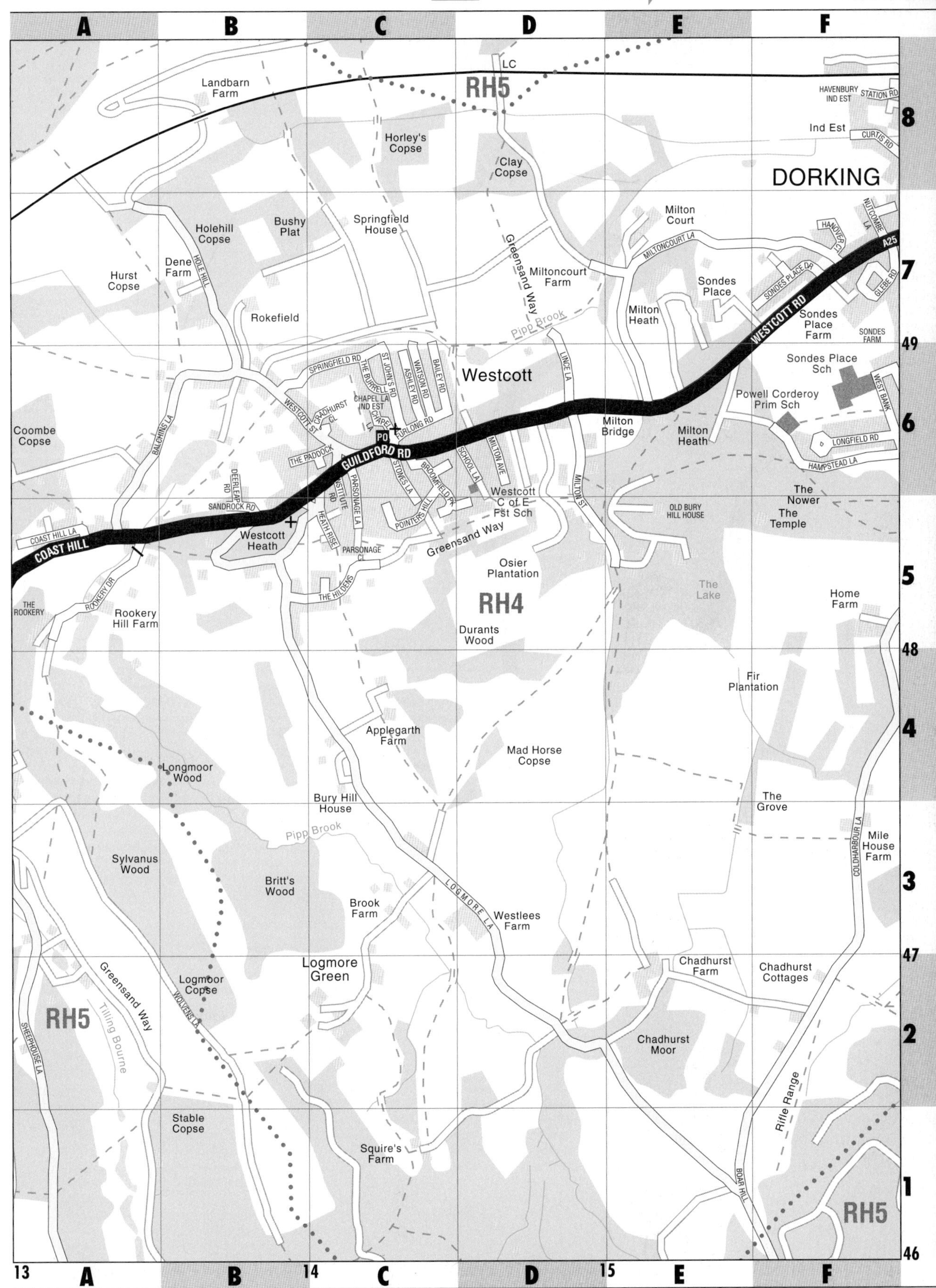

156
136

135
115

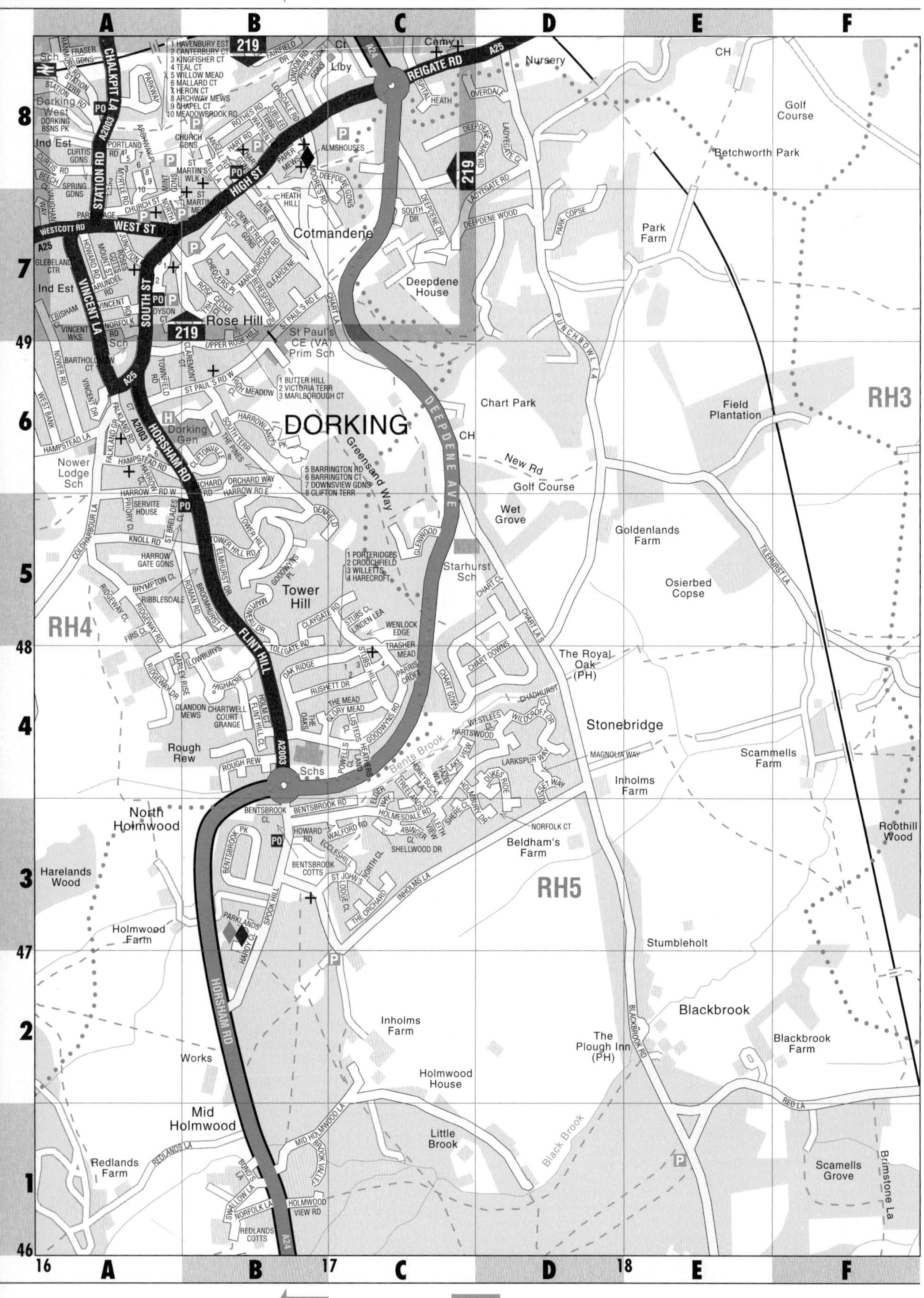

135
157

116
138

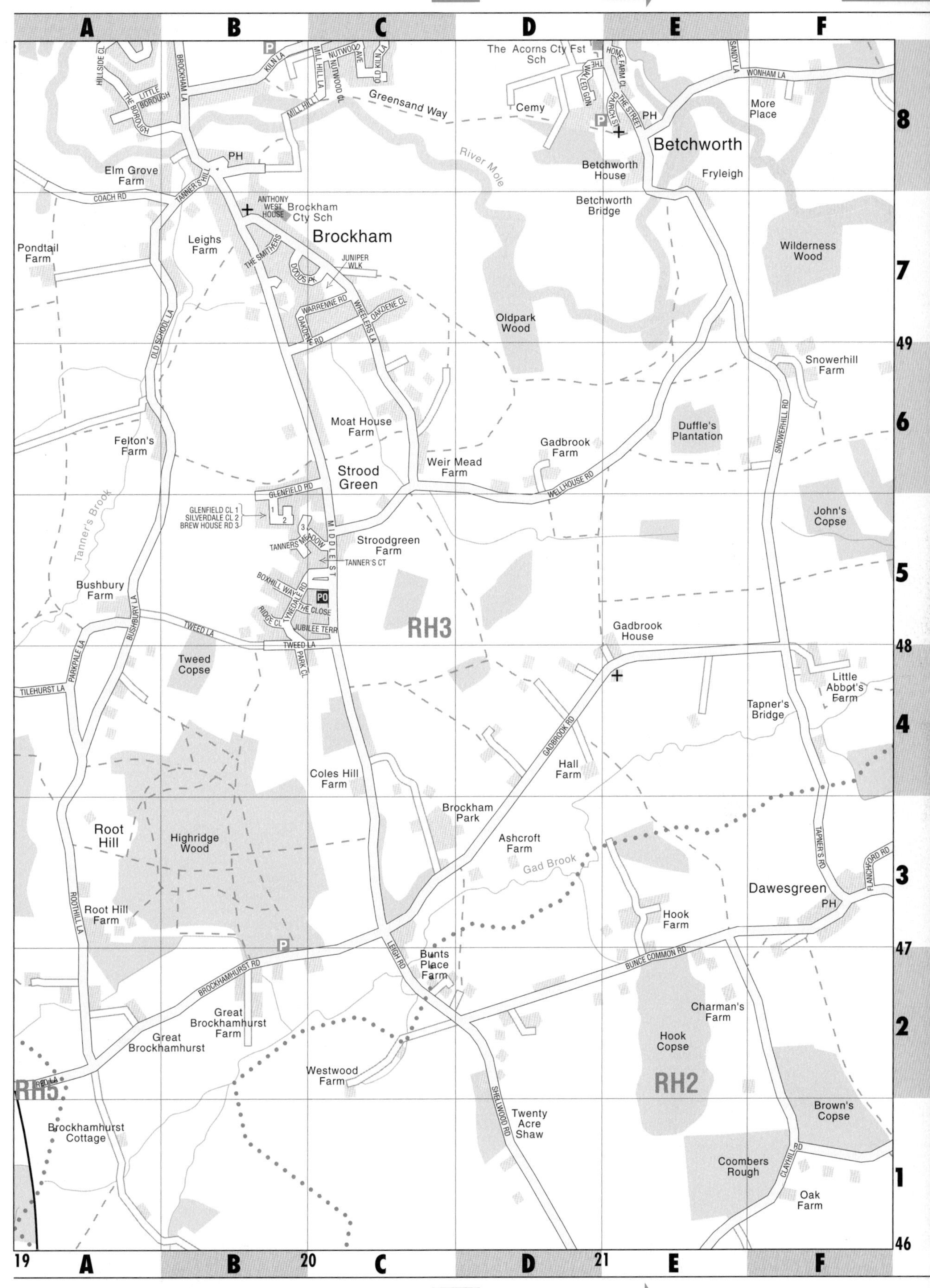

158
138

137
117

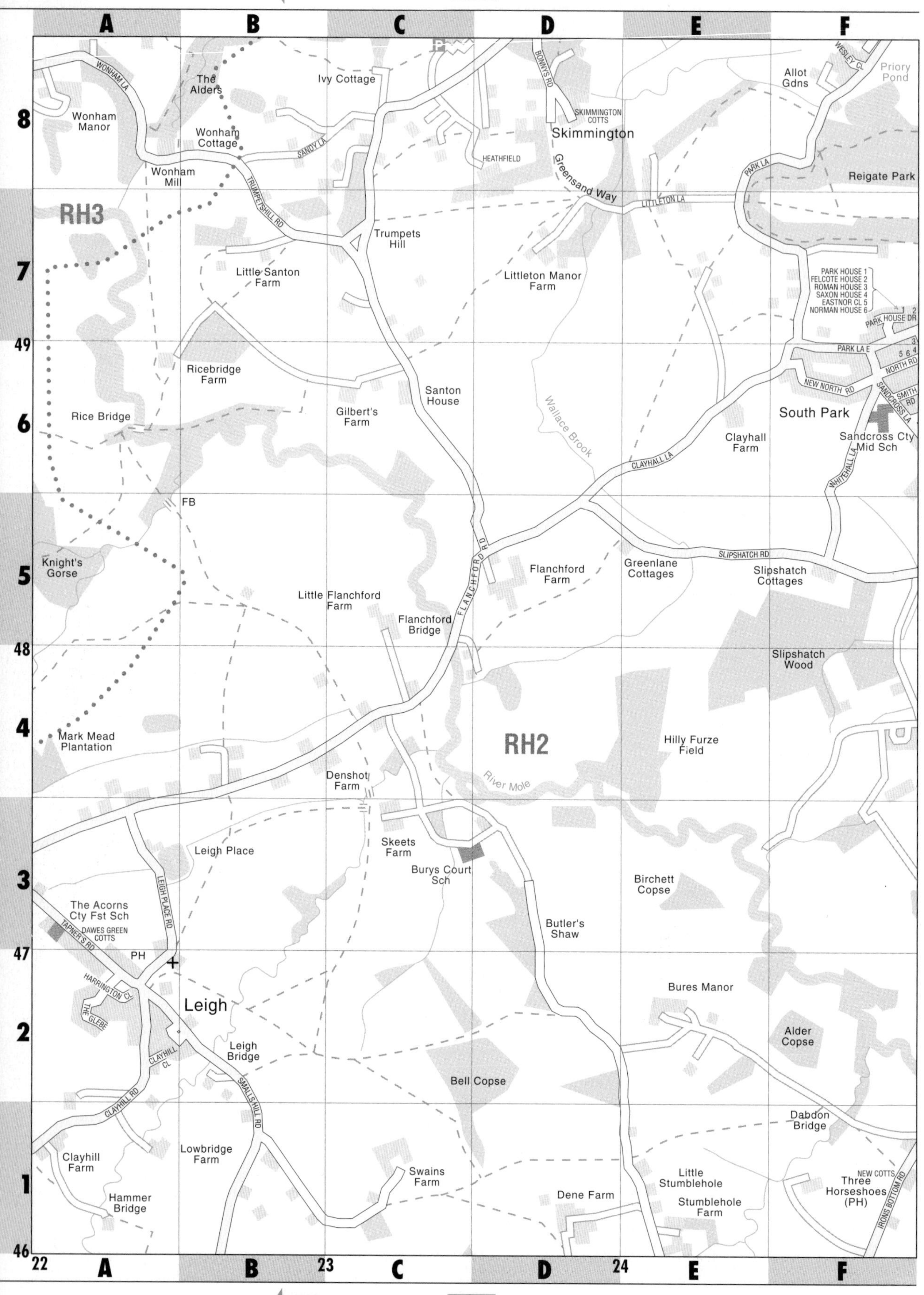

137
159

118
140

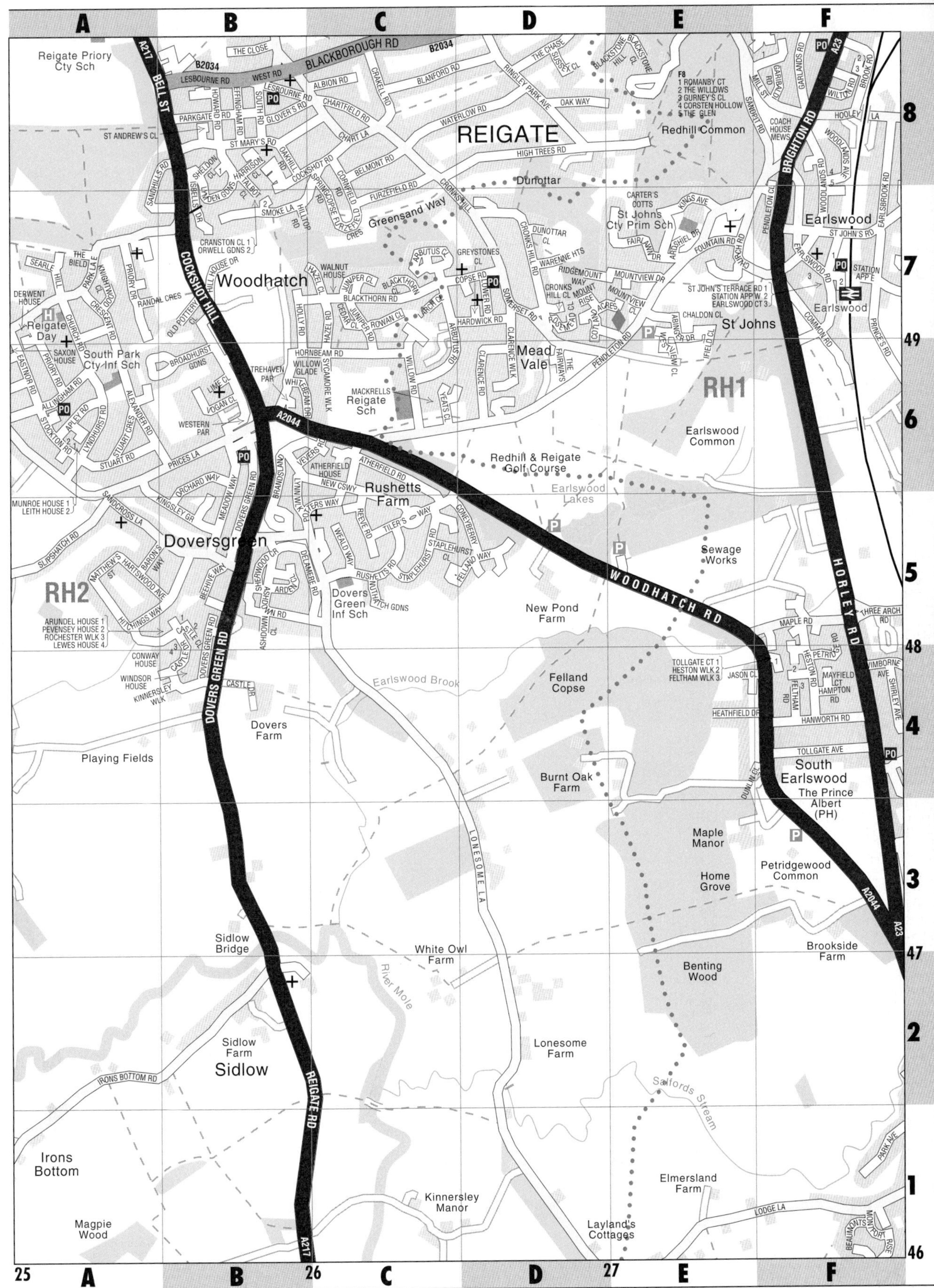

160
140

139
119

139
161

120
142

162
142

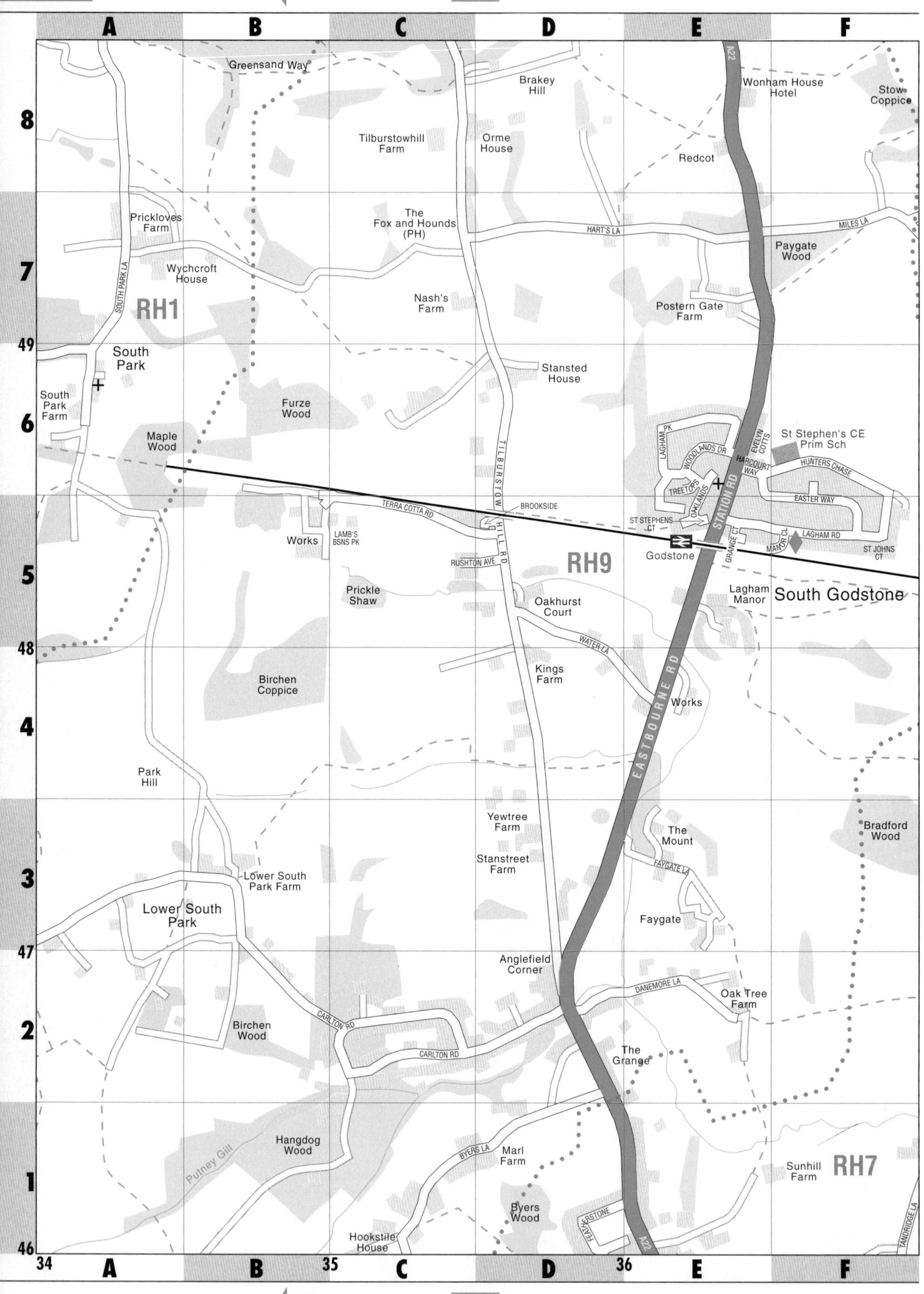
A
B
C
D
E
F
8
7
49
6
5
48
4
3
47
2
1
46
34
35
36
Greensand Way
Brakey Hill
Wonham House Hotel
Stow Coppice
Tilburstowhill Farm
Orme House
Redcot
A22
Prickloves Farm
The Fox and Hounds (PH)
HART'S LA
MILES LA
Paygate Wood
Wychcroft House
SOUTH PARK LA
RH1
Nash's Farm
Postern Gate Farm
South Park
Stansted House
South Park Farm
Furze Wood
Maple Wood
St Stephen's CE Prim Sch
LAGHAM PK
WOODLANDS DR
EVELYN COTTS
HARCOURT WAY
HUNTERS CHASE
TREETOPS
OAKLANDS
EASTER WAY
STATION RD
TILBURSTOW HILL RD
BROOKSIDE
TERRA COTTA RD
ST STEPHENS CT
Works
LAMB'S BSNS PK
LAGHAM RD
GRANGE CT
MANOR CL
ST JOHNS CT
Godstone
RUSHTON AVE
RH9
Prickle Shaw
Oakhurst Court
Lagham Manor
South Godstone
WATER LA
Kings Farm
Birchen Coppice
Works
EASTBOURNE RD
Park Hill
Yewtree Farm
The Mount
Bradford Wood
Stanstreet Farm
FAYGATE LA
Lower South Park Farm
Lower South Park
Faygate
Anglefield Corner
DANEMORE LA
Oak Tree Farm
CARLTON RD
Birchen Wood
CARLTON RD
The Grange
Hangdog Wood
Putney Gill
BYERS LA
Marl Farm
Sunhill Farm
RH7
Byers Wood
FEATHERSTONE
TANDRIDGE LA
Hookstile House
A22

122
144

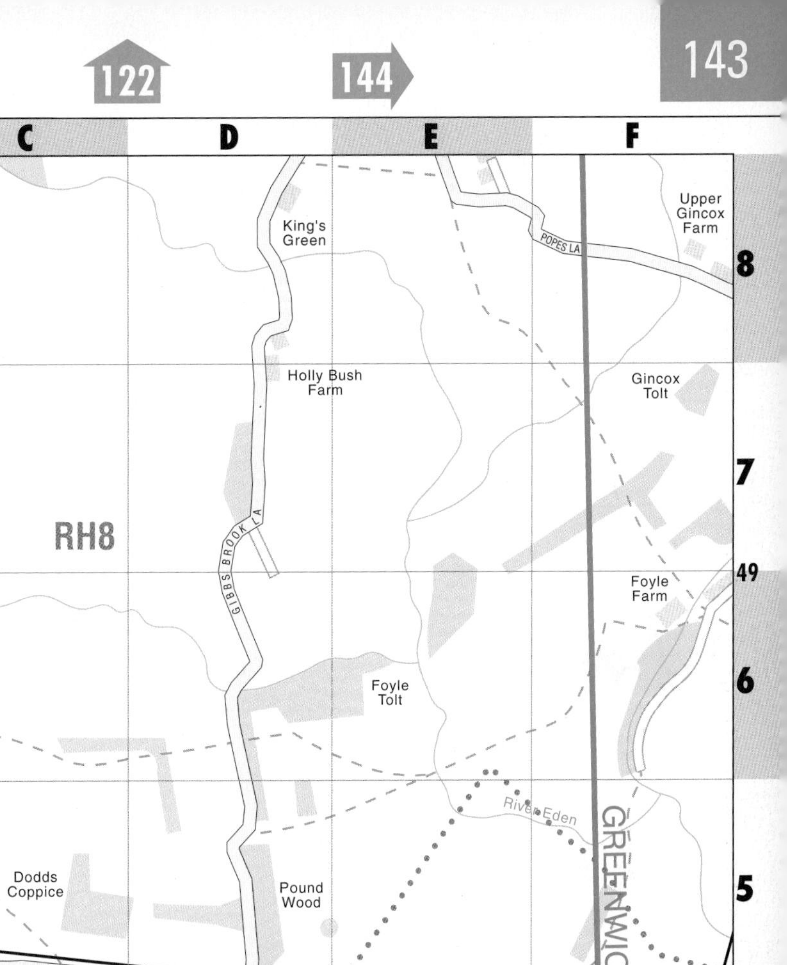

164
144

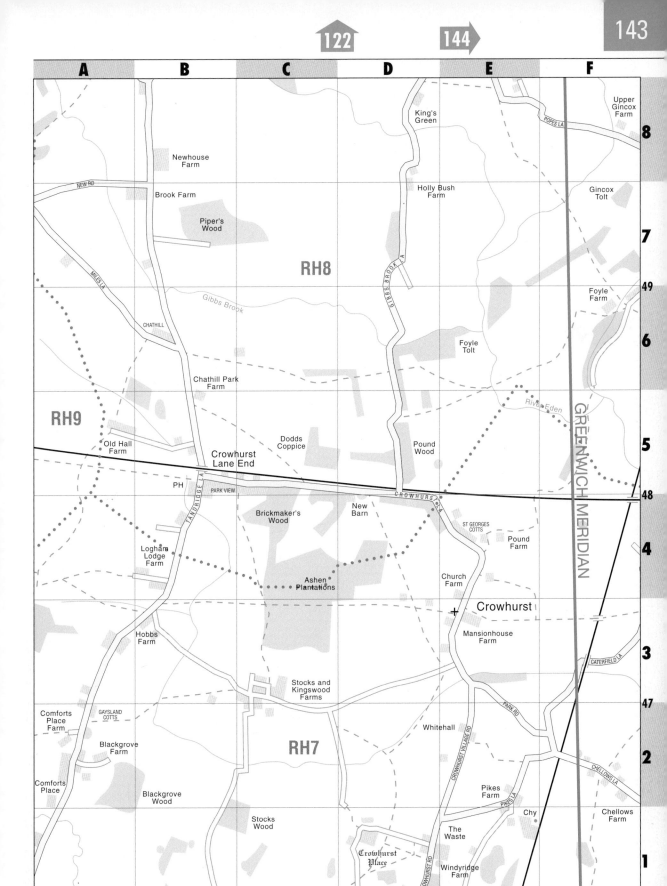

143
123

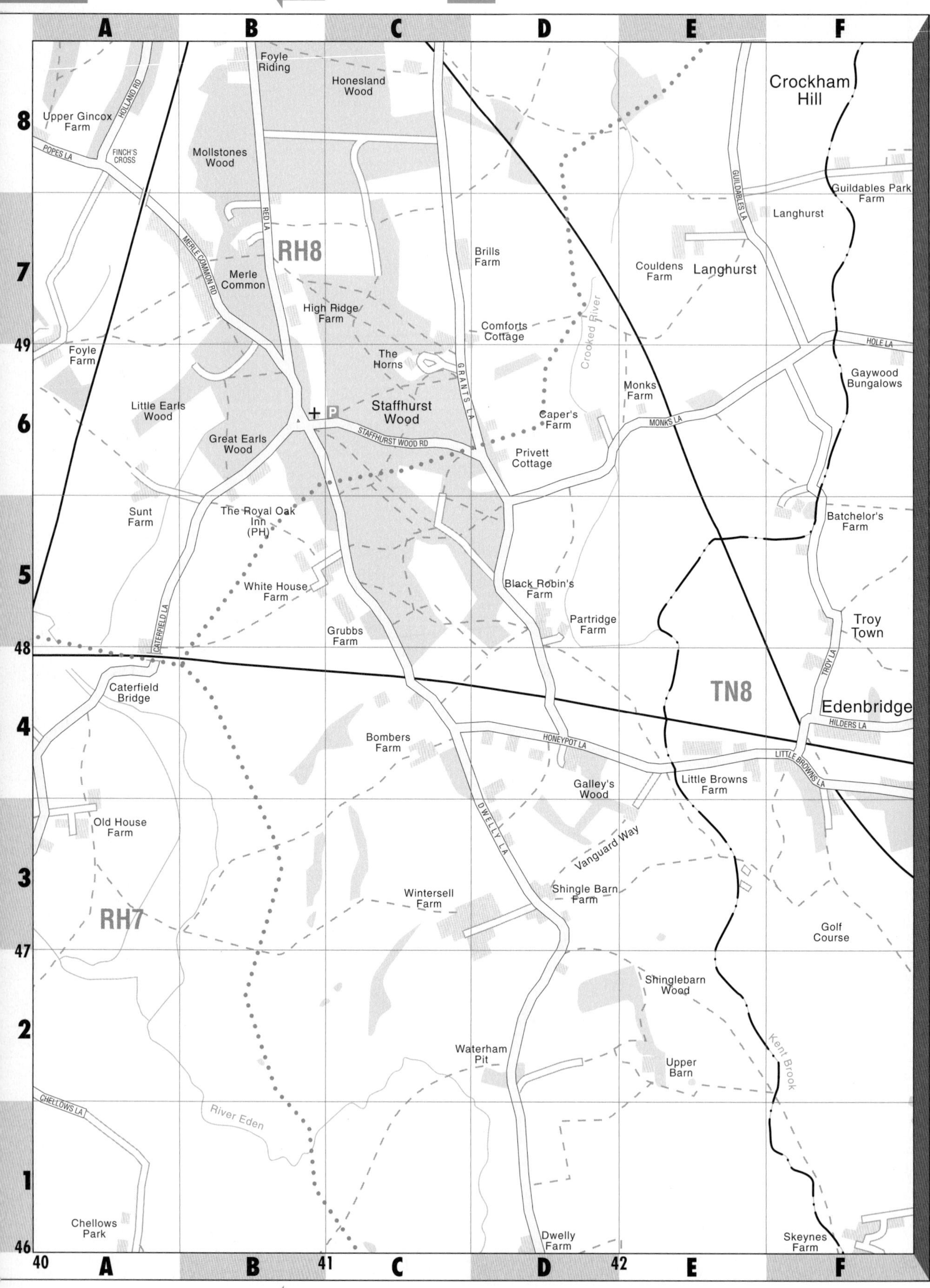

143
165

124
146

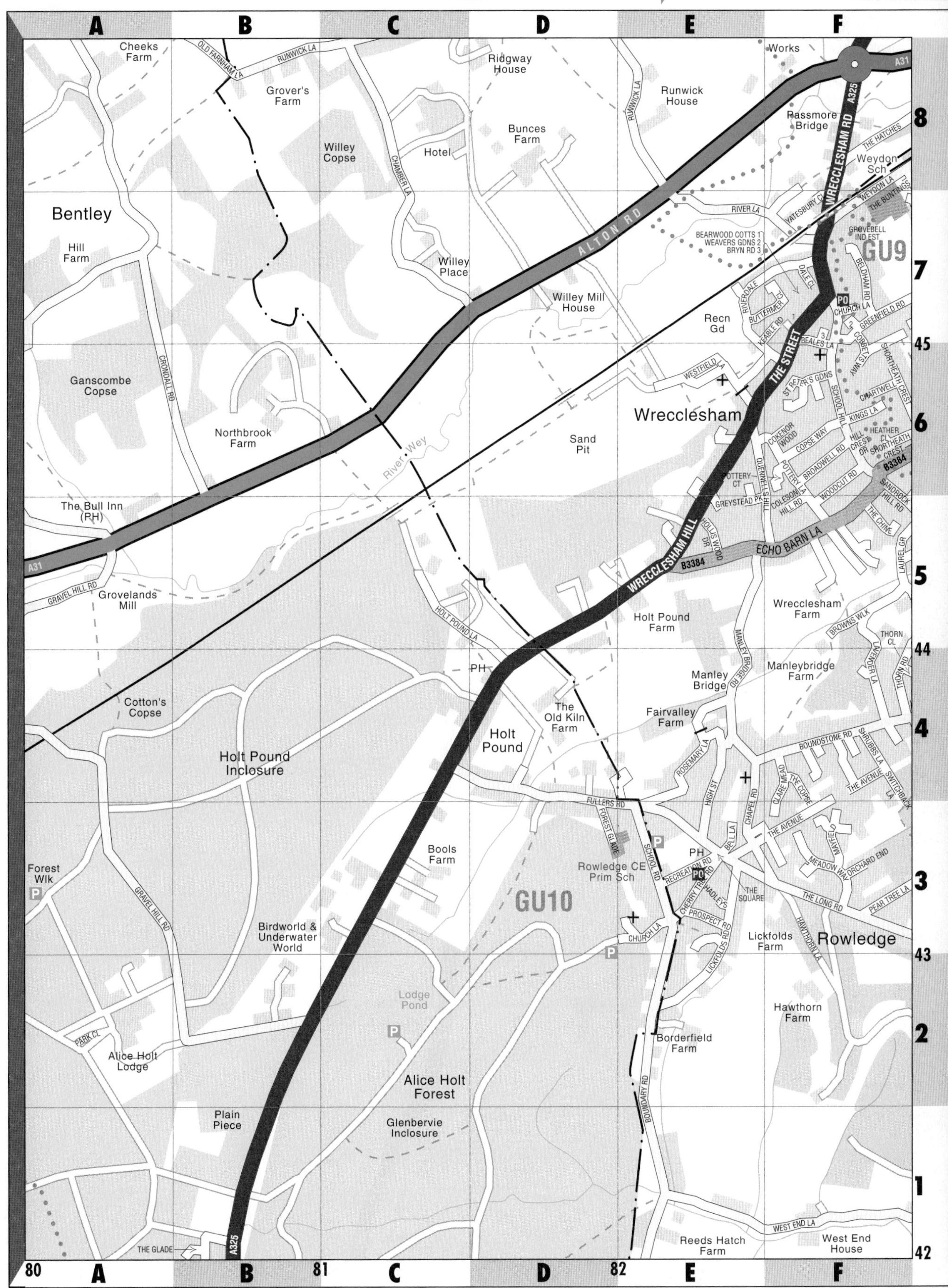

166
146

145
125

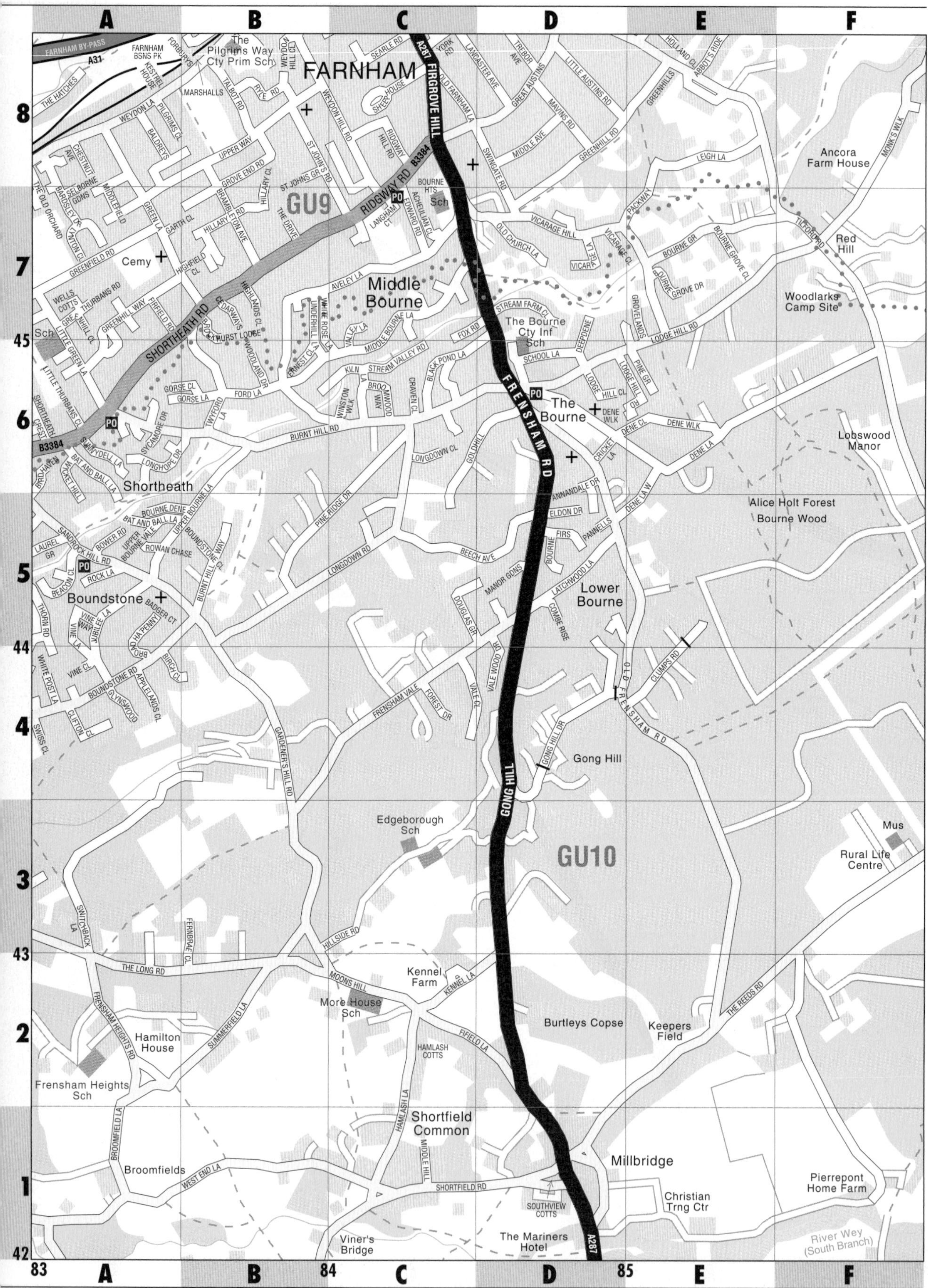

145
167

126
148

168
148

147
127

147
169

128
150

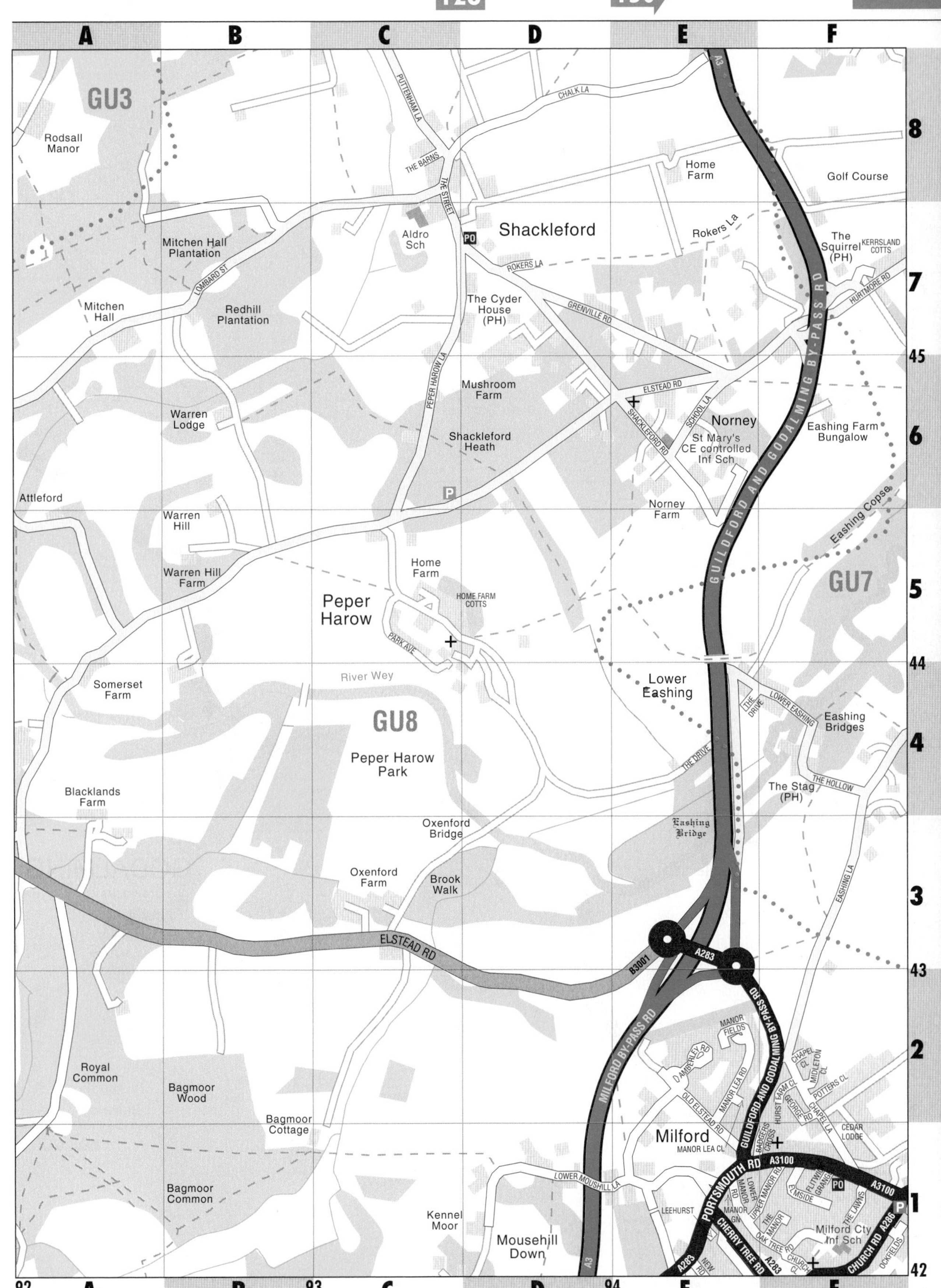

170
150

149
129

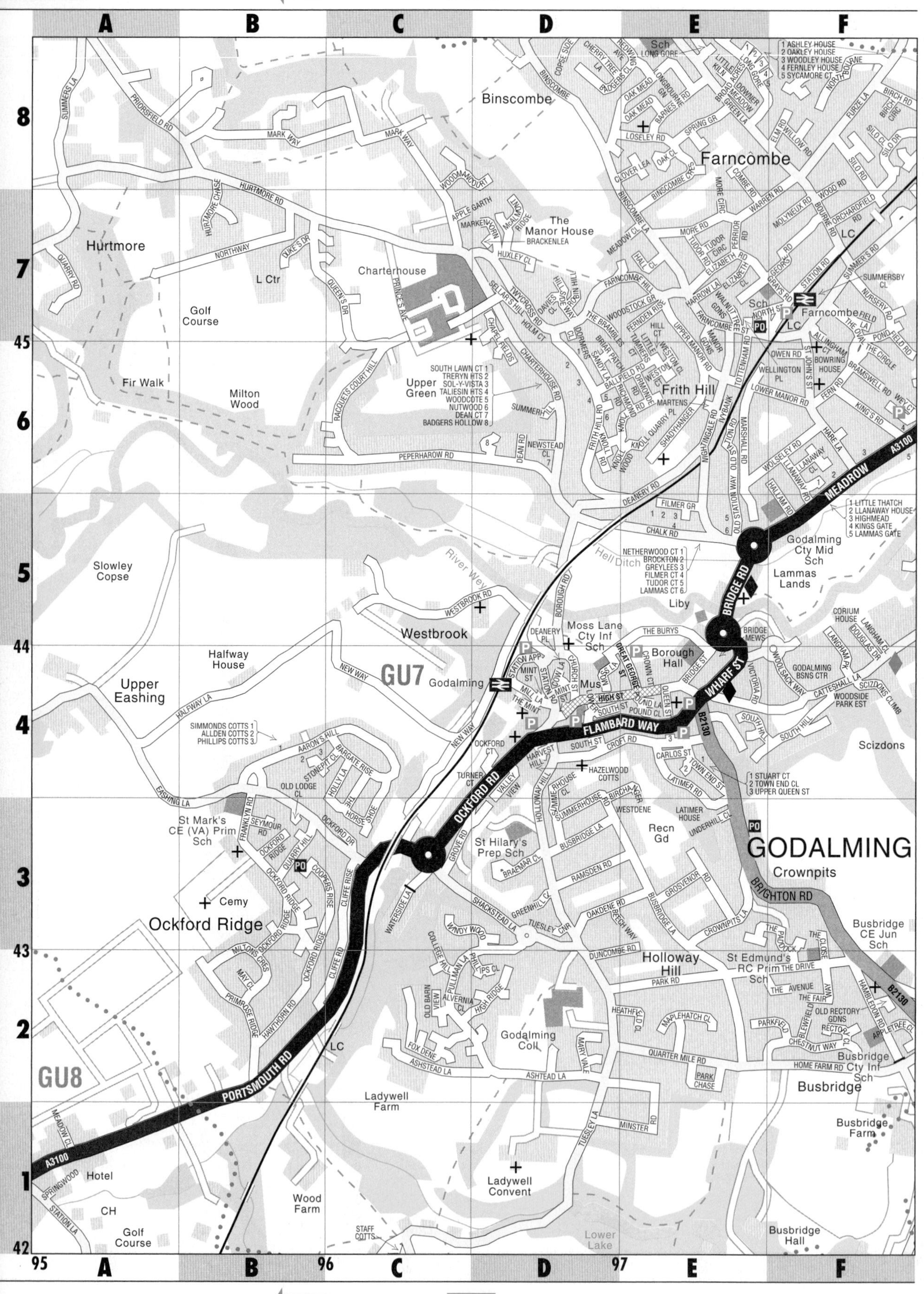
A
B
C
D
E
F
8
7
45
6
5
44
4
3
43
2
1
42
95
96
97
Binscombe
Farncombe
Hurtmore
Charterhouse
The Manor House
L Ctr
Golf Course
Fir Walk
Milton Wood
Upper Green
Frith Hill
Slowley Copse
Westbrook
GU7
Godalming
Halfway House
Upper Eashing
Moss Lane Cty Inf Sch
Borough Hall
Mus
Liby
Godalming Cty Mid Sch
Lammas Lands
Scizdons
St Mark's CE (VA) Prim Sch
Cemy
Ockford Ridge
St Hilary's Prep Sch
Recn Gd
GODALMING
Crownpits
Holloway Hill
St Edmund's RC Prim Sch
Busbridge CE Jun Sch
Godalming Coll
Ladywell Farm
GU8
Busbridge Cty Inf Sch
Busbridge
Busbridge Farm
Hotel
CH
Golf Course
Wood Farm
Ladywell Convent
Lower Lake
Busbridge Hall
A3100
B2130
PORTSMOUTH RD
OCKFORD RD
FLAMBARD WAY
BRIDGE RD
WHARF ST
MEADROW
BRIGHTON RD
1 ASHLEY HOUSE
2 OAKLEY HOUSE
3 WOODLEY HOUSE
4 FERNLEY HOUSE
5 SYCAMORE CT
SOUTH LAWN CT 1
TRERYN HTS 2
SOL-Y-VISTA 3
TALIESIN HTS 4
WOODCOTE 5
NUTWOOD 6
DEAN CT 7
BADGERS HOLLOW 8
1 LITTLE THATCH
2 LLANAWAY HOUSE
3 HIGHMEAD
4 KINGS GATE
5 LAMMAS GATE
NETHERWOOD CT 1
BROCKTON 2
GREYLEES 3
FILMER CT 4
TUDOR CT 5
LAMMAS CT 6
SIMMONDS COTTS 1
ALLDEN COTTS 2
PHILLIPS COTTS 3
1 STUART CT
2 TOWN END CL
3 UPPER QUEEN ST
PRIORSFIELD RD
HURTMORE RD
MARK WAY
NORTHWAY
PEPERHAROW RD
HALFWAY LA
EASHING LA
NEW WAY
WESTBROOK RD
CHALK RD
DEANERY RD
FILMER GR
HIGH ST
SOUTH ST
CROFT RD
CHARTERHOUSE RD
FRITH HILL RD
WARREN RD
STATION RD
CATTESHALL LA
HOLLOWAY HILL
BUSBRIDGE LA
CROWNPITS LA
QUARTER MILE RD
HOME FARM RD
ASHSTEAD LA
TUESLEY LA
PARK RD
DUNCOMBE RD
CLIFFE RD
MEADOW CL
SPRINGWOOD
STATION LA
STAFF COTTS

130
152

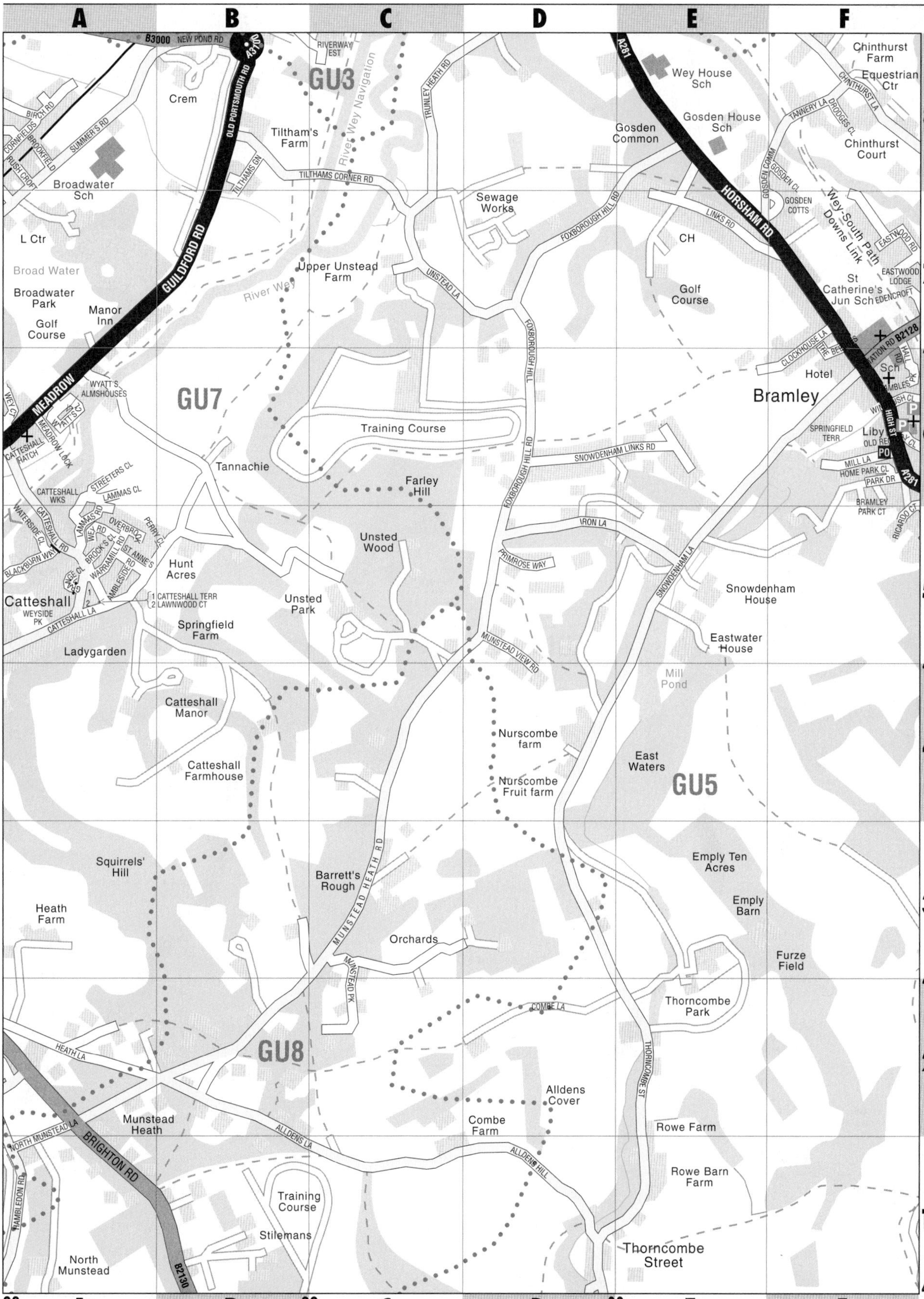

172
152

151
131

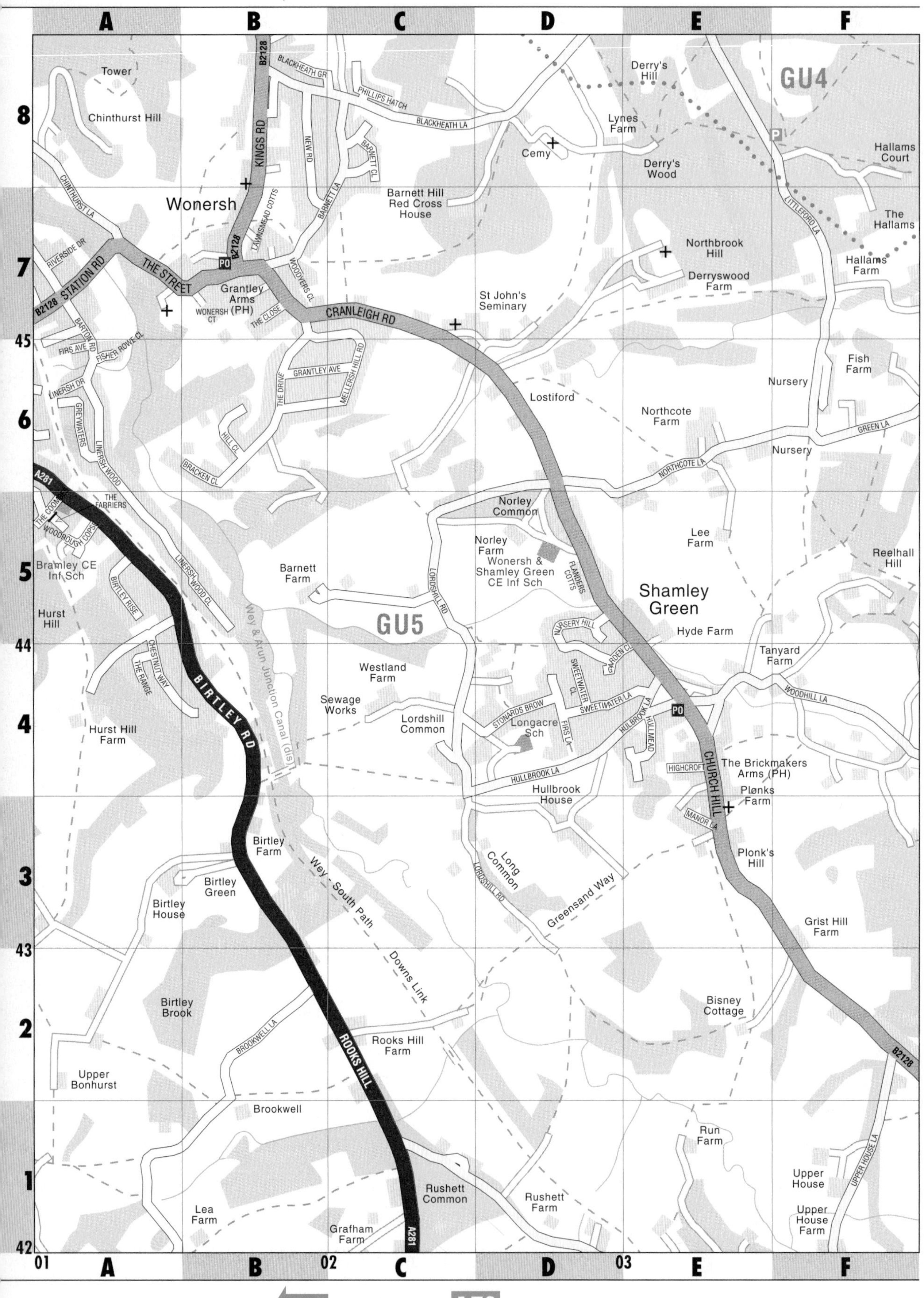

151
173

132
154

174
154

153
133

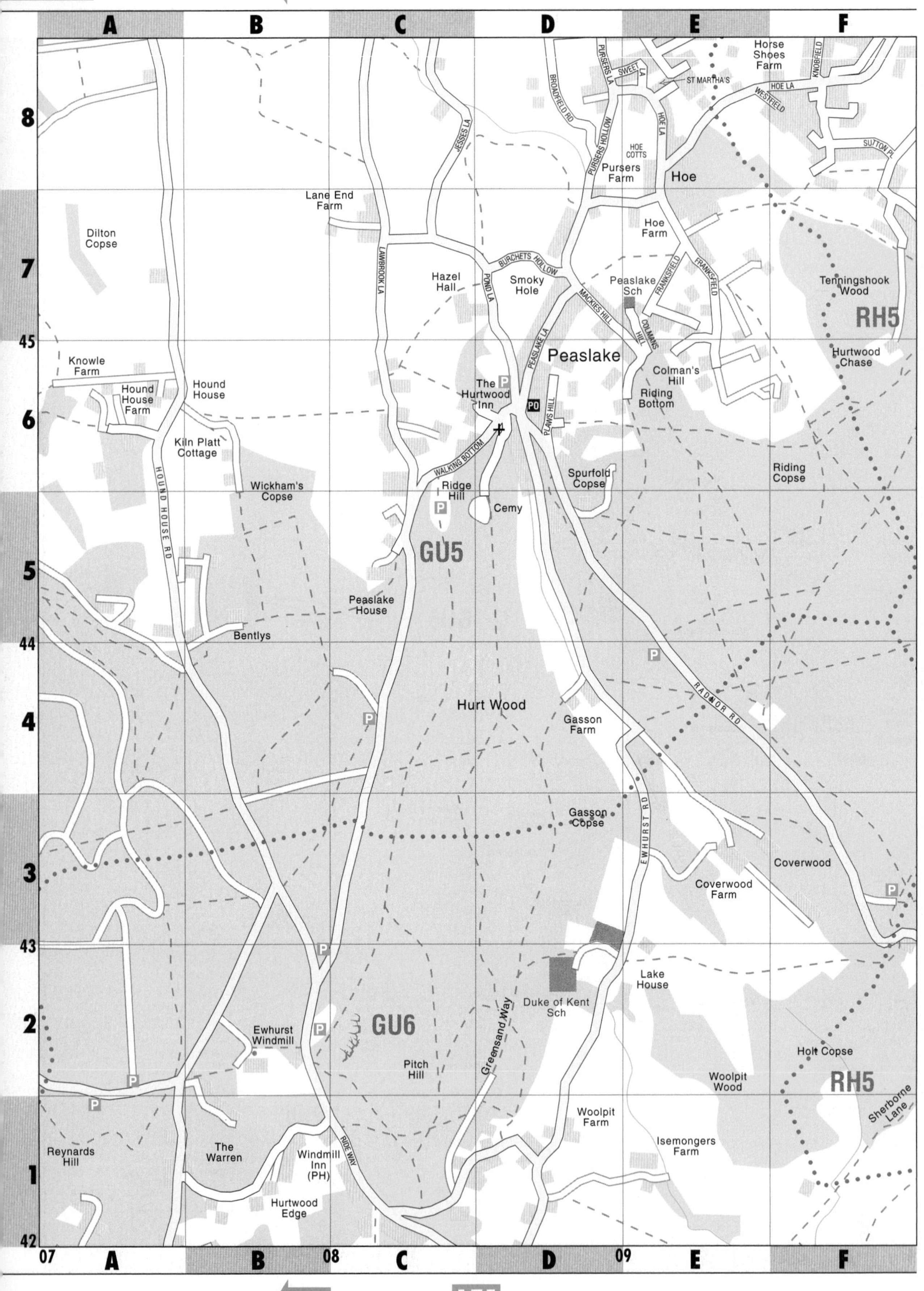

153
175

134
156

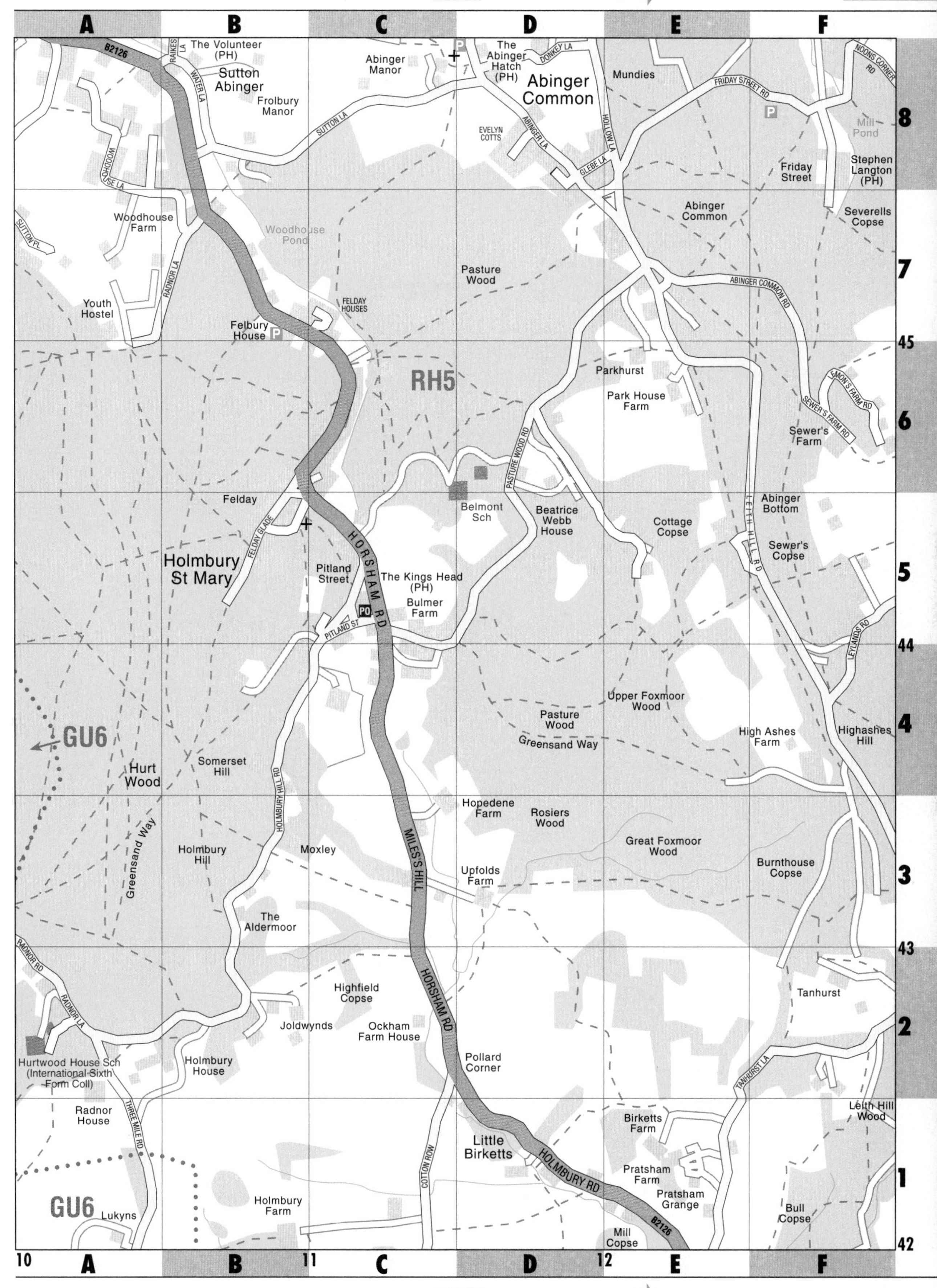

176
156

155
135

RH4
Simons Copse
Home Farm
Broadmoor
BROADMOOR COTT
Severells Copse
Pond Cottage
WHITEBERRY RD
Brookwick Copse
High Field
Collickmoor Farm
Pondfield Copse
Robin Gate Cottage
Robbing Gate
Upper Merriden Cottage
COLDHARBOUR LA
Leylands
LEYLANDS RD
Shootlands Farm
Warren Farm
Tilling Springs
Leylands Farm
Whiteberry Rd Greensand Way
Broadmoor Bottom
The Duke's Warren
Coldharbour Common
Waterden Wood
Whiteberry Hill
Whiteberry Gate
RH5
WOLVENS LA
Crockers Farm
Anstiebury Farm
PH
Anstiebury
PO
Coldharbour
Spring Copse
ANSTIE LA
Wotton Common
Snakes Hill
Kitlands Farm
Kitlands
East Lodge
WEALD VIEW COTTS
The Landslip
Gill Wood
Leith Hill
Leith Hill Tower
ABINGER RD
Cockshot Farm
Mosses Wood
LEITH HILL RD
East Campfield Place
Bushy Copse
TANHURST LA
BROOMEHALL RD
Broome Hall Farm
Smither's Copse
Leith Hill Place Wood
Broome Hall
Leith Hill Place
Leith Hill Place Farm
Nutfold Copse
Great Copse
Hartshurst Farm
Fatting Hovel Copse
SHEEPHOUSE LA
NOONS CORNER RD
A
B
C
D
E
F
8
7
6
5
4
3
2
1
45
44
43
42
13
14
15

155
177

136
158

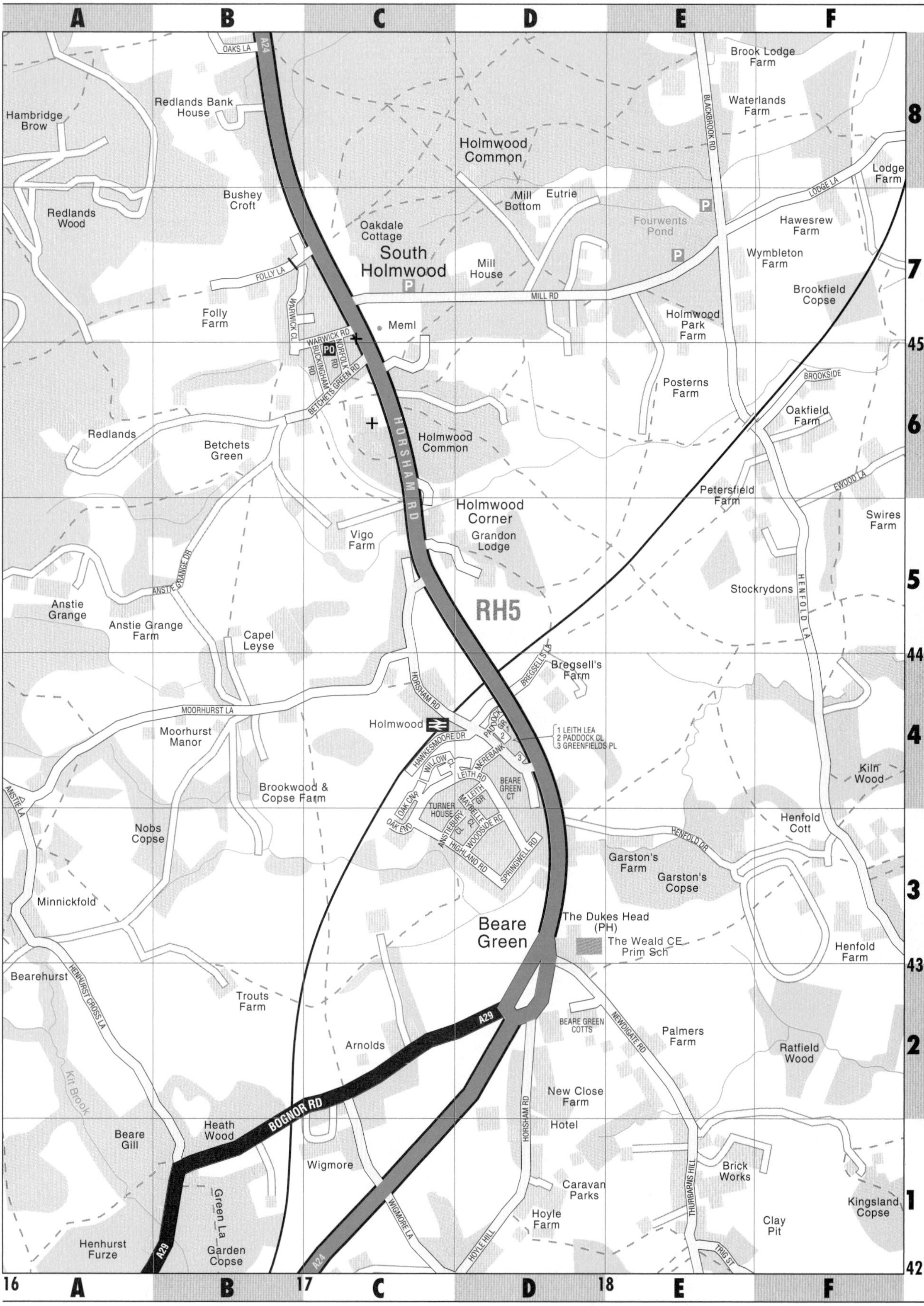

A B C D E F

Oaks La
A24
Brook Lodge Farm
Redlands Bank House
Hambridge Brow
Waterlands Farm
Blackbrook Rd
Holmwood Common
Lodge Farm
Lodge La
Bushey Croft
Mill Bottom
Eutrie
Redlands Wood
Fourwents Pond
Hawesrew Farm
Oakdale Cottage
South Holmwood
Mill House
Wymbleton Farm
Folly La
Brookfield Copse
Mill Rd
Folly Farm
Warwick Cl
Meml
Holmwood Park Farm
Warwick Rd
PO
Buckingham Rd
Norfolk Rd
Betchets Green Rd
Brookside
Posterns Farm
Oakfield Farm
Redlands
Betchets Green
Horsham Rd
Holmwood Common
Petersfield Farm
Ewood La
Holmwood Corner
Swires Farm
Vigo Farm
Grandon Lodge
Anstie Grange Dr
Stockrydons
Anstie Grange
RH5
Henfold La
Anstie Grange Farm
Capel Leyse
Bregsells La
Bregsell's Farm
Horsham Rd
Moorhurst La
Holmwood
Paddock Gr
Hawkesmoore Dr
Moorhurst Manor
1 Leith Lea
2 Paddock Cl
3 Greenfields Pl
Willow Cl
Merebank
Kiln Wood
Anstie La
Brookwood & Copse Farm
Leith Rd
Beare Green Ct
Oak Cnr
Turner House
Leith Gr
Maybelle Cl
Nobs Copse
Oak End
Anstiebury Cl
Woodside Rd
Henfold Cott
Henfold Dr
Highland Rd
Springwell Rd
Garston's Farm
Minnickfold
Garston's Copse
The Dukes Head (PH)
Beare Green
The Weald CE Prim Sch
Henfold Farm
Bearehurst
Henhurst Cross La
Trouts Farm
A29
Beare Green Cotts
Newdigate Rd
Palmers Farm
Arnolds
Ratfield Wood
Kit Brook
New Close Farm
Bognor Rd
Horsham Rd
Heath Wood
Beare Gill
Hotel
Thurbarns Hill
Brick Works
Wigmore
Green La
Caravan Parks
Kingsland Copse
Wigmore La
Hoyle Farm
Clay Pit
Hoyle Hill
Henhurst Furze
A29
Garden Copse
A24
Trig St

8 7 45 6 5 44 4 3 43 2 1 42

16 A B 17 C D 18 E F

178
158

157 137

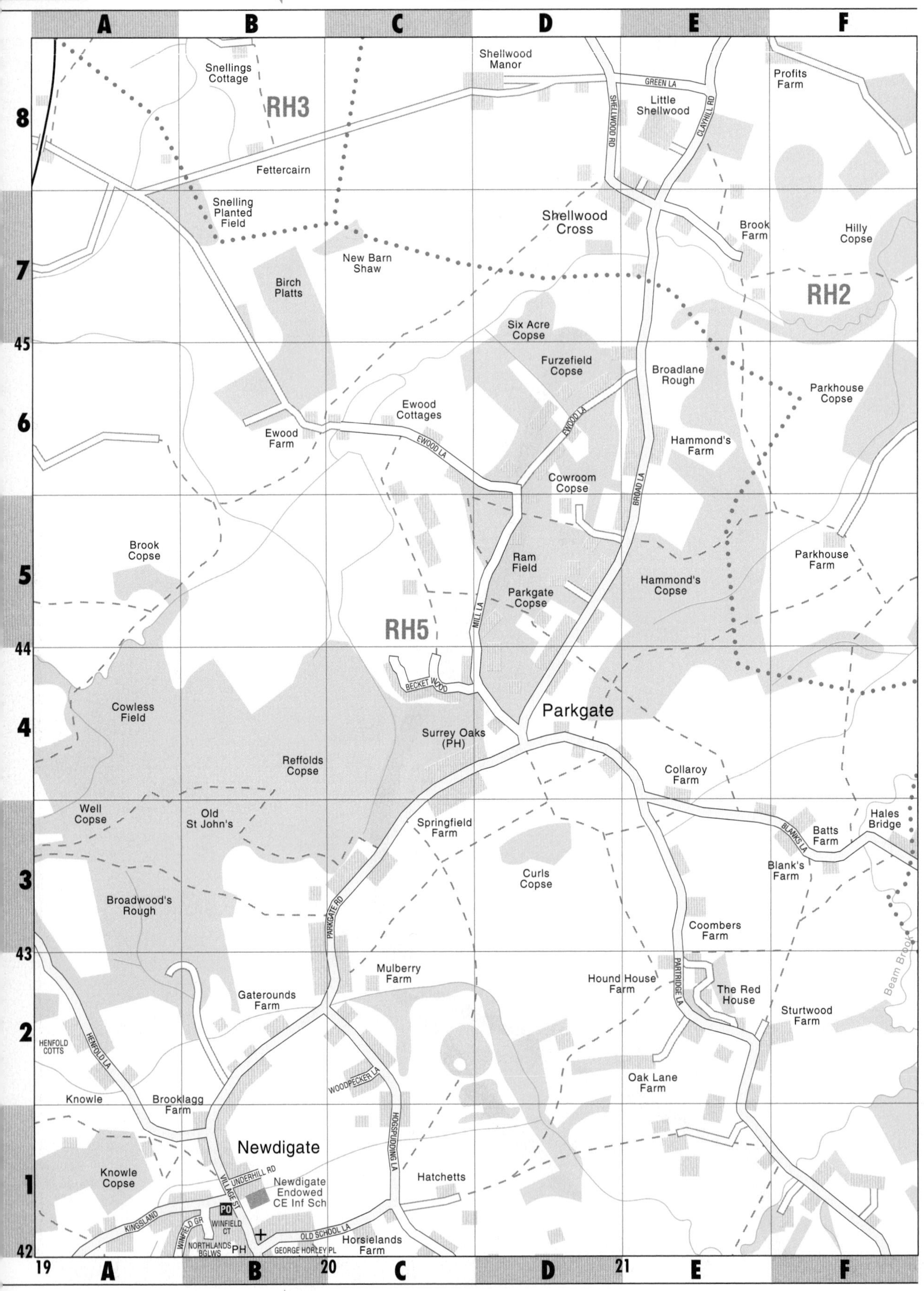

157 179

138
160

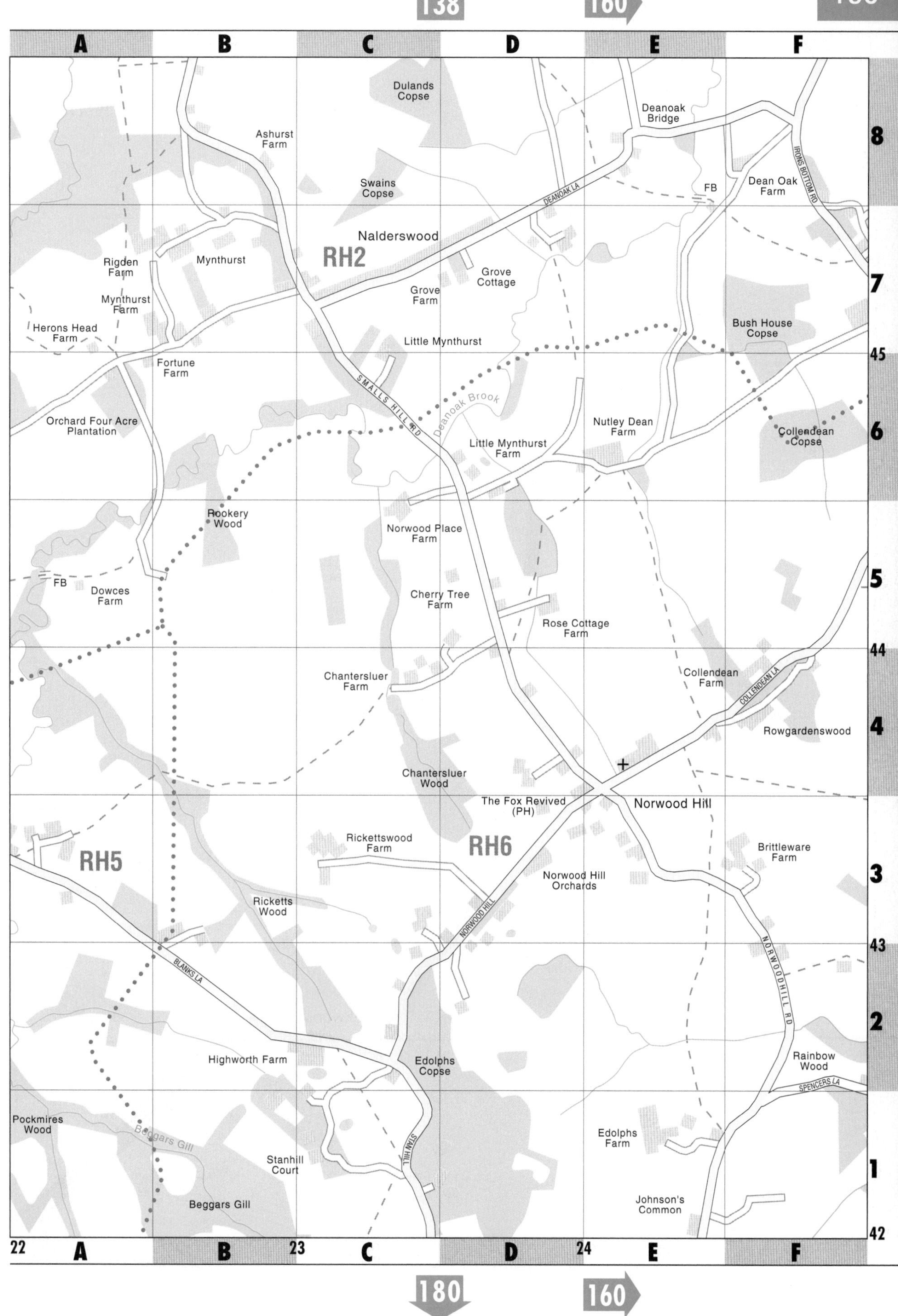

180
160

159
139

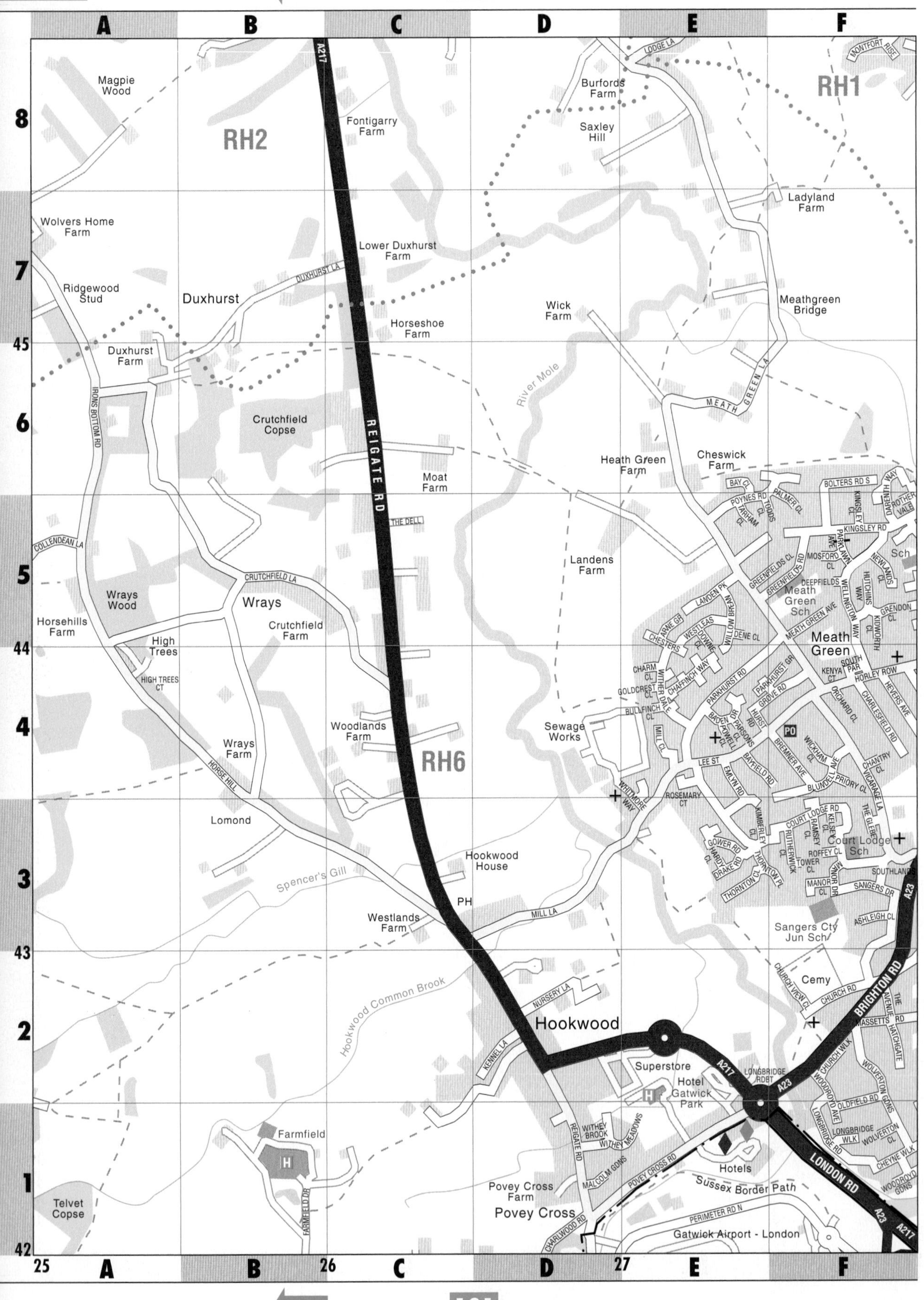

159
181

162

A B C D E F

Horley Lodge La
Salbrook Rd
Redhill Distribution Ctr
Wood Cl
Harwood Pk
A23
Perry Wood
Picketts
The Orchard Bsns Ctr
Job's Farm
Woolborough Farm
Woolborough La
M23
8
Pear Tree Hill
Picketts La
RH1
New House La
Orchard Farm
Astra Bsns Ctr
Beechwood Villas
Empire Villas
Bonehurst Rd
Cross Oak La
Hunters Moon Farm
7
Lake Cottage
Bonehurst Farm
45
Littlelake Farm
Hathersham Farm
6
Bonehurst Bridge
Willow Ct
The Grange
Burstow House
Brookwood House
Longyard House
Haversham House
Skipton Way
Sarel Way
Lake La
Burstow Stream
Hathersham La
Kingsley Rd
Avondale Cl
The Spinney
Bolters Rd
Carlton Ct
Greatlake Farm
Longyards Shaw
Sch
Mallard Cl
Benhams Dr
Benhams Cl
Granary Cl
Kiln La
Bakehouse Rd
1 Fallowfield Way
2 Fairstone Ct
3 Harrowsley Ct
4 Fieldview
5 Woodhayes
6 Rickwood
7 Hayfields
8 Ryelands
9 Whitecroft
10 Brookwood
11 Barleymead
12 Meadowside
5
The Farmhouse (PH)
Chestnut Rd
The Chestnuts
Ladbroke Rd
Waterside
Fern Down
Tanyard Farm
Brook Wood
Yew Tree Cl
Horley Row
Cranbourne
Thatchers Cl
Smithbarn Cl
Collingwood Cl
Langshott
44
Chequers Cl
Cartersmead Cl
Birchwood Cl
Woodcote
The Fieldings
Heritage Lawn
Briars Wood
Hurst
Hazel
Wysemead
Lambyn Croft
Twyner Cl
Chetle
Tanyard Way
Homefield Cl
Greatlake Ct
Wheatfield Way
Honeysuckle Cl
Oakside La
Sewage Works
Chequers Dr
Le May Cl
The Dell
B2036
Grassmere
Harvest Rd
Hedingham
Meridian Gr
Broad Mead
Oakside
Woodlands
Southlands Ave
Herons Wood Ct
Stockfield
Ewelands
Saxley
Copse Cl
4
Lumley Ct
Oakwood Rd
Larksfield
Maize Croft
Raymer Wlk
Langshott Wood
Hevers Ave
Brighton Rd
Yattendon Jun Sch
Cloverfields
Brackenside
Firlands
Langshott La
Broadlands
Middlefield
Copse Rd
Clarence Way
Weatherhill Common
Gatwick Metro Ctr
Heatherlands
Albury Keep
The Meadway
Oaklands
Russet Cl
Acorn Cl
Hilton Ct
Clarence Ct
Horley Cty Inf Sch
Parkview
Parkway
Victoria Cl
Lumley Rd
St Hilda's Cl
Windmill Cl
Langshott
Carlton Tye
Bramley Wlk
Longchamp Cl
Ascot Gd
Sandown Cl
Water View
Weatherhill Cl
Albert Rd
Yattendon Rd
PO
Langshott Cty Inf Sch
Smallfield Rd
3
Queen's Rd
Elizabeth Ct
Station Rd
St Georges Cl
Smallmead
Stonecourt Cl
Harrowsley Green Farm
Kings Rd
Consort Way
High St
Crewdson Rd
Belgravia Ct
Oakwood Sch
Church Rd
Magnolia Ct
Liby
PO
Consort Way E
Station App
Rosemary La
Balcombe Rd
HORLEY
RH6
Wilgers Farm
43
Pine Gdns
Ringley Ave
Victoria Rd
Roslan Ct
Aurum Cl
Silverlea Gdns
Massetts Rd
Hampton Lodge
Russells Cres
The Grove
Grovelands
Fairlawns
Avenue Gdns
Haroldslea Poultry Farm
Peeks Brook La
2
Suffolk Cl
Norfolk Cl
Burt Ct
1 Delta House
2 Delta Bglws
Stafford Rd
Balcombe Gdns
Newstead Hall
Haroldslea
Lincoln Cl
Atkinson Ct
Horley
Stocks Cl
Castle Dr
Newstead Hall
Lechford Rd
Cheyne Wlk
Delta Dr
Upfield
The Drive
Primrose Ave
Hyperion Wlk
Limes Ave
Haroldslea Dr
Haroldslea House
Michael Cres
Fairfield Ave
Haroldslea Cl
Burstow Stream
Crescent Way
Upfield Cl
Bayhorn La
1
Garwick Stream
Riverside
The Ridgeway
Crescent
The Coronet
The Roughs
Bayhorne La
The Crescent
A217
Spiers Way
The Close
Warltersville Way
B2036
M23
42
28 A B 29 C D 30 E F

182

162

141

A B C D E F

8
7
45
6
5
44
4
3
43
2
1
42

M23

Greenmeads Farm
DAYSEYS HILL
Wasp Green Farm
BRICKFIELD RD
WASP GREEN LA
OUTWOOD LA
The Bell Inn
Gay House
Windmill
GAYHOUSE LA
BELLWETHER LA
The Castle (PH)
MILLERS COPSE
MILLER'S LA
Wasp Green
Brightleigh Farm
RH1
Marl House
Copsley Court
Hornecourt Wood
HORNECOURT HILL
LITTLE COLLINS
Outwood
Hornecourt Manor Farm
Rookery Farm
Drivers Green
ROOKERY HILL
Old Hall Farm
Wilmot's Farm
Horne Grange
SCOTT'S HILL
WILMOT'S LA
Church Farm
NORMAN'S RD
CHURCH RD
Horne
Horne House Farm
Burstow Lodge Farm
Burstow Lodge
Hollesley Farm
Little Abbots Farm
CROYDONBARN LA
Weatherhill
CHAPEL RD
COGMAN'S LA
Short Acre Farm
RH6
WEATHERHILL COTTS
HAYES WLK
CHARLOTTE GR
THE CRAVENS
HATHERSHAM CL
RALEIGH DR
CAREY'S WOOD
CAREY'S COPSE
THE WOODLANDS
TUDOR CL
CHURCHILL RD
FIELD WLK
THISTLE WAY
GORSE DR
CLOVER WAY
HEATHER WLK
SMALLFIELD RD
COOPER CL 1
LARKFIELD CL 2
GRASSLANDS 3
WEATHERHILL RD
GRANGEWAY
DYER'S FIELD
WOODSIDE CRES
GRANGE END
NEW RD
ORCHARD RD
MEADOW VIEW
The Plough (PH)
Smallfield Place
ALBERTA DR
VANCOUVER CT
QUEBEC CL
TORONTO DR
ONTARIO CL
WHEELERS LA
Burstow Prim Sch
PO
KINGS MEAD
PLOUGH RD
Rough Beech
Bysshe Court Farm
BRIDGEHAM WAY
Smallfield
PERRYLANDS LA
Green Farm
Rough Beech Farm
BROADBRIDGE LA
Triddles Farm
CHITHURST LA
Bridgeham Grange
RANELAGH COTTS
REDEHALL RD
Redehall Prep Sch
DOWLANDS LA
Broadmead Farm
Saconnex Farm
GEARY CL
Laburnum Court (Caravan Park)
Broadbridge Cottages
Broadbridge Farm
THE HOMESTEAD
Homestead Farm
Dowlands Wood
Roughbeech Wood
Chithurst Farm
LONE OAK
PARK RD
CROSS LA

31 A B 32 C D 33 E F

161

183

142
164

184
164

163
143

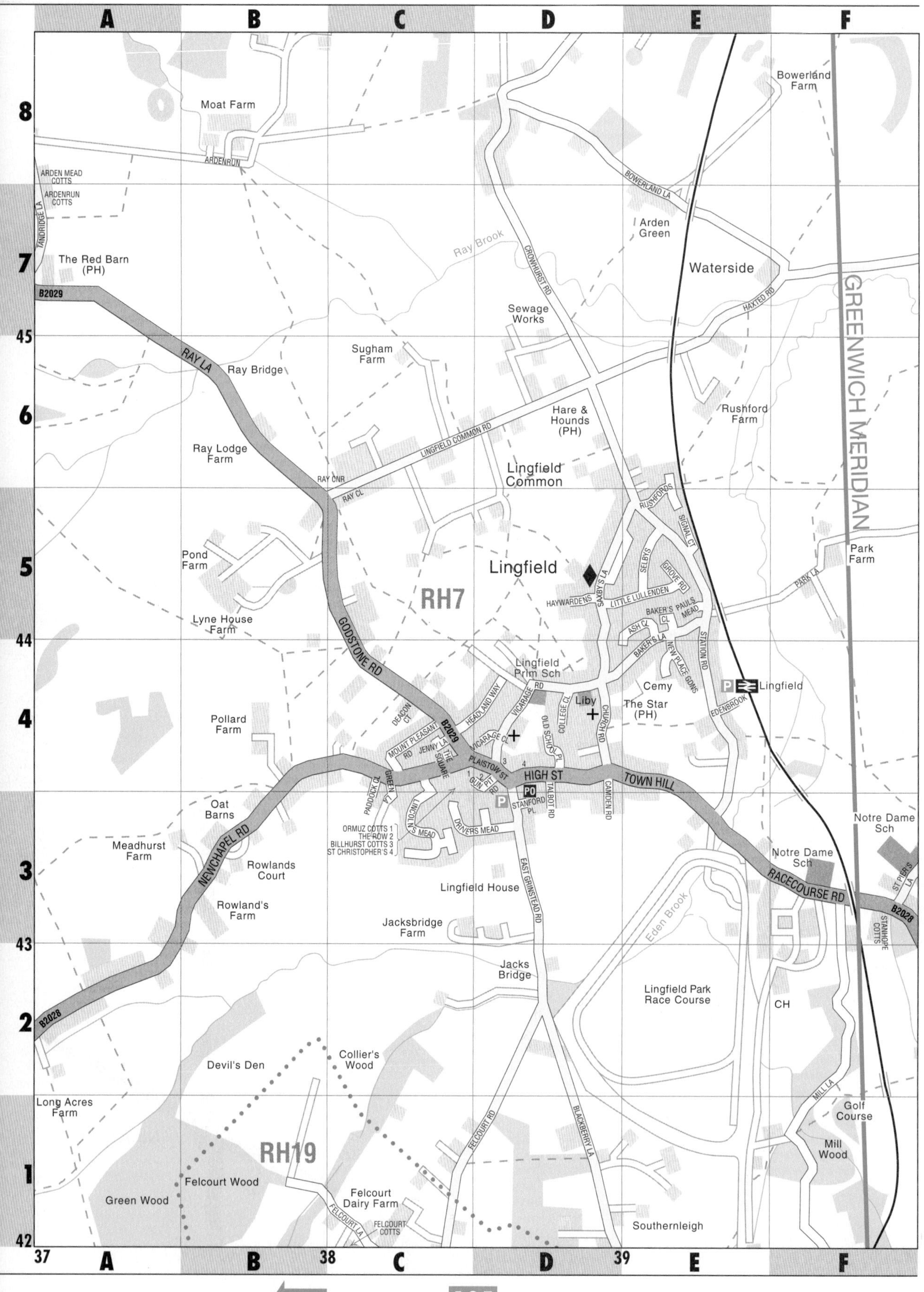

163
185

144

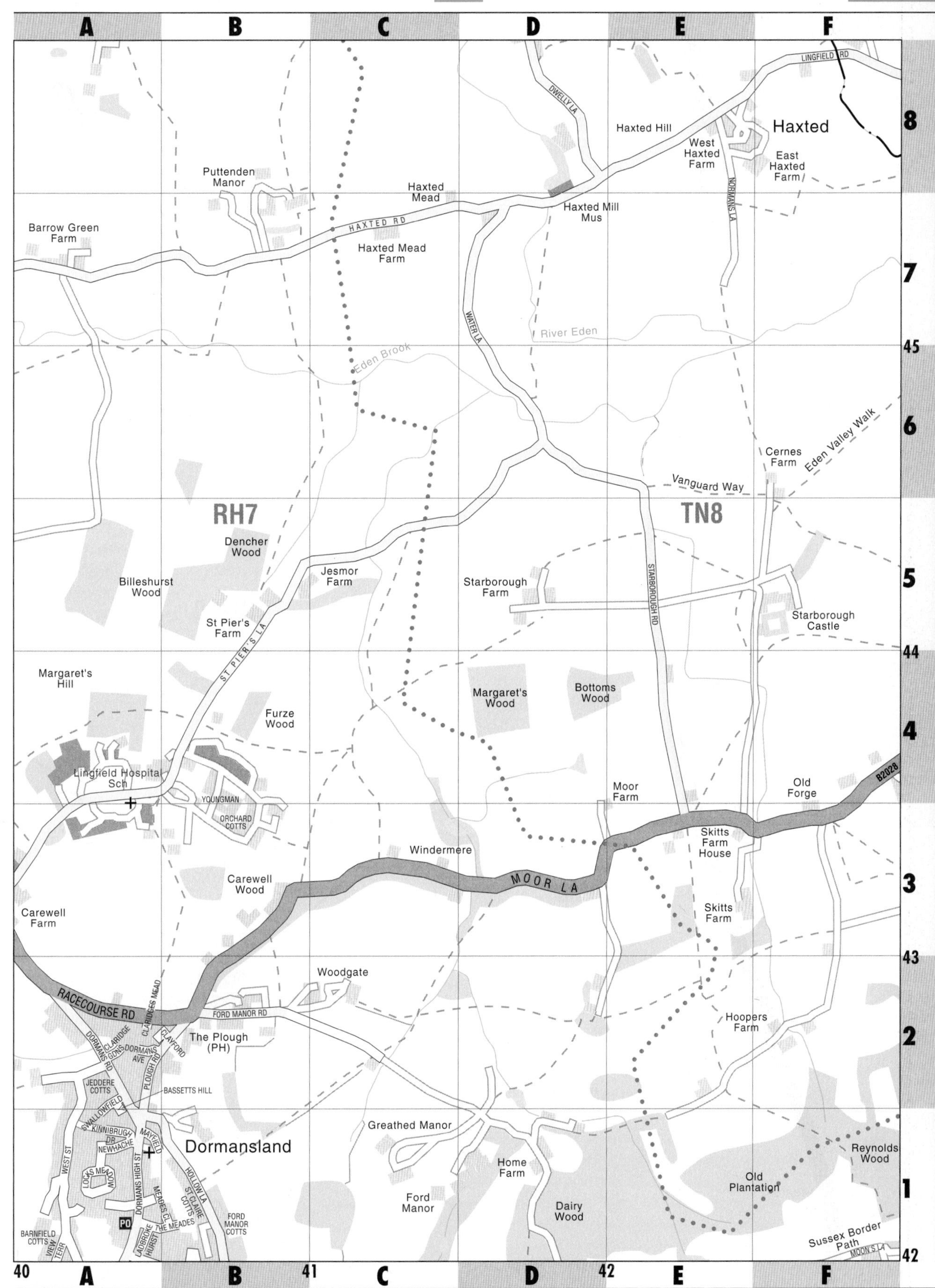
A
B
C
D
E
F
8
7
6
5
4
3
2
1
45
44
43
42
40
41
Haxted
Haxted Hill
West Haxted Farm
East Haxted Farm
LINGFIELD RD
DWELLY LA
NORMANS LA
Puttenden Manor
Haxted Mead
Haxted Mill Mus
HAXTED RD
Barrow Green Farm
Haxted Mead Farm
WATER LA
River Eden
Eden Brook
Cernes Farm
Eden Valley Walk
Vanguard Way
RH7
TN8
Dencher Wood
Billeshurst Wood
Jesmor Farm
Starborough Farm
STARBOROUGH RD
Starborough Castle
St Pier's Farm
ST PIER'S LA
Margaret's Hill
Margaret's Wood
Bottoms Wood
Furze Wood
Lingfield Hospital Sch
YOUNGMAN
ORCHARD COTTS
Moor Farm
Old Forge
B2028
Skitts Farm House
Windermere
MOOR LA
Carewell Wood
Carewell Farm
Skitts Farm
Woodgate
RACECOURSE RD
CLARIDGES MEAD
FORD MANOR RD
Hoopers Farm
The Plough (PH)
DORMANS RD
CLARIDGE GDNS
DORMANS AVE
PLOUGH RD
CLAYFORD
JEDDERE COTTS
BASSETTS HILL
SWALLOWFIELD
KINNIBRUGH DR
NEWHACHE
MAYFIELD
Dormansland
Greathed Manor
Home Farm
Reynolds Wood
Old Plantation
WEST ST
LOCKS MEADOW
DORMANS HIGH ST
MEADES CL
ST CLAIRE COTTS
HOLLOW LA
Ford Manor
Dairy Wood
FORD MANOR COTTS
PO
LADBROKE HURST
THE MEADES
BARNFIELD COTTS
VIEW TERR
Sussex Border Path
MOON'S LA

186

145

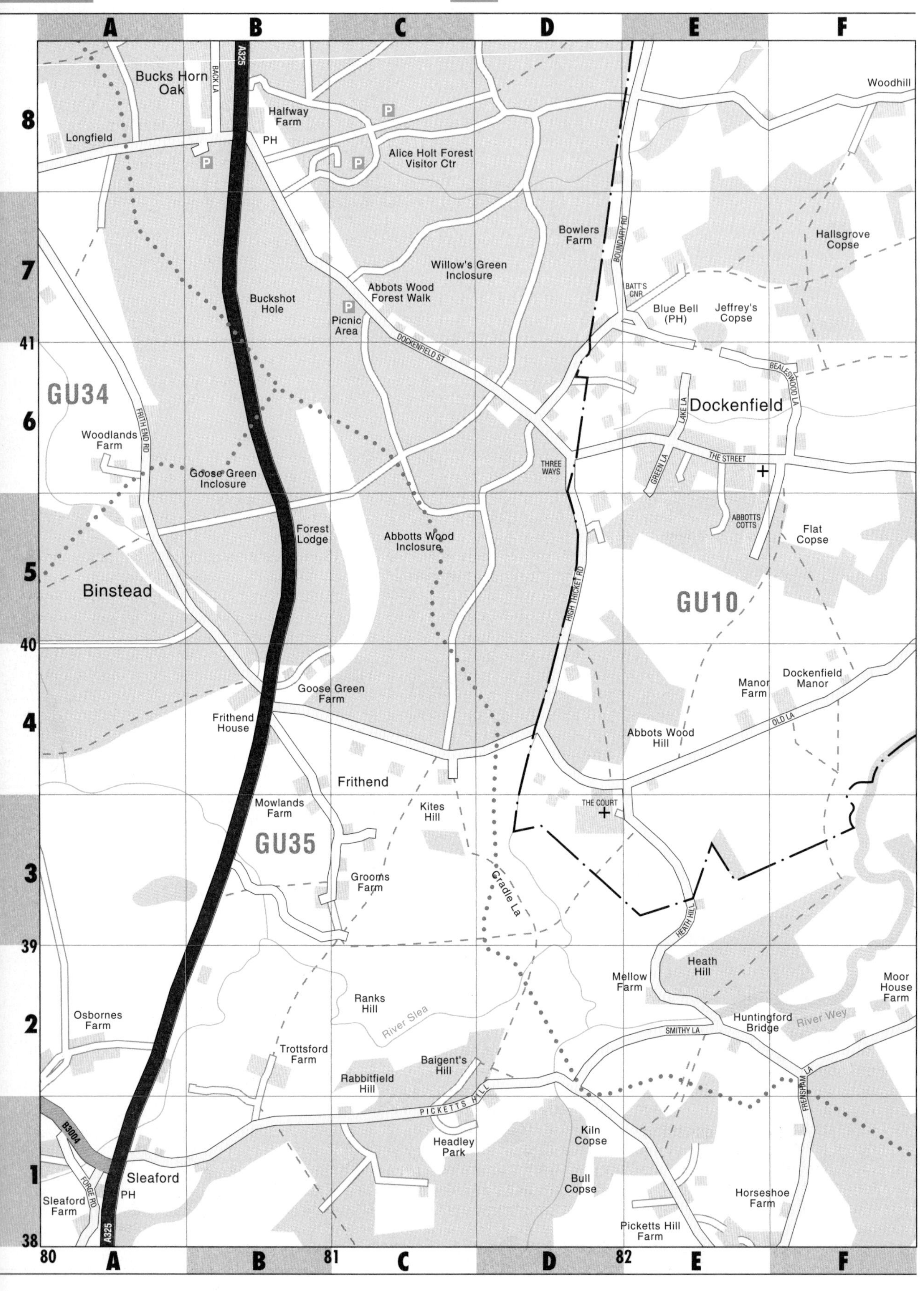
A
B
C
D
E
F
8
7
41
6
5
40
4
3
39
2
1
38
80
81
82
Bucks Horn Oak
BACK LA
A325
Longfield
Halfway Farm
PH
Alice Holt Forest Visitor Ctr
Woodhill
Bowlers Farm
BOUNDARY RD
Hallsgrove Copse
Willow's Green Inclosure
Abbots Wood Forest Walk
Buckshot Hole
Picnic Area
BATT'S CNR
Blue Bell (PH)
Jeffrey's Copse
DOCKENFIELD ST
BEALESWOOD LA
GU34
FRITH END RD
LAKE LA
Dockenfield
Woodlands Farm
Goose Green Inclosure
THREE WAYS
GREEN LA
THE STREET
ABBOTTS COTTS
Forest Lodge
Abbotts Wood Inclosure
Flat Copse
Binstead
HIGH THICKET RD
GU10
Goose Green Farm
Manor Farm
Dockenfield Manor
Frithend House
Abbots Wood Hill
OLD LA
Frithend
Mowlands Farm
Kites Hill
THE COURT
GU35
Grooms Farm
Gradle La
HEATH HILL
Heath Hill
Mellow Farm
Moor House Farm
Ranks Hill
Osbornes Farm
River Slea
Huntingford Bridge
SMITHY LA
River Wey
Trottsford Farm
Baigent's Hill
Rabbitfield Hill
FRENSHAM LA
PICKETTS HILL
B3004
Headley Park
Kiln Copse
Sleaford
FORGE RD
PH
Bull Copse
Sleaford Farm
Horseshoe Farm
Picketts Hill Farm

146
168

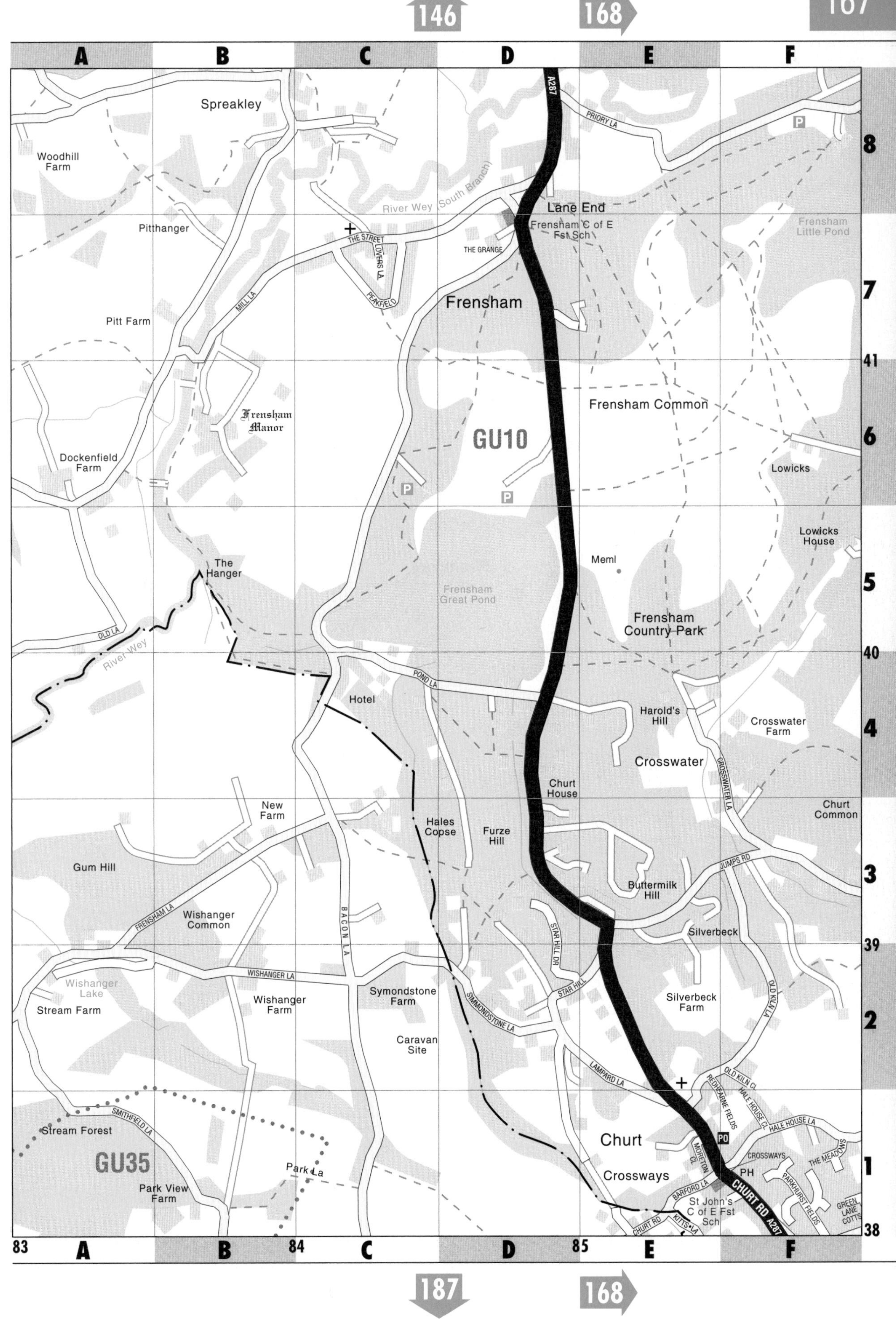

187
168

167
147

167
188

148
170

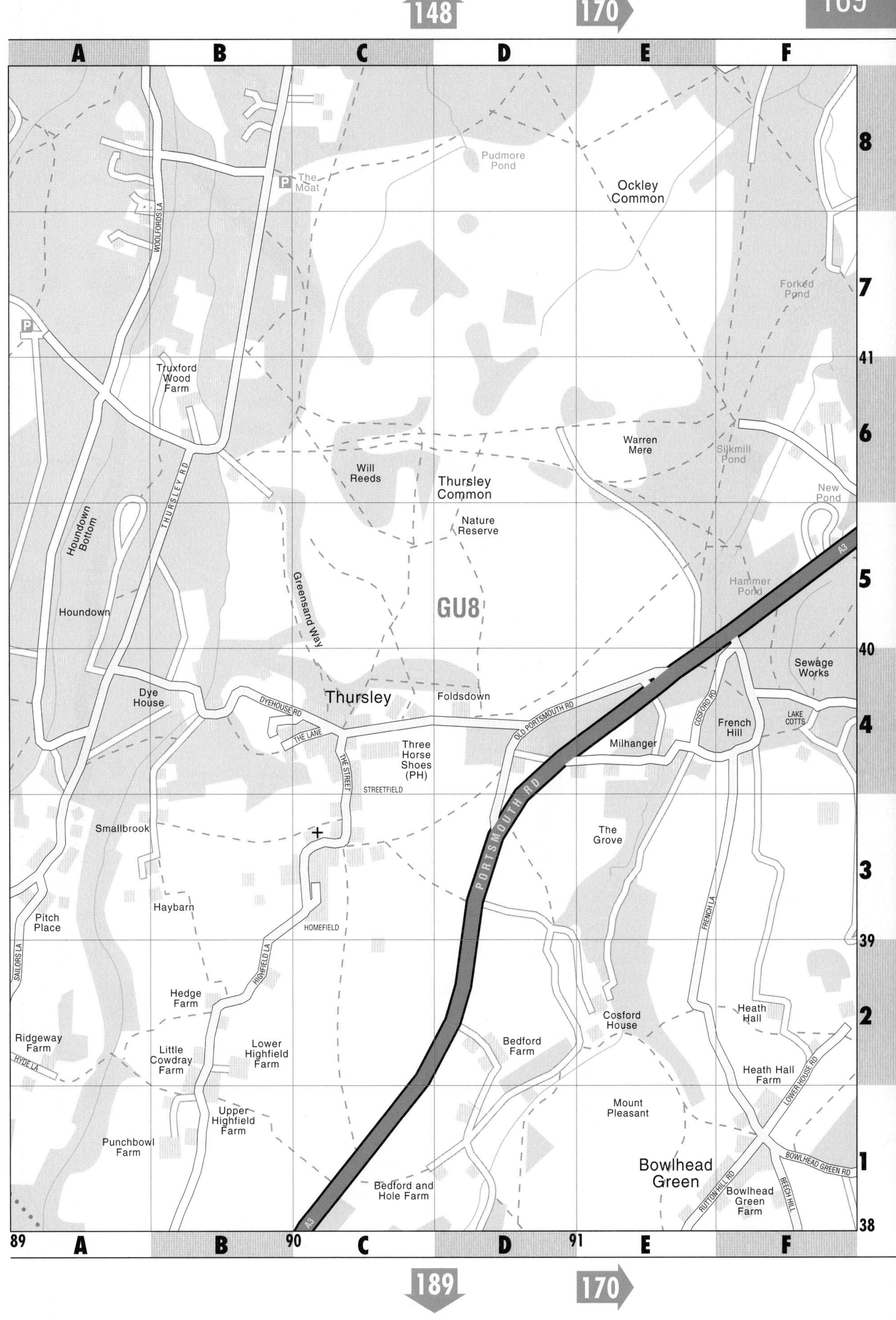
A
B
C
D
E
F
8
7
41
6
5
40
4
3
39
2
1
38
89
90
91
Pudmore Pond
The Moat
Ockley Common
WOOLFORDS LA
Forked Pond
Truxford Wood Farm
Warren Mere
Silkmill Pond
Will Reeds
Thursley Common
New Pond
THURSLEY RD
Houndown Bottom
Nature Reserve
A3
Greensand Way
Hammer Pond
GU8
Houndown
Sewage Works
Dye House
DYEHOUSE RD
Thursley
Foldsdown
OLD PORTSMOUTH RD
COSFORD RD
French Hill
LAKE COTTS
THE LANE
THE STREET
Three Horse Shoes (PH)
Milhanger
STREETFIELD
PORTSMOUTH RD
Smallbrook
The Grove
Haybarn
Pitch Place
HOMEFIELD
FRENCH LA
SAILORS LA
HIGHFIELD LA
Hedge Farm
Cosford House
Heath Hall
Ridgeway Farm
Little Cowdray Farm
Lower Highfield Farm
Bedford Farm
HYDE LA
Heath Hall Farm
LOWER HOUSE RD
Upper Highfield Farm
Mount Pleasant
Punchbowl Farm
Bowlhead Green
BOWLHEAD GREEN RD
RUTTON HILL RD
BEECH HILL
Bowlhead Green Farm
Bedford and Hole Farm

189
170

169
149

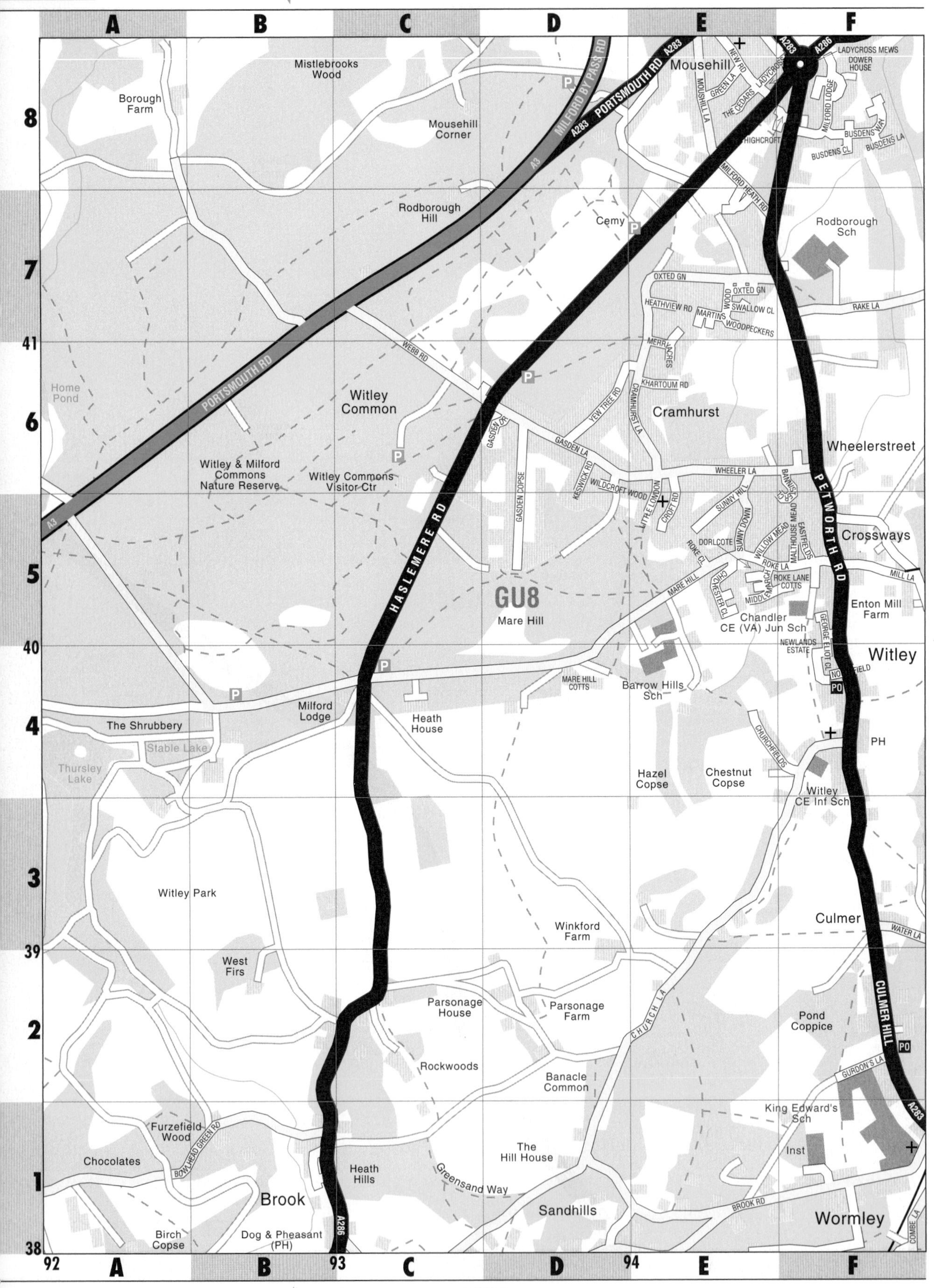

169
190

150
172

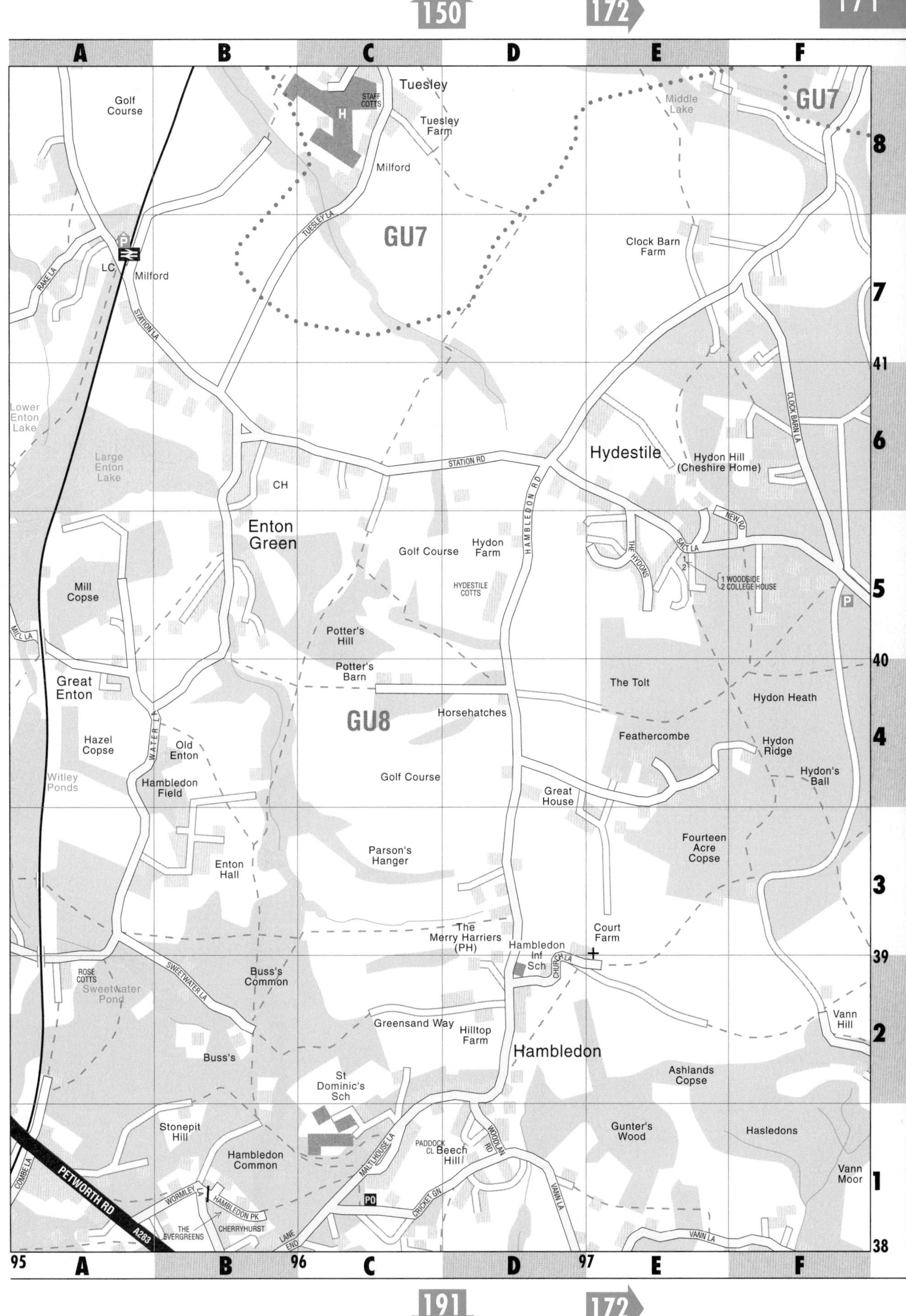

191
172

171
151

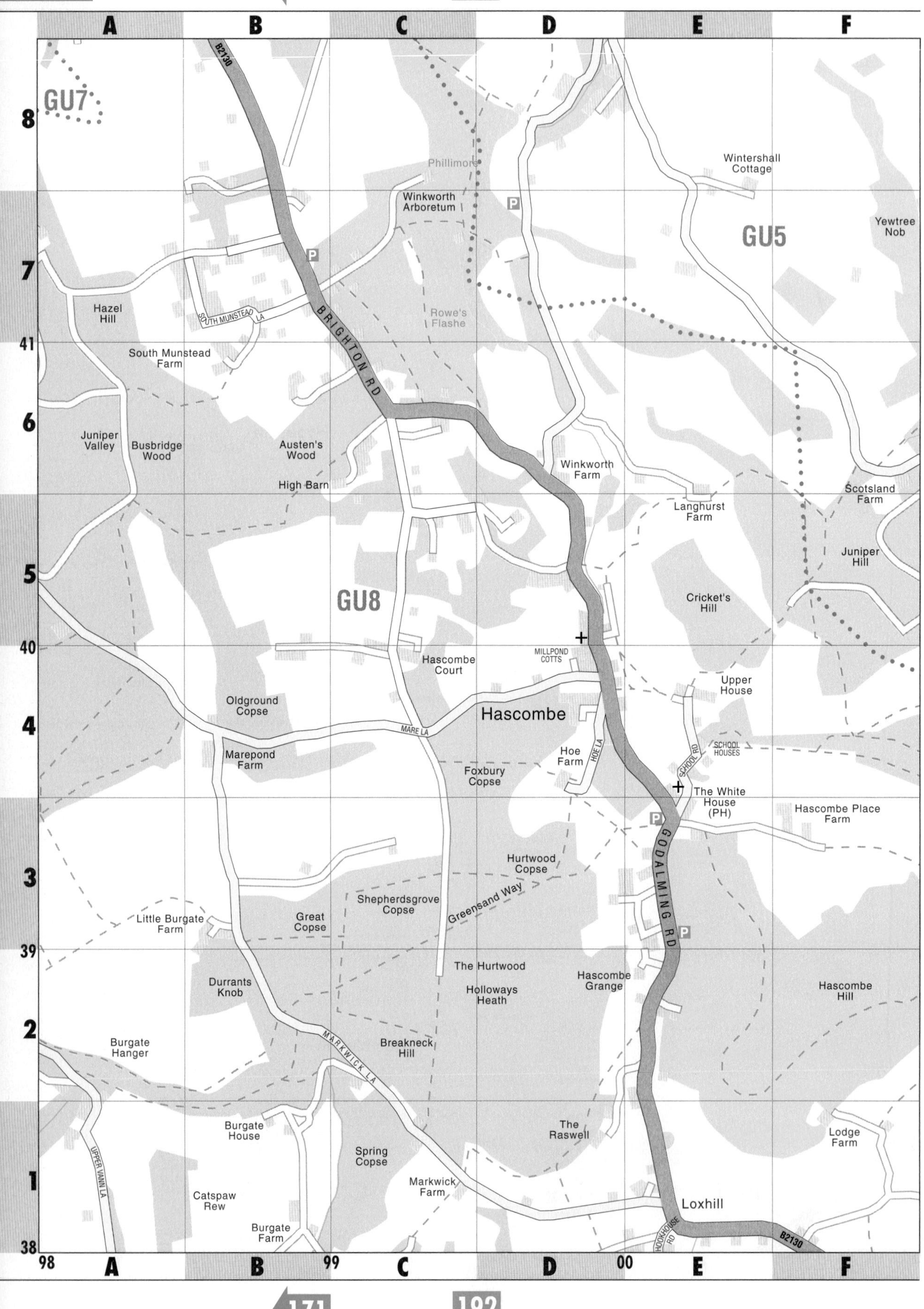

171
192

A B C D E F

Ridgebridge Hill
Gatestreet Farm
A281
Grafham
Run Common
Greensand Way
Grafham Grange
Honeymead Farm
Wey & Arun Junction Canal (disused)
8
East Whipley Farm
EAST WHIPLEY LA
Wintershall
GATE ST
Pinks Hill Farm House
Nurseries
7
Scrubbins Pond
Whipley Manor
Wey-South Path
41
Selhurst Common
GU5
Downs Link
Bridgeham Farm
Great Brook
Goose Green Farm
6
Whipley Manor Farm
Palmers Cross
Scotsland Brook
Tilsey Farm
5
HORSHAM RD
Brooklands Farm
40
PEPPERBOX LA
New Barn
4
Bottle Cottage
Nore Brook
The Leathern Bottle (PH)
Nore Hanger
Rydinghurst Farm
Smithbrook Manor
Rye Farm
Rydinghurst
3
Creek Copse
P
Smithbrook Kilns
B2130
39
ELMBRIDGE RD
B2130
ABBEY CL
FOREST WLK
GU8
Nore
Hunterwood Farm
FURNISS CT
ESSEX DR
CL
LOXFORD
2
Barrihurst
Coney Burroughs
B2130
BARRIHURST LA
CLARK PL
FAIRLOP WLK
DAY CT
JACKSON CL
GU6
Nanhurst
STOVOLDS HILL
RODING CL
ILFORD CT
Fir Field Copse
Lower Barrihurst Farm
Painshill Farm
1
Bayhurst Copse
Grubbins Farm
DUNSFOLD RD
B2130
A281
38

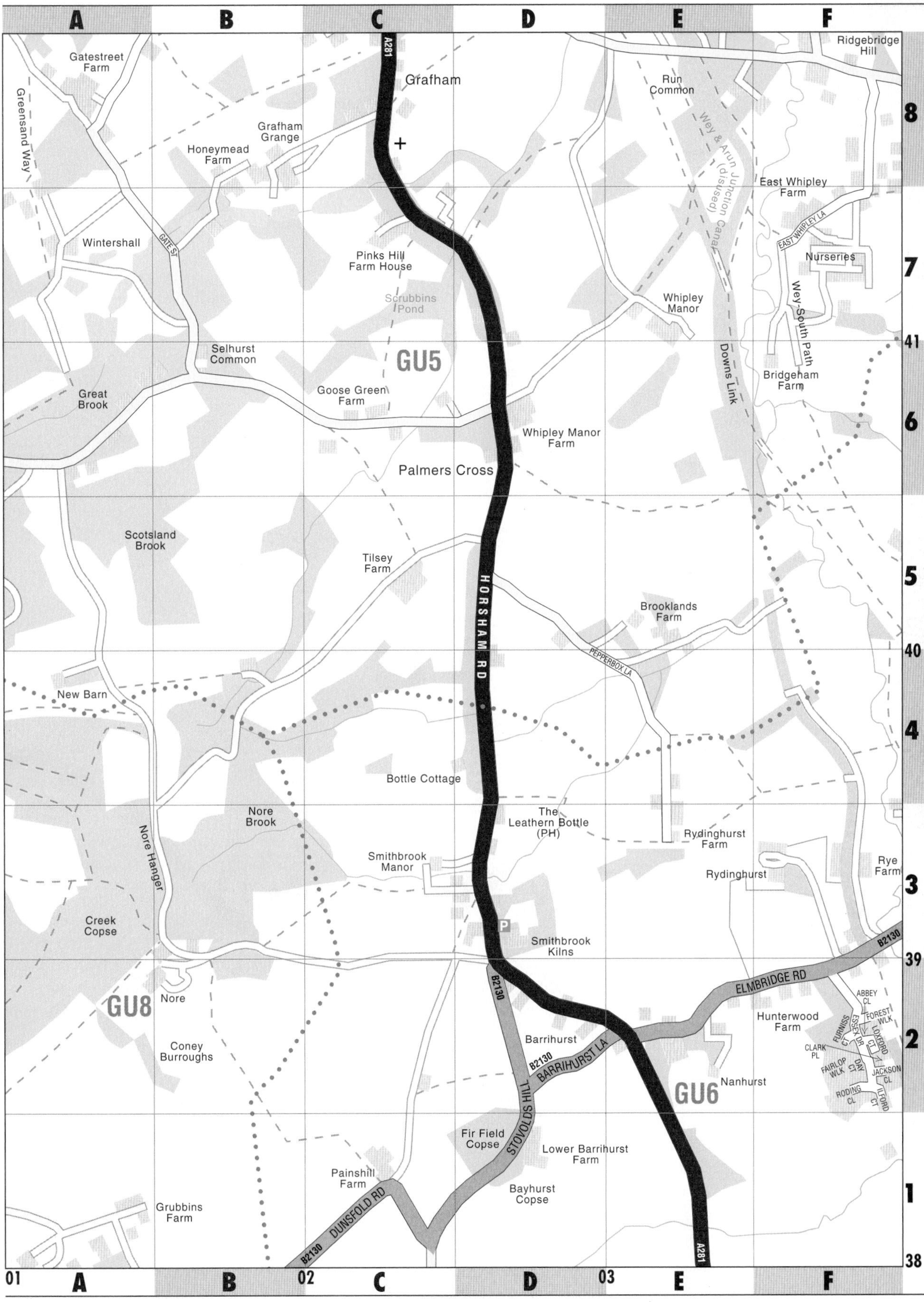

01 A B 02 C D 03 E F

173
153

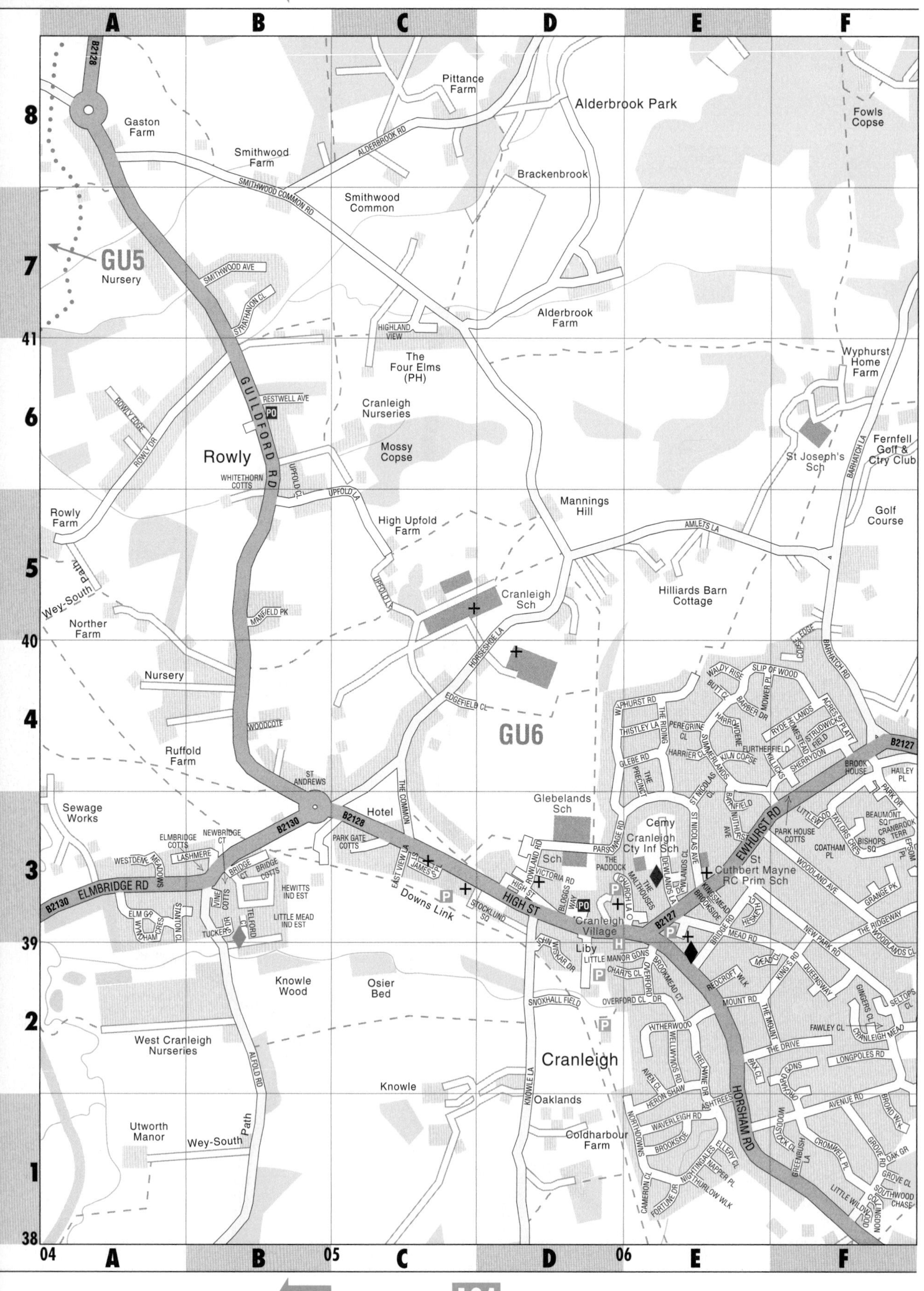

173
194

154
176

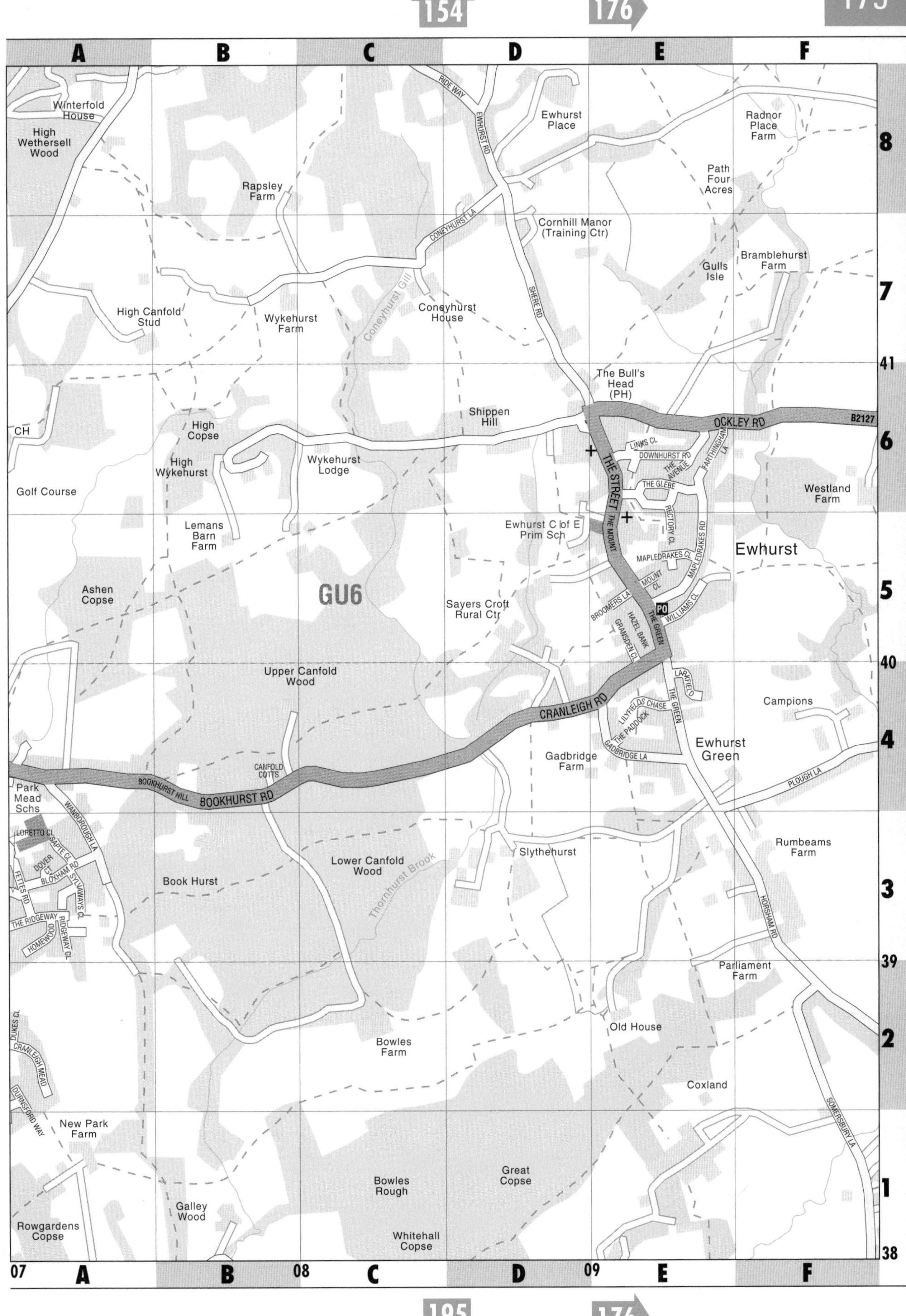

195
176

175
155

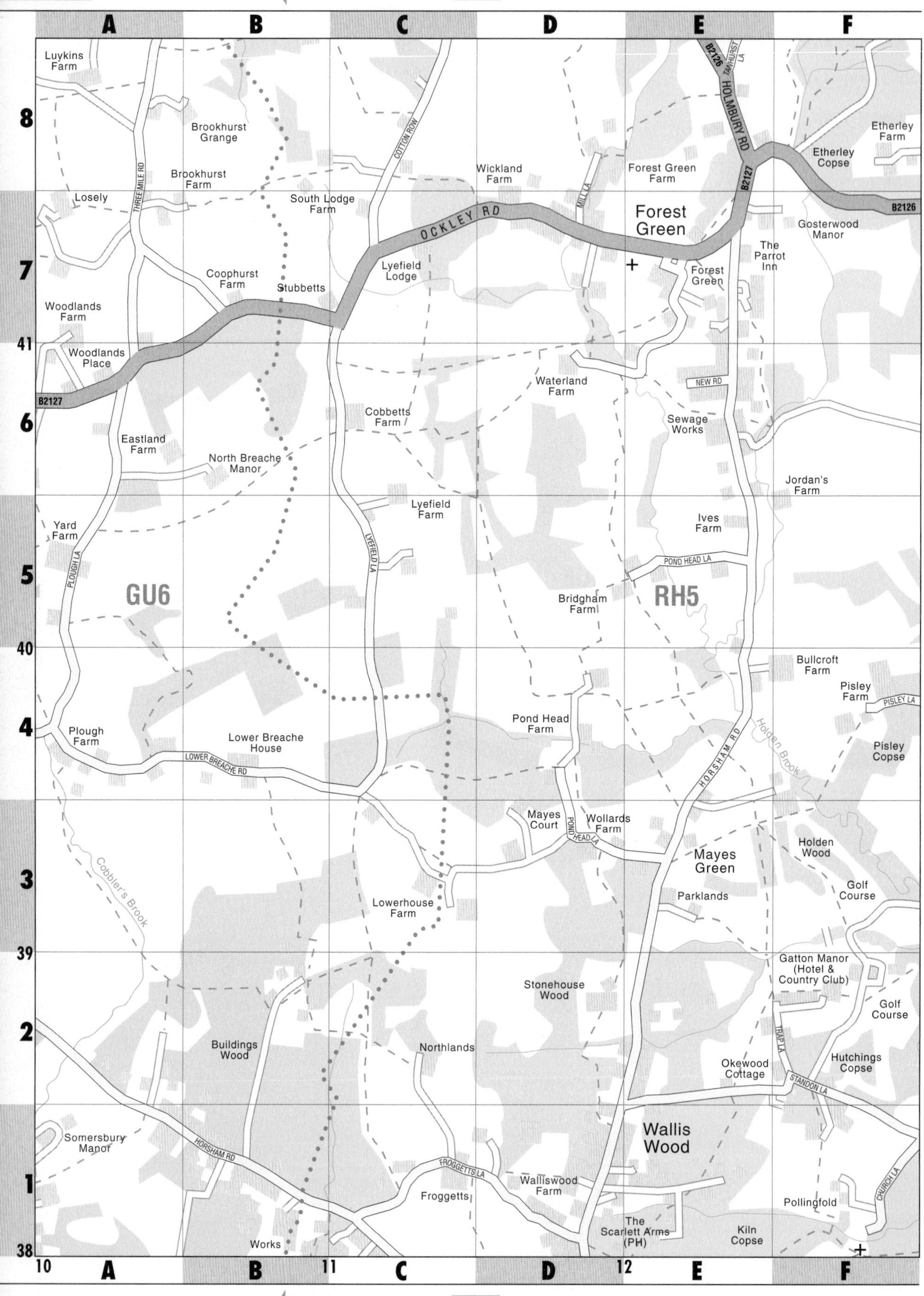

175
196

156
178

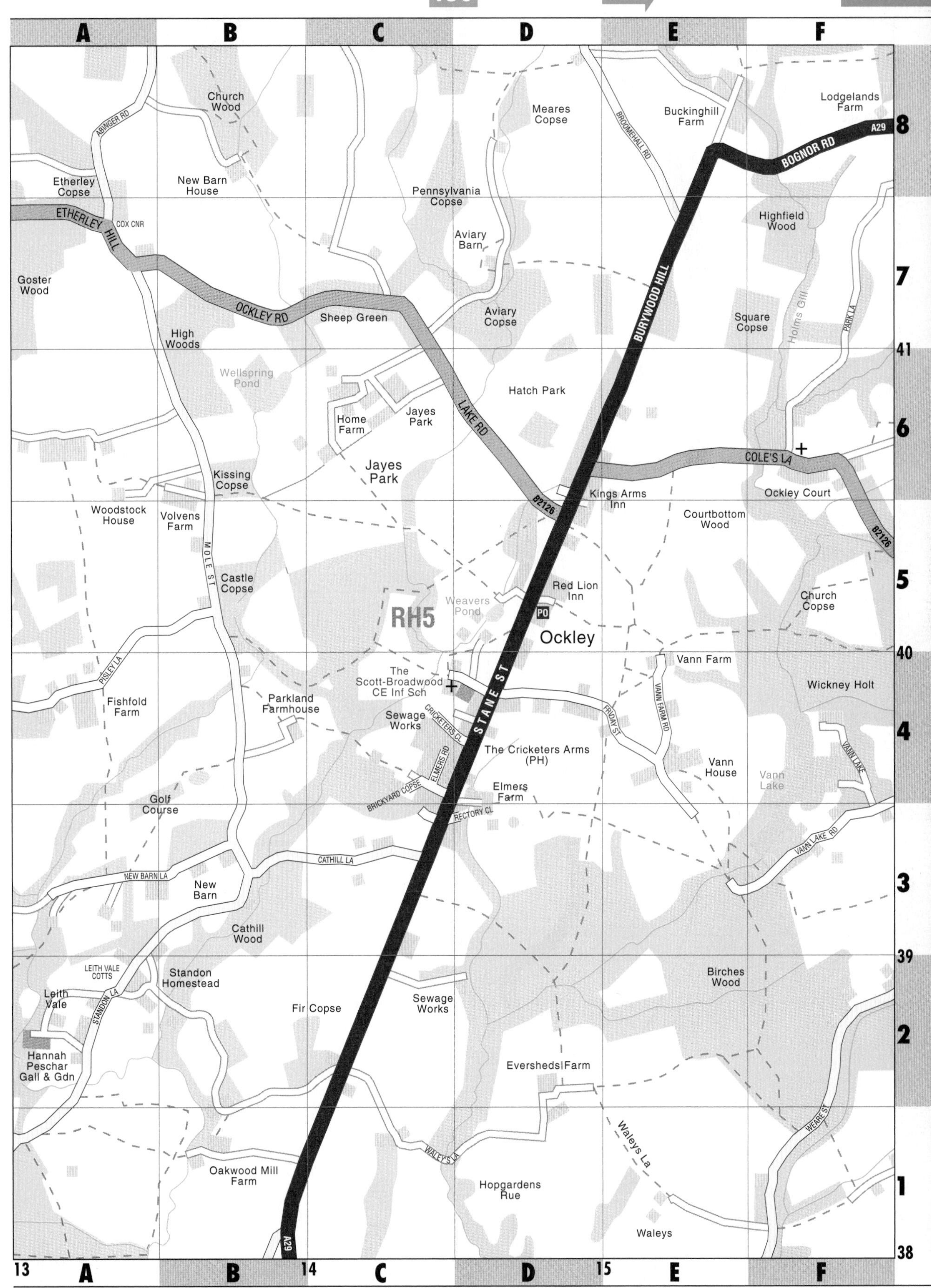

197
178

177
157

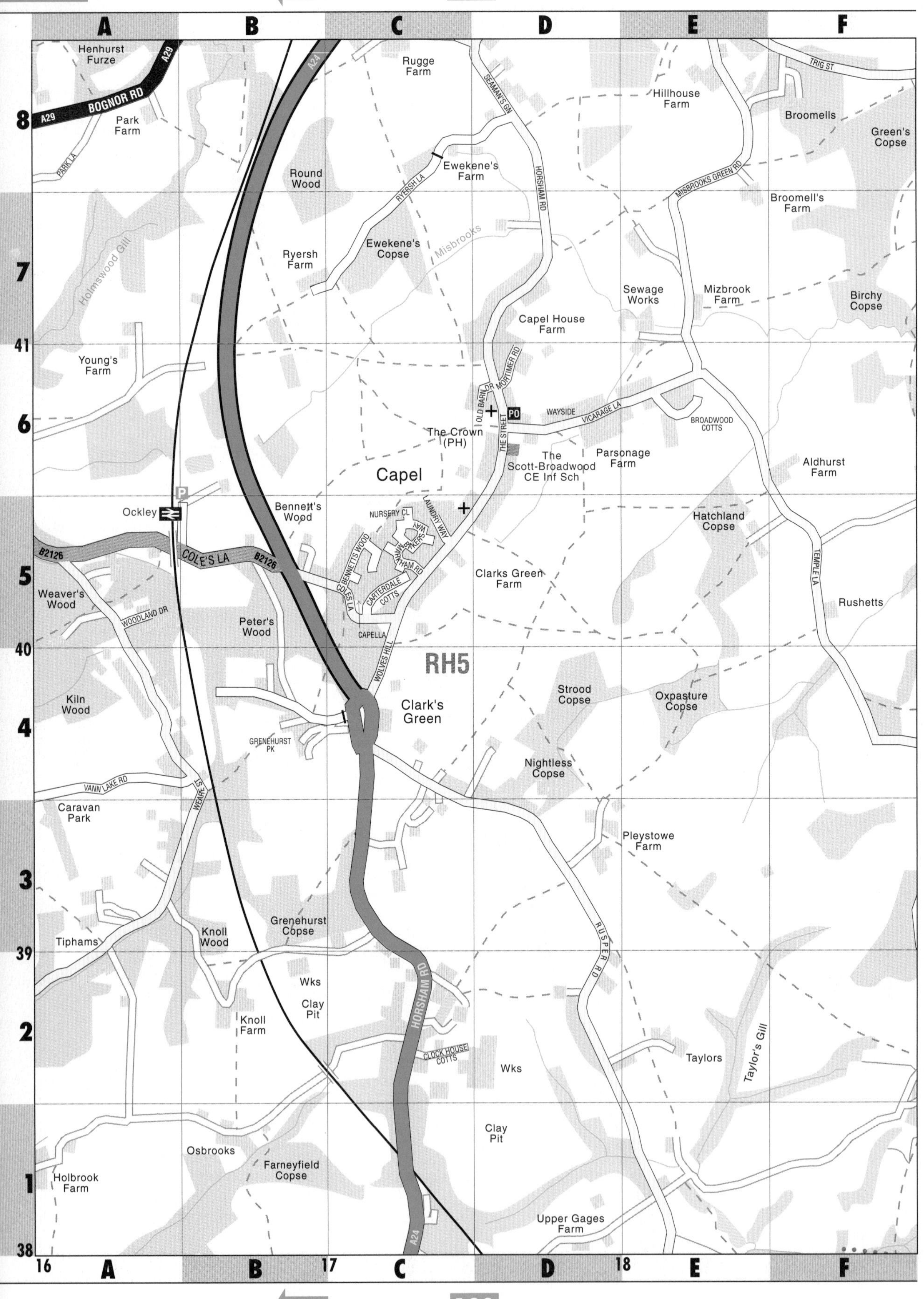

177
198

158
180

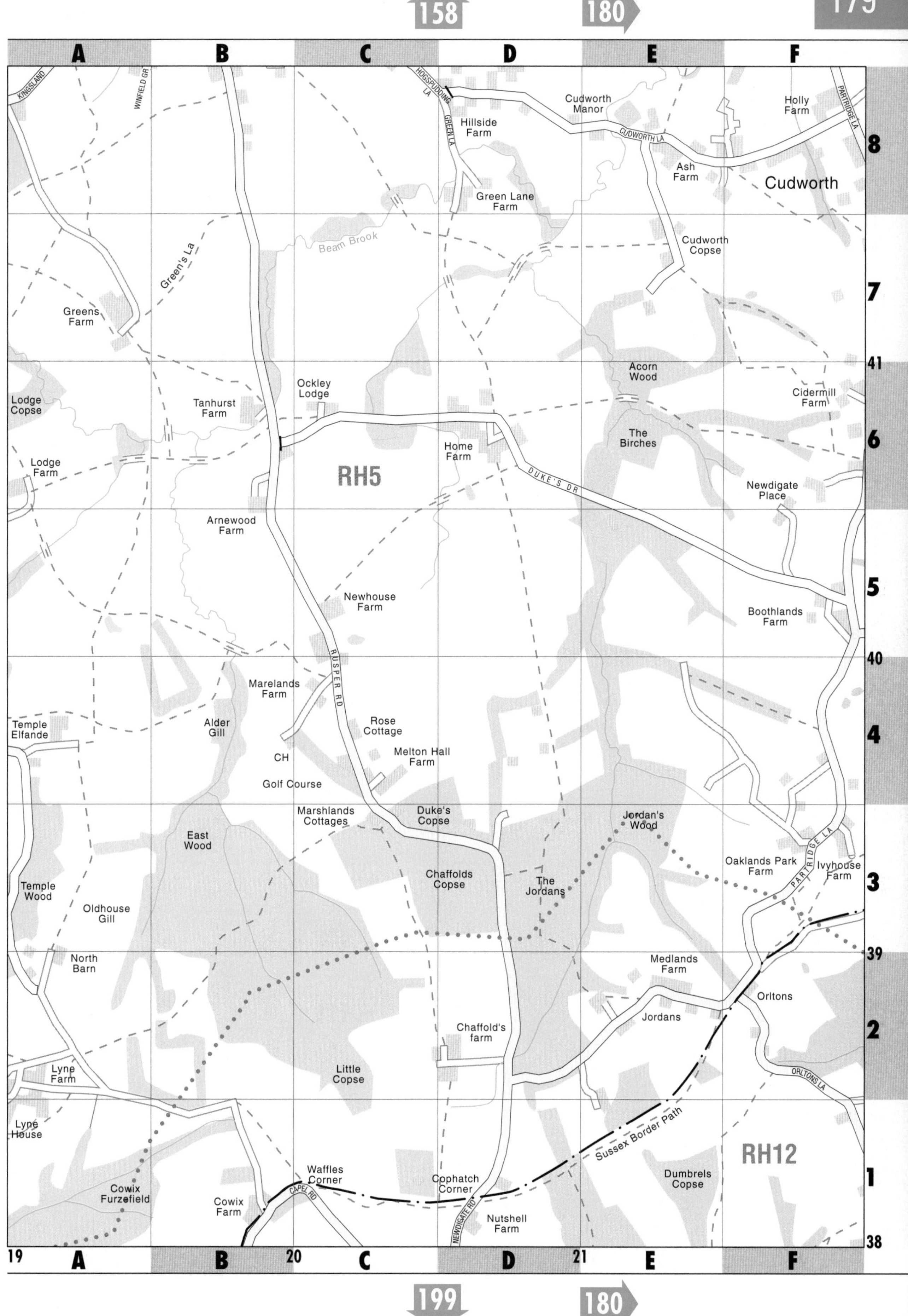

199
180

179
159

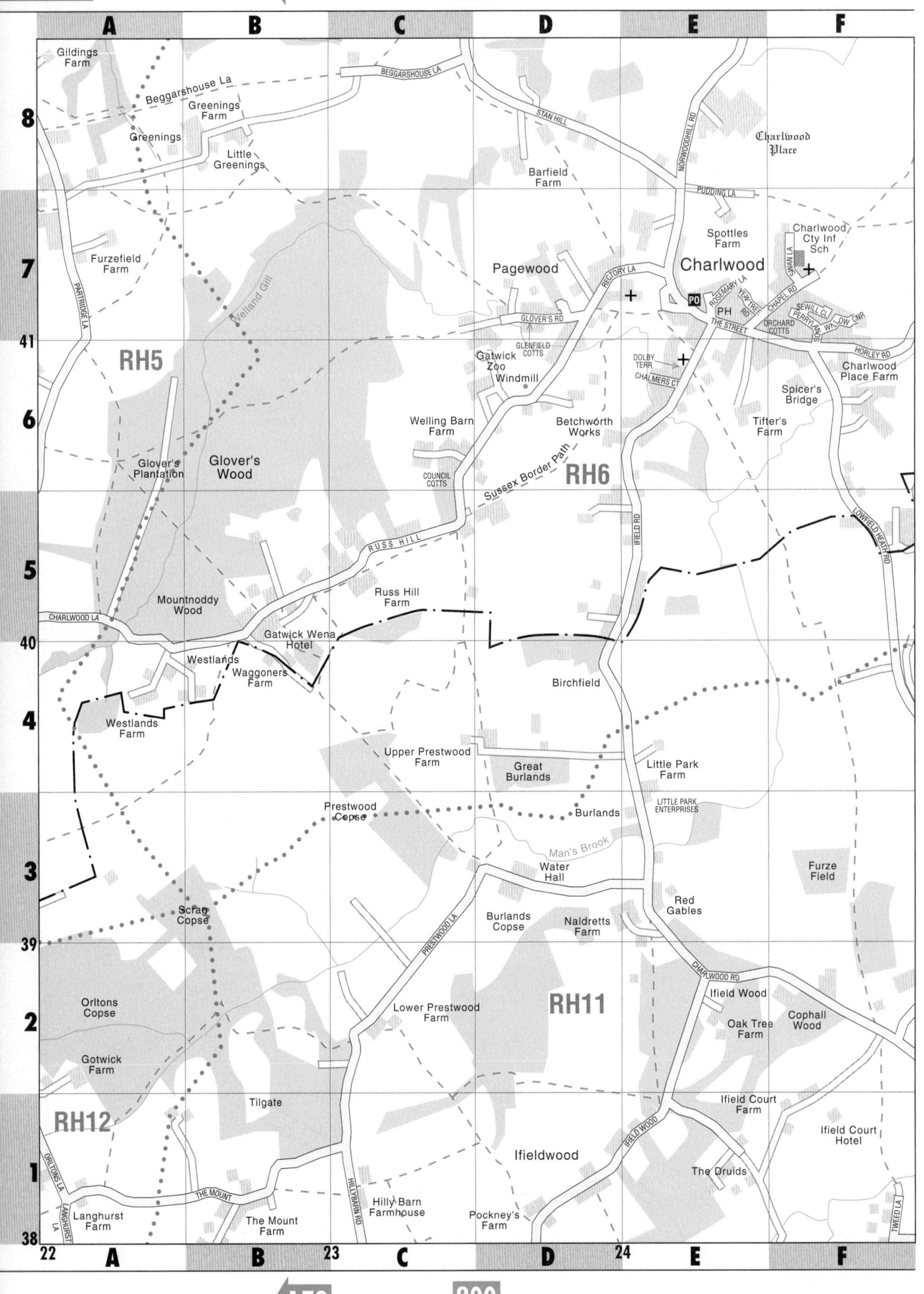

179
200

160
182

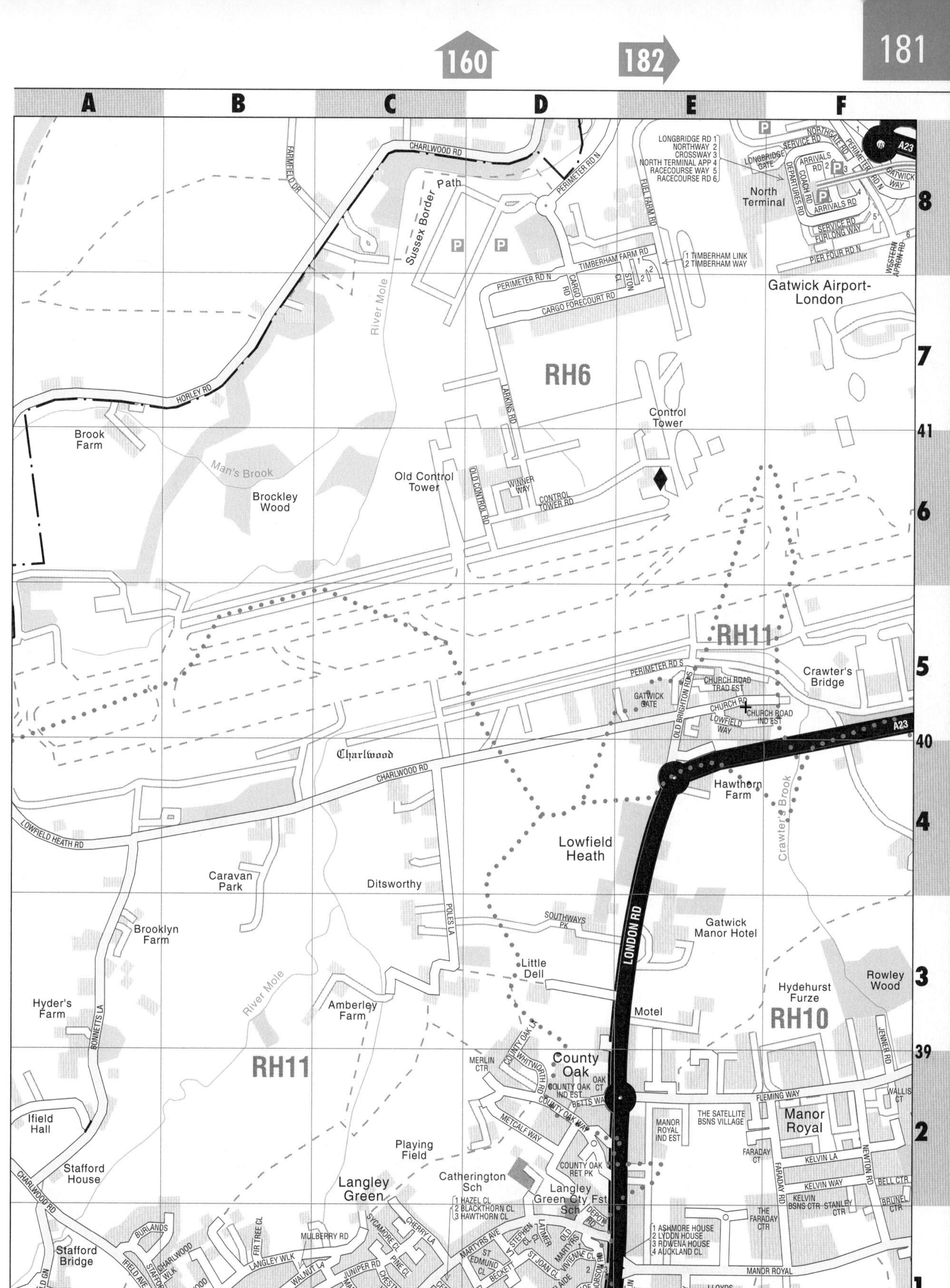

201
182

181
161

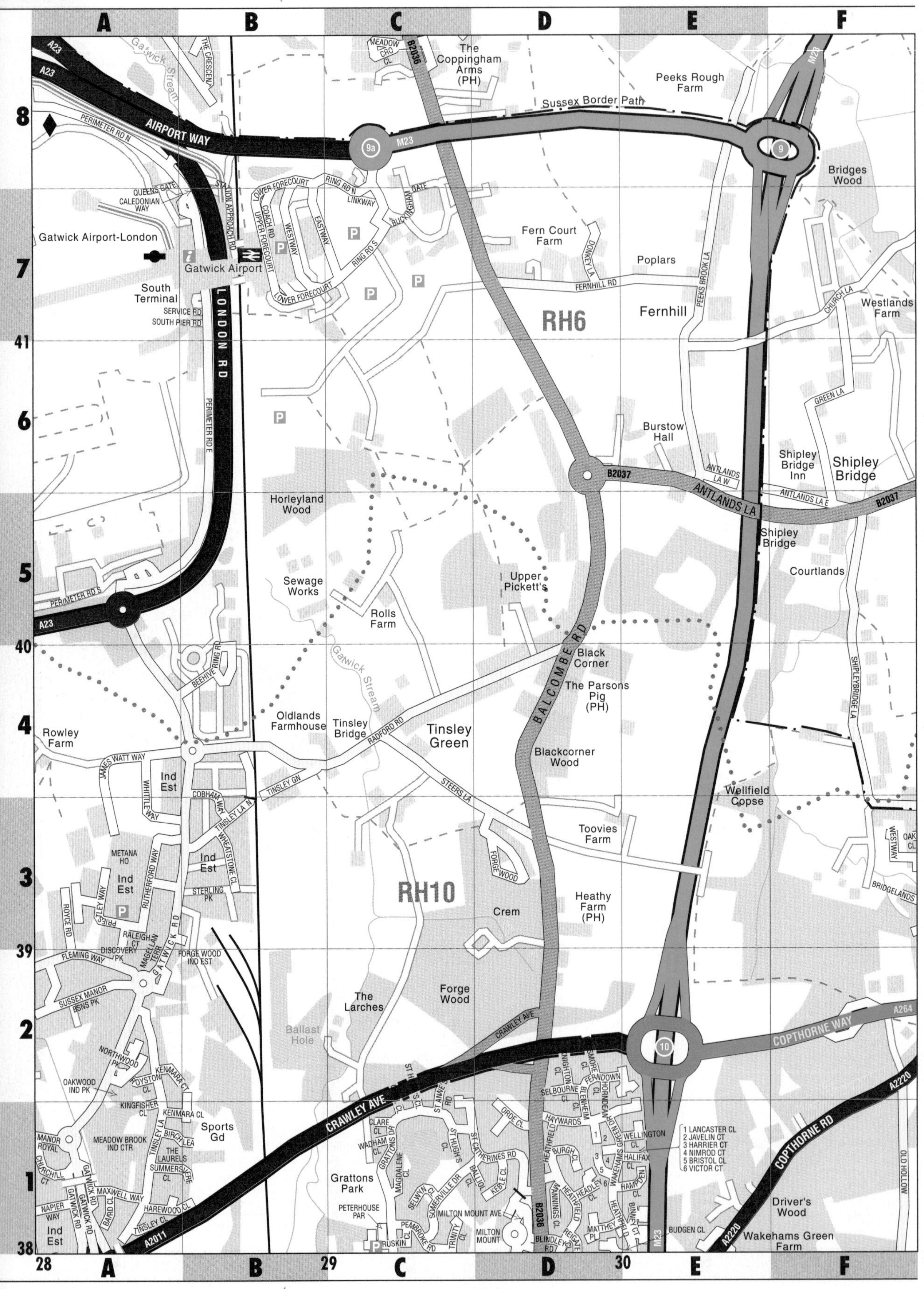

181
202

162
184

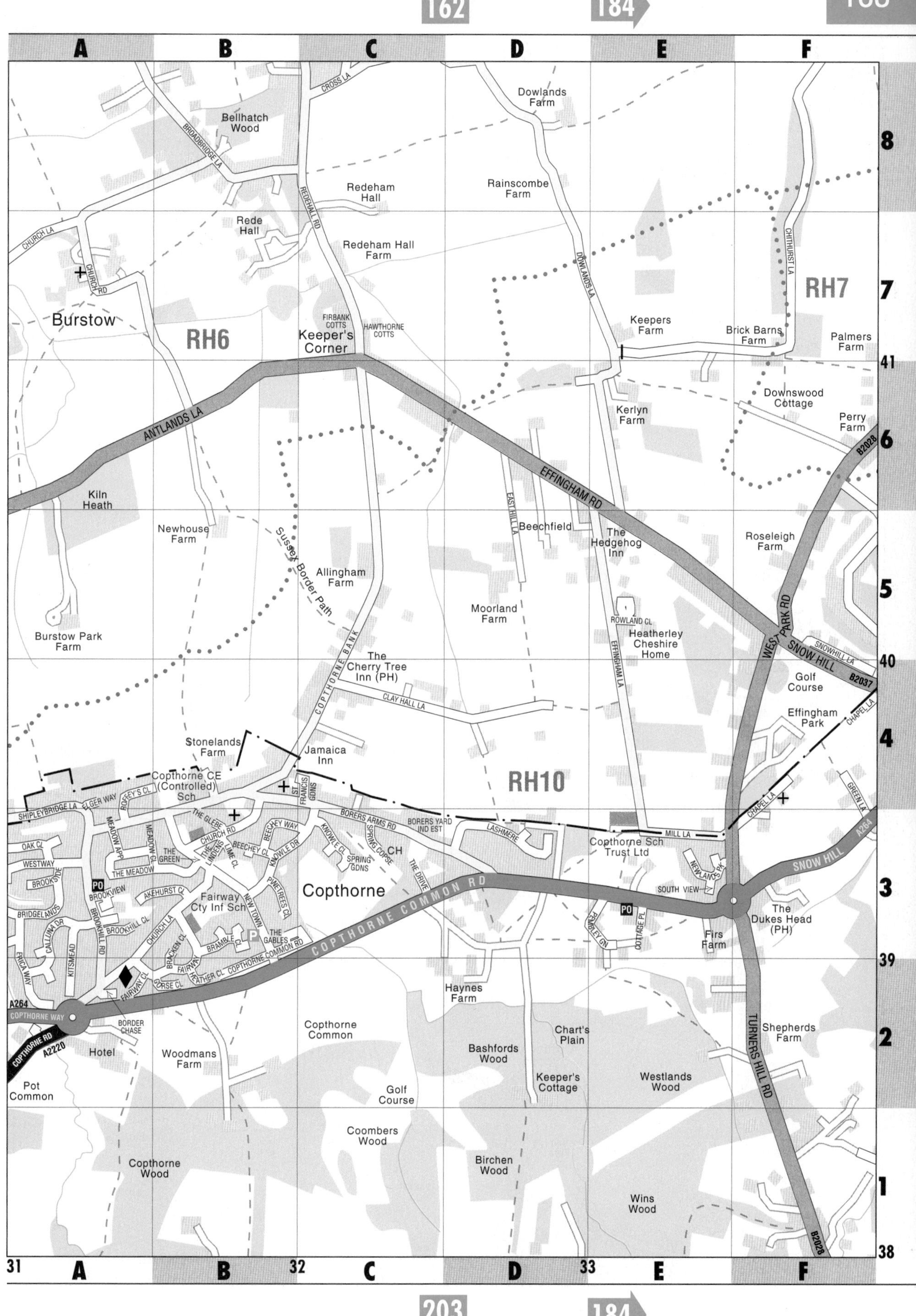

203
184

183
163

183
204

164
186

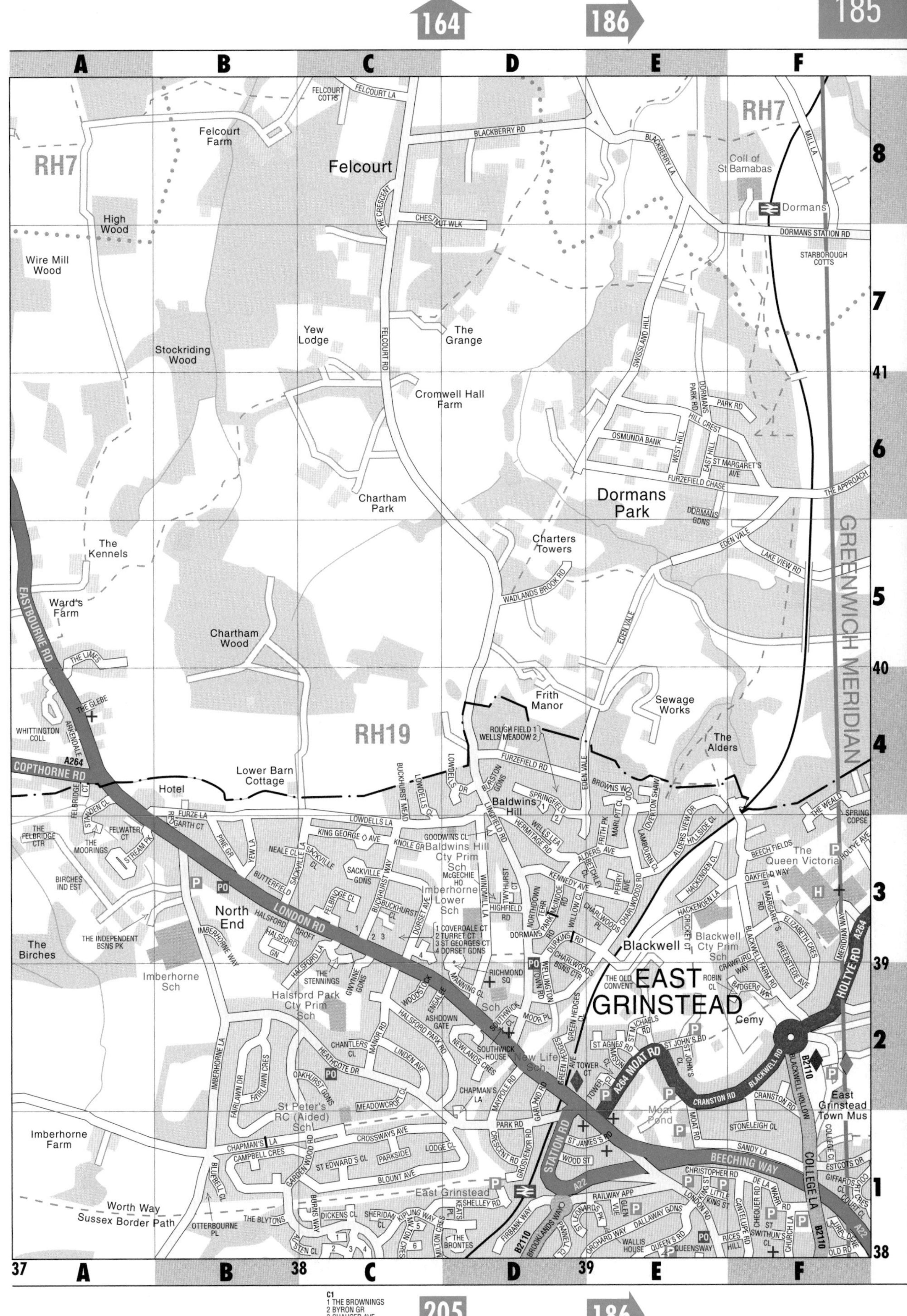

C1
1 THE BROWNINGS
2 BYRON GR
3 CHAUCER AVE
4 TENNYSON RISE
5 THE SAYERS
6 WORDSWORTH RISE

205
186

185
165

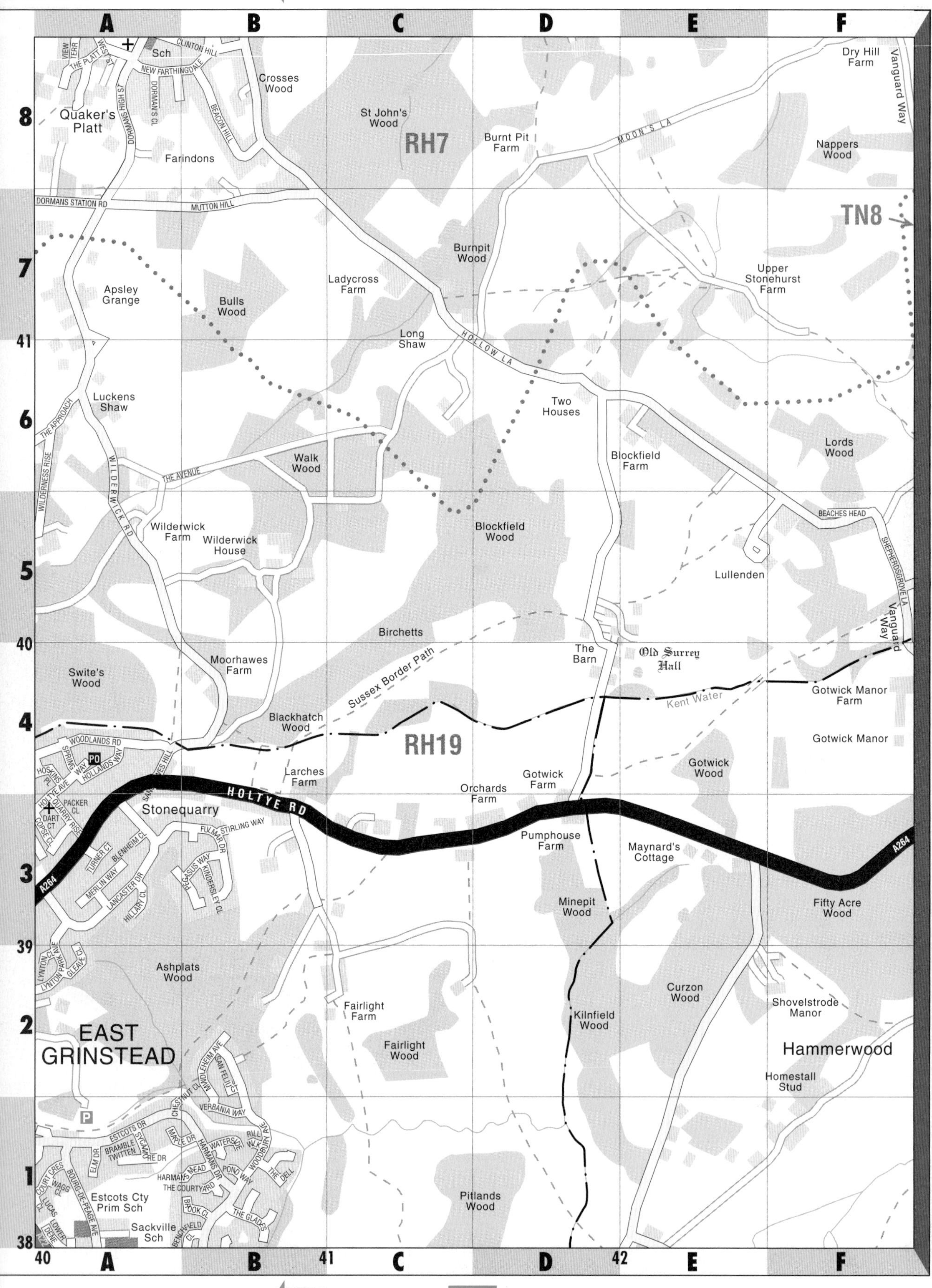

185
206

167
188

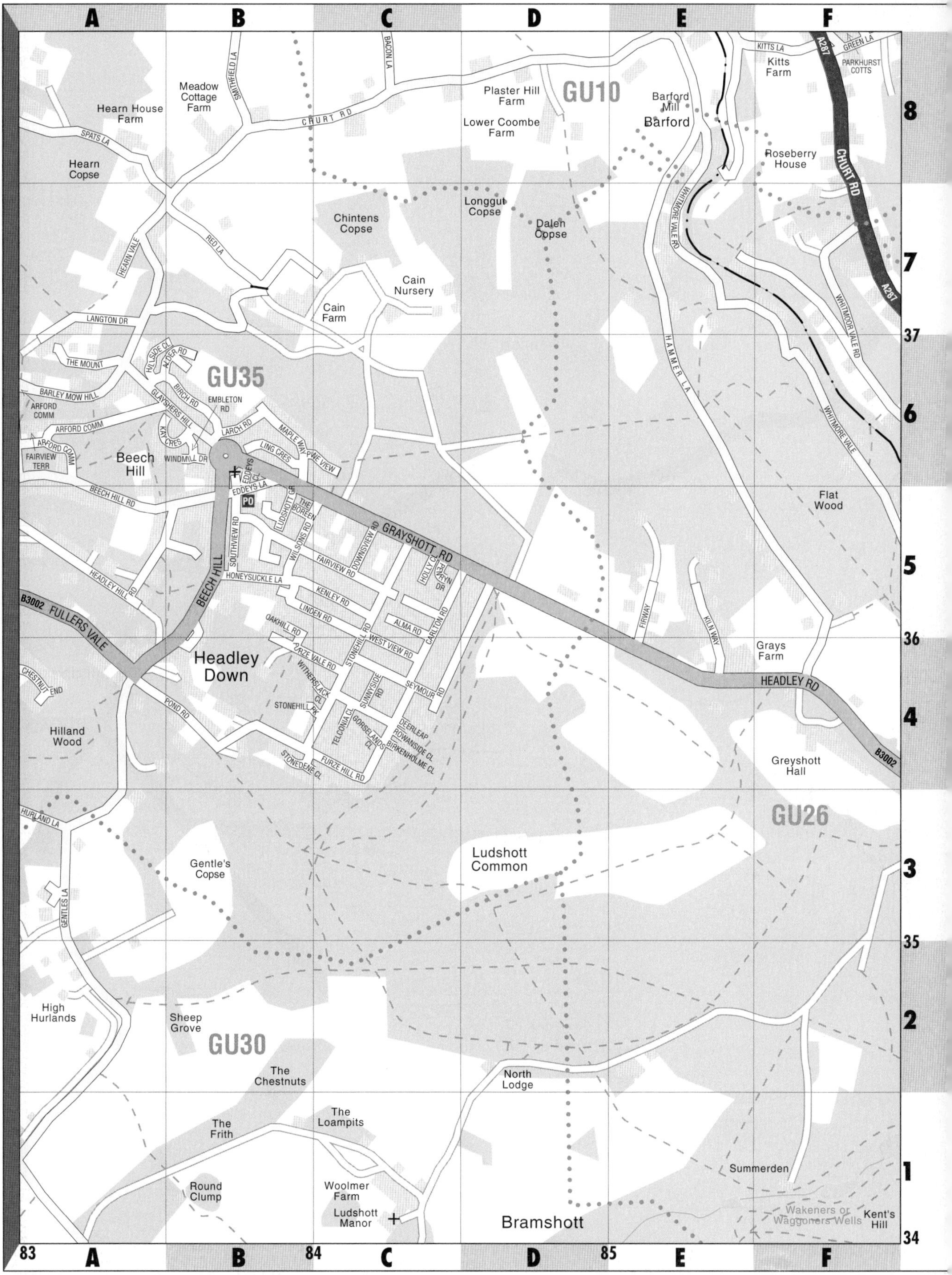

A B C D E F

Meadow Cottage Farm
Hearn House Farm
SMITHFIELD LA
BACON LA
CHURT RD
Plaster Hill Farm
GU10
Lower Coombe Farm
Barford Mill
Barford
KITTS LA
Kitts Farm
A287
GREEN LA
PARKHURST COTTS
SPATS LA
Hearn Copse
Roseberry House
CHURT RD
Chintens Copse
Longgut Copse
Dalen Copse
RED LA
HEARN VALE
WHITMORE VALE RD
Cain Nursery
Cain Farm
A287
WHITMOOR VALE RD
LANGTON DR
HILLSIDE CL
ALDER RD
THE MOUNT
GU35
HAMMER LA
BARLEY MOW HILL
BIRCH RD
EMBLETON RD
ARFORD COMM
GLAYSHERS HILL
ARFORD COMM
LARCH RD
MAPLE WAY
KAY CRES
WHITMORE VALE
ARFORD COMM
LING CRES
PINE VIEW
FAIRVIEW TERR
Beech Hill
WINDMILL DR
EDDEYS CL
EDDEYS LA
BEECH HILL RD
PO
LUDSHOTT GR
THE BOREEN
GRAYSHOTT RD
Flat Wood
SOUTHVIEW RD
WILSONS RD
DOWNSVIEW RD
FAIRVIEW RD
HOLLY CL
PENRYN DR
HEADLEY HILL RD
BEECH HILL
HONEYSUCKLE LA
KENLEY RD
FIRWAY
KILN WAY
B3002 FULLERS VALE
LINDEN RD
ALMA RD
CARLTON RD
OAKHILL RD
WEST VIEW RD
Grays Farm
Headley Down
FURZE VALE RD
STONEHILL RD
CHESTNUT END
WITHERSLACK CL
SUNNYSIDE RD
SEYMOUR RD
HEADLEY RD
POND RD
STONEHILL PK
Hilland Wood
TELCONIA CL
GORSELANDS CL
DEERLEAP
ROWANSIDE CL
BIRKENHOLME CL
STONEDENE CL
FURZE HILL RD
Greyshott Hall
B3002
HURLAND LA
GU26
Gentle's Copse
Ludshott Common
GENTLES LA
High Hurlands
Sheep Grove
GU30
North Lodge
The Chestnuts
The Frith
The Loampits
Round Clump
Woolmer Farm
Summerden
Ludshott Manor
Bramshott
Wakeners or Waggoners Wells
Kent's Hill

8 7 37 6 5 36 4 3 35 2 1 34

83 A B 84 C D 85 E F

188

187
168

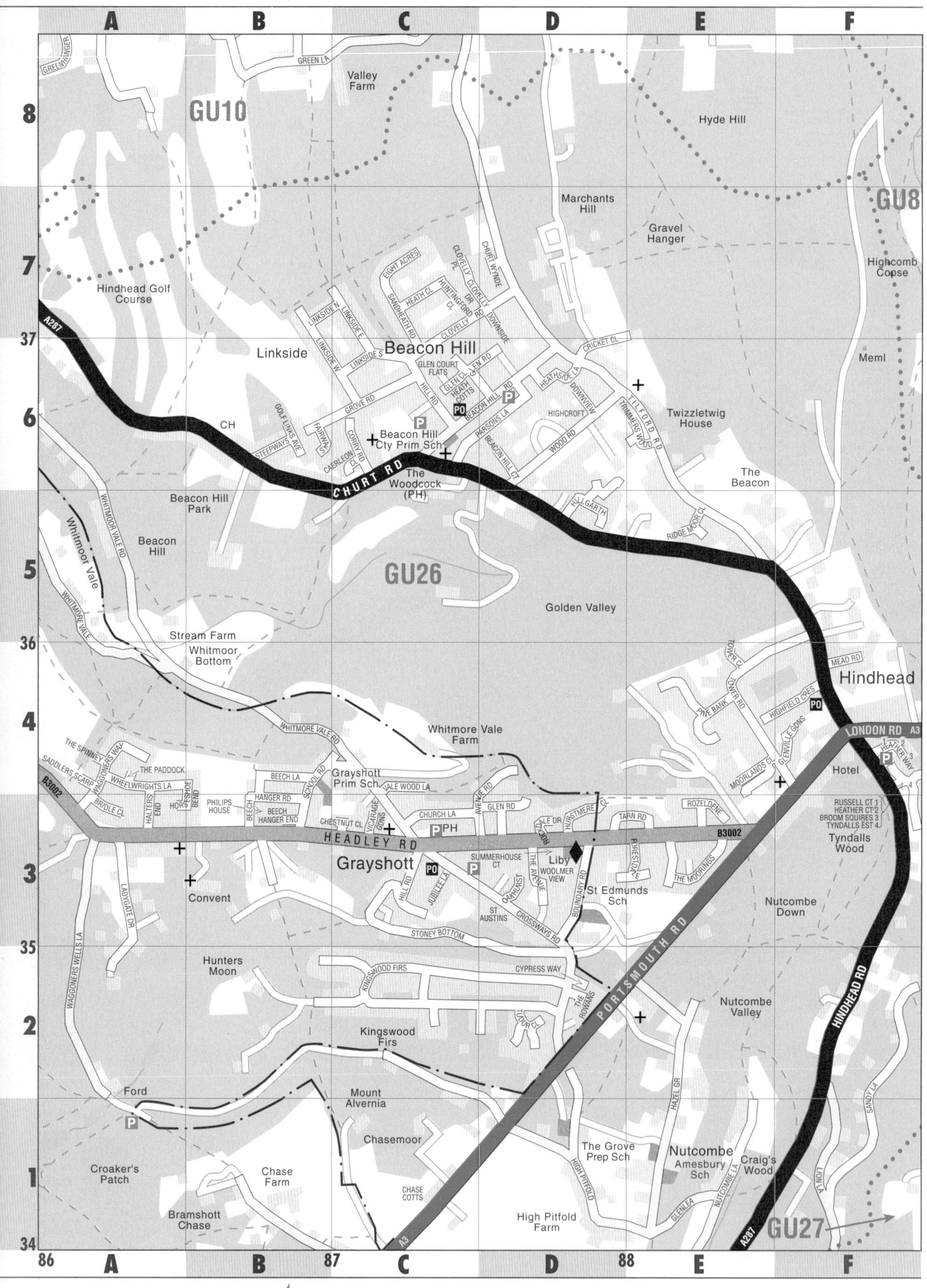

187
207

169
190

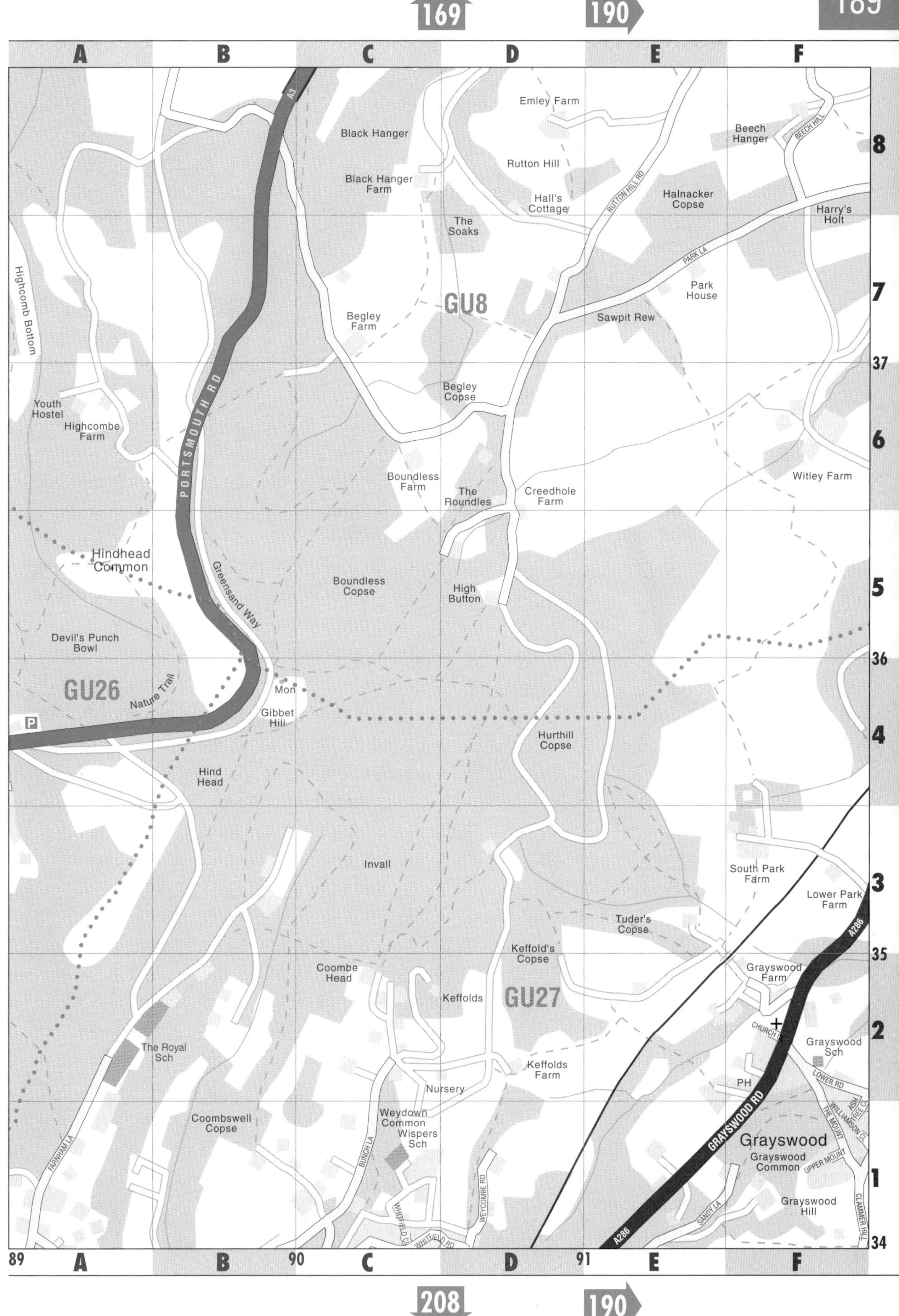

208
190

189
170

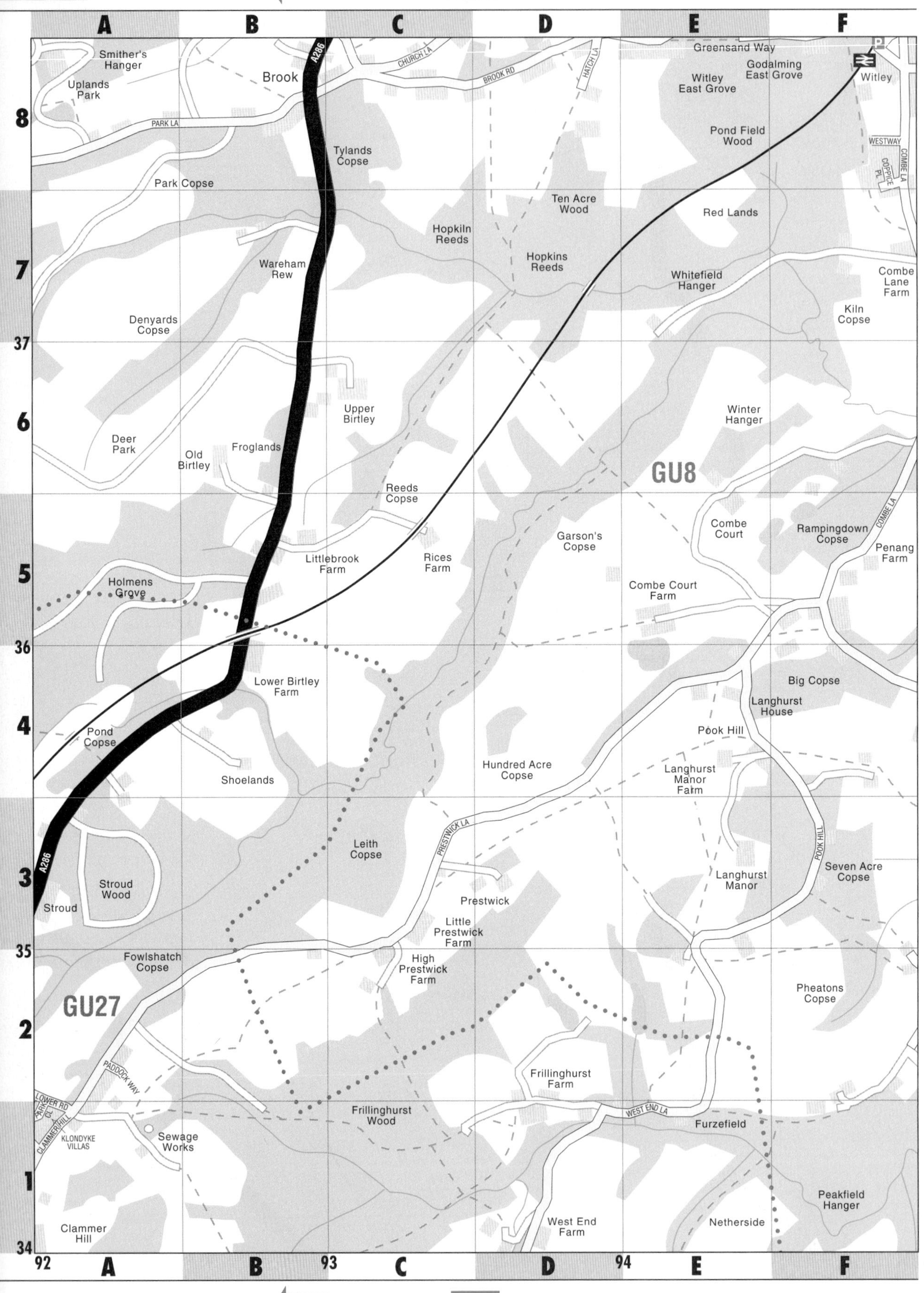

189
209

171

192

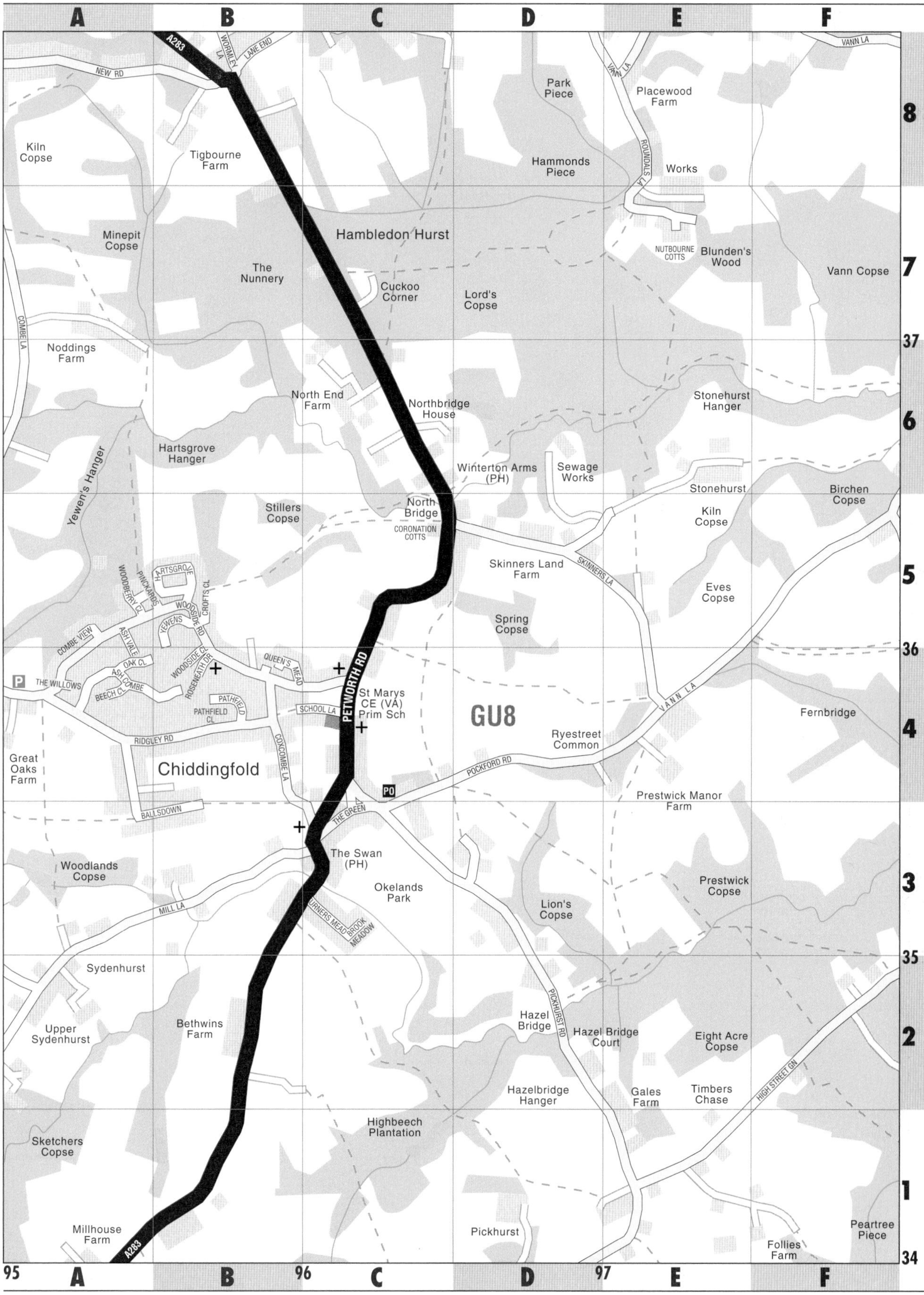

A B C D E F

8 7 37 6 5 36 4 3 35 2 1 34

Kiln Copse
Tigbourne Farm
Park Piece
Placewood Farm
Hammonds Piece
Works
Minepit Copse
Hambledon Hurst
The Nunnery
Cuckoo Corner
Lord's Copse
NUTBOURNE COTTS
Blunden's Wood
Vann Copse
Noddings Farm
North End Farm
Northbridge House
Stonehurst Hanger
Hartsgrove Hanger
Yewen's Hanger
Winterton Arms (PH)
Sewage Works
Stonehurst
Birchen Copse
Stillers Copse
North Bridge
CORONATION COTTS
Kiln Copse
Skinners Land Farm
Eves Copse
Spring Copse
St Marys CE (VA) Prim Sch
GU8
Ryestreet Common
Fernbridge
Great Oaks Farm
Chiddingfold
PO
Prestwick Manor Farm
Woodlands Copse
The Swan (PH)
Okelands Park
Prestwick Copse
Lion's Copse
Sydenhurst
Upper Sydenhurst
Bethwins Farm
Hazel Bridge
Hazel Bridge Court
Eight Acre Copse
Hazelbridge Hanger
Gales Farm
Timbers Chase
Sketchers Copse
Highbeech Plantation
Millhouse Farm
Pickhurst
Follies Farm
Peartree Piece
A283
NEW RD
WORMLEY LA
LANE END
VANN LA
ROUNDALS LA
COMBE LA
SKINNERS LA
HARTSGROVE
PINCKARDS
WOODBERRY CL
CROFTS CL
WOODSIDE RD
YEWENS
COMBE VIEW
ASH VALE
OAK CL
WOODSIDE CL
ROSENEATH DR
QUEEN'S MEAD
PETWORTH RD
THE WILLOWS
ASHCOMBE
BEECH CL
PATHFIELD
PATHFIELD CL
SCHOOL LA
RIDGLEY RD
COXCOMBE LA
POCKFORD RD
BALLSDOWN
THE GREEN
MILL LA
TURNERS MEAD
BROOK MEADOW
PICKHURST RD
HIGH STREET GN
P

95 A B 96 C D 97 E F

210

192

191 172

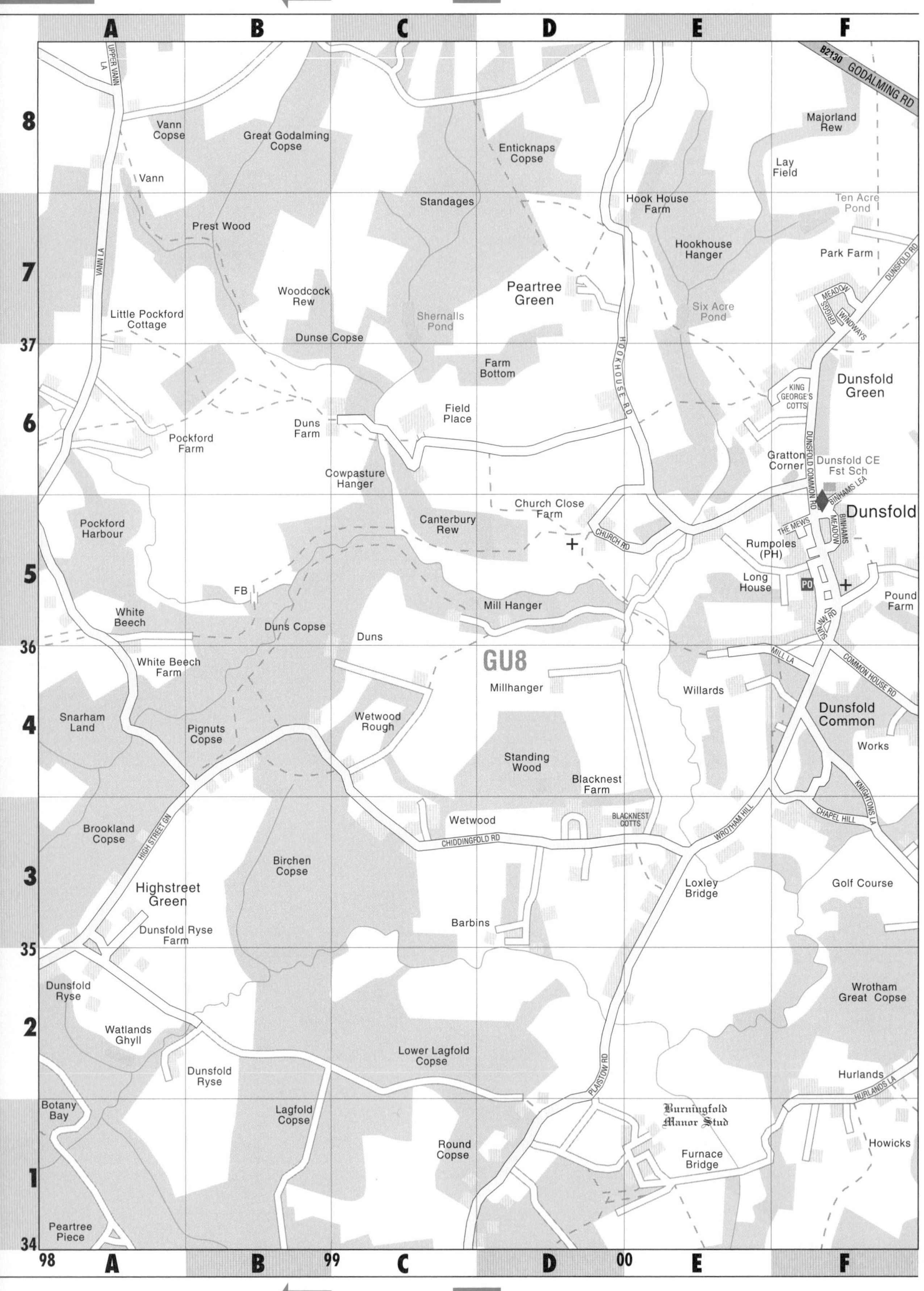

191 211

173
194

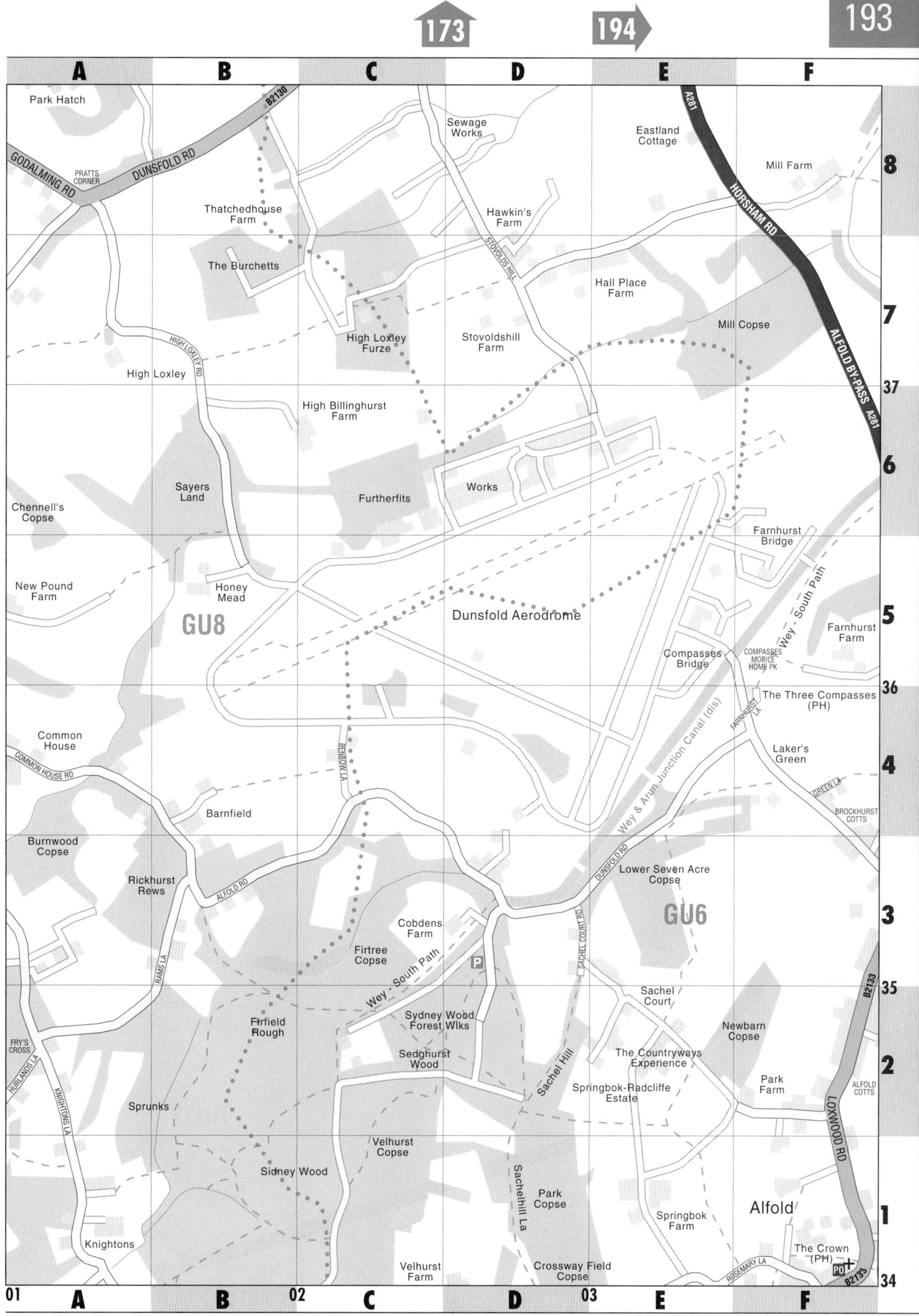

212
194

193
174

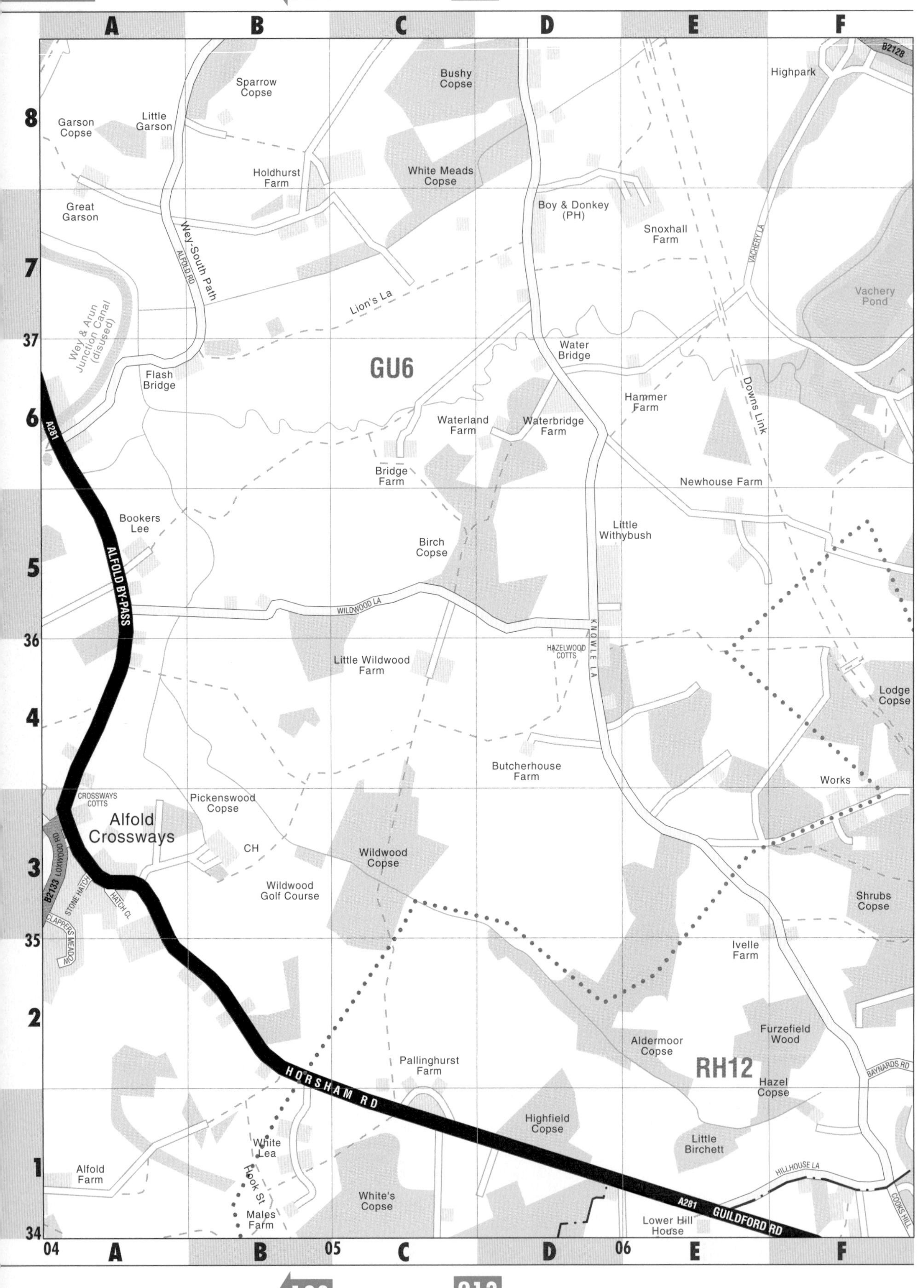

193
213

175
196

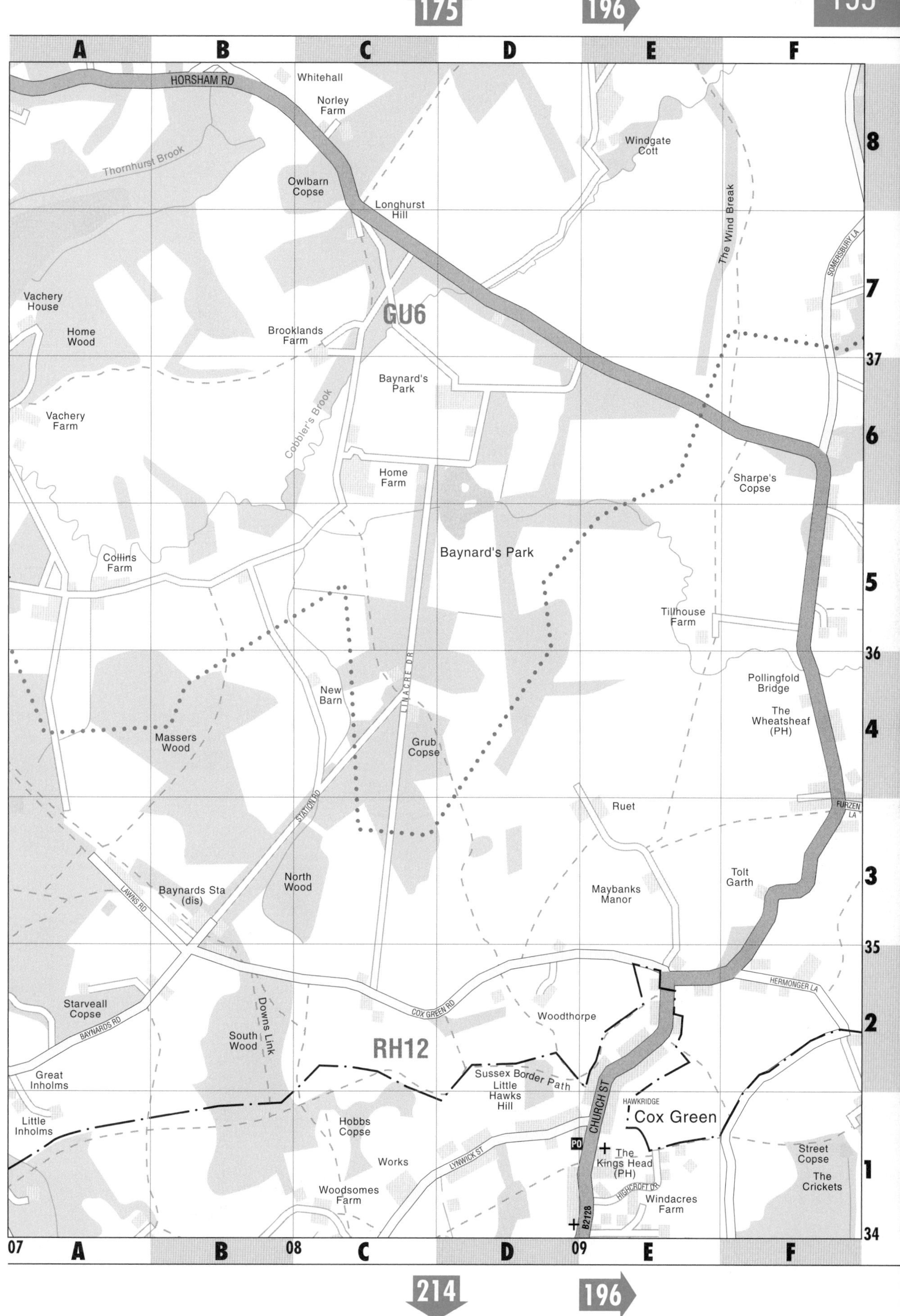

214
196

195
176

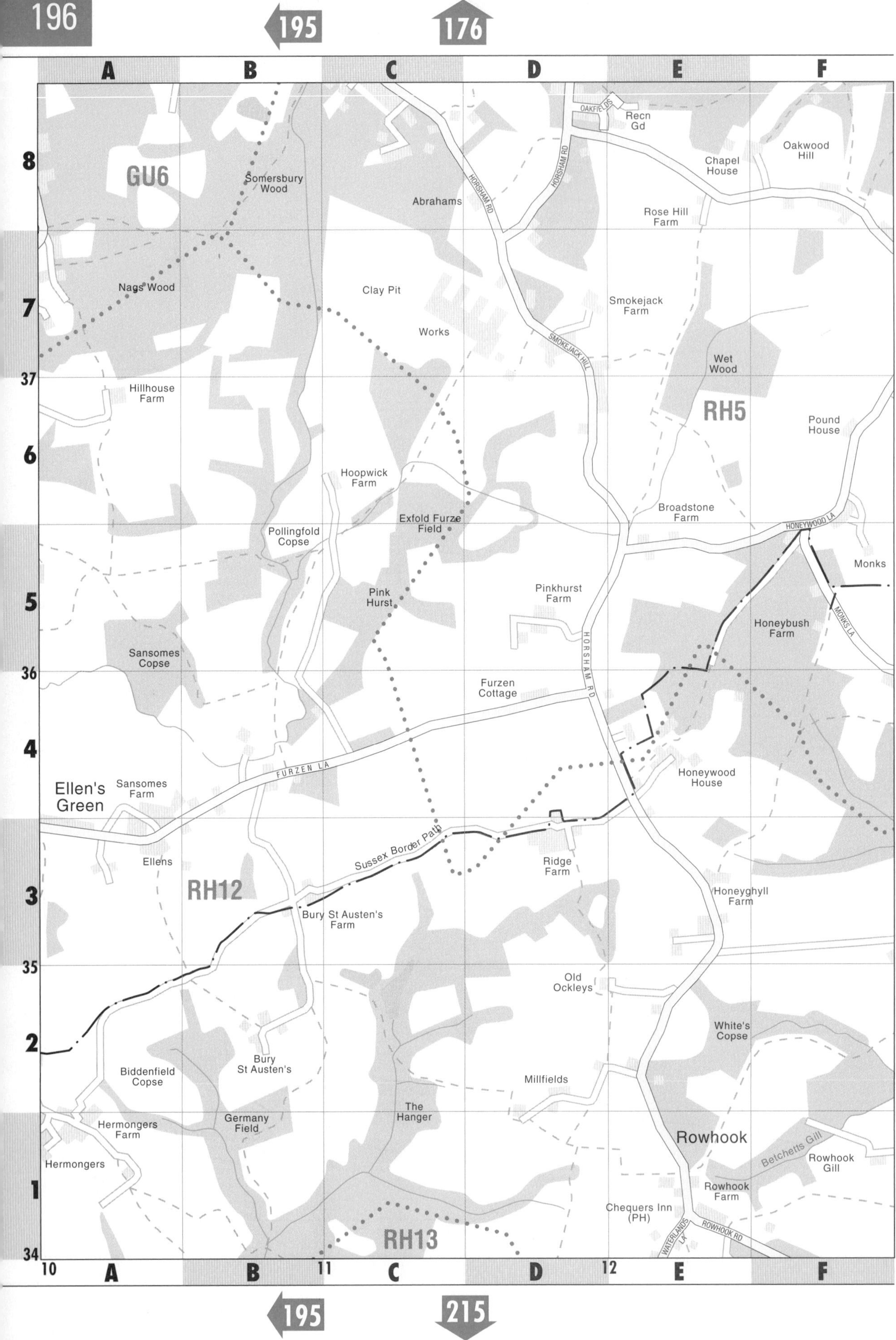

195
215

A B C D E F

Chapel Copse
Hale House
Puttocks Bridge
Paynes Green
Timber Gill
The Punchbowl Inn (PH)
Oakdale Farm
RH5
Woodhams Farm
Oakwoodhill
Boswells Farm
Place Farm
North River
Rowland Wood
Potland Hangers
Ruckmans Farm
Denne Bridge
Sussex Border Path
Tickfold Gill
Denne Farm
Whitelands Copse
Woodbarn
Whitelands Barn
Monks Farm
Northlands Home Farm
Marches Farm
Stone Farm
Joanland Farm
Dawes Farm
Durfold Barn
Hoopers Barn
Tanners Farm
Chatfolds
RH12
Charmans Farm
Chatfolds Bridge
Hoopers Copse
Mayes Park House
Pear Tree Farm
Warnham Lodge
Pound Corner
Westbrook House
Benland Wood
Sands Farm
Cider Mill Farm
Threestile Corner
Rowhook Manor
Old Manor

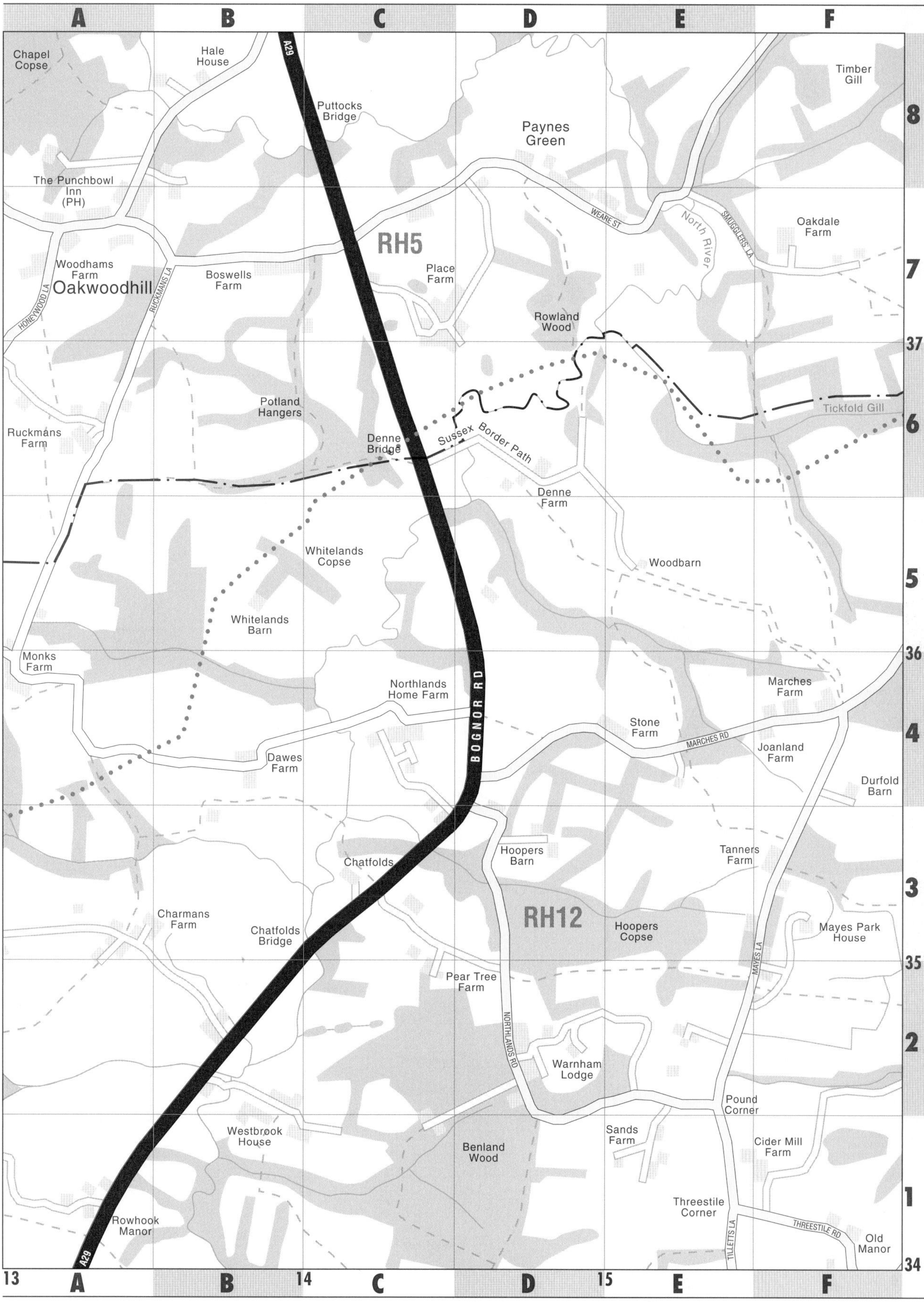

A29
WEARE ST
SMUGGLERS LA
HONEYWOOD LA
RUCKMANS LA
BOGNOR RD
MARCHES RD
MAYES LA
NORTHLANDS RD
THREESTILE RD
TILLETTS LA

8 7 37 6 5 36 4 3 35 2 1 34

13 A B 14 C D 15 E F

197
178

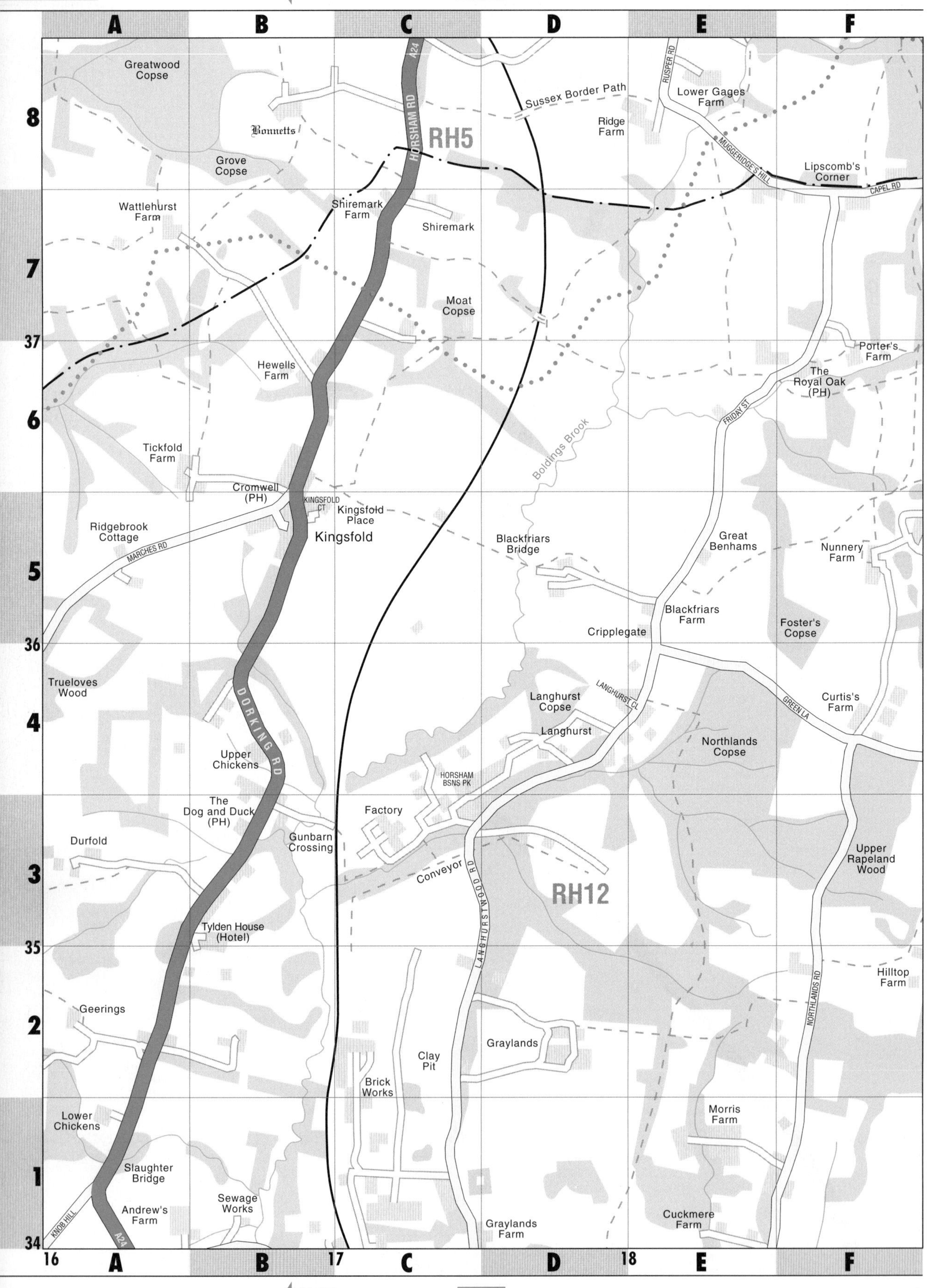
A
B
C
D
E
F
8
7
37
6
5
36
4
3
35
2
1
34
16
17
18
Greatwood Copse
Bonnetts
Grove Copse
Sussex Border Path
RUSPER RD
Lower Gages Farm
Ridge Farm
RH5
HORSHAM RD
A24
MUGGERIDGE'S HILL
Lipscomb's Corner
CAPEL RD
Wattlehurst Farm
Shiremark Farm
Shiremark
Moat Copse
Porter's Farm
The Royal Oak (PH)
Hewells Farm
FRIDAY ST
Boldings Brook
Tickfold Farm
Cromwell (PH)
KINGSFOLD CT
Kingsfold Place
Kingsfold
Ridgebrook Cottage
MARCHES RD
Blackfriars Bridge
Great Benhams
Nunnery Farm
Blackfriars Farm
Cripplegate
Foster's Copse
Trueloves Wood
DORKING RD
Langhurst Copse
LANGHURST CL
Langhurst
GREEN LA
Curtis's Farm
Northlands Copse
Upper Chickens
HORSHAM BSNS PK
The Dog and Duck (PH)
Factory
Durfold
Gunbarn Crossing
Conveyor
LANGHURSTWOOD RD
RH12
Upper Rapeland Wood
Tylden House (Hotel)
Hilltop Farm
NORTHLANDS RD
Geerings
Graylands
Clay Pit
Brick Works
Morris Farm
Lower Chickens
Slaughter Bridge
Andrew's Farm
Sewage Works
KNOB HILL
Graylands Farm
Cuckmere Farm

197
217

179
200

218
200

199
180

F3
1 BERSTEAD WLK
2 DONNINGTON CT
3 HASSOCKS CT
4 PYECOMBE CT
5 TELHAM CT
6 WARBLETON HOUSE
7 CALDBECK HOUSE
8 HALNAKER WLK
9 ICKLESHAM HOUSE

199

D5
1 THE COURTYARD
2 WALSTEAD HOUSE
3 RAVENDENE CT
4 WILLOWFIELD
5 ASHWOOD
6 PARISH HOUSE
7 PERRYFIELD HOUSE
8 HANDSWORTH HOUSE
9 GLENDON HOUSE
10 ALEXANDRA CT

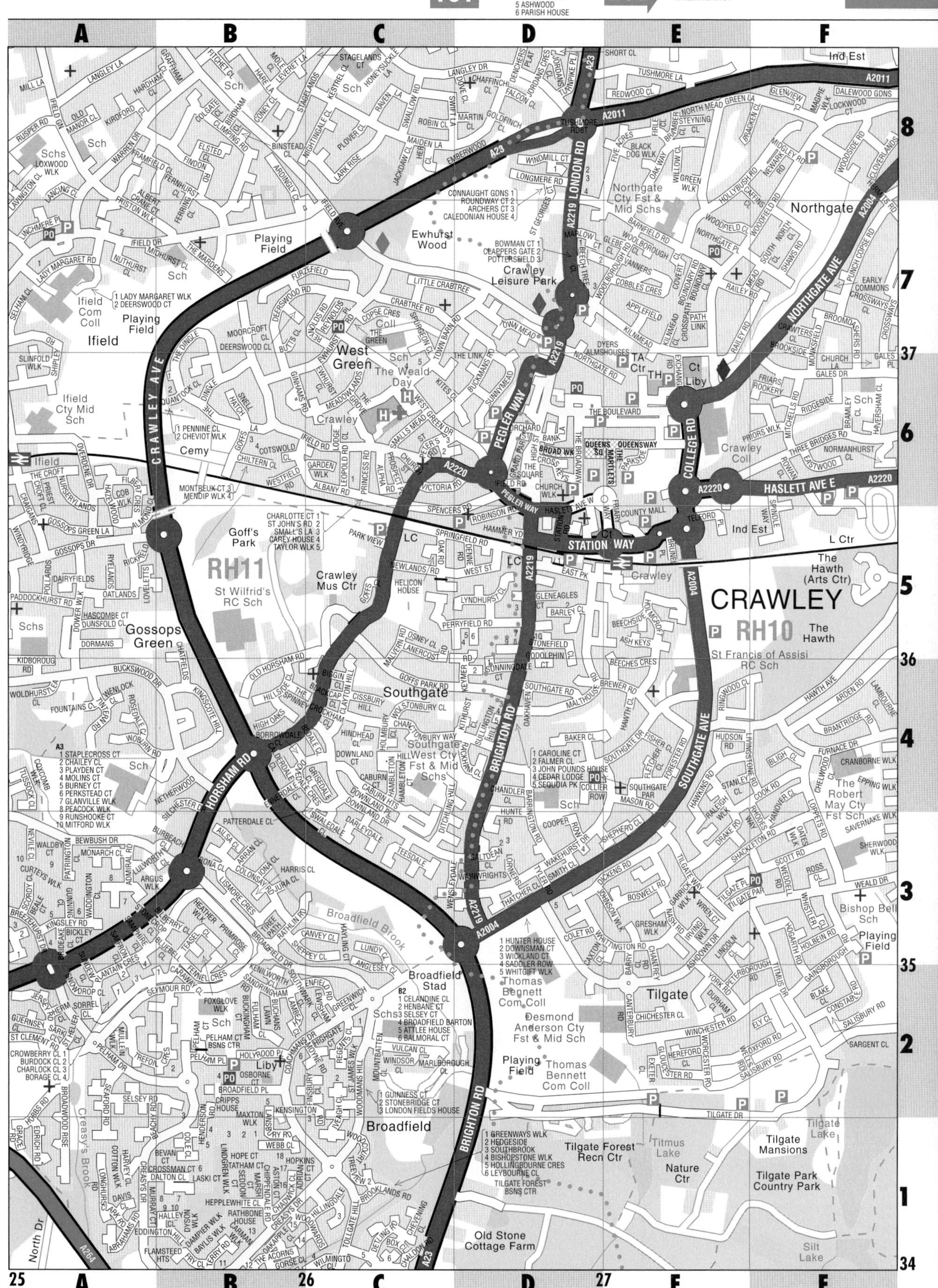

B1
1 STRACHEY CT
2 GREENWOOD CT
3 SHINWELL WLK
4 WILKINSON CT
5 MORRISON CT
6 ADAMSON CT
7 KEIR HARDIE HOUSE
8 SILKIN WLK
9 HERSCHEL WLK
10 JEANS CT
11 PANKHURST CT
12 RAMBLERS WAY
13 SHERATON WLK
14 TIMBERLANDS
15 WOODING GR
16 THOMPSON CT
17 RICHARDSON CT
18 RAMSEY CT

201
182

A
B
C
D
E
F
8
7
37
6
5
36
4
3
35
2
1
34
28
29
30
Hazelwick Sch
Milton Mount Cty Fst & Mid Sch
Pound Hill
Burleys Wood
Three Bridges
Pound Hill Cty Fst & Mid Schs
Crabbet Park
Hotel
Sch
Coll
Three Bridges
Ind Est
Playing Field
CRAWLEY
Worth
RH10
Worth Way
Worth Lodge Farm
Furnace Green
Sch
Maidenbower Cty Fst Sch
Maidenbower
Hotel
Long Wood
Furnace Plain
Tilgate Forest Golf Course
CH
Worthlodge Forest
Flax Field
Brick Field South
Oldhouse Warren
Worth Forest
Whitely Hill
Rugs Corner
RH17
Gatwick Stream
Stanford Brook
NORTHGATE AVE
HAZELWICK AVE
WORTH PARK AVE
HASLETT AVE E
COPTHORNE RD
BALCOMBE RD
CUFFS HILL
TURNERS HILL RD
CRAWLEY LA
GREEN LA
WORTH RD
TILGATE DR
WHITELY HILL
OLD HOLLOW
A2220
A2011
A2004
B2036
M23
1 HYDE HEATH CT
2 CHERRY TREE CL
1 PENSHURST CL
2 THE PADDOCK
3 SHORT GALLOP
4 GREYHOUND SLIP
5 THE CACKSTONES
1 ST IVES
2 ST NICHOLAS CT
3 ST BARNABAS CT
1 GOUDHURST KEEP
2 GOUDHURST CL
3 CROWHURST KEEP
1 TILLOTSON CL
2 MAYFLOWER CL
3 ALBION CL
4 WELLER CL
5 BETHUNE CL
6 THORNDYKE CL
1 STRUDGATE CL
2 HAWKHURST WLK
3 LOWESTOFT WLK
4 BARTON WLK
5 HEMSBY WLK
6 ORMESBY WLK
7 WAVENEY WLK
8 WROXHAM WLK
9 OULTON WLK
10 HICKLING WLK
1 DONCASTER WLK
2 SHARON CL
3 GRAVETYE CL
4 FERRONERS CT
5 BRUNSWICK CT
BALDWIN CL 1
HOUGHTON RD 2
LADYMEAD CL 3
WALKER RD 1
RAWORTH CL 2
STEPNEY CL 3
WRIGHT CL 1
PHILLIPS CL 2

201

183
204

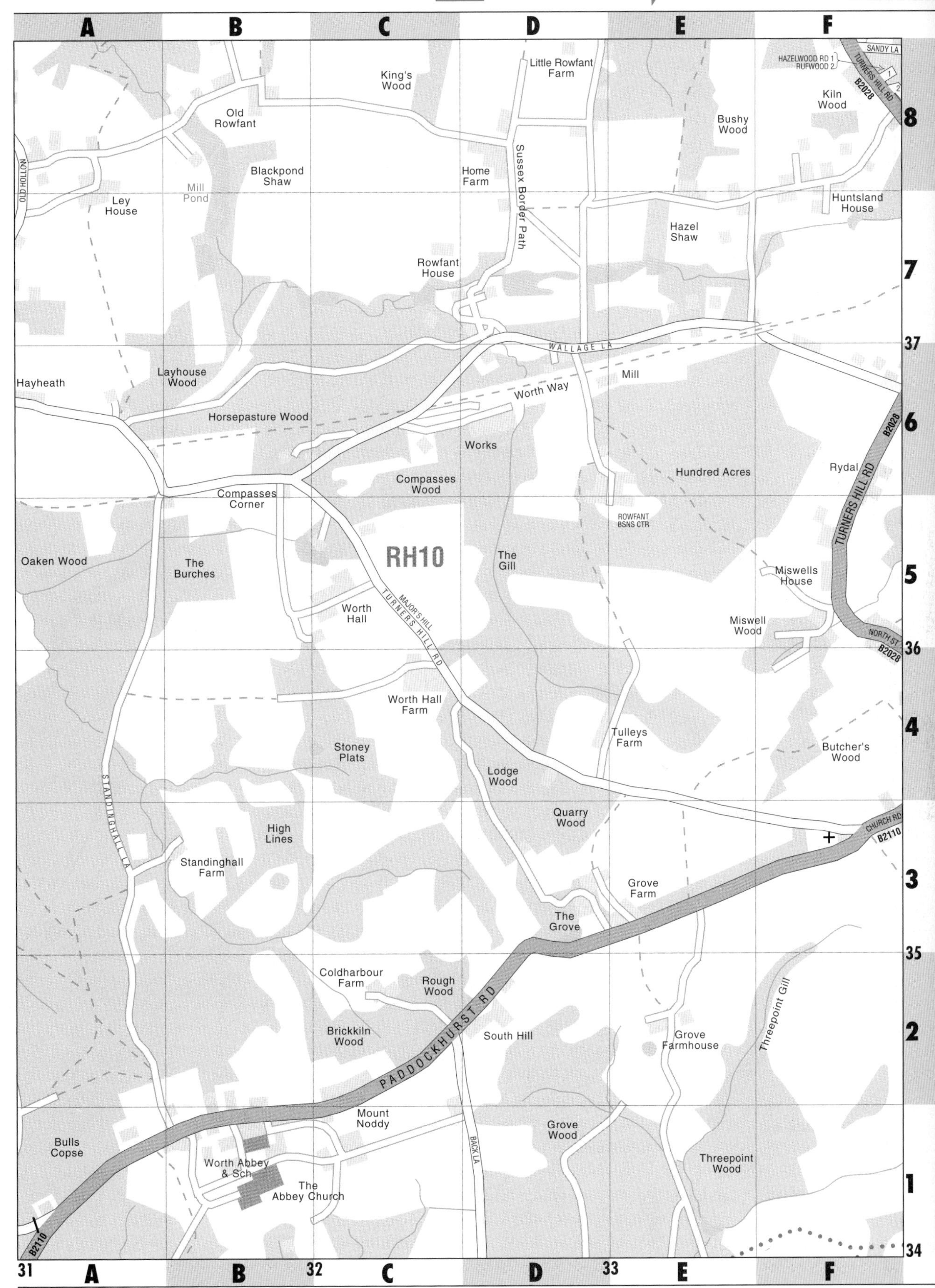
A
B
C
D
E
F
Little Rowfant
Farm
King's
Wood
Old
Rowfant
SANDY LA
HAZELWOOD RD 1
RUFWOOD 2
TURNERS HILL RD
B2028
Kiln
Wood
Bushy
Wood
8
OLD HOLLOW
Blackpond
Shaw
Home
Farm
Sussex Border Path
Mill
Pond
Ley
House
Huntsland
House
Hazel
Shaw
Rowfant
House
7
37
WALLAGE LA
Layhouse
Wood
Mill
Hayheath
Worth Way
Horsepasture Wood
B2028
6
Works
Compasses
Wood
Hundred Acres
Rydal
Compasses
Corner
ROWFANT
BSNS CTR
TURNERS HILL RD
RH10
The
Gill
Oaken Wood
The
Burches
5
Miswells
House
Worth
Hall
MAJOR'S HILL
TURNERS HILL RD
Miswell
Wood
NORTH ST
B2028
36
Worth Hall
Farm
4
Tulleys
Farm
Butcher's
Wood
Stoney
Plats
Lodge
Wood
STANDINGHALL LA
Quarry
Wood
CHURCH RD
B2110
High
Lines
Standinghall
Farm
3
Grove
Farm
The
Grove
35
Coldharbour
Farm
Rough
Wood
Threepoint Gill
PADDOCKHURST RD
2
Brickkiln
Wood
South Hill
Grove
Farmhouse
Mount
Noddy
Grove
Wood
BACK LA
Bulls
Copse
Worth Abbey
& Sch
Threepoint
Wood
The
Abbey Church
1
B2110
34
31
A
32
B
C
D
33
E
F

204

203
184

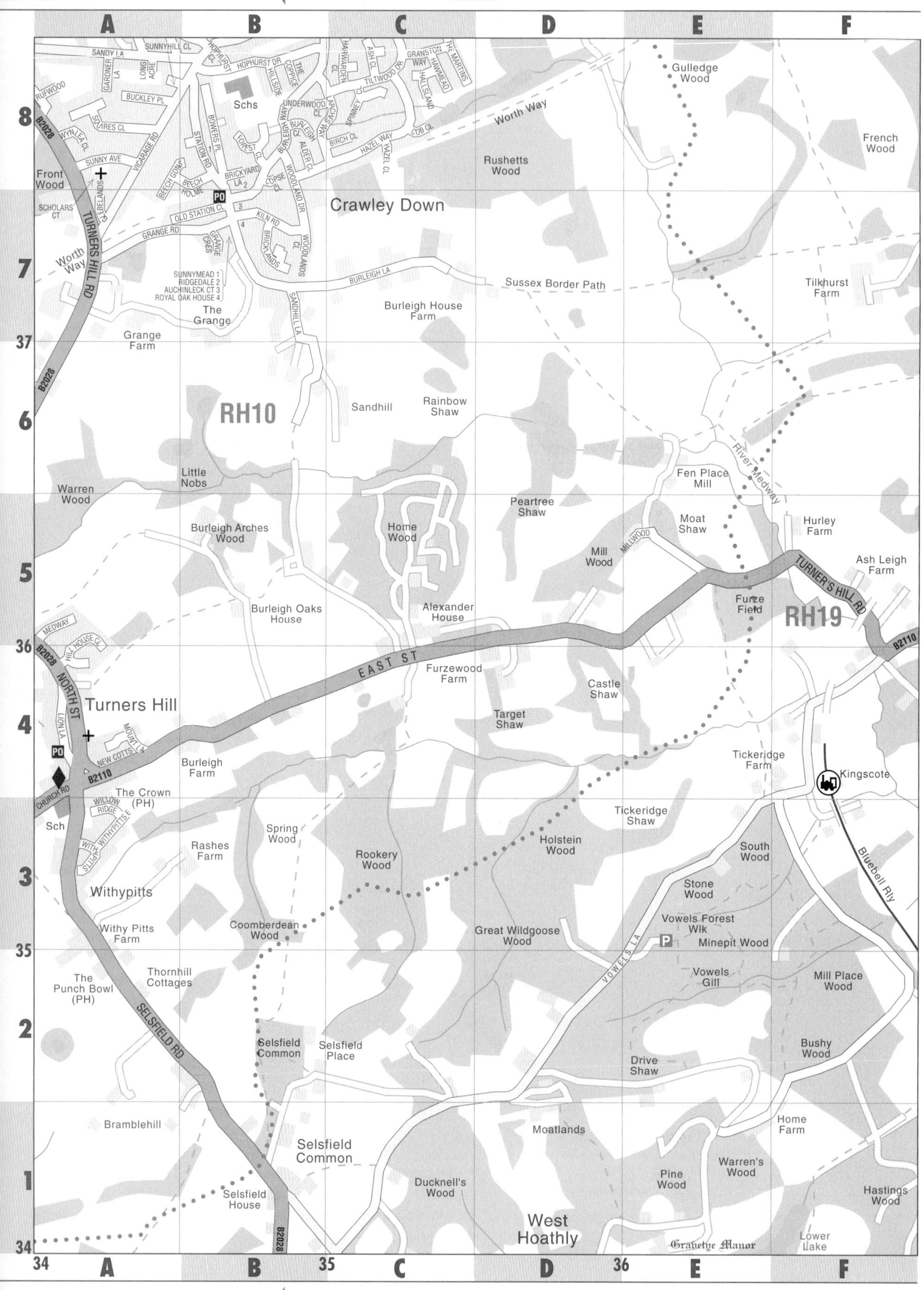
A
B
C
D
E
F
Crawley Down
Schs
Gulledge Wood
Worth Way
Rushetts Wood
French Wood
Front Wood
Sussex Border Path
Tilkhurst Farm
Burleigh House Farm
The Grange
Grange Farm
RH10
Sandhill
Rainbow Shaw
Little Nobs
Warren Wood
Fen Place Mill
River Medway
Peartree Shaw
Moat Shaw
Hurley Farm
Burleigh Arches Wood
Home Wood
Mill Wood
Ash Leigh Farm
Burleigh Oaks House
Alexander House
Furze Field
RH19
EAST ST
Furzewood Farm
Castle Shaw
Turners Hill
Target Shaw
Burleigh Farm
Tickeridge Farm
Kingscote
The Crown (PH)
Tickeridge Shaw
Sch
Spring Wood
Rashes Farm
Holstein Wood
South Wood
Rookery Wood
Withypitts
Stone Wood
Bluebell Rly
Coomberdean Wood
Vowels Forest Wlk
Withy Pitts Farm
Great Wildgoose Wood
Minepit Wood
Thornhill Cottages
The Punch Bowl (PH)
Vowels Gill
Mill Place Wood
Selsfield Common
Selsfield Place
Bushy Wood
Drive Shaw
Bramblehill
Home Farm
Moatlands
Selsfield Common
Warren's Wood
Pine Wood
Ducknell's Wood
Hastings Wood
Selsfield House
West Hoathly
Gravetye Manor
Lower Lake
TURNERS HILL RD
TURNER'S HILL RD
NORTH ST
SELSFIELD RD
VOWELS LA
BURLEIGH LA
SANDHILL LA
B2028
B2110
8
7
37
6
5
36
4
3
35
2
1
34
34
35
36

203

185
206

F8
1 MIDDLE ROW
2 FOREST LODGE
3 SACKVILLE CT
4 GREAT HOUSE CT
5 PORTLAND HOUSE
6 CORNWALL GDNS
7 NORMANDY CL
8 WILLOW MEAD
9 KINGS COPSE
10 REGAL DR
11 BECKETT WAY

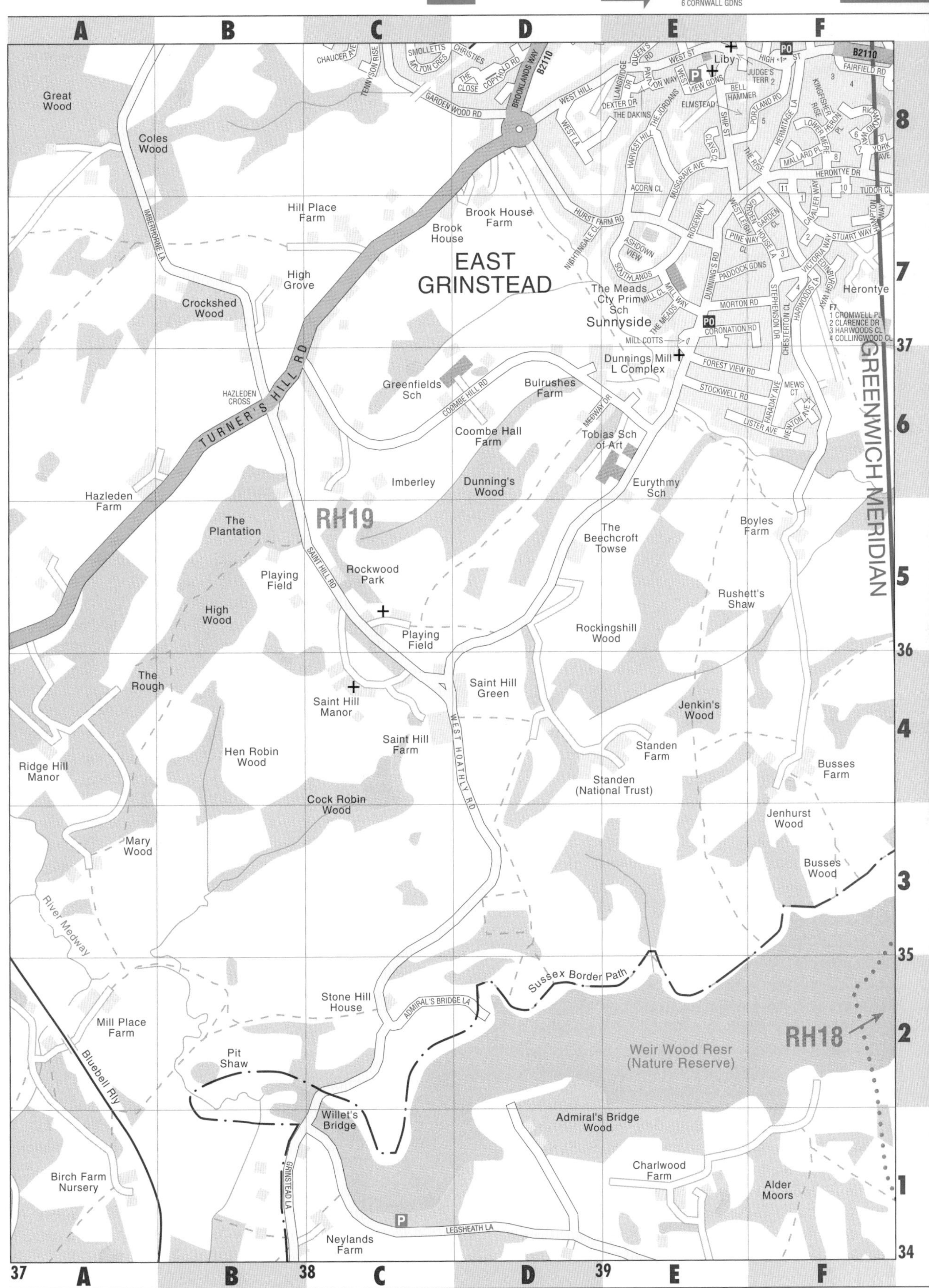

206

205
186

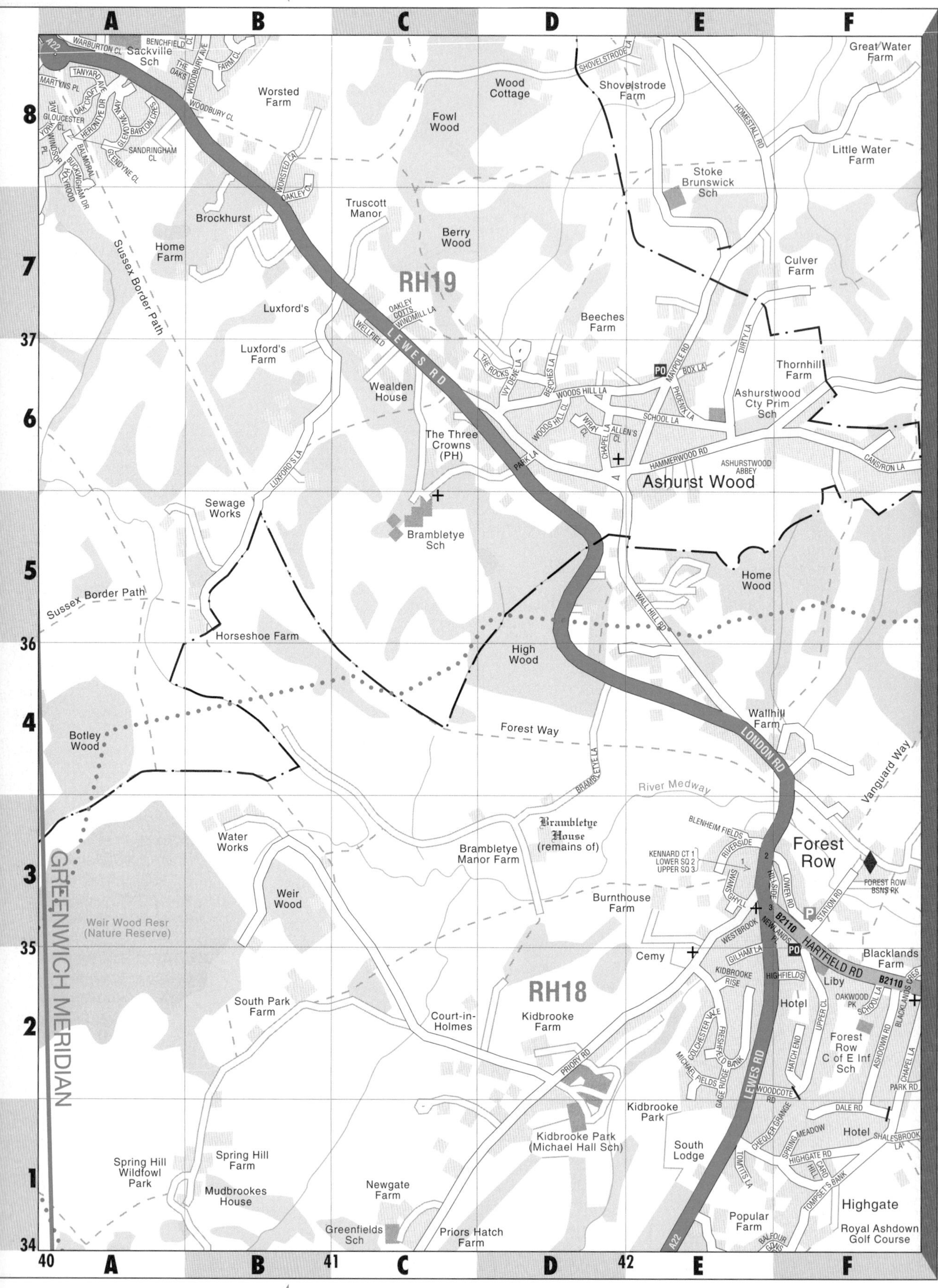
A
B
C
D
E
F
8
7
37
6
5
36
4
3
35
2
1
34
40
41
42
Sackville Sch
Worsted Farm
Wood Cottage
Shovelstrode Farm
Great Water Farm
Fowl Wood
Little Water Farm
Stoke Brunswick Sch
Brockhurst
Truscott Manor
Berry Wood
Home Farm
Sussex Border Path
RH19
Culver Farm
Luxford's
Beeches Farm
Luxford's Farm
LEWES RD
Thornhill Farm
Wealden House
Ashurstwood Cty Prim Sch
The Three Crowns (PH)
Ashurst Wood
ASHURSTWOOD ABBEY
Sewage Works
Brambletye Sch
Home Wood
Sussex Border Path
Horseshoe Farm
High Wood
Wallhill Farm
Botley Wood
Forest Way
LONDON RD
Vanguard Way
River Medway
Brambletye House (remains of)
Water Works
Brambletye Manor Farm
Forest Row
FOREST ROW BSNS PK
Weir Wood
Burnthouse Farm
Weir Wood Resr (Nature Reserve)
Cemy
Blacklands Farm
HARTFIELD RD
RH18
Liby
Hotel
South Park Farm
Court-in-Holmes
Kidbrooke Farm
Forest Row C of E Inf Sch
GREENWICH MERIDIAN
Kidbrooke Park
Hotel
South Lodge
Kidbrooke Park (Michael Hall Sch)
Spring Hill Wildfowl Park
Spring Hill Farm
Mudbrookes House
Newgate Farm
Highgate
Greenfields Sch
Priors Hatch Farm
Popular Farm
Royal Ashdown Golf Course
A22
B2110

205

188
208

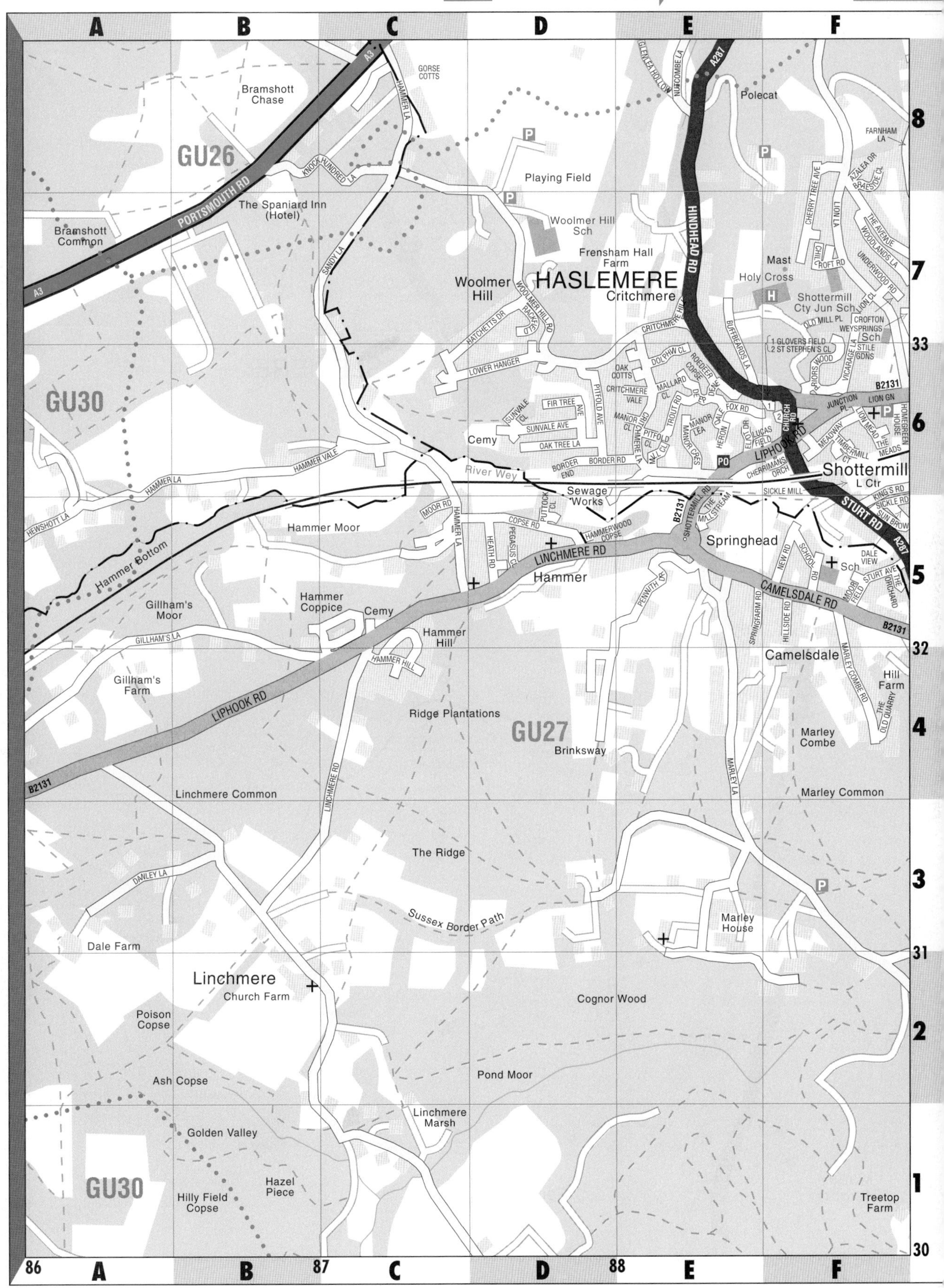
A
B
C
D
E
F
8
7
33
6
5
32
4
3
31
2
1
30
86
87
88
Bramshott Chase
GU26
PORTSMOUTH RD
A3
The Spaniard Inn (Hotel)
Bramshott Common
GU30
Playing Field
Woolmer Hill Sch
Frensham Hall Farm
HASLEMERE
Critchmere
Woolmer Hill
Polecat
HINDHEAD RD
A287
Mast
Holy Cross
Shottermill Cty Jun Sch
Sch
Cemy
River Wey
Sewage Works
Shottermill
L Ctr
Hammer Moor
Hammer Bottom
Springhead
Hammer
LINCHMERE RD
LIPHOOK RD
CAMELSDALE RD
STURT RD
B2131
Gillham's Moor
Hammer Coppice
Cemy
Hammer Hill
Camelsdale
Hill Farm
Gillham's Farm
Ridge Plantations
GU27
Brinksway
Marley Combe
Marley Common
Linchmere Common
The Ridge
Sussex Border Path
Marley House
Dale Farm
Linchmere
Church Farm
Cognor Wood
Poison Copse
Ash Copse
Pond Moor
Golden Valley
Linchmere Marsh
Hazel Piece
Hilly Field Copse
Treetop Farm
GU30

208

207
189

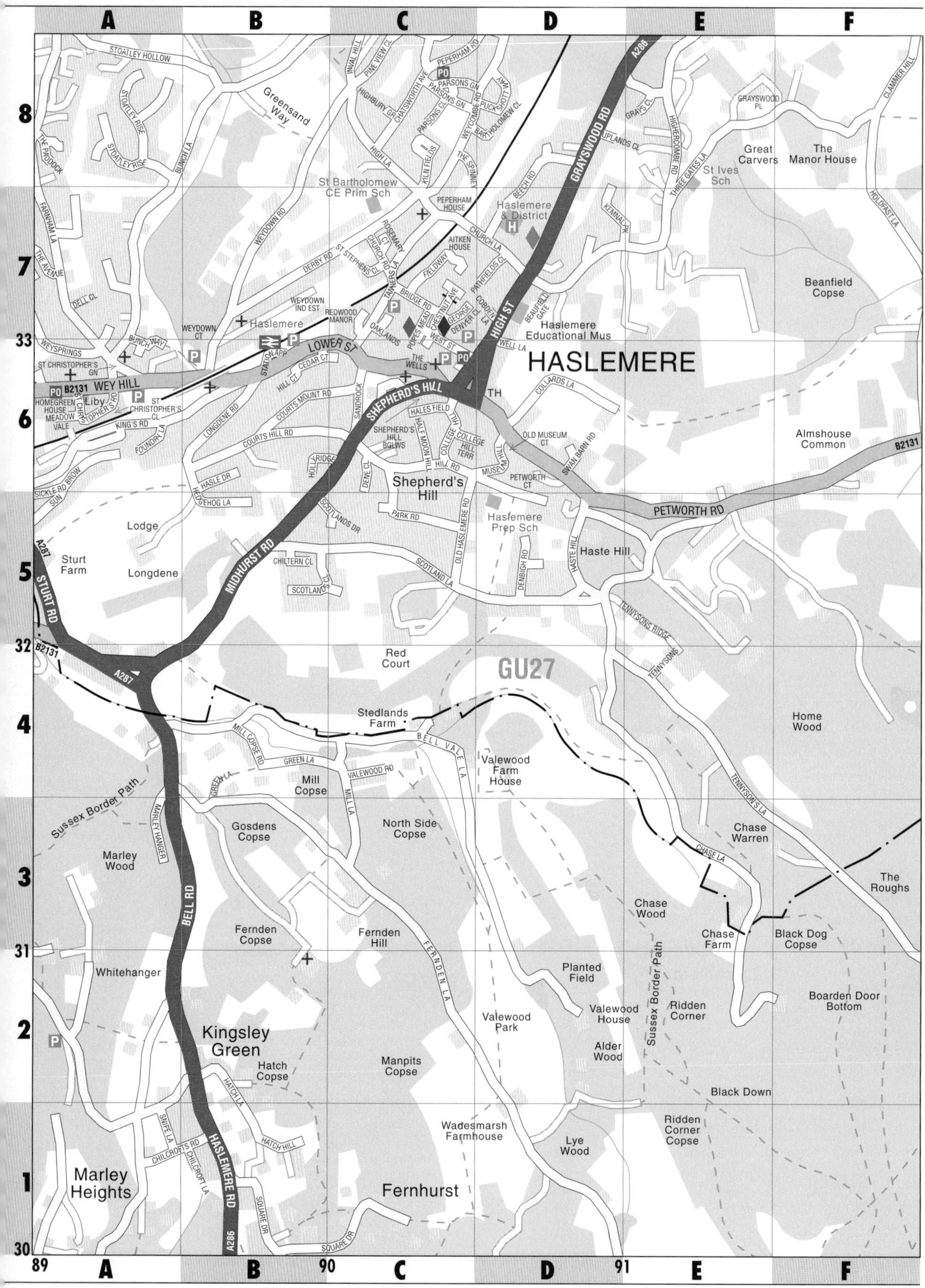
HASLEMERE
GU27
Greensand Way
St Bartholomew CE Prim Sch
Haslemere & District
Haslemere Educational Mus
Great Carvers
The Manor House
St Ives Sch
Beanfield Copse
Almshouse Common
Shepherd's Hill
Haslemere Prep Sch
Haste Hill
Lodge
Sturt Farm
Longdene
Red Court
Stedlands Farm
Home Wood
Valewood Farm House
Mill Copse
North Side Copse
Gosdens Copse
Marley Wood
Sussex Border Path
Chase Warren
The Roughs
Chase Wood
Chase Farm
Black Dog Copse
Fernden Copse
Fernden Hill
Whitehanger
Planted Field
Valewood House
Ridden Corner
Boarden Door Bottom
Valewood Park
Alder Wood
Kingsley Green
Hatch Copse
Manpits Copse
Black Down
Ridden Corner Copse
Wadesmarsh Farmhouse
Lye Wood
Marley Heights
Fernhurst
GRAYSWOOD RD
HIGH ST
SHEPHERD'S HILL
MIDHURST RD
PETWORTH RD
LOWER ST
WEY HILL
STURT RD
BELL RD
HASLEMERE RD
A286
A287
B2131
TENNYSON'S LA
FERNDEN LA
BELL VALE LA
MILL LA
SCOTLAND LA
CHASE LA
COURTS HILL RD
WEYDOWN RD
STOATLEY HOLLOW
STOATLEY RISE
BUNCH LA
PEPERHAM RD
CHURCH LA
HIGHERCOMBE RD
THREE GATES LA
HOLDFAST LA
CLAMMER HILL
A B C D E F
8 7 6 5 4 3 2 1
33 32 31 30
89 90 91

207

190
210

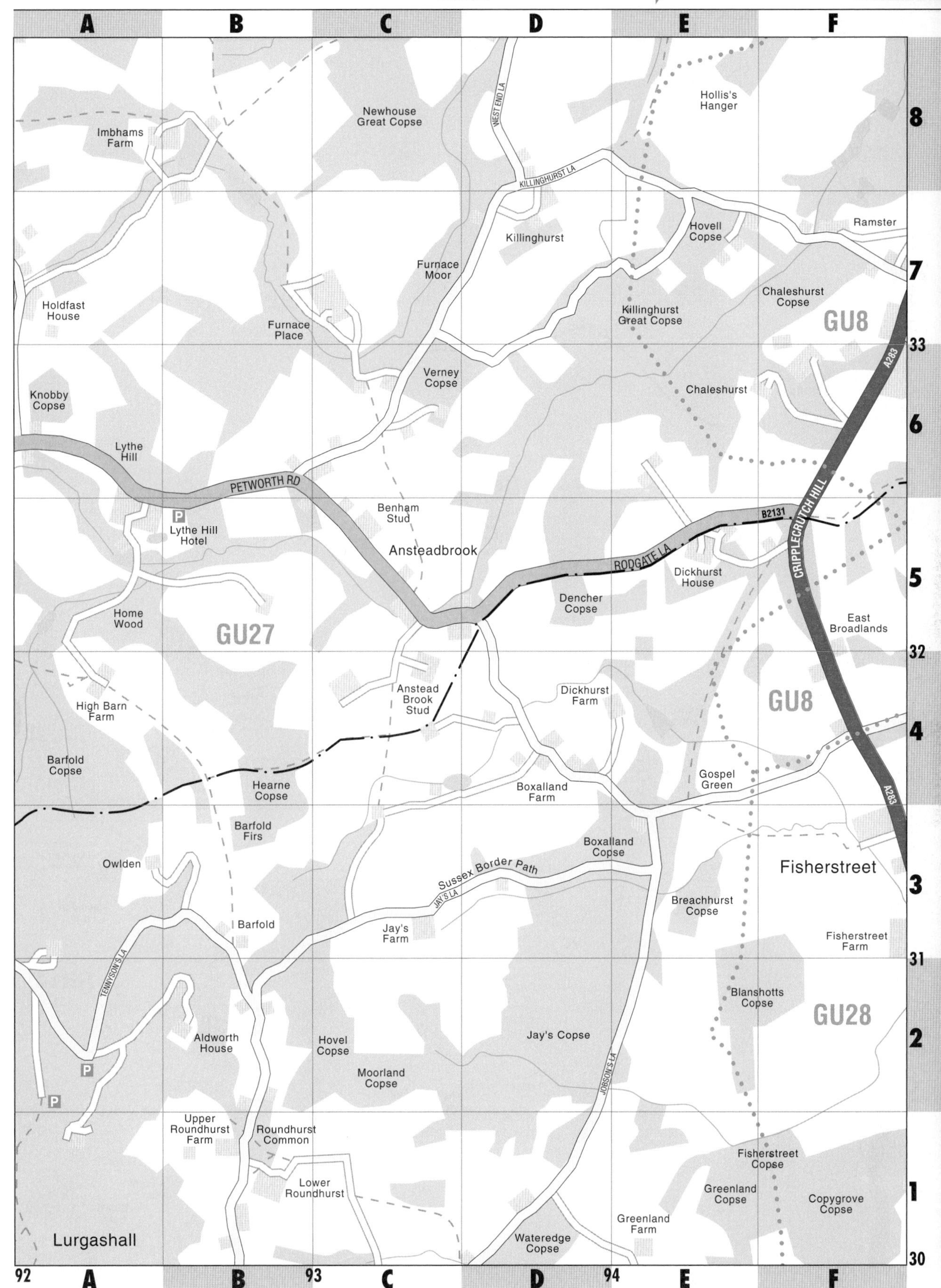
A
B
C
D
E
F
8
7
6
5
4
3
2
1
33
32
31
30
92
93
94
Newhouse Great Copse
Hollis's Hanger
Imbhams Farm
WEST END LA
KILLINGHURST LA
Killinghurst
Hovell Copse
Ramster
Furnace Moor
Holdfast House
Furnace Place
Killinghurst Great Copse
Chaleshurst Copse
GU8
A283
Verney Copse
Chaleshurst
Knobby Copse
Lythe Hill
PETWORTH RD
Benham Stud
B2131
CRIPPLECRUTCH HILL
P
Lythe Hill Hotel
Ansteadbrook
RODGATE LA
Dickhurst House
Dencher Copse
Home Wood
GU27
East Broadlands
Dickhurst Farm
Anstead Brook Stud
High Barn Farm
GU8
Barfold Copse
Gospel Green
Hearne Copse
Boxalland Farm
Barfold Firs
Boxalland Copse
Owlden
Sussex Border Path
Fisherstreet
JAY'S LA
Breachhurst Copse
Barfold
Jay's Farm
Fisherstreet Farm
TENNYSON'S LA
Blanshotts Copse
GU28
Aldworth House
Jay's Copse
Hovel Copse
Moorland Copse
P
P
JOBSON'S LA
Upper Roundhurst Farm
Roundhurst Common
Fisherstreet Copse
Lower Roundhurst
Greenland Copse
Copygrove Copse
Greenland Farm
Lurgashall
Wateredge Copse

210

209
191

A
B
C
D
E
F
8
7
33
6
5
32
4
3
31
2
1
30
95
96
97
Windmill Copse
Great Copse
Sparkes Copse
Tugley Farm
Hungry Corner
PETWORTH RD
A283
Rovehurst Wood
PICKHURST RD
Fisherlane Hanger
Griggs Bottom
Gostrode Farm
Fisher Lane Nursery
Little Tugley
Surrey Copse
Robins Farm
FISHER LA
Sussex Border Path
GOSTRODE LA
Ramsnest Common
White's Hill
Redlands Farm
Works
Surrey Belt
PLAISTOW RD
CH
Surrey Rough
Furze Field
Shillinglee Park Golf Course
GU8
Big Copse
Potlane Farm
Downlands
Walk Copse
Upper North Pond
Shillinglee Park
Downlands Wood
Lower North Pond
Parkgate
Shillinglee Home Farm
Manorhill Copse
Stilland Farm
SHILLINGLEE RD
Gaston's Farm
Newhouse Farm
Turnour's Wood
Deer Tower
New Copse
Nine Acre Rew
Beanfield Copse
Little Hayman's Farm
Eastland Farm
Haymans Farm
Twenty Four Acres
China Bridge
The Lake
RH14
Mill Copse
Park Mill Farm
Frith Lodge
GU28
The Plantation
Frith Wood
Frith Hill
Dale's Farm Hanger
Dale's Farm
Mitchell Park Farm

209

192
212

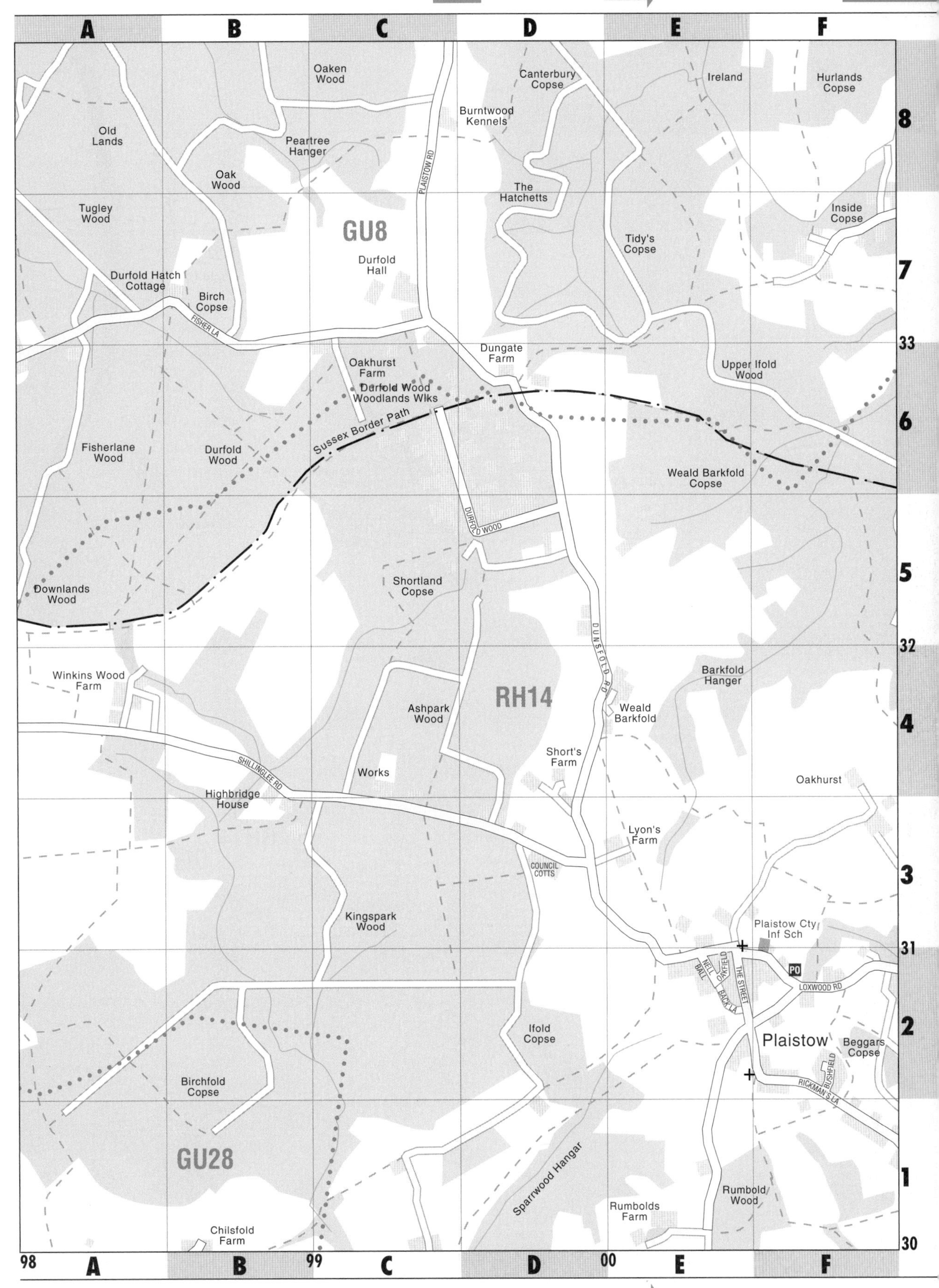
A
B
C
D
E
F
Oaken Wood
Canterbury Copse
Ireland
Hurlands Copse
Old Lands
Peartree Hanger
Burntwood Kennels
8
Oak Wood
PLAISTOW RD
The Hatchetts
Tugley Wood
GU8
Tidy's Copse
Inside Copse
Durfold Hall
Durfold Hatch Cottage
Birch Copse
7
FISHER LA
33
Dungate Farm
Oakhurst Farm
Upper Ifold Wood
Durfold Wood Woodlands Wlks
Sussex Border Path
6
Fisherlane Wood
Durfold Wood
Weald Barkfold Copse
DURFOLD WOOD
5
Downlands Wood
Shortland Copse
DUNSFOLD RD
32
Winkins Wood Farm
Barkfold Hanger
RH14
Ashpark Wood
Weald Barkfold
4
Short's Farm
SHILLINGLEE RD
Works
Oakhurst
Highbridge House
Lyon's Farm
COUNCIL COTTS
3
Kingspark Wood
Plaistow Cty Inf Sch
31
NELL BALL
OAKFIELD
THE STREET
PO
LOXWOOD RD
BACK LA
2
Ifold Copse
Plaistow
Beggars Copse
RUSHFIELD
Birchfold Copse
RICKMAN'S LA
GU28
Sparrwood Hangar
1
Rumbold Wood
Rumbolds Farm
Chilsfold Farm
30
98
99
00

212

211
193

A
B
C
D
E
F
8
7
33
6
5
32
4
3
31
2
1
30
01
02
03
Old Knightons
Old Lock House
Glasshouse Copse
Priorswood
Upper Ifold Farm
GU8
GU6
High Bridge
Turtles Farm
ROSEMARY LA
LOXWOOD RD
B2133
Sydney Wood Cott
Westland Copse
Sir Roger Tichbourne (PH)
Alfold Bars
PIGBUSH LA
THE WALLED GARDEN
Loxwood Hall
Gennets Wood
Oakhurst Farm
OAKHURST LA
Tokens Farm
Thirds Copse
Sydney Farm
Lee House Farm
Gennets Wood
The Rookery
Barberry Furze
Sussex Border Path
Barberry Bridge
Wey-South Path
Gennets Furze
Pawlies Farm
Pond Copse
Hog Wood
Oxoncroft Copse
Gennets Farm
POND COPSE LA
POUND CL
Hog Copse
Furzen Wood
IFOLD BRIDGE LA
Loxwood
POND CL
THE LANE
Hogwood Farm
NICHOLSFIELD
Barn Wood
THISTLEDOWN VALE
GLEBELANDS
PO
STATION RD
HOGWOOD RD
RH14
Loxwood Place Farm
Devil's Hole
POUNDFIELD LA
Ifold
Loxwoodhills Pond
CHALK RD
WYCHWOOD
WILDACRE CL
THE CLOSE
THE RIDE
THE DRIVE
LOXWOOD RD
Charleshurst
Quennells Farm
Spring Copse
IFOLDHURST
Headfoldswood Farm
Corner Copse
PLAISTOW RD
Flitchings Farm
LAKERS LEA
FOXBRIDGE LA
Foxbridge Hanger
Little Headfoldswood Copse
RICKMAN'S LA
Foxbridge Farm
CH
Foxbridge Golf Course
Woodlands Farm

211

194
214

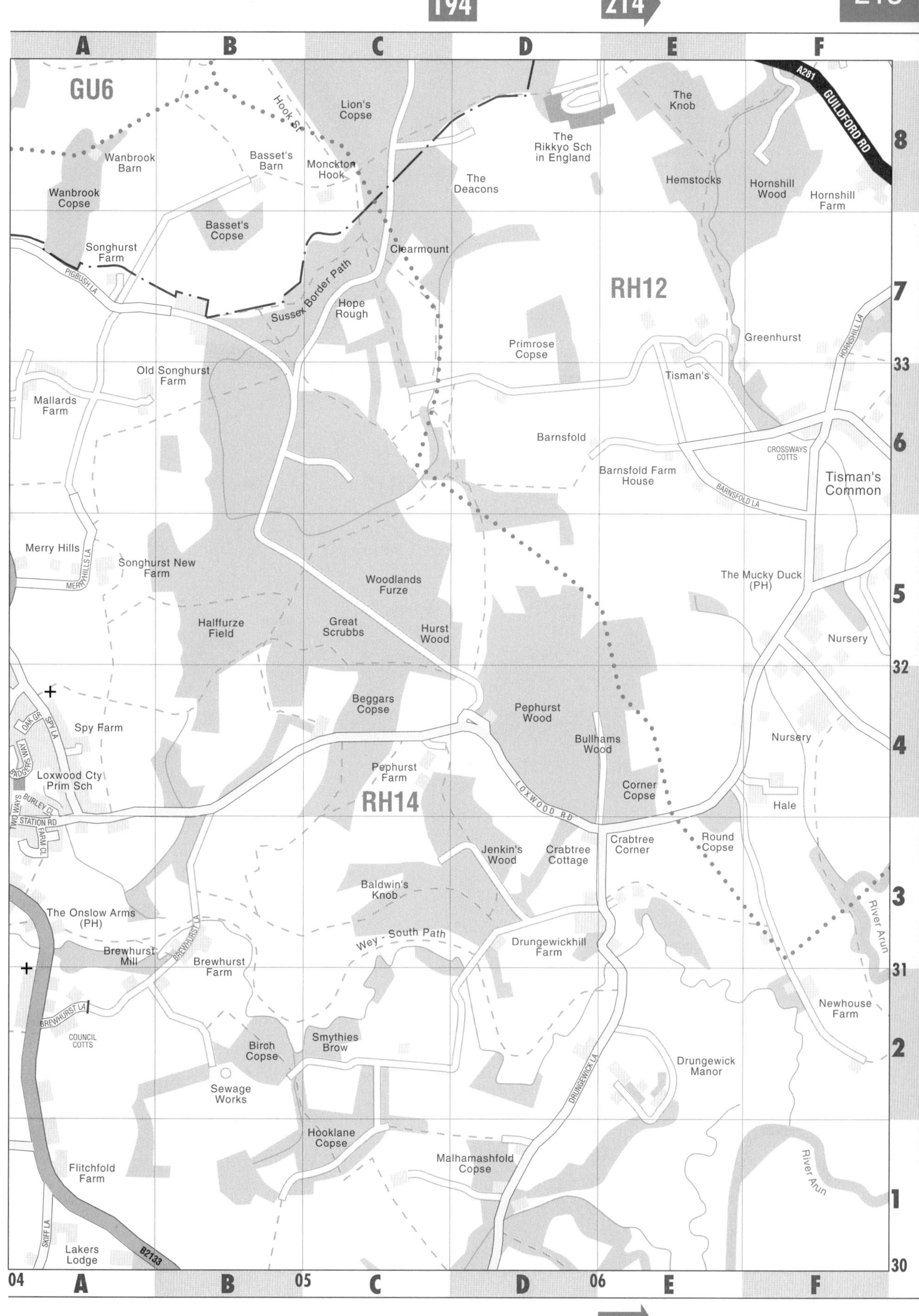
A
B
C
D
E
F
GU6
Lion's Copse
Hook St
The Knob
A281
GUILDFORD RD
The Rikkyo Sch in England
Wanbrook Barn
Basset's Barn
Monckton Hook
The Deacons
Hemstocks
Hornshill Wood
Hornshill Farm
8
Wanbrook Copse
Basset's Copse
Songhurst Farm
Clearmount
PIGBUSH LA
Sussex Border Path
RH12
7
Hope Rough
Greenhurst
HORNSHILL LA
Primrose Copse
33
Old Songhurst Farm
Tisman's
Mallards Farm
Barnsfold
CROSSWAYS COTTS
6
Barnsfold Farm House
Tisman's Common
BARNSFOLD LA
Merry Hills
MERRY HILLS LA
Songhurst New Farm
Woodlands Furze
The Mucky Duck (PH)
5
Halffurze Field
Great Scrubbs
Hurst Wood
Nursery
32
Beggars Copse
Pephurst Wood
Spy Farm
OAK GR
SPY LA
Bullhams Wood
Nursery
4
Pephurst Farm
Loxwood Cty Prim Sch
Corner Copse
RH14
LOXWOOD RD
Hale
BURLEY CL
TWO WAYS
STATION RD
FARM CL
Crabtree Corner
Round Copse
Jenkin's Wood
Crabtree Cottage
Baldwin's Knob
3
River Arun
The Onslow Arms (PH)
Wey - South Path
Drungewickhill Farm
Brewhurst Mill
BREWHURST LA
Brewhurst Farm
31
BREWHURST LA
Newhouse Farm
COUNCIL COTTS
Birch Copse
Smythies Brow
2
Drungewick Manor
DRUNGEWICK LA
Sewage Works
Hooklane Copse
River Arun
Flitchfold Farm
Malhamashfold Copse
1
SKIFF LA
Lakers Lodge
B2133
30
04
A
B
05
C
D
06
E
F

214

213
195

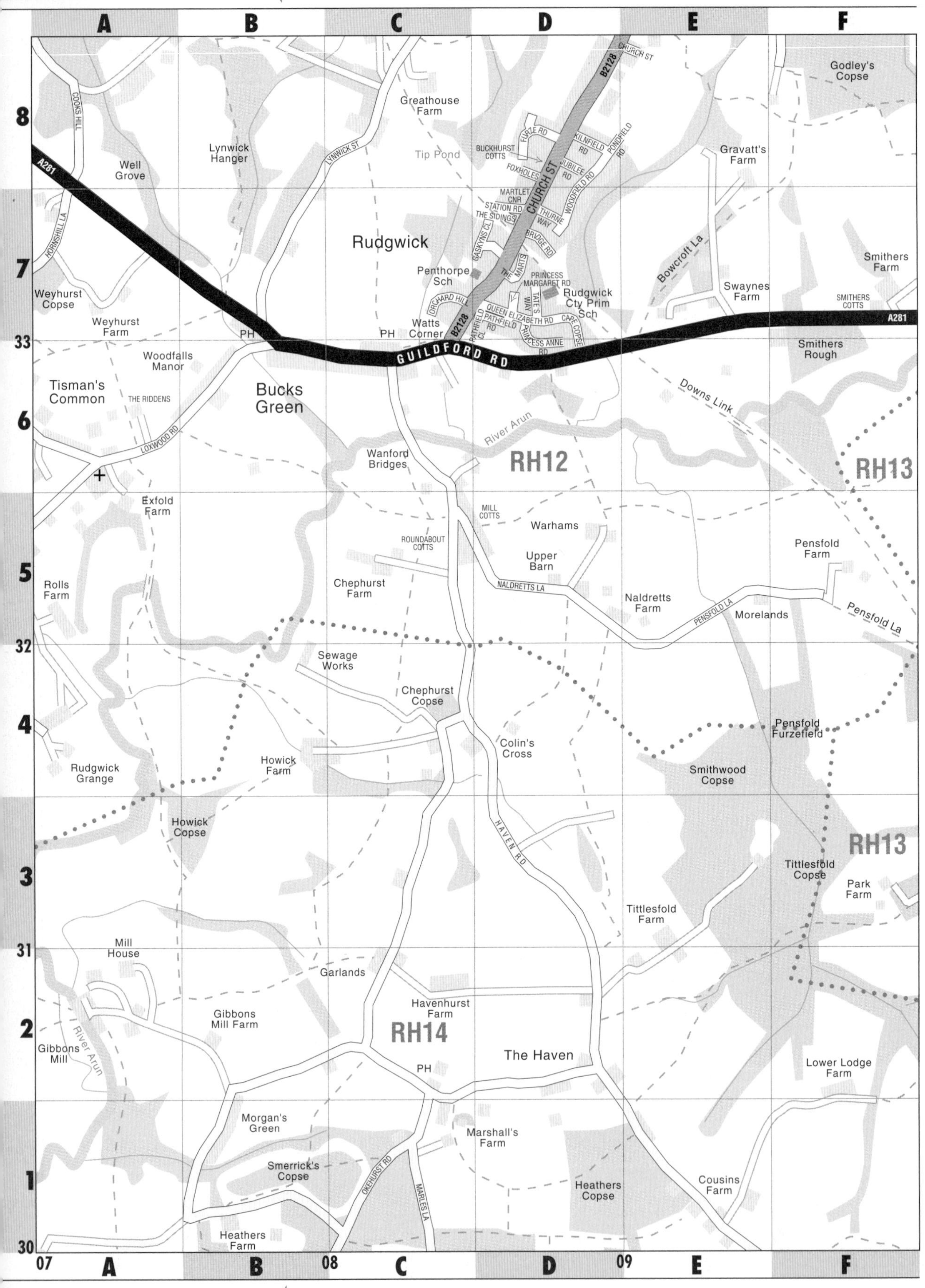
A
B
C
D
E
F
8
7
33
6
5
32
4
3
31
2
1
30
07
08
09
A281
B2128
CHURCH ST
GUILDFORD RD
Godley's Copse
Greathouse Farm
Lynwick Hanger
Well Grove
COOKS HILL
LYNWICK ST
Tip Pond
BUCKHURST COTTS
FURZE RD
KILNFIELD RD
PONDFIELD RD
JUBILEE RD
FOXHOLES
WOODFIELD RD
MARTLET CNR
STATION RD
THE SIDINGS
THURNE WAY
GASKYNS CL
BRIDGE RD
THE MARTS
Gravatt's Farm
Rudgwick
HORNSHILL LA
Bowcroft La
Penthorpe Sch
PRINCESS MARGARET RD
Rudgwick Cty Prim Sch
Swaynes Farm
Smithers Farm
SMITHERS COTTS
ORCHARD HILL
TATE'S WAY
QUEEN ELIZABETH RD
PATHFIELD RD
PATHFIELD CL
CARE COPSE
PRINCESS ANNE RD
Weyhurst Copse
Weyhurst Farm
Watts Corner
PH
Woodfalls Manor
Smithers Rough
Tisman's Common
THE RIDDENS
Bucks Green
Downs Link
LOXWOOD RD
River Arun
Wanford Bridges
RH12
RH13
Exfold Farm
MILL COTTS
Warhams
ROUNDABOUT COTTS
Upper Barn
Pensfold Farm
Rolls Farm
Chephurst Farm
NALDRETTS LA
Naldretts Farm
PENSFOLD LA
Morelands
Pensfold La
Sewage Works
Chephurst Copse
Pensfold Furzefield
Colin's Cross
Smithwood Copse
Rudgwick Grange
Howick Farm
Howick Copse
HAVEN RD
Tittlesfold Copse
Park Farm
Tittlesfold Farm
Mill House
Garlands
Havenhurst Farm
Gibbons Mill Farm
RH14
Gibbons Mill
The Haven
Lower Lodge Farm
Morgan's Green
Marshall's Farm
Smerrick's Copse
OKEHURST RD
MARLES LA
Heathers Copse
Cousins Farm
Heathers Farm

213

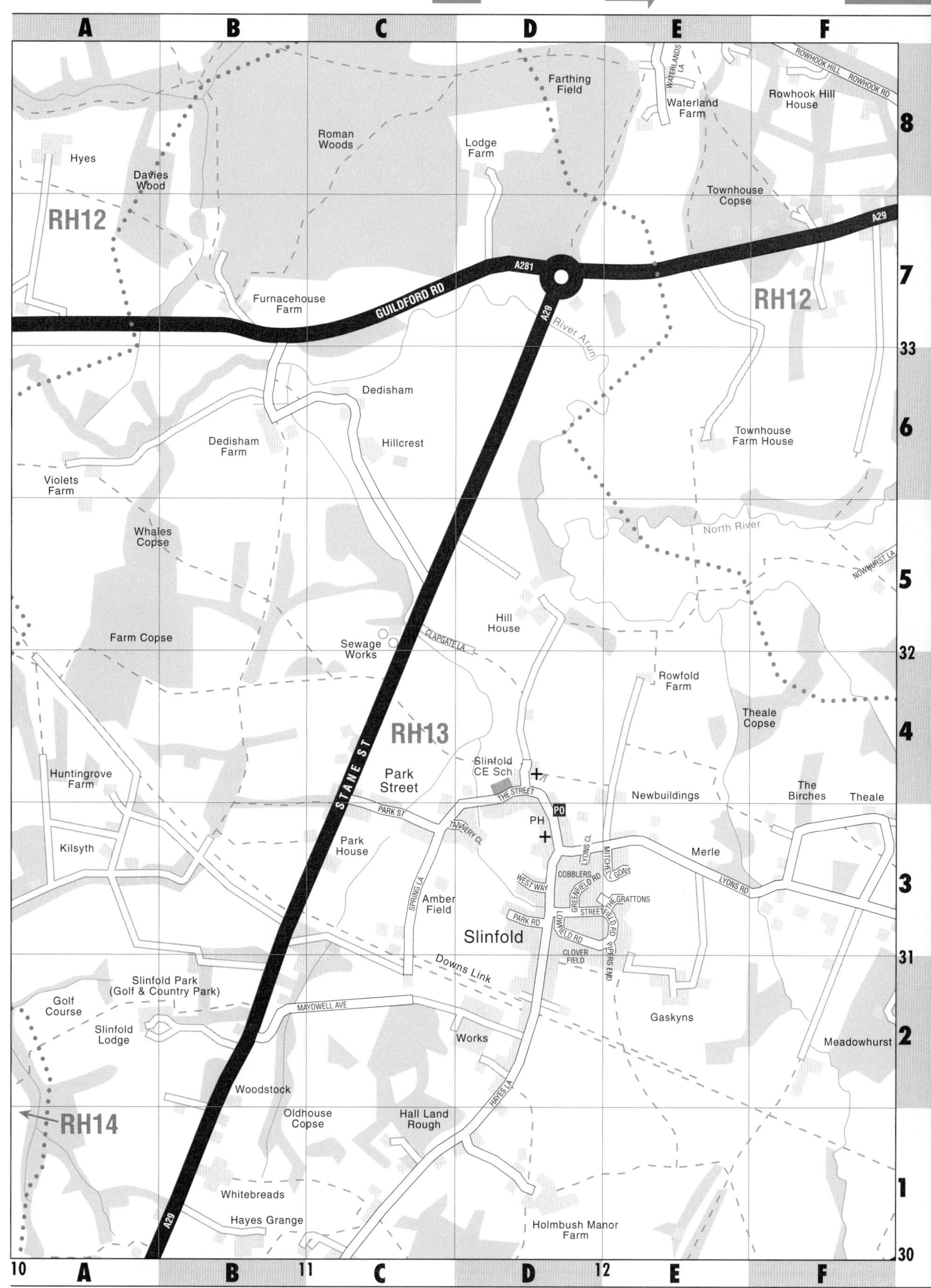
A
B
C
D
E
F
Farthing Field
Waterlands La
Waterland Farm
Rowhook Hill
Rowhook Rd
Rowhook Hill House
Roman Woods
Lodge Farm
Hyes
Davies Wood
RH12
Townhouse Copse
A29
A281
Guildford Rd
Furnacehouse Farm
RH12
A29
River Arun
Dedisham
Dedisham Farm
Hillcrest
Townhouse Farm House
Violets Farm
Whales Copse
North River
Nowhurst La
Farm Copse
Hill House
Sewage Works
Clapgate La
Rowfold Farm
RH13
Theale Copse
Huntingrove Farm
Slinfold CE Sch
Park Street
Stane St
The Street
Park St
Newbuildings
The Birches
Theale
PO
PH
Tannery Cl
Kilsyth
Park House
Lyons Cl
Mitchell Gdns
Merle
Cobblers
Greenfield Rd
West Way
Spring La
Amber Field
The Grattons
Street Field Rd
Lyons Rd
Park Rd
Lowfield Rd
Slinfold
Clover Field
Pipers End
Downs Link
Slinfold Park (Golf & Country Park)
Golf Course
Maydwell Ave
Gaskyns
Slinfold Lodge
Works
Meadowhurst
Woodstock
RH14
Oldhouse Copse
Hall Land Rough
Hayes La
Whitebreads
Hayes Grange
Holmbush Manor Farm
A29
8
7
33
6
5
32
4
3
31
2
1
30
10
11
12

215
197

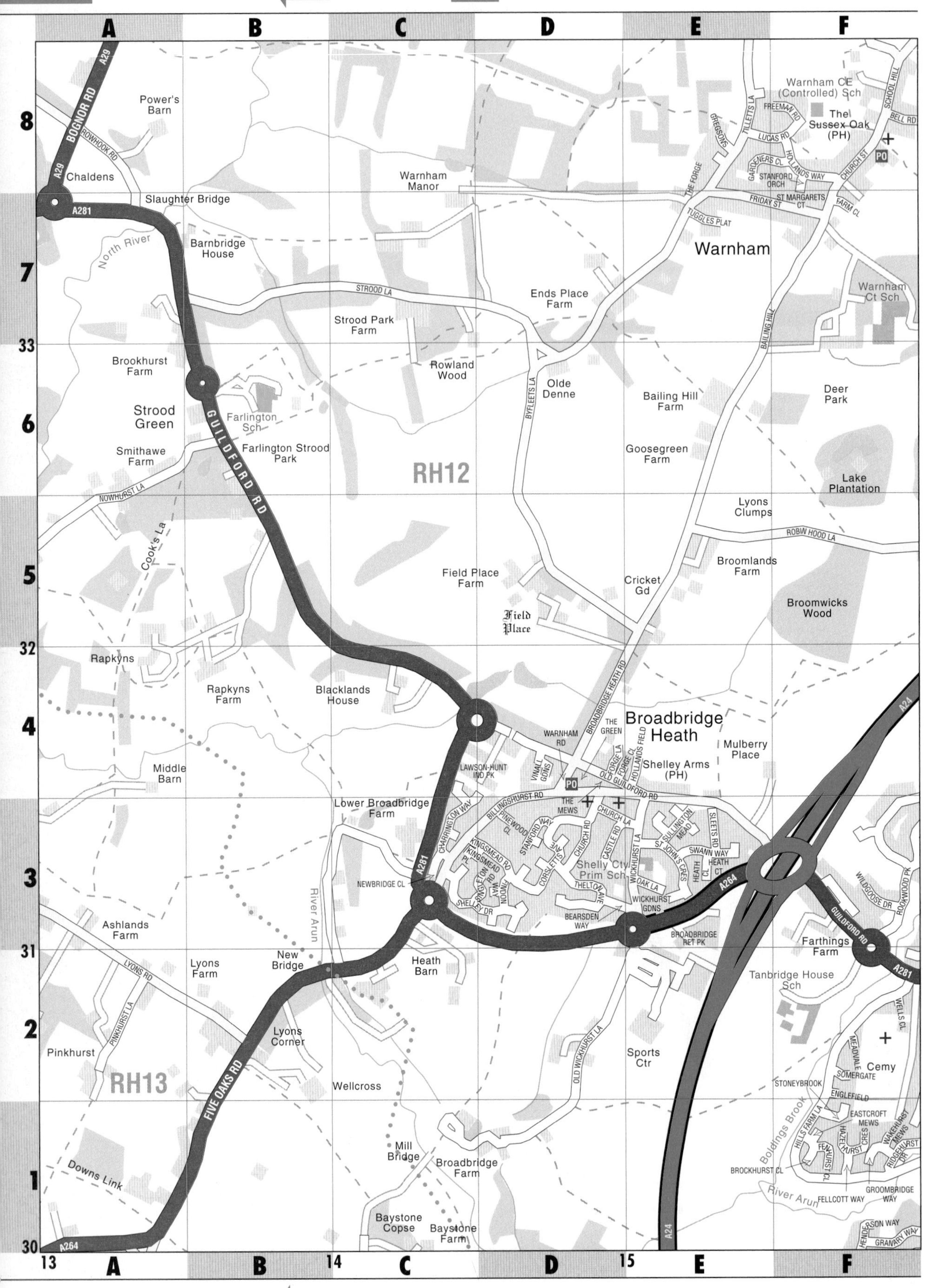
A
B
C
D
E
F
8
7
33
6
5
32
4
3
31
2
1
30
13
14
15
BOGNOR RD
A29
ROWHOOK RD
Power's Barn
Chaldens
Slaughter Bridge
A281
North River
Barnbridge House
STROOD LA
Strood Park Farm
Warnham Manor
Brookhurst Farm
Strood Green
Farlington Sch
GUILDFORD RD
Farlington Strood Park
Smithawe Farm
NOWHURST LA
Cook's La
RH12
Rowland Wood
Ends Place Farm
BYFLEETS LA
Olde Denne
Bailing Hill Farm
Goosegreen Farm
Warnham CE (Controlled) Sch
The Sussex Oak (PH)
SCHOOL HILL
BELL RD
FREEMAN RD
TILLETTS LA
GREGSONS
LUCAS RD
GARDENERS CL
HOLLANDS WAY
STANFORD ORCH
CHURCH ST
ST MARGARETS CT
FRIDAY ST
FARM CL
THE FORGE
TUGGLES PLAT
PO
Warnham
Warnham Ct Sch
BAILING HILL
Deer Park
Lake Plantation
Lyons Clumps
ROBIN HOOD LA
Broomlands Farm
Broomwicks Wood
Field Place Farm
Field Place
Cricket Gd
Rapkyns
Rapkyns Farm
Blacklands House
BROADBRIDGE HEATH RD
WARNHAM RD
THE GREEN
Broadbridge Heath
Mulberry Place
HOLLANDS FIELD
FORGE LA
FORGE CL
Shelley Arms (PH)
OLD GUILDFORD RD
VIMALL GDNS
LAWSON-HUNT IND PK
Middle Barn
Lower Broadbridge Farm
BILLINGSHURST RD
THE MEWS
CHURCH LA
CHARRINGTON WAY
PINEWOOD CL
STANFORD WAY
SULLINGTON MEAD
SLEETS RD
KINGSMEAD RD
KINGSMEAD PL
SINGLETON RD
FINDON WAY
CORSLETTS AVE
CHURCH RD
CASTLE RD
WICKHURST LA
ST JOHN'S CRES
SWANN WAY
HEATH CL
HEATH CT
Shelly Cty Prim Sch
OAK LA
THELTON AVE
SHELLEY DR
WICKHURST GDNS
BEARSDEN WAY
NEWBRIDGE CL
A264
BROADBRIDGE RET PK
River Arun
Ashlands Farm
LYONS RD
Lyons Farm
New Bridge
Heath Barn
Farthings Farm
Tanbridge House Sch
WILDGOOSE DR
ROOKWOOD PK
A24
PINKHURST LA
Pinkhurst
RH13
FIVE OAKS RD
Lyons Corner
Wellcross
OLD WICKHURST LA
Sports Ctr
WELLS CL
MEADVALE
SOMERGATE
Cemy
STONEYBROOK
ENGLEFIELD
EASTCROFT MEWS
WAKEHURST MEWS
Boldings Brook
HILLS FARM LA
HAZELHURST CRES
FENHURST CL
RIDGEHURST DR
Mill Bridge
Broadbridge Farm
Downs Link
BROCKHURST CL
River Arun
FELLCOTT WAY
GROOMBRIDGE WAY
Baystone Copse
Baystone Farm
HENDERSON WAY
GRANARY WAY

215

198
218

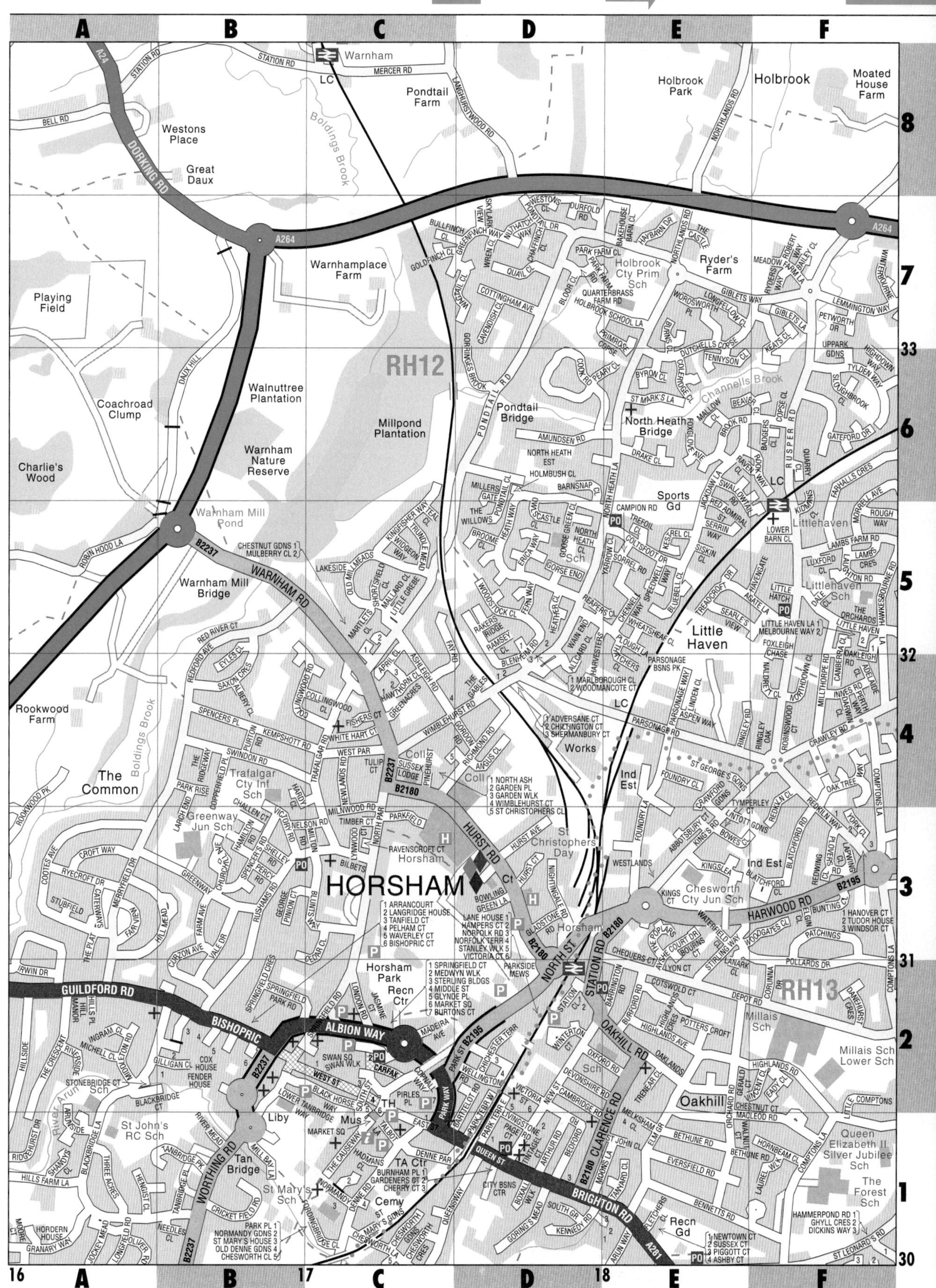

A
B
C
D
E
F
8
7
33
6
5
32
4
3
31
2
1
30
16
17
18
Warnham
STATION RD
MERCER RD
LC
Pondtail Farm
BELL RD
Westons Place
Boldings Brook
LANGHURSTWOOD RD
Holbrook Park
Holbrook
Moated House Farm
NORTHLANDS RD
DORKING RD
Great Daux
A24
A264
Warnhamplace Farm
Playing Field
Ryder's Farm
Holbrook Cty Prim Sch
DAUX HILL
RH12
Walnuttree Plantation
Coachroad Clump
Millpond Plantation
Pondtail Bridge
North Heath Bridge
Channells Brook
Warnham Nature Reserve
Charlie's Wood
Sports Gd
Warnham Mill Pond
Littlehaven
B2237
WARNHAM RD
Warnham Mill Bridge
Little Haven
Rookwood Farm
The Common
Trafalgar Cty Inf Sch
Greenway Jun Sch
Coll
Works
Ind Est
HORSHAM
St Christophers Day
Chesworth Cty Jun Sch
Ind Est
HARWOOD RD
B2195
B2180
HURST RD
NORTH ST
STATION RD
Horsham
Horsham Park
Recn Ctr
GUILDFORD RD
BISHOPRIC
ALBION WAY
CARFAX
PARK WAY
RH13
Millais Sch
Millais Sch Lower Sch
Oakhill
OAKHILL RD
CLARENCE RD
Queen Elizabeth II Silver Jubilee Sch
The Forest Sch
St John's RC Sch
Liby
Mus
TH
TA Ctr
Tan Bridge
WORTHING RD
St Mary's Sch
Cemy
BRIGHTON RD
QUEEN ST
Recn Gd
A281
River Arun

218

217
199

A
B
20
C
D
21
E
F

217

Scale: 7 inches to 1 mile
0 110 yards 220 yards
0 125 m 250 m

One-way Streets

House numbers
1 59
HIGH ST

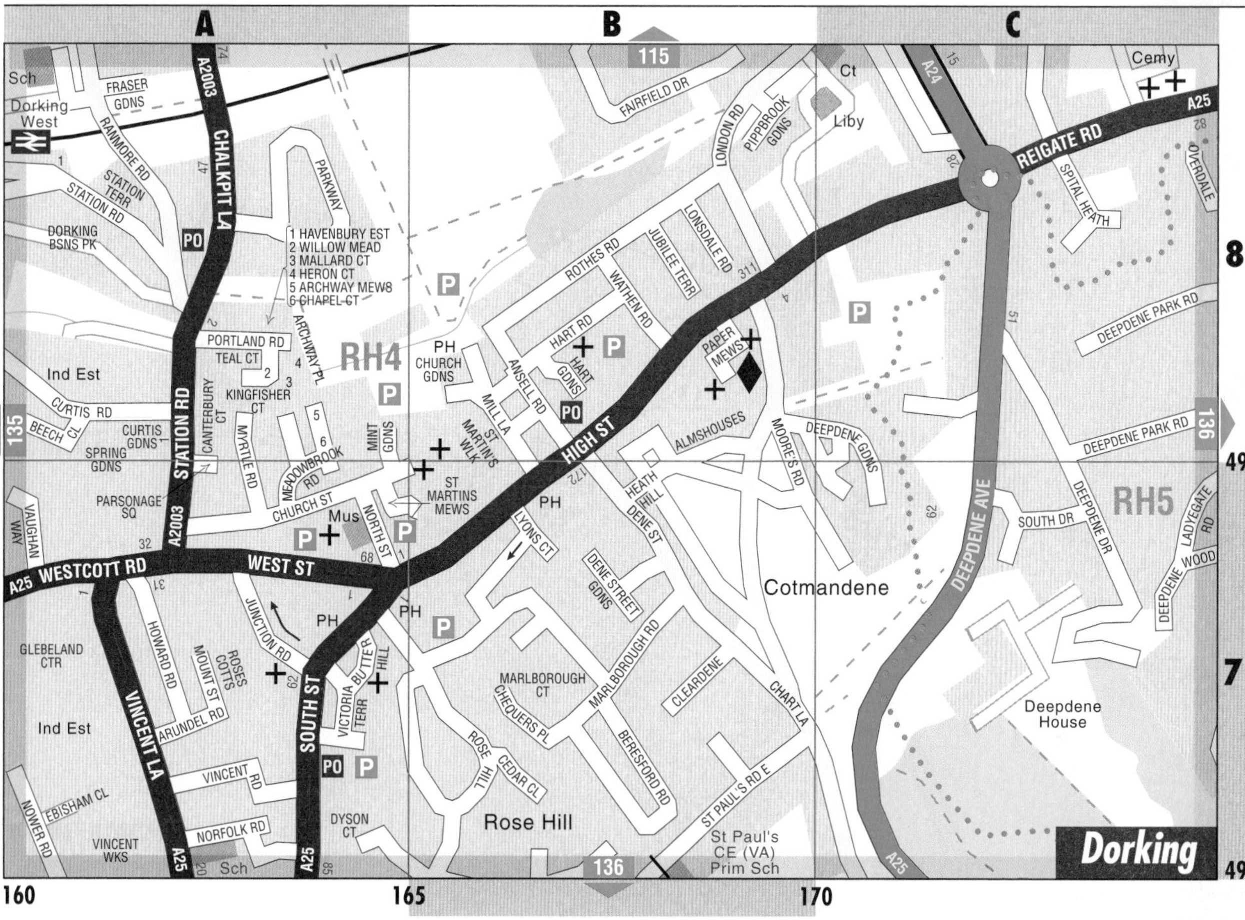

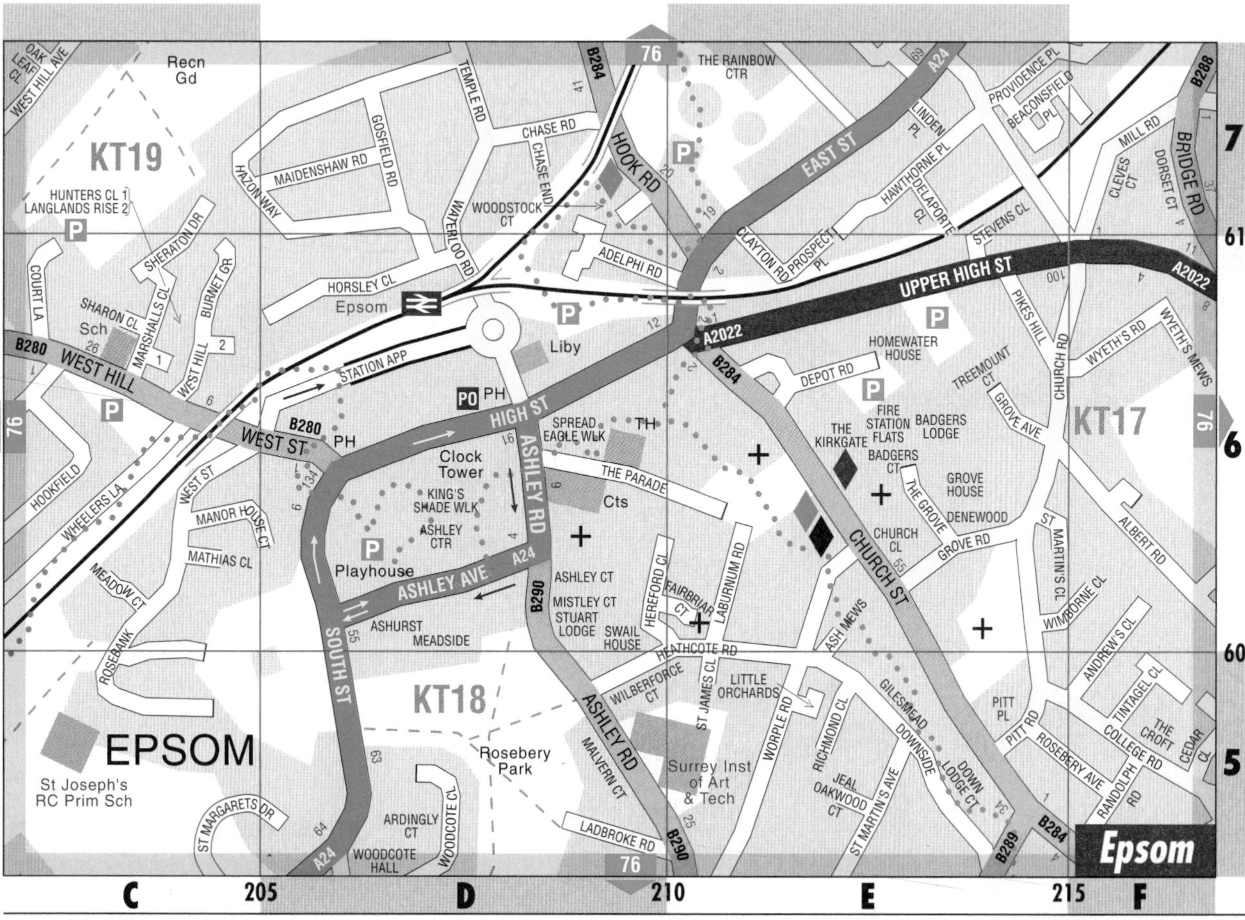

Dorking

A B C
115
8
7
495
490
160 165 170
135 136 136

Sch
Dorking West
FRASER GDNS
RANMORE RD
STATION TERR
STATION RD
DORKING BSNS PK
A2003
CHALKPIT LA
PO
PARKWAY
1 HAVENBURY EST
2 WILLOW MEAD
3 MALLARD CT
4 HERON CT
5 ARCHWAY MEWS
6 CHAPEL CT
ARCHWAY PL
PORTLAND RD
TEAL CT
KINGFISHER CT
RH4
Ind Est
CURTIS RD
BEECH CL
CURTIS GDNS
SPRING GDNS
STATION RD
CANTERBURY CT
MYRTLE RD
MEADOWBROOK RD
MINT GDNS
PARSONAGE SQ
CHURCH ST
Mus
NORTH ST
VAUGHAN WAY
A25 WESTCOTT RD
WEST ST
GLEBELAND CTR
HOWARD RD
MOUNT ST
ROSES COTTS
JUNCTION RD
VINCENT LA
Ind Est
ARUNDEL RD
SOUTH ST
VICTORIA TERR
BUTTER HILL
VINCENT RD
EBISHAM CL
NOWER RD
VINCENT WKS
NORFOLK RD
Sch
DYSON CT
PH
CHURCH GDNS
MILL LA
ST MARTIN'S WLK
ST MARTINS MEWS
ANSELL RD
HART RD
HART GDNS
ROTHES RD
WATHEN RD
JUBILEE TERR
LONSDALE RD
FAIRFIELD DR
LONDON RD
PIPBROOK GDNS
Ct
Liby
HIGH ST
PAPER MEWS
ALMSHOUSES
MOORE'S RD
DEEPDENE GDNS
HEATH HILL
DENE ST
LYONS CT
DENE STREET GDNS
MARLBOROUGH CT
MARLBOROUGH RD
CHEQUERS PL
ROSE HILL
CEDAR CL
BERESFORD RD
CLEARDENE
Cotmandene
CHART LA
ST PAUL'S RD E
Rose Hill
St Paul's CE (VA) Prim Sch
A24
A25
Cemy
REIGATE RD
SPITAL HEATH
OVERDALE
DEEPDENE PARK RD
DEEPDENE AVE
DEEPDENE PARK RD
RH5
SOUTH DR
DEEPDENE DR
LADYGATE RD
DEEPDENE WOOD
Deepdene House

Epsom

C 205 D 210 E 215 F
76
7
610
6
605
5

OAK LEAF CL
WEST HILL AVE
Recn Gd
KT19
HAZON WAY
MAIDENSHAW RD
GOSFIELD RD
TEMPLE RD
CHASE RD
CHASE END
B284
HOOK RD
THE RAINBOW CTR
HUNTERS CL 1
LANGLANDS RISE 2
SHERATON DR
BURNET GR
COURT LA
SHARON CL
Sch
MARSHALLS CL
WEST HILL
WOODSTOCK CT
WATERLOO RD
ADELPHI RD
HORSLEY CL
Epsom
B280 WEST HILL
STATION APP
Liby
PO PH
HIGH ST
SPREAD EAGLE WLK
TH
B280
WEST ST
PH
Clock Tower
KING'S SHADE WLK
ASHLEY CTR
ASHLEY RD
THE PARADE
Cts
HOOKFIELD
WHEELERS LA
WEST ST
MANOR HOUSE CT
MATHIAS CL
MEADOW CT
Playhouse
ASHLEY AVE
A24
ASHLEY CT
MISTLEY CT
STUART LODGE
SWAIL HOUSE
B290
HEREFORD CL
FAIRBRIAR CT
LABURNUM RD
ASHURST
MEADSIDE
SOUTH ST
ROSEBANK
KT18
HEATHCOTE RD
WILBERFORCE CT
ST JAMES CL
LITTLE ORCHARDS
WORPLE RD
RICHMOND CL
EPSOM
St Joseph's RC Prim Sch
ST MARGARETS DR
ARDINGLY CT
WOODCOTE CL
WOODCOTE HALL
Rosebery Park
MALVERN CT
ASHLEY RD
LADBROKE RD
Surrey Inst of Art & Tech
JEAL OAKWOOD CT
ST MARTIN'S AVE
DOWNSIDE
GILESMEAD
DOWN LODGE CT
EAST ST
LINDEN PL
HAWTHORNE PL
DELAPORTE CL
CLAYTON RD
PROSPECT PL
PROVIDENCE PL
BEACONSFIELD PL
STEVENS CL
MILL RD
B288
BRIDGE RD
DORSET CT
CLEVES CT
UPPER HIGH ST
A2022
A2022
B284
DEPOT RD
HOMEWATER HOUSE
FIRE STATION FLATS
THE KIRKGATE
BADGERS LODGE
BADGERS CT
THE GROVE
GROVE HOUSE
DENEWOOD
CHURCH CL
CHURCH ST
ASH MEWS
GROVE RD
TREEMOUNT CT
GROVE AVE
PIKES HILL
CHURCH RD
WYETH'S RD
WYETH'S MEWS
KT17
ST MARTIN'S CL
WIMBORNE CL
ALBERT RD
ANDREW'S CL
TINTAGEL CL
THE CROFT
CEDAR CL
PITT PL
PITT RD
ROSEBERY AVE
COLLEGE RD
RANDOLPH RD
B289
B284

Scale: 7 inches to 1 mile
0 110 yards 220 yards
0 125 m 250 m

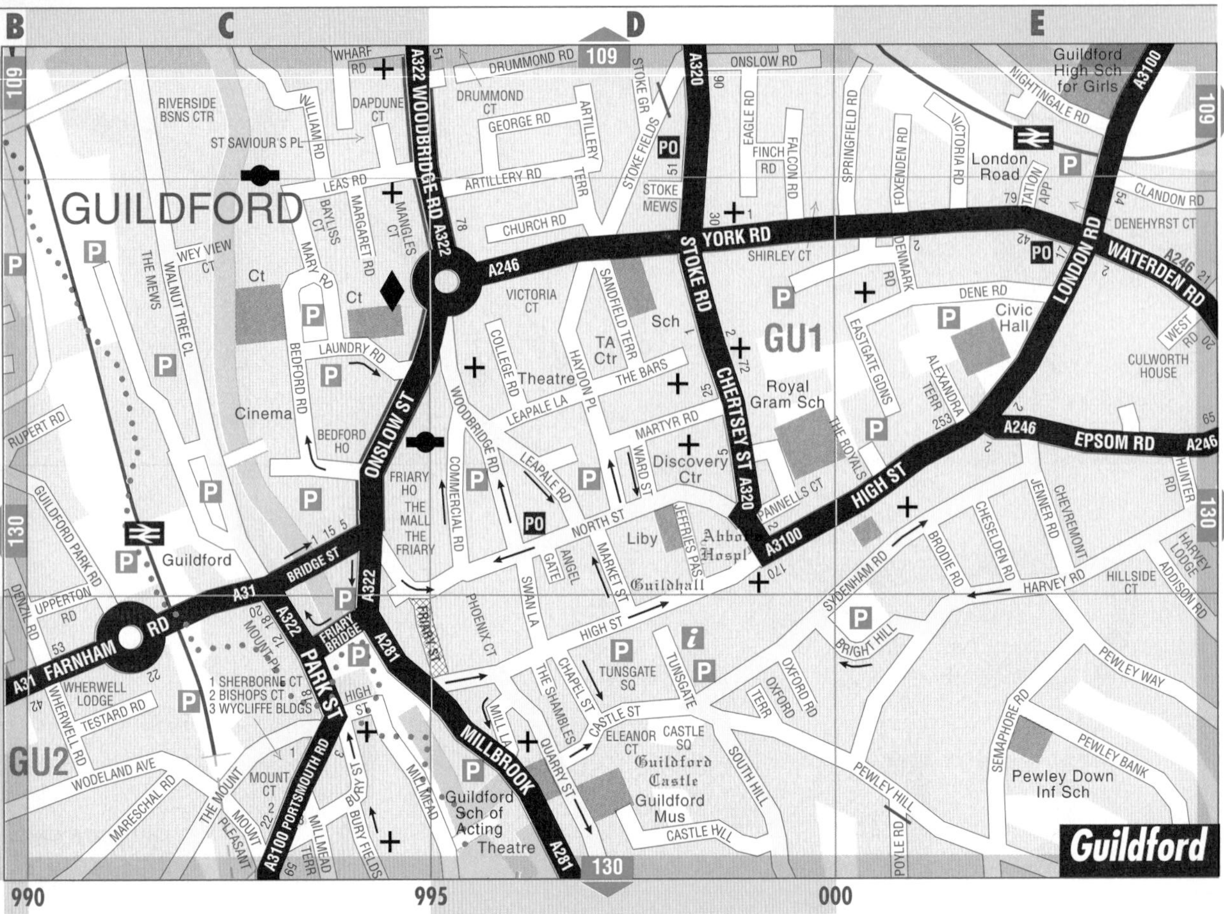

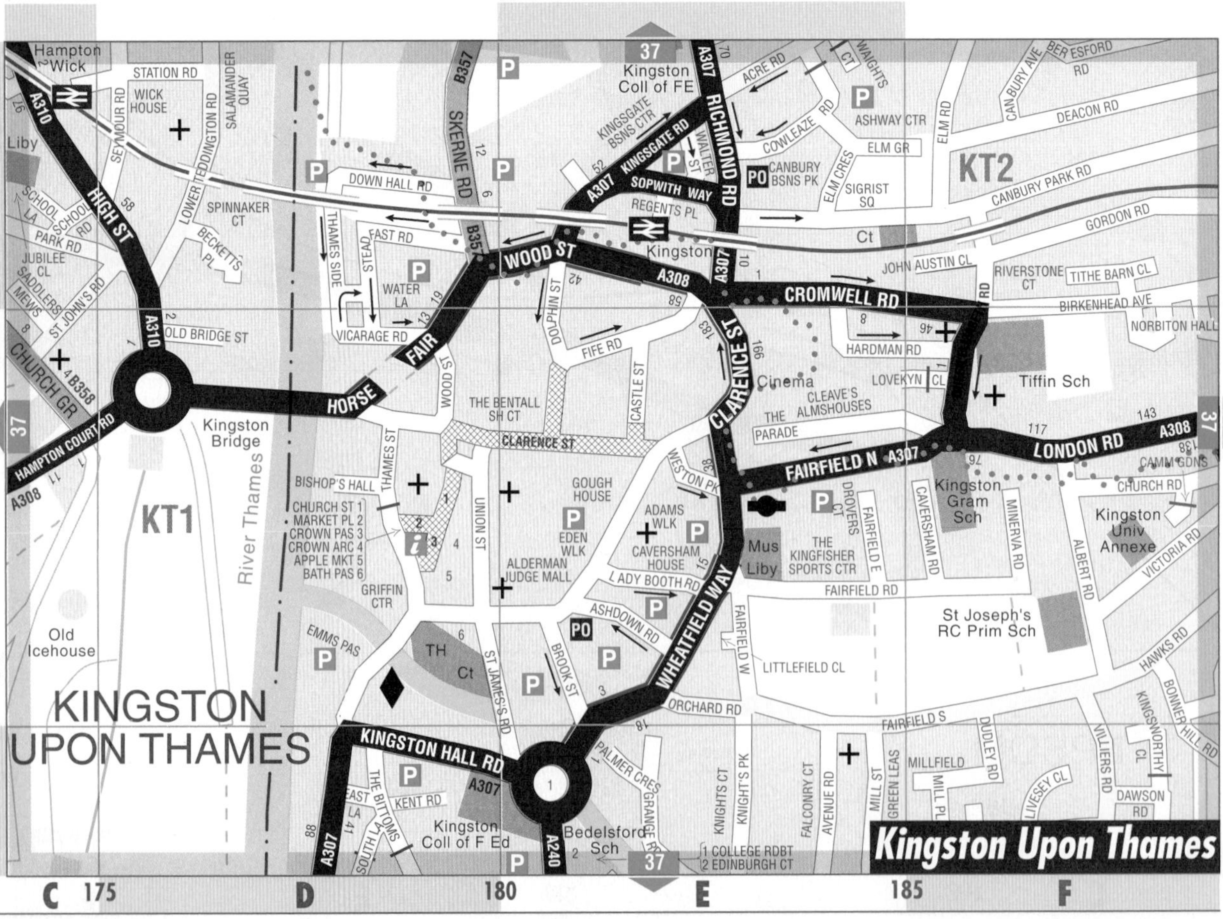

Guildford

Kingston Upon Thames

One-way Streets

House numbers

1 59 HIGH ST

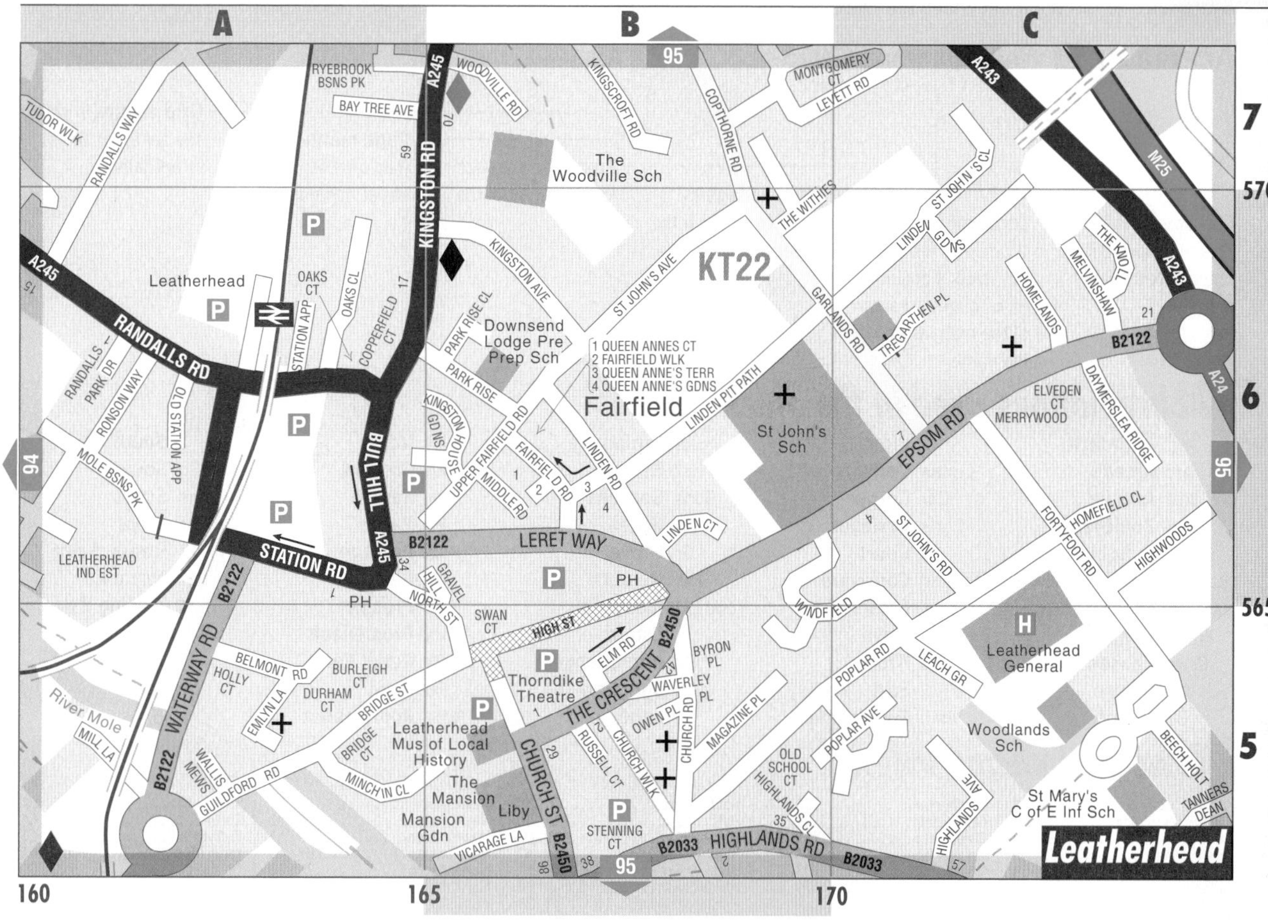

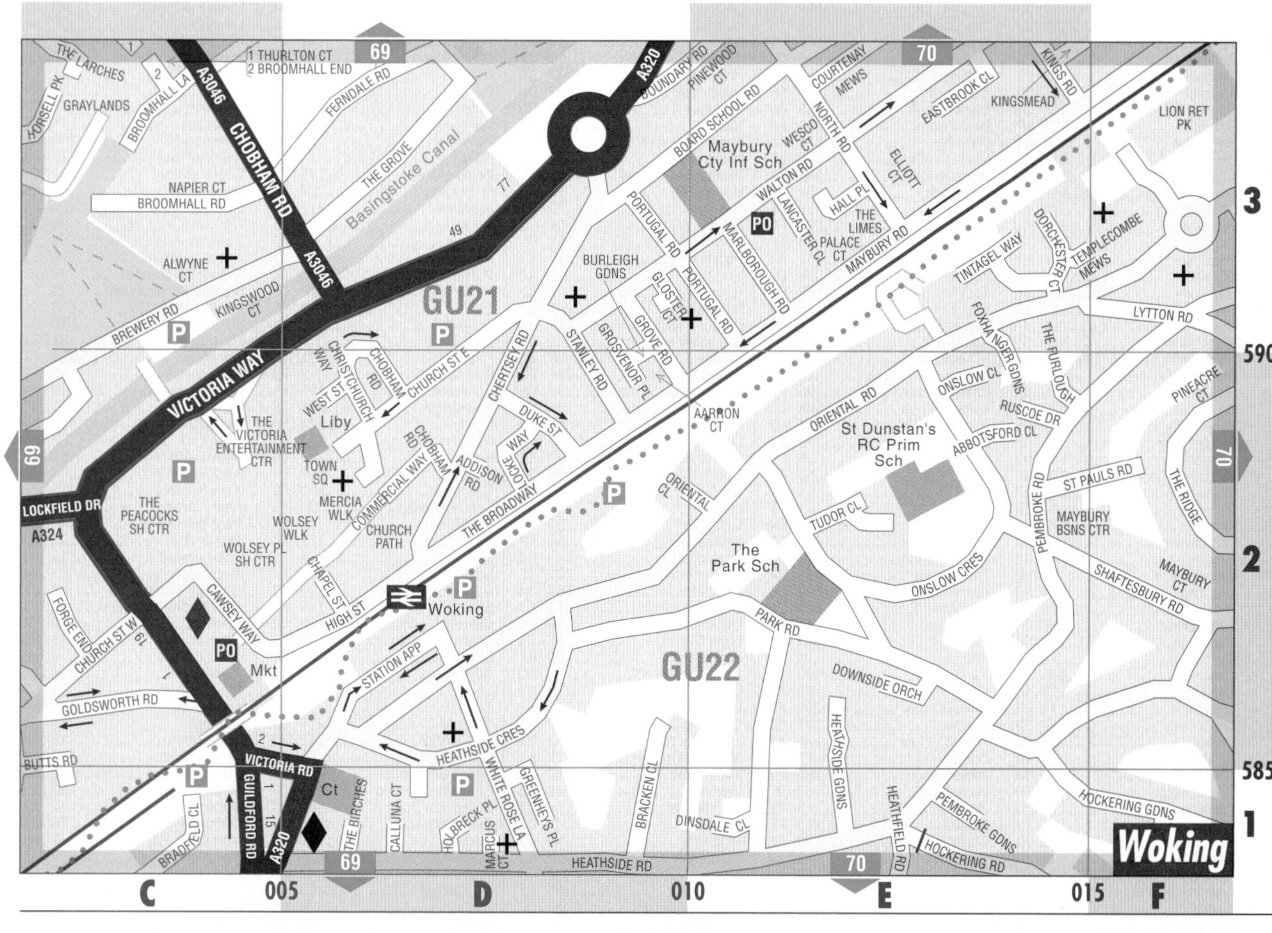

Index

Street names are listed alphabetically and show the locality, the Postcode District, the page number and a reference to the square in which the name falls on the map page

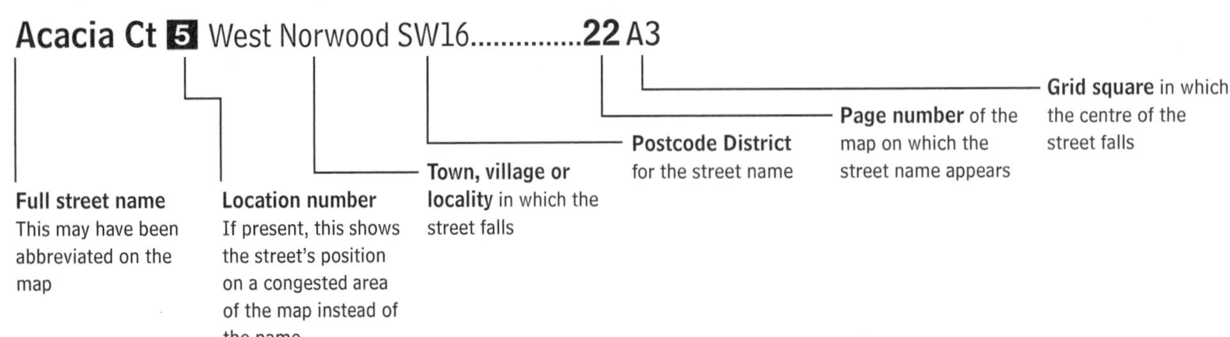

Abbreviations used in the index

App	**Approach**	Cl	**Close**	Espl	**Esplanade**	N	**North**	S	**South**
Arc	**Arcade**	Comm	**Common**	Est	**Estate**	Orch	**Orchard**	Sq	**Square**
Ave	**Avenue**	Cnr	**Corner**	Gdns	**Gardens**	Par	**Parade**	Strs	**Stairs**
Bvd	**Boulevard**	Cotts	**Cottages**	Gn	**Green**	Pk	**Park**	Stps	**Steps**
Bldgs	**Buildings**	Ct	**Court**	Gr	**Grove**	Pas	**Passage**	St	**Street, Saint**
Bsns Pk	**Business Park**	Ctyd	**Courtyard**	Hts	**Heights**	Pl	**Place**	Terr	**Terrace**
Bsns Ctr	**Business Centre**	Cres	**Crescent**	Ind Est	**Industrial Estate**	Prec	**Precinct**	Trad	**Trading Est**
Bglws	**Bungalows**	Dr	**Drive**	Intc	**Interchange**	Prom	**Promenade**	Wlk	**Walk**
Cswy	**Causeway**	Dro	**Drove**	Junc	**Junction**	Ret Pk	**Retail Park**	W	**West**
Ctr	**Centre**	E	**East**	La	**Lane**	Rd	**Road**	Yd	**Yard**
Cir	**Circus**	Emb	**Embankment**			Rdbt	**Roundabout**		

Town and village index

Abinger Common 155 D8
Abinger Hammer 133 F3
Addington 63 A5
Addlestone 52 A6
Albury 132 C4
Aldershot 105 B1
Alfold 193 F1
Alfold Crossways 194 A3
Artington 130 C4
Ascot 29 A6
Ash 106 B3
Ash Vale 106 B7
Ashford 13 F2
Ashstead 75 E1
Ashurst Wood 206 E6
Bagshot 47 D3
Balham 21 A7
Banstead 78 B3
Barnes 7 F6
Beacon Hill 188 C6
Beare Green 157 D3
Beckenham 44 A7
Belmont 59 A2
Bentley 145 A7
Betchworth 137 E8
Biggin Hill 83 E3
Binstead 166 A5
Bisley 68 B3
Blackwater 64 D4
Bletchingley 120 D2
Blindley Heath 163 D8
Bowlhead Green 169 E1
Box Hill 116 A4
Bracknell 27 D6
Bramley 151 F6
Brands Hill 1 A8
Brentford 6 D7
Broadbridge Heath 216 E4
Brockham 137 C7
Bromley 44 E8
Brook 170 B1
Brookwood 88 A7
Buckland 117 A2
Burgh Heath 97 D8
Burstow 183 A7
Byfleet 71 D7
Camberley 65 D6
Capel 178 C6
Carshalton 59 E6
Caterham 100 F4
Catford 24 A7
Charlton 34 D7
Charlwood 180 E7
Cheam 58 F5
Chelsham 82 A2
Chertsey 33 B2
Chessington 56 E4
Chiddingfold 191 B4
Chilworth 131 C3
Chipstead 78 F1
Chiswick 7 D7
Chobham 49 F2
Church Crookham 104 A7
Churt 167 E1
Claygate 55 F3
Cobham 73 B5
Coldharbour 156 E4
Colnbrook 1 D7
Compton 129 B3
Coney Hall 63 F7
Copthorne 183 C3
Coulsdon 79 D3
Cranford 4 C6
Cranleigh 174 D2
Crawley 201 F5
Crawley Down 204 C7
Crondall 124 A5
Crowhurst 143 E3
Crowthorne 45 D5
Croydon 61 D7
Cudworth 179 F8
Dockenfield 166 E6
Domewood 184 A5
Dorking 136 C6
Dormans Park 185 E6
Dormansland 165 B1
Downside 93 B8
Dulwich 22 E5
Dunsfold 192 F5
East Bedfont 14 E7
East Clandon 111 E4
East Ewell 58 D1
East Grinstead 185 E2
East Horsley 112 E8
East Molesey 36 C4
Edenbridge 144 F4
Effingham 113 E8
Egham 12 A4
Ellen's Green 196 A4
Elstead 148 D3
Englefield Green 11 C2
Enton Green 171 B5
Epsom 76 C5
Esher 55 C6
Ewell 58 A1
Ewhurst 175 F5
Fairlands 108 C4
Farley Green 153 E7
Farnborough 85 B3
Farncombe 150 E8
Farnham 125 B1
Faygate 199 F1
Felbridge 184 F4
Felcourt 185 C8
Feltham 15 A7
Fetcham 94 C4
Fickleshole 82 E5
Fisherstreet 209 F3
Flexford 107 C1
Forest Green 176 E7
Forest Hill 23 D7
Forest Row 206 F3
Frensham 167 D7
Frimley 65 F2
Gatton 118 F7
Godalming 150 F3
Godstone 121 B3
Gomshall 133 D4
Grayshott 188 C3
Grayswood 189 F1
Great Bookham 94 B1
Guildford 130 B8
Hackbridge 60 B8
Hale 125 C6
Hambledon 171 D2
Hampton 36 A7
Hamsey Green 81 C4
Harlington 3 C8
Harmondsworth 2 E8
Hascombe 172 D4
Haslemere 208 D6
Hatton 3 F2
Haxted 165 F8
Hayes 44 F3
Headley 96 C2
Headley Down 187 B4
Heath End 125 D6
Hersham 54 D5
Heston 4 F7
Hinchley Wood 55 F8
Hindhead 188 F4
Holmbury St Mary 155 B5
Hookwood 160 D2
Hooley 99 B5
Horley 161 C3
Horne 162 F5
Horsham 217 C3
Horton 1 A4
Hounslow 5 A5
Hydestile 171 E6
Ifold 212 D3
Isleworth 6 B4
Kenley 80 D3
Kingsley Green 208 B2
Kingston Upon Thames 37 C6
Kingswood 97 F6
Knaphill 68 D1
Laleham 33 C6
Lambs Green 199 F6
Langley Vale 96 D8
Leatherhead 95 D5
Leigh 138 B2
Lewisham 24 C8
Lightwater 66 F8
Limpsfield 123 A6
Linchmere 207 B2
Lingfield 164 D5
Little Bookham 93 E3
Littleton 34 A6
Long Ditton 37 C1
Longcross 50 A7
Lower Halliford 34 D2
Lower Kingswood 117 E8
Loxwood 212 F4
Lurgashall 209 A1
Lyne 32 B1
Martyr's Green 92 E7
Merstham 119 D7
Merton 40 B8
Mickleham 115 C7
Milford 149 E1
Mitcham 40 F5
Morden 40 B3
Mortlake 7 C4
Mytchett 85 F3
New Addington 63 D3
New Haw 52 C3
New Malden 38 F5
Newchapel 163 F1
Newdigate 158 B1
Newell Green 8 A1
Normandy 107 A3
North Ascot 28 E8
North Cheam 58 C8
Nutfield 119 F2
Oatlands Park 53 E6
Ockham 92 B6
Ockley 177 D5
Old Windsor 11 A8
Old Woking 90 A7
Ottershaw 51 D5
Outwood 162 B7
Oxshott 74 C6
Oxted 122 E5
Parkgate 158 D4
Peaslake 154 D6
Penge 23 D2
Peper Harow 149 C5
Pirbright 87 F4
Plaistow 211 F2
Poyle 1 E6
Purley 80 A7
Putney 19 D7
Puttenham 128 C4
Pyrford 70 E4
Redhill 118 E2
Reigate 118 B2
Richmond 6 D2
Ripley 91 C6
Roehampton 7 F2
Rowhook 196 E1
Rowledge 145 F3
Rowly 174 B6
Rudgwick 214 C7
Rushmoor 168 C5
Rusper 199 D7
Salfords 140 B1
Sanderstead 80 F6
Sandhurst 64 C7
Seale 127 B4
Selsdon 62 D1
Send 90 C4
Send Marsh 90 F3
Shackleford 149 D7
Shalford 130 E2
Shamley Green 152 E5
Sheerwater 70 D6
Shepperton 34 C3
Shere 133 B4
Sidlow 139 B2
Slinfold 215 D3
Smallfield 162 B2
South Croydon 61 D3
South Godstone 142 F5
South Holmwood 157 C7
South Norwood 42 E5
South Nutfield 140 E7
Staines 12 e4
Stanwell 13 C7
Stoke D'Abernon 73 F3
Stoneleigh 58 A5
Streatham 21 E2
Sunbury 35 B6
Sunningdale 30 B4
Surbiton 37 E2
Sutton 59 C5
Tadworth 97 C5
Tandridge 122 A2
Tatsfield 103 D7
Teddington 17 B3
Thames Ditton 37 B2
The Chart 123 E5
The Sands 126 E2
Thornton Heath 42 B3
Thorpe 32 C6
Thorpe Lea 12 B1
Thursley 169 C4
Tilford 147 D3
Titsey 103 B2
Tolworth 57 B7
Tongham 126 F6
Turners Hill 204 A4
Twickenham 17 B8
Tyler's Green 121 C5
Upper Halliford 34 D5
Upper Tooting 20 F5
Virginia Water 31 C6
Wallington 60 A4
Wallis Wood 176 E1
Walton on the Hill 97 A3
Walton-On-Thames 35 C2
Wanborough 128 C6
Wandsworth 20 C7
Warlingham 81 C1
Warnham 216 E7
Wentworth 30 F3
West Barnes 39 C4
West Byfleet 71 B6
West Clandon 111 B6
West End 67 F6
West Ewell 57 E3
West Hoathly 204 D1
West Horsley 112 B8
West Norwood 22 C5
West Wickham 44 E1
Westcott 135 D6
Westhumble 115 A4
Weybridge 53 A6
Whiteley Village 53 E1
Whyteleafe 80 F1
Wimbledon 19 F2
Windlesham 48 C4
Windsor 9 E8
Winkfield 8 D4
Wisley 71 E3
Witley 170 F4
Woking 69 E1
Wokingham 25 B5
Woldingham 102 A4
Wonersh 152 B7
Wood Street Village 108 B3
Woodham 52 A1
Woodmansterne 78 E4
Worcester Park 57 E6
Wormley 170 F1
Worplesdon 108 D8
Wotton 134 F3
Wraysbury 11 E8
Wrecclesham 145 E6
Yateley 64 A5

1

10th Ave KT20 97 A1
11th Ave KT20 97 F1
12th Ave KT20 97 F1
13th Ave KT20 97 F1
14th Ave KT20 97 F1
15th Ave KT20 97 F1
16th Ave KT20 97 F1
1st Ave KT20 97 E2

2

2nd Ave KT20 97 E2

3

3rd Ave KT20 97 E2

4

4th Ave KT20 97 E2

5

5th Ave KT20 97 E2

6

6th Ave KT20 97 E2

7

7th Ave KT20 97 F2

8

8th Ave KT20 97 E2

9

9th Ave KT20 97 F2

A

Aaron Ct BR3 44 B6
Aaron's Hill GU7 150 B4
Aarron Ct GU21 69 F2
Abbess Cl SW2 22 B7
Abbetts La GU15 65 B3
Abbey Church The RH10 203 B1
Abbey Cl Bracknell RG12 27 D4
Crawley GU6 173 F2
Pyrford GU22 70 E3
Wokingham RG40 25 C7
Abbey Ct Camberley GU15 65 D5
Chertsey KT16 33 B2
Farnham GU9 125 C2
Abbey Dr Laleham TW18 33 C5
Upper Tooting SW17 21 A3
Abbey Gdns KT16 33 A3
Abbey Gn KT16 33 A3
Abbey Ind Est CR4 40 F4
Abbey La BR3 24 A1
Abbey Lodge TW18 12 F3
Abbey Par SW19 20 C1
Abbey Pk BR3 24 A1
Abbey Rd
Chertsey KT16 33 B2
Croydon CR0, CR9 61 B7
Lower Halliford TW17 34 A1
Merton SW19 40 C8
Selsdon CR2 62 D1
Virginia Water GU25 31 D5
Woking GU21 69 D2
Abbey River Cotts KT16 33 C3
Abbey Sch The GU9 125 D1
Abbey St GU9 125 C2
Abbey Way GU14 85 C4
Abbey Wlk KT8 36 B5
Abbey Wood SL5 30 A2
Abbeylands Sch KT15 52 A5
Abbot Cl Byfleet KT14 71 D8
Staines TW18 13 D1
Abbot Rd GU1 130 D7
Abbot's Cl GU2 129 F6
Abbot's Way GU1, GU4 110 D2
Abbots Ct SE25 42 E6
Abbots Dr GU25 31 C5
Abbots Gn CR0, CR2 62 D4
Abbots La CR8 80 C3
Abbots Pk SW2 22 A7
Abbots Way BR3 43 E4
Abbots Wlk CR3 101 B5
Abbots Wood Forest Wlk
GU10 166 C7
Abbotsbury RG12 26 F4
Abbotsbury Ct RH13 217 E3
Abbotsbury Fst Sch SM4 40 B4
Abbotsbury Rd
Coney Hall BR2, BR4 63 F8
Morden SM4, SW19 40 B5
Abbotsfield Rd RH11 200 D4
Abbotsford Cl GU22 70 A2
Abbotshall Rd SE6 24 D6
Abbotsleigh Cl SM2 59 B3
Abbotsleigh Rd SW16 21 C3
Abbotsmede Cl TW1 16 F6
Abbotswood
Guildford GU1 109 F3
Walton-on-T KT13 53 F7
Abbotswood Cl GU1 109 F4
Abbotswood Dr KT13 53 D1
Abbotswood Rd SW16 21 D5
Abbott Ave SW20 39 D8
Abbott Cl TW12 15 E2
Abbott House SW12 20 F8
Abbotts Cotts GU10 166 E5
Abbotts Rd
Cheam SM1, SM3 58 E6
Mitcham CR4, SW16 41 C5
Abbotts Rise RH1 119 A3
Abbotts Tilt KT12 54 E7
Abelia Cl GU24 67 E6
Abell Ct KT15 52 C6
Abercairn Rd SW16 21 C1
Aberconway Rd SM4 40 B5
Abercorn Cl CR2 81 D7
Abercorn Way GU21 69 A1
Aberdare Cl BR4 63 C8
Aberdeen Rd CR0 61 D6
Aberdour KT20 77 F1
Aberfoyle Rd SW16 21 D2
Abingdon Cl Bracknell RG12 27 E4
Merton SW19 20 C2
Woking GU21 69 C1
Abingdon Lodge BR2 44 F7
Abingdon Rd
Sandhurst GU47 45 C1
Thornton Heath SW16 41 E8
Abinger Ave SM2 58 D2
Abinger Cl Dorking RH5 136 C3
Wallington SM6 60 E5
Abinger Common Cty
Sch RH5 134 D1
Abinger Common Rd
RH5 155 F7
Abinger Ct SM6 60 E5
Abinger Dr RH1 139 E7
Abinger Gdns TW7 5 E4
Abinger Hammer
Village Sch RH5 133 F4
Abinger House 2 KT2 18 B1
Abinger La RH5 134 C2
Abinger Rd RH5 156 C3
Abinger Way GU4 110 B6
Aboyne Dr SW20 39 A7
Aboyne Rd SW17 20 D5
Abrahams Rd RH11 201 A1
Acacia Ave Brentford TW8 6 B7
Littleton TW17 34 A4
Sandhurst GU47 45 D1
Woking GU22 89 D7
Acacia Cl Penge SE20 43 A7
Woodham KT15 51 F1
Acacia Ct Bracknell RG12 27 B6
5 West Norwood SW16 22 A3
Acacia Dr Banstead KT17 77 D5
Cheam SM3 40 A1
Woodham KT15 51 F1
Acacia Gdns BR4 63 C8
Acacia Gr Dulwich SE21 22 D6
Kingston u T KT3 38 E6
Acacia House RH2 118 A3
Acacia Mews UB7 2 D8
Acacia Rd Beckenham BR3 43 F6
Guildford GU1 109 D1
Hampton TW12 16 A2
Mitcham CR4 41 B7
South Norwood SW16 41 E8
Staines TW18 13 B3
Academy Cl GU15 65 E8
Academy Gdns CR0 42 F1
Accommodation La UB7 2 C8
Accommodation Rd KT16 50 E6
Ace Par KT9 56 E7
Acer Dr GU24 67 F6
Acer Rd TN16 83 D3
Acheulian Cl GU9 146 C7
Achilles Pl GU21 69 C2
Ackroyd Rd SE23 23 E8
Acorn Cl
East Grinstead RH19 205 E8
1 Hampton TW12 16 B2
Horley RH6 161 C4
Acorn Dr RG40 25 C7
Acorn Gdns SE19 42 F8
Acorn Gr Harlington UB3 3 F7
Kingswood KT20 97 F3
Woking GU22 89 E6
Acorn Keep GU9 125 D8
Acorn Mews GU14 85 A7
Acorn Rd GU17 64 B5
Acorn Way SE23 23 D5
Acorns RH13 218 A4
Acorns Cty Fst Sch The
Betchworth RH3 116 D1
Leigh RH2 138 A3
Acorns The Crawley RH11 201 B1
21 Putney SW19 19 D7
Acorns Way KT10 55 C5
Acre La SM5 60 A6
Acre Rd Kingston u T KT2 37 E8
Mitcham SW19 20 D2
Acres Gdns KT20 97 D8
Acres Platt GU6 174 F4
Action Ct TW15 34 C8
Acuba House SW18 20 B7
Acuba Rd SW18 20 B6
Adair Cl SE25 43 B6
Adair Wlk GU24 87 B6
Adams Cl KT5 37 F3
Adams Croft GU24 87 C7
Adams Ct 2 CR8 80 A7
Adams House 3 SW16 21 C3
Adams Park Rd GU9 125 D3
Adams Rd BR3 43 E4
Adams Way SE25, CR0 43 A3
Adams Wlk 11 KT1 37 E7
Adamson Ct 6 RH11 201 B1
Adamsrill Prim Sch SE26 23 E5
Adamsrill Rd SE23, SE26 23 E4
Adare Wlk SW16, SW2 21 F6
Addington Bsns Ctr CR9 63 E1
Addington Court Golf
Course CR0 63 A2
Addington Ct 7 SW14 7 D4
Addington Golf Course
CR0, CR9 62 E6
Addington Gr SE26 23 E4
Addington High Sch CR0 82 E7
Addington Palace Golf
Course CR0 62 E5
Addington Palace (the
Royal Sch of Church
Music) CR9 62 F4
Addington Rd
Sanderstead CR2 81 A8
Selsdon CR2 62 C1
Thornton Heath CR0 42 A1
West Wickham BR4, CR0 63 D6
West Wickham BR4 63 E8
Addington Village Rd CR0 63 A5
Addiscombe Ave CR0 43 A2
Addiscombe Court Rd
CR0, CR9 61 E8
Addiscombe Rd
Crowthorne RG45 45 C4
Croydon CR0, CR9 61 E8
South Croydon CR0 61 E8
Addison Ave TW3 5 C6
Addison Cl CR3 100 D5
Addison Ct GU1 130 F7
Addison Gdns KT5 37 F5
Addison Rd Caterham CR3 100 D6
Croydon SE25 43 A5
Farnborough GU16 85 E8
Guildford GU1 130 F7
Teddington TW11 17 B2
8 Woking GU21 69 F2
Addison's Cl CR0 62 F8
Addlestone House KT15 52 B7
Addlestone Moor KT15 52 C8
Addlestone Pk KT15 52 B5
Addlestone Rd KT13, KT15 52 E6
Addlestone Sta KT15 52 D6
Adecroft Way KT8 36 C6
Adela Ave KT3 39 B5
Adelaide Cl Crawley RH11 181 D1
Horsham RH12 217 F4
Adelaide Ct 15 BR3 24 A1
Adelaide Pl KT13 53 D6
Adelaide Rd Ashford TW15 13 D3
Heston TW5 4 E6
Kingston u T KT6 37 E4
Richmond TW9 6 F3
Teddington TW11 16 F2
Walton-on-T KT12 54 B7
Adelina Mews SW12 21 D7
Adelphi Cl RH10 202 D4
Adelphi Rd KT17 76 D6
Adenmore Rd SE6 24 A8
Adisham House 7 SE20 23 C1
Adlers La RH5 115 A4
Adlington Pl GU14 85 E2
Admiral Ct SM5 40 E1
Admiral Rd RH11 201 A3
Admiral's Bridge La
RH19 205 C2
Admiral's Wlk The CR5 99 F7
Admirals Ct GU1 110 B2
Admiralty Rd TW11 16 F2
Admiralty Way GU15 64 F4
Adolf St SE6 24 B4
Adrian Ct RH11 201 B1
Advance Rd SE27 22 C4
Adversane Ct RH12 217 D4
Aerodrome Way TW5 4 C8
Aerospace Bvd GU14 105 A7
Agar Cl KT6 56 F8
Agar House 6 KT1 37 E6
Agate House
New Malden KT4 38 E1
12 Penge SE26 23 B3
Agate La RH12 217 F5
Agates La KT21 95 D8
Agincourt Pl SL5 29 C6
Agnes Scott Ct 5 KT13 53 B7
Agnew Rd SE23 23 D8
Agraria Rd GU2 130 B7
Ailsa Ave TW1 6 B2
Ailsa Cl RH11 201 B3
Ailsa Rd TW1 6 B2
Ainger Cl GU12 105 D2
Ainsdale Way GU21 69 A1
Ainsworth Rd CR0, CR9 61 B8
Aintree Cl SL3 1 E6
Aintree House SE26 23 B2
Aintree Rd RH10 202 A4
Air Forces Meml TW20 11 D4
Airborne House 10 SM6 60 B6
Airbourne Forces Mus
GU11 105 A5
Aircraft Espl GU14 85 C1
Airedale Rd SW12 20 F8
Airport Way Horley RH6 182 B8
Stanwell TW19 2 A3
Airport Way Rdbt W RH6 181 F8
Aisne Rd GU16 66 E1
Aitken Cl CR4 40 F2
Aitken House GU27 208 C7
Aitken Rd SE6 24 B6
Akabusi Cl SE25 43 A3
Akehurst Cl RH10 183 B3
Akehurst St SW15 19 A8
Akerman Rd KT6 37 C3
Alamein Rd GU11 105 B3
Alan Hilton Ct KT16 51 D4
Alan Rd SW19 19 E3
Alan Turing Rd GU2 108 D1
Alanbrooke Cl GU21 68 C1
Alanbrooke Rd GU11 105 D6
Albain Cres TW15 13 E6
Albans Cl SW16 21 E5
Albany Cl Esher KT10 55 A2
Mortlake SW14 7 B3
Albany Cres KT10 55 E4
Albany Ct Frimley GU16 65 C1
Kingston u T KT2 17 E2
Oatlands Park KT13 53 E8
Richmond TW10 17 B5
3 Weybridge KT13 53 B6
Albany Ho 6 TW8 6 E8
Albany Mews
Kingston u T KT2 17 D2
Sutton SM1 59 B5
Albany Par 4 TW8 6 E8
Albany Park Ind Est GU15 65 C1
Albany Park Rd
Kingston u T KT2 17 E2
Leatherhead KT22 95 A8
Albany Pk Camberley GU15 65 B1
Frimley GU15 65 C1
Poyle SL3 1 D7
Albany Pl Brentford TW8 6 E8
Egham TW20 12 B4
Albany Rd Brentford TW8 6 D8
Crawley RH11 201 C6
Hersham KT12 54 D6
New Malden KT3 38 D5
Richmond TW10 6 E2
Wimbledon SW19 20 B3
Albany Reach KT7 36 F4
Albany Terr 5 TW10 6 F2
Albanys The RH2 118 A3
Albatross Gdns CR2 81 D8
Albemarle SW19 19 D6
Albemarle Ave TW2 15 F7
Albemarle Gdns KT3 38 D5
Albemarle Lodge SE26 23 E3
Albemarle Pk BR3 44 B8
Albemarle Rd BR2, BR3 44 C8
Albermarle Prim Sch
SW19 19 E6
Albermarle Prim Sch
(Annexe) SW19 19 E7
Albert Ave KT16 33 A6
Albert Carr Gdns SW16 21 E3
Albert Crane Ct RH11 201 A8
Albert Ct 9 SW19 19 E7
Albert Dr Putney SW19 19 E6
Sheerwater GU21, KT14 70 D5
Albert Gr SW20 39 D8
Albert Rd Addlestone KT15 52 D6
Aldershot GU11 105 B2
Ashford TW15 13 F3
Ashstead KT21 75 F1
Bagshot GU19 47 E1
Bracknell RG42 27 B8
Camberley GU15 65 C5
Carshalton SM1 59 D5
Crowthorne RG45 45 B5
Croydon CR0, SE25 43 B5
Englefield Green TW20 11 D2
Epsom KT17 76 F6
Farnborough GU14 85 C2
Hampton TW12 16 C3
Horley RH6 161 A3
Hounslow TW3 5 A3
Kingston u T KT1 37 F7
Merstham RH1 119 C6
Mitcham CR4 40 F6
New Malden KT3 38 F5
Penge SE20 23 D2
Richmond TW10 6 F2
Sutton SM1 59 D5
Teddington TW11 16 F2
Twickenham TW1 16 F7
Warlingham CR6 81 F2
Wokingham RG40 25 B5
Albert Rd N RH2 117 F2
Albert Wlk RG45 45 B5
Alberta Ave SM1 58 F5
Alberta Dr RH6 162 A3
Albertine Cl KT17 77 B3
Albery Cl RH12 217 B4
Albion Cl RH10 202 D5
Albion Ct SM2 59 D3
Albion Par GU21 68 C2
Albion Pl SE25 43 A6
Albion Rd Hounslow TW3 5 A3
Kingston u T KT2 38 C8
Reigate RH2 139 C8
Sandhurst GU47 64 B8
Sutton SM2 59 D3
Twickenham TW2 16 E7
Albion St CR0, CR9 42 B1
Albion Villas Rd
SE23, SE26 23 C5
Albion Way RH12 217 C2
Albury Ave East Ewell SM2 58 C1
Hounslow TW7 5 F7
Albury Cl Hampton TW12 16 B2
Longcross KT16 50 A7
Albury Ct 4 Croydon CR0 61 C6
Mitcham CR4 40 D7
Sutton SM1 59 C6
Albury Keep RH6 161 B4
Albury Lodge 10 SW2 21 F8
Albury Pl RH1 119 C6
Albury Rd Chessington KT9 56 E5
Guildford GU1 131 A8
Albury Rd *continued*
Hersham KT12 53 F4
Merstham RH1 119 C6
Albury St GU5 132 C4
Alcester Ct 4 SM6 60 B6
Alcester Rd SM6 60 B6
Alcock Cl SM6 60 D3
Alcock Rd TW5 4 D7
Alcocks Cl KT20 97 E7
Alcocks La KT20 97 E7
Alcorn Cl SM3 59 A8
Alcot Cl RG45 45 B4
Alden Ct CR0 61 D7
Aldenham Terr RG12 27 C3
Aldenholme KT13 53 E4
Alder Cl Ash Vale GU12 106 A7
Crawley Down RH10 204 B8
Englefield Green TW20 11 E3
Alder Croft CR5 79 F3
Alder Ct 3 SW16 22 A3
Alder Rd
Headley Down GU35 187 B6
Mortlake SW14 7 D4
Alderbrook Prim Sch
SW12 21 B8
Alderbrook Rd
Balham SW12 21 B8
Cranleigh GU6 174 C8
Aldergrove Gdns TW4 4 E5
Alderman Judge Mall 6
KT1 37 E7
Alderman Willey Cl RG41 25 B6
Aldermead TW3 5 B3
Aldermoor Rd SE6 23 F5
Alderney Ave TW5 5 B7
Alders Ave RH19 185 E3
Alders Rd RH2 118 B3
Alders The Feltham TW13 15 E4
Heston TW5 4 F8
Streatham SW16 21 C4
West Byfleet KT14 71 C7
West Wickham BR4 63 B8
Alders View Dr RH19 185 E3
Aldersbrook Dr KT2 17 F2
Aldersey Rd GU1 109 F1
Aldersgrove KT8 36 D4
Aldershot Military Mus
GU11 105 C7
Aldershot Rd Ash GU12 105 F1
Church Crookham GU13 104 A6
Fairlands GU3 108 D5
Guildford GU2, GU3 108 D5
Pirbright GU24, GU3 87 F2
Wood St V GU3 107 E5
Aldershot Sta GU11 105 B1
Alderside Wlk TW20 11 E3
Aldersmead Ave CR0 43 D3
Aldersmead Rd BR3 23 E1
Alderstead La RH1 99 D2
Alderton KT2 38 B8
Alderton Ct KT8 35 F5
Alderton Rd CR0 43 A2
Alderwick Dr TW3 5 D4
Alderwood Cl CR3 100 E2
Aldingbourne Cl RH11 200 F7
Aldis Mews SW17 20 E3
Aldis St SW17 20 E3
Aldous House TW18 12 E4
Aldren Rd SW17 20 C5
Aldrich Cres CR0 63 C2
Aldrich Gdns SM3 58 F7
Aldrich Terr SW18 20 C6
Aldridge Rise KT3 38 E3
Aldrin Pl GU14 84 D4
Aldrington Rd SW16 21 C4
Aldro Sch GU8 149 C7
Aldwick Cl GU14 85 A6
Aldwick Rd CR0 60 F6
Aldworth Cl RG12 27 A5
Aldworth Gdns RG45 45 A5
Aldwych Cl RH10 202 D4
Aldwyn Ct TW20 11 B2
Alexa Ct SM2 59 A4
Alexander Cl TW2 16 F6
Alexander Ct
Beckenham BR3 44 D8
14 Surbiton KT6 37 D2
Alexander Evans Mews
SE23 23 D6
Alexander Godley Cl KT21 95 F8
Alexander Rd Coulsdon CR5 79 B4
Egham TW20 12 C3
Reigate RH2 139 A6
Alexander Wlk RG12 27 B4
Alexanders Wlk CR3 101 A1
Alexandra Ave
Camberley GU15 65 A5
Sutton SM1 59 A7
Warlingham CR6 81 F2
Alexandra Cl Ashford TW15 14 D1
Staines TW18 13 D2
Walton-on-T KT12 54 A8
Alexandra Cotts SE20 23 D2
Alexandra Cres BR1 24 F2
Alexandra Ct Ashford TW15 14 D2
10 Crawley RH10 201 D5
1 Farnborough GU14 85 C1
Alexandra Dr Surbiton KT5 38 A2
West Norwood SE19 22 E3
Alexandra Gdns Chiswick W4 7 E7
Hounslow TW3 5 B5
Knaphill GU21 68 D1
Wallington SM5 60 A2
Alexandra Inf Sch
Kingston u T KT2 18 A1

Alexandra Inf Sch *continued*
Penge BR3 . . . . .23 D1
Alexandra Jun & Inf Sch
TW3 . . . . .5 B5
Alexandra Jun Sch SE26 . .23 D2
Alexandra Lodge
12 Guildford GU1 . . . . .130 F8
1 Weybridge KT13 . . . . .53 B6
Alexandra Pl Croydon CR0 . .42 E1
Guildford GU1 . . . . .130 F7
South Norwood SE25 . . . . . . .42 D4
Alexandra Rd
Addlestone KT15 . . . . .52 D6
Aldershot GU11 . . . . .104 F2
Ash GU12 . . . . .105 F1
Ashford TW15 . . . . .14 E2
Biggin Hill TN16 . . . . .103 B8
10 Brentford TW8 . . . . .6 D8
Croydon CR0 . . . . .42 E2
Englefield Green TW20 . . . . .11 C2
Epsom KT17 . . . . .76 F6
Farnborough GU14, GU11 . . .85 C1
Hounslow TW3 . . . . .5 B5
Kingston u T KT2 . . . . .18 A1
Mitcham SW19 . . . . .20 E1
Mortlake SW14 . . . . .7 D4
Penge SE26 . . . . .23 D2
Richmond TW9 . . . . .6 F5
Thames Ditton KT7 . . . . .36 F4
Twickenham TW1 . . . . .6 C1
Warlingham CR6 . . . . .81 F2
Wimbledon SW19 . . . . .20 A3
Alexandra Sq SM4 . . . . .40 A4
Alexandra Terr GU1 . . . . .130 E8
Alexandra Wlk 8 SE19 . . . .22 E3
Alfold By-Pass Alfold GU6 193 F7
Alfold Crossways GU6 . . . . .194 A5
Alfold Cotts GU6 . . . . .193 F2
Alfold La GU6 . . . . .194 A7
Alfold Rd Alfold GU8 . . . . .193 B3
Cranleigh GU6 . . . . .194 B7
Dunsfold GU8 . . . . .193 B3
Alfonso Cl GU12 . . . . .126 C8
Alford Cl GU4 . . . . .110 A4
Alford Ct 5 SM2 . . . . .59 B3
Alford Gn CR0 . . . . .63 D4
Alfred Butt House SW17 . .20 F5
Alfred Cl RH10 . . . . .202 E5
Alfred Hurley
House SW17 . . . . .20 C4
Alfred Mizen Prim Sch
The CR4 . . . . .41 D6
Alfred Rd Croydon SE25 . . . .43 A4
Farnham GU9 . . . . .125 C1
Feltham TW13 . . . . .15 C6
Kingston u T KT1 . . . . .37 F6
Sutton SM1 . . . . .59 C5
Alfreton Cl SW19 . . . . .19 D5
Alfriston KT5 . . . . .37 F3
Alfriston Ave CR0 . . . . .41 E2
Alfriston Cl KT5 . . . . .37 F3
Alfriston Rd GU16 . . . . .86 C7
Algar Cl TW7 . . . . .6 A4
Algar Rd TW7 . . . . .6 A4
Algarve Rd SW18 . . . . .20 B7
Alice Gough Memorial
Homes RG12 . . . . .27 B6
Alice Holt Forest Visitor
Ctr GU10 . . . . .166 C8
Alice Mews 8 TW11 . . . . . .16 F3
Alice Rd GU11 . . . . .105 B2
Alice Ruston Pl GU22 . . . . .89 C8
Alice Way TW3 . . . . .5 B3
Alicia Ave RH10 . . . . .202 C6
Alington Gr SM6 . . . . .60 D2
Alison Cl Croydon CR0 . . . . .43 D1
Farnborough GU14 . . . . .84 F3
Woking GU21 . . . . .69 E4
Alison Dr GU15 . . . . .65 F5
Alison Way GU11 . . . . .104 F2
Alison's Rd GU11 . . . . .105 B4
All England Lawn Tennis
& Croquet Club The
SW19 . . . . .19 E5
All Hallows Catholic Sch
GU9 . . . . .125 F7
All Saint's Prim Sch SE19 .42 E8
All Saints' Benhilton C of
E Prim Sch SM1 . . . . .59 B7
All Saints C of E Prim Sch
SW19 . . . . .20 C1
All Saints Carshalton CE
Sch SM5 . . . . .60 A5
All Saints CE Inf Sch
GU10 . . . . .147 C3
All Saints Cl RG40 . . . . .25 C7
All Saints Cres GU14 . . . . . .64 E1
All Saints Ct TW5 . . . . .4 D6
All Saints Dr CR2 . . . . .81 A7
All Saints Inf Sch KT22 . . .95 A8
All Saints Rd
Lightwater GU18 . . . . .48 C1
Merton SW19 . . . . .20 C1
Sutton SM1 . . . . .59 C7
All Souls' Rd SL5 . . . . .29 A5
Allan Cl KT3 . . . . .38 D4
Allbrook Cl TW11 . . . . .16 E3
Allbrook House 5 SW15 . .19 A8
Allcard Cl RH12 . . . . .217 D4
Allcot Cl Crawley RH11 . . .200 E3
East Bedfont TW14 . . . . .14 F7
Allcott House TW7 . . . . .5 F4
Allden Ave GU11, GU12 . . .126 D7
Allden Cotts GU7 . . . . .150 B4
Allden Gdns GU12 . . . . . . .126 D7
Alldens Hill GU5, GU8 . . . .151 D1
Alldens La GU8 . . . . .151 B1
Allen Cl Streatham CR4 . . . .41 C8
Sunbury TW16 . . . . .35 B8
Allen House Pk GU22 . . . . .89 C7
Allen Rd
Great Bookham KT23 . . . . . . .94 B1
Penge BR3 . . . . .43 D7
Sunbury TW16 . . . . .35 B7
Thornton Heath CR0 . . . . . . .42 A1
Allen's Cl RH19 . . . . .206 D6
Allenby Ave CR2 . . . . .61 C2
Allenby Rd Biggin Hill TN16 .83 E2
Forest Hill SE23 . . . . .23 E5
Sandhurst GU15 . . . . .65 A6
Allendale GU8 . . . . .148 C3
Allendale Cl
Forest Hill SE26 . . . . .23 D3
Sandhurst GU47 . . . . .45 A2
Allenford House SW15 . . . . .7 F1
Allenswood 12 SW19 . . . . . .19 E7
Allerford Ct SE6 . . . . .24 B5
Allerford Rd SE6 . . . . .24 B4
Allerton Ct SM3 . . . . .58 D8
Allerton House 4 SW19 . .20 C1
Alleyn Cres SE21 . . . . .22 D6
Alleyn Pk SE21 . . . . .22 E5
Alleyn Rd SE21 . . . . .22 E5
Allgood Cl SM4 . . . . .39 D3
Alliance Ct TW15 . . . . .14 C4
Allingham Ct GU7 . . . . . . .150 F7
Allingham Gdns RH12 . . .218 B5
Allingham Rd RH2 . . . . . .139 A6
Allington Ave TW17 . . . . . .34 E6
Allington Cl SW19 . . . . .19 D3
Allington Ct CR0 . . . . .43 C3
Allison Gr SE21 . . . . .22 E7
Alloway Cl 4 GU21 . . . . . . .69 B1
Allsmoor La RG12 . . . . .27 F6
Allum Gr KT20 . . . . .97 B6
Allwood Cl SE26 . . . . .23 D4
Allyington Way RH10 . . . .202 D5
Allyn Cl TW18 . . . . .12 F2
Alma Cl Aldershot GU12 . . .105 D2
Knaphill GU21 . . . . .68 E1
Alma Cres SM1 . . . . .58 E5
Alma Ct CR3 . . . . .100 C6
Alma Gdns GU16 . . . . .86 E8
Alma Ho 7 TW8 . . . . .6 E8
Alma La GU9 . . . . .125 C7
Alma Pl Penge SE19 . . . . . . .22 F1
Thornton Heath CR7 . . . . . . .42 A4
Alma Rd Carshalton SM5 . . .59 E5
Headley Down GU35 . . . . . .187 C5
Reigate RH2 . . . . .118 B3
Thames Ditton KT10, KT7 . . . .36 E1
Alma Sq GU14 . . . . .105 C8
Alma Terr SW18 . . . . .20 D8
Alma Way GU9 . . . . .125 D7
Almer Rd SW20 . . . . .19 A1
Almners Rd Chertsey KT16 .32 C2
Lyne KT16 . . . . .32 B1
Almond Ave Carshalton SM5 59 F8
Woking GU22 . . . . .89 D6
Almond Cl Charlton TW17 . .34 C7
Crawley RH11 . . . . .201 A5
Englefield Green TW20 . . . . .11 B2
Guildford GU1 . . . . .109 D5
Almond Gr TW8 . . . . .6 B7
Almond Rd KT19 . . . . .76 D8
Almond Way CR4 . . . . .41 D5
Almorah Rd TW5 . . . . .4 D6
Alms Heath GU23 . . . . .92 B6
Almsgate GU3 . . . . .129 C2
Almshouse La KT9 . . . . . . .56 D2
Almshouses Dorking RH4 .136 B8
Mickleham RH5 . . . . .115 C8
Sunbury TW16 . . . . .34 F8
Alnwick Gr SM4 . . . . .40 B5
Alpha Ct CR6 . . . . .81 A1
Alpha Rd Chobham GU24 . . .49 F1
Crawley RH11 . . . . .201 C6
Croydon CR0 . . . . .42 E1
Surbiton KT5 . . . . .37 F3
Teddington TW12 . . . . .16 D3
Woking GU22 . . . . .70 C4
Alpha Way TW20 . . . . .32 C8
Alphabet Gdns SM5 . . . . . .40 D3
Alphea Cl SW19 . . . . .20 E1
Alphington Ave GU16 . . . . .65 F1
Alphington Gn GU16 . . . . . .65 F1
Alpine Ave KT5 . . . . .57 C8
Alpine Cl Farnborough GU14 84 D3
South Croydon CR0 . . . . .61 E7
Alpine Rd Redhill RH1 . . . .119 A4
Walton-on-T KT12 . . . . .35 A2
Alpine View SM1 . . . . .59 E5
Alresford Rd GU2 . . . . . . .130 A8
Alric Ave KT3 . . . . .38 F6
Alsace Wlk GU15 . . . . .65 B1
Alsford Cl GU18 . . . . .66 F7
Alsom Ave KT19, KT4 . . . . . .58 A6
Alston Cl KT7 . . . . .37 B2
Alston Rd SW17 . . . . .20 D4
Alt Gr SW19 . . . . .19 E1
Alterton Cl GU21 . . . . .69 A2
Althorne Rd RH1 . . . . .140 A7
Althorp Rd SW17 . . . . .20 F7
Alton Cl TW7 . . . . .5 F5
Alton Ct 19 Beckenham BR3 .24 A1
Egham TW18 . . . . .32 E8
Alton Gdns Beckenham BR3 24 A1
Twickenham TW2 . . . . .16 D8
Alton House 1 RH1 . . . . . .119 A3
Alton Rd Croydon CR0, CR9 .61 A7
Farnham GU10, GU9 . . . . . .145 D7
Richmond TW10, TW9 . . . . . . .6 E3
Roehampton SW15 . . . . .19 A7
Alton Ride GU17 . . . . .64 C6
Altwood Prim Sch CR2 . . .81 A6
Altyre Cl BR3 . . . . .43 F4
Altyre Rd CR0, CR9 . . . . . . .61 D8
Altyre Way BR3 . . . . .43 F4
Alvernia Cl GU7 . . . . .150 C2
Alvernia Lodge SM1 . . . . . .59 C8
Alverstoke Gdns GU11 . . .104 E1
Alverston Gdns SE25 . . . . .42 E4
Alverstone Ave
SW18, SW19 . . . . .20 A6
Alverstone Rd KT3 . . . . . . .38 F5
Alvia Gdns SM1 . . . . .59 C6
Alway Ave KT19 . . . . .57 D5
Alwin Pl GU9 . . . . .125 B7
Alwyn Cl CR0 . . . . .63 B3
Alwyne Ct GU21 . . . . .69 E3
Alwyne Rd SW19 . . . . .19 F2
Alwyns Cl KT16 . . . . .33 A3
Alwyns La KT16 . . . . .33 A3
Amalgamated Dr TW8 . . . . .6 B8
Amanda Ct TW15 . . . . .13 F6
Ambassador RG12 . . . . .26 F4
Ambassador Cl TW3 . . . . . . .4 E5
Amber Ct Aldershot GU12 .105 C2
Mitcham CR4 . . . . .40 E5
Staines TW18 . . . . .12 F3
Amber Hill GU15 . . . . .66 B4
Ambercroft Way CR5 . . . . .100 B8
Amberley Cl
Crawley RH10 . . . . .202 C6
Horsham RH12 . . . . .218 A6
Send Marsh GU23 . . . . .90 F2
Amberley Ct SM2 . . . . .59 C3
Amberley Dr KT15 . . . . .70 F8
Amberley Gdns KT19 . . . . .57 F6
Amberley Gr Croydon CR0 . .42 F2
Forest Hill SE26 . . . . .23 B3
Amberley Grange GU11 . .125 F8
Amberley Rd
Horsham RH12 . . . . .218 A6
Milford GU8 . . . . .149 E2
Amberley Way Heston TW4 . .4 C2
Morden SM4 . . . . .39 F2
Amberside Cl TW2 . . . . .5 D1
Amberwood Dr GU15 . . . . .65 F7
Amberwood Rise KT3 . . . . .38 E3
Amblecote KT11 . . . . .73 E7
Ambleside Catford BR1 . . . .24 D2
Godalming GU7 . . . . .151 A5
13 Putney SW19 . . . . .19 E7
Ambleside Ave
Beckenham BR3 . . . . .43 E4
Streatham SW16 . . . . .21 D4
Walton-on-T KT12 . . . . .35 C1
Ambleside Cl
Crawley RH11 . . . . .200 D5
Farnborough GU14 . . . . .84 E3
Mytchett GU16 . . . . .86 A2
Redhill RH1 . . . . .140 B4
Ambleside Cres GU9 . . . .125 A6
Ambleside Cty Jun Sch
KT12 . . . . .35 C1
Ambleside Dr TW14 . . . . . .14 F7
Ambleside Gdns
Selsdon CR2 . . . . .62 D1
Streatham SW16 . . . . .21 D3
Sutton SM2 . . . . .59 C4
Ambleside Rd GU18 . . . . . .67 B8
Ambleside Sch SM2 . . . . . .58 E2
Ambleside Way TW20 . . . . .12 B1
Ambrey Way CR8, SM6 . . . .60 D2
Amen Cnr SW17 . . . . .21 A2
Amen Corner Bsns Pk
RG12 . . . . .26 D7
Amenity Way SM4 . . . . .39 C2
American Comm Sch
Esher KT11 . . . . .54 C1
Virginia Water TW20 . . . . . . .31 C7
American Magna Carta
Meml TW20 . . . . .11 D6
American Sch in
Switzerland (English
Branch) The TW20 . . . . . .32 C6
Amersham Rd CR0 . . . . . . .42 D3
Amesbury Ave SW2 . . . . . . .21 F6
Amesbury Cl KT4 . . . . .39 C1
Amesbury Rd TW13 . . . . . .15 D6
Amesbury Sch GU26 . . . . .188 E1
Amey Dr KT23 . . . . .94 C3
Amhurst Gdns TW7 . . . . .6 A5
Amis Ave Chessington KT19 .57 B5
Woodham KT15 . . . . .52 A1
Amis Rd GU21 . . . . .88 E8
Amity Gr SW20 . . . . .39 C8
Amlets La GU6 . . . . .174 E5
Ampere Way CR0, CR9 . . . . .41 F1
Amroth Cl SE23 . . . . .23 B7
Amstel Way GU21 . . . . .68 F1
Amundsen Rd RH12 . . . . .217 D6
Amy Johnson Prim Sch
SM6 .60 E3
Amy Rd RH8 . . . . .122 E6
Amyand Cotts 12 TW1 . . . . .6 B1
Amyand Park Gdns 3
TW1 .17 B8
Amyand Park Rd TW1 . . . . .17 A8
Anarth Ct KT13 . . . . .34 E1
Ancaster Cres KT3 . . . . . . .39 A3
Ancaster Dr SL5 . . . . .28 E8
Ancaster Rd BR3 . . . . .43 D6
Anchor Cotts RH7 . . . . . . .163 E8
Anchor Cres GU21 . . . . .68 D2
Anchor Hill GU21 . . . . .68 D2
Anchor Meadow GU14 . . . .84 F4
Anchorage Cl SW19 . . . . . .20 A3
Anderson Ave GU2 . . . . . .109 B5
Anderson Cl KT19 . . . . .76 B7
Anderson Dr TW15 . . . . . . .14 C4
Anderson House SW17 . . .20 D3
Anderson Pl GU19 . . . . .47 E4
Anderson Rd KT13 . . . . . . .53 D7
Anderson's Pl TW3 . . . . .5 B3
Andhurst Ct KT2 . . . . .38 B8
Andon Ct BR3 . . . . .43 E6
Andover Cl
East Bedfont TW14 . . . . .14 F7
Epsom KT19 . . . . .76 D8
Andover Ct TW19 . . . . .13 D8
Andover Rd
Blackwater GU17 . . . . .64 C6
Twickenham TW2 . . . . .16 D7
Andover Way GU11, GU9 .126 B7
Andreck Ct BR3 . . . . .44 C7
Andrew Cl RG40 . . . . .25 E5
Andrew Ct SE23 . . . . .23 D6
Andrew Ewing Prim Sch
TW5 . . . . .4 F7
Andrew Reed House
SW18 . . . . .19 E8
Andrew's Cl KT17 . . . . .76 F6
Andrewartha Rd GU14 . . . .85 E2
Andrewes House SM1 . . . .59 A6
Andrews Cl KT4 . . . . .58 D8
Andrews Rd GU14 . . . . .84 E5
Andromeda Cl RH11 . . . . .200 E4
Anerley Ct SE20 . . . . .23 B1
Anerley Gr SE19 . . . . .22 F1
Anerley Hill SE19 . . . . .22 F2
Anerley Park Rd SE20 . . . .23 B1
Anerley Pk SE20 . . . . .23 B1
Anerley Prim Sch SE20 . . .43 A8
Anerley Rd SE20, SE19 . . . .43 B8
Anerley Sch SE20 . . . . .43 A8
Anerley Sta SE20 . . . . .43 B8
Anerley Station Rd SE20 . .43 B8
Anerley Vale SE19 . . . . .23 A1
Anfield Cl SW12 . . . . .21 C8
Angas Ct 4 KT13 . . . . .53 C5
Angel Ct GU3 . . . . .129 A3
Angel Gate GU1 . . . . .130 D8
Angel Hill SM1 . . . . .59 B7
Angel Hill Dr SM1 . . . . .59 B7
Angel Mews SW15 . . . . .19 A8
Angel Rd KT7 . . . . .37 A1
Angela Ct 2 SE23 . . . . .23 C7
Angelfield TW3 . . . . .5 B2
Angelica Gdns CR0 . . . . . . .43 D1
Angelica Rd Bisley GU24 . .68 A4
Guildford GU2 . . . . .109 A5
Angell Cl RH10 . . . . .202 C5
Angers Cl GU15 . . . . .66 C7
Anglers Reach KT6 . . . . . . .37 D4
Angles Rd SW16 . . . . .21 E4
Anglesea House KT1 . . . . . .37 D5
Anglesea Rd KT1 . . . . .37 D5
Anglesey Ave GU14 . . . . . .84 F7
Anglesey Cl Ashford TW15 .14 A5
Crawley RH11 . . . . .201 C2
Anglesey Court Rd SM5 . . .60 A4
Anglesey Gdns SM5 . . . . . .60 A4
Anglesey Rd GU12 . . . . . .105 D1
Angus Cl Chessington KT9 .57 A5
Horsham RH12 . . . . .217 D4
Angus House 12 SW12 . . . .21 D8
Anlaby Rd TW11 . . . . .16 E3
Ann Parkes Ct TW5 . . . . .4 D5
Annandale Dr GU10 . . . . .146 D6
Annandale Rd Croydon CR0 62 A8
Guildford GU2 . . . . .130 B7
Anne Armstrong Cl
GU11 . . . . .105 D5
Anne Boleyn's Wlk
Cheam SM2, SM3 . . . . .58 E3
Kingston u T KT2 . . . . .17 E3
Anne Way KT8 . . . . .36 B5
Anne's Wlk CR3 . . . . .100 E7
Annella Ct GU11 . . . . .105 D8
Anners Cl TW20 . . . . .32 C6
Annesley Dr CR0 . . . . .62 F7
Annett Cl TW17 . . . . .34 E5
Annett Rd KT12 . . . . .35 A2
Annie Brookes Cl TW18 . . .12 D5
Anningsley Pk KT16 . . . . . .51 C1
Annisdowne RH5 . . . . .133 F1
Annsworthy Ave CR7, SE25 42 D6
Annsworthy Cres CR7 . . . . .42 D7
Ansell Gr SM5 . . . . .41 A1
Ansell Rd Dorking RH4 . . . .136 B8
Frimley GU16 . . . . .65 E1
Upper Tooting SW17 . . . . . . .20 F5
Anselm Cl CR0 . . . . .61 F7
Ansford Rd BR1, SE6 . . . . . .24 D4
Ansley Cl CR2 . . . . .81 B5
Anslie Wlk 8 SW12 . . . . . . .21 B8
Anson Cl CR3, CR8 . . . . . . .100 D7
Anstice Cl W4 . . . . .7 E7
Anstie Grange Dr RH5 . . .157 B5
Anstie La RH5 . . . . .156 F4
Anstiebury Cl RH5 . . . . . . .157 C3
Anston Ct 8 GU2 . . . . .108 E1
Anthony Ct TW7 . . . . .5 F4
Anthony Rd CR0, SE25 . . . . .43 A3
Anthony West House
RH3 . . . . .137 B7
Antigua Wlk SE19 . . . . .22 D3
Antlands La Burstow RH6 .183 B6
Crawley RH6 . . . . .182 E5
Antlands La E RH6 . . . . . . .182 F5
Antlands La W RH6 . . . . . .182 E6
Anton Cres SM1 . . . . .59 A7
Antrobus Cl SM1 . . . . .58 F5
Anvil Cl SW16 . . . . .21 C1
Anvil La KT11 . . . . .73 A5
Anvil Rd TW16 . . . . .35 A6
Anyards Rd KT11 . . . . .73 B5
Anzio Cl GU11 . . . . .105 A2
Apeldoorn Dr CR8, SM6 . . .60 E2
Aperdele Rd KT22 . . . . .75 A1
Aperfield Rd TN16 . . . . . . .83 E2
Apers Ave GU22 . . . . .89 F6
Apex Cl Beckenham BR3 . . . .44 B8
Oatlands Park KT13 . . . . .53 D7
Apex Dr GU16 . . . . .65 D1
Apley Rd RH2 . . . . .139 A6
Aplin Way Hounslow TW7 . . . .5 E6
Lightwater GU18 . . . . .48 A1
Apollo Pl GU21 . . . . .89 A8
Apollo Rise GU14 . . . . .84 D4
Apple Garth GU7 . . . . .150 C7
Apple Gr KT9 . . . . .56 E6
Apple Mkt KT1 . . . . .37 D7
Apple Tree Cl KT23 . . . . . . .94 C3
Apple Tree Way GU47 . . . . .45 D1
Appleby Cl TW2 . . . . .16 D6
Appleby Ct GU15 . . . . .65 B6
Appleby Gdns TW14 . . . . . .14 F7
Appledore RG12 . . . . .26 F3
Appledore Cl Hayes BR2 . . .44 F4
Upper Tooting SW12, SW17 . .20 F6
Appledore Mews GU14 . . .85 A7
Appledown Rise CR5 . . . . . .79 C4
Applefield RH10 . . . . .201 E7
Applegarth Claygate KT10 . .55 F5
New Addington CR0 . . . . .63 B3
Applegarth Ave GU2 . . . . .108 D1
Applegarth Inf & Jun Sch
CR0 . . . . .63 B4
Applelands Cl GU10 . . . . . .146 A4
Appleton Gdns KT3 . . . . . . .39 A3
Appleton Sq CR4 . . . . .40 E8
Appletree Cl
Godalming GU7 . . . . .150 F2
6 Penge SE20 . . . . .43 B8
Appletree Ct GU4 . . . . . . .110 D3
Appletree Pl 4 RG42 . . . . . .27 A8
Appletrees Pl GU22 . . . . . . .89 C8
Appley Dr GU15 . . . . .65 B6
Approach Rd Ashford TW15 14 C2
East Molesey KT8 . . . . .36 A4
Farnham GU9 . . . . .125 C1
Merton SW20 . . . . .39 C7
Purley CR8 . . . . .80 B7
Tatsfield CR6, TN16 . . . . . . .103 B5
Approach The RH19 . . . . .185 F6
April Cl Ashstead KT21 . . . . .75 F1
Camberley GU15 . . . . .65 C2
Feltham TW13 . . . . .15 A5
Horsham RH12 . . . . .217 C4
April Glen SE23 . . . . .23 D5
Aprilwood Cl KT15 . . . . .70 F8
Apsley Ct Crawley RH11 . . .200 F4
Sutton SM2 . . . . .59 C4
Apsley Rd Croydon SE25 . . . .43 B5
Kingston u T KT3 . . . . .38 C6
Aquarius TW1 . . . . .17 B7
Aquarius Ct RH11 . . . . . . .200 E4
Aquila Cl KT21 . . . . .95 E6
Arabella Dr SW15 . . . . .7 E3
Aragon Ave Ewell KT17 . . . .58 B2
Thames Ditton KT7 . . . . .36 F4
Aragon Cl Ashford TW16 . . .14 F1
New Addington CR0 . . . . .63 E1
Aragon Ct Bracknell RG12 . .27 C5
Knaphill GU21 . . . . .68 D2
Aragon Rd Kingston u T KT2 .17 E3
West Barnes SM4 . . . . .39 E2
Aram Ct GU22 . . . . .70 B4
Arbor Cl BR3 . . . . .44 B7
Arbour Cl KT22 . . . . .94 F4
Arbourfield Cl SW2 . . . . . . .21 F7
Arbrook La KT10 . . . . .55 D4
Arbury Terr SE26 . . . . .23 B5
Arbutus Cl RH1 . . . . .139 C7
Arbutus Rd RH1 . . . . .139 C6
Arcade The 11 GU11 . . . . .105 A2
Arch Rd KT12 . . . . .54 D7
Archbishop Lanfranc Sch
The CR0 . . . . .41 E3
Archbishop Tenison's Sch
CR0 . . . . .61 F7
Archbishop's Pl 3 SW2 . . .21 F8
Archdale Pl KT3 . . . . .38 B6
Archdeacon Cambridge's
Prim Sch (C of E) TW2 . . .16 E6
Archer Cl KT2 . . . . .17 E1
Archer Rd SE25 . . . . .43 B5
Archers Ct RH10 . . . . .201 D8
Archway Cl Wallington SM6 .60 E7
Wimbledon SW19 . . . . .20 B4
Archway Mews RH4 . . . . .136 A8
Archway Pl RH4 . . . . .136 A8
Archway St SW13, SW14 . . . .7 E4
Arcturus Rd RH11 . . . . . . .200 E3
Arcus Rd BR1 . . . . .24 E2
Arden 17 SW19 . . . . .19 D7
Arden Cl Bracknell RG12 . . . .28 A7
Reigate RH2 . . . . .139 B5
Arden Mead Cotts RH7 . . .164 A8
Arden Rd RH10 . . . . .201 F4
Ardenrun RH7 . . . . .164 B8
Ardenrun Cotts RH7 . . . . .164 A7
Ardent Cl SE25 . . . . .42 E6
Ardesley Wood KT13 . . . . . .53 E6
Ardfern Ave SW16 . . . . .42 A6
Ardfillan Rd SE6 . . . . .24 D6
Ardgowan Rd SE6 . . . . .24 E7
Ardingly RG12 . . . . .27 A4
Ardingly Cl Crawley RH11 .201 B8
South Croydon CR0 . . . . .62 D7
Ardingly Ct KT18 . . . . .76 D5
Ardleigh Gdns SM3 . . . . . . .40 A2
Ardley Cl SE23, SE6 . . . . . . .23 E5
Ardlui Rd SE27 . . . . .22 C6

Ardmay Gdns KT6 .37 E4
Ardmore Ave GU2 .109 B3
Ardmore House GU2 .109 B3
Ardmore Way GU2 .109 B3
Ardoch Rd SE6 .24 D6
Ardrossan Ave GU15 .66 A5
Ardrossan Gdns KT4 .58 A7
Ardshiel Dr RH1 .139 E7
Ardwell Rd SW2 .21 E6
Arena L Ctr GU15 .65 C6
Arena La GU11 .104 E5
Arena The RG12 .27 A7
Arenal Dr RG45 .45 C3
Arethusa Way GU24 .67 F3
Arford Comm GU35 .187 A6
Argent Cl TW20 .12 C2
Argent Terr GU47 .64 E8
Argosy Gdns TW18 .12 F2
Argosy La TW19 .13 D8
Argus Wlk RH11 .201 A3
Argyle Ave
Isleworth TW2, TW3 .5 A1
Twickenham TW3 .5 A1
Argyle House SM2 .59 C4
Argyle Rd TW3 .5 B2
Argyle St GU24 .87 A6
Argyll Ct 15 SW2 .21 E8
Ariel Way TW4 .4 B4
Arkell Gr SW16 .22 B1
Arkendale RH19 .185 A4
Arkindale Rd SE6 .24 C5
Arklow Mews 3 KT6 .56 E8
Arkwright Dr RG42 .26 D7
Arkwright House 23 SW2 .21 E8
Arkwright Rd Poyle SL3 .1 E5
South Croydon CR2 .61 F2
Arlington Cl Bracknell RG42 27 A8
Sutton SM1 .59 A8
Twickenham TW1 .6 C1
Arlington Ct Reigate RH2 .118 A3
4 Twickenham TW1 .6 C1
Arlington Dr SM5 .59 F8
Arlington Lodge KT13 .53 B6
Arlington Rd Ashford TW15 .13 F3
Richmond TW10 .17 D6
Surbiton KT6 .37 D3
Teddington TW11 .16 F4
Twickenham TW1 .6 C1
Arlington Sq RG12 .27 A7
Arlington Terr GU11 .104 F2
Armadale Rd Feltham TW14 .4 A2
Woking GU21 .69 A2
Armeston KT3 .38 D2
Armfield Cl KT8 .35 F4
Armfield Cres CR4 .40 F7
Armitage Ct SL5 .29 C3
Armitage Dr GU16 .65 F1
Armstrong Cl KT12 .35 A3
Armstrong Mall GU14 .84 D4
Armstrong Rd
Englefield Green TW20 .11 C2
Feltham TW13 .15 E3
Armstrong Way GU14 .84 B1
Armytage Rd TW5 .4 D7
Arnal Cres SW18 .19 E8
Arncliffe RG12 .27 A4
Arndale Way TW20 .12 A3
Arne Cl RH11 .200 F3
Arne Gr RH6 .160 E5
Arnella Ct GU14 .105 D8
Arnewood Cl Oxshott KT22 .74 B5
Roehampton SW15 .19 A7
Arney's La CR4 .41 A3
Arnfield Cl RH11 .200 E5
Arngask Rd SE6 .24 D8
Arnhem Cl GU11 .105 B2
Arnhem Dr CR0 .82 D8
Arnison Rd KT8 .36 D5
Arnold Cres TW7 .5 D2
Arnold Dr KT9 .56 D4
Arnold Rd Mitcham SW17 .20 F1
Sheerwater GU21 .70 B4
Staines TW18 .13 C1
Arnulf St SE6 .24 B4
Arnull's Rd SW16 .22 B2
Arosa Rd 3 TW1 .6 D1
Arragon Gdns
Streatham SW16 .21 E1
West Wickham BR4 .63 B7
Arragon Rd
3 Twickenham TW1 .17 A7
Twickenham TW1 .17 A8
Wandsworth SW18 .20 A7
Arragon Wlk KT14 .71 F6
Arran Cl Crawley RH11 .201 B3
Wallington SM6 .60 C6
Arran Rd SE6 .24 C6
Arran Way KT10 .55 B8
Arrancourt RH12 .217 B2
Arras Ave SM4 .40 C4
Arrivals Rd RH6 .181 F8
Arrol Rd BR3 .43 D6
Arrow Ind Est GU14 .84 F2
Arrow Rd GU14 .84 F2
Artel Croft RH10 .202 A6
Arterberry Rd SW20, SW19 39 D8
Arthur Cl Bagshot GU19 .47 E1
Farnham GU9 .125 B1
Arthur Ct CR0 .61 D7
Arthur Rd Biggin Hill TN16 .83 C3
Crawley RH11 .200 E6
Farnham GU9 .125 C1
Horsham RH13 .217 D1
6 Kingston u T KT2 .18 A1
West Barnes KT3 .39 B4
Wimbledon SW19 .20 A5
Wokingham RG41 .25 A6
Arthur St GU11 .105 B2
Arthur's Bridge Rd GU21 .69 D2
Artillery Rd
1 Aldershot GU11 .105 B2
Farnborough GU11, GU14 .105 D8
7 Guildford GU1 .109 D1
Artillery Terr GU1 .109 D1
Artington Wlk GU2 .130 C6
Arun Way RH13 .217 E1
Arundale KT1 .37 D5
Arundel Ave Ewell KT17 .58 B1
Merton SM4 .39 F5
South Croydon CR2 .62 A1
Arundel Cl Crawley RH10 .202 C6
Croydon CR0, CR9 .61 B7
Hampton TW12 .16 B3
Arundel Ct BR2 .44 E7
Arundel House
Croydon CR0 .61 D5
Reigate RH2 .139 B5
Arundel Rd Belmont SM2 .58 F3
Dorking RH4 .136 A7
Frimley GU15 .66 C4
Hounslow TW4 .4 C4
Kingston u T KT1 .38 C7
Thornton Heath CR0 .42 D3
Arundell Pl 6 GU9 .125 B2
Arunside RH12 .217 A1
Arunside Cty Prim Sch
RH12 .217 A2
Ascalon Ct 19 SW2 .21 F8
Aschurch Rd CR0 .42 F2
Ascot Ct GU11 .105 A1
Ascot Heath Inf Sch SL5 .8 E1
Ascot Heath Jun Sch SL5 .8 E1
Ascot House SE26 .23 B2
Ascot Mews SM6 .60 C2
Ascot Race Course SL5 .28 F6
Ascot Rd
East Bedfont TW14, TW15 .14 B6
Mitcham SW17 .21 A2
Ascot Sta SL5 .29 A5
Ascot Towers SL5 .28 F7
Ascot Wood SL5 .29 A6
Asford Gdns KT11 .73 D3
Ash Church Rd GU12 .106 B2
Ash Cl Ash GU12 .106 B3
Blackwater GU17 .64 C5
Box Hill KT20 .116 C4
Carshalton SM5 .59 F8
Crawley Down RH10 .204 C8
Kingston u T KT3 .38 D7
Lingfield RH7 .164 E5
Merstham RH1 .119 C5
Penge SE20 .43 C7
Pyrford GU22 .71 A4
Woking GU22 .89 E7
Ash Combe GU8 .191 A4
Ash Ct Ottershaw KT16 .51 C5
West Ewell KT19 .57 C6
2 West Norwood SW16 .22 A3
Ash Dr RH1 .140 B7
Ash Gr East Bedfont TW14 .14 E7
Guildford GU2 .109 A2
Heston TW5 .4 D7
Penge SE20 .43 C7
Staines TW18 .13 C2
West Wickham BR4 .44 C1
Ash Grange Cty Prim Sch
GU12 .106 B2
Ash Green La E GU12 .127 C8
Ash Green La W
Ash GU12 .126 F8
Ash, Ash Green GU12 .127 C8
Ash Green Rd GU12 .106 C1
Ash Hill Rd GU12 .106 B3
Ash Keys RH10 .201 E5
Ash La GU8 .148 C2
Ash Lodge 2 TW16 .14 F1
Ash Lodge Cl GU12 .106 A1
Ash Lodge Dr GU12 .106 A1
Ash Manor Sch GU12 .126 F8
Ash Mews KT18 .76 E6
Ash Rd Aldershot GU12 .126 D8
Cheam SM3, SM4 .39 F1
Crawley RH10 .202 A8
Croydon CR0 .63 A8
Littleton TW17 .34 A5
Pirbright GU24, GU3 .88 A1
Woking GU22 .89 E7
Ash St GU12 .106 A1
Ash Sta GU12 .106 B2
Ash Tree Cl
Croydon BR3, CR0 .43 E3
Farnborough GU14 .84 C3
Grayswood GU27 .189 F1
1 Surbiton KT6 .37 E1
Ash Tree Way CR0 .43 E3
Ash Vale GU8 .191 A5
Ash Vale Sta GU12 .106 A7
Ashbourne RG12 .26 F3
Ashbourne Cl Ash GU12 .106 C3
Coulsdon CR5 .79 C1
Ashbourne Rd CR4, SW17 .21 A1
Ashbourne Terr 1 SW19 .20 A1
Ashbrook Rd SL4 .11 B8
Ashburnham Pk KT10 .55 C6
Ashburnham Rd
Crawley RH10 .202 A4
Richmond TW10 .17 B5
Ashburton Ave CR0 .43 B1
Ashburton Cl CR0 .43 A1
Ashburton Gdns CR0 .62 A8
Ashburton Jun & Inf Sch
CR0 .43 B3
Ashburton Rd CR0, CR9 .62 A8
Ashburton Sch CR0 .43 B2
Ashbury Cres GU4 .110 C3
Ashbury Dr GU17 .65 A1
Ashbury Pl SW19 .20 C2
Ashby Ave KT19, KT9 .57 A4
Ashby Ct RH13 .217 E1
Ashby Grange 7 SM6 .60 C4
Ashby Way UB7 .3 A7
Ashby Wlk CR0 .42 C3
Ashcombe Ave KT6 .37 D2
Ashcombe Par GU22 .90 A7
Ashcombe Rd
Dorking RH4 .115 A1
Merstham RH1 .119 C8
Wallington SM5 .60 A4
Wimbledon SW19 .20 A3
Ashcombe Sch The RH4 .115 B1
Ashcombe Sq KT3 .38 C6
Ashcombe Terr KT20 .97 B7
Ashcroft GU4 .130 E2
Ashcroft Pk KT11 .73 E6
Ashcroft Rd KT9 .56 F7
Ashcroft Rise CR5 .79 E3
Ashdale KT23 .94 C1
Ashdale Cl Stanwell TW19 .13 E6
Twickenham TW2 .16 C8
Ashdale Way TW2 .16 B8
Ashdene Cl TW15 .14 C1
Ashdene Cres GU12 .106 A3
Ashdene House TW20 .11 C2
Ashdene Rd GU12 .106 A2
Ashdown Ave GU14 .85 E2
Ashdown Cl
Beckenham BR3 .44 B7
Bracknell RG12 .28 A7
Reigate RH2 .139 B5
Ashdown Dr RH10 .201 E3
Ashdown Gate RH19 .185 D2
Ashdown Gdns CR2 .81 B4
Ashdown Pl KT7 .37 A2
Ashdown Rd Ewell KT17 .77 A6
Forest Row RH18 .206 F2
Kingston u T KT1 .37 E7
Reigate RH2 .139 B5
Ashdown View RH19 .205 E7
Ashdown Way SW17 .21 A6
Ashen Gr SW19 .20 A6
Ashen Vale CR2 .62 D2
Ashenden Rd GU2 .108 F1
Ashfield Ave TW13 .15 B7
Ashfield Cl Beckenham BR3 .24 A1
Richmond TW10 .17 E7
Ashfields RH2 .118 B3
Ashford Ave TW15 .14 B2
Ashford C of E Fst & Mid
Sch TW15 .14 B2
Ashford Cl TW15 .13 E4
Ashford Cres TW15 .13 E5
Ashford High Sch The
TW15 .13 E5
Ashford Hospl TW15 .13 E6
Ashford Ind Est TW15 .14 C4
Ashford Manor Golf Club
TW15 .13 F2
Ashford Park Cty Prim
Sch TW15 .13 D4
Ashford Rd
Feltham TW13, TW15 .14 E4
Littleton TW15, TW17 .14 C1
Staines TW18 .33 D8
Ashford Sta TW15 .13 F5
Ashgrove Rd Ashford TW15 14 D3
Catford BR1 .24 D2
Ashlake Rd SW16 .21 E4
Ashlea Ct CR6 .81 A1
Ashleigh Ave TW20 .12 C1
Ashleigh Cl RH6 .160 F3
Ashleigh Ct SE26 .23 B2
Ashleigh Gdns SM1 .59 B8
Ashleigh House SW14 .7 E4
Ashleigh Point 8 SE26 .23 D5
Ashleigh Rd
Horsham RH12 .217 C4
Mortlake SW14 .7 E4
Penge SE20 .43 B6
Ashley Ave Epsom KT18 .76 D6
Morden SM4 .40 A4
Ashley Cl Frimley GU16 .86 A6
Little Bookham KT23 .93 F2
Oatlands Park KT12, KT13 .34 F1
Ashley Ct 5 Epsom KT18 .76 D6
Knaphill GU21 .68 F1
Ashley Ctr KT18 .76 D6
Ashley Dr Banstead SM7 .78 A5
Blackwater GU17 .64 C4
Hounslow TW7 .5 E8
Twickenham TW2 .16 B7
Walton-on-T KT12 .54 A7
Ashley Gdns
Richmond TW10 .17 D6
Shalford GU4 .130 F2
Ashley House GU7 .150 E8
Ashley Inf Sch KT12 .35 A1
Ashley La CR0 .61 B6
Ashley Park Ave KT12 .53 F8
Ashley Park Cres KT12 .35 A1
Ashley Park Rd KT12 .54 A7
Ashley Rd Epsom KT18 .76 E4
Farnborough GU14 .85 D4
Hampton TW12 .36 A8
Knaphill GU21 .68 F1
Richmond TW9 .6 E4
Thames Ditton KT7 .36 F3
Thornton Heath CR7 .41 F5
Walton-on-T KT12 .54 A8
Westcott RH4 .135 C6
Wimbledon SW19 .20 B2
Ashley Rise KT12 .54 A7
Ashley Way GU24 .67 D6
Ashling Rd CR0, CR9 .43 A1
Ashlyn's Pk KT11 .73 E6
Ashlyns Way KT9 .56 D4
Ashmead Rd TW14 .15 A7
Ashmere Ave BR3 .44 D7
Ashmere Cl SM3 .58 D5
Ashmill Ct CR0 .42 C3
Ashmore Ct TW5 .5 A8
Ashmore House RH11 .181 D1
Ashmore La
Biggin Hill BR2, TN16 .83 C8
Rusper RH12 .199 C6
Ashridge GU14 .84 F7
Ashridge Gn 3 RG42 .27 B8
Ashridge Rd RG40 .25 D8
Ashridge Way
Ashford TW16 .15 A2
Merton SM4, SW20 .39 F5
Ashstead La GU7 .150 C2
Ashstead Sta KT21 .75 E3
Ashtead Ct 15 SW19 .19 D7
Ashtead Hospl The KT21 .95 E8
Ashtead La GU7 .150 D2
Ashtead Woods Rd KT21 .75 C3
Ashton Cl Cheam SM1 .59 A6
Hersham KT12 .54 B4
Ashton Ct BR3 .43 F8
Ashton Gdns TW4 .4 F3
Ashton House SW15 .19 B8
Ashton Rd 2 GU21 .68 F2
Ashtree Ave CR4 .40 D7
Ashtree Ct TW15 .14 B3
Ashtrees GU6 .174 E1
Ashtrees The GU12 .106 B2
Ashurst 3 KT18 .76 D6
Ashurst Cl Horsham RH12 .218 A5
Kenley CR8 .80 D4
Penge SE20 .43 B8
Ashurst Dr Box Hill KT20 .116 B5
Crawley RH10 .202 D6
Littleton TW17 .33 E5
Ashurst Rd Ash Vale GU12 .105 F4
Tadworth KT20 .97 C6
Ashurst Wlk CR0 .62 B8
Ashurstwood
Abbey RH19 .206 E6
Ashurstwood Cty Prim
Sch RH19 .206 E6
Ashvale Rd SW17 .20 F3
Ashview Cl TW15 .13 E3
Ashview Gdns TW15 .13 E3
Ashville Way RG41 .25 A5
Ashway Ctr 5 KT2 .37 E8
Ashwell Ave GU15 .65 F6
Ashwell Ct TW15 .13 E6
Ashwood 5 Crawley RH11 201 D5
Warlingham CR6 .101 C7
Ashwood Gdns CR0 .63 C4
Ashwood Pk
6 Belmont SM2 .59 A3
Fetcham KT22 .94 C4
Woking GU22 .70 A1
Ashwood Rd
Englefield Green TW20 .11 B2
Woking GU22 .70 A1
Ashworth Pl GU2 .108 F1
Aslett St SW18 .20 C8
Asmar Cl CR5 .79 E4
Aspen Cl Guildford GU4 .110 D4
Staines TW18 .12 F5
Stoke D'Abernon KT11 .73 E3
Aspen Ct TW9 .7 A7
Aspen Gdns Ashford TW15 .14 C3
Mitcham CR4 .41 A4
Aspen House Sch SW2 .21 F8
Aspen Sq KT13 .53 D7
Aspen Vale CR3 .80 F1
Aspen Way Banstead KT17 .77 D5
Feltham TW13 .15 B5
Horsham RH12 .217 E4
Aspin Way GU17 .64 B5
Aspinall House SW12 .21 E7
Asprey Gr CR3 .101 A3
Asquith House SM7 .77 F4
Assembly Wlk SM5 .40 E2
Assher Rd KT12 .54 E7
Assheton-Bennett House
KT6 .37 E4
Astleham Rd TW17 .33 E6
Astley House 8 SE27 .22 C4
Aston Cl KT21 .75 C1
Aston Ct RH11 .201 B1
Aston Gn TW5 .4 C5
Aston Rd Claygate KT10 .55 E5
Merton SW20 .39 C7
Aston Way KT18 .76 F3
Astonville St SW18 .20 A7
Astor Cl Addlestone KT15 .52 D6
Kingston u T KT2 .18 B2
Astoria Mansions 18 SW16 21 E5
Astoria Par SW16 .21 E5
Astra Bsns Ctr RH1 .161 A7
Astra Mead RG42 .8 B2
Atalanta Cl CR8 .61 A1
Atbara Ct TW11 .17 B2
Atbara Rd TW11 .17 B2
Atcham Rd TW3 .5 C3
Atfield Gr GU20 .48 D4
Atheldene Rd SW18 .20 C7
Athelney Prim Sch SE6 .24 A5
Athelney St SE6 .24 A5
Athelstan Cl RH10 .202 E6
Athelstan House KT1 .37 F5
Athelstan House Sch
TW12 .36 A8
Athelstan Rd KT1 .37 F5
Athena Cl KT1 .37 F6
Atherfield House RH1 .139 C6
Atherfield Rd RH2 .139 C6
Atherley Way TW4 .15 F8
Atherton Cl Shalford GU4 .130 E3
Stanwell TW19 .2 D1
Atherton Dr SW19 .19 D4
Atherton House CR2 .61 E4
Athlone KT10 .55 E4
Athlone Rd SW2 .22 A8
Atholl House 11 RH1 .118 F1
Atkins Cl GU21 .69 A1
Atkins Dr BR4 .63 D8
Atkins Rd SW4, SW12 .21 D8
Atkinson Ct RH6 .161 B2
Atkinson Morley's
Hospl SW20 .19 B1
Atkinson Rd RH10 .202 C4
Atlanta Ct CR7 .42 C6
Atrebatti Rd GU47 .45 C1
Attebrouche Ct RG12 .27 D2
Attfield Cl GU12 .105 F1
Attleborough Ct SE21 .23 B6
Attlee Cl CR7 .42 C4
Attlee House 5 RH11 .201 B2
Attwood Cl CR2 .81 B5
Atwater Cl SW2 .22 A7
Atwood KT23 .93 E3
Atwood Ave TW9 .7 A5
Atwood House SE21 .22 E5
Aubyn Hill SE27 .22 D4
Auchinleck Ct RH10 .204 B7
Auchinleck Way GU11 .104 E2
Auckland Cl
Crawley RH11 .181 D1
South Norwood SE19 .42 F8
Auckland Gdns SE19 .42 F8
Auckland Hill SE27 .22 C4
Auckland Rd
Caterham CR3 .100 E5
Kingston u T KT1 .37 F5
South Norwood SE19, SE25 .42 F8
Auckland Rise SE19 .42 E8
Audley Cl KT15 .52 B5
Audley Ct Surbiton KT5 .37 F3
Twickenham TW2 .16 D5
Audley Cty Prim Sch CR3 100 F6
Audley Dr CR2, CR6 .81 C4
Audley Firs KT12 .54 C6
Audley House KT15 .52 B5
Audley Pl SM2 .59 B3
Audley Rd TW10 .6 F2
Audley Way SL5 .28 D6
Audrey Cl BR3 .44 B3
Audric Cl KT2 .38 A8
Augur Cl TW18 .12 F3
August La GU5 .153 D7
Augusta Cl KT8 .35 F6
Augusta Rd TW2 .16 C6
Augustine Cl SL3 .1 E4
Augustus Cl TW8 .6 D7
Augustus Ct Hounslow TW3 .5 C3
8 Putney SW19 .19 E7
South Norwood SE19 .22 E1
Streatham SW16 .21 D6
Augustus Gdns GU15 .66 C5
Augustus Rd SW19 .19 E7
Aultone Way
Carshalton SM5 .59 F7
Sutton SM1 .59 C8
Aurelia Gdns CR7 .41 F3
Aurelia Rd CR0, CR7, CR9 .41 F3
Auriol Cl KT19 .57 E7
Auriol Cty Jun Sch KT19 .57 F6
Auriol Park Rd KT19, KT4 .57 E7
Aurum Cl RH6 .161 B2
Austen Cl RH19 .185 B1
Austen Rd
Farnborough GU14 .85 A6
Guildford GU1 .130 F8
Austin Cl Coulsdon CR8 .80 B1
Forest Hill SE23, SE6 .23 F8
Twickenham TW1 .6 C2
Austin House 19 KT6 .37 E4
Austin's Cotts 10 GU9 .125 B2
Austyn Gdns KT5 .38 B1
Autumn Cl SW19 .20 C2
Autumn Dr SM2 .59 B2
Avalon Cl SW20 .39 E7
Avarn Rd SW17 .20 F2
Avebury RG12 .27 A3
Avebury Cl RH12 .218 A7
Avebury Rd SW19 .39 F8
Aveley La GU10, GU9 .146 C7
Aveling Cl Crawley RH10 .202 C4
Purley CR8 .79 F6
Aven Cl GU6 .174 E2
Avening Rd SW18 .20 A8
Avening Terr SW18 .20 A8
Avenue C KT15 .52 E6
Avenue Cl Cranford TW5 .4 B6
Tadworth KT20 .97 B5
Avenue Cres TW5 .4 B7
Avenue Ct Penge SE20 .43 C8
Tadworth KT20 .97 B4
Avenue De Cagny GU24 .87 F5
Avenue Elmers KT6 .37 E4
Avenue Gdns Cranford TW5 .4 B7
Horley RH6 .161 C2
Mortlake SW14 .7 E4
South Norwood SE25 .43 A7
Teddington TW11 .16 F2
Avenue One KT15 .52 E6
Avenue Park Rd
SE21, SE27 .22 B6
Avenue Prim Sch The
SM2 .59 A1
Avenue Rd Banstead SM7 .78 B4
Belmont SM2 .59 A1

Avenue Rd *continued*
Caterham CR3 . . . . . 100 E5
Cobham KT11 . . . . . 73 D3
Cranleigh GU6 . . . . . 174 F1
Egham TW18 . . . . . 12 D3
Epsom KT18 . . . . . 76 D5
Farnborough GU14 . . . . . 85 D3
Feltham TW13 . . . . . 14 F5
Grayshott GU26 . . . . . 188 C3
Hampton TW12 . . . . . 36 B8
Hounslow TW7 . . . . . 5 F6
Kingston u T KT1 . . . . . 37 E6
Mitcham SW16 . . . . . 41 D7
New Malden KT3 . . . . . 38 E5
South Norwood, Annerley SE25 . . . . . 43 A7
South Norwood, Elmers End BR3, SE20 . . . . . 43 D8
Tatsfield TN16 . . . . . 103 E7
Teddington TW11 . . . . . 17 A2
Wallington SM6 . . . . . 60 C3
Wimbledon SW20 . . . . . 39 B7
Avenue S KT5 . . . . . 38 A2
Avenue Sucy GU15 . . . . . 65 B4
Avenue Terr KT3 . . . . . 38 C6
Avenue The
Aldershot GU11, GU12 . . . . . 126 C7
Beckenham BR3 . . . . . 44 C8
Belmont SM2 . . . . . 58 F2
Biggin Hill TN16 . . . . . 103 F5
Brockham RH3, RH5 . . . . . 116 A1
Camberley GU15 . . . . . 65 B5
Chobham GU24 . . . . . 50 A2
Claygate KT10 . . . . . 55 E5
Compton GU3, GU7 . . . . . 129 C1
Coulsdon CR5 . . . . . 79 D4
Cranford TW5 . . . . . 4 A6
Crowthorne RG45 . . . . . 45 B5
Dormansland RH19 . . . . . 186 B6
Egham TW20 . . . . . 12 B4
Ewhurst GU6 . . . . . 175 E6
Godalming GU7 . . . . . 150 F2
Grayshott GU26 . . . . . 188 D3
Hampton TW12 . . . . . 15 F2
Haslemere GU27 . . . . . 207 F7
Horley RH6 . . . . . 160 F2
Hounslow TW3 . . . . . 5 B2
Isleworth TW1 . . . . . 6 C2
Lightwater GU18 . . . . . 48 A1
4 New Malden KT4 . . . . . 39 A1
North Ascot SL5 . . . . . 8 F1
Oxshott KT10, KT22 . . . . . 74 F8
Richmond TW9 . . . . . 6 F5
Rowledge GU10 . . . . . 145 F3
South Croydon CR0 . . . . . 61 E7
South Nutfield RH1 . . . . . 140 E6
Staines TW18 . . . . . 33 B8
Stoneleigh KT17, SM3 . . . . . 58 C3
Sunbury TW16 . . . . . 35 B7
Surbiton KT5 . . . . . 37 F3
Tadworth KT20 . . . . . 97 B5
Twickenham TW1 . . . . . 6 B2
West Wickham BR4 . . . . . 44 E2
Whyteleafe CR3 . . . . . 101 A8
Woodham KT15 . . . . . 52 A1
Worcester Park KT4 . . . . . 57 F8
Worplesdon GU3 . . . . . 88 E1
Avenue Three KT15 . . . . . 52 E7
Avenue Two KT15 . . . . . 52 E6
Averil Gr SW16 . . . . . 22 B2
Avern Gdns KT8 . . . . . 36 B5
Avern Rd KT8 . . . . . 36 B5
Avery Ct SE20 . . . . . 23 B1
Aviary Rd GU22 . . . . . 71 A3
Aviary Way RH10 . . . . . 184 C1
Aviemore Cl BR3 . . . . . 43 F4
Aviemore Way BR3 . . . . . 43 E4
Avington Cl GU1 . . . . . 109 E1
Avington Gr SE20 . . . . . 23 C1
Avoca Rd SW17 . . . . . 21 A4
Avocet Cres GU47 . . . . . 64 E8
Avon Cl Addlestone KT15 . . . 52 A4
Ash GU12 . . . . . 105 F1
Farnborough GU14 . . . . . 84 E7
Sutton SM1 . . . . . 59 C6
Worcester Park KT4 . . . . . 58 A8
Avon Ct GU9 . . . . . 125 C1
Avon House 9 RH1 . . . . . 118 F2
Avon Rd Ashford TW16 . . . . . 14 F1
Farnham GU9 . . . . . 125 C1
Avon Wlk RH11 . . . . . 200 F5
Avondale GU12 . . . . . 105 F7
Avondale Ave
Hinchley Wood KT10 . . . . . 56 A7
New Malden KT4 . . . . . 38 F1
Staines TW18 . . . . . 12 F1
Avondale Cl Hersham KT12 . 54 C5
Horley RH6 . . . . . 161 A5
Avondale Ct SM2 . . . . . 59 C3
Avondale Gdns TW4 . . . . . 4 F2
Avondale High CR3 . . . . . 101 A6
Avondale House 6 SW14 . . . 7 D4
Avondale Rd
Aldershot GU11 . . . . . 126 B8
Ashford TW15, TW19 . . . . . 13 D5
Bromley BR1 . . . . . 24 F2
Catford BR1 . . . . . 24 F2
Mortlake SW14 . . . . . 7 D4
South Croydon CR2 . . . . . 61 C4
Wimbledon SW19 . . . . . 20 B3
Avonmore Ave GU1 . . . . . 109 F2
Avonwick Rd TW3 . . . . . 5 B5
Avro Way Byfleet KT13 . . . . . 52 E1
Wallington SM6 . . . . . 60 E3
Axbridge RG12 . . . . . 27 E4
Axes La RH1 . . . . . 140 D2
Axford House SW2 . . . . . 22 B7
Axwood KT18 . . . . . 76 C4
Aycliffe Ct KT1 . . . . . 38 A7
Ayebridges Ave TW20 . . . . . 12 C1
Ayjay Cl GU11 . . . . . 126 A7
Aylesbury Ct SM1 . . . . . 59 C7
Aylesford Ave BR3 . . . . . 43 E4
Aylesworth Spur SL4 . . . . . 11 B8
Aylett Rd Croydon SE25 . . . . . 43 B5
Isleworth TW7 . . . . . 5 E5
Ayling Ct GU9 . . . . . 125 F7
Ayling Hill GU11 . . . . . 104 F1
Ayling La GU11 . . . . . 125 F8
Aylward Rd Forest Hill SE23 23 D6
Merton SW20 . . . . . 39 F6
Aymer Cl TW18 . . . . . 32 E8
Aymer Dr TW18 . . . . . 32 E8
Aysgarth RG12 . . . . . 27 A3
Aysgarth Ct SM1 . . . . . 59 B7
Aysgarth Rd SE21 . . . . . 22 E8
Ayshe Court Dr RH13 . . . . . 217 E3
Azalea Ct GU22 . . . . . 89 D8
Azalea Dr GU27 . . . . . 207 F8
Azalea Way GU15 . . . . . 66 B6
Azelea Ct CR8 . . . . . 80 B8

B

Babbacombe Cl KT9 . . . . . 56 D5
Babbs Mead GU9 . . . . . 125 A1
Baber Dr TW14 . . . . . 4 C1
Babington Ct SW16 . . . . . 21 D3
Babington Rd SW16 . . . . . 21 D3
Babylon La KT20, RH2 . . . . . 118 B8
Bachelor's La GU23 . . . . . 92 A3
Back Gn KT12 . . . . . 54 C4
Back La Binstead GU10 . . . . . 166 B8
Brentford TW8 . . . . . 6 D8
Crawley RH10 . . . . . 203 D1
East Clandon GU4 . . . . . 111 D4
Elstead GU8 . . . . . 148 D4
Plaistow RH14 . . . . . 211 E2
Richmond TW10 . . . . . 17 C6
Back Rd TW11 . . . . . 16 E2
Bacon Cl GU47 . . . . . 64 D6
Bacon La GU10 . . . . . 167 C3
Badajos Rd GU11 . . . . . 104 F3
Baden Cl TW18 . . . . . 13 B1
Baden Dr RH6 . . . . . 160 E4
Baden Powell Cl KT6 . . . . . 56 F8
Baden Rd GU2 . . . . . 109 B3
Bader Cl CR8 . . . . . 80 D4
Bader Ct GU14 . . . . . 84 F8
Badger Cl Feltham TW13 . . . 15 B5
Guildford GU2 . . . . . 109 B4
Hounslow TW4 . . . . . 4 C4
Badger Ct GU10 . . . . . 146 A5
Badger Dr GU18 . . . . . 48 A1
Badger Way GU10 . . . . . 124 D8
Badgers Cl Ashford TW15 . . 13 F3
Farncombe GU7 . . . . . 150 D8
Horsham RH12 . . . . . 217 F6
Woking GU21 . . . . . 69 C1
Badgers Copse
Frimley GU15 . . . . . 65 E4
Worcester Park KT4 . . . . . 57 F8
Badgers Cross GU8 . . . . . 149 E1
Badgers Ct 4 KT17 . . . . . 76 E6
Badgers Hill GU25 . . . . . 31 C4
Badgers Hollow GU7 . . . . . 150 D6
Badgers La CR6 . . . . . 101 C8
Badgers Lodge 5 KT17 . . . 76 E6
Badgers Way
Bracknell RG12 . . . . . 27 F7
East Grinstead RH19 . . . . . 185 F2
Loxwood RH14 . . . . . 213 A4
Badgers Wlk
Kingston u T KT3 . . . . . 38 E7
Purley CR8 . . . . . 79 C8
Whyteleafe CR3 . . . . . 80 F1
Badgers Wood CR3 . . . . . 100 D2
Badgerwood Dr GU16 . . . . . 65 D2
Badingham Dr KT22 . . . . . 94 E4
Badminton Rd SW12 . . . . . 21 A8
Badshot Lea Cty Inf Sch GU9 . . . . . 126 A6
Badshot Lea Rd GU11, GU9 . . . . . 126 A6
Badshot Pk GU9 . . . . . 126 A6
Bagden Hill KT23 . . . . . 114 D5
Bagot Cl KT21 . . . . . 75 F3
Bagshot Cty Inf Sch GU19 . 47 E2
Bagshot Gn GU19 . . . . . 47 E3
Bagshot Rd Ascot SL5 . . . . . 29 C2
Bracknell RG12 . . . . . 27 C4
Bracknell SL5 . . . . . 48 A8
Brookwood GU21, GU22, GU24, GU3 . . . . . 88 C5
Englefield Green TW20 . . . . . 11 C2
Knaphill GU21, GU22, GU24, GU3 . . . . . 88 C5
Pirbright GU21, GU22, GU24, GU3 . . . . . 88 C5
West End GU24 . . . . . 68 B8
Woking GU21, GU22, GU24, GU3 . . . . . 88 C5
Bagshot Sta GU19 . . . . . 47 E4
Bahram Rd KT19 . . . . . 57 D1
Baigents La GU20 . . . . . 48 D4
Bailes La Flexford GU3 . . . 107 D2
Normandy GU3 . . . . . 107 D3
Bailey Cl Frimley GU16 . . . . . 85 D8
Horsham RH12 . . . . . 217 F7
Bailey House 11 SE26 . . . . . 23 B3
Bailey Pl SE26 . . . . . 23 D2
Bailey Rd RH4 . . . . . 135 C6
Baileys Cl GU17 . . . . . 64 C4
Bailing Hill RH12 . . . . . 216 E7
Baillie Rd GU1 . . . . . 130 F8
Bain Ave GU15 . . . . . 65 B2
Bainbridge cl KT2 . . . . . 17 E3
Baines Cl CR0 . . . . . 61 D5
Bainton Mead GU21 . . . . . 69 A2
Baird Cl RH10 . . . . . 182 A1
Baird Dr GU3 . . . . . 108 B2
Baird Gdns SE19, SE21 . . . . . 22 E4
Baird Rd GU14 . . . . . 85 C6
Bakeham La TW20 . . . . . 11 D1
Bakehouse Barn Cl RH12 217 E7
Bakehouse Rd RH6 . . . . . 161 A5
Baker Cl RH10 . . . . . 201 D4
Baker La CR4 . . . . . 41 A7
Baker St KT13 . . . . . 53 B6
Baker's Cl RH7 . . . . . 164 E5
Baker's La RH7 . . . . . 164 E4
Bakers Ct SE25 . . . . . 42 E6
Bakers End SW20 . . . . . 39 E7
Bakers Gdns SM5 . . . . . 59 E8
Bakers Mead RH9 . . . . . 121 C6
Bakers Way RH5 . . . . . 178 C5
Bakery Mews KT6 . . . . . 38 A1
Bakewell Dr KT3 . . . . . 38 E7
Balaam House SM1 . . . . . 59 A6
Balaclava Rd KT6 . . . . . 37 C2
Balchins La RH4 . . . . . 135 B6
Balcombe Ct RH10 . . . . . 202 D7
Balcombe Gdns RH6 . . . . . 161 C2
Balcombe House 3 SW2 . . 21 F7
Balcombe Rd Crawley, Tinsley Green RH10, RH6 . . 182 D5
Crawley, Worth RH10 . . . . . 202 D5
Horley RH6 . . . . . 161 B2
Baldreys GU9 . . . . . 146 A8
Baldry Gdns SW16 . . . . . 21 F2
Baldwin Cl RH10 . . . . . 202 C3
Baldwin Cres GU4 . . . . . 110 C3
Baldwin House 15 SW2 . . . 22 A7
Baldwins Hill Cty Prim Sch RH19 . . . . . 185 D3
Balfont Cl CR2 . . . . . 81 A6
Balfour Ave GU22 . . . . . 89 F5
Balfour Cres RG12 . . . . . 27 B4
Balfour Gdns RH18 . . . . . 206 E1
Balfour Rd Croydon SE25 . . . 43 A5
Hounslow TW3 . . . . . 5 B4
Merton SW19 . . . . . 20 B1
Wallington SM5 . . . . . 59 F3
Weybridge KT13 . . . . . 53 A6
Balgowan Cl KT3 . . . . . 38 E5
Balgowan Prim Sch BR3 . . 43 E7
Balgowan Rd BR3 . . . . . 43 F7
Balham Gr SW12 . . . . . 21 A8
Balham High Rd
Balham SW12, SW17 . . . . . 21 A7
Upper Tooting SW12 . . . . . 21 A7
Balham Hill SW12 . . . . . 21 B8
Balham New Rd SW12 . . . . . 21 B8
Balham Park Mansions SW12 . . . . . 20 F7
Balham Park Rd SW12, SW17 . . . . . 21 A7
Balham Sta SW12 . . . . . 21 B7
Balham Station Rd SW12 . 21 B7
Balintore Ct 8 GU47 . . . . . 64 D8
Ball and Wicket La GU9 . 125 C7
Ballands N The KT22 . . . . . 94 E5
Ballands' S The KT22 . . . . . 94 E4
Ballantyne Dr KT20 . . . . . 97 F6
Ballantyne Rd GU14 . . . . . 85 A6
Ballard Cl KT2 . . . . . 18 D1
Ballard Ct GU15 . . . . . 66 A8
Ballard Rd GU15 . . . . . 66 A8
Ballards Farm Rd CR2 . . . . . 62 A4
Ballards Gn KT20 . . . . . 97 E8
Ballards La RH8 . . . . . 123 C6
Ballards Rise CR2 . . . . . 62 A4
Ballards Way CR0, CR2 . . . . . 62 B4
Ballater Rd CR2 . . . . . 61 F5
Ballencrieff Rd SL5 . . . . . 29 F2
Ballfield Rd GU7 . . . . . 150 E6
Ballina St SE23 . . . . . 23 D8
Balliol Cl RH10 . . . . . 182 D1
Balliol Way GU47 . . . . . 45 E1
Balloch Rd SE6 . . . . . 24 D6
Ballsdown GU8 . . . . . 191 A3
Balmain Ct TW3 . . . . . 5 B6
Balmoral RH19 . . . . . 206 A8
Balmoral Ave BR3 . . . . . 43 E5
Balmoral Cres
East Molesey KT8 . . . . . 36 A6
Hale GU9 . . . . . 125 B6
Balmoral Ct
11 Belmont SM2 . . . . . 59 A3
6 Crawley RH11 . . . . . 201 B2
North Cheam KT4 . . . . . 58 B8
West Norwood SE27 . . . . . 22 C4
Balmoral Dr Frimley GU16 . . 85 F8
Woking GU22 . . . . . 70 C3
Balmoral Gdns CR2 . . . . . 61 D1
Balmoral Grange TW18 . . . . . 33 B7
Balmoral Rd Ash GU12 . . . 106 B4
Kingston u T KT1 . . . . . 37 F5
North Cheam KT4 . . . . . 58 B8
Balmoral Way SM2 . . . . . 59 A1
Balquhain Cl KT21 . . . . . 75 D2
Baltic Cl SW19 . . . . . 20 D1
Balvernie Gr SW18 . . . . . 20 A8
Bamford Rd BR1 . . . . . 24 D3
Bampfylde Cl SM6 . . . . . 60 C7
Bampton Rd SE23 . . . . . 23 D5
Bampton Way GU21 . . . . . 69 A2
Banavie Gdns BR3 . . . . . 44 C8
Banbury RG12 . . . . . 27 E2
Banbury Cl GU16 . . . . . 86 A7
Banbury Ct 8 SM2 . . . . . 59 A3
Bancroft Cl TW15 . . . . . 14 A3
Bancroft Ct RH2 . . . . . 118 B1
Bancroft Rd
Crawley RH10 . . . . . 202 D5
Reigate RH2 . . . . . 118 B1
Band La 1 TW20 . . . . . 12 A3
Banders Rise GU1 . . . . . 110 C2
Bandon Hill Prim Sch SM6 . . . . . 60 D4
Bandon Rise SM6 . . . . . 60 D5
Banfor Ct SM6 . . . . . 60 C4
Bank Ave CR4 . . . . . 40 D7
Bank La Crawley RH10 . . . . . 201 D6
Kingston u T KT2 . . . . . 17 E1
Roehampton SW15 . . . . . 7 E2
Bank Mews SM1 . . . . . 59 C4
Bank Rd GU11 . . . . . 105 D5
Bank Willow TW10 . . . . . 17 B5
Bank's La KT11, KT24 . . . . . 93 B5
Bankfoot Rd BR1 . . . . . 24 E4
Bankhurst Rd SE4, SE6 . . . . . 23 F8
Banks House TW7 . . . . . 5 E5
Banks Rd RH10 . . . . . 202 C5
Banks Way GU1 . . . . . 109 F4
Bankside Heath End GU9 . . 125 F7
South Croydon CR2 . . . . . 61 F4
Woking GU21 . . . . . 69 B1
Bankside Cl Biggin Hill TN16 83 C1
Carshalton SM5 . . . . . 59 E4
Elstead GU8 . . . . . 148 D3
Isleworth TW7 . . . . . 5 F3
Bankside Dr KT7 . . . . . 56 B8
Bankside Way 6 SE19 . . . . . 22 E2
Banning House 4 SW19 . . . 19 D7
Bannister Cl
Streatham SW2 . . . . . 22 A7
Witley GU8 . . . . . 170 F6
Bannister's Rd GU2 . . . . . 129 F7
Banstead Cty Inf Sch SM7 . 77 F4
Banstead Cty Jun Sch SM7 . . . . . 77 F4
Banstead Downs Golf Club SM2 . . . . . 78 A8
Banstead Rd Banstead SM7 77 D7
Belmont SM7 . . . . . 77 D7
Carshalton SM2, SM5 . . . . . 59 E3
Caterham CR3 . . . . . 100 D5
East Ewell KT17 . . . . . 77 D7
Purley CR8 . . . . . 80 A8
Sutton SM2, SM5 . . . . . 59 E3
Banstead Rd S SM2 . . . . . 59 D1
Banstead Sta SM7 . . . . . 77 F5
Banstead Way SM6 . . . . . 60 E5
Barbara Cl TW17 . . . . . 34 B4
Barber Cl RH10 . . . . . 202 C2
Barber Dr GU6 . . . . . 174 E4
Barberry Way GU17 . . . . . 64 F2
Barbon Cl GU15 . . . . . 66 D3
Barclay Cl KT23 . . . . . 94 B4
Barclay Rd CR0, CR9 . . . . . 61 D7
Barcombe Ave SW2 . . . . . 21 F6
Bardney Rd SM4 . . . . . 40 B5
Bardolph Ave CR0 . . . . . 62 F2
Bardolph Rd TW9 . . . . . 6 F4
Bardon Wlk GU21 . . . . . 69 B2
Bardsley Cl CR0 . . . . . 61 F7
Bardsley Dr GU9 . . . . . 146 A7
Barfield Ct 9 RH1 . . . . . 119 A3
Barfield Sch GU10 . . . . . 126 B3
Barfields RH1 . . . . . 120 C2
Barford La GU10 . . . . . 167 E1
Barfreston Way SE20 . . . . . 43 B8
Bargate Cl KT3 . . . . . 39 A2
Bargate Ct 1 GU2 . . . . . 108 E1
Bargate Rise GU7 . . . . . 150 C4
Barge Cl GU11 . . . . . 105 E5
Bargery Rd SE6 . . . . . 24 B7
Bargrove Cl 8 SE20 . . . . . 23 A1
Bargrove Cres SE6 . . . . . 23 F6
Barham Cl KT13 . . . . . 53 C6
Barham Rd
Croydon CR0, CR2 . . . . . 61 C5
Wimbledon SW20 . . . . . 19 A1
Barhatch La GU6 . . . . . 174 F6
Barhatch Rd GU6 . . . . . 174 F4
Baring Rd CR0, CR9 . . . . . 43 A1
Barker Gn RG12 . . . . . 27 B4
Barker House SE21 . . . . . 22 E5
Barker Rd KT16 . . . . . 32 F2
Barker Wlk SW16 . . . . . 21 D5
Barkham Rd RG41 . . . . . 25 A5
Barkhart Dr RG40 . . . . . 25 C7
Barkhart Gdns RG40 . . . . . 25 C7
Barkis Mead GU47 . . . . . 45 E2
Barley Cl RH10 . . . . . 201 D5
Barley Mow Cl GU21 . . . . . 68 D2
Barley Mow Ct RH3 . . . . . 116 C1
Barley Mow Hill GU35 . . . 187 A6
Barley Mow La GU21 . . . . . 68 D3
Barley Mow Rd TW20 . . . . . 11 C3
Barley Mow Way TW17 . . . 34 A5
Barleymead RH6 . . . . . 161 B4
Barlow Cl SM6 . . . . . 60 E3
Barlow Rd Crawley RH11 . . 200 E3
Hampton TW12 . . . . . 16 A1
Barmeston Rd SE6 . . . . . 24 B6
Barmouth Rd CR0 . . . . . 62 D8
Barn Cl Ashford TW15 . . . . . 14 B3
Bracknell RG12 . . . . . 27 D7
Camberley GU15 . . . . . 65 E6
Epsom KT18 . . . . . 76 C4
Oxshott KT22 . . . . . 74 D6
Woodmansterne SM7 . . . . . 78 D4
Barn Cres CR8 . . . . . 80 D6
Barn Field SM7 . . . . . 78 B5
Barn Meadow La KT23 . . . . . 93 F3
Barn Rd KT15 . . . . . 52 B2
Barnard Cl Frimley GU16 . . . 85 F8
Sunbury TW16 . . . . . 15 B1
Wallington SM6 . . . . . 60 D3
Barnard Ct 1
Knaphill GU21 . . . . . 68 E1
Streatham SW16 . . . . . 21 F5
Barnard Gdns KT3 . . . . . 39 A5
Barnard Rd Chelsham CR6 . 102 B8
Mitcham CR4 . . . . . 41 A7
Barnards Pl CR2 . . . . . 61 B2
Barnato Cl KT14 . . . . . 71 E7
Barnby Rd GU21 . . . . . 68 D2
Barncroft GU9 . . . . . 125 C1
Barnes Bridge Sta SW13 . . . 7 E5
Barnes Cl GU14 . . . . . 85 D4
Barnes Ct CR7 . . . . . 42 C6
Barnes End KT3 . . . . . 39 A4
Barnes High St SW13 . . . . . 7 F5
Barnes Hospl SW14 . . . . . 7 E4
Barnes Rd Farncombe GU7 150 E8
Frimley GU16 . . . . . 85 E8
Barnes Wallis Dr KT13, KT14 . . . . . 71 E8
Barnett Cl Leatherhead KT22 95 B8
Wonersh GU5 . . . . . 152 C8
Barnett Ct RG12 . . . . . 27 C7
Barnett Gn RG12 . . . . . 27 B3
Barnett La Lightwater GU18 . 66 F7
Wonersh GU5 . . . . . 152 C7
Barnett Row GU4 . . . . . 109 D6
Barnett Wood Cty Inf Sch KT21 . . . . . 75 D2
Barnett Wood La
Ashstead KT21, KT22 . . . . . 75 D1
Leatherhead KT22 . . . . . 95 B8
Barnett's Shaw RH8 . . . . . 122 D8
Barnfield Cranleigh GU6 . . . 174 E3
New Malden KT3 . . . . . 38 E3
Barnfield Ave Croydon CR0 . 62 C8
Kingston u T KT2 . . . . . 17 E3
Mitcham CR4 . . . . . 41 B6
Barnfield Cl Coulsdon CR5 100 C8
Wandsworth SW17 . . . . . 20 C5
Barnfield Cotts RH7 . . . . . 165 A1
Barnfield Gdns KT2 . . . . . 17 E3
Barnfield Rd
Crawley RH10, RH11 . . . . . 201 E7
South Croydon CR2 . . . . . 61 E2
Tatsfield TN16 . . . . . 103 D6
Barnfield Way RH8 . . . . . 123 A2
Barnfield Wood Cl BR3 . . . 44 D3
Barnfield Wood Rd BR3 . . . 44 D3
Barnhill Ave BR2 . . . . . 44 F4
Barnlea Cl TW13 . . . . . 15 E6
Barnmead GU24 . . . . . 49 F1
Barnmead Rd BR3 . . . . . 43 E8
Barns The GU8 . . . . . 149 C8
Barnsbury Cl KT3 . . . . . 38 C5
Barnsbury Cres KT5 . . . . . 38 C1
Barnsbury Cty Inf & Jun Schs GU22 . . . . . 89 D6
Barnsbury La KT5 . . . . . 38 C1
Barnscroft SW20 . . . . . 39 B6
Barnsfold La RH12 . . . . . 213 E6
Barnsford Cres GU24 . . . . . 68 A6
Barnsley Cl GU12 . . . . . 86 B2
Barnsnap Cl RH12 . . . . . 217 D6
Barnway TW20 . . . . . 11 C3
Barnwood Cl
Crawley RH10 . . . . . 202 C7
Guildford GU3 . . . . . 108 E3
Barnwood Ct GU2, GU3 . . . 108 E3
Barnwood Cty Inf Sch GU2 . . . . . 108 E2
Barnwood Rd GU2, GU3 . . 108 E3
Barnyard The KT20 . . . . . 97 A3
Baron Cl SM2 . . . . . 59 B1
Baron Ct CR4 . . . . . 40 E5
Baron Gr CR4 . . . . . 40 E5
Baron's Hurst KT18 . . . . . 76 C3
Baron's Way RH2 . . . . . 139 A5
Baron's Wlk CR0 . . . . . 43 E3
Barons Ct SM6 . . . . . 60 D7
Barons The TW1 . . . . . 6 B1
Barons Way TW20 . . . . . 12 D2
Baronsfield Rd TW1 . . . . . 6 B1
Barossa Rd GU15 . . . . . 65 D7
Barr Beacon SE23 . . . . . 23 C8
Barr's La GU21 . . . . . 68 D3
Barracane Dr RG45 . . . . . 45 B5
Barrack Path 8 GU21 . . . . . 68 F1
Barrack Rd
Aldershot GU11 . . . . . 105 A2
Guildford GU2 . . . . . 109 A4
Hounslow TW4 . . . . . 4 E3
Barrards Hall CR2 . . . . . 80 D8
Barrens Brae GU22 . . . . . 70 A1
Barrens Cl GU22 . . . . . 90 A8
Barrens Pk GU22 . . . . . 90 A8
Barrett Cres RG40 . . . . . 25 E6
Barrett Rd KT22, KT23 . . . . . 94 D3
Barrhill Rd SW2 . . . . . 21 E6
Barricane GU21 . . . . . 89 B8
Barrie Cl CR5 . . . . . 79 C3
Barrie Rd GU9 . . . . . 125 A7
Barrihurst La GU6 . . . . . 173 D2
Barringer Sq SW17 . . . . . 21 A4
Barrington Ct
Dorking RH4 . . . . . 136 A6
Staines TW18 . . . . . 12 F2
Barrington Lodge KT13 . . . 53 C5
Barrington Rd Cheam SM3 . 40 A1
Crawley RH10 . . . . . 201 D3
Dorking RH4 . . . . . 136 A6
Horsham RH13 . . . . . 217 E2
Purley CR8 . . . . . 79 C7
Barrington Wlk 8 SE19 . . . 22 E2
Barrow Ave SM5 . . . . . 59 F3

Barrow Ct SE6 ....24 F7
Barrow Green Rd
Oxted RH8 ....122 C6
Tandridge RH9 ....122 C6
Barrow Hedges Cl SM5 ....59 E3
Barrow Hedges Prim Sch SM5 ....59 E3
Barrow Hedges Way SM2, SM5 ....59 E3
Barrow Hill KT4 ....57 E8
Barrow Hill Cl KT4 ....57 E8
Barrow Hills Sch GU8 ....170 E4
Barrow Rd Croydon CR0 ....61 A5
Streatham SW16 ....21 D2
Barrowsfield CR2 ....81 A7
Barry Cl RH10 ....201 E3
Barry Sq RG12 ....27 D2
Barry Terr TW15 ....13 F6
Bars The GU1 ....130 D8
Barsons Cl SE20 ....23 C1
Barston Rd SE27 ....22 C5
Barstow Cres SW2 ....21 F7
Bartholomew Cl GU27 ....208 D8
Bartholomew Ct RH4 ....136 A6
Bartholomew Way RH12 ....218 A7
Bartlett St CR0, CR2 ....61 D5
Barton Cl Addlestone KT15 ....52 A4
Aldershot GU11 ....104 E1
Shepperton TW17 ....34 B3
Barton Cres RH19 ....206 A8
Barton Ct BR2 ....44 D6
Barton Gn KT3 ....38 D7
Barton Pl GU1 ....110 B4
Barton Rd GU5 ....152 A7
Barton The KT11 ....73 D7
Barton Wlk RH10 ....202 B4
Bartons Way GU14 ....84 D7
Barttelot Rd RH12 ....217 D2
Barwell Bsns Pk KT9 ....56 D2
Barwood Ave BR4 ....44 B1
Basden Gr TW13 ....16 A6
Basemoors RG12 ....27 E7
Bashford Way RH10 ....202 D8
Basil Gdns Croydon CR0 ....43 D1
West Norwood SE27 ....22 C3
Basildene Rd TW4, TW5 ....4 D4
Basildon Cl SM2 ....59 B2
Basildon Way RH11 ....200 E2
Basing Cl KT7 ....36 F2
Basing Dr GU11 ....126 B7
Basing House SE6 ....24 A4
Basing Rd SM7 ....77 F4
Basing Way KT7 ....36 F2
Basingfield Rd KT7 ....36 F2
Basinghall Gdns SM2 ....59 B2
Baskerville Rd SW18 ....20 E8
Basset Cl KT15 ....52 C1
Bassett Cl Frimley GU16 ....85 E8
Sutton SM2 ....59 B2
Bassett Gdns TW7 ....5 C7
Bassett Rd Crawley RH10 ....202 D3
Woking GU22 ....70 C3
Bassetts Hill RH7 ....165 A2
Bassingham Rd SW18 ....20 C8
Bat and Ball La
Rowledge GU10 ....146 A5
Wrecclesham GU10, GU9 ....146 A6
Batavia Cl TW16 ....35 C8
Batavia Rd TW16 ....35 B8
Batcombe Mead RG12 ....27 E2
Bateman Gr GU12 ....126 F8
Batemans Ct RH10 ....202 A3
Bates Cres Croydon CR0 ....61 A5
Streatham SW16 ....21 C1
Bates Wlk KT15 ....52 C4
Bateson Way GU21 ....70 C5
Bath Ct 3 SE26 ....23 A5
Bath House Rd CR0, CR9 ....41 E1
Bath Pas KT1 ....37 D7
Bath Rd Camberley GU15 ....65 D6
Cranford TW3, TW4, TW5 ....4 E5
Harlington TW6, UB7, TW5 ....3 D6
Harmondsworth TW6, UB7 ....2 E6
Hounslow TW3, TW4, TW5 ....4 E5
Mitcham CR4 ....40 D6
Poyle SL3, UB7, TW6 ....1 E6
Bathgate Rd SW19 ....19 D5
Bathurst Ave SW19 ....40 B8
Batsworth Rd CR4 ....40 D6
Batt's Cnr GU10 ....166 E7
Batten Ave GU21 ....88 E8
Battenberg Wlk 10 SE19 ....22 E3
Battersby Rd SE6 ....24 D5
Battle Cl SW19 ....20 C2
Battlebridge House RH1 ....119 B5
Battlebridge La RH1 ....119 B5
Batts Hill RH2 ....118 E3
Batty's Barn Cl RG40 ....25 D5
Baty House SW2 ....21 F7
Baudwin Rd SE6 ....24 E6
Bavant Rd SW16 ....41 F7
Bawtree Cl SM2 ....59 C1
Bax Cl GU6 ....174 E2
Baxter Ave RH1 ....118 F1
Baxter Cl RH10 ....202 B4
Bay Cl RH6 ....160 E6
Bay Dr RG12 ....27 E7
Bay Rd RG12 ....27 E8
Bay Tree Ave KT22 ....95 A7
Bayards CR6 ....81 C1
Baydon Ct BR2 ....44 F6
Bayeux KT20 ....97 D5
Bayfield Ave GU16 ....65 E2
Bayfield Rd RH6 ....160 E4
Bayford Cl GU17 ....65 A1
Bayham Rd SM4 ....40 C5
Bayhorne La RH6 ....161 C1
Bayleaf Cl TW12 ....16 D3
Baylis Wlk RH11 ....201 B1
Bayliss Ct 2 GU1 ....130 C8
Baynards Rd RH12 ....195 A2
Bays Cl SE26 ....23 C3
Baysfarm Ct TW6, UB7 ....2 C6
Baywood Cl GU14 ....84 C5
Bazalgette Cl KT3 ....38 D4
Bazalgette Gdns KT3 ....38 D4
Beach Gr TW13 ....16 A6
Beachborough Rd BR1 ....24 C4
Beachy Rd RH11 ....201 A1
Beacon Cl Banstead SM7 ....77 D3
Rowledge GU10 ....146 A5
Beacon Ct Colnbrook SW3 ....1 C7
Horsham RH13 ....218 A4
Beacon Gr SM5 ....60 A6
Beacon Hill
Dormansland RH7 ....186 B8
Woking GU21 ....89 C8
Beacon Hill Ct GU26 ....188 D6
Beacon Hill Cty Prim Sch GU26 ....188 C6
Beacon Hill Rd
Beacon Hill GU26 ....188 D6
Crondall GU10 ....124 E8
Beacon House 10 SE26 ....23 B3
Beacon Rd TW19, TW6 ....3 A1
Beacon Rdbt TW6 ....3 A1
Beacon Sch The KT20 ....77 E2
Beacon View Rd GU8 ....148 C2
Beacon Way SM7 ....77 E3
Beaconsfield Pl KT17 ....76 E7
Beaconsfield Rd
Claygate KT10 ....55 E3
Kingston u T KT3 ....38 D7
Langley Vale KT18 ....96 E8
Old Woking GU22 ....89 F7
Surbiton KT5 ....37 F2
Thornton Heath CR0 ....42 D3
Twickenham TW1 ....6 B1
Beaconshaw BR1 ....24 E1
Beadle Ct CR4 ....40 E6
Beadles La RH8 ....122 D4
Beadlow Cl SM4 ....40 D3
Beadman Pl SE27 ....22 B4
Beadman St SE27 ....22 B4
Beadnell Rd SE23 ....23 D7
Beaford Gr SW20 ....39 F6
Beagle Cl TW13 ....15 B4
Beale Cl RG40 ....25 B7
Beale Ct RH11 ....201 A3
Beale's La KT13 ....53 B7
Beales La GU10 ....145 F7
Beales Rd KT23 ....94 B1
Bealeswood La GU10 ....166 F6
Beam Hollow GU9 ....125 C7
Bean Oak Rd RG40 ....25 F6
Bear La GU9 ....125 C3
Bear Rd TW13 ....15 D4
Beard Rd TW10 ....17 F3
Beard's Hill TW12 ....36 A8
Beard's Rd TW15, TW16 ....14 E2
Beardell St SE19 ....22 F2
Beards Hill Cl TW12 ....36 A8
Beare Green Cotts RH5 ....157 D2
Beare Green Ct RH5 ....157 D4
Bearfield Rd KT2 ....17 E1
Bears Den KT20 ....97 F5
Bears Rail Pk SL4 ....10 F8
Bearsden Way RH12 ....216 D3
Bearwood Cl KT15 ....52 A4
Bearwood Cotts GU10 ....145 F7
Beasley's Ait La TW16, TW17 ....34 F3
Beatrice Ave SW16 ....41 F7
Beatrice Rd Oxted RH8 ....122 E6
1 Richmond TW10 ....6 F2
Beatrix Potter Prim Sch SW18 ....20 C7
Beattie Cl
East Bedfont TW14 ....14 F7
Little Bookham KT23 ....93 F3
Beatty Ave GU1 ....110 A2
Beauchamp Rd
East Molesey KT8 ....36 C4
South Norwood CR7, SE25 ....42 D8
Sutton SM1 ....59 A6
Twickenham TW1 ....17 A8
Beauclare Cl KT21 ....95 D6
Beauclerc Cty Inf Sch TW16 ....35 C6
Beauclere House SM2 ....59 C3
Beauclerk Cl TW13 ....15 E6
Beauclerk House 10 SW16 ....21 E5
Beaufield Gate GU27 ....208 D7
Beaufort Cl Putney SW19 ....19 B8
Reigate RH2 ....117 F2
Woking GU22 ....70 C3
Beaufort Ct TW10 ....17 C4
Beaufort Cty Prim Sch GU21 ....68 F3
Beaufort Gdns Heston TW5 ....4 E6
North Ascot SL5 ....28 E8
South Norwood SW16 ....21 F1
Beaufort House SW20 ....39 D8
Beaufort Rd Farnham GU9 ....125 C3
Kingston u T KT1, KT5, KT6 ....37 E5
Reigate RH2 ....117 F2
Richmond TW10 ....17 C4
Twickenham TW1 ....17 C8
Woking GU22 ....70 C3
Beaufort Way KT17 ....58 A3
Beauforts TW20 ....11 C3
Beaufoy House 3 SE27 ....22 B5
Beaufront Cl GU15 ....66 A7
Beaufront Rd GU15 ....66 B7
Beaulieu Ave SE26 ....23 B4
Beaulieu Cl Bracknell RG12 ....28 A6
Beaulieu Cl *continued*
Hounslow TW4 ....4 F2
Mitcham CR4 ....41 A8
4 Twickenham TW1 ....6 D1
Beaulieu Gdns GU17 ....64 C5
Beaumaris Par GU16 ....85 F8
Beaumont Ave TW9 ....6 F4
Beaumont Cl RH11 ....200 E5
Beaumont Ct Ascot SL5 ....28 F5
Mitcham CR4 ....41 A7
Beaumont Dr TW15 ....14 D3
Beaumont Gdns RG12 ....27 E4
Beaumont Gr GU11 ....104 E2
Beaumont House 1
Streatham SW2 ....21 E7
Wimbledon SW19 ....20 A5
Beaumont Jun Sch GU11 ....104 F2
Beaumont Pl TW7 ....5 F2
Beaumont Prim Sch CR8 ....80 A5
Beaumont Rd Purley CR8 ....80 A6
Putney SW15, SW19 ....19 E8
South Norwood SE19 ....22 C2
Beaumont Sq GU6 ....174 F3
Beaumont Terr 1 SE13 ....24 E8
Beaumonts RH1 ....139 F1
Beaver Cl Hampton TW12 ....36 B8
Horsham RH12 ....217 F6
9 Penge SE20 ....23 A1
Wokingham RG41 ....25 B3
Beaver Water World TN16 ....103 B5
Beavers Cl Farnham GU9 ....125 A2
Guildford GU3 ....108 E2
Beavers Comm Prim Sch TW4 ....4 C4
Beavers Cres TW4 ....4 D3
Beavers Hill GU9 ....124 F2
Beavers La TW4 ....4 C4
Beavers Rd GU9 ....125 A2
Beck Ct BR3 ....43 D6
Beck Gdns GU9 ....125 A6
Beck Ind Est The GU12 ....126 D8
Beck La BR3 ....43 D6
Beck River Pk BR3 ....44 A8
Beck Way BR3 ....44 A6
Beckenham Bsns Ctr BR3 ....23 E2
Beckenham Ct BR3 ....44 A8
Beckenham Gr BR2 ....44 D7
Beckenham Hill Rd BR3, SE6 ....24 C3
Beckenham Hill Sta SE6 ....24 C3
Beckenham Hospl BR3 ....43 F7
Beckenham Junction Sta BR3 ....44 A8
Beckenham La BR1, BR2 ....44 F7
Beckenham Place Pk BR3 ....24 B1
Beckenham Rd
Beckenham BR3 ....43 E8
Penge BR3 ....43 E8
West Wickham BR3, BR4 ....44 C2
Beckenshaw Gdns SM7 ....78 E4
Becket Cl Croydon SE25 ....43 A3
2 Merton SW19 ....40 B8
Becket Wood RH5 ....158 C4
Beckett Ave CR8 ....80 B4
Beckett Cl Streatham SW16 ....21 D6
Wokingham RG40 ....25 E6
Beckett La RH11 ....181 D1
Beckett Way 11 RH19 ....205 F8
Beckett Wlk BR3 ....23 E2
Becketts Cl TW14 ....4 B1
Becketts Pl KT1 ....37 D8
Beckford Ave RG12 ....27 B3
Beckford Rd CR0, SE25 ....42 F3
Beckford Way RH10 ....202 B2
Beckingham Rd GU2 ....109 A2
Beckley Cotts KT23 ....94 C1
Beckmead Sch BR3 ....44 A1
Beckway Rd SW16 ....41 D7
Beckworth Pl KT13 ....53 E8
Beclands Rd SW17 ....21 A2
Becmead Ave SW16 ....21 D4
Becondale Rd SE19 ....22 E3
Bedale Cl RH11 ....201 C4
Beddington Cross CR0 ....41 E2
Beddington Farm Rd
Croydon CR0 ....60 F8
Wallington CR0, CR9 ....41 E1
Beddington Gdns SM5, SM6 ....60 A4
Beddington Gr SM6 ....60 D5
Beddington Inf Sch SM6 ....60 C6
Beddington La CR0 ....60 E8
Beddington Manor SM2 ....59 D4
Beddington Park Cotts SM6 ....60 D7
Beddington Park Prim Sch CR0 ....60 D7
Beddlestead La CR6 ....103 A6
Bedelsford Sch KT1 ....37 E6
Bedfont Cl
East Bedfont TW14 ....3 C1
Mitcham CR4 ....41 A7
Bedfont Ct TW19 ....2 B4
Bedfont Green Cl TW14 ....14 C7
Bedfont Ind Pk N TW15 ....14 C5
Bedfont Inf Sch TW14 ....3 E1
Bedfont Jun Sch TW14 ....3 E1
Bedfont La TW14, TW13 ....14 F8
Bedfont Rd
East Bedfont TW13, TW14 ....14 D6
Feltham TW13, TW14 ....14 D6
Stanwell TW19 ....2 F1
Bedford Ave GU16 ....85 F5
Bedford Cres GU16 ....85 F5
Bedford Ct 6 Richmond TW9 ....6 F3
South Norwood SE19 ....42 F8
Bedford Hill Balham SW12 ....21 B6
Bedford Hill *continued*
Streatham SW16 ....21 B6
Upper Tooting SW12, SW16, SW17 ....21 B6
Bedford House 3 GU1 ....130 C8
Bedford La Frimley GU16 ....85 F6
Sunningdale SL5 ....30 B4
Bedford Pk CR0 ....42 C1
Bedford Pl CR0 ....42 D1
Bedford Rd Guildford GU1 ....130 C8
Horsham RH13 ....217 D1
North Cheam KT4 ....58 C8
Twickenham TW2 ....16 D5
Bedgebury Gdns SW19 ....19 E6
Bedlow Way CR0 ....60 F6
Bedser Cl CR7 ....42 C6
Bedster Gdns KT8 ....36 B6
Bedwardine Rd SE19 ....22 E1
Beech Ave Brentford TW8 ....6 B7
Camberley GU15 ....65 D4
Effingham KT24 ....113 D6
Farnham GU10 ....146 C5
South Croydon CR2 ....61 D1
Tatsfield TN16 ....103 D8
Beech Cl Ashford TW15 ....14 D3
Blindley Heath RH7 ....163 E8
Byfleet KT14 ....71 E7
Carshalton SM5 ....59 F8
Chiddingfold GU8 ....191 A4
Cobham KT11 ....74 A8
Dorking RH4 ....136 A8
Effingham KT24 ....113 D7
Hersham KT12 ....54 C6
Putney SW15 ....19 A8
Stanwell TW19 ....13 D8
Sunbury TW16 ....35 D7
Wimbledon SW19 ....19 C2
Beech Close Ct KT11 ....73 F8
Beech Copse CR2 ....61 E5
Beech Cres KT20 ....116 C5
Beech Ct Beckenham BR3 ....23 F1
4 Guildford GU1 ....130 F8
Teddington TW11 ....17 C2
4 West Norwood SW16 ....22 A3
Beech Dr Blackwater GU17 ....64 D4
Kingswood KT20 ....97 F5
Reigate RH2 ....118 D1
Send Marsh GU23 ....91 A3
Beech Farm Rd CR6 ....102 D8
Beech Fields RH19 ....185 F3
Beech Gdns
Crawley Down RH10 ....204 A8
Woking GU21 ....69 E4
Beech Glen RG12 ....27 B5
Beech Gr Addlestone KT15 ....52 B6
Burgh Heath KT18 ....77 B2
Caterham CR3 ....100 E1
Great Bookham KT23 ....114 A8
Guildford GU2 ....108 F1
Kingston u T KT3 ....38 D6
Mitcham CR4 ....41 D5
Pirbright GU24 ....87 C7
Pirbright GU24 ....87 D7
Beech Hall KT16 ....51 C3
Beech Hanger End GU26 ....188 B3
Beech Hill
Bowlhead Green GU8 ....189 F8
Headley Down GU35 ....187 B5
Woking GU22 ....89 D4
Beech Hill Rd
Headley Down GU35 ....187 A5
Sunningdale SL5 ....29 F3
Beech Holme RH10 ....204 B8
Beech Holt KT22 ....95 C5
Beech House Heston TW5 ....4 E7
New Addington CR0 ....63 B4
Beech House Rd CR0, CR9 ....61 D7
Beech La Flexford GU3 ....107 A1
Grayshott GU26 ....188 B4
Guildford GU2 ....130 C6
Beech Lodge TW18 ....12 E3
Beech Rd Biggin Hill TN16 ....83 C2
East Bedfont TW14 ....14 E8
Epsom KT18 ....76 F4
Farnborough GU14 ....85 A7
Frimley GU16 ....85 F6
Haslemere GU27 ....208 D8
Horsham RH12 ....218 B5
Merstham RH1 ....99 C1
Oatlands Park KT13 ....53 D6
Reigate RH2 ....118 A4
Thornton Heath SW16 ....41 F6
Beech Ride GU47 ....45 B1
Beech Tree Cl RH10 ....201 D7
Beech Tree Dr GU9 ....126 A5
Beech Tree La TW18 ....33 B7
Beech Tree Pl SM1 ....59 B5
Beech Way Epsom KT17 ....76 F4
Godalming GU7 ....150 D3
Selsdon CR2 ....81 D7
Twickenham TW13 ....16 A5
Beech Wlk KT17 ....77 A8
Beech Wood CR3 ....100 F3
Beechcroft Ashstead KT21 ....95 F8
Kingston u T KT2 ....38 B8
Beechcroft Ave Kenley CR8 ....80 D4
Kingston u T KT1, KT3 ....38 C7
Beechcroft Cl Ascot SL5 ....29 D5
Heston TW5 ....4 E7
Streatham SW16 ....21 F3
Beechcroft Ct RG12 ....27 B6
Beechcroft Dr GU2 ....129 D6
Beechcroft Lodge SM2 ....59 C3
Beechcroft Manor KT13 ....53 D7
Beechcroft Mansions SW16 ....21 F3
Beechcroft Rd
Chessington KT9 ....56 F7
Beechcroft Rd *continued*
Mortlake SW14 ....7 C4
Upper Tooting SW17 ....20 E6
Beechcroft Sch SW17 ....20 E6
Beechdene KT20 ....97 B5
Beechen Cliff Way TW7 ....5 F5
Beechen La KT20 ....97 F2
Beechen Pl SE23 ....23 C6
Beeches Ave The SM5 ....59 E3
Beeches Cl Kingswood KT20 ....98 A4
Penge SE20 ....43 C8
Beeches Cres RH10 ....201 E4
Beeches Head RH19 ....186 F5
Beeches La RH19 ....206 D6
Beeches Rd Cheam SM3 ....39 E1
Upper Tooting SW17 ....20 F5
Beeches The Ash Vale GU12 ....85 F1
Banstead SM7 ....78 B3
Bramley GU5 ....151 F6
Fetcham KT22 ....94 E3
Hounslow TW3 ....5 B6
Mitcham CR4 ....40 E4
Staines TW18 ....13 A3
Beeches Wlk SM2, SM5 ....59 E2
Beeches Wood KT20 ....98 A5
Beechey Cl RH10 ....183 B3
Beechey Way RH10 ....183 B3
Beechfield SM7 ....78 B6
Beechfield Ct 7 CR0 ....61 C6
Beechfield Rd SE6 ....23 F7
Beeching Cl GU12 ....106 B3
Beeching Way RH19 ....185 E1
Beechland Cotts KT20 ....117 F7
Beechlawn GU1 ....130 F8
Beechmeads KT11 ....73 D6
Beechmont Ave GU25 ....31 D4
Beechmont Cl BR1 ....24 E3
Beechmore Gdns SM3 ....58 D8
Beechnut Dr GU17 ....64 B6
Beechnut Ind Est 9 GU12 ....105 B1
Beechnut Rd 8 GU12 ....105 B1
Beecholme KT17 ....77 E5
Beecholme Ave CR4 ....41 B8
Beecholme Fst Sch CR4 ....41 B8
Beechrow KT2 ....17 E4
Beechside RH10 ....201 E5
Beechtree Ave TW20 ....11 B2
Beechvale 3 GU22 ....69 F1
Beechway GU1 ....110 B2
Beechwood Ave
Ashford TW16 ....15 A2
Kingswood KT20 ....98 A6
Oatlands Park KT13 ....53 E6
Richmond TW9 ....7 A6
Staines TW18 ....13 B2
Thornton Heath CR7 ....42 B5
Wallington CR5 ....79 B4
Beechwood Cl
Knaphill GU21 ....68 E2
Long Ditton KT6 ....37 D2
North Ascot SL5 ....8 F1
Oatlands Park KT13 ....53 E6
Beechwood Ct
Carshalton SM5 ....59 F6
Chiswick W4 ....7 D8
Sutton SM1 ....59 A5
Walton-on-T KT12 ....54 A7
Beechwood Dr KT11 ....74 A8
Beechwood Gdns CR3 ....101 A5
Beechwood La CR6 ....101 D8
Beechwood Manor KT13 ....53 E6
Beechwood Pk KT22 ....95 C5
Beechwood Rd
Caterham CR3 ....101 A5
Knaphill GU21 ....68 D2
South Croydon CR2 ....61 E2
Wentworth GU25 ....31 B1
Beechwood Villas RH1 ....161 A7
Beechwoods Ct SE19 ....22 F3
Beecot La KT12 ....54 C8
Beeding Cl RH12 ....218 A5
Beedingwood Dr RH12 ....218 F6
Beedon Dr RG12 ....26 E3
Beehive La RG12 ....26 C7
Beehive Rd
Bracknell RG12, RG42 ....26 D7
Staines TW18 ....12 F3
Beehive Ring Rd RH6 ....182 B4
Beehive Way RH2 ....139 B5
Beeleigh Rd SM4 ....40 B5
Beeston Way TW14 ....4 C1
Beeton's Ave GU12 ....106 A4
Beggar's Roost La SM1, SM2 ....59 A4
Beggars La Chobham GU24 ....68 C8
Gomshall RH5 ....133 E4
Beggarshouse La RH6 ....180 C8
Begonia Pl 1 TW12 ....16 A2
Behenna Cl RH11 ....200 E5
Beira St SW12 ....21 B8
Belcroft Cl BR1 ....24 F1
Beldam Bridge Rd GU24 ....68 A6
Beldham Gdns KT8 ....36 B6
Beldham Rd GU10, GU9 ....145 F7
Belenoyd Ct SW16 ....21 F5
Belfast Rd SE25 ....43 B5
Belfield Rd KT19 ....57 E3
Belfry The RH1 ....118 F2
Belgrade Rd TW12 ....36 B8
Belgrave Cl KT12 ....54 B6
Belgrave Cres TW16 ....35 B8
Belgrave Ct GU17 ....64 D3
Belgrave Manor GU22 ....89 E8
Belgrave Rd Barnes SW13 ....7 F7

Belgrave Rd *continued*
Hounslow TW4 .....4 F4
Mitcham CR4 .....40 D6
South Norwood SE25 .....42 F5
Sunbury TW16 .....35 B8
Belgrave Wlk CR4 .....40 D6
Belgravia Ct RH6 .....161 B3
Belgravia Gdns BR1 .....24 E2
Belgravia House 1 TW11 .17 C1
Belgravia Mews KT1 .....37 D5
Bell Bridge Rd KT16 .....32 F1
Bell Cl GU14 .....85 C6
Bell Cnr KT16 .....32 F2
Bell Cres CR5 .....99 B6
Bell Ct KT5 .....57 B8
Bell Ctr RH10 .....181 F2
Bell Dr SW18 .....19 E8
Bell Farm Jun Sch KT12 .54 C6
Bell Foundry La RG40 .....25 C8
Bell Gn SE6 .....23 F4
Bell Green La
BR3, SE26, SE6 .....23 F4
Bell Hammer RH19 .....205 E8
Bell House 15 SW2 .....22 A8
Bell House Gdns RG41 .....25 B6
Bell La Blackwater GU17 .....64 C5
Fetcham KT22 .....94 D4
Rowledge GU10 .....145 E3
Twickenham TW1 .....17 A7
Bell Lane Cl KT22 .....94 D4
Bell Meadow
Dulwich SE19 .....22 E4
Godstone RH9 .....121 C3
Bell Pl GU19 .....47 F3
Bell Rd East Molesey KT8 .....36 D4
Hounslow TW3 .....5 B3
Kingsley Green GU27 .....208 B3
Warnham RH12 .....217 A8
Bell St RH2 .....139 B8
Bell Vale La
Haslemere GU27 .....208 C4
Lurgashall GU27 .....208 C4
Bell View BR3 .....23 F1
Bell Weir Cl TW19 .....12 B6
Bellamy House Heston TW5 .5 A8
Upper Tooting SW17 .....20 D4
Bellamy Rd RH10 .....202 C2
Bellamy St SW12 .....21 B8
Belland Dr GU11 .....104 E1
Bellasis Ave SW2 .....21 E6
Belle Vue Cl
Aldershot GU12 .....105 D2
Staines TW18 .....33 A8
Belle Vue Ent Ctr GU12 .105 E2
Belle Vue Inf Sch GU12 .105 D2
Belle Vue Rd GU12 .....105 D2
Bellever Hill GU15 .....65 E5
Bellevue Pk CR7 .....42 C5
Bellevue Rd
Kingston u T KT1 .....37 E6
Upper Tooting SW17 .....20 F7
Bellew Rd GU16 .....86 B7
Bellew St SW17 .....20 C5
Bellfield CR0 .....62 F3
Bellfields Ct GU1 .....109 C5
Bellfields Rd GU1 .....109 D3
Bellingham Cl GU15 .....66 C4
Bellingham Gn SE6 .....24 A5
Bellingham Rd SE6 .....24 C5
Bellingham Sta SE6 .....24 B5
Bellingham Trad Est SE6 .24 B6
Bellmarsh Rd KT15 .....52 B6
Bellmore Ct 5 CR0 .....42 F1
Bello Cl SE24, SW2 .....22 B7
Belloc Cl RH10 .....202 C7
Belloc Ct RH13 .....218 A3
Bells La SL3 .....1 B4
Belltrees Gr 1 SW16 .....22 A3
Bellwether La RH1 .....162 B7
Belmont KT13 .....53 C4
Belmont Ave
Guildford GU2 .....108 F4
West Barnes KT3 .....39 A5
Belmont Cl GU14 .....84 F7
Belmont Mews GU15 .....65 C3
Belmont Rd Beckenham BR3 43 F7
Belmont SM2 .....59 A1
Camberley GU15 .....65 C4
Crowthorne RG45 .....45 B6
Croydon SE25 .....43 B4
Leatherhead KT22 .....95 A5
Reigate RH2 .....139 C8
Twickenham TW2 .....16 D6
Wallington SM6 .....60 C5
Belmont Rise SM1, SM2 .....58 F3
Belmont Sch RH5 .....155 D6
Belmont Sta SM2 .....59 B1
Belmore Ave GU22 .....70 D3
Belsize Gdns SM1 .....59 B6
Belstone Mews GU14 .....85 A7
Beltane Dr SW19 .....19 D5
Belthorn Cres SW12 .....21 C8
Belton Rd GU15 .....65 E5
Belvedere Ave SW19 .....19 E3
Belvedere Cl Esher KT10 .....55 B5
Guildford GU2 .....109 B3
Teddington TW11 .....16 E3
Weybridge KT13 .....53 A5
Belvedere Ct
Blackwater GU17 .....64 D3
Crawley RH10 .....202 B7
8 Kingston u T KT2 .....18 A1
Belvedere Dr SW19 .....19 E3
Belvedere Gdns KT8 .....36 A4
Belvedere Gr SW19 .....19 E3
Belvedere Rd
Biggin Hill TN16 .....83 F1
Farnborough GU14 .....85 C2
Penge SE19 .....22 F1
Belvedere Sq SW19 .....19 E3
Belvoir Cl GU16 .....65 F1
Belvoir Lodge SE22 .....23 A8
Belvoir Rd SE22 .....23 A8
Benbow La GU8 .....193 C4
Benbrick Rd GU2 .....130 A8
Benbury Cl BR1 .....24 C3
Bence The TW20 .....32 B6
Bench Field CR2 .....61 F5
Benchfield Cl RH19 .....186 B1
Bencombe Rd CR8 .....80 A5
Bencroft Rd SW16 .....21 C1
Bencurtis Pk BR4 .....63 D8
Bendon Valley SW18 .....20 B8
Benedict Dr TW14 .....14 D8
Benedict Fst Sch CR4 .....40 D6
Benedict Prim Sch CR4 .....40 D6
Benedict Rd CR4 .....40 D6
Benedict Wharf CR4 .....40 E6
Benen-Stock Rd TW19 .....2 A2
Benett Gdns SW16 .....41 E7
Benfleet Cl Cobham KT11 .....73 E7
Sutton SM1 .....59 C7
Benham Cl Chessington KT9 56 C4
Coulsdon CR5, CR8 .....80 B1
Benham Gdns TW3, TW4 .....4 F2
Benhams Cl RH6 .....161 A5
Benhams Dr RH6 .....161 A5
Benhill Ave SM1 .....59 C6
Benhill Rd SM1 .....59 D6
Benhill Wood Rd SM1 .....59 C6
Benhilton Gdns SM1 .....59 B7
Benhurst Cl CR2 .....62 D1
Benhurst Ct 13 Penge SE20 .43 B8
Streatham SW16 .....22 A3
Benhurst Gdns CR2 .....62 C1
Benhurst La SW16 .....22 A3
Benin St SE13 .....24 D8
Benjamin Ct TW15 .....14 C1
Benjamin Rd RH10 .....202 D4
Benner La GU24 .....68 A7
Bennet Cl KT1 .....37 C8
Bennett Cl Cobham KT11 .....73 A6
Crawley RH10 .....202 B2
Bennett Ct GU15 .....65 C5
Bennett House 2 SW4 .....21 D8
Bennett St W4 .....7 E8
Bennett Way GU4 .....111 B6
Bennetts Ave CR0 .....62 E8
Bennetts Cl CR4, SW16 .....41 B8
Bennetts Farm Pl KT23 .....93 F2
Bennetts Rd RH13 .....217 E1
Bennetts Way CR0 .....62 F8
Bennetts Wood RH5 .....178 C5
Bens Acre RH13 .....218 A2
Bensbury Cl SW15 .....19 C8
Bensham Cl CR7 .....42 C5
Bensham Gr CR7 .....42 C7
Bensham La CR0, CR7 .....42 B3
Bensham Manor
Rd CR0, CR7 .....42 C5
Bensham Manor Sch CR7 .42 C4
Bensington Ct TW14 .....3 D1
Benson Cl TW3 .....5 A3
Benson Prim Sch CR0 .....62 E7
Benson Rd
Croydon CR0, CR9 .....61 A7
Forest Hill SE23 .....23 C7
Benson's La RH12 .....199 C1
Bentall Sh Ctr The 10 KT2 .37 E7
Benthall Gdns CR8 .....80 C2
Bentham Ave GU21 .....70 C4
Bentley Cl SW19 .....20 A5
Bentley Copse GU15 .....66 B4
Bentley Dr KT13 .....53 A2
Benton's La SE27 .....22 C4
Benton's Rise SE27 .....22 D3
Bentsbrook Cl RH5 .....136 B3
Bentsbrook Cotts RH5 .....136 B3
Bentsbrook Pk RH5 .....136 B3
Bentsbrook Rd RH5 .....136 B3
Benwell Ct TW16 .....35 A8
Benwell Rd GU24 .....88 A8
Benwick Ct SE20 .....43 C8
Benwood Ct SM1 .....59 C7
Beomonds KT16 .....33 A2
Beomonds Row KT16 .....33 A2
Berberis Cl GU1 .....109 C3
Bere Rd RG12 .....27 E3
Beresford Ave
Tolworth KT5 .....38 C2
Twickenham TW1 .....6 C1
Beresford Cl GU16 .....85 F6
Beresford Ct 11 TW1 .....6 C1
Beresford Gdns TW4 .....4 F2
Beresford House SE21 .....22 E5
Beresford Rd Belmont SM2 .58 F3
Dorking RH4 .....136 B7
Kingston u T KT2 .....37 F8
Kingston u T, Norbiton KT3 .....38 C5
Bergenia Ct GU24 .....67 E6
Berkeley Ave TW4 .....4 A5
Berkeley Cl Crawley RH11 .200 E2
Stanwell TW19 .....12 D6
Berkeley Cres GU16 .....86 A8
Berkeley Ct Ashstead KT21 .75 F1
Oatlands Park KT13 .....53 E8
16 Streatham SW2 .....22 A7
Wallington SM6 .....60 C6
Berkeley Dr
East Molesey KT8 .....36 A6
Winkfield SL4 .....9 B7
Berkeley Gdns
Claygate KT10 .....56 A4
Berkeley Gdns *continued*
Pyrford KT14 .....70 F5
Walton-on-T KT12 .....34 F2
Berkeley House 11 TW8 .....6 D8
Berkeley Pl Epsom KT18 .....76 D4
Wimbledon SW19 .....19 D2
Berkeley Prim Sch TW5 .....4 D7
Berkeley Waye TW5 .....4 D7
Berkeleys The KT22 .....94 E3
Berkley Cl TW2 .....16 E5
Berkley Ct Guildford GU1 .109 E1
7 Twickenham TW1 .....17 A8
Berkley Mews TW16 .....35 C6
Berkshire Cl CR3 .....100 D5
Berkshire House SE6 .....24 A4
Berkshire Rd GU15 .....65 F8
Berkshire Sq CR4 .....41 E5
Berkshire Way
Bracknell RG12 .....26 D6
Mitcham CR4 .....41 E5
Bernard Ct GU15 .....65 B4
Bernard Gdns SW19 .....19 F3
Bernard Rd SM5, SM6 .....60 B6
Berne Rd CR7 .....42 C4
Bernel Dr CR0 .....62 F7
Bernersh Cl GU47 .....45 C1
Berney House BR3 .....43 E4
Berney Rd CR0 .....42 D2
Berridge Rd SE19 .....22 E3
Berrington Dr KT24 .....92 F3
Berry Ct TW4 .....4 F2
Berry La Pirbright GU3 .....88 C2
West Norwood SE21, SE27 .22 D4
Woking GU22, GU3 .....88 D4
Berry Meade KT21 .....75 F2
Berry Wlk KT21 .....95 F8
Berry's La KT14 .....71 D8
Berrybank GU47 .....64 E6
Berrycroft RG12 .....27 D8
Berrylands Surbiton KT5 .....37 F3
West Barnes SW20 .....39 C5
Berrylands Ct 7 SM2 .....59 B3
Berrylands Rd KT5 .....37 F3
Berrylands Sta KT5 .....38 B5
Berryman's La SE26 .....23 D4
Berrymeade Wlk RH11 .....200 E5
Berryscourt KT14 .....71 D8
Berryscroft Ct TW18 .....13 C1
Berryscroft Rd TW18 .....13 C1
Berstead Wlk 1 RH11 .....200 F3
Bert Rd CR7 .....42 C4
Bertal Rd SW17 .....20 D4
Bertie Rd SE26 .....23 D2
Bertram Cotts SW19 .....20 A1
Bertram House Sch SW17 21 A6
Bertram Rd KT2 .....18 A1
Bertrand House 11 SW16 .21 E5
Berwyn Ave TW3 .....5 B6
Berwyn Rd
Mortlake SW14, TW10 .....7 B3
Streatham SE24 .....22 B7
Beryl Harding House 3
SW19 .....19 D1
Berystede KT2 .....18 B1
Besley St SW16 .....21 C2
Bessant Dr TW9 .....7 B6
Bessborough Rd SW15 .....19 A7
Bessborough Wks KT8 .....35 F4
Beswick Gdns RG12 .....27 F8
Beta Rd Chobham GU24 .....49 F1
Farnborough GU14 .....85 A5
Woking GU22 .....70 B3
Beta Way TW20 .....32 C8
Betchets Green Rd RH5 .157 C6
Betchley Cl RH19 .....185 E3
Betchworth Cl SM1 .....59 D5
Betchworth Sta RH3 .....116 E3
Betchworth The RH4 .....116 A1
Betchworth Way CR0 .....63 C2
Betchworth Works RH6 .180 D6
Bethany Waye TW14 .....14 E8
Bethel Cl GU9 .....125 D6
Bethel La GU9 .....125 D6
Bethersden Cl BR3 .....23 F1
Bethesda Ct 8 SE20 .....23 C1
Bethlem Royal Hospl The
BR3 .....44 A2
Bethune Cl RH10 .....202 D5
Bethune Rd RH13 .....217 E1
Betjeman Cl CR5 .....79 F2
Betley Ct KT12 .....54 B7
Betony Cl CR0 .....43 D1
Betts Cl BR3 .....43 E7
Betts Way Crawley RH10 .181 D2
Long Ditton KT6 .....37 B1
Penge SE20 .....43 B8
Bettswood Ct 16 SE20 .....43 B8
Betula Cl CR8 .....80 D4
Between Streets KT11 .....73 A5
Beulah Ave CR7 .....42 C7
Beulah Cres CR7 .....42 C7
Beulah Gr CR0 .....42 C3
Beulah Hill SE19, SW16 .....22 C1
Beulah Inf Sch CR7 .....42 C6
Beulah Jun Sch CR7 .....42 C6
Beulah Rd Merton SW19 .....19 F1
South Norwood CR7 .....42 C6
Sutton SM1 .....59 A6
Beulah Wlk CR3 .....101 E7
Bevan Ct Crawley RH11 .201 B1
Croydon CR0 .....61 A5
Beverley Ave Hounslow TW4 .4 F3
Wimbledon SW20 .....38 F8
Beverley Cl
Addlestone KT15 .....52 D5
Ash GU12 .....105 F1
Chessington KT9 .....56 C6
East Ewell KT17 .....77 C8
Beverley Cl *continued*
Frimley GU15 .....66 D6
Oatlands Park KT13 .....53 E8
Beverley Cotts SW15 .....18 E5
Beverley Cres GU14 .....84 F2
Beverley Ct Hounslow TW4 .....4 F3
Kingston u T SW20 .....38 F8
Beverley Gdns Barnes SW13 .7 F4
2 North Cheam KT4 .....39 A1
Beverley House BR1 .....24 D3
Beverley Hts RH2 .....118 B3
Beverley Hyrst 7 CR0 .....61 F8
Beverley La KT2 .....18 E1
Beverley Lodge 6 TW10 .....6 E2
Beverley Mansions TW4 .....4 F3
Beverley Rd Barnes SW13 .....7 F4
Kenley CR3 .....80 F2
Mitcham CR4 .....41 D5
New Malden KT3 .....39 A5
North Cheam KT4 .....58 C8
Penge SE20 .....43 B7
Sunbury TW16 .....34 F8
Teddington KT1 .....37 C8
Beverley Sch KT3 .....39 A4
Beverley Trad Est SM4 .....39 D2
Beverley Way
Kingston u T KT3, SW20, KT2 .38 F8
Wimbledon KT3, SW20 .....39 A6
Beverley Way (Kingston
By Pass) KT3, SW20 .....39 A6
Beverley Way Kingston
Bypass KT3 .....38 F8
Beverstone Rd CR7 .....42 B5
Bevill Allen Cl SW17 .....20 F3
Bevill Cl SE25 .....43 A6
Bevin Sq SW17 .....20 F5
Bevington Rd BR3 .....44 B7
Bew Ct SE21 .....23 A8
Bewbush Dr RH11 .....200 F3
Bewbush Fst Sch RH11 .....200 F3
Bewbush Manor RH11 .....200 E2
Bewbush Mid Sch RH11 .200 F3
Bewlys Rd SE27 .....22 B3
Bexhill Cl TW13 .....15 E6
Bexhill Rd Forest Hill SE4 .....23 F8
Mortlake SW14 .....7 C4
Beynon Rd SM5 .....59 F5
Bglws The CR3 .....100 D4
Bicester Rd TW9 .....7 B4
Bickersteth Rd SW17 .....20 F2
Bickley Ct RH11 .....201 A3
Bickley St SW17 .....20 F3
Bicknell Rd GU16 .....65 E2
Bickney Way KT22 .....94 C5
Bicknoller Cl SM2 .....59 B1
Bidborough Cl BR2 .....44 F4
Biddulph Rd CR2 .....61 C2
Bideford Cl
Farnborough GU14 .....85 A7
Feltham TW13 .....15 F5
Bideford Rd BR1 .....24 F5
Bidhams Cres KT20 .....97 C6
Bidmead Ct KT6 .....56 E7
Bield The RH2 .....139 A7
Bietigheim Way 2 GU15 .....65 C6
Big Common La RH1 .....120 B3
Biggin Ave CR4 .....40 F8
Biggin Cl RH11 .....201 C4
Biggin Hill SE19, SW16 .....22 B1
Biggin Hill Airport TN16 .....83 D5
Biggin Hill Bsns Pk TN16 .83 D4
Biggin Hill Cl KT2 .....17 C3
Biggin Hill Jun & Inf Schs
TN16 .....83 E3
Biggin Way
CR7, SE19, SW16 .....22 C1
Bigginwood Rd SW16 .....42 B8
Bignor Cl RH12 .....218 A7
Bilberry Cl RH11 .....201 B3
Bilbets RH12 .....217 C3
Billesden Rd GU24 .....87 D7
Billet Rd TW18, TW19 .....13 A5
Billhurst Cotts RH7 .....164 D4
Billingshurst Rd RH12 .....216 D3
Billinton Dr RH10 .....202 B5
Billockby Cl KT9 .....56 F4
Billsley Ct SE25 .....42 E5
Bilton Ind Est RG12 .....26 E5
Binbury Row TW18 .....12 E4
Binfield Rd
Bracknell, Dowlesgreen RG40 25 F7
Bracknell, Priestwood RG42 .27 A8
Byfleet KT14 .....71 E7
South Croydon CR2 .....61 F5
Wokingham RG40 .....25 F7
Binfields GU9 .....125 C3
Bingham Cnr CR0 .....43 A1
Bingham Dr Knaphill GU21 .68 F1
Staines TW18 .....13 D1
Bingham Rd CR0, CR9 .....43 B1
Bingley Rd TW16 .....15 A1
Binhams Lea GU8 .....192 F5
Binhams Meadow GU8 .....192 F5
Binley House SW15 .....7 F1
Binney Ct RH10 .....182 E1
Binscombe Cres GU7 .....150 E8
Binscombe Jun Sch GU7 129 E1
Binscombe La GU7 .....150 E7
Binstead Cl RH11 .....201 B8
Binsted Dr GU17 .....64 D5
Binton La GU10 .....126 E3
Birch Ave Caterham CR3 .....100 D3
Leatherhead KT22 .....94 F8
Birch Circ GU7 .....150 F8
Birch Cl Brentford TW8 .....6 B7
Camberley GU15 .....65 E8
Crawley Down RH10 .....204 C8
Hounslow TW3 .....5 D5
Birch Cl *continued*
New Haw KT15 .....52 D2
Rowledge GU10 .....146 A4
Send Marsh GU23 .....90 F2
Teddington TW11 .....17 A3
Woking GU21 .....89 C8
Birch Ct Ashstead KT21 .....75 D2
Sutton SM1 .....59 C5
9 Wallington SM6 .....60 B6
Birch Dr GU17 .....64 D3
Birch Gn TW18 .....13 A4
Birch Gr Bracknell RG12 .....27 C5
Guildford GU1 .....109 C4
Kingswood KT20 .....97 F3
Lewisham SE12 .....24 F8
Upper Halliford TW17 .....34 E7
Woking GU22 .....70 D4
Birch Hill CR0 .....62 D5
Birch Hill Prim Sch RG12 .27 B1
Birch Hill Rd RG12 .....27 B2
Birch La Purley CR8 .....79 E8
West End GU24 .....67 D7
Winkfield RG12, SL5 .....28 B8
Birch Lea RH10 .....182 A1
Birch Platt GU24 .....67 D6
Birch Rd Farncombe GU7 .151 A8
Feltham TW13 .....15 D3
Headley Down GU35 .....187 B6
Windlesham GU20 .....48 E4
Birch Side RG45 .....45 A6
Birch Tree Ave BR4 .....63 F6
Birch Tree View GU18 .....48 A1
Birch Tree Way CR0 .....62 B8
Birch Vale KT11 .....74 A6
Birch Way Ash Vale GU12 .106 A7
Warlingham CR6 .....81 E1
Birch Wlk CR4 .....41 B8
Birchanger GU7 .....150 E4
Birchanger Rd SE25 .....43 A4
Birchcroft Cl CR3 .....100 C2
Birchdale Cl KT14 .....71 C8
Birchend Cl CR2 .....61 D4
Birches Cl Epsom KT18 .....76 E4
Mitcham CR4 .....40 F6
Birches Ind Est RH19 .....185 A3
Birches Rd RH12 .....218 B5
Birches The
Beckenham BR2 .....44 F5
Blackwater GU17 .....64 B5
Crawley RH10 .....202 A7
East Horsley KT24 .....92 E1
Farnborough GU14 .....84 D4
South Norwood SE25 .....42 F7
Twickenham TW4 .....15 F8
Woking GU22 .....69 F1
Birchett Rd
Aldershot GU11 .....105 A2
Farnborough GU14 .....84 E6
Birchetts Cl 2 RG42 .....27 B8
Birchfield Cl
Addlestone KT15 .....52 B6
Coulsdon CR5 .....79 F3
Birchfield Gr KT17 .....58 C1
Birchfields GU15 .....65 C4
Birchgrove KT11 .....73 D5
Birchington Rd KT5 .....37 F2
Birchlands GU47 .....45 E2
Birchlands Ave SW12 .....20 F8
Birchway RH1 .....140 B7
Birchwood Ave
Beckenham BR3 .....43 F5
Hackbridge SM5, SM6 .....60 B7
Birchwood Cl
Crawley RH10 .....202 C3
Horley RH6 .....161 B4
Morden SM4 .....40 B5
Birchwood Dr
Lightwater GU18 .....48 C1
West Byfleet KT14 .....71 A7
Birchwood Gr TW12 .....16 A2
Birchwood La
Caterham CR3 .....100 B2
Oxshott KT10, KT22 .....55 E1
Birchwood Rd
Streatham SW17 .....21 B3
West Byfleet KT14, KT15 .....71 A7
Bird Mews RG40 .....25 B6
Bird Wlk TW2 .....15 F7
Bird-In-Hand Pas SE23 .....23 C6
Birdham Cl RH11 .....201 B8
Birdhaven GU10, GU9 .....146 A6
Birdhurst CR3 .....100 F7
Birdhurst Ave CR2 .....61 D6
Birdhurst Ct SM6 .....60 C3
Birdhurst Gdns CR2 .....61 D6
Birdhurst Rd
Mitcham SW19 .....20 E2
South Croydon CR2 .....61 E5
Birdhurst Rise CR2 .....61 E5
Birds Hill Dr KT22 .....74 D6
Birds Hill Rd KT22 .....74 D6
Birds Hill Rise KT22 .....74 D6
Birdsgrove GU21 .....68 B1
Birdswood Dr GU21 .....88 E7
Birdwood Cl Selsdon CR2 .....81 D8
Teddington TW11 .....16 E4
Birdwood Rd GU15 .....64 F6
Birdworld & Underwater
World GU10 .....145 B3
Birkbeck Hill SE21 .....22 B7
Birkbeck Pl
Sandhurst GU47 .....45 E1
West Norwood SE21 .....22 C6
Birkbeck Rd Penge BR3 .....43 D7
Wimbledon SW19 .....20 B2
Birkbeck Sta SE20 .....43 C6
Birkdale RG12 .....26 E2
Birkdale Ct SL5 .....29 C4

Birkdale Dr RH11 ...200 D5
Birkdale Gdns CR0 ...62 D6
Birkenhead Ave KT2 ...37 F8
Birkenholme Cl GU35 ...187 C4
Birkhall Rd SE6 ...24 D6
Birkheads Rd RH2 ...118 A2
Birkwood Cl SW12 ...21 D8
Birling House 4 SE20 ...23 C1
Birnham Cl GU23 ...91 A3
Birtley Rd GU5 ...152 B4
Birtley Rise GU5 ...152 A5
Biscoe Cl TW5 ...5 A8
Bisenden Rd CR0 ...61 E8
Bisham Cl Carshalton CR4 ...40 F1
Crawley RH10 ...202 D3
Bishams Ct CR3 ...100 F3
Bishop Bell Sch RH10 ...201 F3
Bishop Challoner Sch BR2 ...44 D7
Bishop David Brown Sch GU21 ...70 D6
Bishop Duppa's Almshouses 7 TW10 ...6 E2
Bishop Duppas Pk TW17 ...34 E2
Bishop Fox Way KT8 ...35 F5
Bishop Gilpins Prim Sch SW19 ...19 F3
Bishop Perrin (C of E) Sch TW2 ...16 B7
Bishop Reindorp CE Sch GU1 ...109 C4
Bishop Sumner Dr GU9 ...125 C6
Bishop Thomas Grant Catholic Sec Sch SW16 ...21 F3
Bishop Wand C of E Sec Sch TW16 ...34 F7
Bishop's Cl CR5 ...80 A1
Bishop's Cotts RH3 ...116 B2
Bishop's Hall KT1 ...37 D7
Bishop's La SL4 ...8 B7
Bishop's Mead GU9 ...125 B2
Bishop's Pl SM1 ...59 C5
Bishop's Rd CR0 ...42 B2
Bishopdale RG12 ...27 A5
Bishopric RH12 ...217 B2
Bishopric Ct RH12 ...217 B2
Bishops Cl SM1 ...59 A7
Bishops Ct 1 Ashford TW16 14 F1
Guildford GU2 ...130 C7
Bishops Dr
East Bedfont TW14 ...3 D1
Wokingham RG40 ...25 C7
Bishops Gr Hampton TW12 .15 F4
Windlesham GU20 ...48 C4
Bishops Hill KT12 ...35 A2
Bishops Park Rd SW16 ...41 E8
Bishops Rd GU9 ...125 B7
Bishops Sq GU6 ...174 F3
Bishops Way TW20 ...12 D2
Bishops Wlk CR0, CR9 ...62 E5
Bishops Wood GU21 ...68 F2
Bishopscourt 6 CR0 ...61 F8
Bishopsford Rd SM4 ...40 D3
Bishopsgate Rd SL4, TW20 .11 B5
Bishopsmead Cl
East Horsley KT24 ...112 E7
Epsom KT19 ...57 D1
Bishopsmead Ct KT19 ...57 E1
Bishopsmead Dr KT24 ...112 F6
Bishopsmead Par KT24 ...112 F6
Bishopsthorpe Rd SE26 ...23 D4
Bishopstone Wlk RH11 ...201 C1
Bisley C of E Prim Sch GU24 ...68 A3
Bisley Cl KT4 ...39 C1
Bisley House SW19 ...19 D6
Bitmead Cl RH11 ...200 E5
Bittams La KT15, KT16 ...51 E6
Bittern Cl Crawley RH11 ...200 D5
Sandhurst GU47 ...64 D8
Bitterne Dr GU21 ...69 A2
Bittoms The KT1 ...37 D6
Black Dog Wlk RH10 ...201 E8
Black Horse Way RH12 ...217 C2
Black Lake Cl TW20 ...32 A8
Black Pond La GU10 ...146 C6
Black Prince Cl KT14 ...71 F5
Blackberry Cl
Guildford GU1 ...109 B4
Upper Halliford TW17 ...34 E5
Blackberry Farm Cl TW5 ...4 E7
Blackberry La RH7 ...185 E8
Blackberry Rd RH19, RH7 185 D8
Blackbird Cl GU47 ...64 D8
Blackborough Cl RH2 ...118 C1
Blackborough Rd RH2 ...118 D1
Blackbridge Ct RH12 ...217 B2
Blackbridge La RH12 ...217 A1
Blackbridge Rd GU22 ...89 D7
Blackbrook Rd
Dorking RH5 ...136 E2
South Holmwood RH5 ...157 E8
Blackburn The KT23 ...93 F3
Blackburn Trad Est TW19 ...2 F1
Blackburn Way GU7 ...151 A5
Blackbush Cl SM2 ...59 B3
Blackcap Cl RH11 ...201 C4
Blackcap Pl GU47 ...64 E8
Blackdown Ave GU22 ...70 E4
Blackdown Cl GU22 ...70 D3
Blackdown Prim Sch GU16 ...86 E8
Blackdown Rd GU16 ...86 C8
Blackenham Rd SW17 ...20 F4
Blackett Cl TW18, TW20 ...32 F7
Blackett Rd RH10 ...202 C5
Blackfold Rd RH10 ...202 A5
Blackford Cl CR2 ...61 B2
Blackham House SW19 ...19 E2
Blackheath RH10 ...202 D8
Blackheath Gr GU5 ...152 B8
Blackheath La Albury GU5 132 B3
Wonersh GU5, GU4 ...152 C8
Blackheath Rd GU9 ...125 A7
Blackhills KT10 ...55 A2
Blackhorse La Croydon CR0 43 A2
Lower Kingswood KT20, RH2 ...118 C7
Blackhorse Rd GU21, GU22 88 E6
Blacklands Cres RH18 ...206 F2
Blacklands Meadow RH1 119 E2
Blacklands Rd SE6 ...24 C4
Blackman Gdns GU11 ...126 B8
Blackman's La CR6 ...82 F5
Blackmeadows RG12 ...27 C3
Blackmoor Cl SL5 ...28 D7
Blackmoor Wood SL5 ...28 D7
Blackmore Cres GU21 ...70 C5
Blackmore House SE23 ...23 F7
Blackmore's Gr TW11 ...17 A2
Blackness La GU22 ...89 E8
Blacknest Cotts GU8 ...192 E3
Blacknest Gate Rd SL5 ...30 B6
Blacknest Rd GU25, SL5 ...30 E6
Blackshaw Rd SW17 ...20 D3
Blacksmith Cl KT21 ...95 F8
Blacksmith La GU4 ...131 D3
Blacksmith's La TW18 ...33 C6
Blacksmiths Hill CR2 ...81 B6
Blacksmiths La KT16 ...33 A2
Blackstone Cl
Farnborough GU14 ...84 D6
Reigate RH1 ...139 E8
Blackstone Hill RH1, RH2 .118 E1
Blackstone House SE21 ...22 E5
Blackstroud La E GU18, GU24 ...67 E8
Blackstroud La W GU18 ...67 D8
Blackthorn Cl
Crawley RH11 ...181 C1
Horsham RH13 ...218 A2
Reigate RH2 ...139 C7
Blackthorn Cres GU14 ...84 E8
Blackthorn Ct Heston TW5 ...4 E7
6 West Norwood SW16 ...22 A3
Blackthorn Dr GU18 ...67 B7
Blackthorn Rd
Biggin Hill TN16 ...83 E3
Reigate RH2 ...139 C7
Blackthorne Ave CR0 ...43 C1
Blackthorne Cres SL3 ...1 E5
Blackthorne Ind Pk SL3 ...1 F5
Blackthorne Rd
Great Bookham KT23 ...94 C1
Poyle SL3 ...1 E4
Blackwater Cl GU12 ...106 A1
Blackwater La RH10 ...202 D6
Blackwater Sta GU17 ...64 E4
Blackwater Way GU12 ...126 D8
Blackwater Way Ind Est GU12 ...126 E8
Blackwell Ave GU2 ...108 D1
Blackwell Cty Prim Sch RH19 ...185 E3
Blackwell Farm Rd RH19 185 F3
Blackwell Hollow RH19 ...185 F2
Blackwell Rd RH19 ...185 F2
Blackwood Cl KT14 ...71 C7
Bladen Cl KT13 ...53 E4
Blades Cl KT22 ...95 D7
Bladon Cl GU1 ...110 A2
Bladon Ct Beckenham BR2 ...44 E7
Streatham SW16 ...21 E2
Blagdon Rd KT3 ...38 F5
Blagdon Wlk TW11 ...17 C2
Blair Ave KT10 ...55 C8
Blair Ct Beckenham BR3 ...44 B8
Catford SE6 ...24 F7
Blairderry Rd SW2 ...21 E6
Blaise Cl GU14 ...85 D3
Blake Cl Carshalton SM5 ...40 E1
Crawley RH10 ...201 F2
Crowthorne RG45 ...45 C4
Wokingham RG40 ...25 E8
Blake House BR3 ...24 B2
Blake Rd Croydon CR0 ...61 E8
Mitcham CR4 ...40 E6
Blake's Gn BR4 ...44 C1
Blake's La
East Clandon GU4 ...111 F3
West Horsley GU4 ...111 F3
Blakeden Dr KT10 ...55 F4
Blakehall Rd SM5 ...59 F4
Blakemore Rd
Streatham SW16 ...21 E5
Thornton Heath CR7 ...41 F4
Blakeney Ave BR3 ...43 F8
Blakeney Cl KT19 ...76 D8
Blakeney Rd BR3 ...43 F8
Blakes Ave KT3 ...38 F3
Blakes La KT3 ...38 F4
Blakes Terr KT3 ...39 A4
Blakewood Cl TW13 ...15 C4
Blakewood Ct SE20 ...23 B1
Blanchards Hill GU4 ...109 E8
Blanchland Rd SM4 ...40 B4
Blanchman's Rd CR6 ...81 E1
Blandfield Rd SW12 ...21 A8
Blandford Ave Penge BR3 ...43 E7
Twickenham TW2 ...16 B7
Blandford Cl
Wallington CR0 ...60 E7
Woking GU22 ...70 B2
Blandford Rd Penge BR3 ...43 D7
Teddington TW11 ...16 E3
Blane's La SL5 ...28 C3
Blanford Rd RH2 ...139 C8
Blanks La
Charlwood RH5, RH6 ...159 B2
Cudworth RH5, RH6 ...159 B2
Blashford St SE13 ...24 D8
Blatchford Cl RH13 ...217 F3
Blatchford Ct KT12 ...35 A1
Blatchford Rd RH13 ...217 F3
Blay's La TW20 ...11 B2
Blays Cl TW20 ...11 C2
Blean Gr SE20 ...23 C1
Blegborough Rd SW16 ...21 C2
Blencarn Cl GU21 ...68 F3
Blendworth Point 4 SW15 ...19 B7
Blenheim 26 SW19 ...19 D7
Blenheim Bsns Ctr CR4 ...40 F7
Blenheim Cl
Crawley RH10 ...182 D1
East Grinstead RH19 ...186 A3
Tongham GU10 ...126 E7
Wallington SM6 ...60 C3
West Barnes SW20 ...39 C6
West Byfleet KT14 ...70 F6
Blenheim Cres Hale GU9 .125 A5
South Croydon CR2 ...61 C3
Blenheim Ct Egham TW18 ...12 D4
Farnborough GU14 ...85 D2
Richmond TW9 ...6 F4
South Norwood SE19 ...42 E8
Sutton SM2 ...59 C4
Blenheim Fields RH18 ...206 E3
Blenheim Gdns
Kingston u T KT2 ...18 B1
Sanderstead CR2 ...81 A7
Wallington SM6 ...60 C3
Woking GU22 ...89 B8
Blenheim High Sch KT19 .57 D1
Blenheim House TW3 ...5 A4
Blenheim Park Rd CR2 ...61 C2
Blenheim Pk GU11 ...105 C7
Blenheim Rd Epsom KT19 ...76 E8
Farnborough GU14 ...105 B7
Horsham RH12 ...217 D4
Penge SE20 ...23 C1
Sutton SM1 ...59 B7
West Barnes SW20 ...39 C6
Blenheim Way TW7 ...6 A6
Bleriot Rd TW5 ...4 C7
Bletchingley Cl RH1 ...119 C6
Bletchingley Golf Course RH1 ...120 E3
Bletchingley Rd
Bletchingley RH1, RH9 ...121 B4
Godstone RH1, RH9 ...121 B4
Merstham RH1 ...119 E6
Nutfield RH1 ...120 A2
Nutfield, South Merstham RH1 ...119 E6
Bletchingly Cl CR7 ...42 B5
Bletchmore Cl UB3 ...3 D8
Blewburton Wlk RG12 ...27 E5
Blewfield GU7 ...150 F2
Bligh Cl RH10 ...201 F4
Bligh House 4 SE27 ...22 C4
Blighton La GU10 ...126 E3
Blincoe Cl SW19 ...19 D6
Blind Cnr SE25 ...43 B5
Blindley Ct RH7 ...163 E8
Blindley Rd RH10 ...182 D1
Bloggs Way GU6 ...174 D3
Blomfield Dale RG42 ...26 D7
Blondell Cl UB7 ...2 D8
Bloom Gr SE27 ...22 B5
Bloomfield Cl GU21 ...68 E1
Bloomfield Rd KT1 ...37 E6
Bloomhall Rd SE19 ...22 D3
Bloomsbury Cl KT19 ...57 D1
Bloomsbury Ct Cranford TW5 4 B6
Guildford GU1 ...130 F7
Bloomsbury Way GU17 ...64 D3
Bloor Cl RH12 ...217 D7
Blossom Cl CR2 ...61 F5
Blossom Waye TW5 ...4 E7
Blount Ave RH19 ...185 C1
Bloxham Cres TW12 ...35 F8
Bloxham Rd GU6 ...175 A3
Bloxworth Cl
9 Bracknell RG12 ...27 F5
Wallington SM6 ...60 C7
Blue Anchor Alley 3 TW9 ...6 E3
Blue Ball La TW20 ...11 F3
Blue Barn Way KT13 ...72 A8
Blue Cedars SM7 ...77 D5
Blue Cedars Pl KT11 ...73 D7
Blue Coat Wlk RG12 ...27 D4
Blue Sch The TW7 ...6 A4
Bluebell Cl Crawley RH11 .201 B3
East Grinstead RH19 ...185 B1
Forest Hill SE19, SE26 ...22 F4
Horsham RH12 ...217 E5
Wallington CR4 ...41 B1
Bluebell Ct GU22 ...89 D8
Bluebell Hill RG12 ...27 E8
Bluebell Rise GU18 ...67 B8
Blueberry Gdns CR5 ...79 F3
Bluefield Cl TW12 ...16 A3
Bluegates Stoneleigh KT17 ...58 A3
Wimbledon SW19 ...19 E3
Bluehouse Gdns RH8 ...123 A7
Bluehouse La RH8 ...122 F7
Bluethroat Cl GU47 ...64 E8
Bluff Cove GU11 ...105 C3
Blundel La Oxshott KT11 ...74 B4
Stoke D'Abernon KT11 ...74 B4
Blundell Ave RH6 ...160 F4
Blunden Rd GU14 ...84 F5
Blunt Rd CR0 ...61 D5
Blunts Ave UB7 ...3 A7
Blunts Way RH12 ...217 C3
Blyth Cl TW1 ...5 F1
Blyth Rd BR1, BR2 ...44 F8
Blythe Cl SE23 ...23 F8
Blythe Hill SE23, SE6 ...23 F8
Blythe Hill La SE23, SE6 ...23 F7
Blythe Vale SE23, SE6 ...23 F7
Blythewood La SL5 ...28 E7
Blythwood Dr GU16 ...65 D2
Blythwood Pk BR1 ...44 F8
Blytons The RH19 ...185 B1
Boar Hill RH5 ...135 E1
Board School Rd GU21 ...69 F3
Bocketts Farm Pk KT22 ...94 F2
Bockhampton Rd KT2 ...17 F1
Boddicott Cl SW19 ...19 E6
Bodens Ride SL5 ...28 F1
Bodiam Cl RH10 ...202 C6
Bodiam Ct BR2 ...44 F5
Bodiam Rd SW16 ...21 D1
Bodley Cl KT3 ...38 E4
Bodley Manor Way SE24 ...22 A8
Bodley Rd KT3 ...38 E4
Bodmin Gr SM4 ...40 B4
Bodmin St SW18 ...20 A7
Bodnant Gdns SW20 ...39 B6
Bog La RG12 ...28 A5
Bognor Rd
Beare Green RH5 ...157 B2
Ockley RH5 ...157 B2
Warnham RH12, RH5 ...197 D4
Bois Hall Rd KT15 ...52 D5
Bolderwood Way BR4 ...63 B8
Bolding House La GU24 ...67 F7
Boleyn Ave KT17 ...58 B1
Boleyn Cl Crawley RH10 ...202 D3
Egham TW18 ...12 E3
Boleyn Ct East Molesey KT8 .36 D5
11 Redhill RH1 ...119 A2
Boleyn Dr KT8 ...35 F6
Boleyn Gdns BR4 ...63 B8
Boleyn Wlk KT22 ...94 F7
Bolingbroke Gr SW11 ...20 F8
Bolingbroke House BR3 ...24 B3
Bolney Ct Crawley RH11 ...200 F3
Kingston u T KT6 ...37 C4
Bolsover Gr RH1 ...119 E6
Bolstead Rd CR4 ...41 B8
Bolters La SM7 ...78 A4
Bolters Rd RH6 ...161 A5
Bolters Rd S RH6 ...160 F6
Bolton Cl Chessington KT9 ...56 E4
Penge SE20 ...43 A7
Bolton Gdns Bromley BR1 ...24 F2
Teddington TW11 ...17 A2
Bolton Rd Chessington KT9 .56 E4
Chiswick W4 ...7 C7
Crawley RH10 ...202 C2
Bolton's La
Harlington TW6, UB7 ...3 C7
Pyrford GU22 ...71 A3
Boltons Cl GU22 ...71 A3
Bomer Cl UB7 ...3 A7
Bonchurch Cl SM2 ...59 B3
Bond Fst Sch CR4 ...40 F7
Bond Gdns SM6 ...60 C6
Bond Rd Mitcham CR4 ...40 F7
Surbiton KT6 ...56 F8
Warlingham CR6 ...81 E1
Bond St TW20 ...11 C3
Bond's La RH5 ...136 B1
Bone Mill La RH9 ...121 E1
Bonehurst Rd RH1, RH6 ...161 A7
Bones La RH6, RH7 ...163 B2
Bonner Hill Rd KT1 ...38 A6
Bonners Cl GU22 ...89 F5
Bonnetts La RH11, RH6 ...181 A3
Bonnys Rd RH2 ...138 D8
Bonser Rd TW1 ...16 F6
Bonsey Cl GU22 ...89 E6
Bonsey La GU22 ...89 E6
Bonsey's La GU24, KT16 ...50 F2
Bonsor Dr KT20 ...97 E5
Bonus Pastor RC Sch BR1 24 E4
Bonville Rd BR1 ...24 F3
Bookham Ct
Little Bookham KT23 ...93 F4
Mitcham CR4 ...40 D6
Bookham Gr KT23 ...94 B1
Bookham Ind Pk KT23 ...93 F4
Bookham Rd KT11 ...93 D7
Bookham Sta KT23 ...93 F4
Bookhurst Hill GU6 ...175 A4
Bookhurst Rd GU6 ...175 B4
Booth Dr TW18 ...13 D2
Booth House 2 SW2 ...22 A8
Booth Rd Crawley RH11 ...200 E3
Croydon CR0, CR9 ...61 B8
Boothby House 2 SW16 ...21 C3
Boothroyd House TW7 ...5 F4
Borage Cl RH11 ...201 A3
Border Chase RH10 ...183 A2
Border Cres SE26 ...23 B3
Border End GU27 ...207 D6
Border Gate CR4 ...40 F8
Border Gdns CR0 ...63 B6
Border Rd Forest Hill SE26 ...23 B3
Haslemere GU27 ...207 D6
Bordesley Rd SM4 ...40 B5
Bordon Wlk 6 SW15 ...19 A8
Boreen The GU35 ...187 B5
Borelli Mews GU9 ...125 C2
Borelli Yd GU9 ...125 C2
Borers Arms Rd RH10 ...183 C3
Borers Yard Ind Est RH10 ...183 C3
Borland Rd TW11 ...17 B1
Borough Grange CR2 ...81 A7
Borough Hill CR0, CR9 ...61 B7
Borough Rd
Farncombe GU7 ...150 D5
Godalming GU7 ...150 D5
Hounslow TW7 ...5 F6
7 Kingston u T KT2 ...18 A1
Mitcham CR4 ...40 E7
Tatsfield TN16 ...103 D6
Borough The
Brockham RH3 ...137 A8
Farnham GU9 ...125 B2
Borrowdale Cl
Crawley RH11 ...201 B4
Sanderstead CR2 ...80 F6
Thorpe Lea TW20 ...12 B1
Borrowdale Dr CR2 ...80 F7
Borrowdale Gdns GU15 ...66 D4
Bosbury Rd SE6 ...24 C5
Boscombe Cl TW20 ...32 C8
Boscombe Gdns SW16 ...21 E2
Boscombe House CR0 ...42 D1
Boscombe Rd
Merton SW19 ...40 B8
Mitcham SW17 ...21 A2
North Cheam KT4 ...39 D1
Bosham Rd RH10 ...202 C3
Boshers Gdns TW20 ...11 F2
Bosman Dr GU20 ...48 B6
Bostock Ave RH12 ...218 A5
Bostock House TW5 ...5 A8
Boston Ct
South Norwood SE25 ...42 F5
Sutton SM2 ...59 C3
Boston Gdns W4 ...7 E8
Boston Manor Rd TW8 ...6 C8
Boston Rd CR0 ...42 A3
Boswell House 5 SW16 ...21 C3
Boswell Rd Crawley RH10 .201 E3
Thornton Heath CR7 ...42 C5
Boswood Ct TW4 ...4 F4
Botany Hill GU10 ...126 D1
Botery's Cross RH1 ...120 B2
Bothwell Rd CR0 ...63 C1
Botsford Rd SW20 ...39 E7
Boucher Cl TW11 ...16 F3
Boughton Ave BR2 ...44 F2
Boughton Hall Ave GU23 ...90 F3
Bouldish Farm Rd SL5 ...29 A5
Boulevard The
Crawley RH10, RH11 ...201 E6
4 Upper Tooting SW17 ...21 A6
Boullen Ct SM1 ...59 C6
Boulogne Rd CR0 ...42 C3
Boulters House RG12 ...27 E5
Boulters Rd 2 GU11, GU12 ...105 B2
Boulthurst Way RH8 ...123 B3
Boundaries Mansions 4 SW12 ...21 A7
Boundaries Rd
Balham SW12 ...21 A7
Feltham TW13 ...15 C7
Upper Tooting SW12, SW17 ...21 A7
Boundary Bsns Ct CR4 ...40 D6
Boundary Bsns Ctr GU21 ...70 A4
Boundary Cl
Crawley RH10 ...201 E7
Kingston u T KT1 ...38 B6
Penge SE20 ...43 A7
Boundary Cotts GU4 ...132 A4
Boundary House TW1 ...6 B2
Boundary Rd
Binstead GU10 ...145 E2
Crawley RH10 ...201 E7
Dockenfield GU10 ...166 D7
Farnborough GU14 ...85 C2
Frensham GU10 ...145 E2
Grayshott GU26 ...188 D3
Mitcham SW19 ...20 D2
Staines TW15 ...13 C3
Wallington SM5, SM6 ...60 A3
Woking GU21 ...70 A4
Boundary Rd E KT15 ...52 B2
Boundary Rd N KT15 ...52 B2
Boundary Rd W KT15 ...52 B2
Boundary Way
Addington CR0 ...63 A5
Woking GU21 ...70 A4
Boundfield Rd SE6 ...24 E6
Boundstone Cl GU10 ...146 B5
Boundstone Rd GU10 ...146 A4
Bourbon House SE6 ...24 C4
Bourdon Rd SE20 ...43 C7
Bourg-de-Peage Ave RH19 ...186 A1
Bourke Hill CR5 ...78 F1
Bourley La GU10 ...104 A2
Bourley Rd
Aldershot GU11 ...104 C2
Crondall GU10 ...104 C2
Bourne Ave KT16 ...33 A6
Bourne Cl Chilworth GU4 ...131 B3
West Byfleet KT14 ...71 B6
Bourne Ct Aldershot GU11 126 A8
Chiswick W4 ...7 C8
1 Purley CR8 ...80 A8
Bourne Cty Inf Sch The GU10 ...146 D6
Bourne Dene GU10 ...146 A5
Bourne Dr CR4 ...40 D7
Bourne Firs GU10 ...146 D5
Bourne Gr Ashstead KT21 ...95 D8
Farnham GU10 ...146 E7
Bourne Grove Cl GU10 ...146 E7

Bourne Grove Dr GU10 ... 146 E7
Bourne Hall Mus KT17 ... 57 F2
Bourne House TW15 ... 14 A3
Bourne Hts GU9 ... 146 C8
Bourne La CR3 ... 100 D6
Bourne Meadow
KT16, TW20 ... 32 B5
Bourne Mill Ind Est GU9 . 125 E3
Bourne Mill Rdbt
GU10, GU9 ... 125 E3
Bourne Park Cl CR8 ... 80 E3
Bourne Rd Farncombe GU7 150 F7
Merstham RH1 ... 119 C5
Wentworth GU25 ... 31 D4
Woodham KT15 ... 52 B2
Bourne St CR0, CR9 ... 61 B8
Bourne Vale BR2 ... 44 F1
Bourne View CR8 ... 80 D4
Bourne Way
Addlestone KT15 ... 52 C5
Cheam SM1 ... 58 F5
Coney Hall BR2, BR4 ... 63 F8
West Ewell KT19 ... 57 C6
Woking GU22 ... 89 D5
Bournefield Rd CR3 ... 81 A1
Bournemouth Rd SW19 ... 40 A8
Bourneside GU25 ... 31 A2
Bourneside Gdns SE6 ... 24 C3
Bourneside Rd KT15 ... 52 D5
Bournevale Rd SW16 ... 21 E4
Bourns Ct RH13 ... 217 E3
Bournville Rd SE13, SE6 ... 24 A8
Bousley Rise KT16 ... 51 D4
Bouverie Gdns CR8 ... 79 F5
Bouverie Rd CR5 ... 79 A1
Boveney House RG12 ... 27 E5
Boveney Rd SE23 ... 23 D8
Bovey House 3 RH1 ... 119 A3
Bovill Rd SE23 ... 23 D8
Bovingdon Sq CR4 ... 41 E5
Bowater Rd RH10 ... 202 C3
Bowater Ridge KT13 ... 53 D1
Bowden Cl TW14 ... 14 E7
Bowden Rd SL5 ... 29 D4
Bowen Dr SE19, SE21 ... 22 E5
Bower Ct GU22 ... 70 B3
Bower Hill Cl RH1 ... 140 E6
Bower Hill La RH1 ... 140 D7
Bower Rd GU10 ... 146 A5
Bowerland La RH7 ... 164 E7
Bowers Cl GU4 ... 110 A5
Bowers Farm Dr GU4 ... 110 B5
Bowers La GU4 ... 110 A6
Bowers Pl RH10 ... 204 B8
Bowes Cl RH13 ... 217 E3
Bowes Rd Egham TW18 ... 12 E2
Walton-on-T KT12 ... 54 B8
Bowie Cl SW4 ... 21 D8
Bowland Dr RG12 ... 27 E2
Bowley Cl SE19 ... 22 F2
Bowley La SE19 ... 22 F3
Bowlhead Green Rd GU8 170 B1
Bowling Green Cl SW19 ... 19 B8
Bowling Green Ct GU16 ... 85 E7
Bowling Green La RH12 . 217 D3
Bowling Green Rd GU24 ... 49 E2
Bowlings The GU15 ... 65 C6
Bowman Ct RH10 ... 201 D7
Bowman Mews SW18 ... 19 F7
Bowman's Meadow SM6 ... 60 B7
Bowmans Lea SE23 ... 23 C8
Bowness Cl 7 RH11 ... 200 D5
Bowness Cres KT2, SW15 ... 18 E3
Bowness Dr TW4 ... 4 E3
Bowness Rd SE6 ... 24 B8
Bowring House GU7 ... 150 F6
Bowsley Ct TW13 ... 15 A6
Bowsprit The KT11 ... 73 C4
Bowyer Cres RG40 ... 25 C8
Bowyers Cl KT21 ... 75 F1
Box Cl RH11 ... 201 C1
Box Hill Ctry Pk RH4 ... 115 D3
Box Hill Sch RH5 ... 115 B8
Box La RH19 ... 206 E6
Box Ridge Ave CR8 ... 79 F7
Boxall Rd SE21 ... 22 E8
Boxall Wlk RH13 ... 217 D1
Boxall's Gr GU11 ... 126 A8
Boxall's La GU11 ... 126 B7
Boxford Cl CR2 ... 81 D7
Boxford Ridge RG12 ... 27 B6
Boxgrove Ave GU1 ... 110 A3
Boxgrove Cty Prim Sch
GU1 ... 110 B2
Boxgrove La GU1 ... 110 B2
Boxgrove Rd GU1 ... 110 A2
Boxhill Rd RH4 ... 115 E3
Boxhill Way RH3 ... 137 B5
Boxhill & Westhumble Sta
RH5 ... 115 B4
Boxley Rd SM4, SW19 ... 40 C5
Boxwood Way CR6 ... 81 D2
Boyce House SW16 ... 21 C3
Boyd Cl KT2 ... 18 A1
Boyd Ct RG42 ... 27 A8
Boyd Rd SW19 ... 20 D2
Boyland Rd BR1 ... 24 F3
Boyle Farm Rd KT7 ... 37 A3
Brabazon Ave SM6 ... 60 E3
Brabazon Rd TW5 ... 4 D7
Braboeuf Manor (Coll of
Law) GU2 ... 130 C5
Brabon Rd GU14 ... 84 F5
Brabourne Cl 7 SE19 ... 22 E3
Brabourne Rise BR3 ... 44 D4
Brabrook Ct SM6 ... 60 B5
Bracebridge GU15 ... 65 A5
Bracewood Gdns CR0 ... 61 F7
Bracken Ave Balham SW12 . 21 A8
West Wickham CR0 ... 63 B7
Bracken Bank SL5 ... 28 C8
Bracken Cl Ashford TW16 ... 14 F2
Copthorne RH10 ... 183 B2
Crawley RH10 ... 201 F8
Little Bookham KT23 ... 93 F3
Twickenham TW4 ... 16 A8
Woking GU22 ... 69 F1
Wonersh GU5 ... 152 B6
Bracken End TW7 ... 5 D2
Bracken Gr RH12 ... 218 B5
Bracken Hill Cl BR1 ... 44 F8
Bracken Hill La BR1 ... 44 F8
Bracken Path KT18 ... 76 B6
Bracken Way
Chobham GU24 ... 49 F1
Guildford GU3 ... 108 E3
Brackendale KT1 ... 38 B7
Brackendale Cl
Frimley GU15 ... 65 E3
Hounslow TW5 ... 5 B6
Brackendale Ct 2 BR3 ... 24 A1
Brackendale Rd GU15 ... 65 D4
Brackendene GU12 ... 106 C3
Brackendene Cl GU21 ... 70 A4
Brackenhale Comp Sch
RG12 ... 27 B5
Brackenhill KT11 ... 74 B7
Brackenlea GU7 ... 150 D7
Brackens BR3 ... 24 A1
Brackens The RG45 ... 45 A7
Brackenside RH6 ... 161 B4
Brackenwood
Frimley GU15 ... 66 D5
Sunbury TW16 ... 35 A8
Brackenwood Rd GU21 ... 88 D8
Bracklesham Cl GU14 ... 85 A7
Brackley KT13 ... 53 D5
Brackley Cl SM6 ... 60 E3
Brackley Rd BR3 ... 24 A1
Bracknell Beeches RG12 ... 27 B6
Bracknell Bsns Ctr The
RG12 ... 26 F7
Bracknell Cl GU15 ... 46 F1
Bracknell Coll
Bracknell RG12 ... 27 C7
Bracknell, Wick Hill RG12 ... 27 C8
Bracknell Enterprise Ctr
RG12 ... 27 A7
Bracknell Rd
Bracknell GU19 ... 47 E5
Camberley GU15 ... 47 A1
Crowthorne RG45 ... 45 D6
Winkfield RG42 ... 8 A5
Bracknell Sports & L Ctr
RG12 ... 27 C4
Bracknell Sta RG12 ... 27 B6
Bracknell Wlk RH11 ... 200 E3
Bracondale KT10 ... 55 C5
Bradbury Rd RH10 ... 202 C3
Braddon Rd TW9 ... 6 F4
Bradenhurst Cl CR3 ... 100 F2
Bradfield Cl Guildford GU1 110 A4
Woking GU22 ... 69 E1
Bradfields RG12 ... 27 D4
Bradford Cl SE26 ... 23 B4
Bradford Dr KT19 ... 57 F4
Brading Rd Streatham SW2 . 21 F8
Thornton Heath CR0 ... 41 F3
Bradley Cl SM2 ... 59 B1
Bradley Ct CR0 ... 61 A6
Bradley Dr RG40 ... 25 A2
Bradley La RH4, RH5 ... 115 B3
Bradley Mews SW12 ... 20 F7
Bradley Rd SE19 ... 22 C2
Bradlord House SE21 ... 22 E5
Bradmore Way CR5 ... 79 F1
Bradshaw Cl SW19 ... 20 A2
Bradshaws Cl SE25 ... 43 A6
Bradsole House 13 BR3 ... 24 A1
Bradstock Rd KT17 ... 58 B5
Brae Ct 2 Kingston u T KT2 . 38 A8
South Norwood SE25 ... 42 E8
Braemar Ave
South Croydon CR2 ... 61 C2
Thornton Heath CR7 ... 42 B6
Wimbledon SW18, SW19 ... 20 A6
Braemar Cl Frimley GU16 ... 85 F8
Godalming GU7 ... 150 D3
Braemar Ct
5 Brentford TW8 ... 6 D8
Catford SE6 ... 24 F7
Braemar Gdns BR4 ... 44 C1
Braemar House TW11 ... 17 B3
Braemar Rd Brentford TW8 . 6 D8
North Cheam KT4 ... 58 B7
Braes Mead RH1 ... 140 E8
Braeside Beckenham BR3 ... 24 B3
Woodham KT15 ... 71 B8
Braeside Ave SW19 ... 39 E8
Braeside Cl GU27 ... 207 F8
Braeside Rd SW16 ... 21 C1
Brafferton Rd CR0 ... 61 C6
Braganza Ct GU1 ... 109 F2
Bragg Rd TW11 ... 16 F2
Braid Cl TW13 ... 15 F6
Braidwood Rd SE6 ... 24 D7
Brailsford Cl SW19 ... 20 E1
Brainton Ave TW14 ... 15 C8
Brakey Hill RH1 ... 120 E1
Bramber Cl Crawley RH10 . 201 E8
Horsham RH12 ... 218 B5
Bramble Acres Cl SM2 ... 59 A3
Bramble Bank GU16 ... 86 A6
Bramble Banks SM5 ... 60 A2
Bramble Cl
Copthorne RH10 ... 183 B3
Croydon CR0 ... 63 B6
Guildford GU3 ... 108 E3
Redhill RH1 ... 140 A7
Upper Halliford TW17 ... 34 D6
Bramble Hedge Farm
(Ind Est) KT11 ... 72 C5
Bramble La TW12 ... 15 F2
Bramble Rise KT11 ... 73 C5
Bramble Twitten RH19 ... 186 A1
Bramble Way GU23 ... 90 F3
Bramble Wlk KT18 ... 76 B6
Brambledene Cl GU21 ... 69 C1
Brambledown TW18 ... 33 B8
Brambledown Cl BR2, BR4 . 44 E4
Brambledown Rd
South Croydon CR2 ... 61 E3
Wallington SM5, SM6 ... 60 B3
Bramblegate RG45 ... 45 A6
Brambles Cl Ash GU12 ... 106 B1
Brentford TW7, TW8 ... 6 B7
Caterham CR3 ... 100 E5
Brambles Pk GU5 ... 151 F6
Brambles The
Farncombe GU7 ... 150 D7
8 Wimbledon SW19 ... 19 F3
Brambleton Ave GU9 ... 146 B7
Brambletye Cty Jun Sch
RH1 ... 140 A7
Brambletye La RH18 ... 206 D4
Brambletye Park Rd RH1 140 A7
Brambletye Rd RH10 ... 202 A5
Brambletye Sch RH19 ... 206 C5
Bramblewood RH2 ... 119 B6
Bramblewood Cl SM5 ... 40 E1
Brambling Cl RH13 ... 218 A1
Brambling Rd RH13 ... 218 A1
Bramcote GU15 ... 66 C5
Bramcote Ave CR4 ... 40 F5
Bramcote Ct CR4 ... 40 F5
Bramerton Rd BR3 ... 43 F6
Bramham Gdns KT9 ... 56 D6
Bramley Ave Coulsdon CR5 . 79 C4
Sunbury TW17 ... 34 E6
Bramley CE Inf Sch GU5 . 152 A5
Bramley Cl Chertsey KT16 ... 33 B1
Crawley RH10 ... 201 F6
Croydon CR2 ... 61 C5
Staines TW18 ... 13 C2
Twickenham TW2 ... 5 C1
Bramley Ct Mitcham CR4 ... 40 D7
Redhill RH1 ... 118 E3
Wallington SM6 ... 60 C5
Bramley Hill CR0, CR2 ... 61 C6
Bramley Ho TW3 ... 4 F3
Bramley House
1 Kingston u T KT2 ... 18 B1
Redhill RH1 ... 140 A8
Roehampton SW15 ... 7 F1
Bramley La GU17 ... 64 B5
Bramley Park Ct GU5 ... 151 F6
Bramley Rd
Camberley GU15 ... 65 B2
Carshalton SM1 ... 59 D5
East Ewell SM2 ... 58 D2
Bramley Way
Ashstead KT21 ... 75 F2
Hounslow TW4 ... 4 F2
West Wickham BR4 ... 63 B8
Bramley Wlk RH6 ... 161 C3
Bramleyhyrst CR2 ... 61 C5
Brampton Gdns KT12 ... 54 C5
Brampton Rd CR0 ... 42 F3
Bramshaw Rise KT3 ... 38 E3
Bramshot La
Blackwater GU17 ... 84 A5
Farnborough GU14 ... 84 C6
Bramshott Ct 8 KT6 ... 37 E3
Bramston Rd SW17 ... 20 C5
Bramswell Rd GU7 ... 150 F6
Bramwell Cl TW16 ... 35 D7
Brancaster La CR8 ... 80 C8
Brancaster Rd SW16 ... 21 E5
Brancker Cl SM6 ... 60 E3
Brandon Cl Crawley RH10 . 202 D4
Frimley GU15 ... 66 D4
Brandon House BR3 ... 24 B3
Brandon Rd SM1 ... 59 B6
Brandreth Rd SW17 ... 21 B6
Brandries The SM6 ... 60 D7
Brands Rd SL3 ... 1 B8
Brandsland RH2 ... 139 B6
Brandy Way SM2 ... 59 A3
Brangbourne Rd BR1 ... 24 C3
Brangwyn Cres SW19 ... 40 D7
Branksome Cl
Camberley GU15 ... 65 E6
Walton-on-T KT12 ... 54 D8
Branksome Hill Rd GU47 ... 64 E8
Branksome Park Rd GU15 . 65 E6
Branksome Rd SW19 ... 40 A8
Branksome Way KT3 ... 38 D8
Bransby Rd KT9 ... 56 E4
Branscombe Ct BR2 ... 44 E4
Branstone Ct 9 TW9 ... 6 F6
Branstone Rd TW9 ... 6 F6
Brantridge Rd RH10 ... 201 F4
Brants Bridge RG12 ... 27 E7
Brantwood Ave TW7 ... 6 A3
Brantwood Cl 1 KT14 ... 71 A6
Brantwood Ct KT14 ... 70 F6
Brantwood Dr KT14 ... 70 F6
Brantwood Gdns KT14 ... 71 A6
Brantwood Rd CR2 ... 61 D2
Brassey Cl TW14 ... 15 A7
Brassey Rd RH8 ... 123 A6
Brasted Cl Belmont SM2 ... 59 A1
Forest Hill SE26 ... 23 C4
Brasted Lodge 11 BR3 ... 24 A1
Brathway Rd SW18 ... 20 A8
Bratten Ct CR0 ... 42 D3
Bravington Cl TW17 ... 33 F4
Braxted Pk SW16 ... 21 F2
Bray Cl RH10 ... 202 D4
Bray Ct KT9 ... 56 F5
Bray Gdns GU22 ... 70 E3
Bray Rd Guildford GU2 ... 130 B8
Stoke D'Abernon KT11 ... 73 E3
Braybourne Dr TW7 ... 5 F7
Braybrooke Gdns SE19 ... 22 E1
Braycourt Ave KT12 ... 35 C2
Braye Cl GU47 ... 45 C1
Braywick Ct 9 KT2 ... 18 A1
Braywood Ave TW20 ... 12 A2
Braziers La SL4, SL5 ... 8 D4
Breakfield CR5 ... 79 E3
Breakspeare SE21 ... 22 F5
Breamore Cl SW15 ... 19 A7
Breamwater Gdns TW10 ... 17 B5
Brecon Cl
Farnborough GU14 ... 84 D7
Mitcham CR4 ... 41 E6
North Cheam KT4 ... 58 C8
Brecon House SW18 ... 20 A8
Bredhurst Cl SE20 ... 23 C2
Bredinghurst SE22 ... 23 A8
Bredon Rd CR0 ... 42 F2
Bredune CR8 ... 80 D4
Breech La KT20 ... 97 A2
Breech The GU47 ... 64 E7
Breezehurst Dr RH11 ... 200 F3
Bregsells La RH5 ... 157 D4
Bremans Row SW18 ... 20 C6
Bremer Rd TW18, TW19 ... 13 A5
Bremner Ave RH6 ... 160 F4
Brenchley Cl BR2 ... 44 F3
Brenda Rd SW17 ... 20 F6
Brende Gdns KT8 ... 36 B5
Brendon Cl Esher KT10 ... 55 C4
Harlington UB7 ... 3 C7
Brendon Dr KT10 ... 55 C4
Brendon House SM2 ... 59 C4
Brendon Rd GU14 ... 84 D7
Brenley Cl CR4 ... 41 A6
Brent House BR1 ... 24 D3
Brent Knoll Spec Sch
SE26 ... 23 D5
Brent Lea TW8 ... 6 C7
Brent Rd Brentford TW8 ... 6 C8
South Croydon CR2 ... 62 B2
Brent Way TW8 ... 6 D7
Brentford Bsns Ctr TW8 ... 6 C7
Brentford High St TW8 ... 6 D8
Brentford House 7 TW1 ... 17 B8
Brentford Sch for Girls
TW8 ... 6 D8
Brentford Sta TW8 ... 6 C8
Brentmoor Rd GU24 ... 67 D6
Brentside TW8 ... 6 C8
Brentside Executive Ctr
TW8 ... 6 B8
Brentwaters Bsns Pk TW8 . 6 C7
Brentwood Ct KT15 ... 52 B6
Brereton House 4 SW2 ... 22 A8
Breston Cross KT23 ... 93 F1
Bret Harte Rd GU16 ... 65 E1
Bretherton Ct CR2 ... 61 E4
Bretlands Rd KT16 ... 51 E8
Brett House 1 SW15 ... 19 D8
Brett House Cl 2 SW15 ... 19 D8
Brettgrave KT19 ... 57 C1
Brettingham Cl RH11 ... 200 E3
Brew House Rd RH3 ... 137 B5
Brewer Rd RH10 ... 201 E4
Brewer St RH1 ... 120 C4
Brewers Cl GU14 ... 85 A5
Brewers La 11 TW9 ... 6 D2
Brewery La KT14 ... 71 E6
Brewery Mews Bsns Ctr
TW7 ... 6 A4
Brewery Rd GU21 ... 69 E2
Brewhurst La RH14 ... 213 A2
Breydon Wlk RH10 ... 202 B4
Brian Ave CR2 ... 80 E7
Briane Rd KT19 ... 57 C1
Briar Ave Lightwater GU18 ... 67 A8
South Norwood SW16 ... 21 F1
Briar Banks SM5 ... 60 A2
Briar Cl Crawley RH11 ... 181 C1
Hampton TW12 ... 15 F3
Isleworth TW7 ... 5 F2
West Byfleet KT14 ... 71 C8
Briar Ct Cheam SM3 ... 58 C6
Hampton TW12 ... 16 B3
Briar Gdns BR2 ... 44 F1
Briar Gr CR2 ... 81 A6
Briar Hill CR8 ... 79 E8
Briar La Croydon CR0 ... 63 B6
Wallington SM5 ... 60 A2
Briar Patch GU7 ... 150 D6
Briar Rd Littleton TW17 ... 34 A4
Send GU23 ... 90 B4
Thornton Heath SW16 ... 41 F6
Twickenham TW2 ... 16 E7
Briar Way GU4 ... 110 B5
Briar Wlk KT14 ... 71 A7
Briardale SW19 ... 19 F7
Briarleas Ct GU14 ... 105 D8
Briars Cl GU14 ... 84 D3
Briars Cross RH8 ... 123 D5
Briars Ct KT22 ... 74 D5
Briars The Ash GU12 ... 106 B1
Stanwell TW19 ... 2 A2
Briars Wood RH6 ... 161 C4
Briarswood Cl RH10 ... 202 D8
Briarwood Cl TW13 ... 14 E5
Briarwood Ct 5 KT4 ... 39 A1
Briarwood Rd
Knaphill GU21 ... 88 D8
Stoneleigh KT17 ... 58 A4
Briary Lodge BR3 ... 44 C8
Briavels Ct KT18 ... 76 E4
Brick Farm Cl TW9 ... 7 B6
Brick Kiln La RH8 ... 123 C5
Brickfield Cl TW8 ... 6 C7
Brickfield La UB3 ... 3 D8
Brickfield Rd
Outwood RH1 ... 162 C8
South Norwood CR7, SW16 ... 42 B8
Wimbledon SW19 ... 20 B4
Brickhouse La RH7, RH9 . 163 C4
Bricklands RH10 ... 204 B7
Bricksbury Hill GU9 ... 125 C7
Brickwood Cl SE26 ... 23 B5
Brickwood Rd CR0 ... 61 E8
Brickyard Copse RH5 ... 177 C4
Brickyard La
Crawley Down RH10 ... 204 B8
Wotton RH5 ... 134 D2
Brideake Cl RH11 ... 201 A3
Bridge Barn La GU21 ... 69 D1
Bridge Cl Byfleet KT14 ... 71 F7
Lower Halliford KT12 ... 34 F1
Staines TW18 ... 12 E4
Teddington TW11 ... 16 F4
Woking GU21 ... 69 C2
Bridge Cotts GU6 ... 174 B3
Bridge Ct Cranleigh GU6 ... 174 B3
Leatherhead KT22 ... 95 A5
2 Weybridge KT13 ... 53 B6
Woking GU21 ... 69 D2
Bridge End GU15 ... 65 B4
Bridge Gdns
East Molesey KT8 ... 36 D5
Littleton TW15 ... 14 C1
Bridge La GU25, KT16 ... 31 F3
Bridge Mead GU24 ... 87 F1
Bridge Mews
Godalming GU7 ... 150 E4
Tongham GU10 ... 126 F7
Woking GU21 ... 69 D2
Bridge Par CR8 ... 80 A7
Bridge Pl CR0 ... 42 D1
Bridge Rd Aldershot GU11 . 126 A8
Ascot SL5 ... 29 D4
Bagshot GU19 ... 47 E3
Beckenham BR3 ... 23 F1
Camberley GU15 ... 65 B3
Chertsey KT16 ... 33 B2
Chessington KT9 ... 56 E5
Cobham KT11 ... 73 B4
Cranleigh GU6 ... 174 E3
East Molesey KT8 ... 36 E5
Epsom KT17 ... 76 F7
Farnborough GU14 ... 84 F4
Farncombe GU7 ... 150 E5
Haslemere GU27 ... 208 C7
Hounslow TW3 ... 5 D4
Isleworth TW3, TW7 ... 5 D4
Penge BR3 ... 23 F1
Rudgwick RH12 ... 214 D7
Sutton SM2 ... 59 B4
Twickenham TW1 ... 6 B1
Wallington SM6 ... 60 C5
Weybridge KT13 ... 52 F6
Bridge Row CR0 ... 42 D1
Bridge Sq GU9 ... 125 C2
Bridge St Colnbrook SL3 ... 1 D7
Godalming GU7 ... 150 E4
Guildford GU1 ... 130 C8
Leatherhead KT22 ... 95 A5
Richmond TW10 ... 6 D2
Staines TW18 ... 12 E4
Walton-on-T KT12 ... 34 F2
Bridge View SL5 ... 30 B2
Bridge Way Chipstead CR5 . 98 E8
Twickenham TW2 ... 16 C8
Bridge Wks GU4 ... 110 C4
Bridge Works GU15 ... 65 B3
Bridgefield GU9 ... 125 D2
Bridgefield Cl SM7 ... 77 C4
Bridgefield Rd SM1, SM2 ... 59 A4
Bridgeham Cl KT13 ... 53 A5
Bridgeham Way RH6 ... 162 B2
Bridgehill Cl GU2 ... 109 A3
Bridgelands RH10 ... 183 A3
Bridgeman Rd TW11 ... 17 A2
Bridgemead GU16 ... 85 D8
Bridges Ct RH12 ... 218 A5
Bridges La CR0 ... 60 E6
Bridges Rd SW19 ... 20 B2
Bridges Road Mews SW19 20 B2
Bridgetown Cl 5 SE19 ... 22 E3
Bridgewater Rd KT13 ... 53 D4
Bridgewood Cl SE20 ... 23 B1
Bridgewood Rd
North Cheam KT17, KT4 ... 58 A6
Streatham SW16 ... 21 D1
Bridgford St SW17, SW18 ... 20 C5
Bridle Cl Grayshott GU26 . 188 A3
Kingston u T KT1 ... 37 D5
Sunbury TW16 ... 35 A6
West Ewell KT19 ... 57 D5
Bridle Ct GU11 ... 104 E2
Bridle La
Oxshott KT11, KT22 ... 74 B4
Twickenham TW1 ... 6 B1
Bridle Path CR0 ... 60 E7
Bridle Path The KT17 ... 58 C1
Bridle Rd Addington CR0 ... 63 A6
Claygate KT10 ... 56 B4
Croydon CR0 ... 63 A7

Bridle Rd *continued*
Epsom KT17 76 F6
Bridle Rd The CR8 60 E1
Bridle Way Crawley RH10 202 D7
Croydon CR0 63 A6
Bridle Way The SM6 60 C5
Bridlepath Way TW14 14 E8
Bridleway Cl KT17 58 C1
Bridlington Cl TN16 103 B8
Bridport Rd CR7 42 B6
Brier Lea KT20 97 F1
Brier Rd KT20 97 B8
Brierley CR0 63 B4
Brierley Cl SE25 43 A5
Brierley Rd SW12 21 C6
Brierly Cl GU2 109 A3
Briggs Cl CR4 41 B8
Bright Hill GU1 130 E7
Brightlands Rd RH2 118 C3
Brightman Rd SW18 20 D7
Brighton Cl KT15 52 C5
Brighton Rd
Addlestone KT15 52 C5
Aldershot GU11, GU12 126 C8
Banstead SM2 78 A7
Burgh Heath KT20, SM2, SM7 77 F3
Coulsdon CR5, CR8 79 D4
Crawley RH11 201 D4
Croydon CR2, CR8 61 C3
Godalming GU7 151 A1
Hooley CR5, RH1 99 B6
Horley RH6 160 F2
Horsham RH13 217 E1
Kingston u T KT6 37 D3
Kingswood KT20 97 E5
Lower Kingswood KT20 117 F8
Purley CR8 80 B8
Redhill RH1 139 F8
Redhill RH1 139 F8
Salfords RH1 140 A2
South Croydon CR2 61 C3
Sutton SM2 59 B2
Brightside Ave TW18 13 C1
Brightwell Cl CR0 42 A1
Brightwell Cres SW17 20 F3
Brightwells Rd GU9 125 C2
Brigstock Rd Coulsdon CR5 79 B3
Thornton Heath CR7 42 B5
Brimshot La GU24 49 E2
Brindle Cl GU11 126 B7
Brindles The SM7 77 F2
Brindley House 22 SW12 21 E8
Brine Ct KT6 37 D4
Brinkley Rd KT4 58 B8
Brinkworth Pl SL4 11 B8
Brinn's La GU17 64 C5
Brinsworth Cl TW2 16 D6
Brisbane Ave SW19 40 B8
Brisbane Cl RH11 181 D1
Briscoe Rd SW19 20 D2
Brisson Cl KT10 54 F4
Bristol Cl Crawley RH10 182 D1
Stanwell TW19 2 E1
Bristol Ct 10 TW19 2 E1
Bristol Rd SM4 40 C4
Bristow Cty Inf Sch GU15 65 B2
Bristow Rd
Camberley GU15 65 B3
Hounslow TW3 5 C4
Wallington CR0 60 E6
West Norwood SE19 22 E3
Britannia Ind Est SL3 1 E5
Britannia Rd KT5 37 F2
Britannia Way TW19 13 D8
British Home & Hospl for Incurables SE27 22 B3
Briton Cl CR2 80 E8
Briton Cres CR2 80 E8
Briton Hill Rd CR2 61 F1
Brittain Ct GU47 64 C7
Brittain Rd KT12 54 D5
Britten Cl Ash GU12 106 B2
Crawley RH11 200 F3
Horsham RH13 218 B4
Brittens Cl GU2, GU3 109 A6
Britton Cl SE6 24 D8
Brixton Hill SW2 21 E8
Brixton Hill Pl SW2 21 E8
Broad Acres GU7 150 E8
Broad Cl KT12 54 E7
Broad Green Ave CR0 42 B2
Broad Ha'penny GU10 146 A5
Broad Highway KT11 73 D5
Broad La Bracknell RG12 27 D6
Hampton TW12 16 A2
Parkgate RH2, RH5 158 E6
Broad Oak TW16 14 F2
Broad Oaks KT6 57 B8
Broad Oaks Way BR2 44 F4
Broad St Guildford GU3 108 D3
Teddington TW11 16 F2
West End GU24 67 D6
Wokingham RG40 25 C6
Wood St V GU3 108 D3
Broad St Wlk RG40 25 C6
Broad Wlk
Burgh Heath KT18 97 D8
Caterham CR3 100 F5
Cranleigh GU6 174 F1
Crawley RH10 201 D6
Frimley GU16 65 E2
Heston TW5 4 E6
Lower Kingswood CR5 99 A4
Richmond TW9 6 F7
Broadacre TW18 13 A3
Broadacres GU3 108 E2
Broadbridge Heath Rd RH12 216 D4
Broadbridge La
Burstow RH6 183 B8
Smallfield RH6 162 A2
Broadbridge Ret Pk RH12 216 E3
Broadcoombe CR2 62 D3
Broadfield
Barton 4 RH11 201 B2
Broadfield Cl
Burgh Heath KT20 97 C7
Croydon CR0 60 F8
Broadfield Dr RH11 201 B3
Broadfield East Cty Fst Sch RH11 201 C2
Broadfield East Cty Mid Sch RH11 201 C2
Broadfield North Cty Fst & Mid Sch RH11 201 B2
Broadfield Pl RH11 201 B2
Broadfield Rd Catford SE6 24 E7
Peaslake GU5 154 D8
Broadfields KT8 36 E3
Broadford La GU24 68 E7
Broadford Pk GU4 130 D2
Broadford Rd GU4 130 D2
Broadgates Rd SW18 20 D7
Broadham Green Rd RH8 122 D2
Broadham Pl RH8 122 D4
Broadhurst Ashstead KT21 75 E3
Farnborough GU14 84 C5
Broadhurst Cl 8 TW10 6 F2
Broadhurst Gdns RH2 139 B6
Broadlands
Farnborough GU14 85 E2
Feltham TW13 16 A5
Frimley GU16 85 F8
Horley RH6 161 C4
Broadlands Ave
Shepperton TW17 34 C3
Streatham SW16 21 E6
Broadlands Cl SW16 21 E6
Broadlands Ct
Bracknell RG42 26 E8
Richmond TW9 7 A7
Broadlands Dr
Sunningdale SL5 29 D2
Warlingham CR6 101 C8
Broadlands Mansions 2 SW16 21 E6
Broadlands Way KT3 38 F3
Broadley Gn GU20 48 D4
Broadmead Ashstead KT21 75 F2
Catford SE6 24 A5
Farnborough GU14 84 D3
Horley RH6 161 C4
Merstham RH1 119 C7
Broadmead Ave KT4 39 A2
Broadmead Cl TW12 16 A2
Broadmead Inf Sch CR0 42 D2
Broadmead Jun Sch CR0 42 D3
Broadmead Rd GU22, GU23 90 B5
Broadmeads GU23 90 B5
Broadmere Cty Prim Sch The GU21 70 D6
Broadmoor Cott RH5 156 A8
Broadmoor Cty Prim Sch RG45 45 D4
Broadmoor Hospl RG45 45 E5
Broadoaks Cres KT14 71 B6
Broadview Est TW19 14 A8
Broadview Rd SW16 21 D1
Broadwater Cl
Hersham KT12 54 A5
Sheerwater GU21 70 D7
Wraysbury TW19 11 E8
Broadwater House 1 KT13 53 B7
Broadwater Inf Sch SW17 20 E4
Broadwater Jun Sch SW17 20 E4
Broadwater Rd SW17 20 E4
Broadwater Rd N KT12 54 A5
Broadwater Rd S KT12 54 A5
Broadwater Rise GU1 131 A8
Broadwater Sch GU7 151 A8
Broadway Bracknell RG12 27 C7
Knaphill GU21 68 C1
Staines TW18 13 B2
Tolworth KT6 38 B1
Winkfield SL4 9 B7
Broadway Ave
Thornton Heath CR0 42 D4
Twickenham TW1 6 B1
Broadway Cl CR2 81 B5
Broadway Ct
Beckenham BR3 44 C6
Wimbledon SW19 19 F2
Broadway Gdns CR4 40 E4
Broadway House GU21 68 C1
Broadway Mkt SW17 20 F4
Broadway Rd
Lightwater GU18 48 C2
Windlesham GU18, GU20 48 C2
Broadway The Cheam SM3 58 E4
Crawley RH10 201 D6
Laleham TW18 33 C7
Mortlake SW13 7 E5
Sandhurst GU47 64 B8
Sutton SM1 59 C6
Thames Ditton KT10 36 E1
Tolworth KT6 38 A1
Wallington SM6 60 E6
Wimbledon SW19 19 F2
Woking GU21 69 F2
Woodham KT15 52 A1
Broadwell Ct TW5 4 D6
Broadwell Rd GU10 145 F6
Broadwood Cl RH12 218 A5
Broadwood Cotts RH5 178 E6
Broadwood Rise RH11 201 A2
Brock Rd RH11 181 B1
Brock Way GU25 31 C5
Brock's Cl GU7 151 A5
Brockbridge House SW15 7 F1
Brockenhurst KT8 35 F3
Brockenhurst Ave KT4 38 E1
Brockenhurst Cl GU21 69 F5
Brockenhurst Rd
Aldershot GU11 126 B8
Ascot SL5 29 B3
Bracknell RG12 28 A6
Croydon CR0 43 B2
Brockenhurst Way SW16 41 D7
Brockham Cl SW19 19 F3
Brockham Cres CR0 63 D3
Brockham Ct 6 SM2 59 B3
Brockham Cty Sch RH3 137 B7
Brockham Dr SW2 21 F8
Brockham Hill Pk KT20 116 C4
Brockham House 14 SW2 21 F8
Brockham La RH3, RH4 116 A1
Brockhamhurst Rd RH3 137 B2
Brockholes Cross KT24 113 A6
Brockhurst Cl RH12 216 F1
Brockhurst Cotts GU6 193 F4
Brockhurst Lodge GU9 146 B7
Brocklebank Ct CR6 81 A1
Brocklebank Rd SW18 20 C8
Brocklesby Rd SE25 43 B5
Brockley Combe KT13 53 D6
Brockley Pk SE23 23 E8
Brockley Rise SE23 23 E8
Brockley View SE23 23 E8
Brockman Rise BR1 24 D4
Brocks Dr Cheam SM3 58 E7
Fairlands GU3 108 C5
Brockshot Cl 1 TW8 6 D8
Brockton GU7 150 E5
Brockway Cl GU1 110 B2
Brockwell Park Gdns SE24 22 B8
Brockworth KT2 38 B8
Broderick House SE21 22 E5
Brodie House 7 SM6 60 B6
Brodie Rd GU1 130 E8
Brodrick Gr KT23 94 A1
Brodrick Rd SW17 20 E6
Brograve Gdns BR3 44 B7
Broke Ct GU4 110 C4
Brokes Cres RH2 118 A3
Brokes Rd RH2 118 A3
Bromford Cl RH8 123 A2
Bromleigh Ct SE21, SE22 23 B6
Bromley Ave BR1 24 E1
Bromley Cres BR2 44 F6
Bromley Ct BR1 24 F1
Bromley Gdns BR2 44 F6
Bromley Gr BR2 44 D7
Bromley Hill BR1 24 E2
Bromley Pk BR1 44 F8
Bromley Rd Beckenham BR3 44 B8
Beckenham BR2, BR3 44 D7
Catford SE6, BR1 24 B5
Bromley Road Infs Sch BR3 44 B8
Brompton Cl Hounslow TW4 4 F2
Penge SE20 43 A7
Bromwich House 3 TW10 6 E1
Bronson Rd SW20 39 E7
Bronte Ct 14 RH1 119 A2
Brontes The RH19 185 D1
Brook Ave GU9 125 F7
Brook Cl Ash GU12 106 B3
East Grinstead RH19 186 B1
Epsom KT19 57 E2
Sandhurst GU47 45 E1
Stanwell TW19 13 F8
West Barnes SW20 39 B6
Wokingham RG41 25 A8
Brook Ct Beckenham BR3 43 F8
6 Brentford TW8 6 D8
Cheam SM3 58 C6
Mortlake SW14 7 E4
Brook Dr Ashford TW16 14 E2
Bracknell RG12 27 E5
Brook Farm Rd KT11 73 D4
Brook Gdns Barnes SW13 7 F4
Farnborough GU14 84 F2
Kingston u T KT2 38 C8
Brook Gn Bracknell RG42 26 F8
Chobham GU24 49 F1
Brook Hill
Farley Green GU5 153 D8
Oxted RH8 122 C5
Brook House
Cranleigh GU6 174 F4
Heath End GU9 125 D6
4 Twickenham TW1 17 A8
Brook La Chobham GU24 68 D8
Farley Green GU5 132 E1
Faygate RH12 218 C8
Send GU23 90 E5
Brook La Bns Ctr 4 TW8 6 D8
Brook La N 3 TW8 6 D8
Brook Mead KT19 57 E4
Brook Meadow GU8 191 C3
Brook Rd Bagshot GU19 47 E2
Brook GU8 190 D8
Camberley GU15 65 B4
Chilworth GU4 131 C3
Horsham RH12 217 E6
Merstham RH1 119 C7
Redhill RH1 139 F8
Surbiton KT6 56 E8
Thornton Heath CR7 42 C5
Twickenham TW1 6 A1
Brook Rd *continued*
Wormley GU8 170 E1
Brook Rd S TW8 6 D8
Brook St KT1 37 E7
Brook Trad Est The GU12 105 E2
Brook Valley RH5 136 B1
Brook Way KT22 75 A1
Brookdale Rd Catford SE6 24 B8
2 Lewisham SE6 24 B8
Brooke Ct 7 KT2 17 D4
Brooke Forest GU3 108 C5
Brookehowse Rd SE6 24 B5
Brookers Cl KT21 75 D2
Brookers Cnr RG45 45 C5
Brookers House KT21 75 D2
Brookers Row RG45 45 C6
Brookfield Farncombe GU7 151 A8
Woking GU21 69 B3
Brookfield Ave SM1, SM5 59 E7
Brookfield Cl
Ottershaw KT16 51 D4
Redhill RH1 140 A3
Brookfield Gdns KT10 55 F4
Brookfield Rd GU12 105 F3
Brookfields Ave CR4 40 E4
Brookhill Cl RH10 183 A3
Brookhill Rd RH10 183 A3
Brookhouse Rd GU14 84 F3
Brookhurst Rd KT15 52 B4
Brooklands GU11 104 E1
Brooklands Ave SW18 20 B6
Brooklands Cl
Charlton TW16 34 E8
Cobham KT11 73 E4
Heath End GU9 125 D7
Brooklands Coll KT13 52 F4
Brooklands Ct
Kingston u T KT1 37 D5
Mitcham CR4 40 D7
New Haw KT15 52 D1
Reigate RH2 118 B3
Brooklands Ind Est KT13 52 E1
Brooklands La KT13 52 F4
Brooklands Mus KT13 53 A2
Brooklands Rd
Crawley RH11 201 C1
Heath End GU9 125 E7
Thames Ditton KT7 37 A1
Weybridge KT13 53 B3
Weybridge KT13, KT14 72 A8
Brooklands Sch RH2 118 B3
Brooklands The TW7 5 D6
Brooklands Way
East Grinstead RH19 205 D8
Heath End GU9 125 E7
Redhill RH1 118 E3
Brookley Cl GU10 126 C3
Brookleys GU24 49 F1
Brooklyn SE20 23 A1
Brooklyn Ave SE25 43 B5
Brooklyn Cl Carshalton SM5 59 E8
Woking GU22 89 E8
Brooklyn Ct GU22 89 E8
Brooklyn Gr SE25 43 B5
Brooklyn Rd Croydon SE25 43 B5
Woking GU22 89 E8
Brookmead CR4 41 C3
Brookmead Ct
Cranleigh GU6 174 E2
Farnham GU9 125 B1
Brookmead Rd CR0 41 C3
Brooks Cl KT13 53 A1
Brooks House 6 SW2 22 A7
Brooks La W4 7 A8
Brooks Rd W4 7 A8
Brooksby Cl GU17 64 B5
Brookscroft CR0 62 E1
Brookside
Beare Green RH5 157 F6
Chertsey KT16 32 E2
Colnbrook SL3 1 C7
Copthorne RH10 183 A3
Cranleigh GU6 174 E1
Cranleigh GU6 174 E3
Crawley RH10 201 F7
Guildford GU4 109 D6
Hale GU9 125 D6
Sandhurst GU47 64 C8
South Godstone RH9 142 D5
Wallington SM5 60 A5
Wokingham RG41 25 A7
Brookside Ave TW15 13 D3
Brookside Cl TW13 15 A5
Brookside Cres 1 KT4 39 A1
Brookside Way CR0 43 D3
Brookview RH10 183 A3
Brookview Rd SW16, SW17 21 C3
Brookwell La GU5 152 B2
Brookwood RH6 161 B4
Brookwood Ave SW13 7 F5
Brookwood Cl BR2 44 F5
Brookwood Cty Fst & Mid Sch GU24 88 A7
Brookwood Hospl GU21 68 C1
Brookwood House RH6 161 B6
Brookwood Lye Rd GU21, GU22 88 C7
Brookwood Rd
Farnborough GU14 85 D4
Hounslow TW3 5 B6
Wandsworth SW18 20 A7
Brookwood Sta GU24 88 A6
Broom Acres GU47 45 B1
Broom Bank CR6 102 C8
Broom Cl Blackwater GU17 64 E4
Esher KT10 55 B5
Teddington KT1, TW11 17 D1
Broom Field GU18 67 A7
Broom Gdns CR0 63 A7
Broom Hall KT22 74 D5
Broom La GU24 49 E3
Broom Lock TW11 17 C2
Broom Pk KT1 17 D1
Broom Rd Croydon CR0 63 A7
Richmond TW11 17 C3
Teddington KT1, TW11 17 C2
Broom Squires GU26 188 F4
Broom Water TW11 17 C3
Broom Water W TW11 17 C3
Broom Way KT13 53 E6
Broomcroft Cl GU22 70 D3
Broomcroft Dr GU22 70 D3
Broomdashers Rd RH10 201 F7
Broome Cl RH12 217 D5
Broome Ct 3 TW9 7 A6
Broome Lodge TW18 13 B3
Broome Rd TW12 35 F8
Broome St KT18 96 C1
Broomehall Rd
Coldharbour RH5 156 D2
Ockley RH5 177 E8
Broomers La GU6 175 E5
Broomfield Elstead GU8 148 E4
Guildford GU2 108 E2
Staines TW18 13 A2
Sunbury TW16 35 A8
Broomfield Cl
Guildford GU3 108 E3
Sunningdale SL5 30 B2
Broomfield Cotts KT20 97 E8
Broomfield Ct KT13 53 B4
Broomfield Dr SL5 30 B3
Broomfield La GU10 146 A1
Broomfield Pk
Sunningdale SL5 30 B2
Westcott RH4 135 C6
Broomfield Rd
Beckenham BR3 43 F6
Richmond TW9 6 F6
Surbiton KT5 37 F1
Teddington TW11 17 C2
Woodham KT15 71 B8
Broomfield Ride KT22 74 D7
Broomfields KT10 55 C5
Broomhall Bldgs SL5 30 B2
Broomhall End GU21 69 E3
Broomhall La
Sunningdale SL5 30 A3
Woking GU21 69 E3
Broomhall Rd
South Croydon CR2 61 D2
Woking GU21 69 E3
Broomhill GU10 124 D8
Broomhill Rd GU14 84 D5
Broomhurst Ct RH4 136 B5
Broomlands La RH8 123 E8
Broomleaf Cnr GU9 125 D2
Broomleaf Rd GU9 125 E2
Broomleigh Bsns Pk SE6 23 F3
Broomloan La SM1 59 A8
Broomsquires Rd GU19 47 F2
Broomwood Cl CR0 43 D4
Broomwood Way GU10 146 C6
Broseley Gr SE26 23 E3
Broster Gdns SE25 42 F6
Brough Cl KT2 17 D3
Brougham Pl GU9 125 B7
Broughton Ave TW10 17 C4
Broughton Mews GU16 65 F1
Broughton Rd CR7 42 A3
Brow The RH1 140 A4
Browell House GU4 110 D2
Browells La TW13 15 B6
Brown Bear Ct TW13 15 D4
Brown Cl SM6 60 E3
Brown's Hill RH1 141 D2
Brown's Rd KT5, KT6 37 F2
Browne House 9 SE26 23 B3
Browngraves Rd UB7 3 C7
Brownhill Rd SE6 24 C8
Browning Ave
Carshalton SM1 59 E6
North Cheam KT4 39 B1
Browning Cl
Crawley RH10 202 C7
Frimley GU15 66 C4
Hampton TW12 15 F4
Browning Rd KT22 94 D2
Browning Way TW5 4 D6
Brownings The 1 RH19 185 C1
Brownlow Rd Redhill RH1 118 E1
South Croydon CR0 61 F6
Brownrigg Cres RG12 27 E8
Brownrigg Rd TW15 14 A4
Browns La KT24 113 D8
Browns Wlk GU10 145 F5
Browns Wood RH19 185 E4
Brownsover Rd GU14 84 C4
Brox La
Addlestone KT15, KT16 51 D2
Ottershaw KT15, KT16 51 D2
Woodham KT15, KT16 51 D2
Brox Rd KT16 51 D4
Broxholm Rd SE27, SW16 22 A5
Broxted Rd SE23, SE6 23 F6
Bruce Ave TW17 34 C3
Bruce Cl KT14 71 E6
Bruce Dr CR2 62 D2
Bruce Hall Mews SW17 21 A4
Bruce Lawns SW17 21 A4
Bruce Rd Mitcham CR4 21 A1
South Norwood SE25 42 D5
Brudenell Rd SW17 21 A4

Brumana Cl KT13 53 B4
Brumfield Rd KT19 57 C5
Brunel Cl Cranford TW5 4 B7
South Norwood SE19 22 F2
Brunel Ct SW13 7 F5
Brunel Ctr RH10 181 F2
Brunel Dr RG45 45 C8
Brunel House 25 SW2 21 E8
Brunel Pl RH10 201 E5
Brunel Univ Coll Osterley Campus TW7 5 F7
Brunel Univ Coll (Twickenham Campus) TW1 6 B3
Brunel Univ (Runnymede Campus) TW20 11 C5
Brunel Wlk 3 TW4 16 A8
Brunner Ct KT16 51 C5
Brunner House SE6 24 C4
Brunswick RG12 27 A2
Brunswick Cl
Crawley RH10 202 A4
Thames Ditton KT7 36 F1
Twickenham TW2 16 D5
Walton-on-T KT12 54 C8
Brunswick Ct
Crawley RH10 202 A4
Kingston u T KT2 17 D2
2 Penge SE19 23 A1
Brunswick Dr GU24 87 D7
Brunswick Gr KT11 73 C6
Brunswick Mews SW16 21 D2
Brunswick Pl SE19 23 A1
Brunswick Rd
Kingston u T KT2 38 A8
Pirbright, Alexander Barracks GU24 87 C6
Pirbright, Blackdown Barracks GU16, GU24 86 E6
Sutton SM1 59 B6
Bruntile Cl GU14 85 D1
Brushwood Rd RH12 218 B6
Bruton Rd SM4 40 C5
Bruton Way RG12 27 E2
Bryan Cl TW16 15 A1
Bryanston Ave TW2 16 B7
Bryanstone Ave GU2 109 A4
Bryanstone Cl GU2 108 F4
Bryanstone Ct SM1 59 C7
Bryanstone Gr GU2 108 F5
Bryce Cl RH12 218 A5
Bryce Gdns GU11 126 C7
Bryden Cl SE26 23 E3
Brympton Cl RH4 136 A5
Bryn Rd GU10 145 F7
Brynford Cl GU21 69 E4
Bryony House RG42 26 E8
Bryony Rd GU1 110 B4
Bryony Way TW16 15 A2
Buchan Country Park RH11 200 E1
Buchan The GU15 66 A8
Buchanan House
Dulwich SE21 22 E5
Wandsworth SW18 20 A8
Buchans Lawn RH11 201 B2
Bucharest Rd SW18 20 C8
Buckfast Rd SM4 40 B5
Buckhurst Ave CR4, SM5 40 F1
Buckhurst Cl
East Grinstead RH19 185 C3
Redhill RH1 118 F3
Buckhurst Cotts RH12 214 D8
Buckhurst Gr RG40 25 F5
Buckhurst Hill RG12 27 F5
Buckhurst La SL5 30 A6
Buckhurst Mead RH19 185 C4
Buckhurst Moors RG12 26 C6
Buckhurst Rd Ascot SL5 29 F7
Frimley GU16 85 F6
Buckhurst Way RH19 185 C3
Buckingham Ave
East Molesey KT8 36 B7
Feltham TW14 4 B1
South Norwood CR7 42 A8
Buckingham Cl
Guildford GU1 109 F2
Hampton TW12 15 F3
Buckingham Ct
Belmont SM2 59 A2
Crawley RH11 201 B2
Staines TW18 13 A4
Wokingham RG40 25 C6
Buckingham Dr RH19 206 A8
Buckingham Gate RH6 182 C7
Buckingham Gdns
Hampton KT8 36 B7
South Norwood CR7 42 A7
Buckingham La SE23 23 E8
Buckingham Prim Sch TW12 15 F3
Buckingham Rd
Hampton TW12, TW13 15 F3
Kingston u T KT1 37 F5
Mitcham CR4 41 E4
Richmond TW10 17 D6
South Holmwood RH5 157 C6
Buckingham Way SM6 60 C2
Buckland Cl GU14 85 C7
Buckland Cnr RH2 117 D2
Buckland Ct RH3 117 A2
Buckland Cty Jun & Inf Sch TW18 13 C1
Buckland Inf Sch KT9 56 F6
Buckland La RH3 117 B5
Buckland Rd
Chessington KT9 56 F5
East Ewell SM2 58 D2
Lower Kingswood KT20 117 F7
Reigate RH2 117 D2
Buckland Way KT4 39 C1
Buckland Wlk SM4 40 C5
Bucklands Rd TW11 17 C2
Bucklebury RG12 27 A2
Buckleigh Ave SW20 39 F6
Buckleigh Rd SW16 21 E1
Buckleigh Way SE19 22 F1
Bucklers' Way SM5 59 F7
Buckles Way SM7 77 E3
Buckley Pl RH10 204 A8
Buckmans Rd RH11 201 D6
Bucknills Cl KT18 76 C5
Bucks Cl KT14 71 B5
Buckswood Dr RH11 201 A4
Buckthorn Cl RG40 25 E7
Buddhapadipa Temple The SW19 19 D4
Budebury Rd TW18 13 A3
Budge La CR4 40 F2
Budge's Cotts RG40 25 E8
Budge's Gdns RG40 25 E7
Budge's Rd RG40 25 D7
Budgen Cl RH10 182 D1
Budgen Dr RH1 119 A3
Budham Way RG12 27 B3
Buff Ave SM7 78 B4
Buffbeards La GU27 207 E6
Buffers La KT22 95 A8
Bug Hill CR6 101 D7
Bugkingham Way GU16 65 F1
Bulbrook Row RG12 27 E7
Bulganak Rd CR7 42 C5
Bulkeley Cl TW20 11 C3
Bull Hill KT22 95 A6
Bull La Bracknell RG42 27 B8
Woking GU4 89 F1
Bullard Rd TW11 16 F2
Bullbeggars La
Godstone RH9 121 C3
Woking GU21 69 B3
Bullbrook Dr RG12 27 F8
Buller Ct GU14 85 C1
Buller Rd CR7 42 D6
Bullers Rd GU9 125 E6
Bullfinch Cl Horley RH6 160 E4
Horsham RH12 217 C7
Sandhurst GU47 64 E8
Bullfinch Ct 3 SE21 22 D6
Bullfinch Rd CR2 62 D1
Bullrush Cl CR0 42 E3
Bulls Alley SW14 7 D5
Bullswater Common Rd GU24, GU3 88 A2
Bullswater La GU24 88 A2
Bulstrode Ave TW3 5 A4
Bulstrode Gdns TW3 5 A4
Bulstrode Rd TW3 5 A4
Bunbury Way KT17 77 B4
Bunce Common Rd RH2, RH3 137 E2
Bunce Dr CR3 100 D4
Bunch La GU27 208 B8
Bunch Way GU27 208 A6
Bundy's Way TW18 12 F2
Bungalow Rd SE25 42 E5
Bungalows The SW16 21 B1
Bunting Cl Horsham RH13 217 F3
Mitcham CR4 40 F4
Buntings The GU9 145 F8
Bunyan Cl RH11 200 E3
Bunyard Dr GU21 70 C5
Burbage Gn RG12 27 F4
Burbage Rd SE21, SE24 22 D8
Burbeach Cl RH11 201 B3
Burberry Cl KT3 38 E7
Burbidge Rd TW17 34 A5
Burchets Hollow GU5 154 D7
Burchetts Way TW17 34 B3
Burcote 6 KT13 53 D4
Burcote Rd SW18 20 D8
Burcott Gdns KT15 52 D4
Burcott Rd CR8 80 A5
Burden Way GU2 109 A5
Burdenshot Hill GU22, GU3 89 B3
Burdenshott Ave TW10 7 B3
Burdenshott Rd
Guildford GU4 109 C8
Woking GU22, GU3, GU4 89 A2
Burdett Ave SW20 39 A8
Burdett Cl RH10 202 D5
Burdett Rd Richmond TW9 6 F4
Thornton Heath CR0 42 D3
Burdock Cl Crawley RH11 201 A2
Croydon CR0 43 D1
Lightwater GU18 67 B8
Burdon La SM2 58 F2
Burdon Pk SM2 58 F2
Burfield Cl SW17 20 D4
Burfield Dr CR6 101 C8
Burfield Rd SL4, TW19 11 B8
Burford Ct RG40 25 E5
Burford La KT17 77 C8
Burford Lea GU8 148 E4
Burford Rd Camberley GU15 65 B4
Forest Hill SE6 23 F6
Horsham RH13 217 E2
New Malden KT4 39 A2
Sutton SM1 59 A8
Burford Way CR0 63 C4
Burges Way TW18 13 A3
Burgess Cl TW13 15 E4
Burgess Mews SW19 20 B2
Burgess Rd SM1 59 B6
Burgh Cl RH10 182 D1
Burgh Heath Rd KT17, KT18 76 F4
Burgh Mount SM7 77 F4
Burgh Wood SM7 77 F4
Burghead Cl GU47 64 D7
Burghfield KT17 76 F4
Burghill Rd SE26 23 E4
Burghley Ave KT3 38 D8
Burghley House SW19 19 E5
Burghley Pl CR4 40 F5
Burghley Rd SW19 19 E4
Burgoyne Rd Ashford TW16 14 F2
Camberley GU15 66 A6
South Norwood SE25 42 F5
Burham Cl SE20 23 C1
Burhill Cty Inf Sch KT12 54 D4
Burhill Rd KT12 54 C3
Buriton House 9 SW15 19 B7
Burke Cl SW15 7 E3
Burlands RH11 181 A1
Burlea Cl KT12 54 B5
Burleigh Ave SM6 60 B7
Burleigh Cl
Addlestone KT15 52 B5
Crawley Down RH10 204 B8
Burleigh Ct KT22 95 A5
Burleigh Cty Inf Sch RH10 204 B8
Burleigh Gdns
Ashford TW15 14 C3
Woking GU21 69 F2
Burleigh La
Crawley Down RH10 204 C7
North Ascot SL5 28 E8
Burleigh Pk KT11 73 E7
Burleigh Rd
Addlestone KT15 52 B5
Cheam SM3, SM4 39 E1
Frimley GU16 85 D8
North Ascot SL5 28 E7
Burleigh Way RH10 204 B8
Burleigh Wlk SE6 24 C7
Burley Cl Loxwood RH14 213 A4
Mitcham SW16 41 D7
Burley Orchard KT16 33 A3
Burley Way GU17 64 C6
Burleys Rd RH10 202 C6
Burlingham Cl GU4 110 D3
Burlington Ave TW9 7 A6
Burlington Cl TW14 14 D8
Burlington Ct 6
Aldershot GU11 105 A1
Blackwater GU17 64 D3
Chiswick W4 7 C7
Burlington Jun Sch KT3 38 F5
Burlington La W4 7 E8
Burlington Rd
Hounslow TW7 5 D6
New Malden KT3 38 F5
South Norwood CR7 42 D7
Burlsdon Way RG12 27 E8
Burma Rd KT16 49 F8
Burma Terr 11 SE19 22 E3
Burmarsh Ct SE20 43 C8
Burmester House SW17 20 C5
Burmester Rd SW17 20 C5
Burn Cl KT15 52 D6
Burn Moor Chase RG12 27 E2
Burnaby Cres W4 7 C8
Burnaby Gdns W4 7 B8
Burnbury Rd SW12 21 C7
Burne-Jones Dr GU47 64 D6
Burnell Ave TW10 17 C3
Burnell House 19 SW2 22 A7
Burnell Rd SM1 59 B6
Burnet Ave GU1, GU4 110 B4
Burnet Cl GU24 67 E6
Burnet Gr KT19 76 C6
Burney Ave KT5 37 F4
Burney Cl KT23 94 C2
Burney Ct 6 RH11 201 A3
Burney House 6 SW16 21 C3
Burney Rd RH5 115 A4
Burnham Cl GU21 68 D1
Burnham Dr
North Cheam KT4 58 D8
Reigate RH2 118 A2
Burnham Gdns
Cranford TW5 4 B6
Croydon CR0 42 F2
Burnham Manor GU15 66 A8
Burnham Pl RH13 217 D1
Burnham Rd Knaphill GU21 68 D1
Morden SM4 40 B5
Burnham St KT2 38 A8
Burnham Way SE26 23 F3
Burnhams Rd KT23 93 E3
Burnhill Rd BR3 44 A7
Burns Ave TW14 4 A1
Burns Cl Farnborough GU14 84 F6
Horsham RH12 217 E7
Mitcham SW17 20 D2
Burns Ct SM6 60 B3
Burns Dr SM7 77 E5
Burns Rd RH10 202 C8
Burns Way Crawley RH12 200 C1
East Grinstead RH19 185 C1
Heston TW5 4 D6
Burnsall Cl GU14 85 B6
Burnside KT21 75 F1
Burnside Cl TW1 6 A1
Burnt Ash Prim Sch BR1 24 F3
Burnt Hill Rd GU10, GU9 146 B6
Burnt Hill Way GU10 146 B5
Burnt House La RH12 200 A7
Burnt Pollard La GU24 48 E1
Burntcommon Cl GU23 90 F2
Burntcommon La GU23 91 A2
Burntwood Cl
Caterham CR3 101 A6
Wandsworth SW18 20 E7
Burntwood Ct SW17 20 C5
Burntwood Grange Rd SW18 20 E7
Burntwood La
Caterham CR3 101 A6
Wandsworth SW17 20 D6
Burntwood Sch SW17 20 D6
Burntwood View SE19 22 F3
Burnwood Park Rd KT12 54 B6
Burpham Court Farm Park GU4 109 F7
Burpham La GU4 110 A5
Burpham Prim Sch GU4 110 A5
Burr Hill La GU24 49 F2
Burr Rd SW18 20 A8
Burrell Cl CR0 43 E3
Burrell Ct RH11 200 F4
Burrell House 5 TW1 17 B8
Burrell Rd GU16 85 C8
Burrell Row BR3 44 A7
Burrell The RH4 135 C6
Burrells BR3 44 B7
Burritt Rd KT1 38 A7
Burrow Hill Gn GU24 49 E2
Burrow Hill Sch GU16 65 F1
Burrow Wlk SE21 22 C8
Burrows Cl Guildford GU2 108 F2
Little Bookham KT23 93 F3
Burrows Cross GU5 133 C2
Burrows Hill Cl TW19, TW6 2 C3
Burrows La GU5 133 C3
Burrwood Gdns GU12 106 A4
Burstead Cl KT11 73 D7
Burston Gdns RH19 185 D4
Burstow House RH6 161 B6
Burstow Prim Sch RH6 162 B3
Burstow Rd SW20 39 E8
Burtenshaw Rd KT7 37 A3
Burton Cl Chessington KT9 56 D3
Horley RH6 161 A2
Windlesham GU20 48 D4
Burton Ct KT7 37 A3
Burton Gdns TW5 4 F6
Burton House SE26 23 B3
Burton Rd KT2 17 E1
Burton's Rd TW12 16 C4
Burtons Ct RH12 217 C2
Burtwell La SE21, SE27 22 D4
Burwash Rd RH10 202 A5
Burway Cres KT16 33 A5
Burwood Ave CR8 80 B5
Burwood Cl Guildford GU1 110 D2
Hersham KT12 54 C4
Reigate RH2 118 D1
Tolworth KT6 38 A1
Burwood Ct SE23 23 C8
Burwood Park Sch KT12 53 F5
Burwood Rd
Hersham KT12, KT13 54 B4
Hersham KT12 54 D5
Bury Cl GU21 69 D3
Bury Fields GU2 130 C7
Bury Gr SM4 40 B4
Bury La GU21 69 C3
Bury St GU2 130 C7
Burys Court Sch RH2 138 C3
Burys The GU7 150 E5
Burywood Hill RH5 177 E7
Busbridge CE Jun Sch GU7 150 F2
Busbridge Cty Inf Sch GU7 150 F2
Busbridge La GU7 150 E3
Busby House SW16 21 C4
Busch Cl TW7 6 B6
Busch Cnr TW7 6 B6
Busdens Cl GU8 170 F8
Busdens La GU8 170 F8
Busdens Way GU8 170 F8
Bush Cl KT15 52 C5
Bush La GU23 90 D3
Bush Rd Littleton TW17 33 F4
Richmond TW9 6 F8
Bush Wlk RG40 25 C6
Bushbury La RH3 137 A5
Bushell Cl SW2 21 F6
Bushell House 3 SE27 22 C4
Bushetts Gr RH1, RH2 119 B6
Bushey Cl CR3, CR8 80 F3
Bushey Croft RH8 122 C5
Bushey Ct SW20 39 B7
Bushey Down SW12 21 B6
Bushey Fst Sch KT3 39 B6
Bushey La SM1 59 A6
Bushey Mid Sch SW20 39 B6
Bushey Rd Croydon CR0 63 A8
Merton SW20 39 D7
Sutton SM1 59 A6
Sutton SM1 59 B6
West Barnes SW20 39 D7
Bushey Way BR3 44 D4
Bushfield RH14 211 F2
Bushfield Dr RH1 140 A4
Bushnell Rd SW17 21 B5
Bushwood Rd TW9 7 A8
Bushy Ct KT1 37 C8
Bushy Hill Dr GU1 110 C3
Bushy Hill Jun Sch GU1 110 D2
Bushy Park Gdns TW12 16 D3
Bushy Park Rd TW11 17 B1
Bushy Rd
Fetcham KT22, KT23 94 B5
Teddington TW11 16 F1
Bushy Shaw KT21 75 C2
Business Ctr The RG41 25 B4
Busk Cres GU14 84 F3
Bute Ave TW10 17 E6
Bute Ct SM6 60 C5
Bute Gdns SM6 60 C5
Bute Gdns W SM6 60 C5
Bute Rd Thornton Heath CR0 42 A1
Wallington SM6 60 C6
Butler Rd Bagshot GU19 47 F2
Crowthorne RG45 45 B6
Butlers Dene Rd CR3 102 A7
Butlers Hill KT24 112 B5
Butlers Rd RH13 218 B4
Butt Cl GU6 174 E4
Butter Hill Dorking RH4 136 A7
Hackbridge SM5, SM6 60 A6
Buttercup Cl RG40 26 A6
Buttercup Sq TW19 13 D7
Butterfield Camberley GU15 65 B4
East Grinstead RH19 185 B3
Butterfield Cl TW1 5 F1
Butterfly Wlk CR6 101 C7
Buttermer Cl GU10 145 F7
Buttermere Cl
East Bedfont TW14 14 F7
Farnborough GU14 84 E4
Horsham RH12 218 B6
West Barnes SM4 39 D3
Buttermere Ct GU12 105 F4
Buttermere Dr GU15 66 D4
Buttermere Gdns
Bracknell RG12 27 C6
Sanderstead CR8 80 D6
Buttermere Way TW20 12 B1
Buttersteep Rise GU20, SL5 28 C1
Butterworth Ct SW16 21 E5
Butts Cl RH11 201 B7
Butts Cotts Feltham TW13 15 F5
4 Woking GU21 69 A1
Butts Cres TW13 16 A5
Butts House TW13 16 A5
Butts Rd Catford BR1 24 E3
Woking GU21 69 E2
Butts The TW8 6 D8
Buxton Ave CR3 100 E6
Buxton Cres SM3 58 E6
Buxton Dr KT3 38 D7
Buxton La CR3 100 E6
Buxton Rd Ashford TW15 13 D3
Mortlake SW14 7 E4
Thornton Heath CR7 42 B4
Byards Croft SW16 41 D8
Byatt Wlk TW12 15 E2
Bychurch End 9 TW11 16 F3
Bycroft St SE20 23 D1
Bycroft Way RH10 202 B8
Bye Ways TW2 16 B5
Byerley Way RH10 202 E7
Byers La RH9 142 C1
Byeway The SW14 7 C4
Byeways The KT5 38 B4
Byfield Ct KT3 39 A5
Byfield Rd TW7 6 A4
Byfleet Cnr KT14 71 A6
Byfleet Cty Prim Sch KT14 71 D8
Byfleet Ind Est KT14 71 D8
Byfleet & New Haw Sta KT15 52 D1
Byfleet Rd
New Haw KT14, KT15 52 D2
Weybridge KT11, KT13, KT14 72 C7
Byfleet Tech Ctr The KT14 71 D8
Byfleets La RH12 216 D6
Byfrons The GU14 85 D2
Bygrove CR0 63 B3
Bygrove Ct SW19 20 D2
Bygrove Rd SW19 20 D2
Bylands GU22 70 A1
Byne Rd Carshalton SM5 59 E8
Penge SE20, E26 23 C3
Bynes Rd CR2 61 D3
Byrd Rd RH11 200 F3
Byrefield Rd GU2 108 F4
Byrne Ct 1 CR8 80 A7
Byrne Rd SW12 21 B6
Byron Ave Carshalton SM1 59 D6
Coulsdon CR5 79 F3
Cranford TW4 4 B5
Frimley GU15 66 B3
West Barnes KT3 39 A4
Byron Ave E SM1 59 D6
Byron Cl Crawley RH10 202 B7
Forest Hill SE26 23 E4
Hampton TW12 15 F4
Horsham RH12 217 E6
Knaphill GU21 68 E2
Walton-on-T KT12 35 E1
Byron Ct Dulwich SE21 23 A7
1 Richmond TW10 17 D4
South Norwood CR7 42 C7
Byron Dr RG45 45 B3
Byron Gdns SM1 59 D6
Byron Gr 2 RH19 185 C1
Byron House BR3 24 B2
Byron Inf Sch CR5 79 F2
Byron Jun Sch CR5 79 F2
Byron Pl KT22 95 B5
Byron Rd Addlestone KT15 52 E6
South Croydon CR2 62 B1
Byton Rd SW17 20 F2
Byttom Hill RH5 115 C8
Byward Ave TW14 4 C1
Byway The SM2 59 D2
Byways The Ashstead KT21 75 D1
Worcester Park KT19 57 F6
Bywood RG12 27 A2
Bywood Ave CR0 43 D3

Bywood Cl CR8 80 B4
Bywood Terr CR0 43 C3
Byworth Cl GU9 124 F2
Byworth Rd GU9 124 F2

C

Cabbell Pl KT15 52 C6
Cabell Rd GU2 108 E2
Cabin Moss RG12 27 E2
Cable House Sch GU21 69 E4
Cabrera Ave GU25 31 D3
Cabrera Cl GU25 31 D3
Cabrol Rd GU14 85 A5
Caburn Ct RH11 201 C4
Caburn Hts RH11 201 C4
Cackstones The RH10 202 D7
Cadbury Cl Ashford TW16 14 E1
Isleworth TW7 6 A6
Cadbury Rd TW16 14 E2
Caddy Cl 4 TW20 12 A3
Cadley Terr SE23 23 C6
Cadmer Cl KT3 38 E5
Cadnam Cl GU11 126 C6
Cadnam Point 14 SW15 19 B7
Cadogan Cl Beckenham BR3 44 D7
Teddington TW11 16 E3
Cadogan Ct SM2 59 B4
Cadogan Ho 11 GU1 130 F8
Cadogan Rd KT6 37 D4
Cadogen Rd GU11 105 D7
Caen Wood Rd KT21 75 C1
Caenshill Rd KT13 53 A3
Caenswood Hill KT13 53 A1
Caenwood Cl KT13 53 A4
Caerleon Cl GU26 188 C6
Caernarvon GU16 85 F8
Caernarvon Cl CR4 41 E6
Caernarvon Ct 3 KT5 37 F4
Caesar Ct GU11 104 E2
Caesar's Camp Rd GU15 66 A8
Caesar's Cl GU15 66 A8
Caesar's Way TW17 34 D3
Caesars Ct GU9 125 C7
Caesars Wlk CR4 40 F4
Caffins Cl RH10 201 E8
Caillard Rd KT14 71 E8
Cain Rd RG12, RG42 26 E7
Cain's La TW14 3 E2
Cairn Cl GU15 66 B3
Cairndale Cl BR1 24 F1
Cairngorm Pl GU14 84 E7
Cairo New Rd CR0, CR9 61 B8
Caister House 10 SW12 21 B8
Caistor Mews SW12 21 B8
Caistor Rd SW12 21 B8
Caithness Dr KT18 76 D5
Caithness Rd CR4 21 B1
Calbourne Rd SW12 21 A8
Caldbeck Ave KT4 39 B1
Caldbeck House 7 RH11 200 F3
Calder Rd SM4 40 C4
Calder Way SL3 1 E4
Calderdale Cl RH11 201 B4
Caldwell Rd GU20 48 D5
Caledon Pl GU1 110 A4
Caledon Rd SM5, SM6 60 A6
Caledonia Rd TW19 13 E7
Caledonian House RH10 201 D8
Caledonian Way RH6 182 B8
Calfridus Way RG12 27 F6
California Ct SM2 59 B1
California Rd KT3 38 C6
Callander Rd SE6 24 C6
Calley Down Cres
CR0, CR9 63 D1
Callis Farm Cl TW19 2 E1
Callisto Cl RH11 200 E3
Callow Field CR8 80 A6
Callow Hill GU25, TW20 31 C7
Calluna Ct GU22 69 F1
Calluna Dr RH10 183 A3
Calmont Rd BR1 24 E2
Calonne Rd SW19 19 D4
Calshot Rd TW6 3 B5
Calshot Way Frimley GU16 86 A7
Harlington TW6 3 A5
Calthorpe Gdns SM1 59 C7
Calton Gdns GU11 126 C7
Calverley Cl BR3 24 B2
Calverley Rd KT17 58 A4
Calvert Cl GU12 105 D1
Calvert Cres RH4 115 B1
Calvert Ct 5 TW9 6 F3
Calvert Rd Dorking RH4 115 B2
Effingham KT24 113 B7
Calvin Cl GU15 66 B4
Calvin Wlk RH11 200 E3
Camac Rd TW2 16 D7
Camber Cl RH10 202 C6
Camberley Ave SW20 39 B7
Camberley Cl SM3 58 D7
Camberley Ct 8 SM2 59 B3
Camberley Cty Inf Sch
GU15 65 C5
Camberley Heath Golf
Course GU15 66 B5
Camberley Rd TW6 3 A4
Camberley Sta GU15 65 D5
Camberley Towers GU15 65 D5
Cambisgate SW19 19 E3
Camborne Cl TW6 3 A4
Camborne Cres TW6 3 A4
Camborne Rd Belmont SM2 59 B3
Croydon CR0 43 A2
Sutton SM2 59 B3
Wandsworth SW18 20 A8

Camborne Rd *continued*
West Barnes SM4 39 D4
Camborne Rd S TW6 3 A4
Camborne Way
Harmondsworth TW6 3 A4
Heston TW5 5 A6
Cambray Rd SW12 21 C7
Cambria BR3 44 B7
Cambria Cl TW3 5 A3
Cambria Ct Feltham TW14 15 B8
Staines TW18 12 E4
Cambria Gdns TW19 13 E8
Cambria House SE26 23 A4
Cambrian Cl
Camberley GU15 65 B5
West Norwood SE27 22 B5
Cambrian Rd
Farnborough GU14 84 D7
Richmond TW10 6 F1
Cambridge Ave KT3, SW20 38 F7
Cambridge Cl
Harmondsworth UB7 2 D8
Hounslow TW4 4 E3
Knaphill GU21 68 F1
Wimbledon SW20 39 B8
Cambridge Cotts TW9 7 A8
Cambridge Cres TW11 17 A3
Cambridge Ct SW20 39 B8
Cambridge Gdns KT1 38 A7
Cambridge Gr SE20 43 B8
Cambridge Grove Rd
Kingston u T KT1 38 A6
5 Kingston u T KT1 38 A7
Cambridge House 2
TW11 17 A3
Cambridge House Sch
SW20 39 C8
Cambridge Meadows
GU9 125 A1
Cambridge Park Ct TW1 17 D8
Cambridge Pk TW1 6 C1
Cambridge Pl GU9 125 C2
Cambridge Rd
Aldershot GU11 104 F2
Barnes SW13 7 F5
Carshalton SM5 59 E5
Crowthorne RG45 45 C4
Croydon SE20, SE25 43 B6
East Molesey KT8 35 F5
Hampton TW12 15 F1
Horsham RH13 217 D2
Hounslow TW4 4 E3
Kingston u T KT1 38 A7
Littleton TW15, TW17 14 C1
Mitcham CR4 41 C6
New Malden KT3 38 E5
Richmond TW9 7 A7
Sandhurst GU47 45 E1
Teddington TW11 17 A3
Twickenham TW1 6 D1
Walton-on-T KT12 35 B3
Wimbledon SW20 39 B8
Cambridge Rd E GU14 85 D1
Cambridge Rd W GU14 85 C1
Cambridge Sq GU15 65 C6
Cambridge Wlk 3 GU15 65 C6
Camden Ave TW13 15 C7
Camden Gdns
South Norwood CR7 42 B6
Sutton SM1 59 B5
Camden Hill Rd SE19 22 E2
Camden Jun Sch SM5 59 F6
Camden Rd Carshalton SM5 59 F6
Lingfield RH7 164 D4
Sutton SM1 59 B5
Camden Way CR7 42 B6
Cameford Ct 20 SW12 21 E8
Camel Cl KT2 17 D3
Camellia Ct
21 Beckenham BR3 24 A1
West End GU24 67 F6
Camellia Pl TW2 16 B8
Camelot Cl Biggin Hill TN16 83 C3
Wimbledon SW19 20 A4
Camelot Ct RH11 200 E6
Camelsdale Cty Fst Sch
GU27 207 F5
Camelsdale Rd
Kingsley Green GU27 207 F5
Linchmere GU27 207 F5
Cameron Cl GU6 174 E1
Cameron Ct 3 SW19 19 E7
Cameron House BR1 44 F8
Cameron Lodge TW3 5 C3
Cameron Rd
Farnborough GU11 105 D7
Forest Hill SE6 23 F6
Thornton Heath CR0 42 B3
Cameron Sq CR4 40 E8
Camgate Est TW19 13 F8
Camilla Cl Ashford TW16 14 F2
Great Bookham KT23 94 B2
Camilla Dr RH5 115 A5
Camille Cl SE25 43 A6
Camlan Rd BR1 24 F4
Camm Gdns
5 Kingston u T KT1 37 F7
Thames Ditton KT7 36 F2
Camomile Ave CR4 40 F8
Camp End Rd KT11, KT13 72 C8
Camp Farm Rd GU11 105 D5
Camp Hill GU10, GU9 147 C8
Camp Rd
Farnborough GU14 105 C8
Wimbledon SW19 19 C3
Woldingham CR3 101 E6
Camp View SW19 19 B3
Campbell Ave GU22 89 F6

Campbell Cl
Aldershot GU11 126 C7
Streatham SW16 21 D4
Twickenham TW2 16 D7
Campbell Cres RH19 185 B1
Campbell Ct Dulwich SE21 23 A7
Leatherhead KT22 95 B5
Campbell House 6 SM6 60 B6
Campbell Pl GU16 65 F3
Campbell Rd
Aldershot GU11 105 A3
Caterham CR3 100 D6
Crawley RH10 202 C5
Thornton Heath CR0 42 B3
Twickenham TW2 16 D6
Weybridge KT13 53 A3
Campden Rd CR0, CR2 61 E5
Campen Cl SW19 19 E6
Camphill Ct KT14 71 A7
Camphill Ind Est KT14 71 B8
Camphill Rd KT14, KT15 71 B7
Campion Cl
Blackwater GU17 64 F3
South Croydon CR2 61 E6
Campion Dr KT20 97 B7
Campion House
Bracknell RG42 26 E8
6 Redhill RH1 119 A4
Campion House
(Seminary) TW7 5 D6
Campion Rd
Horsham RH12 217 E5
Hounslow TW7 5 F6
Campion Way RG40 25 E7
Camrose Ave TW13 15 C4
Camrose Cl Croydon CR0 43 E2
Morden SM4 40 A5
Can Hatch KT20 77 E1
Canada Ave RH1 140 A5
Canada Dr RH1 140 A5
Canada House RH1 140 A5
Canada Rd Byfleet KT14 71 D8
Cobham KT11 73 C6
Frimley GU16 86 E8
Canadian Ave SE6 24 B7
Canal Cl GU11 105 D5
Canal Cotts GU12 106 A4
Canal Wlk Croydon CR0 42 F3
Forest Hill SE26 23 C3
Canberra Cl Crawley RH11 181 D1
Horsham RH12 217 F4
Canberra Pl RH12 217 F5
Canberra Rd TW6 3 A4
Canbury Ave KT2 37 F8
Canbury Bsns Pk 3 KT2 37 E8
Canbury Ct KT2 17 E1
Canbury Mews SE26 23 A5
Canbury Park Rd KT2 37 F8
Candlerush Cl GU22 70 B2
Candover Cl UB7 2 D7
Candy Croft KT23 94 B2
Cane Cl SM6 60 E3
Canewdon Cl GU22 89 E8
Canford Dr KT15 52 B8
Canford Gdns KT3 38 E3
Canham Rd SE25 42 E6
Canmore Gdns SW16 21 C1
Canning Rd
Aldershot GU12 105 D2
Croydon CR0, CR9 61 F8
Cannizaro Rd SW19 19 D3
Cannon Cl Hampton TW12 16 B2
Sandhurst GU47 64 F8
West Barnes SW20 39 C6
Cannon Cres GU24 68 E8
Cannon Gr KT22 94 E6
Cannon Hill RG12 27 C3
Cannon Hill La
Merton KT3, SM4, SW20 39 E5
West Barnes KT3,
SM4, SW20 39 E5
Cannon House SE26 23 B2
Cannon Side KT22 94 E5
Cannon Way
East Molesey KT8 36 B5
Fetcham KT22 94 E6
Canon's Hill CR5, CR8 80 A1
Canon's Wlk CR0 62 D7
Canonbie Rd SE23 23 C8
Canonbury Cotts RH12 199 F6
Canons Cl RH2 117 F2
Canons L Ctr The CR4 40 F5
Canons La KT20 97 F8
Canopus Way TW19 13 E8
Cansiron La RH19 206 F6
Cantelupe Rd RH19 185 F1
Canter The RH10 202 E7
Canterbury Cl BR3 44 B8
Canterbury Ct
Ashford TW15 13 F4
Dorking RH4 136 A8
South Croydon CR2 61 C3
Canterbury Gr SE27, SW16 22 A5
Canterbury Mews KT22 74 C6
Canterbury Rd Ash GU12 106 A3
Crawley RH10 201 E2
Farnborough GU14 85 D2
Feltham TW13 15 E6
Guildford GU2 108 F3
Morden SM4 40 C3
Thornton Heath CR0, CR7 42 A2
Cantley Cres RG41 25 A8
Cantley Gdns SE19 42 F8
Canute Ct SW16 22 A5
Canvey Cl RH11 201 C3
Cape Copse RH12 214 D7
Capel KT5 37 F2
Capel Ave SM6 60 F5

Capel CE (VA) Fst Sch
RH5 178 D6
Capel Ct SE20 43 C8
Capel La RH11 200 F5
Capel Lodge
5 Richmond TW9 6 F6
15 Streatham SW2 21 F8
Capel Rd RH12 199 A8
Capella House RH5 178 C5
Capern Rd SW18 20 C7
Capital Ind Est CR4 40 F4
Capital Pk GU22 90 B6
Caplan Est CR4 41 C8
Capper Rd GU15 65 A7
Capri Rd CR0 42 F2
Capricorn Cl RH11 200 E4
Capsey Rd RH11 200 E6
Capstans Wharf 7 GU21 68 F1
Capstone Rd BR1 24 F4
Caradon Cl GU21 69 B1
Caradon Ct 7 TW1 6 C1
Caraway Cl RH11 201 B2
Caraway Pl Guildford GU2 109 A6
Hackbridge SM6 60 B7
Carberry Rd 11 SE19 22 E2
Carbery La SL5 29 B6
Card Hill RH18 206 F1
Cardamom Cl GU2 109 A5
Cardigan Cl GU21 68 F1
Cardigan Rd Richmond TW10 6 E1
Wimbledon SW19 20 C2
Cardinal Ave
Kingston u T KT2 17 E2
West Barnes SM4 39 E3
Cardinal Cl
West Barnes SM4 39 E3
Worcester Park KT19, KT4 58 A6
Cardinal Cres KT3 38 C7
Cardinal Dr KT12 35 D1
Cardinal Newman RC Sch
KT12 54 D7
Cardinal Rd TW13 15 B7
Cardinal Road Inf Sch
TW13 15 B7
Cardinal's Wlk
Ashford TW16 14 E2
Hampton TW12 16 C1
Cardingham GU21 69 B2
Cardington Sq TW4 4 D3
Cardwell Cres SL5 29 C4
Cardwells Keep GU2 109 A4
Carew Cl CR5 100 B8
Carew Ct SM2 59 B2
Carew House SW16 22 A5
Carew Manor Sch SM6 60 D7
Carew Rd Ashford TW15 14 C2
Mitcham CR4 41 A7
Thornton Heath CR7 42 B5
Wallington SM6 60 C4
Carey House RH11 201 C6
Carey Rd RG40 25 C5
Carey's Copse RH6 162 B3
Carey's Wood RH6 162 B3
Carfax RH12 217 C2
Carfax Ave GU10 126 F8
Cargate Ave GU11 105 A1
Cargate Gr GU11 105 A1
Cargate Hill GU11 104 F1
Cargate Terr GU11 104 F1
Cargill Rd SW18 20 C7
Cargo Forecourt Rd RH6 181 D7
Cargo Rd RH6 181 D7
Cargreen Rd SE25 42 F5
Carholme Rd SE23 23 F7
Carisbrook Ct 1 SW16 21 F5
Carisbrooke GU16 85 F8
Carisbrooke Ct SM2 58 F3
Carisbrooke Rd CR4 41 E5
Carleton Ave SM6 60 D2
Carleton Cl KT10 36 D1
Carlingford Gdns CR4 21 A1
Carlingford Rd SM4 39 D3
Carlinwark Dr GU15 65 F7
Carlisle Cl KT2 38 A8
Carlisle Inf Sch TW12 16 B2
Carlisle Rd Cheam SM1 58 F4
Hampton TW12 16 B1
Rushmoor GU10 168 C6
Carlisle Way SW17 21 A3
Carlos St GU7 150 E4
Carlton Ave Feltham TW14 4 C1
South Croydon CR2 61 E3
Carlton Cl Chessington KT9 56 D4
Frimley GU15 66 B3
Woking GU21 70 A5
Carlton Cres SM3 58 E6
Carlton Ct Horley RH6 161 A5
12 Penge SE20 43 B8
South Norwood SE19 42 F8
Staines TW18 13 A3
Carlton Gn RH1 118 E4
Carlton House Cheam SM1 58 F4
Hounslow TW4 5 A1
Carlton Park Ave SW20 39 D7
Carlton Rd Ashford TW16 14 F1
Blindley Heath RH9 142 C2
Headley Down GU35 187 C5
Kingston u T KT3 38 E7
Mortlake SW14 7 C3
Redhill RH1 118 E4
South Croydon CR2 61 D3
Walton-on-T KT12 35 B2
Woking GU21 70 A5
Carlton Terr SE26 23 C5
Carlton Tye RH6 161 C3
Carlwell St SW17 20 E3
Carlyle Cl KT8 36 B7
Carlyle Ct RG45 45 C5

Carlyle Rd Croydon CR0 62 A8
Staines TW18 13 A1
Carlyon Cl
Farnborough GU14 85 C4
Mytchett GU16 85 F4
Carlys Cl BR3 43 D7
Carmalt Gdns KT12 54 C5
Carman Wlk RH11 201 B1
Carmarthen Cl GU14 85 A7
Carmel Cl 9 GU22 69 E1
Carmichael Ct SW13 7 F5
Carmichael House 17
SE21 22 E4
Carmichael Mews SW18 20 D8
Carmichael Rd SE25 43 A5
Carminia Rd SW17 21 B6
Carnac St SE21, SE27 22 D5
Carnation Dr RG42 8 B2
Carnegie Cl KT6 56 F8
Carnegie Pl SW19 19 D5
Carnforth Cl KT19 57 B4
Carnforth Rd SW16 21 D1
Carnoustie RG12 26 E2
Carole House 14 SE20 43 B8
Carolina Rd CR7 42 C8
Caroline Cl Hounslow TW7 5 E7
South Croydon CR0 61 E6
Streatham SW16 21 F5
Caroline Ct Ashford TW15 14 B2
Catford SE6 24 D4
Crawley RH11 201 D4
17 Surbiton KT6 37 D2
Caroline Dr RG41 25 A7
Caroline Pl UB3 3 E7
Caroline Rd SW19 19 F1
Carolyn Cl GU21 88 F8
Carpenter Cl KT17 57 F2
Carpenters Ct TW2 16 E6
Carrick Cl TW7 6 A4
Carrick Gate KT10 55 C7
Carrington Ave TW3 5 B2
Carrington Cl Croydon CR0 43 E2
Redhill RH1 118 F2
Carrington Lodge 3 TW10 6 E2
Carrington Pl KT10 55 C6
Carrington Rd TW10 7 A3
Carrinton La GU12 106 A8
Carroll Ave GU1 110 B1
Carroll Cres SL5 28 F5
Carrow Rd KT12 54 D7
Carshalton Beeches Sta
SM5 59 F4
Carshalton Coll SM5 59 F7
Carshalton Gr SM1 59 D5
Carshalton High Sch for
Boys SM5 59 E8
Carshalton High Sch for
Girls SM5 59 E7
Carshalton Lodge KT13 53 E7
Carshalton Park Rd SM5 59 F5
Carshalton Pl SM5 60 A5
Carshalton Rd
Camberley GU15 47 A1
Carshalton SM1, SM5 59 D5
Mitcham CR4 41 A4
Sutton SM1, SM5 59 D5
Wallington SM7 78 F6
Woodmansterne SM7 78 F6
Carshalton Sta SM5 59 F6
Carson Rd SE21 22 D6
Carstairs Rd SE6 24 C5
Carswell Rd SE6 24 C8
Cartbridge Cl GU23 90 B4
Carter Cl SM6 60 D3
Carter Rd Crawley RH10 202 D3
Mitcham SW19 20 D2
Carter's Cotts RH1 139 E7
Carter's Rd KT17 76 F4
Carterdale Cotts RH5 178 C5
Carters Cl KT4 39 D1
Carters La GU22 90 D7
Carters Wlk GU9 125 D8
Cartersmead Cl RH6 161 B4
Carthouse Cotts GU4 110 C4
Carthouse La GU21 68 E5
Cartmel Cl RH2 118 E3
Cartmel Ct BR2 44 E7
Cartmel Gdns SM4 40 C4
Carwarden House Sch
GU15 66 A3
Caryl House 6 SW19 19 D7
Carylls Cotts RH12 199 F1
Cascades CR0 62 F1
Caselden Cl KT15 52 C5
Casewick Rd SE27 22 B4
Casher Rd RH10 202 C3
Cassel Hospl The TW10 17 D4
Cassilis Rd TW1 6 B1
Cassino Cl GU11 105 B2
Cassiobury Ave TW14 14 F8
Cassland Rd CR7 42 D5
Casslee Rd SE6 23 F8
Cassocks Sq TW17 34 D2
Castillon Rd SE6 24 E6
Castlands Rd SE6 23 F6
Castle Ave KT17 58 B2
Castle Cl Beckenham BR2 44 E6
Bletchingley RH1 120 C2
Charlton TW16 14 E1
Frimley GU15 65 F4
Reigate RH2 139 B5
Wimbledon SW19 19 D5
Castle Ct Belmont SM2 59 A4
Forest Hill SE26 23 E4
Morden SM4 40 D4

Castle Dr Horley RH6 ...161 C2
Reigate RH2 ...139 B4
Castle Gdns RH4 ...115 F1
Castle Gn KT13 ...53 E7
Castle Grove Rd GU24 ...68 E7
Castle Hill Farnham GU9 ..125 B3
Guildford GU1 ...130 D7
Castle Hill Ave CR0 ...63 C2
Castle Hill Prim Sch CR0 .63 C4
Castle Hill Rd TW20 ...11 C5
Castle House 10 SM2 ...59 A3
Castle Par KT17 ...58 A3
Castle Rd Aldershot GU11 .104 E4
Broadbridge Heath RH12 ..216 D3
Camberley GU15 ...65 F4
Epsom KT18 ...76 B4
Isleworth TW7 ...5 F5
Kingswood CR5 ...98 E6
Oatlands Park KT13 ...53 E7
Woking GU21 ...69 F5
Castle Sq Bletchingley RH1 120 C2
Guildford GU1 ...130 D7
Castle St Bletchingley RH1 .120 C2
Farnham GU9 ...125 B3
Guildford GU1 ...130 D7
Kingston u T KT2 ...37 E7
Castle The RH12 ...217 E7
Castle View KT18 ...76 B5
Castle View Rd KT13 ...53 B6
Castle Way Ewell KT17 ...58 A2
Feltham TW13 ...15 C4
Wimbledon SW19 ...19 D5
Castle Wlk TW16 ...35 C6
Castle Yd 17 TW10 ...6 D2
Castlecombe Dr SW19 ...19 D8
Castlecraig Ct GU47 ...64 D7
Castledine Rd SE20 ...23 B1
Castlefield Rd RH2 ...118 A1
Castlegate TW9 ...6 F4
Castlemaine Ave
Ewell KT17 ...58 B2
South Croydon CR0, CR2 ...61 F5
Castleman House SL5 ...29 D4
Castleton Cl Banstead SM7 .78 A4
Croydon CR0 ...43 E3
Castleton Ct KT5 ...37 F4
Castleton Dr SM7 ...78 A5
Castleton Rd CR4 ...41 D5
Caswell Cl GU14 ...84 F6
Catalina Rd TW6 ...3 A4
Catalpa Cl GU1 ...109 C3
Catena Rise GU18 ...48 B1
Cater Gdns GU3 ...108 F3
Caterfield La
Crowhurst RH7 ...143 F3
Oxted RH7, RH8 ...144 A5
Caterham By-Pass CR3 ..101 B4
Caterham Cl GU24 ...87 E6
Caterham Dene Hospl
CR3 ...100 F4
Caterham
Dr CR3, CR5, CR8 ...100 C8
Caterham Sch CR3 ...100 F1
Caterham Sch Prep CR3 .100 F1
Caterham Sta CR3 ...101 A3
Caterways RH12 ...217 A3
Catford Bridge Sta SE6 ...24 A8
Catford Broadway SE6 ...24 B8
Catford Cty Sch SE6 ...24 C5
Catford Cty Sch (Annexe)
BR1 ...24 E4
Catford Hill SE6 ...24 A7
Catford Rd SE6 ...24 A8
Catford Sta SE6 ...24 A8
Cathedral Cl GU2 ...130 B8
Cathedral Hill Ind Est
GU2 ...109 A2
Cathedral View GU2 ...108 F1
Catherine Baird Ct 12
SW12 ...21 B8
Catherine Cl KT14 ...71 F5
Catherine Ct 3 SW19 ...19 F3
Catherine Dr TW16 ...14 F2
Catherine Drive TW9 ...6 E3
Catherine Gdns TW3 ...5 D3
Catherine Howard Ct 6
KT13 ...53 B7
Catherine Rd KT6 ...37 D4
Catherine Wheel Rd TW8 ..6 D7
Catherington Sch RH11 .181 D2
Cathill La RH5 ...177 C3
Cathles Rd SW12 ...21 C8
Catlin Cres TW17 ...34 D4
Catlin Gdns RH9 ...121 B5
Catling Cl SE23 ...23 D5
Caton Ct BR2 ...44 E7
Cator Cl CR0 ...82 E8
Cator Cres CR0 ...82 E8
Cator La BR3 ...43 F8
Cator Park Girls Sch BR3 .23 E1
Cator Rd Penge SE20, SE26 .23 D2
Wallington SM5 ...59 F5
Catteshall Hatch GU7 ...151 A6
Catteshall La GU7 ...150 F4
Catteshall Rd GU7 ...151 A5
Catteshall Terr GU7 ...151 A5
Catteshall Wks GU7 ...151 A6
Causeway TW14, TW4 ...4 B3
Causeway Ct 1 GU21 ...68 F1
Causeway Est TW20 ...12 C4
Causeway The
Carshalton SM5 ...60 A8
Claygate KT10 ...55 F3
Egham TW18, TW20 ...12 D4
Horsham RH12 ...217 C1
Causeway The *continued*
Sutton SM2 ...59 C2
Teddington TW11 ...16 F2
Wimbledon SW19 ...19 C3
Cavalier Way RH19 ...205 F7
Cavalry Cres TW4 ...4 D3
Cavalry Ct GU11 ...104 E2
Cavans Rd GU11 ...105 C6
Cave Rd TW10 ...17 C4
Cavell Rd RH10 ...202 C5
Cavendish Ave KT3 ...39 B5
Cavendish Cl Ashford TW16 14 F2
Horsham RH12 ...217 D7
Cavendish Ct Ashford TW16 14 F2
Blackwater GU17 ...64 D3
Poyle SL3 ...1 E6
Cavendish Dr KT10 ...55 E5
Cavendish Gdns RH1 ...119 A2
Cavendish House TW1 ...6 A1
Cavendish Jun & Inf Sch
W4 ...7 E7
Cavendish Meads SL5 ...29 D3
Cavendish Mews GU11 ..105 A1
Cavendish Rd
Aldershot GU11 ...105 A1
Ashford TW16 ...14 F2
Balham SW12 ...21 B8
Chiswick W4 ...7 C6
Mitcham SW19 ...20 E1
New Malden KT3 ...38 F5
Redhill RH1 ...119 A2
Sutton SM2 ...59 C3
Thornton Heath CR0 ...42 B1
Weybridge KT13 ...53 C3
Woking GU22 ...89 D8
Cavendish Terr TW13 ...15 A6
Cavendish Way BR4 ...44 B1
Cavenham Cl GU22 ...89 E8
Caverleigh Way KT4 ...39 B2
Caversham Ave SM3 ...58 E8
Caversham House 8 KT1 .37 E7
Caversham Rd KT1 ...37 F7
Caves Farm Cl GU47 ...64 A8
Cawnpore St SE19 ...22 E3
Cawsey Way GU21 ...69 E2
Cawston Ct BR1 ...24 F1
Caxton Ave KT15 ...52 A4
Caxton Cl RH10 ...201 E3
Caxton Gdns GU2 ...109 B2
Caxton House RH8 ...123 F3
Caxton La RH8 ...123 E4
Caxton Rd SW19 ...20 C3
Caxton Rise RH1 ...119 A2
Caxtons Ct GU1 ...110 A3
Caygill Cl BR2 ...44 F5
Cayley Cl SM6 ...60 E3
Cearn Way CR5 ...79 F4
Cecil Cl Ashford TW15 ...14 C1
Chessington KT9 ...56 D6
Cecil Ct 9 CR0 ...61 F8
Cecil Lodge KT9 ...56 D6
Cecil Mansions 2 SW17 ..21 A6
Cecil Pl CR4 ...40 F4
Cecil Rd Ashford TW15 ...14 C2
Cheam SM1, SM2 ...58 F4
Hounslow TW3 ...5 C5
Merton SW19 ...20 B1
Thornton Heath CR0 ...41 F3
Cedar Ave Blackwater GU17 64 D5
Cobham KT11 ...73 C4
Twickenham TW2 ...5 C1
Cedar Cl Aldershot GU12 ..126 E8
Bagshot GU19 ...47 E3
Crawley RH11 ...181 C1
Dorking RH4 ...136 B7
East Molesey KT8 ...36 E5
Epsom KT17 ...76 F5
Esher KT10 ...54 F3
Horsham RH12 ...217 C3
Kingston u T KT2 ...18 D4
Laleham TW18 ...33 C6
Reigate RH2 ...139 C7
Wallington SM5 ...59 F4
Warlingham CR6 ...101 E8
West Norwood SE21 ...22 C6
Wokingham RG40 ...25 C6
Cedar Ct 8 Brentford TW8 ..6 D8
Egham TW20 ...12 A4
Haslemere GU27 ...208 B6
Mortlake SW14 ...7 C3
Ottershaw KT16 ...51 C5
Sanderstead CR2 ...81 A8
Stoneleigh KT17 ...58 A3
Sutton SM2 ...59 C4
Wimbledon SW19 ...19 D5
Cedar Dr Fetcham KT22 ...94 E4
Sunningdale SL5 ...30 A2
Cedar Gdns Sutton SM2 ...59 C4
Woking GU21 ...69 B1
Cedar Gr Bisley GU24 ...68 A4
Weybridge KT13 ...53 C6
Cedar Hill KT18 ...76 C3
Cedar House
Charlton TW16 ...14 F1
New Addington CR0 ...63 B4
Cedar Hts TW10 ...17 E7
Cedar La GU16 ...85 D8
Cedar Lodge
Crawley RH11 ...201 D4
Milford GU8 ...149 F2
Cedar Rd Cobham KT11 ...73 B5
Cranford TW5 ...4 C5
Croydon CR0, CR9 ...61 E8
East Bedfont TW14 ...14 D7
East Molesey KT8 ...36 E5
Farnborough GU14 ...85 C3
Sutton SM2 ...59 C4
Teddington TW11 ...17 A3
Cedar Rd *continued*
Weybridge KT13 ...53 A6
Woking GU22 ...89 C7
Cedar Terr TW9 ...6 E3
Cedar Tree Gr SE27 ...22 B3
Cedar Way Charlton TW16 ..14 E1
Guildford GU1 ...109 C4
Cedar Wlk Claygate KT10 ...55 F4
Kenley CR8 ...80 C3
Kingswood KT20 ...97 E7
Cedarcroft Rd KT9 ...56 F6
Cedars 2 Bracknell RG12 ...27 F5
Woodmansterne SM7 ...78 F5
Cedars Ave CR4 ...41 A6
Cedars Ct GU1 ...110 A4
Cedars House 5 SW27 ...22 B3
Cedars Prim Sch The TW5 .4 A7
Cedars Rd Barnes SW13 ...7 F5
Beckenham BR3 ...43 F7
Morden SM4 ...40 A5
Teddington KT8 ...37 C8
Wallington CR0 ...60 E6
Cedars The
Ashstead KT21, KT22 ...95 D6
Byfleet KT14 ...71 F7
Guildford GU1 ...110 A4
Milford GU8 ...170 E8
Reigate RH2 ...118 D1
Teddington TW11 ...16 F2
Wallington SM6 ...60 C6
Cedarville Gdns SW16 ...21 F2
Cedarways GU9 ...146 B7
Celandine Cl
1 Crawley RH11 ...201 B2
Crowthorne RG45 ...45 C6
Celandine Rd KT12 ...54 E6
Celia Cres TW15 ...13 D2
Celia Ct 7 TW9 ...6 F6
Celtic Ave BR2 ...44 E6
Celtic Rd KT14 ...71 F5
Cemetery La TW17 ...34 B2
Cemetery Pales
Brookwood GU24 ...88 A6
Pirbright GU24 ...87 F5
Centaurs Bsns Pk TW7 ...6 A8
Central Ave
East Molesey KT8 ...35 F4
Isleworth TW3, TW7 ...5 C3
Wallington SM6 ...60 E5
Central Ct KT15 ...52 B6
Central Hill SE19, SE27 ...22 D2
Central La SL4 ...9 B7
Central Par Feltham TW14 ..15 C8
Heston TW5 ...5 A7
Kingston u T KT6 ...37 E3
New Addington CR0, CR9 ...63 C1
Penge SE20 ...23 D1
Central Pk Est TW4 ...4 D3
Central Rd Morden SM4 ...40 B4
North Cheam KT4 ...58 A8
Central Sq KT8 ...35 F5
Central Terr BR3 ...43 D6
Central Veterinary
Laboratory KT15 ...52 B2
Central Way Feltham TW14 ..4 B2
Oxted RH8 ...122 D8
Sutton SM5 ...59 E3
Winkfield SL4 ...9 B7
Central Wlk RG40 ...25 C6
Centre The Feltham TW13 ..15 B6
Walton-on-T KT12 ...34 F1
Centurion Cl 4 GU47 ...64 D8
Centurion Ct SM6 ...60 B8
Century Rd TW20 ...12 C3
Century Way GU24 ...87 D8
Cerne Rd SM4 ...40 C3
Cerotus Pl KT16 ...32 F2
Chadacre Rd KT17 ...58 B5
Chadhurst Cl RH5 ...136 D4
Chadwick Ave SW19 ...20 A2
Chadwick Cl
Crawley RH11 ...201 B1
Teddington TW11 ...17 A2
Chadworth Way KT10 ...55 D5
Chaffers Mead KT21 ...75 F3
Chaffinch Ave CR0 ...43 D3
Chaffinch Cl
Crawley RH11 ...201 D8
Croydon CR0 ...43 D3
Horsham RH12 ...217 D7
5 Sandhurst GU47 ...64 D8
Tolworth KT6 ...57 A7
Chaffinch Rd BR3 ...43 E8
Chaffinch Way RH6 ...160 E4
Chagford Ct SW19 ...20 E1
Chailey Cl
3 Crawley RH11 ...201 A3
Heston TW5 ...4 D6
Chailey Pl KT12 ...54 E6
Chalcot Cl SM2 ...59 A3
Chalcot Mews SW16 ...21 E5
Chalcott Gdns KT6 ...37 C1
Chaldon Cl RH1 ...139 E7
Chaldon Common Rd
CR3 ...100 C2
Chaldon Rd Caterham CR3 100 D4
Crawley RH11 ...201 C1
Chaldon Way CR5 ...79 E1
Chale Wlk SM2 ...59 B2
Chalet Ct CR7 ...42 B4
Chalfont Dr GU14 ...85 C2
Chalfont Rd SE25 ...42 F6
Chalford Cl KT8 ...36 A5
Chalford Ct KT6 ...37 F2
Chalford Rd SE21 ...22 D4
Chalgrove Ave SM4 ...40 A4
Chalgrove Rd SM2 ...59 D3
Chalice Cl SM6 ...60 D4
Chalk La Ashstead KT21 ...96 A8
East Horsley KT24 ...112 F4
Epsom KT18 ...76 E3
Shackleford GU8 ...149 D8
Chalk Paddock KT18 ...76 D4
Chalk Pit Rd Banstead SM7 78 A2
Langley Vale KT18, KT21 ...96 C8
Sutton SM1 ...59 C5
Chalk Rd Farncombe GU7 .150 E5
Ifold RH14 ...212 C3
Chalkenden Cl SE20 ...23 B1
Chalkley Cl CR4 ...41 A7
Chalkpit La Dorking RH4 ..136 A8
Oxted RH8 ...122 D8
Woldingham CR3, RH8 ...102 C1
Chalkpit Terr RH4 ...115 A1
Chalkpit Wood RH8 ...122 D8
Chalky La KT9 ...56 D1
Challen Ct RH12 ...217 B3
Challenge Ct KT22 ...95 B8
Challenge Rd TW15 ...14 D5
Challice Way SW2 ...21 F7
Challin St SE20 ...43 C8
Challis Pl RG42 ...26 E8
Challock Cl TN16 ...83 C3
Challoner Ct BR2 ...44 D7
Challoners Cl KT8 ...36 D5
Chalmers Ct RH6 ...180 E6
Chalmers Rd Ashford TW15 14 B3
Banstead SM7 ...78 C4
Chalmers Rd E TW15 ...14 C3
Chalmers Way TW14 ...4 B2
Chalner House 21 SW2 ...22 A7
Chamber La GU10 ...145 C7
Chamberlain Cres BR4 ...44 B2
Chamberlain Way KT6 ...37 E2
Chamberlain Wlk TW13 ...15 E4
Chambers House 2 SW16 .21 C4
Chambers Rd GU12 ...106 B6
Chamomile Gdns GU14 ...84 C5
Champion Cres SE26 ...23 E4
Champion Rd SE26 ...23 E4
Champness Cl 9 SE27 ...22 D4
Champneys Cl SM2 ...58 F3
Chancellor Gdns CR2 ...61 B2
Chancellor Gr SE21 ...22 C5
Chancery La BR3 ...44 B7
Chanctonbury Chase
RH1 ...119 A1
Chanctonbury Dr SL5 ...29 E1
Chanctonbury Gdns SM2 ..59 B3
Chanctonbury Way RH11 201 C4
Chandler CE (VA) Jun
Sch GU8 ...170 F5
Chandler Cl
Crawley RH10, RH11 ...201 D4
Hampton TW12 ...36 A8
Chandler Ct
2 Tolworth KT5 ...38 B1
8 Wallington SM6 ...60 B4
Chandlers KT20 ...97 B6
Chandlers Cl TW14 ...14 F8
Chandlers Field Sch KT8 .36 A4
Chandlers Rd GU12 ...106 B4
Chandlers Way 11 SE24 ...22 A8
Chandon Lodge SM2 ...59 C3
Chandos Rd TW18 ...12 D3
Channel Cl TW5 ...5 A6
Channings GU21 ...69 E4
Channon Ct 3 KT6 ...37 E4
Chantlers Cl RH19 ...185 C2
Chanton Dr SM2 ...58 C1
Chantrey Cl KT21 ...95 C8
Chantrey Rd RH10 ...201 E3
Chantry Cl Farnham GU9 ..125 A2
Horley RH6 ...160 F4
Chantry Cotts GU4 ...131 B3
Chantry Ct GU16 ...65 D1
Chantry Hurst KT18 ...76 D4
Chantry La GU5 ...132 F4
Chantry Rd Bagshot GU19 ..47 D2
Chertsey KT16 ...33 C2
Chessington KT9 ...57 A5
Chilworth GU4 ...131 B3
Chantry View Rd GU1 ...130 E6
Chantry Way CR4 ...40 D6
Chantry Wood Nature
Trail GU1 ...130 E5
Chantrys Ct GU9 ...125 A2
Chantrys The GU9 ...125 A1
Chapel Ave KT15 ...52 B6
Chapel Cl Bracknell RG12 ..27 D6
Milford GU8 ...149 F2
Chapel Ct RH4 ...136 A7
Chapel Farm Park RH5 ...115 A5
Chapel Fields GU7 ...150 D7
Chapel Gn CR8 ...80 A6
Chapel Gr Addlestone KT15 .52 B6
Burgh Heath KT18 ...97 C8
Chapel Hill Dunsfold GU8 .192 F3
Effingham KT24 ...113 D8
Chapel La
Ashurst Wood RH19 ...206 D6
Bagshot GU19 ...47 D2
Copthorne RH10 ...183 F4
Farnborough GU14 ...84 F8
Forest Row RH18 ...206 F2
Great Bookham KT23 ...114 D5
Milford GU8 ...149 F2
Pirbright GU24 ...88 A4
Westcott RH4 ...135 C6
Westhumble RH5 ...114 D5
Chapel Lane Ind Est RH4 135 C6
Chapel Park Rd KT15 ...52 B6
Chapel Rd Camberley GU15 .65 B5
Charlwood RH6 ...180 F7
Hounslow TW3 ...5 B4
Limpsfield RH8 ...123 C5
Chapel Rd *continued*
Redhill RH1 ...118 F1
Rowledge GU10 ...145 E3
Smallfield RH6 ...162 B4
Tadworth KT20 ...97 D4
Twickenham TW1 ...17 B8
Warlingham CR6 ...81 D1
West Norwood SE27 ...22 B4
Chapel Sq Sandhurst GU15 .64 F6
Thorpe GU25 ...31 E5
Chapel St
Farnborough GU14 ...85 D6
Guildford GU1 ...130 D7
6 Woking GU21 ...69 F2
Chapel View CR2 ...62 C3
Chapel Way KT18, KT20 ...77 C1
Chapelhouse Cl GU2 ...108 E1
Chaplain's Hill RG45 ...45 D4
Chaplin Cres TW16 ...14 E2
Chapman House 2 SE27 ..22 B5
Chapman Rd
Crawley RH10 ...202 C2
Thornton Heath CR0 ...42 A1
Chapman's La
East Grinstead RH19 ...185 B1
East Grinstead RH19 ...185 D1
Chapter Way TW12 ...16 A4
Chara Pl W4 ...7 D8
Charcot House SW15 ...7 F1
Chargate Cl KT12 ...54 A4
Charing Ct BR2 ...44 E7
Charlbury Cl 7 RG12 ...27 F5
Charlecombe Ct TW18 ...13 B3
Charlecote Cl GU14 ...85 D3
Charlecote Gr SE26 ...23 B5
Charles Ct 5 TW11 ...16 E3
Charles Darwin Sch TN16 83 F3
Charles Dickens Ct SE25 ..43 A5
Charles Hill GU10 ...147 E6
Charles Mills Ct SW16 ...21 E2
Charles Rd Merton SW19 ..40 A8
Staines TW18 ...13 D2
Charles Sq RG12 ...27 C7
Charles St Chertsey KT16 ...32 F1
Croydon CR0, CR9 ...61 C7
Hounslow TW3 ...4 F5
Mortlake SW13, SW14 ...7 E5
Charles Staunton House
SE27 ...22 D4
Charlesfield Rd RH6 ...160 F4
Charleston Cl TW13 ...15 A5
Charleston Ct RH10 ...202 B3
Charleville Cir SE19, SE26 .23 A3
Charlmont Rd SW17 ...20 F2
Charlock Cl RH11 ...201 A2
Charlock Way GU1 ...110 B4
Charlotte Cl GU9 ...125 D8
Charlotte Ct RH11 ...201 C6
Charlotte Gr RH6 ...162 A4
Charlotte Mews 3 KT10 ..55 B6
Charlotte Rd Barnes SW13 ..7 F6
Wallington SM6 ...60 C4
Charlotte Sq 5 TW10 ...6 F1
Charlton Ave KT12 ...54 B6
Charlton Ct GU47 ...45 D1
Charlton Dr TN16 ...83 D2
Charlton Gdns CR5 ...79 C1
Charlton Ho 5 TW8 ...6 E8
Charlton Kings KT13 ...53 E7
Charlton La TW17 ...34 D5
Charlton Rd TW17 ...34 C7
Charlwood CR0 ...62 F2
Charlwood Cl KT23 ...94 B3
Charlwood Cty Inf Sch
RH6 ...180 F7
Charlwood Dr KT22 ...74 D4
Charlwood House 1 SW2 .21 F7
Charlwood La RH5 ...180 A5
Charlwood Rd
Crawley RH6, RH11 ...181 C4
Hookwood RH6, RH11 ...181 C8
Rusper RH11, RH6 ...180 E2
Charlwood Sq CR4 ...40 D6
Charlwood Wlk RH11 ...181 B1
Charlwoods Bsns Ctr
RH19 ...185 D2
Charlwoods Pl RH19 ...185 E3
Charlwoods Rd RH19 ...185 E3
Charm Cl RH6 ...160 E4
Charman Rd RH1 ...118 E1
Charmans Cl RH12 ...218 B5
Charminster Ave SW19 ...40 B7
Charminster Ct 3 KT6 ...37 D2
Charminster Rd KT4 ...39 D1
Charmouth Ct TW10 ...6 F2
Charnwood SL5 ...29 F3
Charnwood Ave SW19 ...40 B7
Charnwood Cl KT3 ...38 E5
Charnwood Rd SE25 ...42 D5
Charrington Rd 2
CR0, CR9 ...61 C8
Charrington Way RH12 ..216 C3
Charsley Rd SE6 ...24 B6
Chart Cl Bromley BR2 ...44 E8
Croydon CR0 ...43 C3
Dorking RH5 ...136 D5
Mitcham CR4 ...40 F5
Chart Downs RH5 ...136 D4
Chart Gdns RH5 ...136 C4
Chart House Rd GU12 ...106 A7
Chart La Dorking RH4, RH5 136 C7
Reigate RH2 ...139 C8
Chart La S RH5 ...136 D5
Charta Rd TW20 ...12 C2
Charta Rd E TW20 ...12 C2
Charta Rd S TW20 ...12 C2
Charta Rd W TW20 ...12 C3
Charter Cres TW4 ...4 E3

Charter Ct KT3 . . . . .38 E6
Charter Rd KT1 . . . . .38 B6
Charter Sq KT1 . . . . .38 B7
Charterhouse GU7 . . . . . .150 C7
Charterhouse Cl RG12 . . . .27 E4
Charterhouse Rd GU7 . . .150 D6
Charters Cl SE19 . . . . .22 E3
Charters La SL5 . . . . .29 D4
Charters Rd SL5 . . . . .29 E2
Charters Sch SL5 . . . . .29 D2
Charters Way SL5 . . . . .29 F2
Chartfield Rd RH2 . . . . . . .139 C8
Chartham Gr SE27 . . . . .22 B5
Chartham Rd SE25 . . . . . . .43 B6
Charts Cl GU6 . . . . .174 E2
Chartway RH2 . . . . .118 B1
Chartwell Frimley GU16 . . . .85 F6
25 Putney SW19 . . . . .19 D7
Wrecclesham GU9 . . . . .145 F6
Chartwell Cl 2 CR0 . . . . . .42 D1
Chartwell Court Grange
RH4 . . . . .136 B4
Chartwell Gdns
Cheam SM3 . . . . .58 E6
Farnborough GU11 . . . . . . .105 C7
Chartwell Lodge 5 BR3 . . .24 A1
Chartwell Pl Cheam SM3 . . .58 F6
Epsom KT18 . . . . .76 E5
Chartwell Way 4 SE20 . . . .43 B8
Charwood SW16 . . . . .22 A4
Charwood Rd RG40 . . . . . . .25 F7
Chase Bridge Inf Sch TW2 .5 E1
Chase Bridge Jun Sch TW2 5 E1
Chase Cotts GU26 . . . . . . .188 C1
Chase Ct Isleworth TW7 . . . . .6 A5
Merton SW20 . . . . .39 E7
Chase End KT19 . . . . .76 D7
Chase Gdns TW2 . . . . .16 D8
Chase La GU27 . . . . .208 E3
Chase Rd KT17, KT19 . . . . . .76 D7
Chase The Ashstead KT21 . .75 C1
Coulsdon CR5 . . . . .79 D5
Crawley RH10 . . . . .202 A5
Crowthorne RG45 . . . . .45 A6
East Horsley KT24 . . . . .92 F1
Farnborough GU14 . . . . .85 D6
Guildford GU2 . . . . .130 A8
Kingswood KT20 . . . . .98 B6
Oxshott KT22 . . . . .74 C4
Reigate RH2 . . . . .139 D8
South Norwood SW16 . . . . . .22 A1
Sunbury TW16 . . . . .35 B8
Wallington CR0, SM6 . . . . . . .60 F5
Chasefield Cl GU1, GU4 . .110 A4
Chasefield Rd SW17 . . . . . .20 F4
Chaseley Ct KT13 . . . . .34 E1
Chasemore Cl CR4 . . . . . . .40 F2
Chasemore Gdns CR0 . . . .61 A5
Chaseside Ave SW20 . . . . .39 E7
Chaseside Gdns KT16 . . . . .33 B2
Chasewater Ct 5 GU11 . .105 A1
Chatelet Cl RH6 . . . . .161 B4
Chatfield Cl GU14 . . . . .85 C2
Chatfield Ct CR3 . . . . .100 D5
Chatfield Dr GU4 . . . . .110 C3
Chatfield Rd CR0 . . . . .42 B1
Chatfields RH11 . . . . .201 B4
Chatham Ave BR2 . . . . .44 F2
Chatham Cl SM3 . . . . .39 F2
Chatham Rd KT1, KT2 . . . . .38 A7
Chathill RH8 . . . . .143 B6
Chatley Heath
Semaphore Tower KT11 . .72 D1
Chatsfield KT17 . . . . .58 A1
Chatsworth Ave
Haslemere GU27 . . . . .208 C8
Merton SW20 . . . . .39 F7
Chatsworth Cl BR2, BR4 . . .63 F8
Chatsworth Cres TW3, TW7 .5 D4
Chatsworth Gdns KT3 . . . . .38 F4
Chatsworth Gr GU9 . . . . . .125 B6
Chatsworth House KT6 . . .37 D4
Chatsworth Hts GU15 . . . . .66 B7
Chatsworth Inf Sch TW3 . . .5 C3
Chatsworth Jun Sch TW3 . .5 C3
Chatsworth Lodge BR4 . . .63 C8
Chatsworth Pl Mitcham CR4 40 F6
Oxshott KT22 . . . . .74 D6
Teddington TW11 . . . . .17 A4
Chatsworth Rd Cheam SM3 58 E6
Chiswick W4 . . . . .7 C8
Croydon CR0, CR9 . . . . .61 D7
Farnborough GU14 . . . . .85 E3
Chatsworth Way SE27 . . . .22 C5
Chattern Hill TW15 . . . . . . .14 B4
Chattern Rd TW15 . . . . .14 C4
Chatterton Ct TW9 . . . . .6 F5
Chatton Row GU24 . . . . . . .68 A2
Chaucer Ave Cranford TW4 . .4 B5
3 East Grinstead RH19 . . .185 C1
Richmond TW9 . . . . .7 A5
Weybridge KT13 . . . . .53 A3
Chaucer Cl Banstead SM7 . .77 E5
Wokingham RG40 . . . . .25 F6
Chaucer Ct GU2 . . . . .130 C7
Chaucer Gdns SM1 . . . . . . .59 A7
Chaucer Gn CR0 . . . . .43 C2
Chaucer Gr GU15 . . . . .65 D5
Chaucer House Sutton SM1 59 A7
2 West Norwood SE27 . . . . .22 C4
Chaucer Rd Ashford TW15 . .13 F4
Crawley RH10 . . . . .202 C8
Crowthorne RG45 . . . . .45 B4
Farnborough GU14 . . . . .84 F6
Sutton SM1 . . . . .59 A6
Chaucer Way KT15 . . . . . . .52 A4
Chavey Down Rd RG42 . . . . .8 B2
Chaworth Cl KT16 . . . . .51 C4
Chaworth Rd KT16 . . . . . . .51 C4
Chawridge La SL4 . . . . .8 C7
Cheam Cl Bracknell RG12 . .27 D4
Burgh Heath KT20 . . . . .97 B6
Cheam Common Inf Sch
KT4 . . . . .58 B8
Cheam Common Jun Sch
KT4 . . . . .58 B8
Cheam Common Rd KT4 . .58 C7
Cheam Court Flats SM3 . . .58 E4
Cheam Fields Prim Sch
SM3 .58 E5
Cheam High Sch SM3 . . . .58 E6
Cheam Mansions SM3 . . . .58 E3
Cheam Park Farm Inf Sch
SM3 .58 E7
Cheam Park Farm Jun Sch
SM3 .58 E7
Cheam Park Way SM3 . . . .58 E4
Cheam Rd Belmont SM2 . . .58 C1
Cheam SM1 . . . . .59 A4
East Ewell KT17, SM2 . . . . . .58 C1
Ewell SM2 . . . . .58 C1
Cheam Sta SM2 . . . . .58 E3
Cheapside GU21 . . . . .69 D5
Cheapside C of E Prim Sch
SL5 .29 E8
Cheapside Rd SL5 . . . . .29 D7
Cheddar Rd TW6 . . . . .3 A5
Cheeseman Cl
Hampton TW12 . . . . .15 E2
Wokingham RG40 . . . . .25 D7
Chelford Rd BR1, E6 . . . . . .24 D3
Chellows La RH7 . . . . .143 F2
Chelmsford Cl SM2 . . . . . . .59 A2
Chelsea Cl Hampton TW12 . .16 C3
New Malden KT4 . . . . .39 A2
Chelsea Fields SW19 . . . . .40 D8
Chelsea Gdns SM3 . . . . . . .58 E6
Chelsfield Gdns SE26 . . . . .23 C5
Chelsham Common Rd
CR6 .82 A3
Chelsham Court Rd CR6 . .82 E2
Chelsham Rd Croydon CR2 .61 D4
Warlingham CR6 . . . . .81 F2
Chelsham Terr CR6 . . . . . . .81 F1
Cheltenham Ave 9 TW1 . .17 A8
Cheltenham Cl KT3 . . . . . . .38 C6
Cheltenham Villas CR7 . . . .42 A3
Chelwood Cl
Crawley RH10 . . . . .201 F4
Ewell KT17 . . . . .76 F7
Chelwood Gdns TW9 . . . . . .7 A5
Cheney Ct SE23 . . . . .23 D7
Cheniston Cl KT14 . . . . .71 A6
Cheniston Ct SL5 . . . . .30 A2
Chennells Way RH12 . . . . .217 E5
Chennestone Cty Prim
Sch TW16 . . . . .35 B7
Chepstow Cl RH10 . . . . . .202 E6
Chepstow Rd CR0 . . . . .61 F8
Chequer Grange RH18 . . .206 E1
Chequer Rd RH19 . . . . . . .185 F1
Chequer Tree Cl GU21 . . . .68 E3
Chequers Cl Horley RH6 . .161 A4
Walton on t H KT20 . . . . .97 A2
Chequers Ct
7 Croydon CR0 . . . . .42 F1
Horsham RH13 . . . . .217 E2
Walton on t H KT20 . . . . .97 A2
Chequers Dr RH6 . . . . .161 A4
Chequers La KT20 . . . . .97 A2
Chequers Pl RH4 . . . . .136 B7
Cherbury Cl RG12 . . . . .27 E5
Cherimoya Gdns KT8 . . . . .36 B6
Cherington Way SL5 . . . . . .28 E7
Cheriton Ave BR2 . . . . .44 F4
Cheriton Ct
South Norwood SE25 . . . . . . .42 E4
Walton-on-T KT12 . . . . .35 C1
Cheriton Sq SW17 . . . . .21 A6
Cheriton Way GU17 . . . . . . .64 D5
Cherkley Hill KT22, RH5 . . .95 D1
Cherrimans Orch GU27 . . .207 F6
Cherry Cl Banstead KT17 . . .77 D5
Carshalton SM5 . . . . .59 F8
Merton SM4 . . . . .39 E5
7 Streatham SW2 . . . . .22 A8
Cherry Cres TW8 . . . . .6 B7
Cherry Ct RH13 . . . . .217 D1
Cherry Green Cl RH1 . . . .140 B7
Cherry Hill Gdns CR0 . . . . .60 F6
Cherry La RH11 . . . . .181 C1
Cherry Lodge 7 GU12 . . .105 B1
Cherry Orch Ashstead KT21 76 B1
Staines TW18 . . . . .13 A3
Cherry Orchard Gdns
6 Croydon CR0 . . . . .61 D8
East Molesey KT8 . . . . .35 F6
Cherry Orchard Rd
Croydon CR0 . . . . .42 E1
East Molesey KT8 . . . . .36 A6
Cherry St GU21 . . . . .69 E1
Cherry Tree Ave
Guildford GU2 . . . . .108 F1
Haslemere GU27 . . . . .207 F7
Staines TW18 . . . . .13 B2
Cherry Tree Cl
Crawley RH10 . . . . .202 D8
Farnborough GU14 . . . . .84 C5
Farnham GU9 . . . . .125 C3
Sandhurst GU47 . . . . .45 D1
Cherry Tree Ct CR5 . . . . . . .79 F1
Cherry Tree Dr
Bracknell RG12 . . . . .27 D6
Streatham SW16 . . . . .21 E5
Cherry Tree Gn CR2 . . . . . . .81 B5
Cherry Tree La GU7 . . . . .150 D8
Cherry Tree Rd
Milford GU8 . . . . .149 E1
Rowledge GU10 . . . . .145 E3
Cherry Tree Wlk
Beckenham BR3 . . . . .43 F5
Coney Hall BR4 . . . . .63 F6
Cherry Way Horton SL3 . . . . .1 C4
Upper Halliford TW17 . . . . . .34 E5
West Ewell KT19 . . . . .57 D4
Cherrydale Rd GU15 . . . . . .66 D5
Cherryhill Gr GU11 . . . . . .104 F1
Cherryhurst GU8 . . . . .171 B1
Cherrywood Ave TW20 . . . .11 B1
Cherrywood Cl KT2 . . . . . . .18 A1
Cherrywood Ct 1 TW11 . .17 A3
Cherrywood La SM4, SW20 39 E5
Cherrywood Rd GU14 . . . . .85 B7
Chertsey Bridge
Rd KT16, TW18 . . . . .33 D2
Chertsey Bvd KT16 . . . . . . .32 F1
Chertsey Cl CR8 . . . . .80 B4
Chertsey Cres CR0 . . . . . . .63 C1
Chertsey Ct SW14 . . . . .7 B4
Chertsey Dr SM3 . . . . .58 E8
Chertsey House TW13 . . . .16 A5
Chertsey La TW18 . . . . .12 F2
Chertsey Rd
Addlestone KT15 . . . . .52 B8
Ashford TW15
&TW16 TWTW16 . . . . .14 D2
Burrowhill GU20, GU24 . . . . .49 C6
Byfleet KT14 . . . . .71 D8
Chertsey KT15 . . . . .52 B8
Chobham GU24, KT16, GU21 .50 D1
Feltham TW13 &TW16 TW16 .14 E4
Feltham, Ashford Common
TW13, TW16 . . . . .14 D2
Lower Halliford TW17 . . . . . .34 A2
Shepperton TW17 . . . . .33 F2
Twickenham TW2 . . . . .16 D7
Windlesham GU20 . . . . .48 E5
Woking GU21 . . . . .69 F3
Chertsey St Guildford GU1 130 D8
Upper Tooting SW17 . . . . . . .21 A3
Chertsey Sta KT16 . . . . .32 F1
Chertsey Wlk KT16 . . . . . . .33 A2
Chervil Cl TW13 . . . . .15 A5
Cherwell Cl SL3 . . . . .1 B8
Cherwell Ct Teddington KT1 17 D1
West Ewell KT19 . . . . .57 C6
Cherwell Wlk RH11 . . . . . .200 F5
Cheselden Rd GU1 . . . . . .130 E8
Cheseman St SE26 . . . . . . .23 B5
Chesfield Rd KT2 . . . . .17 E1
Chesham Cl SM2 . . . . .58 E1
Chesham Cres SE20 . . . . . . .43 C8
Chesham Ct SW18 . . . . .20 D8
Chesham Mews 14 GU1 . .130 F8
Chesham Rd
Guildford GU1 . . . . .130 F8
Kingston u T KT1, KT2 . . . . . .38 A7
Penge SE20 . . . . .43 C8
Cheshire Cl
Mitcham CR4, SW16 . . . . . . .41 E6
Ottershaw KT16 . . . . .51 D4
Cheshire Gdns KT9 . . . . . . .56 D4
Cheshire House
Cheam SM4 . . . . .40 B2
Ottershaw KT16 . . . . .51 D4
Chesney Cres CR0 . . . . .63 C3
Chessholme Ct TW16 . . . . .14 E1
Chessholme Rd TW15 . . . . .14 C2
Chessington Cl KT19 . . . . .57 C4
Chessington Comm Coll
KT9 .56 D3
Chessington Hall
Gdns KT9 . . . . .56 D4
Chessington Hill Pk KT9 . .57 A5
Chessington North Sta
KT9 .56 E5
Chessington Par KT9 . . . . .56 D5
Chessington Park KT9 . . . .57 A6
Chessington Rd Ewell KT19 57 D3
West Ewell KT19 . . . . .57 D3
Chessington South Sta
KT9 .56 D3
Chessington Way BR4 . . . .63 B8
Chessington World of
Adventures KT9 . . . . .56 C1
Chester Ave Richmond TW10 .6 F1
Twickenham TW2 . . . . .15 F7
Chester Cl Ash GU12 . . . . .106 B2
Ashford TW15 . . . . .14 D3
Dorking RH4 . . . . .115 C1
Guildford GU2 . . . . .108 F3
1 Richmond TW10 . . . . .6 F1
Sutton SM1 . . . . .59 A8
Chester Gdns SM4 . . . . . . .40 C3
Chester House KT1 . . . . . . .38 B7
Chester Rd Ash GU12 . . . .106 B2
Effingham KT24 . . . . .113 B7
Harlington TW6 . . . . .3 A4
Hounslow TW4 . . . . .4 B4
Wimbledon SW19, SW20 . . . .19 C2
Chester Way GU10 . . . . . . .126 F6
Chesterblade La RG12 . . . .27 E2
Chesterfield Cl RH19 . . . .184 C4
Chesterfield Ct KT6 . . . . . .37 E4
Chesterfield Dr KT10 . . . . .56 A8
ChesterfieldHouse 6
SW16 . . . . .21 C3
Chesterfield Rd
Ashford TW15 . . . . .13 E3
Chiswick W4 . . . . .7 C8
West Ewell KT19 . . . . .57 D3
Chesters RH6 . . . . .160 E5
Chesters Rd GU15 . . . . .66 B5
Chesters The KT3 . . . . .38 E8
Chesterton Cl RH19 . . . . .205 F7
Chesterton Ct RH13 . . . . .218 A4
Chesterton Dr
Merstham RH1 . . . . .119 E7
Stanwell TW19 . . . . .13 F7
Chesterton Terr KT1 . . . . . .38 A7
Chestnut Ave
Aldershot GU12 . . . . .126 E8
Camberley GU15 . . . . .66 A6
Coney Hall BR4 . . . . .63 E6
Farnham GU9 . . . . .146 A8
Guildford GU2 . . . . .130 C5
Hampton TW12 . . . . .16 A1
Hampton, Hampton Court
KT8 &KT11 . . . . .36 F7
Haslemere GU27 . . . . .208 C7
11 Mortlake SW14 . . . . .7 D4
Tatsfield TN16 . . . . .103 E5
Thames Ditton KT10 . . . . . . .36 D1
Wentworth GU25 . . . . .30 F5
Weybridge KT13 . . . . .53 C3
Whiteley Village KT12 . . . . . .53 E2
Worcester Park KT19 . . . . . . .57 E6
Chestnut Cl
Addlestone KT15 . . . . .52 D5
Ashford, Chattern Hill TW15 .14 B4
Ashford, Felthamhill TW16 . . .14 F2
Blackwater GU17 . . . . .64 E4
Carshalton SM5 . . . . .40 F1
Catford SE6 . . . . .24 C4
East Grinstead RH19 . . . . . .186 A1
Englefield Green TW20 . . . . .11 C2
Grayshott GU26 . . . . .188 C3
Harlington UB7 . . . . .3 B7
Kingswood KT20 . . . . .98 A4
Redhill RH1 . . . . .140 B7
Send Marsh GU23 . . . . .91 A3
West Norwood SE27, SW16 . .22 A4
Chestnut Copse RH8 . . . .123 B2
Chestnut Cres KT12 . . . . . .53 E2
Chestnut Ct
Aldershot GU12 . . . . .105 D2
Beckenham BR3 . . . . .24 A1
5 Croydon CR0 . . . . .61 C6
Feltham TW13 . . . . .15 D3
Horsham RH13 . . . . .217 E2
Hounslow TW3 . . . . .5 A4
Kingston u T KT3 . . . . .38 E6
Chestnut Dr TW20 . . . . .11 D2
Chestnut End GU35 . . . . .187 A4
Chestnut Gdns RH12 . . . .217 C5
Chestnut Gr Balham SW12 .21 A7
Isleworth TW7 . . . . .6 A3
Kingston u T KT3 . . . . .38 D6
Mitcham CR4 . . . . .41 D5
South Croydon CR2 . . . . .62 C3
Staines TW18 . . . . .13 C2
Woking GU22 . . . . .89 E7
Chestnut Grove Sch SW12 21 A7
Chestnut House SE27 . . . . .22 C5
Chestnut La Chobham GU24 49 C4
Weybridge KT13 . . . . .53 B5
Chestnut Manor Cl TW18 .13 B3
Chestnut Mead RH1 . . . . .118 E2
Chestnut Pl Ashtead Kt21 . .95 E8
Ewell KT17 . . . . .77 A8
Chestnut Rd Ashford TW15 .14 B4
Farnborough GU14 . . . . .85 A5
Guildford GU1 . . . . .109 D1
Horley RH6 . . . . .161 B5
Kingston u T KT2 . . . . .17 E1
Merton SW20 . . . . .39 D7
Twickenham TW2 . . . . .16 E6
West Norwood SE21, SE27 . .22 C5
Chestnut Way
Bramley GU5 . . . . .152 A4
Feltham TW13 . . . . .15 B5
Godalming GU7 . . . . .150 F2
Chestnut Wlk
Crawley RH11 . . . . .181 C1
Felcourt RH19 . . . . .185 C8
Upper Halliford TW17 . . . . . .34 E5
Whiteley Village KT12 . . . . . .53 E2
Chestnuts The Horley RH6 161 A5
Penge BR3 . . . . .43 D6
Walton-on-T KT12 . . . . .54 A8
Cheston Ave CR0 . . . . .43 F1
Chesworth Cl RH13 . . . . .217 C1
Chesworth Cres RH13 . . .217 C1
Chesworth Cty Jun Sch
RH13 . . . . .217 E3
Chesworth Gdns RH13 . . .217 C1
Chesworth La RH12, RH13 217 C1
Cheswycks Sch GU16 . . . . .86 B5
Chetwode Cl RG40 . . . . . . .25 E6
Chetwode Dr KT20 . . . . . . .77 D1
Chetwode Pl GU11 . . . . . .126 C7
Chetwode Rd
Burgh Heath KT20 . . . . .97 C8
Upper Tooting SW17 . . . . . . .20 F5
Chetwode Terr GU11 . . . .104 E1
Chetwood Rd RH11 . . . . . .200 D2
Chevening Cl RH11 . . . . . .201 C1
Chevening Rd SE19 . . . . . .22 D2
Chevington Villas RH1 . . .120 F3
Cheviot Cl Banstead SM7 . .78 B4
Farnborough GU14 . . . . .84 E7
Frimley GU15 . . . . .66 C4
Harlington UB3 . . . . .3 D7
Sutton SM2 . . . . .59 D2
Cheviot Gdns SE27 . . . . . . .22 B4
Cheviot Rd SE27 . . . . .22 B3
Cheviot Wlk RH11 . . . . . . .201 B6
Chevremont GU1 . . . . .130 E8
Chewter Cl GU19 . . . . .47 F3
Chewter La GU20 . . . . .48 B6
Cheyham Gdns SM2 . . . . . .58 D1
Cheyham Way SM2 . . . . . . .58 E1
Cheylesmore Dr GU16 . . . .66 D3
Cheyne Ave TW2 . . . . .15 F7
Cheyne Ct Banstead SM7 . . .78 B4
4 Wallington SM6 . . . . .60 B4
Cheyne Hill KT5 . . . . .37 F5
Cheyne Rd TW15 . . . . .14 D2
Cheyne Way GU14 . . . . .84 F8
Cheyne Wlk Croydon CR0 . .62 A8
Horley RH6 . . . . .161 A1
Cheynell Wlk RH11 . . . . . .200 F4
Chichele Gdns CR0 . . . . . . .61 E6
Chichele Rd RH8 . . . . .122 E7
Chichester Cl
Crawley RH10 . . . . .201 E2
Dorking RH4 . . . . .115 B1
Hampton TW12 . . . . .15 F2
Witley GU8 . . . . .170 E5
Chichester Ct Ewell KT17 . .57 F2
Stanwell TW19 . . . . .13 E7
Chichester Dr CR8 . . . . .79 F7
Chichester Mews SE27 . . .22 A4
Chichester Rd Ash GU12 .106 A3
Dorking RH4 . . . . .115 B2
South Croydon CR0 . . . . .61 E7
Chichester Terr RH12 . . . .217 D2
Chichester Way TW14 . . . .15 C8
Chiddingfold Rd GU8 . . . .192 C3
Chiddingly Cl RH10 . . . . . .202 B5
Chiddingstone Cl SM2 . . . .59 A1
Chilberton Dr RH1 . . . . . .119 C5
Chilbolton TW20 . . . . .11 E3
Chilbrook Rd KT11 . . . . . . .73 A1
Chilchester Ct BR3 . . . . . . .44 B6
Chilcombe House 7
SW15 . . . . .19 A8
Chilcroft La GU27 . . . . . . .208 B1
Chilcroft Rd GU27 . . . . . . .207 F7
Chilcrofts Rd GU27 . . . . . .208 A1
Child Cl RG40 . . . . .25 D8
Childebert Rd SW17 . . . . . .21 B6
Childerly KT1 . . . . .38 A6
Childrens Trust
(Tadworth Court) The
KT20 .97 D6
Childs Hall Cl KT23 . . . . . . .93 F2
Childs Hall Dr KT23 . . . . . . .93 F2
Childs Hall Rd KT23 . . . . . .93 F2
Childs La 10 SE19 . . . . .22 E2
Chilham Cl GU16 . . . . .85 F8
Chillerton Rd SW17 . . . . . . .21 B3
Chillingford House SW17 .20 C4
Chillingham Way GU15 . . .65 C4
Chillingworth Gdns TW1 . .16 F5
Chilmans Dr KT23 . . . . . . .94 B2
Chilmark Gdns
Merstham RH1 . . . . .119 E6
New Malden KT3 . . . . .39 A3
Chilmark Rd SW16 . . . . . . .41 D8
Chilmead 1 RH1 . . . . .118 F2
Chilmead La RH1 . . . . . . .119 D3
Chilsey Green Rd KT16 . . . .32 E2
Chiltern GU22 . . . . .89 C5
Chiltern Ave
Farnborough GU14 . . . . .84 D4
Twickenham TW2 . . . . .16 A7
Chiltern Cl Crawley RH11 .201 B6
Farnborough GU14 . . . . .84 D4
Haslemere GU27 . . . . .208 B5
North Cheam KT4 . . . . .58 C8
South Croydon CR0 . . . . .61 E7
Chiltern Dr KT5 . . . . .38 B4
Chiltern Gdns BR2 . . . . . . .44 F5
Chiltern Rd Sandhurst GU47 45 A1
Sutton SM2 . . . . .59 C1
Chilterns The SM2 . . . . . . .59 B2
Chilthorne Cl SE6 . . . . .23 F8
Chiltington Ct RH12 . . . . .217 D4
Chilton Ct KT12 . . . . .54 A6
Chilton Rd TW9 . . . . .7 A4
Chiltons Cl SM7 . . . . .78 B4
Chilworth CE Inf Sch
GU4 . . . . .131 D3
Chilworth Ct
8 Putney SW19 . . . . .19 D7
13 Redhill RH1 . . . . .118 F2
Chilworth Gdns SM1 . . . . .59 C7
Chilworth Rd GU4, GU5 . .132 A4
Chilworth Sta GU4 . . . . . .131 E3
Chimneys Ct SW19 . . . . . . .19 C1
Chinchilla Dr TW4 . . . . .4 C5
Chine The GU10 . . . . .145 F5
Chingford Ave GU14 . . . . . .85 D5
Chingley Cl BR1 . . . . .24 E2
Chinthurst La
Shalford GU4, GU5 . . . . . . .130 F2
Wonersh GU5 . . . . .152 A7
Chinthurst Pk GU4 . . . . . .130 E1
Chinthurst Sch KT20 . . . . .97 C4
Chippendale Cl GU17 . . . . .64 E4
Chippendale Rd RH11 . . . .201 B1
Chippenham 4 KT1 . . . . . . .37 F7
Chipstead Ave CR7 . . . . . . .42 B5
Chipstead Cl Belmont SM2 .59 B2
Coulsdon CR5 . . . . .79 A3
Penge SE19 . . . . .22 F1
Redhill RH1 . . . . .140 A7
Chipstead Ct GU21 . . . . . . .68 E2
Chipstead House 4 SW2 . .21 E7
Chipstead La CR5, KT20 . . .98 B3
Chipstead Sta CR5 . . . . . . .78 F1
Chipstead Valley Prim Sch
CR5 .79 A3
Chipstead Valley Rd
Chipstead CR5 . . . . .79 B3
Coulsdon CR5 . . . . .79 B3

Chipstead Way CR5, SM7 . .78 F3
Chirton Wlk GU21 . . . . .69 A1
Chisbury Cl RG12 . . . . .27 E3
Chisholm Rd Croydon CR0 . .61 E8
18 Richmond TW10 . . . . .6 F1
Chislehurst Rd TW10 . . . . . .6 E2
Chislet Cl BR3 . . . . .24 A1
Chiswick Cl CR0 . . . . .60 F7
Chiswick Comm Sch W4 . . .7 D7
Chiswick House W4 . . . . . .7 E7
Chiswick La S W4 . . . . .7 F8
Chiswick Mall W4 . . . . .7 F8
Chiswick Quay W4 . . . . .7 C6
Chiswick Sq W4 . . . . .7 E8
Chiswick Sta W4 . . . . .7 C7
Chiswick Staithe W4 . . . . . .7 C6
Chiswick Village W4 . . . . . . .7 B8
Chithurst La RH6, RH7 . . .162 F2
Chittenden Cotts
GU23, KT14 . . . . .71 E3
Chitterfield Gate UB7 . . . . . .3 A7
Chitty's Wlk GU3 . . . . .108 F5
Chive Ct GU14 . . . . .84 C4
Chivelston 27 SW19 . . . . . . .19 D7
Chivenor Gr KT2 . . . . .17 D3
Chobham Cl KT16 . . . . .51 B4
Chobham Common
(Nature Reserve) KT16 . . .49 F6
Chobham Gdns SW19 . . . .19 D6
Chobham Golf Course
GU21 . . . . .68 C5
Chobham La KT16, GU24 . . .50 A8
Chobham Park La GU24 . . .50 B2
Chobham Rd
Chobham GU21 . . . . .69 E3
Frimley GU16 . . . . .66 A2
Knaphill GU21 . . . . .68 D3
Ottershaw KT16 . . . . .51 B4
1 Woking GU21 . . . . .69 F2
Woking, Horsell Common
GU21, GU24 . . . . .69 D5
Chobham St Lawrence
Cof E Prim Sch GU24 . . . .68 E8
Choir Gn GU21 . . . . .68 E2
Cholmley Rd KT7 . . . . .37 B3
Cholmeley Wlk TW9 . . . .6 C2
Chrislaine Cl TW19 . . . . .2 D1
Chrismas Ave GU12 . . . . .105 C1
Chrismas Pl GU12 . . . . . . .105 C1
Christ Church C of E
Prim Sch Purley CR8 . . . . .61 B1
Streatham SW2 . . . . .21 F7
Christ Church C of E Sch
KT16 . . . . .51 D4
Christ Church CE Inf Sch
KT3 . . . . .38 E6
Christ Church CE Jun Sch
KT3 . . . . .38 D6
Christ Church CE Prim
Sch KT5 . . . . .38 A3
Christ Church Mount
KT19 . . . . .76 B7
Christ Church Prim Sch
SE23 . . . . .23 D6
Christ Church Rd
Beckenham BR3 . . . . .44 A7
Epsom KT18 . . . . .76 A6
Surbiton KT5 . . . . .37 F3
Christ the King RC Fst Sch
TW19 . . . . .2 E1
Christ's Sch (East Side)
SW14 . . . . .7 D4
Christ's Sch (West Side)
TW10 . . . . .6 F2
Christabel Cl TW7 . . . . .5 E4
Christchurch Ave 4 TW11 17 A3
Christchurch C of E Fst
Sch GU25 . . . . .31 B6
Christchurch Cl SW19 . . . .20 D1
Christchurch Cotts GU25 . .31 B6
Christchurch Dr GU47 . . . .64 D6
Christchurch Gdns KT19 . .76 B8
Christchurch House 2
SW2 . . . . .21 E7
Christchurch Hts 9 RH2 .118 F1
Christchurch Pk SM2 . . . . .59 C3
Christchurch Pl KT19 . . . . .76 B8
Christchurch Rd
Harlington TW6 . . . . .3 A4
Mitcham SW19 . . . . .20 D1
Mortlake SW14 . . . . .7 C2
Purley CR8 . . . . .80 B8
Streatham SW2 . . . . .21 F7
Virginia Water GU25 . . . . . .31 C5
Christchurch Way 2 GU21 69 F2
Christian Fields SW16 . . . .22 A1
Christie Cl Guildford GU1 .109 D4
Lightwater GU18 . . . . .48 C1
Little Bookham KT23 . . . . . .93 F3
Christie Dr SE25 . . . . .43 A4
Christie House BR4 . . . . . . .44 B1
Christies RH19 . . . . .205 D8
Christine Cl GU12 . . . . . . .105 F1
Christmas Hill GU4 . . . . . .130 F2
Christmaspie Ave GU3 . . .107 B1
Christopher Ct
Ashford TW15 . . . . .13 E3
6 Croydon CR0 . . . . .43 A1
Tadworth KT20 . . . . .97 C4
Christopher Rd RH19 . . . .185 E1
Christy Rd TN16 . . . . .83 C4
Chrystie La KT23 . . . . .94 B1
Chuck's La KT20 . . . . .97 B3
Chudleigh Ct 4 GU14 . . . . .85 B4
Chudleigh Gdns SM1 . . . . .59 C7
Chudleigh Rd TW1, TW2 . . .16 F8
Chulsa Rd SE26 . . . . .23 B3
Chumleigh Wlk KT5 . . . . . .37 F5
Church Almshouses 8 TW9 6 F3
Church App Dulwich SE21 . .22 D5
Thorpe TW20 . . . . .32 C6
Church Ave Beckenham BR3 44 A8
Farnborough GU14 . . . . .85 C3
Mortlake SW14 . . . . .7 D4
Church Circ GU14 . . . . .85 C1
Church Cl Addlestone KT15 .52 B6
6 Epsom KT17 . . . . .76 E6
Fetcham KT22 . . . . .94 D3
Grayswood GU27 . . . . .189 F2
Hounslow TW4 . . . . .4 F5
Laleham TW18 . . . . .33 C6
Lower Kingswood KT20 . . . .117 F8
Milford GU8 . . . . .149 F1
Pirbright GU24 . . . . .87 F6
Woking GU21 . . . . .69 E3
Church Ct Forest Hill SE26 . .23 E3
Reigate RH2 . . . . .118 B1
Church Dr BR4 . . . . .63 E7
Church Farm La SM3 . . . . .58 E4
Church Field House KT11 .73 B5
Church Gdns Dorking RH4 136 B8
Leatherhead KT22 . . . . .95 B7
Church Gn Elstead GU8 . . .148 C3
Hersham KT12 . . . . .54 C4
Church Gr KT1 . . . . .37 C7
Church Hill
Aldershot GU11, GU12 . . . .126 C8
Camberley GU15 . . . . .65 E5
Caterham CR3 . . . . .100 F3
Merstham RH1 . . . . .99 B1
Nutfield RH1 . . . . .119 F2
Purley CR8 . . . . .60 E1
Shamley Green GU5 . . . . . .152 E4
Shere GU5 . . . . .133 A4
Tatsfield TN16 . . . . .103 D5
Wallington SM5 . . . . .59 F5
Wimbledon SW19 . . . . .19 F3
Woking GU21 . . . . .69 D3
Church Hill House Hospl
RG12 . . . . .27 A3
Church Hill Rd
Cheam SM1, SM3 . . . . .58 E6
Kingston u T KT6 . . . . .37 E4
Church La Albury GU5 . . . .132 C4
Ascot SL5 . . . . .29 D5
Ash GU12 . . . . .106 B2
Binstead GU10 . . . . .145 E3
Bisley GU21, GU24 . . . . .68 A4
Bletchingley RH1 . . . . .120 D3
Broadbridge Heath RH12 . .216 D3
Brook GU8 . . . . .190 C8
Burgh Heath KT18, SM7 . . . . .77 E2
Burstow RH6 . . . . .182 F7
Caterham CR3 . . . . .100 A3
Chelsham CR6 . . . . .82 C3
Chessington KT9 . . . . .56 F4
Copthorne RH10 . . . . .183 B3
Cranleigh GU6 . . . . .174 E3
Crawley RH10 . . . . .201 F6
Crondall GU10 . . . . .124 D8
East Grinstead RH19 . . . . .185 F1
Farnborough GU14 . . . . .84 E4
Godstone RH9 . . . . .121 D3
Grayshott GU26 . . . . .188 C3
Hambledon GU8 . . . . .171 D2
Haslemere GU27 . . . . .208 D7
Headley KT18 . . . . .96 D2
Hooley CR5 . . . . .99 B5
Merton SW19 . . . . .39 F8
Oxted RH8 . . . . .122 E6
Pirbright GU24 . . . . .87 D4
Send GU23 . . . . .90 C1
Shere GU5 . . . . .133 A4
Sunningdale SL5 . . . . .30 B4
Teddington TW11 . . . . .16 F3
Thames Ditton KT7 . . . . .37 A3
Twickenham TW1 . . . . .17 A7
Upper Tooting SW17 . . . . . .21 A3
Upper Tooting,
Furzedown SW17 . . . . .21 B4
Wallington SM6 . . . . .60 D7
Wallis Wood RH5 . . . . .176 F1
Warlingham CR6 . . . . .81 D2
Weybridge KT13 . . . . .53 A6
Witley GU8 . . . . .170 E2
Wormley GU8 . . . . .170 E2
Worplesdon GU3 . . . . .108 E8
Wrecclesham GU10 . . . . . .145 F7
Church La E GU11 . . . . . . .126 B8
Church La W GU11 . . . . . .105 A1
Church Lane Ave CR5 . . . . .99 B5
Church Lane Dr CR5 . . . . .99 B5
Church Meadow KT6 . . . . .56 C8
Church Mews KT15 . . . . . . .52 C6
Church Par TW15 . . . . .13 F4
Church Pas GU9 . . . . .125 B2
Church Path
Aldershot GU14 . . . . .105 C8
Ash GU12 . . . . .106 A3
Croydon CR0, CR9 . . . . .61 C8
Merton SW19 . . . . .40 A7
Mitcham CR4 . . . . .40 E6
7 Woking GU21 . . . . .69 F2
Church Pl CR4 . . . . .40 E6
Church Rd Addlestone KT15 .52 B5
Aldershot GU11 . . . . .126 C8
Ascot SL5 . . . . .29 A5
Ashford TW15 . . . . .13 F4
Ashstead KT21 . . . . .75 D1
Bagshot GU19 . . . . .47 D3
Barnes SW13 . . . . .7 F5
Beckenham BR2 . . . . .44 E6
Biggin Hill TN16 . . . . .83 E2
Church Rd *continued*
Bracknell RG12 . . . . .27 C7
Broadbridge Heath RH12 . .216 D3
Burstow RH6 . . . . .183 A7
Byfleet KT14 . . . . .71 E6
Caterham CR3 . . . . .100 F3
Cheam SM3 . . . . .58 E4
Claygate KT10 . . . . .55 F3
Copthorne RH10 . . . . .183 B3
Crawley, Lowfield
Heath RH11 . . . . .181 E5
Crawley, Worth RH10 . . . . .202 E6
Croydon CR0, CR9 . . . . .61 C7
Dunsfold GU8 . . . . .192 D5
East Molesey KT8 . . . . .36 D6
Egham TW20 . . . . .12 A3
Epsom KT17 . . . . .76 E6
Feltham TW13 . . . . .15 D3
Fetcham KT23 . . . . .94 A3
Frimley GU16 . . . . .65 D1
Guildford GU1 . . . . .130 D8
Haslemere GU27 . . . . .208 C7
Haslemere,
Shottermill GU27 . . . . .207 F6
Heston TW5 . . . . .4 B8
Heston TW5 . . . . .5 A7
Horley RH6 . . . . .160 F2
Horley RH6 . . . . .161 A3
Horne RH6 . . . . .162 F5
Horsham RH12 . . . . .218 B5
Hounslow TW7 . . . . .5 E7
Kenley CR8 . . . . .80 D4
Kingston u T KT1 . . . . .37 F7
Leatherhead KT22 . . . . .95 B5
Lingfield RH7 . . . . .164 D4
Little Bookham KT23 . . . . . . .93 F4
Long Ditton KT6 . . . . .37 C1
Lower Halliford TW17 . . . . . .34 B2
Milford GU8 . . . . .149 F1
Mitcham CR4, SW19 . . . . . . .40 D7
New Malden KT4 . . . . .38 E1
Purley CR8 . . . . .60 E1
Redhill RH1 . . . . .139 E7
Reigate RH2 . . . . .139 A7
Richmond TW10, TW9 . . . . . .6 E2
Richmond, Ham
Common TW10 . . . . .17 E4
Sandhurst GU15 . . . . .64 F7
Sandhurst, Owlsmoor GU47 . .45 E1
South Norwood SE19 . . . . . .22 E1
Sunningdale SL5 . . . . .30 A3
Teddington TW11 . . . . .16 F3
Turners Hill RH10 . . . . .204 A3
Wallington SM6 . . . . .60 D7
Warlingham CR6 . . . . .81 D2
West End GU24 . . . . .67 F7
West Ewell KT19 . . . . .57 D3
Whyteleafe CR3 . . . . .100 F8
Wimbledon SW19 . . . . .19 E4
Windlesham GU20 . . . . .48 C4
Winkfield SL4 . . . . .8 C5
Winkfield, Chavey Down SL5 .28 B8
Woking, Horsell GU21 . . . . .69 E4
Woking, St John's GU21 . . . .89 A8
Woldingham CR3 . . . . .101 E4
Church Rd E
Crowthorne RG45 . . . . .45 B5
Farnborough GU14 . . . . .85 D2
Church Rd W GU14 . . . . . . .85 C1
Church Rise
Chessington KT9 . . . . .56 F4
Forest Hill SE23 . . . . .23 D6
Church Road Ind Est
RH11 . . . . .181 E5
Church Road Trad Est
RH11 . . . . .181 E5
Church Row GU23 . . . . .91 C6
Church Side Epsom KT18 . .76 B6
Gatton RH2 . . . . .118 F6
Church Sq TW17 . . . . .34 B2
Church St
Aldershot GU11 . . . . .104 F2
Betchworth RH3 . . . . .137 E8
Chiswick W4 . . . . .7 F8
Cobham KT11 . . . . .73 B4
Crawley RH11 . . . . .201 C6
Crowthorne RG45 . . . . .45 B4
Croydon CR0, CR9 . . . . .61 C8
Dorking RH4 . . . . .136 A7
Effingham KT24 . . . . .113 D8
Epsom KT17, KT18 . . . . .76 E6
Esher KT10 . . . . .55 B6
Ewell KT17 . . . . .58 A2
Godalming GU7 . . . . .150 D4
Hampton TW12 . . . . .36 C8
Isleworth TW7 . . . . .6 B5
Kingston u T KT1 . . . . .37 D7
Leatherhead KT22 . . . . .95 B5
Old Woking GU22 . . . . .90 C6
Reigate RH2 . . . . .118 B1
Rudgwick RH12 . . . . .214 E8
Rudgwick, Cox Green RH12 .195 E1
Staines TW18 . . . . .12 E4
Sunbury TW16 . . . . .35 B6
Twickenham TW1 . . . . .17 A7
Walton-on-T KT12 . . . . .35 A2
Warnham RH12 . . . . .216 F8
Weybridge KT13 . . . . .53 A6
Church St E GU21 . . . . .69 F2
Church St W GU21 . . . . . . .69 E2
Church Stretton Rd TW3 . . . .5 C2
Church Terr 20 TW10 . . . . . .6 D2
Church Vale SE23 . . . . .23 D6
Church View GU12 . . . . . .106 A2
Church View Cl RH6 . . . . .160 F2
Church Villa TW16 . . . . . . .35 B6
Church Way Oxted RH8 . . .122 F3
South Croydon CR2 . . . . .81 A8
Church Wlk
Bletchingley RH1 . . . . .120 D2
Brentford TW8 . . . . .6 C8
Caterham CR3 . . . . .101 A3
Chertsey KT16 . . . . .33 A3
Crawley RH10 . . . . .201 D6
Horley RH6 . . . . .160 F2
Leatherhead KT22 . . . . .95 B5
Mitcham SW16 . . . . .41 C7
Reigate RH2 . . . . .118 C1
18 Richmond TW10 . . . . .6 D2
Thames Ditton KT7 . . . . .36 F3
Walton-on-T KT12 . . . . .35 A1
West Barnes SW20 . . . . .39 C6
Weybridge KT13 . . . . .53 B8
Churchcroft Cl SW12 . . . . .21 A8
Churchdown BR1 . . . . .24 E4
Churchfield Rd
Reigate RH2 . . . . .117 F2
Walton-on-T KT12 . . . . .35 A1
Weybridge KT13 . . . . .53 A6
Churchfields
East Molesey KT8 . . . . .36 A6
Guildford GU4 . . . . .110 A6
Witley GU8 . . . . .170 E4
Woking GU21 . . . . .69 E3
Churchfields Ave
Feltham TW13 . . . . .16 A5
Weybridge KT13 . . . . .53 B6
Churchfields Prim Sch
BR3 . . . . .43 D6
Churchfields Rd BR3 . . . . .43 E7
Churchill Ave
Aldershot GU12 . . . . .126 C8
Horsham RH12 . . . . .217 B3
Churchill Cl
East Bedfont TW14 . . . . . . .14 F7
Farnborough GU14 . . . . .85 B8
Fetcham KT22 . . . . .94 E4
Warlingham CR6 . . . . .81 D2
Churchill Cres GU14 . . . . . .85 B8
Churchill Ct
Crawley RH10 . . . . .182 A1
Staines TW18 . . . . .13 C2
Churchill Dr KT13 . . . . .53 C6
Churchill House SM7 . . . . .77 F4
Churchill Rd
Guildford GU1 . . . . .130 F8
North Ascot SL5 . . . . .28 F7
Smallfield RH6 . . . . .162 B3
South Croydon CR2 . . . . . . .61 C3
Churchill Way TW16 . . . . . .15 A2
Churchley Rd SE26 . . . . . . .23 B4
Churchley Villas SE26 . . . . .23 B4
Churchmore Rd SW16 . . . .41 D8
Churchside Cl TN16 . . . . . .83 C2
Churchview Rd TW2 . . . . . .16 D6
Churston Cl 17 SW2 . . . . . .22 A7
Churston Dr SM4 . . . . .39 E4
Churt Rd Beacon Hill GU26 188 C6
Headley Down GU10, GU35 .187 C8
Churt Wynde GU26 . . . . . .188 D7
Chuters Cl KT14 . . . . .71 F7
Chuters Gr KT17 . . . . .76 F7
Cibber Rd SE23 . . . . .23 D6
Cinder Path GU22 . . . . .89 C8
Cinderford Way BR1 . . . . . .24 E4
Cinnamon Gdns GU2 . . . .109 A6
Cintra Ct SE19 . . . . .22 F2
Cintra Pk SE19 . . . . .22 F1
Circle Gdns Byfleet KT14 . . . .71 F6
Merton SW19 . . . . .40 A7
Circle Hill Rd RG45 . . . . . . .45 C5
Circle Rd KT12 . . . . .53 E2
Circle The GU7 . . . . .150 F6
Cissbury Cl RH12 . . . . . . .218 A6
Cissbury Hill RH11 . . . . . .201 C4
Cissbury House 6 SE26 . . . .23 A5
City Bsns Ctr RH13 . . . . . .217 D1
City of London
Freemen's Sch KT21 . . . .96 A8
City Prospect 5 SE19 . . . .22 E2
City Wharf House KT7 . . . .37 B3
Clacket La TN16 . . . . .103 E2
Clairvale Rd TW5 . . . . .4 E6
Clairview Rd SW16, SW17 . .21 B4
Clairville Ct 1 RH2 . . . . . .118 D1
Clairville Point 12 SE23 . . .23 D5
Clammer Hill GU27 . . . . . .189 F1
Clandon Ave TW20 . . . . .12 C1
Clandon CE Inf Sch GU4 .111 A4
Clandon Cl KT17 . . . . .58 A4
Clandon Ct GU14 . . . . .85 B3
Clandon House 12 KT2 . . . .18 B2
Clandon Mews RH4 . . . . .136 B4
Clandon Pk GU4 . . . . .111 A3
Clandon Rd Guildford GU1 130 E8
Send Marsh GU4, GU23 . . . . .91 A1
West Clandon GU4, GU23 . .111 A8
Clandon Regis Golf
Club GU4 . . . . .111 B4
Clandon Sta GU4 . . . . .111 B6
Clanfield House 12 SW15 . .19 A7
Clanfield Ride GU17 . . . . . .64 D5
Clapgate La RH13 . . . . . . .215 C5
Clappers
Gate RH10, RH11 . . . . . . .201 D7
Clappers La GU24 . . . . .68 D8
Clappers Meadow GU6 . .194 A3
Clare Ave RG40 . . . . .25 C7
Clare Cl Crawley RH10 . . . .182 C1
West Byfleet KT14 . . . . .71 A6
Clare Cotts RH1 . . . . .120 B3
Clare Cres KT22 . . . . .75 B1
Clare Ct Wimbledon SW19 . .19 E2
Woldingham CR3 . . . . .102 A4
Clare Gdns TW20 . . . . .12 A3
Clare Hill KT10 . . . . .55 B5
Clare Hill Golf Course
KT10 . . . . .55 B4
Clare Hill (No 1) KT10 . . . .55 B5
Clare Hill (No 2) KT10 . . . .55 B5
Clare House Prim Sch
BR3 . . . . .44 C7
Clare Lawn Ave SW14 . . . . .7 D2
Clare Mead GU10 . . . . . . .145 F4
Clare Rd Hounslow TW4 . . . . .4 F4
Stanwell TW19 . . . . .13 E8
Clare Wood KT22 . . . . .75 B1
Claredale GU22 . . . . .89 E8
Claredale Ct SM2 . . . . .59 C3
Clarefield Ct SL5 . . . . .30 A2
Claremont TW17 . . . . .34 B3
Claremont Ave
Camberley GU15 . . . . .65 F5
Esher KT10 . . . . .54 F4
Hersham KT12 . . . . .54 D6
Sunbury TW16 . . . . .35 B8
West Barnes KT3 . . . . .39 B4
Woking GU22 . . . . .89 E8
Claremont Cl
Hamsey Green CR2 . . . . .81 B4
Hersham KT12 . . . . .54 D5
4 Streatham SW2 . . . . .21 F7
Claremont Ct RH4 . . . . . .136 B6
Claremont Dr Esher KT10 . .55 B4
Shepperton TW17 . . . . .34 B3
Claremont End KT10 . . . . . .55 B4
Claremont Fan Court Sch
KT10 . . . . .55 A3
Claremont Gdns KT6 . . . . .37 E4
Claremont Gr W4 . . . . .7 E7
Claremont Hospl KT6 . . . . .37 D3
Claremont La KT10 . . . . . .55 B5
Claremont Landscape Gdn
KT10 . . . . .54 F3
Claremont Park Rd KT10 . .55 B4
Claremont Rd
Claygate KT10 . . . . .55 E3
Croydon CR0 . . . . .43 A1
Egham TW18 . . . . .12 D3
Kingston u T KT6 . . . . .37 E4
Redhill RH1 . . . . .119 A4
Teddington TW11 . . . . .16 F4
Twickenham TW1 . . . . .6 C1
West Byfleet KT14 . . . . .71 A7
Claremont Terr KT7 . . . . . . .37 B2
Claremount Cl KT18 . . . . . .77 C2
Claremount Gdns KT18 . . .77 D2
Clarence Ave
Kingston u T KT3 . . . . .38 D7
Streatham SW4 . . . . .21 D8
Clarence Cl
Aldershot GU12 . . . . .105 D2
Hersham KT12 . . . . .54 B6
Clarence Ct RH6 . . . . .161 D4
Clarence Dr
Camberley GU15 . . . . .66 B7
2 East Grinstead RH19 . . . .205 F7
Englefield Green TW20 . . . . .11 C4
Clarence House KT12 . . . . .54 B5
Clarence La SW15 . . . . .7 F1
Clarence Rd
Biggin Hill TN16 . . . . .83 F1
Hersham KT12 . . . . .54 B6
Horsham RH13 . . . . .217 E1
Reigate RH1 . . . . .139 D6
Richmond TW9 . . . . .7 A6
Sutton SM1 . . . . .59 B5
Teddington TW11 . . . . .17 A2
Thornton Heath CR0 . . . . . . .42 D2
Wallington SM6 . . . . .60 B5
Wimbledon SW19 . . . . .20 B2
Clarence St Egham TW20 . . .11 F2
Kingston u T KT1, KT2 . . . . . .37 E7
4 Richmond TW9 . . . . .6 E3
Staines TW18 . . . . .12 E4
Clarence Terr TW3 . . . . .5 B3
Clarence Way RH6 . . . . . .161 D4
Clarence Wlk RH1 . . . . . . .139 D6
Clarendon Cres TW2 . . . . .16 D5
Clarendon Ct
Blackwater GU17 . . . . .64 D3
1 Richmond TW9 . . . . .7 A6
Clarendon Cty Prim Sch
TW15 . . . . .13 F4
Clarendon Gate KT16 . . . . .51 D4
Clarendon Gr CR4 . . . . .40 F6
Clarendon Rd
Ashford TW15 . . . . .13 F4
Croydon CR0, CR9 . . . . .61 B8
Mitcham SW19 . . . . .20 E1
Redhill RH1 . . . . .118 F2
Wallington SM6 . . . . .60 C4
Clarendon Sch TW12 . . . . .16 B2
Clarens St SE6 . . . . .23 F6
Clares The CR3 . . . . .101 A3
Claret Gdns SE25 . . . . .42 E5
Clareville Rd CR3 . . . . . . .101 A3
Clarewood Dr GU15 . . . . . .65 E6
Clarice Way SM6 . . . . .60 E2
Claridge Gdns RH7 . . . . . .165 A2
Claridges Mead RH7 . . . . .165 A2
Clark Pl GU6 . . . . .173 F2
Clark Rd RH11 . . . . .201 A1
Clark Way TW5 . . . . .4 D7
Clarke Cres GU15 . . . . .64 E7
Clarke's Ave KT4, SM3 . . . .58 D8
Clarks Hill GU10 . . . . .124 D1
Clarks La CR6, TN16 . . . . .103 C4
Claudia Pl SW19 . . . . .19 E7
Claverdale Rd SW2 . . . . . . .22 A8
Clavering Ave RG12 . . . . .27 A2
Clavering Cl TW1 . . . . .17 A4
Claverton KT21 . . . . .75 E2
Clay Ave CR4 . . . . .41 B7

Clay Hall La RH10 ... 183 C4
Clay La
Guildford, Burpham GU4 ... 110 A5
Guildford, Jacobswell GU4 ... 109 E7
Headley KT18 ... 96 B3
Horne RH7 ... 163 D3
Nutfield RH1 ... 140 D7
South Nutfield RH1 ... 140 D7
Wokingham RG40 ... 25 F5
Claycart Rd
Aldershot GU11 ... 104 D4
Aldershot GU11 ... 104 E3
Claydon Ct TW18 ... 13 A4
Claydon Dr CR0 ... 60 E6
Claydon Gdns GU17 ... 65 A1
Claydon Rd GU21 ... 69 A3
Clayford RH7 ... 165 B2
Claygate Cres CR0 ... 63 D4
Claygate La
Hinchley Wood KT10 ... 56 A8
Thames Ditton KT7 ... 37 A1
Claygate Lodge Cl KT10 ... 55 E3
Claygate Prim Sch KT10 ... 55 E3
Claygate Rd RH4 ... 136 B5
Claygate Sta KT10 ... 55 E4
Clayhall House 3 RH2 ... 118 A2
Clayhall La RH2 ... 138 E6
Clayhanger GU1, GU4 ... 110 C3
Clayhill Cl Bracknell RG12 ... 28 A6
Leigh RH2 ... 138 A2
Clayhill Rd RH2 ... 137 F1
Claylands Ct SE19 ... 22 D3
Claymore Cl SM3, SM4 ... 40 A2
Claypole Dr TW5 ... 4 E6
Clays Cl RH19 ... 205 E8
Clayton Dr GU2 ... 108 F4
Clayton Gr RG12 ... 27 E8
Clayton Hill RH11 ... 201 C4
Clayton House KT7 ... 37 B1
Clayton Mead RH9 ... 121 B4
Clayton Rd
Chessington KT10, KT9 ... 56 D6
Ewell KT17 ... 76 E6
Farnborough GU14 ... 64 F1
Isleworth TW7 ... 5 E4
Clear Water Pl KT6 ... 37 C3
Cleardene RH4 ... 136 B7
Cleardown GU22 ... 70 B1
Clears Cotts RH2 ... 117 E3
Clears The RH2 ... 117 E3
Clearsprings GU18 ... 67 A8
Cleave Prior CR5 ... 98 E8
Cleave's Almshouses 1
KT2 ... 37 E7
Cleaveland Rd KT6 ... 37 D4
Cleaverholme Cl SE25 ... 43 B3
Cleeve Ct TW14 ... 14 E7
Cleeve Hill SE23 ... 23 B7
Cleeve House RG12 ... 27 E5
Cleeve Rd KT22 ... 95 A7
Cleeve The GU1 ... 110 A1
Cleeves Ct 6 RH1 ... 119 A2
Clement Cl CR8 ... 80 B3
Clement Rd Penge BR3 ... 43 D7
Wimbledon SW19 ... 19 E3
Clements Ct TW4 ... 4 D3
Clements House KT22 ... 95 A8
Clements Mead KT22 ... 95 A8
Clements Rd KT12 ... 54 B8
Clensham Ct SM3 ... 59 A8
Clensham La SM1 ... 59 A8
Clerics Wlk TW17 ... 34 D3
Clerks Croft RH1 ... 120 D2
Clevedon KT13 ... 53 D5
Clevedon Ct
Farnborough GU14 ... 85 D3
Frimley GU16 ... 86 A8
West Norwood SE21 ... 22 D5
Clevedon Gdns TW5 ... 4 B6
Clevedon Rd
Kingston u T KT1 ... 38 A7
Penge SE20 ... 43 D8
Twickenham TW1 ... 6 D1
Cleveland Ave
Hampton TW12 ... 15 F1
Merton SW20 ... 39 F7
Cleveland Cl KT12 ... 54 B7
Cleveland Dr TW18 ... 33 B8
Cleveland Gdns
Barnes SW13 ... 7 F5
Worcester Park KT4 ... 57 F8
Cleveland Pk TW19 ... 2 E1
Cleveland Rd Barnes SW13 ... 7 F5
Isleworth TW7 ... 6 A3
New Malden KT3 ... 38 E5
Worcester Park KT4 ... 57 E8
Cleveland Rise SM4 ... 39 D2
Cleves Ave KT17 ... 58 B2
Cleves Cl KT11 ... 73 B5
Cleves Cres CR0 ... 82 C8
Cleves Ct Epsom KT17 ... 76 F7
Kingston u T KT6 ... 37 E3
Knaphill GU21 ... 68 D2
Cleves Rd TW10 ... 17 C5
Cleves Sch KT13 ... 53 F6
Cleves Way Ashford TW16 ... 14 F2
Hampton TW12 ... 15 F1
Cleves Wood KT13 ... 53 E6
Clewborough Dr GU15 ... 66 B6
Clewborough House Sch
GU15 ... 66 B6
Clews La GU24 ... 68 B3
Clifden Centre(Richmond
Adult & Community Coll)
TW1 ... 16 F7
Clifden House 7 TW8 ... 6 D8
Clifden Rd Brentford TW8 ... 6 D8
Twickenham TW1 ... 16 F7
Cliff End CR8 ... 80 B7
Cliffe Rd Croydon CR2 ... 61 D5
Godalming GU7 ... 150 C2
Cliffe Rise GU7 ... 150 C3
Cliffe Wlk 2 SM1 ... 59 C5
Clifford Ave
Mortlake SW14, TW10, TW9 ... 7 B4
Wallington SM6 ... 60 C6
Clifford Ct SW18 ... 20 D8
Clifford Gr TW15 ... 14 A4
Clifford House BR3 ... 24 B2
Clifford Manor Rd GU4 ... 130 E5
Clifford Rd Croydon SE25 ... 43 A5
Hounslow TW4 ... 4 D4
Richmond TW10 ... 17 D6
Clifton Av SM2 ... 78 B8
Clifton Ave TW13 ... 15 C5
Clifton Cl Caterham CR3 ... 100 D4
Chertsey KT15 ... 52 B8
Rowledge GU10 ... 146 A4
Clifton Ct Beckenham BR3 ... 44 B8
South Norwood SE25 ... 42 E4
8 Stanwell TW19 ... 2 E1
Clifton Gdns GU16 ... 85 F6
Clifton Hill Sch CR3 ... 100 D4
Clifton Lodge (Brunel Univ
Coll Twickenham Campus)
TW1 ... 6 B2
Clifton Mews SE25 ... 42 E5
Clifton Par TW13 ... 15 C4
Clifton Park Ave SW20 ... 39 C7
Clifton Pl SM7 ... 78 A4
Clifton Rd Coulsdon CR5 ... 79 C4
Crawley RH10 ... 202 C5
Harlington TW6 ... 3 B4
Hounslow TW7 ... 5 E5
Kingston u T KT2 ... 37 F8
South Norwood SE25 ... 42 E5
Teddington TW11 ... 16 E4
Wallington SM6 ... 60 B5
Wimbledon SW19 ... 19 D2
Wokingham RG41 ... 25 A8
Clifton Terr RH4 ... 136 B6
Clifton Way GU21 ... 68 F2
Cliftons La RH2 ... 117 D2
Cliftonville RH4 ... 136 B6
Climping Rd RH11 ... 201 B8
Cline Rd GU1 ... 130 F7
Clinton Ave KT8 ... 36 C5
Clinton Cl GU21 ... 68 D1
Clinton Hill RH7 ... 186 A8
Clinton House
New Malden KT3 ... 38 D1
6 Surbiton KT6 ... 37 D2
Clinton Rd KT22 ... 95 C4
Clintons Gn RG42 ... 27 A8
Clippesby Cl KT9 ... 56 F4
Clipstone Rd TW3 ... 5 A4
Clive Ct Streatham SW16 ... 21 D3
Tolworth KT6 ... 57 A8
Clive Gn RG12 ... 27 B4
Clive House 3 Croydon CR0 ... 42 F1
Redhill RH1 ... 118 E3
Clive Rd Aldershot GU12 ... 105 D1
Esher KT10 ... 55 B6
Feltham TW14 ... 4 A1
Mitcham SW19 ... 20 E2
Teddington TW1 ... 17 A4
West Norwood SE21, SE27 ... 22 D5
Clive Way RH10 ... 202 C6
Cliveden Pl TW17 ... 34 C3
Cliveden Rd SW19 ... 39 F8
Clock Barn La GU8 ... 171 F6
Clock House Cl KT14 ... 71 F7
Clock House Cotts RH5 ... 178 C2
Clock House Ct BR3 ... 43 E7
Clock House Mead KT11 ... 74 B5
Clock House Rd BR3 ... 43 E7
Clock House Sta BR3 ... 43 E8
Clock Tower Rd TW7 ... 5 F4
Clockhouse Cl SW19 ... 19 C6
Clockhouse Ct GU1 ... 109 C5
Clockhouse La
Ashford TW14, TW15 ... 14 B5
Bramley GU5 ... 151 F7
East Bedfont TW14, TW15 ... 14 B5
Clockhouse La E TW20 ... 12 B1
Clockhouse La W TW20 ... 12 A1
Clockhouse Rd GU14 ... 85 B4
Clodhouse Hill GU22 ... 88 D5
Cloister Cl TW11 ... 17 B3
Cloister Gdns SE25 ... 43 B3
Cloisters The Frimley GU16 ... 65 D1
Old Woking GU22 ... 90 B6
Clone The 5 KT2 ... 18 B1
Clonmel
Rd TW11, TW12, TW2 ... 16 D4
Clonmore St SW18 ... 19 F7
Close The Beckenham BR3 ... 43 E5
Bracknell RG12 ... 27 C5
Brockham RH3 ... 137 B5
Cheam SM3 ... 39 F2
Croydon SE25 ... 43 A3
East Grinstead RH19 ... 205 D8
Esher KT10 ... 55 B3
Farnham GU9 ... 125 D1
Frimley GU16 ... 85 C8
Godalming GU7 ... 150 F3
Horley RH6 ... 161 C1
Hounslow TW7 ... 5 D5
Ifold RH14 ... 212 D3
Kingston u T KT3 ... 38 C7
Lightwater GU18 ... 48 A1
Mitcham CR4 ... 40 F5
Mortlake TW9 ... 7 B4
North Ascot SL5 ... 28 D7
Purley CR8 ... 61 B1
Purley, Russell Hill CR8 ... 60 F1
Close The *continued*
Reigate RH2 ... 139 B8
Sandhurst GU47 ... 64 E8
Surbiton KT6 ... 37 E3
Virginia Water GU25 ... 31 D4
Wallington SM5 ... 59 E2
West Byfleet KT14 ... 71 A6
Wonersh GU5 ... 152 B7
Closeworth Rd GU14 ... 105 E8
Cloudesdale Rd SW17 ... 21 B6
Clouston Cl SM6 ... 60 E5
Clouston Rd GU14 ... 84 F5
Clovelly Ave CR6 ... 101 B8
Clovelly Dr GU26 ... 188 D7
Clovelly Pl GU26 ... 188 C7
Clovelly Rd
Beacon Hill GU26 ... 188 C7
Hounslow TW3 ... 5 B5
Clover Cl RG40 ... 25 E7
Clover Ct GU22 ... 89 D8
Clover Field RH12 ... 215 D4
Clover Hill CR5 ... 99 B6
Clover House TW3 ... 5 C6
Clover Lea GU7 ... 150 E8
Clover Rd GU2 ... 108 E2
Clover Way Carshalton CR4 ... 41 A1
Smallfield RH6 ... 162 C3
Cloverfields RH6 ... 161 B4
Cloverlands RH10 ... 201 F8
Clovers Cotts RH12 ... 199 F1
Clovers End RH12 ... 218 A5
Clovers Way RH12 ... 218 D7
Clowders Rd SE6 ... 23 F5
Clowser Cl 4 SM1 ... 59 C5
Club La RG45 ... 45 D5
Club Row GU24 ... 87 D8
Clubhouse Rd GU11 ... 104 F5
Clump Ave KT20 ... 116 C4
Clumps Rd GU10 ... 146 E4
Clumps The TW15 ... 14 D4
Clyde Ave CR2 ... 81 B4
Clyde Cl RH1 ... 119 A2
Clyde Ct RH1 ... 119 A2
Clyde Rd Croydon CR0 ... 61 F8
Stanwell TW19 ... 13 E7
Sutton SM1 ... 59 A5
Wallington SM6 ... 60 C4
Clyde Terr SE23 ... 23 C6
Clyde Vale SE23 ... 23 C6
Clydesdale Cl TW7 ... 5 F4
Clydesdale Gdns TW10 ... 7 B3
Clymping Dene TW14 ... 15 B8
Clytha Ct SE27 ... 22 C4
Clyve Way TW18 ... 32 E8
Coach House Cl GU16 ... 65 E3
Coach House La SW19 ... 19 D5
Coach Rd Brockham RH3 ... 137 A7
Brockham, Pixham RH4 ... 115 E1
Crawley, North
Terminal RH6 ... 181 F8
Crawley, South
Terminal RH6 ... 182 B7
North Ascot SL5 ... 8 E1
Ottershaw KT16 ... 51 C4
Coachlads Ave 3 GU2 ... 108 F1
Coachmans Dr RH11 ... 201 B2
Coalbrook Mansions
SW12 ... 21 B7
Coaldale Wlk SE21 ... 22 C8
Coast Hill RH4, RH5 ... 134 F4
Coast Hill La RH4 ... 135 A5
Coates Wlk 15 TW8 ... 6 E8
Coatham Pl GU6 ... 174 F3
Cob Cl RH10 ... 204 C8
Cob Wlk RH11 ... 201 A6
Cobb's Rd TW4 ... 4 F3
Cobbets Ridge GU10 ... 147 C8
Cobbett Cl RH10 ... 202 C8
Cobbett Rd Guildford GU2 ... 108 F2
Twickenham TW2 ... 16 A7
Cobbetts Cl GU21 ... 69 B2
Cobbetts Farm GU24 ... 68 A4
Cobbetts Hill KT13 ... 53 B3
Cobbetts Way GU10, GU9 ... 145 F6
Cobbetts Wlk GU24 ... 68 A4
Cobbler's Wlk TW11 ... 16 F1
Cobblers RH12 ... 215 D4
Cobbles Cres RH10 ... 201 E7
Cobden La GU27 ... 208 D7
Cobden Mews SE26 ... 23 B3
Cobden Rd SE25 ... 43 A4
Cobham Ave KT3 ... 39 A4
Cobham Bus Mus KT11 ... 72 B7
Cobham Cl SM6 ... 60 E4
Cobham Ct CR4 ... 40 D7
Cobham Gate KT11 ... 73 B5
Cobham Park Rd KT11 ... 73 C2
Cobham Rd
Fetcham KT11, KT22, KT23 ... 94 C6
Heston TW5 ... 4 C7
Kingston u T KT1, KT2 ... 38 A7
Cobham & Stoke
D'Abernon Sta KT11 ... 73 E2
Cobham Way
Crawley RH10 ... 182 B4
East Horsley KT24 ... 92 E1
Cobnor Cl RH11 ... 200 F4
Cobs Way KT15 ... 52 C1
Coburg Cres SW2 ... 22 A7
Cochrane Ct KT23 ... 94 A2
Cochrane Pl GU20 ... 48 D5
Cochrane Rd SW19 ... 19 F1
Cock La KT22 ... 94 C5
Cock's La Newell Green SL4 ... 8 A6
Winkfield RG42 ... 8 A6
Cock-A-Dobby GU47 ... 45 A1
Cocks Cres KT3 ... 38 F5
Cockshot Hill RH2 ... 139 B7
Cockshot Rd RH2 ... 139 C8
Codrington Ct GU21 ... 68 F1
Codrington Hill SE23, SE4 ... 23 E8
Cody Cl Ash Vale GU12 ... 105 F5
Wallington SM6 ... 60 D3
Cody Rd GU14 ... 84 F3
Coe Ave SE25 ... 43 A3
Coe Cl GU11 ... 105 A1
Cogman's La RH6 ... 162 D4
Cokenor Wood GU10 ... 145 F6
Cokers La SE21 ... 22 D7
Colborne Way KT4 ... 58 C8
Colburn Ave CR3 ... 100 F3
Colburn Cres GU1 ... 110 A4
Colburn Way SM1 ... 59 D7
Colby Rd Dulwich SE19 ... 22 E3
Walton-on-T KT12 ... 35 A1
Colchester Vale RH18 ... 206 E2
Colchester Villas CR7 ... 42 A3
Colcokes Rd SM7 ... 78 A3
Cold Harbour La GU14 ... 84 F8
Coldharbour Cl TW20 ... 32 C6
Coldharbour La
Bletchingley RH1 ... 120 F1
Dorking RH4, RH5 ... 135 F3
Egham TW20 ... 32 D6
Purley CR8 ... 61 A1
Pyrford GU22 ... 70 F4
South Holmwood RH5 ... 156 F6
West End GU24 ... 67 F8
Coldharbour Rd
Croydon CR0 ... 61 A5
Pyrford GU22, KT14 ... 70 F4
Coldharbour Sch CR9 ... 61 A5
Coldharbour Way CR0 ... 61 A5
Coldshott RH8 ... 123 A2
Cole Cl RH11 ... 201 B1
Cole Court Lodge 8 TW1 ... 17 A8
Cole Gdns TW5 ... 4 A7
Cole Park Gdns TW1 ... 6 A1
Cole Park Rd TW1 ... 6 B1
Cole Park View 2 TW1 ... 6 A1
Cole Rd TW1 ... 6 A1
Cole's La RH5 ... 178 B5
Colebrook KT16 ... 51 D4
Colebrook Cl SW19 ... 19 D8
Colebrook Rd SW16 ... 41 E8
Colebrook Rise BR2 ... 44 E7
Colebrooke Pl KT16 ... 51 C3
Colebrooke Rd RH1 ... 118 E3
Coleford Bridge Rd
Farnborough GU16 ... 85 D4
Mytchett GU14, GU16 ... 85 E4
Coleford Cl GU16 ... 85 F3
Coleford Paddocks GU16 ... 85 F4
Colekitchen La GU5 ... 133 D6
Coleman Cl SE25 ... 43 A7
Coleman Ct SW18 ... 20 A8
Coleman Rd GU12 ... 105 D1
Coleridge Ave SM1 ... 59 E6
Coleridge Cl
Crowthorne RG45 ... 45 C4
Horsham RH12 ... 217 E6
Coleridge Cres SL3 ... 1 E6
Coleridge Ct 2 TW10 ... 17 D4
Coleridge Rd Ashford TW15 ... 13 F4
Croydon CR0 ... 43 C2
Coles La RH5 ... 178 C5
Colesburg Rd BR3 ... 43 F7
Colescroft Hill CR8 ... 80 A4
Coleshill Rd TW11 ... 16 E2
Colesmead Rd RH1 ... 118 F4
Coleson Hill Rd GU10 ... 145 F5
Colet Rd RH10 ... 201 D3
Coleville Rd GU14 ... 84 F5
Coley Ave GU22 ... 70 A2
Colfe Rd SE23 ... 23 E7
Colgate Cl RH11 ... 201 B8
Colin Cl Coney Hall BR4 ... 63 F7
Croydon CR0 ... 62 F7
Colin Ct SW16 ... 21 D6
Colin Rd CR3 ... 101 A4
Coliston Rd SW18 ... 20 A8
Coll of Liberal Arts SM1 ... 59 B5
Coll of St Barnabas RH7 ... 185 F8
Coll of Tech Three
Bridges Outpost RH10 ... 202 A7
Collamore Ave SW18 ... 20 E7
Collards La GU27 ... 208 D6
College Ave Egham TW20 ... 12 B2
Epsom KT17 ... 76 F5
College Cl Addlestone KT15 ... 52 D7
Camberley GU15 ... 65 D7
East Grinstead RH19 ... 185 F1
Lingfield RH7 ... 164 D4
Twickenham TW2 ... 16 D7
College Cres Redhill RH1 ... 119 A4
Sandhurst GU47 ... 64 E8
College Ct CR0 ... 62 A8
College Fields Bsns Ctr
SW19 ... 40 E8
College Gdns Dulwich SE21 ... 22 E7
Farnham GU9 ... 125 B2
New Malden KT3 ... 38 F4
Upper Tooting SW17 ... 20 E6
College Gn SE19 ... 22 E1
College Hill
Godalming GU7 ... 150 C2
Haslemere GU27 ... 208 C6
College Hill Terr GU27 ... 208 C6
College House GU8 ... 171 E5
College La
East Grinstead RH19 ... 185 F1
Woking GU22 ... 89 C8
College Rd Ash GU12 ... 106 B3
Bracknell RG12 ... 27 D5
Crawley RH10 ... 201 E6
Croydon CR0, CR9 ... 61 D8
College Rd *continued*
Dulwich SE19, SE21 ... 22 E6
Epsom KT17 ... 76 F5
Ewell KT17 ... 77 B5
Guildford GU1 ... 130 D8
Hounslow TW7 ... 5 F6
Mitcham SW19 ... 20 D2
Sandhurst GU47 ... 64 E8
Woking GU22 ... 70 B3
College Rdbt 1 KT1 ... 37 E6
College Ride Bagshot GU19 ... 47 C2
Camberley GU15 ... 65 D7
College Town Inf Sch
GU47 ... 64 E8
College Town Jun Sch
GU47 ... 64 E8
College Way TW15 ... 13 F4
College Wlk KT1 ... 37 E6
Collendean La RH6 ... 159 F4
Collens Field GU24 ... 87 F4
Collette Ct SE25 ... 42 E4
Colley La RH2 ... 117 E3
Colley Manor Dr RH2 ... 117 D2
Colley Way RH2 ... 117 E4
Collier Cl Farnborough GU14 ... 84 D5
West Ewell KT19 ... 57 B4
Collier Row RH10 ... 201 D4
Collier Way GU4 ... 110 D3
Collier's Wood Sta SW19 ... 20 D1
Colliers CR3 ... 101 A2
Colliers Cl GU21 ... 69 B2
Colliers Water La CR7 ... 42 A4
Collingdon GU6 ... 174 F1
Collingsbourne KT15 ... 52 B6
Collingtree Rd SE26 ... 23 C4
Collingwood GU14 ... 85 E2
Collingwood Ave KT5 ... 38 C1
Collingwood Cl
4 East Grinstead RH19 ... 205 F7
Horley RH6 ... 161 B4
Horsham RH12 ... 217 C4
3 Penge SE20 ... 43 B8
Twickenham TW2, TW4 ... 16 A8
Collingwood Coll GU15 ... 66 A8
Collingwood Cres GU1 ... 110 A2
Collingwood Mount GU15 ... 66 A7
Collingwood Pl
Camberley GU15 ... 66 B8
Walton-on-T KT12 ... 54 B7
Collingwood Rd
Crawley RH10 ... 202 D5
Horsham RH12 ... 217 B4
Mitcham CR4 ... 40 E6
Sutton SM1 ... 59 A6
Collingwood Rise GU15 ... 66 A7
Collins Gdns GU12 ... 106 B2
Collins Rd RH11 ... 200 E4
Collis Prim Sch TW11 ... 17 B2
Collyer Ave CR0 ... 60 E6
Collyer Rd CR0 ... 60 E6
Collyer's Sixth Form Coll
RH12 ... 217 D4
Colman Cl KT18 ... 77 C2
Colman House RH1 ... 118 F3
Colman Way RH1 ... 118 E4
Colmans Hill GU5 ... 154 E7
Colmer Rd SW16 ... 21 E1
Coln Trad Est SL3 ... 1 F6
Colnbrook By-Pass
Brands Hill SL3, UB7 ... 1 D7
Colnbrook SL3, UB7 ... 1 D7
Harmondsworth UB7 ... 2 C7
Colnbrook C of E Comb
Sch SL3 ... 1 D7
Colnbrook Ct Poyle SL3 ... 1 F6
Upper Tooting SW17 ... 20 D4
Colndale Rd SL3 ... 1 E5
Colne Bank SL3, TW19 ... 1 C4
Colne Ct KT19 ... 57 C6
Colne Dr KT12 ... 54 D7
Colne House 2 RH1 ... 118 F2
Colne Lodge KT12 ... 54 D7
Colne Rd TW1, TW2 ... 16 E7
Colne Reach TW19 ... 1 F2
Colne Way Ash GU12 ... 106 A1
Wraysbury TW19 ... 12 B6
Colne Wlk RH11 ... 200 F5
Colnebridge Cl TW18 ... 12 E3
Coloma Convent Girls Sch
CR9 ... 62 D7
Colonel's La KT16 ... 33 A3
Colonial Ave TW2 ... 5 C1
Colonial Rd TW14 ... 14 E8
Colonsay Rd RH11 ... 201 B3
Colony Gate GU16 ... 66 D2
Colson Rd CR0, CR9 ... 61 E8
Colson Way SW16 ... 21 C4
Colston Ave SM1, SM5 ... 59 E6
Colston Ct SM5 ... 59 F6
Colston Rd SW14 ... 7 C3
Coltash Rd RH10 ... 202 A5
Coltsfoot Dr
Guildford GU1, GU4 ... 110 B4
Horsham RH12 ... 217 E5
Coltsfoot La RH8 ... 123 A2
Columbia Ave KT4 ... 38 F2
Columbia Ct KT3 ... 38 F2
Columbine Ave CR2 ... 61 B3
Columbus Dr GU14 ... 84 C4
Colville Gdns GU18 ... 67 C8
Colvin Cl SE26 ... 23 C3
Colvin Rd CR7 ... 42 A4
Colwood Gdns SW19 ... 20 D1
Colworth Rd CR0 ... 43 A1
Colwyn Cl Crawley RH11 ... 200 F4

Colwyn Cl *continued*
Streatham SW16 21 C3
Colwyn Cres TW3 5 C6
Colyton Cl GU21 69 C1
Combe House SW14 7 C5
Combe Hurst KT2 18 C3
Combe La
Bramley GU5, GU8 151 D2
Chiddingfold GU8 191 A7
Farnborough GU14 85 A6
Shere KT24, GU4 133 B8
Whiteley Village KT12 53 F2
Wormley GU8 170 F1
Combe Martin Coll KT2 18 C3
Combe Rd GU7 150 E8
Combe Rise GU10 146 D5
Combe View GU8 191 A5
Combemartin Rd SW18 19 E7
Combermere Rd SM4 40 B4
Comeragh Cl GU22 89 A7
Comet Rd TW19 13 D8
Comforts Farm Ave RH8 123 A3
Comfrey Cl
Farnborough GU14 84 C5
Wokingham RG40 25 E8
Commerce Rd TW8 6 C7
Commerce Way CR0 60 F8
Commercial Rd
Aldershot GU12 126 C8
Guildford GU1 130 D8
Staines TW18 13 A2
Commercial Way GU21 69 F2
Commodore Ct GU14 105 B8
Common Cl GU21 69 D5
Common House Rd GU8 192 F4
Common La Claygate KT10 56 A3
New Haw KT15 52 C2
Common Rd Claygate KT10 56 A3
Redhill RH1 139 F7
Common Side KT18 76 A4
Common The GU6 174 C3
Commonfield Rd SM7 78 B6
Commonfields GU24 67 F6
Commonside KT22, KT23 94 A5
Commonside Cl SM2 78 B8
Commonside Ct SW16 21 E2
Commonside E CR4 41 B6
Commonwealth Lodge Sch CR8 79 D7
Commonwealth Rd CR3 101 A4
Community Cl TW5 4 B6
Como Rd SE23 23 E6
Compass Hill TW10 6 D1
Compasses Mobile Home Pk GU6 193 F5
Compassion Cl RH11 200 E5
Comper Cl RH11 200 E4
Comport Gn CR0 82 E7
Compton Cl Bracknell RG12 26 E3
Esher KT10 55 D5
Sandhurst GU47 45 C1
Compton Cres
Chessington KT9 56 E4
Chiswick W4 7 C8
Compton Ct
7 Guildford GU1 130 F8
Sutton SM1 59 C6
9 West Norwood SE19 22 E3
Compton Hts GU3 129 D6
Compton Place Bsns Ctr GU15 65 A4
Compton Rd Croydon CR0 43 B1
Wimbledon SW19 19 F2
Compton Way GU10 126 B1
Comptons Brow La RH13 218 A3
Comptons La RH12, RH13 217 F3
Comsaye Wlk RG12 27 C4
Conal Ct SW16 21 D3
Conaways Cl KT17 58 A1
Concorde Bsns Pk TN16 83 D4
Concorde Cl TW3 5 B5
Concorde House KT15 52 B6
Condor Ct GU2 130 C7
Condor Rd TW18 33 C6
Conduit La CR0 62 A5
Conduit The RH1 120 D6
Coney Acre SE21 22 C7
Coney Cl RH11 201 B8
Coney Croft RH12 218 B5
Coney Hall Par BR4 63 E7
Coney Hill Rd BR4 63 F8
Coney Hill Sch BR2 63 F7
Coneyberry RH2 139 D5
Coneybury RH1 120 E1
Coneybury Cl CR6 101 B8
Coneyhurst La GU6 175 D7
Conford Dr GU4 130 E2
Coniers Way GU1, GU4 110 B4
Conifer Cl RH2 118 A3
Conifer Ct 23 SW19 19 D7
Conifer Dr GU15 66 A6
Conifer Gdns
Streatham SW16 21 F5
Sutton SM1 59 B8
Conifer La TW20 12 C3
Conifers KT13 53 F6
Conifers Cl Horsham RH12 218 B6
Teddington TW11 17 C1
Conifers The RG45 45 A7
Coningsby RG12 27 C5
Coningsby Ct CR4 41 A7
Coningsby Rd CR2 61 C2
Conisborough Cres SE6 24 C5
Conista Ct GU21 68 F3
Coniston Cl Barnes SW13 7 F7
Coniston Cl *continued*
Chiswick W4 7 C7
Crawley RH11 200 D4
Farnborough GU14 84 E3
Frimley GU15 66 C3
Horsham RH12 218 B6
West Barnes SM4 39 D3
Coniston Ct
Beckenham BR3 44 C8
Chessington KT9 56 E7
Lightwater GU18 48 B1
Penge SE26 23 B2
3 Wallington SM6 60 B6
Weybridge KT13 53 B4
Coniston Dr GU9 125 A6
Coniston Gdns SM2 59 D4
Coniston Rd Catford BR1 24 E2
Coulsdon CR5 79 C3
Croydon CR0 43 A2
Old Woking GU22 90 B7
Twickenham TW2 5 B1
Coniston Way
Chessington KT9 56 E7
Redhill RH2 118 E2
Thorpe Lea TW20 12 B1
Connaught Ave
Ashford TW15 13 E4
Hounslow TW4 4 E3
Mortlake SW14 7 C3
Connaught Bsns Ctr
Mitcham CR4 40 F4
Wallington CR9 60 F4
Connaught Cl SM1 59 D8
Connaught Cres GU24 87 F7
Connaught Gdns
Crawley RH10 201 D8
Morden SM4 40 C5
Connaught Rd
Aldershot GU12 105 D2
Bagshot GU19 47 C3
Brookwood GU24 87 F7
Camberley GU15 65 F5
Carshalton SM1 59 D8
New Malden KT3 38 E5
4 Richmond TW10 6 F2
Teddington TW11, TW12 16 D3
Connaught Sch The GU12 126 E7
Connell House 6 SM6 60 C4
Connington 2 KT1 38 A7
Connop Way GU16 65 F3
Conquest Rd KT15 52 A5
Conrad Dr KT4 39 D1
Consfield Ave KT3 39 A4
Consort Dr GU15 66 C7
Consort Mews TW7 5 D2
Consort Way RH6 161 A3
Consort Way E RH6 161 B2
Constable Gdns TW7 5 D2
Constable Rd RH10 201 F2
Constable Way GU47 64 E6
Constable Wlk SE21 22 E5
Constance Cres BR2 44 F1
Constance Rd Sutton SM1 59 C6
Thornton Heath CR0 42 B2
Twickenham TW2 16 B8
Constantine House SW2 22 B7
Constitution Hill GU22 89 E8
Contley House Hotel RG40 25 B8
Control Tower Rd
Crawley RH6 181 D6
Harlington TW6 3 B4
Convent Cl BR3 24 C1
Convent Hill SE19 22 C2
Convent of the Sacred Heart Digby-Stuart Coll SW15 7 F2
Convent Rd TW15 14 B3
Conway Cl GU16 65 F1
Conway Dr Ashford TW15 14 C2
Farnborough GU14 84 D4
Sutton SM2 59 B4
Conway Gdns CR4 41 E5
Conway House
Reigate RH2 139 A4
6 Streatham SW2 21 E7
Conway Rd Feltham TW13 15 D3
Harlington TW6 3 B4
Twickenham TW4 16 A8
Wimbledon SW20 39 C8
Conway Wlk TW12 15 F2
Conyer's Rd SW16 21 D3
Conyers Cl KT12 54 D5
Cook Rd Crawley RH10 201 F4
Horsham RH12 217 D6
Cookes La SM3 58 E4
Cookham Cl GU47 45 C1
Cookham Rd RG12 26 E7
Cooks Hill RH12 214 A8
Cooks Mead RH12 199 D7
Coolarne Rise GU15 66 A6
Coolgardie Rd TW15 14 C3
Coolham Ct RH11 200 F6
Coolhurst La RH13 218 A1
Coombe Ave CR0 61 E6
Coombe Bank KT2, KT3 38 E8
Coombe Cl Crawley RH11 181 D1
Frimley GU16 85 D8
Hounslow TW3 5 A3
Coombe Cotts RH3 116 D4
Coombe Cres TW12 15 E1
Coombe Ct Beckenham BR3 43 F8
Tadworth KT20 97 C4
Coombe Dr KT15 51 F4
Coombe End KT2 18 D1
Coombe Gdns
New Malden KT3 38 F5
Wimbledon SW20 39 A8
Coombe Girls Sch KT3 38 D7
Coombe Hill Glade KT2 18 E1
Coombe Hill Golf Course KT2 18 C1
Coombe Hill Inf Sch KT3 38 D8
Coombe Hill Jun Sch KT3 38 D8
Coombe Hill Rd
East Grinstead RH19 205 D6
Kingston u T KT2 18 E1
Coombe House Chase KT3 38 D8
Coombe La
South Croydon CR0 62 B5
Wimbledon SW20 39 B8
Worplesdon GU3 108 D7
Coombe La W KT2 18 E1
Coombe Lane Flyover SW20 38 F8
Coombe Manor GU24 68 B4
Coombe Neville KT2 18 D1
Coombe Pine RG12 27 D3
Coombe Pk KT2 18 D3
Coombe Rd Croydon CR0 61 E6
Forest Hill SE26 23 B4
Hampton TW12 15 F2
Kingston u T KT3 38 E6
Kingston u T, Norbiton KT2 38 A8
South Croydon CR0, CR2 61 E6
Coombe Ridings KT2 18 C3
Coombe Rise KT2 38 C8
Coombe The RH3 116 D4
Coombe Way KT14 71 F7
Coombe Wlk SM1 59 B7
Coombe Wood Golf Course KT2 18 C1
Coombe Wood Hill CR8 80 C6
Coombe Wood Rd KT2 18 C3
Coombefield Cl KT3 38 E4
Coombelands La KT15 52 A4
Coomber Way CR0, CR4 41 D2
Coombes The GU5 152 A5
Cooper Cl RH6 162 A3
Cooper Cres SM5 59 F7
Cooper Ct GU14 85 C4
Cooper House
Hounslow TW4 4 F4
7 West Norwood SW27 22 B3
Cooper Rd
Croydon CR0, CR9 61 B6
Guildford GU1 130 F8
Windlesham GU20 48 D4
Cooper Row RH10 201 D3
Cooper's Hill La TW20 11 D4
Cooper's Hill Rd
Nutfield RH1 120 A1
South Nutfield RH1 141 B5
Cooper's Terr GU9 125 C3
Cooper's Yd SE19 22 E2
Coopers Cl TW18 12 E3
Coopers Hill Dr GU24 87 C7
Coopers Rise GU7 150 C3
Cootes Ave RH12 217 A3
Copeland House SW17 20 D4
Copelands BR3 23 F1
Copelands Cl GU15 66 D4
Copeman Cl SE26 23 C3
Copenhagen Way KT12 54 B7
Copenhagen Wlk RG45 45 B4
Copers Cope Rd BR3 23 F1
Copleigh Dr KT20 97 E7
Copley Cl Knaphill GU21 88 E8
Redhill RH1 118 E3
Copley Pk SW16 21 F2
Copley Way KT20 97 D7
Copnall Way RH12 217 C2
Coppard Gdns KT9 56 C4
Copped Hall Dr GU15 66 C6
Copped Hall Way GU15 66 C6
Coppedhall 1 SE21 22 D6
Copper Beech Cl GU22 89 B6
Copper Beeches TW7 5 D6
Copper Cl SE19 22 F1
Copper Mill Dr TW7 5 F5
Copper Mill La SW17 20 C4
Copperfield Ave GU47 45 E2
Copperfield Cl CR2, CR8 80 C8
Copperfield Ct KT22 95 A6
Copperfield Pl RH12 217 B4
Copperfield Rise KT15 51 F4
Copperfields
Beckenham BR3 44 C8
Fetcham KT22 94 C5
Coppermill Rd TW19 1 B2
Coppice Cl Guildford GU2 108 D2
Heath End GU9 125 E6
West Barnes SW20 39 C6
Coppice Dr TW19 11 D8
Coppice La RH2 117 F3
Coppice Pl GU8 190 F8
Coppice Rd RH12 218 A5
Coppice The Ashford TW15 14 B2
Crawley Down RH10 204 B8
Coppice Wlk RH10 202 A7
Coppin House SW2 22 B7
Copping Cl CR0 61 E6
Coppins The CR0 63 B4
Coppsfield KT8 36 A6
Copse Ave Heath End GU9 125 E8
West Wickham BR4 63 B7
Copse Cl Camberley GU15 66 A6
Chilworth GU4 131 C3
Crawley Down RH10 204 B8
East Grinstead RH19 186 A3
Horsham RH12 217 F6
Copse Cres RH11 201 C7
Copse Dr RG41 25 A7
Copse Edge Cranleigh GU6 174 F4
Elstead GU8 148 C3
Copse Edge Ave KT17 76 F6
Copse End GU15 66 A6
Copse Glade KT6 37 D1
Copse Hill Purley CR8 79 E6
Sutton SM2 59 B3
Wimbledon SW20 19 B1
Copse La RH6 161 D4
Copse Rd Cobham KT11 73 B6
Knaphill GU21 68 F1
Linchmere GU27 207 D5
Reigate RH1 139 D7
Copse Side GU7 129 D1
Copse The Caterham CR3 101 A1
Farnborough GU14 84 D3
Fetcham KT22, KT23 94 B4
Rowledge GU10 145 F4
South Nutfield RH1 140 E7
Copse View CR2 62 E2
Copse Way GU10 145 F6
Copse Wood Ct RH1 118 E3
Copsem Dr KT10 55 B4
Copsem La Esher KT10 55 C3
Oxshott KT22 55 C1
Copsem Way KT10 55 C4
Copsen Wood KT22 74 C8
Copsleigh Ave RH1 140 A3
Copsleigh Cl RH1 140 A3
Copsleigh Way RH1 140 A3
Copt Hill La KT20 97 F7
Copthall Gdns TW1 16 F7
Copthall Way KT15 52 A1
Copthorne Ave SW12 21 D8
Copthorne Bank RH10, RH6 183 C4
Copthorne CE (Controlled) Sch RH10 183 B3
Copthorne Chase TW15 13 F4
Copthorne Cl TW17 34 C3
Copthorne Common Rd RH10 183 C3
Copthorne Dr GU18 48 B1
Copthorne Rd
Copthorne RH10 182 F1
Crawley RH10 202 E8
Domewood RH10, RH19 184 D4
Felbridge RH10, RH19 184 D4
Leatherhead KT22 95 B7
Copthorne Rise CR8 80 D6
Copthorne Sch Trust Ltd RH10 183 E3
Copthorne Way RH10 182 F2
Copyhold Rd RH19 205 D8
Corban Rd TW3 5 A4
Corbet Cl CR4, SM6 60 A8
Corbet Rd KT17 57 E1
Corbett Cl CR0 82 D7
Corbett Ct SE6 23 F4
Corbett Dr GU18 66 F7
Corbiere Ct SW19 19 D2
Corby Cl RH11 200 E3
Corby Dr TW20 11 C2
Cordelia Croft RG42 27 E8
Cordelia Gdns
Ash Vale GU12 85 F1
Stanwell TW19 13 E8
Cordelia Rd TW19 13 E8
Corderoy Pl KT16 32 F3
Cordrey Gdns CR5 79 E4
Cordrey House KT15 52 B8
Cordwalles Cty Jun Sch GU15 65 F8
Cordwalles Rd GU15 65 F8
Corfe Cl KT21 75 C1
Corfe Gdns GU16 65 F1
Corfe Way GU14 85 E1
Coriander Cl GU14 84 C4
Coriander Cres GU2 109 A6
Corium House GU7 150 F5
Cork Tree House 3 SW27 22 B3
Corkran Rd KT6 37 E2
Corkscrew Hill BR4 63 D7
Cormongers La RH1 119 D2
Cormorant Cl SM1 58 F5
Cormorant Ct 12 SE21 22 D6
Cormorant Pl GU47 64 E7
Cornbunting Cl GU47 64 D8
Cornelia Cl GU14 84 D3
Corner Farm Cl KT20 97 C5
Corner Fielde SW2 21 F7
Cornerside TW15 14 C1
Cornerstone Sch The KT18 76 C6
Corney Rd W4 7 E8
Cornfield Rd RH2 139 C8
Cornfields GU7 151 A8
Cornflower La CR0 43 D1
Cornford Gr SW12 21 B6
Cornhill Cl KT15 52 B8
Cornish Gr SE20 43 B8
Cornwall Ave Byfleet KT14 71 F5
Claygate KT10 55 F3
Cornwall Cl GU15 65 F7
Cornwall Gdns 6 RH19 205 F8
Cornwall Rd Belmont SM2 59 A2
Thornton Heath CR0, CR9 61 B8
Twickenham TW1 17 A7
Cornwall Way TW18 12 E2
Cornwallis Cl CR3 100 C5
Coronation Cotts GU8 191 C5
Coronation Rd
Aldershot GU11 126 B7
Ascot SL5 29 A2
Bracknell SL5 29 A2
East Grinstead RH19 205 E7
Coronation Sq RG40 25 D7
Coronet Cl RH10 202 E7
Coronet The RH6 161 C1
Corporation Ave TW4 4 E3
Corpus Christi RC Prim Sch KT3 38 C6
Corrib Dr SM1 59 E5
Corrie Gdns GU25 31 C2
Corrie Rd Addlestone KT15 52 D6
Old Woking GU22 90 C7
Corrigan Ave CR5 79 A5
Corry Rd GU26 188 C6
Corsair Cl TW19 13 E8
Corsair Rd TW19 13 E8
Corscombe Cl KT2 18 C3
Corsehill St SW16 21 C2
Corsham Way RG45 45 B5
Corsletts Ave RH12 216 D3
Corsten Hollow 4 RH1 139 F8
Corunna Dr RH13 217 F2
Cosdach Ave SM6 60 D3
Cosedge Cres CR0, CR9 61 B5
Cosford Rd GU8 169 E4
Coteford St SW17 21 A4
Cotelands CR0 61 E7
Cotford Rd CR7 42 C5
Cotherstone KT19 57 D2
Cotherstone Rd SW2 21 F7
Cotland Acres RH1 139 D7
Cotsford Ave KT3 38 D4
Cotswold Cl Crawley RH11 201 B6
Farnborough GU14 84 E7
Hinchley Wood KT10 55 F8
Kingston u T KT2 18 C2
Staines TW18 13 A3
Cotswold Ct RH13 217 E2
Cotswold Rd
Hampton TW12 16 A2
Sutton SM2 59 B1
Cotswold St SE27 22 B4
Cotswold Way KT4 58 C8
Cottage Cl Horsham RH12 218 B6
Ottershaw KT16 51 C4
Cottage Farm Way TW20 32 C6
Cottage Gdns GU14 84 F4
Cottage Gr KT6 37 D3
Cottage Pl RH10 183 E3
Cottage Rd KT19 57 D3
Cottenham Dr SW20 19 B1
Cottenham Par SW20 39 B7
Cottenham Park Rd SW20 39 B8
Cottenham Pl SW20 19 B1
Cottenhams RH7 163 E8
Cotterill Rd KT6 37 F1
Cottesbrooke Cl SL3 1 D6
Cottesloe Cl GU24 67 F3
Cottesmore RG12 27 A2
Cottimore Ave KT12 35 B1
Cottimore Cres KT12 35 B2
Cottimore La
Walton-on-T KT12 35 B2
Walton-on-T KT12 35 D1
Cottimore Terr KT12 35 B2
Cottingham Ave RH12 217 D7
Cottingham Rd SE20 23 D1
Cottington Rd TW13 15 D4
Cotton Hill BR1 24 D4
Cotton House 18 SW12 21 E8
Cotton Row RH5 176 C8
Cotton Wlk RH11 201 A1
Cottongrass Cl CR0 43 D1
Cottrell Flats GU14 105 D8
Cotts Wood Dr GU4 110 A6
Couchmore Ave KT10 55 E8
Coulsdon C of E Prim Sch CR5 79 F1
Coulsdon Coll CR5 100 A8
Coulsdon Court Municipal Golf Course CR5 79 F3
Coulsdon Court Rd CR5 79 F3
Coulsdon High Sch CR5 100 B7
Coulsdon House 5 SW2 21 E7
Coulsdon La CR5 99 A8
Coulsdon Pl CR3 100 D5
Coulsdon Rd
Caterham CR3, CR5 100 B7
Coulsdon CR3, CR5 100 B7
Coulsdon Rise CR5 79 E2
Coulsdon South Sta CR5 79 D3
Coulthurst Ct SW16 21 E1
Council Cotts
Charlwood RH6 180 C6
Loxwood RH14 213 A2
Plaistow RH14 211 D3
West End GU24 67 F7
Countisbury Gdns KT15 52 B5
Countisbury House SE26 23 A5
Country Way TW13, TW16 15 C3
Countryways Experience The GU6 193 E2
County Mall RH10 201 E5
County Oak Ind Est RH10 181 D2
County Oak La RH11 181 D3
County Oak Ret Pk RH11 181 D2
County Oak Way RH10, RH11 181 D3
County Rd CR7 42 B7
Courier House 17 SW2 22 A8
Courland Rd KT15 52 B7
Course Rd SL5 29 A6
Court Ave CR5 100 A8
Court Bushes Rd CR3 101 B7
Court Cl
East Grinstead RH19 185 F1
Twickenham TW13, TW2 16 B5
Court Close Ave TW13, TW2 16 B5
Court Cres Chessington KT9 56 D4
East Grinstead RH19 185 F1
Court Downs Rd BR3 44 B7
Court Dr Carshalton SM1 59 E6

Court Dr *continued*
Croydon CR0 .60 F6
Court Farm Ave KT19 .57 D5
Court Farm Gdns KT19 .76 C8
Court Farm Ind Est TW19 .2 F1
Court Farm Rd CR6 .81 A2
Court Gdns GU15 .65 D5
Court Green Hts GU22 .89 C7
Court Haw SM7 .78 E4
Court Hill Sanderstead CR2 .80 E7
Woodmansterne CR5 .78 F2
Court House Mansions
KT19 .76 D7
Court La Dulwich SE21 .22 F8
Epsom KT19 .76 C6
Court Lane Gdns SE21 .22 E8
Court Lodge Cty Inf Sch
RH6 .160 F3
Court Lodge Rd RH6 .160 F3
Court Rd
10 Aldershot GU11 .105 A2
Banstead SM7 .78 A4
Caterham CR3 .100 E4
South Norwood SE25 .42 F6
Tyler's Green RH9 .121 C4
Court The
Dockenfield GU10 .166 D3
Guildford GU2 .130 C7
Warlingham CR6 .81 E1
Court Way TW1, TW2 .16 F8
Court Wood La CR0 .62 F1
Courtenay Ave SM2 .59 A2
Courtenay Dr BR3 .44 D7
Courtenay Mews GU21 .70 A3
Courtenay Rd
Heath End GU9 .125 E7
North Cheam KT4, SM3 .58 C7
Penge BR3, SE20 .23 D2
Woking GU21 .70 A3
Courtfield Rd TW15 .14 B2
Courtfield Rise BR4 .63 D7
Courthope Rd SW19 .19 E3
Courthope Villas SW19 .19 E1
Courtland Ave SW16 .21 F1
Courtlands Beckenham BR3 .44 B7
Richmond TW10 .7 A2
10 Sutton SM2 .59 B3
Walton-on-T KT12 .35 A2
Courtlands Ave Esher KT10 55 A4
Hampton TW12 .15 F2
Richmond TW9 .7 B5
West Wickham BR2 .44 F1
Courtlands Cl CR2 .62 A1
Courtlands Cres SM7 .78 A3
Courtlands Dr KT19 .57 F4
Courtlands Rd KT5 .38 A2
Courtleas KT11 .74 A6
Courtney Cl SE19 .22 E2
Courtney Cres SM5 .59 F2
Courtney Pl Cobham KT11 .73 F7
Croydon CR0 .61 A7
Courtney Rd
Croydon CR0, CR9 .61 A7
Harlington TW6 .3 A4
Mitcham SW19 .20 E1
Courts Hill Rd GU27 .208 B6
Courts Mount Rd GU27 .208 B6
Courts The SW16 .21 E1
Courtside SE23 .23 C5
Courtwood Prim Sch CR0 .62 F1
Courtyard The
Addlestone KT15 .52 C6
Cranleigh GU6 .153 E1
1 Crawley RH10 .201 D5
Crawley, Whitevane
Hill RH13 .218 E4
East Grinstead RH19 .186 B1
Coutts Ave KT9 .56 E5
Coval Gdns SW14 .7 B3
Coval La SW14 .7 B3
Coval Rd SW14 .7 C3
Cove Cty Inf Sch GU14 .84 E6
Cove Cty Jun Sch GU14 .84 E5
Cove Manor Cty Inf Sch
GU14 .84 E6
Cove Manor Cty Jun Sch
GU14 .84 F6
Cove Rd GU14 .84 F4
Cove Sch GU14 .84 E5
Coveham Cres KT11 .73 A6
Coventry Rd SE25 .43 A5
Coverack Cl CR0 .43 E2
Coverdale Ct RH19 .185 C3
Coverdale Gdns CR0 .61 F7
Covert Cl RH10 .201 E7
Covert La RG12 .27 C5
Covert The Ascot SL5 .29 B2
Farnborough GU14 .84 E8
Coverton Rd SW17 .20 E3
Coverts Cl GU9 .125 E4
Coverts Rd KT10 .55 F3
Coves Farm Wood RG42 .26 D7
Covey Cl Farnborough GU14 .85 A8
Merton SW19 .40 B7
Covey The RH10 .202 E8
Covington Gdns SW16 .22 B1
Covington Way
South Norwood SW16 .22 A1
South Norwood SW16 .22 B1
Streatham SW16 .21 F2
Cow La GU7 .150 D4
Cowden St SE6 .24 A4
Cowdray Cl RH10 .202 C5
Cowdrey Rd SW19 .20 C3
Cowfold Cl RH11 .200 F3
Cowick Rd SW17 .20 F4
Cowleaze Rd KT2 .37 E8
Cowley Ave KT16 .32 F2
Cowley Cl CR2 .62 C2
Cowley Cres KT12 .54 C6
Cowley La KT16 .32 F2
Cowley Rd SW14 .7 E4
Coworth Cl SL5 .30 B4
Coworth Park Sch GU24 .49 B6
Coworth Rd SL5 .30 A4
Cowper Ave SM1 .59 D6
Cowper Cl KT16 .32 F3
Cowper Gdns SM6 .60 C4
Cowper Rd Richmond TW10 .17 F3
Wimbledon SW19 .20 C2
Cowshot Cres GU24 .87 D7
Cowslip La RH5 .115 B7
Cox Cnr RH5 .177 A7
Cox Green Rd
Cranleigh RH12 .195 C2
Ewhurst RH12 .195 C2
Cox House RH12 .217 B2
Cox La Chessington KT9 .56 F6
West Ewell KT19 .57 C5
Coxbridge GU9 .124 F1
Coxcomb Wlk RH11 .201 A4
Coxcombe La GU8 .191 B4
Coxdean KT18 .97 C8
Coxgreen GU47 .64 D6
Coxley Rise CR8 .80 C6
Coxs Ave TW17 .34 E6
Coxwell Rd SE19 .22 E1
Crab Hill BR3 .24 D1
Crab Hill La RH1 .140 F4
Crabbet Rd RH10 .202 B7
Crabtree Cl KT23 .94 C1
Crabtree Cnr TW20 .32 B8
Crabtree Dr KT22 .95 C2
Crabtree La Churt GU10 .168 A2
Great Bookham KT23 .94 C1
Headley KT22 .96 C1
Westhumble RH5 .115 A5
Crabtree Office Village
TW20 .32 C8
Crabtree Rd
Camberley GU15 .65 B2
Crawley RH11 .201 C7
Thorpe TW20 .32 C7
Crabwood RH8 .122 E7
Craddocks Ave KT21 .75 F3
Craddocks Par KT21 .75 E2
Cradhurst Cl RH4 .135 C6
Craig Rd TW10 .17 C4
Craigans RH11 .201 A5
Craigen Ave CR0 .43 B1
Craigmore Tower GU22 .89 E8
Craignair Rd SW2 .22 A8
Craignish Ave SW16 .41 F7
Craigside Kingston u T KT2 .38 B8
Purley CR8 .79 F5
Craigwell Ave TW13 .15 A5
Craigwell Cl TW18 .32 E8
Crail Cl RG41 .25 A3
Crake Pl GU47 .64 D8
Crakell Rd RH2 .139 C8
Cramhurst La GU8 .170 E6
Cramond Ct TW14 .14 E7
Crampshaw La KT21 .95 F7
Crampton Rd SE20 .23 C2
Cranborne Ave KT6, KT9 .57 A7
Cranborne Wlk RH10 .201 F4
Cranbourne Cl
Horley RH6 .161 B5
Thornton Heath SW16 .41 E6
Cranbourne Cotts SL4 .9 B5
Cranbourne Sch SL5 .9 A4
Cranbrook Ct 9 TW8 .6 D8
Cranbrook Dr
Thames Ditton KT10 .36 C1
Twickenham TW2 .16 B7
Cranbrook House SE19 .42 D8
Cranbrook Rd Hounslow TW4 4 F3
South Norwood CR7 .42 C7
Wimbledon SW19 .19 E1
Cranbrook Terr GU6 .174 F3
Crane Ave TW7 .6 A2
Crane Ct Sandhurst GU47 .64 D8
West Ewell KT19 .57 C6
Crane House Catford BR1 .24 D3
Feltham TW13 .16 A5
Crane Inf Sch TW13 .15 F6
Crane Jun Sch TW13 .15 F6
Crane Lodge Rd TW5 .4 B8
Crane Mead Ct TW1 .16 F8
Crane Park Rd TW2 .16 B6
Crane Rd Stanwell TW19 .3 A1
Twickenham TW2 .16 E7
Crane Way TW2 .16 C8
Cranebrook TW2 .16 C6
Craneford Cl TW2 .16 F8
Craneford Way TW2 .16 F8
Cranes Dr KT5 .37 F5
Cranes Park Ave KT5, KT6 .37 F5
Cranes Park Cres KT5 .37 F5
Cranes Pk KT5, KT6 .37 E4
Craneswater TW6 .3 F7
Cranfield Ct 6 GU21 .68 F1
Cranfield Rd E SM5 .60 A2
Cranfield Rd W SM5 .60 A2
Cranford Ave TW19 .13 F8
Cranford Cl Purley CR8 .80 C6
Stanwell TW19 .13 E8
Wimbledon SW20 .19 B1
Cranford Comm Sch TW5 .4 B8
Cranford Ct SM1 .59 C6
Cranford Jun & Inf Schs
TW4 .4 B5
Cranford La Cranford UB3 .4 A7
Harlington UB3 .3 E7
Hatton TW6 .3 F6
Hatton, Hatton Cross TW6 .3 F4
Cranford La *continued*
Heston TW5 .4 D7
Cranford Lodge SW19 .19 E6
Cranford Rise KT10 .55 C5
Cranleigh Cl Penge SE20 .43 B7
Sanderstead CR2 .81 A7
Cranleigh Ct
Farnborough GU14 .84 F4
Mitcham CR4 .40 D6
Richmond TW9 .7 A4
Cranleigh Cty Inf Sch
GU6 .174 E3
Cranleigh Gdns
Kingston u T KT2 .17 F2
Sanderstead CR2 .81 A7
South Norwood SE25 .42 E6
Sutton SM1 .59 B8
Cranleigh House SW20 .39 B7
Cranleigh Mead GU6 .174 F2
Cranleigh Rd
Ewhurst GU6 .175 D4
Feltham TW13 .14 F4
Merton SW19 .40 A6
Thames Ditton KT10 .36 C1
Wonersh GU5 .152 C7
Cranleigh Sch GU6 .174 C5
Cranleigh Village Hospl
GU6 .174 D3
Cranley Cl GU1 .110 A1
Cranley Gdns SM6 .60 C3
Cranley Pl GU21 .68 D1
Cranley Rd Guildford GU1 .109 F1
Hersham KT12 .53 F5
Cranmer Cl
Warlingham CR6 .81 E2
West Barnes SM4 .39 E3
Weybridge KT13 .53 A3
Cranmer Ct Hampton TW12 .16 B3
Kingston u T KT2 .17 D4
Cranmer Farm Cl CR4 .40 F5
Cranmer Gdns CR6 .81 E2
Cranmer Mid Sch CR4 .40 F5
Cranmer Rd
Croydon CR0, CR9 .61 C7
Hampton TW12 .16 B3
Kingston u T KT2 .17 E3
Mitcham CR4 .40 F5
Cranmer Terr SW17 .20 D3
Cranmer Wlk RH10 .202 C5
Cranmore Ave TW7 .5 C7
Cranmore Cl GU11 .104 E1
Cranmore Ct GU16 .85 F4
Cranmore Gdns GU11 .104 E1
Cranmore La
Aldershot GU11 .104 E1
West Horsley KT24 .112 C6
Cranmore Rd Catford BR1 .24 F5
Mytchett GU16 .86 A4
Cranmore Sch KT24 .112 C6
Cranston Cl
Hounslow TW3, TW4 .4 E5
Reigate RH2 .139 B8
Cranston Rd
East Grinstead RH19 .185 F2
Forest Hill SE23 .23 E6
Cranstoun Cl GU3 .108 F5
Crantock Rd SE6 .24 C6
Cranwell Ct CR0 .62 D8
Cranwell Gr
Lightwater GU18 .66 F8
Littleton TW17 .33 F5
Cranwell Rd TW6 .3 B5
Craster Rd SW2 .21 F8
Cravan Ave TW13 .15 A6
Craven Cl GU10 .146 C6
Craven Gdns SW19 .20 B3
Craven House
10 Farnham GU9 .125 B2
2 Mortlake SW14 .7 D4
Craven Rd Crawley RH10 .202 B5
Croydon CR0 .43 B1
Kingston u T KT2 .37 F8
Cravens The RH6 .162 A3
Crawford Cl TW7 .5 E5
Crawford Gdns
Camberley GU15 .65 B5
Horsham RH13 .217 E4
Crawfurd Way RH19 .185 F3
Crawley Ave
Crawley RH10 .182 C1
Crawley, Ifield RH10, RH11 .201 A6
Crawley Chase RG42 .8 B2
Crawley Coll
Crawley RH10 .201 E6
Crawley, Three
Bridges RH10 .202 A6
Crawley Coll (West
Green Annexe) RH11 .201 C7
Crawley Down CE
(Controlled) Sch RH10 .204 B8
Crawley Down Rd
East Grinstead RH19 .184 F4
Felbridge RH19 .184 F4
Crawley Dr GU15 .65 F6
Crawley Hill GU15 .65 F5
Crawley Hospl RH11 .201 C6
Crawley La RH10 .202 C7
Crawley Leisure Pk
RH11 .201 D7
Crawley Mus Ctr RH11 .201 C5
Crawley Rd Crawley RH12 .200 B1
Faygate RH12 .218 D7
Horsham RH12 .218 B5
Crawley Ridge GU15 .65 F6
Crawley Ridge Cty Inf Sch
GU15 .65 F6
Crawley Ridge Cty Jun Sch
GU15 .65 F7
Crawley Sta RH10 .201 E5
Crawley Wood Cl GU15 .65 F5
Crawshaw Rd KT16 .51 D4
Crawters Cl RH10 .201 F7
Cray Ave KT21 .75 F2
Crayke Hill KT9 .56 E3
Crayonne Cl TW16 .34 E8
Crealock St SW18 .20 B8
Creasys Dr RH11 .201 B1
Credenhill St SW16 .21 C2
Crediton Way KT10 .56 A5
Credon Cl GU14 .84 F5
Cree's Meadow GU20 .48 D3
Creek Rd KT8 .36 E5
Creek The TW16 .35 A4
Creeland Gr SE6 .23 F7
Cremorne Gdns KT19 .57 D2
Crerar Cl GU14 .84 D3
Crescent Ct KT6 .37 D4
Crescent Day Hospl CR0 .63 C1
Crescent Gdns SW19 .20 A5
Crescent Gr CR4 .40 E5
Crescent La GU12 .106 B5
Crescent Rd
Beckenham BR3 .44 B7
Bletchingley RH1 .120 C2
Caterham CR3 .101 A3
East Grinstead RH19 .185 D1
Kingston u T KT2 .18 B1
Reigate RH2 .139 A7
Shepperton TW17 .34 C4
Wimbledon SW20 .39 D8
Wokingham RG40 .25 C5
Crescent The
Ashford TW15 .13 F3
Barnes SW13 .7 F5
Beckenham BR3 .44 A8
Belmont SM2 .78 A8
Bracknell RG12 .27 C5
Carshalton SM1 .59 D5
Chertsey KT16 .33 A6
East Molesey KT8 .36 A5
Egham TW20 .11 F2
Epsom KT18 .76 A4
Farnborough GU14 .85 C3
Felcourt RH19 .185 C8
Guildford GU2 .109 A3
Harlington UB7 .3 D7
Heath End GU9 .125 D8
Horley RH6 .182 B8
Horsham RH12 .217 A2
Kingston u T KT6 .37 E4
Kingston u T, Norbiton KT3 .38 C7
Leatherhead KT22 .95 B5
Lower Halliford TW17 .34 F2
Reigate RH2 .118 B1
Thornton Heath CR0, SE25 .42 D3
West Wickham BR4 .44 E3
Weybridge KT13 .53 A7
Wimbledon SW19 .20 A5
Woldingham CR3 .102 A4
Crescent Way Horley RH6 .161 A1
South Norwood SW16 .22 A1
Crescent Wood Rd
SE21, SE26 .23 A5
Cressage Ho 9 TW8 .6 E8
Cressall Cl KT22 .95 B7
Cressall Mead KT22 .95 B7
Cressingham Gr SM1 .59 C6
Cresswell Rd Croydon SE25 43 A5
Feltham TW13 .15 E4
Twickenham TW1 .6 D1
Crest Hill GU5 .133 E1
Crest Rd South Croydon CR2 .62 B3
West Wickham BR2 .44 F2
Crest The Surbiton KT5 .38 A4
10 West Norwood SW27 .22 B3
Cresta Dr KT15 .51 F1
Creston Ave GU21 .68 E3
Creston Way KT4 .39 D1
Crestwood Way TW4 .4 E2
Creswell GU21 .68 D2
Crewdson Rd RH6 .161 B3
Crewe's Ave CR6 .81 C3
Crewe's Cl CR6 .81 C2
Crewe's Farm La CR6 .81 E2
Crewe's La CR6 .81 D3
Crichton Ave SM6 .60 D6
Crichton Rd SM5 .59 F3
Cricket Cl GU26 .188 D6
Cricket Ct RH19 .185 E3
Cricket Field Gr RG45 .45 D4
Cricket Field Rd RH12 .217 B1
Cricket Gn
Hambledon GU8 .171 C1
Mitcham CR4 .40 F5
Cricket Green Sch CR4 .40 E6
Cricket Hill RH1 .140 F7
Cricket La Farnham GU10 .146 D6
Penge BR3 .23 E3
Cricket View KT13 .53 B5
Cricket Way KT13 .53 E8
Cricketers Cl
Chessington KT9 .56 D6
Ockley RH5 .177 C4
Cricketers La
Windlesham GU20 .48 D4
Winkfield RG42 .8 A3
Cricketers Wlk SE26 .23 C3
Cricklade Ave SW2 .21 F6
Crieff Ct 3 TW11, KT8 .17 C1
Criffel Ave SW2 .21 D7
Crimea Rd Aldershot GU11 105 B2
Frimley GU16 .86 D8
Crimp Hill
Englefield Green SL4, TW20 .11 A6
Old Windsor SL4, TW20 .11 A6
Cripley Rd GU14 .84 D6
Cripplecrutch Hill
Chiddingfold GU27 .209 F5
Fisherstreet GU27 .209 F5
Cripps House RH11 .201 B2
Crispen Rd TW13 .15 E4
Crispin Cl Ashstead KT21 .75 F1
Wallington SM6 .60 E8
Crispin Cres SM6 .60 D8
Critchmere Hill GU27 .207 E7
Critchmere La GU27 .207 E6
Critchmere Vale GU27 .207 E6
Critten La KT24, RH5 .113 D2
Crittenden Lodge BR4 .44 A1
Crocker Cl SL5 .28 F8
Crockers La RH7 .163 D4
Crockerton Rd SW17 .20 F6
Crockford Cl KT15 .52 C6
Crockford Park Rd KT15 .52 C5
Crockham Cl RH11 .201 C4
Crocknorth Rd KT24 .113 A2
Crocus Cl CR0 .43 D1
Croffets KT20 .97 D6
Croft Ave Dorking RH4 .115 B1
West Wickham BR4 .44 C1
Croft Cl Harlington UB7 .3 C7
Wokingham RG41 .25 A2
Croft Rd Aldershot GU11 .126 B8
Carshalton SM1 .59 E5
Godalming GU7 .150 E4
Merton SW19 .20 C1
South Norwood SW16 .22 A1
Witley GU8 .170 E5
Wokingham RG40 .25 A1
Woldingham CR3 .102 A5
Croft The Crawley RH11 .201 A6
Epsom KT17 .76 F5
Heston TW5 .4 E7
Croft Way Frimley GU16 .65 F2
Horsham RH12 .217 A3
Richmond TW10 .17 B5
Crofter's Cl GU47 .64 A8
Crofters Cl TW7 .5 D2
Crofters Mead CR0 .62 F2
Croftleigh Ave CR8 .80 B3
Crofton KT21 .75 E1
Crofton Ave Chiswick W4 .7 D7
Walton-on-T KT12 .54 C7
Crofton Cl Bracknell RG12 .27 E4
Ottershaw KT16 .51 C3
Crofton Terr TW9 .6 F3
Crofts Cl GU8 .191 B5
Crofts The TW17 .34 E5
Croftside The SE25 .43 A6
Croham Cl CR2 .61 E4
Croham Hurst Golf Course
CR2 .62 A3
Croham Hurst Sch CR2 .61 F5
Croham Manor Rd CR2 .61 E4
Croham Mount CR2 .61 E3
Croham Park Ave CR0, CR2 61 F5
Croham Rd
Croydon CR0, CR2 .61 E5
South Croydon CR2 .61 E5
Croham Valley Rd CR2 .62 B3
Croindene Rd SW16 .41 E8
Cromer Ct SW16 .21 E5
Cromer Rd Croydon SE25 .43 B6
Harlington TW6 .3 A5
Mitcham SW17 .21 A2
Cromford Way KT3 .38 D8
Crompton Fields RH10 .181 E1
Crompton Way RH10 .181 E1
Cromwell Ave KT3 .38 F4
Cromwell Cl KT12 .35 B1
Cromwell Ct 15 KT2 .18 A1
Cromwell Gr CR3 .100 C6
Cromwell House CR0 .61 B7
Cromwell Pl
Cranleigh GU6 .174 F1
1 East Grinstead RH19 .205 F7
Mortlake SW14 .7 C4
Cromwell Rd Ascot SL5 .29 B4
Beckenham BR3 .43 E6
Camberley GU15 .65 D7
Caterham CR3 .100 C6
Feltham TW13 .15 B7
Hounslow TW3 .5 A3
Kingston u T KT2 .37 E8
Redhill RH1 .118 F1
Teddington TW11 .17 A2
Thornton Heath CR0 .42 D2
Wimbledon SW19 .20 B3
Worcester Park KT19, KT4 .57 E7
Cromwell St TW3 .5 A3
Cromwell Way GU14 .85 C7
Cromwell Wlk 1 RH1 .118 F1
Crondall Ct GU15 .65 B4
Crondall House SW15 .19 A7
Crondall La GU10, GU9 .124 D2
Crondall Rd GU10 .145 A6
Cronks Hill RH1, RH2 .139 D7
Cronks Hill Cl RH1 .139 D7
Cronks Hill Rd RH1 .139 D7
Crooksbury Rd
Farnham GU10 .126 C2
Tilford GU10 .147 D8
Crosby Cl TW13 .15 E4
Crosby Hill Dr GU15 .65 F7
Crosby Way GU9 .125 A1
Crosby Wlk SE24 .22 A8
Cross Deep TW1 .17 A6
Cross Deep Gdns TW1 .16 F6
Cross Farm Cty Inf Sch
GU16 .85 E6
Cross Fell RG12 .27 A5

Cross Gates Cl RG12 .....27 F6
Cross Gdns GU16 .....85 F6
Cross Keys RH10 .....201 D6
Cross La Burstow RH6 .....162 C1
Frimley GU16 .....85 F6
Ottershaw KT16 .....51 C4
Cross Lances Rd TW3 .....5 B3
Cross Lanes GU1 .....130 F8
Cross Oak La RH1, RH6 .....161 C7
Cross Rd Ash GU12 .....106 B3
Belmont SM2 .....59 A1
Carshalton SM1 .....59 D5
Croydon CR0 .....42 D1
Feltham TW13 .....15 E4
Kingston u T KT2 .....17 F1
Merton SW19 .....20 A1
Oatlands Park KT13 .....53 D7
Purley CR8 .....80 B6
Tadworth KT20 .....97 C5
Wentworth SL5 .....30 A1
Cross St
6 Aldershot GU11 .....105 A2
Farnborough GU14 .....105 C8
Hampton TW12 .....16 C3
Mortlake SW13 .....7 E4
Wokingham RG40 .....25 C6
Crossacres GU22 .....70 E4
Crossfield Pl KT13 .....53 B3
Crossland Rd Redhill RH1 .....119 A1
Thornton Heath CR7 .....42 B3
Crosslands KT16 .....51 E6
Crosslands Rd KT19 .....57 D4
Crossley Cl TN16 .....83 D4
Crossman Ct RH11 .....201 B1
Crossman Houses 19
SW12 .....21 E8
Crosspath RH10 .....201 E7
Crossroads The KT24 .....113 D7
Crosswater La GU10 .....167 F4
Crossway Bracknell RG12 .....27 C7
Crawley RH6 .....181 F8
Walton-on-T KT12 .....54 B8
West Barnes KT3, SW20 .....39 C5
Crossways Aldershot GU12 .....105 C1
Charlton TW16 .....14 F1
Churt GU10 .....167 F1
Crawley RH10 .....202 A7
Effingham KT24 .....113 D8
Egham TW20 .....12 D2
South Croydon CR0, CR2 .....62 F3
Sutton SM2 .....59 D2
Tatsfield TN16 .....103 C7
Crossways Ave RH19 .....185 C1
Crossways Cl RH10 .....201 F7
Crossways Cotts
Alfold Crossways GU6 .....194 A3
Rudgwick RH12 .....213 F6
Crossways Ct TN16 .....103 C7
Crossways La RH2 .....118 D7
Crossways Rd
Beckenham BR3 .....44 A5
Grayshott GU26 .....188 D3
Mitcham CR4 .....41 B6
Crossways The
Abinger Hammer RH5 .....134 B3
Coulsdon CR5 .....100 A8
Guildford GU2 .....129 F7
Heston TW5 .....4 F7
Lower Kingswood RH2 .....118 C7
Merstham RH1 .....119 C6
Crosswell Cl TW17 .....34 C7
Crouch Cl BR3 .....24 A2
Crouch La SL4 .....8 F7
Crouch Oak La KT15 .....52 C6
Crouchfield RH4 .....136 C4
Crouchmans Cl SE21, SE26 .....23 A5
Crowberry Cl RH11 .....201 A2
Crowborough Cl CR6 .....81 E1
Crowborough Dr CR6 .....81 E1
Crowborough Rd SW17 .....21 A3
Crowhurst SE25 .....43 A6
Crowhurst Cl RH10 .....202 E6
Crowhurst Keep RH10 .....202 E6
Crowhurst La
Crowhurst RH7, RH8 .....143 D4
Tandridge RH7 .....143 D5
Crowhurst Mead RH9 .....121 C5
Crowhurst Rd
Crowhurst RH7 .....164 D7
Lingfield RH7 .....164 D7
Crowhurst Village Rd
RH7 .....143 E2
Crowland Rd CR7 .....42 D5
Crowland Wlk SM4 .....40 C3
Crowley Cres CR0 .....61 A5
Crowmarsh Gdns SE23 .....23 C8
Crown Arc KT1 .....37 D7
Crown Cl Colnbrook SW3 .....1 C7
Walton-on-T KT12 .....35 C2
Crown Cotts Bracknell SL5 .....28 C4
Englefield Green TW20 .....11 A1
Crown Ct Godalming GU7 .....150 E4
4 Twickenham TW1 .....17 B8
Crown Dale SE19, SE27 .....22 C3
Crown Dr GU9 .....126 A5
Crown Hill Ct SL5 .....29 B4
Crown Hts GU1 .....130 E6
Crown La Farnham GU9 .....126 A5
Merton SM4, SW19 .....40 A6
South Norwood SE19, SW16 .....22 A3
Wentworth GU25 .....31 D3
Crown Lane Gdns SE27 .....22 A3
Crown Lane Prim Sch
SE27 .....22 B3
Crown Meadow SL3 .....1 B7
Crown Par Morden SM4 .....40 A5
South Norwood SE19 .....22 B2
Crown Pas KT1 .....37 D7
Crown Pl GU47 .....45 E1
Crown Point SE19 .....22 B2
Crown Rd Kingston u T KT3 .....38 C8
Morden SM4, SW19 .....40 B5
Sutton SM1 .....59 B6
Twickenham TW1 .....6 B1
Wentworth GU25 .....31 C3
Crown Rise KT16 .....32 F1
Crown Row RG12 .....27 D3
Crown St TW20 .....12 A4
Crown Terr TW9 .....6 F3
Crown Wood Cty Prim
Sch RG12 .....27 E3
Crown Yard TW3 .....5 C4
Crownbourne Ct SM1 .....59 B6
Crownpits La GU7 .....150 E3
Crowntree Cl TW7 .....5 F8
Crowther Rd SE25 .....43 A5
Crowthorne C of E Sch
RG45 .....45 C5
Crowthorne Cl SW18 .....19 F7
Crowthorne Lodge RG12 .....27 B5
Crowthorne Rd
Bracknell RG40, RG12 .....26 F2
Bracknell,
Easthampstead RG12 .....27 A5
Sandhurst GU47 .....45 B2
Crowthorne Rd N RG12 .....27 B6
Croxall House KT12 .....35 C3
Croxden Wlk SM4 .....40 C3
Croxted Cl SE21 .....22 C8
Croyde Cl GU14 .....85 A7
Croydon Airport Ind Est
CR9 .....60 F4
Croydon Coll CR9 .....61 D8
Croydon Coll Annexe CR0 .....42 D1
Croydon Coll (Selhurst
Tertiary Ctr) SE25 .....42 D4
Croydon Flyover The
CR0, CR9 .....61 C7
Croydon General Hospl
CR9 .....42 C1
Croydon Gr CR0 .....42 B1
Croydon High Sch CR2 .....62 C1
Croydon La Banstead SM7 .....78 D6
Wallington SM7 .....78 D6
Croydon La S SM7 .....78 B5
Croydon Rd Beckenham BR3 .....43 E6
Caterham CR3 .....101 A5
Chelsham CR6 .....102 D5
Coney Hall BR2, BR4 .....63 F7
Croydon CR0 .....60 D7
Harlington TW6 .....3 B4
Mitcham CR0, CR4, CR9 .....41 C4
Penge SE20 .....43 C8
Reigate RH2 .....118 C2
Tatsfield TN16 .....103 F3
Titsey CR6 .....102 D5
Wallington CR0, SM5, SM6 .....60 D7
Croydon Rd Ind Est BR3 .....43 D5
Croydon Water Palace
CR9 .....61 A4
Croydonbarn La
RH6, RH9 .....163 B4
Croylands Dr KT6 .....37 E2
Croysdale Ave TW16 .....35 A6
Crozier Dr CR2 .....62 B1
Cruikshank Lea GU47 .....64 E6
Crunden Rd CR2 .....61 D3
Crundwell Ct GU9 .....125 D3
Crusader Gdns CR0 .....61 E7
Crusoe Rd CR4 .....20 F1
Crutchfield La Sidlow RH6 .....160 B5
Walton-on-T KT12 .....54 B8
Crutchley Rd Catford SE6 .....24 E6
Wokingham RG40 .....25 D7
Crystal Ct SE19 .....22 F3
Crystal Palace National
Sports Ctr SE19 .....23 A2
Crystal Palace Par SE19 .....22 F3
Crystal Palace Park Rd
SE19, SE26 .....23 B3
Crystal Palace Sta SE19 .....23 A2
Crystal Palace Station Rd
SE19 .....23 A2
Crystal Terr SE19 .....22 D2
Crystal View Ct BR1 .....24 D4
Cubitt St CR0 .....60 F5
Cubitt Way GU21 .....68 D1
Cuckfield Cl RH11 .....200 F3
Cuckmere Cres RH11 .....200 F5
Cuckoo La GU24 .....67 D6
Cuckoo Vale GU24 .....67 D6
Cuda's Cl KT19 .....57 F6
Cuddington Ave KT19, KT4 .....57 F7
Cuddington Cl KT20 .....97 D7
Cuddington Croft Cty Fst
& Mid Sch SM2 .....58 D2
Cuddington Cty Prim Sch
KT4 .....57 F7
Cuddington Glade KT19 .....76 A7
Cuddington Golf Course
SM2 .....77 E7
Cuddington Park Cl SM7 .....77 F6
Cuddington
Way SM2, SM7 .....77 D8
Cudham Dr CR0 .....82 C8
Cudham Rd TN16 .....103 E8
Cudham St SE6 .....24 C8
Cudworth La RH5 .....179 E8
Cuffs Hill RH10 .....202 E2
Culham Ho RG12 .....27 E5
Culham House RG12 .....27 E5
Cull's Rd GU3 .....107 B1
Cullens Mews 4 GU11 .....105 A1
Cullerne Cl KT17 .....57 F1
Cullesden Rd CR8 .....80 B4
Culmer Hill GU8 .....170 F2
Culmington Rd CR2 .....61 C2
Culsac Rd 1 KT6 .....56 E8
Culver Dr RH8 .....122 E5
Culver Rd GU47 .....45 D1
Culverden Ct 5 KT13 .....53 D7
Culverden Rd SW12 .....21 C6
Culverden Terr KT13 .....53 D7
Culverhay KT21 .....75 E3
Culverhouse Gdns SW16 .....21 F5
Culverlands Cres GU12 .....106 A3
Culverley Rd SE6 .....24 C7
Culvers Ave SM5, CR4 .....59 F8
Culvers House Prim Sch
CR4 .....41 A1
Culvers Retreat SM5 .....59 F8
Culvers Way SM5 .....59 F8
Culverstone Cl BR2 .....44 F4
Culworth House GU1 .....130 E8
Cumber House SW18 .....20 A7
Cumberland
Ave GU2, GU3 .....109 A6
Cumberland Cl Epsom KT19 .....57 E1
2 Twickenham TW1 .....6 B1
6 Wimbledon SW20 .....19 D1
Cumberland Ct 4 CR0 .....42 D1
Cumberland Dr
Bracknell RG12 .....27 E8
Chessington KT9 .....56 F7
Hinchley Wood KT10 .....56 A8
Cumberland House KT2 .....18 B1
Cumberland Lodge SL4 .....10 D4
Cumberland Pl Catford SE6 .....24 F7
Sunbury TW16 .....35 A5
Cumberland Rd
Ashford TW15 .....13 D5
Barnes SW13 .....7 F6
Beckenham BR2 .....44 F6
Croydon SE25 .....43 B3
Frimley GU15 .....66 C4
Richmond TW9 .....7 A7
Cumberland St TW18 .....12 D3
Cumberlands CR8 .....80 D4
Cumberlow Ave SE25 .....43 A6
Cumbernauld Gdns TW16 .....14 F3
Cumbernauld Wlk RH11 .....200 E2
Cumbrae Gdns KT6 .....56 D8
Cumbria Ct GU14 .....85 E1
Cumnor Gdns KT17 .....58 A4
Cumnor House Sch CR2 .....61 B2
Cumnor Rd SM2 .....59 C4
Cumnor Rise CR8 .....80 C2
Cumnor Way RG12 .....27 E5
Cunliffe Cl KT18 .....96 B3
Cunliffe Rd KT19 .....57 F6
Cunliffe St SW16 .....21 C2
Cunningham Ave GU1 .....110 B2
Cunningham Cl BR4 .....63 B8
Cunningham Rd SM7 .....78 D4
Cunnington Rd GU14 .....85 E2
Cunworth Ct RG12 .....26 F3
Curfew Bell Rd KT16 .....32 F2
Curl Way RG41 .....25 A5
Curlew Cl CR2 .....81 D8
Curlew Ct KT6 .....57 A7
Curlew Gdns GU4 .....110 D3
Curley Hill Rd GU18 .....66 F7
Curling Cl CR5 .....100 A7
Curling Vale GU2 .....130 A7
Curly Bridge Cl GU14 .....84 F8
Curnick's La SE27 .....22 C4
Curran Ave SM6 .....60 A7
Currie Hill Cl SW19 .....19 F4
Currie House 18 SW12 .....21 D8
Curteys Wlk RH11 .....201 A3
Curtis Cl GU15 .....66 C7
Curtis Field Rd SW16 .....22 A4
Curtis Gdns RH4 .....136 A8
Curtis Rd Dorking RH4 .....136 A8
Twickenham TW4 .....15 F8
West Ewell KT19 .....57 C6
Curvan Cl KT17 .....57 F1
Curzon Ave RH12 .....217 B3
Curzon Cl KT13 .....53 A6
Curzon Rd
Thornton Heath CR7 .....42 A3
Weybridge KT13 .....53 A5
Cusack Cl TW1 .....16 F4
Cuthbert Gdns SE25 .....42 E6
Cuthbert Rd Ash GU12 .....106 B6
Thornton Heath CR0, CR9 .....61 B8
Cuttinglye La RH10 .....184 A1
Cuttinglye Rd RH10 .....184 C2
Cutts Rd GU11 .....105 D7
Cyclamen Cl 4 TW12 .....16 A2
Cyclamen Way KT19 .....57 C5
Cygnet Ave TW14 .....15 D8
Cygnet Cl GU21 .....69 B3
Cygnets Cl RH1 .....119 A3
Cygnets The Feltham TW13 .....15 E4
Staines TW18 .....12 F3
Cypress Ave TW2 .....16 C8
Cypress Ct Sutton SM1 .....59 A4
7 West Norwood SW16 .....22 A3
Cypress Gr GU12 .....105 F7
Cypress Hill Ct GU14 .....64 F1
Cypress Inf Sch SE25 .....42 E7
Cypress Jun Sch SE25 .....42 E7
Cypress Lodge SE25 .....42 E7
Cypress Rd Guildford GU1 .....109 C4
South Norwood SE25 .....42 E7
Cypress Way
Banstead KT17 .....77 D5
Blackwater GU17 .....64 B5
Grayshott GU26 .....188 D2
Cypress Wlk TW20 .....11 B2
Cyprus Rd GU16 .....86 D8

D

D'abernon Cl KT10 .....55 A6
D'Abernon Dr KT11 .....73 E3
D'arcy Rd SM3 .....58 D6
Dacre Rd CR0 .....41 E2
Dacres Rd SE23 .....23 D5
Daffodil Cl Croydon CR0 .....43 D1
7 Hampton TW12 .....16 A2
Daffodil Dr GU24 .....68 A3
Dafforne Rd SW17 .....21 A5
Dagden Rd GU4 .....130 E3
Dagley La GU4 .....130 D3
Dagmar Rd
4 Kingston u T KT2 .....18 A1
South Norwood SE25 .....42 E4
Dagnall Pk CR0, SE25 .....42 E4
Dagnall Rd SE25 .....42 E4
Dagnan Rd SW12 .....21 C8
Dahlia Gdns CR4 .....41 D5
Dahomey Rd SW16 .....21 C2
Daimler Way SM6 .....60 E3
Dainford Cl BR1 .....24 D3
Dairy Cl CR7 .....42 C7
Dairyfields RH11 .....201 A5
Dairymans Wlk GU4 .....110 B6
Daisy Cl CR0 .....43 D1
Dakin Cl RH10 .....202 C2
Dakins The RH19 .....205 E8
Dalcross RG12 .....27 E3
Dalcross Rd TW4, TW5 .....4 E5
Dale Ave TW4 .....4 E4
Dale Cl Addlestone KT15 .....52 B5
Horsham RH12 .....217 F5
Sunningdale SL5 .....30 A4
Wrecclesham GU10 .....145 F7
Dale Ct 3 KT2 .....17 F1
Dale Gdns GU47 .....64 A8
Dale Lodge Rd SL5 .....30 A4
Dale Park Ave SM5 .....59 F8
Dale Park Rd SE19 .....42 D8
Dale Rd Ashford TW16 .....14 F1
Cheam SM1 .....58 F6
Forest Row RH18 .....206 F1
Purley CR8 .....80 B7
Walton-on-T KT12 .....34 F2
Dale View
Haslemere GU27 .....207 F5
Headley KT18 .....96 B4
Woking GU21 .....69 B1
Dalebury Rd SW17 .....20 F6
Dalegarth Gdns CR8 .....80 D6
Daleham Ave TW20 .....12 A2
Daleside Rd
Streatham SW17 .....21 B3
West Ewell KT19 .....57 D4
Dalewood Gdns
Crawley RH10 .....201 F8
North Cheam KT4 .....58 B8
Dalkeith Rd SE21 .....22 C8
Dallas Rd Cheam SM3 .....58 E4
Forest Hill SE26 .....23 B5
Dallaway Gdns RH19 .....185 E1
Dalley Ct GU47 .....64 D7
Dallington Cl KT12 .....54 C4
Dalmain Prim Sch SE23 .....23 E7
Dalmain Rd SE23 .....23 D7
Dalmally Rd CR0 .....43 A2
Dalmeny Ave SW16 .....42 A7
Dalmeny Cres TW3 .....5 D3
Dalmeny Rd
North Cheam KT4 .....58 B7
Wallington SM5 .....60 A3
Dalmore Ave KT10 .....55 F4
Dalmore Rd SE21 .....22 C6
Dalston Cl GU15 .....66 D3
Dalton Ave CR4 .....40 E7
Dalton Cl RH11 .....201 B1
Dalton House 7 SW12 .....21 B8
Dalton St SE27 .....22 B5
Damascene Wlk SE21 .....22 C7
Damask Cl GU24 .....67 E6
Damer House 9 TW10 .....6 F1
Dampier Wlk RH11 .....201 B1
Dan Bryant House 5
SW12 .....21 C8
Danbrook Rd SW16 .....21 E1
Danbury Mews SM5, SM6 .....60 B6
Dancer Rd TW9 .....7 A4
Dane Ct GU22 .....70 F4
Dane Rd Ashford TW15 .....14 D2
Merton SW19 .....40 C8
Warlingham CR6 .....81 D2
Danebury CR0 .....63 B4
Danebury Prim Sch SW15 .....18 F8
Danebury Wlk GU16 .....85 F8
Daneby Rd SE6 .....24 C6
Danecourt Gdns CR0 .....61 F7
Danehurst TW8 .....6 C7
Danehurst Cl TW20 .....11 E2
Danehurst Cres RH13 .....217 F2
Danehurst Ct KT17 .....76 F6
Danemore La RH9 .....142 E2
Danes Cl KT22 .....74 C5
Danes Hill GU22 .....70 B1
Danes Hill Jun Sch KT22 .....74 C6
Danes Hill Sch KT22 .....74 D6
Danes Way KT22 .....74 D5
Danesbury Rd TW13 .....15 B7
Danescourt Cres SM1 .....59 C8
Danesfield GU23 .....90 F4
Danesfield Sch KT12 .....54 C8
Daneshill RH1 .....118 E2
Daneshill Cl RH1 .....118 E2
Danesmead KT11 .....74 A8
Danesrood GU1 .....130 F8
Daneswood Ave SE6 .....24 C5
Daneswood Cl KT13 .....53 C5
Danetree Cl KT19 .....57 C3
Danetree Rd KT19 .....57 D3
Danetree Sch KT19 .....57 C4
Daniel Cl SW17, SW19 .....20 E2
Daniel Ct 3 BR3 .....24 A1
Daniel Way SM7 .....78 B5
Daniell Way CR0, CR9 .....41 F1
Daniels La CR6 .....81 F4
Danley La GU27 .....207 A3
Danses Cl GU4 .....110 D3
Danvers Way CR3 .....100 C4
Dapdune Ct GU1 .....109 C1
Dapdune Rd GU1 .....109 D1
Daphne Ct KT4 .....57 E8
Daphne St SW18 .....20 C8
Darby Cl CR3 .....100 C5
Darby Cres TW16 .....35 C7
Darby Gdns TW16 .....35 C7
Darby Green La GU17 .....64 B6
Darby Green Rd GU17 .....64 B5
Darcy Ave SM6 .....60 C6
Darcy Cl CR5 .....100 B8
Darcy Pl KT21 .....75 F2
Darcy Rd Ashstead KT21 .....75 F2
Isleworth TW7 .....6 A6
Thornton Heath SW16 .....41 E7
Darell Prim Sch TW9 .....7 A4
Darell Rd TW9 .....7 A4
Darent House BR1 .....24 D3
Darenth Way RH6 .....160 F6
Darfield Rd GU1 .....110 A4
Dargate Cl SE19 .....22 F1
Dark La GU3 .....128 B4
Darlaston Rd SW19 .....19 E1
Darley Cl Addlestone KT15 .....52 C5
Croydon CR0 .....43 E3
Darley Dene Ct KT15 .....52 C6
Darley Dene Inf Sch KT15 .....52 C5
Darley Dr KT3 .....38 D7
Darley Gdns SM4 .....40 B3
Darleydale RH11 .....201 C3
Darleydale Cl GU47 .....45 D2
Darlington Ct SE6 .....24 F7
Darlington House 2 KT6 .....37 D2
Darlington Rd SE27 .....22 B3
Darmaine Cl CR2 .....61 C3
Darnley Pk KT13 .....53 B7
Darracott Cl GU15 .....66 B8
Darrell Ct BR2 .....44 E6
Dart Cl SL3 .....1 B8
Dart Ct RH19 .....186 A3
Dart Rd GU14 .....84 D6
Dartmouth Ave GU21 .....70 D5
Dartmouth Cl RG12 .....27 E6
Dartmouth Gn GU21 .....70 D5
Dartmouth House CR0 .....42 B2
Dartmouth Path GU21 .....70 D5
Dartmouth Pl Chiswick W4 .....7 E8
Forest Hill SE23 .....23 C6
Dartmouth Rd SE23, SE26 .....23 C5
Dartnell Ave KT14 .....71 C7
Dartnell Cl KT14 .....71 B7
Dartnell Cres KT14 .....71 B7
Dartnell Ct KT14 .....71 C7
Dartnell Park Rd KT14 .....71 C8
Dartnell Pl KT14 .....71 B7
Dartnell Rd CR0 .....42 F2
Darvel Cl GU21 .....69 A3
Darvills La GU9 .....125 C2
Darwall Dr SL5 .....28 D7
Darwin Cl RH12 .....217 F4
Darwin Gr GU11 .....105 C3
Daryngton Dr GU1 .....110 B1
Dashwood Cl
Bracknell RG12 .....27 D8
West Byfleet KT14 .....71 C7
Dashwood Ct TW3 .....5 C3
Dashwood House SE21 .....22 F5
Dassett Rd SE27 .....22 B3
Datchet Rd Forest Hill SE6 .....23 F6
Horton SL3 .....1 A4
Daux Hill RH12 .....217 B6
Davenant Rd CR0, CR9 .....61 B6
Davenport Cl TW11 .....17 A2
Davenport Lodge TW5 .....4 E7
Davenport Rd RG12 .....27 E8
Daventry Cl SL3 .....1 F6
Daventry Ct RG42 .....27 B8
David Cl UB3 .....3 E7
David House SE25 .....43 A6
David Livingstone Prim
Sch CR7 .....42 C8
David Rd SL3 .....1 F5
David's Rd SE23 .....23 C7
Davidson Inf Sch CR0 .....42 F2
Davidson Jun Sch CR0 .....42 F2
Davidson Lodge CR0 .....42 E2
Davidson Rd CR0, SE25 .....42 F3
Davies Cl Croydon CR0, SE25 .....43 A3
Farncombe GU7 .....150 D7
Davies Walk TW7 .....5 D6
Davis Cl RH11 .....201 A1
Davis Gdns GU47 .....64 E7
Davis Rd Chessington KT9 .....57 A6
Weybridge KT13 .....52 F1
Davos Cl GU22 .....89 E8
Davy Cl RG40 .....25 C5
Dawell Dr TN16 .....83 C2
Dawes Ave TW7 .....6 A3
Dawes Ct KT10 .....55 B6
Dawes Green Cotts RH2 .....138 A3
Dawley Ride SL3 .....1 E6
Dawlish Ave SW18 .....20 B6
Dawn Cl TW4 .....4 E4
Dawn Redwood Cl SL3 .....1 A4

Dawn Wlk BR2 44 D7
Dawnay Cl SL5 28 F8
Dawnay Gdns SW18 20 D6
Dawnay Rd Camberley GU15 65 B7
Great Bookham KT23 94 C1
Wandsworth SW17, SW18 20 D6
Dawney Hill GU24 87 F5
Dawneys Rd GU24 87 E5
Dawsmere Cl GU15 66 C5
Dawson Rd Byfleet KT14 71 E8
Kingston u T KT1 37 F6
Dax Ct TW16 35 C6
Day Ct GU6 173 F2
Day's Acre CR2 61 F1
Daybrook Rd SW19 40 B6
Daymerslea Ridge KT22 95 C6
Daysbrook Rd SW2 21 F7
Dayseys Hill RH1 162 A8
Dayspring GU2 109 B5
Daytone House SW20 39 D8
De Broome Rd TW13 15 C7
De Burgh House 10 SW19 20 C1
De Burgh Pk SM7 78 B4
De Frene Rd SE23, SE26 23 E5
De Havilland Dr KT13 71 E8
De Havilland Rd Heston TW5 4 C7
Wallington SM6 60 E3
De Havilland Way TW19 2 E1
De La Warr Rd RH19 185 F1
De Lara Way GU21 69 D1
De Montfort Par 1 SW16 21 E5
De Montfort Rd SW16 21 E6
De Ros Pl TW20 12 A2
de Stafford Sch CR3 100 F6
De'arn Gdns CR4 40 E6
De-Vitre Gn RG40 25 F7
Deacon Cl Downside KT11 93 B8
Wallington CR8 60 E2
Wokingham RG40 25 C8
Deacon Ct RH7 164 C4
Deacon Field GU2 109 A2
Deacon Rd KT2 37 F8
Deacons Wlk TW12 16 A4
Deadbrook La GU12 105 E3
Deal Rd SW17 21 A2
Dean Cl GU22 70 E3
Dean Ct Farncombe GU7 150 D6
10 Kingston u T KT2 18 A1
Dean Gr RG40 25 C7
Dean La CR3, CR5, RH1 99 D3
Dean Par GU15 65 F8
Dean Rd Croydon CR0 61 D6
Farncombe GU7 150 D6
Hampton TW12 16 A3
Isleworth TW3 5 B2
Dean Wlk KT23 94 B1
Deanery Pl GU7 150 D4
Deanery Rd GU7 150 E6
Deanfield Gdns CR0 61 D6
Deanhill Ct SW14 7 B3
Deanhill Rd SW14 7 B3
Deanoak La Leigh RH2 159 D8
Sidlow RH2 159 D8
Deans Cl Chiswick W4 7 B8
South Croydon CR0 61 F7
Walton on t H KT20 97 B3
Deans Ct GU20 48 D4
Deans Gate Cl SE23 23 D5
Deans La Nutfield RH1 120 A2
Walton on t H KT20 97 B2
Deans Rd Merstham RH1 119 C5
Sutton SM1 59 B7
Deans Wlk CR5 80 A1
Deansfield CR3 100 F2
Deansgate RG12 27 B2
Dearmer House 6 SW2 22 A8
Debden Cl KT2 17 D3
Deborah Cl TW7 5 E6
Deburgh Rd SW19 20 C1
Decon Pl CR3 100 C4
Dedham House SE6 24 C4
Dedisham Cl RH10 202 A5
Dedswell Dr GU4 111 A6
Dee Rd TW9 6 F3
Dee Way KT19 57 E1
Deedman Cl GU12 106 A2
Deep Dene GU27 207 E6
Deep Well Dr GU15 65 E5
Deepcut Bridge Rd GU16 86 C7
Deepdale Bracknell RG12 27 A5
Wimbledon SW19 19 D4
Deepdale Ave BR2 44 F5
Deepdene GU10 146 D7
Deepdene Ave
Dorking RH4, RH5 136 C6
South Croydon CR0 61 F7
Deepdene Avenue Rd RH4 115 C1
Deepdene Ct BR2 44 E6
Deepdene Dr RH5 136 C7
Deepdene Gdns
Dorking RH4, RH5 136 C8
Streatham SW2 21 F8
Deepdene Lodge 8 SW2 21 F8
Deepdene Park Rd RH5 136 D8
Deepdene Point 9 SE26 23 D5
Deepdene Vale RH4 115 C1
Deepdene Wood RH5 136 D7
Deepfield Rd RG12 27 D7
Deepfield Way CR5 79 E3
Deepfields RH6 160 F5
Deeprose Cl GU3 109 B5
Deepwell Cl TW7 6 A6
Deer Leap GU18 67 A8
Deer Park Cl KT2 18 B1
Deer Park Gdns CR4 40 D5
Deer Park Rd SW19 40 C7
Deer Park Way BR4 63 F8
Deer Rock Hill RG12 27 C3
Deer Rock Rd GU15 65 F8
Deerbarn Rd GU2 109 B2
Deerbrook Rd SE24, SW2 22 B7
Deerhurst KT2 38 B8
Deerhurst Cl TW13 15 B4
Deerhurst Rd SW16 21 F3
Deerings Rd RH2 118 C1
Deerleap GU35 187 C4
Deerleap Rd RH4 135 B6
Deers Farm GU23, KT14 71 E3
Deerswood Cl
Caterham CR3 101 A3
Crawley RH11 201 B7
Deerswood Ct RH11 201 A7
Deerswood Lower Sch RH11 201 A8
Deerswood Rd RH11 201 B7
Deerswood Upper Sch RH11 201 A8
Deeside Rd SW17 20 D5
Defiant Way SM6 60 E3
Defoe Ave TW9 7 A7
Defoe Cl SW17, SW19 20 E2
Delabole Rd RH1 119 E6
Delamare Cres CR0 43 C3
Delamere Rd Reigate RH2 139 C5
Wimbledon SW20 39 D8
Delaporte Cl KT17 76 E7
Delcombe Ave KT4 39 C1
Delderfield KT21 95 D6
Delfont Cl RH10 202 D4
Delia St SW18 20 B8
Dell Cl Fetcham KT22 94 E4
Haslemere GU27 208 A7
Mickleham RH5 115 C8
Wallington SM6 60 D6
Dell Close Cotts RH5 115 C8
Dell Gr GU16 65 F2
Dell House CR2 61 C2
Dell La KT17 58 A5
Dell Rd KT17 58 A4
Dell The Brentford TW8 6 C8
Burgh Heath KT20 97 C6
East Grinstead RH19 186 B1
Englefield Green SL4 11 A5
Feltham TW14 15 B8
Heath End GU9 125 D7
Horley RH6 161 B4
Reigate RH2 118 A2
Sidlow RH6 160 C5
South Norwood SE19 42 F8
Woking GU21 69 C1
Dell Wlk KT3 38 E7
Dellbow Rd TW14 4 B2
Dellfield Cl BR3 44 C8
Delmey Cl CR0 61 F7
Delphian Ct 5 SW16 22 A4
Delta Bglws RH6 161 A1
Delta Cl Chobham GU24 49 F1
Worcester Park KT4 57 F7
Delta Dr RH6 161 A1
Delta House RH6 161 A1
Delta Rd Chobham GU24 49 F1
Woking GU21 70 A3
Worcester Park KT19, KT4 57 E7
Delta Way TW20 32 C8
Delves KT20 97 D6
Delville Cl GU14 84 D3
Demesne Rd SM6 60 D6
Dempster Cl KT6 37 C1
Dempster House GU9 125 D8
Den Cl BR2, BR3 44 D6
Den Rd BR2 44 D6
Denbigh Cl SM1 58 F5
Denbigh Gdns TW10 6 F2
Denbigh Rd
Haslemere GU27 208 D5
Hounslow TW3 5 B5
Denby Dene GU12 106 B2
Denby Rd KT11 73 C7
Denchers Plat RH11 181 D1
Dencliffe TW15 14 A3
Dendy St SW12 21 A7
Dene Ave TW3 4 F4
Dene Cl 2 Bracknell RG12 27 C8
Farnham GU10 146 E6
Haslemere GU27 208 C6
Hayes BR2 44 F1
Horley RH6 160 E5
Worcester Park KT4 57 F8
Dene Ct GU1 110 B3
Dene Gdns KT7 56 A8
Dene La GU10 146 E6
Dene La W GU10 146 E5
Dene Pl GU21 69 C1
Dene Rd Ashtead KT21 95 F8
Farnborough GU14 84 F3
Guildford GU1 130 E8
Dene St RH4 136 B7
Dene Street Gdns RH4 136 B7
Dene The
Abinger Hammer RH5 134 B3
Belmont SM2 77 F8
East Molesey KT12, KT8 35 F4
South Croydon CR0 62 D6
Dene Tye RH10 202 D7
Dene Wlk GU10 146 E6
Denefield Dr CR8 80 D4
Denehurst Gdns
Mortlake TW10 7 A3
Twickenham TW2 16 D8
Denehyrst Ct GU1 130 E8
Denewood 8 KT17 76 E6
Denfield RH4 136 C5
Denham Cres CR4 40 F5
Denham Ct SE26 23 B5
Denham Gr RG12 27 C3
Denham Rd Egham TW20 12 A4
Ewell KT17 76 F7
Feltham TW14 15 C8
Denholm Gdns GU1, GU4 110 A4
Denison Rd Feltham, Lower Feltham TW13 14 F4
Mitcham SW19 20 D2
Denleigh Gdns KT7 36 E3
Denly Way GU18 48 C1
Denman Dr Ashford TW15 14 B2
Claygate KT10 56 A5
Denmans RH10 202 D7
Denmark Ave SW19 19 E1
Denmark Ct Morden SM4 40 A4
2 Weybridge KT13 53 B7
Denmark Gdns SM5 59 F7
Denmark Rd
Carshalton SM5 59 F7
Croydon SE25 43 B4
Guildford GU1 130 E8
Kingston u T KT1 37 E6
Twickenham TW2 16 D5
Wimbledon SW19 19 D2
Denmark Sq GU12 105 E2
Denmark St
Aldershot GU12 105 D2
Wokingham RG40 25 C5
Denmead Ct RG12 27 E3
Denmead House SW15 7 F1
Denmead Lower Sch TW12 16 B1
Denmead Rd CR0 42 B1
Denmead Upper Sch TW12 16 B1
Denmore Ct SM6 60 B5
Dennan Rd KT6 37 F1
Denne Par RH12, RH13 217 C1
Denne Rd Crawley RH11 201 D5
Horsham RH12 217 C1
Dennett Rd CR0 42 A2
Denning Ave CR0 61 A5
Denning Cl TW12 15 F3
Denningtons The KT4 57 E8
Dennis Cl Ashford TW15 14 D1
Redhill RH1 118 E3
Dennis House SM1 59 A6
Dennis Park Cres SW20 39 E8
Dennis Rd KT8 36 C5
Dennis Reeve Cl CR4 40 F8
Dennis Way GU1 109 E6
Dennistoun Cl GU15 65 D5
Densole Cl BR3 43 E8
Denton Cl RH1 140 A4
Denton Gr KT12 54 E8
Denton Rd Twickenham TW1 6 D1
Wokingham RG40 25 C6
Denton Way Frimley GU16 65 D2
Woking GU21 69 A2
Dents Gr KT20 117 F7
Denvale Wlk GU21 69 A1
Denwood SE23 23 D5
Denzil Rd GU2 130 B8
Departures Rd RH6 181 F8
Depot Rd Crawley RH11 181 D1
Epsom KT17 76 E6
Horsham RH13 217 E2
Hounslow TW3, TW7 5 D4
Derby Arms Rd KT18 76 F2
Derby Cl KT18 97 B8
Derby Hill SE23 23 C6
Derby Hill Cres SE23 23 C6
Derby Rd Cheam SM1, SM2 58 F4
Guildford GU2 108 F1
Haslemere GU27 208 B7
Hounslow TW3 5 B3
Merton SW19 20 A1
Mortlake SW14 7 B3
Surbiton KT5, KT6 38 A1
Thornton Heath CR0 42 B1
Derby Stables Rd KT18 76 F2
Derek Ave Hackbridge SM6 60 B6
West Ewell KT19 57 B5
Derek Cl KT19 57 B5
Derek Horn Ct GU15 65 B6
Deri Dene Cl 2 TW19 2 E1
Dering Pl CR0 61 C6
Dering Rd CR0, CR9 61 C6
Derinton Rd SW17 21 A4
Deronda Rd SE24, SW2 22 B7
Deroy Cl SM5 59 F4
Deroy Ct SM5 59 F4
Derrick Ave CR2 61 C1
Derrick House 13 SW2 22 A7
Derrick Rd BR3 43 F5
Derry Cl GU12 105 F5
Derry Rd Farnborough GU14 84 F8
Wallington CR0, SM6 60 E7
Derrydown GU22 89 C6
Derwent Ave
Ash Vale GU12 105 F4
Kingston u T SW15 18 E4
Derwent Cl
Addlestone KT15 52 D5
Claygate KT10 55 F4
Crawley RH11 200 F5
East Bedfont TW14 14 F7
Farnborough GU14 84 E4
Hale GU9 125 A6
Horsham RH12 218 B6
Derwent Dr CR8 80 E6
Derwent House
Penge SE20 43 B7
Reigate RH2 139 A7
Derwent Lodge KT4 58 B8
Derwent Rd
Lightwater GU18 67 B8
Penge SE20 43 B7
Thorpe Lea TW20 12 B1
Derwent Rd *continued*
Twickenham TW2 5 B1
West Barnes SM4 39 D3
Derwent Wlk SM6 60 B3
Desborough Cl TW17 34 A2
Desborough Ct SE25 43 B5
Desford Way TW15 13 F6
Desmond Anderson Cty Fst Sch RH10 201 E2
Desmond Anderson Cty Mid Sch RH10 201 E2
Despard House SW2 22 A6
Detherick Ct TW3 5 C3
Detillens La RH8 123 A6
Detling Rd RH11 201 C1
Dettingen Rd GU16 86 E8
Deutsche Schule TW10 17 D7
Devana End SM5 59 F7
Devas Rd SW20 39 C8
Devenish La GU20, SL5 29 D1
Devenish Rd
Ascot GU20, SL5 29 D2
Sunningdale GU20, SL5 29 D2
Deverill Ct SE20 43 C8
Devey Cl KT2 18 D3
Devil's La TW20 12 C2
Devitt Cl KT21 76 A3
Devoil Cl GU4 110 B5
Devoke Way KT12 54 D8
Devon Ave TW2 16 C7
Devon Bank GU2 130 C6
Devon Cl Kenley CR8 80 E3
Sandhurst GU47 64 D7
Devon Cres RH1, RH2 118 D1
Devon House
Caterham CR3 100 F3
Knaphill GU21 68 D2
Penge SE20 23 B1
Devon Rd Belmont SM2 58 E2
Hersham KT12 54 C6
Merstham RH1 119 C5
Devon Way Chessington KT9 56 C6
West Ewell KT19 57 B5
Devon Waye TW5 4 F7
Devoncroft Gdns TW1 17 A8
Devonshire Ave
Sheerwater GU21 70 D6
Sutton SM2 59 C3
Devonshire Ct
Croydon CR0 44 A1
Feltham TW13 15 B6
6 Richmond TW9 6 F6
Devonshire Dr
Camberley GU15 65 F7
Long Ditton KT6 56 D8
Devonshire Gdns W4 7 C7
Devonshire House
14 Balham SW12 21 B8
Hounslow TW3 5 C4
Sutton SM2 59 C3
Devonshire Pl GU11 104 F1
Devonshire Prim Sch SM2 59 C3
Devonshire Rd Chiswick W4 7 E8
Feltham TW13 15 E4
Forest Hill SE23 23 C8
Hackbridge SM5, SM6 60 A6
Horsham RH13 217 D2
Mitcham SW17, SW19 20 E1
Sutton SM2 59 C3
Thornton Heath CR0 42 D2
Weybridge KT13 53 A6
Devonshire St W4 7 E8
Devonshire Way CR0, CR9 62 F8
Devonshires The KT18 76 F5
Dewar Cl RH11 200 E5
Dewar House SW17 20 E3
Dewey St SW17 20 F3
Dewlands RH9 121 C4
Dewlands Cl GU6 174 E3
Dewlands La GU6 174 E3
Dewsbury Gdns KT4 58 A7
Dexter Dr RH19 205 E8
Diamedes Ave TW19 13 D7
Diamond Ct 4 RH1 119 A2
Diamond Est SW17 20 E5
Diamond Hill GU15 65 E7
Diamond Ridge GU15 65 E7
Diana Gdns KT6 56 F8
Dianthus Cl KT16 32 E2
Dianthus Ct GU22 69 D1
Dianthus Pl RG42 8 B2
Dibdin Cl SM1 59 A7
Dibdin Rd SM1 59 A8
Diceland Rd SM7 77 F3
Dick Sheppard Sch SE24 22 A8
Dick Turpin Way TW14 3 F3
Dickens Cl
East Grinstead RH19 185 C1
Richmond TW10 17 E6
Dickens Dr KT15 51 F4
Dickens Rd RH10 201 E3
Dickenson's La SE25 43 A3
Dickenson's Pl SE25 43 A3
Dickerage Hill KT3 38 C6
Dickerage La KT3 38 C6
Dickerage Rd KT1, KT2, KT3 38 C7
Dickins Way RH13 217 F1
Dickinson Rd TW13 15 D3
Digby Pl CR0 61 F7
Digby Way KT14 71 F7
Digdens Rise KT18 76 C4
Dillwyn Cl SE26 23 E4
Dilston Rd KT22 95 A8
Dilton Gdns SW15 19 B7
Dingle Rd TW15 14 B3
Dingle The RH11 201 B6
Dingley La SW16 21 D6
Dingwall Ave CR0, CR9 61 C8
Dingwall Rd
Croydon CR0, CR9 61 D8
Wallington SM5 59 F2
Wandsworth SW18 20 C8
Dinsdale Cl GU22 70 A1
Dinsdale Gdns SE25 42 E4
Dinsmore Rd SW12 21 B8
Dinton Rd Kingston u T KT2 17 F1
Mitcham SW17, SW19 20 D2
Dione Wlk RH11 200 E4
Dippenhall Rd GU10 124 C2
Dippenhall St GU10 124 A5
Dirdene Cl KT17 76 F7
Dirdene Gdns KT17 76 F7
Dirdene Gr KT17 76 F7
Dirtham La KT24 113 B6
Dirty La RH19 206 E7
Discovery Pk RH10 182 A2
Disraeli Ct SL3 1 B8
Distillery Wlk 14 TW8 6 E8
Ditches La CR3, CR5 99 E6
Ditchling RG12 27 A2
Ditchling Hill RH11 201 C4
Ditton Cl KT7 37 A2
Ditton Grange Cl KT6 37 D1
Ditton Grange Dr KT6 37 D1
Ditton Hill KT6 56 D8
Ditton Hill Rd KT6 37 C1
Ditton Lawn KT7 37 A1
Ditton Pl 7 SE20 43 B8
Ditton Rd KT6 37 E1
Ditton Reach KT7 37 B3
Dittoncroft Cl CR0 61 E6
Dixon Dr KT13 52 F1
Dixon Pl BR4 44 B1
Dixon Rd SE25 42 F6
Dobbins Pl RH11 200 E5
Doble Ct CR2 81 A8
Dobson Rd RH11 181 D1
Dock Rd TW8 6 D7
Dockenfield St GU10 166 C6
Dockett Eddy La TW17 33 F1
Dockett Moorings KT16 33 F1
Dockwell Cl TW14 4 A3
Dockwell's Ind Est TW14 4 C2
Doctors Cl SE26 23 C3
Doctors La CR3 100 A3
Dodbrooke Rd SE27 22 B5
Dodd's La KT14 71 A5
Dodds Cres KT14 71 B5
Dodds Pk RH3 137 B7
Doel Cl SW19 20 C1
Dogflud Way GU9 125 C3
Doggett Rd Catford SE6 24 A8
Lewisham SE6 24 A8
Doghurst Ave UB7 3 B7
Doghurst Dr UB7 3 B7
Doghurst La CR5 98 F7
Doland Ct SW17 20 F2
Dolby Terr RH6 180 E6
Dollis Cl RH10 202 C5
Dollis Ct GU9 125 D3
Dollis Dr GU9 125 D3
Dolphin Cl
Haslemere GU27 207 E6
Kingston u T KT6 37 D4
Dolphin Ct Merton SW19 20 A1
Stanwell TW19 13 A5
2 Wallington SM6 60 B4
Dolphin Ct N TW19 13 A5
Dolphin Rd TW16 34 E8
Dolphin Rd N TW16 34 E8
Dolphin Rd S TW16 34 E8
Dolphin Rd W TW16 34 E8
Dolphin Sq W4 7 E7
Dolphin St KT2 37 E8
Doman Rd GU15 65 A4
Dome Hill CR3 120 E8
Dome Hill Peak CR3 100 E1
Dome Hill Pk SE26 22 F4
Dome Way RH1 118 F2
Dominion Rd CR0 42 F2
Donald Lynch House CR4 40 F7
Donald Rd CR0, CR9 41 F2
Donald Woods Gdns KT5 57 C8
Doncaster Wlk RH10 202 A4
Doncastle Rd RG12 26 F6
Donkey La
Abinger Common RH5 155 D8
Crawley RH6 182 D7
Donnafields GU24 68 A3
Donne Cl RH10 202 B8
Donne Gdns GU22 70 E4
Donne Pl CR4 41 B5
Donnington Cl GU15 65 B4
Donnington Ct 2 RH11 200 F3
Donnington Rd KT4 58 A8
Donnybrook RG12 27 A2
Donnybrook Rd SW16 21 D1
Donovan Cl KT19 57 D1
Donyngs Place Recn Ctr RH1 118 E2
Doods Brow Sch RH1 119 F2
Doods Park Rd RH2 118 C1
Doods Pl RH2 118 D2
Doods Rd RH2 118 C2
Doods Way RH2 118 D2
Doomsday Garden RH13 218 A1
Doone Cl TW11 17 A2
Dora Rd SW19 20 A4
Dora's Green La GU10 124 C5
Doradus Ct 20 SW19 19 D7
Doral Way SM5 59 F5
Doran Dr RH2 118 D1
Doran Gdns RH2 118 D1

Dorcas Ct GU15 65 B3
Dorchester Ct
Reigate RH2 118 C2
Staines TW18 13 A4
5 Streatham SW16 21 E6
Woking GU22 70 A3
Dorchester Dr TW14 3 E1
Dorchester Gr W4 7 E8
Dorchester Mews
New Malden KT3 38 D5
Twickenham TW1 6 C1
Dorchester Prim Sch KT4 39 C1
Dorchester Rd Cheam SM4 40 C2
Morden CR4 40 C2
North Cheam KT4 39 C1
Weybridge KT13 53 B7
Dore Gdns SM4 40 B2
Doreen Cl GU14 84 E7
Dorian Dr SL5 29 E8
Doric Dr KT20 97 F7
Dorien Rd SW20 39 D7
Dorin Ct Pyrford GU22 70 E4
Warlingham CR6 101 B7
Doris Rd TW15 14 D2
Dorking Bsns Pk RH4 136 A8
Dorking Cl KT4 58 D8
Dorking (Deepdene) Sta
RH4 115 C1
Dorking General Hospl
RH4 136 B6
Dorking Mus RH4 136 A7
Dorking Rd Chilworth GU4 131 E3
Epsom KT18 76 B4
Great Bookham KT23 114 C8
Leatherhead KT22 95 B3
Lower Kingswood KT20 116 F7
Tadworth KT20 97 C3
Walton on t H KT20 97 C3
Warnham RH12, RH5 198 B4
Dorking Sta RH4 115 C1
Dorking West Sta RH4 136 A8
Dorlcote GU8 170 E5
Dorlcote Rd SW18 20 E8
Dorling Dr KT17 76 F7
Dorly Cl TW17 34 E4
Dorman's Cl RH7 186 A8
Dormans RH11 201 A5
Dormans Ave RH7 165 A2
Dormans Gdns RH19 185 E6
Dormans High St RH7 186 A8
Dormans Park Rd
Dormans Park RH19 185 E6
East Grinstead RH19 185 D3
Dormans Rd RH7 165 A2
Dormans Sta RH7 185 F8
Dormans Station Rd
Dormans Park RH7 185 F7
Dormansland RH7 185 F7
Dormansland Prim Sch
RH7 186 A8
Dormer Cl RG45 45 A5
Dormers Cl GU7 150 D7
Dormy House The GU25 30 F3
Dorney Gr KT13 53 B8
Dorney Way TW4 4 E2
Dornford Gdns CR5 100 C8
Dornton Rd
South Croydon CR2 61 D5
Upper Tooting SW12, SW17 21 C6
Dorrien Wlk SW16 21 D6
Dorrington Ct SE25 42 E7
Dorrit Cres GU3 108 E3
Dorryn Ct SE26 23 D3
Dorset Ave RH19 185 C3
Dorset Ct Camberley GU15 65 F8
Epsom KT17 76 F7
Dorset Dr GU22 70 B2
Dorset Gdns
East Grinstead RH19 185 C3
Thornton Heath SW16 41 F5
Dorset House 2 SE20 43 B8
Dorset Rd Ash GU12 106 B5
Ashford TW15 13 D5
Belmont SM2 59 A1
Merton SW19 40 A7
Mitcham CR4 40 E7
Penge BR3 43 D6
Dorset Sq KT19 57 D1
Dorset Way Byfleet KT14 52 D1
Twickenham TW2 16 D7
Dorset Waye TW5 4 F7
Dorsten Sq RH11 200 F3
Dorton Way GU23 91 B6
Douai Cl GU14 85 C4
Douai Gr TW12 36 C8
Douglas Ave KT3 39 B5
Douglas Cl Guildford GU4 109 D6
Wallington SM6 60 E4
Douglas Ct CR3 100 D5
Douglas Dr Croydon CR0 63 A7
Godalming GU7 150 F5
Douglas Gr GU10 146 C5
Douglas Gracey
House SW18 19 E8
Douglas Houghton
House 11 RH1 118 F2
Douglas House
Little Bookham KT23 94 A3
Twickenham TW1 6 B2
Douglas Mews SM7 77 F3
Douglas Pl GU14 85 A5
Douglas Rd
Addlestone KT15 52 B7
Hounslow TW3 5 B4
Kingston u T KT1 38 B7
Douglas Rd *continued*
Reigate RH2 118 B2
Stanwell TW19 2 D1
Surbiton KT6 37 F1
Thames Ditton KT10 55 B8
Douglas Robinson Ct
SW16 21 E1
Douglas Sq SM4 40 A3
Doultons The TW18 13 A2
Dounesforth Gdns SW18 20 B7
Dove Cl Crawley RH11 201 D8
Selsdon CR2 81 D8
Dove Ct TW19 13 E8
Dovecote Cl KT13 53 B7
Dovecote Gdns 8 SW14 7 D4
Dovedale Cl Guildford GU1 110 A4
Sandhurst GU47 45 D2
Dovedale Cres RH11 201 B4
Dovedale Rise CR4 20 F1
Dovehouse Gn 1 KT13 53 D6
Dover Ct GU6 175 A3
Dover Gdns SM5 59 F7
Dover House
7 Beckenham BR3 24 A1
15 Penge SE20 43 B8
Dover House Rd SW15 19 B8
Dover Rd SE19 22 D2
Dover Terr TW9 7 A5
Dovercourt Ave CR7 42 A5
Dovercourt La SM1 59 C7
Dovercourt Rd SE21, SE22 22 E8
Doverfield Rd
Guildford GU4 110 A4
Streatham SW2 21 E8
Dovers Green Inf Sch
RH2 139 C5
Dovers Green Rd RH2 139 B4
Doversmead GU21 68 E3
Doveton Rd CR2 61 D5
Dowanhill Rd SE6 24 D7
Dowdeswell Cl SW15 7 E3
Dowding Ct RG45 45 C6
Dowding Rd TN16 83 D4
Dowell House SE21 22 F5
Dower Ave SM6 60 B2
Dower House GU8 170 F8
Dower Wlk RH11 201 A5
Dowes House 18 SW16 21 E5
Dowlands La RH10, RH6 183 D7
Dowlans Cl KT23 114 A8
Dowlans Rd KT23 114 B8
Dowler Ct 2 KT2 37 F8
Dowman Cl 2 SW19 20 B1
Down Hall Rd KT2 37 D8
Down La GU3 129 B4
Down Lodge Ct KT18 76 E5
Down Rd Guildford GU1 110 B1
Teddington TW11 17 B2
Down St KT8 36 A4
Down Yhonda GU8 148 C3
Downderry Prim Sch BR1 24 E4
Downderry Rd BR1 24 E4
Downe Cl RH6 160 E5
Downe Golf Course BR6 83 E7
Downe Rd CR4 40 F7
Downer Meadow GU7 150 E8
Downes Cl TW1 6 B1
Downfield 7 KT4 39 A1
Downfield House KT3 38 D1
Downham Enterprise Ctr
SE6 24 F6
Downham La BR1 24 D3
Downham Way BR1 24 E4
Downhurst Rd GU6 175 E6
Downing Ave GU2 129 F8
Downing House 8 SW19 20 A1
Downing St GU9 125 B2
Downland Cl
Burgh Heath KT18 77 B1
Wallington CR5 79 B5
Downland Ct RH11 201 C4
Downland Dr RH11 201 C3
Downland Gdns KT18 77 B1
Downland Pl RH11 201 C4
Downland Way KT18 77 B1
Downlands Rd CR8 79 F6
Downmill Rd RG12 26 F7
Downs Ave KT18 76 F4
Downs Bridge Rd
BR2, BR3 44 D8
Downs Court Rd CR8 80 B6
Downs Ct Purley CR8 61 B1
2 Redhill RH1 119 A4
10 Wimbledon SW19 19 D1
Downs Est KT17 77 C5
Downs Hill BR2, BR3 44 D8
Downs Hill Rd KT18 76 E5
Downs La KT22 95 B3
Downs Rd
Ashstead KT18, KT21 96 C7
Beckenham BR3 44 B7
Coulsdon CR5 79 D1
Epsom KT17, KT18 76 E3
Mickleham RH5 115 C7
Purley CR8 80 B8
South Norwood CR7 42 C8
Sutton SM2 78 C8
Downs Side SM2 77 F8
Downs The
Leatherhead KT22 95 C2
Wimbledon SW19, SW20 19 D1
Downs View Dorking RH4 115 D1
Hounslow TW7 6 A6
Tadworth KT20 97 B6
Downs View Lodge 9 KT6 37 E3
Downs View Rd KT23 114 C8
Downs Way Epsom KT18 76 F3
Great Bookham KT23 94 C1
Downs Way *continued*
Oxted RH8 122 E8
Tadworth KT20 97 B6
Downs Way Cty Inf Sch
RH8 122 E8
Downs Wood KT18 77 B2
Downsend Lodge Pre Prep
Sch KT22 95 B6
Downsend Sch KT22 95 D7
Downsend Sch (Epsom
Lodge) KT17 76 F7
Downshire Way
Bracknell RG12, RG42 27 A7
Bracknell RG12 27 B6
Downside
Beacon Hill GU26 188 D7
Epsom KT18 76 E5
Twickenham TW1 16 F5
Downside Bridge Rd KT11 73 B4
Downside Cl SW19 20 C2
Downside Common Rd
KT11 73 C1
Downside Ct RH1 119 C6
Downside Orch GU22 70 A2
Downside Rd
Downside KT11 73 B2
Guildford GU4 131 B8
Sutton SM2 59 E4
Downsman Ct RH10 201 D3
Downsview Ave GU22 89 F6
Downsview Ct GU1 109 C5
Downsview Gdns
Dorking RH4 136 B6
South Norwood SE19 22 C1
Downsview Prim Sch
SE19 22 C1
Downsview Rd
Headley Down GU35 187 C5
Horsham RH12 218 B6
South Norwood CR7, SE19 22 C1
Downsway Guildford GU1 110 E1
South Croydon CR2 80 E8
Whyteleafe CR3 80 F2
Downsway Cl KT20 97 A6
Downsway The SM2 59 C2
Downswood RH2 118 D4
Downton Ave SW2 21 F6
Downview Cl
Beacon Hill GU26 188 D6
Downside KT11 93 B8
Doyle Rd SE25 43 A5
Dr Johnson Ave SW17 21 B5
Dragon La KT13 53 A1
Dragoon Ct GU11 104 E2
Drake Ave Caterham CR3 100 C5
Mytchett GU16 86 A1
Staines TW18 12 F3
Drake Cl Bracknell RG12 27 B4
Horsham RH12 217 E6
Drake Ct Dulwich SE19 22 F3
Kingston u T KT5 37 F5
Drake Rd Chessington KT9 57 A5
Crawley RH10 201 E3
Horley RH6 160 E3
Mitcham CR4 41 A3
Thornton Heath CR0, CR9 41 F2
Drake's Cl KT10 55 A6
Drakefield Rd SW17 21 A5
Drakes Ct SE23 23 C7
Drakes Way GU22 89 D5
Drakewood Rd SW16 21 D1
Drax Ave SW20 19 A1
Draxmont SW19 19 E2
Dray Ct GU2 130 B8
Draycot Rd KT6 38 A1
Draycott RG12 27 E4
Drayhorse Dr GU19 47 E2
Draymans Way TW7 5 F4
Drayton Cl Bracknell RG12 27 D7
Fetcham KT22 94 E3
Hounslow TW4 4 F2
Drayton Ct Tolworth KT5 57 B8
West Byfleet KT14 71 A6
Drayton Rd CR0, CR9 61 B8
Dresden Way KT13 53 C5
Drew House 12 SW16 21 E5
Drew Pl CR3 100 D4
Drewstead Rd SW16 21 D6
Drift The
East Horsley KT11, KT24 92 E3
Martyr's Green KT11, KT24 92 E3
Drift Way SL3 1 C7
Driftway The Banstead SM7 77 C4
Leatherhead KT22 95 C4
Mitcham CR4 41 A8
Driftway (Worple Road)
The KT22 95 B4
Driftwood Dr CR8 80 C2
Drill Hall Rd KT16 33 A2
Drive Rd CR5 99 F7
Drive Spur KT20 98 B6
Drive The Artington GU3 130 B5
Ashford TW15 14 D1
Banstead SM7 77 E3
Beckenham BR3 44 A8
Belmont SM2 77 F7
Cobham KT11 73 F5
Copthorne RH10 183 C3
Coulsdon CR5, CR8 79 E5
Cranleigh GU6 174 F2
Farnham GU9 146 B7
Feltham TW14 15 C8
Fetcham KT22 94 E5
Godalming GU7 150 F2
Guildford GU2 108 F1
Guildford GU2 130 A7
Headley KT18, KT22 96 A3
Horley RH6 161 B1
Drive The *continued*
Hounslow TW3, TW7 5 D5
Ifold RH14 212 D2
Kingston u T KT2 18 C1
Leatherhead KT22, KT18 95 F4
Morden SM4 40 D4
Shackleford GU7, GU8 149 E4
South Norwood CR7 42 D5
Thames Ditton KT10 36 C1
Thorpe GU25 31 F4
Wallington CR8, SM6 60 D1
West Ewell KT19 57 F4
West Wickham BR4 44 D2
Wimbledon SW19, SW20 19 C1
Woking GU22 89 B7
Wonersh GU5 152 B6
Drivers Mead RH7 164 D3
Drodges Cl GU5 151 F8
Droitwich Cl Bracknell RG12 27 E6
Forest Hill SE26 23 A5
Drove Rd GU4 132 A7
Drovers Ct 3 KT1 37 E7
Drovers Rd CR2 61 D5
Drovers Way Ash GU12 106 C1
Bracknell RG12 27 F6
Hale GU9 125 A6
Druid's Cl KT21 95 F7
Druids Way BR2 44 D5
Drumaline Ridge KT4 57 E8
Drummond Cl RG12 27 F8
Drummond Ct 4 GU1 109 D1
Drummond Ctr CR9 61 C8
Drummond Gdns KT19 76 B8
Drummond Rd
Crawley RH11 200 E5
Croydon CR0, CR9 61 C8
Guildford GU1 109 D1
Drummonds Pl TW9 6 E3
Drungewick La RH14 213 D2
Drury Cl RH10 202 D4
Drury Cres CR0, CR9 61 A8
Dry Arch Rd SL5 29 F3
Dryden RG12 27 A2
Dryden Ct 11 TW10 17 D4
Dryden Rd
Farnborough GU14 84 F6
Wimbledon SW19 20 C2
Drynham Pk KT13 53 E7
Du Cane Ct SW12 21 A7
Ducavel House SW2 21 F7
Duck's Wlk TW1 6 C2
Dudley Cl KT15 52 C7
Dudley Dr SM4 39 E2
Dudley Gr KT18 76 C5
Dudley Rd Ashford TW15 13 F4
East Bedfont TW14 14 D7
Kingston u T KT1 37 F6
Richmond TW9 7 A5
Walton-on-T KT12 35 A2
Wimbledon SW19 20 A2
Dudset La TW5 4 A6
Duffield Rd KT20 97 B3
Duffins Orch KT16 51 C3
Duke Cl RH10 202 C2
Duke Of Cambridge Cl
TW2 5 D1
Duke Of Cornwall Ave
GU15 46 D1
Duke Of Edinburgh Rd
SM1 59 D8
Duke of Kent Sch GU6 154 D2
Duke St Richmond TW10, TW9 6 D2
Sutton SM1 59 D6
Woking GU21 69 F2
Duke's Ave W4 7 D8
Duke's Dr Farncombe GU7 150 B7
Newdigate RH5 179 D6
Duke's Hill GU19 47 E5
Duke's La
Old Windsor SL4, SL5 10 B3
Winkfield SL5 9 F1
Duke's Ride RG45 45 B5
Dukes Ave Hounslow TW4 4 E3
Kingston u T KT2, TW10 17 D4
New Malden KT3 38 F6
Richmond KT2, TW10 17 D4
Dukes Cl Ashford TW15 14 C4
Cranleigh GU6 175 A2
Hale GU9 125 A6
Hampton TW12 15 F3
Dukes Covert GU19 47 E6
Dukes Ct Addlestone KT15 52 C6
Beckenham BR3 43 E6
Dukes Green Ave TW14 4 A2
Dukes Hill CR3, CR6 101 E7
Dukes Pk GU11 105 D6
Dukes Rd KT12 54 D5
Dukes Ride RH5 136 D4
Dukes Way BR4 63 E7
Dukes Wlk GU9 125 A6
Dukes Wood RG45 45 B5
Dukeshill Rd RG42 27 B8
Dukesthorpe Rd SE26 23 D4
Dulverton Ct 12 KT6 37 E4
Dulverton Rd CR2 62 C1
Dulwich and Sydenham
Hill Golf Course SE21 22 F6
Dulwich Bsns Ctr SE23 23 D7
Dulwich Coll
(Endowed) SE21 22 E6
Dulwich Coll Picture
Gal SE21 22 E8
Dulwich Coll Prep
Sch SE21 22 E5
Dulwich Comm SE21 22 E7
Dulwich Ct SE22 23 B7
Dulwich Oaks The SE21 22 F5
Dulwich Village SE21 22 E8
Dulwich Wood Ave SE19 22 E3
Dulwich Wood Pk
SE21, SE19 22 E4
Dumbarton Ct 16 SW2 21 E8
Dumbleton Cl KT2 38 B8
Dumphreys House 5
SW4 21 D8
Dumville Dr RH9 121 B4
Dunally Pk TW17 34 D2
Dunbar Ave Beckenham BR3 43 E5
Thornton Heath CR7, SW16 42 A7
Dunbar Ct Carshalton SM1 59 D5
Walton-on-T KT12 35 C1
Dunbar Rd Frimley GU16 85 F7
Kingston u T KT3 38 C5
Dunbar St SE27 22 C5
Dunboe Pl TW17 34 C2
Dunbridge House SW15 7 F1
Duncan Dr Guildford GU1 110 A2
Wokingham RG40 25 E5
Duncan Gdns TW18 13 A2
Duncan Rd
Burgh Heath KT20 97 E8
Richmond TW9 6 E3
Duncombe Ct TW18 12 F1
Duncombe Hill SE23 23 E8
Duncombe House 7
SW19 19 D7
Duncombe Rd GU7 150 D2
Duncroft Cl RH2 117 F1
Dundaff Cl GU15 66 A5
Dundas Cl RG12 27 B5
Dundas Gdns KT8 36 B6
Dundee Rd SE25 43 B4
Dundela Gdns KT17, KT4 58 B6
Dundonald Prim Sch
SW19 19 F1
Dundonald Rd SW19 19 F1
Dundrey Cres RH1 119 E6
Dundry House 8 SE26 23 A5
Dunedin Dr CR3 100 E2
Dunelm Gr SE27 22 C5
Dunfee Way KT14 71 E7
Dunfield Gdns SE6 24 B3
Dunfield Rd SE6 24 B3
Dungates La RH3 117 A2
Dunheved Cl CR7 42 A3
Dunheved Rd N CR7 42 A3
Dunheved Rd S CR7 42 A3
Dunheved Rd W CR7 42 A3
Dunhill Point 12 SW15 19 B7
Dunkeld Rd SE25 42 D5
Dunkirk St 12 SE27 22 C4
Dunleary Cl TW4 15 F8
Dunley Dr CR0 63 C4
Dunlin Cl RH1 139 F4
Dunlin Ct 11 SE21 22 D6
Dunlin Rise GU4 110 D3
Dunmail Dr CR2, CR8 80 E6
Dunmore GU2 108 D2
Dunmore Rd SW20 39 D8
Dunmow Cl TW13 15 E4
Dunnets GU21 68 E2
Dunning's Rd RH19 205 E7
Dunnings Mill L Complex
RH19 205 E6
Dunnock Ct 10 SE21 22 D6
Dunnymans Rd SM7 77 F4
Dunoon Gdns SE23 23 D8
Dunoon Rd SE23 23 C8
Dunottar Cl RH1 139 D7
Dunraven Ave RH1 140 B2
Dunraven House 11 TW9 6 F6
Dunraven Lower Sch
SW16 21 F5
Dunraven Upper Sch
SW16 21 F5
Dunsborough Cotts GU23 91 C7
Dunsbury Cl SM2 59 B2
Dunsdon Ave GU2 130 B8
Dunsfold CE Prim Sch
GU8 192 F6
Dunsfold Cl RH11 201 A5
Dunsfold Common Rd
GU8 192 F6
Dunsfold Ct 9 SM2 59 B3
Dunsfold House
10 Kingston u T KT2 18 B2
7 Streatham SW2 21 F8
Dunsfold Rd Alfold GU6 193 E3
Alfold Crossways GU6 193 E3
Bramley GU5, GU8 173 C1
Dunsfold GU6, GU8 193 B8
Plaistow GU8, RH14 211 D4
Dunsfold Rise CR5 79 D6
Dunsfold Way CR0 63 C3
Dunsmore Rd KT12 35 B3
Dunstable Rd
East Molesey KT8 35 F5
Richmond TW10, TW9 6 E3
Dunstall Pk GU14 85 A7
Dunstall Rd SW19, SW20 19 C2
Dunstall Way KT8 36 B6
Dunstan Ct TW18 13 A4
Dunstan Rd CR5 79 D2
Dunstan's Rd SE22 23 A8
Dunster Ave SM4 39 D1
Dunster House SE6 24 B5
Dunton Cl KT6 37 E1
Dunton Ct SE26 23 B6
Dunton House 14 SW16 21 E5
Duntshill Rd SW18 20 B7
Dunvegan Cl KT8 36 B5
Dunvegan House 12 RH1 118 F1
Dupont Rd SW20 39 D7
Duppas Ave CR0 61 B6
Duppas Cl TW17 34 D4
Duppas Ct CR0 61 B7

Duppas Hill La CR0 61 B6
Duppas Hill Rd CR0 61 B6
Duppas Hill Terr CR0, CR9 61 B7
Duppas Jun Sch CR0 61 B5
Duppas Rd CR0, CR9 61 B7
Dura Den Cl BR3 24 B1
Durand Cl SM5 40 F1
Durban Rd Beckenham BR3 43 F7
West Norwood SE27 22 D4
Durbin Rd KT9 56 F6
Durfold Dr RH2 118 C1
Durfold Rd RH12 217 D7
Durfold Wood RH14 211 D5
Durfold Wood
Woodlands Wlks GU8 211 C6
Durford Cres SW15 19 B7
Durham Ave BR2 44 F5
Durham Cl Crawley RH10 201 E2
Guildford GU2 108 F3
Wimbledon SW20 39 B7
Durham Ct
Leatherhead KT22 95 A5
Teddington TW11 16 E4
Durham Hill BR1 24 F4
Durham Rd Beckenham BR2 44 F6
Feltham TW14 15 C8
Sandhurst GU47 45 E2
Wimbledon SW20 39 B8
Durkins Rd RH19 185 D3
Durleston Park Dr KT23 94 C2
Durley Mead RG12 27 F4
Durlston Rd KT2 17 E2
Durnford House SE6 24 B5
Durning Rd SE19 22 D3
Durnsford Ave
SW18, SW19 20 A6
Durnsford Rd SW18, SW19 20 B5
Durnsford Way GU6 175 A2
Durrell Way TW17 34 D3
Durrington Ave SW20 19 C1
Durrington Park Rd SW20 39 C8
Dutch Barn Cl TW19 2 D1
Dutch Gdns KT2 18 B2
Dutchells Copse RH12 217 E7
Dutton House SW2 22 B7
Duval Pl GU19 47 E3
Duxford 10 KT1 38 A7
Duxhurst La RH2 160 B7
Dwelly La Haxted TN8 165 D8
Limpsfield TN8 144 D3
Dyehouse Rd GU8 169 C4
Dyer House TW12 36 B8
Dyer's Field RH6 162 B3
Dyers Almshouses RH10 201 D7
Dykes Ct 11 SW2 21 F7
Dykes Path GU22 70 C4
Dykes Way BR2 44 F6
Dymes Path SW19 19 D6
Dynevor Pl GU3 108 C5
Dynevor Rd TW10 6 E2
Dysart Ave KT2, TW10 17 C4
Dysart Sch KT2 17 D4
Dyson Ct RH4 136 A7
Dyson Wlk RH11 201 B1

E

Eady Cl RH13 217 F2
Eagle Cl Crowthorne RG45 45 A7
Wallington SM6 60 E4
Eagle Ct 9 SE21 22 D6
Eagle Hill SE19 22 D2
Eagle House Sch GU47 45 B2
Eagle Rd Farnborough GU14 85 B2
Guildford GU1 109 D1
Eagle Trad Est CR4 40 F3
Eagles Dr TN16 83 D1
Eagles Nest GU47 45 A1
Ealing Rd TW8 6 E8
Eardley Prim Sch SW16 21 C2
Eardley Rd SW16 21 C2
Earl Rd SW14 7 C3
Earle Gdns KT2 17 E1
Earles Meadow RH12 218 B6
Earleswood KT11 73 E7
Earleydene SL5 29 B1
Earls Gr GU15 65 E6
Earlsbrook Rd RH1 139 F7
Earlsfield Prim Sch SW18 20 C6
Earlsfield Rd SW18 20 C8
Earlsfield Sta SW18 20 C7
Earlsthorpe Rd SE26 23 D4
Earlswood RG12 27 B2
Earlswood Ave CR7 42 A4
Earlswood Cl RH13 218 A4
Earlswood Ct RH1 139 F7
Earlswood Cty Inf &
Nurs Sch RH1 140 A8
Earlswood House 2 SW2 21 F7
Earlswood Rd RH1 139 F7
Earlswood Sta RH1 139 F7
Early Commons RH10 201 F7
Easby Cres SM4 40 B3
Easedale House TW7 5 F2
Eashing La
Godalming GU7, GU8 150 A3
Shackleford GU7, GU8 149 F3
Eashing Point 5 SW15 19 B7
Easington Pl GU1 130 F8
East Ave Heath End GU9 125 D6
Wallington CR0 60 F5
Whiteley Village KT12 53 F1
East Croydon Sta CR9 61 D8
East Dr Beckenham BR3 44 C4
Wallington SM5 59 F2
Wentworth GU25 31 B3
East Flexford La GU3 128 F6
East Gdns
Mitcham SW17, SW19 20 E2
Woking GU22 70 C2
East Gn GU17 64 C4
East Grinstead Rd RH7 164 D3
East Grinstead Sta RH19 185 D1
East Grinstead Town Mus
RH19 185 F2
East Hill Biggin Hill TN16 83 B1
Dormans Park RH19 185 E6
Oxted RH8 122 F6
South Croydon CR2 61 E1
Woking GU22 70 C2
East Hill Ct RH8 122 E5
East Hill La RH10 183 D5
East Hill Rd RH8 122 E6
East La Kingston u T KT1 37 D6
West Horsley KT24 92 D2
East Meads GU2 130 A8
East Park La RH7 163 C1
East Pk RH10, RH11 201 D5
East Pl SE27 22 C4
East Ramp TW6 3 B6
East Rd East Bedfont TW14 14 D8
Kingston u T KT2 37 E8
Merton SW19 20 C2
Reigate RH2 117 F2
Weybridge KT13 53 D3
Wimbledon SW19 20 C2
East Resr (Nature Reserve)
RH9 121 B5
East Ring GU10 127 A7
East Shalford La GU4 131 A3
East Sheen Ave SW14 7 D3
East Sheen Prim Sch SW14 7 E3
East St Brentford TW8 6 C7
Ewell KT17 76 E7
Farnham GU9 125 C3
Great Bookham KT23 94 B2
Horsham RH12 217 C1
Rusper RH12 199 E7
Turners Hill RH10, RH19 204 C4
East Station Rd GU12 105 B1
East Stratton Cl RG12 27 F4
East Surrey Coll RH1 119 A4
East Surrey Hospl RH1 118 E1
East Surrey Hospl The
RH1 140 A5
East Surrey Mus CR3 101 A3
East View La GU6 174 C3
East Way CR0 62 E7
East Whipley La
Rowly GU5 173 F7
Shamley Green GU5 173 F8
East Wlk RH2 118 B1
Eastbank Rd TW12 16 C3
Eastbourne Gdns SW14 7 C4
Eastbourne Rd
Blindley Heath RH9 142 E4
Chiswick W4 7 C8
Felbridge RH7 184 E8
Feltham TW13 15 D6
Godstone RH9 121 D2
Mitcham SW17 21 A2
Newchapel RH7, RH9 163 F5
South Godstone RH9 142 E4
Eastbrook Cl GU21 70 A3
Eastbury Gr W4 7 E8
Eastbury La GU3 129 A3
Eastbury Rd KT2 17 E1
Eastchurch Rd TW6 3 E4
Eastchurch Road Rdbt TW6 3 E5
Eastcote Ave KT8 36 A4
Eastcroft Ct GU1 131 A8
Eastcroft Mews RH12 216 F1
Eastcroft Rd KT19 57 E3
Eastdean Ave KT18 76 B6
Easter Way RH9 142 F5
Eastern Ave KT16 33 A6
Eastern Ind Area RG12 27 D7
Eastern La RG45 45 F4
Eastern Perimeter Rd TW14 3 F5
Eastern Rd
Aldershot GU12 105 E2
Bracknell RG12 27 D7
Eastern View TN16 83 C2
Eastfield Rd RH1 140 C8
Eastfields GU8 170 F5
Eastfields High Sch CR4 41 B7
Eastfields Rd CR4 41 A7
Eastgate SM7 77 F5
Eastgate Gdns GU1 130 E8
Easthampstead Park Sch
RG12 26 D3
Easthampstead Rd
Bracknell RG12 27 A7
Wokingham RG40 25 E4
Eastheath Ave RG41 25 A4
Eastheath Gdns RG41 25 B3
Eastlands Cl RH8 122 D8
Eastlands Cres SE21, SE22 22 F8
Eastlands Way RH8 122 D8
Eastleigh Cl SM2 59 B3
Eastleigh Rd TW6 3 F4
Eastleigh Way TW14 15 A7
Eastleigh Wlk 10 SW15 19 A8
Eastmead
Farnborough GU14 85 B3
Woking GU21 69 B2
Eastmearn Rd SE21, SE27 22 C6
Eastmont Rd KT10 55 F8
Eastney Rd CR0 42 B1
Eastnor Cl RH2 138 F6
Eastnor Rd RH2 139 A6
Easton House 4 SE27 22 B5
Eastry Ave BR2 44 F3
Eastway Crawley RH6 182 B7
Epsom KT19 76 D8
Eastway *continued*
Guildford GU2 108 F1
Merton SM4, SW20 39 E5
Wallington SM6 60 C6
Eastwell Cl BR3 23 E1
Eastwick Ct 2 SW19 19 D7
Eastwick Cty Inf Sch KT23 94 B3
Eastwick Cty Mid Sch
KT23 94 B3
Eastwick Dr KT23 94 B4
Eastwick Park Ave KT23 94 B3
Eastwick Rd
Great Bookham KT23 94 B2
Hersham KT12 54 B5
Eastwood Crawley RH10 201 F6
3 Weybridge KT13 53 D4
Eastwood Lodge GU5 151 F7
Eastwood Rd GU5 151 F7
Eastwood St SW16 21 C2
Eastworth Rd KT15, KT16 33 A1
Eaton Ct Guildford GU1 110 A3
Sutton SM2 59 D4
Eaton Dr KT2 18 A1
Eaton Ho GU1 130 F7
Eaton Park Rd KT11 73 F5
Eaton Pk KT11 73 E5
Eaton Rd Camberley GU15 65 B4
Isleworth TW3, TW7 5 D3
Sutton SM2 59 D4
Eatonville Rd SW17 20 F6
Eatonville Villas SW17 20 F6
Ebba's Way KT18 76 B4
Ebbage Ct 5 GU22 69 E1
Ebbisham Ct KT18 76 C4
Ebbisham La KT20 97 A4
Ebbisham Rd Epsom KT18 76 B5
North Cheam KT4 58 C8
Ebenezer Wlk CR4 41 C8
Ebisham Cl RH4 136 A7
Ebor Cotts SW15 18 E5
Ebsworth St SE23 23 D8
Ecclesbourne Inf Sch CR7 42 C4
Ecclesbourne Jun Sch
CR7 42 C4
Ecclesbourne Rd CR7 42 C4
Eccleshill Beckenham BR2 44 F5
Dorking RH5 136 C3
Echelford Cty Mid Sch
TW15 14 B3
Echelforde Dr TW15 14 A4
Echo Barn La GU10 145 F5
Echo Pit Rd GU1, GU4 130 E6
Ecob Cl GU3 108 F5
Ecton Rd KT15 52 B6
Ector Rd SE6 24 E6
Eddeys Cl GU35 187 B6
Eddeys La GU35 187 B6
Eddington Hill RH11 201 B1
Eddington Rd RG12 26 E3
Eddisbury House 7 SE26 23 A5
Eddy Rd GU12 105 C1
Eddystone Wlk TW19 13 E8
Ede Cl TW4 4 F4
Ede Ct KT17 76 F7
Ede's Cotts KT21 95 D8
Eden Cl KT15 52 B1
Eden Grove Rd KT14 71 E6
Eden Park Ave BR3 44 A4
Eden Park Sch BR3 43 F4
Eden Park Sta BR3 44 A4
Eden Rd Crawley RH11 200 F4
Croydon CR0 61 D6
Penge BR3 43 E8
West Norwood SE27 22 B3
Eden St KT1, KT2 37 E7
Eden Vale
Dormans Park RH19 185 E5
East Grinstead RH19 185 E5
Eden Way Beckenham BR3 44 A3
Warlingham CR6 81 E1
Eden Wlk 5 KT1 37 E7
Edenbrook RH7 164 E4
Edencourt Rd SW16 21 B2
Edencroft GU5 151 F7
Edenfield Gdns KT4 57 F7
Edenham High Sch CR0 43 F2
Edenhurst Pl SM2 59 A4
Edenside Rd KT23 93 F3
Edensor Gdns W4 7 E7
Edensor Rd W4 7 E7
Edenvale Cl CR4 21 A1
Edenvale Rd CR4 21 A1
Ederline Ave SW16 42 A7
Edgar Cl RH10 202 E5
Edgar Ct KT3 38 E6
Edgar Rd
South Croydon CR2 61 D2
Tatsfield TN16 103 D6
Twickenham TW4 15 F8
Edgbarrow Rise GU47 45 A2
Edgbarrow Sch RG45 45 A3
Edgbarrowhill Star RG45 45 A3
Edgcumbe Park Dr RG45 45 A5
Edge Cl KT13 53 A3
Edge Hill SW19 19 D1
Edge Hill Ct SW19 19 D1
Edge Point Cl SE27 22 B3
Edgeborough Ct 6 GU1 130 F8
Edgeborough Sch GU10 146 C3
Edgecombe Cl KT2 18 C1
Edgecombe House SW19 19 E8
Edgecoombe CR2 62 D2
Edgecumbe Ct 2 CR0 43 A1
Edgedale Cl RG45 45 B5
Edgefield Cl
Cranleigh GU6 174 C4
Redhill RH1 140 A4
Edgehill Ct KT12 35 C1
Edgehill House 2 RH1 118 F1
Edgehill Rd Mitcham CR4 41 B8
Purley CR2, CR8 61 B1
Edgeley KT23 93 E3
Edgell Cl GU25 31 F6
Edgell Rd TW18 12 F3
Edgemoor Rd GU16 66 C3
Edgewood Cl RG45 45 A7
Edgewood Gn CR0 43 D1
Edgeworth Cl CR3 81 A1
Edgington Rd SW16 21 D2
Edinburgh Cl GU12 106 A5
Edinburgh Ct Catford SE6 24 F7
2 Kingston u T KT1 37 E6
West Barnes SM4 39 D4
Edinburgh Dr TW15, TW18 13 D2
Edinburgh Rd SM1 59 D8
Edinburgh Way RH19 205 F7
Edith Gdns KT5 38 B2
Edith Rd
Thornton Heath SE25 42 D4
Wimbledon SW19 20 B2
Edmonds Ct 4 RG12 27 C8
Edmund Rd CR4 40 E6
Edna Rd SW20 39 D7
Edrich Rd RH11 201 A1
Edridge House 9 SE27 22 B5
Edridge Rd CR0, CR9 61 D7
Edward Alleyn House
SE21 22 E8
Edward Ave
Camberley GU15 65 A5
Morden CR4, SM4 40 D4
Edward Cl TW12 16 C3
Edward Ct TW18 13 C2
Edward II Ave KT14 71 F5
Edward Pauling House
TW14 14 F8
Edward Pauling Prim Sch
TW13 14 E6
Edward Pinner Ct 5 KT6 56 E8
Edward Rd Biggin Hill TN16 83 E1
Coulsdon CR5 79 D4
Croydon CR0 42 E2
Farnham GU9 146 C7
Hampton TW12 16 C3
Hatton TW14 3 E2
Penge SE20 23 D2
Windlesham GU20 48 D4
Edward St 2 GU11 105 A2
Edward Way TW15 13 F6
Edwards Cl KT4 58 D8
Edwin Cl KT24 92 D2
Edwin Rd
Twickenham TW1, TW2 16 E7
West Horsley KT24 92 D2
Edwin Stray House TW13 16 A5
Edwina Ct SM1 59 B6
Eelmoor Plain Rd GU11 104 D5
Eelmoor Rd
Aldershot GU11 104 D5
Farnborough GU14 84 F2
Eelmoor Road Trad Est
GU14 85 A2
Effingham Cl SM2 59 B3
Effingham Common
Rd KT24 93 C2
Effingham Ct
Mitcham SW19 20 E1
Woking GU22 89 E8
Effingham House 9 KT2 18 B2
Effingham House Golf
Club KT24 113 D7
Effingham Junction Sta
KT24 93 A4
Effingham La RH10 183 E4
Effingham Lodge 1 KT6 37 E4
Effingham Pl KT24 113 D8
Effingham Rd
Burstow RH10, RH6 183 D6
Domewood RH10, RH6 183 D6
Reigate RH2 139 B8
Thames Ditton KT6, KT7 37 C2
Thornton Heath CR0 41 F2
Effort St SW17 20 E3
Effra Ct SE19 22 E1
Effra Rd SW19 20 B2
Egbury House SW15 7 F1
Egerton Ct
5 Guildford GU2 108 E1
5 Richmond TW10 6 E2
Egerton House W4 7 C8
Egerton Pl KT13 53 C4
Egerton Rd Guildford GU2 129 F8
New Malden KT3 38 F5
Sandhurst GU15 64 F7
Sandhurst GU15 65 A7
South Norwood SE25 42 E6
Twickenham TW2 16 E8
Weybridge KT13 53 C4
Eggar's Ct GU12 105 B1
Eggar's Hill GU11 126 A8
Egham By-Pass TW20 12 A4
Egham Cl Cheam SM3 58 E8
Putney SW19 19 E6
Egham Cres SM3 58 D8
Egham Ct KT6 37 D4
Egham Hill Egham TW20 11 F3
Englefield Green TW20 11 D2
Egham Hill Rdbt TW20 11 F3
Egham Mus TW20 12 A3
Egham Sta TW20 12 A3
Egleston Rd SM4 40 B3
Egley Dr GU22 89 D5
Egley Rd GU22 89 D6
Eglinton Rd GU10 168 B7
Eglise Rd CR6 81 E2
Egmont Ave KT6 37 F1
Egmont Park Rd KT20 97 A2
Egmont Rd New Malden KT3 38 F5
Surbiton KT6 38 A1
Sutton SM2 59 C3
Walton-on-T KT12 35 B2
Egmont Way KT20 97 E8
Egremont Rd SE27 22 A5
Eight Acres GU26 188 C7
Eighteenth Rd CR4 41 E5
Eileen Rd SE25 42 D4
Eisenhower House KT8 37 C8
Eland Pl CR9 61 B7
Eland Rd Aldershot GU12 105 D1
Croydon CR0, CR9 61 B7
Elberon Ave CR0 41 C3
Elborough Rd SE25 43 A4
Elborough St SW18 20 A7
Elbow Meadow SL3 1 F6
Elcho Rd GU24 87 D8
Elder Cl GU1, GU4 110 A4
Elder Gdns 9 SE27 22 C4
Elder Oak Cl SE20 43 B8
Elder Rd Bisley GU24 68 A4
West Norwood SE27 22 C3
Elder Way RH5 136 C3
Elderberry Gr 10 SE27 22 C4
Eldergrove GU14 85 E2
Eldersley Cl RH1 118 F3
Eldersley Gdns RH1 118 F3
Elderslie Cl BR3 44 B3
Elderton Rd SE26 23 E4
Eldertree Pl CR4 41 C8
Eldertree Way CR4 41 C8
Elderwood SE27 22 C3
Eldon Ave Croydon CR0 62 C8
Heston TW5 5 A7
Eldon Ct KT13 53 C5
Eldon Dr GU10 146 D5
Eldon Pk SE25 43 B5
Eldon Rd CR3 100 D6
Eldrick Ct TW14 14 D7
Eldridge Cl TW14 15 A7
Eleanor Ave KT19 57 D1
Eleanor Ct GU1 130 D7
Eleanor Gr SW13, SW14 7 E4
Eleanor House 6 SW19 40 B8
Elfin Gr TW11 16 F3
Elfrida Cres SE6 24 A4
Elfrida Inf & Jun Sch SE6 24 A4
Elgar Ave Crowthorne RG45 45 B7
Thornton Heath SW16 41 E6
Tolworth KT5, KT6 38 B2
Elgar House Kenley CR8 80 C5
Twickenham TW2 5 D1
Elgar Way RH13 218 B4
Elger Way RH10 183 A4
Elgin Ave TW15 14 C2
Elgin Cl RH13 217 F3
Elgin Cres Caterham CR3 101 A5
Harlington TW6 3 E5
Elgin Ct 6 CR0 61 C6
Elgin Gdns GU1 110 A2
Elgin Rd Croydon CR0 61 F8
Sutton SM1 59 C7
Wallington SM6 60 C4
Weybridge KT13 53 B5
Elgin Way GU16 85 F8
Eliot Bank SE23, SE26 23 B6
Eliot Bank Prim Sch SE23 23 B6
Eliot Cl GU15 66 B7
Eliot Dr GU27 207 E6
Eliot House 10 TW10 6 F1
Elizabeth Ave
Bagshot GU19 47 F2
Staines TW18 13 D2
Elizabeth Cl Bracknell RG12 27 C5
Cheam SM1 58 F8
Farncombe GU7 150 E7
Elizabeth Cotts 5 TW9 7 A6
Elizabeth Cres RH19 185 F3
Elizabeth Ct Horley RH6 161 A3
Sunbury TW16 35 C6
Teddington TW11 16 E3
West Barnes SM4 39 E2
Whyteleafe CR3 80 F1
Elizabeth Gdns Ascot SL5 29 B4
Sunbury TW16 35 C6
Elizabeth Hart Ct KT13 52 F5
Elizabeth House CR3 101 A3
Elizabeth Rd
Farncombe GU7 150 E7
Wokingham RG40 25 D6
Elizabeth Way
Feltham TW13 15 C4
South Norwood SE19 22 D1
Elizabethan Cl TW19 13 D8
Elizabethan Way
Crawley RH10 202 C5
Stanwell TW19 13 D8
Elkins Gdns GU4 110 A4
Ellacombe House 1 SW2 22 A8
Elland Rd KT12 54 D8
Ellenborough Cl RG12 27 D8
Ellenbridge Way CR2 61 E2
Elleray Ct GU12 106 A5
Elleray Rd TW11 16 F2
Ellerdine Rd TW3 5 D3
Ellerker Gdns TW10 6 E1
Ellerman Ave TW2, TW4 15 F7
Ellerslie Ct 6 SM6 60 B4
Ellerton Rd Surbiton KT6 37 F1
Wandsworth SW17, SW18 20 D7
Wimbledon SW20 19 A1
Ellery Cl GU6 174 E1
Ellery Rd SE19 22 D1

Elles Ave GU1 110 C1
Elles Cl GU14 85 B3
Elles Rd GU14 84 F2
Ellesfield Ave RG12 26 E5
Ellesmere Ave BR3 44 B7
Ellesmere Ct Chiswick W4 7 D8
Penge SE20 43 B7
Weybridge KT12 53 E4
Ellesmere Dr CR2 81 B5
Ellesmere Pl KT12 53 E5
Ellesmere Rd
Twickenham TW1 6 C1
Weybridge KT13 53 E4
Ellice Rd RH8 122 F6
Ellies Mews TW15 13 E6
Ellingham GU22 89 E8
Ellingham Prim Sch KT9 56 D3
Ellingham Rd KT9 56 D4
Ellington Rd Feltham TW13 14 F4
Hounslow TW3 5 B5
Ellington Way KT18 77 B2
Elliot Cl RH10 202 C4
Elliot Park GU12 105 E2
Elliot Rise SL5 28 D7
Elliott Ct GU21 70 A3
Elliott Gdns TW17 34 A5
Elliott Rd CR7 42 B5
Ellis Ave GU2 129 F7
Ellis Cl CR5 99 F7
Ellis Farm Cl GU22 89 D5
Ellis Rd Coulsdon CR5 99 F7
Crowthorne RG45 45 B6
Mitcham CR4 40 F3
Ellisfield Dr SW15 19 A8
Ellison Rd Barnes SW13 7 F5
Streatham SW16 21 E1
Ellison Way
Tongham GU10 126 F7
Wokingham RG40 25 B6
Ellman Rd RH11 200 F4
Ellora Rd SW16 21 D3
Ellson Cl RH10 202 C4
Ellswood Ct 18 KT6 37 D2
Elm Bank Gdns SW13 7 E5
Elm Bank Mansions SW13 7 E5
Elm Bridge La GU22 90 A8
Elm Cl Box Hill KT20 116 C5
Carshalton SM5 40 F1
Leatherhead KT22 95 B5
Send Marsh GU23 91 A3
South Croydon CR2 61 E4
Stanwell TW19 13 D7
Tolworth KT5 38 C2
Twickenham TW13, TW2 16 B6
Warlingham CR6 81 D2
West Barnes SW20 39 C5
Woking GU21 69 D4
Elm Cotts RH5 115 C8
Elm Court Sch SE27 22 C6
Elm Cres Heath End GU9 125 D7
Kingston u T KT2 37 E8
Elm Ct Catford SE6 24 B7
5 Charlton TW16 14 F1
Knaphill GU21 68 D2
Mitcham CR4 40 F7
Sandhurst GU47 45 E2
Elm Dr Chobham GU24 49 F1
East Grinstead RH19 186 A1
Leatherhead KT22 95 B4
Sunbury TW16 35 C7
Winkfield SL4 9 B7
Elm Gdns Burgh Heath KT18 97 C8
Claygate KT10 55 F4
Mitcham CR4 41 D5
Elm Gr Bisley GU24 68 A3
Caterham CR3 100 E5
Cranleigh GU6 174 A3
Epsom KT18 76 C5
Heath End GU9 125 C7
Horsham RH13 217 E1
Kingston u T KT2 37 E8
Sutton SM1 59 B6
Wimbledon SW19 19 E1
Elm Grove Par SM6 60 A7
Elm Grove Rd
Cobham KT11 73 D3
Farnborough GU14 85 B4
Elm Hill Bglws GU3 106 E3
Elm House 2 KT2 17 F1
Elm La Ash GU10 126 F8
Forest Hill SE6 23 F6
Ockham GU23 92 A8
Elm Park Rd SE25 42 F6
Elm Pk Streatham SW2 21 F8
Sunningdale GU20, SL5 29 E1
Elm Pl GU11 126 C8
Elm Rd Beckenham BR3 43 F7
Carshalton CR4, SM6 41 A1
Chessington KT9 56 E6
Claygate KT10 55 F4
East Bedfont TW14 14 D8
Farncombe GU7 150 F8
Heath End GU9 125 D7
Kingston u T KT2 37 F8
Kingston u T KT3 38 D6
Leatherhead KT22 95 B5
Mortlake SW14 7 C3
Purley CR8 80 B6
Redhill RH1 118 E1
South Norwood CR7 42 D5
Stoneleigh KT17 57 F4
Warlingham CR6 81 D2
Woking GU21 69 D1
Woking, Horsell GU21 69 F4
Elm Rd W SM4 39 F2
Elm Tree Ave KT10 36 E2
Elm Tree Cl
Addlestone KT16 51 E8
Ashford TW15 14 B3
Elm View GU12 106 B3
Elm Way North Cheam KT4 58 C7
West Ewell KT19 57 D5
Elm Wlk SW20 39 D5
Elm Wood Prim Sch SE27 22 D5
Elmbank Ave
Englefield Green TW20 11 B2
Guildford GU2 130 A8
Elmbourne Rd SW17 21 B5
Elmbridge Ave KT5 38 C3
Elmbridge Cotts GU6 174 B3
Elmbridge La GU22 89 F8
Elmbridge Rd GU6 173 F2
Elmbrook Cl TW16 35 B8
Elmbrook Rd SM1 58 F6
Elmcourt Rd SE21, SE27 22 B6
Elmcroft
Little Bookham KT23 94 A3
12 Woking GU22 69 E1
Elmcroft Cl Chessington KT9 56 E7
Feltham TW14 3 F1
Frimley GU16 85 F7
Elmcroft Dr Ashford TW15 14 A3
Chessington KT9 56 E7
Elmdene KT5 38 C1
Elmdene Cl BR3 43 F4
Elmdon Rd Hatton TW6 3 F4
Hounslow TW5 4 E5
Elmer Cotts KT22 95 A4
Elmer Gdns TW7 5 D4
Elmer Mews KT22 95 A5
Elmer Rd SE6 24 C8
Elmer's Dr TW11 17 B2
Elmers End Rd
Beckenham BR3 43 D5
Penge BR3, SE20 43 C6
Elmers End Sta BR3 43 D5
Elmers Rd
Croydon CR0, SE25 43 A2
Ockley RH5 177 C4
Elmerside Rd BR3 43 E5
Elmfield KT23 94 A4
Elmfield Ave Mitcham CR4 41 A8
Teddington TW11 16 F3
Elmfield House GU4 110 C3
Elmfield Mansions 5
SW17 21 A6
Elmfield Rd SW17 21 B6
Elmfield Way CR2 61 F2
Elmgate Ave TW13 15 C5
Elmgrove Cl GU21 88 D8
Elmgrove Rd Croydon CR0 43 B2
Weybridge KT13 53 A7
Elmhurst Ave CR4 21 B1
Elmhurst Ballet Sch GU15 65 D5
Elmhurst Ct Croydon CR0 61 D5
Guildford GU1 130 F8
Elmhurst Dr RH4 136 B5
Elmhurst Lodge SM2 59 C3
Elmhurst Sch for Boys
CR2 61 D5
Elmore Rd CR5 99 A6
Elmpark Gdns CR2 62 C1
Elms Cotts CR4 40 F7
Elms Ct SW19 20 B1
Elms Rd Aldershot GU11 105 A2
Wokingham RG40 25 B5
Elms The Ash GU10 126 F8
Ashford TW15 14 A3
Claygate KT10 55 F3
Croydon CR0 42 C1
Mortlake SW13 7 F4
Elmscott Rd BR1 24 F3
Elmshorn KT17 77 C3
Elmside Guildford GU2 130 A8
Milford GU8 149 F1
New Addington CR0 63 B4
Elmsleigh Ct SM1 59 B7
Elmsleigh Ctr The TW18 12 F4
Elmsleigh House TW2 16 D6
Elmsleigh Rd
Farnborough GU14 84 F4
Staines TW18 12 F3
Twickenham TW2 16 D6
Elmslie Cl KT18 76 C5
Elmstead RH19 205 E8
Elmstead Cl KT19 57 E5
Elmstead Gdns KT4 58 A7
Elmstead Rd KT14 71 A5
Elmsway TW15 14 A3
Elmswood KT23 93 F3
Elmsworth Ave TW3 5 B5
Elmtree Cl KT14 71 E6
Elmtree Rd TW11 16 E3
Elmwood Ave TW13 15 B5
Elmwood Cl Ashstead KT21 75 D2
Hackbridge SM6 60 B8
Stoneleigh KT17 58 A3
Elmwood Ct KT21 75 D2
Elmwood Dr KT17 58 A3
Elmwood Inf Sch CR0 42 B3
Elmwood Jun Sch CR0 42 B2
Elmwood Rd Chiswick W4 7 C8
Knaphill GU21 88 D8
Mitcham CR4 40 F6
Redhill RH1 119 B5
Thornton Heath CR0 42 B2
Elmworth Gr SE21 22 D6
Elphinstone Ct SW16 21 E2
Elsdon Rd GU21 69 A1
Elsenham St SW18, SW19 19 F6
Elsenwood Cres GU15 66 A6
Elsenwood Dr GU15 66 A7
Elsinore Ave TW19 13 E8
Elsinore Rd SE23 23 E7
Elsinore Way TW9 7 B4
Elsley Cl GU16 85 F6
Elsrick Ave SM4 40 A4
Elstan Way CR0 43 E2
Elstead Ct SM4 39 E1
Elstead Gn GU8 148 D4
Elstead House 12 SW2 21 F8
Elstead Rd Milford GU8 149 C3
Seale GU10 127 B3
Shackleford GU7, GU8 149 E6
The Sands GU10 127 A2
Elsted Cl RH11 201 B8
Elston Pl GU12 126 C8
Elston Rd GU11, GU12 126 C8
Elstree Hill BR1 24 E1
Elsworth Cl TW14 14 E7
Elsworthy KT7 36 E3
Elthorne Ct TW13 15 C7
Elton Rd Kingston u T KT2 38 A8
Purley CR8 79 C7
Elveden Cl GU22 71 B2
Elveden Ct KT22 95 C6
Elveden Rd KT11 73 C8
Elvington Gn BR2 44 F4
Elvino Rd SE26 23 E3
Elwell Cl TW20 12 A2
Elwill Way BR3 44 D5
Ely Cl Crawley RH10 201 F2
Frimley GU16 86 A7
Kingston u T SW20 38 F7
Ely Ct KT1 38 A6
Ely House 7 RH1 118 F1
Ely Rd Hatton TW6 3 F5
Hounslow TW4 4 C4
Thornton Heath CR0 42 D4
Elystan Cl SM6 60 C2
Embankment The
Twickenham TW1 17 A7
Wraysbury TW19 11 C7
Embassy Ct
Kingston u T KT6 37 D4
7 Wallington SM6 60 B4
Embassy Gdns BR3 43 F8
Ember Cl KT15 52 D5
Ember Ctr KT12 54 E8
Ember Farm Ave KT8 36 D3
Ember Farm Way KT8 36 D4
Ember Gdns KT10, KT8 36 E2
Ember House BR1 24 D3
Ember La KT10, KT8 36 D2
Embercourt
Rd KT10, KT7, KT8 36 E3
Emberwood RH11 201 D8
Embleton Rd GU35 187 B6
Embleton Wlk TW12 15 F3
Emerton Rd KT22 94 C6
Emery Down Cl RG12 28 A6
Emley Rd KT15 52 B6
Emlyn La KT22 95 A5
Emlyn Rd Horley RH6 160 E4
Redhill RH1 140 A7
Emmanuel Cl GU2 109 A4
Emmanuel House SE21 22 D5
Emmanuel Rd SW12 21 D7
Emmbrook Rd RG41 25 A8
Emmbrook Sch The RG41 25 A8
Emmeline Ct KT12 35 C2
Emmetts Cl GU21 69 D2
Empire Villas RH1 161 B7
Empress Ave GU14 85 B5
Emsworth Cl RH10 202 C3
Emsworth St SW2 21 F6
Ena Rd SW16 41 E6
Endale Cl SM5 59 F8
Endeavour Way
Wallington CR0 41 E2
Wimbledon SW19 20 B4
Enderley House SE19 42 F8
Endlesham Ct 3 SW12 21 A8
Endlesham Rd SW12 21 A8
Endsleigh Cl CR2 62 C1
Endsleigh Gdns
Hersham KT12 54 C5
Kingston u T KT6 37 C3
Endsleigh Mansions 4
SW16 21 E5
Endsleigh Rd RH1 119 C6
Endway KT5 38 B2
Enfield Rd Ash GU12 106 B5
Crawley RH11 201 C2
Harlington TW6 3 E5
Enfield Road Rdbt TW6 3 E5
Engadine Cl CR0 61 F7
Engadine St SW18 20 A7
Engalee RH19 185 C2
Englefield RH12 216 F2
Englefield Cl
Englefield Green TW20 11 C2
Thornton Heath CR0 42 C3
Englefield Green Cty Inf
Sch TW20 11 C3
Englefield Rd GU21 68 D2
Engleheart Dr TW14 3 F1
Engleheart Rd SE6 24 C8
Englehurst TW20 11 C2
Englemere Pk SL5 28 D5
Englemere Pond Nature
Trail SL5 28 C6
Englesfield GU15 66 D5
Engliff La GU22 71 A3
Enid Wood House RG12 27 C7
Enmore Ave SE25 43 A4
Enmore Gdns SW14 7 D2
Enmore Rd SE25 43 A4
Ennerdale RG12 27 A5
Ennerdale Cl Cheam SM1 58 F6
Crawley RH11 201 B4
Ennerdale Cl *continued*
East Bedfont TW14 14 F7
Ennerdale Gr GU9 125 A6
Ennerdale Rd TW9 6 F5
Ennismore Ave GU1 109 F1
Ennismore Gdns KT7 36 E3
Ennor Ct KT4 58 C6
Ensham Sch SW17 20 F3
Ensham Sec Sch (Annexe)
SW17 20 E4
Ensign Cl Purley CR8 61 A1
Stanwell TW19 13 D7
Ensign Way TW19 13 D7
Enterdent Cotts RH9 121 D2
Enterdent Rd RH9 121 D2
Enterprise Cl CR0 42 A1
Enterprise Est GU1 109 E5
Enterprise House KT12 35 B2
Enterprise Way TW11 16 F2
Envis Way GU3 108 C4
Eothen Cl CR3 101 A3
Epping Way RG12 27 F5
Epping Wlk RH10 201 F4
Epsom Bsns Pk KT17 76 E8
Epsom Cl GU15 65 C8
Epsom Coll KT17 77 A5
Epsom Cty Prim Sch KT19 76 D8
Epsom Downs Cty Inf Sch
KT18 96 D8
Epsom Downs Metro Ctr
KT20 97 B7
Epsom Downs Sta KT17 77 B4
Epsom & Ewell High Sch
KT19 57 C5
Epsom General Hospl
KT18 76 C4
Epsom La N KT18, KT20 97 B7
Epsom La S KT20 97 C5
Epsom Pl GU6 174 F3
Epsom Rd
Ashstead KT18, KT21 76 A2
Cheam SM4 39 F2
Crawley RH10 202 A4
Croydon CR0 61 A6
East Clandon GU4 111 D3
Ewell KT17 76 F8
Guildford GU4 110 F2
Guildford GU1 130 F8
Guildford, Merrow
GU1, GU4 110 C1
Leatherhead KT22 95 C6
Morden SM4 39 F2
West Clandon GU4 111 D3
West Horsley GU4, KT24 112 C6
Epsom Sq TW6 3 F5
Epsom Sta KT18 76 D6
Epworth Rd TW7, TW8 6 B7
Eresby Dr BR3 44 A1
Erica Cl GU24 67 E6
Erica Ct GU22 69 D1
Erica Dr RG40 25 D5
Erica Gdns CR0 63 B7
Erica Way Copthorne RH10 183 A2
Horsham RH12 217 D5
Eridge Cl RH10 202 C6
Erin Cl BR1 24 E1
Erindale Ct BR3 44 A8
Eriswell Cres KT12 53 F4
Eriswell Rd KT12 53 F5
Erkenwald Cl KT16 32 E3
Ermine Cl TW4 4 C5
Ermyn Cl KT21 95 D6
Ermyn Way KT21, KT22 95 D6
Erncroft Way TW1 5 F1
Ernest Ave SE27 22 B4
Ernest Bevin Sch SW17 20 E6
Ernest Cl Beckenham BR3 44 A4
Farnham GU10, GU9 146 B6
Ernest Cotts KT17 57 F3
Ernest Gdns W4 7 B8
Ernest Gr BR3 43 F4
Ernest Rd KT1 38 B7
Ernest Sq KT1 38 B7
Ernle Rd SW20 19 C1
Erridge Rd SW19 40 A7
Errol Gdns KT3 39 A5
Erskine Cl Carshalton SM1 59 E7
Crawley RH11 200 E2
Erskine Rd SM1, SM5 59 D7
Esam Way SE27, SW16 22 A3
Escombe Dr GU2, GU3 109 B6
Escot Rd TW16 14 E1
Escott Pl KT16 51 D4
Esher Ave Cheam SM3 58 D7
Walton-on-T KT12 35 A1
Esher Church Sch KT10 55 C5
Esher Cl KT10 55 B5
Esher Coll KT7 36 E2
Esher Cres TW6 3 F5
Esher Gdns SW19 19 D6
Esher Gn KT10 55 B6
Esher Green Dr KT10 55 B7
Esher Mews CR4 40 F6
Esher Park Ave KT10 55 C5
Esher Place Ave KT10 55 B6
Esher Rd
Camberley GU15 47 A1
East Molesey KT8 36 D4
Hersham KT10, KT12 54 E6
Esher Sta KT10 55 D8
Eskdale Gdns CR8 80 D5
Eskdale Way GU15 66 D4
Eskmont Ridge SE19 22 E1
Esme House SW15 7 F3
Esparto St SW18 20 B8
Essame Cl RG40 25 D6
Essenden Rd CR2 61 E3
Essendene Cl CR3 100 E4
Essendene Lodge Sch
CR3 100 E4
Essendene Rd CR3 100 E5
Essex Ave TW7 5 E4
Essex Cl Addlestone KT15 52 C6
Frimley GU16 86 A7
West Barnes SM4 39 D2
Essex Ct Barnes SW13 7 F5
South Norwood SE19 22 D2
Essex Dr GU6 173 F2
Essex Gr SE19 22 D2
Essex House 5 CR0 61 D8
Essex Tower 5 SE20 43 B8
Estcots Cty Prim Sch
RH19 186 A1
Estcots Dr RH19 186 A1
Estcourt Rd CR0, SE25 43 B3
Estella Ave KT3, SW20 39 B5
Estoria Cl SW2 22 A8
Estreham Rd SW16 21 D2
Estridge Cl TW3 5 A3
Eswyn Rd SW17 20 F3
Ethel Rd TW15 13 E3
Ethelbert Rd SW20 39 D8
Ethelbert St SW12 21 B7
Ethelworth Ct 4 SW2 22 A7
Etherley Hill RH5 177 A7
Etherow St SE22 23 A8
Etherstone Gn SW16 22 A4
Etherstone Rd SW16 22 A4
Eton Ave Heston TW5 5 A8
New Malden KT3 38 D5
Eton Cl SW18 20 B8
Eton Ct TW18 12 F3
Eton Pl GU9 125 B7
Eton Rd UB3 3 F7
Eton St TW10 6 E2
Ettrick Ct GU14 105 B8
Etwell Pl KT5 37 F3
Eureka Rd KT1 38 A7
Europa Park Rd GU1 109 C2
Eurythmy Sch RH19 205 E6
Eustace Cres RG40 25 D8
Eustace Rd GU4 110 D3
Euston Rd CR0 42 A1
Evans Cl RH10 202 D5
Evans Gr TW13 16 A6
Evans Rd SE6 24 E6
Eve Rd Isleworth TW7 6 A3
Sheerwater GU21 70 B4
Evedon RG12 27 B2
Evelina Rd SE20 23 D1
Eveline Rd CR4 40 F8
Evelyn Ave GU11 126 B8
Evelyn Cl Twickenham TW2 16 B8
Woking GU22 89 D7
Evelyn Cotts
Abinger Common RH5 155 D8
South Godstone RH9 142 E6
Evelyn Cres TW16 34 F8
Evelyn Ct CR0 43 A2
Evelyn Gdns Richmond TW9 6 E3
Tyler's Green RH9 121 C5
Evelyn Rd Richmond TW9 6 E4
Richmond, Ham TW10 17 C5
Wimbledon SW19 20 B2
Evelyn Terr TW9 6 E4
Evelyn Way
Stoke D'Abernon KT11 73 F3
Sunbury TW16 34 F8
Wallington SM6 60 D6
Evelyn Woods Rd GU11 105 C7
Evendon's Cl RG41 25 A3
Evendon's La RG41 25 A3
Evening Hill BR3 24 C1
Evenlode Way GU47 64 D8
Everard La CR3 101 B5
Everest Ct
South Norwood SE19 42 E8
Woking GU21 68 E3
Everest Rd Camberley GU15 65 D8
Crowthorne RG45 45 B6
Stanwell TW19 13 E8
Everglade TN16 83 D1
Everglades BR2 44 E6
Evergreen Ct TW19 13 D8
Evergreen Rd GU16 66 A3
Evergreen Way TW19 13 D8
Evergreens The GU8 171 B1
Everlands Cl 6 GU22 69 E1
Eversfield Ct 2 RH2 118 C1
Eversfield Rd
Horsham RH13 217 E1
Reigate RH2 118 B1
Richmond TW9 6 F5
Eversley Cres TW7 5 D6
Eversley Pk SW19 19 B3
Eversley Rd
Kingston u T KT5 37 F4
South Norwood SE19 22 D1
Eversley Way Croydon CR0 63 A7
Thorpe TW20 32 C7
Everton Rd CR0 43 A1
Evesham Cl Belmont SM2 59 A3
Reigate RH2 117 F2
Evesham Gn SM4 40 B3
Evesham Rd
Morden SM4 40 B3
Reigate RH2 117 F2
Evesham Rd N RH3 117 F2
Evesham Wlk GU47 45 D1
Ewart Rd SE23 23 D8
Ewelands RH6 161 C4
Ewell By-Pass KT17 58 A2
Ewell Castle Sch KT17 58 A2
Ewell Court Ave KT19 57 E5
Ewell Downs Rd KT17 77 A7
Ewell East Sta KT17 58 B1

Ewell Grove Cty Inf Sch KT17 57 F1
Ewell House KT17 57 F1
Ewell House Gr KT17 57 F1
Ewell Park Gdns KT17 58 A3
Ewell Park Way KT17 58 B2
Ewell Rd Cheam SM2, SM3 58 D4
Surbiton KT5, KT6 37 F2
Thames Ditton KT6, KT7 37 B2
Tolworth KT6 38 B1
Ewell West Sta KT19 57 E2
Ewelme Rd SE23 23 C7
Ewen Cres SW2 22 A8
Ewhurst Ave CR2 61 F2
Ewhurst C of E Fst Sch GU6 175 E5
Ewhurst Cl Crawley RH11 201 C6
East Ewell SM2 58 C2
Ewhurst Ct CR4 40 D6
Ewhurst Rd Cranleigh GU6 174 E3
Crawley RH11 201 C7
Ewhurst GU5, GU6 154 E3
Ewins Cl GU12 106 A2
Ewood La
Beare Green RH5 157 F6
Parkgate RH5 158 C6
Ewshot Hill Cross GU10 124 D7
Exbury Rd SE6 24 A6
Excalibur Cl RH11 200 E5
Excelsior Cl KT1 38 A7
Exchange Rd Ascot SL5 29 C4
Crawley RH10 201 E6
Exchange The 6 CR8 80 A8
Exeforde Ave TW15 14 A4
Exeter Cl RH10 201 E2
Exeter Ct Kingston u T KT6 37 E4
Mitcham SW19 20 E1
Exeter House TW13 16 A6
Exeter Rd Ash GU12 106 A3
Croydon CR0 42 F2
Feltham TW13 15 F5
Harlington TW6 3 E4
Exeter Way TW6 3 E5
Explorer Ave TW19 13 E7
Eyebright Cl CR0 43 D1
Eyhurst Cl KT20 97 F3
Eyhurst Spur KT20 97 F3
Eyles Cl RH12 217 B4
Eylewood Rd SE27 22 C3
Eynella Rd SE21 22 F8
Eyston Dr KT13 53 A1

F

Fabyc House TW9 7 A7
Factory Cotts GU10 124 D2
Factory La CR0, CR9 61 B8
Fagg's Rd Feltham TW14 4 A2
Hatton TW14 4 A2
Fair Green Ct 1 CR4 40 F6
Fair La CR5, RH2 98 D1
Fair Oak Cl KT22 74 D7
Fair St TW3 5 C4
Fair View RH12 217 A3
Fairacre Hounslow TW7 5 D6
Kingston u T KT3 38 E6
Fairacres Burgh Heath KT20 97 C6
Cobham KT11 73 E7
New Addington CR0 62 F2
Fairbairn Cl CR8 80 A6
Fairbourne KT11 73 D6
Fairbourne Cl GU21 69 A1
Fairbourne La CR3 100 C4
Fairbourne Way GU2 109 A4
Fairbriar Ct 9 KT18 76 E6
Fairchildes Ave CR0 82 D7
Fairchildes Cotts CR6 82 F6
Fairchildes Prim Sch CR9 82 E7
Fairchildes Rd CR6 82 E4
Faircroft SE26 23 C4
Faircross RG12 27 B6
Fairdene CR5 98 F6
Fairdene Rd CR5 79 D2
Fairfax RG42 27 A8
Fairfax Ave Ewell KT17 58 B2
Redhill RH1 118 F2
Fairfax Cl KT12 35 B1
Fairfax Mews GU14 85 D2
Fairfax Rd
Farnborough GU14 85 C7
Old Woking GU22 90 B7
Teddington TW11 17 B1
Fairfield App TW19 11 D8
Fairfield Ave Horley RH6 161 A1
Staines TW18 12 F4
Twickenham TW2 16 B7
Fairfield Cl
Great Bookham KT23 94 B1
Mitcham SW19 20 E1
West Ewell KT19 57 E5
Fairfield Ct RH4 115 B1
Fairfield Dr Dorking RH4 136 B8
Frimley GU16 65 E3
Fairfield E KT1 37 E7
Fairfield Ind Est KT1 37 F6
Fairfield La GU24 68 A7
Fairfield N KT1, KT2 37 E7
Fairfield Path CR0, CR9 61 D7
Fairfield Pk KT11 73 D5
Fairfield Pl KT1 37 E6
Fairfield Rd
Beckenham BR3 44 A7
East Grinstead RH19 205 F8
Kingston u T KT1 37 E7
Leatherhead KT22 95 B6
South Croydon CR0, CR9 61 E7
Fairfield Rise GU2 108 F2
Fairfield S KT1 37 F7
Fairfield The GU9 125 C2
Fairfield W KT1 37 E7
Fairfield Way Coulsdon CR5 79 D5
West Ewell KT19 57 E5
Fairfield Wlk KT22 95 B6
Fairfields SE6 24 B8
Fairfields Rd TW3 5 C4
Fairford SE6 24 A7
Fairford Ave CR0 43 D4
Fairford Cl Croydon CR0 43 E4
Pyrford KT14 70 F5
Reigate RH2 118 C3
Fairford Ct SM2 59 B3
Fairford Gdns KT4 57 F7
Fairgreen Rd CR7 42 B4
Fairhaven TW20 11 F3
Fairhaven Ave CR0 43 D3
Fairhaven Ct Croydon CR2 61 C5
1 Egham TW20 11 F3
Fairhaven Rd RH1 119 A5
Fairholme
East Bedfont TW14 14 E8
2 New Malden KT3 38 E5
Fairholme Cres KT21 75 C2
Fairholme Gdns GU9 125 C1
Fairholme Jun & Inf Schs TW14 14 D7
Fairholme Rd
Ashford TW15 13 F3
Cheam SM1 58 F4
Thornton Heath CR0 42 A2
Fairings The KT12 54 B6
Fairlands Ave
Fairlands GU3 108 C5
Sutton SM1 59 A8
Thornton Heath CR7 42 A4
Fairlands Ct GU3 108 C5
Fairlands Rd GU3 108 D5
Fairlawn
Little Bookham KT23 93 F3
Weybridge KT13 53 E5
Fairlawn Cl Claygate KT10 55 F4
Feltham TW13 15 F4
Kingston u T KT2 18 C2
Fairlawn Cres RH19 185 B2
Fairlawn Dr
East Grinstead RH19 185 B2
Redhill RH1 139 E7
Reigate RH1 139 E7
Fairlawn Gr SM7 78 D6
Fairlawn Pk Forest Hill SE26 23 E3
Woking GU21 69 E4
Fairlawn Prim Sch SE23 23 C8
Fairlawn Prim Sch Annexe SE23 23 C7
Fairlawn Rd Merton SW19 19 F1
Sutton SM2, SM5 78 C8
Fairlawnes SM6 60 B5
Fairlawns Addlestone KT15 52 B5
Guildford GU1 110 C1
Horley RH6 161 B2
Sunbury TW16 35 A6
Twickenham TW1 6 C1
Woodham KT15 70 F8
Fairlawns Cl TW18 13 B2
Fairleas BR3 44 B7
Fairlie Gdns SE23 23 C8
Fairlight TW12 16 B3
Fairlight Cl KT4 58 C6
Fairlight Rd SW17 20 D4
Fairline Ct BR3 44 C7
Fairlop Wlk GU6 173 F2
Fairmead Tolworth KT5, KT6 38 B1
Woking GU21 69 C1
Fairmead Cl Heston TW5 4 D7
Kingston u T KT3 38 D6
Sandhurst GU47 64 E7
Fairmead Rd CR0 42 A2
Fairmeads KT11 73 F6
Fairmile Ave Cobham KT11 73 F6
Streatham SW16 21 D3
Fairmile Hts KT11 74 A6
Fairmile La KT11 73 E5
Fairmile Park Copse KT11 73 F6
Fairmile Park Rd KT11 73 F6
Fairoak Cl CR8 80 B4
Fairoak La
Chessington KT9, KT22, KT10 75 B8
Oxshott KT10, KT22, KT9 74 E8
Fairoaks Airport GU24 50 E1
Fairoaks Ct KT15 52 B5
Fairs Rd KT22 95 A8
Fairstone Ct RH6 161 B4
Fairview KT17 77 C8
Fairview Ave GU22 69 F1
Fairview Cl Forest Hill SE26 23 E3
Woking GU22 69 F1
Fairview Cotts GU25 31 D3
Fairview Ct Ashford TW15 14 A3
Kingston u T KT2 38 B8
Staines TW18 13 A2
Fairview Dr TW17 33 F4
Fairview Gdns GU9 125 D6
Fairview House 17 SW2 21 F8
Fairview Pl SW2 21 F8
Fairview Rd Ash GU12 106 B3
Carshalton SM1, SM5 59 E5
Ewell KT17 76 F8
Headley Down GU35 187 C5
Thornton Heath SW16 41 F8
Wokingham RG40 25 C5
Fairview Terr GU35 187 A6
Fairwater Dr KT15 52 D2
Fairwater House TW11 17 A4
Fairway Chertsey KT16 33 B1
Copthorne RH10 183 B2
Crawley RH11 200 D4
Fairway *continued*
Guildford GU1 110 D1
Sutton SM5 78 C8
West Barnes SW20 39 C6
Fairway Cl
Copthorne RH10 183 A2
Croydon BR3, CR0 43 E4
Hounslow TW4 4 D2
West Ewell KT19 57 C6
Woking GU23 89 B7
Fairway Cty Inf Sch RH10 183 B3
Fairway Est TW4 4 C2
Fairway Gdns BR3 44 D3
Fairway Hts GU15 66 B6
Fairway The
East Molesey KT8 36 B6
Frimley GU15 66 A3
Godalming GU7 150 F2
Heath End GU9 125 D7
Kingston u T KT3 38 D8
Leatherhead KT22 75 A1
Pirbright GU22, GU24 88 C3
Weybridge KT13 72 A8
Fairways Ashford TW15 14 B2
Beacon Hill GU26 188 B6
4 Hounslow TW7 5 E6
Kenley CR8 80 C2
Teddington TW11 17 D1
Fairways The RH1 139 D6
Fairwell La KT24 112 B7
Fairwyn Rd SE26 23 E4
Fakenham Way GU47 45 D2
Falaise TW20 11 F3
Falaise Cl GU11 105 B3
Falcon Cl Chiswick W4 7 C8
Crawley RH11 201 D8
Lightwater GU18 66 F8
Falcon Ct Frimley GU16 65 D1
Sheerwater GU21 70 C6
8 West Norwood SE21 22 D6
Falcon Dr TW19 2 E1
Falcon Rd Guildford GU1 109 D1
Hampton TW12 15 F1
Falcon Way Feltham TW14 4 B2
Sunbury TW16 34 E7
Falcon Wood KT22 94 F8
Falconhurst 4
Kingston u T KT6 37 E4
Oxshott KT22 74 D4
Falconry Ct KT1 37 E6
Falcons Cl TN16 83 D2
Falconwood
East Horsley KT24 92 F3
Englefield Green TW20 11 E3
Falconwood Rd CR0 63 A3
Falcourt Cl SM1 59 B5
Falkland Ct GU14 105 E8
Falkland Gr RH4 136 A6
Falkland House SE6 24 C4
Falkland Park Ave SE25 42 E7
Falkland Rd RH4 136 A6
Falklands Dr RH13 218 B4
Falkner Rd GU9 125 B2
Fallow Deer Cl RH13 218 B4
Fallowfield Way RH6 161 B4
Fallsbrook Rd SW16 21 C2
Falmer Cl RH11 201 D4
Falmouth Cl GU15 66 A4
Falmouth Rd KT12 54 C6
Falstone GU21 69 B1
Fambridge Cl SE26 23 F4
Famet Ave CR8 80 C6
Famet Cl CR8 80 C6
Famet Gdns CR8 80 C5
Famet Wlk CR8 80 C6
Fanchford Rd RH2 117 E1
Fanes Cl RG42 26 F8
Fanfare The GU22 70 C4
Fanshawe Rd TW10 17 C4
Faraday Ave RH19 205 F6
Faraday Ct RH10 181 F2
Faraday Ctr The RH10 181 F1
Faraday House
2 Balham SW12 21 B8
5 Hampton TW12 16 B2
Faraday Rd Crawley RH10 181 F2
East Molesey KT8 36 A5
Farnborough GU14 85 C6
Wimbledon SW19 20 B2
Faraday Way CR0, CR9 41 F1
Farcrosse Cl GU47 64 C8
Fareham House 18 SW15 19 A7
Fareham Rd TW14 15 C8
Farewell Pl CR4 40 E8
Farhalls Cres RH12 217 F6
Faringdon Cl GU47 45 C1
Faringdon Dr RG12 27 D4
Farington Acres KT13 53 D7
Faris Barn Dr KT15 70 F8
Faris La KT15 70 F8
Farleigh Ave BR2 44 F2
Farleigh Court Rd CR6 82 B5
Farleigh Ct Croydon CR2 61 C5
2 Guildford GU2 108 E1
Farleigh Cty Prim Sch CR6 81 E2
Farleigh Dean Cres CR0 82 B8
Farleigh House 7 KT2 18 B2
Farleigh Rd
Warlingham CR6 81 E2
Woodham KT15 71 A8
Farleton Cl KT13 53 D4
Farley Copse RG42 26 E8
Farley Croft BR2 44 E7
Farley Ct GU14 85 D2
Farley Heath Rd GU5 153 C6
Farley House SE26 23 B5
Farley Moor RG42 26 D8
Farley Pk RH8 122 D5
Farley Pl SE25 43 A5
Farley Rd Lewisham SE6 24 C8
South Croydon CR2 62 B2
Farleycroft 1 CR0 43 A1
Farleys Cl KT24 92 C1
Farlington Pl SW15 19 B8
Farlington Sch RH12 216 B6
Farlton Rd SW18 20 B8
Farm App RH9 163 C5
Farm Ave Horsham RH12 217 B3
Streatham SW16 21 E4
Farm Cl Ascot SL5 29 C4
Bracknell RG42 26 F8
Byfleet KT14 71 F7
Chertsey KT16 32 A3
Coney Hall BR4 63 F7
Crawley RH10 202 A7
Crowthorne RG45 45 C7
East Grinstead RH19 206 B8
East Horsley KT24 112 F7
Egham TW18 12 E3
Fairlands GU3 108 C6
Fetcham KT22 94 E3
Guildford GU1 109 D4
Lower Halliford TW17 34 A2
Loxwood RH14 213 A3
Sutton SM2 59 D3
Wallington SM6 60 C1
Warnham RH12 216 F7
Farm Dr Croydon CR0 62 F8
Purley CR8 79 D8
Farm Fields CR2 80 F8
Farm La Addlestone KT15 52 A3
Ashstead KT21, KT18 76 B2
Croydon CR0 62 F8
East Horsley KT24 112 F7
Purley CR8 60 C1
Send GU23 90 C3
Wallington CR8 60 C1
Farm Rd Aldershot GU12 105 E3
Frimley GU16 65 F2
Morden SM4 40 B4
Old Woking GU22 90 B7
Staines TW18 13 B2
Sutton SM2 59 D3
Thames Ditton KT10 55 B8
Twickenham TW4 15 E7
Warlingham CR6 101 E8
Farm View KT20 117 F8
Farm Way North Cheam KT4 58 C7
Stanwell TW19 1 F1
Farm Wlk GU12 127 C8
Farmdale Rd SM2, SM5 59 E3
Farmer's Rd TW18 12 E3
Farmfield Dr RH6 181 B8
Farmfield Hospl RH6 160 B1
Farmfield Rd BR1 24 E3
Farmhouse Cl GU22 70 D4
Farmhouse Rd SW16 21 C1
Farmington Ave SM1 59 D7
Farmleigh Cl RH10 202 C8
Farmleigh Gr KT12 53 F5
Farmstead Rd SE6 24 B4
Farmview KT11 73 D3
Farnaby Rd BR1, BR2 44 E8
Farnan Rd SW16 21 E3
Farnborough Ave CR2 62 E3
Farnborough Bsns Ctr GU14 84 F2
Farnborough Coll of Tech GU14 85 C2
Farnborough Cres
Coney Hall BR2 44 F1
South Croydon CR2 62 E2
Farnborough Gate Ret Pk GU14 85 C7
Farnborough Grange Cty Jun Sch GU14 85 A7
Farnborough Grange Inf Sch GU14 85 A8
Farnborough Hill Sch GU14 85 C5
FarnboroughHouse 1 SW15 19 A7
Farnborough Ind Est GU14 85 A3
Farnborough North Sta GU14 85 D6
Farnborough Rd
Aldershot GU11 104 E3
Farnborough GU14 85 C5
Heath End GU11, GU9 125 D7
Farnborough (Sixth Form) Coll GU14 85 B6
Farnborough St GU14 85 D6
Farnborough Sta GU14 85 B5
Farncombe C of E Inf Sch GU7 150 E7
Farncombe Hill GU7 150 E7
Farncombe St GU7 150 E7
Farncombe Sta GU7 150 F7
Farnell Mews KT13 53 B7
Farnell Rd Isleworth TW7 5 D4
Stanwell TW18 13 A5
Farnell's Almshouses TW7 5 F5
Farnham Bsns Ctr GU9 125 C3
Farnham Bsns Pk GU9 125 B1
Farnham By-Pass GU10, GU9 125 C2
Farnham Castle GU9 125 B3
Farnham Cl RG12 27 D7
Farnham Coll GU9 125 C1
Farnham Com Hospl GU9 125 E4
Farnham Ct SM3 58 E4
Farnham Gdns SW20 39 B7
Farnham La GU27 208 A7
Farnham Park Cl GU9 125 B6
Farnham Park Dr GU9 125 B6
Farnham Rd
Elstead GU10, GU8 148 C4
Guildford, Guildford Park GU1, GU2, GU3 130 B7
Guildford, Onslow Village GU2, GU3 129 E6
Farnham Rd Hospl GU2 130 B7
Farnham Sta GU9 125 C2
Farnham Trad Est GU9 125 F4
Farnhurst La GU6, GU8 193 F4
Farningham RG12 27 E3
Farningham Cres CR3 101 A4
Farningham Ct SW16 21 D1
Farningham Rd CR3 101 A4
Farnley GU21 68 F2
Farnley Rd CR7, SE25 42 D5
Farnsworth House 8 SW27 22 B3
Farquhar Rd Dulwich SE19 22 F3
Wimbledon SW19 20 A5
Farquharson Rd CR0 42 C1
Farrell Cl GU15 65 C3
Farren Rd SE23 23 E6
Farrer's Pl CR0 62 D6
Farriers KT18 96 C3
Farriers Cl KT17 76 E7
Farriers Ct Belmont SM2 58 E3
Wimbledon SW19 19 E1
Farriers Rd KT17 76 E8
Farriers The GU5 152 A5
Farthingfield House GU9 125 C3
Farthingham La GU6 175 E6
Farthings GU21 68 E3
Farthings The 1 KT2 38 A8
Farwig La BR1 44 F8
Fassett Rd KT1 37 E5
Fauconberg Ct W4 7 C8
Fauconberg Rd W4 7 C8
Faulkner Pl GU19 47 F4
Faulkner's Rd KT12 54 C5
Faversham Rd
Beckenham BR3 43 F7
Forest Hill SE6 23 F7
Morden SM4 40 B3
Sandhurst GU47 45 D1
Fawcett Cl SW16 22 A4
Fawcett Rd CR0, CR9 61 C7
Fawcus Cl KT10 55 E4
Fawler Mead RG12 27 F5
Fawley Cl GU6 174 F2
Fawns Manor Cl TW14 14 C7
Fawns Manor Rd TW14 14 D7
Fawsley Cl SL3 1 E7
Fay Rd RH12 217 C5
Faygate Bsns Ctr RH12 199 F1
Faygate La
Blindley Heath RH9 142 E3
Faygate RH12 199 F4
Rusper RH12 199 F4
Faygate Rd SW2 21 F6
Faygate Sta RH12 199 F1
Fayland Ave SW16 21 C3
Fearn Cl KT24 112 E6
Fearnley Cres TW12 15 F2
Featherbed La CR0 63 A1
Feathers La TW19 12 A6
Featherstone RH7 142 D1
Featherstone Ave SE23 23 C6
Fee Farm Rd KT10 55 F3
Felbridge Ave RH10 202 D7
Felbridge Cl
East Grinstead RH19 185 C3
Frimley GU16 65 F1
Streatham SW16 22 A4
Sutton SM2 59 B2
Felbridge Ct
East Grinstead RH19 185 A4
Harlington UB3 3 D8
Felbridge Ctr The RH19 185 A3
Felbridge Cty Prim Sch RH19 184 F4
Felbridge Rd RH19 184 D3
Felcot Rd RH19 184 C4
Felcote House RH2 138 F7
Felcott Cl KT12 54 C7
Felcott Rd KT12 54 C7
Felcourt Cotts RH19 185 C8
Felcourt La RH19 164 C1
Felcourt Rd
Dormans Park RH19, RH7 185 C7
Felcourt RH19, RH7 185 C7
Felday Glade RH5 155 B5
Felday Houses RH5 155 C7
Felday Rd RH5 133 F3
Felix Dr GU4 111 A7
Felix La TW17 34 F3
Felix Rd KT12 35 A3
Fell Rd CR0, CR9 61 C7
Felland Way RH2 139 D5
Fellbrook TW10 17 B5
Fellcott Way RH12 216 F1
Fellow Gn GU24 67 F6
Fellow Green Rd GU24 67 F6
Fellowes Ct UB3 3 D8
Fellowes Rd SM1, SM5 59 E8
Fellows Rd GU14 85 D1
Felmingham Rd SE20 43 C7
Felnex Trad Est SM6 60 A8
Felsberg Rd SW2 21 E8
Felside Ct KT13 53 A5
Felstead Rd KT19 76 D8
Feltham Arena TW14 15 A8
Feltham Ave KT8 36 E5

Feltham Corporate Ctr TW13 15 B5
Feltham Hill Jun & Inf Schs TW13 14 F5
Feltham Hill Rd
Ashford TW15 14 C2
Feltham TW13 15 B4
Feltham Rd Ashford TW15 14 C4
Mitcham CR4 41 A7
Redhill RH1 139 F4
Feltham Sch The TW13 15 C6
Feltham Sta TW13 15 B7
Feltham Wlk RH1 139 F4
Felthambrook Ind Ctr TW13 15 B5
Felthambrook Ind Est TW13 15 B5
Felthambrook Way TW13 15 B3
Feltonfleet SchTrust Ltd KT11 72 E6
Felwater Ct RH19 185 A3
Fenby Cl RH13 218 C4
Fenchurch Rd RH10 202 B4
Fencote RG12 27 D3
Fendall Rd KT19 57 C5
Fender House RH12 217 B2
Fengates Rd RH1 118 E1
Fenhurst Cl RH12 216 F1
Fenn's Way GU21 69 E4
Fennel Cl Croydon CR0 43 D1
Farnborough GU14 84 B4
Guildford GU1 110 B4
Fennel Cres RH11 201 B2
Fennells Mead KT17 57 F2
Fenner House KT12 54 A6
Fenning Ct CR4 40 E5
Fenns La GU24 67 E5
Fenns Yd GU9 125 B2
Fennscombe Ct GU24 67 F6
Fenstanton Prim Sch SW2 22 A7
Fenton Ave TW18 13 C3
Fenton Cl RH1 119 A1
Fenton House TW5 5 A8
Fenton Rd RH1 119 A1
Fentum Rd GU2 109 A3
Fenwick Cl GU21 69 B1
Ferguson Ave KT5 37 F4
Ferguson Cl BR2, BR3 44 D6
Fermandy La RH10 184 A1
Fermor Rd SE23 23 E7
Fern Ave CR4 41 D5
Fern Cl Crowthorne RG45 45 A7
Frimley GU16 66 C3
Warlingham CR6 81 E1
Fern Cotts RH5 133 E4
Fern Gr TW14 15 B8
Fern Lodge 13 SW16 22 A3
Fern Rd GU7 150 F6
Fern Towers CR3 101 A2
Fern Way RH12 217 D5
Fern Wlk TW15 13 D3
Fernbank Ave KT12 35 E2
Fernbank Cres SL5 28 D8
Fernbank Pl SL5 28 D7
Fernbank Rd
Addlestone KT15 52 A5
North Ascot SL5 28 D8
Fernbrae Cl GU10 146 B3
Ferndale GU3 108 E3
Ferndale Ave
Addlestone KT16 51 E7
Hounslow TW4 4 E4
Ferndale Rd Ashford TW15 13 E3
Banstead SM7 77 F3
Croydon SE25 43 B4
Woking GU21 69 F3
Fernden La GU27 208 C2
Fernden Rise GU7 150 E7
Ferndown Crawley RH10 182 D2
Horley RH6 161 A5
5 Kingston u T KT6 37 E4
Ferndown Cl
Guildford GU1 131 A8
Sutton SM2 59 D4
Ferndown Gdns
Cobham KT11 73 C6
Farnborough GU14 84 E4
Fernery The TW18 12 E3
Ferney Ct KT14 71 D8
Ferney Meade Way TW7 6 A5
Ferney Rd KT14 71 D7
Fernfell Golf & Ctry Club GU6 174 F6
Fernham Rd CR7 42 C6
Fernhill KT22 74 D5
Fernhill Cl
Crawley Down RH10 184 B1
Farnborough GU17 64 F1
Hale GU9 125 B6
Woking GU22 89 D7
Fernhill Ct KT2 17 D3
Fernhill Cty Prim Sch GU14 64 F1
Fernhill Dr GU9 125 B6
Fernhill Gdns KT2 17 E3
Fernhill La
Farnborough GU17 64 F1
Hale GU9 125 B6
Woking GU22 89 C7
Fernhill Pk GU22 89 D7
Fernhill Rd
Blackwater GU14, GU17 64 E2
Crawley RH6 182 D7
Farnborough, Hawley GU14, GU17 64 E2
Fernhill Rd *continued*
Farnborough, West Heath GU14, GU17 84 E6
Fernhill Sch GU14 64 F1
Fernhill Wlk GU17 64 F1
Fernhurst Cl RH11 201 B8
Fernhurst Rd Ashford TW15 14 C4
Croydon CR0 43 B1
Ferniehurst GU15 65 F4
Fernihough Cl KT13 72 A8
Fernlands Cl KT16 51 E7
Fernlea KT23 94 B3
Fernlea Rd Balham SW12 21 B7
Mitcham CR4 41 A8
Fernleigh Cl Croydon CR0 61 A6
Walton-on-T KT12 54 B7
Fernleigh Rise GU16 86 C7
Fernley House GU7 150 E8
Ferns Cl CR2 62 B1
Ferns Mead GU9 125 B1
Ferns The GU9 125 C7
Fernside Ave TW13 15 B4
Fernside Rd SW12 21 A8
Fernthorpe Rd SW16 21 C2
Fernwood
New Addington CR0, CR2 62 E2
Putney SW19 19 F7
Fernwood Ave SW16 21 D4
Feroners Cl RH10 202 A4
Ferrard Cl SL5 28 D8
Ferraro Cl TW5 5 A8
Ferrers Ave SM6 60 D6
Ferrers Rd SW16 21 D3
Ferriby Ct RG12 27 C7
Ferring Cl RH11 201 B8
Ferrings SE21 22 E5
Ferris Ave CR0 62 F7
Ferroners Ct RH10 202 A4
Ferry Ave TW18 12 E1
Ferry La Barnes SW13 7 F8
Brentford TW8 6 E8
Chertsey KT16 33 A3
Guildford GU2, GU3 130 C5
Laleham TW18 33 C6
Lower Halliford TW17 34 A1
Richmond TW9 6 F8
Wraysbury TW19 12 B5
Ferry Rd East Molesey KT8 36 A6
Richmond TW11 17 B3
Thames Ditton KT7 37 B3
Twickenham TW1 17 B7
Ferry Sq 1 TW8 6 E8
Ferry Wks TW17 34 A1
Ferrymoor TW10 17 B5
Fetcham Common La KT22 94 B6
Fetcham Park Dr KT22 94 E4
Fetcham Village Cty Inf Sch KT22 94 D5
Fettes Rd GU6 175 A3
Fiddicroft Ave SM7 78 C5
Field Cl Chessington KT9 56 C5
Cranford TW4 4 B6
East Molesey KT8 36 B4
Guildford GU4 110 D3
Hamsey Green CR2 81 B5
Harlington UB7 3 C7
Field Ct Oxted RH8 122 E8
Wimbledon SW19 20 A5
Field End Coulsdon CR5 79 D5
Farnham GU9 125 F4
West End GU24 67 F6
Field House Cl SL5 29 A1
Field La Brentford TW8 6 C7
Farncombe GU7 150 F7
Frimley GU16 65 E1
Teddington TW11 17 A3
Field Pk RG12 27 D8
Field Pl KT3 38 F3
Field Rd Farnborough GU14 64 F1
Feltham TW14 4 B1
Field Stores App GU11 105 C3
Field View Egham TW20 12 C3
Feltham TW13 14 D5
Field Way Aldershot GU12 105 E3
New Addington CR0 63 B4
Send Marsh GU23 90 F2
Tongham GU10 126 F7
Field Wlk RH6 162 C4
Fieldcommon La KT12 35 F1
Fielden Pl RG12 27 D7
Fieldend Horsham RH12 218 B5
Teddington TW11 16 F4
Fieldend Rd SW16 41 C8
Fielders Gn GU1 110 A1
Fieldhouse Rd SW12 21 C7
Fieldhouse Villas SM7 78 E4
Fieldhurst Cl KT15 52 B5
Fielding Ave TW2 16 C5
Fielding Gdns RG45 45 B4
Fielding House W4 7 E8
Fielding Rd GU47 64 E6
Fieldings The
Forest Hill SE23 23 C7
Horley RH6 161 C4
Woking GU21 68 F3
Fieldsend Rd SM3 58 E5
Fieldside Rd BR1 24 D3
Fieldview Horley RH6 161 B4
Wandsworth SW17, SW18 20 D7
Fieldway GU27 208 C7
Fife Rd Kingston u T KT2 37 E7
Mortlake SW14 7 C2
Fife Way KT23 94 A2
Fifehead Cl TW15 13 E2
Fifield La GU10 146 C2
Fifield Path SE23 23 D5
Fifth Cross Rd TW2 16 D6
Figge's Rd CR4 21 A1
Filbert Cres RH11 201 A6
Filby Rd KT9 56 F4
Filey Cl Biggin Hill TN16 103 B8
Crawley RH11 200 F4
Sutton SM2 59 C3
Filmer Ct GU7 150 E5
Filmer Gr GU7 150 E5
Finborough Rd SW17 20 F2
Finch Ave SE27 22 D4
Finch Cl GU21 68 C2
Finch Dr TW14 15 D8
Finch Rd 9 GU1 109 D1
Finch's Cross RH8 144 A8
Finchampstead Rd RG41, RG40 25 B3
Finchdean House SW15 18 F8
Finches Rise GU1 110 C3
Findhorn Cl GU47 64 D7
Findings The GU14 84 E8
Findlay Dr GU3 108 F5
Findon Ct KT15 51 F5
Findon Rd RH11 201 B8
Findon Way RH12 216 D3
Finlay Gdns KT15 52 C6
Finlays Cl KT9 57 A5
Finmere RG12 27 C2
Finnart Cl KT13 53 C6
Finney Dr GU20 48 D4
Finney La TW7 6 A6
Finsbury Cl RH11 201 C2
Finstock Gn RG12 27 F5
Finton House Sch SW17 20 F6
Fintry Pl GU14 84 E7
Fintry Wlk GU14 84 E7
Finucane Ct TW9 6 F4
Fiona Cl KT23 94 A3
Fir Acre Rd GU12 106 A6
Fir Cl KT12 35 A2
Fir Dr GU17 64 D3
Fir Gr KT3 38 F3
Fir Grange Ave KT13 53 B5
Fir Rd Cheam SM3 39 F1
Feltham TW13 15 D3
Fir Tree Alley 10 GU11 105 A2
Fir Tree Ave GU27 207 D6
Fir Tree Cl Ascot SL5 29 A2
Banstead KT17 77 C4
Crawley RH11 181 B1
Esher KT10 55 C5
Leatherhead KT22 95 C4
Streatham SW16 21 C3
Worcester Park KT19 57 F6
Fir Tree Gdns CR0 63 A6
Fir Tree Gr SM5 59 F3
Fir Tree Rd
Banstead KT17, SM7 77 D5
Guildford GU1 109 D4
Hounslow TW4 4 E3
Leatherhead KT22 95 C4
Fir Tree Wlk RH2 118 D1
Fir Wlk KT17, SM3 58 D4
Firbank Cotts RH6 183 C7
Firbank Dr GU21 89 B8
Firbank La GU21 89 B8
Firbank Pl TW20 11 B2
Firbank Way RH19 185 D1
Fircroft Cl GU22 69 F1
Fircroft Ct 9 GU22 69 F1
Fircroft Prim Sch SW17 20 F5
Fircroft Rd Chessington KT9 56 F6
Upper Tooting SW17 20 F5
Firdene KT5 38 C1
Fire Bell Alley KT6 37 E3
Fire Station Cotts CR8 79 F6
Fire Station Flats 3 KT17 76 E6
Fire Station Rd GU11 105 B3
Fireball Hill SL5 29 D2
Firefly Cl SM6 60 E3
Firfield Rd
Addlestone KT15 52 A6
Farnham GU9 146 A7
Firfields KT13 53 B4
Firgrove GU21 89 B8
Firgrove Ct
7 Farnborough GU14 85 B4
Farnham GU9 125 C1
Firgrove Hill GU9 125 C1
Firgrove Par 5 GU14 85 B4
Firgrove Rd 6 GU14 85 B4
Firhill Rd SE6 24 A5
Firlands Bracknell RG12 27 C4
Horley RH6 161 B4
Weybridge KT13 53 E4
Firlands Ave GU15 65 D5
Firle Cl RH10 201 E8
Firmston House 9 SW14 7 D4
Firs Ave Bramley GU5 152 A6
Mortlake SW14 7 C3
Firs Cl Claygate KT10 55 E4
Dorking RH4 136 A5
Farnborough GU14 85 C2
Forest Hill SE23 23 E8
Mitcham CR4 41 B8
Firs Dr TW5 4 B7
Firs La GU5 152 D4
Firs Rd CR8 80 B4
Firs The Artington GU3 130 B5
Bisley GU24 68 A3
6 Bracknell RG12 27 F5
Caterham CR3 100 D5
Claygate KT10 55 E4
2 Forest Hill SE26 23 B3
Forest Hill SE26 23 C3
Sutton SM2 59 B3
Wimbledon SW20 19 A1
Firsby Ave CR0 43 E1
Firsdene Cl KT16 51 D4
First Ave East Molesey KT8 36 A5
Mortlake SW14 7 E4
Walton-on-T KT12 35 B3
West Ewell KT19 57 E2
Woodham KT15 52 B2
First Cl KT8 36 C6
First Cross Rd TW2 16 E6
First Quarter Bsns Pk KT19 76 E8
Firstway SW20 39 C7
Firsway GU2 109 A2
Firswood Ave KT19 57 F5
Firtree Ave CR4 41 A7
Firtree Ct BR2 44 F6
Firway GU26 187 E5
Firwood Cl GU21 88 E8
Firwood Ct GU15 65 C5
Firwood Dr GU15 65 C5
Firwood Rd GU25 30 E3
Fisher Cl Crawley RH10 201 E4
Croydon CR0 42 F1
Hersham KT12 54 B6
Fisher La Chiddingfold GU8 210 E7
Dunsfold GU8 211 B7
Fisher Rowe Cl GU5 152 A6
Fisherdene KT10 56 A3
Fisherman Cl TW10 17 C4
Fishermen's Cl GU11 105 E5
Fishers Ct Horsham RH12 217 C4
4 Teddington TW11 16 F3
Fishers Wood SL5 30 C1
Fishponds Cl RG41 25 A4
Fishponds Est RG41 25 A4
Fishponds Rd
Upper Tooting SW17 20 F4
Wokingham RG41 25 A4
Fiske Ct 1 Merton SW19 20 C1
Sutton SM2 59 C3
Fitch Ct CR4 41 A7
Fitchet Cl RH11 201 B8
Fitz Wygram Cl TW12 16 C3
Fitzalan Rd Claygate KT10 55 E3
Horsham RH12, RH13 218 A4
Fitzgeorge Ave KT2, KT3 38 D8
Fitzgerald Ave SW14 7 E4
Fitzgerald Rd Mortlake SW14 7 D4
Thames Ditton KT7 37 A3
Fitzherbert House 11 TW10 6 F1
Fitzjames Ave CR0 62 A8
Fitzjohn Cl GU4 110 C4
Fitzrobert Pl TW20 12 A2
Fitzroy Cres W4 7 D7
Fitzroy Gdns SE19 22 E1
Fitzwilliam Ave TW9 6 F5
Fitzwilliam House TW9 6 D3
Fitzwilliam Hts SE23 23 C6
Five Acres RH10 201 E8
Five Oaks Cl GU21 88 E8
Five Oaks Rd Broadbridge Heath RH12, RH13 216 B2
Slinfold RH12, RH13 216 B2
Fiveacre Cl CR7 42 A3
Flag Cl CR0 43 D1
Flambard Way GU7 150 D4
Flamborough Cl TN16 103 B8
Flamsteed Hts RH11 201 B1
Flanchford House 2 RH2 118 A2
Flanchford Rd Leigh RH2 138 D5
Reigate RH2 138 D5
Reigate RH2 138 D5
Flanders Cotts GU5 152 D5
Flanders Cres SW17, SW19 20 F2
Flanders Ct TW20 12 C3
Flatford House SE6 24 C4
Flats The GU17 64 C4
Flaxley Rd SM4 40 B2
Flaxmore Ct CR7 42 D7
Fleece Rd KT6 37 C1
Fleet Cl KT8 35 F4
Fleet Rd Aldershot GU11 104 D6
Blackwater GU17 84 A4
Church Crookham GU13, GU14 104 D6
Farnborough GU14 84 C4
Fleet Terr SE6 24 C8
Fleetside KT8 36 A4
Fleetway TW20 32 C6
Fleetwood Cl
Chessington KT9 56 D3
South Croydon CR0 61 F7
Tadworth KT20 97 D7
Fleetwood Ct 7
Stanwell TW19 2 E1
2 West Byfleet KT14 71 A6
Fleetwood Rd KT3 38 B6
Fleetwood Sq KT3 38 B6
Fleming Cl GU14 85 D6
Fleming Ct CR0 61 A5
Fleming Mead CR4, SW19 20 F1
Fleming Way
Crawley RH10, RH11 181 F2
Isleworth TW7 5 F3
Flemish Fields KT16 33 A2
Fletcher Cl Crawley RH10 201 E4
Ottershaw KT15, KT16 51 E4
Fletcher Gdns RG42 26 D8
Fletcher Rd KT16 51 D4
Fletchers Cl RH13 217 E1
Fleur Gates 7 SW19 19 D8
Flexford Gn RG12 26 E3
Flexford Rd GU3 107 C1
Flexlands Sch GU24 68 F8
Flimwell Cl BR1 24 E3
Flint Cl Banstead SM7 78 B5
Crawley RH10 202 B3
Great Bookham KT23 94 C1
Redhill RH1 118 F2
Flint Hill RH4, RH5 136 B5
Flint Hill Cl RH4 136 B4
Flintgrove RG12 27 D8
Flintlock Cl TW19 2 A3
Flitwick Grange GU8 149 F1
Flock Mill Pl SW18 20 B7
Flood La 4 TW1 17 A7
Flora Gdns CR0 82 C8
Floral Ct KT21 75 C1
Floral House KT16 32 F1
Florence Ave Morden SM4 40 C4
Woodham KT15 71 A8
Florence Cl KT12 35 B2
Florence Cotts
Kingston u T SW15 18 E5
Winkfield SL4 8 C7
Florence Ct SW19 19 E2
Florence Gdns
Chiswick W4 7 C8
Staines TW18 13 B1
Florence House 5 KT2 17 F1
Florence Rd Feltham TW13 15 B7
6 Kingston u T KT2 17 F1
Penge BR3 43 E7
Sandhurst GU47 64 E7
South Croydon CR2 61 D2
Walton-on-T KT12 35 B2
Wimbledon SW19 20 B2
Florence Terr SW15 18 E5
Florence Way SW12 20 F7
Florian Ave SM1 59 D6
Florida Ct Beckenham BR2 44 F5
Staines TW18 13 A3
Florida Rd Shalford GU4 130 E3
South Norwood CR7 42 B8
Florys Ct 7 SW19 19 E7
Flower Cres KT16 51 C4
Flower La
Tyler's Green RH9 121 D6
Woldingham RH9 121 D6
Flower Wlk GU2 130 C6
Flowersmead SW17 21 A6
Floyd's La GU22 71 A3
Foden Rd GU11 105 A1
Foley Mews KT10 55 E4
Foley Rd Biggin Hill TN16 83 D1
Claygate KT10 55 E3
Folly Hill Farnham GU9 125 A5
Hale GU9 125 A5
Folly Hill Cty Inf Sch GU9 125 A6
Folly La RH5 157 B7
Folly La N GU9 125 B6
Folly La S GU9 125 A6
Follyfield Rd SM7 78 A5
Fontaine Ct BR3 43 F8
Fontaine Rd SW16 21 F1
Fontenoy Rd SW12, SW17 21 C6
Fonthill Cl SE20 43 A7
Fonthill Ct SE23 23 C8
Fontley Way SW15 19 A8
Fontmell Cl TW15 14 A3
Fontmell Pk TW15 14 A3
Fontwell Rd RH10 202 A3
Forbes Chase GU47 64 D7
Forbes Cl RH10 202 B2
Forbes Ct SE19 22 E3
Forburys GU9 146 B8
Ford Cl Ashford TW15 13 E2
Littleton TW17 34 A4
Thornton Heath CR7 42 B4
Ford La GU10, GU9 146 B6
Ford Manor Cotts RH7 165 B1
Ford Manor Rd RH7 165 B2
Ford Rd Ashford TW15 13 F4
Bisley GU24 67 F4
Chertsey KT16 33 B1
Chobham GU24 49 C1
Old Woking GU22 90 B7
Fordbridge Ct TW15 13 E2
Fordbridge Rd
Ashford TW15 13 F3
Sunbury TW16 35 A5
Upper Halliford TW16, TW17 34 F3
Fordel Rd SE6 24 D7
Fordingbridge Cl
Chertsey KT16 33 B1
Horsham RH12 217 C1
Fordington House SE26 23 B5
Fordmill Rd SE6 24 A6
Fordwater Rd KT15, KT16 33 B1
Fordwater Trad Est KT16 33 C1
Fordwells Dr RG12 27 F5
Fordyce House 3 SW16 21 C4
Foreman Pk GU12 106 B2
Foreman Rd GU12 106 B1
Forest Cl Bracknell SL5 28 C6
Crawley Down RH10 204 B8
East Horsley KT24 92 F2
Horsham RH12 218 B4
Woking GU22 70 D4
Forest Cres KT21 76 A3
Forest Croft SE23 23 B6
Forest Dene Ct SM2 59 C4
Forest Dr Charlton TW16 14 F1
Farnham GU10 146 C4
Kingswood KT20 98 A6
Forest End Rd GU47 64 A8
Forest Glade GU10 145 D3
Forest Gn RG12 27 D7
Forest Hill Bsns Ctr SE23 23 C6
Forest Hill Ct SE26 23 B5
Forest Hill Ind Est SE23 23 C6
Forest Hill Rd SE23 23 C8
Forest Hill Sec Sch SE23 23 D5
Forest Hill Sta SE23 23 C6
Forest Hills GU15 65 B4
Forest La KT24 92 F3

Forest Lodge 2
East Grinstead RH19 . . . . . .205 F8
Forest Hill SE23 . . . . .23 C5
Forest Oaks RH13 . . . . . . .218 B4
Forest Rd Cheam SM3, SM4 .40 A2
Crawley RH12 . . . . .218 D5
Crowthorne RG45 . . . . .45 C5
East Horsley KT24 . . . . .92 F2
Feltham TW13 . . . . .15 C6
North Ascot RG42 . . . . .8 D2
Richmond TW9 . . . . .7 A7
Windsor SL4 . . . . .9 E7
Winkfield RG42, SL5 . . . . . . .8 D2
Woking GU22 . . . . .70 D4
Forest Ridge BR3 . . . . .44 A6
Forest Row Bsns Pk
RH18 . . . . .206 F4
Forest Row C of E Inf
Sch RH18 . . . . .206 F2
Forest Sch The RH13 . . . .217 F1
Forest Side KT4 . . . . .38 F1
Forest View RH10 . . . . . . .202 A3
Forest View Rd RH19 . . . .205 E6
Forest Way KT21 . . . . .76 A3
Forest Wlk GU6 . . . . .173 F2
Forestdale GU26 . . . . .188 E3
Forestdale Ctr The CR0 . . .62 F3
Forestdale Prim Sch CR0 .62 F2
Forester Rd RH10 . . . . . . .201 E4
Foresters Cl Knaphill GU21 .68 F1
Wallington SM6 . . . . .60 D3
Foresters Dr CR8, SM6 . . . .60 D2
Foresters Prim Sch SM6 . .60 D4
Foresters Sq RG12 . . . . . . .27 E6
Foresters Way RG45 . . . . . .45 E8
Forestfield Crawley RH10 .202 B3
Horsham RH13 . . . . .218 A3
Forestholme Cl SE23 . . . . .23 C6
Forge Ave CR5 . . . . .100 B7
Forge Cl
Broadbridge Heath RH12 . .216 D4
Farnham GU9 . . . . .125 D3
Forge Dr KT10 . . . . .56 A3
Forge End GU21 . . . . .69 E2
Forge La
Broadbridge Heath RH12 . .216 D4
Cheam SM2, SM3 . . . . .58 E3
Crawley RH10 . . . . .202 A7
Farnborough GU11 . . . . . . .105 A6
Feltham TW13 . . . . .15 E3
Sunbury TW16 . . . . .35 A6
Forge Lane Inf Sch TW13 .15 E3
Forge Lane Jun Sch TW13 15 E3
Forge Rd Crawley RH10 . . .202 A7
Headley GU35 . . . . .166 A1
Forge Steading SM7 . . . . . .78 B4
Forge The Harlington UB3 . . .3 D8
Warnham RH12 . . . . .216 E7
Forge Wood RH10 . . . . . .182 D3
Forge Wood Ind Est
RH10 . . . . .182 B2
Forgefield TN16 . . . . .83 D3
Forman Ct TW1 . . . . .16 F7
Forrest Gdns SW16 . . . . . . .41 F6
Forrester Path SE26 . . . . . .23 C4
Forster House SE6 . . . . . . .24 D5
Forster Park Sch SE6 . . . . .24 E5
Forster Rd Beckenham BR3 .43 E6
Streatham SW2 . . . . .21 E8
Thornton Heath CR0 . . . . . . .42 C2
Forsyte Cres SE19 . . . . .42 E8
Forsyte Ct KT2 . . . . .38 B8
Forsyth Path GU21 . . . . . . .70 D6
Forsyth Rd GU21 . . . . .70 C5
Forsythe Shades BR3 . . . . .44 C8
Forsythia Pl GU1 . . . . .109 C3
Fort La RH2 . . . . .118 B5
Fort Narrien GU15 . . . . .64 F7
Fort Rd Box Hill KT20 . . . . .116 B4
Guildford GU1 . . . . .130 E6
Fortescue Ave TW2 . . . . . .16 C5
Fortescue Rd
Mitcham SW19 . . . . .20 D1
Weybridge KT13 . . . . .52 F6
Forth Cl GU14 . . . . .84 D6
Fortrose Cl GU47 . . . . .64 D7
Fortrose Gdns SW12, SW2 .21 E7
Fortune Dr GU6 . . . . .174 E1
Fortyfoot Rd KT22 . . . . . . .95 C6
Forum The KT8 . . . . .36 B5
Forval Cl CR4 . . . . .40 F4
Foss Ave CR0, CR9 . . . . . . .61 A5
Foss Rd SW17 . . . . .20 D4
Fosse Way KT14 . . . . .70 F6
Fosseway RG45 . . . . .45 A5
Fossewood Dr GU15 . . . . . .65 D7
Fosterdown RH9 . . . . .121 B6
Fosters Gr GU20 . . . . .48 B6
Fosters La GU21 . . . . .68 C2
Foulser Rd SW17 . . . . .21 A5
Foulsham Rd CR7 . . . . .42 D6
Foundation Units GU1 . . .109 F5
Founders Gdns SE19 . . . . .22 C1
Foundry Cl RH13 . . . . .217 E4
Foundry Ct KT16 . . . . .33 A2
Foundry La
Haslemere GU27 . . . . .208 A6
Horsham RH12, RH13 . . . . .217 E3
Horton SL3 . . . . .1 B4
Foundry Mews KT16 . . . . . .33 A2
Fountain Ct
New Malden KT3 . . . . .38 C5
Penge SE26 . . . . .23 C2
Fountain Dr Dulwich SE19 . .22 F4
Wallington SM5 . . . . .59 F2
Fountain Rd Redhill RH1 . .139 E7
South Norwood CR7 . . . . . . .42 C7
Upper Tooting SW17 . . . . . . .20 D4
Fountains Ave TW13 . . . . . .15 F5
Fountains Cl
Crawley RH11 . . . . .201 A4
Feltham TW13 . . . . .15 F5
Fountains Garth RG12 . . . .27 A6
Four Acres Cobham KT11 . . .73 E6
Guildford GU1, GU4 . . . . . .110 C3
Four Seasons Cres SM3 . . .58 F8
Four Square Ct TW4 . . . . . . .5 A1
Four Wents KT11 . . . . .73 C5
Fourth Cross Rd TW2 . . . .16 D6
Fourth Dr CR5 . . . . .79 D3
Fowler Cl RH10 . . . . .202 C4
Fowler Rd
Farnborough GU14 . . . . .84 F3
Mitcham CR4 . . . . .41 A7
Fowler's Rd GU11 . . . . . . .105 D6
Fowlers La RG42 . . . . .27 B8
Fowlers Mead GU24 . . . . . .49 E2
Fowlerscroft GU3 . . . . .129 B2
Fox Cl Crawley RH11 . . . . . .181 B1
Weybridge KT13 . . . . .53 D5
Woking GU22 . . . . .70 D4
Fox Covert Fetcham KT22 . .94 D3
Lightwater GU18 . . . . .67 A8
Fox Covert Cl SL5 . . . . .29 C4
Fox Dene GU7 . . . . .150 C2
Fox Gr KT12 . . . . .35 B2
Fox Heath GU14 . . . . .84 C3
Fox Hill SE19 . . . . .22 F1
Fox Hill Gdns SE19 . . . . . . .22 F1
Fox Hill Prim Sch RG12 . . .27 B4
Fox Hills La GU12 . . . . . . .106 C3
Fox Hills Rd KT16 . . . . .51 B5
Fox La KT23 . . . . .93 F3
Fox La N KT16 . . . . .32 F1
Fox La S KT16 . . . . .32 F1
Fox Rd Bracknell RG12 . . . . .27 C5
Farnham GU10 . . . . .146 C7
Haslemere GU27 . . . . .207 E6
Fox Way GU10 . . . . .124 D8
Fox Yd GU9 . . . . .125 B2
Foxacre CR3 . . . . .100 E5
Foxborough Hill GU5 . . . .151 D6
Foxborough Hill Rd
GU5 . . . . .151 D6
Foxbourne Rd SW17 . . . . . .21 A6
Foxbridge La RH14 . . . . . .212 C1
Foxburrows Ave GU2 . . . .108 F2
Foxcombe CR0 . . . . .63 B4
Foxcombe Rd 6 SW15 . . . .19 A7
Foxdown Cl GU15 . . . . .65 C5
Foxearth Cl TN16 . . . . .83 E1
Foxearth Rd CR2 . . . . .62 C2
Foxearth Spur CR2 . . . . . . .62 C2
Foxenden Rd GU1 . . . . . . .109 E1
Foxes Dale BR2 . . . . .44 D6
Foxes Path GU4 . . . . .89 F1
Foxglove Ave
Beckenham BR3 . . . . .24 B1
Horsham RH12 . . . . .217 E6
Foxglove Cl TW19 . . . . .13 D7
Foxglove Gdns
Guildford GU4 . . . . .110 C3
Purley CR8 . . . . .79 F8
Foxglove La KT9 . . . . .57 A6
Foxglove Way CR4 . . . . .41 B1
Foxglove Wlk RH11 . . . . . .201 B3
Foxgrove Dr GU21 . . . . .70 A4
Foxgrove Rd BR3 . . . . .24 C1
Foxhanger Gdns GU22 . . . .70 A3
Foxheath RG12 . . . . .27 E4
Foxhill Cres GU15 . . . . .66 B8
Foxhills GU21 . . . . .69 C2
Foxhills Cl KT16 . . . . .51 C4
Foxholes Rudgwick RH12 . .214 D8
Weybridge KT13 . . . . .53 D5
Foxhurst Rd GU12 . . . . . . .106 A4
Foxlake Rd KT14 . . . . .71 F7
Foxleigh Chase RH12 . . . .217 F5
Foxley Cl Blackwater GU17 .64 C5
Redhill RH1 . . . . .140 A4
Foxley Ct SM2 . . . . .59 C3
Foxley Gdns CR8 . . . . .80 B6
Foxley Hall CR8 . . . . .80 A6
Foxley Hill Rd CR8 . . . . . . .80 A7
Foxley La CR8 . . . . .60 E1
Foxley Rd Purley CR8 . . . . . .80 B5
Thornton Heath CR7 . . . . . . .42 B5
Foxoak Hill KT12, KT13 . . . .53 E1
Foxon Cl CR3 . . . . .100 E6
Foxon La CR3 . . . . .100 E6
Foxon Lane Gdns CR3 . . .100 E6
Foxtail House TW3 . . . . .5 C6
Foxton KT1 . . . . .38 A6
Foxwarren KT10 . . . . .55 F2
Foxwood Cl TW13 . . . . .15 B5
Frailey Cl GU22 . . . . .70 B3
Frailey Hill GU22 . . . . .70 B3
Framfield Cl RH11 . . . . . .201 A8
Framfield Rd CR4 . . . . .21 A1
Frampton Cl SM2 . . . . .59 A3
Frampton Rd TW4 . . . . .4 E2
France Hill Dr GU15 . . . . . .65 C5
France Hill Sch GU15 . . . . .65 C2
Frances Ct SE25 . . . . .42 F7
Franche Court Rd SW17 . .20 C5
Francis Ave TW13 . . . . .15 A5
Francis Barber Cl SW16 . .21 F4
Francis Chichester Cl SL5 .29 B4
Francis Cl Littleton TW17 . .34 A5
West Ewell KT19 . . . . .57 D6
Francis Cnr KT24 . . . . .133 B8
Francis Ct Guildford GU2 . .109 B3
Kingston u T KT5 . . . . .37 E5
Francis Edwards Way
RH11 . . . . .200 E2
Francis Gr SW19 . . . . .19 F2
Francis Rd Caterham CR3 .100 D5
Hounslow TW4 . . . . .4 D5
Thornton Heath CR0 . . . . . . .42 B2
Wallington SM6 . . . . .60 C4
Francis Way GU15 . . . . .66 C4
Franciscan Prim Sch
SW17 . . . . .21 A3
Franciscan Rd SW17 . . . . .21 A4
Frangate KT24 . . . . .112 E8
Frank Dixon Cl SE21 . . . . .22 E7
Frank Dixon Way SE21 . . . .22 E7
Frank Towell Ct TW14 . . . .15 A7
Frankland House 4 SW12 .21 B8
Franklands Dr KT15 . . . . . .51 F3
Franklin Cl Kingston u T KT1 38 A6
West Norwood SE27 . . . . . . .22 B5
Franklin Cres CR4 . . . . .41 C5
Franklin Ct 2 GU2 . . . . . .108 F1
Franklin House BR2 . . . . . .44 E7
Franklin Ind Est SE20 . . . .43 C8
Franklin Rd Crawley RH10 202 C5
Penge SE20 . . . . .43 C8
Walton-on-T KT12 . . . . .35 A3
Franklin Way CR0, CR9 . . . .41 E2
Franklyn Rd
Godalming GU7 . . . . .150 B3
Walton-on-T KT12 . . . . .35 B3
Franks Ave KT3 . . . . .38 C5
Franks House TW7 . . . . .6 B3
Franks Rd GU2 . . . . .109 A3
Franksfield GU5 . . . . .154 E7
Fransfield Gr SE26 . . . . . .23 B5
Frant Cl SE20 . . . . .23 C1
Frant Rd CR0, CR7 . . . . . . .42 B4
Franthorne Way SE6 . . . . .24 B5
Fraser Gdns RH4 . . . . .136 A8
Fraser Mead GU47 . . . . . . .64 E6
Fraser Rd RG42 . . . . .27 B8
Frederick Cl SM1 . . . . .58 F5
Frederick Gdns SM1 . . . . . .58 F5
Frederick Pl RG41 . . . . . . .25 A6
Frederick Rd SM1 . . . . .58 F5
Frederick Sanger Rd
GU2 . . . . .129 D8
Frederick St GU11 . . . . . .105 A2
Free Prae Rd KT16 . . . . . . .33 A1
Freeborn Way RG12 . . . . . .27 E7
Freedown La SM2 . . . . .78 C6
Freehold Ind Ctr TW4 . . . . .4 C2
Freelands Ave CR2 . . . . . . .62 D2
Freelands Rd KT11 . . . . . . .73 B5
Freeman Cl TW17 . . . . .34 E5
Freeman Dr KT8 . . . . .35 F5
Freeman House 13 SW2 . . .21 E8
Freeman Rd
Morden CR4, SM4 . . . . .40 D4
Warnham RH12 . . . . .216 F8
Freemantle Rd GU19 . . . . . .47 F4
Freemantles Sch (Specl
Sch) KT16 . . . . .32 E2
Freemason's Rd CR0 . . . . .42 E1
Freesia Dr GU24 . . . . .68 A3
Freethorpe Cl SE19 . . . . . .42 E8
French Gdns
Blackwater GU17 . . . . .64 D4
Cobham KT11 . . . . .73 C5
French La GU8 . . . . .169 E3
French St TW16 . . . . .35 C7
Frenchaye KT15 . . . . .52 C5
Frenches Ct 4 RH1 . . . . .119 A3
Frenches Rd RH1 . . . . . . .119 B4
Frenches The RH1 . . . . . .119 A3
Frenchlands Hatch KT24 .112 E8
Frensham RG12 . . . . .27 D3
Frensham C of E Fst Sch
GU10 . . . . .167 D7
Frensham Ct CR4 . . . . .40 D6
Frensham Ctry Pk GU10 .167 E5
Frensham Dr
New Addington CR0 . . . . .63 C3
Roehampton SW15 . . . . .19 A6
Frensham Heights Rd
GU10 . . . . .146 A2
Frensham Heights Sch
GU10 . . . . .146 A2
Frensham House 7 KT6 . .37 E4
Frensham La GU35, GU10 .166 F2
Frensham Rd
Crowthorne RG45 . . . . .45 B7
Farnham GU10, GU9 . . . . . .146 D6
Purley CR8 . . . . .80 B5
Frensham Vale GU10 . . . .146 C4
Frensham Way KT17 . . . . . .77 C3
Fresham House BR2 . . . . . .44 F6
Freshborough Ct 1 GU1 .130 F8
Freshfield KT20 . . . . .117 E8
Freshfield Bank RH18 . . .206 E2
Freshfield Cl RH10 . . . . . .202 A5
Freshfields CR0 . . . . .43 F1
Freshford St SW17, SW18 . .20 C5
Freshmount Gdns KT19 . . .76 B8
Freshwater Cl SW17 . . . . .21 A2
Freshwater Rd SW17 . . . . .21 A2
Freshwood Cl BR3 . . . . . . .44 B8
Freshwood Way SM6 . . . . .60 C2
Frewin Rd SW18 . . . . .20 D7
Friar Mews SE27 . . . . .22 B5
Friar's Gate GU2 . . . . . . .130 A7
Friars Ave SW15 . . . . .18 F5
Friars Croft GU4 . . . . .110 C4
Friars Ct Farnham GU9 . . .125 D7
5 Wallington SM6 . . . . .60 B6
Friars Keep RG12 . . . . .27 B5
Friars La TW9 . . . . .6 D2
Friars Orch KT22 . . . . .94 D6
Friars Rd GU25 . . . . .31 D5
Friars Rise GU22 . . . . .70 A1
Friars Rookery RH10 . . . .201 F6
Friars Stile Pl 9 TW10 . . . . .6 E1
Friars Stile Rd TW10 . . . . . . .6 E1
Friars Way KT16 . . . . .33 A3
Friars Wood CR0 . . . . .62 E2
Friary Bridge GU1 . . . . . . .130 C7
Friary Ct GU21 . . . . .68 F1
Friary Ho 4 GU1 . . . . . . .130 C8
Friary Pas GU1 . . . . .130 C7
Friary Rd Ascot SL5 . . . . . .29 B3
Wraysbury TW19 . . . . .11 C8
Friary St GU1 . . . . .130 C7
Friary The 5 GU1 . . . . . . .130 C8
Friary Way RH10 . . . . .201 E5
Friday Rd CR4 . . . . .20 F1
Friday St Faygate RH12 . . .198 E6
Ockley RH5 . . . . .177 E4
Rusper RH12 . . . . .198 E6
Warnham RH12 . . . . .216 E7
Friday Street Rd RH5 . . . .155 E8
Friend Ave GU12 . . . . .105 D1
Friends Cl RH11 . . . . .181 D1
Friends' Rd CR0, CR9 . . . . .61 D7
Friends Rd CR8 . . . . .80 B7
Friendship Way RG12 . . . . .27 B6
Friern Rd SE22 . . . . .23 A8
Frimley Ave SM6 . . . . .60 F5
Frimley Bsns Pk GU16 . . . .85 B8
Frimley CE Jun Sch GU16 .85 E7
Frimley Cl
New Addington CR0 . . . . .63 C3
Putney SW19 . . . . .19 E6
Frimley Cres CR0 . . . . .63 C3
Frimley Gdns CR4 . . . . .40 E6
Frimley Green Rd GU16 . . .85 A6
Frimley Grove Gdns GU16 .65 E1
Frimley Hall Dr GU15 . . . . .65 F6
Frimley High St GU16 . . . . .85 D8
Frimley House CR4 . . . . . . .40 E6
Frimley Park Hospl GU16 .65 D2
Frimley Rd Ash Vale GU12 .106 A8
Camberley GU15 . . . . .65 B3
Chessington KT9 . . . . .56 E5
Frimley GU15, GU16 . . . . . . .65 C1
Frinton Rd SW17 . . . . .21 A2
Friston Wlk RH11 . . . . . . .201 A7
Frith End Rd GU34, GU35 .166 A6
Frith Hill Rd
Farncombe GU7 . . . . .150 D6
Frimley GU16 . . . . .66 B1
Frith Knowle KT12 . . . . .54 B5
Frith Pk RH19 . . . . .185 E3
Frith Rd CR0, CR9 . . . . .61 C8
Fritham Cl KT3 . . . . .38 E3
Friths Dr RH2 . . . . .118 B4
Frithwald Rd KT16 . . . . . . .32 F2
Frobisher RG12 . . . . .27 C2
Frobisher Cl CR8 . . . . .80 C2
Frobisher Cres TW19 . . . . .13 E8
Frobisher Ct Belmont SM2 . .58 F3
Forest Hill SE23 . . . . .23 B6
Frobisher Gdns
Guildford GU1 . . . . .110 A2
Stanwell TW19 . . . . .13 E8
Frodsham Way GU47 . . . . .45 E2
Frog Grove La GU3 . . . . . .107 F4
Frog Hall RG40 . . . . .25 F5
Frog Hall Dr RG40 . . . . . . .25 E5
Frog La Bracknell RG12 . . . .27 A6
Woking GU4 . . . . .89 E2
Froggetts La RH5 . . . . . . .176 C1
Frogmore Cl SM3 . . . . .58 E7
Frogmore Comm Coll
GU46 . . . . .64 A5
Frogmore Ct GU17 . . . . . . .64 C4
Frogmore Cty Infs Sch
GU17 . . . . .64 B5
Frogmore Cty Jun Sch
GU17 . . . . .64 B5
Frogmore Gdns SM3 . . . . . .58 E6
Frogmore Gr GU17 . . . . . . .64 C4
Frogmore Park Dr GU17 . .64 D4
Frogmore Rd GU17 . . . . . . .64 C5
Frome Cl GU14 . . . . .84 D6
Fromondes Rd SM3 . . . . . .58 E5
Fromow Gdns GU20 . . . . . .48 D4
Froxfield Down 6 RG12 . . .27 F4
Fruen Rd TW14 . . . . .14 F8
Fry Cl RH11 . . . . .201 B1
Fry's Cross GU8 . . . . .193 A2
Fryern Wood CR3 . . . . . . .100 C3
Frylands Ct CR0 . . . . .82 C8
Fryston Ave Croydon CR0 . .62 A8
Wallington CR5 . . . . .79 B5
Fuchsia Way GU24 . . . . . . .67 E6
Fuel Farm Rd RH6 . . . . . .181 E8
Fulbourn 4 KT1 . . . . .38 A7
Fulbourne Cl RH1 . . . . . . .118 E3
Fulford Rd Caterham CR3 .100 D6
West Ewell KT19 . . . . .57 D3
Fulham Cl RH11 . . . . .201 B2
Fullbrook Ave KT15 . . . . . .71 A8
Fullbrook Cty Sec Sch
KT15 . . . . .71 A8
Fullbrooks Ave KT4 . . . . . .38 F1
Fuller's Wood CR0 . . . . . . .63 A6
Fullers Ave KT6 . . . . .56 F8
Fullers Farm Rd KT24 . . .112 B1
Fullers Rd Binstead GU10 .145 D3
Rowledge GU10 . . . . .145 D3
Fullers Vale GU35 . . . . . .187 A5
Fullers Way N KT6 . . . . . . .56 F7
Fullers Way S KT9 . . . . .56 E7
Fullers Wood La RH1 . . . .119 C1
Fullerton Cl KT14 . . . . .71 F5
Fullerton Dr KT14 . . . . .71 E5
Fullerton Rd Byfleet KT14 . .71 F5
Croydon CR0 . . . . .42 F2
Sutton SM5 . . . . .59 E2
Fullerton Way KT14 . . . . . .71 E5
Fullmer Way KT15 . . . . .51 F1
Fulmar Cl 1 RH11 . . . . . .200 D5
Fulmar Ct 5 SE21 . . . . .22 D6
Fulmar Dr RH19 . . . . .186 B3
Fulmer Cl TW12 . . . . .15 E3
Fulstone Cl TW4 . . . . .4 F3
Fulvens GU5 . . . . .133 E1
Fulwell Golf Course TW12 16 C4
Fulwell Park Ave TW2 . . . .16 C6
Fulwell Rd TW11, TW12 . . .16 D4
Fulwell Sta TW11 . . . . .16 D4
Fulwood Gdns TW1 . . . . .6 A1
Fulwood Wlk SW19 . . . . . . .19 E7
Furlong Cl CR4 . . . . .41 B1
Furlong Rd RH4 . . . . .135 C6
Furlong Way RH6 . . . . . . .181 F8
Furlough The GU22 . . . . . . .70 A2
Furmage St SW18 . . . . .20 B8
Furnace Dr RH10 . . . . . . .201 F4
Furnace Farm Rd RH10 . .202 A4
Furnace Par RH10 . . . . . . .202 A4
Furnace Pl RH10 . . . . .202 A4
Furnace Rd RH19 . . . . . . .184 C3
Furneaux Ave SE27 . . . . . .22 B3
Furness Rd SM4 . . . . .40 B3
Furniss Ct GU6 . . . . .173 F2
Furnival Cl GU25 . . . . .31 D3
Furrows Pl CR3 . . . . .100 F4
Furrows The KT12 . . . . .54 C8
Furse Cl GU15 . . . . .66 C4
Further Green Rd SE6 . . . .24 E7
Furtherfield GU6 . . . . .174 E4
Furtherfield Cl CR0 . . . . . .42 A3
Furze Cl Ash Vale GU12 . . .106 A7
Redhill RH1 . . . . .118 F2
Furze Ct CR0 . . . . .62 A8
Furze Field KT22 . . . . .74 E6
Furze Gr KT20 . . . . .97 F6
Furze Hill Kingswood KT20 . .97 F6
Purley CR8 . . . . .79 F8
Furze Hill Cres RG45 . . . . .45 C4
Furze Hill Rd GU35 . . . . . .187 C4
Furze La
East Grinstead RH19 . . . . . .185 B4
Farncombe GU7, GU3 . . . . .150 F8
Purley CR8 . . . . .79 F8
Furze Rd Addlestone KT15 . .51 F4
Rudgwick RH12 . . . . .214 D8
South Norwood CR7 . . . . . . .42 C6
Furze Vale Rd GU35 . . . . .187 B4
Furzebank SL5 . . . . .29 D5
Furzedown Cl TW20 . . . . . .11 E2
Furzedown Dr SW17 . . . . . .21 B3
Furzedown Prim Sch
SW17 . . . . .21 A2
Furzedown Rd
Streatham SW17 . . . . .21 B3
Sutton SM2 . . . . .78 C8
Furzefield RH11 . . . . .201 C7
Furzefield Chase RH19 . .185 E6
Furzefield Cres RH2 . . . . .139 C7
Furzefield Cty Prim Sch
RH1 . . . . .119 D7
Furzefield Rd
East Grinstead RH19 . . . . . .185 D4
Horsham RH12 . . . . .218 B5
Reigate RH2 . . . . .139 C7
Furzehill RH1 . . . . .118 E2
Furzeland House 2 KT3 . .38 E2
Furzemoors RG12 . . . . .27 B4
Furzen La
Ellen's Green RH12, RH5 . . .196 B4
Wallis Wood RH12, RH5 . . .196 B4
Furzewood TW16 . . . . .35 A8
Fyfield Cl
Beckenham BR2, BR3 . . . . . .44 D5
Blackwater GU17 . . . . .64 D5

G

Gable Ct Forest Hill SE26 . . .23 B4
9 Redhill RH1 . . . . .119 A2
Gable End GU14 . . . . .85 B4
Gable Lodge BR4 . . . . .44 C1
Gables Ave TW15 . . . . .13 F3
Gables Cl Ash Vale GU12 . .106 A5
Farnborough GU14 . . . . .85 A4
Old Woking GU22 . . . . .89 F7
Gables Ct GU22 . . . . .89 F7
Gables The Banstead SM7 . .77 F2
Copthorne RH10 . . . . .183 B3
Elstead GU8 . . . . .148 C3
Horsham RH12 . . . . .217 D4
Oxshott KT22 . . . . .74 C7
Weybridge KT13 . . . . .53 C5
Gabriel Cl TW13 . . . . .15 D4
Gabriel Dr GU15 . . . . .66 B4
Gabriel Rd RH10 . . . . .202 C2
Gabriel St SE23 . . . . .23 E8
Gadbridge La GU6 . . . . . . .175 E4
Gadbrook Rd RH3 . . . . . . .137 D4
Gadesden Rd KT19 . . . . . . .57 C4
Gaffney Cl GU11 . . . . .105 D7
Gage Cl RH10 . . . . .184 C1
Gage Ridge RH18 . . . . .206 E2
Gainsborough RG12 . . . . . .27 C3
Gainsborough Cl
Beckenham BR3 . . . . .24 A1
Camberley GU15 . . . . .65 F7
Farnborough GU14 . . . . .85 D2
Thames Ditton KT10 . . . . . . .36 E1
Gainsborough Ct
Dulwich SE21 . . . . .22 E6

Gainsborough Ct *continued*
Walton-on-T KT12 . . . . .54 A6
Gainsborough Dr
North Ascot SL5 . . . . .28 D7
Sanderstead CR2 . . . . .81 A6
Gainsborough Gdns TW7 . .5 D2
Gainsborough Mews SE26 23 B5
Gainsborough Rd
Crawley RH10 . . . . .201 F3
Epsom KT19 . . . . .57 C1
New Malden KT3 . . . . .38 D2
Richmond TW9 . . . . .6 F4
Gaist Ave CR3 . . . . .101 B5
Galahad Ho RH1 . . . . .119 A2
Galahad Rd RH11 . . . . . . .200 E6
Galba Ct 1 TW8 . . . . .6 D7
Gale Cl Hampton TW12 . . . . .15 E2
Mitcham CR4 . . . . .40 D6
Gale Cres SM7 . . . . .78 A2
Gale Dr GU18 . . . . .48 A1
Gales Cl GU4 . . . . .110 D3
Gales Dr RH10 . . . . .201 F6
Gales Pl RH10 . . . . .201 F6
Galgate Cl 4 SW19 . . . . . . .19 E7
Gallery Rd Dulwich SE21 . . .22 D7
Pirbright GU24 . . . . .87 D8
Galleymead Rd SL3 . . . . .1 F6
Gallop The
South Croydon CR2 . . . . .62 B3
Sutton SM2 . . . . .59 D2
Gallwey Rd GU11 . . . . .105 C3
Galpin's Rd CR4, CR7 . . . . . .41 F5
Galsworthy Rd
Chertsey KT16 . . . . .33 A2
Kingston u T KT2 . . . . .38 B8
Galton Rd SL5 . . . . .29 F3
Galvani Way CR0, CR9 . . . . .41 F1
Galvins Cl GU2 . . . . .109 A4
Gambles La GU23 . . . . .91 C2
Gambole Rd SW17 . . . . .20 E4
Gander Green Cres TW12 .36 A8
Gander Green La
KT4, SM1, SM3 . . . . .58 F7
Gangers Hill CR3, RH9 . . .121 F7
Ganghill GU1 . . . . .110 A3
Gannet Ct 4 SE21 . . . . .22 D6
Ganymede Ct RH11 . . . . . .200 E3
Gap Rd SW19 . . . . .20 B3
Gapemouth Rd GU16, GU24 86 E5
Garbetts Way GU10 . . . . . .126 F6
Garbrand Wlk KT17 . . . . . . .57 F2
Garden Ave CR4 . . . . .21 B1
Garden Cl Addlestone KT15 .52 D6
Ashford TW15 . . . . .14 C2
Banstead SM7 . . . . .78 A4
East Grinstead RH19 . . . . . .205 F7
Farnborough GU14 . . . . .84 E3
Hampton TW12 . . . . .15 F3
Leatherhead KT22 . . . . .95 C3
Putney SW15 . . . . .19 B8
Shamley Green GU5 . . . . . .152 D4
Wallington SM6 . . . . .60 E5
Garden Ct 5 Belmont SM2 .59 A3
4 Richmond TW9 . . . . .6 F6
South Croydon CR0 . . . . .61 F7
Garden Flats SW16 . . . . . . .21 E5
Garden House La RH19 . .205 F7
Garden La SW2 . . . . .21 F7
Garden Pl RH12 . . . . .217 C4
Garden Rd Mortlake TW9 . . . .7 A4
Penge SE20 . . . . .43 C8
Walton-on-T KT12 . . . . .35 B2
Garden The KT24 . . . . .113 D7
Garden Wlk Beckenham BR3 43 F8
Crawley RH11 . . . . .201 C6
Hooley CR5 . . . . .99 B4
Horsham RH12 . . . . .217 C4
Garden Wood Rd RH19 . .205 C8
Gardener's Hill Rd GU10 .146 B4
Gardener's Wlk KT23 . . . . . .94 B1
Gardeners Cl RH12 . . . . . .216 E8
Gardeners Ct RH13 . . . . . .217 D1
Gardeners Gn RH12 . . . . . .199 C6
Gardeners Rd CR0 . . . . .42 B1
Gardenfields KT20 . . . . .97 E8
Gardenia Ct 1 BR3 . . . . . . .24 A1
Gardenia Dr GU24 . . . . .67 F6
Gardens The
Beckenham BR3 . . . . .44 D7
Esher KT10 . . . . .55 A6
Hatton TW14 . . . . .3 D1
Pirbright GU24 . . . . .87 F5
Tongham GU10 . . . . .126 F7
Gardner House TW13 . . . . .15 F6
Gardner Ind Est SE26 . . . . . .23 F3
Gardner La RH10 . . . . .204 A8
Gardner Pl TW14 . . . . .4 B1
Gardner Rd GU1 . . . . .109 D1
Garendon Gdns SM4 . . . . . .40 B2
Garendon Rd SM4 . . . . .40 B2
Gareth Cl KT4 . . . . .58 D8
Gareth Ct SW16 . . . . .21 D5
Garfield Prim Sch SW19 . .20 C2
Garfield Rd
Addlestone KT15 . . . . .52 C6
Camberley GU15 . . . . .65 C5
2 Twickenham TW1 . . . . . . .17 A7
Wimbledon SW19 . . . . .20 C2
Garibaldi Rd RH1 . . . . . . .139 F8
Garland Rd RH19 . . . . . . .185 D2
Garland Way CR3 . . . . . . .100 D5
Garlands Rd
Leatherhead KT22 . . . . .95 C6
Redhill RH1 . . . . .118 F1
Garlichill Rd KT17, KT18 . . .77 B2
Garlies Rd SE23 . . . . .23 E5
Garnet House KT4 . . . . . . .38 D1
Garnet Rd CR7 . . . . .42 D5
Garrad's Rd SW16 . . . . .21 D4
Garrard Rd SM7 . . . . .78 A3
Garrat La SW17, SW18 . . . .20 C5
Garratt Cl CR0 . . . . .60 E6
Garratt La SW17, SW18 . . . .20 C5
Garratt Park Sec Sch
SW18 . . . . .20 C5
Garratt Terr SW17 . . . . .20 E4
Garratts La SM7 . . . . .78 A3
Garraway House SE21 . . . .22 F5
Garrett Cl RH10 . . . . .202 C4
Garrick Cl Hersham KT12 . . .54 B6
1 Richmond TW9 . . . . .6 D2
Staines TW18 . . . . .13 A1
Garrick Cres CR0 . . . . .61 E8
Garrick Gdns KT8 . . . . .36 A6
Garrick House Chiswick W4 .7 E8
2 Kingston u T KT1 . . . . .37 E5
7 Streatham SW16 . . . . .21 C3
Garrick Rd TW9 . . . . .7 A5
Garrick Way GU16 . . . . .85 E7
Garrick Wlk RH10 . . . . . . .201 E3
Garrick's Ait KT8 . . . . .36 C7
Garrison Cl TW4 . . . . .4 F2
Garrison La KT9 . . . . .56 E3
Garrones The RH10 . . . . . .202 E7
Garside Cl TW12 . . . . .16 B2
Garson La TW19 . . . . .11 D8
Garson Rd KT10 . . . . .54 F4
Garson's La SL4 . . . . .8 A7
Garston Gdns CR8 . . . . . . .80 D4
Garston La CR8 . . . . .80 D4
Garstons The KT23 . . . . . . .94 A2
Garswood RG12 . . . . .27 D3
Garth Cl Farnham GU9 . . . .146 A7
Kingston u T KT2 . . . . .17 F3
West Barnes SM4 . . . . .39 D2
Garth Ct W4 . . . . .7 D8
Garth High Sch SM4 . . . . . .40 D3
Garth Hill Sch RG12 . . . . . .27 C8
Garth Rd Chiswick W4 . . . . . .7 D8
Kingston u T KT2 . . . . .17 F3
West Barnes SM4 . . . . .39 D2
Garth The Ash GU10, GU12 105 F1
Cobham KT11 . . . . .73 E6
Farnborough GU14 . . . . .85 D4
Hampton TW12 . . . . .16 B2
Garthorne Rd SE23 . . . . . . .23 D8
Garthside TW10 . . . . .17 E3
Gartmoor Gdns SW19 . . . . .19 F7
Garton Cl RH11 . . . . .200 E5
Garvens SE19 . . . . .22 E3
Gascoigne Rd
New Addington CR0 . . . . .63 C2
Weybridge KT13 . . . . .53 B7
Gasden Copse GU8 . . . . . .170 D5
Gasden Dr GU8 . . . . .170 D6
Gasden La GU8 . . . . .170 D6
Gaskyns Cl RH12 . . . . .214 D7
Gassiot Rd SW17 . . . . .20 F4
Gassiot Way SM1 . . . . .59 D7
Gasson Wood Rd RH11 . .200 E4
Gaston Bell Cl TW9 . . . . .6 F4
Gaston Bridge Rd
Shepperton TW17 . . . . .34 D3
Upper Halliford TW17 . . . . . .34 E4
Gaston Rd CR4 . . . . .41 A6
Gaston Way TW17 . . . . .34 D4
Gatcombe Ct BR3 . . . . .24 A1
Gate Ct 4 KT13 . . . . .53 B7
Gate House 4 KT6 . . . . .37 E1
Gate St GU5 . . . . .173 B7
Gateford Dr RH12 . . . . . . .217 F6
Gatehouse Cl KT2 . . . . .18 C1
Gates Cl RH10 . . . . .202 C2
Gates Green Rd BR4 . . . . . .63 F7
Gatesden Rd KT22 . . . . .94 C4
Gateside Rd SW17 . . . . .20 F5
Gatestone Ct 9 SE19 . . . . .22 E2
Gatestone Rd SE19 . . . . . . .22 E2
Gateway The GU21 . . . . . . .70 C5
Gateways Guildford GU1 . .131 B8
Kingston u T KT6 . . . . .37 E4
Gateways Ct SM6 . . . . .60 B5
Gateways The TW9 . . . . .6 D3
Gatfield Gr TW13 . . . . .16 A6
Gatfield House TW13 . . . . .16 A6
Gatley Ave KT19 . . . . .57 B5
Gatley Dr GU1 . . . . .109 F4
Gatton Bottom
Gatton RH2, RH1 . . . . .118 E7
Lower Kingswood RH1, RH2 119 B8
Merstham RH1, RH2 . . . . . .119 B8
Gatton Cl Reigate RH2 . . . .118 C4
Sutton SM2 . . . . .59 B2
Gatton Park Ct RH1 . . . . . .118 F4
Gatton Park Rd RH1, RH2 118 E4
Gatton Point RH1 . . . . .119 A5
Gatton Rd Reigate RH2 . . .118 C4
Upper Tooting SW17 . . . . . . .20 E4
Gatwick Airport Sta RH6 .182 B7
GatwickAirport-London
RH6 . . . . .181 F7
Gatwick Gate RH11 . . . . . . .181 E5
Gatwick Metro Ctr RH6 . .161 B4
Gatwick Park Hospl RH6 .160 E2
Gatwick Rd
Crawley RH10, RH6 . . . . . . .182 A3
Wandsworth SW18 . . . . .19 F8
Gatwick Way RH6 . . . . . . .181 F8
Gatwick Zoo RH6 . . . . .180 D6
Gauntlet Cres CR3, CR8 . .100 D7
Gauntlett Rd SM1 . . . . .59 D5
Gavell Rd KT11 . . . . .73 A6
Gaveston Cl KT14 . . . . .71 F6
Gaveston Rd KT22 . . . . .95 A7
Gavina Cl SM4 . . . . .40 E4
Gayfere Rd KT17 . . . . .58 A5
Gayhouse La RH1 . . . . . . .162 E8
Gayler Cl RH1 . . . . .120 F2
Gaynesford Rd
Forest Hill SE23 . . . . .23 D6
Wallington SM5 . . . . .59 F3
Gaysland Cotts RH7 . . . . .143 A2
Gayton Cl KT21 . . . . .75 E1
Gayton Ct New Malden KT3 .38 F4
Reigate RH2 . . . . .118 A2
Gaywood Cl SW2 . . . . .22 A7
Gaywood Rd KT21 . . . . .75 F1
Geary Cl RH6 . . . . .162 B1
Gedge Ct CR4 . . . . .40 E5
Geffers Ride SL5 . . . . .28 E7
Gemini Cl RH11 . . . . .200 E4
Gemma Ct BR3 . . . . .43 F7
Genesis Bsns Pk GU21 . . . .70 C4
Genesis Cl TW19 . . . . .13 F7
Geneva Cl TW17 . . . . .34 E7
Geneva Rd Kingston u T KT1 37 E5
Thornton Heath CR7 . . . . . . .42 C4
Genoa Rd SE20 . . . . .43 C8
Gentles La GU30, GU35 . . .187 A3
Genyn Rd GU2 . . . . .130 B8
George Abbot Sch GU1 . .110 A3
George Denyer Cl GU27 .208 C7
George Eliot Cl GU8 . . . . .170 F5
George Gdns GU11 . . . . . .126 C7
George Groves Rd SE20 . . .43 A8
George Horley Pl RH5 . . .158 B1
George House 8 SE26 . . . .23 B3
George Pinion Ct RH12 . .217 B3
George Rd Farncombe GU7 150 F7
Guildford GU1 . . . . .109 D1
Kingston u T KT2 . . . . .18 C1
Milford GU8 . . . . .149 F2
New Malden KT3 . . . . .38 F4
George Sq SW19 . . . . .40 A6
George St
Croydon CR0, CR9 . . . . .61 D8
Hounslow TW3, TW5 . . . . .4 F5
Pirbright GU24 . . . . .87 A6
Richmond TW10 . . . . .6 D2
Staines TW18 . . . . .12 F4
George Wyver Cl SW18 . . .19 E8
George's Rd TN16 . . . . . . .103 D7
Georgeham Rd GU47 . . . . . .45 D2
Georgelands GU23 . . . . . . .91 B6
Georges Terr CR3 . . . . . . .100 D5
Georgetown Cl 4 SE19 . . .22 E3
Georgia Rd
Kingston u T KT3 . . . . .38 C5
South Norwood CR7 . . . . .42 B8
Georgian Cl
Camberley GU15 . . . . .65 E7
Crawley RH10 . . . . .202 D5
Staines TW18 . . . . .13 B4
Georgian Ct CR0, CR9 . . . . .42 D1
Georgina Ct 5 TW1 . . . . . . .6 C8
Gerald Ct RH13 . . . . .217 E2
Gerald's Gr SM7 . . . . .77 D5
Geraldine Rd W4 . . . . .7 A8
Gerard Ave TW4 . . . . .16 A8
Gerard Rd SW13 . . . . .7 F6
Germander Dr GU24 . . . . . .68 A4
Gerrards Mead SM7 . . . . . .77 F3
Ghent St SE6 . . . . .24 A6
Ghyll Cres RH13 . . . . . . .217 F1
Gibb's Acre GU24 . . . . .87 F4
Gibbet La GU15 . . . . .66 A7
Gibbon Rd KT2 . . . . .17 F1
Gibbons Cl Crawley RH10 .202 C3
Sandhurst GU47 . . . . .64 C8
Gibbs Ave SE19 . . . . .22 D3
Gibbs Brook La
Crowhurst RH7, RH8 . . . . . .143 D7
Oxted RH7, RH8 . . . . .143 D7
Gibbs Cl SE19 . . . . .22 D3
Gibbs House
6 Balham SW12 . . . . .21 B8
Bromley BR1 . . . . .44 F8
Gibbs Sq SE19 . . . . .22 D3
Giblets La RH12 . . . . .217 F7
Giblets Way RH12 . . . . . . .217 E7
Gibraltar Cres KT19 . . . . . .57 E1
Gibson Cl Chessington KT9 .56 C5
Isleworth TW7 . . . . .5 D4
Gibson Ct KT10 . . . . .55 F7
Gibson House SM1 . . . . . . .59 A6
Gibson Pl TW19 . . . . .2 C1
Gibson Rd SM1 . . . . .59 B5
Gibson's Hill
South Norwood SW16 . . . . . .22 A1
South Norwood SW16 . . . . . .22 A2
Gidd Hill CR5 . . . . .79 A3
Giffard Dr GU14 . . . . .84 F5
Giffard Way GU2 . . . . .109 A4
Giffards Cl RH19 . . . . .185 F1
Giffards Meadow GU9 . . .125 E1
Giggs Hill Rd KT7 . . . . .37 A2
Giggshill Gdns KT7 . . . . . . .37 A1
Gilbert Cl 1 SW19 . . . . .40 B8
Gilbert Rd Frimley GU15 . . .65 C2
Merton SW19 . . . . .20 C1
Gilbert Scott Jun & Inf
Sch CR2 . . . . .62 E3
Gilbert St TW3 . . . . .5 C4
Gilbey Rd SW17 . . . . .20 E3
Gilders Rd KT9 . . . . .56 F4
Giles Coppice SE19 . . . . . . .22 F4
Giles Travers Cl TW20 . . . .32 C6
Gilesmead KT18 . . . . .76 E5
Gilham La RH18 . . . . .206 E2
Gilham's Ave SM7 . . . . .77 E7
Gill Ave GU2 . . . . .129 E8
Gillett Ct RH13 . . . . .218 B4
Gillett House RH13 . . . . . .218 B4
Gillett Rd CR7 . . . . .42 D5
Gillette Cnr TW7 . . . . .6 A7
Gillham's La GU27 . . . . . . .207 A5
Gilliam Gr CR8 . . . . .61 A1
Gillian Ave GU11, GU12 . . .126 D8
Gillian Cl GU12 . . . . .126 D8
Gillian Park Rd SM3 . . . . . .39 F1
Gilliat Dr GU4 . . . . .110 D3
Gilligan Cl RH12 . . . . .217 B2
Gilmais KT23 . . . . .94 C2
Gilmore Cres TW15 . . . . . . .14 A2
Gilpin Ave SW14 . . . . .7 D3
Gilpin Cl CR4 . . . . .40 E7
Gilpin Cres TW2 . . . . .16 B8
Gilpin Way UB3 . . . . .3 D7
Gilsland Rd CR7 . . . . .42 D5
Gilton Rd SE6 . . . . .24 E5
Gimcrack Hill KT22 . . . . . . .95 B5
Gingers Cl GU6 . . . . .174 F2
Ginhams Rd RH11 . . . . . . .201 B6
Gipsy Hill SE19, SE27 . . . . .22 E3
Gipsy Hill Sta SE19 . . . . . . .22 E3
Gipsy La Bracknell RG12 . . .27 D7
Wokingham RG40 . . . . .25 C4
Gipsy Rd SE21, SE27 . . . . . .22 D4
Gipsy Road Gdns SE27 . . . .22 C4
Girdwood Rd SW18, SW19 .19 E8
Girling Way TW14 . . . . .4 A4
Girton Cl GU47 . . . . .45 E1
Girton Gdns CR0 . . . . .63 A7
Girton Rd SE26 . . . . .23 D3
Gittens Cl BR1 . . . . .24 F4
Giunevere Ho RH1 . . . . . . .119 A2
Glade Cl KT6 . . . . .56 D8
Glade Gdns CR0 . . . . .43 E2
Glade House SL5 . . . . .29 D4
Glade Spur KT20 . . . . .98 B6
Glade The Ascot SL5 . . . . . .29 C4
Belmont SM2 . . . . .58 E2
Binstead GU10 . . . . .145 B1
Coulsdon CR5, CR8 . . . . . . .100 A8
Crawley RH10 . . . . .202 A4
Croydon CR0 . . . . .43 D3
Fetcham KT22 . . . . .94 B5
Heath End GU9 . . . . .125 D7
Horsham RH13 . . . . .218 A3
Kingswood KT20 . . . . .98 B6
Mytchett GU16 . . . . .86 A2
Sheerwater KT14 . . . . .70 E6
Staines TW18 . . . . .13 B2
Stoneleigh KT17 . . . . .58 A4
West Wickham BR4 . . . . .63 B7
Glades The RH19 . . . . .186 B1
Gladeside CR0 . . . . .43 D3
Gladeside Ct CR6 . . . . . . .101 B7
Gladiator St SE23 . . . . .23 E8
Gladiator Way
GU11, GU14 . . . . .105 A8
Gladioli Cl 6 TW12 . . . . . . .16 A2
Gladsmuir Cl KT12 . . . . . . .54 C8
Gladstone Ave Feltham TW14 4 B1
Twickenham TW2 . . . . .16 D8
Gladstone Ct 5 SW19 . . . . .20 A1
Gladstone Gdns TW3 . . . . . .5 C6
Gladstone Mews 3 SE20 . . .23 C1
Gladstone Pl KT8 . . . . .36 E4
Gladstone Rd
Ashstead KT21 . . . . .75 D1
Croydon CR0 . . . . .42 D2
Horsham RH12 . . . . .217 D3
Kingston u T KT1 . . . . .38 A6
Merton SW19 . . . . .20 A1
Surbiton KT6 . . . . .56 E8
Glamis Cl GU16 . . . . .85 F7
Glamis Ho 10 RH2 . . . . . . .118 F1
Glamorgan Cl CR4, SW16 . .41 E6
Glamorgan Rd KT1 . . . . .17 C1
Glanfield Rd BR3 . . . . .43 F5
Glanty The TW20 . . . . .12 B4
Glanville House 4 SW12 . . .21 C8
Glanville Wlk 8 RH11 . . . .201 A3
Glasbrook Ave TW2 . . . . . . .15 F7
Glasford St SW17 . . . . .20 F2
Glassmill La BR2 . . . . .44 F7
Glassonby Wlk GU15 . . . . . .66 C5
Glastonbury Prim Sch
SM4 .40 B2
Glastonbury Rd Cheam CR4 40 A2
Morden SM4 . . . . .40 A2
Glayshers Hill GU35 . . . . .187 B6
Glazebrook Cl SE21 . . . . . . .22 D6
Glazebrook Rd TW11 . . . . . .16 F1
Glaziers La GU3 . . . . .107 C2
Gleave Cl RH19 . . . . .186 A2
Glebe Ave CR4 . . . . .40 E7
Glebe Cl Crawley RH10 . . . .201 E7
Great Bookham KT23 . . . . . . .94 A1
Lightwater GU18 . . . . .48 C1
Sanderstead CR2 . . . . .80 F8
Glebe Cotts Feltham TW13 .16 A5
West Clandon GU4 . . . . . . .111 B3
Glebe Ct Guildford GU1 . . .109 F1
Mitcham CR4 . . . . .40 F6
Glebe Gdns Byfleet KT14 . . .71 E5
New Malden KT3 . . . . .38 E2
Glebe House TW13 . . . . .16 A5
Glebe Hyrst CR2 . . . . .80 F7
Glebe La
Abinger Common RH5 . . . . .155 D8
Rushmoor GU10 . . . . .168 C5
Glebe Path CR4 . . . . .40 F6
Glebe Rd Ashstead KT21 . . .75 D1
Belmont SM2 . . . . .58 E2
Cranleigh GU6 . . . . .174 E4
Dorking RH4 . . . . .135 F7
Egham TW20 . . . . .12 C2
Glebe Rd *continued*
Farnborough GU14 . . . . .84 F5
Merstham CR5 . . . . .99 B3
Staines TW18 . . . . .13 B3
Wallington SM5 . . . . .59 F4
Warlingham CR6 . . . . .81 D2
Glebe Sch BR4 . . . . .63 D8
Glebe Side TW1 . . . . .5 F1
Glebe Sq CR4 . . . . .40 F6
Glebe The Blackwater GU17 .64 E4
Copthorne RH10 . . . . .183 B3
Ewhurst GU6 . . . . .175 E6
Felbridge RH19 . . . . .185 A4
Horley RH6 . . . . .160 F3
Leigh RH2 . . . . .138 A2
New Malden KT4 . . . . .38 F1
Streatham SW16 . . . . .21 D4
Glebe Way Coney Hall BR4 . .63 E7
Feltham TW13 . . . . .16 A5
Sanderstead CR2 . . . . .80 F8
West Wickham BR4 . . . . .63 D8
Glebeland Ctr RH4 . . . . . . .136 A7
Glebeland Gdns TW17 . . . . .34 C3
Glebeland Rd GU15 . . . . . . .64 F4
Glebelands Claygate KT10 . .55 F2
Crawley Down RH10 . . . . . .204 A7
East Molesey KT8 . . . . .36 B5
Loxwood RH14 . . . . .212 F4
Glebelands Rd
East Bedfont TW14 . . . . .15 A8
Wokingham RG40 . . . . .25 C7
Glebelands Sch GU6 . . . . .174 D3
Glebewood RG12 . . . . .27 C4
Gledhow Wood KT20 . . . . . .98 B5
Gleeson Mews KT15 . . . . . . .52 C6
Glen Albyn Rd SW19 . . . . . .19 D6
Glen Ave TW15 . . . . .14 A4
Glen Cl Beacon Hill GU26 . .188 C6
Kingswood KT20 . . . . .97 E4
Littleton TW17 . . . . .34 A5
Glen Court Flats GU26 . . . .188 C6
Glen Ct Addlestone KT15 . . . .51 F5
Bromley BR1 . . . . .24 F1
10 Penge SE20 . . . . .43 B8
Staines TW18 . . . . .12 F1
Glen Dale Mews BR3 . . . . . .44 B8
Glen Gdns CR0, CR9 . . . . . . .61 A6
Glen Innes GU47 . . . . .45 E1
Glen Rd Beacon Hill GU26 .188 C6
Chessington KT9 . . . . .56 F7
Grayshott GU26 . . . . .188 D3
Glen Road End SM6 . . . . . . .60 B2
Glen The Addlestone KT15 . . .51 F5
Ascot SL5 . . . . .29 D5
Beckenham BR2 . . . . .44 E7
Croydon CR0 . . . . .62 D7
Redhill RH1 . . . . .139 F8
Glen Vue RH19 . . . . .185 E1
Glen Wlk TW7 . . . . .5 D2
Glena Mount SM1 . . . . .59 C6
Glenalmond House TW15 .13 E5
Glenavon Cl KT10 . . . . .56 A4
Glenavon Ct KT4 . . . . .58 B8
Glenbow Rd BR1 . . . . .24 E3
Glenbuck Ct 6 KT6 . . . . . . .37 E3
Glenbuck Rd KT6 . . . . .37 E3
Glenburnie Rd SW17 . . . . . .20 F5
Glencairn Rd SW16 . . . . . . .21 E1
Glencoe Cl GU16 . . . . .86 A8
Glencoe Rd KT13 . . . . .53 A7
Glendale Cl
Horsham RH12 . . . . .218 A6
Woking GU21 . . . . .69 C1
Glendale Dr GU4 . . . . .110 C5
Glendale Rise CR8 . . . . .80 B4
Glendene Ave KT24 . . . . . . .92 E1
Glendon House 9 RH10 . .201 D5
Glendower Gdns 10 SW14 . .7 D4
Glendower Rd SW14 . . . . . . .7 D4
Glendyne Cl RH19 . . . . . . .206 A8
Glendyne Way RH19 . . . . . .206 A8
Gleneagle Lodge BR3 . . . . .44 A8
Gleneagle Mews SW16 . . . .21 D3
Gleneagle Rd SW16 . . . . . . .21 D3
Gleneagles Cl TW19 . . . . . . .2 D1
Gleneagles Ct
Crawley RH10, RH11 . . . . . .201 D5
3 Teddington TW11 . . . . . . .17 A3
Gleneagles Dr GU14 . . . . . .84 C3
Gleneagles House RG12 . .26 E3
Gleneldon Mews SW16 . . . .21 E4
Gleneldon Rd SW16 . . . . . .21 E4
Glenfarg Rd SE6 . . . . .24 D7
Glenfield Cl RH3 . . . . .137 B5
Glenfield Cotts RH6 . . . . .180 D7
Glenfield House RG12 . . . . .27 C5
Glenfield Rd Ashford TW15 .14 C2
Banstead SM7 . . . . .78 B4
Brockham RH3 . . . . .137 B6
Streatham SW12 . . . . .21 C7
Glenhaven Dr TW19 . . . . . . .2 A2
Glenheadon Cl KT22 . . . . . .95 D4
Glenheadon Rise KT22 . . . . .95 D4
Glenhurst BR3 . . . . .44 C8
Glenhurst Cl GU17 . . . . .64 E4
Glenhurst Ct SE19 . . . . .22 F3
Glenhurst Rd TW8 . . . . .6 C8
Glenhurst Rise SE19 . . . . . .22 C1
Glenister Park Rd SW16 . . .21 D1
Glenlea GU26 . . . . .188 E1
Glenlea Hollow
GU26, GU27 . . . . .207 E8
Glenlion Ct 2 KT13 . . . . . . .53 D7
Glenmill TW12 . . . . .15 F3
Glenmore Cl KT15 . . . . .52 B7
Glenmore House 6 TW10 . .6 E1
Glenmount Rd GU16 . . . . . .86 A2
Glenn Ave CR8 . . . . .80 B8

Glennie Ct SE21 ... 23 A7
Glennie Rd SE27, SW16 ... 22 A5
Glentanner Way SW17 ... 20 D5
Glenthorne Ave CR0, CR9 ... 43 C1
Glenthorne Cl SM3 ... 40 A1
Glenthorne Gdns SM3 ... 40 A1
Glenthorne High Sch SM3 40 A1
Glenthorne Rd KT1 ... 37 F5
Glenthorpe Rd SM4 ... 39 D4
Glenview Cl RH10 ... 201 F8
Glenville Gdns GU26 ... 188 F4
Glenville Mews SW18 ... 20 A8
Glenville Rd KT2 ... 38 A8
Glenwood Bracknell RG12 ... 27 D5
Dorking RH5 ... 136 C5
Virginia Water GU25 ... 31 C8
Glenwood Rd
Forest Hill SE6 ... 24 A7
Hounslow TW3 ... 5 D4
Stoneleigh KT17 ... 58 A4
Glenwood Way CR0 ... 43 D3
Globe Farm La GU17 ... 64 B5
Glorney Mead GU9 ... 126 A6
Glory Mead RH4, RH5 ... 136 C4
Glossop Rd CR2 ... 61 D2
Gloster Cl GU12 ... 105 F5
Gloster Ct GU21 ... 69 F3
Gloster Rd New Malden KT3 38 E5
Old Woking GU22 ... 90 A7
Gloucester Cl
East Grinstead RH19 ... 206 A8
Frimley GU16 ... 85 E6
Thames Ditton KT7 ... 37 A1
Gloucester Cres TW18 ... 13 D2
Gloucester Ct Richmond TW9 7 A7
8 Surbiton KT6 ... 37 D2
Gloucester Dr TW18, TW19 12 D5
Gloucester Gdns
Bagshot GU19 ... 47 E3
Sutton SM1 ... 59 B8
Gloucester Lodge 5 CR0 ... 61 F8
Gloucester Rd
Aldershot GU11 ... 126 C7
Bagshot GU19 ... 47 E3
Crawley RH10 ... 201 E2
Croydon CR0 ... 42 E2
Feltham TW13 ... 15 C7
Guildford GU2 ... 108 F3
Hampton TW12 ... 16 B1
Hounslow TW4 ... 4 E3
Kingston u T KT1, KT2 ... 38 B7
Redhill RH1 ... 118 F2
Richmond TW9 ... 7 A7
Teddington TW11 ... 16 E3
Thornton Heath CR0 ... 42 E2
Twickenham TW2 ... 16 C7
Glover's Rd
Charlwood RH6 ... 180 D7
Reigate RH2 ... 139 B8
Glovers Field GU27 ... 207 F6
Gloxinia Wlk TW12 ... 16 A2
Glyn ADT Tech Sch KT17 ... 76 F8
Glyn Cl Ewell KT17 ... 58 A2
South Norwood SE19, SE25 ... 42 E8
Glyn Ct SE27 ... 22 A5
Glyn Rd KT4, SM3 ... 58 D8
Glyndale Grange SM2 ... 59 B4
Glynde Pl RH12 ... 217 C2
Glynswood Frimley GU15 ... 65 F3
Rowledge GU10 ... 146 A4
Glynwood Ct SE23 ... 23 C6
Goat Rd CR4 ... 40 F2
Goat Wharf TW8 ... 6 E8
Goaters Rd SL5 ... 28 C7
Goatsfield Rd TN16 ... 103 C7
Godalming Ave SM6 ... 60 F5
Godalming Bsns Ctr GU7 150 F4
Godalming Coll GU7 ... 150 D2
Godalming Cty Mid Sch
GU7 ... 150 F5
Godalming Rd
Dunsfold GU8 ... 193 A8
Hascombe GU8 ... 172 E3
Godalming Sta GU7 ... 150 D4
Goddard Cl Crawley RH10 ... 202 B3
Littleton TW17 ... 33 F6
Goddard House SW19 ... 19 D6
Goddard Rd BR3 ... 43 E5
Goddards La GU15 ... 65 B3
Godfrey Ave TW2 ... 16 D8
Godfrey Way TW4 ... 15 F8
Godley Rd Byfleet KT14 ... 71 F6
Wandsworth SW18 ... 20 D7
Godolphin Cl SM2 ... 77 F8
Godolphin Ct RH10, RH11 201 D5
Godolphin House 7 SW2 ... 22 A7
Godolphin Rd KT13 ... 53 D4
Godric Cres CR0 ... 63 D1
Godson Rd CR0, CR9 ... 61 A7
Godstone Farm RH9 ... 121 C3
Godstone Fst Sch RH9 ... 121 B3
Godstone Green Rd RH9 ... 121 B4
Godstone Hill
Tyler's Green RH9 ... 121 C5
Woldingham CR3, RH9 ... 121 B7
Godstone House 1 KT2 ... 18 B2
Godstone Mount 3 CR8 ... 80 B7
Godstone Rd
Bletchingley RH1 ... 120 F2
Caterham CR3 ... 101 A3
Kenley CR3, CR8 ... 80 D4
Lingfield RH7 ... 164 C4
Oxted RH8, RH9 ... 122 C5
Purley CR8 ... 80 D4
Sutton SM1 ... 59 C6
Twickenham TW1 ... 6 B1
Whyteleafe CR3 ... 80 D4
Godstone Sta RH9 ... 142 E5
Godwin Cl KT19 ... 57 C4
Goffs Cl RH11 ... 201 C5
Goffs La RH11 ... 201 B6
Goffs Park Rd RH11 ... 201 C4
Goffs Rd TW15 ... 14 D2
Gogmore Farm Cl KT16 ... 32 F2
Gogmore La KT16 ... 33 A2
Goidel Cl SM6 ... 60 D6
Gold Cup La SL5 ... 28 D8
Goldcliff Cl SM4 ... 40 A2
Goldcrest Cl RH6 ... 160 E4
Goldcrest Way
New Addington CR0 ... 63 D3
Wallington CR8 ... 60 D1
Golden Ct 10 TW9 ... 6 D2
Golden Mews SE20 ... 43 C8
Golden Orb Wood RG42 ... 26 D8
Goldfinch Cl
Crawley RH11 ... 201 D8
Horsham RH12 ... 217 C7
Goldfinch Gdns GU4 ... 110 D2
Goldfinch Rd CR0, CR2 ... 62 E1
Goldfort Wlk GU21 ... 68 E3
Goldhill GU10 ... 146 C6
Golding Cl Chessington KT9 56 C4
Crawley RH10 ... 202 C5
Goldings The GU21 ... 68 F3
Goldney Rd GU15 ... 66 C4
Goldrings Rd KT22 ... 74 C6
Goldsmith Way RG45 ... 45 B4
Goldsmiths Cl GU21 ... 69 C1
Goldstone Farm View
KT23 ... 114 A8
Goldsworth Orch 6 GU21 69 A1
Goldsworth Park Ctr
GU21 ... 69 A2
Goldsworth Park Trad Est
GU21 ... 69 B3
Goldsworth Prim Sch
GU21 ... 69 C1
Goldsworth Rd GU21 ... 69 D2
Goldsworth Road Ind Est
GU21 ... 69 D2
Goldwell Rd CR7 ... 41 F5
Gole Rd GU24 ... 87 D6
Golf Cl Pyrford GU22 ... 70 E5
South Norwood SW16 ... 42 A8
Golf Club Dr KT2 ... 18 D1
Golf Club Rd
Weybridge KT13 ... 53 C1
Woking GU22 ... 89 B7
Golf Dr GU15 ... 65 F4
Golf Links Ave GU26 ... 188 B6
Golf Rd CR8 ... 80 D1
Golf Side Belmont SM2 ... 77 E8
Twickenham TW2 ... 16 D5
Golf Side Cl KT3 ... 38 E7
Goliath Cl SM6 ... 60 E3
Gomer Gdns TW11 ... 17 A2
Gomer Pl TW11 ... 17 A2
Gomshall Ave SM6 ... 60 E5
Gomshall Gdns CR8 ... 80 E4
Gomshall La GU5 ... 133 B4
Gomshall Rd KT17, SM2 ... 58 C1
Gomshall Sta GU5 ... 133 E4
Gong Hill Dr GU10 ... 146 D4
Gong Hill Frensham Rd
GU10 ... 146 D4
Gonston Cl SW19 ... 19 E6
Gonville Prim Sch CR7 ... 41 F4
Gonville Rd CR7 ... 41 F4
Good Shepherd RC Prim
Sch Catford BR1 ... 24 F4
New Addington CR0 ... 63 B3
Goodbehere House 7
SE27 ... 22 C4
Goodchild Rd RG40 ... 25 D6
Goodden Cres GU14 ... 84 F3
Goodenough Rd SW19 ... 19 F1
Goodenough Way CR5 ... 99 F7
Goodhart Way BR4 ... 44 E3
Goodhew Rd CR0, SE25 ... 43 A3
Gooding Cl KT3 ... 38 C4
Goodings Gn RG40 ... 25 F6
Goodland House 1 KT3 ... 38 E2
Goodman Cres SW2 ... 21 D6
Goodman Pl TW18 ... 12 F4
Goodson House SM4 ... 40 C2
Goodways Dr RG12 ... 27 D7
Goodwin Cl Crawley RH11 200 F3
Mitcham CR4 ... 40 D6
Goodwin Gdns CR0, CR2 ... 61 B4
Goodwin Rd CR0 ... 61 B5
Goodwins Cl RH19 ... 185 D3
Goodwood Cl
Camberley GU15 ... 65 C8
Crawley RH10 ... 202 A3
Morden SM4 ... 40 A5
Goodwood House SE26 ... 23 B2
Goodwood Par BR3 ... 43 E5
Goodwood Pl GU14 ... 85 E3
Goodwood Rd RH1 ... 118 F3
Goodwyns Pl RH4 ... 136 B5
Goodwyns Rd RH4 ... 136 C4
Goose Gn GU5 ... 133 C4
Goose Green Cl RH12 ... 217 D5
Goose La GU22 ... 89 B5
Goose Rye Rd Woking GU3 89 A2
Worplesdon GU3 ... 88 E1
Goossens Cl 1 SM1 ... 59 C5
Gordon Ave
Camberley GU15 ... 65 C4
Isleworth TW1 ... 6 B2
Mortlake SW14 ... 7 E3
South Croydon CR2, CR8 ... 61 C1
Gordon Cl
Addlestone KT16 ... 51 E7
Staines TW18 ... 13 B2
Gordon Cres
Camberley GU15 ... 65 C4
Croydon CR0 ... 42 F1
Gordon Dr
Addlestone KT16 ... 51 E7
Shepperton TW17 ... 34 D2
Gordon Rd
Aldershot GU11 ... 105 A1
Ashford TW15 ... 13 E5
Beckenham BR3 ... 43 F6
Camberley GU15 ... 65 C5
Caterham CR3 ... 100 D6
Chiswick W4 ... 7 B8
Claygate KT10 ... 55 E3
Crowthorne RG45 ... 45 D3
Farnborough GU14 ... 105 D8
Horsham RH12 ... 217 D4
Hounslow TW3 ... 5 C3
Kingston u T KT2 ... 37 F8
Redhill RH1 ... 119 A4
Richmond TW9 ... 6 F5
Shepperton TW17 ... 34 D3
Surbiton KT5 ... 37 F2
Wallington SM5 ... 59 F4
Gordon's Sch GU24 ... 67 E7
Gordondale Rd
SW18, SW19 ... 20 A6
Gordons Way RH8 ... 122 D7
Gore Rd SW20 ... 39 C7
Goring Rd TW18 ... 12 E3
Goring's Mead RH13 ... 217 D1
Gorling Cl RH11 ... 200 E5
Gorrick Sq RG41 ... 25 B3
Gorringe Park Ave
CR4, SW17 ... 21 A1
Gorringe Park Mid Sch
CR4 ... 41 A8
Gorringes Brook RH12 ... 217 D6
Gorse Bank GU18 ... 67 A8
Gorse Cl Burgh Heath KT20 97 B7
Copthorne RH10 ... 183 B2
Crawley RH11 ... 201 B1
Wrecclesham GU10 ... 146 B6
Gorse Cotts GU27 ... 207 C8
Gorse Ct GU4 ... 110 C3
Gorse Dr RH6 ... 162 C3
Gorse End RH12 ... 217 D5
Gorse Hill La GU25 ... 31 D5
Gorse Hill Rd GU25 ... 31 D5
Gorse La Chobham GU24 ... 49 E3
Wrecclesham GU10 ... 146 B6
Gorse Pl RG42 ... 8 B1
Gorse Rd Croydon CR0 ... 63 A7
Frimley GU16 ... 65 E2
Gorse Rise SW17 ... 21 A3
Gorselands GU9 ... 125 C7
Gorselands Cl Ash GU12 106 A5
Headley Down GU35 ... 187 C4
West Byfleet KT14 ... 71 C8
Gorsewood Rd GU21 ... 88 E7
Gort Cl GU11 ... 105 E7
Gosberton Rd SW12 ... 21 A7
Gosbury Hill KT9 ... 56 E6
Gosden Cl Crawley RH10 ... 202 A5
Shalford GU5 ... 151 F8
Gosden Comm GU5 ... 151 E8
Gosden Cotts GU5 ... 151 F7
Gosden Hill Rd GU4 ... 110 C5
Gosden House Sch GU5 151 E8
Gosden Rd GU24 ... 67 F6
Gosfield Rd KT19 ... 76 D7
Gosnell Cl GU16 ... 66 D3
Gosport House 9 SW15 ... 19 A7
Gossops Dr RH11 ... 201 A5
Gossops Green Cty Fst
Sch RH11 ... 201 A5
Gossops Green Cty Mid
Sch RH11 ... 201 A5
Gossops Green La RH11 201 A5
Gossops Par RH11 ... 200 F5
Gostling Rd TW2 ... 16 A7
Goston Gdns CR7 ... 42 A6
Gostrode La GU8 ... 210 A6
Gothic Ct Harlington UB3 ... 3 D8
Sandhurst GU47 ... 64 B7
Gothic Rd TW2 ... 16 D6
Goudhurst Cl RH10 ... 202 E6
Goudhurst House 10
SE20 ... 23 C1
Goudhurst Keep RH10 ... 202 E6
Goudhurst Rd BR1 ... 24 F3
Gough House 4 KT1 ... 37 E7
Gough's La RG12 ... 27 D8
Gough's Meadow GU47 ... 64 B7
Gould Ct Dulwich SE19 ... 22 E3
Guildford GU4 ... 110 D3
Gould Rd East Bedfont TW14 14 E8
Twickenham TW2 ... 16 E7
Goulding Gdns CR7 ... 42 C7
Government House Rd
GU11, GU14 ... 105 B7
Government Rd
Aldershot GU11 ... 105 E4
Farnborough GU11 ... 105 E4
Governor's Rd GU15 ... 64 F6
Govett Ave TW17 ... 34 C4
Govett Gr GU20 ... 48 D5
Gower Pk GU47 ... 64 D7
Gower Rd Horley RH6 ... 160 E3
Hounslow TW7 ... 5 F8
Weybridge KT13 ... 53 D4
Gower The TW20 ... 32 C6
Gowland Pl BR3 ... 43 F7
Graburn Way KT8 ... 36 D6
Grace Bennett Cl GU14 ... 85 A7
Grace Bsns Ctr CR4 ... 40 F3
Grace House SE26 ... 23 B3
Grace Path SE26 ... 23 C4
Grace Rd Crawley RH11 ... 201 A1
Thornton Heath CR0 ... 42 C3
Grace Reynolds Wlk 4
GU15 ... 65 C6
Gracedale Rd SW16, SW17 21 B3
Gracefield Gdns SW16 ... 21 E5
Gracious Pond Rd GU24 ... 50 B4
Gradient The SE26 ... 23 A4
Graemesdyke Ave SW14 ... 7 B3
Graffham Cl RH11 ... 201 B8
Grafton Cl Twickenham TW4 15 F7
West Byfleet KT14 ... 70 F6
Worcester Park KT4 ... 57 E7
Grafton Ct TW14 ... 14 D7
Grafton Park Rd KT4 ... 57 E8
Grafton Rd Kingston u T KT3 38 E6
Thornton Heath CR0 ... 42 A1
Worcester Park KT19, KT4 ... 57 E7
Grafton Way KT8 ... 35 F5
Graham Ave CR4 ... 41 A8
Graham Cl CR0 ... 63 A8
Graham Gdns KT6 ... 37 E1
Graham House
5 Balham SW12 ... 21 B8
Little Bookham KT23 ... 94 A3
Redhill RH1 ... 118 E3
Graham Rd Hampton TW12 16 A4
Merton SW19 ... 19 F1
Mitcham CR4 ... 41 A8
Purley CR8 ... 80 A6
Windlesham GU20 ... 48 C4
Grainford Ct RG40 ... 25 C5
Grainger Rd TW7 ... 5 F5
Grampian Cl UB3 ... 3 D7
Grampian Rd GU47 ... 45 A2
Granada St SW17 ... 20 F3
Granard Rd SW11, SW12 ... 20 F8
Granary Cl RH6 ... 161 A5
Granary Way RH12 ... 217 A1
Grand Ave Camberley GU15 65 C6
Tolworth KT5 ... 38 B3
Grand Avenue Prim Sch
KT5 ... 38 C3
Grand Avenue Prim Sch
(Upper Sch) KT5 ... 38 C3
Grand Dr KT3, SM4, SW20 ... 39 C5
Grand Par Crawley RH10 ... 201 D6
Mortlake SW14 ... 7 C3
Tolworth KT6 ... 38 A1
Grand Stand Rd
KT17, KT18 ... 77 A2
Grand View Ave TN16 ... 83 C3
Granden Rd SW16 ... 41 E7
Grandfield Ct W4 ... 7 D8
Grandis Cotts GU23 ... 91 B5
Grandison Rd KT4 ... 58 C7
Grange Ave
Crowthorne RG45 ... 45 B6
South Norwood SE25 ... 42 E7
Twickenham TW2 ... 16 E6
Grange Cl Ashstead KT22 ... 95 D7
Bletchingley RH1 ... 120 D2
Crawley RH10 ... 202 A8
East Molesey KT8 ... 36 B5
Godalming GU7 ... 151 A5
Guildford GU2 ... 109 B5
Heston TW5 ... 4 F8
Merstham RH1, RH2 ... 119 B7
Grange Cres RH10 ... 204 B7
Grange Ct Egham TW20 ... 11 F3
Hackbridge SM6 ... 60 B7
Littleton TW17 ... 34 A5
Merstham RH2 ... 119 B7
South Godstone RH9 ... 142 E5
Staines TW18 ... 13 A3
Sutton SM2 ... 59 B3
Walton-on-T KT12 ... 54 A8
Grange Cty Inf Sch The
KT15 ... 52 A1
Grange Dr Merstham RH1 119 B7
Woking GU21 ... 69 E4
Grange End RH6 ... 162 A3
Grange Farm Rd GU12 ... 106 A3
Grange Gdns
Banstead SM7 ... 78 B6
South Norwood SE25 ... 42 E7
Grange Hill SE25 ... 42 E7
Grange La SE21 ... 22 F6
Grange Lodge SW19 ... 19 D2
Grange Mansions KT17 ... 57 F3
Grange Meadow SM7 ... 78 B6
Grange Mills SW12 ... 21 C7
Grange Park Pl SW20 ... 19 B1
Grange Park Rd CR7 ... 42 D6
Grange Pk Cranleigh GU6 174 F3
Woking GU21 ... 69 F5
Grange Pl TW18 ... 33 C7
Grange Rd Ash GU12 ... 106 B1
Ashstead KT21, KT22 ... 95 D7
Belmont SM2 ... 59 A3
Bracknell RG12 ... 27 C8
Camberley GU15 ... 65 E5
Caterham CR3 ... 101 A2
Chessington KT9 ... 56 E6
Crawley Down RH10 ... 204 A7
East Molesey KT8 ... 36 B5
Egham TW20 ... 11 F3
Farnborough GU14 ... 85 B7
Guildford GU2, GU3 ... 109 B5
Hersham KT12 ... 54 E6
Kingston u T KT1 ... 37 E6
Rushmoor GU10 ... 168 C7
South Croydon CR2 ... 61 C2
South Norwood SE19, SE25 ... 42 D7
Sutton SM2 ... 59 A3
Tongham GU10 ... 126 E6
Woking GU21 ... 69 E5
Woodham KT15 ... 52 B1
Grange Specl Sch The
GU11 ... 126 B8
Grange The Chobham GU24 49 E1
Croydon CR0 ... 62 F8
Frensham GU10 ... 167 D7
Horley RH6 ... 161 A6
New Malden KT3 ... 39 A4
Walton-on-T KT12 ... 54 B8
Wimbledon SW19 ... 19 D2
Worcester Park KT19 ... 57 D6
Grange Vale SM2 ... 59 B3
Grangecliffe Gdns SE25 ... 42 E7
Grangefields Rd GU4 ... 109 D6
Grangemill Rd SE6 ... 24 A6
Grangemill Way SE6 ... 24 A6
Grangemount KT22 ... 95 D7
Grangeway RH6 ... 162 A3
Grangewood La BR3 ... 23 F2
Gransden Cl GU6 ... 175 E5
Granston Way RH10 ... 204 C8
Grant Cl TW17 ... 34 B3
Grant Pl 2 CR0 ... 42 F1
Grant Rd Crowthorne RG45 45 C4
Croydon CR0 ... 42 F1
Grant Way TW7, TW8 ... 6 A8
Grant Wlk SL5 ... 29 E1
Grantchester 3 KT1 ... 38 A7
Grantham Cl GU47 ... 45 E1
Grantham House TW16 ... 14 E1
Grantham Rd W4 ... 7 E7
Grantley Ave GU5 ... 152 B6
Grantley Cl GU4 ... 130 E2
Grantley House SW19 ... 19 D7
Grantley Rd
Cranford TW4, TW5 ... 4 C5
Guildford GU2 ... 109 A2
Granton Rd SW16 ... 41 C8
Grants Cotts KT10 ... 55 D8
Grants La TN8, RH8 ... 144 C6
Grantwood Cl RH1 ... 140 B4
Granville Ave
Feltham TW13 ... 15 A6
Hounslow TW3, TW4 ... 5 A2
Granville Cl Byfleet KT14 ... 71 F6
South Croydon CR0 ... 61 E8
Weybridge KT13 ... 53 C4
Granville Gdns SW16 ... 21 F1
Granville Rd
Limpsfield RH8 ... 123 A7
Merton SW19 ... 20 A1
Wandsworth SW18 ... 19 F8
Weybridge KT13 ... 53 C4
Woking GU22 ... 89 F7
Granwood Ct 5 TW7 ... 5 E6
Grasmere Ave
Kingston u T SW15 ... 18 E4
Merton SW19 ... 40 A6
Twickenham TW3 ... 5 B1
Grasmere Cl
East Bedfont TW14 ... 14 F7
Guildford GU1 ... 110 B2
Thorpe Lea TW20 ... 12 B1
Grasmere Ct SE26 ... 23 A3
Grasmere Gdns RH12 ... 218 B6
Grasmere Rd Bromley BR1 24 F1
Croydon SE25 ... 43 B4
Farnborough GU14 ... 84 E4
Hale GU9 ... 125 A6
Lightwater GU18 ... 48 B1
Purley CR8 ... 80 B8
Streatham SW16 ... 21 F3
Grasmere Way KT14 ... 71 F7
Grassfield Cl CR5 ... 99 C8
Grasslands RH6 ... 162 A3
Grassmere RH6 ... 161 C4
Grassmount
Forest Hill SE23 ... 23 B6
Wallington CR8 ... 60 C1
Grassway SM6 ... 60 C6
Grately House 10 SW15 ... 19 B7
Grattons Dr RH10 ... 182 C1
Grattons The RH13 ... 215 E3
Gravel Hill
Leatherhead KT22 ... 95 B6
South Croydon CR0, CR2 ... 62 E4
Gravel Hill Rd GU10 ... 145 A3
Gravel Pits GU5 ... 133 C4
Gravel Pits La GU5 ... 133 C4
Gravel Rd
Farnborough GU14 ... 105 D8
Hale GU9 ... 125 B7
Twickenham TW2 ... 16 E7
Graveley 7 KT1 ... 38 A7
Gravelly Hill CR3 ... 120 F7
Gravenel Gdns SW17 ... 20 E3
Graveney Gr SE20 ... 23 C1
Graveney Rd
Crawley RH10 ... 202 C5
Upper Tooting SW17 ... 20 E4
Graveney Sch SW17 ... 21 B3
Gravetts La GU3 ... 108 E5
Gravetye Cl RH10 ... 202 A4
Gray Ct 8 KT2 ... 17 D4
Gray Pl KT16 ... 51 D4
Gray's La KT21 ... 95 F8
Grayham Cres KT3 ... 38 D5
Grayham Rd KT3 ... 38 D5
Graylands GU21 ... 69 E3
Graylands Ct GU21 ... 69 E3
Graylands Ct 5 GU1 ... 130 F8
Grays Cl GU27 ... 208 E8
Grays La TW15 ... 14 B4
Grays Rd GU7 ... 150 F7
Grays Wood RH6 ... 161 C3
Grayscroft Rd SW16 ... 21 D1

Grayshott Dr GU17 ... 64 C5
Grayshott Prim Sch GU26 ... 188 D3
Grayshott Rd GU26, GU35 . 187 C5
Grayswood CE (VA) Fst Sch GU27 ... 189 F2
Grayswood Dr GU16 ... 86 A2
Grayswood Gdns SW20 ... 39 B7
Grayswood Pl GU27 ... 208 E8
Grayswood Point 14 SW15 . 19 A7
Grayswood Rd
Grayswood GU27 ... 189 F1
Haslemere GU27 ... 189 F1
Grazely Ct SE19 ... 22 E3
Great Austins GU9 ... 146 D8
Great Bookham Cty Mid Sch KT23 ... 94 A1
Great Brownings SE21 ... 22 F4
Great Chertsey Rd
Chiswick SW14, W4 ... 7 D6
Feltham TW13, TW2 ... 16 A5
Great Elshams SM7 ... 78 A3
Great George St GU7 ... 150 E4
Great Goodwin Dr GU1 .. 110 B3
Great Hollands Inf Sch RG12 ... 26 F4
Great Hollands Jun Sch RG12 ... 26 E4
Great Hollands Rd RG12 .. 26 F3
Great Hollands Sq RG12 .. 26 F3
Great House Ct 4 RH19 .. 205 F8
Great Oaks Pk GU4 ... 110 C5
Great Quarry GU1 ... 130 D6
Great South-West Rd
East Bedfont TW14, TW6, TW4, TW5 ... 3 D2
Feltham TW6, TW14 ... 3 D2
Hatton TW6, TW14 ... 3 D2
Hounslow TW5 ... 4 B4
Great Tattenhams KT18 ... 77 C1
Great West Rd
Brentford TW8 ... 6 B8
Cranford TW5 ... 4 F6
Heston TW5 ... 4 F6
Hounslow TW5, TW7 ... 5 C6
Great West Road Cedars Rd W4 ... 7 C8
Great West Road Chiswick W4 ... 7 F8
Great West Road Ellesmere Rd W4 ... 7 D8
Great West Road Hogarth La W4 ... 7 E8
Great West Trad Est TW8 ... 6 B8
Great Woodcote Dr CR8 .. 60 D1
Great Woodcote Pk CR8, SM6 ... 60 E1
Greatfield Cl GU14 ... 85 B8
Greatfield Rd GU14 ... 85 B8
Greatford Dr GU1 ... 110 D1
Greatham Rd RH10 ... 202 C3
Greatham Wlk 8 SW15 ... 19 A7
Greathed Manor RH7 ... 165 C1
Greathurst End KT23 ... 93 F3
Greatlake Ct RH6 ... 161 B4
Greatstone House 13 SE20 23 C1
Greatwood Cl KT16 ... 51 C2
Greaves Pl SW17 ... 20 E4
Grebe Cres RH13 ... 218 A1
Grebe Terr 4 KT1 ... 37 E6
Grecian Cres SE19, SW16 .. 22 B2
Green Acre GU11 ... 104 F1
Green Acres CR0 ... 61 F7
Green Bsns Ctr The TW20 . 12 C4
Green Cl Beckenham BR2 ... 44 E6
Carshalton SM5 ... 59 F8
Feltham TW13 ... 15 E3
Green Court Ave CR0 ... 62 B8
Green Court Gdns CR0 ... 62 B8
Green Croft RG40 ... 25 E8
Green Cross La GU10 ... 168 A1
Green Ct TW16 ... 14 F2
Green Curve SM7 ... 77 F4
Green Dene
East Horsley KT24 ... 112 E3
West Horsley KT24 ... 112 E3
Green Dr Send Marsh GU23 . 90 F4
Wokingham RG40 ... 25 E4
Green Dragon Jun & Inf Sch TW8 ... 6 E8
Green End KT9 ... 56 E6
Green Farm Rd GU19 ... 47 F3
Green Finch Cl RG45 ... 45 A6
Green Hedges 8 TW1 ... 6 C1
Green Hedges Ave RH19 . 185 D2
Green Hedges Cl RH19 .. 185 D2
Green Hill BR6 ... 83 F7
Green Hill Cl GU15 ... 66 C6
Green Hill Rd GU15 ... 66 C6
Green House The 5 SW19 . 19 E7
Green La
Addlestone KT15, KT16 ... 51 E7
Alfold Crossways GU6 ... 193 F4
Ascot SL5 ... 29 E8
Ashford TW16 ... 14 F2
Ashstead KT22 ... 95 D6
Ashstead, Lower Ashstead KT21 ... 75 D1
Bagshot GU19 ... 47 F2
Blackwater GU17 ... 64 B4
Blackwater, Hawley GU17 ... 64 E4
Burstow RH6 ... 182 F6
Byfleet KT14 ... 71 F7
Caterham CR3 ... 100 C5
Cheam SM4 ... 40 B3
Green La *continued*
Chertsey KT15, KT16 ... 51 E7
Chessington KT9 ... 56 E3
Chobham GU24 ... 49 F1
Churt GU10 ... 168 A1
Cobham KT11 ... 73 E7
Copthorne RH10 ... 183 F4
Crawley, Northgate RH10 .. 201 E8
Crawley, Worth RH10 ... 202 D6
Cudworth RH5 ... 179 D8
Dockenfield GU10 ... 166 E6
East Molesey KT8 ... 36 B4
Egham TW20 ... 12 B3
Egham TW18 ... 32 E8
Farncombe GU7, GU3 ... 150 E8
Farnham GU9 ... 146 A7
Farnham, Weybourne GU9 .. 125 F5
Faygate RH12 ... 198 F4
Feltham TW13 ... 15 E3
Guildford GU1 ... 110 B1
Heath End GU9 ... 125 F5
Hersham KT12 ... 54 B5
Hounslow TW4 ... 4 C3
Kingsley Green GU27 ... 208 B4
Leatherhead KT22 ... 95 D6
Leigh RH2 ... 158 E8
Lingfield RH7 ... 164 C4
Lower Kingswood KT20 ... 97 F1
Milford GU8 ... 170 E8
Morden SM4 ... 40 B3
New Malden KT3 ... 38 C4
North Cheam KT4 ... 39 A1
Penge SE20 ... 23 D1
Purley CR8 ... 60 D1
Redhill RH1 ... 118 E3
Redhill, Whitebushes RH1 .. 140 A4
Reigate RH2 ... 117 F1
Sandhurst GU47 ... 64 C7
Shamley Green GU5 ... 153 A7
Shepperton TW17 ... 34 C4
South Norwood CR7, SW16 .. 42 B8
South Nutfield RH1 ... 140 F1
Streatham SW16 ... 21 F1
Tilford GU10 ... 147 E6
West Clandon GU4 ... 111 B8
West Horsley GU23, KT24 ... 92 B3
Wood St V GU3 ... 108 A3
Green La E GU3 ... 128 B8
Green La W GU12 ... 127 E8
Green Lane Ave KT12 ... 54 C5
Green Lane Cl
Addlestone KT16 ... 51 E8
Byfleet KT14 ... 71 F7
Camberley GU15 ... 65 C7
Green Lane Cotts GU10 .. 167 F1
Green Lane Cty Inf Sch GU7 ... 129 E1
Green Lane Gdns CR7 ... 42 C7
Green Lane Prim Sch KT4 39 B2
Green Lanes KT19 ... 57 E2
Green Leaf Ave SM6 ... 60 D6
Green Leas Ashford TW16 .. 14 F2
Kingston u T KT1 ... 37 E6
Green Leas Cl TW16 ... 14 F2
Green Man La TW14 ... 4 A3
Green Mead KT10 ... 54 F4
Green Pk TW18 ... 12 E5
Green Rd KT16, TW20 ... 32 B5
Green Sch for Girls The TW7 ... 6 A6
Green St TW16 ... 35 A7
Green The Bracknell RG12 .. 27 B5
Broadbridge Heath RH12 .. 216 D4
Burgh Heath KT20 ... 97 E8
Carshalton SM6 ... 60 A8
Chiddingfold GU8 ... 191 C3
Claygate KT10 ... 55 F4
Copthorne RH10 ... 183 B3
Crawley RH11 ... 201 C7
Ewell KT17 ... 77 A7
Ewhurst GU6 ... 175 E4
Farnham GU9 ... 126 A6
Feltham TW13 ... 15 B6
Fetcham KT22 ... 94 D3
Frimley GU16 ... 85 F6
Hale GU9 ... 125 C6
Heston TW5 ... 5 A8
Kingston u T KT3 ... 38 C7
Merton SM4 ... 39 E5
New Addington CR0 ... 62 F2
7 Richmond TW9 ... 6 D2
Staines TW18 ... 13 D3
Sutton SM1 ... 59 B7
The Sands GU10 ... 126 E1
Twickenham TW2 ... 16 E6
Tyler's Green RH9 ... 121 C4
Warlingham CR6 ... 81 D1
Whiteley Village KT12 ... 53 E1
Wimbledon SW19 ... 19 D3
Woldingham CR3 ... 102 A4
Green View
Chessington KT9 ... 56 F3
Godstone RH9 ... 121 B4
Green Way
Aldershot GU12 ... 105 E3
Redhill RH1 ... 118 E3
Sunbury TW16 ... 35 A5
Green Wlk Crawley RH10 .. 201 E8
Hampton TW12 ... 15 F2
Green Wood SL5 ... 28 C8
Green Wrythe Cres SM5 .. 40 E1
Green Wrythe La SM4, SM5 ... 40 E2
Green Wrythe Prim Sch SM5 ... 40 D3
Green's School La GU14 .. 85 A4
Greenacre Knaphill GU21 ... 68 E3
Whyteleafe CR3 ... 101 B7
Greenacre Ct TW20 ... 11 C2
Greenacre Pl SM6 ... 60 B8
Greenacre Sch for Girls SM7 ... 78 B6
Greenacres Crawley RH10 . 202 A5
Farnham GU10 ... 126 C2
Great Bookham KT23 ... 94 A3
Horsham RH12 ... 217 C4
Oxted RH8 ... 122 E8
Greenaway Terr TW19 ... 13 E7
Greenbank Way GU15 ... 65 D2
Greenbush La GU6 ... 174 F1
Greencroft
2 Farnborough GU14 ... 85 B4
Guildford GU1 ... 110 B1
Greencroft Rd TW5 ... 4 F6
Greene Fielde End TW18 . 13 D1
Greenfield Ave KT5 ... 38 B3
Greenfield House 23 SW19 ... 19 D7
Greenfield Link CR5 ... 79 E4
Greenfield Rd
Farnham GU9, GU10 ... 146 A7
Slinfold RH13 ... 215 D3
Wrecclesham GU9 ... 145 F7
Greenfield Sch GU22 ... 89 E8
Greenfield Way RG45 ... 45 A7
Greenfields Cl Horley RH6 160 E5
Horsham RH12 ... 218 A6
Greenfields Pl RH5 ... 157 D4
Greenfields Rd
Horley RH6 ... 160 F5
Horsham RH12 ... 218 A5
Greenfields Sch
East Grinstead RH19 ... 205 D6
Forest Row RH18 ... 206 C1
Greenfields Way RH12 ... 218 A6
Greenfinch Way RH12 ... 217 D7
Greenford Rd SM1 ... 59 B6
Greenham House TW7 ... 5 D4
Greenham Wlk GU21 ... 69 C1
Greenham Wood RG12 ... 27 C3
Greenhanger GU10 ... 188 A8
Greenhayes Ave SM7 ... 78 A4
Greenhayes Cl RH2 ... 118 C1
Greenhayes Gdns SM7 ... 78 A4
Greenhayes Sch BR4 ... 63 C8
Greenheys Pl GU22 ... 69 F1
Greenhill SM1 ... 59 C8
Greenhill Ave CR3 ... 101 B6
Greenhill Cl
Godalming GU7 ... 150 D3
Wrecclesham GU9 ... 146 A7
Greenhill Gdns GU4 ... 110 C3
Greenhill La CR6 ... 81 F2
Greenhill Rd GU9 ... 146 D8
Greenhill Way
Farnham GU9 ... 146 A7
Wrecclesham GU9 ... 146 A7
Greenhills GU9 ... 146 E8
Greenholme GU15 ... 66 D5
Greenhow RG12 ... 27 B4
Greenhurst La RH8 ... 123 A3
Greenhurst Rd SE27 ... 22 A3
Greenlake Terr TW18 ... 13 A1
Greenlands Rd
Camberley GU15 ... 65 B1
Staines TW18 ... 13 A4
Weybridge KT13 ... 53 C7
Greenlaw Gdns KT3 ... 38 F2
Greenlea Pk SW19 ... 40 E8
Greenleaf Cl 8 SW2 ... 22 A8
Greenleas GU16 ... 65 E2
Greenleaves Ct TW15 ... 14 B2
Greenmead Cl SE25 ... 43 A4
Greenmeads GU22 ... 89 E5
Greeno Cres TW17 ... 34 A4
Greenoak Rise TN16 ... 83 C1
Greenoak Way SW19 ... 19 D4
Greenock Rd SW16 ... 41 D8
Greensand Cl RH1 ... 119 D7
Greensand Rd RH1 ... 119 A2
Greenside Cl Catford SE6 .. 24 D6
Guildford GU4 ... 110 C3
Greenside Cotts GU23 ... 91 C6
Greenside Rd CR0 ... 42 A2
Greenside Wlk TN16 ... 83 B1
Greensleeves Manor SM2 . 59 B4
Greenstede Ave RH19 ... 185 F2
Greenvale Prim Sch CR2 .. 81 D8
Greenvale Rd GU21 ... 68 D1
Greenvale Spec Sch SE23 . 23 E5
Greenview Ave CR0 ... 43 E3
Greenview Ct TW15 ... 13 F4
Greenway
Great Bookham KT23 ... 94 B4
Horsham RH12 ... 217 B3
Tatsfield TN16 ... 103 C7
Wallington SM6 ... 60 C3
West Barnes SW20 ... 39 C5
Greenway Cl KT14 ... 71 A6
Greenway Dr TW18 ... 33 D8
Greenway Gdns CR0 ... 62 F7
Greenway Jun Sch RH12 . 217 B3
Greenway The Epsom KT18 . 76 A5
Hounslow TW4 ... 4 F3
Oxted RH8 ... 123 B2
Greenways
Beckenham BR3 ... 44 A7
Egham TW20 ... 11 E3
Forest Hill SE26 ... 23 C4
Hinchley Wood KT10 ... 55 E6
Sandhurst GU47 ... 45 B1
Walton on t H KT20 ... 97 B2
Greenways Dr SL5 ... 29 E1
Greenways The 1 TW1 ... 6 A1
Greenways Wlk RH11 ... 201 C1
Greenwich Cl RH11 ... 201 C2
Greenwood
4 Bracknell RG12 ... 27 F5
8 Putney SW19 ... 19 D8
Greenwood Cl
Hinchley Wood KT7 ... 37 A1
Merton SM4 ... 39 E5
Woodham KT15 ... 70 F8
Greenwood Ct 2 RH11 .. 201 B1
Greenwood Dr RH1 ... 140 A4
Greenwood Gdns CR3 ... 101 A2
Greenwood La TW12 ... 16 B3
Greenwood Pk KT2 ... 18 E1
Greenwood Prim Sch CR4 41 D6
Greenwood Rd
Crowthorne RG45 ... 45 B6
Hinchley Wood KT7 ... 56 A8
Isleworth TW7 ... 5 F4
Knaphill GU21 ... 88 E7
Mitcham CR4 ... 41 D6
Pirbright GU24 ... 87 C7
Thornton Heath CR0, CR9 ... 42 C2
Greenwood The GU1 ... 110 A1
Gregan Ct GU11 ... 104 F1
Gregory Cl Crawley RH10 . 202 C2
Woking GU21 ... 69 C2
Gregory Ct CR8 ... 80 B6
Gregsons RH12 ... 216 E8
Grena Gdns TW9 ... 6 F3
Grena Rd TW10, TW9 ... 6 F3
Grenaby Ave CR0 ... 42 D2
Grenaby Rd CR0 ... 42 D2
Grenadier Rd GU12 ... 106 B4
Grenadiers Way GU14 ... 84 C3
Grendon Cl RH6 ... 160 F5
Grenehurst Pk RH5 ... 178 B4
Grenfell Rd CR4, SW17 ... 20 F2
Grennell Cl SM1 ... 59 D8
Grennell Rd SM1 ... 59 C8
Grenside Rd KT13 ... 53 B7
Grenville Cl Cobham KT11 .. 73 E6
Tolworth KT5 ... 38 C1
Grenville Ct SE19 ... 22 F3
Grenville Gdns GU16 ... 85 E6
Grenville Mews TW12 ... 16 B3
Grenville Rd
New Addington CR0 ... 63 C2
Shackleford GU8 ... 149 D7
Gresham Ave CR6 ... 81 E1
Gresham Cl RH8 ... 122 F7
Gresham Ct
Farnborough GU14 ... 105 C8
Hounslow TW3 ... 5 C6
Staines TW18 ... 13 A3
Gresham House
2 Teddington TW11 ... 16 F3
3 Thames Ditton KT7 ... 37 A2
Gresham Ind Est GU12 ... 105 E2
Gresham Prim Sch CR2 ... 81 A8
Gresham Rd Croydon SE25 . 43 A5
Hampton TW12 ... 16 A2
Hounslow TW3, TW5 ... 5 C6
Limpsfield RH8 ... 122 F6
Penge BR3 ... 43 E7
Staines TW18 ... 13 A3
Gresham Way
Frimley GU16 ... 85 E6
Wimbledon SW19 ... 20 A5
Gresham Way Est SW19 ... 20 B5
Gresham Wlk RH10 ... 201 E3
Gressenhall Rd SW18 ... 19 F8
Greta Bank KT24 ... 92 C1
Greville Ave CR2 ... 62 D1
Greville Cl Ashstead KT21 .. 95 E8
Guildford GU2 ... 108 E1
Twickenham TW1 ... 17 B8
Greville Ct Ashstead KT21 .. 75 E1
Fetcham KT23 ... 94 C2
Greville Cty Prim Sch The KT21 ... 75 F2
Greville Park Ave KT21 ... 75 E1
Greville Park Rd KT21 ... 75 E1
Greville Rd TW10 ... 6 F1
Grey Alders KT17 ... 77 C5
Grey Court Sch TW10 ... 17 C5
Greycot Rd BR3 ... 24 A3
Greyfields Cl CR8 ... 80 B6
Greyfriars 10 SE26 ... 23 A5
Greyfriars Dr Ascot SL5 ... 29 B3
Bisley GU24 ... 68 A4
Greyfriars Rd GU23 ... 91 A3
Greyhound Cl GU12 ... 105 F1
Greyhound La SW16 ... 21 D2
Greyhound Rd SM1 ... 59 C5
Greyhound Slip RH10 ... 202 D7
Greyhound Terr SW16 ... 41 C8
Greylees GU7 ... 150 E5
Greys Ct GU11 ... 104 E2
Greystead Pk GU10 ... 145 E5
Greystead Rd SE23 ... 23 C8
Greystoke Ct RG45 ... 45 A4
Greystone Cl CR2 ... 81 C8
Greystones Cl RH1 ... 139 D7
Greystones Dr RH2 ... 118 C3
Greyswood St SW16 ... 21 B2
Greythorne Rd GU21 ... 69 A1
Greywaters GU5 ... 152 A6
Grice Ave TN16 ... 83 C6
Grier Cl RH11 ... 200 E5
Grierson House SW16 ... 21 C4
Grierson Rd SE23 ... 23 D8
Griesse Cl GU10 ... 126 E7
Griffin Ct Ashstead KT21 ... 95 E8
8 Brentford TW8 ... 6 E8
Great Bookham KT23 ... 94 B1
Griffin Ctr KT1 ... 37 D7
Griffin Ctr The TW14 ... 4 B1
Griffin Pk (Brentford FC) TW8 ... 6 D8
Griffin Way
Great Bookham KT23 ... 94 A1
Sunbury TW16 ... 35 A7
Griffiths Cl KT4 ... 58 B8
Griffiths Rd SW19 ... 20 B1
Griffon Cl GU14 ... 84 D3
Griggs Meadow GU8 ... 192 F7
Grimwade Ave CR0 ... 62 A7
Grimwood Rd TW1 ... 16 F8
Grindall Cl CR0 ... 61 B6
Grindley Gdns CR0 ... 42 F3
Grindstone Cres GU21 ... 68 B1
Grindstone Handle Cnr GU21 ... 68 C1
Grinstead La RH19 ... 205 B1
Grisedale Cl
Crawley RH11 ... 201 C4
Sanderstead CR8 ... 80 E5
Grisedale Gdns CR8 ... 80 E5
Grizedale Terr SE23 ... 23 B6
Grobars Ave GU21 ... 69 C4
Groom Cres SW18 ... 20 D8
Groombridge Cl KT12 ... 54 B5
Groombridge House SE20 23 D1
Groombridge Way RH12 . 216 F1
Groomfield Cl SW17 ... 21 A4
Grooms The RH10 ... 202 D8
Grosslea SM4 ... 40 D4
Grosvenor Ave
Mortlake SW14 ... 7 E4
Richmond TW10 ... 6 E2
Wallington SM5, SM6 ... 60 A4
Grosvenor Ct
Blackwater GU17 ... 64 D3
Guildford GU4 ... 110 B4
Morden SM4 ... 40 A5
Penge SE19 ... 22 F2
2 Richmond TW10 ... 6 F1
1 Sutton SM2 ... 59 C4
Teddington TW11 ... 17 A2
Wimbledon SW19 ... 19 E2
Grosvenor Gdns
Kingston u T KT2 ... 17 D2
Mortlake SW14 ... 7 E4
Wallington SM6 ... 60 C3
Grosvenor Hill SW19 ... 19 E2
Grosvenor Ho 8 GU1 ... 130 F8
Grosvenor Pl 1
Oatlands Park KT13 ... 53 D7
9 Woking GU21 ... 69 F2
Grosvenor Rd
Aldershot GU11 ... 105 A1
Brentford TW8 ... 6 D8
Croydon SE25 ... 43 A5
East Grinstead RH19 ... 185 D1
Godalming GU7 ... 150 E3
Hounslow TW3, TW4 ... 4 F4
Langley Vale KT18, KT21 ... 96 E8
Richmond TW10 ... 6 E2
Staines TW18 ... 13 A1
Twickenham TW1 ... 17 A7
Wallington SM6 ... 60 B5
West End GU24 ... 68 D6
West Wickham BR4 ... 63 B8
Groton Rd SW18 ... 20 B6
Grotto Rd Twickenham TW1 . 16 F6
Weybridge KT13 ... 53 B7
Grove Ave Epsom KT17 ... 76 E6
Sutton SM1, SM2 ... 59 A4
Twickenham TW1 ... 16 F7
Grove Cl Cranleigh GU6 ... 174 F1
Forest Hill SE23 ... 23 E7
8 Kingston u T KT1 ... 37 F5
Old Windsor SL4 ... 11 B8
Grove Cnr KT23 ... 94 B1
Grove Cres Feltham TW13 .. 15 E4
Kingston u T KT1 ... 37 E6
Walton-on-T KT12 ... 35 B2
Grove Cross Rd GU16 ... 65 D1
Grove Ct East Molesey KT8 . 36 D4
Egham TW20 ... 12 A3
Forest Hill SE26 ... 23 E4
Hounslow TW3 ... 5 A3
8 Kingston u T KT1 ... 37 E6
Kingston u T KT3 ... 38 E6
Penge SE20 ... 23 B1
Grove Cty Prim Sch The GU16 ... 65 E2
Grove End GU19 ... 47 F5
Grove End La KT10 ... 36 D1
Grove End Rd GU9 ... 146 B8
Grove Farm Ct CR4 ... 40 F4
Grove Gdns TW11 ... 17 A4
Grove Heath La GU23 ... 91 D4
Grove Heath N GU23 ... 91 B5
Grove Heath Rd GU23 ... 91 B4
Grove House
7 Epsom KT17 ... 76 E6
Old Windsor SL4 ... 11 C8
6 Redhill RH1 ... 118 F1
Walton-on-T KT12 ... 35 B2
Grove House Froebel Ed Inst SW15 ... 7 F1
Grove House Prim Sch SE27 ... 22 B6
Grove Jun & Inf Sch W4 ... 7 C8
Grove La Kingston u T KT1 .. 37 E5
Wallington CR5 ... 79 B5
Winkfield RG42 ... 8 B4
Grove Park Bridge W4 ... 7 C7
Grove Park Gdns W4 ... 7 C7
Grove Park Rd W4 ... 7 B7
Grove Park Terr W4 ... 7 B8
Grove Pl KT13 ... 53 C5
Grove Prep Sch The GU26 ... 188 D1
Grove Rd Ash GU12 ... 106 A3
Ashstead KT21 ... 95 F8

Grove Rd *continued*
Barnes SW13 7 F5
Beacon Hill GU26 188 C6
Camberley GU15 65 F5
Cheam SM2 59 A4
Chertsey KT16 32 F3
Cranleigh GU6 174 F1
East Molesey KT8 36 D5
Epsom KT17, KT18 76 E6
Godalming GU7 150 C3
Guildford GU1 110 C1
Horley RH6 160 F4
Hounslow TW3 5 A3
Hounslow TW7 5 E6
Kingston u T KT6 37 D4
Lingfield RH7 164 E5
Merton SW19 20 C1
Mitcham CR4 41 B7
Richmond TW10 6 F1
9 Richmond TW10 6 F2
Shepperton TW17 34 C3
Sutton SM2 59 A4
Tatsfield TN16 103 C7
Thornton Heath CR7 42 A5
Twickenham TW2 16 D5
Woking GU21 69 F3
Grove Rd Prim Sch TW3 5 A3
Grove Shaw KT20 97 E3
Grove Terr TW11 17 A4
Grove The Addlestone KT15 52 B5
Aldershot GU11 105 A1
Biggin Hill TN16 83 E1
Caterham CR3 100 C6
Coulsdon CR5 79 D5
Crawley RH11 201 C6
Egham TW20 12 A3
Epsom KT17 76 E6
Farnborough GU14 85 D1
Frimley GU16 65 D1
Horley RH6 161 B2
Hounslow TW7 5 E6
North Ascot SL5 28 C8
Teddington TW11 17 A4
1 Twickenham TW1 6 B1
Walton-on-T KT12 35 B2
West Wickham BR4 63 C7
Woking GU21 69 F3
Grove Way KT10 36 C1
Grove Wood Hill CR5 79 D5
Grovebarns TW18 13 A2
Grovebell Ind Est GU9 145 F7
Grovefields Ave GU16 65 D1
Grovehill Ct BR1 24 F2
Grovehill Rd RH1 118 F1
Groveland Ave SW16 21 F1
Groveland Rd BR3 43 F6
Groveland Way KT3 38 D4
Grovelands
East Molesey KT8 36 A5
Farnham GU10 146 E7
Horley RH6 161 B2
Kingston u T KT1 37 D5
Grovelands Rd CR8 79 F7
Grovelands Sch KT12 35 B3
Groveley Rd TW13, TW16 14 F3
Groveside KT23 114 A8
Groveside Cl
Carshalton SM5 59 E8
Great Bookham KT23 114 A8
Grovestile Waye TW14 14 D8
Grovewood 9 TW9 7 A6
Grovewood Ct 6 TW7 5 E6
Grub St RH8 123 C6
Guardian Ct GU8 148 C3
Guards Ct SL5 30 B2
Guerdon Pl RG12 27 D2
Guernsey Cl
Crawley RH11 201 A2
Guildford GU4 110 A6
Heston TW5 5 A7
Guernsey Farm Dr GU21 69 D4
Guernsey Gr SE24 22 C8
Guildables La RH8, TN8 144 E7
Guildcroft GU1 110 A1
Guildersfield Rd SW16 21 E1
Guildford Ave TW13 15 A6
Guildford Business Park Rd GU2 109 B2
Guildford Castle GU1 130 D7
Guildford Cath GU2 109 B1
Guildford Coll Markenfield House GU1 109 D1
Guildford Cty Sch GU2 130 B7
Guildford & Godalming By-Pass Rd
Compton GU3 129 E6
Guildford GU2 129 E6
Shackleford GU7 149 F6
Guildford Golf Club GU1 110 C1
Guildford High Sch for Girls GU1 109 E1
Guildford Ind Est GU2 109 A2
Guildford Lodge Dr KT24 112 F6
Guildford Mus GU1 130 D7
Guildford Park Ave GU2 130 B8
Guildford Park Rd GU2 130 C8
Guildford Rd
Abinger Hammer RH5 134 C3
Addlestone KT16 51 C5
Aldershot GU11, GU12 126 D7
Ash GU12, GU3 106 D3
Bagshot GU19 47 E3
Bisley GU24 67 F7
Broadbridge Heath RH12 216 B6
Chertsey KT16 32 F1
Cranleigh GU6 174 B6
Farncombe GU7 151 B7
Guildford Rd *continued*
Farnham GU10, GU9 125 F4
Farnham, Runfold GU10 126 B4
Fetcham KT22 94 F3
Frimley GU16 85 F6
Great Bookham KT23 94 A1
Horsham RH12 217 A2
Lightwater GU18, GU19 48 B1
Mytchett GU16 86 B5
Normandy GU3 107 B4
Ottershaw KT16 51 C5
Pirbright GU3 88 C2
Rowhook RH12, RH13 215 C7
Rowly GU6 174 B6
Rudgwick RH12 214 C6
Shamley Green GU5 153 A1
Slinfold RH12, RH13 215 C7
Thornton Heath CR0 42 D3
West End GU24 67 F7
West End, Castle Green GU21, GU24 68 D6
Westcott RH4 135 C6
Windlesham GU19 47 F2
Woking GU22, GU4 89 E8
Woking, Westfield GU22, GU4 89 D4
Wotton RH5 134 C3
Guildford Rd E GU14 85 C1
Guildford Rd W GU14 85 C1
Guildford Road Trad Est GU9 125 D3
Guildford Sch of Acting GU2 130 D7
Guildford St Chertsey KT16 33 A2
Staines TW18 13 A2
Guildford Sta GU1 130 C8
Guildford Way SM6 60 E5
Guildown Ave GU2 130 B6
Guildown Rd GU2 130 C6
Guileshill La GU23 91 F5
Guilford Ave KT5 37 F6
Guillemont Fields GU14 84 D5
Guillemont Jun Sch GU14 84 D7
Guillemot Path 2 RH11 200 D5
Guinevere Rd RH11 200 E6
Guinness Ct Crawley RH11 201 C2
4 Knaphill GU21 68 F1
3 South Croydon CR0 61 F8
Gull Cl SM6 60 E3
Gulliver Ct CR0 61 B3
Gumbrells Cl GU3 108 C5
Gumley Gdns TW7 6 A4
Gumley House Convent Sch for Girls TW7 6 A4
Gun Hill GU11 105 B3
Gun Pit Rd RH7 164 D4
Gunnell Cl SE25 43 A3
Gunnell Ct CR4 40 E8
Gunners Rd SW18 20 D6
Gunning Cl RH11 201 A3
Gunters Mead KT22 74 C8
Gunton Rd SW17 21 A2
Gurdon's La GU8 170 F2
Gurney Cres CR0 41 F1
Gurney Rd SM5 60 A6
Gurney's Cl 3 RH1 139 F8
Guy Rd CR0, SM6 60 D7
Guyatt Gdns CR4 41 A7
Gwydor Rd BR3 43 D6
Gwydyr Rd BR2 44 F6
Gwynne Ave CR0 43 D2
Gwynne Gdns RH19 185 C2
Gwynne House 6 SW2 21 F7
Gwynne Rd CR3 100 D4
Gwynne Vaughan Ave GU2 109 B5

H

H Jones Cres GU11 105 C3
Habershon Dr GU16 66 D2
Haccombe Rd SW19 20 C2
Hackbridge Inf Sch SM6 41 A1
Hackbridge Jun Sch SM5 41 A1
Hackbridge Park Gdns SM5 59 F8
Hackbridge Rd SM5, SM6 60 A8
Hackbridge Sta SM6 60 B8
Hackenden Cl RH19 185 E3
Hackenden La RH19 185 E3
Hacketts La GU22 70 F4
Hackhurst La RH5 133 F4
Hackington Cres BR3 24 A2
Haddenham Ct SW17 20 D4
Haddington Rd BR1 24 D4
Haddon Cl New Malden KT3 38 F4
Oatlands Park KT13 53 D6
Haddon Rd SM1 59 B6
Hadfield Rd TW19 2 D1
Hadleigh Cl SW20 39 F7
Hadleigh Dr SM2 59 B2
Hadleigh Gdns GU16 85 E6
Hadley Ct SL3 1 E6
Hadley Pl KT13 53 A3
Hadley Rd CR4 41 D5
Hadley Wood Rise CR8 80 B5
Hadleys GU10 145 E3
Hadlow Pl SE19 23 A1
Hadmans Cl RH12 217 C1
Hadrian Cl Stanwell TW19 13 E8
Wallington SM6 60 E3
Hadrian Ct 1 SM2 59 B3
Hadrian Way
Stanwell TW19 13 D8
Stanwell TW19 13 E8
Hadrians GU9 125 E4
Hafton Rd SE6 24 E6
Haggard Rd TW1 17 B8
Haig Pl SM4 40 A3
Haig Rd Aldershot GU12 105 C1
Biggin Hill TN16 83 E2
Sandhurst GU15 64 F6
Haigh Cres RH1 140 B7
Hailes Cl SW19 20 C2
Hailey Pl GU6 174 F4
Hailsham Ave SW2 21 F6
Hailsham Cl
Sandhurst GU47 45 D1
Surbiton KT6 37 D2
Hailsham Rd SW17 21 A2
Haines Ct KT13 53 D5
Haines Wlk SM4 40 B2
Haining Gdns GU16 86 A3
Hainthorpe Rd SE27 22 B4
Halcyon Ct TW18 33 B7
Haldane Pl SW18 20 B7
Hale Cty Prim Sch GU9 125 B7
Hale End RG12 27 F5
Hale Ends GU22 89 B6
Hale House Cl GU10 167 F1
Hale House La GU10 168 B2
Hale Pit Rd KT23 94 C1
Hale Pl GU9 125 E5
Hale Rd Farnham GU9 125 D4
Hale GU9 125 D5
Hale Rdbt GU9 125 E5
Hale Reeds GU9 125 E6
Hale St TW18 12 E4
Hale Way GU16 85 D8
Halebourne La GU24 49 A2
Hales Ct 5 TW11 17 A3
Hales Field GU27 208 C6
Hales House 3 SW12 21 B8
Hales Oak KT23 94 C1
Halesowen Rd SM4 40 B2
Haleswood KT11 73 C5
Halewood RG12 26 F3
Half Acre TW8 6 D8
Half Acre Mews TW8 6 D8
Half Moon Hill GU27 208 C6
Half Moon St GU19 47 E3
Half Way Cotts GU10 124 C3
Halford Rd TW10 6 E2
Halfpenny Cl GU4 131 D3
Halfpenny Cross KT11 73 A2
Halfpenny Ct SL5 30 B2
Halfpenny La
Guildford GU4 131 C5
Sunningdale SL5 30 A2
Halfway La GU7 150 B4
Haliburton Rd TW1, TW7 6 A3
Halifax Cl Crawley RH10 182 E1
Farnborough GU14 84 F3
Halifax St SE26 23 B5
Halimote Rd GU11 105 A1
Haling Down Pas CR8 61 C1
Haling Gr CR2 61 C3
Haling Manor High Sch CR2 61 B3
Haling Manor High Sch (Pampisford Wing) CR2 61 B2
Haling Park Gdns CR2 61 B4
Haling Park Rd CR2 61 C4
Haling Rd CR2 61 D4
Hall Cl Camberley GU15 65 E6
Farncombe GU7 150 E7
Hall Ct TW11 16 F3
Hall Dene Cl GU1 110 C2
Hall Dr SE26 23 C3
Hall Farm Dr TW2 16 D8
Hall Grove (Sch) GU19 48 A5
Hall Hill RH8 122 D4
Hall La UB3 3 D7
Hall Pl GU21 70 A3
Hall Place Dr KT13 53 E5
Hall Rd Bramley GU5 151 F6
Isleworth TW7 5 D2
Wallington SM6 60 B2
Hall Sch Wimbledon SW15 19 A5
Hall Way CR8 80 B6
Hallam Rd GU7 150 F5
Halland Cl RH10 202 A7
Hallane House SE27 22 C3
Halley Cl RH11 201 B1
Halley Dr SL5 28 D7
Halley's App GU21 69 A1
Halley's Ct 1 GU21 69 A1
Halley's Wlk KT15 52 C3
Hallgrove Bottom GU19 47 F5
Halliards The KT12 35 A3
Halliford Cl TW17 34 E6
Halliford Rd
Sunbury TW16 35 A5
Upper Halliford TW16, TW17 34 F5
Halliford Sch TW17 34 C2
Hallington Cl GU21 69 B2
Hallmark Cl GU47 64 E8
Hallmead Rd SM1 59 B7
Hallowell Ave CR0 60 E6
Hallowell Cl CR4 41 A6
Hallowfield Way CR4 40 E6
Halls Farm Cl GU21 68 D2
Hallsland RH10 204 C8
Hallsland Way RH8 122 F3
Halnaker Wlk 9 RH11 200 F3
Halsford Croft RH19 185 B3
Halsford Gn RH19 185 B3
Halsford La RH19 185 C3
Halsford Park Cty Prim Sch RH19 185 C2
Halsford Park Rd RH19 185 C2
Halters End GU26 188 A3
Ham Cl TW10 17 C5
Ham Comm TW10 17 D5
Ham Farm Rd KT2, TW10 17 E4
Ham Gate Ave
Richmond TW10 17 E4
Richmond, Richmond Park TW10 18 A4
Ham House TW10 17 D3
Ham La Elstead GU8 148 E4
Englefield Green TW20 11 B4
Ham Ridings TW10 17 F3
Ham St TW10 17 C5
Ham The TW8 6 C7
Ham View CR0 43 E3
Hamble Ave GU17 64 D5
Hamble Cl GU21 69 A2
Hamble Ct KT1 17 D1
Hamble Wlk GU21 69 A2
Hambleden Ct RG12 27 E5
Hambledon Ct 9 SM6 60 B4
Hambledon Gdns SE25 42 F6
Hambledon Hill KT18 76 C3
Hambledon House 2 KT2 18 B2
Hambledon Inf Sch GU8 171 D2
Hambledon Pk GU8 171 B1
Hambledon Pl
Dulwich SE21 22 F7
Little Bookham KT23 94 A4
Hambledon Rd
Caterham CR3 100 D4
Godalming GU8, GU7 171 D5
Hambledon GU8, GU7 171 D5
Hydestile GU8, GU7 171 D5
Wandsworth SW18 19 F8
Hambledon Vale KT18 76 C3
Hambleton Cl Frimley GU16 66 B3
North Cheam KT4 58 C8
Hambleton Ct RH11 201 C4
Hambleton Hill RH11 201 C4
Hambridge Way SW2 22 A8
Hambro Rd SW16 21 D3
Hambrook Rd SE25 43 B6
Hamers House 10 SW2 22 A8
Hamesmoor Rd GU16 85 F4
Hamesmoor Way GU16 85 F4
Hamfield Cl RH8 122 C8
Hamilton Ave Cheam SM3 58 E8
Cobham KT11 73 A6
Pyrford GU22 70 E3
Tolworth KT6, SM3 57 A8
Hamilton Cl TW13 14 F3
Hamilton Cl GU19 47 E2
Hamilton Cl Chertsey KT16 32 F1
Epsom KT19 76 C7
Guildford GU2 109 A6
Purley CR8 80 B7
Hamilton Cres TW3 5 B2
Hamilton Ct Catford SE6 24 F7
Cobham KT11 73 A6
Croydon CR0 43 A1
Farnborough GU17 64 E1
Great Bookham KT23 94 B2
Hamilton Dr
Guildford GU2 109 A6
Sunningdale SL5 29 E2
Hamilton House
Chiswick W4 7 E8
10 Richmond TW9 7 A6
Hamilton Mews KT13 53 A6
Hamilton Par TW13 15 A4
Hamilton Pl
Guildford GU2 109 A6
Kingswood KT20 97 F4
Sunbury TW16 15 B1
Hamilton Rd Brentford TW8 6 D8
Feltham TW13 14 F4
Horsham RH12 217 B3
Merton SW19 20 B1
South Norwood CR7 42 D6
Twickenham TW2 16 E7
West Norwood SE27 22 D4
Hamilton Road Ind Est SE27 22 D4
Hamilton Road Mews 1 SW19 20 B1
Hamilton Way SM6 60 D2
Hamlash Cotts GU10 146 C2
Hamlash La GU10 146 C1
Hamlet Rd SE19 23 A1
Hamlet St RG42 27 E8
Hamlyn Gdns SE19 22 E1
Hamm Court Est KT13 52 F8
Hamm Moor La KT15 52 E6
Hammelton Ct BR1 44 F8
Hammelton Rd BR1 44 F8
Hammer Hill GU27 207 C4
Hammer La
Grayshott GU10, GU26 187 E6
Haslemere GU27, GU30 207 A6
Haslemere GU26 207 C8
Linchmere GU27 207 C5
Hammer Vale GU27 207 B6
Hammer Yd RH10 201 D5
Hammerfield Dr RH5 133 F3
Hammerpond Rd RH13 217 F1
Hammersley Rd GU11 105 C7
Hammerwood Copse GU27 207 D5
Hammerwood Rd RH19 206 E6
Hammond Ave CR4 41 B7
Hammond Cl
Hampton TW12 36 A8
Woking GU21 69 C4
Hammond Cty Jun Sch GU18 48 A1
Hammond Rd GU21 69 C4
Hammond Way GU18 48 B1
Hamond Cl CR2 61 B2
Hampden Ave BR3 43 E7
Hampden Cl RH10 182 E1
Hampden Rd
Beckenham BR3 43 E7
Kingston u T KT1 38 A6
Hamper's La RH13 218 A2
Hampers Ct RH13 217 D2
Hampshire Cl GU12 126 D7
Hampshire Ct
Addlestone KT15 52 C5
Barnes SW13 7 F5
Hampshire Rd GU15 65 F8
Hampstead La RH4 135 F6
Hampstead Rd RH4 136 A6
Hampton Cl SW20 19 C1
Hampton Court Ave KT8 36 E3
Hampton Court Cres KT8 36 D6
Hampton Court Palace KT8 36 F6
Hampton Court Par KT8 36 E5
Hampton Court Rd KT1, KT8 37 B6
Hampton Court Sta KT8 36 E5
Hampton Court Way KT10, KT7, KT8 36 E3
Hampton Farm Ind Est TW13 15 E5
Hampton Gr KT17 76 F8
Hampton Hill Bsns Pk TW12 16 C3
Hampton Hill Jun Mix Sch TW12 16 C3
Hampton Inf Sch TW12 16 A1
Hampton Jun Sch TW12 36 A8
Hampton La TW13 15 E4
Hampton Lodge RH6 161 A2
Hampton Rd Hale GU9 125 B6
North Cheam KT4 58 B8
Redhill RH1 139 F4
Teddington TW11, TW12 16 E3
Thornton Heath CR0 42 C3
Twickenham TW2 16 D5
Hampton Rd E TW13 15 F5
Hampton Rd W TW13 15 E5
Hampton Road Ind Pk CR0 42 C3
Hampton Sch TW12 16 A3
Hampton Sta TW12 36 A8
Hampton Way RH19 205 F7
Hampton Wick Inf Sch KT1 17 D1
Hampton Wick Sta KT1 37 C8
Hamsey Green Cty Inf Sch CR6 81 B3
Hamsey Green Cty Jun Sch CR6 81 B3
Hamsey Green Gdns CR6 81 C3
Hamsey Way CR2 81 B4
Hanbury Dr TN16 83 B6
Hanbury Path GU21 70 D5
Hanbury Rd RH11 200 E5
Hanbury Way GU15 65 C3
Hancock Rd SE19 22 D2
Hancocks Mount SL5 29 D3
Hancombe Rd GU47 45 A1
Handcroft Rd CR0 42 B1
Handel House TW2 5 D1
Handside Cl KT4 39 D1
Handsworth House 8 RH10 201 D5
Hanford Cl SW18 20 A7
Hanger Hill KT13 53 B5
Hanley Pl BR3 24 A1
Hannah Cl BR3 44 C6
Hannah Ct SW19 19 D1
Hannah Peschar Gall & Gdn RH5 177 A2
Hannay Wlk SW16 21 D6
Hannen Rd SE27 22 B5
Hannibal Rd TW19 13 E8
Hannibal Way CR0 60 F4
Hanning Lodge TW3 5 C3
Hanover Ave TW13 15 A6
Hanover Cl Cheam SM3 58 F6
Crawley RH10 201 F3
Englefield Green TW20 11 B2
Frimley GU16 65 E1
Merstham RH1 119 C7
Richmond TW9 7 A7
Hanover Ct Dorking RH4 135 F7
Horsham RH13 217 F3
1 Penge SE19 23 A1
Woking GU22 89 E8
Hanover Gdns
Bracknell RG12 26 F2
Farnborough GU14 84 E6
Hanover House KT6 38 A1
Hanover Rd SW19 20 C1
Hanover St CR0, CR9 61 B7
Hanover Terr TW7 6 A6
Hanover Wlk KT13 53 E7
Hansler Gr KT8 36 D5
Hanson Cl Balham SW12 21 B8
Beckenham BR3 24 B2
Camberley GU15 66 B7
Guildford GU1 109 F4
Mortlake SW14 7 C4
Hanworth Cl RG12 27 C3
Hanworth La KT16 32 F1
Hanworth Rd
Bracknell RG12 27 A2
Feltham TW13 15 B7
Hampton TW12 16 A3
Hounslow TW3, TW4 5 B2
Redhill RH1 139 F4
Sunbury TW16 15 A1
Twickenham TW4 15 F8

Hanworth Terr TW3 . . . . .5 B3
Hanworth Trad Est
Chertsey KT16 . . . . .32 F1
Feltham TW13 . . . . .15 E5
Harberson Rd SW12 . . . . . .21 B7
Harbin House 5 SW2 . . . . .22 A7
Harbledown Rd CR2 . . . . . .81 A8
Harborough Rd SW16 . . . . .21 F4
Harbour Cl GU14 . . . . .85 A8
Harbourfield Rd SM7 . . . . .78 B4
Harbridge Ave SW15 . . . . .19 A8
Harbury Rd SM5 . . . . .59 E3
Harcourt Ave SM6 . . . . .60 B6
Harcourt Cl Egham TW20 . .12 C2
Isleworth TW7 . . . . .6 A4
Harcourt Field SM6 . . . . . .60 B6
Harcourt Lodge 2 SM6 . . .60 B6
Harcourt Rd Bracknell RG12 27 B4
Camberley GU15 . . . . .65 B5
Merton SW19 . . . . .20 A1
Thornton Heath CR7 . . . . . . .42 A3
Wallington SM6 . . . . .60 B6
Harcourt Way RH9 . . . . . .142 E6
Hardcastle Cl SE25 . . . . . . .43 A3
Hardcourts Cl BR4 . . . . . . .63 B7
Hardel Rise SW2 . . . . .22 B8
Hardel Wlk SE24, SW2 . . . .22 A8
Hardell Cl TW20 . . . . .12 A3
Hardham Cl RH11 . . . . . . .201 A8
Harding Cl Kingston u T KT2 .37 F8
South Croydon CR0 . . . . .61 F7
Harding Ct SE25 . . . . .42 F7
Harding House SM6 . . . . . .60 C2
Harding Pl SE23 . . . . .23 E8
Harding Rd KT18 . . . . .96 E8
Hardings La SE20 . . . . .23 D2
Hardman Rd KT2 . . . . .37 E7
Hardwell Way RG12 . . . . . .27 E5
Hardwick Cl KT22 . . . . .74 C4
Hardwick La KT16 . . . . .32 D1
Hardwick Rd RH1 . . . . . . .139 D7
Hardwicke Ave TW5 . . . . . . .5 A6
Hardwicke Rd
Reigate RH2 . . . . .118 A2
Richmond TW10 . . . . .17 C4
Hardy Cl Crawley RH10 . . .202 C7
Dorking RH5 . . . . .136 B3
Horley RH6 . . . . .160 E3
Horsham RH12 . . . . .217 B4
Hardy Gn RG45 . . . . .45 B4
Hardy Rd SW19 . . . . .20 B1
Hardys Cl KT8 . . . . .36 E5
Hare Hill KT15 . . . . .51 F4
Hare Hill Cl GU22 . . . . .71 A4
Hare La Claygate KT10 . . . . .55 E4
Crawley RH11 . . . . .201 B8
Farncombe GU7 . . . . .150 F6
Horne RH7 . . . . .163 D5
Harebell Hill KT11 . . . . .73 E5
Harecroft
Dorking RH4, RH5 . . . . .136 C4
Fetcham KT23 . . . . .94 C3
Haredon Cl SE23 . . . . .23 D8
Harefield KT10 . . . . .55 E7
Harefield Ave SM2 . . . . .58 E2
Harefield Rd SW16 . . . . . . .21 F1
Harelands Cl GU21 . . . . . . .69 C2
Harelands La GU21 . . . . . . .69 C2
Harendon KT20 . . . . .97 D6
Hares Bank CR0 . . . . .63 D1
Harestone Dr CR3 . . . . . . .100 F2
Harestone Hill CR3 . . . . . .100 F2
Harestone La CR3 . . . . . . .100 E2
Harestone Valley Rd CR3 .100 F2
Harewood Cl
Crawley RH10 . . . . .182 A1
Reigate RH2 . . . . .118 C4
Harewood Gdns CR2 . . . . .81 C4
Harewood Rd
Guildford GU4 . . . . .110 C4
Hounslow TW7 . . . . .5 F6
Mitcham SW19 . . . . .20 E2
South Croydon CR2 . . . . .61 E4
Harfield Rd TW16 . . . . .35 D7
Harkness Cl KT17 . . . . .77 C3
Harland Ave CR0 . . . . .62 A7
Harland Fst Sch CR4 . . . . .40 D7
Harlech Ct 1 SE23 . . . . . . .23 C7
Harlech Gdns TW5 . . . . .4 C7
Harlech Rd GU17 . . . . .64 D4
Harlequin Ave TW8 . . . . .6 A8
Harlequin Cl TW7 . . . . .5 E2
Harlequin Rd TW11 . . . . . . .17 B1
Harlington Cl UB7 . . . . .3 C7
Harlington Cnr UB3 . . . . . . .3 D6
Harlington Rd
E TW13, TW14 . . . . .15 C7
Harlington Rd W TW14 . . . .4 B1
Harlow Ct 4 RH2 . . . . . . .118 D1
Harman Pl CR8 . . . . .80 B8
Harmans Dr RH19 . . . . . . .186 B1
Harmans Mead RH19 . . . .186 B1
Harmans Water Cty Inf
Sch RG12 . . . . .27 E4
Harmans Water Cty Jun
Sch RG12 . . . . .27 E4
Harmans Water Rd RG12 .27 D4
Harmar Cl RG40 . . . . .25 E6
Harmes Way GU14 . . . . . .105 D7
Harmondsworth La UB7 . . . .2 E8
Harmondsworth Prim Sch
UB7 . . . . .2 D8
Harmony Cl Crawley RH11 200 E4
Wallington SM6 . . . . .60 E2
Harms Gr GU4 . . . . .110 C4
Harold Rd Carshalton SM1 . .59 D6
Crawley RH10 . . . . .202 E5
South Norwood SE19 . . . . . . .22 D1
Haroldslea RH6 . . . . .161 E2
Haroldslea Cl RH6 . . . . . . .161 C1
Haroldslea Dr RH6 . . . . . .161 D1
Harpenden Rd SE27, SW16 .22 B6
Harper Dr RH10 . . . . .202 C2
Harper's Rd GU12 . . . . . . .106 C2
Harpesford Ave GU25 . . . . .31 C4
Harps Oak La RH1, RH2 . . .99 A2
Harpurs KT20 . . . . .97 D5
Harrier Cl GU6 . . . . .174 E4
Harrier Ct RH10 . . . . .182 D1
Harriet Gdns CR0 . . . . .62 A8
Harriet Tubman Cl SW2 . . .22 A8
Harrington Cl Leigh RH2 . .138 A2
Wallington CR0 . . . . .60 E8
Harrington Ct 7 CR0 . . . . .61 D8
Harrington Rd SE25 . . . . . .43 B5
Harriotts Cl KT22 . . . . .95 C7
Harriotts La KT21, KT22 . . .95 C8
Harris City Tech Coll SE19 .42 F8
Harris Cl Crawley RH11 . . .201 B3
Hounslow TW5 . . . . .5 A6
Harris Lodge SE6 . . . . .24 C7
Harris Way TW16 . . . . .34 E8
Harrison Cl RH2 . . . . .139 B8
Harrison Ct TW17 . . . . .34 B4
Harrison's Rise CR0, CR9 . .61 B7
Harrodian Sch SW13 . . . . . . .7 F7
Harrogate Ct 2 SE26 . . . . .23 A5
Harrow Bottom Rd GU25 . .31 F3
Harrow Cl Chertsey KT15 . . .52 B8
Chessington KT9 . . . . .56 D3
Dorking RH4 . . . . .136 A6
Harrow Gate Gdns RH4 . .136 A5
Harrow Gdns CR6 . . . . .81 F3
Harrow La GU7 . . . . .150 E7
Harrow Lodge SM2 . . . . . . .59 D4
Harrow Rd Ashford TW15 . .14 A6
Carshalton SM1, SM2, SM5 . .59 E4
Warlingham CR6 . . . . .81 F3
Harrow Rd E RH4 . . . . . . .136 B6
Harrow Rd W RH4 . . . . . . .136 A6
Harrow Way TW17 . . . . . . .34 C7
Harrowdene GU6 . . . . .174 E4
Harrowdene Ct SW19 . . . . .19 E3
Harrowdene Gdns TW11 . .17 A1
Harrowlands Pk RH4 . . . .136 B6
Harrowsley Ct RH6 . . . . . .161 B4
Hart Cl Bletchingley RH1 . . .120 E2
1 Bracknell RG42 . . . . .27 B8
Farnborough GU14 . . . . .84 E8
Hart Dene Cl GU19 . . . . . . .47 E3
Hart Dyke Cl RG41 . . . . . . .25 B2
Hart Gdns RH4 . . . . .136 B8
Hart House SW2 . . . . .22 A7
Hart Rd Byfleet KT14 . . . . . .71 E6
Dorking RH4 . . . . .136 B8
Hart The GU9 . . . . .125 B2
Hart's La RH9 . . . . .142 D7
Harte Rd TW3 . . . . .4 F5
Hartfield Cres SW19 . . . . . .19 F1
Hartfield Gr SE20 . . . . .43 C8
Hartfield Rd
Chessington KT9 . . . . .56 D5
Forest Row RH18 . . . . .206 F2
Merton SW19 . . . . .20 A1
Hartford Rd KT19 . . . . .57 B4
Hartford Rise GU15 . . . . . . .65 D6
Hartham Cl TW7 . . . . .6 A6
Hartham Rd TW7 . . . . .6 A6
Harting Ct RH11 . . . . .200 F3
Hartington Ct W4 . . . . .7 B7
Hartington Pl RH2 . . . . . . .118 A3
Hartington Rd Chiswick W4 . .7 C6
Twickenham TW1 . . . . .6 B1
Hartland Cl KT15 . . . . .52 C2
Hartland Pl GU14 . . . . .85 A7
Hartland Rd
Addlestone KT15 . . . . .52 A3
Cheam SM4 . . . . .40 B2
Hampton TW12 . . . . .16 B4
Isleworth TW7 . . . . .6 A4
Hartland Way Croydon CR0 .62 E8
Morden SM4 . . . . .39 F2
Hartlands The TW5 . . . . .4 B8
Hartley Cl GU17 . . . . .64 B5
Hartley Down CR5, CR8 . . . .79 F5
Hartley Farm CR8 . . . . .79 F4
Hartley Hill CR8 . . . . .79 F4
Hartley Old Rd CR8 . . . . . . .79 F5
Hartley Rd CR0 . . . . .42 C2
Hartley Way CR5, CR8 . . . . .79 F4
Harts Gdns GU2 . . . . .109 B4
Harts Leap Cl GU47 . . . . . . .45 B1
Harts Leap Rd GU47 . . . . . .64 A8
Harts Yd 14 GU9 . . . . .125 B2
Hartscroft CR0 . . . . .62 E2
Hartsgrove GU8 . . . . .191 B5
Hartshill GU2 . . . . .108 D2
Hartshill Wlk GU21 . . . . . . .69 B3
Hartspiece Rd RH1 . . . . . .140 B7
Hartswood RH5 . . . . .136 D4
Hartswood Ave RH2 . . . . . .139 A5
Hartswood House 10 SW2 .21 E7
Harvard Hill W4 . . . . .7 B8
Harvard Rd Hounslow TW7 . . .5 E6
Sandhurst GU47 . . . . .45 E1
Harvest Bank Rd BR4 . . . . .63 F7
Harvest Ct Beckenham BR3 .24 A1
Littleton TW17 . . . . .34 A5
Harvest Hill
East Grinstead RH19 . . . . . .205 E8
Godalming GU7 . . . . .150 D4
Harvest La KT7 . . . . .37 A3
Harvest Rd Crawley RH10 .202 C4
Harvest Rd *continued*
Englefield Green TW20 . . . . . .11 D2
Feltham TW13 . . . . .15 A5
Harvest Ride
RG12, RG42, SL5 . . . . .28 A8
Harvester Rd KT19 . . . . . . .57 D1
Harvesters RH12 . . . . .217 D5
Harvesters Cl TW7 . . . . .5 D2
Harvestside RH6 . . . . .161 C4
Harvey Cl RH11 . . . . .201 A1
Harvey Dr TW12 . . . . .36 A8
Harvey Lodge GU1 . . . . . .130 E8
Harvey Rd
Farnborough GU14 . . . . .84 C5
Guildford GU1 . . . . .130 E8
Twickenham TW4 . . . . .15 F8
Walton-on-T KT12 . . . . .35 A2
Harwarden Cl RH10 . . . . . .204 C8
Harwood Ave CR4 . . . . .40 E6
Harwood Gdns SL4 . . . . . . .11 B8
Harwood Pk RH1 . . . . .161 A8
Harwood Rd RH12, RH13 .218 A3
Harwoods Cl 3 RH19 . . . . .205 F7
Harwoods La RH19 . . . . . .205 F7
Hascombe Ct RH11 . . . . . .201 A5
Hascombe House 11 SW15 19 B7
Haseley End SE23 . . . . .23 C8
Haseltine Prim Sch SE6 . . .23 F4
Haseltine Rd SE26 . . . . . . .23 F4
Haslam Ave SM3, SM4 . . . . .39 E1
Hasle Dr GU27 . . . . .208 B6
Haslemere Ave
Cranford TW5 . . . . .4 C5
Mitcham CR4, SW19 . . . . . . .40 D7
Wimbledon SW18 . . . . .20 B6
Haslemere Cl Frimley GU16 66 C3
Hampton TW12 . . . . .15 F3
Wallington SM6 . . . . .60 E5
Haslemere & District
Hospl GU27 . . . . .208 D7
Haslemere Educational
Mus GU27 . . . . .208 D7
Haslemere Fst Sch CR4 . . .40 D7
Haslemere & Heathrow Est
The TW4 . . . . .4 B4
Haslemere Ind Est
Feltham TW14 . . . . .4 A2
Wimbledon SW18 . . . . .20 B6
Haslemere Prep Sch
GU27 . . . . .208 D5
Haslemere Rd Brook GU8 .170 C5
Kingsley Green GU27 . . . . .208 B1
Thornton Heath CR7 . . . . . . .42 B4
Witley GU8 . . . . .170 C5
Haslemere Sta GU27 . . . .208 B6
Haslett Ave E RH10 . . . . . .202 A6
Haslett Ave W
RH10, RH11 . . . . .201 D5
Haslett Rd TW17 . . . . .34 E7
Hassall Ct GU22 . . . . .90 A6
Hassocks Cl SE23, SE26 . . . .23 B5
Hassocks Ct 3 RH11 . . . . .200 F3
Hassocks Rd SW16 . . . . . . .41 D8
Haste Hill GU27 . . . . .208 D5
Hastings Cl GU16 . . . . .86 A7
Hastings Dr KT6 . . . . .37 C3
Hastings Pl 1 CR0 . . . . .42 F1
Hastings Rd Crawley RH10 202 C6
Croydon CR0 . . . . .42 F1
Hatch Cl Addlestone KT15 . .52 B7
Alfold Crossways GU6 . . . . .194 A3
Hatch End
Forest Row RH18 . . . . .206 F2
Windlesham GU20 . . . . .48 C4
Hatch Gdns KT20 . . . . .97 D7
Hatch Hill GU27 . . . . .208 B1
Hatch La
Harmondsworth TW6, UB7 . . .2 D7
Kingsley Green GU27 . . . . .208 B2
Ockham GU23 . . . . .72 B1
Ockham GU23 . . . . .92 B7
South Nutfield RH1 . . . . . . .140 F3
Wormley GU8 . . . . .190 D8
Hatch Pl TW10 . . . . .17 F3
Hatch Rd SW16 . . . . .41 E7
Hatch Ride RG45 . . . . .45 B7
Hatch Ride Cty Prim Sch
RG45 . . . . .45 B7
Hatches The Farnham GU9 145 F8
Frimley GU16 . . . . .85 F6
Hatchet La SL4, SL5 . . . . .9 B5
Hatchett Rd TW14 . . . . .14 C7
Hatchetts Dr GU27 . . . . . . .207 D7
Hatchford Park Sch KT11 .72 E1
Hatchgate RH6 . . . . .160 F2
Hatchgate Copse RG12 . . .26 E3
Hatchlands RH12 . . . . .218 A7
Hatchlands Pk GU4 . . . . . .111 F5
Hatchlands Rd RH1 . . . . . .118 E1
Hatfield Cl Belmont SM2 . . .59 B2
Mitcham CR4 . . . . .40 D5
West Byfleet KT14 . . . . .71 B7
Hatfield Gdns GU14 . . . . . .85 E3
Hatfield House 16 KT6 . . . .37 E4
Hatfield Mead SM4 . . . . . . .40 A4
Hatfield Prim Sch SM4 . . .39 E3
Hatfield Rd KT21 . . . . .95 F8
Hatfield Wlk RH11 . . . . . . .200 E2
Hathaway Ct 10 RH1 . . . . .119 A2
Hathaway Rd CR0 . . . . .42 B2
Hatherleigh Cl
Chessington KT9 . . . . .56 D5
Morden SM4 . . . . .40 A5
Hatherleigh House SM4 . .40 A5
Hatherley Rd TW9 . . . . .6 F6
Hatherop Rd TW12 . . . . . . .15 F1
Hathersham Cl RH6 . . . . . .162 A4
Hathersham La RH1, RH6 .161 F6
Hathersley House 3 SW2 .22 A8
Hatherwood KT21 . . . . .95 E6
Hatton Cross Rdbt TW6 . . . .3 F4
Hatton Cross Sta TW6 . . . . .3 F3
Hatton Gdns CR4 . . . . .40 F4
Hatton Gn TW14 . . . . .4 A3
Hatton Hill GU20 . . . . .48 C5
Hatton Rd
East Bedfont TW14 . . . . .14 D8
Hatton TW14, TW6 . . . . .3 E2
Thornton Heath CR0 . . . . . . .42 A1
Havana Rd SW18, SW19 . . .20 A6
Havelock Cotts GU22 . . . . .89 D5
Havelock Hall 3 CR0 . . . . .42 F1
Havelock House
4 Croydon CR0 . . . . .42 F1
Farnborough GU14 . . . . . . .105 C8
Forest Hill SE23 . . . . .23 C7
Havelock Rd Croydon CR0 . .61 F8
Wimbledon SW19 . . . . .20 C3
Wokingham RG41 . . . . .25 A6
Havelock St RG41 . . . . .25 A6
Havelock Wlk SE23 . . . . . . .23 C6
Haven Cl SW19 . . . . .19 D5
Haven Ct BR3 . . . . .44 C7
Haven Gdns RH10 . . . . . . .184 B1
Haven Rd Ashford TW15 . . . .14 B5
Rudgwick RH12, RH14 . . . .214 D3
Haven The Ashford TW16 . . .15 A1
Richmond TW9 . . . . .7 A4
Haven Way GU9 . . . . .125 D4
Havenbury Est RH4 . . . . .136 A8
Havenbury Ind Est RH4 . .135 F8
Havengate RH12 . . . . .217 F5
Haverfield Gdns TW9 . . . . . .7 A7
Haverhill Rd SW12 . . . . . . .21 C7
Havers Ave KT12 . . . . .54 D5
Haversham Cl
Crawley RH10 . . . . .201 F6
Twickenham TW1 . . . . .6 D1
Haversham Dr RG12 . . . . . .27 B3
Haversham House RH6 . .161 B5
Havisham Pl SW16 . . . . . . .22 B1
Hawarden Gr SE24 . . . . . . .22 C8
Hawarden Rd CR3 . . . . . . .100 C6
Hawes Down Schs BR4 . . .44 D1
Hawes La BR4 . . . . .63 E8
Hawes Rd KT20 . . . . .97 D7
Haweswater House TW1 . . .5 F2
Hawk La RG12 . . . . .27 D5
Hawk's Hill KT22 . . . . .94 F4
Hawke Rd SE19 . . . . .22 E2
Hawkedale Fst Sch TW16 .34 F6
Hawker Cl SM6 . . . . .60 E3
Hawker Ct 14 KT2 . . . . .18 A1
Hawker Rd GU12 . . . . .105 F5
Hawkes Cl RG41 . . . . .25 A7
Hawkes Leap GU20 . . . . . . .48 B6
Hawkes Rd CR4 . . . . .40 F8
Hawkesbourne Rd RH12 .217 F5
Hawkesfield Rd SE23, SE6 .23 F6
Hawkesley Cl TW1 . . . . . . .17 A4
Hawkesmoor Rd RH11 . . .200 E4
Hawkesmoore Dr RH5 . . .157 C4
Hawkesworth Dr GU19 . . . .47 E1
Hawkewood Rd TW16 . . . .35 A6
Hawkfield Ct TW7 . . . . .5 E5
Hawkhirst Rd CR8 . . . . .80 E3
Hawkhurst KT11 . . . . .74 A5
Hawkhurst Gdns KT9 . . . . .56 E6
Hawkhurst Rd SW16 . . . . . .41 D8
Hawkhurst Way
New Malden KT3 . . . . .38 D4
West Wickham BR4 . . . . .63 B8
Hawkhurst Wlk RH10 . . . .202 B4
Hawkins Cl RG12 . . . . .28 A7
Hawkins Rd Crawley RH10 201 E4
Teddington TW11 . . . . .17 B2
Hawkins Way Catford SE6 . .24 A3
Wokingham RG40 . . . . .25 E6
Hawkley Gdns SE27 . . . . . .22 B6
Hawkridge RH12 . . . . .195 E1
Hawkridge Ct RG12 . . . . . .27 E6
Hawks Hill Cl KT22 . . . . . . .94 F4
Hawks Rd KT1 . . . . .37 F7
Hawksbrook La BR3 . . . . . .44 C3
Hawkshead Cl BR1 . . . . . . .24 E1
Hawkshill Cl KT10 . . . . .55 A4
Hawkshill Way KT10 . . . . . .55 A4
Hawksview KT11 . . . . .73 F6
Hawksway TW18 . . . . .12 F5
Hawkswell Cl GU21 . . . . . . .68 F2
Hawkswell Wlk GU21 . . . . .68 F3
Hawkswood Ave GU16 . . . .65 F2
Hawkswood House RG42 . .26 E8
Hawkwood Dell KT23 . . . . .94 A1
Hawkwood Rise KT23 . . . . .94 A1
Hawley Cl TW12 . . . . .15 F2
Hawley Ct GU14 . . . . .84 E8
Hawley Cty Prim Sch
GU17 . . . . .64 E3
Hawley Garden Cotts
GU17 . . . . .64 D4
Hawley Gn GU17 . . . . .64 E3
Hawley La GU14 . . . . .85 B8
Hawley Lodge GU14 . . . . . .64 F2
Hawley Place Sch GU17 . . .64 E1
Hawley Rd GU14, GU17 . . . .64 F3
Hawley Way TW15 . . . . . . .14 B3
Hawmead RH10 . . . . .204 C8
Haworth Rd RH10 . . . . . . .202 C5
Hawth (Arts Ctr) The
RH10 . . . . .201 F5
Hawth Ave RH10 . . . . .201 F4
Hawth Cl RH10 . . . . .201 E4
Hawthorn Ave CR7 . . . . . . .42 B8
Hawthorn Cl Banstead SM7 .77 E5
Bracknell RG42 . . . . .27 A8
Hawthorn Cl *continued*
Cranford TW5 . . . . .4 B7
Crawley RH11 . . . . .181 C1
Hampton TW12 . . . . .16 A3
Horsham RH12 . . . . .217 C4
Redhill RH1 . . . . .140 A4
Woking GU22 . . . . .89 E7
Hawthorn Cres
Selsdon CR2 . . . . .81 C8
Upper Tooting SW17 . . . . . . .21 A3
Hawthorn Ct Richmond TW9 .7 B6
8 West Norwood SW16 . . . .22 A3
Hawthorn Dr BR4 . . . . .63 E6
Hawthorn Gr SE20 . . . . . . .43 B8
Hawthorn Hatch TW8 . . . . . .6 B7
Hawthorn La
Newell Green SL4 . . . . .8 A7
Rowledge GU10 . . . . .145 F3
Hawthorn Rd Brentford TW8 .6 B7
Carshalton SM1, SM2, SM5 . .59 E4
Frimley GU16 . . . . .65 F2
Godalming GU7 . . . . .150 B2
Send Marsh GU23 . . . . .91 A3
Wallington SM5, SM6 . . . . . . .60 B3
Woking GU22 . . . . .89 D7
Hawthorn Way Bisley GU24 68 A3
Redhill RH1 . . . . .140 B8
Upper Halliford TW17 . . . . . .34 D5
Woodham KT15 . . . . .52 C1
Hawthorndene Cl BR2 . . . .63 F8
Hawthorndene Rd BR2 . . . .63 F8
Hawthorne Ave
Biggin Hill TN16 . . . . .83 D4
Mitcham CR4 . . . . .40 D7
Wallington SM5 . . . . .60 A3
Winkfield SL4 . . . . .9 B6
Hawthorne Cl
Aldershot GU12 . . . . .126 E7
Sutton SM1 . . . . .59 C8
Hawthorne Cotts RH6 . . .183 C7
Hawthorne Cres GU17 . . . .64 E4
Hawthorne Ct TW19 . . . . . .13 D8
Hawthorne Dr SL4 . . . . .9 B7
Hawthorne Pl KT17 . . . . . . .76 E7
Hawthorne Rd TW20 . . . . .12 C4
Hawthorne Way
Guildford GU4 . . . . .110 B5
Stanwell TW19 . . . . .13 D8
Winkfield SL4 . . . . .9 B7
Hawthorns Sch (Pendell
Court) The RH1 . . . . .120 B4
Hawthorns The
Belmont SM2 . . . . .59 A4
Ewell KT17 . . . . .58 A3
Oxted RH8 . . . . .123 A2
Poyle SL3 . . . . .1 F6
Haxted Mill Mus TN8 . . . .165 D8
Haxted Rd
Haxted RH7, TN8 . . . . .165 C7
Lingfield RH7, TN8 . . . . .165 C7
Haybarn Dr RH12 . . . . .217 E7
Haycroft Cl CR8 . . . . .80 B1
Haycroft Rd KT6 . . . . .56 E7
Hayden Ct KT15 . . . . .71 B8
Haydn Ave CR8 . . . . .80 A4
Haydon House 2 TW11 . . .17 C1
Haydon Park Rd SW19 . . . .20 B3
Haydon Pl GU1 . . . . .130 D8
Haydon's Rd Merton SW19 .20 C2
Wimbledon SW19 . . . . .20 C2
Haydons Road Sta SW19 . .20 C3
Hayes Barton GU22 . . . . . . .70 D3
Hayes Chase BR4 . . . . .44 E3
Hayes Cres SM3 . . . . .58 D6
Hayes Ct Streatham SW12 . .21 E7
Wimbledon SW19 . . . . .19 E2
Hayes Hill BR2 . . . . .44 E1
Hayes Hill Rd BR2 . . . . .44 F1
Hayes La
Beckenham BR2, BR3 . . . . . .44 D5
Kenley CR8, CR3 . . . . .80 B3
Purley CR8 . . . . .80 B3
Slinfold RH13 . . . . .215 D2
Hayes Mead Rd BR2 . . . . . .44 E1
Hayes Prim Sch The CR8 . .80 B3
Hayes Sta BR2 . . . . .44 F1
Hayes The KT18 . . . . .96 E8
Hayes Way BR3 . . . . .44 D5
Hayes Wlk RH6 . . . . .162 A4
Hayesend House SW17 . . .20 C4
Hayesford Park Dr BR2 . . .44 F4
Hayfields RH6 . . . . .161 C4
Haygarth Pl SW19 . . . . .19 D3
Haygreen Cl KT2 . . . . .18 B2
Haylett Gdns KT1 . . . . .37 D5
Hayling Ave TW13 . . . . .15 A5
Hayling Ct Cheam SM3 . . . .58 C6
Crawley RH11 . . . . .201 C3
Haymeads Dr KT10 . . . . . . .55 C4
Haymer Gdns KT4 . . . . .58 A7
Hayne Rd BR3 . . . . .43 F8
Haynes La SE19 . . . . .22 E2
Haynt Wlk SW20 . . . . .39 E6
Hays Bridge Bsns Ctr
RH9 . . . . .163 C6
Hays Bridge Houses RH9 163 B7
Hays Wlk SM2 . . . . .58 D1
Haysleigh Gdns SE20 . . . . .43 A7
Haysleigh House SE20 . . . .43 B7
Haywain The RH8 . . . . . . .122 D5
Hayward Cl SW19 . . . . .40 B8
Hayward Rd KT7 . . . . .36 F2
Haywardens RH7 . . . . .164 D5
Haywards RH10 . . . . .182 D1
Haywood RG12 . . . . .27 C2
Hazel Ave
Farnborough GU14 . . . . .84 F3
Guildford GU1 . . . . .109 C5

Hazel Bank Ewhurst GU6 . .175 E5
South Norwood SE25 . . . . . . .42 E7
Tolworth KT5 . . . . .38 C1
Hazel Cl Brentford TW8 . . . . . .6 B7
Crawley RH11 . . . . .181 C1
Crawley Down RH10 . . . . . .204 C8
Croydon CR0 . . . . .43 D1
Englefield Green TW20 . . . . .11 B2
Mitcham CR4 . . . . .41 D5
Reigate RH2 . . . . .139 C7
Twickenham TW2 . . . . .16 C8
Hazel Ct Guildford GU1 . . .109 D5
Warlingham CR6 . . . . .81 E1
9 West Norwood SW16 . . . .22 A3
Hazel Dr GU23 . . . . .90 F2
Hazel Gr Forest Hill SE26 . . .23 D4
Haslemere GU26 . . . . .188 E2
Staines TW18 . . . . .13 C2
Hazel Mead KT17 . . . . .58 A1
Hazel Par KT22 . . . . .94 C5
Hazel Rd Ash GU12 . . . . . .127 C8
Mytchett GU16 . . . . .86 A2
Reigate RH2 . . . . .139 C7
Hazel Way Chipstead CR5 . . .78 F1
Crawley Down RH10 . . . . . .204 C8
Fetcham KT22 . . . . .94 C4
Hazel Wlk RH5 . . . . .136 C4
Hazelbank Ct KT16 . . . . . . .33 C1
Hazelbank Rd Catford SE6 .24 E6
Chertsey KT16 . . . . .33 C2
Hazelbury Cl SW19 . . . . . . .40 A7
Hazeldene KT15 . . . . .52 C5
Hazeldene Ct CR8 . . . . .80 D4
Hazelhurst Beckenham BR3 .44 D8
Horley RH6 . . . . .161 C4
Hazelhurst Cl GU4 . . . . . .110 B6
Hazelhurst Cres RH12 . . .216 F1
Hazelhurst Ct SE6 . . . . .24 C3
Hazelhurst Dr RH10 . . . . .202 E6
Hazelhurst Rd SW17 . . . . . .20 D4
Hazelhurst Sch SW20 . . . . .39 D8
Hazell Hill RG12 . . . . .27 C6
Hazell Rd GU9 . . . . .124 F1
Hazelmere Cl Hatton TW14 . .3 E1
Leatherhead KT22 . . . . .95 B8
Hazelmere Ct 10 SW2 . . . . .21 F7
Hazelwick Ave RH10 . . . . .202 B8
Hazelwick Mill La RH10 .202 A8
Hazelwick Rd RH10 . . . . .202 A7
Hazelwick Sch RH10 . . . .202 A8
Hazelwood RH11 . . . . .201 A5
Hazelwood Ave SM4 . . . . . .40 B5
Hazelwood Cl RH10 . . . . .203 F8
Hazelwood Cotts
Cranleigh GU6 . . . . .194 D4
Godalming GU7 . . . . .150 D4
Hazelwood Ct KT6 . . . . .37 E3
Hazelwood Gr CR2 . . . . . . .81 B6
Hazelwood House BR2 . . . . .44 E6
Hazelwood La CR5 . . . . . . .98 F8
Hazelwood Lodge BR4 . . . .44 C2
Hazelwood Rd
Knaphill GU21 . . . . .68 E1
Oxted RH8 . . . . .123 B3
Hazelwood Sch RH8 . . . . . .123 A4
Hazledean Rd CR0, CR9 . . .61 D8
Hazleden Cross RH19 . . . .205 B6
Hazledene Rd W4 . . . . .7 C8
Hazlemere Gdns KT4 . . . . .39 A1
Hazlewood GU8 . . . . .148 E4
Hazlitt Cl TW13 . . . . .15 E4
Hazon Way KT19 . . . . .76 C7
Headcorn Pl CR7 . . . . .41 F5
Headcorn Rd Bromley BR1 .24 F3
Thornton Heath CR7 . . . . . .41 F5
Headington Cl RG40 . . . . . .25 D8
Headington Dr RG40 . . . . .25 D8
Headington Rd SW18 . . . . .20 C6
Headlam Rd SW4 . . . . .21 D8
Headland Way RH7 . . . . .164 D4
Headley Ave CR0, SM6 . . . . .60 F5
Headley Cl
Chessington KT19 . . . . .57 A4
Crawley RH10 . . . . .182 D1
Headley Common
Rd KT18, KT20 . . . . .116 D7
Headley Ct SE26 . . . . .23 C3
Headley Dr
Burgh Heath KT18 . . . . .97 B8
New Addington CR0 . . . . . . .63 C3
Headley Gr
Burgh Heath KT20 . . . . .97 C7
Headley KT20 . . . . .116 D7
Headley Heath App KT20 116 B4
Headley Hill Rd GU35 . . .187 A5
Headley Rd Ashstead KT18 .96 C6
Grayshott GU26 . . . . .188 C3
Headley KT18 . . . . .96 A4
Hindhead GU26 . . . . .188 C3
Langley Vale KT21 . . . . .96 C8
Leatherhead KT18, KT22 . . . .95 E4
Mickleham RH5 . . . . .115 E7
Headon Ct GU9 . . . . .125 D1
Headway Cl TW10 . . . . .17 C4
Headway The KT17 . . . . . .57 F2
Hearn Vale GU35 . . . . . . .187 A7
Hearn Wlk RG12 . . . . .27 E8
Hearne Rd W4 . . . . .7 A8
Hearnville Prim Sch SW12 21 A7
Hearnville Rd SW12 . . . . . .21 A7
Hearsey Gdns GU17 . . . . . .64 C6
Heath Bsns Ctr The TW3 . . .5 C3
Heath Cl Banstead SM7 . . . .78 B5
Beacon Hill GU26 . . . . .188 C7
Broadbridge Heath RH12 . .216 E3
Harlington UB3 . . . . .3 D7
Heath End GU9 . . . . .125 C7
Stanwell TW19 . . . . .2 C1
Heath Cl *continued*
Virginia Water GU25 . . . . . . .31 D5
Wokingham RG41 . . . . .25 B4
Heath Cnr GU15 . . . . .66 A3
Heath Cotts GU26 . . . . . . .188 C6
Heath Ct RH12 . . . . .216 E3
Heath Dr Brookwood GU24 .88 A7
Send GU23 . . . . .90 B5
Sutton SM2 . . . . .59 C2
Walton on t H KT18 . . . . . . .97 A2
West Barnes SW20 . . . . .39 C5
Heath End Sch GU9 . . . . .125 E6
Heath Gdns TW1 . . . . .16 F6
Heath Gr Ashford TW16 . . . .14 F1
Penge SE20 . . . . .23 C1
Heath Hill
Dockenfield GU10 . . . . .166 E3
Dorking RH4 . . . . .136 B7
Heath Hill Rd N RG45 . . . . .45 B5
Heath Hill Rd S RG45 . . . . .45 B4
Heath House
Thornton Heath CR7 . . . . . . .42 A4
Weybridge KT13 . . . . .53 A6
Heath La Albury GU5 . . . . .132 E2
Crondall GU10 . . . . .124 B7
Godalming GU7, GU8 . . . . .151 A2
Heath End GU9 . . . . .125 C7
Heath Mead SW19 . . . . .19 D5
Heath Mill La GU3 . . . . . . .88 C2
Heath Rd Bagshot GU19 . . . .47 E3
Caterham CR3 . . . . .100 D3
Isleworth TW3, TW7 . . . . .5 C3
Linchmere GU27 . . . . .207 D5
Oxshott KT22 . . . . .74 C7
South Norwood CR7 . . . . . . .42 C6
Twickenham TW1 . . . . .16 F7
Weybridge KT13 . . . . .53 A5
Woking GU21 . . . . .69 F4
Heath Ridge Gn KT11 . . . . .74 A6
Heath Rise Camberley GU15 65 D5
Hayes BR2 . . . . .44 F3
Virginia Water GU25 . . . . . . .31 D5
Westcott RH4 . . . . .135 C5
Heath The CR3 . . . . .100 C3
Heath View KT24 . . . . .92 F2
Heath Way RH12 . . . . .217 D5
Heathacre SL3 . . . . .1 E6
Heatham Pk TW2 . . . . .16 F8
Heathbridge KT13 . . . . .53 A4
Heathcote KT20 . . . . .97 D5
Heathcote Cl GU12 . . . . . .106 A3
Heathcote Dr RH19 . . . . .185 C2
Heathcote Rd Ash GU12 . .106 B3
Camberley GU15 . . . . .65 D5
Epsom KT18 . . . . .76 E6
Twickenham TW1 . . . . .6 B2
Heathcroft Ave TW16 . . . . .14 F1
Heathdale Ave TW4 . . . . .4 E4
Heathdene KT20 . . . . .77 E1
Heathdene Rd
Streatham SW16 . . . . .21 F1
Wallington SM5, SM6 . . . . . .60 B3
Heathdown Rd GU22 . . . . .70 D4
Heathedge SE23, SE26 . . . . .23 B6
Heather Cl Aldershot GU11 104 E1
Ash GU12 . . . . .106 B5
Copthorne RH10 . . . . .183 B2
Guildford GU2 . . . . .109 B3
Hampton TW12 . . . . .35 F8
Horsham RH12 . . . . .217 D5
Isleworth TW7 . . . . .5 D2
Kingswood KT20 . . . . .97 E5
Lewisham SE13 . . . . .24 D7
Woking GU21 . . . . .69 C4
Woodham KT15 . . . . .52 B1
Wrecclesham GU9 . . . . .145 F6
Heather Cotts GU12 . . . . .106 A8
Heather Ct
10 Aldershot GU11 . . . . . . .105 A1
Hindhead GU26 . . . . .188 F4
Heather Dr SL5 . . . . .30 B2
Heather Gdns Belmont SM2 59 A4
Farnborough GU14 . . . . .84 E2
Heather Mead GU16 . . . . . .65 F2
Heather Mead Ct GU16 . . .65 F2
Heather Pl 4 KT10 . . . . . . .55 B6
Heather Ridge Arc GU15 . .66 C4
Heather Ridge Cty Inf Sch
GU15 . . . . .66 D4
Heather Way
Chobham GU24 . . . . .49 E3
Hindhead GU26 . . . . .188 F4
South Croydon CR2 . . . . .62 D2
Heather Wlk
Crawley RH11 . . . . .201 B3
Pirbright GU24 . . . . .87 D7
Smallfield RH6 . . . . .162 C3
Twickenham TW4 . . . . .16 A8
Whiteley Village KT12 . . . . . .53 F1
Heatherdale Cl KT2 . . . . . . .18 B1
Heatherdale Rd GU15 . . . .65 D4
Heatherdene KT24 . . . . . . .92 D2
Heatherdene Cl CR4 . . . . . .40 E5
Heatherdene Mansions 2
TW1 .6 D1
Heatherlands
Ashford TW16 . . . . .15 A2
Horley RH6 . . . . .161 B4
Heatherley Cl GU15 . . . . . .65 B5
Heatherley Rd GU15 . . . . . .65 B5
Heathermount RG12 . . . . . .27 E5
Heathermount Dr RG45 . . .45 A6
Heathermount Sch SL5 . . .29 D3
Heathers Land RH4 . . . . .136 C4
Heathers The TW19 . . . . . . .13 F8
Heatherset Cl KT10 . . . . . . .55 C5
Heatherset Gdns SW16 . . .21 F1
Heatherside Dr GU25 . . . . .31 A3
Heatherside Rd KT19 . . . . .57 D3
Heathervale Rd KT15 . . . . .52 B1
Heatherway
Crowthorne RG45 . . . . .45 A5
Felbridge RH19 . . . . .184 F7
Heatherwood Hospl SL5 . .28 E6
Heathfield Cobham KT11 . . .74 A5
Crawley RH10 . . . . .202 D8
Reigate RH2 . . . . .138 D8
Heathfield Ave Ascot SL5 . .29 E4
Wandsworth SW18 . . . . .20 D8
Heathfield Cl
Godalming GU7 . . . . .150 E2
Woking GU22 . . . . .70 A1
Heathfield Ct Ashford TW15 13 E5
Penge SE20 . . . . .23 C1
Wandsworth SW18 . . . . .20 D8
Heathfield Dr
Mitcham SW19 . . . . .20 E1
Redhill RH1 . . . . .139 E4
Heathfield Gdns CR0 . . . . .61 D6
Heathfield Inf Sch TW2 . . .16 A7
Heathfield Jun Sch TW2 . .16 A7
Heathfield N TW1, TW2 . . . .16 F8
Heathfield Rd Bromley BR1 .24 F1
Croydon CR0 . . . . .61 D6
Hersham KT12 . . . . .54 E6
Wandsworth SW18 . . . . .20 D8
Woking GU22 . . . . .70 A1
Heathfield S TW1, TW2 . . . .16 F8
Heathfield Sch SL5 . . . . . .28 B7
Heathfield Sq SW18 . . . . . .20 D8
Heathfield Vale CR2 . . . . . .62 E2
Heathhurst Rd CR2 . . . . . . .61 E2
Heathland Sch The TW4 . . . .4 F1
Heathland St GU11 . . . . . .105 A2
Heathlands Tadworth KT20 .97 D5
Upper Tooting SW12 . . . . . . .21 B6
Weybridge KT13 . . . . .53 C5
Heathlands Cl
Sunbury TW16 . . . . .35 A7
Twickenham TW1 . . . . .16 F7
Woking GU21 . . . . .69 E5
Heathlands Country Mkt
RG40 . . . . .25 E1
Heathlands Ct
Hounslow TW4 . . . . .4 E2
Mitcham CR4 . . . . .41 A6
Heathlands Rd RG40 . . . . . .25 E2
Heathlands Sch SW19 . . . .19 C5
Heathlands Way TW4 . . . . . .4 E2
Heathmere Prim Sch
SW15 . . . . .19 A7
Heathmoors RG12 . . . . .27 C4
Heathpark Dr GU20 . . . . . . .48 E4
Heathrise GU23 . . . . .91 B4
Heathrow GU5 . . . . .133 C4
Heathrow Airport London
TW6 .3 A5
Heathrow Bvd UB7 . . . . .2 F7
Heathrow Causeway Est
TW4 .4 B4
Heathrow Central Sta TW6 .3 B4
Heathrow Cl TW6 . . . . .2 B6
Heathrow International
Trad Est TW4 . . . . .4 B4
Heathrow Sch UB7 . . . . .2 F8
Heathrow Terminal 4 Sta
TW6 .3 C1
Heathshot 8 TW10 . . . . .6 E1
Heathside
Hinchley Wood KT10 . . . . . . .55 E7
Twickenham TW4 . . . . .15 F8
Weybridge KT13 . . . . .53 B5
Heathside Cl KT10 . . . . . . .55 E7
Heathside Cres GU22 . . . . .69 F2
Heathside Ct KT20 . . . . . . .97 C4
Heathside Gdns GU22 . . . .70 A2
Heathside La GU26 . . . . . .188 D6
Heathside Park Rd GU22 . .70 A1
Heathside Pk GU15 . . . . . . .66 C7
Heathside Rd GU22 . . . . . . .69 F1
Heathside Sch KT13 . . . . . .52 F4
Heathvale Bridge
Rd GU12 . . . . .106 A6
Heathview Ct SW19 . . . . . .19 D6
Heathview Gdns SW15 . . . .19 C8
Heathview Rd
Thornton Heath CR7 . . . . . . .42 A5
Witley GU8 . . . . .170 E7
Heathway Camberley GU15 .65 D5
Caterham CR3 . . . . .100 D2
Croydon CR0 . . . . .62 F7
East Horsley KT24 . . . . .93 A3
North Ascot SL5 . . . . .28 E8
Heathway Cl GU15 . . . . . . .65 D5
Heathwood KT20 . . . . .97 C4
Heathwood Ct
Hounslow TW3 . . . . .5 B3
Streatham SW12 . . . . .21 C7
Heathwood Point 7 SE26 .23 D5
Heathyfields Rd GU9 . . . .125 A6
Heaton Rd CR4 . . . . .21 A1
Heavers Farm Prim Sch
SE25 . . . . .42 F4
Hebdon Rd SW17 . . . . .20 F5
Heddon Cl TW7 . . . . .6 A3
Heddon Wlk 1 GU14 . . . . .85 A7
Hedge Cnr KT20 . . . . .97 C4
Hedge Croft Cotts GU23 . .91 B6
Hedge Wlk SE6 . . . . .24 B4
Hedgecourt Pl RH19 . . . . .184 E4
Hedgehog La GU27 . . . . . .208 B5
Hedgerley Ct GU21 . . . . . . .69 C2
Hedgeside RH11 . . . . .201 C1
Hedgeway GU2 . . . . .130 A7
Hedingham Cl RH6 . . . . . .161 C4
Hedley Rd TW4 . . . . .16 A8
Heelas Rd RG41 . . . . .25 A5
Heenan Cl GU16 . . . . .85 E7
Heighton Gdns CR0 . . . . . .61 B5
Heights Cl Banstead SM7 . . .77 E3
Wimbledon SW20 . . . . .19 B1
Heights The BR3 . . . . .24 C1
Helder Gr SE12 . . . . .24 F8
Helder St CR2 . . . . .61 D4
Heldmann Cl TW7 . . . . .5 D3
Helen Ave TW14 . . . . .15 B8
Helen Cl KT8 . . . . .36 B5
Helen Ct GU14 . . . . .85 B4
Helena Cl SM6 . . . . .60 E3
Helford Wlk 3 GU21 . . . . . .69 A1
Helgiford Gdns TW16 . . . . .14 E1
Helicon House RH11 . . . .201 C5
Helix Ho TW7 . . . . .6 B5
Helksham Cl GU47 . . . . . . .45 D1
Helme Cl SW19 . . . . .19 F3
Helmsdale Bracknell RG12 . .27 E4
3 Woking GU21 . . . . .69 B1
Helmsdale Rd SW16 . . . . . .21 D1
Helston Cl GU16 . . . . .86 A7
Helvellyn Cl TW20 . . . . . . .12 C1
Helvetia St SE6 . . . . .23 F6
Hemingford Rd SM3 . . . . . .58 C6
Hemlock Cl KT20 . . . . .97 E4
Hemming Cl 7 TW12 . . . . .36 A8
Hempshaw Ave SM7 . . . . . .78 F3
Hemsby Rd KT9 . . . . .56 F4
Hemsby Wlk RH10 . . . . . .202 B4
Henage Cnr GU24 . . . . .49 E2
Henbane Ct 2 RH11 . . . . .201 B2
Henbit Cl KT20 . . . . .97 B8
Henchley Dene GU4 . . . . .110 D4
Henderson Ave GU2 . . . . .109 B5
Henderson Hospl SM2 . . . .59 B2
Henderson Rd
Biggin Hill TN16 . . . . .83 C7
Crawley RH11 . . . . .201 B1
Thornton Heath CR0 . . . . .42 D3
Wandsworth SW18 . . . . .20 E8
Henderson Way RH12 . . .216 F1
Hendfield Ct 5 SM6 . . . . . .60 B4
Hendham Rd SW17 . . . . . . .20 F6
Hendon Terr TW15 . . . . . . .14 D2
Hendon Way TW19 . . . . .2 D1
Hendrick Ave SW12 . . . . . . .20 F8
Heneage Cres CR0 . . . . . . .63 C1
Henfield Rd SW19, SW20 . .39 F8
Henfold Cotts RH5 . . . . . .158 A2
Henfold Dr RH5 . . . . .157 E3
Henfold La RH5 . . . . .157 F5
Hengelo Gdns CR4 . . . . . . .40 D5
Hengist Cl RH12 . . . . .217 A1
Hengist Way BR2, BR3 . . . . .44 E5
Hengrave Rd SE23 . . . . . . .23 D8
Hengrove Cres TW15 . . . . .13 D5
Henhurst Cross La RH5 . .157 A2
Henley Ave SM3 . . . . .58 E7
Henley Bank GU2 . . . . . . .130 A7
Henley Cl Crawley RH10 . .202 D3
Farnborough GU14 . . . . .84 E8
Hounslow TW7 . . . . .5 F6
Henley Ct Mitcham CR4 . . . .41 A6
Old Woking GU22 . . . . .90 A7
Henley Dr Frimley GU16 . . . .85 E7
Kingston u T KT2 . . . . .18 F1
Henley Gate GU24, GU3 . .107 C8
Henley Lodge SE25 . . . . . . .42 F5
Henley Way TW13 . . . . .15 D3
Henley Wood CR6 . . . . .82 A2
Hennel Cl SE23 . . . . .23 C5
Hennessy Ct GU21 . . . . . . .70 C6
Henry Cavendish Prim Sch
SW12 . . . . .21 C7
Henry Doulton Dr SW17 . .21 B4
Henry Hatch Ct SM2 . . . . . .59 C3
Henry Peters Dr TW11 . . . .16 E3
Henry Tyndale Sch GU14 . .85 D6
Hensford Gdns SE26 . . . . .23 B4
Henshaw Cl RH11 . . . . . . .200 F4
Henslow Way GU21 . . . . . . .70 D5
Henson Rd RH10 . . . . .202 B7
Hensworth Rd TW15 . . . . .13 D3
Henty Cl RH11 . . . . .200 E3
Hepburn Gdns BR2 . . . . . . .44 F1
Hepple Cl TW7 . . . . .6 B5
Hepplewhite Cl RH11 . . . .201 B1
Hepworth Croft GU47 . . . . .64 E6
Hepworth Ct SM3 . . . . .40 A1
Hepworth Rd SW16 . . . . . . .21 E1
Hepworth Way KT12 . . . . . .34 F1
Heracles Cl SM6 . . . . .60 E3
Herald Ct 5 GU12 . . . . . . .105 B1
Herald Gdns SM6 . . . . .60 B7
Herbert Cl RG12 . . . . .27 B4
Herbert Cres GU21 . . . . . . .68 E1
Herbert Gdns W4 . . . . .7 B8
Herbert Rd Kingston u T KT1 37 F6
Merton SW19 . . . . .19 F1
Herbs End GU14 . . . . .84 C5
Hereford Cl Crawley RH10 .201 E2
Epsom KT18 . . . . .76 D6
Guildford GU2 . . . . .108 F3
Staines TW18 . . . . .33 B8
Hereford Copse GU22 . . . . .89 B8
Hereford Ct 6 CR0 . . . . . . .42 F1
Hereford Gdns TW2 . . . . . .16 C7
Hereford Ho 9 GU11 . . . .105 A1
Hereford La GU9 . . . . .125 B7
Hereford Rd TW13 . . . . .15 C7
Hereford Way KT9 . . . . .56 D5
Hereward Ave CR8 . . . . . . .61 A1
Hereward Rd SW17 . . . . . . .20 F4
Heriot Rd KT16 . . . . .33 A2
Heritage Ct 2 TW20 . . . . . .12 A3
Heritage House 22 SW19 . .19 D7
Heritage Lawn RH6 . . . . .161 C4
Herlwyn Gdns SW17 . . . . . .20 F4
Herm Cl Crawley RH11 . . . .201 A2
Hounslow TW7 . . . . .5 C7
Hermes House BR3 . . . . . . .43 E8
Hermes Way SM6 . . . . .60 D3
Hermitage Cl
Claygate KT10 . . . . .56 A4
Farnborough GU14 . . . . .85 D1
Frimley GU16 . . . . .65 F1
Littleton TW17 . . . . .34 A5
Hermitage Ct TW18 . . . . . . .12 F3
Hermitage Cty Jun Sch
The GU21 . . . . .88 E8
Hermitage Dr SL5 . . . . .28 E7
Hermitage Gdns SE19 . . . .22 C1
Hermitage La Croydon CR0 .43 A3
East Grinstead RH19 . . . . . .205 F8
Streatham SW16 . . . . .21 F1
Hermitage Par SL5 . . . . . . .29 A6
Hermitage Rd
East Grinstead RH19 . . . . . .185 D3
Kenley CR8 . . . . .80 C3
Knaphill GU21 . . . . .88 D8
South Norwood SE19 . . . . . . .22 D2
Hermitage The Barnes SW13 7 F6
Feltham TW13 . . . . .14 F5
Forest Hill SE23 . . . . .23 C7
Kingston u T KT1 . . . . .37 D5
Richmond TW10 . . . . .6 E2
Hermitage Woods Cres
GU21 . . . . .88 E7
Hermits Rd RH10 . . . . .201 F7
Hermonger La RH12 . . . . .195 F2
Herndon Cl TW20 . . . . .12 A4
Herne Rd KT6 . . . . .56 E8
Heron Cl Cheam SM1 . . . . . .58 F5
Crawley RH11 . . . . .201 C8
Guildford GU2 . . . . .109 B4
Mytchett GU16 . . . . .85 F4
North Ascot SL5 . . . . .28 D8
Heron Ct Dorking RH4 . . . .136 A8
5 Kingston u T KT1 . . . . .37 E6
Stanwell TW19 . . . . .13 E7
6 West Norwood SE21 . . . . .22 D6
Heron Dale KT15 . . . . .52 D5
Heron House KT1 . . . . .37 C8
Heron Pl RH19 . . . . .205 F8
Heron Rd Croydon CR0 . . . . .61 E8
Isleworth TW1 . . . . .6 B3
Heron Shaw GU6 . . . . .174 E1
Heron Sq 25 TW10 . . . . .6 D2
Heron Way RH13 . . . . .218 A1
Heron Way Cty Prim Sch
RH13 . . . . .218 A1
Heron Wlk GU21 . . . . .70 C5
Heron Wood Rd GU12 . . . .126 D7
Heron's Way RG40 . . . . .25 E7
Herondale Bracknell RG12 . .27 C2
Haslemere GU27 . . . . .207 E6
Selsdon CR2 . . . . .62 D2
Herondale Ave SW18 . . . . .20 E7
Heronfield TW20 . . . . .11 C2
Heronry The KT12 . . . . .54 A4
Herons Cl RH10 . . . . .184 B5
Herons Croft KT13 . . . . . . .53 D4
Herons L Ctr The GU27 . . .207 F6
Herons Lea RH10 . . . . . . .184 A4
Herons Pl TW7 . . . . .6 B4
Herons Way GU24 . . . . .87 D6
Herons Wood Ct RH6 . . . .161 B4
Heronscourt GU18 . . . . . . .67 C8
Herontye Dr RH19 . . . . . .206 A8
Herrett St GU12 . . . . .126 D8
Herretts Gdns GU12 . . . . .105 D1
Herrick Cl Crawley RH10 . .202 C8
Frimley GU16 . . . . .66 C3
Herrick Ct 4 TW10 . . . . . . .17 D4
Herrings La GU20 . . . . .48 D4
Herschel Wlk 9 RH11 . . .201 B1
Herschell Rd SE23 . . . . . . .23 E8
Hersham Cl SW15 . . . . .19 A8
Hersham Gdns KT12 . . . . . .54 C6
Hersham Rd Hersham KT12 54 D6
Walton-on-T KT12 . . . . .54 B7
Hersham Sta KT12 . . . . . . .54 E7
Hersham Trad Est KT12 . . .54 E8
Hershell Ct SW14 . . . . .7 B3
Hertford Ave SW14 . . . . .7 E3
Hertford Lodge 10 SW19 . .19 E7
Hertford Sq CR4 . . . . .41 E5
Hertford Way CR4 . . . . .41 E5
Hesiers Hill CR6 . . . . .82 E2
Hesiers Rd CR6 . . . . .82 F3
Hesketh Cl GU6 . . . . .174 E3
Heslop Ct 2 SW12 . . . . . . .21 A7
Heslop Rd SW12 . . . . .20 F7
Hessle Gr KT17 . . . . .76 F8
Hester Terr TW9 . . . . .7 A4
Hesterman Way CR0, CR9 . .41 F1
Heston Ave TW5 . . . . .4 E7
Heston Comm Sch TW5 . . . .5 A7
Heston Grange TW5 . . . . . . .4 F8
Heston Grange La TW5 . . . .4 F8
Heston Ind Mall TW5 . . . . . .4 F7
Heston Inf Sch TW5 . . . . . . .5 A7
Heston Jun Sch TW5 . . . . . .5 A7
Heston Phoenix
Distribution Pk TW5 . . . . . .4 C8
Heston Rd Heston TW5 . . . . .5 A7
Redhill RH1 . . . . .139 F4
Heston Wlk RH1 . . . . .139 F4
Hetherington Rd TW17 . . .34 C7
Hethersett Cl RH2 . . . . . . .118 C4
Hetley Gdns 1 SE19 . . . . . .22 F1

Heverfield Ct CR4 20 F1
Hevers Ave RH6 161 A4
Hewers Way KT20 97 C7
Hewitt Cl CR0 63 A7
Hewitts Ind Est GU6 174 B3
Hewlett Pl GU19 47 F3
Hewshott La GU30 207 A5
Hexal Rd SE6 24 E5
Hexham Cl Crawley RH10 202 E6
Sandhurst GU47 45 D2
Hexham Gdns TW7 6 A7
Hexham Rd Cheam SM4 40 B1
West Norwood SE27 22 C6
Hextalls La RH1 120 E6
Heybridge Ave SW16 21 F2
Heydon Ct BR4 63 E8
Heyford Ave SW20 39 F6
Heyford Rd CR4 40 F7
Heymede KT22 95 C4
Heythorp St SW18 19 F6
Heythorpe Cl GU21 68 F2
Heyward Ct SM2 59 A4
Heywod Dr GU19 47 D3
Hibernia Gdns TW3 5 A2
Hibernia Rd TW3 5 A3
Hickey's Almshouses 7 TW9 6 F3
Hickling Wlk RH10 202 B4
Hickmans Cl RH9 121 C3
Hicks La GU17 64 B5
Hidaburn Ct 7 SW16 21 C4
Hidcote Gdns SW20 39 B6
Hidcote House SM2 59 C3
Hidecote Cl GU22 70 B3
Higgins Wlk TW12 15 E2
Higgs La GU19 47 D3
High Ashton 11 KT2 18 B1
High Ashurst (Outdoor Ctr) RH5 116 A7
High Barn Rd KT24, RH5 113 E3
High Beech Bracknell RG12 27 F5
South Croydon CR2 61 E3
High Beeches
Banstead KT17, SM7 77 D5
Frimley GU16 65 D2
High Beeches Cl CR8 60 D1
High Broom Cres BR4 44 B2
High Cedar Dr SW20 19 B1
High Close Sch RG40 25 C7
High Coombe Pl KT2 18 D1
High Down Rd SM2 78 B8
High Dr
Kingston u T KT2, KT3 38 C7
Oxshott KT22 74 D5
Woldingham CR3 102 A5
High Fields SL5 29 F4
High Foleys KT10 56 B3
High Gables BR2 44 E7
High Garth KT10 55 C4
High Hill Rd Chelsham CR6 82 C5
Fickleshole CR6 82 C5
High La Haslemere GU27 208 C8
Warlingham CR3, CR6 101 F8
High Level Dr SE26 23 A4
High Limes 2 SE19 22 E2
High Loxley Rd GU8 193 B7
High Mead BR4 63 E8
High Meadow Cl RH4 136 B6
High Meadow Pl KT16 32 F3
High Oaks RH11 201 B4
High Par The SW16 21 E5
High Park Ave
East Horsley KT24 92 F1
Richmond TW9 7 A6
High Park Rd
Farnham GU9 125 C3
Richmond TW9 7 A6
High Path SW19 40 C8
High Path Rd GU1 110 C1
High Pewley GU1 130 E7
High Pine Cl KT13 53 C5
High Pines CR6 101 C8
High Pitfold GU26 188 D1
High Rd Byfleet KT14 71 E6
Chipstead CR5, RH2 98 F4
Kingswood CR5, RH2 98 F4
Lower Kingswood CR5, RH2 98 F4
High Ridge GU7 150 D2
High St Addlestone KT15 52 B6
Aldershot GU11 105 A2
Aldershot GU11, GU12 105 B1
Ascot SL5 29 A6
Ascot, Sunninghill SL5 29 D4
Bagshot GU19 47 E3
Banstead SM7 78 B4
Beckenham BR3 44 A7
Bletchingley RH1 120 D2
Bracknell RG12 27 B7
Bracknell RG12 27 C7
Bramley GU5 151 F6
Brentford TW8 6 E8
Brentford, Brentford End TW8 6 D7
Camberley GU15 65 D6
Carshalton SM5 60 A6
Caterham CR3 100 E4
Cheam SM1, KT17 58 E4
Chobham GU24 68 E8
Claygate KT10 55 F4
Cobham KT11 73 B4
Colnbrook SL3 1 C7
Cranford TW5 4 B7
Cranleigh GU6 174 D3
Crawley RH10 201 D6
Crowthorne RG45 45 C4
Croydon CR0, CR9 61 C7
High St *continued*
Croydon, Woodside SE25 43 A5
Dorking RH4 136 B8
East Grinstead RH19 205 F8
East Molesey KT8 36 A5
4 Egham TW20 11 F3
Epsom KT17, KT18 76 D6
Esher KT10 55 B6
Ewell KT17 58 A2
Farnborough GU14 105 D8
Feltham TW13 15 A6
Godalming GU7 150 D4
Godstone RH9 121 C4
Great Bookham KT23 94 B2
Guildford GU1, GU2 130 D7
Hampton TW12 16 C2
Harlington UB3 3 D8
Harmondsworth UB7 2 D8
Haslemere GU27 208 D7
Heston TW5 4 B7
Horley RH6 161 B3
Hounslow TW3 5 B4
Kingston u T KT1 37 D6
Knaphill GU21 68 C2
Leatherhead KT22 95 B5
Limpsfield RH8 123 B7
Lingfield RH7 164 D4
Merstham RH1 119 B7
New Malden KT3 38 E5
Nutfield RH1 119 F2
Old Woking GU22 90 B6
Oxshott KT22 74 D5
Oxted RH8 122 D5
Penge SE19, SE20, BR3 23 C1
Purley CR8 80 A8
Redhill RH1 118 F2
Reigate RH2 118 A1
Ripley GU23 91 C6
Rowledge GU10 145 E4
Rusper RH12 199 D7
Sandhurst GU47 64 A8
Sandhurst, Little Sandhurst GU47 45 A1
Shepperton TW17 34 C3
South Norwood CR7, SE25 42 D5
South Norwood,Woodside SE25 43 A6
Staines TW18 12 F4
Stanwell TW19 2 D1
Sunningdale SL5 30 A4
Sutton SM1, SM2 59 B5
Sutton SM1 59 B6
Tadworth KT20 97 C4
Teddington TW11 17 A3
Teddington, Hampton Hill TW12 16 C2
Teddington, Hampton Wick KT1 37 D8
Thames Ditton KT7 37 A3
Twickenham TW2 16 C8
Tyler's Green RH9 121 C4
Walton-on-T KT12 35 A1
West End GU24 67 F7
West Wickham BR4 44 B1
Weybridge KT13 53 A6
Wimbledon SW19 19 D3
Woking GU21 69 F2
Woking, Horsell GU21 69 C3
High St Mews SW19 19 E3
High Standing CR3 100 C2
High Street Collier's Wood SW17, SW19 20 D2
High Street Gn GU8 191 F2
High Street Harlington TW6 3 D7
High The SW16 21 E5
High Thicket Rd GU10 166 D5
High Tree Cl KT15 52 A5
High Trees Croydon CR0 43 E1
Streatham SW2 22 A7
High Trees Cl CR3 100 F5
High Trees Ct
Caterham CR3 100 F4
Sidlow RH6 160 A4
High Trees Rd RH2 139 D8
High View Belmont SM2 77 F8
Gomshall GU5 133 C4
5 Penge SE19 22 F1
High View Ave CR0, SM6 60 F5
High View Cl
Farnborough GU14 85 A4
South Norwood SE19, SE25 42 F7
High View Lodge 18 GU11 105 A2
High View Prim Sch SM6 60 E5
High View Rd
Farnborough GU14 85 A4
Guildford GU2 129 E6
Lightwater GU18 66 F8
South Norwood SE19 22 D2
Highacre RH4 136 B4
Highams Hill RH11 200 F5
Highams La GU20, GU24 49 A5
Highbarrow Rd CR0 43 A1
Highbirch Cl RH12 218 B5
Highbury Ave CR7 42 B7
Highbury Cl
New Malden KT3 38 C4
West Wickham BR4 63 B8
Highbury Cres GU15 66 A8
Highbury Gr GU27 208 C8
Highbury Rd SW19 19 E3
Highclere Ascot SL5 29 D4
Guildford GU1 110 A4
Highclere Cl
Bracknell RG12 27 E7
Kenley CR8 80 C4
Highclere Ct GU21 68 C2
Highclere Dr GU15 66 A7
Highclere Gdns GU21 68 D2
Highclere Rd
Aldershot GU12 126 D8
Kingston u T KT3 38 D6
Knaphill GU21 68 C2
Highclere St SE26 23 E4
Highcliffe BR3 44 B8
Highcliffe Dr SW15 7 F1
Highcotts La GU4, GU23 91 A1
Highcroft
Beacon Hill GU26 188 D6
Milford GU8 170 F8
Purley CR8 79 F5
Shamley Green GU5 152 E4
2 Surbiton KT5 37 F4
Highcroft Ct KT23 94 A4
Highcroft Dr RH12 195 E1
Highcross Way 4 SW15 19 A7
Highdaun Dr SW16 41 F5
Highdene 6 GU22 69 F1
Highdown KT4 57 F8
Highdown Ct RH10 202 B3
Highdown Way RH12 217 F6
Higher Alham RG12 27 E2
Higher Dr
Belmont KT17, SM7 77 D6
East Horsley KT24 112 E8
Purley CR8 80 A6
Higher Gn KT17 77 A6
Highercombe Rd GU27 208 E8
Highfield Bracknell RG12 26 F3
Feltham TW14 15 A7
Shalford GU4 130 F1
Woodmansterne SM7 78 E2
Highfield Ave GU11 126 A8
Highfield Cl
Aldershot GU11 126 B8
Englefield Green TW20 11 C2
Farnborough GU14 84 F4
Farnham GU9 146 B7
Long Ditton KT6 37 C1
Oxshott KT22 74 D8
Wokingham RG40 25 B6
Highfield Cres GU26 188 F4
Highfield Ct
Englefield Green TW20 11 D2
Mitcham CR4 40 E5
Highfield Dr
Beckenham BR2 44 F5
West Ewell KT19 57 F4
West Wickham BR4 63 C7
Highfield Gdns GU11 126 B8
Highfield Hill SE19 22 E1
Highfield Inf Sch BR2 44 E5
Highfield Jun Sch BR2 44 E5
Highfield La
Puttenham GU3 128 A3
Thursley GU8 169 B2
Highfield Path GU14 84 F4
Highfield Rd
Biggin Hill TN16 83 C3
Carshalton SM1 59 E5
Caterham CR3 101 A5
Chertsey KT16 33 A1
East Grinstead RH19 185 D3
Farnborough GU14 84 F4
Feltham TW13 15 A7
Hounslow TW7 5 F6
Purley CR8 61 A1
Tolworth KT5 38 C2
Upper Halliford TW16 34 F4
Walton-on-T KT12 35 A1
West Byfleet KT14 71 A6
Highfield Sch SW18 20 E8
Highfields Ashstead KT21 95 D8
East Horsley KT24 112 F7
Fetcham KT22 94 D3
Forest Row RH18 206 F2
Sutton SM1 59 A8
Highgate Ct Crawley RH11 201 C2
Farnborough GU14 85 C5
Highgate House 11 SE26 23 A5
Highgate La GU14 85 C5
Highgate Rd RH18 206 F1
Highgate Wlk SE23 23 C6
Highgrove 2 GU14 85 B7
Highgrove Ct BR3 24 A1
Highgrove House GU4 110 C3
Highland Cotts SM6 60 C6
Highland Croft BR3 24 B2
Highland Lodge 2 SE19 22 F1
Highland Pk TW13 14 F4
Highland Rd
Aldershot GU12 105 D2
Beare Green RH5 157 D3
Bromley BR1, BR2 44 F8
Camberley GU15 65 E8
Purley CR8 80 A5
West Norwood SE19 22 E2
Highland View GU6 174 C7
Highlands Ave
Horsham RH13 217 E2
Leatherhead KT22 95 C5
Highlands Cl
Farnham GU9 146 B7
Hounslow TW3 5 B6
Leatherhead KT22 95 B5
Highlands Cres RH13 217 E2
Highlands Ct SE19 22 E2
Highlands Heath SW15 19 C8
Highlands La GU22 89 E5
Highlands Pk KT22 95 D4
Highlands Rd
Heath End GU9 125 C7
Horsham RH13 217 F2
Leatherhead KT22 95 C5
Reigate RH2 118 D2
Highlands The KT24 92 E2
Highmead GU7 150 F6
Highpoint KT13 53 A5
Highridge Cl KT18 76 E5
Highridge Ct KT18 76 E5
Highview CR3 100 E2
Highview Cres GU15 46 F1
Highview Ct
2 Putney SW19 19 E7
2 Reigate RH2 118 D1
Highview High Sch SM6 60 E5
Highway RG45 45 A5
Highway The SM2 59 C2
Highwayman's Ridge GU20 48 B6
Highwold CR5 79 A1
Highwood Cl CR8 80 C2
Highwoods Caterham CR3 100 E2
Leatherhead KT22 95 C6
Hilary Ave CR4 41 A6
Hilary Dr RG45 45 B6
Hilbert Rd SM3 58 D7
Hilborough Cl SW19 20 C1
Hildenborough Gdns BR1 24 F2
Hildenbrough House BR3 23 F1
Hildenlea Pl BR2 44 E7
Hildenley Cl RH1 119 D7
Hildens The RH4 135 C5
Hilder Gdns GU14 85 D3
Hilders La TN8 144 F4
Hilders The KT21 76 B2
Hilditch House 7 TW10 6 F1
Hildreth St SW12 21 B7
Hildreth Street Mews SW12 21 B7
Hilgay GU1 109 F1
Hilgay Cl GU1 109 F1
Hilgay Ct GU1 109 F1
Hill Cl Purley CR8 80 C6
Woking GU21 69 D3
Wonersh GU5 152 B6
Hill Copse View RG12 27 E8
Hill Cres Kingston u T KT5 37 F4
North Cheam KT4 58 C8
Hill Crest
Dormans Park RH19 185 E6
Elstead GU8 148 D4
Hill Crest Dr GU10 145 F6
Hill Ct Farncombe GU7 150 E6
Haslemere GU27 208 B6
8 Kingston u T KT2 18 B1
14 Kingston u T KT6 37 E4
Hill Dr SW16 41 F6
Hill Field Rd TW12 35 F8
Hill Gr TW13 15 F6
Hill House Cl RH10 204 A5
Hill House Dr
Hampton TW12 36 A8
Reigate RH2 139 B7
Weybridge KT13 72 A8
Hill House Rd SW16 21 F3
Hill La KT20 97 E6
Hill Manor RH12 217 A2
Hill Mead RH12 217 B3
Hill Park Dr KT22 94 F8
Hill Rd Beacon Hill GU26 188 C6
Carshalton SM5 59 E4
Fetcham KT23 94 B5
Grayshott GU26 188 C3
Haslemere GU27 208 C6
Heath End GU9 125 D7
Mitcham CR4 21 B1
Purley CR8 79 F7
Sutton SM1 59 B5
Hill Rise Dorking RH4 115 A1
Forest Hill SE23 23 B7
Hinchley Wood KT10 56 B8
Richmond TW10 6 D2
Hill St TW10 6 D2
Hill The CR3 100 F3
Hill Top SM3, SM4 39 F2
Hill View CR4 41 E5
Hill View Cl Purley CR8 80 B8
Tadworth KT20 97 C6
Hill View Cres GU2 108 F3
Hill View Ct 15 GU22 69 E1
Hill View Rd Claygate KT10 56 A3
Farnham GU9 124 F2
Twickenham TW1 6 A1
Woking GU22 69 F1
Hillacre CR3 100 E2
Hillard Ct SM6 60 D4
Hillars Heath Rd CR5 79 E4
Hillary Cl
East Grinstead RH19 186 A3
Farnham GU9 146 B7
Hillary Cres KT12 35 C1
Hillary Ct TW19 13 E7
Hillary House 10 RH1 118 F2
Hillary Rd GU9 146 B7
Hillbarn CR2 80 E8
Hillberry RG12 27 C2
Hillbrook Gdns KT13 53 A3
Hillbrook Prim Sch & Hillcroft Sch Annexe SW17 21 A4
Hillbrook Rd SW17 21 A4
Hillbrook Rise GU9 125 B6
Hillbrow New Malden KT3 38 F6
3 Reigate RH2 118 C1
7 Richmond TW10 6 E1
Hillbrow Cl GU3 108 B2
Hillbrow Cotts RH9 121 C3
Hillbrow Ct RH9 121 C3
Hillbrow Rd Catford BR1 24 E2
Esher KT10 55 C6
Hillbury Cl CR6 81 C1
Hillbury Gdns CR6 81 C1
Hillbury Rd
Upper Tooting SW17 21 B5
Warlingham CR3, CR6 81 B1
Hillcote Ave SW16 22 A1
Hillcrest Heath End GU9 125 D8
Weybridge KT13 53 B6
Hillcrest Ave KT16 51 E6
Hillcrest Cl Beckenham BR3 43 F3
Crawley RH10 202 D6
Epsom KT18 76 F4
Forest Hill SE26 23 A4
Hillcrest Ct Sutton SM2 59 D4
Weybridge KT13 53 B6
Hillcrest Gdns KT10 55 F7
Hillcrest House GU4 110 C3
Hillcrest Par CR5 79 B5
Hillcrest Rd
Biggin Hill TN16 83 D3
Camberley GU15 66 B7
Guildford GU2 108 F2
Kenley CR3 80 F2
Wallington CR8 60 F1
Hillcrest View BR3 43 F3
Hillcroft Ave CR5, CR8 79 D6
Hillcroft Coll KT6 37 E3
Hillcroft Cty Prim Sch
Caterham CR3 100 E4
Whyteleafe CR3 100 F6
Hillcroome Rd SM2 59 D4
Hillcross Ave Merton SM4 39 E4
West Barnes SM4 39 E4
Hillcross Mid Sch SM4 39 F5
Hilldale Rd SM1 58 F6
Hilldeane Rd CR8 61 A1
Hilldown Ct SW16 21 E1
Hilldown Rd
Streatham SW16 21 F1
West Wickham BR2 44 F1
Hilley Field La KT22 94 C6
Hillfield Ave SM4 40 E4
Hillfield Cl Guildford GU1 110 C3
Redhill RH1 119 A1
Hillfield Rd RH1 119 A1
Hillford Pl RH1 140 A3
Hillgarth GU26 188 D5
Hillgate Pl SW12 21 B8
Hillhouse La RH12 194 F1
Hillhurst Gdns CR3 100 E7
Hillier Gdns CR0 61 A5
Hillier House GU2 130 B7
Hillier Lodge TW12 16 D3
Hillier Mews GU1 110 A1
Hillier Pl KT9 56 C4
Hillier Rd GU1 110 A1
Hillier's La CR0, SM6 60 E7
Hillingdale Biggin Hill TN16 83 B1
Crawley RH11 201 C1
Hillingdon Ave TW19 13 E7
Hillmead RH11 200 F6
Hillmont Rd KT10 55 E7
Hillmore Gr SE26 23 E3
Hillmount 13 GU22 69 E1
Hillrise Brands Hill SL3 1 A8
Walton-on-T KT12 34 F2
Hills Farm La RH12 216 F1
Hills Pl RH12 217 A2
Hillsborough Ct GU14 84 E8
Hillsborough Pk GU15 66 C5
Hillside Ascot SL5 29 C4
Banstead SM7 77 E4
Crawley Down RH10 204 B8
Forest Row RH18 206 E3
Horsham RH12 217 A2
Sandhurst GU15 64 F7
Wentworth GU25 31 C3
Wimbledon SW19 19 D2
Woking GU22 89 D7
Hillside Ave CR8 80 B6
Hillside Cl Banstead SM7 77 E3
Brockham RH3 137 A8
Crawley RH11 201 B4
East Grinstead RH19 185 E3
Headley Down GU35 187 A6
Knaphill GU21 68 D2
Merton SM4 39 E5
Hillside Cres GU16 85 F7
Hillside Ct Guildford GU1 130 E8
7 Kingston u T KT2 18 B1
Hillside Gdns
Addlestone KT15 51 F5
Brockham RH3, RH5 116 A1
Streatham SW2 22 A6
Wallington SM6 60 C3
Hillside La Coney Hall BR2 63 F8
Heath End GU9 125 D8
Hillside Pk SL5 29 F1
Hillside Rd
Aldershot GU11 126 A8
Ash GU12 106 B3
Ashtead KT21 75 F2
Beckenham BR2 44 F6
Belmont SM2 58 F3
Coulsdon CR5 79 F1
Croydon CR0 61 B6
East Ewell KT17 58 C1
Farnham GU10 146 C3
Heath End GU9 125 E7
Kingston u T KT5 38 A4
Linchmere GU27 207 F5
Streatham SW2 22 A6
Tatsfield TN16 103 E8
Warlingham CR3, CR6 81 A1
Whyteleafe CR3, CR6 81 A1
Hillside Way GU7 150 D7
Hillsmead Way CR2 81 B6
Hillspur Cl GU2 108 F2
Hillspur Rd GU2 108 F2
Hilltop Cl Ascot SL5 29 E7

Hilltop Cl *continued*
Guildford GU3 . . . . 108 F5
Leatherhead KT22 . . . . 95 C4
Hilltop Ct SE19 . . . . 42 D8
Hilltop La CR3, RH1 . . . . . . 100 A1
Hilltop Rd Kenley CR3 . . . . . 80 F2
Reigate RH2 . . . . 139 B7
Hilltop Rise KT23 . . . . 94 C1
Hilltop Wlk CR3 . . . . 101 E6
Hillview Whyteleafe CR3 . . . . 80 F2
Wimbledon SW20 . . . . 19 B1
Hillview Ct SE19 . . . . 22 E4
Hillview Dr RH1 . . . . 140 A8
Hillview Rd SM1 . . . . 59 D7
Hillworth BR3 . . . . 44 B7
Hillworth Rd SW2 . . . . 22 A8
Hilly Mead SW19 . . . . 19 E1
Hillybarn Rd RH11 . . . . . . 180 C1
Hilsea Point 7 SW15 . . . . . 19 B7
Hilton Ct RH6 . . . . 161 C4
Hilton Way CR2 . . . . 81 B4
Himley Rd SW17 . . . . 20 F2
Hinchcliffe Cl SM6 . . . . 60 F3
Hinchley Cl KT10 . . . . 55 F7
Hinchley Dr KT10 . . . . 55 F7
Hinchley Way KT10 . . . . 56 A7
Hinchley Wood Prim Sch
KT10 . . . . 56 A8
Hinchley Wood Sch KT10 . 56 A8
Hinchley Wood Sta KT10 . . 55 F7
Hindell Cl GU14 . . . . 85 A8
Hindhead Cl RH11 . . . . . . 201 C4
Hindhead Point 6 SW15 . . 19 B7
Hindhead Rd GU26, GU27 . 188 F2
Hindhead Way SM6 . . . . 60 E5
Hindsley's Pl SE23 . . . . 23 C6
Hinkler Cl SM6 . . . . 60 E3
Hinstock Cl GU14 . . . . 85 A3
Hinton Ave TW4 . . . . 4 D3
Hinton Cl RG45 . . . . 45 B7
Hinton Dr RG45 . . . . 45 B7
Hinton Rd SM6 . . . . 60 C4
Hipley Ct GU1 . . . . 131 A8
Hipley St GU22 . . . . 90 B7
Hitchcock Cl TW17 . . . . 33 F6
Hitchings Way RH2 . . . . . . 139 A5
Hither Green Hospl SE13 . 24 D8
Hither Green La SE13 . . . . . 24 E8
Hitherbury Cl GU2 . . . . . . 130 C6
Hitherfield Prim Sch SW2 22 A6
Hitherfield Rd SW16, SW27 22 A5
Hitherhooks Hill RG42 . . . . 26 E8
Hithermoor Rd TW19 . . . . . . 2 A2
Hitherwood GU6 . . . . 174 E2
Hitherwood Cl RH2 . . . . . . 118 E3
Hitherwood Ct SE21 . . . . . . 22 F4
Hitherwood Dr SE19, SE21 . 22 F4
Hoadly Rd SW16 . . . . 21 D6
Hobart Gdns CR7 . . . . 42 D6
Hobart Pl 14 TW10 . . . . 6 F1
Hobart Rd KT4 . . . . 58 B7
Hobbs Cl KT14 . . . . 71 B6
Hobbs Ind Est RH7 . . . . . . 184 D7
Hobbs Rd Crawley RH11 . . 201 A2
5 West Norwood SE27 . . . . 22 C4
Hobill Wlk KT5 . . . . 37 F3
Hocken Mead RH10 . . . . . . 202 D8
Hockering Gdns GU22 . . . . 70 B1
Hockering Rd GU22 . . . . 70 B1
Hockford Cl GU3 . . . . 88 B1
Hodge La SL5 . . . . 9 A3
Hodges Cl GU19 . . . . 47 E1
Hodgkin Cl RH10 . . . . 202 C5
Hodgson Gdns GU1, GU4 . 110 A4
Hoe Bridge Sch GU22 . . . . 90 C8
Hoe Cotts GU5 . . . . 154 E8
Hoe La Hascombe GU8 . . . . 172 D4
Peaslake GU5, RH5 . . . . . . 154 F8
Hoebridge Golf Ctr GU22 . 90 C8
Hoebrook Glade GU22 . . . . 89 E6
Hogarth Ave TW15 . . . . 14 C2
Hogarth Bsns Pk W4 . . . . . . 7 E8
Hogarth Cl GU47 . . . . 64 E6
Hogarth Cres
Mitcham CR4, SW19 . . . . . . 40 D8
Thornton Heath CR0 . . . . . . 42 C2
Hogarth Ct Dulwich SE19 . . . 22 F4
Heston TW5 . . . . 4 E7
Hogarth Gdns TW5 . . . . 5 A7
Hogarth House 6 SE27 . . . 22 C4
Hogarth La W4 . . . . 7 E8
Hogarth Rd RH10 . . . . 201 F3
Hogarth Roundabout W4 . . 7 E8
Hogarth Way TW12 . . . . 36 C8
Hoghatch La GU9 . . . . 125 A6
Hogoak La SL4 . . . . 8 A8
Hogscross La CR5 . . . . 98 F5
Hogshill La KT11 . . . . 73 C5
Hogsmill Way KT19 . . . . 57 C6
Hogspudding La RH5 . . . . 158 C1
Hogtrough La
Nutfield RH1 . . . . 140 D8
Oxted RH8 . . . . 122 B6
Hogwood Rd RH14 . . . . . . 212 C3
Holbeach Mews SW12 . . . . 21 B7
Holbeach Prim Sch SE6 . . 24 A8
Holbeach Rd SE6 . . . . 24 B8
Holbeck RG12 . . . . 26 F3
Holbein Rd RH10 . . . . 201 F3
Holberry House 5 SE21 . . . 22 E4
Holborn Way CR4 . . . . 40 F7
Holbreck Pl GU22 . . . . 69 F1
Holbrook Cl GU9 . . . . 125 F8
Holbrook Ct TW20 . . . . 12 C3
Holbrook Cty Prim Sch
RH12 . . . . 217 E7
Holbrook House 5 SW2 . . . 21 F7
Holbrook Meadow TW20 . . 12 C2
Holbrook School La
RH12 . . . . 217 E7
Holbrook Way GU11 . . . . . 126 B7
Holcon Ct RH1 . . . . 119 A4
Holder Rd Aldershot GU12 . 105 E1
Crawley RH10 . . . . 202 B3
Holderness Way SE27 . . . . . 22 B3
Holdernesse Rd
Isleworth TW7 . . . . 6 A6
6 Upper Tooting SW17 . . . . 21 A6
Holdfast La GU27 . . . . 208 F7
Holdsworth House 5
SW2 . . . . 22 A8
Hole Hill RH4 . . . . 135 B7
Holford Rd GU1 . . . . 110 C1
Holland Ave Belmont SM2 . . 59 A2
Wimbledon SW20 . . . . 38 F8
Holland Cl Coney Hall BR2 . . 63 F8
Farnham GU9 . . . . 146 E8
Redhill RH1 . . . . 118 F1
Holland Cres RH8 . . . . 123 A2
Holland Cty Jun Sch
RH8 . . . . 123 A1
Holland Dr SE23 . . . . 23 E5
Holland Gdns TW20 . . . . . . 32 F7
Holland La RH8 . . . . 123 A2
Holland Pines RG12 . . . . . . 26 F2
Holland Rd Croydon SE25 . . 43 A4
Oxted RH8 . . . . 123 A1
Holland Way BR2 . . . . 63 F8
Hollands Field RH13 . . . . . 216 E4
Hollands The
Feltham TW13 . . . . 15 D4
New Malden KT4 . . . . 38 F1
Hollands Way
East Grinstead RH19 . . . . . 186 A4
Warnham RH12 . . . . 216 F8
Holles Cl TW12 . . . . 16 A3
Hollies Ave KT14 . . . . 70 F6
Hollies Cl
South Norwood SW16 . . . . . 22 A2
Twickenham TW1 . . . . 16 F6
Hollies Ct KT15 . . . . 52 C5
Hollies Way 2 SW12 . . . . . . 21 A8
Hollin Ct RH10, RH11 . . . . . 181 E1
Hollingbourne Cres
RH11 . . . . 201 C1
Hollingsworth Rd CR0, CR2 62 B4
Hollington Cres KT3 . . . . . . 39 A3
Hollingworth Cl KT8 . . . . . . 35 F5
Hollingworth Ct 7 KT6 . . . 37 D2
Hollis Wood Dr GU10 . . . . 145 E5
Hollman Gdns SW16 . . . . . . 22 B2
Hollow Cl GU2 . . . . 130 B8
Hollow La
Dormansland RH19, RH7 . . 186 D6
Virginia Water GU25 . . . . . . 31 C6
Wotton RH5 . . . . 134 D2
Hollow The Crawley RH11 . 200 F5
Shackleford GU7 . . . . 149 F4
Holloway Dr GU25 . . . . 31 E5
Holloway Hill
Godalming GU7 . . . . 150 D4
Lyne KT16 . . . . 51 D8
Holloway La UB7 . . . . 2 E8
Holloway St TW3 . . . . 5 B4
Holly Acre GU22 . . . . 89 C4
Holly Ave Frimley GU16 . . . . 66 B3
Walton-on-T KT12 . . . . 35 D1
Woodham KT15 . . . . 52 A1
Holly Bank Rd GU22 . . . . . . 89 B7
Holly Bush Ind Pk GU12 . 105 E5
Holly Bush La
Farnborough GU11 . . . . . . 105 E6
Hampton TW12 . . . . 15 F1
Holly Cl Aldershot GU12 . . . 105 C2
Crawley RH10 . . . . 202 A8
Englefield Green TW20 . . . . 11 B2
Farnborough GU14 . . . . 85 A4
Feltham TW13 . . . . 15 E3
Headley Down GU35 . . . . . 187 C5
Horsham RH12 . . . . 218 B5
Longcross KT16 . . . . 50 A7
Woking GU21 . . . . 89 B8
Holly Cott KT7 . . . . 37 A1
Holly Cres BR3 . . . . 43 F4
Holly Ct 9 Belmont SM2 . . . 59 A3
Leatherhead KT22 . . . . 95 A5
Holly Gn KT13 . . . . 53 D6
Holly Grove Cl TW3 . . . . 4 F3
Holly Hedge Cl GU16 . . . . . . 65 E2
Holly Hedge Rd
Cobham KT11 . . . . 73 B5
Frimley GU16 . . . . 65 E2
Holly Hill Dr SM7 . . . . 78 A3
Holly Hock GU24 . . . . 68 A4
Holly Hough KT20 . . . . 116 B5
Holly House
Bracknell RG12 . . . . 27 B3
Brentford TW8 . . . . 6 C8
Holly La Banstead SM7 . . . . . 78 C2
Godalming GU7 . . . . 150 C4
Woodmansterne SM7 . . . . . . 78 C2
Worplesdon GU3 . . . . 108 D7
Holly La E SM7 . . . . 78 B3
Holly La W SM7 . . . . 78 B2
Holly Lea GU4 . . . . 109 D7
Holly Lodge Mid Sch
GU12 . . . . 105 F8
Holly Rd Aldershot GU12 . . 105 D1
Farnborough GU14 . . . . 85 A4
Hampton TW12 . . . . 16 C2
Hounslow TW3 . . . . 5 B3
Reigate RH2 . . . . 139 B7
Twickenham TW1 . . . . 17 A7
Holly Ridge GU24 . . . . 67 E6
Holly Spring Cty Inf Sch
RG12 . . . . 27 E7
Holly Spring Cty Jun Sch
RG12 . . . . 27 E7
Holly Spring La RG12 . . . . . 27 D8
Holly Tree Rd CR3 . . . . 100 E5
Holly Way Blackwater GU17 . 64 D4
Mitcham CR4 . . . . 41 D6
Holly Wlk SL4 . . . . 9 E4
Hollybank GU24 . . . . 67 F6
Hollybank Cl TW12 . . . . 16 A3
Hollybank Rd KT14 . . . . 71 A5
Hollybush Rd
Crawley RH10 . . . . 201 E8
Kingston u T KT2 . . . . 17 E2
Hollybush Ride GU19, GU20 47 F6
Hollycombe TW20 . . . . 11 D4
Hollycroft Cl
Harmondsworth UB7 . . . . 3 A8
South Croydon CR2 . . . . 61 E5
Hollycroft Gdns UB7 . . . . 3 A8
Hollydene BR1 . . . . 44 F8
Hollyfield Rd KT5 . . . . 37 F2
Hollyfield Sch KT6 . . . . 37 E4
Hollyfields Cl GU15 . . . . 65 B5
Hollymead SM5 . . . . 59 F7
Hollymead Rd CR5 . . . . 79 A1
Hollymeoak Rd CR5 . . . . . . 79 B1
Hollymoor La KT19 . . . . 57 D1
Hollymount Prim Sch
SW20 . . . . 39 C8
Hollyridge GU27 . . . . 208 B6
Hollytree Cl SW19 . . . . 19 D7
Hollytree Gdns GU16 . . . . . 85 D8
Hollywoods CR0 . . . . 62 F2
Holm Cl KT15 . . . . 70 E7
Holm Ct Dorking RH4 . . . . . 136 B4
Farncombe GU7 . . . . 150 D7
Holman Ct KT17 . . . . 58 A2
Holman Rd KT19 . . . . 57 C5
Holmbank Dr TW17 . . . . 34 E5
Holmbrook Cl GU14 . . . . . . 84 C4
Holmbrook Gdns GU14 . . . . 84 C4
Holmbury Ave RG45 . . . . . . 45 A7
Holmbury Cl RH11 . . . . . . 201 C4
Holmbury Ct Mitcham SW19 20 E1
Upper Tooting SW17 . . . . . . 20 F5
Holmbury Dr RH5 . . . . 136 C4
Holmbury Gr CR0 . . . . 62 F3
Holmbury Hill Rd RH5 . . . . 155 B3
Holmbury Rd RH5 . . . . 155 D1
Holmbush Cl RH12 . . . . . . 217 D6
Holmcroft Crawley RH10 . . 201 E5
Walton on t H KT20 . . . . 97 B2
Holmdene Cl BR3 . . . . 44 C7
Holme Chase KT13 . . . . 53 C4
Holme Cl RG45 . . . . 45 A7
Holmes Cl Ascot SL5 . . . . . . 29 C3
Woking GU23 . . . . 89 F6
Wokingham RG41 . . . . 25 A4
Holmes Cres RG41 . . . . 25 A4
Holmes Rd Merton SW19 . . . 20 C1
Twickenham TW1 . . . . 16 F6
Holmesdale 2 KT13 . . . . . . 53 D4
Holmesdale Ave SW14 . . . . . 7 B3
Holmesdale Cl
Guildford GU1 . . . . 110 B2
South Norwood SE25 . . . . . . 42 F6
Holmesdale Rd
Dorking RH5 . . . . 136 C3
Reigate RH2 . . . . 118 B2
Richmond TW9 . . . . 6 F6
South Norwood SE25 . . . . . . 42 E5
South Nutfield RH1 . . . . . . 140 F7
Teddington TW11 . . . . 17 C2
Thornton Heath CR0 . . . . . . 42 D4
Holmethorpe Ave RH1 . . . 119 B4
Holmethorpe Ind Est
RH1 . . . . 119 B4
Holmewood Cl RG41 . . . . . . 25 A2
Holmewood Gdns SW2 . . . . 21 F8
Holmewood Rd
South Norwood SE25 . . . . . . 42 E6
Streatham SW2 . . . . 21 F8
Holmgrove House CR8 . . . . 80 A7
Holming End RH12 . . . . . . 218 B5
Holmoaks House BR3 . . . . . 44 C7
Holmsdale Cty Inf Sch
RH2 . . . . 118 B3
Holmshaw Cl SE26, SE6 . . . 23 E4
Holmsley Cl KT3 . . . . 38 F2
Holmsley House SW15 . . . . 18 F8
Holmwood 2 KT5 . . . . 37 F3
Holmwood Ave CR2 . . . . 80 F6
Holmwood Cl
Addlestone KT15 . . . . 52 A5
Cheam SM2 . . . . 58 D3
East Horsley KT24 . . . . 112 E6
Holmwood Gdns SM6 . . . . . 60 B4
Holmwood Rd
Chessington KT9 . . . . 56 E5
East Ewell KT17, SM2 . . . . . 58 C2
Holmwood Sta RH5 . . . . . 157 C4
Holmwood View Rd RH5 . 136 B1
Holne Chase SM4 . . . . 40 A3
Holroyd Rd KT10 . . . . 55 F2
Holstein Ave KT13 . . . . 53 A6
Holsworthy Way KT9 . . . . . . 56 C5
Holt Cl GU14 . . . . 85 C7
Holt La RG41 . . . . 25 B7
Holt Pound La GU10 . . . . . 145 C5
Holt Sch The RG41 . . . . 25 B7
Holt The Morden SM4 . . . . . 40 A5
Wallington SM6 . . . . 60 C6
Holt Wood CR6 . . . . 82 A3
Holton Heath 8 RG12 . . . . . 27 F5
Holtwood Rd KT22 . . . . 74 C6
Holtye Ave RH19 . . . . 186 A3
Holtye Rd RH19 . . . . 186 B3
Holtye Wlk RH10 . . . . 202 A4
Holy Cross Catholic Prim
Sch SE6 . . . . 24 C7
Holy Cross Hospl GU27 . . 207 F7
Holy Cross RC Convent
Sch KT3 . . . . 38 E4
Holy Cross RC Prep Sch
KT2 . . . . 18 C1
Holy Family RC Prim Sch
The KT15 . . . . 52 A5
Holy Ghost RC Prim Sch
SW12 . . . . 21 A8
Holy Trinity C of E Inf Sch
SW17 . . . . 20 F6
Holy Trinity C of E Prim
Sch Forest Hill SE23 . . . . . 23 C6
Streatham SW2 . . . . 21 F8
West End GU24 . . . . 68 A7
Wimbledon SW19 . . . . 20 B2
Holy Trinity CE Aided Sch
SL5 . . . . 30 A3
Holy Trinity CE Jun Sch
TW10 . . . . 7 A3
Holy Trinity CE Sch The
RH11 . . . . 201 A4
Holy Trinity Church of
England Jun Sch SM6 . . . 60 C6
Holy Trinity Sch GU1 . . . . 130 F7
Holybourne Ave SW15 . . . . 19 A8
Holyhead Ct KT1 . . . . 37 D5
Holyhook Cl RG45 . . . . 45 A6
Holyoake Ave GU21 . . . . . . 69 C2
Holyoake Cres GU21 . . . . . . 69 C2
Holyrood RH19 . . . . 206 A8
Holyrood Pl RH11 . . . . 201 B2
Holywell Cl
Farnborough GU14 . . . . 85 A7
Stanwell TW19 . . . . 13 E7
Holywell Way TW19 . . . . . . 13 E7
Homan House 6 SW4 . . . . 21 D8
Hombrook Dr RG42 . . . . 26 E8
Hombrook House RG42 . . . 26 E8
Home Cl Carshalton SM5 . . . 59 F8
Crawley RH10 . . . . 202 C8
Fetcham KT22 . . . . 94 D6
Home Ct KT6 . . . . 37 D4
Home Farm Cl
Betchworth RH3 . . . . 137 E8
Burgh Heath KT18 . . . . 77 D2
Esher KT10 . . . . 55 B4
Farnborough GU14 . . . . 85 D6
Ottershaw KT16 . . . . 51 A3
Thames Ditton KT7 . . . . 36 F2
Upper Halliford TW17 . . . . . 34 E5
Home Farm Cotts GU8 . . . 149 C5
Home Farm Gdns KT12 . . . . 54 C8
Home Farm Rd GU7 . . . . . 150 F2
Home Meadow SM7 . . . . . . 78 A3
Home Park Cl GU5 . . . . . . 151 F6
Home Park Rd SW19 . . . . . . 19 F4
Home Park Wlk KT1 . . . . . . 37 D5
Home Pk RH8 . . . . 123 A4
Homebeech House 7
GU22 . . . . 69 E1
Homecoppice House 1
BR1 . . . . 24 F1
Homecourt TW14 . . . . 15 A7
Homecroft Rd SE26 . . . . 23 C3
Homefield Morden SM4 . . . . 40 A5
Thursley GU8 . . . . 169 C3
Homefield Cl Horley RH6 . 161 B4
Leatherhead KT22 . . . . 95 C6
Woodham KT15 . . . . 70 E7
Homefield Gdns
Burgh Heath KT20 . . . . 97 C7
Mitcham CR4, SW19 . . . . . . 40 D7
Homefield House SE23 . . . 23 D5
Homefield Pk SM1, SM2 . . . 59 B4
Homefield Prep Sch SM1 . 59 A5
Homefield Rd
Coulsdon CR3, CR5 . . . . . . 100 B7
Walton-on-T KT12 . . . . 35 E2
Warlingham CR6 . . . . 101 C8
Wimbledon SW19 . . . . 19 E3
Homegreen House GU27 208 A6
Homeland Dr SM2 . . . . 59 B2
Homelands KT22 . . . . 95 C6
Homelands Dr SE19 . . . . . . 22 E1
Homelea Cl GU14 . . . . 85 B8
Homeleigh Cres GU12 . . . . 106 A8
Homeleigh Ct 8 SW16 . . . . 21 E5
Homemead SW12 . . . . 21 B6
Homemead Rd CR0 . . . . 41 C3
Homepark House GU9 . . . 125 C2
Homer Rd CR0 . . . . 43 D3
Homersham Rd KT1 . . . . . . 38 B7
Homesdale Rd CR3 . . . . . . 100 D4
Homestall GU2 . . . . 108 D2
Homestall Rd RH19 . . . . . . 206 E8
Homestead GU6 . . . . 174 F4
Homestead Gdns KT10 . . . . 55 E5
Homestead Rd
Caterham CR3 . . . . 100 D4
Staines TW18 . . . . 13 B2
Homestead Way CR0 . . . . . 82 D7
Homesteads The BR3 . . . . . 24 B2
Homewalk House SE26 . . . 23 C4
Homewater House 1
KT17 . . . . 76 E6
Homewaters Ave TW16 . . . 34 F8
Homewood GU6 . . . . 175 A3
Homewood Cl TW12 . . . . . . 15 F2
Homewood Gdns SE25 . . . . 42 E4
Homewoods 2 SW12 . . . . . . 21 C8
Homeworth House 8
GU22 . . . . 69 E1
Homildon House 10 SE26 . . 23 A5
Homington Ct KT2 . . . . 17 E1
Homstead The RH6 . . . . . . 162 B1
Hone Hill GU47 . . . . 64 B8
Hones Yard Bsns Pk
GU9 . . . . 125 D2
Honey Hill RG40 . . . . 26 A1
Honeybrook
Rd SW12, SW4 . . . . 21 C8
Honeycrock La RH1 . . . . . 140 B2
Honeyhill Rd RG42 . . . . 27 A8
Honeypot La TN8 . . . . 144 D4
Honeypots Rd GU22 . . . . . . 89 D5
Honeysuckle Bottom
KT24 . . . . 112 E2
Honeysuckle Cl
Crowthorne RG45 . . . . 45 A7
Horley RH6 . . . . 161 C4
Honeysuckle Gdns CR0 . . . 43 D1
Honeysuckle La
Crawley RH11 . . . . 181 C1
Dorking RH5 . . . . 136 C4
Headley Down GU35 . . . . . 187 B5
Honeysuckle Wlk RH12 . . 218 A5
Honeywood La
Ockley RH5 . . . . 196 F5
Rowhook RH5 . . . . 196 F5
Honeywood Rd
Horsham RH13 . . . . 218 A4
Isleworth TW7 . . . . 6 A3
Honeywood Wlk SM5 . . . . . 59 F6
Honister Hts CR8 . . . . 80 E5
Honister Wlk GU15 . . . . 66 D4
Honley Rd SE6 . . . . 24 B8
Honnor Rd TW18 . . . . 13 D1
Honor Oak Rd SE23 . . . . . . 23 C8
Hood Ave SW14 . . . . 7 C2
Hood Cl CR0, CR9 . . . . 42 B1
Hood Rd SW20 . . . . 18 F1
Hook Heath Ave GU22 . . . . 89 C8
Hook Heath Gdns GU22 . . . 88 F6
Hook Heath Rd GU22 . . . . . 89 B6
Hook Hill CR2 . . . . 61 E1
Hook Hill La GU22 . . . . 89 C6
Hook Hill Pk GU22 . . . . 89 B6
Hook House 9 SW27 . . . . . 22 B3
Hook La Gomshall GU5 . . . 133 C2
Puttenham GU3 . . . . 128 D3
West End GU24 . . . . 67 C6
Hook Mill La GU18 . . . . 48 D2
Hook Rd Chessington KT6 . . 56 E7
Epsom KT19, KT17 . . . . 57 C2
Ewell KT19 . . . . 76 D8
Surbiton KT6, KT9 . . . . 56 E7
Hook Rise N Surbiton KT6 . . 56 E7
Tolworth KT6, KT9 . . . . 57 B8
Hook Rise S KT6, KT9 . . . . . 57 B8
Hook Rise South KT6 . . . . . 56 E7
Hook Underpass KT6 . . . . . 56 E7
Hooke Rd KT24 . . . . 92 F2
Hookfield KT18, KT19 . . . . . 76 C6
Hookfield Mews KT19 . . . . . 76 C6
Hookhouse Rd GU8 . . . . . 192 D6
Hookley Cl GU8 . . . . 148 E3
Hookley La GU8 . . . . 148 E3
Hookstile La GU9 . . . . 125 C1
Hookstone La GU24 . . . . . . 67 F8
Hookwood Bglws RH8 . . . 123 B6
Hookwood Cnr RH8 . . . . . 123 B7
Hookwood Cotts KT18 . . . . 96 C3
Hooley La RH1 . . . . 139 F8
Hoover House SE6 . . . . 24 C4
Hope Ave RG12 . . . . 27 E2
Hope Cl SM1 . . . . 59 C5
Hope Ct RH11 . . . . 201 B1
Hope Fountain GU15 . . . . . 65 F4
Hope Grant's Rd GU11 . . . 105 A4
Hope La GU9 . . . . 125 B6
Hope Pk BR1 . . . . 24 F1
Hope St GU8 . . . . 148 D4
Hopeman Cl GU47 . . . . 64 D7
Hopes Cl TW5 . . . . 5 A8
Hopfield GU21 . . . . 69 E3
Hopfield Ave KT14 . . . . 71 E6
Hophurst Cl RH10 . . . . 204 B8
Hophurst Dr RH10 . . . . 204 B8
Hophurst Hill RH10, RH19 184 D2
Hophurst La RH10 . . . . 184 B1
Hopkins Ct RH11 . . . . 201 B1
Hoppety The KT20 . . . . 97 D5
Hoppingwood Ave KT3 . . . . 38 E6
Hopton Gdns KT3 . . . . 39 A3
Hopton Rd SW16 . . . . 21 E3
Hopwood Cl SW17 . . . . 20 C5
Horace Rd KT1 . . . . 37 F6
Horatio Ave RG42 . . . . 27 E8
Horatius Way CR0 . . . . 60 F4
Hordern House RH12 . . . . 217 A1
Horewood Rd RG12 . . . . 27 B3
Horley Cty Inf Sch RH6 . . 161 A3
Horley Lodge La RH1 . . . . 161 A8
Horley Rd Crawley RH6 . . . 181 B7
Hookwood RH6 . . . . 181 B7
Redhill RH1 . . . . 139 F5
Horley Row RH6 . . . . 161 A4
Horley Sta RH6 . . . . 161 B2
Hormer Cl GU47 . . . . 45 D1
Horn Rd GU14 . . . . 84 E5
Hornbeam Cl
Farnborough GU14 . . . . 84 C5
Horsham RH13 . . . . 217 F1
Sandhurst GU47 . . . . 45 D1
Hornbeam Cres TW8 . . . . 6 B7
Hornbeam Rd
Guildford GU1 . . . . 109 C3
Reigate RH2 . . . . 139 C6
Hornbeam Terr SM5 . . . . . . 40 E1
Hornbeam Wlk KT12 . . . . . . 53 F2

Hornby Ave RG12 27 D2
Hornchurch Cl KT2 17 D3
Hornchurch Hill CR3 80 F1
Horndean Cl
Crawley RH10 182 D2
3 Roehampton SW15 19 A7
Horndean Rd RG12 27 F3
Horne Rd TW17 34 A5
Hornecourt Hill RH6 162 F7
Horner La CR4 40 D7
Hornhatch GU4 131 B3
Hornhatch Cl GU4 131 B3
Hornhatch La GU4 131 B2
Horniman Dr SE23 23 C8
Horniman Grange 7 SE23 23 C7
Horniman Mus & Gdns SE23 23 B7
Horniman Prim Sch SE23 23 B7
Hornshill La RH12 213 F7
Horsa Cl SM6 60 E3
Horse Fair KT1 37 D7
Horse Gate Ride SL5 29 A3
Horse Hill RH6 160 B4
Horsebrass Dr GU19 47 E2
Horsecroft SM7 77 F2
Horsell Birch Woking GU21 69 A4
Woking GU21 69 B4
Horsell C of E Sch GU21 69 B4
Horsell Common Rd GU21 69 C5
Horsell Ct KT16 33 B2
Horsell Moor GU21 69 D2
Horsell Park Cl GU21 69 D3
Horsell Pk GU21 69 E3
Horsell Rise GU21 69 E4
Horsell Rise Cl GU21 69 D4
Horsell Vale GU21 69 E3
Horsell Village Cty Inf Sch GU21 69 D4
Horsell Way GU21 69 C3
Horseshoe Bend GU26 188 B3
Horseshoe Cl
Camberley GU15 65 F8
Crawley RH10 202 D7
Horseshoe Cres GU15 65 F8
Horseshoe La
Ash Vale GU12 106 A7
Cranleigh GU6 174 D4
Horseshoe La E GU1 110 C2
Horseshoe La W GU1 110 B1
Horseshoe Ridge KT13 72 C8
Horseshoe The
Banstead SM7 77 F4
Coulsdon CR5, CR8 79 D6
Godalming GU7 150 C3
Horsham Bsns Pk RH12 198 C4
Horsham Hospl RH12 217 C3
Horsham Mus RH12 217 C1
Horsham Rd Alfold GU6 193 F8
Beare Green RH5 157 C4
Beare Green, Holmwood Cnr RH5 157 C6
Bramley GU5, GU4 151 E7
Bramley, Palmers Cross GU5, GU6 173 D5
Capel RH5 178 C2
Capel RH5 178 D8
Cranleigh GU6 174 E1
Cranleigh GU6, RH12 194 C1
Crawley RH11 201 B4
Crawley, Palmers Cross GU5, GU6 173 D5
Dorking RH4 136 A6
Dorking, Mid Holmwood RH5 136 B2
East Bedfont TW14 3 C1
Ellen's Green GU6 176 B1
Ewhurst GU6 175 F3
Holmbury St M GU5, RH5, GU6 155 C5
Rowhook RH5, RH12 196 D5
Rusper RH12 199 B5
Sandhurst GU47 45 D1
Shalford GU4 130 E3
South Holmwood RH5 157 C6
Wallis Wood RH12, RH5 196 D5
Wallis Wood, Mayes Green RH5, GU6 176 E4
Horsham Sta RH13 217 D2
Horsley Cl KT19 76 D6
Horsley Dr Kingston u T KT2 17 D3
New Addington CR0 63 C3
Horsley Rd KT11, KT24 93 B7
Horsley Sta KT24 92 E2
Horsneile La RG42 27 B8
Horton Country Park KT19 57 A3
Horton Hill KT19 76 C8
Horton Hospl KT19 76 B8
Horton La KT19, KT18 57 B2
Horton Park Children's Farm KT19 57 A1
Horton Rd Colnbrook SL3 1 A6
Horton SL3 1 A6
Poyle SL3, TW19 1 E4
Stanwell TW19 2 A2
Horton Trad Est SL3 1 C4
Horton Way CR0 43 D4
Horvath Cl KT13 53 D6
Hosack Rd SW12, SW17 21 A6
Hoskins Pl RH19 186 A4
Hoskins Place Ind Est GU15 65 B3
Hoskins Rd RH8 122 E6
Hospital Bridge Rd TW2 16 B7
Hospital Hill GU11 105 A3
Hospital of the Holy Trinity (Almshouses) CR9 61 C8
Hospital Rd
Aldershot GU11 105 B3
Hounslow TW3 5 A4
Hospital Way SE13 24 D7
Hotham Cl KT8 36 A6
Hotham Rd SW19 20 C1
Houblon Rd TW10 6 E2
Houghton Cl TW12 15 E2
Houghton Rd RH10 202 C3
Houlder Cres CR0 61 B4
Houlton Ct GU19 47 F2
Hound House Rd GU5 154 A5
Hounslow Ave TW3 5 B2
Hounslow Bsns Pk TW3 5 B3
Hounslow Central Sta TW3 5 B4
Hounslow East Sta TW3 5 C5
Hounslow Ed Ctr (Specl Sch) The TW4 4 E4
Hounslow Gdns TW3 5 B2
Hounslow Heath Jun & Inf Schs TW4 4 E4
Hounslow Manor Sch TW3 5 C4
Hounslow Rd
Feltham, Hanworth TW13 15 D4
Feltham, North Feltham TW14 4 B1
Twickenham TW2, TW3 5 C1
Hounslow Sta TW3 5 B2
Hounslow Town Prim Sch TW3 5 D4
Hounslow West Sta TW3 4 E5
Houseman Rd GU14 84 F6
Houston Ct 3 CR0 42 E1
Houston Rd SE23, SE6 23 E5
Houstoun Ct TW5 4 F7
Hove Gdns SM1 40 B1
Hovenden House 6 SE21 22 E4
How La CR5 79 A1
Howard Ave KT17 58 A1
Howard Cl Ashford TW16 14 F2
Ashtead KT21 75 F1
Hampton TW12 16 C2
Leatherhead KT22 95 C4
Walton on t H KT20 97 A2
West Horsley KT24 92 D2
Howard Cole Way GU11 104 E2
Howard Ct Beckenham BR3 44 C7
Effingham KT24 113 D8
Reigate RH2 118 B2
Howard Dr GU14 84 B4
Howard Gdns GU1 110 A2
Howard House Penge SE20 43 C8
Reigate RH2 118 B2
Howard of Effingham Sch KT24 113 E8
Howard Prim Sch CR0 61 C6
Howard Rd Coulsdon CR5 79 D5
Crawley RH11 200 D2
Croydon SE25 43 A3
Dorking RH4 136 A7
Dorking, North Holmwood RH5 136 C3
East Horsley KT24 93 A4
Great Bookham KT23 114 C8
Horsham RH13 218 A4
Isleworth TW7 5 F4
New Malden KT3 38 F5
Penge SE20 43 C8
Reigate RH2 139 B8
Surbiton KT5 37 F3
Wokingham RG40 25 C5
Howard Ridge GU4 110 A5
Howard St KT7 37 B3
Howards Cl GU22 90 A7
Howards Crest Cl BR3 44 C7
Howards La KT15 51 F3
Howards Rd GU22 89 F7
Howberry Rd CR7 42 D7
Howden Ct SE25 42 F7
Howden Rd SE25 42 F7
Howe Dr CR3 100 D5
Howell Hill Cl KT17 77 C8
Howell Hill Gr KT17 58 C1
Howgate Rd SW14 7 D4
Howitts Cl KT10 55 A5
Howland House 9 SW16 21 E5
Howley Rd CR0, CR9 61 C7
Howmic Ct 1 TW1 6 C1
Howorth Ct RG12 27 E5
Howson Terr TW10 6 E1
Hoylake Cl RH11 200 D5
Hoylake Gdns CR4 41 C6
Hoyle Hill RH5 157 D1
Hoyle Rd SW17 20 E3
Harmondsworth Moor Ctry Pk UB7 2 B7
Hubbard Dr KT9 56 C4
Hubbard Rd SE27 22 C4
Hubberholme RG12 27 A6
Huddleston Cres RH1 119 D7
Hudson Ct Guildford GU2 108 F1
4 Merton SW19 40 B8
Hudson Rd Crawley RH10 201 E4
Harlington UB7 3 D8
Hudsons KT20 97 D6
Huggins Pl SW2 21 F7
Hugh Herland KT1 37 E6
Hughenden Rd KT4 39 A2
Hughes Ct CR0 42 A1
Hughes Rd Ashford TW15 14 C2
Wokingham RG40 25 E7
Hughes Wlk CR0 42 C2
Hullbrook La GU5 152 D4
Hullmead GU5 152 E4
Hulton Cl KT22 95 C4
Hulverston Cl SM2 59 B2
Humber Way GU47 64 D8
Humbolt Cl GU2 108 F1
Hummer Rd TW20 12 A4
Humphrey Cl KT22 94 C5
Humphries Yd RG12 27 C5
Hungerford Cl GU47 64 C8
Hungerford Sq 3 KT13 53 D6
Hungry Hill La GU23 91 D3
Hunstanton Cl
Colnbrook SW3 1 C7
Crawley RH11 200 D5
Hunston Rd SM4 40 B1
Hunter Cl SW12 21 A7
Hunter House RH10 201 D3
Hunter Rd
Crawley RH10, RH11 201 D4
Farnborough GU14 84 F3
Guildford GU1 130 E8
South Norwood CR7 42 D6
Wimbledon SW20 39 C8
Hunters Chase RH9 142 F6
Hunters Cl KT19 76 C6
Hunters Ct 5 TW9 6 D2
Hunters Meadow SE19 22 E4
Hunters Rd KT9 56 E6
Hunters The BR3 44 C8
Hunters Way CR0 61 E6
Huntersfield Cl RH2 118 B4
Hunting Cl KT10 55 A6
Hunting Gate Dr KT9 56 E3
Hunting Gate Mews
Sutton SM1 59 B7
Twickenham TW2 16 E7
Huntingdon Cl CR4, SW16 41 E5
Huntingdon Ct SW14 7 C4
Huntingdon Gdns
Chiswick W4 7 C7
North Cheam KT4 58 C7
Huntingdon Rd
Redhill RH1 118 F1
Woking GU21 68 F2
Huntingfield CR0 62 F3
Huntingfield Way TW20 12 D2
Huntingford Cl GU26 188 C7
Huntley House 7 SE21 22 E4
Huntley Way SW20 39 A7
Huntly Rd SE25 42 E5
Hunts Cl GU2 108 D2
Hunts Hill Rd GU3 107 A4
Hunts Slip Rd SE21 22 E6
Huntsgreen Ct RG12 27 C6
Huntsman Cl TW13 15 B4
Huntsman's Mews GU16 85 F3
Huntsmans Cl
Fetcham KT22 94 D3
Warlingham CR6 101 C8
Huntsmans Ct CR3 100 C6
Huntsmans Meadow SL5 28 F8
Huntsmoor Rd KT19 57 D5
Huntspill St SW17 20 C5
Huntsworth Ct SE6 24 A7
Hurland La GU30, GU35 187 A3
Hurlands Bsns Ctr GU9 125 F4
Hurlands Cl GU10, GU9 125 F4
Hurlands La GU8 192 F2
Hurlands Pl GU9 125 F4
Hurley Cl KT12 54 B8
Hurley Ct RG12 27 E5
Hurley Gdns GU4 110 A4
Hurlford GU21 69 A2
Hurlstone Rd SE25 42 E4
Hurn Court Rd TW5 4 D5
Hurn Ct TW5 4 D5
Hurnford Cl CR2 61 E1
Huron Rd SW17 21 A5
Hursley Ct 11 KT6 37 D2
Hurst Ave RH12 217 D3
Hurst Cl Chessington KT9 57 A5
Crawley RH11 200 F4
Hayes BR2 44 F1
Headley KT18 96 C3
Woking GU22 89 C7
Hurst Croft GU1 130 E6
Hurst Ct Beckenham BR3 24 A1
Horsham RH12 217 D3
South Norwood SE25 42 F5
Hurst Dr KT20 97 A1
Hurst Farm Cl GU8 149 F2
Hurst Farm Rd RH19 205 D7
Hurst Gr KT12 34 F1
Hurst Green Cl RH8 123 A3
Hurst Green Cty Prim Sch RH8 123 A3
Hurst Green Rd RH8 122 F3
Hurst Green Sta RH8 122 F3
Hurst Hill Cotts GU5 152 B4
Hurst House 7 SE26 23 B3
Hurst La East Molesey KT8 36 C6
Headley KT18 96 D4
Thorpe TW20 32 A7
Hurst Lodge 4 KT13 53 D4
Hurst Lodge Sch SL5 29 F2
Hurst Park Cty Prim Sch KT8 36 A6
Hurst Rd Aldershot GU11 105 C4
Croydon CR0 61 D5
East Molesey KT8, KT12 36 C6
Epsom KT19 76 D8
Farnborough GU14 85 B8
Horley RH6 160 E4
Horsham RH12 217 D3
Walton-on-T KT8&KT12 35 D5
Hurst View Rd CR2 61 E3
Hurst Way Pyrford GU22 70 E5
South Croydon CR2 61 E4
Hurstbourne KT10 55 F4
Hurstbourne House SW15 7 F1
Hurstbourne Priors CR2 61 E4
Hurstbourne Rd SE23 23 E7
Hurstcourt Rd SM1 59 B8
Hurstdene Ave Hayes BR2 44 F1
Staines TW18 13 B2
Hurstfield Rd KT8 36 A6
Hurstlands RH8 123 A3
Hurstleigh Cl RH1 118 F3
Hurstleigh Dr RH1 118 F3
Hurstmere Cl GU26 188 D3
Hurstview Grange CR0 61 B3
Hurstwood SL5 29 A3
Hurtmore Chase GU7 150 B7
Hurtmore Rd
Farncombe GU7 150 B7
Shackleford GU7 150 B7
Hurtwood House Sch (International Sixth Form Coll) RH5 155 A2
Hurtwood Rd KT12 35 F2
Hussar Ct GU11 104 E2
Hussars Cl TW4 4 E4
Hutchingson's Rd CR0 82 C8
Hutchins House 8 SW4 21 D8
Hutchins Way RH6 160 F5
Hutsons Cl RG40 25 D8
Hutton Cl GU20 48 D3
Hutton Rd GU12 106 A6
Huxley Cl GU7 150 D7
Huxley Rd GU2 129 D8
Hyacinth Cl 3 TW12 16 A2
Hyacinth Rd SW15 19 A7
Hyde Cl TW16 14 E2
Hyde Ct TW4 4 F2
Hyde Dr RH11 200 E5
Hyde Farm Sch SW12 21 D7
Hyde Heath Ct RH10 202 D8
Hyde La
Beacon Hill GU10, GU8 168 E1
Thursley GU8 169 A2
Hyde Rd Richmond TW10 6 F2
Sanderstead CR2, CR8 80 E6
Hyde Terr TW15, TW16 14 E2
Hyde Wlk SM4 40 A2
Hydestile Cotts GU8 171 D5
Hydethorpe Rd SW12 21 C7
Hydons The GU8 171 E5
Hylands Cl Crawley RH10 202 A5
Epsom KT18 76 C4
Hylands Mews KT18 76 C4
Hylands Rd KT18 76 C4
Hylton Lodge KT12 54 C5
Hyndewood 10 SE23 23 D5
Hyperion Ct RH11 200 E4
Hyperion House 1 SW2 21 F8
Hyperion Pl KT19 57 D2
Hyperion Wlk RH6 161 B1
Hyrstdene CR0 61 B6
Hythe Cl RG12 27 E4
Hythe End Rd TW19 12 A5
Hythe Field Ave TW20 12 D2
Hythe Park Rd TW20 12 D2
Hythe Rd Egham TW18 12 D3
South Norwood CR7, SE25 42 D7
Hythe Sch The TW18 12 D3
Hythe The TW18 12 E3

I

Ian Ct SE23 23 C6
Iberian Ave CR0, SM6 60 E6
Iberian Way GU15 66 B6
Ibis La W4 7 C6
Ibotson Ct SL3 1 E6
Ibsley Gdns SW15 19 A7
Ibstock Place Sch SW15 7 E1
Icehouse Wood RH8 122 F4
Icklesham House 9 RH11 200 F3
Icklingham Gate KT11 73 C7
Icklingham Rd KT11 73 D6
Iden Cl BR2 44 E6
Idlecombe Rd SW17 21 A2
Idmiston Rd
New Malden KT4 38 F2
West Norwood SE21, SE27 22 C6
Idmiston Sq KT4 38 F2
Ifield Ave RH11 201 C7
Ifield Cl RH1 139 E7
Ifield Com Sch RH11 201 A7
Ifield Cty Mid Sch RH11 201 A6
Ifield Fst Sch RH11 201 A8
Ifield Gn RH11 181 A1
Ifield Rd Charlwood RH6 180 E5
Crawley RH11 201 D6
Crawley, West Green RH11 201 C6
Ifield St RH11 200 F8
Ifield Sta RH11 201 A6
Ifield Wood RH11 180 E1
Ifold Bridge La RH14 212 D4
Ifold Rd RH1 140 A7
Ifoldhurst RH14 212 C2
Ightham House BR3 23 F1
Ikona Ct KT13 53 C5
Ildersly Gr SE21 22 D6
Ilex Cl
Englefield Green TW20 11 B1
Sunbury TW16 35 C7
Ilex House KT15 52 A1
Ilex Way SW16 22 A3
Ilford Ct GU6 173 F2
Ilfracombe Rd BR1 24 F5
Ilkley Cl SE19 22 D2
Illingworth Cl CR4 40 D6
Illingworth Gr RG12 27 F8
Imber Cl KT7 36 D1
Imber Court Trad Est KT8 36 D3
Imber Cross KT7 36 F3
Imber Gr KT10 36 D2
Imber Park Rd KT10 36 D1
Imberhorne La RH19 185 B2
Imberhorne Lower Sch RH19 185 D3
Imberhorne Sch RH19 185 B3
Imberhorne Way RH19 185 B3
Imjin Cl GU11 105 B3
Immanuel & St Andrew C of E Prim Sch SW16 21 E2
Impact Ct SE20 43 B7
Imperial Gdns CR4 41 B6
Imperial House GU25 31 E4
Imperial Rd TW14 14 E8
Imperial Way CR0, CR9 61 A4
Impington 8 KT1 38 A7
Imran Ct GU12 126 C8
Ince Rd KT12 53 E4
Inchmery Rd SE6 24 C7
Inchwood Bracknell RG12 27 C1
Croydon BR4, CR0 63 B6
Independent Bsns Pk The RH19 185 A3
Ingatestone Rd SE25 43 B5
Ingham Cl CR2 62 D2
Ingham Rd CR2 62 D2
Ingle Dell GU15 65 D4
Ingle House SW12 21 D7
Ingleboro Dr CR8 80 D6
Ingleby Way SM6 60 D3
Inglehurst KT15 52 B1
Inglemere Ct CR4, SW17 20 F1
Inglemere Rd
Forest Hill SE23 23 D5
Mitcham CR4, SW17 20 F1
Ingleside SL3 1 F6
Ingleside Cl BR3 24 A1
Ingleton RG12 27 A6
Ingleton Rd SM5 59 E2
Inglewood Addlestone KT16 51 F7
New Addington CR0 62 E2
Woking GU21 69 B1
Inglewood Ave GU15 66 D5
Inglewood Ct 2 BR1 24 F1
Inglis Rd CR0 42 F1
Ingram Cl RH12 217 A2
Ingram High Sch for Boys CR7 42 C8
Ingram House KT8 37 C8
Ingram Rd CR7 42 C8
Ingrams Almshouses TW7 6 A5
Ingrams Cl KT12 54 C5
Ingrebourne House BR1 24 D3
Inholms La RH5 136 C3
Inkerman Rd GU21 68 E1
Inkerman Way GU21 68 E1
Inman Rd SW18 20 C8
Inner Park Rd SW19 19 D6
Inner Ring E TW6 3 B4
Inner Ring W TW6 3 A4
Innes Cl SW20 39 E7
Innes Lodge SE23 23 D5
Innes Rd RH12 217 F4
Innes Yd CR0, CR9 61 C7
Innings La RG12 27 E8
Innisfail Gdns GU11 125 F8
Inst of Oceanographic Sciences GU8 170 F1
Institute Rd
Aldershot GU12 105 D1
Westcott RH4 135 C6
Instone Cl SM6 60 E3
Instow Gdns GU14 85 A7
Inval Hill GU27 208 C8
Inveresk Gdns KT4 58 A7
Inverness Ct SE6 24 F7
Inverness Rd Hounslow TW3 5 A3
North Cheam KT4 39 D1
Inverness Way GU47 64 D7
Invicta Cl TW14 14 F7
Invicta Ct KT9 56 F5
Invincible Rd GU14 85 A3
Inwood Ave Coulsdon CR5 100 A7
Hounslow TW3 5 C4
Inwood Bsns Pk TW3 5 B3
Inwood Cl CR0 62 E8
Inwood Ct 1 KT12 54 C8
Inwood Rd TW3 5 C3
Iona Cl Crawley RH11 201 B3
Forest Hill SE13, SE4, SE6 24 A8
Ipsley Lodge GU10 126 E5
Ipswich Rd SW17 21 A2
Irene Rd KT11 74 B5
Ireton Ave KT13 53 F8
Iris Cl Croydon CR0 43 D1
Surbiton KT6 37 F2
Iris Rd Bisley GU24 68 A4
West Ewell KT19 57 B5
Iron La GU5 151 D5
Irons Bottom Rd RH2 159 F8
Irvine Ct CR7 42 A3
Irvine Dr GU14 84 E8
Irvine Pl GU25 31 E4
Irving Wlk RH10 201 E3
Irwin Dr RH12 217 A2
Irwin Rd GU2 130 A7
Isabel Cotts KT18 76 B5
Isabella Ct 8 TW10 6 F1
Isbells Dr RH2 139 B7
Isham Rd SW16 41 E7
Isis Ct W4 7 B7
Isis St SW18 20 C6
Isis Way GU47 64 D8
Island Cl TW18 12 E4
Island Cotts The KT11 73 B1
Island Farm Ave KT8 35 F4
Island Farm Rd KT8 36 A4
Island House SW19 40 C5

Island Rd CR4, SW19 20 F1
Islay Gdns TW4 4 D2
Isleworth Bsns Complex TW7 5 F5
Isleworth Sta TW7 5 F5
Isleworth & Syon Sch for Boys TW7 5 E7
Isleworth Town Sch TW7 6 A5
Itchingwood Common Rd RH8 123 E2
Ivanhoe Cl RH11 181 D1
Ivanhoe House 11 SW12 21 B8
Ivanhoe Rd TW4 4 D4
Iveagh Cl RH11 201 C1
Iveagh Ct Beckenham BR3 44 B6
Bracknell RG12 27 C4
Iveagh Rd GU2 130 B7
Ively Rd GU14 84 D1
Ively Rdbt GU14 84 E2
Iverna Gdns TW14 3 D2
Ivers Way CR0 63 B3
Ivestor Terr SE23 23 C8
Ivor Cl GU1 131 A8
Ivory Ct TW13 15 A7
Ivory Wlk RH11 200 E3
Ivy Cl TW16 35 C7
Ivy Dene La RH19 206 D6
Ivy Dr GU18 67 A7
Ivy Gdns CR4 41 D6
Ivy House CR0 43 D1
Ivy La Farnham GU9 125 B2
Hounslow TW4 4 F3
Woking GU22 70 B1
Ivy Mill Cl RH9 121 B3
Ivy Mill La
Bletchingley RH1, RH9 121 B3
Godstone RH1, RH9 121 B3
Ivy Rd Aldershot GU12 105 E2
Hounslow TW3 5 B3
Tolworth KT6 38 A1
Upper Tooting SW17 20 E3
Ivybank GU7 150 E6
Ivybridge Cl 3 TW1 17 A8
Ivybridge Jun & Inf Sch TW1 5 F1
Ivychurch Cl SE20 23 C1
Ivydale Rd SM5 59 F8
Ivyday Gr SW16 21 F5
Ivydene
East Molesey KT12, KT8 35 F4
Knaphill GU21 68 B1
Ivydene Cl Redhill RH1 140 B4
Sutton SM1 59 C6
Ivymount Rd SE27 22 A5

J

Jackass La RH9 121 F4
Jackdaw Cl RH11 201 C8
Jackdaw La RH12 217 E6
Jackman's La GU21 89 B8
Jackson Cl Bracknell RG12 27 B4
Crawley GU6 173 F2
Epsom KT18 76 D5
Jackson's Pl CR0 42 E1
Jackson's Way CR0 63 B7
Jacob Cl RG42 26 D7
Jacob Rd GU15 65 A7
Jacobean Cl RH10 202 C5
Jacobs Well Rd GU4 109 D6
Jaggard Way SW12 20 F8
Jail La TN16 83 E3
Jamaica Rd CR7 42 B3
James Boswell 1 SW16 22 A4
James Dixon Prim Sch SE20 23 B1
James Est CR4 40 F7
James Rd Camberley GU15 65 B2
Shalford GU3 130 C1
James St TW3 5 D4
James Watt Way RH10 182 A4
James Way GU15 65 B2
Jameston RG12 27 C1
Jamieson House TW4 15 F8
Jamnagar Cl TW18 12 F2
Janoway Hill GU21 89 C8
Japonica Cl GU21 69 C1
Japonica Ct GU12 105 F1
Jarrett Cl SW2 22 B7
Jarrow Cl SM4 40 B4
Jarvis Rd CR2 61 D4
Jasmin Rd KT19 57 B5
Jasmine Cl Redhill RH1 140 A4
Woking GU21 68 F3
Jasmine Ct Horsham RH12 217 C2
11 Wallington SM6 60 B4
Jasmine Gdns CR0 63 B7
Jasmine Gr SE20 43 B8
Jasmine Way KT7 36 E5
Jason Cl Redhill RH1 139 E4
Weybridge KT13 53 C5
Jasons Dr GU4 110 C4
Jasper House KT4 38 D1
Jasper Rd Dulwich SE19 22 F2
West Norwood SE19 22 F2
Javelin Ct RH10 182 D1
Jawahar Bagh SW16 22 B2
Jay Ave KT15 52 E7
Jay's La Fisherstreet GU27 209 C3
Lurgashall GU27 209 C3
Jays Nest Cl GU17 64 D4
Jayson Ct 7 CR0 43 A1
Jeal Oakwood Ct KT18 76 E5
Jean House SW17 20 E3
Jean Humbert House 2 SE27 22 D4
Jeans Ct 10 RH11 201 B1
Jeddere Cotts RH7 165 A2
Jeffries Pas GU1 130 D8
Jeffries Rd KT24 112 C5
Jeffs Cl TW12 16 B2
Jeffs Rd SM1 58 F6
Jefton Ct SM6 60 C4
Jemmett Cl KT2 38 B8
Jengar Cl SM1 59 B6
Jenkins' Hill London Rd GU19 47 D2
Jenkins Pl GU11 105 D8
Jenner Dr GU24 68 A6
Jenner Rd Crawley RH10 181 F3
Guildford GU1 130 E8
Jennett Rd CR0, CR9 61 A7
Jennifer Rd BR1 24 F5
Jennings Cl KT15 52 C2
Jenny La RH7 164 C4
Jenson Way SE19 22 F1
Jeppo's La CR4 40 F5
Jerome Cnr GU47 45 E2
Jersey Cl Addlestone KT16 51 F7
Guildford GU4 110 B6
Jersey Rd Crawley RH11 201 A2
Hounslow TW5, TW7 5 D7
Mitcham SW17 21 B2
Jerviston Gdns SW16 22 A2
Jesmond Cl CR4 41 B6
Jesmond Rd CR0 42 F2
Jessamy Rd KT13 53 B8
Jesses La GU5 154 C8
Jessie's Hollow GU5 133 C1
Jessiman Terr TW17 34 A4
Jessops Way CR0, CR4 41 C3
Jeston House 10 SE27 22 B5
Jevington RG12 27 C1
Jewell House 3 SW12 21 C8
Jewels Hill Biggin Hill TN16 83 A6
West Wickham CR6 83 A6
Jews Wlk SE26 23 B4
Jeypore Rd SW18 20 C8
Jig's La S RG42 27 E8
Jillian Cl TW12 16 A1
Jobson's La
Fisherstreet GU27 209 D2
Lurgashall GU27 209 D1
Jocelyn Rd TW9 6 E4
Jock's La RG42 26 E8
Jockey Mead RH12 217 A1
Jodrell Cl TW7 6 A6
Joe Hunte Ct 2 SW27 22 B3
John Austin Cl KT2 37 F8
John Baird Ct SE26 23 D4
John Baird House 14 SE20 23 C1
John Barter House TW3 4 F5
John Busch Sch TW7 6 B6
John Cl GU11, GU9 125 E8
John Cobb Rd KT13 53 A3
John Dee House 3 SW14 7 D4
John Fisher Sch The CR8 60 E1
John Gale Ct KT17 57 F2
John Kaye Ct TW17 34 A4
John Kirk House 5 SW16 21 E5
John Nightingale Sch KT8 35 F6
John Nike Way RG12 26 C7
John Paul II RC Sec Sch SW19 19 D8
John Pounds House RH11 201 D4
John Ruskin Sixth Form Coll CR2 62 E3
John Russell Cl GU2 109 A4
John St Croydon SE25 43 A5
Hounslow TW3, TW5 4 E4
John Wesley Ct 5 TW1 17 A7
John Wiskar Dr GU6 174 D2
John's Rd TN16 103 D7
John's Terr CR0 42 E1
Johns La SM4 40 C4
Johns Wlk CR3 101 A8
Johnsdale RH8 122 F6
Johnson Rd Heston TW5 4 C7
Thornton Heath CR0 42 D2
Johnson Wlk RH10 201 E3
Johnson's Cl SM5 59 F7
Johnsons Dr TW12 36 C8
Johnston Gr GU2 109 A5
Johnston Wlk GU2 109 A5
Joinville Pl KT15 52 D6
Jolesfield RH11 200 F3
Jolliffe Rd RH1 99 C1
Jones Cnr SL5 28 E8
Jones Wlk 6 TW10 6 F1
Jonquil Gdns 5 TW12 16 A2
Jonson Cl CR4 41 B6
Jordan Cl CR2 80 F8
Jordans Cl Crawley RH11 201 D8
Guildford GU1 110 A2
Redhill RH1 140 A4
Stanwell TW19 13 C8
Jordans Cres RH11 181 D1
Jordans The RH19 205 E8
Josef Perrin House 1 SE27 22 D4
Joseph Hood Fst Sch SW20 39 E6
Joseph Locke Way KT10 55 A8
Joseph's Rd GU1 109 D2
Josephine Ave KT20 117 F8
Josephine Cl KT20 117 F8
Jubilee Ave North Ascot SL5 28 E8
Twickenham TW2 16 C7
Wokingham RG41 25 B7
Jubilee Cl
Farnborough GU14 84 D4
North Ascot SL5 28 E8
Stanwell TW19 13 C8
Teddington KT1 37 C8
Jubilee Cres KT15 52 D5
Jubilee Ct Bracknell RG12 27 C6
Hounslow TW3 5 B4
Staines TW18 13 A4
Thornton Heath CR7 42 A5
Jubilee Dr GU12 106 A6
Jubilee Hall Rd GU14 85 C4
Jubilee House 5 TW12 36 A8
Jubilee La
Grayshott GU26 188 C3
Rowledge GU10 146 A5
Jubilee Rd Aldershot GU11 126 B7
Cheam SM3 58 D3
Mytchett GU16 86 A2
Rudgwick RH12 214 D8
Jubilee Terr
Brockham RH3 137 C5
Dorking RH4 136 B8
Jubilee Villas KT10 36 E1
Jubilee Way
Chessington KT4, KT9 57 B7
East Bedfont TW14 15 A7
Merton SW19 40 B8
Tolworth KT4, KT9 57 B7
Jubilee Wks SW19 40 C7
Jubilee Wlk RH10 202 A6
Judge Wlk KT10 55 E4
Judge's Terr RH19 205 E8
Julian Cl GU21 69 C1
Julian Hill KT13 53 B3
Julian House SE21 22 E4
Julian Taylor Path SE23 23 B6
Julians Prim Sch SW16 22 A4
Julien Rd CR5 79 D4
Juliet Gdns RG42 27 F8
Julius Ct TW8 6 E7
Julius Hill RG42 27 F8
Jumps Rd GU10 168 B3
Junction Pl GU27 207 F6
Junction Rd Ashford TW15 14 D3
Croydon CR2 61 D5
Dorking RH4 136 A7
Lightwater GU18 48 B1
June Cl CR5 79 B5
June La RH1 140 B2
Junewood Cl KT15 70 F8
Juniper RG12 27 E4
Juniper Cl Biggin Hill TN16 83 E2
Chessington KT9 56 F5
Guildford GU1 109 C6
Reigate RH2 139 C7
Juniper Ct Belmont SM2 59 A4
Hounslow TW3 5 B3
Juniper Dr GU24 68 A4
Juniper Gdns Ashford TW16 14 F2
Mitcham CR4 41 C8
Juniper Hall (Field Study Ctr) RH5 115 C6
Juniper Pl GU4 130 D2
Juniper Rd Crawley RH11 181 C1
Farnborough GU14 84 C5
Reigate RH2 139 C7
Juniper Terr GU4 130 D2
Juniper Wlk RH3 137 C7
Jura Cl RH11 201 B3
Justin Cl TW8 6 D7
Jutland Gdns CR5 99 F7
Jutland Pl TW20 12 C3
Jutland Rd SE6 24 C8
Juxon Cl RH11 200 F4

K

Kaithwood House RH12 218 B5
Kangley Bridge Ctr SE26 23 F3
Kangley Bridge Rd
Forest Hill SE26 23 F3
Penge SE26 23 F3
Karen Ct BR1 44 F8
Kashmir Cl KT15 52 D2
Katharine Rd 1 TW1 17 A7
Katharine St CR0, CR9 61 C7
Katherine Cl KT15 52 A4
Katherine Ct SE23 23 C7
Kathleen Moore Ct BR4 63 C8
Kay Ave KT15 52 E7
Kay Cres GU35 187 B6
Kaye Ct GU1 109 C5
Kaye Don Way KT13 53 A1
Kayemoor Rd SM2 59 E4
Kaynes Pk SL5 28 E8
Keable Rd GU10 145 E7
Kearton Cl CR8 80 C2
Keates Gn RG42 27 B8
Keats Ave RH1 119 B3
Keats Cl Horsham RH12 217 F7
Mitcham SW17, SW19 20 D2
Keats House BR3 24 B2
Keats Pl RH19 185 D1
Keats Way Crowthorne RG45 45 B6
Croydon CR0 43 C3
Keble Cl Crawley RH10 182 D1
New Malden KT4 38 F1
Keble St SW17 20 C4
Keble Way GU47 45 E2
Kedeston Ct SM3 40 B1
Keedonwood Rd
Bromley BR1 24 F3
Catford BR1 24 F3
Keeley Rd CR0, CR9 61 C8
Keeling House 2 TW11 16 E3
Keen's Rd CR0 61 C6
Keens Cl SW16 21 D3
Keens La GU2, GU3 108 F5
Keens Park Rd GU3 108 F5
Keep Hatch Cty Inf Sch RG40 25 D7
Keep Hatch Cty Jun Sch RG40 25 D7
Keep The Catford SE6 24 B7
Kingston u T KT2 17 F1
Keepers Cl GU4 110 D4
Keepers Combe RG12 27 D3
Keepers Mews TW11 17 C2
Keepers Terr GU25 31 B4
Keepers Wlk GU25 31 D4
Keephatch Rd RG40 25 E7
Keevil Dr SW19 19 E8
Keir Hardie House 7 RH11 201 B1
Keith Lucas Rd GU14 84 F2
Keith Park Cres TN16 83 C7
Keldholme RG12 27 A6
Kelling Gdns CR0 42 B2
Kellino St SW17 20 F4
Kelly Cl TW17 34 E7
Kelmscott 5 SE23 23 D5
Kelsey Cl RH6 160 F3
Kelsey Gate BR3 44 B7
Kelsey La BR3 44 A6
Kelsey Park Ave BR3 44 B7
Kelsey Park Rd BR3 44 A7
Kelsey Park Sch BR3 44 A6
Kelsey Sq BR3 44 A7
Kelsey Way BR3 44 A6
Kelso Cl RH10 202 E7
Kelso Ct SE20 23 B1
Kelso Rd SM5 40 C2
Kelvedon Ave KT12 53 F3
Kelvedon Cl KT2 18 A2
Kelvin Ave KT22 94 F8
Kelvin Bsns Ctr RH10 181 F2
Kelvin Cl KT19 57 A4
Kelvin Ct Chiswick W4 7 C7
Isleworth TW7 5 E5
8 Penge SE20 43 B8
8 Twickenham TW1 6 B1
Kelvin Dr TW1 6 B1
Kelvin Gdns CR0 41 E2
Kelvin Gr Chessington KT6 56 E7
Forest Hill SE26 23 B5
Kelvin Grove Prim Sch
Forest Hill SE26 23 B5
Forest Hill SE23 23 E7
Kelvin La RH10 181 F2
Kelvin Way RH10 181 F2
Kelvinbrook KT8 36 B6
Kelvington Cl CR0 43 E2
Kelyway House 20 SW2 22 A8
Kemble Cl KT13 53 D6
Kemble Cotts KT15 52 A6
Kemble Rd
Croydon CR0, CR9 61 B7
Forest Hill SE23 23 D7
Kembleside Rd TN16 83 C1
Kemerton Rd
Beckenham BR3 44 B7
Croydon CR0 42 F2
Kemishford GU22 89 A4
Kemnal Pk GU27 208 D7
Kemp Ct GU19 47 F2
Kemp Gdns CR0 42 C3
Kempshott Rd
Horsham RH12 217 B4
Streatham SW16 21 E1
Kempston House SM2 59 B2
Kempton Ave TW16 35 B8
Kempton Ct
Farnborough GU14 84 F2
Sunbury TW16 35 B8
Kempton Park Race Course TW16 15 C1
Kempton Park Sta TW16 15 B1
Kempton Wlk CR0 43 E3
Kemsing Cl Coney Hall BR2 63 F8
Thornton Heath CR7 42 C5
Kemsley Rd TN16 103 D8
Kendal Cl
East Bedfont TW14 14 F7
Farnborough GU14 84 E4
Redhill RH2 118 D2
Kendal Ct 7 CR0 42 E1
Kendal Gdns SM1 59 C8
Kendal Gr GU15 66 D4
Kendal House
5 Croydon CR0 42 E1
Penge SE20 43 B7
Kendale Cl RH10 202 C2
Kendale Rd BR1 24 E3
Kendall Ave Penge BR3 43 E7
South Croydon CR2 61 D2
Kendall Ave S CR2 61 D1
Kendall Ct 4 SE19 22 F1
Kendall House SE12 24 F8
Kendall Rd Isleworth TW7 6 A5
Penge BR3 43 E7
Kendor Ave KT19 76 C8
Kendra Hall Rd CR2 61 B3
Kendrey Gdns TW2 16 E8
Kendrick Cl RG40 25 C5
Kenilford Rd SW12 21 B8
Kenilworth Ave
Bracknell RG12 27 D8
Oxshott KT11 74 B5
Wimbledon SW19 20 A4
Kenilworth Cl
Banstead SM7 78 B3
Crawley RH11 201 B2
Kenilworth Ct TW2 16 E6
Kenilworth Dr KT12 54 D7
Kenilworth Gdns TW18 13 C3
Kenilworth Rd
Ashford TW15, TW19 13 D5
Farnborough GU14 84 C5
Penge SE20 43 D8
Kenilworth Rd *continued*
Stoneleigh KT17 58 A5
Kenilworth Terr 3 SM2 59 A3
Kenley Cl CR3 100 E7
Kenley Gdns CR7 42 B5
Kenley House 5 CR0 43 A1
Kenley La CR8 80 D3
Kenley Prim Sch CR3 80 E3
Kenley Rd
Headley Down GU35 187 C5
Kingston u T KT1, KT3 38 B7
Merton SW19 40 A6
Twickenham TW1 6 B1
Kenley Sta CR8 80 C5
Kenley Wlk SM3 58 D6
Kenlor Rd SW17 20 D3
Kenmara Cl RH10 182 A1
Kenmara Ct RH10 182 A2
Kenmare Dr CR4 20 F1
Kenmare Rd CR7 42 A3
Kenmore Cl Frimley GU16 85 D8
Richmond TW9 7 A7
Kenmore Rd CR8 80 B5
Kennard Ct RH18 206 E3
Kennedy Ave RH19 185 D3
Kennedy Cl CR4 41 A7
Kennedy Ct TW15 14 C3
Kennedy Rd RH13 217 D1
Kennel Ave SL5 28 F8
Kennel Cl
Fetcham KT22, KT23 94 C3
North Ascot SL5 8 F2
Kennel Gn SL5 28 E8
Kennel La Fetcham KT22 94 C4
Frensham GU10 146 C2
Hookwood RH6 160 D2
Windlesham GU20 48 C5
Kennel Ride SL5 8 F1
Kennel Wood SL5 28 F8
Kennel Wood Cres CR0 82 D8
Kennels La GU14 84 C2
Kennet Cl Ash GU12 106 A1
Crawley RH11 200 F5
Farnborough GU14 84 E6
Kennet House 6 RH1 118 F2
Kennet Rd TW7 5 F4
Kennet Sq CR4 40 E8
Kenneth Rd SM7 78 D4
Kennoldes SE21 22 D6
Kenrick Sq RH1 120 E1
Kensington Ave CR7 42 A8
Kensington Avenue Inf Sch CR7 42 A8
Kensington Avenue Jun Sch CR7 42 A8
Kensington Rd RH11 201 C2
Kensington Terr CR2 61 D3
Kent Cl Mitcham CR4, SW16 41 E5
Staines TW18 13 D2
Kent Dr TW11 16 E3
Kent Gate Way
Addington CR0 63 B5
New Addington CR0, CR2 62 F4
Kent Hatch Rd
Limpsfield RH8, TN8 123 D4
The Chart RH8, TN8 123 D4
Kent House La BR3 23 E3
Kent House Rd
Forest Hill SE26, BR3 23 E2
Penge SE26, BR3 23 E2
Kent House Sta BR3 43 E8
Kent House Station App BR3 43 D8
Kent Lodge 9 SW19 19 D7
Kent Rd East Molesey KT8 36 C5
Kingston u T KT1 37 D6
Richmond TW9 7 A7
West Wickham BR4 44 B1
Windlesham GU20 48 D5
Woking GU22 70 C3
Kent Tower SE20 23 B1
Kent Way KT6 56 F8
Kentigern Dr RG45 45 E5
Kenton Ave TW16 35 F7
Kenton Cl Bracknell RG12 27 D7
Frimley GU16 65 F1
Kenton Ct SE26 23 E4
Kenton Way GU21 68 F2
Kentwyns Rise RH1 140 F8
Kenwood Cl UB7 3 A8
Kenwood Dr
Beckenham BR3 44 C6
Hersham KT12 54 B5
Kenwood Pk KT13 53 D4
Kenwood Ridge CR8 80 B2
Kenworth Gr GU18 48 A1
Kenwyn Rd SW20 39 C8
Kenya Ct RH6 160 F4
Kenyngton Dr TW16 15 A3
Kenyngton Manor Prim Sch TW16 15 A2
Kenyons KT24 112 B7
Keogh Barracks GU16 86 B1
Keogh Cl GU12 86 B2
Keppel Rd RH4 115 B1
Keppel Spur SL4 11 B8
Kepple Pl GU19 47 F3
Kerria Way GU24 67 F6
Kerrill Ave CR5 100 A8
Kerrsland Cotts GU7 149 F7
Kerry Terr GU21 70 B3
Kersey Dr CR2 81 D7
Kershaw House 7 SE27 22 B5
Keston Ave
Coulsdon CR5, CR8 100 B8

Keston Ave *continued*
Woodham KT15 71 A8
Keston Avenue Jun & Inf Schs CR5 100 A8
Keston Rd CR7 42 A3
Kestrel Ave TW18 12 F5
Kestrel Cl Crawley RH11 201 C8
Crondall GU10 124 D7
Guildford GU4 110 D3
Horsham RH12 217 E5
Kingston u T KT2 17 D4
Kestrel House GU9 146 A8
Kestrel Way CR0 63 D2
Keswick Ave
Kingston u T KT2, SW15 18 E3
Merton SW19 40 A7
Upper Halliford TW17 34 E6
Keswick Cl Crawley RH11 200 D4
Frimley GU15 66 D4
Sutton SM1 59 C6
Keswick Dr GU18 67 B8
Keswick Rd
Fetcham KT22, KT23 94 C2
Thorpe Lea TW20 12 B1
Twickenham TW2 5 C1
West Wickham BR4 63 E8
Witley GU8 170 D6
Kettering Ct CR7 42 C5
Kettering St SW16 21 C2
Kettlewell Cl GU21 69 E4
Kettlewell Dr GU21 69 E5
Kettlewell Hill GU21 69 E4
Ketton Gn RH1 119 D7
Kevan Dr GU23 90 E2
Kevin Cl TW4 4 D5
Kew Bridge Rd TW8 6 F8
Kew Cres SM3 58 F7
Kew Foot Rd TW9 6 E4
Kew Gardens Rd TW9 7 A6
Kew Gardens Sta TW9 7 A6
Kew Gn TW9 6 F8
Kew Lodge 10 TW9 6 F6
Kew Observatory TW9 6 C4
Kew Palace TW9 6 E7
Kew Rd TW9, W4 6 F5
Kew Ret Pk TW9 7 B6
Key Cross GU10 147 D5
Keymer Cl TN16 83 D3
Keymer Rd Crawley RH11 201 D4
Streatham SW2 21 F6
Keynsham Rd SM4 40 B1
Keynsham Way GU47 45 D2
Keynsham Wlk SM4 40 B1
Keysham Ave TW5 4 A6
Keywood Dr TW16 15 A2
Khama Rd SW17 20 E4
Khartoum Rd
Upper Tooting SW17 20 D4
Witley GU8 170 E6
Kibble Gn RG12 27 C3
Kidborough Down KT23 114 A8
Kidborough Rd RH11 200 F4
Kidbrooke Park (Michael Hall Sch) RH18 206 D1
Kidbrooke Rise RH18 206 E2
Kidderminster Rd CR0 42 C2
Kidmans Cl RH12 217 F5
Kidworth Cl RH6 160 F5
Kielder Wlk GU15 66 C4
Kier Pk SL5 29 C6
Kilberry Cl TW7 5 D6
Kilcorral Cl KT17 77 A5
Kilasser Ct KT20 97 C4
Killearn Rd SE6 24 D7
Killester Gdns KT17, KT4 58 B6
Killick House SM1 59 B6
Killicks GU6 174 F4
Killieser Ave SW2 21 E6
Killigrew House TW16 14 E1
Killinghurst La GU27,GU8 209 D8
Killross Rd TW14 14 D7
Kilmarnock Pk RH2 118 B2
Kilmartin Ave SW16 42 A6
Kilmartin Gdns GU16 65 F1
Kilmington Cl RG12 27 E2
Kilmiston Ave TW17 34 C3
Kilmiston House TW17 34 C3
Kilmore Dr GU15 66 B4
Kilmorey Gdns TW1 6 B3
Kilmorey Rd TW1 6 B3
Kilmorie Prim Sch SE23 23 E6
Kilmorie Rd SE23 23 E6
Kilmuir Cl GU47 64 D7
Kiln Cl UB3 3 D8
Kiln Copse GU6 174 E4
Kiln Fields GU27 208 C8
Kiln La Bracknell RG12 27 A7
Brockham RH3 116 C1
Ewell KT17 76 E8
Farnham GU10, GU9 146 C6
Horley RH6 161 A5
Ripley GU23 91 B3
Sunningdale SL5 30 A4
Kiln Meadows GU3 108 C5
Kiln Mews SW17 20 D3
Kiln Rd RH10 204 B7
Kiln Way Aldershot GU11 126 B7
Grayshott GU26 187 E5
Kiln Wlk RH1 140 A4
Kilnfield Rd RH12 214 D8
Kilnmead RH10, RH11 201 E7
Kilnmead Cl RH10 201 E7
Kilnside KT10 56 A3
Kilnwood La
Crawley RH12 200 B3
Faygate RH12 199 F3
Kilross Rd TW14 14 E7
Kilrue La KT12 53 F6
Kilrush Terr GU21 70 A3
Kilsha Rd KT12 35 C3
Kimber Ct GU4 110 D3
Kimber Ctr The SW18 20 A8
Kimber Rd SW18 20 B8
Kimberley RG12 27 C1
Kimberley Cl RH6 160 E3
Kimberley Pl 5 CR8 80 A8
Kimberley Rd
Crawley RH10 202 B7
Penge BR3 43 D7
Thornton Heath CR0, CR7 42 B3
Kimberley Ride KT11 74 B6
Kimberley Wlk KT12 35 B2
Kimbers La GU9 125 D3
Kimble Rd Mitcham SW17 20 D2
Mitcham SW17 20 D3
Kimbolton Cl SE12 24 F8
Kimmeridge RG12 27 E3
Kimpton Bsns Ctr SM3 58 F8
Kimpton House SW15 19 A8
Kimpton Ind Est SM3 58 F8
Kimpton Rd SM3 58 F8
Kinburn Dr TW20 11 E3
Kindell House 4 SW14 7 D4
Kindersley Cl RH19 186 B3
Kinfauns Rd SW2 22 A6
King Acre Ct TW18 12 E5
King Alfred Ave SE6 24 A4
King Athelstan Prim Sch KT1 37 F6
King Charles Cres KT5 37 F2
King Charles' Rd KT5, KT6 37 F3
King Charles Wlk 6 SW19 19 E7
King Edward Dr KT6 56 E7
King Edward's Gr TW11 17 C2
King Edward's Sch GU8 170 F1
King Edwards Rd SL5 28 E8
King Edwards Rise SL5 28 E8
King Garth Mews SE23 23 C6
King Gdns CR0 61 B5
King George Ave
East Grinstead RH19 185 C3
Walton-on-T KT12 35 D1
King George Cl TW16 14 E3
King George Sq TW10 6 F1
King George V1 Ave TN16 83 D3
King George VI Ave CR4 40 F5
King George's Cotts GU8 192 F6
King George's Dr KT15 52 A1
King George's Lodge GU2 109 A4
King George's Trad Est KT9 57 A6
King Henry's Dr
New Addington CR0 82 E8
West Wickham CR0 82 E8
King Henry's Rd KT1, KT3 38 B6
King St Chertsey KT16 33 A1
East Grinstead RH19 185 E1
Richmond TW10, TW9 6 D2
Twickenham TW1 17 A7
King Street Par 6 TW1 17 A7
King William IV Gdns SE20 23 C2
King's Ave Ashford TW16 14 F2
Hounslow TW3, TW5 5 B6
King's Cl Staines TW18 13 D1
Thames Ditton KT7 37 A2
King's Coll Sch SW19 19 D2
King's Court Prim Sch SL4 11 B8
King's Ct
Aldershot GU10, GU12 126 E8
Beckenham BR3 44 B6
Wimbledon SW19 20 A2
King's Dr KT7 37 B2
King's Head La KT14 71 D8
King's House Jun Sch TW10 6 F2
King's House Sch TW10 6 F2
King's Keep GU47 45 B1
King's La SM1, SM2 59 D5
King's Paddock TW12 36 C8
King's Pas KT2 37 D8
King's Rd Aldershot GU11 104 F1
Ascot SL5 29 D4
Cranleigh GU6 174 F2
Crowthorne RG45 45 C5
Croydon SE25 43 A6
Egham TW20 12 A4
Farncombe GU7 150 F6
Haslemere GU27 208 A6
Horsham RH12, RH13 217 E3
Kingston u T KT2 18 E1
Long Ditton KT6 37 C1
Mortlake SW14 7 D4
Teddington TW11, TW12 16 D3
Twickenham TW1 6 B1
Wimbledon SW19 20 A2
King's Ride Bracknell SL5 28 D5
Camberley GU15 65 D7
King's Shade Wlk 1 KT18 76 D6
King's Terr 8 TW7 6 A4
King's Way GU24 87 D8
King's Wlk GU15 64 F6
Kingcup Cl CR0 43 D1
Kingcup Dr GU24 68 A4
Kingfield Cl GU22 89 F7
Kingfield Dr GU22 89 F7
Kingfield Gdns GU22 89 F7
Kingfield Rd GU22 89 F7
Kingfield Sch GU22 90 A7
Kingfisher Cl
Crawley RH10 182 A1
Farnborough GU14 84 D6
Hersham KT12 54 E5
Putney SW19 19 E6
Kingfisher Ct Cheam SM1 58 F5
Dorking RH4 136 A8
East Molesey KT8 36 E5
Isleworth TW3 5 B2
Sheerwater GU21 70 C5
Kingfisher Dr
Guildford GU4 110 C3
Redhill RH1 119 A3
Staines TW18 12 F4
Teddington TW10 17 B4
Kingfisher Gdns CR2 62 D1
Kingfisher Lodge TW11 17 A4
Kingfisher Rise RH19 205 F8
Kingfisher Sports Ctr The KT1 37 E7
Kingfisher Way
Beckenham CR0 43 D4
Horsham RH12 217 C5
Kingfisher Wlk GU12 105 F2
Kingham Cl SW18 20 C8
Kings Ave Ash GU10, GU12 126 F8
Bromley BR1 24 F2
Byfleet KT14 71 D7
New Malden KT3 38 F5
Redhill RH1 139 E7
Streatham SW12, SW4 21 D8
Wallington SM5 59 F3
Kings Chase KT8 36 C6
Kings Cl KT12 35 B1
Kings Copse 9 RH19 205 F8
Kings Cres GU15 65 C8
Kings Cross La RH1 140 E6
Kings Ct Horsham RH13 217 E3
16 Kingston u T KT2 18 A1
11 Roehampton SW15 19 A8
Tadworth KT20 97 C5
3 Wallington SM6 60 B4
Kings Dr KT5 38 A3
Kings Dr The KT12 53 F2
Kings Farm Ave TW10 7 A3
Kings Gate GU7 150 F6
Kings Hall Rd BR3 43 E8
Kings Keep KT6 37 E5
Kings La
Englefield Green TW20 11 A2
Windlesham GU20 48 E5
Wrecclesham GU10 145 F6
Kings' Manor Sch GU2 108 E1
Kings Mead
Smallfield RH6 162 B3
South Nutfield RH1 140 E7
Kings Mead Pk KT10 55 E3
Kings Mill La
Salfords RH1 140 D5
South Nutfield RH1 140 D5
Kings Rd Belmont SM2 59 A1
Biggin Hill TN16 83 C2
Feltham TW13 15 C7
Horley RH6 161 A3
Mitcham CR4 41 A6
Richmond TW10, TW9 6 F2
Shalford GU4 130 E2
Walton-on-T KT12 35 B1
West End GU24 68 A6
Woking GU21 70 A3
Wonersh GU5 152 B8
Woodham KT15 71 B8
Kings Ride Gate TW10 7 A3
Kings Way CR0 60 F5
Kings Wlk CR2 81 B5
Kings's Rd 2 GU1 109 D1
Kingsbridge House 11 SE20 43 B8
Kingsbridge Rd
Walton-on-T KT12 35 B2
West Barnes SM4 39 D2
Kingsbrook KT22 75 A1
Kingsbury Cres TW18 12 D4
Kingsbury Dr SL4 11 B8
Kingsclear Pk GU15 65 D4
Kingsclere Cl SW15 19 A8
Kingscliffe Gdns SW19 19 F7
Kingscote Hill RH11 201 B4
Kingscote Rd
Croydon CR0, CR9 43 B2
Kingston u T KT3 38 D6
Kingscote Sta RH19 204 F4
Kingscourt Rd SW16 21 E5
Kingscroft Cty Inf Sch TW18 13 A3
Kingscroft Cty Jun Sch TW18 13 A2
Kingscroft La RG42 8 A6
Kingscroft Rd
Leatherhead KT22 95 B7
Woodmansterne SM7 78 E4
Kingsdale Rd SE20 23 D1
Kingsdale Sch SE21 22 E5
Kingsdene KT20 97 B5
Kingsdown 1 SW19 19 D1
Kingsdown Ave CR2, CR8 61 C2
Kingsdown Rd Cheam SM3 58 E5
Ewell KT17 77 A6
Kingsdowne Rd KT6 37 F2
Kingsfield GU5 153 E7
Kingsfield Bsns Pk RH1 140 A8
Kingsfold Ct RH12 198 B5
Kingsford Ave SM6 60 E3
Kingsgate Bsns Ctr KT2 37 E8
Kingsgate Rd KT2 37 E8
Kingshill Ave KT4 39 B2
Kingslake Ct 2 GU21 68 E1
Kingsland RH5 158 A1
Kingsland Ct RH10 202 A6
Kingslea Horsham RH13 217 E3
Leatherhead KT22 95 A7
Kingslee Ct 12 SM2 59 B3
Kingsleigh Pl CR4 40 F6
Kingsleigh Wlk BR2 44 F5
Kingsley Ave Banstead SM7 78 A4
Camberley GU15 65 D3
Carshalton SM1 59 D6
Englefield Green TW20 11 B2
Hounslow TW3 5 C5
Kingsley Cl
Crowthorne RG45 45 B3
Horley RH6 160 F5
Kingsley Ct
Walton-on-T KT12 54 A7
Worcester Park KT4 57 F8
Kingsley Dr KT4 57 F8
Kingsley Gr RH2 139 B5
Kingsley House 8 KT6 37 E4
Kingsley Inf Sch CR9 42 A1
Kingsley Jun Sch CR9 42 A1
Kingsley Rd Crawley RH11 201 A3
Farnborough GU14 84 F6
Horley RH6 160 F5
Hounslow TW3 5 C5
Thornton Heath CR0 42 A1
Wimbledon SW19 20 B3
Kingslyn Cres SE19 42 E8
Kingsmead Biggin Hill TN16 83 D3
Cranleigh GU6 174 E3
Farnborough GU14 85 B4
Frimley GU16 85 E7
Richmond TW10 6 F1
Weybridge KT13 53 D4
Woking GU21 70 A3
Kingsmead Ave
Mitcham CR4 41 C6
North Cheam KT4 58 B7
Sunbury TW16 35 C7
Tolworth KT6 57 A8
Kingsmead Cl
Horsham RH12 218 B6
Teddington TW11 17 B2
West Ewell KT19 57 D3
Kingsmead Ct BR1 24 F1
Kingsmead Lodge SM2 59 D4
Kingsmead Pl RH12 216 C3
Kingsmead Rd
Broadbridge Heath RH12 216 D3
Streatham SW2 22 A6
Kingsmead Sh Ctr GU14 85 B3
Kingsmere SE6 24 B7
Kingsmere Rd
Bracknell RG42 26 F8
Putney SW19 19 D6
Kingsnympton Pk KT2 18 B2
Kingsridge SW19 19 E6
Kingsthorpe Rd SE26 23 D4
Kingston Ave Cheam SM3 58 E7
East Horsley KT24 92 E1
Feltham TW14 3 F1
Leatherhead KT22 95 B6
Kingston Bsns Ctr KT9 56 F7
Kingston By - Pass KT6 57 B8
Kingston By-Pass
KT6, KT7, KT9 56 C7
Kingston Cl TW11 17 B2
Kingston Coll of F Ed KT1 37 D6
Kingston Coll of F Ed (M V Annex) KT2 37 E8
Kingston Cres
Beckenham BR3 43 F8
Staines TW15 13 D2
Kingston Gdns CR0 60 E7
Kingston Gram Sch KT2 37 F7
Kingston Hall Rd KT1 37 D6
Kingston Hill KT2 18 C2
Kingston Hill Pl KT2, TW10 18 C4
Kingston Hospl KT2 38 B8
Kingston House Gdns KT22 95 B6
Kingston La
Teddington TW11 17 B2
West Horsley KT24 112 A8
Kingston Lodge 1 KT3 38 E5
Kingston Mus KT1 37 E7
Kingston Poly (Gipsy Hill Ctr) KT2 18 D3
Kingston Rd
Ashford TW15, TW17 13 F2
Ashstead KT22, KT9 75 A3
Camberley GU15 47 A1
Ewell KT17, KT19, KT4, KT5, KT6 57 D6
Kingston u T KT1, KT3 38 C5
Leatherhead KT22 75 A1
Merton SW19, SW20 39 E7
New Malden KT3 38 C5
Putney SW15, SW19 19 B7
Roehampton SW15, SW19 19 B7
Staines TW15, TW18 13 B2
Teddington TW11 17 B2
Tolworth KT17, KT19, KT4, KT5, KT6 57 D6
Worcester Park KT17, KT19, KT4, KT5, KT6 57 D6
Kingston Rise KT15 52 A1
Kingston Sq SE19 22 D3
Kingston Sta KT2 37 E8
Kingston Univ
Kingston u T KT2 18 D3
Kingston u T KT1 37 E6
Kingston Univ Annex KT1 37 F7
Kingston Univ Roehampton Vale Ctr SW15 18 F5
Kingston Vale SW15 18 E5
Kingstons Ind Est GU12 105 E2
Kingsway Aldershot GU11 104 E1
Blackwater GU17 64 E5
Coney Hall BR4 63 F7
Mortlake SW14, TW9 7 B4
Stanwell TW19 13 E7
West Barnes KT3 39 C4
Woking GU21 69 D1
Kingsway Ave Selsdon CR2 62 D2
Woking GU21 69 D1
Kingsway Bsns Pk GU21 70 C5
Kingsway Bsns Pk The TW12 35 F8
Kingsway Rd SM3 58 E3
Kingsway Terr KT13 53 A2
Kingsway The KT17 57 F1
Kingswear House SE23 23 C6
Kingswick Cl SL5 29 D5
Kingswick Dr SL5 29 D5
Kingswood Ave
Beckenham BR2, BR3 44 E5
Hampton TW12 16 B2
Hamsey Green CR2 81 C4
Hounslow TW3, TW5 4 F5
Thornton Heath CR7 42 A4
Kingswood Cl
Englefield Green TW20 11 D4
Guildford GU1 110 C2
New Malden KT3 38 F3
Surbiton KT6 37 E2
Weybridge KT13 53 B3
Kingswood Ct
6 Richmond TW10 6 F2
Woking GU21 69 E3
Kingswood Cty Prim Sch KT20 117 F7
Kingswood Dr
Belmont SM2 59 B2
Carshalton SM5 40 F1
Dulwich SE19, SE21 22 F4
Kingswood Firs GU26 188 C2
Kingswood Golf Course KT20 98 A3
Kingswood Hall of Residence TW20 11 D4
Kingswood House 3 KT2 18 B2
Kingswood House Sch KT18 76 C6
Kingswood La CR6 81 C4
Kingswood Pk KT20 97 E6
Kingswood Prim Sch SE27 22 D3
Kingswood Rd
Beckenham BR2 44 E6
Merton SW19 39 F8
Penge SE20 23 C2
Streatham SW2 21 E8
Tadworth KT20 97 B6
Kingswood Rise TW20 11 D4
Kingswood Sta KT20 97 F6
Kingswood Way
Hamsey Green CR2 81 C6
Selsdon CR2 81 D7
Wallington SM6 60 E5
Kingsworth Cl BR3 43 E4
Kingsworthy Cl KT1 37 F6
Kinloss Rd SM5 40 C2
Kinnaird Ave Bromley BR1 24 F2
Chiswick W4 7 C7
Kinnaird Cl BR1 24 F2
Kinnear Ct SW20 39 D8
Kinnersley Wlk RH2 139 B4
Kinnibrugh Dr RH7 165 A1
Kinross Ave Ascot SL5 28 F4
Worcester Park KT4 58 A8
Kinross Cl TW16 14 F3
Kinross Ct SL5 28 F4
Kinross Dr TW16 14 F3
Kinsey House SE21 22 E4
Kintyre Cl SW16 41 F6
Kintyre Ct 17 SW2 21 E8
Kinver Rd SE26 23 C4
Kipings KT20 97 D5
Kipling Cl RH10 202 C8
Kipling Ct RH13 218 A4
Kipling Dr SW17 20 D2
Kipling Way RH19 185 C1
Kirby Cl KT19 57 F5
Kirby Rd GU21 69 D2
Kirby Way KT12 35 C3
Kirdford Cl RH11 201 A8
Kirk Rise SM1 59 B7
Kirkby Ct GU16 65 E1
Kirkdale SE26 23 B5
Kirkfield GU2 109 A4
Kirkgate The 2 KT17 76 E6
Kirkham Cl GU47 45 D2
Kirkland Ave GU21 68 F3
Kirkleas Rd KT6 37 E1
Kirklees Rd CR7 42 A4
Kirkley Rd SW19 40 A8
Kirkly Cl CR2 61 E2
Kirkstall Gdns SW2 21 E7
Kirkstall Rd SW2 21 E7
Kirksted Rd SM4 40 B1
Kirkstone Cl GU15 66 D4
Kirkstone Way BR1 24 E1
Kirrane Cl KT3 38 F4
Kirriemuir Gdns GU12 106 D3
Kirtley Rd SE26 23 E4
Kitchener Rd
Farnborough GU11 105 D6
South Norwood CR7 42 D6
Kitchenride Cnr KT16 51 A6
Kites Cl RH11 201 C6
Kithurst Cl RH11 201 D4
Kitley Gdns SE19 42 F8
Kitsmead RH10 183 A2

Kitsmead La KT16 50 D8
Kittiwake Cl
Crawley RH11 200 D4
Selsdon CR0, CR2 62 E1
Kittiwake Pl SM1 58 F5
Klondyke Villas GU27 190 A1
Knaggs House 1 TW11 16 E3
Knapdale Cl SE23 23 B6
Knaphill Cty Inf Sch GU21 68 B1
Knaphill Cty Jun Sch GU21 68 C1
Knapmill Rd SE6 24 B6
Knapmill Way SE6 24 B6
Knapp Rd TW15 13 F4
Knapton Mews SW17 21 A2
Knaresborough Dr SW18 20 B7
Kneller Gdns TW7 5 D1
Kneller Rd New Malden KT3 38 E2
Twickenham TW2 5 D1
Knepp Cl RH10 202 C6
Knight's Hill SE19, SE27 22 B4
Knight's Hill Sq SE27 22 B4
Knight's Pk KT1 37 E6
Knighton Cl Crawley RH10 182 D2
Croydon CR2 61 B2
Knighton Park Rd SE26 23 D3
Knighton Rd RH1 140 A7
Knightons La GU8 193 A2
Knights Cl TW20 12 D2
Knights Ct Kingston u T KT1 37 E6
Penge BR3 43 E8
Knights Pl RH1 119 A2
Knights Rd GU9 125 E7
Knights Way GU15 66 C4
Knightsbridge Cres TW18 13 B2
Knightsbridge Ho 10 GU1 130 F8
Knightsbridge Rd GU15 65 E7
Knightswood
Bracknell RG12 27 B1
Woking GU21 68 F1
Knightwood Cl RH2 139 A7
Knightwood Cres KT3 38 E3
Knipp Hill KT11 73 F6
Knob Hill RH12 198 A1
Knobfield RH5 154 F8
Knockhundred La GU26 207 C8
Knole Cl Crawley RH10 202 D7
Croydon CR0 43 C3
Knole Gr RH19 185 C3
Knole Wood SL5 29 C1
Knoll Ct SE19 22 F3
Knoll Park Rd KT16 32 F1
Knoll Quarry GU7 150 E6
Knoll Rd Camberley GU15 65 D6
Dorking RH4 136 A5
Farncombe GU7 150 E6
Knoll The Beckenham BR3 44 B8
Cobham KT11 74 A6
Leatherhead KT22 95 C6
Knoll Wood GU7 150 D6
Knollmead KT4, KT5 38 C1
Knollmead Prim Sch KT4 57 C8
Knolls Cl KT4 58 B7
Knolls The KT17 77 C3
Knolly's Cl SE27, SW16 22 A5
Knolly's Rd SE27, SW16 22 A5
Knollys Rd GU11 104 F3
Knott Park House KT22 74 C4
Knowl Hill GU22 70 B1
Knowl Hill Sch The GU24 87 E5
Knowle Cl RH10 183 C3
Knowle Dr RH10 183 B3
Knowle Gdns KT14 70 F6
Knowle Gn TW18 13 A3
Knowle Gr GU25 31 C2
Knowle Grove Cl GU25 31 C2
Knowle Hill GU25 31 C2
Knowle La GU6, RH12 194 D4
Knowle Lodge CR3 101 A4
Knowle Park Ave TW18 13 B3
Knowle Pk KT11 73 E4
Knowle Rd TW2 16 E7
Knowlton Gn BR2 44 F4
Knox Rd GU2 109 B6
Kohat Ct GU11 104 F2
Kohat Rd SW19 20 B3
Kohima Cl GU11 105 B3
Koonowla Cl TN16 83 D4
Kooringa CR6 101 B8
Korda Cl TW17 33 F6
Kreisel Wlk TW9 6 F8
Kristina Ct SM2 59 A4
Krooner Rd GU15 65 B3
Kuala Gdns SW16 41 F8
Kyle Cl RG12 27 B6
Kynaston Ave CR7 42 C4
Kynaston Cres CR0, CR7 42 C4
Kynaston Ct CR3 100 E2
Kynaston House 7 SW2 21 F7
Kynaston Rd CR0, CR7 42 C4
Kynersley Cl SM5 59 F7

L

La Retraite RC Girls Sch SW12 21 C8
Laburnam Ct 12 SW16 22 A3
Laburnum Ave SM1 59 E7
Laburnum Cl 2
Aldershot GU11 105 A1
Guildford GU1 109 C4
Laburnum Cres TW16 35 B8
Laburnum Ct CR4 41 A7
Laburnum Gdns CR0 43 D1
Laburnum Gr Brands Hill SL3 1 B8
Hounslow TW3 4 F3
Kingston u T KT3 38 D7
Laburnum Pas 1 GU11 105 A1
Laburnum Pl TW20 11 B2
Laburnum Rd
Aldershot GU11 105 A2
Chertsey KT16 33 A1
Epsom KT18 76 E6
Heath End GU9 125 E7
Merton SW19 20 C1
Mitcham CR4 41 A7
Woking GU22 89 D7
Laburnum Way TW19 13 F7
Laburnums The GU17 64 B5
Lacey Ave CR5 100 A7
Lacey Cl TW20 12 D1
Lacey Dr Coulsdon CR5 100 B7
Hampton TW12 35 F8
Lackford Rd CR5 78 F1
Lacock Cl SW19 20 C2
Lacy Gn CR5 100 A7
Ladas Rd SE27 22 C3
Ladbroke Cotts 2 RH1 119 A2
Ladbroke Ct 7 RH1 119 A3
Ladbroke Gr RH1 119 A2
Ladbroke Hurst RH7 165 A1
Ladbroke Rd Epsom KT18 76 D5
Horley RH6 161 B5
Redhill RH1 119 A3
Ladbrook Rd SE25 42 D5
Ladderstile Ride
Kingston u T KT2 18 C3
Richmond KT2, TW10 18 B3
Ladlands SE22 23 A8
Lady Booth Rd 7 KT1 37 E7
Lady Eleanor Holles Sch The (Jun Girls) TW12 16 B3
Lady Eleanor Holles Sch The (Senior Girls) TW12 16 B3
Lady Hay KT4 57 F8
Lady Margaret Rd
Crawley RH11 201 A7
Sunningdale SL5 29 F2
Lady Margaret Wlk RH11 201 A7
Ladybank RG12 27 B1
Ladycross GU8 170 E8
Ladycross Mews GU8 170 E8
Ladyegate Cl RH5 136 D8
Ladyegate Rd RH5 136 D8
Ladygate Dr GU26 188 A3
Ladygrove CR2 62 D2
Ladygrove Dr GU4 110 B6
Ladymead GU1 109 C2
Ladymead Cl RH10 202 C3
Ladymead Retail Ctr GU1 109 E2
Ladythorpe Cl KT15 52 B6
Ladywood Ave GU14 84 C4
Ladywood Rd KT6 57 A8
Laffan's Rd GU11 104 E6
Lafone Ave TW13 15 C6
Lafone House 11 SW2 21 E8
Lagham Pk RH9 142 E6
Lagham Rd RH9 142 F5
Laglands Cl RH2 118 C3
Laings Ave CR4 40 F7
Laings Cnr CR4 40 F8
Lainlock Pl TW3 5 B6
Lainson St SW18 20 A8
Laird Ct GU19 47 E1
Lairdale Cl SE21 22 C8
Laitwood Rd SW12 21 B7
Lake Cl Byfleet KT14 71 D7
6 Wimbledon SW19 19 F3
Lake Cotts GU8 169 F4
Lake End Way RG45 45 A4
Lake Gdns Hackbridge SM6 60 B7
Richmond TW10 17 B6
Lake House 4 SW27 22 B3
Lake La Dockenfield GU10 166 E6
Horley RH1, RH6 161 C6
Lake Rd Croydon CR0 62 F8
Frimley GU16 86 B6
Ockley RH5 177 D6
Virginia Water GU25 31 B5
Wimbledon SW19 19 F3
Lake Side The GU17 64 D4
Lake View RH5 136 C4
Lake View Rd
Copthorne RH19 184 C4
Domewood RH19 184 C4
Dormans Park RH19 185 F5
Dormansland RH19 185 F5
Lakehall Gdns CR7 42 B4
Lakehall Rd CR7 42 B4
Lakehurst Rd KT19 57 E5
Lakeland Dr GU16 65 E1
Lakeman Ct CR7 42 C7
Lakers Lea RH14 212 F1
Lakers Rise SM7 78 E3
Lakes Cl GU4 131 B3
Lakeside Beckenham BR3 44 B6
3 Bracknell RG42 27 C8
Hackbridge SM6 60 B6
Horsham RH12 217 C5
10 Kingston u T KT2 18 B1
Knaphill GU21 88 E8
Oatlands Park KT13 53 E8
Redhill RH1 119 A3
West Ewell KT19 57 E4
Lakeside Cl Ash Vale GU12 105 F4
Knaphill GU21 88 E8
South Norwood SE25 43 A7
Lakeside Cty Prim Sch GU16 65 F1
Lakeside Dr KT10 55 C4
Lakeside Est SL3 2 A8
Lakeside Gdns GU14 84 D7
Lakeside Grange KT13 53 C7
Lakeside Rd
Ash Vale GU11, GU12 105 F4
Lakeside Rd *continued*
Colnbrook SL3 1 F7
Farnborough GU14 105 A7
Lakeview Rd SE27 22 B3
Laleham C of E Prim Sch TW18 33 C7
Laleham Ct GU21 69 E3
Laleham Lea Prep Sch CR8 60 E1
Laleham Rd Catford SE6 24 C8
Lewisham SE6 24 C8
Littleton TW17 34 A4
Shepperton TW17 34 B3
Staines TW18 12 F2
Lamb's Bsns Pk RH9 142 C5
Lamberhurst Rd SE27 22 A3
Lamberhurst Wlk RH10 202 A5
Lambert Ave TW9 7 B4
Lambert Cl TN16 83 D3
Lambert Cotts RH1 120 E2
Lambert Cres GU17 64 C4
Lambert Rd SM7 78 B5
Lambert's Pl CR0 42 D1
Lambert's Rd KT6 37 F4
Lambeth Cl RH11 201 B2
Lambeth Inst Strand Ctr SW2 21 F8
Lambeth Prospect SE19 22 D2
Lambeth Rd CR0 42 B1
Lambly Hill GU25 31 E6
Lamborne Cl GU47 45 A1
Lambourn Cl RH19 185 E3
Lambourne Ave SW19 19 F4
Lambourne Cl RH10 201 F4
Lambourne Cres GU21 70 D6
Lambourne Dr
Bagshot GU19 47 D2
Cobham KT11 73 D4
Lambourne Gr
Bracknell RG12 27 E7
Kingston u T KT1 38 B7
Lambourne Way GU10 126 F7
Lambs Cres RH12 217 F5
Lambs Farm Cl RH12 218 A5
Lambs Farm Rd RH12 218 A6
Lambs Green Rd RH12 199 F6
Lambton Rd SW20 39 C8
Lambyn Croft RH6 161 C4
Lamerock Rd BR1 24 F4
Lammas Ave CR4 41 A7
Lammas Cl GU7 151 A6
Lammas Ct
Farncombe GU7 150 E5
Stanwell TW19 12 D5
Lammas Dr TW18 12 D4
Lammas Gate GU7 150 F6
Lammas Gn SE26 23 B5
Lammas Hill KT10 55 A5
Lammas La KT10 55 A6
Lammas Rd
Godalming GU7 151 A5
Richmond TW10 17 C4
Lammermoor Rd SW12 21 B8
Lampard La GU10 167 E2
Lampeter Cl 4 GU22 69 E1
Lampton Ave TW5 5 B6
Lampton Ct TW5 5 B6
Lampton House Cl SW19 19 D4
Lampton Park Rd TW3 5 B5
Lampton Rd TW3, TW5 5 B5
Lampton Sch TW5 5 A6
Lanain Ct SE12 24 F8
Lanark Cl Frimley GU16 65 E2
Horsham RH13 217 E2
Lancaster Ave
Farnham GU9 146 D8
Mitcham CR4 41 E4
West Norwood SE21, SE27 22 C6
Wimbledon SW19 19 D3
Lancaster Cl
Ash Vale GU12 105 F5
Beckenham BR2 44 F5
Crawley RH10 182 D1
Englefield Green TW20 11 D3
Kingston u T KT2 17 D3
Stanwell TW19 2 E1
Woking GU21 70 A3
Lancaster Cotts 1 TW10 6 E1
Lancaster Ct
1 Banstead SM7 77 F5
1 Belmont SM2 59 A3
Epsom KT19 57 D1
Stanwell TW19 13 E7
Walton-on-T KT12 35 B2
Lancaster Dr
Camberley GU15 65 D6
East Grinstead RH19 186 A3
Lancaster Gdns
Kingston u T KT2 17 D3
Wimbledon SW19 19 E3
Lancaster House
Bracknell RG12 27 B4
Wandsworth SW18 20 B8
Lancaster Mews 2 TW10 6 E1
Lancaster Pk TW10 6 E2
Lancaster Pl Hounslow TW5 4 D5
Twickenham TW1 17 A8
Wimbledon SW19 19 D3
Lancaster Rd
South Norwood SE25 43 A6
Wimbledon SW19 19 E3
Lancaster Way GU14 85 C7
Lancelot Cl RH11 200 E6
Lancelot Ho RH1 119 A2
Lancer Ct GU11 104 E2
Lanchester Dr RG45 45 C7
Lancing Cl RH11 201 A8
Lancing Ct RH12 218 A4
Lancing Rd Feltham TW13 14 F6
Thornton Heath CR0 41 F2
Landen Ct RG40 25 B4
Landen Pk RH6 160 E5
Landgrove Rd SW19 20 A3
Landon Way TW15 14 B2
Landscape Rd CR6 101 B8
Landsdowne Cl KT5 57 B8
Landseer Cl Mitcham SW19 40 D8
Sandhurst GU47 64 E6
Landseer Rd
Cheam SM1, SM2 59 A4
New Malden KT3 38 D2
Lane Cl KT15 52 B5
Lane Ct SW11 20 F8
Lane End Epsom KT18 76 B5
Hambledon GU8 191 B8
Lane End Dr GU21 68 C2
Lane House RH13 217 D2
Lane The Chertsey KT16 33 A6
Ifold RH14 212 C4
Thorpe GU25 31 E6
Thursley GU8 169 C4
Lanercost Cl SW2 22 A6
Lanercost Rd
Crawley RH11 201 C5
Streatham SW2 22 A6
Lanesborough Prep Sch GU1 109 F1
Lang Cl KT23 94 B4
Langaller La KT22 94 B6
Langborough Rd RG40 25 C5
Langbourne Prim Sch SE21 22 E5
Langbourne Way KT10 56 A4
Langcroft Cl SM5 59 F7
Langdale Ave CR4 40 F6
Langdale Cl
Farnborough GU14 84 E4
Mortlake SW14 7 B3
Woking GU21 69 C3
Langdale Dr SL5 28 E7
Langdale Rd
Crawley RH11 200 D4
Thornton Heath CR7 42 A5
Langdon Cl GU15 66 C4
Langdon Pl SW14 7 C4
Langdon Rd SM4 40 C4
Langdon Wlk SM4 40 C4
Langham Cl GU7 150 F4
Langham Ct Farnham GU9 146 C7
12 Twickenham TW1 6 C1
Wimbledon SW20 39 C7
Langham Dene CR8 80 B4
Langham Gdns TW10 17 C4
Langham House Cl TW10 17 D4
Langham Pk GU7 150 F4
Langham Pl Chiswick W4 7 E8
Egham TW20 11 F3
Langham Rd
Teddington TW11 17 B2
Wimbledon SW20 39 C8
Langholm Cl SW12 21 D8
Langhorn Dr TW2 16 E8
Langhurst Cl RH12 198 E4
Langhurst La RH12 200 A8
Langhurstwood Rd RH12 198 D3
Langland Gdns CR0 62 F8
Langlands Rise KT19 76 C6
Langley Ave
North Cheam KT4, SM3 58 D8
Surbiton KT6 37 E1
Langley Cl Guildford GU1 109 D2
Langley Vale KT18 96 D8
Langley Cres UB3 3 F7
Langley Ct RH2 118 B2
Langley Dr
Aldershot GU11 126 A8
Camberley GU15 65 D6
Crawley RH11 201 D8
Langley Gr KT3 38 E7
Langley Green Cty Fst Sch RH11 181 D1
Langley Green Cty Mid Sch RH11 201 C8
Langley La RH11 201 A8
Langley Oaks Ave CR2 62 A1
Langley Par RH11 181 C1
Langley Park Golf Course BR3 44 C2
Langley Park Rd
SM1, SM2 59 C3
Langley Park Sch for Boys BR3 44 B3
Langley Park Sch for Girls BR3 44 C3
Langley Pl RH11 181 C1
Langley Rd Beckenham BR3 43 E5
Isleworth TW7 5 F5
Merton SW19 40 A8
Selsdon CR2 62 D2
Staines TW18 12 F2
Surbiton KT6 37 E2
Langley Vale Rd
KT18, KT21 76 E1
Langley Way BR4 44 E2
Langley Wlk
Crawley RH11 181 B1
Woking GU22 89 E8
Langmans Way GU21 68 E3
Langmead St SE27 22 C4
Langport Ct KT12 35 C1
Langridge Dr RH19 205 E8
Langridge House RH12 217 B2
Langridge Mews TW12 15 F2
Langroyd Rd SW17 20 F6
Langshott RH6 161 D4
Langshott Cl KT15 70 F8
Langshott Cty Inf Sch RH6 161 C3
Langshott La RH6 161 C4
Langsmead RH7 163 E8
Langstone Cl RH10 202 C3
Langthorne Ct SE6 24 C4
Langton Ave KT17 76 F8
Langton Cl Addlestone KT15 52 B7
Woking GU21 68 F2
Langton Dr GU35 187 A7
Langton House 5 SW16 21 C4
Langton Pl SW18 20 A7
Langton Rd KT8 36 C5
Langton Rise SE22, SE23 23 B8
Langton Way Egham TW20 12 C2
South Croydon CR0 61 E6
Langwood Chase TW11 17 C2
Lanherne House 5 SW19 19 D1
Lanigan Dr TW3 5 B2
Lankton Cl BR3 44 C8
Lansbury Ave TW14 4 B1
Lansbury Rd RH11 201 B1
Lansdell Rd CR4 41 A7
Lansdown GU1 110 A1
Lansdown Cl
Horsham RH12 218 B6
Knaphill GU21 88 F8
Walton-on-T KT12 35 C1
Lansdowne Cl
Twickenham TW1 16 F7
Wimbledon SW20 19 D1
Lansdowne Copse 1 KT4 58 A8
Lansdowne Ct Purley CR8 61 B1
2 Worcester Park KT4 58 A8
Lansdowne Hill SE27 22 B5
Lansdowne Pl SE19 22 F1
Lansdowne Rd
Aldershot GU11 105 A1
Croydon CR0 42 D1
Frimley GU16 86 A8
Hounslow TW3 5 B4
Purley CR8 80 A7
Staines TW18 13 B1
West Ewell KT19 57 D3
Wimbledon SW19, SW20 19 C1
Lansdowne Wood Cl 11 SE27 22 B5
Lanswood Ct KT4 58 A8
Lantern Ct SW20 39 D8
Lanyon Cl RH12 218 A6
Lanyon Mews RH12 218 A6
Lapse Wood Wlk SE22 23 B7
Lapwing Cl Horsham RH13 217 F3
Selsdon CR0, CR2 62 E1
Lapwing Ct KT6 57 A7
Lapwing Gr GU4 110 D3
Lara Cl KT9 56 E3
Larbert Rd SW16 21 C1
Larby Pl KT17 57 E1
Larch Ave Ascot SL5 29 E4
Guildford GU1 109 C4
Wokingham RG41 25 A7
Larch Cl Camberley GU15 65 E8
Kingswood KT20 98 C6
Reigate RH1 139 C7
Upper Tooting SW12 21 B6
Warlingham CR6 101 E8
Larch Cres KT19 57 B4
Larch End RH12 217 B4
Larch Rd GU35 187 B6
Larch Tree Way CR0 63 A7
Larch Way GU14 84 C3
Larches Ave SW14 7 D3
Larches The
Horsham RH12 218 C6
Woking GU21 69 E3
Larches Way
Blackwater GU17 64 B5
Crawley Down RH10 204 C8
Larchvale Ct 4 SM2 59 B3
Larchwood 5 RG12 27 F5
Larchwood Cl SM7 77 E4
Larchwood Dr TW20 11 B2
Larchwood Glade GU15 66 A7
Larchwood Rd GU21 88 D8
Larcombe Cl CR0 61 F6
Larges Bridge Dr RG12 27 D6
Larges La RG12 27 C7
Largewood Ave KT6 57 A8
Lark Ave TW18 12 F5
Lark Rise Crawley RH11 201 C8
East Horsley KT24 112 E4
Larkbere Rd SE26 23 E4
Larkfield Cobham KT11 73 A6
Ewhurst GU6 175 E4
Larkfield Cl Coney Hall BR2 63 F8
Farnham GU9 124 F2
Larkfield Ct RH6 162 A3
Larkfield Rd Farnham GU9 124 F2
Richmond TW9 6 E3
Larkhall Cl KT12 54 C4
Larkham Cl TW13 14 E5
Larkin Cl CR5 79 F2
Larkins Rd RH6 181 D7
Larks Way GU21 68 C3
Larksfield
Englefield Green TW20 11 C1
Horley RH6 161 B4
Larkspur Cl GU11 126 A7
Larkspur Ct SM6 60 B3
Larkspur Way
Dorking RH5 136 D4
West Ewell KT19 57 C5
Larkswood Cl GU47 45 A1
Larkswood Dr RG45 45 B5

Lascombe La GU3 ....128 B4
Lashmere Copthorne RH10 183 D3
Cranleigh GU6 ....174 B3
Laski Ct RH11 ....201 B1
Lasswade Ct KT16 ....32 F2
Lasswade Rd KT16 ....32 F2
Lastingham Ct TW18 ....13 A2
Latchmere Cl KT2, TW10 ...17 E3
Latchmere Jun & Inf Schs KT2 ....17 F2
Latchmere La
Kingston u T KT2, TW10 ....17 F3
Richmond KT2, TW10 ....17 F3
Latchmere Rd KT2 ....17 F2
Latchwood La GU10 ....146 D5
Lateward Rd TW8 ....6 D8
Latham Ave GU16 ....65 E2
Latham Cl Biggin Hill TN16 ..83 C3
5 Twickenham TW1 ....17 A8
Latham Rd TW1 ....16 F8
Latham's Way CR0 ....60 F8
Lathwood House 6 SE26 ..23 B3
Latimer RG12 ....27 B1
Latimer Cl Crawley RH11 .181 D1
North Cheam KT4 ....58 B6
Woking GU22 ....70 B3
Latimer House GU7 ....150 E3
Latimer Rd
Croydon CR0, CR9 ....61 B7
Godalming GU7 ....150 E4
Teddington TW11 ....16 F3
Wimbledon SW19 ....20 B2
Wokingham RG41 ....25 B5
Latton Cl Esher KT10 ....55 B6
Walton-on-T KT12 ....35 E2
Latymer Cl KT13 ....53 C6
Laud Dr RH10 ....202 D5
Laud St CR0, CR9 ....61 C7
Laud Way RG40 ....25 E6
Lauder Cl GU16 ....65 E2
Lauderdale GU14 ....84 D3
Lauderdale Dr TW10 ....17 D5
Lauderdale House TW18 ..12 F3
Laughton Rd RH12 ....217 F5
Launceston Ct CR7 ....42 A3
Laundry La GU47 ....64 E5
Laundry Rd GU1 ....130 C8
Laundry Way RH5 ....178 C5
Lauradale RG12 ....27 A5
Laurel Ave
Englefield Green TW20 ....11 B3
Twickenham TW1 ....16 F7
Laurel Cl Camberley GU15 ..65 D4
Crawley RH10 ....202 A3
Farnborough GU14 ....84 C3
Poyle SL3 ....1 E7
Upper Tooting SW17 ....20 E3
Laurel Cres Croydon CR0 ...63 A7
Sheerwater GU21 ....70 D6
Laurel Ct SE25 ....42 E4
Laurel Dene RH19 ....185 F1
Laurel Dr RH8 ....122 F4
Laurel Gdns
Aldershot GU11 ....126 A7
Hounslow TW4 ....4 E3
Woodham KT15 ....52 B1
Laurel Gr Forest Hill SE26 ..23 E4
Penge SE20 ....23 C1
Rowledge GU10 ....145 F5
Wrecclesham GU10 ....146 A5
Laurel House SM4 ....40 B4
Laurel Manor SM2 ....59 C3
Laurel Rd Teddington TW12 .16 D3
Wimbledon SW20 ....39 B8
Laurel Wlk RH13 ....217 F1
Laureldene GU3 ....107 B1
Laurels The Banstead SM7 ..77 F2
Cobham KT11 ....73 E4
Crawley RH10 ....182 A1
Heath End GU9 ....125 F7
6 Oatlands Park KT13 ....53 D7
Laurier Rd CR0 ....42 F2
Lauriston Cl GU21 ....68 D2
Lauriston Rd SW19 ....19 D2
Lauser Rd TW19 ....13 C8
Laustan Cl GU1 ....110 C2
Lavant Cl RH11 ....200 F5
Lavender Ave Mitcham CR4 .40 F8
North Cheam KT4, SM3 ....58 C7
Lavender Cl
Caterham CR3 ....100 C2
Coulsdon CR5 ....99 C8
Redhill RH1 ....140 B4
Wallington SM5 ....60 B6
Lavender Ct KT8 ....36 B6
Lavender Gr CR4 ....40 E8
Lavender La GU10 ....145 F4
Lavender Park Rd KT14 ...71 A6
Lavender Pk SL5 ....28 C6
Lavender Rd
Carshalton SM1 ....59 D6
Thornton Heath CR0 ....41 F3
Wallington SM5 ....60 A6
West Ewell KT19 ....57 B4
Woking GU22 ....70 B3
Lavender Vale SM6 ....60 D4
Lavender Way CR0 ....43 D3
Lavengro Rd SE27 ....22 C6
Laverock Sch RH8 ....122 E7
Laverstoke Gdns SW15 ...19 A8
Lavington Cl RH11 ....201 A7
Lavington Rd CR0 ....60 F6
Lavinia Ct BR1 ....24 E1
Lawbrook La
Gomshall GU5 ....154 C7
Lawbrook La *continued*
Peaslake GU5 ....154 C7
Lawday Link GU9 ....125 A7
Lawday Pl GU9 ....125 A7
Lawday Place La GU9 ...125 A7
Lawdon Gdns CR0 ....61 B6
Lawford Cl SM6 ....60 E2
Lawford Gdns CR8 ....80 C3
Lawford Rd W4 ....7 C7
Lawford's Hill Cl GU3 ....88 C3
Lawford's Hill Rd GU3 ....88 C3
Lawman Ct 2 TW9 ....6 F6
Lawn Cl KT3 ....38 E7
Lawn Cres TW9 ....7 A5
Lawn Rd Beckenham BR3 ...23 F1
Guildford GU2 ....130 C6
Lawns Rd RH12 ....195 A3
Lawns The Belmont SM2 ...58 E3
Farnborough GU14 ....84 E3
Milford GU8 ....149 F1
North Ascot SL5 ....28 D6
Purley CR8 ....61 B1
South Norwood SE19 ....42 D8
1 Wimbledon SW19 ....19 F3
Lawnsmead Cotts GU5 ..152 B7
Lawnwood Ct GU7 ....151 A5
Lawrence Ave KT3 ....38 E2
Lawrence Cl
Guildford GU4 ....110 B6
Wokingham RG40 ....25 D6
Lawrence Cres GU20 ....48 D4
Lawrence Est TW4 ....4 C3
Lawrence Gr RG42 ....26 D8
Lawrence La RH3 ....117 B3
Lawrence Lodge GU15 ....65 D7
Lawrence Rd
Hampton TW12 ....15 F1
Hounslow TW4 ....4 C3
Richmond TW10 ....17 C4
South Norwood SE25 ....42 F5
Lawrence Way GU15 ....64 F4
Lawrence Weaver Cl SM4 .40 A3
Lawrie Park Ave SE26 ....23 B3
Lawrie Park Cres SE26 ....23 B3
Lawrie Park Gdns SE26 ...23 B3
Lawrie Park Rd
Forest Hill SE19, SE26 ....23 C3
Penge SE19, SE26 ....23 C3
Laws Cl RH11 ....200 E5
Laws Terr GU11 ....105 C3
Lawson Cl SW19 ....19 D5
Lawson Ct 18 KT6 ....37 D2
Lawson Way SL5 ....30 B3
Lawson-Hunt Ind Pk RH12 ....216 C4
Laxton Ct CR7 ....42 C5
Laxton Gdns RH1 ....119 D7
Layard Rd CR7 ....42 D7
Layburn Cres SL3 ....1 B8
Layhams Rd
Coney Hall BR2, BR4, CR6 ...63 F5
West Wickham BR2 ....63 F1
Layton Cres CR0 ....61 B5
Layton Ct KT13 ....53 B6
Layton Pl TW9 ....7 A6
Layton Rd TW3 ....5 B3
Layton's La TW16 ....34 F7
Le Chateau CR0 ....61 D7
Le Marchant Rd
GU15, GU16 ....65 F3
Le May Cl RH6 ....161 A4
Le Personne Rd CR3 ....100 D5
Lea Cl Ash GU12 ....106 A1
Crawley RH11 ....200 F5
Farnham GU9 ....126 A6
Lea Croft RG45 ....45 B6
Lea Ct GU9 ....125 F7
Lea Rd Beckenham BR3 ....44 A7
Camberley GU15 ....65 B2
Lea The TW20 ....12 C1
Lea Way GU12 ....105 F3
Leach Gr KT22 ....95 C5
Leacroft Staines TW18 ....13 B4
Sunningdale SL5 ....30 A4
Leacroft Ave SW12 ....20 F8
Leacroft Cl Kenley CR8 ....80 C3
Staines TW18 ....13 B4
Leaf Cl KT7, KT8 ....36 E4
Leaf Gr SE27, SW16 ....22 A3
Leafield Cl
South Norwood SW16 ....22 B2
Woking GU21 ....69 B1
Leafield Copse RG12 ....27 F5
Leafield Rd
Merton SW19, SW20 ....39 F6
Sutton SM1 ....59 A8
Leafy Way CR0 ....61 F8
Leamington Ave SM4 ....39 F5
Leamington Cl TW3 ....5 C2
Leamington Ct 4 SE26 ...23 A5
Leander Ct 5 KT6 ....37 D2
Leander Rd 4
Streatham SW2 ....21 F8
Thornton Heath CR7 ....41 F5
Leapale La GU1 ....130 D8
Leapale Rd GU1 ....130 D8
Leas Cl KT9 ....56 F3
Leas La CR6 ....81 D1
Leas Rd Guildford GU1 ....130 C8
Warlingham CR6 ....81 D1
Leaside KT23 ....94 A4
Leather Cl CR4 ....41 A7
Leatherhead By-Pass Rd KT22 ....95 D5
Leatherhead General Hospl KT22 ....95 C5
Leatherhead Golf Club KT22 ....75 A3
Leatherhead Ind Est KT22 .95 A6
Leatherhead Mus of Local History KT22 ....95 B5
Leatherhead Rd
Ashstead KT21, KT22 ....95 E7
Chessington KT9 ....75 C6
Fetcham KT22, KT23 ....94 C2
Great Bookham KT22, KT23 ..94 C2
Oxshott KT22 ....74 D4
Leatherhead Sta KT22 ....95 A6
Leaveland Cl BR3 ....44 A5
Leaves Gn RG12 ....27 D3
Leaves Green Cres BR2 ...83 C8
Leaves Green Rd BR2 ....83 D8
Leavesden Rd KT13 ....53 B5
Leazes Ave CR3 ....100 A4
Lebanon Ave TW13 ....15 D3
Lebanon Ct 11 TW1 ....17 B8
Lebanon Dr KT11 ....74 A6
Lebanon Gdns TN16 ....83 D2
Lebanon Pk TW1 ....17 B8
Lebanon Rd CR0 ....42 E1
Lechford Rd RH6 ....161 A1
Leckford Rd SW18 ....20 C7
Leckhampton Pl SW2 ....22 A8
Leconfield Ave SW13, SW15 .7 F4
Ledbury Pl CR0 ....61 C6
Ledbury Rd
Croydon CR0, CR9 ....61 D6
Reigate RH2 ....118 A2
Ledger Cl GU1 ....110 B3
Ledger Dr KT15 ....51 F4
Ledgers Rd CR6 ....82 B1
Ledrington Rd SE19 ....23 A2
Lee Ct GU11 ....126 C8
Lee Hollow GU5 ....133 C1
Lee Rd Aldershot GU11 ....104 E2
Merton SW19 ....40 B8
Lee St RH6 ....160 E4
Leech La KT18, KT22 ....96 C1
Leechcroft Rd SM6 ....60 A7
Leechpool La RH12, RH13 218 A4
Leechpool Lane Cty Prim Sch RH13 ....218 A4
Leechpool & Owlbeech Nature Reserve RH13 ..218 C4
Leeds Ct Carshalton SM5 ...59 F7
Catford SE6 ....24 B5
Leegate Cl GU21 ....69 B3
Leehurst GU8 ....149 E1
Lees The CR0 ....62 F8
Leeson House 8 TW1 ....17 B8
Leeward Gdns SW19 ....19 F2
Leewood Way KT24 ....113 D8
Legge Cres GU11 ....104 E1
Legion Ct SM4 ....40 A3
Legrace Ave TW4, TW5 ....4 D5
Legsheath La RH19 ....205 D1
Leicester RG12 ....27 E2
Leicester Ave CR4 ....41 E5
Leicester Cl KT4 ....58 C6
Leicester House 2 KT7 ...37 A2
Leicester Rd CR0 ....42 E2
Leigh Cl Addlestone KT15 ...51 F3
New Malden KT3 ....38 D5
Leigh Court Cl KT11 ....73 D5
Leigh Cres CR0 ....63 C3
Leigh Ct CR0 ....82 E8
Leigh Hill Rd KT11 ....73 D5
Leigh House 4 KT2 ....18 B2
Leigh La GU9 ....146 E8
Leigh Orchard Cl SW16 ...21 F5
Leigh Pl KT11 ....73 C5
Leigh Place La RH9 ....121 E3
Leigh Place Rd RH2 ....138 A3
Leigh Rd Betchworth RH3 .137 C2
Cobham KT11 ....73 B5
Isleworth TW3 ....5 D3
Leigham Ave SW16 ....21 E5
Leigham Court Rd
SE27, SW16, SW21 ....22 A4
Leigham Dr TW7 ....5 E7
Leigham Hall 3 SW16 ....21 E5
Leigham Hall Par 2 SW16 21 E5
Leigham Vale
SE27, SW16, SW2 ....22 A6
Leighlands RH10 ....202 C8
Leighton Gdns
Sanderstead CR2 ....81 B6
Thornton Heath CR0 ....42 B1
Leighton House 7 KT6 ...37 E3
Leighton St CR0 ....42 B1
Leighton Way KT18 ....76 D5
Leinster Ave SW14 ....7 C3
Leisure La KT14 ....71 B7
Leith Cl RG45 ....45 A7
Leith Gr RH5 ....157 D4
Leith Hill Rd
Abinger Common RH5 ....155 F5
Wotton RH5 ....156 A3
Leith Hill Tower RH5 ....156 B3
Leith House Reigate RH2 .139 A6
16 Streatham SW2 ....21 F8
Leith Lea RH5 ....157 D4
Leith Rd Beare Green RH5 .157 D4
Ewell KT17 ....76 E7
Leith Towers 11 SM2 ....59 B3
Leith Vale Cotts RH5 ....177 A2
Leith View RH5 ....136 C3
Leith View Rd RH12 ....218 A5
Leithcote Gdns SW16 ....21 F4
Leithcote Path SW16 ....21 F5
Lela Ave TW4, TW5 ....4 C5
Lemington Gr RG12 ....27 B3
Lemmington Way RH12 ..218 A7
Lemon's Farm Rd RH5 ...155 F6
Lendore Rd GU16 ....85 D8
Lenelby Rd KT6 ....38 A1
Leney Cl RG40 ....25 D8
Lenham Rd
South Norwood CR7 ....42 D7
Sutton SM1 ....59 C5
Lennard Ave BR4 ....63 E8
Lennard Cl BR4 ....63 E8
Lennard Rd
Penge BR3, SE20, SE26 ....23 E2
Thornton Heath CR0 ....42 C1
Lennox Ct 18 RH1 ....119 A2
Lennox Gdns CR0 ....61 B6
Lenten Cl GU5 ....133 D1
Lentmead Rd BR1 ....24 F5
Lenton Rise TW9 ....6 E4
Leo Ct 4 TW8 ....6 D7
Leof Cres SE6 ....24 B3
Leominster Rd SM4 ....40 C3
Leominster Wlk SM4 ....40 C3
Leonard Ave SM4 ....40 C4
Leonard Cl GU16 ....85 D8
Leonard Rd CR4, SW16 ....41 C8
Leonardslee Ct RH10 ....202 B3
Leopold Ave
Farnborough GU14 ....85 B5
Wimbledon SW19 ....19 F3
Leopold Rd Crawley RH11 .201 C6
Wimbledon SW19 ....19 F4
Leopold Terr SW19 ....20 A3
Leppington RG12 ....27 B2
Leret Way KT22 ....95 B6
Lesbourne Rd RH2 ....139 B8
Lescombe Cl SE23 ....23 E5
Lescombe Rd SE23, SE6 ...23 E5
Lesley Ct 8 SM6 ....60 B6
Leslie Gdns SM2 ....59 A3
Leslie Gr CR0 ....42 E1
Leslie Park Rd CR0 ....42 E1
Leslie Rd Chobham GU24 ..49 E1
Dorking RH4 ....115 D1
Lessing St SE23 ....23 E8
Lessingham Ave SW17 ....21 A4
Lessness Rd SM4 ....40 C4
Lestor Ct TW7 ....5 F4
Letchworth Ave TW14 ....14 F8
Letchworth Ct RH11 ....200 E3
Letchworth St SW17 ....20 F4
Letcombe Sq RG12 ....27 F5
Levana Cl SW19 ....19 E7
Levehurst House SE27 ....22 C3
Levendale Rd SE23, SE6 ...23 F6
Leveret Cl CR0 ....82 D8
Leveret La RH11 ....201 B8
Leverkusen Rd RG12 ....27 B6
Levern Dr GU9 ....125 C6
Leverson St SW16 ....21 C2
Levett House 8 SW16 ....21 C3
Levett Rd KT22 ....95 B7
Levylsdene GU1 ....110 D1
Lewes Cl RH10 ....202 C6
Lewes Ct 3 CR4 ....40 F6
Lewes House RH2 ....139 B5
Lewes Rd
Ashurst Wood RH19 ....206 C6
East Grinstead RH19 ....206 C6
Forest Row RH18 ....206 E2
Lewesdon Cl 18 SW19 ....19 D7
Lewin Ct SW16 ....21 E2
Lewin Rd Mortlake SW14 ...7 D4
Streatham SW16 ....21 D2
Lewins Rd KT18 ....76 B5
Lewis Cl KT15 ....52 C6
Lewis Rd Mitcham CR4 ....40 E7
18 Richmond TW10 ....6 D2
Sutton SM1 ....59 B6
Lewis Sports & L Ctr SE19 42 F8
Lewisham Cl RH11 ....201 C2
Lewisham Way GU47 ....45 D2
Lexden Rd CR4 ....41 D5
Lexington Ct CR8 ....80 C8
Lexton Gdns SW12 ....21 D7
Ley Rd GU14 ....85 A8
Leyborne Pk TW9 ....7 A6
Leybourne Ave KT14 ....71 F6
Leybourne Cl Byfleet KT14 .71 F6
Crawley RH11 ....201 C1
Leyburn Gdns CR0 ....61 E8
Leycester Cl GU20 ....48 B6
Leyfield KT4 ....38 F1
Leylands La TW19 ....2 A2
Leylands Rd
Abinger Common RH5 ....155 F5
Wotton RH5 ....156 A6
Leys Rd KT22 ....74 D7
Leys The KT12 ....54 E6
Leyside RG45 ....45 A5
Leyton Rd SW19 ....20 C1
Liberty Ave SW19 ....40 D8
Liberty Hall Rd KT15 ....52 A5
Liberty La KT15 ....52 B5
Liberty Mid Sch CR4 ....40 E7
Liberty Rise KT15 ....52 A4
Licensed Victuallers Sch SL5 ....28 C6
Lichfield Ct
Kingston u T KT6 ....37 E4
Richmond TW9 ....6 E3
Lichfield Gdns TW10, TW9 ..6 E2
Lichfield Rd Hounslow TW4 ..4 C4
Richmond TW9 ....6 F6
Lichfield Terr 1 TW9 ....6 E2
Lichfield Way CR2 ....62 D2
Lichfields RG12 ....27 E7
Lickfolds Rd GU10 ....145 E3
Liddel Way SL5 ....28 F5
Liddell Ct 3 CR8 ....80 A7
Liddington Hall Dr GU3 ..108 E4
Liddington Hall Est GU3 .108 E4
Liddington New Rd GU3 .108 E4
Lidiard Rd SW18 ....20 C6
Lido Rd GU1 ....109 D2
Lidsey Cl RH10 ....202 C4
Lidstone Cl GU21 ....69 B2
Lightwater Ctry Pk GU18 ..47 F1
Lightwater Meadow GU18 .67 B8
Lightwater Rd GU18 ....67 C8
Lightwater Village Cty Inf Sch GU18 ....48 A1
Lightwood RG12 ....27 D3
Lilac Ave GU22 ....89 D7
Lilac Cl GU1 ....109 C5
Lilac Gdns CR0 ....63 A7
Lilian Rd CR4, SW16 ....41 C8
Lilian Rolfe House 5 SE27 ....22 D4
Lilleshall Rd SM4 ....40 D3
Lilley Dr KT20 ....98 B5
Lillie Rd TN16 ....83 D1
Lilliput Childrens Ctr KT12 ....54 C5
Lily Hill Dr RG12 ....27 E7
Lily Hill Rd RG12 ....27 F7
Lilyfields Chase GU6 ....175 E4
Lime Ave Camberley GU15 ..66 A6
Horsham RH12 ....218 A4
Winkfield SL4 ....9 F5
Lime Cl Carshalton SM5 ....59 F8
Copthorne RH10 ....183 B3
Crawley RH11 ....181 C1
Reigate RH2 ....139 B6
West Clandon GU4 ....111 B7
Lime Cres TW16 ....35 C7
Lime Ct CR4 ....40 D7
Lime Gr Addlestone KT15 ...52 A6
Guildford GU1 ....109 B5
Kingston u T KT3 ....38 E6
Twickenham TW1 ....6 A1
Warlingham CR6 ....81 E1
West Clandon GU4 ....111 B7
Woking GU22 ....89 E6
Lime Lodge 3 TW16 ....14 F1
Lime Meadow Ave CR2 ...81 B6
Lime St GU11 ....104 F2
Lime St Rdbt GU11 ....104 F2
Lime Tree Ave KT10, KT7 ...36 E1
Lime Tree Cl KT23 ....94 A3
Lime Tree Ct KT21 ....75 E1
Lime Tree Gr CR0 ....62 F7
Lime Tree Rd TW5 ....5 B6
Lime Tree Wlk
Coney Hall BR4 ....63 F6
Thorpe GU25 ....31 E5
Lime Wlk RG12 ....27 C5
Limebush Cl KT15 ....52 C2
Limecroft Cl KT19 ....57 D3
Limecroft Rd GU21 ....68 B2
Limekiln Pl SE19 ....22 F1
Limerick Cl Bracknell RG42 .27 A8
Streatham SW12 ....21 C8
Limerick Ct 1 SW12 ....21 C8
Limerick House GU22 ....70 A1
Limes Ave Barnes SW13 ....7 F5
Carshalton SM5 ....40 F1
Croydon CR0, CR9 ....61 A7
Horley RH6 ....161 B1
Penge SE20 ....23 B1
Limes Cl TW15 ....14 A3
Limes Ct BR3 ....44 B7
Limes Field Rd SW14 ....7 E4
Limes Rd Beckenham BR3 ..44 B7
Egham TW20 ....11 F3
Farnborough GU14 ....84 C5
Thornton Heath CR0 ....42 D2
Weybridge KT13 ....53 A6
Limes The Belmont SM2 ....59 A4
Dormans Park RH19 ....185 A5
East Molesey KT8 ....36 B5
Woking GU21 ....70 A3
Woking, Horsell GU21 ....69 D4
Limetree Cl SW2 ....21 F7
Limetree Pl CR4 ....41 B8
Limetree Wlk 2 SW17 ....21 A3
Limeway Terr RH4 ....115 A1
Limewood Cl GU21 ....88 D7
Limpsfield Ave
Putney SW19 ....19 D6
Thornton Heath CR7 ....41 F4
Limpsfield CE Inf Sch RH8 ....123 C6
Limpsfield Chart Golf Club RH8 ....123 C6
Limpsfield Grange Sch RH8 ....123 A8
Limpsfield Rd
Chelsham CR6 ....102 B8
Hamsey Green CR2, CR6 ...81 C3
Sanderstead CR2, CR6 ....81 C3
Warlingham CR2, CR6 ....81 C3
Linacre Dr
Cranleigh GU6, RH12 ....195 C4
Ewhurst GU6, RH12 ....195 C4
Lince La RH4 ....135 D6
Linchmere Pl RH11 ....201 A7
Linchmere Rd
Lewisham SE12 ....24 F8
Linchmere GU27 ....207 C4
Linchmere, Hammer GU27 .207 D5
Lincoln Ave
Twickenham TW2 ....16 C6
Wimbledon SW19 ....19 D5
Lincoln Cl Ash Vale GU12 .105 F5
Crawley RH10 ....201 E3
Croydon SE25 ....43 B3
Frimley GU15 ....66 B4
Horley RH6 ....161 A2
Lincoln Ct TW12 ....15 F3
Lincoln Dr GU22 ....70 E3

Lincoln Lodge BR3 44 B7
Lincoln Rd Croydon SE25 43 B6
Dorking RH4 115 C1
Feltham TW13 15 F5
Guildford GU2 108 F3
Kingston u T KT3 38 C6
Mitcham CR4 41 E4
North Cheam KT4 39 B1
Lincoln Terr 4 SM2 59 A3
Lincoln Way TW16 34 E8
Lincoln Wlk KT19 57 D1
Lincolns Mead RH7 164 C3
Lincombe Rd BR1 24 F5
Lind Rd SM1 59 C5
Linda Ct KT9 56 D6
Lindale SW19 19 E6
Lindale Cl GU25 30 F5
Lindbergh Rd SM6 60 E3
Linden 3 RG12 27 F4
Linden Ave Coulsdon CR5 79 B3
East Grinstead RH19 185 C2
Hounslow TW3 5 B2
Thornton Heath CR7 42 B5
Linden Bridge Sch KT4 57 E7
Linden Cl Crawley RH10 202 A3
Horsham RH12 217 E4
Tadworth KT20 97 D7
Thames Ditton KT7 37 A2
Woodham KT15 71 A8
Linden Cres KT1 37 F7
Linden Ct Beckenham BR3 44 B6
Camberley GU15 65 F7
Englefield Green TW20 11 B2
Leatherhead KT22 95 B6
Penge SE20 23 B1
Linden Dr CR3 100 C3
Linden Gdns KT22 95 C6
Linden Gr Kingston u T KT3 38 E6
Penge SE20 23 C2
Teddington TW11 16 F3
Walton-on-T KT12 53 F8
Warlingham CR6 81 E1
Linden Lea RH4 136 C5
Linden Leas BR4 63 D8
Linden Lodge Sch SW19 19 E7
Linden Pit Path KT22 95 B6
Linden Pl Ewell KT17 76 E7
Mitcham CR4 40 E5
Staines TW18 13 A4
Linden Rd Guildford GU1 109 D1
Hampton TW12 36 A8
Headley Down GU35 187 C5
Leatherhead KT22 95 B6
Weybridge KT13 53 C2
Linden Way
Send Marsh GU23 90 F3
Shepperton TW17 34 C4
Wallington CR8 60 C1
Woking GU22 89 F6
Lindenhill Rd RG42 26 F8
Lindens Cl KT24 113 E7
Lindens The Chiswick W4 7 D6
Copthorne RH10 183 B3
Farnham GU9 125 D1
New Addington CR0 63 C4
Lindfield Gdns GU1 109 F2
Lindfield Rd CR0 42 F3
Lindgren Wlk RH11 201 B1
Lindisfarne Rd SW20 19 A1
Lindley Ct Teddington KT1 37 C8
West Byfleet KT14 71 B7
Lindley Pl TW9 7 A6
Lindley Rd
Tyler's Green RH9 121 C5
Walton-on-T KT12 54 D7
Lindon Bennett Sch TW13 15 D3
Lindores Rd SM5 40 E1
Lindsay Cl Chessington KT9 56 E3
Epsom KT18 76 C6
Stanwell TW19 2 D2
Lindsay Dr TW17 34 D3
Lindsay Rd Hampton TW12 16 B4
North Cheam KT4 58 B8
Woodham KT15 71 B8
Lindsey Cl CR4, SW16 41 E5
Lindsey Gdns TW14 14 D8
Lindum Dene GU11 105 A1
Lindum Rd TW11 17 C1
Lindums The BR3 23 F2
Lindway SE27 22 B3
Linersh Dr GU5 152 A6
Linersh Wood GU5 152 A6
Linersh Wood Cl GU5 152 B5
Lines Rd GU11 105 D7
Linfield Cl KT12 54 B5
Linford Ct CR4 40 E8
Ling Cres GU35 187 B6
Ling Dr GU18 66 F7
Ling's Coppice SE21 22 D6
Lingfield Ave KT1, KT5 37 F5
Lingfield Common Rd
RH7 164 C6
Lingfield Ct SW19 19 D2
Lingfield Dr RH10 202 E7
Lingfield Gdns CR5 100 B8
Lingfield Hospital Sch
RH7 165 A4
Lingfield House SE26 23 B2
Lingfield Park Race
Course RH7 164 E2
Lingfield Prim Sch RH7 164 D4
Lingfield Rd
Dormans Park RH19 185 D3
East Grinstead RH19 185 D3
Edenbridge TN8 165 F8
Haxted TN8 165 F8
North Cheam KT4 58 C7
Wimbledon SW19 19 D2
Lingfield Sta RH7 164 E4
Lingwell Rd SW17 20 E5
Lingwood RG12 27 C3
Lingwood Gdns TW7 5 E7
Link La SM6 60 E4
Link Prim Day Sch The
CR0 60 E6
Link Rd Addlestone KT15 52 E6
Carshalton CR4, SM6 41 A1
East Bedfont TW14 14 F8
Link Sec Day Sch The CR0 60 F6
Link The Crawley RH11 201 D6
Teddington TW11 16 F2
Link Way Richmond TW10 17 B6
Staines TW18 13 B2
Link's Rd KT17 77 A5
Linkfield KT8 36 B6
Linkfield Cnr RH1 118 E2
Linkfield Gdns RH1 118 E1
Linkfield La RH1 118 F3
Linkfield Rd TW7 5 F5
Linkfield St RH1 118 E1
Linklater's Cotts GU14 84 B6
Links Ave SM4 40 A5
Links Brow KT22 94 E4
Links Cl Ashstead KT21 75 C2
Ewhurst GU6 175 E6
Links Gdns SW16 22 A1
Links Green Way KT11 74 A5
Links Pl KT21 75 D2
Links Prim Sch SW17 21 A2
Links Rd Ashford TW15 13 E3
Ashstead KT21 75 C2
Bramley GU5 151 E7
Mitcham SW16, SW17 21 A2
West Wickham BR4 44 C1
Links The North Ascot SL5 28 E7
Walton-on-T KT12 54 A8
Links View Ave RH3, RH5 116 A1
Links View Rd Croydon CR0 63 A7
Hampton TW12 16 E1
Links Way Beckenham BR3 44 A3
Effingham KT24 113 E7
Farnborough GU14 84 C3
Mitcham SW17 21 A2
Linkscroft Ave TW15 14 B2
Linkside KT3 38 E7
Linkside E GU26 188 C7
Linkside N GU26 188 B7
Linkside S GU26 188 C6
Linkside W GU26 188 B6
Linkway Camberley GU15 65 C4
Crawley RH6 182 C7
Crowthorne RG45 45 A5
Guildford GU2 108 F2
West Barnes SW20 39 B5
West Barnes KT3, SW20 39 B6
Woking GU22 70 C2
Linkway The SM2 59 C2
Linley Ct 1 Dulwich SE21 22 E4
Sutton SM1 59 C6
Linnell Rd RH1 140 B8
Linnet Cl CR2 62 D1
Linnet Gr GU4 110 D3
Linnet Mews SW12 21 A8
Linsford Bsns Pk GU16 85 F3
Linsford La GU16 85 F3
Linslade Cl TW4 4 E2
Linstead Rd GU14 84 E8
Linstead Way SW18, SW19 19 E8
Linton Cl CR4, SM5 40 F2
Linton Glade CR0 62 E1
Linton Gr SE27 22 C3
Linton's La KT17 76 E7
Lintott Ct TW19 2 D1
Lintott Gdns RH13 217 E3
Lion and Lamb Way 7
GU9 125 B2
Lion and Lamb Yd 5
GU9 125 B2
Lion Ave TW1 16 F7
Lion Cl Haslemere GU27 207 F7
Littleton TW17 33 E6
Lion Ctr The TW13 15 E5
Lion Gate Gdns TW9 6 F4
Lion Gn GU27 207 F6
Lion Green Rd CR5 79 D3
Lion La Haslemere GU27 207 F7
Turners Hill RH10 204 A4
Lion Mead GU27 207 F6
Lion Park Ave KT9 57 A6
Lion Rd Thornton Heath CR0 42 C4
Twickenham TW1, TW2 16 F7
Lion Ret Pk GU22 70 B3
Lion Way TW8 6 D7
Lion Wharf Rd TW7 6 B4
Liphook Cres SE23 23 C8
Liphook Rd
Haslemere GU27 207 F6
Linchmere GU27 207 B4
Lipsham Cl SM7 78 D6
Lisbon Ave TW2 16 C6
Liscombe RG12 27 B2
Liscombe House RG12 27 B2
Liskeard Dr 2 GU14 85 A6
Lisle Cl SW17 21 B4
Lismore 9 SW19 19 F3
Lismore Cl TW7 6 A5
Lismore Cres RH11 201 B3
Lismore Rd CR2 61 E4
Lissoms Rd CR5 79 A1
Lister Ave RH19 205 F6
Lister Cl SW19 40 E8
Lister Ct 1 CR8 80 B7
Litchfield Ave SM4 39 F2
Litchfield Rd SM1 59 C6
Litchfield Way GU2 129 F7
Lithgow's Rd TW14, TW6 3 F3
Little Acre BR3 44 A6
Little Austins Rd GU9 146 D8
Little Birch Cl KT15 52 D2
Little Bookham St KT23 93 F2
Little Bornes SE21 22 E4
Little Borough RH3 137 A8
Little Brownings SE23 23 B6
Little Browns La TN8 144 F4
Little Collins RH1 162 B7
Little Common La RH1 120 C3
Little Comptons RH13 217 F2
Little Crabtree RH11 201 C7
Little Cranmore La KT24 112 C6
Little Ct BR4 63 E8
Little Dimocks SW12 21 B6
Little Elms UB3 3 D7
Little Ferry Rd TW1 17 B7
Little Gn GU8 148 D4
Little Grebe RH12 217 C5
Little Green La
Addlestone KT16 51 E7
Wrecclesham GU9 146 A6
Little Halliards KT12 35 A3
Little Hatch RH12 217 F5
Little Haven La RH12 217 F5
Little Heath La KT11 74 A5
Little Heath Rd GU24 49 E2
Little Hide GU1 110 B3
Little Kiln GU7 150 E8
Little King St RH19 185 E1
Little London Shere GU5 132 F2
Witley GU8 170 E5
Little Lullenden RH7 164 E5
Little Manor Gdns GU6 174 E2
Little Mead GU21 68 F3
Little Mead Ind Est GU6 174 B3
Little Moor GU47 45 C1
Little Moreton Cl KT14 71 B7
Little Orch Woking GU21 70 A5
Woodham KT15 71 A8
Little Orchard Way GU4 130 E1
Little Orchards KT18 76 E5
Little Paddock GU15 66 A8
Little Park Dr TW13 15 E6
Little Park Enterprises
RH6 180 E3
Little Platt GU2 108 D2
Little Queens Rd TW11 16 F2
Little Ringdale RG12 27 E5
Little Roke Ave CR8 80 B5
Little Roke Rd CR8 80 C5
Little St GU2 109 B5
Little St Leonards SW14 7 C4
Little Sutton La SL3 1 B8
Little Tangley Flats GU5 131 C1
Little Thatch GU7 150 F6
Little Thurbans Cl GU9 146 A6
Little Tumners Ct GU7 150 E6
Little Warren Cl GU4 131 B7
Little Wellington St 9
GU11 105 A2
Little Wildwood GU6 174 F1
Little Woodcote La
CR8, SM5, SM6 79 B8
Littlebourne 2 SE13 24 E8
Littlebrook Cl CR0 43 D3
Littlecote Cl SW19 19 E8
Littlecroft Rd 2 TW20 11 F3
Littledale Cl RG12 27 E6
Littlefield Cl Ash GU12 106 A1
Fairlands GU3 108 D5
9 Kingston u T KT1 37 E7
Littlefield Cotts GU3 108 B6
Littlefield Ct UB7 2 D7
Littlefield Gdns GU12 106 A1
Littlefield Way GU3 108 D5
Littleford La GU4, GU5 152 F7
Littlehaven Cty Inf Sch
RH12 217 F5
Littleheath Rd CR2 62 B2
Littlemead KT10 55 D6
Littlers Cl SW19 40 D8
Littlestone Cl BR3 24 A2
Littleton C of E Fst Sch
TW17 34 A6
Littleton Cross GU3 130 A4
Littleton House 4 RH2 118 A2
Littleton La Artington GU3 130 A3
Littleton TW17, TW18 33 E4
Reigate RH2 138 E7
Littleton Rd TW15, TW17 14 C1
Littleton St SW18 20 C6
Littlewick Cotts GU21 68 F4
Littlewick Rd GU21 68 E3
Littlewood GU6 174 F3
Littlewood House CR2 81 B5
Littleworth Ave KT10 55 D5
Littleworth Common Rd
KT10 55 D7
Littleworth La KT10 55 D6
Littleworth Pl KT10 55 D6
Littleworth Rd
Hinchley Wood KT10 55 E6
Puttenham GU10, GU8 148 C8
The Sands GU10 126 F1
Liverpool Rd
Kingston u T KT2 18 A1
South Norwood CR7 42 C6
Livesey Cl KT1 37 F6
Livingstone Ct TW19 13 E7
Livingstone Rd
Caterham CR3 100 D5
Crawley RH10 201 E4
Horsham RH13 217 D1
Hounslow TW3 5 C3
South Norwood CR7 42 D7
Llanaway Cl GU7 150 F6
Llanaway House GU7 150 F6
Llanaway Rd GU7 150 F6
Llangar Gr RG45 45 A5
Llanthony Rd SM4 40 D4
Llanvair Cl SL5 29 A3
Llanvair Dr SL5 28 F3
Llewellyn Ct SE20 43 C8
Lloyd Ave
Thornton Heath SW16 41 E8
Wallington CR5 79 B5
Lloyd Ct 6 SE27 22 B5
Lloyd House BR3 24 B2
Lloyd Park Ave CR0 61 F6
Lloyd Rd KT4, SM3 58 D7
Lloyds Ct RH10 181 E1
Lloyds Way BR3 43 F4
Lobelia Rd GU24 68 A4
Lochinvar St SW12 21 B8
Lochinver RG12 27 B2
Lock Cl GU21, KT15 70 E7
Lock La GU22, GU23, KT14 71 C3
Lock Rd Farnborough GU11 105 D5
Guildford GU1 109 D4
Richmond TW10 17 C4
Lock's La CR4 41 A7
Locke King Rd KT13 53 A3
Locke Way GU21 69 F2
Locke-King Cl KT13 53 A3
Lockesley Sq KT6 37 D3
Lockfield Cotts GU21 69 A1
Lockfield Dr GU21 68 F2
Lockhart Rd KT11 73 C6
Lockhurstthatch La GU5 153 E6
Locks Meadow RH7 165 A1
Locks Ride SL5 8 C2
Locksley Dr GU21 68 F2
Locksmeade Rd TW10 17 C4
Lockswood GU24 88 B7
Lockton Chase SL5 28 D6
Lockton House RG40 25 C6
Lockwood Cl
Farnborough GU14 84 E8
Forest Hill SE26 23 D4
Horsham RH12 218 A5
Lockwood Ct RH10 201 F8
Lockwood Path GU21 70 E6
Lockwood Way KT9 57 A5
Lodden Lodge SM2 59 C3
Loddon Cl GU15 66 A6
Loddon Rd GU14 84 D6
Loddon Way GU12 106 A1
Loder Cl GU21 70 D6
Lodge Ave CR0, CR9 61 A7
Lodge Cl Brentford TW7 6 B6
Carshalton CR4 41 A1
Crawley RH11 201 C6
Dorking RH5 136 C3
E Ewell KT17 58 C1
East Grinstead RH19 185 D1
Englefield Green TW20 11 D3
Fetcham KT22 94 D5
Stoke D'Abernon KT11 73 F3
Lodge Gdns BR3 43 F4
Lodge Hill CR8 80 A4
Lodge Hill Cl GU10 146 D6
Lodge Hill Rd GU10 146 E7
Lodge La Beckenham BR3 44 B5
New Addington CR0, R9 63 B3
Salfords RH1 139 F1
South Croydon CR0 63 A4
South Holmwood RH5 157 F8
Lodge Pl SM1 59 B5
Lodge Rd Fetcham KT22 94 D5
Sutton SM1 59 B5
Thornton Heath CR0 42 B2
Wallington SM6 60 B5
Lodge Sch CR8 79 D8
Lodge Way Ashford TW15 13 E6
Charlton TW17 34 C7
Lodgebottom Rd
KT22, RH5 116 A8
Lodsworth GU14 84 D3
Lofthouse Pl KT9 56 C4
Logan Cl TW4 4 F4
Logmore La RH4 135 D3
Lois Dr TW17 34 B4
Lollesworth La KT24 112 C8
Loman Rd GU16 86 A4
Lomas Cl CR0 63 C3
Lombard Bsns Pk
Merton SW19 40 B7
Thornton Heath CR9 41 F2
Lombard Rd SW19 40 B7
Lombard St GU8 149 B7
Lombardy Cl GU21 68 F2
Lomond Gdns CR2 62 E3
Loncin Mead Ave KT15 52 C2
London Butterfly House
TW8 6 B6
London Cross KT24 112 F4
London Fields House
RH11 201 C2
London Inst The SW17 21 B3
London La Bromley BR1 24 F1
Shere GU5 133 A5
London Rd Ascot SL5 29 D5
Ashford TW15, TW18,
TW19, TW14 13 D5
Bagshot GU15, GU19 47 C1
Blackwater GU15, GU17 64 E4
Bracknell RG42 26 B7
Bracknell RG12, SL5 28 C6
Bracknell, Binfield
RG12, RG42 26 C7
Brands Hill SL3 1 B8
Brentford TW7, TW8 6 B6
Bromley BR1 24 F1
Camberley GU15 65 C6
Caterham CR3 100 D4
London Rd *continued*
Cheam KT17 58 C6
Crawley RH10 181 E3
Dorking RH4 115 C3
East Grinstead RH19 185 C3
Englefield Green TW20 11 C1
Ewell KT17 58 C6
Forest Hill SE22, SE23 23 C7
Forest Row RH18 206 E4
Guildford GU1 109 F1
Guildford, Burpham
GU1, GU4 110 B4
Hackbridge SM6, CR4 60 B7
Hindhead GU26 188 F4
Horsham RH12 217 C2
Hounslow TW3, TW7, TW1,
TW8 5 D5
Isleworth TW7, TW8 6 B6
Kingston u T KT1, KT2 37 F7
Mitcham CR4, SW17 40 F6
Morden SM4 40 A5
North Cheam KT4, SM3, SM4 58 C6
Redhill RH1 119 A3
Reigate RH2 118 A2
Send Marsh GU23 90 E1
Stoneleigh KT17, KT4, SM3 58 C6
Sunningdale, Blacknest SL5 30 B6
Sunningdale, Shrubs Hill SL5 30 C4
Thornton Heath CR0,
CR7, SW16 42 A3
Twickenham TW1 17 A7
Virginia Water GU25 31 B7
Wentworth SL5, GU25 30 C4
Westhumble RH4 115 C3
Windlesham GU19, GU20 48 C7
Wokingham RG42, RG12 26 C7
London Rd N RH1 99 B2
London Rd S
Merstham RH1 119 B6
Redhill RH1 119 B6
London Road Sta GU1 109 E1
London St KT16 33 A2
Lone Oak RH6 162 B1
Loneacre GU20 48 E4
Lonesome La
Reigate RH1, RH2 139 D3
Salfords RH1, RH2 139 D3
Lonesome Prim Sch CR4 41 B7
Lonesome Way CR4 41 C8
Long Acre RH10 204 A8
Long Beech Dr GU14 84 C3
Long Bridge GU9 125 C2
Long Cl RH10 202 D6
Long Copse Cl KT23 94 B4
Long Ditton Cty Inf Sch
KT6 37 C1
Long Dyke GU1 110 B3
Long Garden Mews 3
GU9 125 B2
Long Garden Way GU9 125 B2
Long Garden Wlk 4 GU9 125 B2
Long Garden Wlk E 2
GU9 125 B2
Long Garden Wlk W 1
GU9 125 B2
Long Gore GU7 150 E8
Long Grove Rd KT19 57 B1
Long Hill The Sands GU10 126 E1
Woldingham CR3 101 F6
Long Hill Rd RG12, SL5 28 A7
Long Houses GU24 87 D3
Long La Croydon CR0 43 C3
Stanwell TW15, TW19 13 F7
Long Lodge Dr KT12 54 C7
Long Meadow Cl BR3, BR4 44 C2
Long Mickle GU47 45 B1
Long Rd The GU10 146 A2
Long Reach Ockham GU23 92 B3
West Horsley KT24 92 B3
Long Shaw KT22 95 A7
Long Wlk Burgh Heath KT18 97 D8
Kingston u T KT3 38 C6
Long Wlk The SL4 10 D7
Long's Way RG40 25 E7
Longacre GU12 106 A2
Longacre Pl SM5 60 A4
Longacre Sch GU5 152 D4
Longbourne Gn GU7 150 E8
Longbourne Way KT16 32 F3
Longboyds KT11 73 B4
Longbridge Gate RH6 181 E8
Longbridge Rd
Crawley RH6 181 F8
Horley RH6 160 F1
Longbridge Rdbt RH6 160 E2
Longbridge Wlk RH6 160 F1
Longchamp Cl RH6 161 C3
Longcroft Ave SM7 78 C5
Longcross Rd KT16, GU24 50 C7
Longcross Sta GU25 30 F1
Longdene Rd GU27 208 B6
Longdown GU10 146 C6
Longdown La N KT17 77 A6
Longdown La S KT17, KT18 77 A4
Longdown Lodge GU47 64 B8
Longdown Rd Catford SE6 24 A4
Ewell KT17 77 A6
Farnham GU10 146 C5
Guildford GU4 131 B6
Sandhurst GU47 45 B1
Longfellow Cl RH12 217 E7
Longfellow Rd KT4 39 B1
Longfield BR1 44 F8
Longfield Ave CR4, SM6 41 A1
Longfield Cl GU14 85 B8

Longfield Cres
Burgh Heath KT20 .97 C7
Forest Hill SE23, SE26 .23 C5
Longfield Dr Mitcham SW19 40 E8
Mortlake SW14 .7 B2
Longfield Rd Ash GU12 .106 A2
Dorking RH4 .135 F6
Horsham RH12 .217 A1
Longfield St SW18 .20 A8
Longford Ave Feltham TW14 .3 F1
Stanwell TW19 .13 E7
Longford Cl
Camberley GU15 .65 D4
Hampton TW12 .16 A4
Longford Ct KT19 .57 C6
Longford Gdns SM1 .59 C8
Longford House
Catford BR1 .24 D3
Hampton TW12 .16 A4
Longford Ind Est TW12 .16 B2
Longford Rd TW2 .16 B7
Longford Rdbt TW6, UB7 .2 B6
Longford Sch TW14 .14 F8
Longford Way TW19 .13 E7
Longford Wlk 9 SW2 .22 A8
Longheath Dr KT23 .93 E3
Longheath Gdns CR0 .43 C4
Longhedge House SE26 .23 A4
Longhill Rd SE6 .24 D5
Longhope Dr GU10 .146 A6
Longhurst Rd
Crawley RH11 .201 A1
Croydon CR0 .43 B3
East Horsley KT24 .112 E6
Longlands Ave CR5 .79 A5
Longlands Ct CR4 .41 A8
Longlands Way GU15 .66 D5
Longleat Sq GU14 .85 E3
Longleat Way TW14 .14 D8
Longley Rd Farnham GU9 .125 D1
Thornton Heath CR0 .42 B2
Upper Tooting SW17 .20 F2
Longmead GU1 .110 C1
Longmead Bsns Ctr KT19 .76 D8
Longmead Cl CR3 .100 E5
Longmead House SE27 .22 C3
Longmead Rd Epsom KT19 .57 E1
Thames Ditton KT7 .36 F2
Upper Tooting SW17 .20 F3
Longmeadow
Frimley GU15, GU16 .65 F3
Little Bookham KT23 .93 F2
Longmere Gdns KT20 .97 C8
Longmere Rd RH10 .201 D8
Longmoors RG42 .26 E8
Longmore Rd KT12 .54 E6
Longpoles Rd GU6 .174 F2
Longridge Gr GU22 .70 E5
Longs Cl GU22 .71 A3
Longs Ct 2 TW9 .6 F3
Longsdon Way CR3 .101 A3
Longshot Ind Est RG12 .26 E7
Longshot La RG12 .26 E7
Longside Cl TW20 .32 C8
Longstaff Cres SW18 .20 A8
Longstaff Rd SW18 .20 A8
Longstone Rd SW17 .21 B3
Longthornton Rd SW16 .41 D7
Longton Ave SE26 .23 A4
Longton Gr SE26 .23 B4
Longwater Rd RG12 .27 C3
Longwood Dr SW15 .19 B8
Longwood Rd CR8 .80 D3
Longwood View RH10 .202 A3
Longyard House RH6 .161 B5
Lonsdale Gdns CR7, SW16 .41 F5
Lonsdale Mews 4 TW9 .7 A6
Lonsdale Rd Barnes SW13 .7 F7
Croydon SE25 .43 B5
Dorking RH4 .136 B8
Weybridge KT13 .53 A3
Look Out Discovery Ctr
The RG12 .27 D1
Loop Rd Epsom KT18 .76 C3
Old Woking GU22 .89 F7
Loppets Rd RH10 .201 F3
Loraine Gdns KT21 .75 E2
Loraine House 1 SM5 .60 B6
Loraine Rd W4 .7 B8
Lord Chancellor Wlk KT2 .38 C8
Lord Knyvett Cl TW19 .2 D1
Lordell Pl SW19 .19 C2
Lords Cl Feltham TW13 .15 E6
West Norwood SE21 .22 C6
Lordsbury Field SM6 .60 C1
Lordsgrove Cl KT20 .97 B7
Lordshill Rd GU5 .152 C5
Lordship La SE21, SE22 .23 A8
Loretto Cl GU6 .175 A3
Lorian Dr RH2 .118 C2
Loriners RH10 .201 D3
Loring Rd TW7 .5 F5
Lorne Ave CR0 .43 D2
Lorne Gdns Croydon CR0 .43 D2
Knaphill GU21 .88 D8
Lorne Rd 2 TW10 .6 F2
Lorne The KT23 .94 A1
Lorraine Ct BR3 .44 C8
Lorraine Cty Inf Sch GU15 65 E8
Lorraine Rd GU15 .65 F8
Lory Ridge GU19 .47 E4
Loseberry Rd KT10 .55 D5
Loseley Ho GU3 .129 E3
Loseley Rd GU7 .150 E8
Lothian Rd GU24 .87 A6
Lothian Wood KT20 .97 B5
Lotus Rd TN16 .83 F1
Loubet St SW17 .20 F2
Loudwater Cl TW16 .35 A5
Loudwater Rd TW16 .35 A5
Loughborough RG12 .27 E3
Louis Fields GU3 .108 C5
Louisa Ct TW2 .16 E6
Louisa House SW15 .7 F3
Louise Margaret
Maternity Hospl GU11 .105 B3
Louise Margaret Rd
GU11 .105 C3
Louisville Rd SW17 .21 A5
Lovat Wlk TW5 .4 E7
Lovatt Ct SW12 .21 B7
Love La Cheam SM3 .58 E4
Croydon SE25 .43 B6
Godstone RH9 .121 C3
Long Ditton KT6 .56 D8
Mitcham CR4 .40 E6
Morden SM4 .40 B2
Sutton CR4 .40 B2
Walton on t H KT20 .97 A1
Loveday House 2 SW2 .22 A7
Lovedean Ct RG12 .27 E3
Lovekyn Cl KT2 .37 F7
Lovel La SL5 .9 B3
Lovel Rd SL5 .9 A4
Lovelace Cl KT24 .93 A4
Lovelace Dr GU22 .70 F3
Lovelace Gdns
Hersham KT12 .54 C5
Surbiton KT6 .37 D2
Lovelace Prim Sch KT9 .56 C5
Lovelace Rd Bracknell RG12 26 E5
Surbiton KT6 .37 D2
West Norwood SE21 .22 C7
Lovelands La
Lower Kingswood KT20 .118 B8
West End GU24 .68 C6
Loveletts RH11 .201 A5
Lovell House 4 SW19 .40 C8
Lovell Rd TW10 .17 C5
Lovells Cl GU18 .48 B1
Lovelock Cl CR8 .80 C2
Lovers La GU10 .167 C7
Lovett Dr SM5 .40 D2
Lovett House 9 GU9 .125 B2
Lovett Rd TW20 .12 C4
Low Cross Wood La SE21 .22 F5
Low La GU9 .126 B6
Lowbury RG12 .27 E5
Lowburys RH4 .136 B4
Lowdells Cl RH19 .185 C4
Lowdells Dr RH19 .185 D4
Lowdells La RH19 .185 C3
Lower Addiscombe Rd
CR0 .42 E1
Lower Barn Cl RH12 .217 F5
Lower Barn Rd CR8 .80 D6
Lower Breache Rd GU6 .176 B4
Lower Bridge Rd RH1 .118 F1
Lower Broadmoor Rd
RG45 .45 D4
Lower Charles St GU15 .65 C6
Lower Church La 13 GU9 .125 B2
Lower Church St CR0, CR9 .61 B8
Lower Coombe St
CR0, CR9 .61 C6
Lower Court Rd KT19 .76 C8
Lower Ct KT19 .76 D8
Lower Dene RH19 .186 A1
Lower Downs Rd SW20 .39 D8
Lower Dunnymans 4 SM7 77 F5
Lower Eashing GU7 .149 F4
Lower Edgeborough Rd
GU1 .130 F8
Lower Farm Rd KT23, KT24 93 C3
Lower Farnham Rd
GU11, GU12 .126 C7
Lower Forecourt RH6 .182 B7
Lower George St 18 TW10 .6 D2
Lower Gn KT12 .54 D5
Lower Gn W CR4 .40 E6
Lower Green Rd
Esher KT10 .55 C8
Thames Ditton KT10 .55 C8
Lower Grove Rd TW10 .6 F2
Lower Guildford Rd GU21 .68 D1
Lower Ham La GU8 .148 E4
Lower Ham Rd KT2 .17 D2
Lower Hampton
Rd TW12, TW16 .35 D7
Lower Hanger GU27 .207 D6
Lower Hill Rd KT19 .76 B7
Lower House Rd GU8 .169 F2
Lower Manor Rd
Farncombe GU7 .150 F6
Milford GU8 .149 E1
Lower Marsh La KT1, KT5 .38 A5
Lower Mere RH19 .205 F8
Lower Mill Field GU19 .47 D2
Lower Morden La SM4 .39 E3
Lower Mortlake Rd TW9 .6 F4
Lower Moushill La GU8 .149 D1
Lower Nelson St 4 GU11 105 A2
Lower Northfield 5 SM7 .77 F5
Lower Park Rd CR5 .78 E1
Lower Peryers KT24 .112 E7
Lower Pillory Down SM5 .79 B7
Lower Rd Effingham KT24 .113 D8
Fetcham KT22, KT23, KT24 .94 C3
Forest Row RH18 .206 F3
Grayswood GU27 .189 F2
Great Bookham KT22,
KT23, KT24 .94 C3
Purley CR8 .80 B6
Lower Rd *continued*
Reigate RH1 .139 D7
Sutton SM1 .59 C6
Lower Richmond Rd
SW14, TW9 .7 B4
Lower Sandfields GU23 .90 D3
Lower Sawleywood 2
SM7 .77 F5
Lower Shott KT23 .94 B1
Lower South St GU7 .150 D4
Lower South View GU9 .125 C3
Lower Sq RH18 .206 E3
Lower St Haslemere GU27 .208 C6
Shere GU5 .133 A4
Lower Sunbury Rd TW12 .36 A7
Lower Sydenham Sta SE6 .23 F3
Lower Tanbridge Way
RH12 .217 B2
Lower Teddington Rd
KT1 .37 D8
Lower Village Rd SL5 .29 C4
Lower Weybourne La
Farnham GU9 .126 A6
Heath End GU9 .125 F6
Lower Wood Rd KT10 .56 B4
Lowestoft Wlk RH10 .202 B4
Loweswater Wlk GU15 .66 D4
Lowfield Cl GU18 .67 A8
Lowfield Heath Rd
Charlwood RH6 .180 F5
Crawley RH6 .180 F5
Lowfield Rd RH13 .215 D3
Lowfield Way RH11 .181 E5
Lowicks Rd GU10 .168 C6
Lowlands Rd
Blackwater GU17 .64 C4
Stanwell TW19 .2 D2
Lowndes Bldgs GU9 .125 B3
Lowood Ct SE19 .22 F3
Lowry Cl GU47 .64 D6
Lowry Cres CR4 .40 E7
Lowther Hill SE23 .23 E8
Lowther Rd Barnes SW13 .7 F6
Kingston u T KT2 .37 F8
Lowthorpe 5 GU21 .69 A1
Loxford Ct GU6 .173 F2
Loxford Rd CR3 .100 F2
Loxford Way CR3 .100 F2
Loxley Cl SE26 .23 D3
Loxley Rd Hampton TW12 .15 F4
Wandsworth SW18 .20 D7
Loxton Rd SE23 .23 E7
Loxwood Cl TW14 .14 E7
Loxwood Cty Prim Sch
RH14 .213 A4
Loxwood Rd Alfold GU6 .193 F2
Alfold Crossways GU6 .193 F2
Ifold RH14 .212 A2
Loxwood RH12, RH14 .213 D4
Loxwood, Alfold Bars
GU6, RH14 .212 F8
Plaistow RH14 .212 A2
Rudgwick RH12 .214 A6
Loxwood Wlk RH11 .201 A8
Lucan Dr TW18 .13 D1
Lucas Cl RH19 .186 A1
Lucas Ct SE26 .23 E3
Lucas Field GU27 .207 E6
Lucas Green GU24 .67 D4
Lucas Green Rd GU24 .67 E5
Lucas Rd Penge SE20 .23 C2
Warnham RH12 .216 F8
Lucerne Cl GU22 .89 E8
Lucerne Ct 8 BR3 .24 A1
Lucerne Dr RH10 .202 D4
Lucerne Rd CR7 .42 C5
Lucie Ave TW15 .14 B2
Lucien Rd
Upper Tooting SW17 .21 A4
Wimbledon SW18 .20 B6
Lucille House SE26 .23 B2
Luckley Oakfield Sch
RG40 .25 B3
Luckley Path RG40 .25 C6
Luckley Rd RG41 .25 B3
Luckley Wood RG41 .25 B3
Lucraft House 12 SW2 .21 E8
Luddington Ave
GU25, TW20 .31 F7
Ludford Cl CR0 .61 B6
Ludgrove Sch RG40 .25 D3
Ludlow RG12 .27 B2
Ludlow Cl GU16 .86 A7
Ludlow Rd Feltham TW13 .15 A4
Guildford GU2 .130 B8
Ludovick Wlk SW15 .7 E3
Ludshott Gr GU35 .187 B5
Luke Rd GU11 .125 E8
Luke Rd E GU11 .125 F8
Lullarook Cl TN16 .83 C3
Lullington Rd SE20 .23 A1
Lulworth Ave TW5, TW7 .5 C7
Lulworth Cl Crawley RH11 201 B3
Farnborough GU14 .85 A7
Lulworth Cres CR4 .40 E7
Lumley Ct RH6 .161 A4
Lumley Gdns SM3 .58 E5
Lumley House KT3 .38 D1
Lumley Rd Cheam SM1, SM3 58 E5
Horley RH6 .161 A3
Luna Rd CR7 .42 C6
Lunar Cl TN16 .83 D3
Lundy Cl RH11 .201 C3
Lunghurst Rd CR3 .102 A5
Lunham Rd SE19 .22 E2
Lupin Cl Bagshot GU19 .47 C1
Croydon CR0 .43 D1
Streatham SW2 .22 B6
Lupin Ride RG45 .45 B7
Lupus Ct SE19 .42 D8
Luscombe Ct BR2 .44 E7
Lushington Dr KT11 .73 B5
Lushington House KT12 .35 C3
Lushington Rd SE6 .24 B3
Lusted Hall La
Biggin Hill TN16 .103 C7
Tatsfield TN16 .103 C7
Lusteds Cl RH4 .136 C4
Lutea House SM2 .59 C3
Luther Rd TW11 .16 F3
Lutwyche Rd SE23, SE6 .23 F6
Lutyens Cl RH11 .200 E4
Luxford Cl RH12 .217 F5
Luxford's La
Ashurst Wood RH19 .206 B6
Forest Row RH19 .206 B6
Lyall Ave SE21 .22 F4
Lyall Pl GU9 .125 B7
Lycett House 10 SW2 .21 E8
Lych Way GU21 .69 D3
Lyconby Gdns CR0 .43 E2
Lydbury RG12 .27 F6
Lydden Gr SW18 .20 B8
Lydden Rd SW18 .20 B8
Lydele Cl GU21 .69 F4
Lydford Cl
2 Farnborough GU14 .85 A7
Frimley GU16 .86 A7
Lydhurst Ave SW2 .21 F6
Lydney RG12 .27 B2
Lydney Cl SW19 .19 E6
Lydon House RH11 .181 D1
Lye Copse Ave GU14 .85 B8
Lye The KT20 .97 C5
Lye View Cotts GU21 .89 A8
Lyefield La GU6, RH5 .176 C5
Lyfield KT11, KT22 .74 B5
Lyford Rd SW18 .20 E7
Lyham Rd SW2 .21 E8
Lyle Cl CR4 .41 A2
Lymbourne Cl SM2 .59 A1
Lymden Gdns RH2 .139 B7
Lyme Regis Rd SM7 .77 F2
Lymer Ave SE19 .22 F3
Lymescote Gdns SM1 .59 A8
Lyminge Gdns SW17, SW18 20 E7
Lymington Cl SW16 .41 D7
Lymington Ct SM1 .59 C7
Lymington Gdns KT19 .57 F5
Lyn Ct GU1 .131 A8
Lynch Rd GU9 .125 E2
Lynchen Cl TW5 .4 B6
Lynchford La GU11, GU14 .105 E8
Lynchford Rd GU14 .105 D8
Lyncroft Gdns Ewell KT17 .57 F2
Isleworth TW3 .5 C2
Lyndale Ct 3 RH1 .119 A4
Lyndale Rd RH1 .119 A4
Lynde House KT12 .35 C3
Lynden Gate SW15 .19 B8
Lynden Hurst CR0 .61 F8
Lyndhurst Ave
Aldershot GU11 .126 C6
Blackwater GU17 .64 C6
Mitcham SW16 .41 D7
Sunbury TW16 .35 A6
Tolworth KT5 .38 B1
Twickenham TW2, TW4 .16 A7
Lyndhurst Cl
Bracknell RG12 .28 A6
Crawley RH11 .201 D5
South Croydon CR0 .61 F7
Woking GU21 .69 D4
Lyndhurst Ct 7 SM2 .59 A3
Lyndhurst Dr KT3 .38 F2
Lyndhurst Farm Cl RH19 .184 D4
Lyndhurst House 2 SW15 .19 A8
Lyndhurst Rd Ascot SL5 .29 A5
Coulsdon CR5 .79 A3
Reigate RH2 .139 A6
Thornton Heath CR7 .42 A5
Lyndhurst Sch GU15 .65 B5
Lyndhurst Way
Addlestone KT16 .51 E8
Belmont SM2 .59 A2
Lyndon Ave SM6 .60 A7
Lyndon Yd SW17 .20 B4
Lyndsey Cl GU14 .84 B4
Lyne Cl GU25 .31 F3
Lyne Crossing
Rd KT16, TW20 .32 B3
Lyne Ct GU25 .31 F2
Lyne La
Chertsey KT16, TW20 .32 A3
Lyne KT16 .32 A2
Lyne & Longcross Inf Sch
KT16 .51 B8
Lyne Place Manor GU25 .31 F2
Lyne Rd GU25 .31 E3
Lynegrove Ave TW15 .14 C3
Lyneham Rd RG45 .45 B5
Lynfield Ct SE23 .23 D8
Lynmouth Ave SM4 .39 D2
Lynmouth Gdns TW5 .4 D6
Lynn Cl TW15 .14 D3
Lynn Ct Streatham SW16 .21 D3
Whyteleafe CR3 .80 F1
Lynn Rd SW12 .21 B8
Lynn Way GU14 .84 F7
Lynn Wlk RH2 .139 B6
Lynne Cl CR2 .81 C8
Lynne Ct Forest Hill SE23 .23 F8
13 Guildford GU1 .130 F8
South Croydon CR2 .61 E6
Wimbledon SW20 .39 B8
Lynne Wlk KT10 .55 C5
Lynscott Way CR2 .61 B2
Lynsted Ct BR3 .43 E7
Lynton KT7 .37 A2
Lynton Cl Chessington KT9 .56 E6
East Grinstead RH19 .186 A2
Farnham GU9 .146 A7
Isleworth TW7 .5 F3
Lynton Ct SM2 .59 C4
Lynton Park Ave RH19 .186 A2
Lynton Prep Sch KT17 .76 F8
Lynton Rd New Malden KT3 .38 D4
Thornton Heath CR0, CR7 .42 A3
Lynwick St Rudgwick RH12 214 C8
Rudgwick RH12 .214 C8
Rudgwick, Cox Green RH12 .195 D1
Lynwood GU2 .130 B8
Lynwood Ave Egham TW20 .11 E2
Epsom KT17 .76 F5
Wallington CR5 .79 B4
Lynwood Chase 1 RG12 .27 C8
Lynwood Cl GU21 .70 D6
Lynwood Cres SL5 .29 E3
Lynwood Ct RH12 .217 C3
Lynwood Dr Mytchett GU16 .86 A3
North Cheam KT4 .58 A8
Lynwood Flats SL5 .29 E4
Lynwood Gdns CR0 .60 F6
Lynwood Rd Epsom KT17 .76 F5
Redhill RH1 .119 A3
Thames Ditton KT7 .36 F1
Upper Tooting SW17 .20 F4
Lynx Hill KT24 .112 F8
Lyon Cl RH10 .202 C2
Lyon Ct RH13 .217 E2
Lyon Rd Crowthorne RG45 .45 C6
Merton SW19 .40 C8
Walton-on-T KT12 .54 E8
Lyon Way GU16 .65 C1
Lyon Way Ind Est GU16 .65 C1
Lyons Cl RH13 .215 D3
Lyons Ct RH4 .136 B7
Lyons Dr GU2 .109 A6
Lyons Rd RH13 .215 E3
Lyonsdene KT20 .117 F8
Lyric Cl RH10 .202 D4
Lyric Mews SE26 .23 D4
Lyric Rd SW13 .7 F6
Lysander Rd CR0 .60 F4
Lysias Rd SW12 .21 B8
Lysons Ave GU12 .105 F8
Lysons Rd GU11 .105 A1
Lyster Mews KT11 .73 C6
Lytchet Minster Cl 4
RG12 .27 F4
Lytchgate Cl CR2 .61 E3
Lytcott Dr KT8 .35 F6
Lytham RG12 .26 E3
Lytham Ct SL5 .29 C4
Lytton Dr RH10 .202 D7
Lytton Gdns SM6 .60 D6
Lytton House 3 TW12 .16 B2
Lytton Rd GU22 .70 B3
Lyveden Rd SW17, SW19 .20 F2
Lywood Cl KT20 .97 C5

M

Mabbotts KT20 .97 D6
Mabel St GU21 .69 D2
Maberley Cres SE19 .23 A1
Maberley Ct SE19 .23 A1
Maberley Rd Penge SE19 .23 A1
Penge, Elmers End BR3 .43 D6
Macadam Ave RG45 .45 C7
MacArthur House 4 SW2 .21 E8
Macaulay Ave KT10 .55 E8
Macaulay Ct CR3 .100 E6
Macaulay Rd CR3 .100 E6
Macbeth Ct RG42 .27 E8
Macclesfield Rd CR0, SE25 43 C4
Macdonald Ct TW3 .5 C3
Macdonald Rd
Heath End GU9 .125 B7
Lightwater GU18 .67 A8
Macfarlane La TW7 .6 A8
MacGregor House SW12 .21 D7
Mackenzie Rd BR3 .43 D7
Mackie House SW2 .22 A8
Mackie Rd 18 SW2 .22 A8
Mackies Hill GU5 .154 D7
Macklin House SE23 .23 B6
Mackrells RH1 .139 C6
Macleod Rd RH13 .217 F1
Macmillan House SM7 .77 F4
Macphail Cl RG40 .25 E8
Maddison Cl TW11 .16 F2
Maddox La KT23 .93 E3
Maddox Pk KT23 .93 E4
Madehurst Ct RH11 .200 F3
Madeira Ave Bromley BR1 .24 E1
Horsham RH12 .217 C2
Madeira Cl KT14 .71 A6
Madeira Cres KT14 .70 F6
Madeira Rd Mitcham CR4 .40 F5
Streatham SW16 .21 E3
West Byfleet KT14 .71 A6
Madeira Wlk RH1, RH2 .118 D2
Madeline Rd SE20 .23 A1
Madgehole La GU5 .153 B3
Madingley RG12 .27 B1
Madingley Ct TW1 .6 C2
Madison Gdns BR2 .44 F6
Madox Brown End GU47 .64 E6
Madrid Rd GU2 .130 B8
Maesmaur Rd TN16 .103 D6
Mafeking Ave TW8 .6 E8
Mafeking Rd TW19 .12 B6

Magazine Cotts GU4 131 C3
Magazine Pl KT22 95 B5
Magazine Rd CR3 100 B5
Magdala Rd Isleworth TW7 6 A4
South Croydon CR2 61 D3
Magdalen Cl KT14 71 E5
Magdalen Cres KT14 71 E5
Magdalen Ct SE25 43 A4
Magdalen Rd SW18 20 D7
Magdalene Cl RH10 182 C1
Magdalene Rd
Littleton TW17 33 F6
Sandhurst GU47 45 F2
Magellan Terr RH10 182 A2
Magna Carta La TW19 11 E7
Magna Carta Sec Sch TW20 12 D2
Magna Rd TW20 11 B2
Magnolia Cl
Kingston u T KT2 18 B2
Sandhurst GU47 45 D1
Magnolia Ct
3 Belmont SM2 59 B3
Horley RH6 161 A3
Penge SE26 23 C3
Richmond TW9 7 B6
Wallington SM6 60 B5
Magnolia Dr TN16 83 E3
Magnolia Rd W4 7 B8
Magnolia Way
Dorking RH5 136 D4
West Ewell KT19 57 C5
Magnolia Wharf W4 7 B8
Magpie Cl Coulsdon CR5 79 C1
Crondall GU10 124 D8
Magpie Wlk RH10 201 F8
Maguire Dr Frimley GU16 66 C3
Richmond TW10 17 C4
Mahonia Cl GU24 67 F6
Maida Rd GU11 105 B4
Maiden La RH11 201 C8
Maiden's Gn SL4 8 B6
Maidenbower Cty Fst Sch RH10 202 C4
Maidenbower Dr RH10 202 D4
Maidenbower La RH10 202 C4
Maidenbower Pl RH10 202 C4
Maidenbower Sq RH10 202 C4
Maidenshaw Rd KT19 76 D7
Maids of Honour Row 4 TW9 6 D2
Maidstone Cres GU24 87 D6
Main Dr RG12, SL5 28 B8
Main Rd TN16 83 C5
Main St Chertsey KT15 52 E7
Feltham TW13 15 D3
Mainprize Rd RG12 27 E7
Mainstone Cl GU16 86 C7
Mainstone Rd GU24 67 F3
Mainwaring Ct CR4 41 A7
Mais House SE26 23 B6
Maise Webster Cl TW19 13 D8
Maisonettes The SM1 58 F5
Maitland Cl Hounslow TW4 4 F4
Walton-on-T KT12 54 E8
West Byfleet KT14 71 A6
Maitland Rd
Farnborough GU14 105 B8
Penge SE26 23 D2
Maitlands Cl GU10 126 F6
Maizecroft RH6 161 C4
Majestic Way CR4 40 F7
Major's Farm Rd SL3 1 A8
Major's Hill RH10 203 C5
Malacca Farm GU4 111 B7
Malan Cl TN16 83 E2
Malcolm Cl SE20 23 C1
Malcolm Dr KT6 37 E1
Malcolm Gdns RH6 160 D1
Malcolm Prim Sch SE20 23 C1
Malcolm Rd Coulsdon CR5 79 D4
Croydon CR0, SE25 43 A3
Penge SE20 23 C1
Wimbledon SW19 19 E2
Malden Ave SE25 43 B6
Malden Ct KT3 39 B6
Malden Golf Course KT3 38 F7
Malden Green Ave KT4 39 A1
Malden Hill KT3 38 F6
Malden Hill Gdns KT3 38 F6
Malden Manor Prim Sch KT3 38 E2
Malden Manor Sta KT3 38 E2
Malden Parochial CE Prim Sch KT4 38 E1
Malden Pk KT3 38 F3
Malden Rd Cheam KT4, SM3 58 D5
New Malden KT3, KT4 38 F2
Malden Way KT3 39 A5
Malden Way (Kingston By Pass) KT3, KT5 38 E4
Maldon Ct SM6 60 C5
Maldon Rd SM6 60 B5
Malet Cl TW20 12 D2
Maley Ave SE27 22 B6
Malham Cl RH10 202 C3
Malham Fell RG12 27 A5
Malham Rd SE23 23 D7
Malham Road Ind Est SE23 23 D7
Mall The Brentford TW8 6 D8
Croydon CR9 61 C8
6 Guildford GU1 130 C8
Hersham KT12 54 D5
Kingston u T KT6 37 D4
Mortlake SW14 7 C2
Mall The (Prep Sch) TW2 16 D5
Mallard Cl Aldershot GU12 105 F2
Mallard Cl *continued*
Haslemere GU27 207 E6
Horley RH6 161 A5
Horsham RH12 217 C5
Redhill RH1 119 A4
Twickenham TW4 16 A8
Mallard Ct Dorking RH4 136 A8
6 Richmond TW10 6 D1
Mallard Pl
East Grinstead RH19 205 F8
Twickenham TW1 17 A5
Mallard Rd CR2 62 D1
Mallard Way SM6 60 C2
Mallard Wlk BR3, CR0 43 D4
Mallard's Reach KT13 53 D8
Mallards The Frimley GU16 65 F2
Laleham TW18 33 B7
Mallards Way GU18 67 A8
Malling Cl CR0 43 C3
Malling Gdns SM4 40 C3
Malling House 9 BR3 24 A1
Malling Way BR2 44 F2
Mallinson Rd SM6 60 D7
Mallow Cl Burgh Heath KT20 97 B8
Croydon CR0 43 D1
Horsham RH12 217 E6
Mallow Cres GU4 110 C4
Mallowdale Rd RG12 27 E2
Malloy Ct GU21 70 A3
Malmains Cl BR3 44 D5
Malmains Way BR3 44 D5
Malmesbury Fst Sch SM4 40 C2
Malmesbury Mid Sch SM4 40 C3
Malmesbury Rd SM4 40 C3
Malmstone Ave RH1 119 D6
Malt Hill TW20 11 E3
Malt House SL4 11 B8
Malt House Cl SL4 11 B8
Malta Rd GU16 86 E8
Maltby Rd KT9 57 A4
Malthouse Ct GU4 130 E4
Malthouse Dr TW13 15 D3
Malthouse La
Pirbright GU24, GU3 88 C2
West End GU24 67 F7
Malthouse Mead GU8 170 F5
Malthouse Rd RH10, RH11 201 D4
Malthouses The GU6 174 E3
Malting Way TW7 5 F4
Maltings Cl SW13 7 E5
Maltings The Byfleet KT14 71 F6
Oxted RH8 122 F4
Staines TW18 12 E4
Maltlhouse La GU8 171 C1
Malton House SE25 42 E5
Malus Cl KT15 51 F3
Malus Dr KT15 51 F3
Malvern Cl Mitcham CR4 41 C6
Ottershaw KT16 51 C4
Penge SE20 43 A7
Surbiton KT6 37 E1
Malvern Ct Belmont SM2 59 A3
Brands Hill SL3 1 A8
Epsom KT18 76 D5
3 Surbiton KT6 37 E1
Malvern Dr TW13 15 D3
Malvern Rd Crawley RH11 201 C5
Farnborough GU14 84 D7
Hampton TW12 16 A1
Harlington UB3 3 E7
Surbiton KT6 37 E1
Thornton Heath CR7 42 A5
Malyons The TW17 34 D3
Manatee Pl SM6 60 D7
Manby Lodge Cty Inf Sch KT13 53 C5
Manchester Rd CR7 42 C6
Mandeville Cl
Guildford GU2 109 A4
Merton SW19 39 E8
Mandeville Ct TW20 12 A4
Mandeville Dr KT6 37 D1
Mandeville Rd
Isleworth TW7 6 A5
Littleton TW17 34 A4
Mandora Rd GU11 105 B4
Mandrake Rd SW17 20 F5
Manfield Cty Fst Sch GU12 106 B2
Manfield Pk GU6 174 B5
Manfield Rd GU12 106 A2
Mangles Ct 1 GU1 130 C8
Mangles Rd GU1 109 D3
Manley Bridge Rd
Rowledge GU10 145 E4
Wrecclesham GU10 145 E4
Mann's Cl TW7 5 F2
Mannamead KT18 96 E8
Mannamead Cl KT18 96 E8
Manning Cl RH19 185 D2
Manning Pl TW10 6 F1
Mannings Cl RH10 182 D1
Manningtree Cl SW19 19 E7
Manoel Rd TW2 16 D6
Manor Ave Caterham CR3 100 E3
Hounslow TW4 4 D5
Manor Chase KT13 53 B5
Manor Cl
East Horsley KT24 112 E7
Haslemere GU27 207 E6
Horley RH6 160 F3
New Malden KT4 38 E1
Pyrford GU22 70 F3
South Godstone RH9 142 F5
Tongham GU10 126 F7
Warlingham CR6 81 E2
Manor Cotts GU21 68 E5
Manor Cres Byfleet KT14 71 F6
Guildford GU2 109 B3
Haslemere GU27 207 E6
Pirbright GU24 87 D7
Surbiton KT5 38 A3
Manor Ct Horsham RH12 218 A5
Kingston u T KT2 38 A8
Streatham SW16 21 E5
Twickenham TW2 16 C6
Weybridge KT13 53 B6
Manor Dr Feltham TW13 15 D3
Hinchley Wood KT10 56 A7
Horley RH6 160 F3
Sunbury TW16 35 A7
Surbiton KT5 38 A3
West Ewell KT19 57 E4
Woodham KT15 52 A1
Manor Dr N KT3, KT4 38 D2
Manor Dr The KT4 38 F1
Manor Farm Ave TW17 34 B3
Manor Farm Bsns Ctr GU10 126 F5
Manor Farm Cl GU12 105 F1
Manor Farm Ct TW20 12 A3
Manor Farm La TW20 12 A3
Manor Farm Rd CR7, SW16 42 A7
Manor Fields
Horsham RH12, RH13 218 A4
Milford GU8 149 E2
Seale GU10 127 B4
Manor Fst Sch The KT14 71 E5
Manor Gdns
Effingham KT24 113 D7
Farncombe GU7 150 E7
Farnham GU10 146 D5
Guildford GU2 109 B3
Hampton TW12 16 C1
Merton SW19, SW20 39 F7
Richmond TW10, TW9 6 F3
South Croydon CR2 61 F4
Sunbury TW16 35 A7
Manor Gn GU8 149 E1
Manor Gr Beckenham BR3 44 B7
Richmond TW9 7 A4
Manor Green Rd KT19 76 C7
Manor Hill SM7 78 F4
Manor House SM6 60 B5
Manor House Ct KT18 76 C6
Manor House Dr SL5 9 A1
Manor House Flats GU10 126 F6
Manor House Sch KT23 113 E8
Manor House The GU15 65 D6
Manor House Way TW7 6 B4
Manor La Feltham TW13 15 A6
Harlington UB3 3 D8
Lewisham SE12 24 F8
Lower Kingswood KT20 118 A6
Shamley Green GU5 152 E3
Sunbury TW16 35 B7
Sutton SM1 59 C5
Manor Lea GU27 207 E6
Manor Lea Cl GU8 149 E2
Manor Lea Rd GU8 149 E2
Manor Leaze TW20 12 B3
Manor Lodge GU2 109 B3
Manor Mount SE23 23 C7
Manor Park Cl BR4 44 B1
Manor Park Ctr (Coll of Tech) GU11 105 B1
Manor Park Ind Est GU12 105 C1
Manor Park Prim Sch SM1 59 C5
Manor Park Rd Sutton SM1 59 C5
West Wickham BR4 44 B1
Manor Pk Richmond TW9 6 F3
Staines TW18 12 D5
Manor Pl
East Bedfont TW14 15 A7
Great Bookham KT23 94 A1
Mitcham CR4 41 C6
Staines TW18 13 B3
Sutton SM1 59 B6
Manor Rd
Aldershot GU11, GU12 126 A8
Ash GU10, GU12 126 F8
Ashford TW15 14 A3
Beckenham BR3 44 B7
Belmont SM2 58 F2
Croydon SE25 43 A6
East Grinstead RH19 185 C2
East Molesey KT8 36 D5
Farnborough GU14 85 D3
Farnham GU9 125 E4
Guildford GU2 109 B3
Horsham RH12 218 A5
Merstham RH1 119 C6
Merton SW20 39 F7
Mitcham CR4, SW16 41 C6
Reigate RH2 117 F3
Richmond TW10, TW9 6 F3
Send Marsh GU23 90 F4
Tatsfield TN16 103 E7
Teddington TW11 17 B3
Twickenham TW2 16 D6
Wallington SM5, SM6 60 B5
Walton-on-T KT12 34 F2
West Wickham BR4 63 B8
Woking GU21 69 C3
Wokingham RG41 25 A2
Manor Rd N
Hackbridge SM5, SM6 60 B6
Hinchley Wood KT7 56 A8
Manor Rd S KT10 55 E6
Manor Royal RH10, RH11 181 E1
Manor Royal Ind Est RH10 181 E2
Manor The GU8 149 F1
Manor Way Bagshot GU19 47 F3
Beckenham BR3 44 A6
Egham TW20 11 F2
Guildford GU2 129 F6
Mitcham CR4, SW16 41 C6
New Malden KT4 38 F1
Old Woking GU22 90 B6
Oxshott KT22 74 C3
Purley CR8 79 E7
South Croydon CR2 61 F4
Woodmansterne SM7 78 F3
Manor Way The SM6 60 B6
Manor Wlk
1 Aldershot GU12 105 B1
Weybridge KT13 53 B5
Manor Wood Rd CR8 79 E6
Manorcroft Sch TW20 12 A2
Manorcrofts Rd TW20 12 A2
Manordene Cl KT7 37 A1
Manorfields RH11 200 D2
Manorgate Rd KT2 38 A8
Manorhouse La KT23 113 E8
Mansard Beeches SW17 21 A3
Mansard Manor SM2 59 C3
Manse Cl UB3 3 D8
Mansel Cl GU2 109 B6
Mansel Rd SW19 19 F2
Mansell Way CR3 100 D5
Mansfield Cl SL5 28 D7
Mansfield Cres RG12 27 B3
Mansfield Dr RH1 119 D6
Mansfield Pl SL5 28 D8
Mansfield Rd
Chessington KT9 56 D5
South Croydon CR2 61 D4
Wokingham RG41 25 A5
Manship Rd CR4 41 A8
Manston Cl SE20 43 C8
Manston Dr RG12 27 C3
Manston Gr KT2 17 D3
Manston Rd GU4 110 A5
Mantilla Rd SW17 21 A4
Mantlet Cl SW16 21 C1
Manville Ct GU4 130 E1
Manville Gdns SW17 21 B5
Manville Rd SW17 21 B5
Many Gates SW12 21 B6
Manygate La TW17 34 C3
Maori Rd GU1 130 F8
Mapel Ct 3 RG12 27 F5
Maple Cl Ash Vale GU12 106 A7
Blackwater GU17 64 C5
Crawley RH11 181 C1
Hampton TW12 15 F2
Horsham RH12 218 A5
Mitcham CR4 41 B8
Whyteleafe CR3 80 F2
Maple Ct Catford SE6 24 B7
2 Croydon CR0 61 C6
Englefield Green TW20 11 B2
Kingston u T KT3 38 D6
11 West Norwood SW16 22 A3
Woking GU21 69 C3
Maple Dr Crowthorne RG45 45 C7
East Grinstead RH19 186 A1
Lightwater GU18 66 F8
Maple Gdns TW15, TW19 13 E6
Maple Gr Brentford TW8 6 B7
Guildford GU1 109 D3
Woking GU22 89 E6
Maple Gr Bsns Ctr TW4 4 C3
Maple Ho 8 RH2 118 F1
Maple House 2 KT6 37 E4
Maple Ind Est TW13 15 A5
Maple Inf Sch KT6 37 D4
Maple Leaf Cl
Biggin Hill TN16 83 D3
Farnborough GU14 84 F3
Maple Mews SW16 21 F3
Maple Pl KT17 77 D5
Maple Rd Ashstead KT21 95 D8
Kingston u T KT6 37 D4
Penge SE20 43 C8
Redhill RH1 139 F5
Send Marsh GU23 91 A3
Whyteleafe CR3 80 F2
Maple Way Feltham TW13 15 B5
Headley Down GU35 187 B6
Hooley CR5 99 B6
Maple Wlk Aldershot GU12 126 D8
Sutton SM2 59 B1
Mapledale Ave CR0 62 B7
Mapledrakes Cl GU6 175 E5
Mapledrakes Rd GU6 175 E5
Maplehatch Cl GU7 150 E2
Maplehurst Beckenham BR2 44 E7
Fetcham KT22 94 D4
Maplehurst Cl KT1 37 E5
Mapleleaf Cl CR2 81 D8
Maples The Banstead SM7 78 B5
Ottershaw KT16 51 C4
4 Teddington KT8 17 C1
Maplestead Rd SW2 21 F8
Maplethorpe Rd CR7 42 B5
Marble Hill TW1 17 C8
Marble Hill Cl TW1 17 B8
Marble Hill Gdns TW1 17 B8
Marbles Way KT20 97 D8
March Rd
6 Twickenham TW1 17 A8
Weybridge KT13 53 A5
Marcheria Cl RG12 27 B3
Marches Rd RH12 197 E4
Marchmont House 10 SW16 21 C3
Marchmont Rd
Richmond TW10 6 F2
Wallington SM6 60 C3
Marchside Cl TW5 4 D6
Marcus Ct Brentford TW8 6 E7
Woking GU22 69 F1
Marcuse Rd CR3 100 D4
Mardale GU15 66 C4
Mardell Rd CR0 43 D4
Marden Ave BR2 44 F3
Marden Cres CR0 41 F3
Marden Lodge Cty Prim Sch CR3 101 B6
Marden Rd CR0 41 F3
Mardens The RH11 201 B7
Mare Hill GU8 170 E5
Mare Hill Cotts GU8 170 D4
Mare La GU8 172 C4
Mares Field House GU4 110 D2
Mareschal Rd GU2 130 C7
Maresfield CR0 61 E7
Mareth Cl GU11 105 B2
Marfleet Cl SM5 59 E8
Margaret Cl TW18 13 D2
Margaret Lockwood Cl KT5 37 F5
Margaret Rd GU1 130 C8
Margaret Roper RC Prim Sch CR8 61 A1
Margaret Way CR8 100 B8
Margery Gr KT20 117 E6
Margery La KT20, RH2 118 A6
Margin Dr SW19 19 D4
Marham Gdns
Morden SM4 40 C3
Wandsworth SW17, SW18 20 E7
Maria Theresa Cl KT3 38 D4
Marian Ct SM1 59 B5
Marian Rd CR4, SW16 41 C8
Marian Vian Prim Sch BR3 43 E4
Mariette Way SM6 60 E2
Marigold Cl RG45 45 A6
Marigold Ct GU1 109 E4
Marigold Dr GU24 68 A4
Marigold Way CR0 43 D1
Marina Ave KT3 39 B4
Marina Cl KT16 33 C1
Marina Way TW11 17 D1
Mariner Gdns TW10 17 C5
Mariners Dr
Farnborough GU14 85 C6
Normandy GU3 107 B4
Marion Ave TW17 34 B4
Marion Ct SW17 20 E3
Marion Rd Crawley RH10 202 B3
Thornton Heath CR0 42 D4
Marist RC Prim Sch KT14 70 F6
Marius Mansions 3 SW17 21 A6
Marius Rd SW17 21 A6
Marjoram Cl
Farnborough GU14 84 B4
Guildford GU2 109 A5
Marjorie Fosters Way GU24 87 D8
Marjory Kinnon Sch TW14 3 E2
Mark Oak La KT22 94 A6
Mark St RH2 118 B2
Mark Way GU7 150 B8
Markedge La CR5, RH2 98 F2
Markenfield Rd GU1 109 D1
Markenhorn GU7 150 D7
Market Par Croydon SE25 43 A5
Feltham TW13 15 E6
Market Pl Brentford TW8 6 C7
Kingston u T KT1 37 D7
Wokingham RG40 25 C5
Market Rd TW9 7 A4
Market Sq Horsham RH12 217 C1
Reigate RH2 118 A1
Staines TW18 12 E4
Market St Bracknell RG12 27 B7
Guildford GU1 130 D8
Market The SM1, SM4, SM5 40 C1
Marketfield Rd 14 RH2 118 F1
Marketfield Way RH1 119 A1
Markfield CR0 81 F8
Markfield Rd CR3 101 B2
Markham Ct GU15 65 D6
Markham House 9 SE21 22 E4
Markham Mews RG40 25 C6
Markham Rd RH5 178 C5
Markhole Cl TW12 15 F1
Marks Rd Warlingham CR6 81 E1
Wokingham RG41 25 A8
Marksbury Ave TW9 7 A4
Markville Gdns CR3 101 A2
Markway The TW16 35 C7
Markwell Cl SE26 23 B4
Markwick La GU8 172 C2
Marlang Ct BR3 44 D8
Marlborogh Rd TW7, TW8 6 B7
Marlborough 11 SW19 19 D7
Marlborough Cl
Crawley RH11 201 C2
Hersham KT12 54 D7
Horsham RH12 217 D5
Mitcham SW19 20 E2
Marlborough Ct
Dorking RH4 136 B7
Wallington SM6 60 C3
Wokingham RG40 25 D7
Marlborough Cty Inf Sch GU11 105 C7
Marlborough Dr KT13 53 C7
Marlborough Gdns KT6 37 D2
Marlborough House SW19 19 D5

Marlborough Jun & Inf Sch TW7 6 A6
Marlborough Rd
Ashford TW15 13 E3
Dorking RH4 136 B7
Feltham TW13 15 D6
Hampton TW12 16 A2
Mitcham SW19 20 E2
Richmond TW10 6 F1
South Croydon CR2 61 C3
Sutton SM1 59 A8
Woking GU21 70 A3
Marlborough Rise GU15 65 E6
Marlborough Trad Est TW9 7 B6
Marlborough View GU14 84 C5
Marld The KT21 75 F1
Marler Rd SE23 23 F7
Marles La RH14 214 C1
Marlesford Ct SM6 60 C6
Marley Cl KT15 51 F4
Marley Combe Rd GU27 207 F4
Marley Croft TW18 12 E5
Marley Hanger GU27 208 A3
Marley La GU27 207 E4
Marley Rise RH4 136 A4
Marlfield Ct KT3 38 F2
Marlin Cl TW16 14 E2
Marling Ct TW12 15 F2
Marlingdene Cl TW12 16 A2
Marlings Cl CR3 80 E2
Marlins Cl 3 SM1 59 C5
Marlow Cl SE20 43 B6
Marlow Cres TW1 5 F1
Marlow Ct RH10 201 D7
Marlow Dr SM3 58 D7
Marlow House TW11 17 A4
Marlow Rd SE20, SE25 43 B7
Marlowe Ct Dulwich SE19 22 F3
6 Kingston u T KT2 17 D4
Marlowe House KT1 37 D5
Marlowe Lodge CR0 62 E8
Marlowe Sq CR4 41 C5
Marlowe Way CR0 60 E8
Marlpit Ave CR5 79 E2
Marlpit Cl RH19 185 E4
Marlpit La CR5 79 E2
Marlyns Cl GU4 110 A4
Marlyns Dr GU1, GU4 110 A4
Marmion House 13 SW12 21 B8
Marmot Rd TW4 4 D4
Marncrest Ct KT12 54 B5
Marnell Way TW4 4 D4
Marneys Cl KT18 76 A4
Marnfield Cres SW2 21 F7
Maroons Way SE6 24 A3
Marqueen Towers SW16 21 F1
Marquis Ct 1 KT1 37 E5
Married Quarters CR3 100 C5
Marriott Cl TW14 3 D1
Marriott House SE6 24 C4
Marriott Lodge Cl KT15 52 C6
Marrowbrook Cl GU14 85 A4
Marrowbrook La GU14 85 A3
Marrowells KT13 53 F7
Marryat Pl SW19 19 E4
Marryat Rd SW19 19 E3
Marsh Ave Epsom KT19 57 E1
Mitcham CR4 41 A7
Marsh Ct Crawley RH11 201 B1
3 Merton SW19 40 C8
Marsh Farm Rd TW2 16 F7
Marsh La KT15 52 B6
Marshall Cl
Farnborough GU14 84 F7
Frimley GU16 66 D2
Hounslow TW4 4 F2
Sanderstead CR2 81 A6
Marshall House 3 KT3 38 E5
Marshall Par GU22 70 F4
Marshall Pl KT15 52 C2
Marshall Rd Crawley RH10 202 C4
Farncombe GU7 150 E6
Sandhurst GU47 64 D6
Marshall's Rd SM1 59 B6
Marshalls GU9 146 B8
Marshalls Cl KT19 76 C6
Marsham Ct 19 SW19 19 D7
Marshfields C of E Fst Sch KT16 51 E4
Marshwood Rd GU18 67 D8
Marston KT19 76 C8
Marston Ave KT9 56 E4
Marston Ct KT12 35 C1
Marston Dr
Farnborough GU14 85 B7
Warlingham CR6 81 E1
Marston House RH1 118 F2
Marston Rd Farnham GU9 124 F2
Richmond TW11 17 B3
Woking GU21 69 B2
Marston Way
North Ascot SL5 28 E7
South Norwood SE19 22 C1
Martel Cl GU15 66 C7
Martell Rd SE21 22 D5
Martens Pl GU7 150 E6
Martin Cl Crawley RH11 201 D8
Selsdon CR2 62 D1
Warlingham CR6 81 B3
Martin Cres CR0 42 A1
Martin Ct SW19 20 A1
Martin Gr SM4, SW19 40 A6
Martin House 5 KT3 38 E5
Martin Rd GU2 109 A3
Martin Way Frimley GU16 65 E2
Martin Way *continued*
Merton SW19, SW20, SM4 39 E6
Woking GU21 69 A1
Martin's Heron Sta RG12 27 F5
Martin's Rd BR2 44 F7
Martindale SW14 7 C2
Martindale Ave GU15 66 C4
Martindale Cl GU4 110 D3
Martindale Rd
Balham SW12 21 B8
Hounslow TW4 4 E4
Woking GU21 69 A1
Martineau Cl KT10 55 D6
Martineau Dr RH4 136 B5
Martingale Cl TW16 35 A5
Martingale Ct GU11 104 E2
Martingales Cl TW10 17 D5
Martins Cl Blackwater GU17 64 D4
Guildford GU1 110 C2
West Wickham BR4 63 D8
Martins Dr RG41 25 B7
Martins La RG12 27 E6
Martins The
Crawley Down RH10 204 C8
Forest Hill SE26 23 B3
Martins Wood GU8 170 E7
Martinsyde GU22 70 C2
Martlet Cnr RH12 214 D7
Martlets Cl RH12 217 C5
Martlets The RH10 201 E6
Marton Cl SE6 24 A5
Marts The RH12 214 D7
Martyns Pl RH19 206 A8
Martyr Rd GU1 130 D8
Martyrs Ave RH11 181 D1
Martyrs La GU21 70 B7
Marvell Cl RH10 202 C8
Marwell Cl BR4 63 F8
Mary Adelaide Cl SW15 18 E5
Mary Rd GU1 130 C8
Mary Rose Cl TW12 36 A8
Mary Vale GU7 150 D2
Mary's Terr TW1 17 A8
Marygold House TW3 5 C6
Maryhill Cl CR8 80 C2
Maryland Ct KT1 38 B7
Maryland Rd CR7 42 B8
Maryland Way TW16 35 A7
Marymount International Sch KT2 18 C1
Masefield Ct 10 KT6 37 D2
Masefield Gdns RG45 45 B3
Masefield Rd
Crawley RH11 200 E3
Hampton TW13 15 F4
Masefield Way TW19 13 F7
Maskall Cl SW2 22 A7
Maskani Wlk SW16 21 C1
Maskell Rd SW17 20 C5
Maskell Way GU14 84 D3
Mason Cl
East Grinstead RH19 185 E2
Hampton TW12 35 F8
Wimbledon SW20 39 D8
Mason Ct 3 SE19 22 F1
Mason Rd Crawley RH10 201 E4
Farnborough GU14 84 E6
Mason Way GU11 126 B7
Mason's Ave CR0, CR9 61 C7
Mason's Bridge Rd
Redhill RH1 140 C3
Salfords RH1 140 C3
Mason's Pl CR4 40 F8
Masonic Hall Rd KT16 32 F3
Masons Paddock RH4 115 A1
Massetts Rd RH6 161 A2
Massingberd Way SW17 21 B4
Master Cl RH8 122 E6
Mastin House SW18 20 A7
Maswell Park Cres TW3 5 C2
Maswell Park Rd TW3 5 C3
Matham Rd KT8 36 D4
Mathew Terr GU11 105 C2
Mathews Cl GU14 105 E8
Mathias Cl KT18 76 C6
Mathisen Way SL3 1 E6
Mathon Ct GU1 109 F1
Matilda Cl SE19 22 D1
Matlock Cres SM3 58 E6
Matlock Gdns SM1, SM3 58 E6
Matlock Pl SM1, SM3 58 E6
Matlock Rd CR3 100 E6
Matlock Way KT3 38 D8
Matthew Arnold Cl
Cobham KT11 73 A5
Staines TW18 13 C2
Matthew Arnold Sch The TW18 13 C2
Matthew Ct CR4 41 D4
Matthew Rd GU9 125 E8
Matthew's Gdns CR0 82 D8
Matthew's St RH2 139 A5
Matthews Ct SL5 29 D5
Matthews Dr RH10 202 C3
Matthews La TW18 12 F4
Matthews Rd GU15 65 C8
Matthewsgreen Rd RG41 25 A8
Matthey Pl RH10 182 D1
Matthias Ct 12 TW10 6 E1
Maultway Cl GU15 66 B8
Maultway Cres GU15 66 B8
Maultway N GU15 47 B1
Maultway The
Camberley GU15, GU16 66 D6
Frimley GU15, GU16 66 D6
Maunsell Pk RH10 202 B6
Maurice Ave CR3 100 D5
Maurice Ct 3 TW8 6 D7
Mavery Ct BR1 24 F1
Mavins Rd GU9 146 D8
Mavis Ave KT19 57 E5
Mavis Cl KT19 57 E5
Mawbey Rd KT16 51 D4
Mawson Cl SW20 39 E7
Mawson La W4 7 F8
Maxine Cl GU47 45 B1
Maxton Wlk RH11 201 B2
Maxwell Cl CR0 41 E1
Maxwell Ct SE21 23 A7
Maxwell Dr KT14 71 C8
Maxwell Rd TW15 14 C2
Maxwell Way RH10 182 A1
May Cl Chessington KT9 56 F4
Godalming GU7 150 B2
2 Sandhurst GU47 64 D8
May Cotts CR5 98 B2
May Cres GU12 105 E1
May Ct 2 SW19 40 C8
May Rd TW2 16 E7
May's Hill Rd BR2 44 E6
Maybelle Cl RH5 157 D3
Mayberry Pl KT5 37 F2
Maybourne Cl SE26 23 B3
Maybourne Grange CR0 61 E8
Maybourne Rise GU22 89 D3
Maybury Bsns Ctr Woking GU22 70 A2
Maybury Cl
Burgh Heath KT20 97 E8
Frimley GU16 85 D8
Maybury Ct GU22 70 B2
Maybury Cty Inf Sch GU21 70 A3
Maybury Hill GU21, GU22 70 B2
Maybury Rd GU21 70 A3
Maybury Rough GU22 70 B2
Maybury St SW17 20 E3
Maycroft BR2 44 F1
Maycross Ave SM4 40 A5
Mayday Hospl CR7 42 B3
Mayday Rd CR0, CR7 42 B3
Maydwell Ave RH13 215 C2
Mayefield Rd CR7 41 F4
Mayell Cl KT22 95 C4
Mayes Cl CR6 81 D1
Mayes La RH12 197 F3
Mayfair Ave
New Malden KT4 39 A1
Twickenham TW2 16 C8
Mayfair Cl Beckenham BR3 44 B8
Surbiton KT6 37 E1
Mayfair Ct Beckenham BR3 44 B8
4 South Croydon CR0 61 F8
Mayfield Crawley RH10 202 D6
Dormansland RH7 165 A1
Hersham KT12 54 C6
Rowledge GU10 145 F3
Mayfield Ave KT15 52 C1
Mayfield Cl Ashford TW15 14 B2
Farnham GU9 126 B6
Hersham KT12 54 A6
Hinchley Wood KT7 37 B1
Penge SE20 43 B8
Redhill RH1 140 A3
Weybridge KT15 52 C1
Mayfield Cres CR7 41 F5
Mayfield Ct Redhill RH1 139 F4
Sutton SM2 59 C3
Mayfield Cty Inf Sch GU14 85 B6
Mayfield Cty Jun Sch GU14 85 A6
Mayfield Gdns Egham TW18 12 F2
Walton-on-T KT12 54 A6
Mayfield Gr KT23 114 A8
Mayfield Rd
Camberley GU15 65 B1
Farnborough GU14 84 F7
Hersham KT12 54 A6
Merton SW19 39 F8
South Croydon CR2 61 D2
Sutton SM2 59 D4
Weybridge KT13 52 F5
Mayflower Cl RH10 202 D5
Mayford Cl Balham SW12 20 F8
Penge BR3 43 D6
Woking GU22 89 D5
Mayford Rd SW12 21 A8
Mayhurst Ave GU22 70 C3
Mayhurst Cl GU22 70 C3
Mayhurst Cres GU22 70 C3
Maynard Ct TW18 13 A4
Maynooth Gdns CR4 40 F2
Mayo Rd
Thornton Heath CR0 42 D4
Walton-on-T KT12 35 A2
Mayow Rd SE23, SE26 23 D4
Maypole Rd
Ashurst Wood RH19 206 E6
East Grinstead RH19 185 D2
Mayroyd Ave KT6 57 A8
Mays Cl KT13 52 F1
Mays Cnr GU23 90 D3
Mays Gr GU23 90 D4
Mays Rd
Teddington TW11, TW12 16 D3
Wokingham RG40 25 E6
Maysfield Rd GU23 90 D4
Maytree Cl GU1 109 C5
Maytree Ct CR4 41 A6
Maytree Wlk SW2 22 A6
Maytrees GU21 68 C2
Maywater Cl CR2 80 D8
Maywood Cl BR3 24 B1
Maywood Dr GU15 66 A7
Maze Rd TW9 7 A7
McAlmont Ridge GU7 150 D7
McCarthy Rd TW13 15 D3
McCormick House 9 SW2 22 A7
McDonald House 1 KT2 17 F1
Mcdonald's Almshouses GU9 125 A1
McDonough Cl KT9 56 E6
McDougall Ct TW9 7 A5
McGechie Ho RH19 185 D3
McIndoe Rd RH19 185 D3
McIntosh Cl SM6 60 E3
McIver Cl RH19 184 F4
McKay Cl GU11 105 C3
McKay Rd SW20 19 C2
Mckay Trad Est SL3 1 E5
McKinlay Ct BR3 43 F7
Mcleod Ct SE21 23 A7
McLeod House SE23 23 C6
McMillan Ct SE6 24 F7
McNaughton Cl GU14 84 D3
McRae La CR4 40 F2
Meachen Ct RG40 25 C6
Mead Ave RH1 140 A1
Mead Cl Cranleigh GU6 174 E2
Egham TW20 12 B2
Redhill RH1 119 A4
Mead Cres Carshalton SM1 59 E6
Little Bookham KT23 94 A2
Mead Ct Egham TW20 12 C2
Woking GU21 68 E3
Mead Cty Inf Sch The KT19 57 F6
Mead Dr CR5 79 E5
Mead End KT21 75 F3
Mead La Chertsey KT16 33 C1
Farnham GU9 125 B2
Mead Path SW17 20 D2
Mead Pl CR0 42 C1
Mead Rd Caterham CR3 100 F4
Cranleigh GU6 174 E3
Crawley RH10 201 F7
Hersham KT12 54 E6
Hindhead GU26 188 F4
Richmond TW10 17 C5
Mead The Ashstead KT21 95 E8
Beckenham BR3 44 C8
Dorking RH4 136 C4
Farnborough GU14 85 B3
Wallington SM6 60 D4
West Wickham BR4 44 D1
Mead Way Coulsdon CR5 79 F1
Croydon CR0 62 E8
Guildford GU4 110 C6
Hayes BR2, BR4 44 F3
Meadcroft House 4 KT3 38 E2
Meade Cl W4 7 A8
Meade Ct Bagshot GU19 47 F3
Walton on t H KT20 97 A3
Meades Cl RH7 165 B1
Meades The RH7 165 A1
Meadfoot Rd SW16 41 C8
Meadhurst Pk TW16 14 E2
Meadhurst Rd KT16 33 B1
Meadhurst Sports Club TW16 14 F3
Meadlands Dr TW10 17 D6
Meadlands Prim Sch TW10 17 C4
Meadow App RH10 183 A3
Meadow Ave CR0 43 D3
Meadow Bank
East Horsley KT24 112 E8
Farnham GU9 125 B1
Meadow Bglws GU4 131 B3
Meadow Brook Ind Ctr RH10 182 A1
Meadow Cl Ash Vale GU12 85 F1
Blackwater GU17 64 D4
Catford SE6 24 A3
Copthorne RH10 183 A3
Farncombe GU7 150 E7
Hersham KT12 54 F6
Hinchley Wood KT10 55 F7
Horsham RH12 218 A5
Milford GU8 150 A1
Purley CR8 79 D6
Richmond TW10 17 E7
Sutton SM1 59 C8
Twickenham TW4 16 A8
West Barnes SW20 39 C5
Meadow Cotts GU24 67 F7
Meadow Croft Cl RH6 182 C8
Meadow Ct Epsom KT18 76 C6
Farnborough GU14 84 F4
Staines TW18 12 E5
Meadow Dr GU23 90 F4
Meadow Farm La RH12 217 F7
Meadow Gdns TW18 12 D3
Meadow Hill
Coulsdon CR5, CR8 79 C6
New Malden KT3 38 E3
Purley CR5, CR8 79 C6
Meadow House GU4 110 D2
Meadow La KT22 94 C5
Meadow Pl W4 7 E7
Meadow Rd Ashford TW15 14 D3
Ashstead KT21 75 E2
Bromley BR2 44 E7
Carshalton SM1 59 E5
Claygate KT10 55 E4
Farnborough GU14 85 B7
Feltham TW13 15 E6
Guildford GU4 110 A5
Merton SW19 20 C1
Wentworth GU25 30 E4
Wokingham RG41 25 A5
Meadow Rise Coulsdon CR5 79 D6
Knaphill GU21 68 C2
Meadow Stile CR0, CR9 61 C7
Meadow The RH10 183 A3
Meadow Vale GU27 208 A6
Meadow Vale Prim Sch RG42 26 F8
Meadow View RH6 162 C3
Meadow View Rd CR7 42 B4
Meadow Way
Addlestone KT15 52 B6
Aldershot GU12 105 F3
Blackwater GU17 64 C5
Bracknell RG42 27 A8
Burgh Heath KT20 77 E2
Chessington KT9 56 E5
Great Bookham KT23 94 B4
Reigate RH2 139 B5
Rowledge GU10 145 F3
West End GU24 67 F6
West Horsley KT24 92 D2
Wokingham RG41 25 A5
Meadow Waye TW5 4 E7
Meadow Wlk
Hackbridge SM6 60 B7
Walton on t H KT20 97 B3
West Ewell KT17, KT19 57 F3
Wokingham RG41 25 A6
Meadowbank KT5 37 F3
Meadowbank Gdns TW4, TW5 4 B6
Meadowbank Rd GU18 48 C1
Meadowbrook RH8 122 D5
Meadowbrook Cl SL3 1 F6
Meadowbrook Rd RH4 136 A7
Meadowcroft Cl
Crawley RH11 200 F5
East Grinstead RH19 185 C2
Meadowcroft Cty Fst Sch KT16 51 F7
Meadowfield Cl KT3 39 C5
Meadowlands
Cobham KT11 73 A6
Crawley RH11 201 C6
Oxted RH8 123 A1
West Clandon GU4 111 B5
Meadowlea Cl UB7 2 D8
Meadows End TW16 35 A8
Meadows Leigh Cl KT13 53 C7
Meadows The Ash GU12 106 B2
Churt GU10 167 F1
Guildford GU2 130 C6
Sandhurst GU47 64 E5
Warlingham CR6 81 E2
Meadowside
Great Bookham KT23 94 A4
Horley RH6 161 B4
Twickenham TW1 17 D8
Walton-on-T KT12 54 C8
Meadowside Rd SM2 58 E2
Meadowview TW19 1 F2
Meadowview Rd
Catford SE6 24 A3
Reigate RH2 118 F4
West Ewell KT19 57 E2
Meadrow GU7 150 F6
Meadrow Lock GU7 151 A6
Meads Cty Prim Sch The RH19 205 E7
Meads Rd GU1 110 B1
Meads The Cheam SM3 58 E7
East Grinstead RH19 205 E7
Haslemere GU27 207 F6
Weybridge KT13 53 D4
Meadside 4 Epsom KT18 76 D6
7 Woking GU22 69 F1
Meadside Cl BR3 43 E8
Meadsview Ct 3 GU14 85 B4
Meadvale RH12 216 F2
Meadvale Rd CR0 43 A3
Meadway Ashford TW15 14 A4
Beckenham BR3 44 C8
Effingham KT24 113 E7
Epsom KT19 76 C7
Esher KT10 55 B2
Frimley GU16 65 F2
Haslemere GU27 207 F6
Oxshott KT22 74 E5
Staines TW18 13 A1
Tolworth KT5 38 C1
Twickenham TW2 16 D7
Warlingham CR6 81 C3
West Barnes SW20 39 C5
Meadway Cl TW18 13 A1
Meadway Dr
New Haw KT15 52 C3
Woking GU21 69 D4
Meadway The RH6 161 C3
Meaford Way SE20 23 B1
Meare Cl KT20 97 D4
Meath Green Ave RH6 160 F5
Meath Green Cty Jun Sch RH6 160 F5
Meath Green La
Horley RH1, RH6 160 E6
Salfords RH1, RH6 160 E6
Meath Sch KT16 51 D3
Medawar Rd GU2 129 D8
Medcroft Gdns SW14 7 C3
Mede Cl TW19 11 D7
Mede Ct TW18 12 E5
Mede Field KT22 94 D3
Medfield St SW15 19 B8
Medhurst Cl GU24 49 F2
Medina Ave KT10 55 E7
Medlake Rd TW20 12 C2
Medland Cl CR4 41 A1
Medlar Cl Crawley RH11 181 C1
Guildford GU1 109 C3
Medlar Dr GU17 64 F3
Medora Rd SW2 21 F8

Medway RH10 204 A5
Medway Cl CR0 43 C3
Medway Ct Horsham RH12 218 B5
South Norwood SE25 42 E4
Medway Dr
East Grinstead RH19 205 D6
Farnborough GU14 84 E7
Medway Rd RH11 200 F5
Medwyn Wlk RH12 217 C2
Melbourne Cl SM6 60 C5
Melbourne Ct Penge SE20 23 A1
Twickenham TW2 16 D7
Melbourne Mews SE6 24 C8
Melbourne Rd
Merton SW19 40 A8
Teddington TW11 17 C2
Wallington SM6 60 C5
Melbourne Way RH12 217 F5
Melbury Cl Chertsey KT16 33 A2
Claygate KT10 56 B4
West Byfleet KT14 71 A5
Melbury Gdns SW20 39 B8
Melbury House TW2 16 D6
Meldone KT3 38 D1
Meldone Cl KT5 38 B3
Meldrum Cl RH8 123 A3
Melfield Gdns SE6 24 C3
Melfont Ave CR7 42 B6
Melford Cl KT9 56 F5
Melford Ct Dulwich SE22 23 A8
Sutton SM2 59 C3
Melford Rd SE21, SE22 23 A7
Melfort Rd CR7, SW16 42 B6
Meliot Rd SE6 24 D6
Melksham Cl RH13 217 E1
Meller Cl SM6 60 E7
Mellersh Hill Rd GU5 152 C6
Mellish Ct KT6 37 E3
Mellison Rd SW17 20 E3
Mellor Cl KT12 35 F2
Mellor Ct [2] SW19 20 C1
Mellor House [2] SE21 22 E4
Mellow Cl SM7 78 C5
Mellows Rd SM6 60 D5
Melody Rd TN16 83 C1
Melrose RG12 27 B1
Melrose Ave
Farnborough GU14 84 C5
Mitcham CR4 21 B1
Thornton Heath SW16 42 A6
Twickenham TW2 16 B8
Wimbledon SW19 20 A5
Melrose Gdns
Hersham KT12 54 C5
Kingston u T KT3 38 D6
Melrose Rd Barnes SW13 7 F5
Biggin Hill TN16 83 C3
Coulsdon CR5 79 B4
Merton SW19 40 A8
Weybridge KT13 53 A5
Melrose Sch CR4 40 E6
Melrose Tudor SM6 60 E5
Melsa Rd SM4 40 C3
Melton Ct [8] Croydon CR0 61 F8
[2] Twickenham TW1 17 B8
Melton Fields KT19 57 D2
Melton Pl KT19 57 D2
Melton Rd RH1 119 C5
Melville Ave Frimley GU16 65 F1
South Croydon CR0, CR2 61 F5
Wimbledon SW20 19 A1
Melvin Ct [11] TW9 7 A6
Melvin Rd SE20 43 C8
Melvinshaw KT22 95 C6
Membury Cl GU16 86 A7
Membury Wlk RG12 27 F5
Memorial Cl TW5 4 F8
Memory Cotts KT20 97 E8
Mendip Cl Forest Hill SE26 23 C4
Harlington UB3 3 D7
North Cheam KT4 58 C8
Mendip Rd Bracknell RG12 27 E4
Farnborough GU14 84 E7
Mendip Wlk RH11 201 B6
Menin Way GU9 125 D1
Menlo Gdns SE19 22 D1
Meon Cl Farnborough GU14 84 D6
Tadworth KT20 97 B5
Meon Ct TW7 5 E5
Meopham Rd CR4, SW16 41 C8
Merantum Way
Merton SW19 40 C8
Mitcham SW19 40 C8
Mercer Cl Crawley RH10 202 C3
Thames Ditton KT7 36 F2
Mercer Rd RH12 217 C8
Merchiston Rd SE6 24 D6
Mercia Wlk [5] GU21 69 F2
Mercury Cl RH11 200 E3
Mercury Ctr TW14 4 B2
Mere Cl SW15, SW19 19 D8
Mere End CR0 43 D2
Mere Rd Oatlands Park KT13 53 D7
Shepperton TW17 34 B3
Tadworth KT20 97 B4
Walton on t H KT20 97 B4
Merebank RH5 157 D4
Merebank La CR0, SM6 60 F5
Merefield Gdns KT20 97 D8
Meretune Ct SM4 39 F6
Merevale Cres SM4 40 C3
Mereway Industry TW2 16 E7
Mereway Rd TW2 16 E7
Mereworth Cl BR2 44 F4
Mereworth Dr RH10 202 D8
Meridian Ct Catford SE6 24 F7
Croydon CR0 61 A6
Sunningdale SL5 29 B1
Meridian Gr RH6 161 C4
Meridian Way RH19 185 F3
Merland Cl KT20 97 C7
Merland Gn KT20 97 C7
Merland Rise KT18, KT20 97 C8
Merland Rise Cty Prim Sch KT20 97 C8
Merle Common Rd RH8 144 B7
Merlewood RG12 27 D4
Merlewood Cl CR3 100 D7
Merlin Cl Brands Hill SL3 1 B8
Crawley RH11 200 E6
Mitcham CR4 40 E6
South Croydon CR0 61 E6
Merlin Clove RG42 8 B2
Merlin Ct Beckenham BR2 44 F5
Frimley GU16 65 D1
Sheerwater GU21 70 C5
Merlin Ctr RH11 181 D2
Merlin Gr BR3 44 A4
Merlin Way
East Grinstead RH19 186 A3
Farnborough GU14 84 D3
Merling Cl KT9 56 D5
Merlins Cl GU9 125 C1
Merrick House RH2 118 C1
Merricks Ct SW14 7 B3
Merrilands Rd KT4 39 C1
Merrilyn Cl KT10 56 A4
Merrist Wood Coll (Agricultural) GU3 108 C7
Merritt Gdns KT9 56 C4
Merrivale Gdns GU21 69 C2
Merrow Bsns Ctr GU4 110 D4
Merrow CE Fst Sch GU4 110 D3
Merrow Chase GU1 110 D1
Merrow Common Rd GU4 110 D4
Merrow Copse GU1 110 B2
Merrow Croft GU1 110 C2
Merrow Ct Guildford GU1 110 D1
Mitcham CR4 40 D7
Merrow La GU4 110 C5
Merrow Rd SM2 58 D2
Merrow St GU1, GU4 110 D2
Merrow Way CR0 63 C4
Merrow Woods GU1 110 B3
Merryacres GU8 170 E6
Merryfield Dr RH12 217 A3
Merryhill Rd RG42 27 B8
Merryhills Cl TN16 83 D3
Merryhills La RH14 213 A5
Merrylands KT16 51 E7
Merrylands Ct KT23 93 F4
Merrylands Farm KT23 94 A3
Merrylands Rd KT23 93 F3
Merryman Dr RG45 45 A7
Merrymeet SM7 78 F5
Merryweather Ct [1] KT3 38 E4
Merrywood KT22 95 C6
Merrywood Gr KT20 117 E5
Merrywood Pk
Frimley GU15 65 F4
Reigate RH2 118 B3
Merryworth Cl GU12 105 F1
Mersham Pl Penge SE20 43 B8
South Norwood CR7 42 D7
Mersham Rd CR7 42 D7
Merstham Cty Prim Sch RH1 119 C6
Merstham Rd RH1 120 A5
Merstham Sta RH1 119 C7
Merton Abbey Prim Sch SW19 40 B8
Merton Cl GU47 45 F2
Merton Gdns KT20 97 D8
Merton Hall Gdns SW20 39 E8
Merton Hall Rd SW19, SW20 39 E8
Merton High St SW19 20 C1
Merton House SW18 20 A7
Merton Ind Pk SW19 40 C8
Merton Mansions SW20 39 D7
Merton Park Fst Sch SW19 40 A7
Merton Park Par SW19 39 F8
Merton Park Sta SW19 40 A8
Merton Pl [9] SW19 20 C1
Merton Rd Croydon SE25 43 A4
Merton SW19 20 B1
Wandsworth SW18 20 A7
Merton Road Ind Est SW18 20 A8
Merton Tech Coll SM4 39 F4
Merton Tech Coll (Annexe) SW19 40 A8
Merton Way
East Molesey KT8 36 C6
Leatherhead KT22 95 A8
Merton Wlk KT22 75 A1
Mervyn Rd TW17 34 C2
Metana Ho RH10 182 A3
Metcalf Rd TW15 14 B3
Metcalf Way RH11 181 D2
Metcalfe Wlk TW13 15 E4
Meteor Way SM6 60 E3
Meteorological Off (HQ) RG12 27 D7
Metro Bsns Ctr The SE26 23 F3
Metro Ctr SM4 39 D2
Metro Ind Ctr TW7 5 E5
Meudon Ave GU14 85 B3
Meudon Ct KT6 37 D4
Meville Ct GU2 130 C6
Mews Ct RH19 205 F6
Mews The Banstead SM7 78 B4
Broadbridge Heath RH12 216 D4
Dunsfold GU8 192 F5
Mews The *continued*
[16] Farnham GU9 125 B2
Guildford GU1 130 C8
Mewsend TN16 83 D1
Meyer House [1] SW12 21 B8
Meyrick Cl GU21 68 E3
Mezel Hill Cotts SL4 10 C3
Miall Wlk SE26 23 E4
Michael Cres RH6 161 A1
Michael Fields RH18 206 E2
Michael Rd SE25 42 E6
Michaelmas Cl SW20 39 C6
Michaelson House [4] SE21 22 E4
Michel's Row [2] TW9 6 F4
Micheldever Way RG12 27 F4
Michelet Cl GU18 48 B1
Michelham Gdns
Burgh Heath KT20 97 C7
Twickenham TW1 16 F5
Michell Cl RH12 217 A2
Michels Almshouses [11] TW10 6 E2
Michelsdale Dr [3] TW9 6 E3
Mickle Hill GU47 45 A1
Micklefield Prep Sch RH2 118 A2
Mickleham Dr KT22, RH5 95 C1
Mickleham Gdns SM3 58 E4
Mickleham Hall RH5 115 C7
Mickleham Way CR0 63 D3
Mid Holmwood La RH5 136 B1
Mid St Nutfield RH1 119 F1
South Nutfield RH1 140 F7
Middle Ave GU9 146 D8
Middle Bourne La GU10 146 C7
Middle Church La [12] GU9 125 B2
Middle Cl Coulsdon CR5 100 A7
Ewell KT17 76 E7
Frimley GU15 66 C6
Middle Farm Cl KT24 113 D8
Middle Farm Pl KT24 113 D8
Middle Gn TW18 13 D1
Middle Gordon Rd GU15 65 D5
Middle Green Cl [3] KT5 37 F3
Middle Hill
Aldershot GU11 105 A3
Englefield Green TW20 11 D3
Frensham GU10 146 C1
Middle La Ewell KT17 76 E7
Teddington TW11 16 F2
Middle Mill KT5 37 F6
Middle Old Pk GU9 124 F4
Middle Rd
Leatherhead KT22 95 B6
Mitcham SW16 41 D7
Middle Row [1] RH19 205 F8
Middle St Brockham RH3 137 C5
Croydon CR0, CR9 61 C7
Horsham RH12 217 C2
Shere GU5 133 A4
Middle Way SW16 41 D7
Middlefield Farnham GU9 146 A7
Horley RH6 161 C4
Middlefields CR0 62 E2
Middlemarch GU8 170 E5
Middlemead Cl KT23 94 A2
Middlemead Rd KT23 93 F2
Middlemoor Rd GU16 85 E8
Middlesex Ct KT15 52 C6
Middlesex House [6] SE20 23 C1
Middlesex Rd CR4 41 E4
Middleton Gdns GU14 84 E6
Middleton Rd
Camberley GU15 65 F7
Carshalton CR4, SM5 40 D2
Downside KT11 93 C8
Epsom KT19 57 D1
Horsham RH12 217 A2
Morden SM4 40 D2
Middleton Way RH11 200 E5
Midgarth Cl KT22 74 D6
Midgley Rd RH10 201 F8
Midholm Rd CR0 62 E8
Midhope Cl GU22 89 E8
Midhope Gdns GU22 89 E8
Midhope Rd GU22 89 E8
Midhurst SE26 23 C2
Midhurst Ave CR0 42 A2
Midhurst Cl RH11 201 A7
Midhurst Rd GU27 208 B5
Midleton Cl GU8 149 F2
Midleton Industrial Estate Rd GU2 109 B2
Midleton Rd
Guildford GU2 109 A2
Guildford GU2 109 B2
Kingston u T KT3 38 C7
Midmoor Rd
Streatham SW12 21 C7
Wimbledon SW19 39 E8
Midsummer Ave TW4 4 F3
Midsummer Wlk GU21 69 D3
Midway Cheam SM3, SM4 39 F2
Walton-on-T KT12 54 B8
Midway Ave
Chertsey KT16 33 A6
Chertsey KT16 33 B6
Thorpe TW20 32 B6
Midway Cl TW19 13 B5
Miena Way KT21 75 D2
Mike Hawthorn Dr GU9 125 C3
Milbanke Ct RG12 26 F7
Milbanke Way RG12 26 F7
Milborne Rd RH10 202 C2
Milborough Cres SE12 24 E8
Milbourne La KT10 55 C5
Milbourne Lodge Jun Sch KT10 55 C4
Milbourne Lodge Sch KT10 55 D4
Milbrook KT10 55 C4
Milburn House SW20 39 B7
Milburn Wlk KT18 76 E4
Milden Cl GU16 86 A6
Milden Gdns GU16 85 F6
Mile Path GU22 89 B7
Mile Rd
Carshalton CR4, SM6 41 A1
Wallington CR0, CR4, CR9, SM6 41 C1
Miles Ct CR9 61 B8
Miles La Cobham KT11 73 E6
South Godstone RH9 142 F7
Tandridge RH8, RH9 143 A7
Miles Pl GU18 66 F7
Miles Rd Ash GU12 106 B3
Epsom KT19 76 D7
Mitcham CR4 40 E6
Miles's Hill
Holmbury St M RH5 155 C3
Peaslake RH5 155 C3
Milestone Cl Ripley GU23 91 B5
Sutton SM2 59 D3
Milestone Rd SE19 22 F2
Milford By Pass Rd GU8 149 D2
Milford Gdns CR0 43 D4
Milford Gr SM1 59 C6
Milford Heath Rd GU8 170 E8
Milford Hospl GU7 171 C8
Milford Lodge GU8 170 F8
Milford Mews SW16 21 F5
Milford Rd GU8 148 E4
Milford Sta GU8 171 A7
Milking La
Biggin Hill, Downe BR6 83 E7
Biggin Hill, Leaves Green BR2 83 D8
Mill Bay La RH12 217 B1
Mill Cl Bagshot GU19 47 D3
Carshalton SM5 60 A8
East Grinstead RH19 205 E7
Great Bookham KT23 94 A3
Haslemere GU27 207 E6
Horley RH6 160 E4
Wokingham RG41 25 A7
Mill Copse Rd GU27 208 B4
Mill Cotts
East Grinstead RH19 205 E7
Rudgwick RH12 214 D5
Mill Farm Ave TW16 14 E1
Mill Farm Cres TW4 15 E7
Mill Farm Rd RH13 218 A4
Mill Field GU19 47 D3
Mill Gdns SE26 23 B5
Mill Gn CR4 41 A2
Mill Green Bsns Pk CR4 41 A2
Mill Green Rd CR4 41 A2
Mill Hill RH3 137 B8
Mill Hill La RH3 116 B1
Mill House La KT16 32 B5
Mill La Ascot SL5 30 A7
Bracknell RG12 26 F5
Bramley GU5 151 F6
Byfleet KT14 71 F6
Carshalton SM5 60 A7
Chiddingfold GU8 191 B3
Chilworth GU4, GU5 131 F4
Copthorne RH10 183 E3
Crawley RH11 201 A8
Croydon CR0 61 A7
Dorking RH4 136 B8
Dunsfold GU8 192 F4
Ewell KT17 57 F2
Felbridge RH19 184 E5
Felcourt RH7 164 F2
Fetcham KT22 95 A5
Forest Green RH5 176 D7
Frensham GU10 167 B7
Godalming GU7 150 D4
Guildford GU1 130 D7
Hookwood RH6 160 D3
Horton SL3 1 C4
Kingsley Green GU27 208 C3
Merstham RH1 119 D4
Ockham GU23 91 D8
Oxted RH8 122 F2
Parkgate RH5 158 D5
Pirbright GU24 87 E3
Shalford GU3 130 C1
The Chart RH8 123 F4
Thorpe KT16, TW20 32 C5
Witley GU8 170 F5
Mill Lane Trad Est CR0 60 F7
Mill Mead TW18 12 F4
Mill Pl KT1 37 F6
Mill Plat Isleworth TW7 6 A5
Isleworth TW7 6 B4
Mill Plat Ave TW7 6 A5
Mill Pond Rd GU20 48 B6
Mill Rd Cobham KT11 73 C4
Crawley RH10 202 B7
Epsom KT17 76 F7
Ewell KT17 76 F7
Kingswood KT20 97 D4
Merton SW19 20 C1
South Holmwood RH5 157 D7
Thames Ditton KT10 55 A8
Twickenham TW2 16 C6
Mill Ride SL5 28 D8
Mill Shaw RH8 122 F3
Mill St Colnbrook SL3 1 D7
Kingston u T KT1 37 E6
Redhill RH1 139 F8
Mill Stream GU9 125 E6
Mill Vale BR2 44 F7
Mill View Cl KT17 57 F3
Mill View Gdns CR0 62 D7
Mill Way
East Grinstead RH19 205 E7
Feltham TW14 4 B2
Headley KT22 96 A2
Millais RH13 218 A3
Millais Cl RH11 200 F2
Millais Ct RH13 218 A4
Millais Rd KT3 38 E2
Millais Sch RH13 217 F2
Millais Sch Lower Sch RH13 217 F2
Millais Way KT19 57 C6
Millan Cl KT15 52 B1
Milland House [11] SW15 19 A7
Millbank SM6 60 D5
Millbank The RH11 200 F6
Millbourne Rd TW13 15 E4
Millbrook Guildford GU1 130 D7
Oatlands Park KT13 53 E6
Millbrook Way SL3 1 E5
Millcombe Cl [5] GU21 69 B1
Millcroft House SE6 24 B4
Miller House [9] SW2 21 E8
Miller Rd Guildford GU4 110 C4
Mitcham SW19 20 D2
Thornton Heath CR0 42 A1
Miller's Ct TW20 12 D2
Miller's La RH1 162 C7
Millers Cl TW18 13 B3
Millers Copse
Langley Vale KT18 96 D8
Outwood RH1 162 B7
Millers Gate RH12 217 D6
Millers Mead Ct SW19 20 D1
Millfarm Bsns Pk TW4 15 E8
Millfield Charlton TW16 34 D8
Kingston u T KT1 37 F6
Millfield La KT20 98 A2
Millfield Rd TW4 15 F7
Millford GU21 69 B2
Millford Cty Inf Sch GU8 149 F1
Millgate Ct GU9 125 D3
Millhedge Cl KT11 73 E3
Millholme Wlk GU15 66 C4
Millhouse Pl SE27 22 B4
Millins Cl GU47 45 E1
Millmead Byfleet KT14 71 F7
Guildford GU2 130 C7
Wokingham RG41 25 A7
Millmead Terr GU2 130 C7
Millpond Cotts GU8 172 D4
Millpond Ct KT15 52 E5
Mills Ho GU12 105 D3
Mills Spur SL4 11 B8
Mills's Rd KT12 54 C5
Millside SM5 59 F8
Millside Ct KT23 94 A2
Millside Pl TW7 6 B5
Millstream The GU27 207 E5
Millthorpe Rd RH12 217 F4
Millview Cl RH2 118 D3
Millway RH2 118 D1
Millwood RH10 204 E5
Millwood Rd TW3, TW7 5 C2
Milman Cl RG12 28 A7
Milne Cl RH11 200 E3
Milne Pk E CR0 82 D8
Milne Pk W CR0 82 D8
Milner App CR3 101 A6
Milner Cl CR3 101 A5
Milner Dr Cobham KT11 73 F7
Twickenham TW2 16 D8
Milner Rd Caterham CR3 101 A6
Kingston u T KT1 37 D6
Merton SW19 40 B8
Morden CR4, SM4 40 D4
South Norwood CR7 42 D6
Milnthorpe Rd W4 7 D8
Milnwood Rd RH12 217 C3
Milstead Cl KT20 97 B5
Milton Ave Carshalton SM1 59 E6
Croydon CR0 42 D2
Westcott RH4 135 D6
Milton Cl Bracknell RG12 27 B3
Carshalton SM1 59 D7
Horton SL3 1 A4
Milton Cres RH19 205 C8
Milton Ct Kingston u T KT2 17 E4
Twickenham TW2 16 E5
Wokingham RG40 25 B7
Milton Dr Littleton TW17 33 E5
Wokingham RG40 25 B7
Milton Gdns Epsom KT18 76 E5
Stanwell TW19 13 F7
Wokingham RG40 25 B6
Milton Grange GU12 106 A5
Milton House
[12] Beckenham BR3 24 A1
[5] Kingston u T KT2 18 B2
Sutton SM1 59 A7
Milton Lodge TW1 16 F8
Milton Mount RH10 182 D1
Milton Mount Ave RH10 202 D8
Milton Mount Cty Fst & Mid Sch RH10 202 C8
Milton Rd Addlestone KT15 52 A4
Caterham CR3 100 D6
Crawley RH10 202 C7
Croydon CR0 42 D2
Egham TW20 11 F3
Hampton TW12 36 B8
Horsham RH12 217 C3
Mitcham CR4 21 A1

Milton Rd *continued*
Mortlake SW14 7 D4
Sutton SM1 59 A6
Wallington SM6 60 D4
Walton-on-T KT12 54 D7
Wimbledon SW19 20 C2
Wokingham RG40, RG41 25 B6
Milton St RH4 135 D6
Milton Way KT23 94 C2
Miltoncourt La RH4 135 E7
Miltons Cres GU7 150 B2
Milverton House SE23 23 E5
Milward Gdns RG12 26 C7
Mina Rd SW19 40 A8
Minard Rd SE6 24 E7
Minchin Cl KT22 95 A5
Mincing La GU24 49 F2
Minden Rd Cheam SM3 58 F8
Penge SE20 43 B8
Mindleheim Ave RH19 186 B2
Minehead Rd SW16 21 F3
Minehurst Rd GU16 85 F4
Minerva Cl TW19 2 A2
Minerva Rd KT1 37 F7
Minimax Cl TW14 4 A1
Mink Ct TW4 4 C5
Minley Cl GU14 84 E4
Minley Rd Blackwater GU17 84 A7
Farnborough GU14 84 D5
Minniedale KT5 37 F4
Minorca Ave GU16 66 E2
Minorca Rd Frimley GU16 66 E1
Weybridge KT13 53 A6
Minshull Pl 24 BR3 24 A1
Minstead Cl RG12 27 F6
Minstead Gdns SW15 18 F8
Minstead Way KT3 38 E3
Minster Ave SM1 59 A8
Minster Ct Camberley GU15 65 D7
Camberley, York Town GU15 64 F4
Minster Dr CR0 61 E6
Minster Gdns KT8 35 F5
Minster Rd GU7 150 E1
Minsterley Ave
TW16, TW17 34 E5
Minstrel Gdns KT5 37 F5
Mint Gdns RH4 136 A8
Mint La KT20 118 A6
Mint Rd
Wallington SM5, SM6 60 B6
Woodmansterne SM7 78 C3
Mint St GU7 150 D4
Mint The GU7 150 D4
Mint Wlk Croydon CR0, CR9 61 C7
Knaphill GU21 68 E2
Warlingham CR6 81 D2
Miranda Wlk RH11 200 E4
Mirfield Ct SE20 43 A7
Misbrooks Green
Rd RH5 178 E8
Missenden Cl TW14 14 F7
Missenden Gdns SM4 40 C3
Mission Sq 13 TW8 6 E8
Mistletoe Cl CR0 43 D1
Mistley Ct 6 KT18 76 D6
Misty's Field KT12 35 C1
Mitcham Garden Village
CR4 41 A4
Mitcham Ind Est CR4 41 A8
Mitcham Junc CR4 41 A4
Mitcham La SW16 21 C3
Mitcham Pk CR4 40 F5
Mitcham Rd
Camberley GU15 47 A1
Thornton Heath CR0, CR9 41 F3
Upper Tooting SW17 20 F3
Mitcham Sta CR4 40 E5
Mitchell Gdns RH13 215 E3
Mitchell's Row GU4 130 E2
Mitchells Cl GU4 130 E3
Mitchells Cotts GU4 131 E1
Mitchells Rd RH10 201 F6
Mitchley Ave CR2, CR8 80 D6
Mitchley Gr CR2 81 A6
Mitchley Hill CR2 80 F6
Mitchley View CR2 81 A6
Mitford Cl KT9 56 C4
Mitford Wlk 11 RH11 201 A3
Mitre Cl Shepperton TW17 34 D3
Sutton SM2 59 D3
Mixbury Gr KT13 53 D4
Mixnams La KT16 33 A6
Mizen Cl KT11 73 D5
Mizen Way KT11 73 D4
Moat Ct Ashstead KT21 75 E2
Ottershaw KT16 51 C4
Moat Rd RH19 185 E2
Moat Side TW13 15 C4
Moat The KT3 38 E8
Moat Wlk RH10 202 C7
Moats La RH1 140 F3
Moberly Rd SW4 21 D8
Model Cotts SW14 7 C4
Moffat Ct
Upper Tooting SW17 20 E4
Wimbledon SW19 20 A3
Moffat Rd
South Norwood CR7 42 D7
Upper Tooting SW17 20 F4
Moffatts Cl GU47 64 A8
Mogador Cotts KT20 117 D7
Mogador Rd KT20 117 E7
Mogden La TW7 5 F2
Moir Cl CR2 62 A2
Moira Ct SW17 21 A6
Mole Abbey Gdns KT8 36 B6
Mole Bsns Pk KT22 95 A6
Mole Cl Crawley RH11 201 B8
Farnborough GU14 84 D6
Mole Ct KT19 57 C6
Mole House KT12 54 E5
Mole Rd Fetcham KT22 94 D6
Hersham KT12 54 D5
Mole St RH5 177 B5
Mole Valley Pl KT21 95 D8
Molember Ct KT7 36 E5
Molember Rd KT8 36 E4
Moles Cl RG40 25 D5
Moles Hill KT22 74 D8
Molesey Ave KT12, KT8 35 F4
Molesey Cl KT12 54 E6
Molesey Dr SM3 58 E7
Molesey Hospl KT8 36 A4
Molesey Park Ave KT8 36 B4
Molesey Park Cl KT8 36 C4
Molesey Park Rd KT8 36 C4
Molesey Rd
East Molesey KT12 35 E2
Hersham KT12 54 D5
Molesham Cl KT8 36 B6
Molesham Way KT8 36 B6
Molesley Rd Hersham KT12 54 E8
Walton-on-T KT12 54 E8
Molesworth Rd KT11 73 A6
Moliner Ct 4 BR3 24 A1
Molins Ct 5 RH11 201 A3
Mollie Davis Ct SE19 22 F2
Mollison Dr SM6 60 E3
Molly Huggins Cl SW12 21 C8
Molly Millar Bridge RG41 25 B4
Molly Millar's La RG41 25 A4
Molyneux Dr SW17 21 B4
Molyneux Rd
Farncombe GU7 150 F7
Weybridge KT13 53 A5
Windlesham GU20 48 D4
Monahan Ave CR8 79 F8
Monarch Cl Coney Hall BR4 63 F6
Crawley RH11 201 A3
East Bedfont TW14 14 E8
Monarch Mews
SE27, SW16 22 A3
Monarch Par CR4 40 F7
Monaveen Gdns KT8 36 B6
Monby Lodge Inf Sch
KT13 53 C5
Mondial Way UB7 3 C7
Money Ave CR3 100 E5
Money Rd CR3 100 D5
Monivea Rd BR3 23 F1
Monk's Wlk
Farnham GU10, GU9 146 F8
Reigate RH2 118 B1
Monkleigh Rd SM4, SW20 39 E5
Monks Ave KT8 35 F4
Monks Cl Ascot SL5 29 B3
Farnborough GU14 85 C4
Monks Cres
Addlestone KT15 52 B5
Walton-on-T KT12 35 B1
Monks Ct RH2 118 B1
Monks Dr SL5 29 B3
Monks Gn KT22 94 D6
Monks La
Limpsfield RH8, TN8 144 E6
Rowhook RH5 196 F5
Monks Orchard Rd
Beckenham BR3, CR0 44 A1
Croydon BR3, CR0 44 A1
Monks Orchard Sch CR0 43 D4
Monks Rd Banstead SM7 78 A3
Virginia Water GU25 31 D5
Monks Way Beckenham BR3 44 A3
Harmondsworth UB7 2 E8
Staines TW18 13 D1
Monks' Well GU10 147 C8
Monks Wlk SL5 29 B3
Monksdene Gdns SM1 59 B7
Monksfield RH10 201 F7
Monkshanger GU9 125 E2
Monkshood Cl RG40 25 E7
Monkswell La CR5 98 B2
Monkton La GU9 125 E5
Monkton Pk GU9 125 F4
Monmouth Ave KT1 17 C1
Monmouth Cl CR4, SW16 41 E5
Mono La TW13 15 B6
Monro Dr GU2 109 B4
Monroe Dr SW14 7 B2
Mons Cl GU11 105 E7
Mons Wlk TW20 12 C3
Monsell Gdns TW18 12 E3
Monson Rd RH1 118 F4
Montacute Cl GU14 85 D4
Montacute Rd
Forest Hill SE23, SE6 23 F8
Morden SM4 40 D3
New Addington CR0 63 C2
Montagu Gdns SM6 60 C6
Montague Ave CR2 80 E7
Montague Cl
Camberley GU15 65 B5
Lightwater GU18 48 A1
Walton-on-T KT12 35 A2
Wokingham RG40 25 E7
Montague Dr CR3 100 C5
Montague House (Coll &
Liby) RG40 25 C6
Montague Rd Hounslow TW3 5 B4
Merton SW19 20 B1
Richmond TW10 6 E1
Thornton Heath CR0 42 B1
Montana Cl CR2 61 D1
Montana Gdns
Beckenham SE6 23 F3
5 Sutton SM1 59 C5
Montana Rd
Upper Tooting SW17 21 A5
Wimbledon SW20 39 C8
Montem Rd Forest Hill SE23 23 F8
New Malden KT3 38 E5
Montford Rd TW16 35 A5
Montfort Pl SW19 19 D7
Montfort Rise RH1 139 F1
Montgomerie Dr GU2 109 A6
Montgomery Ave KT10 55 E8
Montgomery Cl
Mitcham CR4 41 E5
Sandhurst GU47 64 B8
Montgomery Ct
Chiswick W4 7 C8
Leatherhead KT22 95 C7
Montgomery House 5
SW14 7 D4
Montgomery Rd
Farnborough GU14 84 F3
2 Woking GU22 69 E1
Montpelier Ct BR2 44 F5
Montpelier Rd
Purley CR2, CR8 61 B1
South Croydon CR2, CR8 61 B1
Sutton SM1 59 C6
Montpelier Row TW1 17 C8
Montrave Rd SE20 23 C1
Montrell Rd SW2 21 E7
Montreux Ct RH11 201 B6
Montrose Ave TW2 16 B8
Montrose Cl Ashford TW15 14 C3
Frimley GU16 65 E2
Montrose Gdns
Mitcham CR4 40 F7
Oxshott KT22 74 D7
Sutton SM1 59 B8
Montrose Rd TW14 3 D1
Montrose Way SE23 23 D7
Montrose Wlk KT13 53 B7
Montrouge Cres KT17 77 C3
Montserrat Cl SE19 22 D3
Monument Bridge Ind Est
E GU21 70 B4
Monument Bridge
Ind Est W GU21 70 A4
Monument Hill KT13 53 B6
Monument Hill Cty Prim
Sch GU22 70 C4
Monument Rd
Sheerwater GU21 70 B4
Weybridge KT13 53 B7
Monument Way E GU21 70 B4
Monument Way W GU21 70 A4
Moon Ct KT22 94 D6
Moon's La RH19, RH7, TN8 186 E8
Moons Hill GU10 146 C2
Moons La RH13 217 E1
Moor Cl GU47 45 E1
Moor House Sch RH8 122 F3
Moor La Chessington KT9 56 E5
Harmondsworth UB7 2 C8
Lingfield RH7, TN8 165 D3
Staines TW18 12 D6
Stanwell TW19 12 D6
Woking GU22 89 F5
Moor Lane Jun Sch KT9 56 F5
Moor Mead Rd TW1 6 A1
Moor Park Cres RH11 200 D5
Moor Park Gdns KT2 18 E1
Moor Park House RG12 26 E3
Moor Park La GU10, GU9 126 A2
Moor Park Way GU9 125 F2
Moor Pl
East Grinstead RH19 185 D2
Windlesham GU20 48 B5
Moor Rd Farnborough GU14 85 A8
Frimley GU16 85 F8
Linchmere GU27 207 C5
Moorcroft RH9 121 C3
Moorcroft Cl RH11 201 B7
Moorcroft Rd SW16 21 E5
Moordale Ave RG42 26 E8
Moore Cl Addlestone KT15 52 B5
Ash GU10 126 F8
Mitcham CR4 41 B7
Mortlake SW14 7 C4
Wallington SM6 60 E3
Moore Ct RH12 217 A1
Moore Grove Cres TW20 11 F1
Moore House 1 SE27 22 C4
Moore Rd Pirbright GU24 87 B6
South Norwood SE19 22 C2
Moore Way SM2 59 A2
Moore's Rd RH4, RH5 136 B8
Mooreland Rd BR1 24 F1
Moores Gn RG40 25 E8
Moorfield GU27 207 F5
Moorfield Ctr The GU1 109 D5
Moorfield Rd
Chessington KT9 56 E5
Guildford GU1 109 E5
Moorfields Cl TW18 32 E8
Moorfields Ct 6 SW16 21 C4
Moorhayes Dr TW18 33 C6
Moorhead Rd RH12 218 B5
Moorholme GU22 89 E8
Moorhouse Rd RH8 123 F5
Moorhurst La RH5 157 B4
Moorings The
East Grinstead RH19 185 A3
Hindhead GU26 188 E3
Moorland Cl
Crawley RH10 202 C3
Twickenham TW4 16 A8
Moorland Rd UB7 2 C8
Moorlands KT12 54 A7
Moorlands Cl GU26 188 E4
Moorlands Pl GU15 65 B5
Moorlands Rd GU15 65 B4
Moorlands The GU22 89 F6
Moormead Dr KT19 57 E5
Moormede Cres TW18 12 F4
Moors La GU8 148 C3
Moors The GU10 126 F7
Moorside Cl GU14 65 A1
Moorside Rd BR1 24 F4
Moorsom Way CR5 79 D2
Moray Ave GU47 64 D7
Moray House 11 KT6 37 E4
Mordaunt Dr RG45 45 B3
Morden Cl Bracknell RG12 27 F5
Burgh Heath KT20 97 D7
Morden Court Par SM4 40 A5
Morden Ct SM4 40 B5
Morden Farm Mid Sch
SM4 39 E2
Morden Fst Sch SM4 40 A4
Morden Gdns CR4 40 D5
Morden Hall Park SW19 40 C6
Morden Hall
Rd SM4, SW19 40 C5
Morden House SM4 40 A5
Morden Park Sch Sports
Ctr SM4 39 F4
Morden Rd Merton SW19 40 B7
Mitcham CR4, SM4, SW19 40 D5
Morden Road Sta SW19 40 B7
Morden South Sta SM4 40 A4
Morden Sta SW19 40 B6
Morden Way SM3 40 A2
Mordred Rd SE6 24 E6
More Circ GU7 150 E7
More Cl CR8 80 A8
More House Sch GU10 146 C2
More La KT10 55 B7
More Rd GU7 150 E7
Morecambe Cl RH11 200 F4
Morecoombe Cl KT2 18 B1
Morecote Cl GU4 130 E2
Moreland Ave SL3 1 C7
Moreland Cl SL3 1 C7
Morella Cl GU25 31 D5
Morella Rd SW11, SW12 20 F8
Moremead Rd SE6 24 A4
Morena St SE6 24 B8
Moresby Ave KT5 38 B2
Moreton Ave TW7 5 E6
Moreton Cl GU10 167 E1
Moreton Green Fst Sch
SM4 40 D4
Moreton House SW17 20 D4
Moreton Rd
North Cheam KT4 58 B8
South Croydon CR2 61 D5
Morgan Ct TW15 14 B3
Moring Rd SW17 21 A4
Morkyns Wlk SE21 22 E5
Morland Ave CR0 42 E1
Morland Cl Hampton TW12 15 F3
Mitcham CR4 40 E6
Morland Rd
Aldershot GU11 126 C6
Croydon CR0 42 F2
Penge SE20 23 D2
Sutton SM1 59 C5
Morland's Rd GU11 105 D5
Morley Ct Beckenham BR3 44 D8
Beckenham BR2 44 F5
Sunningdale SL5 29 F3
Morley House SW2 21 E8
Morley Rd Cheam SM3 39 F1
Farnham GU9 125 D1
South Croydon CR2 61 F1
Twickenham TW1 6 D1
Morningside Rd KT4 58 C8
Mornington Cl TN16 83 D2
Mornington Cres TW5 4 B6
Mornington Rd TW15 14 C3
Mornington Wlk TW10 17 C4
Morrell Ave
Horsham RH12 217 F6
Horsham RH12 218 A6
Morris Cl BR3, CR0 43 E4
Morris Gdns SW18 20 A8
Morris Rd
Farnborough GU14 105 D8
Isleworth TW7 5 F4
South Nutfield RH1 140 E7
Morrish Rd SW2 21 E8
Morrison Ct 5 RH11 201 B1
Morrison House SW2 22 A7
Morriss Ct 3 RH2 118 F1
Morston Cl KT20 97 B7
Mortaine Rd TW15 13 D5
Mortimer Cl SW16 21 D6
Mortimer Cres KT4 57 D7
Mortimer Lodge 11 SW19 19 E7
Mortimer Rd
Biggin Hill TN16 83 C7
Capel RH5 178 D6
Mitcham CR4 40 F8
Mortimer Sch SW16 21 D6
Mortlake Cl CR0 60 E7
Mortlake Dr CR4 40 E8
Mortlake High St SW14 7 D4
Mortlake Rd SW14, TW9 7 A6
Mortlake Sta SW14 7 C4
Morton KT20 97 D6
Morton Cl Frimley GU16 85 F7
Woking GU21 69 D4
Morton Gdns SM6 60 C5
Morton House SE27 22 D3
Morton Rd
East Grinstead RH19 205 E7
Morden CR4, SM4 40 D4
Woking GU21 69 D4
Morval Cl GU14 84 E4
Morven Rd SW17 20 F5
Moselle Cl GU14 84 D5
Moselle Rd TN16 83 F1
Mosford Cl RH6 160 F5
Mospey Cres KT17 76 F4
Moss Gdns CR2 62 D3
Moss La GU7 150 D4
Moss Lane Cty Inf Sch
GU7 150 D4
Mossfield KT11 73 A6
Mosslea Rd Kenley CR3 80 F2
Penge SE20 23 C2
Mossville Gdns SM4, SW20 39 F5
Mostyn Rd SW19 39 F7
Mostyn Terr RH1 140 A8
Motspur Park Sta KT3 39 B4
Motspur Pk KT3 39 A3
Motts Hill La
Tadworth KT20 97 A4
Walton on t H KT20 97 A4
Mouchotte Cl TN16 83 C7
Moulton Ave TW3, TW5 4 F5
Mount Adon Pk SE21, SE22 23 A8
Mount Angelus Rd SW15 18 F8
Mount Ararat Rd TW10 6 E2
Mount Arlington BR2 44 E7
Mount Ash Rd SE26 23 B5
Mount Ave CR3 100 C3
Mount Cl Crawley RH10 202 D7
Ewhurst GU6 175 E5
Fetcham KT22 94 F4
Kenley CR8 80 D3
Wallington SM5 60 A2
Woking GU22 89 C6
Mount Cl The GU25 31 D3
Mount Ct Guildford GU2 130 C7
6 Kingston u T KT2 18 B1
West Wickham BR4 63 E8
Mount Dr The RH2 118 D3
Mount Ephraim La SW16 21 D5
Mount Ephraim Rd SW16 21 E5
Mount Felix KT12 34 F2
Mount Gdns SE26 23 B5
Mount Hermon Cl GU22 69 E1
Mount Hermon Rd GU22 69 E1
Mount La Bracknell RG12 27 C7
Turners Hill RH10 204 A4
Mount Lee TW20 11 F3
Mount Nod Rd SW16, SW2 21 F5
Mount Park Ave CR2 61 B2
Mount Pk SM5 60 A2
Mount Pl GU1 130 C7
Mount Pleasant
Biggin Hill TN16 83 D2
Bracknell RG12 27 C6
Effingham KT24 113 E7
Ewell KT17 57 F1
Farnham GU9 125 A1
Guildford GU2 130 C7
Sandhurst GU47 45 A1
West Horsley KT24 112 B6
West Norwood SE27 22 C4
Weybridge KT13 53 A7
Wokingham RG41 25 A6
Mount Pleasant Cl GU18 48 A1
Mount Pleasant Rd
Aldershot GU12 105 C2
Caterham CR3 101 A4
Kingston u T KT3 38 C6
Lingfield RH7 164 C4
Mount Prim Sch The KT3 38 C6
Mount Rd Chessington KT9 56 F5
Chobham GU24 69 B7
Cranleigh GU6 174 E2
Feltham TW13 15 E5
Kingston u T KT3 38 D6
Mitcham CR4 40 E7
South Norwood SE19 22 D2
Wimbledon SW18, SW19 20 B6
Woking GU22 89 B6
Mount Rise Forest Hill SE23 23 C6
Reigate RH1 139 D7
Mount St RH4 136 A7
Mount The Cranleigh GU6 174 E2
Esher KT10 55 A4
Ewell KT17 57 F1
Ewhurst GU6 175 E5
Fetcham KT22 94 E4
Grayswood GU27 189 F1
Guildford GU2 130 C7
Headley Down GU35 187 A6
Lower Kingswood KT20 97 F1
New Malden KT3 38 F6
North Cheam KT4 58 B6
Oatlands Park KT13 53 E8
Rusper RH11, RH12 180 B1
Rusper RH12 200 B8
Wallington CR5 79 B5
Warlingham CR6 101 A8
Wentworth GU25 31 D3
Woking GU21, GU22 69 D1
Mount View GU11 105 A1
Mount View Rd KT10 56 B3
Mount Villas SE27 22 B5
Mount Way SM5 60 A2
Mountacre Cl SE26 23 A4
Mountbatten Cl
Crawley RH11 201 C2
6 West Norwood SE19 22 E3
Mountbatten Ct 15 GU11 105 A2
Mountbatten Gdns BR3 43 E5
Mountbatten Rise GU47 45 A1
Mountcombe Cl KT6 37 E2

Mountearl Gdns
SW16, SW2 21 F5
Mountfield Cl SE6 24 D8
Mounthurst Rd BR2 44 F2
Mounts Hill SL4, SL5 9 C3
Mountsfield Cl TW19 2 A2
Mountside Caterham CR3 100 F3
Guildford GU2 130 C7
Mountview 5 SW16 21 F5
Mountview Cl RH1 139 E7
Mountview Dr RH1 139 E7
Mountwood KT8 36 B6
Mountwood Cl CR2 62 B1
Moushill La GU8 170 E8
Mowat Ct KT4 57 F8
Mowbray Ave KT14 71 E6
Mowbray Cres TW20 12 A3
Mowbray Ct SE19 42 F8
Mowbray Dr RH11 200 F4
Mowbray Gdns RH4 115 B1
Mowbray Rd
Richmond TW10 17 C5
South Norwood SE19 42 F8
Mower Cl RG40 25 F7
Mower Pl GU6 174 E4
Moyne Ct 3 GU21 68 F1
Moyne Rd RH11 201 C2
Moyser Rd SW16, SW17 21 B3
Muchelney Rd SM4 40 C3
Muckhatch La TW20 32 B7
Mudie House 8 SW2 21 E8
Muggeridge's Hill
Capel RH12, RH5 198 E8
Rusper RH12, RH5 198 E8
Muirdown Ave SW14 7 D3
Muirfield Cl RH11 200 D5
Muirfield House RG12 26 E3
Muirfield Rd GU21 69 A1
Muirkirk Rd SE6 24 C7
Mulberries The GU9 125 F4
Mulberry Ave TW19 13 E7
Mulberry Bsns Pk RG41 25 A4
Mulberry Cl Ash GU12 106 A4
Crowthorne RG45 45 C4
Horsham RH12 217 C5
1 Sandhurst GU47 64 D8
Streatham SW16 21 C4
Weybridge KT13 53 B7
Woking GU21 69 E5
Mulberry Cres TW8 6 C7
Mulberry Ct Ashstead KT21 75 D1
1 Bracknell RG12 27 F4
Guildford GU4 110 D3
4 Surbiton KT6 37 D2
Twickenham TW1 16 F5
Wokingham RG40 25 C6
Mulberry La CR0 42 F1
Mulberry Mews 2 SM6 60 C4
Mulberry Rd RH11 181 B1
Mulberry Trees TW17 34 D2
Mulgrave Chambers SM2 59 B4
Mulgrave Manor SM2 59 B4
Mulgrave Rd Belmont SM2 59 A4
Croydon CR0, CR9 61 D7
Frimley GU16 65 F2
Sutton SM2 59 A4
Mulgrave Way GU21 68 E1
Mulholland Cl CR4 41 B7
Mullards Cl CR4 40 F1
Mullein Wlk RH11 201 A2
Mullens Rd TW20 12 C3
Mullins Path SW14 7 D4
Mulroy Dr GU15 66 A6
Multon Rd SW18 20 D8
Muncaster Cl TW15 14 A4
Muncaster Rd TW15 14 B3
Muncies Mews SE6 24 C6
Munday's Boro GU3 128 A4
Munday's Boro Rd GU3 128 B4
Munnings Dr GU47 64 E6
Munnings Gdns TW7 5 D2
Munro Way GU14 105 D8
Munroe House RH2 139 A6
Munslow Gdns SM1 59 D6
Munstead Ct SM2 59 C3
Munstead Heath Rd
Bramley GU5, GU7, GU8 151 C3
Godalming GU5, GU7, GU8 151 C3
Munstead Pk GU8 151 C2
Munstead View GU3 130 C4
Munstead View Rd GU5 151 D5
Munster Ave TW4 4 E2
Munster Ct TW11 17 C2
Munster Rd TW11 17 C2
Murdoch Cl TW18 13 A3
Murdoch Rd RG40 25 D5
Murfett Cl SW19 19 E6
Murray Ave TW3 5 B2
Murray Ct Ascot SL5 29 C3
Crawley RH11 201 A1
Horsham RH13 218 B4
Murray Gn GU21 70 C5
Murray House KT16 51 D4
Murray Rd
Farnborough GU14 84 F3
Ottershaw KT15, KT16 51 D5
Richmond TW10 17 C6
Wimbledon SW19 19 D2
Wokingham RG41 25 A6
Murray's La KT14 71 E5
Murray's Rd GU11 105 D5
Murrell Rd GU12 106 A3
Murrellhill La RG42 26 C8
Murrells La GU15 65 B3
Murrells Wlk KT23 94 A3
Murreys The KT21 75 D1
Muschamp Inf Sch SM5 59 E8
Muschamp Jun Sch SM5 59 E8
Muschamp Rd SM1, SM5 59 E8
Museum Hill GU27 208 D6
Museum of Richmond
TW10 6 D2
Musgrave Ave RH19 205 E8
Musgrave Rd TW7 5 F6
Mushroom Castle La RG42 8 B2
Musical Museum The TW8 6 E8
Musquash Way TW4 4 C5
Mustard Mill Rd TW18 12 F4
Mutton Hill RH7 186 B7
Mutton Oaks RG12 26 D8
Muybridge Rd KT3 38 C7
Mychell House 8 SW19 20 C1
Mychett Cty Fst Sch GU16 85 F4
Mychett Heath GU16 86 A3
Myers Way GU16 66 D2
Mylis Cl SE26 23 B4
Mylne Sq RG40 25 D6
Mylor Cl GU21 69 E5
Mynn's Cl KT18 76 B5
Mynterne Ct 10 SW19 19 D7
Myrna Cl SW19 20 E1
Myrtle Ave TW14 3 E2
Myrtle Cl Lightwater GU18 67 B8
Poyle SL3 1 E6
Myrtle Dr GU17 64 D5
Myrtle Gr KT3 38 C7
Myrtle Rd Croydon CR0 63 A7
Dorking RH4 136 A8
Hampton TW12 16 C2
Hounslow TW3 5 C5
Sutton SM1 59 C5
Mytchett Lake Rd GU16 86 A1
Mytchett Place Rd
Mytchett GU12, GU16 86 C1
Normandy GU12, GU16, GU24 86 C1
Mytchett Rd GU12, GU16 85 F3
Myton Rd SE21 22 D5

N

Naafi Rdbt GU11 105 B2
Nadine Ct SM6 60 C2
Nailsworth Cres RH1 119 D6
Nairn Cl GU16 65 E2
Nairn Ct 3 Wallington SM6 60 C4
Wimbledon SW19 20 B2
Naldrett Cl RH12 217 F4
Naldretts La RH12 214 D5
Nallhead Rd TW13 15 C3
Namba Roy Cl SW16 21 F4
Namton Dr CR7, SW16 41 F5
Napier Cl Crowthorne RG45 45 D5
Farnborough GU11 105 E7
Napier Ct Caterham CR3 100 E5
10 Croydon CR0 61 F8
1 Surbiton KT6 37 D2
Woking GU21 69 E3
Napier Dr GU15 66 A8
Napier Gdns GU1 110 B2
Napier Lodge TW15 14 D2
Napier Rd Ashford TW15 14 D1
Crowthorne RG45 45 C4
Croydon SE25 43 B5
Harmondsworth TW6 2 D6
Isleworth TW7 6 A3
South Croydon CR2 61 D3
Napier Way RH10 182 A1
Napier Wlk TW15 14 D1
Napoleon Ave GU14 85 B6
Napoleon Rd TW1 17 B8
Napper Cl SL5 28 D7
Napper Pl GU6 174 E1
Narrow La CR6 101 B8
Naseby RG12 27 B1
Naseby Cl TW7 5 E6
Naseby Rd SE19 22 D2
Nash Cl Farnborough GU14 84 F4
Sutton SM1 59 D7
Nash Dr 6 RH1 119 A3
Nash Gdns North Ascot SL5 28 E7
Redhill RH1 118 F3
Nash Rd RH10 201 E3
Nassau Rd SW13 7 F6
Nasturtium Dr GU24 68 A4
Natal Rd
South Norwood CR7 42 D6
Streatham SW16 21 D2
Natalie Cl TW14 14 D8
Natalie Mews TW2 16 D5
National Physical
Laboratory TW11 16 E2
National Wks TW4 4 F4
Nayland House SE6 24 C4
Neale Cl RH19 185 B3
Neath Gdns SM4 40 C3
Neb La RH8 122 D4
Needles Bank RH9 121 B4
Needles Cl RH12 217 B1
Neelem Ct GU14 85 C1
Neil Cl TW15 14 C3
Neil Wates Cres 18 SW2 22 A7
Nelgarde Rd Catford SE6 24 A8
Lewisham SE6 24 A8
Nell Ball RH14 211 E2
Nell Gwynn Ave TW17 34 D3
Nell Gwynne Ave SL5 29 D5
Nell Gwynne Cl SL5 29 D5
Nello James Gdns SE27 22 D4
Nelson Cl Aldershot GU12 105 D1
Biggin Hill TN16 83 E2
Bracknell RG12 27 E7
Crawley RH10 202 C5
East Bedfont TW14 14 F7
Heath End GU9 125 D8
Thornton Heath CR0 42 B1
Nelson Cl *continued*
Walton-on-T KT12 35 B1
Nelson Ct Carshalton SM5 59 F7
Chertsey KT16 33 A1
Nelson Gdns
Guildford GU1 110 A2
Twickenham TW3, TW4 5 A1
Nelson Grove Rd SW19 40 C8
Nelson Ho 19 GU11 105 A2
Nelson Hospl SW20 39 F7
Nelson Prim Sch TW2 5 B1
Nelson Rd Ashford TW15 13 E3
Caterham CR3 100 D4
Harmondsworth TW6 2 F6
Heath End GU9 125 D8
Horsham RH12 217 C3
Merton SW19 20 C1
New Malden KT3 38 D4
Twickenham TW2, TW4 16 B8
Nelson St 3 GU11 105 A2
Nelson Trad Est SW19 40 B8
Nelson Way GU15 64 F4
Nene Gdns TW13 15 F6
Nene Rd TW6, UB7 3 B6
Nepean St 4 SW15 19 A8
Neptune Cl RH11 200 E4
Neptune Rd TW6 3 C6
Nesbit Ct RH11 200 E3
Nesbitt Sq SE19 22 E1
NESCOT Epsom's Coll of
FE & HE KT17 77 A8
Nether Mount GU2 130 B7
Netheravon Rd S W4 7 F8
Netherby Pk KT13 53 E5
Netherby Rd SE23 23 C8
Nethercote Ave GU21 68 F2
Netherfield Rd SW17 21 A5
Netherlands The CR5 99 C8
Netherleigh Pk RH1 140 E6
Nethern Court Rd CR3 102 A4
Netherne La CR5 99 C5
Netherton RG12 27 A5
Netherton Rd TW1 6 B2
Netherwood RH11 201 B4
Netherwood Ct GU7 150 E5
Netley Cl Cheam SM3 58 D5
New Addington CR0 63 C3
Netley Dr KT12 35 F2
Netley Gdns SM4 40 C2
Netley Rd Brentford TW8 6 E8
Morden SM4 40 C2
Netley Rd (W) TW6 3 D6
Netley St GU14 105 C8
Nettlecombe RG12 27 D3
Nettlecombe Cl SM2 59 B2
Nettlefold Pl SE27 22 B5
Nettles Terr 3 GU1 109 D1
Nettlestead Cl BR3 23 F1
Nettleton Rd TW6 3 B6
Nettlewood Rd SW16 21 D1
Neuchatel Rd SE6 23 F6
Nevada Cl
Farnborough GU14 84 D3
Kingston u T KT3 38 C5
Nevelle Cl RG42 26 D8
Nevile Cl RH11 201 A3
Neville Ave KT3 38 D8
Neville Cl Banstead SM7 78 B5
Esher KT10 54 F4
Hounslow TW3 5 B5
Neville Ct 10 SW12 21 C8
Neville Duke Rd GU14 84 F8
Neville Rd Croydon CR0 42 D2
Kingston u T KT1 38 A7
Richmond TW10 17 C6
Neville Wlk SM5 40 E2
Nevis Rd SW17 21 A6
New Barn La Kenley CR3 80 E3
Wallis Wood RH5 177 A3
New Barns Ave CR4 41 D5
New Beckenham Sta BR3 23 F1
New Belmont House 4
SE23 23 C7
New Berry La KT12 54 D5
New Chapel Sq TW13 15 B7
New Church Ct 3 SE19 23 A1
New Cl Feltham TW13 15 E3
Mitcham SW19 40 C6
New Colebrooke Ct SM5 60 A3
New Cotts
Betchworth RH3 116 D4
Sidlow RH2 138 F1
Turners Hill RH10 204 A4
New Cross Rd GU2 109 B3
New Cswy RH2 139 C6
New Ct KT15 52 C7
New Dawn Cl GU14 84 D3
New Epsom & Ewell
Cottage Hospl The KT19 75 E8
New Farthingdale RH7 186 B8
New Forest Cotts GU22 89 F7
New Forest Ride RG12 27 F4
New Green Pl SE19 22 E2
New Haw Jun Sch KT15 52 A1
New Haw Rd KT15 52 C4
New Heston Rd TW5 4 F7
New House Farm La GU3 108 C2
New House La RH1 161 E8
New Inn La GU4 110 B4
New Kelvin Ave TW11 16 E2
New La GU22, GU4 89 F3
New Life Sch RH19 185 D2
New Lodge Dr RH8 122 F7
New Malden Sta KT3 38 E6
New Meadow SL5 28 D8
New Mile Rd SL5 29 C7
New Moorhead Dr RH12 218 C6
New North Rd RH2 138 F6
New Par TW15 13 F4
New Park Ct 26 SW2 21 E8
New Park Par 14 SW2 21 E8
New Park Rd Ashford TW15 14 C3
Cranleigh GU6 174 F2
Streatham SW2 21 E8
Streatham, Streatham Hill
SW12, SW2 21 E7
New Pl CR0 63 A4
New Place Gdns RH7 164 E4
New Pond Rd
Artington GU3 129 E1
Compton GU3 129 E1
New Poplars The GU12 106 A1
New Rd Albury GU5 132 D3
Bagshot GU19 47 F3
Blackwater GU17 64 E4
Bracknell RG12 27 D7
Brentford TW8 6 D8
Carshalton CR4 41 A1
Chilworth GU4 131 B3
Crowthorne RG45 45 C5
East Bedfont TW14 3 D1
East Clandon GU4 111 E4
East Molesey KT8 36 A6
Egham TW18 12 C4
Esher KT10 55 C6
Feltham TW14 15 B7
Feltham TW13 15 E3
Forest Green RH5 176 E6
Gomshall GU5 133 C4
Harlington TW6, UB7 3 C7
Hounslow TW3 5 B3
Hydestile GU8 171 F5
Kingston u T KT2 18 A1
Limpsfield RH8 123 B5
Linchmere GU27 207 F5
Littleton TW17 34 B6
Milford GU8 170 E8
North Ascot SL5 8 F1
Oxshott KT10, KT22 74 F8
Richmond TW10 17 C4
Sandhurst GU47 64 A8
Smallfield RH6 162 B3
Tadworth KT20 97 C4
Tandridge RH8, RH9 143 A7
Tongham GU10 126 F6
Weybridge KT13 53 C5
Windlesham GU19, GU20 48 A4
Wonersh GU5 152 B8
Wormley GU8 191 A8
New Rd Units TW3 5 B3
New Residences KT16 51 C7
New Scotland Hill Cty
Prim Sch GU47 45 A2
New Sq TW14 14 C7
New St Crawley RH10 202 A7
Horsham RH13 217 D2
Staines TW18 13 A4
New Town RH10 183 B3
New Victoria Hospl The
KT3 38 E8
New Way GU7 150 C4
New Wickham La TW20 12 B1
New Wokingham Rd RG45 45 A6
New Woodlands Sch BR1 24 E4
New Zealand Ave KT12 34 F1
Newall Rd TW6 3 C6
Newark Cl Guildford GU4 110 B6
Ripley GU23 91 A6
Newark Ct KT12 35 C1
Newark La
Ripley GU22, GU23 91 A6
Woking GU22 90 F8
Newark Rd Crawley RH10 201 F8
South Croydon CR2 61 D4
Windlesham GU20 48 B6
Newbolt Ave SM3 58 D5
Newborough Gn KT3 38 D5
Newborough House
SW19 20 D1
Newbridge Cl RH12 216 C3
Newbridge Ct
Cranleigh GU6 174 B3
Upper Tooting SW17 20 C4
Newbridge Point 3 SE23 23 D5
Newbury Gdns KT19 57 F6
Newbury Rd TW6 2 F6
Newchapel Rd
Lingfield RH7 164 B3
Newchapel RH7 163 F2
Newcome Gdns SW16 21 E4
Newcome Pl GU12 126 D7
Newcome Rd GU9 125 E6
Newdigate Endowed CE
Inf Sch RH5 158 B1
Newdigate House 6 KT2 18 B2
Newdigate Rd
Beare Green RH5 157 E2
Rusper RH12 199 C8
Newenham Rd KT23 94 A1
Newent Cl SM5 40 F1
Newfield Ave GU14 84 E6
Newfield Cl TW12 36 A8
Newfield Rd GU12 106 A6
Newfoundland Rd GU16 86 D8
Newgate CR0 42 C1
Newgate Cl TW13 15 E5
Newhache RH7 165 A1
Newhall Gdns KT12 54 C8
Newhaven Cres TW15 14 D3
Newhaven Rd SE25 42 D4
Newhouse 5 KT3 38 E2
Newhouse Cl KT3 38 E2
Newhouse Wlk SM4 40 C2
Newland House Sch TW1 16 F4
Newland House Sch
Annex TW1 16 F4
Newlands Ave
Thames Ditton KT7 36 E1
Woking GU22 89 F6
Newlands Cl Hersham KT12 54 E6
Horley RH6 160 F5
Newlands Cnr GU4 132 A7
Newlands Cres RH19 185 D2
Newlands Croft SE20 23 D2
Newlands Ct
Addlestone KT15 52 B5
Caterham CR3 100 C6
Streatham SW16 21 E3
Newlands Dr Ash GU12 106 B4
Poyle SL3 1 E4
Newlands Estate GU8 170 F5
Newlands Flats GU1 109 F2
Newlands Pk
Copthorne RH10 183 E3
Forest Hill SE20, SE26 23 D3
Penge SE26 23 D3
Newlands Pl RH18 206 F3
Newlands Rd
Camberley GU15 65 B1
Crawley RH11 201 C5
Horsham RH12 217 C4
Thornton Heath SW16 41 E7
Newlands The SM6 60 D3
Newlands Way KT9 56 C5
Newlands Wood CR0 62 F2
Newman Cl RH10 202 C4
Newman Rd CR0 41 F1
Newmans Ct GU9 125 A7
Newmarket Rd RH10 202 A4
Newminster Rd SM4 40 C3
Newnham Cl CR7 42 C7
Newnham House SE6 24 C5
Newport Jun Sch GU12 105 D1
Newport Rd
Aldershot GU12 105 D1
Harmondsworth TW6 3 A6
Newquay Rd SE6 24 C6
Newry Rd TW1 6 A2
Newsham Rd 1 GU21 68 F2
Newstead Cl GU7 150 D6
Newstead Hall RH6 161 D1
Newstead House CR3 101 B1
Newstead Rd SE12 24 F8
Newstead Rise CR3 101 B1
Newstead Way SW19 19 E4
Newstead Wlk SM4, SM5 40 C2
Newton Ave RH19 205 F6
Newton Rd Crawley RH10 181 F2
Farnborough GU14 85 D6
Isleworth TW7 5 F5
Merton SW19 19 E1
Purley CR8 79 C7
Newton Way GU10 126 F7
Newton Wood Rd KT21 75 F3
Newtown Ct RH13 217 E1
Newtown Rd GU47 64 B8
Nicholas Gdns GU22 70 F3
Nicholas House SE26 23 B2
Nicholas Lodge KT10 55 A8
Nicholas Rd CR0 60 E6
Nicholass Ct 2 CR8 80 B7
Nicholes Rd TW3 5 A3
Nichols Cl KT9 56 C4
Nicholsfield RH14 212 F4
Nicholson Rd CR0 42 F1
Nicholson Wlk 3 TW20 12 A3
Nicol Cl 6 TW1 6 B1
Nicola Cl CR2 61 C4
Nicosia Rd SW18 20 E8
Niederwald Rd SE26 23 E4
Nightingale Ave KT24 92 D2
Nightingale Cl
Carshalton SM5 60 A8
Chiswick W4 7 C8
Cobham KT11 73 D8
Crawley RH11 201 C8
East Grinstead RH19 205 D7
Farnborough GU14 84 C6
Nightingale Cres
Bracknell RG12 27 D4
West Horsley KT24 92 C2
Nightingale Ct
2 Knaphill GU21 68 F1
Penge SE19 22 F2
8 Redhill RH1 119 A2
Nightingale Dr
Mytchett GU16 86 A3
West Ewell KT19 57 B4
Nightingale Gdns GU47 64 B8
Nightingale La
Balham SW11, SW12 20 F8
Richmond TW10 17 E8
Nightingale Rd Ash GU12 106 C3
Carshalton SM5 60 A8
East Horsley KT24 92 F2
East Molesey KT8 36 B4
Esher KT10 54 F4
Farncombe GU7 150 E6
Guildford GU1 109 E1
Hampton TW12 16 A2
Horsham RH12 217 D3
Selsdon CR2 62 D1
Walton-on-T KT12 35 B2
Nightingale Sq SW12 21 A8
Nightingale Way RH1 120 E2
Nightingales GU6 174 E1
Nightingales The TW19 13 F7
Nightjar Cl GU10 124 D8
Nimbus Rd KT19 57 D1
Nimrod Ct RH10 182 D1
Nimrod Rd SW16, SW17 21 B3

Nine Elms Cl TW14 ... 14 F7
Nine Mile Ride
Bracknell RG12, RG40 ... 26 F1
Crowthorne RG12, RG40 ... 26 F1
Nineacres Way CR5 ... 79 E3
Ninehams Cl CR3 ... 100 D7
Ninehams Gdns CR3 ... 100 D7
Ninehams Rd
Caterham CR3 ... 100 D6
Tatsfield TN16 ... 103 D6
Nineteenth Rd CR4 ... 41 E5
Ninfield Ct RH11 ... 200 F2
Niton Rd TW9 ... 7 A4
Niven Cl RH10 ... 202 D5
Nobel Dr TW6 ... 3 E7
Noble Cnr TW5 ... 5 A6
Noble Ct CR4 ... 40 D7
Noble St KT12 ... 54 C7
Nobles Way TW20 ... 11 E2
Noel Ct TW4 ... 4 F4
Noel Terr SE23 ... 23 C6
Noke Dr RH1 ... 119 A2
Nonsuch Court Ave KT17 ... 58 B1
Nonsuch Ct SM3 ... 58 E4
Nonsuch High Sch for Girls
SM3 ... 58 D3
Nonsuch Ind Est KT17 ... 76 E8
Nonsuch Prim Sch KT17 ... 58 B5
Nonsuch Wlk SM2 ... 58 D1
Noons Corner Rd RH5 ... 156 A8
Norbiton Ave KT1, KT2 ... 38 A7
Norbiton Common
Rd KT1, KT3 ... 38 B6
Norbiton Hall KT2 ... 37 F7
Norbiton Sta KT1 ... 38 A8
Norbury Ave Isleworth TW3 ... 5 D3
South Norwood CR7, SW16 ... 42 B7
Norbury Cl SW16 ... 42 B8
Norbury Court Rd SW16 ... 41 E7
Norbury Cres SW16 ... 42 A7
Norbury Cross SW16 ... 41 E6
Norbury Hill SW16 ... 22 B1
Norbury Manor Girls
High Sch CR7 ... 42 A8
Norbury Rd Reigate RH2 ... 117 F1
South Norwood CR7 ... 42 C6
Norbury Rise SW16 ... 41 E6
Norbury Sta SW16 ... 41 F8
Norbury Trad Est SW16 ... 41 F7
Norbury Way KT23 ... 94 C2
Norcroft Gdns SE22 ... 23 A8
Norcutt Rd TW2 ... 16 E7
Norfolk Ave CR2 ... 62 A1
Norfolk Cl Crawley RH11 ... 200 E2
Horley RH6 ... 161 A2
5 Twickenham TW1 ... 6 B1
Norfolk Cotts RH1 ... 140 E7
Norfolk Ct Dorking RH5 ... 136 D3
Horsham RH12 ... 218 B5
Surbiton KT5 ... 37 F3
Norfolk Farm Cl GU22 ... 70 D3
Norfolk Farm Rd GU22 ... 70 D3
Norfolk House
2 Croydon CR0 ... 61 D8
11 Merton SW19 ... 20 C1
Penge SE20 ... 43 C8
Norfolk House Rd SW16 ... 21 E5
Norfolk La RH5 ... 136 B1
Norfolk Rd Claygate KT10 ... 55 E5
Dorking RH4 ... 136 A7
Feltham TW13 ... 15 C7
Horsham RH12, RH13 ... 217 D2
Mitcham SW19 ... 20 E2
South Holmwood RH5 ... 157 C6
South Norwood CR7 ... 42 C6
Norfolk Terr RH12, RH13 ... 217 D2
Norgrove St SW12 ... 21 A8
Norheads La
Biggin Hill TN16 ... 83 B2
Chelsham TN16 ... 83 B2
Norhyrst Ave SE25 ... 42 F6
Nork Gdns SM7 ... 77 E5
Nork Rise SM7 ... 77 D3
Nork Way KT17, SM7 ... 77 D4
Norlands La
Egham TW18, TW20 ... 32 E7
Thorpe TW18, TW20 ... 32 E7
Norley Vale SW15 ... 19 A7
Norman Ave Ewell KT17 ... 76 F7
Feltham TW13 ... 15 F6
South Croydon CR2, CR8 ... 61 C1
Twickenham TW1 ... 17 C8
Norman Colyer Ct KT19 ... 57 D1
Norman Cres TW5 ... 4 D7
Norman Ct Farnham GU9 ... 125 C1
9 Hampton TW12 ... 36 A8
Streatham SW16 ... 22 A3
Norman House
Feltham TW13 ... 15 F6
Lower Halliford TW17 ... 34 A2
Reigate RH2 ... 138 F6
Norman Keep RG42 ... 27 F8
Norman Rd Ashford TW15 ... 14 D2
Merton SW19 ... 20 C1
Sutton SM1 ... 59 A5
Thornton Heath CR7 ... 42 B4
Norman's Rd RH1, RH6 ... 162 C5
Normandy RH12 ... 217 C1
Normandy Cl
Crawley RH10 ... 202 C4
7 East Grinstead RH19 ... 205 F8
Forest Hill SE26 ... 23 E5
Frimley GU16 ... 86 E8
Normandy Gdns RH12 ... 217 C1
Normandy Wlk TW20 ... 12 C3
Normanhurst TW15 ... 14 A3
Normanhurst Cl RH10 ... 201 F6
Normanhurst Dr TW1 ... 6 B2
Normanhurst Rd
Streatham SW2 ... 21 F6
Walton-on-T KT12 ... 54 D8
Normans La TN8 ... 165 E7
Normansfield Ave
KT1, KT8 ... 17 C1
Normansfield Hospl KT8 ... 17 C1
Normanton RH2 ... 117 D2
Normanton Ave
SW18, SW19 ... 20 A6
Normanton Rd CR2 ... 61 E4
Normanton St SE23 ... 23 D6
Normington Cl SW16 ... 22 A3
Norrels Dr KT24 ... 92 F1
Norrels Ride KT24 ... 92 F2
Norreys Ave RG40 ... 25 D7
Norris Hill Rd GU13, GU14 104 A8
Norris Rd TW18 ... 12 F4
Norstead Pl SW15 ... 19 A6
North Acre SM7 ... 77 F3
North Ash RH12 ... 217 C4
North Ave Heath End GU9 ... 125 D7
8 Richmond TW9 ... 7 A6
Wallington SM5 ... 60 A3
Whiteley Village KT12 ... 53 E2
North Camp Sta GU12 ... 105 F8
North Cl Ash GU12 ... 105 E1
Crawley RH10 ... 201 F7
Dorking RH5 ... 136 C3
East Bedfont TW14 ... 3 D1
Farnborough GU14 ... 85 A8
Merton SM4 ... 39 E5
North Comm KT13 ... 53 C6
North Crofts SE21 ... 23 B7
North Dene TW5 ... 5 B6
North Down CR2 ... 80 E7
North Downs Cres CR0 ... 63 B1
North Downs Golf Course
CR3 ... 102 A2
North Downs Rd CR0 ... 63 C1
North Dr Beckenham BR3 ... 44 B5
Hounslow TW3, TW7 ... 5 C5
Pirbright GU24 ... 87 C6
Streatham SW16 ... 21 C4
Wentworth GU25 ... 30 E4
North End CR0, CR9 ... 61 C8
North End La SL5 ... 30 B2
North Farm Rd GU14 ... 84 F8
North Farnborough Cty
Inf Sch GU14 ... 85 D5
North Feltham Trad Est
TW14 ... 4 B3
North Gate Rd GU14 ... 85 C2
North Gdns SW19 ... 20 D1
North Gn RG12 ... 27 D8
North Gr KT16 ... 32 F3
North Hatton Rd TW6 ... 3 D6
North Heath Cl RH12 ... 217 D5
North Heath Cty Prim
Sch RH12 ... 217 D5
North Heath Est RH12 ... 217 D6
North Heath La RH12 ... 217 E6
North Holmes Cl RH12 ... 218 B5
North Hyde La TW5 ... 4 F8
North La
Aldershot GU11, GU12 ... 105 D2
Teddington TW11 ... 16 F2
North Lodge Dr SL5 ... 28 C7
North Mead Crawley RH10 201 E8
Redhill RH1 ... 118 F4
North Minden House
GU16 ... 86 D7
North Moors GU1 ... 109 E6
North Munstead La GU8 ... 151 A1
North Par Chessington KT9 ... 56 F5
Horsham RH12 ... 217 C3
North Park La RH9 ... 121 A5
North Pl Mitcham SW19 ... 20 F1
Teddington TW11 ... 16 F2
North Pole La BR2 ... 63 F4
North Rd Ash Vale GU12 ... 105 F4
Brentford TW8 ... 6 E8
Crawley RH10 ... 202 A7
East Bedfont TW14 ... 3 D1
Guildford GU2 ... 109 B4
Hersham KT12 ... 54 C5
Heston TW5 ... 4 C8
Kingston u T KT6 ... 37 D3
Mitcham SW17, SW19 ... 20 C2
Reigate RH2 ... 138 F6
Richmond TW9 ... 7 A5
West Wickham BR4 ... 44 B1
Wimbledon SW17, SW19 ... 20 C2
Winkfield SL5 ... 28 B8
Woking GU21 ... 70 A3
North Sheen Sta TW10 ... 7 A3
North Side GU10 ... 126 F7
North St Carshalton SM5 ... 59 F6
Dorking RH4 ... 136 A7
Egham TW20 ... 11 F2
Farncombe GU7 ... 150 E7
Guildford GU1 ... 130 D8
Horsham RH12, RH13 ... 217 D3
Isleworth TW7 ... 6 A4
Leatherhead KT22 ... 95 A6
Redhill RH1 ... 118 F2
Turners Hill RH10 ... 204 A4
Winkfield SL4 ... 9 A6
North Station App RH1 ... 140 F7
North Terminal App RH6 ... 181 F8
North View SW19 ... 19 C3
North View Cres KT18 ... 77 C2
North Weald La KT2 ... 17 D3
North Weylands Ind Est
KT12 ... 54 E8
North Wlk CR0 ... 63 C5
North Worple Way SW14 ... 7 D4
Northampton Cl RG12 ... 27 E6
Northampton Rd CR0, CR9 ... 62 A8
Northanger Rd SW16 ... 21 E2
Northborough Rd SW16 ... 41 E7
Northbourne GU7 ... 150 F8
Northbrook Coll of
Design & Tech RH12 ... 217 C4
Northbrook Copse RG12 ... 27 F3
Northbrook Rd
Aldershot GU11 ... 126 B8
Thornton Heath CR0 ... 42 D4
Northcliffe Cl KT4 ... 57 E7
Northcote KT15 ... 52 D6
Northcote Ave
Isleworth TW7 ... 6 A2
Tolworth KT5 ... 38 B2
Northcote Cl KT24 ... 92 C2
Northcote Cres KT24 ... 92 C2
Northcote La GU5 ... 152 E6
Northcote Pk KT22 ... 74 C4
Northcote Rd
Ash Vale GU12 ... 106 A7
Farnborough GU14 ... 84 F6
Isleworth TW1, TW7 ... 6 A2
Kingston u T KT3 ... 38 D6
Thornton Heath CR0 ... 42 D3
West Horsley KT24 ... 92 C2
Northcott RG12 ... 27 A1
Northcroft Cl TW20 ... 11 B3
Northcroft Gdns TW20 ... 11 B3
Northcroft Rd
Englefield Green TW20 ... 11 B3
West Ewell KT19 ... 57 E3
Northcroft Villas TW20 ... 11 B3
Northdown Cl RH12 ... 217 F4
Northdown Ct RH9 ... 121 C5
Northdown La GU1 ... 130 E6
Northdown Rd
Belmont SM2 ... 59 A1
Woldingham CR3 ... 102 A2
Northdown Terr RH19 ... 185 D3
Northdowns GU6 ... 174 E1
Northend Ct KT23 ... 94 C1
Northern Perimeter Rd
Harlington TW6 ... 3 E6
Hatton TW6 ... 3 E6
Northern Perimeter Road
(W) TW6 ... 2 D6
Northernhay Wlk SM4 ... 39 E5
Northey Ave Belmont SM2 ... 58 E1
East Ewell SM2 ... 58 E1
Northfield Lightwater GU18 ... 67 B8
Shalford GU4 ... 130 E1
Witley GU8 ... 170 F4
Northfield Cl GU12 ... 105 D1
Northfield Cres SM3 ... 58 E6
Northfield Ct TW18 ... 33 B8
Northfield Pl KT13 ... 53 B3
Northfield Rd Cobham KT11 73 B6
Heston TW5 ... 4 D7
Staines TW18 ... 33 B8
Northfields KT21 ... 95 E8
Northgate Ave RH10 ... 201 F7
Northgate Cty Fst Sch
RH10 ... 201 E7
Northgate Cty Mid Sch
RH10 ... 201 E7
Northgate Dr GU15 ... 66 A7
Northgate Pl RH10 ... 201 E7
Northgate Rd
Crawley RH10, RH11 ... 201 D6
Crawley, North
Terminal RH6 ... 181 F8
Northington Cl RG12 ... 27 F3
Northlands Bglws RH5 ... 158 B1
Northlands Rd
Faygate RH12 ... 198 F2
Horsham RH12 ... 217 E7
Warnham RH12 ... 197 D2
Northmead GU14 ... 85 B4
Northmead GM Jun Sch
GU2 ... 109 B4
Northmoor 4 SE23 ... 23 D5
Northolt Rd TW6 ... 2 E6
Northover BR1 ... 24 F5
Northrop Rd TW6 ... 3 E6
Northspur Rd SM1 ... 59 A7
Northstead Rd SW2 ... 22 A6
Northumberland Ave TW7 ... 6 A7
Northumberland Cl TW19 ... 2 E1
Northumberland
Cres TW14 ... 3 E1
Northumberland Gdns
Hounslow TW7 ... 6 A7
Mitcham CR4 ... 41 D4
Northumberland Pl 26
TW10 ... 6 D2
Northway Crawley RH6 ... 181 F8
Farncombe GU7 ... 150 B7
Guildford GU2 ... 109 A3
Merton SM4, SW20 ... 39 E5
Wallington SM6 ... 60 C6
Northway Rd CR0 ... 42 F2
Northwood Ave
Knaphill GU21 ... 68 D1
Purley CR8 ... 80 B6
Northwood Pk RH10 ... 182 A2
Northwood Rd
Forest Hill SE23 ... 23 F7
Harmondsworth TW6 ... 2 D6
South Norwood CR7 ... 42 C7
Wallington SM5 ... 60 A4
Northwood Way 1 SE19 ... 22 E2
Norton Ave KT5 ... 38 B2
Norton Cl GU3 ... 88 D1
Norton Ct BR3 ... 43 F8
Norton Gdns SW16 ... 41 E7
Norton House 4 KT3 ... 38 E5
Norton Pk SL5 ... 29 C4
Norton Rd Frimley GU15 ... 66 C4
Wokingham RG40 ... 25 C5
Norwegian Sch SW19 ... 19 C1
Norwich Ave GU15 ... 65 E3
Norwich Rd Crawley RH10 202 B5
South Norwood CR7 ... 42 C6
Norwood Cl
Effingham KT24 ... 113 E7
Twickenham TW2 ... 16 D6
Norwood Cres TW6 ... 3 C6
Norwood Farm La KT11 ... 73 B8
Norwood Heights Sh Ctr
SE19 ... 22 E2
Norwood High St SE27 ... 22 C4
Norwood Hill RH6 ... 159 D3
Norwood Hospl SE19 ... 22 D2
Norwood Junction Sta
SE25 ... 43 A5
Norwood Park Rd SE27 ... 22 C3
Norwood Rd
Effingham KT24 ... 113 E7
Streatham SE24, SE27 ... 22 B7
West Norwood SE24, SE27 ... 22 B7
Norwood Sch
West Norwood SE27 ... 22 C3
West Norwood SE27 ... 22 C4
Norwoodhill Rd RH6 ... 159 F2
Noseby Ct KT12 ... 54 C8
Notley End TW20 ... 11 C1
Notre Dame Jun Sch
RH7 ... 164 F3
Notre Dame Sch RH7 ... 164 F3
Notson Rd SE25 ... 43 B5
Nottingham Cl GU21 ... 68 F1
Nottingham Ct 5 GU21 ... 68 F1
Nottingham Rd
Croydon CR2 ... 61 C5
Isleworth TW7 ... 5 F5
Upper Tooting SW17 ... 20 F7
Nova Mews SM4 ... 39 E2
Nova Rd CR0 ... 42 C2
Nower Lodge Sch RH4 ... 136 A6
Nower Rd RH4 ... 136 A6
Nowhurst La RH12 ... 216 A5
Noyna Rd SW17 ... 20 F5
Nuffield Ct TW5 ... 4 F7
Nuffield Dr GU47 ... 45 E1
Nuffield Hospl GU2 ... 108 E1
Nugee Ct RG45 ... 45 B5
Nugent Ct Guildford GU2 ... 109 B4
Streatham SW16 ... 21 C4
Nugent Rd Guildford GU2 ... 129 D8
South Norwood SE25 ... 42 F6
Numa Ct TW8 ... 6 D7
Nunappleton Way RH8 ... 123 A3
Nuneaton RG12 ... 27 E3
Nuneham SW16 ... 21 D4
Nuns Wlk GU25 ... 31 D4
Nuptown La SL4 ... 8 A8
Nursery Ave CR0 ... 62 D8
Nursery Cl Capel RH5 ... 178 C5
Croydon CR0 ... 62 D8
Ewell KT17 ... 57 E1
Feltham TW14 ... 15 B8
Frimley GU16 ... 85 F7
Walton on t H KT20 ... 97 B2
Woking GU21 ... 69 C3
Woodham KT15 ... 51 F1
Nursery Cotts GU21 ... 88 F8
Nursery Gdns
Chilworth GU4 ... 131 B3
Hounslow TW4 ... 4 F2
Staines TW18 ... 13 B1
Sunbury TW16 ... 34 F7
Nursery Hill GU5 ... 152 D5
Nursery La Hookwood RH6 160 D2
North Ascot SL5 ... 28 E8
Nursery Rd
Farncombe GU7 ... 150 F7
Knaphill GU21 ... 68 D2
Merton SW19 ... 40 B7
Mitcham CR4 ... 40 E6
South Norwood CR7, SE25 ... 42 D5
Sunbury TW16 ... 34 F7
Sutton SM1 ... 59 C6
Walton on t H KT20 ... 97 B2
Wimbledon SW19 ... 19 E1
Nurserylands RH11 ... 201 A6
Nutborn House SW19 ... 19 D2
Nutbourne GU9 ... 125 E7
Nutbourne Cotts GU8 ... 191 E7
Nutbourne Ct TW18 ... 12 F1
Nutcombe La Dorking RH4 135 F7
Haslemere GU26, GU27 ... 188 E1
Nutcroft Gr KT22 ... 94 E6
Nutfield Church Prim Sch
RH1 ... 140 F8
Nutfield Cl SM5 ... 59 E7
Nutfield Ct Camberley GU15 65 D7
Nutfield RH1 ... 119 F2
Nutfield Marsh Rd RH1 ... 119 E4
Nutfield Rd Coulsdon CR5 ... 79 A3
Merstham RH1 ... 119 C5
Nutfield RH1 ... 119 C1
Redhill RH1 ... 119 C1
Thornton Heath CR7 ... 42 B5
Nutfield Sta RH1 ... 140 E7
Nuthatch Cl GU10 ... 124 D7
Nuthatch Gdns RH2 ... 139 C5
Nuthatch Way RH12 ... 217 D7
Nuthurst RG12 ... 27 E4
Nuthurst Ave
Cranleigh GU6 ... 174 E3
Streatham SW2 ... 21 F6
Nuthurst Cl RH11 ... 201 A7
Nutley RG12 ... 27 A1
Nutley Ct RH2 ... 118 A1
Nutley La RH2 ... 117 F2
Nutmeg Ct GU14 ... 84 C5
Nutshell La GU9 ... 125 C6
Nutty La TW17 ... 34 C6
Nutwell St SW17 ... 20 E3
Nutwood GU7 ... 150 D6
Nutwood Ave RH3 ... 137 C8
Nutwood Cl RH3 ... 137 C8
Nyefield Pk KT20 ... 97 A1
Nylands Ave TW9 ... 7 A5
Nymans Cl RH12 ... 218 A7
Nymans Ct RH10 ... 202 B3
Nymans Gdns SW20 ... 39 B6
Nyon Gr SE23, SE6 ... 23 F6

O

O'Connor Rd GU11 ... 105 E7
Oak Ave Croydon CR0 ... 63 B8
Egham TW20 ... 12 D1
Hampton TW12, TW13 ... 15 E2
Heston TW5 ... 4 E7
Sandhurst GU47 ... 45 D1
Oak Bank CR0 ... 63 C4
Oak Cl Box Hill KT20 ... 116 B5
Chiddingfold GU8 ... 191 A4
Copthorne RH10 ... 183 A3
Farncombe GU7 ... 150 E8
Oak Cnr RH5 ... 157 C4
Oak Cottage Cl Catford SE6 24 F7
Wood St V GU3 ... 108 C2
Oak Cotts GU27 ... 207 E6
Oak Croft RH19 ... 206 A8
Oak Ct Crawley RH10 ... 181 D2
Farnham GU9 ... 125 B1
Oak Dell RH10 ... 202 C7
Oak Dr KT20 ... 116 B5
Oak End RH5 ... 157 C3
Oak End Way KT15 ... 70 F7
Oak Farm Cl GU17 ... 64 C5
Oak Farm Com Sch GU14 ... 84 F6
Oak Gdns CR0 ... 63 A8
Oak Glade KT19 ... 76 A7
Oak Gr Cranleigh GU6 ... 174 F1
Loxwood RH14 ... 213 A4
Sunbury TW16 ... 15 B1
West Wickham BR4 ... 44 C1
Oak Grange Rd GU4 ... 111 B6
Oak Grove Cres GU15 ... 64 F6
Oak Grove Rd SE20 ... 43 C7
Oak Hill Epsom KT18 ... 76 D3
Guildford GU4 ... 110 C6
Surbiton KT6 ... 37 E2
Wood St V GU3 ... 108 B3
Oak Hill Cres KT6 ... 37 E2
Oak Hill Gr KT6 ... 37 E3
Oak Hill Rd KT6 ... 37 E3
Oak House SE20 ... 43 B7
Oak La
Broadbridge Heath RH12 ... 216 E3
Englefield Green TW20 ... 11 C5
Isleworth TW7 ... 5 E3
Twickenham TW1 ... 17 A8
Woking GU22 ... 70 B3
Oak Leaf Cl KT19 ... 76 C7
Oak Lodge
4 Charlton TW16 ... 14 F1
Crowthorne RG45 ... 45 C5
Oak Lodge Cl KT12 ... 54 C5
Oak Lodge Dr
Salfords RH1 ... 140 A1
West Wickham BR4 ... 44 B2
Oak Lodge Prim Sch BR4 ... 44 B2
Oak Lodge Sch SW12 ... 21 A8
Oak Mead GU7 ... 150 E8
Oak Park Gdns SW19 ... 19 D7
Oak Pk KT14 ... 70 E6
Oak Rd Caterham CR3 ... 100 E5
Cobham KT11 ... 73 E4
Crawley RH11 ... 201 C5
Farnborough GU14 ... 85 C3
Kingston u T KT3 ... 38 D7
Leatherhead KT22 ... 95 A8
Reigate RH2 ... 118 B2
Oak Ridge RH4 ... 136 B4
Oak Row CR4 ... 41 C7
Oak Tree Cl
Aldershot GU12 ... 126 E8
Ash Vale GU12 ... 85 B1
Guildford, Burpham GU4 ... 110 C6
Guildford, Jacobswell GU4 ... 109 C6
Knaphill GU21 ... 68 B1
Wentworth GU25 ... 31 D3
Oak Tree Dr
Englefield Green TW20 ... 11 C3
Guildford GU1 ... 109 C5
Oak Tree La GU27 ... 207 D6
Oak Tree Rd Knaphill GU21 ... 68 B1
Milford GU8 ... 149 F1
Oak Tree View GU9 ... 125 E6
Oak Tree Way RH13 ... 217 F4
Oak Way Ashstead KT21 ... 76 A3
Crawley RH10 ... 201 E8
Croydon CR0 ... 43 D3
East Bedfont TW14 ... 14 E7
Reigate RH2 ... 139 D8
Oak Wlk RH12 ... 199 F1
Oak's Rd GU21 ... 69 E2
Oakapple Cl Crawley RH11 201 B1
Hamsey Green CR2 ... 81 B5
Oakbank Fetcham KT22 ... 94 D4
Woking GU22 ... 89 E8
Oakbank Ave KT12 ... 35 F2
Oakbrook BR3 ... 44 B7
Oakcombe Cl KT3 ... 38 E8

Oakcroft Bsns Ctr KT9 ... 56 F6
Oakcroft Cl KT14 ... 70 F5
Oakcroft House 3 KT3 ... 38 E2
Oakcroft Rd
Chessington KT9 ... 56 F6
Pyrford KT14 ... 70 F5
Oakcroft Villas KT9 ... 56 F6
Oakdale Beckenham BR3 ... 44 C7
Bracknell RG12 ... 27 D3
Oakdale Rd Epsom KT19 ... 57 D2
Streatham SW16 ... 21 E3
Weybridge KT13 ... 53 A7
Oakdale Way CR4 ... 41 A2
Oakdene Chobham GU24 ... 49 F1
Kingswood KT20 ... 97 E7
Sunningdale SL5 ... 29 F3
1 West Norwood SE19 ... 22 E3
Oakdene Ave KT7 ... 37 A1
Oakdene Cl Brockham RH3 137 C7
Great Bookham KT23 ... 114 C8
Oakdene Ct KT12 ... 54 B7
Oakdene Dr KT5 ... 38 C1
Oakdene Lodge SE20 ... 23 B1
Oakdene Mews SM3 ... 39 F1
Oakdene Par KT11 ... 73 B5
Oakdene Rd
Brockham RH3 ... 137 C7
Cobham KT11 ... 73 B5
Godalming GU7 ... 150 D3
Little Bookham KT23 ... 93 F3
Redhill RH1 ... 118 F1
Shalford GU3 ... 130 C1
Oaken Coppice KT21 ... 96 A8
Oaken Copse GU15 ... 66 C7
Oaken Copse Cres GU14 ... 85 B7
Oaken Dr KT10 ... 55 F4
Oaken La KT10 ... 55 E5
Oakengates RG12 ... 27 A1
Oakenshaw Cl KT6 ... 37 E2
Oakfield Plaistow RH14 ... 211 E2
Woking GU21 ... 68 E3
Oakfield Cl New Malden KT3 38 F4
Weybridge KT13 ... 53 C6
Oakfield Ct Croydon CR2 ... 61 C4
Wokingham RG41 ... 25 A5
Oakfield Cty Jun Sch
KT22 ... 94 D4
Oakfield Dr RH2 ... 118 B3
Oakfield Gdns
Beckenham BR3 ... 44 A4
Carshalton SM5 ... 40 F1
3 Dulwich SE19 ... 22 E3
Oakfield Glade KT13 ... 53 C6
Oakfield Rd Ashford TW15 ... 14 B3
Ashstead KT21 ... 75 E1
Blackwater GU17 ... 64 F3
Cobham KT11 ... 73 B5
Penge SE20 ... 23 B1
Thornton Heath CR0 ... 42 C1
Wimbledon SW19 ... 19 D5
Oakfield Sch Dulwich SE21 ... 22 D7
Pyrford GU22 ... 70 F4
Oakfield Way RH19 ... 185 F3
Oakfields Camberley GU15 ... 65 B5
Crawley RH10 ... 202 D7
Guildford GU3 ... 108 F3
Wallis Wood RH5 ... 196 D8
Walton-on-T KT12 ... 35 A1
West Byfleet KT14 ... 71 B5
Oakhall Ct TW16 ... 14 F3
Oakhall Dr TW16 ... 14 F3
Oakham Cl SE6 ... 23 F6
Oakham Dr BR2 ... 44 F5
Oakhaven RH10, RH11 ... 201 D4
Oakhill KT10 ... 56 A4
Oakhill Cl KT21 ... 75 C1
Oakhill Ct 8 Surbiton KT6 ... 37 E3
Wimbledon SW19 ... 19 D1
Oakhill Gdns KT13 ... 53 E8
Oakhill Lodge CR8 ... 80 A6
Oakhill Rd Addlestone KT15 ... 51 F4
Ashtead KT21 ... 75 C1
Beckenham BR3 ... 44 C7
Headley Down GU35 ... 187 B5
Horsham RH13 ... 217 E2
Reigate RH2 ... 139 B8
Sutton SM1 ... 59 C7
Thornton Heath SW16 ... 41 F8
Oakhurst Chobham GU24 ... 49 E2
Grayshott GU26 ... 188 D3
Oakhurst Cl 4 TW11 ... 16 E3
Oakhurst Gdns RH19 ... 185 C2
Oakhurst Grange Sch
CR3 ... 100 D1
Oakhurst La RH14 ... 212 E7
Oakhurst Rd KT19 ... 57 D4
Oakhurst Rise SM5 ... 59 E1
Oakington 6 KT1 ... 38 A7
Oakington Dr TW16 ... 35 C7
Oakland Ave GU9 ... 125 E7
Oakland Way KT19 ... 57 E4
Oaklands Croydon CR0 ... 61 B5
Fetcham KT22 ... 94 D3
Haslemere GU27 ... 208 C7
Horley RH6 ... 161 C3
Horsham RH13 ... 217 E2
Purley CR8 ... 80 C5
South Godstone RH9 ... 142 E5
Twickenham TW2 ... 16 C8
Oaklands Ave Hounslow TW7 ... 5 F8
Thames Ditton KT10 ... 36 D1
Thornton Heath CR7 ... 42 A5
West Wickham BR4 ... 63 B7
Oaklands Cl
Chessington KT9 ... 56 C6
North Ascot SL5 ... 8 F1
Shalford GU4 ... 130 E1
Oaklands Ct KT15 ... 52 B7
Oaklands Cty Jun Sch
RG45 ... 45 A6
Oaklands Dr North Ascot SL5 ... 8 F1
Redhill RH1 ... 140 B7
Wokingham RG41 ... 25 A5
Oaklands Gdns CR8 ... 80 C5
Oaklands Inf Sch
Biggin Hill TN16 ... 83 C3
Crowthorne RG45 ... 45 A6
Oaklands La
Biggin Hill TN16 ... 83 C5
Crowthorne RG45 ... 45 B7
Oaklands Pk RG41 ... 25 A4
Oaklands Rd Bromley BR1 ... 24 E1
Mortlake SW14 ... 7 D4
Oaklands Sch TW3 ... 5 D4
Oaklands Way
Tadworth KT20 ... 97 C5
Wallington SM6 ... 60 D3
Oaklawn Rd Ashstead KT22 ... 74 E2
Leatherhead KT22 ... 74 E2
Oaklea GU12 ... 106 A5
Oaklea Ct CR2 ... 61 D2
Oakleigh Epsom KT18 ... 76 E5
Lightwater GU18 ... 67 C8
Oakleigh Ave KT6 ... 57 B8
Oakleigh Ct Oxted RH8 ... 122 E6
Penge SE20 ... 23 B1
Oakleigh Rd RH12 ... 217 F4
Oakleigh Way Mitcham CR4 41 B8
1 Tolworth KT6 ... 38 B1
Oakley Ave CR0 ... 60 E6
Oakley Cl Addlestone KT15 ... 52 D6
East Grinstead RH19 ... 206 B7
Hounslow TW7 ... 5 D6
Oakley Cotts RH19 ... 206 C7
Oakley Ct Carshalton CR4 ... 41 A2
15 Redhill RH1 ... 119 A2
Oakley Dell GU4 ... 110 C3
Oakley Gdns SM7 ... 78 B4
Oakley House GU7 ... 150 E8
Oakley Rd Camberley GU15 ... 65 B4
Croydon SE25 ... 43 B4
Whyteleafe CR6 ... 81 A1
Oakman House 29 SW19 ... 19 D7
Oakmead Gn KT18 ... 76 C4
Oakmead Pl CR4 ... 40 E8
Oakmead Rd
Upper Tooting SW12 ... 21 B7
Wallington CR0 ... 41 D3
Oakridge GU24 ... 67 F6
Oakridge La BR1 ... 24 D3
Oakridge Rd BR1 ... 24 E4
Oaks Ave Feltham TW13 ... 15 E6
North Cheam KT4 ... 58 B6
West Norwood SE19, SE27 ... 22 E3
Oaks Cl Horsham RH12 ... 218 B6
Leatherhead KT22 ... 95 A6
Oaks Ct KT22 ... 95 A6
Oaks La South Croydon CR0 ... 62 C7
South Holmwood RH5 ... 157 B8
Oaks Rd Purley CR8 ... 80 B5
Reigate RH2 ... 118 D2
South Croydon CR0 ... 62 C6
Stanwell TW19 ... 2 D1
Oaks Sports Ctr SM5 ... 78 F8
Oaks The Bracknell RG12 ... 27 D7
Dorking RH4 ... 136 B4
East Grinstead RH19 ... 206 B8
Epsom KT18 ... 76 F5
Farnborough GU14 ... 84 D3
Staines TW18 ... 12 F4
West Byfleet KT14 ... 71 A5
Wimbledon SW19 ... 19 E2
Oaks Track SM5, SM6 ... 60 B1
Oaks Way
Burgh Heath KT18 ... 97 B8
Long Ditton KT6 ... 37 D1
Purley CR8 ... 80 C5
Wallington SM5 ... 59 F3
Oaksford Ave SE26 ... 23 B5
Oakshade Rd Catford BR1 ... 24 D4
Oxshott KT22 ... 74 C5
Oakshaw RH8 ... 122 D8
Oakshaw Rd SW18 ... 20 B8
Oakside Ct RH6 ... 161 C4
Oakside La RH6 ... 161 C4
Oaktree Way GU47 ... 45 A1
Oaktrees Ash GU12 ... 105 F1
Hale GU9 ... 125 B6
Oakview RG40 ... 25 B4
Oakview Gr CR0 ... 43 E1
Oakview Rd SE6 ... 24 B3
Oakway Aldershot GU12 ... 126 E8
Beckenham BR2 ... 44 D7
Knaphill GU21 ... 88 E8
West Barnes SW20 ... 39 C5
Oakway Dr GU16 ... 65 E1
Oakwood Guildford GU2 ... 109 A6
Wallington SM6 ... 60 B2
Oakwood Ave
Beckenham BR2, BR3 ... 44 C7
Mitcham CR4 ... 40 D7
Purley CR8 ... 80 C7
Oakwood Cl
East Horsley KT24 ... 112 E8
Redhill RH1 ... 119 A1
South Nutfield RH1 ... 140 F7
Oakwood Ct
Beckenham BR3 ... 44 C7
Bisley GU24 ... 68 A3
Oakwood Dr
East Horsley KT24 ... 112 E8
West Norwood SE19 ... 22 E2
Oakwood Gdns
Knaphill GU21 ... 68 B1
Sutton SM1 ... 59 A8
Oakwood Ind Pk RH10 ... 182 A2
Oakwood Independent Sch
CR8 ... 80 B6
Oakwood Pk RH18 ... 206 F2
Oakwood Pl CR0 ... 42 A3
Oakwood Rd
Bletchingley RH1 ... 120 A6
Bracknell RG12 ... 27 E7
Horley RH6 ... 161 B4
Knaphill GU21 ... 88 E8
Thornton Heath CR0, CR7 ... 42 A3
Thorpe GU25 ... 31 C4
Wimbledon SW20 ... 39 A8
Windlesham GU20 ... 48 E4
Oakwood Rise CR3 ... 100 E2
Oakwood Sch RH6 ... 161 C3
Oareborough RG12 ... 27 E4
Oast House Cl TW19 ... 11 E8
Oast House Cres GU9 ... 125 D6
Oast House La GU9 ... 125 D6
Oast La GU11 ... 126 B7
Oast Rd RH8 ... 122 F4
Oates Cl BR2 ... 44 D6
Oates Wlk RH10 ... 201 F3
Oatfield Rd KT20 ... 97 B6
Oatlands Crawley RH11 ... 201 A5
Horley RH6 ... 161 C4
Oatlands Ave
Oatlands Park KT13 ... 53 E6
Weybridge KT13 ... 53 E6
Oatlands Chase KT12, KT13 53 E7
Oatlands Cl KT13 ... 53 D6
Oatlands Ct 3 SW19 ... 19 D7
Oatlands Cty Inf Sch KT13 53 D6
Oatlands Dr
Oatlands Park KT13, KT12 ... 53 D7
Weybridge KT13, KT12 ... 53 D7
Oatlands Gn KT13 ... 53 D7
Oatlands Mere KT13 ... 53 D7
Oatlands Rd KT20 ... 97 E8
Oban Rd SE25 ... 42 D5
Obelisk Way GU15 ... 65 C6
Oberon Way
Crawley RH11 ... 200 E3
Littleton TW17 ... 33 E6
Oberursel Way GU11 ... 104 F2
Observatory Rd SW14 ... 7 C3
Observatory Wlk 4 RH1 ... 118 F1
Occam Rd GU2 ... 129 D8
Ockenden Cl GU22 ... 69 F1
Ockenden Gdns GU22 ... 69 F1
Ockenden Rd GU22 ... 69 F1
Ockfields GU8 ... 149 F1
Ockford Ct GU7 ... 150 D4
Ockford Dr GU7 ... 150 C3
Ockford Rd GU7 ... 150 D4
Ockford Ridge GU7 ... 150 B2
Ockham Dr KT24 ... 92 D3
Ockham La Downside KT11 ... 92 D7
Martyr's Green GU23 ... 92 D7
Ockham GU23 ... 92 D7
Ockham Rd N
Ockham GU23 ... 92 C3
West Horsley KT24 ... 92 C3
Ockham Rd S KT24 ... 112 E7
Ockley Ct GU4 ... 110 B6
Ockley House 8 KT2 ... 18 B2
Ockley Rd Ewhurst GU6 ... 175 F6
Forest Green GU6, RH5 ... 176 C7
Ockley RH5 ... 177 B7
Streatham SW16 ... 21 E5
Thornton Heath CR0, CR9 ... 41 F2
Wotton GU6, RH5 ... 176 C7
Ockley Sta RH5 ... 178 A5
Ockleys Mead RH9 ... 121 C5
Octagon Rd KT12 ... 53 E1
Octavia RG12 ... 27 A1
Octavia Cl CR4 ... 40 E4
Octavia Rd TW7 ... 5 F4
Octavia Way TW18 ... 13 A2
October Ct BR2 ... 44 F6
Odard Rd KT8 ... 36 A5
Odette House 6 SE27 ... 22 D4
Odiham Rd
Crondall GU9, GU10 ... 124 D7
Heath End GU10, GU9 ... 124 D7
Ogden House TW13 ... 15 E4
Okeburn Rd SW17 ... 21 A3
Okehurst Rd RH14 ... 214 C1
Okingham Cl GU47 ... 45 D1
Olaf Palme House TW13 ... 15 B5
Old Acre KT14 ... 71 A5
Old Ave
Sheerwater GU21, KT14 ... 70 E6
Weybridge KT13 ... 53 C3
Old Avenue Cl KT14 ... 70 E6
Old Barn Cl SM2 ... 58 E3
Old Barn Dr RH5 ... 178 D6
Old Barn La Churt GU10 ... 168 B1
Kenley CR3 ... 80 F3
Old Barn Rd KT18 ... 76 C2
Old Barn View GU7 ... 150 C2
Old Bisley Rd GU16 ... 66 C3
Old Bracknell Cl RG12 ... 27 B6
Old Bracknell La E RG12 ... 27 B6
Old Bracknell La W RG12 ... 27 B6
Old Brickfield Rd GU11 ... 126 B7
Old Bridge St KT1 ... 37 D7
Old Brighton Rd S RH11 ... 181 E5
Old Bromley Rd BR1 ... 24 D3
Old Charlton Rd TW17 ... 34 C4
Old Chertsey Rd GU24 ... 50 C1
Old Chestnut Ave KT10 ... 55 B4
Old Church La GU9 ... 146 D7
Old Church Path KT10 ... 55 B6
Old Claygate La KT10 ... 56 A5
Old Common Rd KT11 ... 73 B7
Old Compton La GU9 ... 125 F2
Old Control Rd RH6 ... 181 D6
Old Convent The RH19 ... 185 E2
Old Cote Dr TW5 ... 5 A8
Old Cotts GU3 ... 130 C2
Old Court Rd GU2 ... 130 A8
Old Crawley Rd RH12 ... 218 C7
Old Cross Tree Way
GU12 ... 127 C8
Old Ct KT21 ... 95 E8
Old Dean Rd GU15 ... 65 D7
Old Deer Park Gdns TW9 ... 6 E4
Old Denne Gdns RH12 ... 217 C1
Old Devonshire Rd SW12 ... 21 B8
Old Dock Cl TW9 ... 7 A8
Old Elstead Rd GU8 ... 149 E2
Old Esher Cl KT12 ... 54 D5
Old Esher Rd KT12 ... 54 E5
Old Farleigh Rd
Chelsham CR0, CR2, CR6 ... 81 E6
Selsdon CR0, CR6, CR22 ... 81 E6
Old Farm Cl TW4 ... 4 F3
Old Farm Pl GU12 ... 105 F5
Old Farm Rd
Guildford GU1 ... 109 D4
Hampton TW12 ... 15 F2
Old Farmhouse Dr KT22 ... 74 D4
Old Farnham La
Bentley GU10 ... 124 A1
Farnham GU9 ... 146 C8
Old Ford House CR0 ... 60 E7
Old Forge Cres TW17 ... 34 B3
Old Fox Cl CR3 ... 100 B6
Old Frensham Rd
Farnham GU10 ... 146 E4
Frensham GU10 ... 146 E4
Old Green La GU15 ... 65 C7
Old Guildford Rd
Mytchett GU12, GU16 ... 86 C4
Warnham RH12 ... 216 E4
Old Haslemere Rd GU27 ... 208 C5
Old Heath Way GU9 ... 125 C7
Old Hill GU22 ... 89 D7
Old Horsham Rd RH11 ... 201 B4
Old Hospital Cl
SW12, SW17 ... 20 F7
Old House Cl Ewell KT17 ... 57 F1
Wimbledon SW19 ... 19 E3
Old House Gdns 9 TW1 ... 6 C1
Old Kiln GU9 ... 125 A2
Old Kiln Cl GU10 ... 167 F2
Old Kiln Court Yd 15 GU9 125 B2
Old Kiln La Brockham RH3 137 C8
Churt GU10 ... 167 F2
Old Kingston Rd KT4 ... 57 C7
Old La Aldershot GU11 ... 126 A7
Aldershot, North
Town GU12 ... 105 E3
Dockenfield GU10 ... 166 F4
East Horsley KT11 ... 93 A5
Martyr's Green KT11 ... 92 E7
Ockham GU23, KT11 ... 72 B1
Oxted RH8 ... 122 F5
Tatsfield TN16 ... 103 D6
Old Lands Hill RG12 ... 27 D8
Old Lane Gdns KT11 ... 93 A5
Old Lodge Cl GU7 ... 150 B3
Old Lodge La CR8 ... 80 A3
Old Lodge Pl 7 TW1 ... 6 B1
Old London Rd
Epsom KT17, KT18 ... 77 A2
Mickleham RH5 ... 115 C8
Old Malden La KT4 ... 57 E8
Old Malt Way GU21 ... 69 D2
Old Manor Cl RH11 ... 201 A8
Old Manor Dr TW7 ... 5 C1
Old Manor Gdns GU4 ... 131 C3
Old Martyrs RH11 ... 181 D1
Old Merrow St GU4 ... 110 D3
Old Mill La RH1 ... 119 B7
Old Mill Pl GU27 ... 207 F7
Old Millmeads RH12 ... 217 C5
Old Museum Ct GU27 ... 208 D6
Old Nursery Pl TW15 ... 14 B3
Old Oak Ave CR5 ... 98 E8
Old Orch Byfleet KT14 ... 71 F7
Sunbury TW16 ... 35 C7
Old Orchard The GU9 ... 146 A8
Old Palace La TW9 ... 6 C2
Old Palace Rd
Croydon CR0, CR9 ... 61 C7
Guildford GU2 ... 130 A8
Weybridge KT13 ... 53 B7
Old Palace Sch CR9 ... 61 B7
Old Palace Terr 8 TW9 ... 6 D2
Old Palace Yd 2 TW9 ... 6 D2
Old Park Cl GU9 ... 125 A6
Old Park La Farnham GU9 ... 125 A4
Hale GU9 ... 124 F6
Old Park Mews TW5 ... 4 F7
Old Parvis Rd KT14 ... 71 C7
Old Pasture Rd GU16, GU15 65 F3
Old Pharmacy Ct RG45 ... 45 C4
Old Pond Cl GU15 ... 65 C1
Old Portsmouth Rd
Artington GU2, GU3, GU7 ... 130 C3
Frimley GU15 ... 66 A5
Shalford GU2, GU3, GU7 ... 130 C3
Thursley GU8 ... 169 D4
Old Pottery Cl RH2 ... 139 B7
Old Quarry The GU27 ... 207 F4
Old Rd Addlestone KT15 ... 51 F3
Buckland RH3 ... 116 F1
East Grinstead RH19 ... 185 F1
Old Rectory Cl
Bramley GU5 ... 151 F6
Walton on t H KT20 ... 97 A3
Old Rectory Dr GU12 ... 106 B2
Old Rectory Gdns
Farnborough GU14 ... 85 D4
Old Rectory Gdns *continued*
Godalming GU7 ... 150 F2
Old Rectory La KT24 ... 92 E1
Old Redstone Dr RH1 ... 140 A8
Old Reigate Rd
Brockham RH3 ... 116 C1
Dorking RH4 ... 115 F2
Old Sawmill La RG45 ... 45 C6
Old School Cl Ash GU12 ... 106 A3
Merton SW19 ... 40 A7
Penge BR3 ... 43 E7
Old School Ct
Leatherhead KT22 ... 95 B5
Wraysbury TW19 ... 11 E8
Old School La
Brockham RH3 ... 137 A7
Newdigate RH5 ... 158 B1
Old School Mews KT13 ... 53 D6
Old School Pl
Lingfield RH7 ... 164 D4
Woking GU22 ... 89 F6
Old School Sq KT7 ... 36 F3
Old Schools La KT17 ... 57 F2
Old St Mary's KT24 ... 112 B6
Old Station App KT22 ... 95 A6
Old Station Cl RH10 ... 204 B7
Old Station Rd GU7 ... 150 E6
Old Station Way GU7 ... 150 E5
Old Surrey Mews
The RH9 ... 121 C5
Old Swan Yd SM5 ... 59 F6
Old Town CR0, CR9 ... 61 B7
Old Town Mews GU9 ... 125 A2
Old Tye Ave TN16 ... 83 E3
Old Westhall Cl CR6 ... 101 C8
Old Wickhurst La RH12 ... 216 D2
Old Woking Rd
Old Woking GU22 ... 90 C8
Pyrford GU22, KT14 ... 70 D3
West Byfleet KT14 ... 71 A6
Woking GU22 ... 90 C8
Old Wokingham Rd
Bracknell RG45 ... 45 C7
Crowthorne RG45 ... 45 C7
Oldacre GU24 ... 67 F7
Oldbury RG12 ... 26 F6
Oldbury Cl Frimley GU16 ... 85 F8
Horsham RH12 ... 218 A7
Oldbury Rd KT16 ... 32 E2
Olde Farm Dr GU17 ... 64 B5
Olden La CR8 ... 80 A7
Oldfield Gdns KT21 ... 95 D8
Oldfield House SW16 ... 21 B4
Oldfield House Sch TW12 ... 35 F8
Oldfield Rd Hampton TW12 ... 35 F8
Horley RH6 ... 160 F1
Wimbledon SW19 ... 19 E2
Oldfields Rd SM1, SM3 ... 59 A8
Oldfields Trad Est SM1 ... 59 A7
Oldfieldwood GU22 ... 70 B2
Oldham House 10 SE21 ... 22 E4
Oldhouse La Bisley GU24 ... 68 A5
West End GU24 ... 68 A5
Windlesham GU18 ... 48 C2
Olding House 6 SW12 ... 21 C8
Oldridge Rd SW12 ... 21 B8
Oldstead RG12 ... 27 D4
Oldstead Rd BR1 ... 24 D4
Oldwood Chase GU14 ... 84 C3
Oleander Cl RG45 ... 45 A7
Olive Rd 3 SW19 ... 20 C1
Oliver Ave SE25 ... 42 F6
Oliver Cl Addlestone KT15 ... 52 B6
Brentford W4 ... 7 B8
Oliver Ct TW7 ... 5 F4
Oliver Gr SE25 ... 42 F5
Oliver Rd Ascot SL5 ... 29 B5
Horsham RH12 ... 217 A1
Kingston u T KT3 ... 38 C7
Sutton SM1 ... 59 D6
Olivier Rd RH10 ... 202 D5
Ollerton RG12 ... 27 A1
Olley Cl SM6 ... 60 E4
Olveston Wlk SM4, SM5 ... 40 D3
Olyffe Dr BR3 ... 44 C8
Omega Rd GU21 ... 70 A3
Omega Way TW20 ... 32 C8
One Tree Cnr GU1 ... 131 B8
One Tree Hill Rd GU4 ... 131 B7
Ongar Cl KT15 ... 51 F4
Ongar Hill KT15 ... 52 A4
Ongar Pl KT15 ... 52 A4
Ongar Place Inf Sch KT15 ... 52 A4
Ongar Rd KT15 ... 52 A5
Onslow Ave Belmont SM2 ... 77 F8
Richmond TW10 ... 6 E2
Onslow Avenue Mansions
TW10 ... 6 E2
Onslow Cl
Thames Ditton KT7 ... 36 E1
Woking GU22 ... 70 A2
Onslow Cres GU22 ... 70 A2
Onslow Cty Inf Sch GU2 ... 129 F7
Onslow Dr SL5 ... 9 A1
Onslow Gdns
Sanderstead CR2 ... 81 A7
Thames Ditton KT7 ... 36 E1
Wallington SM6 ... 60 C3
Onslow House 1 KT2 ... 37 F8
Onslow Lodge TW18 ... 12 F1
Onslow Mews KT16 ... 33 A3
Onslow Rd Guildford GU1 ... 109 D1
Hersham KT12 ... 54 A5
New Malden KT3 ... 39 A5
Richmond TW10 ... 6 E1

Onslow Rd continued
Sunningdale SL5 30 B2
Thornton Heath CR0 42 A1
Onslow St GU1 130 C8
Onslow Way Pyrford GU22 70 F4
Thames Ditton KT7 36 E1
Ontario Cl RH6 162 A2
Onyx House KT4 38 D1
Opal House KT4 38 D1
Openview SW17, SW18 20 D6
Opladen Way RG12 27 E4
Opossum Dr TW4 4 C4
Opus Park GU4 109 D6
Oracle Ctr RG12 27 C7
Orangery The TW10 17 C6
Orchard Ave Ashford TW15 14 C2
Carshalton CR4 41 A1
Croydon CR0 43 E1
Hatton TW14 3 D2
Heston TW5 4 E7
Hinchley Wood KT7 56 A8
Kingston u T KT3 38 E6
Woodham KT15 70 F8
Orchard Bsns Ctr SE26 23 F3
Orchard Bsns Ctr The RH1 161 A8
Orchard Cl Ash Vale GU12 106 A5
Ashford TW15 14 C2
Ashstead KT21 95 D7
Banstead SM7 78 B5
East Horsley KT24 92 F3
Farnborough GU17 64 F1
Farnham GU9 126 A6
Fetcham KT22 94 D5
Flexford GU3 107 B1
Guildford GU1 110 B1
Horley RH6 160 F4
Leatherhead KT22 94 F8
Walton-on-T KT12 35 B2
West Barnes SW20 39 C5
West End GU24 67 D6
West Ewell KT19 57 B4
Woking GU22 70 B3
Wokingham RG40 25 D6
Orchard Cotts
Charlwood RH6 180 F7
Lingfield RH7 165 B3
Orchard Ct Barnes SW13 7 F4
Bracknell RG12 27 C7
Croydon BR3 44 A1
Harmondsworth UB7 2 C7
Hounslow TW7 5 D7
Wallington SM6 60 B5
Walton-on-T KT12 34 F1
Orchard Cty Fst Sch The KT8 36 D5
Orchard Dene KT14 71 A6
Orchard Dr Sunbury TW17 34 E6
Woking GU21 69 F4
Orchard End
Caterham CR3 100 E5
Fetcham KT22 94 C3
Oatlands Park KT13 53 E8
Rowledge GU10 145 F3
Orchard Gate
Sandhurst GU47 64 B8
Thames Ditton KT10 36 D1
Orchard Gdns
Aldershot GU11 126 C8
Chessington KT9 56 E6
Cranleigh GU6 174 F2
Effingham KT24 113 E7
Epsom KT18 76 C4
Sutton SM1 59 A5
Orchard Gr Croydon CR0 43 E2
Penge SE20 23 A1
Orchard Hill
Rudgwick RH12 214 C7
Windlesham GU20 48 D3
Orchard House
Guildford GU4 110 D2
Tongham GU10 126 F7
Orchard House Cheyne Ctr (Hospl) BR4 63 C7
Orchard Jun & Inf Sch The TW3 5 A3
Orchard La
Thames Ditton KT8 36 D3
Wimbledon SW20 39 B8
Orchard Lea Cl GU22 70 E4
Orchard Mains GU22 89 C8
Orchard Pl RG40 25 C6
Orchard Rd Brentford TW8 6 C8
Chessington KT9 56 E6
Dorking RH4 136 B6
Farnborough GU14 85 A4
Farnham GU9 126 A4
Guildford, Burpham GU4 110 B5
Guildford, Onslow Village GU2 129 F7
Hampton TW12 15 F1
Hamsey Green CR2 81 B5
Horsham RH13 217 E2
Hounslow TW4 5 A2
Kingston u T KT1 37 E7
Mortlake TW9 7 A4
Reigate RH2 118 B1
Shalford GU4 130 E3
Shere GU5 133 A4
Smallfield RH6 162 C3
Sunbury TW16 15 B1
Sutton SM1 59 A6
Twickenham TW1 6 B2
Orchard Rise Croydon CR0 43 F1
Kingston u T KT2 38 C8
Orchard Rise continued
Mortlake TW10 7 B3
Orchard School Sports Ctr SE20 43 A8
Orchard St
Crawley RH10, RH11 201 D6
Thames Ditton KT7 37 B2
Orchard The Banstead SM7 78 A4
Dorking RH5 136 C3
Ewell KT17 57 F1
Ewell KT17, KT19 57 F3
Haslemere GU27 207 F5
Hounslow TW3 5 C5
Lightwater GU18 67 B8
Thorpe GU25 31 E4
Weybridge KT13 53 B6
Woking GU22 89 E5
Orchard Way
Addlestone KT15 52 B4
Aldershot GU11, GU12 126 C8
Ashford TW15 13 F6
Beckenham BR3, CR0 43 E3
Camberley GU15 65 B2
Carshalton SM1 59 D6
Croydon BR3, CR0 43 E3
Dorking RH4 136 B6
East Grinstead RH19 185 E1
Esher KT10 55 C4
Flexford GU3 107 B1
Lower Kingswood KT20 97 F1
Oxted RH8 123 A2
Reigate RH2 139 B6
Send GU23 90 C2
Orchard Way Prim Sch CR0 43 E2
Orchardfield Rd GU7 150 F7
Orchardleigh KT22 95 B5
Orchards Cl KT14 71 A5
Orchards The
Ashford TW15 14 D3
[4] Crawley RH11 200 D5
Horsham RH12 217 F5
Orchid Dr GU24 68 A4
Orchid Mead SM7 78 B5
Orde Cl RH10 182 D1
Ordnance Cl TW13 15 A6
Ordnance Rd GU11 105 C3
Ordnance Rdbt GU11 105 B2
Oregano Way GU2 109 A6
Oregon Cl KT3 38 C5
Orestan La KT24 113 C8
Orford Ct Wallington SM6 60 C5
West Norwood SE27 22 B6
Orford Gdns TW1 16 F6
Orford Rd SE6 24 B5
Oriel Cl Crawley RH10 182 C1
Mitcham CR4 41 D6
Oriel Ct [6] CR0 42 D1
Oriel Hill GU15 65 D4
Oriel Jun & Inf Sch TW13 15 E5
Oriental Cl GU22 70 A2
Oriental Rd Ascot SL5 29 D5
Woking GU22 70 A3
Orion RG12 27 A1
Orion Ct RH11 200 D4
Orion Ctr The CR0 60 E8
Orlando Gdns KT19 57 D1
Orlean Ct KT12 54 C8
Orleans Cl KT10 55 D8
Orleans Ct [10] TW1 17 B8
Orleans Inf Sch TW1 17 B8
Orleans Park Sec Sch TW1 17 B8
Orleans Rd
South Norwood SE19 22 D2
[10] Twickenham TW1 17 C8
Orltons La RH12 179 F2
Ormanton Rd SE26 23 A4
Orme Rd KT1, KT3 38 B7
Ormeley Rd SW12 21 B7
Ormerod Gdns CR4 41 A8
Ormesby Wlk RH10 202 B4
Ormond Ave
Hampton TW12 36 B8
[22] Richmond TW10 6 D2
Ormond Cres TW12 36 B8
Ormond Dr TW12 16 B1
Ormond Rd TW10 6 D2
Ormonde Ave KT19 57 D1
Ormonde Lodge (West London Ins of Higher Education) TW1 6 B2
Ormonde Rd
Farncombe GU7 150 E6
Mortlake SW14 7 C4
Woking GU21 69 C3
Wokingham RG41 25 A5
Ormsby SM2 59 B3
Ormside Way RH1 119 B4
Ormuz Cotts RH7 164 C4
Orpin Rd RH1 119 C5
Orpwood Cl TW12 15 F2
Orwell Cl GU14 84 E6
Orwell Gdns RH2 139 B7
Orwell House [7] RH1 118 F2
Osborn La SE23 23 E8
Osborn Rd GU9 125 D4
Osborne Ave TW19 13 F7
Osborne Cl Beckenham BR3 43 E5
Feltham TW13 15 D3
Frimley GU16 85 F8
Osborne Ct Crawley RH11 201 B2
Farnborough GU14 105 C8
[10] Surbiton KT6 37 E3
Osborne Dr GU18 67 A8
Osborne Gdns CR7 42 C7
Osborne Pl SM1 59 D5
Osborne Rd Egham TW20 11 F2
Osborne Rd continued
Farnborough GU14 105 C8
Hounslow TW3, TW4 4 F4
Kingston u T KT2 17 E1
Redhill RH1 119 A4
South Norwood CR7 42 C7
Walton-on-T KT12 35 A1
Wokingham RG40 25 C6
Osbourne Terr [1] SW17 21 A3
Osier Pl TW20 12 C2
Osier Way
Banstead KT17, SM7 77 E5
Mitcham CR4 40 F4
Oslac Rd SE6 24 B3
Oslo Ct SW19 20 D1
Osman's Cl RG42 8 B1
Osmond Gdns SM6 60 C5
Osmund Cl RH10 202 E6
Osmunda Bank RH19 185 E6
Osnaburgh Hill GU15 65 B5
Osney Cl RH11 201 C5
Osney Wlk SM4, SM5 40 D3
Osprey Cl Cheam SM1 58 F5
Fetcham KT22 94 C5
Osprey Gdns CR0, CR2 62 E1
Ospringe Cl [9] SE20 23 C1
Ostade Rd SW2 21 F8
Osterley Ave TW7 5 D7
Osterley Cl RG40 25 F5
Osterley Cres TW7 5 F6
Osterley Ct TW7 5 D6
Osterley Lodge [1] TW7 5 E6
Osterley Rd TW7 5 E6
Osterley Sta TW7 5 D7
Osterly Gdns CR7 42 C7
Oswald Cl KT22 94 C5
Oswald Rd KT22 94 C5
Osward CR0 62 F1
Osward Rd SW12, SW17 20 F6
Otford Cl SE20 43 C8
Othello Gr RG42 27 E8
Otho Ct [5] TW8 6 D7
Otter Cl Crowthorne RG45 45 A7
Ottershaw KT16 51 B4
Otter Mdw KT22 94 F8
Otterbourne Pl RH19 185 B1
Otterbourne Rd [1] CR0, CR9 61 C8
Otterburn Gdns TW7 6 A7
Otterburn St SW17 20 F2
Otterden St SE6 24 A4
Ottermead La KT16 51 C4
Ottershaw House CR4 40 D7
Ottershaw Pk KT16 51 A3
Ottways Ave KT21 95 D8
Ottways La KT21, KT22 95 D8
Otway Cl RH11 200 F4
Oulton Wlk RH10 202 B4
Our Lady of the Rosary RC Sch TW18 13 A2
Our Lady Queen of Heaven RC Prim Sch SW19 19 D8
Our Lady Queen Of Heaven RC Sch RH11 201 B8
Our Lady & St Philip Neri Prim Sch SE26 23 E4
Our Lady & St Philip Neri RC Sch Forest Hill SE23 23 D5
Forest Hill SE26 23 E4
Our Lady's Prep Sch RG45 45 B5
Our Ladys RC First Sch KT16 33 A1
Ouseley Rd
Upper Tooting SW12 20 F7
Wraysbury TW19 11 D8
Outdowns KT24 113 B5
Outram Pl KT13 53 C5
Outram Rd CR0 61 F8
Outwood House [6] SW2 21 F8
Outwood La
Bletchingley RH1 141 D7
Chipstead CR5, KT20 98 C6
Kingswood CR5, KT20 98 C6
Outwood RH1 141 D1
Oval Prim Sch CR0 42 E1
Oval Rd CR0 42 E1
Oval The Banstead SM7 78 A5
Farncombe GU7 150 F7
Guildford GU2 130 A8
Wood St V GU3 108 B2
Overbrae BR3 24 A3
Overbrook Godalming GU7 151 A5
West Horsley KT24 112 B6
Overbury Ave BR3 44 C6
Overbury Cres CR0 63 C1
Overbury Ct BR3 44 C6
Overdale Ashstead KT21 75 E3
Bletchingley RH1 120 C2
Dorking RH5 136 D8
Overdale Ave KT3 38 D7
Overdale Rise GU16 65 E3
Overdene Dr RH11 201 A6
Overdown Rd SE6 24 B4
Overford Cl GU6 174 E2
Overford Dr GU6 174 E2
Overhill CR6 101 C8
Overhill Rd
Dulwich SE21, SE22 23 A8
Wallington CR8 61 A1
Overhill Way BR3 44 D4
Overlord Cl GU15 65 C8
Overstand Cl BR3 44 A4
Overstone Gdns CR0 43 F2
Overthorpe Cl GU21 68 E2
Overton Cl Aldershot GU11 126 C6
Hounslow TW7 5 F6
Overton House SW15 18 F8
Overton Rd SM2 59 A3
Overton Shaw RH19 185 E4
Overton's Yd CR0, CR9 61 C7
Oveton Way KT23 94 B1
Ovett Cl SE19 22 E2
Ovingdon Ct GU21 68 F3
Owen Cl CR0 42 D3
Owen House Feltham TW14 15 A8
[6] Twickenham TW1 17 B8
Owen Pl KT22 95 B5
Owen Rd Farncombe GU7 150 F6
Windlesham GU20 48 D5
Owen Wlk [7] SE20 23 A1
Owens Way SE23 23 E8
Owl Cl CR2 62 D1
Owlbeech Ct RH13 218 B4
Owlbeech Pl RH13 218 B4
Owlbeech Way RH13 218 B4
Owletts RH10 202 D7
Owlscastle Cl RH12 217 D5
Owlsmoor Cty Prim Sch GU47 45 E1
Owlsmoor Rd GU47 45 D1
Ownstead Gdns CR2 80 F8
Ownsted Hill CR0 63 D1
Oxdowne Cl KT11 74 B5
Oxenden Ct GU10 126 E8
Oxenden Rd GU10, GU12 126 F8
Oxenhope RG12 27 A5
Oxford Ave Harlington TW6 3 F7
Merton SW20 39 E7
Oxford Cl
Littleton TW15, TW17 14 C1
Mitcham CR4 41 C6
Oxford Cres KT3 38 D3
Oxford Ct Epsom KT18 76 E5
[17] Kingston u T KT6 37 E4
Oxford Gdns W4 7 A8
Oxford Rd
Carshalton SM2, SM5 59 E5
Crawley RH10 201 F2
Farnborough GU14 85 C1
Guildford GU1 130 D7
Horsham RH13 217 E2
Redhill RH1 118 E2
Sandhurst GU47 45 E2
South Norwood SE19 22 D2
Teddington TW11, TW12 16 D3
Wallington SM6 60 C5
Wokingham RG41 25 A6
Oxford Terr GU1 130 D7
Oxford Way TW13 15 D4
Oxleigh Cl KT3 38 E4
Oxlip Cl CR0 43 D1
Oxshott Rd Ashstead KT22 74 F3
Leatherhead KT22 75 A2
Oxshott Rise KT11 73 E5
Oxshott Sta KT22 74 C6
Oxshott Way KT11 73 E4
Oxted Cl CR4 40 D6
Oxted Cty Sch RH8 122 F7
Oxted Gn GU8 170 E7
Oxted Hospl RH8 122 D7
Oxted Rd Tandridge RH9 121 D4
Tyler's Green RH9 121 D4
Oxted Sta RH8 122 E6
Oxtoby Way SW16 41 D8
Oyster La KT14 71 E7

P

Pacific Cl TW14 14 F7
Packer Cl RH19 186 A3
Packham Ct KT4 58 C7
Packway GU9 146 E7
Padbrook RH8 123 A6
Padbury Cl TW14 14 D7
Padbury Oaks UB7 2 B6
Paddock Cl
Beare Green RH5 157 D4
Camberley GU15 66 A6
Cobham KT11 73 C5
Forest Hill SE26 23 D4
Hambledon GU8 171 C1
Lingfield RH7 164 C4
New Malden KT4 38 E1
Oxted RH8 122 F4
Paddock Ct SW20 39 C5
Paddock Gdns
East Grinstead RH19 205 E7
South Norwood SE19 22 E2
Paddock Gr RH5 157 D4
Paddock House GU4 110 D2
Paddock Sch SW15 7 F3
Paddock The
Addington CR0 63 A4
Bracknell RG12 27 C6
Cranleigh GU6 174 D3
Crawley RH10 202 D7
Crowthorne RG45 45 A6
Ewhurst GU6 175 E4
Godalming GU7 150 F3
Grayshott GU26 188 A4
Guildford GU1 110 D2
Haslemere GU27 208 A8
Westcott RH4 135 C6
Paddock Way
Grayswood GU27 190 A2
Oxted RH8 122 F4
Sheerwater GU21 70 B5
Paddock Wlk CR6 101 B8
Paddockhurst Rd
Crawley RH11 201 A5
Crawley RH10 203 C2
Paddocks Cl KT21 75 E1
Paddocks Mead GU21 68 F3
Paddocks Rd GU4 110 A5
Paddocks The
Flexford GU3 107 C1
Great Bookham KT23 94 B1
Oatlands Park KT13 53 E7
Woodham KT15 52 B1
Paddocks Way
Ashstead KT21 75 E1
Chertsey KT16 33 B1
Padstow Wlk
Crawley RH11 200 F4
East Bedfont TW14 14 F7
Padua Rd SE20 43 C8
Padwick Rd RH13 218 A2
Page Cl TW12 15 E2
Page Cres CR0 61 B5
Page Croft KT15 52 B8
Page Ct RH13 217 D1
Page Rd TW14 3 D1
Page's Croft RG40 25 D5
Page's Yd W4 7 E8
Pageant Wlk CR0 61 E7
Pagehurst Rd CR0 43 B2
Paget Ave SM1 59 D7
Paget Cl Camberley GU15 66 B7
Hampton TW12 16 D4
Paget La TW7 5 E4
Paget Pl Kingston u T KT2 18 C2
Thames Ditton KT7 36 F1
Pagewood Cl RH10 202 D4
Pagoda Ave TW9 6 F4
Paice Gn RG40 25 D7
Pain's Cl CR4 41 B7
Paines Hill RH8 123 C4
Paisley Rd SM5 40 D1
Pakenham Cl SW12 21 A7
Pakenham Rd RG12 27 D2
Palace Ct
South Norwood CR7 42 D5
Streatham SW2 22 A6
Woking GU21 70 A3
Palace Dr KT13 53 B7
Palace Gn CR0 62 F3
Palace Gr SE19 22 F1
Palace Rd East Molesey KT8 36 D6
Kingston u T KT1 37 D5
Penge SE19 22 F1
Streatham SE27, SW16, SW2 22 A6
Woodham KT15 52 B2
Palace Sq SE19 22 F1
Palace View CR0 62 F6
Palestine Gr SW19 40 D8
Palewell Common Dr SW14 7 D2
Palewell Pk SW14 7 D3
Palgrave House [4] TW2 16 C8
Pallingham Dr RH10 202 C3
Palm Ct BR3 43 F6
Palm Gr GU1 109 C5
Palmer Ave KT4, SM3 58 C6
Palmer C of E Jun Sch The RG40 25 D7
Palmer Cl Crowthorne RG45 45 A8
Heston TW5 5 A6
Horley RH6 160 F5
Redhill RH1 140 A8
West Wickham BR4 63 D8
Palmer Cres
Kingston u T KT1 37 E6
Ottershaw KT16 51 D4
Palmer Rd RH10 202 C3
Palmer School Rd RG40 25 C6
Palmer's Lodge GU2 130 B8
Palmers Gr KT8 36 A5
Palmers Rd Mortlake SW14 7 C4
Thornton Heath SW16 41 F7
Palmersfield Rd SM7 78 B5
Palmerston Cl
Farnborough GU14 84 D3
Woking GU21 70 A5
Palmerston Ct [9] KT6 37 D2
Palmerston Gr [4] SW19 20 A1
Palmerston House SM7 77 F4
Palmerston Rd
Carshalton SM5 60 A6
Hounslow TW3 5 C6
Merton SW19 20 A1
Mortlake SW14 7 C3
Sutton SM1 59 C5
Thornton Heath CR0 42 D4
Twickenham TW2 5 E1
Pampisford Rd
Croydon CR2, CR8 61 B2
Purley CR2, CR8 61 B2
Pams Way KT19 57 D5
Pan's Gdns GU15 65 F4
Pandora Ct [4] KT6 37 E3
Pangbourne Ct SW17 20 C4
Pankhurst Cl TW7 5 F4
Pankhurst Ct [11] RH11 201 B1
Pankhurst Dr RG12 27 D4
Pankhurst Rd KT12 35 C2
Panmuir Rd SW20 39 B8
Panmure Rd SE26 23 B5
Pannell Cl RH19 185 D1
Pannells GU10 146 D5
Pannells Cl KT16 32 F1
Pannells Ct GU1 130 D8
Pantile Rd KT13 53 D6
Pantiles Cl GU21 69 B1
Paper Mews RH4 136 B8
Papercourt La GU23 90 F6
Papplewick Sch SL5 29 A2
Papworth Way SW2 22 A8
Parade Cl GU23 90 C4
Parade Mews SE27, SW2 22 B6
Parade The Ash GU12 106 A4
Ashford TW16 14 F1
Burgh Heath KT20 97 E8
Claygate KT10 55 E4

Parade The *continued*
Coulsdon CR5 80 A1
Epsom KT18 76 D6
2 Kingston u T KT2 37 E7
Wallington CR0 60 F5
Wentworth GU25 31 D3
Paradise Rd TW10 6 E2
Paragon Gr KT5 37 F3
Parbury Rise KT9 56 E4
Parchmore Rd CR7 42 C6
Parchmore Way CR7 42 B7
Pares Cl GU21 69 D3
Parfew Ct SE22 23 B6
Parfitts Cl GU9 125 A2
Parfour Dr CR8 80 C3
Parham Rd RH11 200 F7
Parish Church C of E Inf & Jun Schs CR9 61 B7
Parish Cl Ash GU12 106 B1
Hale GU9 125 A6
Parish Ct KT6 37 E3
Parish House 6 RH11 201 D5
Parish La SE20, SE26 23 D1
Parish Rd GU14 105 B8
Park Ave Bromley BR1 24 F2
Camberley GU15 65 D4
Caterham CR3 100 E3
Egham TW20 12 C1
Isleworth TW3 5 B1
Mitcham CR4 21 B1
Mortlake SW14 7 D3
Peper Harow GU8 149 C5
Salfords RH1 139 F1
Staines TW18 13 A2
Upper Halliford TW17 34 E6
Wallington SM5 60 A4
West Wickham BR4 63 C8
Wokingham RG40 25 B6
Park Ave E KT17 58 A4
Park Ave W KT17 58 A4
Park Avenue Mews CR4 21 B1
Park Barn Dr GU2, GU3 108 E2
Park Barn E GU2 108 F2
Park Chase
Godalming GU7 150 E2
Guildford GU1 109 E1
Park Cl Binstead GU10 145 A2
Brockham RH3 137 B4
Esher KT10 55 A4
Fetcham KT22 94 D3
Grayswood GU27 190 A1
Hampton TW12 36 C8
Isleworth TW3, TW7 5 C2
Kingston u T KT2 38 A8
Oatlands Park KT13 53 F8
Wallington SM5 59 F4
Woodham KT15 52 C1
Park Close Cotts TW20 10 F3
Park Copse RH5 136 D7
Park Corner Dr KT24 112 E7
Park Cotts 10 TW1 6 B1
Park Cres Sunningdale SL5 29 F3
Twickenham TW2 16 D7
Park Ct Beckenham BR3 44 B6
Farnham GU9 125 D3
New Malden KT3 38 D5
Teddington KT1 37 C8
Upper Tooting SW12 21 A7
Wallington SM6 60 E5
West Norwood SE21 22 D5
Woking GU22 69 F1
Park Dr Bramley GU5 151 F6
Cranleigh GU6 174 F3
Mortlake SW14 7 D3
Sunningdale SL5 29 F3
Weybridge KT13 53 B5
Woking GU22 69 F1
Park End BR1 44 F8
Park Farm Cl RH12 217 D7
Park Farm Ind Est GU15 65 C1
Park Farm Rd
Horsham RH12 217 D7
Kingston u T KT2 17 E1
Park Gate Cotts GU6 174 C3
Park Gate Ct
Teddington TW12 16 C3
11 Woking GU22 69 E1
Park Gdns KT2 17 F3
Park Gn KT23 94 A3
Park Hall Rd Dulwich SE21 22 D5
Reigate RH2 118 A3
West Norwood SE21 22 D5
Park Hall Road Trad Est SE21 22 D5
Park Hill Forest Hill SE23 23 C7
Richmond TW10 6 F1
Wallington SM5 59 F4
Park Hill Cl SM5 59 E5
Park Hill Ct
South Croydon CR0 61 E8
Upper Tooting SW17 20 F5
Park Hill Inf Sch CR0 61 E7
Park Hill Jun Sch CR0 61 E7
Park Hill Rd
Beckenham BR2 44 E7
Ewell KT17 76 F8
South Croydon CR0, CR2 61 E7
Wallington SM6 60 B3
Park Hill Rise CR0 61 F7
Park Hill Sch KT2 18 A1
Park Ho 8 GU11 105 A1
Park Horsley KT24 113 A6
Park House Penge SE26 23 A3
Reigate RH2 138 F7
Park House Cotts GU6 174 F3
Park House Dr RH2 138 F7
Park House Gdns TW1 6 C2
Park House Mid Sch SW19 19 F4
Park La Ashstead KT21 96 A8
Ashurst Wood RH19 206 D6
Brook GU8 190 A8
Camberley GU15 65 C5
Cheam SM3 58 E4
Cranford TW5 4 A7
Croydon CR0, CR9 61 D7
Guildford GU4 110 D3
Hooley CR5 99 D6
Horton SL3 1 A4
Lingfield RH7 164 F5
Ockley RH5 177 F7
Reigate RH2 138 E8
Richmond TW9 6 D3
Teddington TW11 16 F2
Wallington SM5, SM6 60 A5
Winkfield SL4 9 B7
Park La E RH2 139 A7
Park Lawn CR7 42 C7
Park Lawn Rd KT13 53 C6
Park Ley Rd CR3 101 D6
Park Mansions SE26 23 C5
Park Mead Cty Inf Sch GU6 175 A3
Park Mead Jun Sch GU6 175 A3
Park Mews TW19 13 F8
Park Pl Hampton TW12 16 C2
Horsham RH12 217 C1
4 Woking GU22 69 F1
Park Prim Sch GU11 126 C7
Park Rd Albury GU5 132 E2
Aldershot GU11 126 B8
Ashford TW15 14 B3
Ashstead KT21 75 E1
Banstead SM7 78 C3
Beckenham BR3 23 F1
Bracknell RG12 27 D8
Burstow RH6 162 C1
Camberley GU15 65 C4
Caterham CR3 100 E4
Cheam SM3 58 E4
Chiswick W4 7 D8
Crowhurst RH7 143 E2
Dormans Park RH19 185 F6
East Grinstead RH19 185 D1
East Molesey KT8 36 C5
Egham TW20 12 A4
Esher KT10 55 B6
Farnborough GU11, GU14 105 E8
Farnham GU9 125 D4
Faygate RH12 199 F1
Feltham TW13 15 D4
Fickleshole CR6 82 E5
Forest Row RH18 206 F2
Godalming GU7 150 E2
Guildford GU1 109 D1
Hackbridge SM6 60 B8
Hampton TW12 16 C3
Haslemere GU27 208 C5
Isleworth TW3, TW7 5 C2
Isleworth TW7 6 B5
Kenley CR8 80 C4
Kingston u T KT2, TW10 18 A1
Limpsfield RH8 122 F7
Lower Halliford TW17 34 A1
Mitcham SW19 20 E2
New Malden KT3 38 D5
Redhill RH1 118 F3
Richmond TW10 6 F1
Sandhurst GU47 64 C8
Slinfold RH13 215 D3
South Norwood SE25 42 E5
Stanwell TW19 2 C1
Sunbury TW16 15 B1
Surbiton KT5 37 C8
Teddington TW11 16 F2
Teddington, Hampton Wick KT1 37 C8
Twickenham TW1 6 C1
Wallington SM6 60 B5
Woking GU22 70 A2
Wokingham RG40 25 B6
Woodmansterne CR5, KT20, SM7 78 C3
Park Rise Forest Hill SE23 23 E7
Horsham RH12 217 B4
Leatherhead KT22 95 B6
Park Rise Cl KT22 95 B6
Park Rise Rd SE23 23 E7
Park Road House 3 KT2 18 A1
Park Row GU9 125 B3
Park Sch The GU22 70 A2
Park Sheen SW14 7 B3
Park Side KT15 52 C1
Park Sq 1 KT10 55 B6
Park St Bagshot GU19 47 E3
Camberley GU15 65 C5
Croydon CR0, CR9 61 C8
Guildford GU1, GU2 130 C7
Horsham RH12 217 D2
Poyle SL3 1 D6
Slinfold RH13 215 C3
Teddington TW11 16 E2
Park Terr Carshalton SM5 59 E7
New Malden KT4 39 A1
Park Terr E RH13 217 D1
Park Terr W RH13 217 D1
Park The Forest Hill SE23 23 C7
Great Bookham KT23 94 A3
Wallington SM5 59 F5
Park View Addlestone KT15 52 C5
Bagshot GU19 47 D3
Crawley RH11 201 C5
Great Bookham KT23 94 A2
Horley RH6 161 A3
Morden CR4 40 D4
Park View *continued*
New Malden KT3 38 F6
Purley CR8 80 B8
Tandridge RH8 143 B5
Park View Ct GU22 89 F8
Park View Rd
Salfords RH1 140 A1
Woldingham CR3 101 F5
Park Way Crawley RH10 202 C7
East Molesey KT8 36 B6
Feltham TW14 15 B8
Great Bookham KT23 94 A4
Horsham RH12 217 C2
Park Wood Cl SM7 77 D4
Park Wood Rd SM7 77 D4
Park Wood View SM7 77 D4
Park Works Rd RH1 119 E2
Parkcroft Rd SE12 24 F8
Parkdale Cres KT4 57 D7
Parke Rd TW16 35 A5
Parker Cl RH10 202 D5
Parker Ct SW19 19 E1
Parker Rd CR0, CR9 61 C6
Parker's Cl KT21 95 E8
Parker's Hill KT21 95 E8
Parker's La Ashstead KT21 95 F8
Winkfield RG42 8 B5
Parkers Ct GU19 47 E3
Parkfield Godalming GU7 150 F2
Horsham RH12 217 C3
3 Hounslow TW7 5 E6
Parkfield Ave
Feltham TW13 15 A5
Mortlake SW14 7 E3
Parkfield Cl RH11 200 F6
Parkfield Cres TW13 15 A5
Parkfield Par TW13 15 A5
Parkfield Rd TW13 15 A5
Parkfields Croydon CR0 43 F1
Oxshott KT22 74 D8
Parkfields Ave SW20 39 B7
Parkfields Cl SM5 60 A6
Parkfields Rd TW10 17 F3
Parkgate Cl KT2 18 B2
Parkgate Gdns SW14 7 D2
Parkgate Rd
Newdigate RH5 158 C3
Parkgate RH5 158 C3
Reigate RH2 139 B8
Wallington SM5, SM6 60 B5
Parkham Ct BR2 44 E7
Parkhill Cl GU17 64 D4
Parkhill Rd GU17 64 D4
Parkhurst KT19 57 C1
Parkhurst Cotts GU10 187 F8
Parkhurst Fields GU10 167 F1
Parkhurst Gr RH6 160 F4
Parkhurst Rd
Carshalton SM1 59 D6
Guildford GU2 109 B2
Horley RH6 160 E4
Parkin House SE20 23 D1
Parkland Dr RG12 27 E8
Parkland Gdns 12 SW19 19 D7
Parkland Gr Ashford TW15 14 A4
Heath End GU9 125 F8
Hounslow TW7 5 F6
Parkland Rd TW15 14 A4
Parklands Addlestone KT15 52 C5
Dorking RH5 136 B3
Great Bookham KT23 94 A4
Kingston u T KT5 37 F4
Oxted RH8 122 E4
Redhill RH1 119 A3
Parklands Cl SW14 7 C2
Parklands Ct TW5 4 D5
Parklands Pl GU1 110 B1
Parklands Rd SW16, SW17 21 B3
Parklands Way KT4 57 E8
Parklawn Ave Epsom KT18 76 B6
Horley RH6 160 F5
Parkleigh Ct SW19 40 B7
Parkleigh Rd SW19 40 B7
Parkleys
Kingston u T KT2, TW10 17 D4
Richmond KT2, TW10 17 D4
Parkpale La RH3 137 A4
Parkshot TW9 6 E3
Parkside Beckenham BR3 44 B7
Cheam SM3 58 E4
Crawley RH10 201 E6
East Grinstead RH19 185 C1
Hale GU9 125 C6
Teddington TW12 16 C3
Wimbledon SW19 19 D4
Parkside Ave SW19 19 D3
Parkside Cl
East Horsley KT24 92 F2
Penge SE20 23 C1
Parkside Cres KT5 38 C3
Parkside Ct KT13 53 A6
Parkside Gdns
Coulsdon CR5 79 B2
Wimbledon SW19 19 D4
Parkside Hospl SW19 19 D5
Parkside Mews RH12 217 D2
Parkside Pl KT24 92 F2
Parkside Prep Sch KT11 74 A1
Parkside Rd Hounslow TW3 5 B2
Sunningdale SL5 30 A4
Parkstone Dr GU15 65 C4
Parkthorne Rd SW12 21 D8
Parkview Lodge BR3 44 B6
Parkview Rd CR0, CR9 43 A1
Parkview Vale GU4 110 C3
Parkway Camberley GU15 65 C3
Crowthorne RG45 45 A5
Dorking RH4 136 A8
Parkway *continued*
Guildford GU1 109 E2
Horley RH6 161 A3
New Addington CR0, CR9 63 C1
Oatlands Park KT13 53 D6
West Barnes SM4, SW20 39 D5
Parkway Sch The TW5 4 A7
Parkway The TW5 4 B7
Parkway Trad Est TW5 4 C8
Parkwood BR3 24 A1
Parkwood Ave KT10 36 C1
Parkwood Gr TW16 35 A6
Parkwood Rd
Biggin Hill TN16 103 F6
Hounslow TW7 5 F6
Nutfield RH1 119 E2
Wimbledon SW19 19 F3
Parley Dr GU21 69 C1
Parliament Mews SW14 7 C5
Parliamentary Rd GU24 87 A6
Parnall House 11 SE19 22 E4
Parnell Cl RH10 202 D4
Parnham Ave GU18 67 D8
Parr Ave KT17 58 B2
Parr Cl KT22 94 F7
Parr Ct TW13 15 C4
Parr's Pl TW12 16 A1
Parris Croft RH4 136 C4
Parrs Cl CR2 61 D2
Parry Cl Horsham RH13 218 C4
Stoneleigh KT17 58 A3
Parry Dr KT13 53 A1
Parry Rd SE25 42 E6
Parsley Gdns CR0 43 D1
Parson's Mead CR0 42 B1
Parson's Mead Sch KT21 95 E8
Parson's Pightle CR5 100 A7
Parsonage Bsns Pk RH12 217 E4
Parsonage Cl
Warlingham CR6 81 F3
Westcott RH4 135 C5
Parsonage Farm Cty Inf Sch GU14 84 C5
Parsonage La RH4 135 C6
Parsonage Rd
Cranleigh GU6 174 D3
Englefield Green TW20 11 D3
Horsham RH12, RH13 217 E4
Parsonage Sq RH4 136 A7
Parsonage Way
Frimley GU16 65 E1
Horsham RH12 217 E4
Parsons Cl
Haslemere GU27 208 C8
Horley RH6 160 E4
Parsons Field GU47 64 B8
Parsons Gn GU27 208 C8
Parsons Green Ct GU1 109 D3
Parsons House 21 SW12 21 E8
Parsons La GU26 188 D6
Parsons Mead KT8 36 C6
Parsonsfield Cl SM7 77 D4
Parsonsfield Rd SM7 77 D4
Parthia Cl KT20 97 B8
Partridge Cl
Crondall GU10 124 D8
Frimley GU16 65 E1
Partridge Knoll CR8 80 B6
Partridge La
Newdigate RH5 179 F3
Parkgate RH5 158 E2
Partridge Mead SM7 77 C4
Partridge Rd 8 TW12 16 A2
Partridge Way GU4 110 D3
Parvis Rd Byfleet KT14 71 D7
West Byfleet KT14 71 D7
Paschal Rd GU15 65 F8
Passfields SE6 24 C5
Passingham House TW5 5 A8
Pastens Rd RH8 123 C4
Pasture Rd SE6 24 F7
Pasture The RH10 202 C6
Pasture Wood Rd RH5 155 D6
Patching Cl RH11 200 F7
Patchings RH13 217 F3
Paterson Cl GU16 66 C3
Pates Manor Dr TW14 14 D8
Path Link RH10 201 E7
Path The SW19 40 B8
Pathfield GU8 191 B4
Pathfield Cl
Chiddingfold GU8 191 B4
Rudgwick RH12 214 D7
Pathfield Rd
Rudgwick RH12 214 D7
Streatham SW16 21 D2
Pathfields GU5 133 A4
Pathfields Cl GU27 208 D7
Pathfinders The GU14 84 C3
Pathway The GU23 90 F2
Patmore La KT12 53 F4
Patricia Gdns SM2 78 A8
Patrington Cl RH11 201 A3
Patten Ash Dr RG40 25 E7
Patten Rd SW18 20 E8
Pattenden Rd SE23, SE6 23 F7
Patterdale Cl Catford BR1 24 E2
Crawley RH11 201 C4
Patterson Ct SE19 22 F2
Patterson Rd SE19 22 F2
Paul Cl GU11 125 E8
Paul Gdns CR0 61 F8
Paul Vanson Ct KT12 54 D4
Paul's Pl KT21 96 B8
Pauline Cres TW2 16 C7
Pauls Mead RH7 164 E5
Paved Ct 9 TW9 6 D2
Pavement The 11 SE27 22 C4
Pavilion Gdns TW18 13 B1
Pavilion Rd GU11 104 E1
Pavilion Way RH19 205 E8
Pavilions End The GU15 65 D3
Paviors GU9 125 C3
Pawley Cl GU10 126 F7
Pawleyne Cl SE20 23 C1
Pawson's Rd CR0 42 C4
Pax Cl RH11 200 E4
Paxton Cl Richmond TW9 6 F5
Walton-on-T KT12 35 C2
Paxton Ct Forest Hill SE26 23 E4
Mitcham CR4 40 F7
Paxton Gdns GU21 70 E7
Paxton Pl SE27 22 E4
Paxton Prim Sch SE19 22 E2
Paxton Rd SE23 23 E5
Payley Dr RG40 25 E8
Payne Cl RH10 202 D8
Paynesfield Ave SW14 7 D4
Paynesfield Rd
Tatsfield TN16 103 D7
Tatsfield TN16 103 D8
Peabody Est SE24 22 C8
Peabody Hill SE21 22 C7
Peabody Rd GU11, GU14 105 D8
Peacemaker Cl RH11 200 E4
Peach St RG40 25 C6
Peach Tree Cl GU14 85 A7
Peaches Cl SM2 58 E3
Peacock Ave TW14 14 D7
Peacock Cotts RG12 26 C5
Peacock Gdns CR0, CR2 62 E1
Peacock La RG12 26 D6
Peacock Wlk 9 RH11 201 A3
Peacocks Sh Ctr The GU21 69 E2
Peak Hill SE26 23 C4
Peak Hill Ave SE26 23 C4
Peak Hill Gdns SE26 23 C4
Peak Rd GU2 109 A4
Peak The SE26 23 C5
Peakfield GU10 167 C7
Peaks Hill CR8 60 E1
Peaks Hill Rise CR8 60 E1
Peall Rd CR0 41 F3
Pear Ave TW17 34 E6
Pear Tree Cl
Addlestone KT15 52 A5
Mitcham CR4 40 E7
Pear Tree Ct GU15 66 B8
Pear Tree Hill RH1 161 A8
Pear Tree La GU10 145 F3
Pear Tree Rd
Addlestone KT15 52 A5
Ashford TW15 14 C3
Pearce Cl CR4 41 A7
Pearce House 7 SW2 21 E8
Pearcefield Ave 5 SE23 23 C7
Pearfield Rd SE23 23 E5
Pearl Ct GU21 68 E3
Pearmain Cl TW17 34 B4
Pears Rd TW3 5 C4
Pearson Ct SM4 40 B4
Pearson Rd RH10 202 C6
Peartree Ave SW17 20 C5
Peartree Cl CR2 81 B5
Peary Cl RH12 217 D6
Peaslake La GU5 154 D6
Peaslake Sch GU5 154 E7
Peat Comm GU8 148 C2
Peatmore Ave GU22 71 A3
Peatmore Cl GU22 71 A3
Peatmore Dr GU24 87 C6
Pebble Cl KT20 116 E6
Pebble Hill KT24 112 C2
Pebble Hill Cotts RH8 123 B6
Pebble La KT18, KT21 96 A5
Pebblehill Rd
Betchworth KT20, RH3 116 E5
Box Hill KT20, RH3 116 E5
Pebworth Ct 8 RH1 119 A3
Pebworth Lodge SE25 42 F5
Peckarmans Wood SE21, SE26 23 A5
Peek Cres SW19 19 D3
Peeks Brook La
Crawley RH6 182 E7
Horley RH6 161 F2
Peel Ave GU16 86 A7
Peel Ct GU14 105 C8
Peel Ctr The RG12 27 B7
Pegasus Ave GU12 105 E2
Pegasus Cl GU27 207 D5
Pegasus Ct Crawley RH11 200 E4
Farnborough GU14 85 E1
Kingston u T KT1 37 D6
Pegasus Rd
Croydon CR0, CR9 61 A4
Farnborough GU14 84 F7
Pegasus Way RH19 186 B3
Pegg Rd TW5 4 D7
Peggotty Pl GU47 45 E2
Pegler Way RH11 201 D6
Pegwell Cl RH11 200 F4
Peket Cl TW18 32 E8
Peldon Ct TW10 6 F2
Pelham Ct Crawley RH11 201 B2
Great Bookham KT23 94 C1
Horsham RH12 217 B2
Staines TW18 13 B3
Pelham Ct Bsns Ctr RH11 201 B2
Pelham Dr RH11 201 A2
Pelham House CR3 100 F3
Pelham Pl RH11 201 B2

Pelham Prim Sch SW19 20 A1
Pelham Rd Merton SW19 20 A1
Penge BR3, SE20 43 C7
Pelham Way KT23 94 C1
Pelhams Cl KT10 55 A6
Pelhams Wlk KT10 55 A6
Pelinore Rd SE6 24 E6
Pelling Hill SL4 11 B7
Pelton Ave SM2 59 B1
Pelton Ct CR2 61 C4
Pemberley Chase KT19 57 B5
Pemberley Cl KT19 57 B5
Pemberton House SE26 23 A4
Pemberton Pl KT10 55 C7
Pemberton Rd KT8 36 C5
Pembley Gn RH10 183 E3
Pembridge Ave TW4 15 F7
Pembroke RG12 27 A1
Pembroke Ave
Hersham KT12 54 D6
Surbiton KT5 38 B4
Pembroke Broadway GU15 65 C5
Pembroke Cl Ascot SL5 29 D4
Banstead SM7 78 B2
Pembroke Ct GU22 70 B3
Pembroke Gdns GU22 70 A1
Pembroke Mews SL5 29 D4
Pembroke Pl TW7 5 E5
Pembroke Rd
Crawley RH10 182 C1
Mitcham CR4 41 A7
South Norwood SE25 42 E5
Woking GU22 70 A2
Pembroke Villas TW9 6 D3
Pembrook Lodge 2 SW16 21 F5
Pembury Ave
New Malden KT4 39 A2
North Cheam KT4 39 A2
Pembury Cl Hayes BR2 44 F2
Wallington CR5 79 A5
Pembury Ct UB3 3 D8
Pembury Pl GU12 105 C1
Pembury Rd SE25 43 A5
Pemdevon Rd CR0 42 A2
Penarth Ct SM2 59 C3
Penates KT10 55 D6
Penberth Rd SE6 24 C7
Penceat Ct SE20 43 C7
Pendarves Rd SW20 39 C8
Pendell Ave UB3 3 F7
Pendell Rd RH1 120 B4
Pendennis Cl KT14 71 A5
Pendennis Rd SW16 21 E4
Penderel Rd TW3 5 A2
Penderry Rise SE6 24 D6
Pendine Pl RG12 27 B4
Pendle House 13 SE26 23 A5
Pendle Rd SW16 21 B3
Pendlebury RG12 27 A2
Pendleton Cl RH1 139 F7
Pendleton Rd RH1 139 E6
Pendragon Rd BR1 24 F5
Pendragon Way GU15 66 D3
Penerley Rd SE6 24 B7
Penfold Cl CR0, CR9 61 A7
Penfold Croft GU9 125 F4
Penfold Ct CR4 41 A7
Penfold Rd RH10 202 B2
Penge East Sta SE20 23 C2
Penge La SE20 23 D1
Penge Rd SE20, SE25 43 A6
Penge West Sta SE20 23 B2
Pengilly Rd GU9 125 B1
Penhurst GU21 69 F5
Peninsula Cl GU15 66 B7
Peninsular Cl TW14 3 E1
Penistone Rd SW16 21 E1
Penn Cl RH11 181 D1
Pennards The TW16 35 C6
Pennefather's Rd GU11 104 F3
Penner Cl SW19 19 E6
Penners Gdns KT6 37 E2
Pennine Cl RH11 201 B6
Pennine Way
Farnborough GU14 84 E7
Harlington UB7 3 D7
Pennings Ave GU2, GU3 108 F3
Pennington Cl 10 SE27 22 D4
Pennington Dr KT13 53 E7
Pennington Lodge 18 KT5 37 E4
Penns Wood GU14 85 D1
Penny Dr GU3 108 B2
Penny La TW17 34 E2
Penny Mews SW12 21 B8
Penny Royal SM6 60 D4
Pennycroft CR0 62 E2
Pennyfield KT11 73 A6
Pennymead Dr KT24 112 F8
Pennymead Rise KT24 112 F8
Pennypot La GU24 68 C7
Penrhyn Cl GU11 105 B1
Penrhyn Cres SW14 7 C3
Penrhyn Gdns KT1 37 D5
Penrhyn Rd KT1 37 E6
Penrith Cl Beckenham BR3 44 B8
Redhill RH2 118 E2
Penrith Pl SE27 22 B6
Penrith Rd New Malden KT3 38 D5
South Norwood CR7 42 C7
Penrith St SW16 21 C2
Penrose Ct TW20 11 C2
Penrose Rd KT22 94 C5
Penryn Dr GU35 187 C5
Penryn House 5 RH1 119 A3
Pensfold La RH12, RH13 214 E5
Pensford Ave TW9 7 A5
Pensford Cl RG45 45 B7
Penshurst Cl RH10 202 D7
Penshurst Gn BR2 44 F4
Penshurst Rd CR7 42 B4
Penshurst Rise GU16 85 F8
Penshurst Way SM2 59 A3
Penshurst Wlk BR2 44 F4
Pentelow Gdns TW14 4 A1
Penthorpe Sch RH12 214 C7
Pentland Ave TW17 34 A4
Pentland Pl GU14 84 E7
Pentlands BR3 44 C8
Pentlands Cl CR4 41 B6
Pentney Rd
Streatham SW12 21 C7
Wimbledon SW19, SW20 39 E8
Penton Ave TW18 32 F8
Penton Ct TW18 12 F2
Penton Hall TW18 33 A8
Penton Hall Dr TW18 33 A8
Penton Hook Marina
Chertsey KT16 33 A6
Egham TW18 32 F7
Penton Hook Rd TW18 33 A8
Penton House SM2 59 C3
Penton Rd TW18 12 F1
Pentreath Ave GU2 129 F8
Penwerris Ave TW5, TW7 5 C7
Penwerris Ct TW7 5 C7
Penwith Dr GU27 207 E5
Penwith Rd SW18 20 B6
Penwith Wlk GU22 89 D8
Penwood End GU22 89 B6
Penwood Gdns RG12 26 D3
Penwood House SW15 7 F1
Penwortham Prim Sch SW17 21 B2
Penwortham Rd
South Croydon CR2 61 D1
Streatham SW16 21 C2
Peper Harow La GU8 149 C6
Peperham House GU27 208 C7
Peperham Rd GU27 208 C8
Peperharow Rd GU7 150 C6
Peppard Rd RH10 202 D3
Pepper Cl CR3 100 E2
Pepperbox La GU5 173 E4
Peppermint Cl CR0 41 E2
Pepys Cl Ashstead KT21 76 A2
Brands Hill SL3 1 B8
Pepys Rd SW20 39 C8
Perak Ct KT5 38 C2
Percheron Cl TW7 5 F4
Percheron Dr GU21 88 C8
Percival Rd Feltham TW13 14 F6
Mortlake SW14 7 C3
Percival Way KT19 57 D6
Percy Ave TW15 14 A3
Percy Bilton Ct TW5 5 B6
Percy Bryant Rd TW16 14 E1
Percy Ct 1 KT5 37 F3
Percy Gdns
3 Isleworth TW7 6 A4
New Malden KT4 38 E1
Percy House 4 SW16 21 C4
Percy Rd Carshalton CR4 41 A2
Croydon SE25 43 A4
Guildford GU2 109 B3
Hampton TW12 16 A1
Horsham RH12 217 B3
Isleworth TW7 6 A3
Penge SE20 43 D8
Twickenham TW2 16 C7
Percy Way TW2 16 C7
Peregrine Cl
Bracknell RG12 27 B4
Cranleigh GU6 174 E4
Peregrine Gdns CR0 62 E8
Peregrine Rd TW16 34 F7
Peregrine Way
SW19, SW20 19 C1
Performing Arts & Tech
Sch SE25 42 D3
Perifield SE21 22 C7
Perimeter Rd E RH6 182 B6
Perimeter Rd N RH6 181 D7
Perimeter Rd S RH6 181 E5
Perkins Ct TW15 13 F3
Perkins Way RG41 25 A5
Perkstead Ct 7 RH11 201 A3
Perleybrooke La GU21 69 A2
Perowne St GU11 104 F2
Perram Wks GU4 110 C4
Perran Rd SE24, SW2 22 B6
Perran Wlk 16 TW8 6 E8
Perrin Cl TW15 13 F3
Perrin Ct GU21 70 B4
Perring Ave GU14 84 F8
Perrior Rd GU7 150 E7
Perry Ave RH19 185 E3
Perry Cl GU7 151 B5
Perry Hill SE23, SE6 23 F5
Perry House 24 SW2 21 E8
Perry How KT4 38 F1
Perry Oaks RG12 27 E7
Perry Oaks Dr TW6, UB7 2 C5
Perry Rise SE23, SE6 23 E5
Perry Vale SE23 23 D6
Perry Way Bracknell RG12 27 E7
Farnham GU9 125 B7
Lightwater GU18 66 F7
Perryfield House 7
RH10 201 D5
Perryfield Rd RH11 201 D5
Perryfield Way TW10 17 B6
Perrylands RH6 180 F7
Perrylands La RH6 162 A2
Perrymount Prim Sch
SE23 23 D6
Perryn Ct 2 TW1 17 A8
Perrywood Bsns Pk RH1 140 B1
Persant Rd SE6 24 E6
Perseverance Cotts GU23 91 C6
Persfield Mews KT17 57 F1
Persfield Rd KT17 58 A1
Pershore Gr SM5 40 D3
Perth Cl Crawley RH11 181 D1
Wimbledon SW20 39 A7
Perth Rd BR3 44 C7
Perth Way RH12 217 F4
Perystreete SE23 23 C6
Petauel Rd TW11 16 E3
Petavel Rd TW11 16 E2
Peter Ave RH8 122 D6
Peter Kennedy Ct CR0 43 F3
Peter's Path SE26 23 B4
Peterborough Rd
Carshalton CR4, SM4, SM5 40 E3
Crawley RH10 201 E2
Guildford GU2 108 F3
Peterhouse Cl GU47 45 F2
Peterhouse Par RH10 182 C1
Peterlee Wlk RH11 200 E2
Petersfield Ave
TW15, TW18 13 C2
Petersfield Cres CR5 79 E4
Petersfield Rd TW18 13 C3
Petersfield Rise SW15 19 B7
Petersham Ave KT14 71 E7
Petersham Cl Byfleet KT14 71 E7
Cheam SM1 59 A5
Richmond TW10 17 D6
Petersham Rd TW10 17 E7
Peterstow Cl SW19 19 E6
Peterwood Pk CR9 60 F8
Peterwood Way CR0 60 F8
Petrel Ct 7 SE21 22 D6
Petridge Rd RH1 139 F4
Petters Rd KT21 75 F3
Petts La TW17 34 A5
Petworth Cl Coulsdon CR5 99 C8
Frimley GU16 85 F8
Petworth Ct Crawley RH11 200 F3
Haslemere GU27 208 D6
Petworth Dr RH12 217 F7
Petworth Gdns SW20 39 B6
Petworth Rd
Chiddingfold GU8 191 C4
Chiddingfold,
Ansteadbrook GU27 209 B6
Witley GU8 170 F5
Wormley GU8 171 A1
Pevensey Cl
Crawley RH10 202 C5
Hounslow TW7 5 C7
Pevensey Ct SW16 22 A5
Pevensey House RH2 139 B5
Pevensey Rd Feltham TW13 15 E7
Upper Tooting SW17 20 D4
Pevensey Way GU16 86 A8
Peverel Rd RH11 200 E5
Peveril Dr TW11 16 D3
Pewley Bank GU1 130 E7
Pewley Down Inf Sch
GU1 130 E7
Pewley Hill GU1 130 E7
Pewley Point GU1 130 F7
Pewley Way GU1 130 F7
Pewsey Vale RG12 27 F4
Peyton's Cotts RH1 119 F3
Pharaoh Cl CR4 40 F2
Pheasant Cl CR8 80 B6
Philanthropic Rd RH1 140 B8
Philip Gdns CR0 62 F8
Philip Rd TW18 13 D2
Philip Southcote Sch
KT15 52 C8
Philips House GU26 188 B3
Phillips Cl Ash GU10 126 E8
Crawley RH10 202 C2
Godalming GU7 150 D2
Phillips Cotts GU7 150 B4
Phillips Hatch GU5 152 C8
Philpot La GU24 69 C7
Phipp's Bridge Rd
CR4, SW19 40 D6
Phoenix Bsns Pk RG12 26 C7
Phoenix Cl BR4 63 E8
Phoenix Coll SM4 40 C4
Phoenix Ct
13 Aldershot GU11 105 A2
Croydon SE25 43 A4
Guildford GU1 130 D7
Phoenix La RH19 206 E6
Phoenix Pl TW18 13 A3
Phoenix Rd SE20 23 C2
Phoenix Way TW5 4 D8
Phyllis Ave KT3 39 B4
Phyllis House CR0 61 B6
Piccards The GU2 130 C5
Pickering RG12 27 A5
Pickering Gdns SE25 42 F3
Picket Post Cl RG12 27 F6
Pickets St SW12 21 B8
Picketts Hill GU35 166 C1
Picketts La RH1 161 C8
Pickford St GU11 105 B2
Pickhurst Gn BR2 44 F2
Pickhurst Inf Sch BR2 44 F3
Pickhurst Jun Sch BR2 44 F3
Pickhurst La BR2, BR3, BR4 44 E2
Pickhurst Mead BR2 44 F2
Pickhurst Pk BR2 44 F4
Pickhurst Rd GU8 191 D2
Pickhurst Rise BR4 44 D1
Pickins Piece SL3 1 A5
Pickwick Cl TW4 4 E2
Pickwick Rd SE21 22 E8
Picquets Way KT20, SM7 77 F2
Picton Cl GU15 66 B7
Picton House 1 SW4 21 E8
Pier Rd TW14 4 B2
Pierrefondes Ave GU14 85 B5
Pierrepoint SE25 42 E6
Pierson House 12 SE19 22 E4
Pigbush La RH14 213 A7
Pigeon La TW12 16 A4
Pigeonhouse La
Lower Kingswood CR5 98 C3
Winkfield SL4, SL5 8 E4
Piggott Ct RH13 217 E1
Pigott Ct RG40 25 D6
Pigott Rd RG40 25 E8
Pike Cl GU11 105 C2
Pikes Hill KT17 76 E6
Pikes La RH7 143 E2
Pikethorne SE23 23 D6
Pilgrim Cl SM4 40 B2
Pilgrim Hill SE27 22 C4
Pilgrim House GU1 130 D7
Pilgrim's Way CR2 61 F5
Pilgrims Cl Farnham GU9 146 A8
Shere GU5 133 A4
Westhumble RH5 115 B4
Pilgrims La Caterham CR3 100 B1
Tatsfield RH8 103 D3
Titsey RH8 103 D3
Pilgrims Pl RH2 118 A3
Pilgrims View GU12 127 C8
Pilgrims Way GU24 68 A3
Pilgrims' Way
Guildford GU4 130 E5
Reigate RH2 118 A3
Pilgrims Way Shere GU5 133 A4
Westhumble RH5 115 B4
Pilgrims Way Cotts RH3 116 C2
Pilgrims Way Cty Prim
Sch The GU9 146 B8
Pilsden Cl SW19 19 D7
Pilton Est The CR9 61 B8
Pimms Cl GU4 110 A5
Pinckards GU8 191 B5
Pincott La KT24 112 B6
Pincott Rd SW19 40 C8
Pine Ave Camberley GU15 65 D3
West Wickham BR4 44 B1
Pine Bank GU26 188 E4
Pine Cl Ash Vale GU12 106 A6
Crawley RH11 181 C1
Kenley CR8 80 D2
Penge SE20 43 C8
Sandhurst GU15 64 E7
Woking GU21 69 C3
Woodham KT15 71 B8
Pine Coombe CR0 62 D6
Pine Cres SM5 78 D8
Pine Croft Rd RG41 25 A2
Pine Ct Bracknell RG12 27 E5
2 Weybridge KT13 53 C5
Pine Dean KT23 94 B2
Pine Dr GU17 64 E3
Pine Gdns Horley RH6 161 A2
Surbiton KT5 38 A3
Pine Gr
East Grinstead RH19 185 B3
Farnham GU10 146 E6
Weybridge KT13 53 C5
Wimbledon SW19 19 F3
Windlesham GU20 48 D4
Pine Grove Mews 3 KT13 53 C5
Pine Hill KT18 76 D4
Pine Mount Rd GU15 65 D4
Pine Pl KT17 77 D5
Pine Rd GU22 89 C7
Pine Ridge SM5 60 A2
Pine Ridge Cty Inf Sch
GU15 47 A1
Pine Ridge Dr GU10 146 C5
Pine Ridge Golf Ctr GU16 66 D2
Pine Shaw RH10 202 D7
Pine Tree Cl TW5 4 B6
Pine Tree Hill GU22 70 D3
Pine Trees Bsns Pk TW18 12 E3
Pine View GU35 187 C6
Pine View Cl
Chilworth GU4 131 F3
Farnham GU9 126 A5
Haslemere GU27 208 C8
Pine Way TW20 11 B2
Pine Way Cl RH19 205 E7
Pine Wlk Caterham CR3 100 F5
Cobham KT11 73 D5
East Horsley KT24 112 F7
Great Bookham KT23 94 B2
Surbiton KT5 38 A3
Sutton SM5 59 D1
Woodmansterne CR5, SM7 78 F2
Pine Wood TW16 35 A8
Pineacre Ct GU22 70 B2
Pinecote Dr SL5 29 F2
Pinefields KT15 52 B6
Pinefields Cl RG45 45 B4
Pinehill Rd RG45 45 C3
Pinehill Rise GU47 64 C8
Pinehurst Ascot SL5 29 D4
Horsham RH12 217 C4
8 Woking GU22 69 F1
Pinehurst Ave GU14 85 B2
Pinehurst Cl KT20 98 A5
Pinehurst Cotts GU14 85 B2
Pinel Cl GU25 31 E5
Pines Ct 14 SW19 19 D7
Pines Cty Inf Sch RG12 27 A2
Pines Cty Jun Sch RG12 27 A2
Pines The Camberley GU15 65 F7
Dorking RH4 136 B6
Guildford GU3 108 E3
Horsham RH12 218 C5
Purley CR8 80 C6
South Norwood SE19, SW16 22 B2
Sunbury TW16 35 A6
Pinetrees Cl RH10 183 B3
Pinewood Ave
Crowthorne RG45 45 C6
Woodham KT15 52 C1
Pinewood Cl
Broadbridge Heath RH12 216 D3
South Croydon CR0 62 E7
Woking GU21 70 A4
Pinewood Cres GU14 84 C5
Pinewood Ct
Addlestone KT15 52 D6
Woking GU21 70 A3
Pinewood Dr TW18 13 A3
Pinewood Gdns GU19 47 C3
Pinewood Gr KT15 52 B1
Pinewood Inf Sch GU14 84 D7
Pinewood Mews TW19 2 D1
Pinewood Pk
Farnborough GU14 84 C7
Woodham KT15 71 B8
Pinewood Pl KT19 57 D6
Pinewood Rd
Feltham TW13 15 B5
Normandy GU12 106 D3
Wentworth GU25 31 A5
Pinfold Rd SW16 21 E4
Pinglestone Cl TW6, UB7 2 E7
Pinkcoat Cl TW13 15 B5
Pinkerton Pl SW16 21 D4
Pinkhurst La RH13 216 A2
Pioneers Ind Pk CR9 41 E1
Piper Rd KT1 38 A6
Piper's End GU25 31 D6
Pipers Cl KT11 73 D3
Pipers End RH13 215 E3
Pipers Gdns CR0 43 E2
Pipers Patch 1 GU14 85 B4
Pipewell Rd SM5 40 E3
Pippbrook Gdns RH4 136 B8
Pippin Cl CR0 43 F1
Pippins Ct TW15 14 B2
Piquet Rd BR3, SE20 43 C7
Pirbright Cres CR0 63 C4
Pirbright Cty Prim Sch
GU24 87 E5
Pirbright House 11 KT2 18 B2
Pirbright Rd
Farnborough GU14 85 C3
Normandy GU3 107 B6
Wandsworth SW18 20 A7
Pirbright Terr GU24 87 F4
Pirles Pl RH12 217 C2
Pisley La RH5 177 A4
Pit Farm Rd GU1 110 A1
Pit Wood Gn KT20 97 C7
Pitcairn Rd CR4 20 F1
Pitchfont La CR6, RH8 102 F2
Pitfold Ave GU27 207 D6
Pitfold Cl GU27 207 E6
Pitlake CR0, CR9 61 B8
Pitland St RH5 155 C5
Pitson Cl KT15 52 D6
Pitt Cres SW19 20 B4
Pitt Pl KT17 76 E5
Pitt Rd Epsom KT17 76 E5
Thornton Heath CR0, CR7 42 C4
Pitt Way GU14 84 F5
Pitts Rd GU11 105 B4
Pittville Gdns SE25 43 A6
Pixfield Ct BR2 44 F7
Pixham Firs RH4 115 C2
Pixham La RH4 115 C2
Pixholme Ct RH4 115 C2
Pixholme Gr RH4 115 C1
Pixton Way CR0, CR2 62 E2
Place Ct GU11 126 C7
Place Farm Rd RH1 120 D4
Placehouse La CR5 80 A1
Plaistow Cty Inf Sch
RH14 211 F3
Plaistow Rd
Chiddingfold GU8 210 D6
Dunsfold GU8 192 D2
Ifold RH14 212 D1
Loxwood RH14 212 D1
Plaistow St RH7 164 D4
Plane St SE26 23 B5
Plane Tree Cres TW13 15 B5
Plane Tree Wlk 4 SE19 22 E2
Planes The KT16 33 C2
Plantagenet Cl KT19 57 D6
Plantagenet Pk RG42 27 F8
Plantain Cres RH11 201 A2
Plantation La CR6 101 E8
Plantation Row GU15 65 B5
Plassy Rd SE6 24 B8
Plat The RH12 217 A3
Platt Meadow GU4 110 D3
Platt The RH7 186 A8
Platt's Eyot TW12 36 A7
Plaws Hill GU5 154 D6
Playden Ct 4 RH11 201 A3
Playgreen Way SE6 24 A4
Playground Cl BR3 43 D7
Pleasant Gr CR0 62 F7
Pleasant Pl KT12 54 D4
Pleasure Pit Rd KT21 76 B1
Plesman Way SM6 60 E2
Plevna Rd TW12 36 B8

Pleydell Ave SE19 .22 F1
Plough Cl RH11 .200 F8
Plough Ind Est KT22 .95 A7
Plough La Downside KT11 .73 A2
Ewhurst GU6 .176 A5
Horsham RH12 .217 E5
Purley CR0, CR8, SM6 .60 F1
Wallington, Bandonhill
CR0, SM6 .60 E5
Wallington, Russell Hill SM6 .60 F2
Wimbledon SW17, SW19 .20 C4
Wokingham RG40 .25 F6
Plough Lane Cl CR0, SM6 .60 E5
Plough Rd
Dormansland RH7 .165 A2
Smallfield RH6 .162 C3
West Ewell KT19 .57 D3
Ploughlands RG42 .26 F8
Ploughmans End TW7 .5 D2
Plover Cl Crawley RH11 .201 C8
Staines TW18 .12 F5
Plovers Rd RH13 .217 F3
Plovers Rise GU24 .87 E7
Plowman House SW19 .19 D6
Plummer La CR4 .40 F7
Plummer Rd SW4 .21 D8
Plumpton Way SM5 .59 E7
Plumtree Cl SM6 .60 D3
Pocket Cl RG12 .26 D7
Pockford Rd GU8 .191 D4
Pocklington Ct SW15 .19 A7
Point (L Ctr) The RG12 .27 B7
Point Royal RG12 .27 B4
Pointers Hill RH4 .135 C5
Pointers Rd KT11 .72 E2
Pointers The KT21 .95 E7
Polden Cl GU14 .84 E7
Polecroft La SE6 .23 F6
Poles La RH11, RH6 .181 C3
Polesden Gdns SW20 .39 B7
Polesden La Ripley GU23 .91 A6
Send Marsh GU23 .90 F5
Polesden Lacey KT23 .114 B5
Polesden Rd KT23 .114 B6
Polesden View KT23 .114 B8
Polesteeple Hill TN16 .83 D2
Police Station Rd KT12 .54 C4
Pollard Gr GU15 .66 C4
Pollard House KT4 .58 C6
Pollard Rd Morden SM4 .40 D4
Woking GU22 .70 B3
Pollardrow Ave RG42 .26 F8
Pollards RH11 .201 A5
Pollards Cres SW16 .41 E6
Pollards Dr RH13 .217 F2
Pollards Hill E SW16 .41 F6
Pollards Hill N SW16 .41 F6
Pollards Hill S SW16 .41 F6
Pollards Hill W SW16 .41 F6
Pollards Oak Cres RH8 .123 A3
Pollards Oak Rd RH8 .123 A3
Pollards Wood Hill RH8 .123 B5
Pollards Wood Rd
Limpsfield RH8 .123 B4
Thornton Heath SW16 .41 E6
Polsted La GU3 .129 C3
Polsted Rd SE6 .23 F8
Poltimore Rd GU2 .130 B7
Polworth Rd SW16 .21 E3
Polyanthus Way RG45 .45 B8
Pond Cl Hersham KT12 .54 A4
Loxwood RH14 .212 F4
Pond Copse La RH14 .212 F5
Pond Cottage La BR3, BR4 .44 A1
Pond Cotts SE21 .22 E7
Pond Farm Cl KT20 .97 B3
Pond Head La
Forest Green RH5 .176 E5
Wallis Wood RH5 .176 D3
Pond Hill Gdns SM3 .58 E4
Pond House GU4 .110 D2
Pond La Frensham GU10 .167 C5
Peaslake GU5 .154 D7
Pond Meadow GU2 .108 E2
Pond Meadow Sch GU2 .108 E2
Pond Moor Rd RG12 .27 B4
Pond Piece KT22 .74 B6
Pond Rd Egham TW20 .12 C2
Headley Down GU35 .187 B4
Woking GU22 .89 B7
Pond Way
East Grinstead RH19 .186 B1
Teddington TW11 .17 C2
Pond Wood Rd RH10 .202 A8
Pondfield House SE27 .22 C3
Pondfield Rd
Farncombe GU7 .150 F7
Kenley CR8 .80 B3
Rudgwick RH12 .214 D8
West Wickham BR2 .44 E1
Ponds La GU5 .153 F8
Ponds The KT13 .53 E4
Pondside Cl UB3 .3 D7
Pondtail Cl RH12 .217 D6
Pondtail Dr RH12 .217 D7
Pondtail Rd RH12 .217 D6
Ponsonby Rd SW15 .19 B8
Pontefract Rd BR1 .24 F3
Ponton House SW2 .22 A7
Pony Chase KT11 .73 F6
Pook Hill GU8 .190 F3
Pool Cl BR3 .24 A3
Pool Ct SE6 .24 A6
Pool End Cl TW17 .34 A4
Pool Rd Aldershot GU11 .126 C7
East Molesey KT12, KT8 .35 F4
Poole Court Rd TW5 .4 E5
Poole Ct TW5 .4 E5
Poole Rd West Ewell KT19 .57 D4
Woking GU21 .69 E1
Pooley Ave TW20 .12 B3
Pooley Green Cl TW20 .12 C3
Pooley Green Rd TW20 .12 C3
Pope Cl East Bedfont TW14 .14 F7
Mitcham SW17, SW19 .20 D2
Pope Ct 10 KT2 .17 D4
Pope's Ave TW2 .16 E6
Pope's Gr TW1, TW2 .16 F6
Popes Cl SL3 .1 C7
Popes Gr CR0 .62 F7
Popes La RH8 .143 F8
Popes Mead GU27 .208 C7
Popeswood Rd RG42 .26 D8
Popham Cl Bracknell RG12 .27 F4
Feltham TW13 .15 F5
Popham Gdns TW9 .7 B4
Poplar Ave
Leatherhead KT22 .95 C5
Mitcham CR4 .40 F8
Windlesham GU20 .48 B6
Poplar Cl Crawley RH11 .181 C1
Mytchett GU16 .86 A3
Poyle SL3 .1 E6
Poplar Cotts GU3 .108 E4
Poplar Cres KT19 .57 C4
Poplar Ct
4 Streatham SW16 .21 F5
13 Twickenham TW1 .6 C1
Wimbledon SW19 .20 A3
Poplar Dr KT17, SM7 .77 D5
Poplar Farm Cl KT19 .57 C4
Poplar Fst Sch SW19 .40 A6
Poplar Gdns KT3 .38 D7
Poplar Gr Kingston u T KT3 .38 D6
Woking GU22 .89 E8
Poplar La BR3 .44 B4
Poplar Rd Ashford TW15 .14 C3
Cheam SM3 .39 F1
Leatherhead KT22 .95 C5
Merton SW19 .40 A7
Shalford GU4 .130 E2
Poplar Rd S SM4, SW19 .40 A6
Poplar Way TW13 .15 B5
Poplar Wlk Caterham CR3 .100 E4
Croydon CR0 .42 C1
Heath End GU9 .125 D7
Poplars Cl GU14 .84 C5
Poplars The Ascot SL5 .29 A4
Horsham RH13 .217 E3
Poppy La CR0, CR9 .43 C1
Poppy Pl RG40 .25 B6
Poppyhills Rd GU15 .65 F8
Porchester SL5 .29 A5
Porchester Mead BR3 .24 B2
Porchester Rd KT1 .38 B7
Porchfield Cl SM2 .59 B1
Porlock House 5 SE26 .23 A5
Porridge Pot Alley GU2 .130 C7
Port Way GU24 .68 A3
Portal Cl SE27 .22 A5
Porteridges RH4 .136 C4
Portesbery Hill Dr GU15 .65 E6
Portesbery Rd GU15 .65 E6
Portesbery Sch GU15 .65 D6
Porthcawe Rd SE26 .23 F4
Portia Gr RG42 .27 E8
Portland Ave KT3 .38 F2
Portland Cotts CR0 .41 D2
Portland Cres TW13, TW15 .14 D4
Portland Dr RH1 .119 D6
Portland House
5 East Grinstead RH19 .205 F8
Merstham RH1 .119 D6
20 Streatham SW2 .22 A7
Portland House
Mews KT18 .76 D5
Portland Pl Croydon SE25 .43 A5
Ewell KT17 .76 E7
Portland Rd Ashford TW15 .13 E5
Croydon SE25 .43 B4
Dorking RH4 .136 A8
East Grinstead RH19 .205 F8
Kingston u T KT1 .37 F6
Mitcham CR4 .40 E7
Portland Terr TW9 .6 D3
Portley La CR3 .100 E6
Portley Wood Rd CR3 .101 A7
Portman Ave SW14 .7 D4
Portman Cl 5 RG42 .27 A8
Portman Rd KT1 .37 F7
Portmore Park Rd KT13 .53 A6
Portmore Quays KT13 .52 F6
Portmore Way KT13 .53 A7
Portnall Dr GU25 .30 F4
Portnall Rd GU25 .30 F4
Portnall Rise GU25 .30 F3
Portnalls Cl CR5 .79 B3
Portnalls Rd CR5 .79 B2
Portnalls Rise CR5 .79 C3
Portobello
House 6 SW27 .22 B3
Porton Ct KT6 .37 C3
Portsea House 3 SW15 .19 B7
Portsmouth Ave KT7 .37 A2
Portsmouth Rd
Camberley GU15 .66 A7
Cobham KT10, KT11 .73 C7
Downside KT11 .72 F6
Esher KT10 .55 A4
Esher KT10 .55 D7
Godalming GU7, GU8 .150 B2
Guildford GU2 .130 C6
Haslemere GU26 .188 E2
Hinchley Wood KT10, KT7 .55 E8
Hindhead GU26 .188 E2
Kingston u T KT1, KT6 .37 C3
Portsmouth Rd *continued*
Milford GU8 .149 E1
Ockham GU23 .91 D7
Putney SW15 .19 C8
Ripley GU23 .91 B4
Send Marsh GU23 .91 B4
Thames Ditton KT6, KT7 .37 C3
Thursley GU8 .169 D3
Wisley GU23, KT11 .72 C3
Witley GU8 .170 B6
Portswood Pl SW15 .7 F1
Portugal Gdns TW2 .16 C6
Portugal Rd GU21 .69 F3
Portway KT17 .58 A2
Portway Cres KT17 .58 A2
Post House La KT23 .94 A2
Post La TW2 .16 D7
Postford Mill Cotts GU4 .131 F5
Postmill Cl CR0, CR9 .62 D7
Potley Hill Cty Prim Sch
GU46 .64 A5
Potley Hill Rd GU46 .64 A5
Potter Cl CR4 .41 B7
Potter's La SW16 .21 D2
Potterhill Ct TW11 .17 B1
Potteries La GU16 .85 F4
Potteries The
Farnborough GU14 .84 D6
Ottershaw KT16 .51 E4
Potterne Cl 5
SW15, SW19 .19 D8
Potters Cl Croydon CR0 .43 E1
Milford GU8 .149 F2
Potters Cres GU12 .106 B2
Potters Croft RH13 .217 E2
Potters Gate GU9 .125 A2
Potters Gate CE Prim Sch
GU9 .125 A2
Potters Gr KT3 .38 C5
Potters La GU23 .90 B2
Potters Way RH2 .139 C5
Pottersfield RH10 .201 D7
Pottery Ct GU10 .145 F6
Pottery La GU10 .145 F6
Pottery Rd TW8 .6 E8
Poulett Gdns TW1 .17 A7
Poullett House SW2 .22 B7
Poulton Ave SM1, SM5 .59 D7
Pound Cl Godalming GU7 .150 E4
Long Ditton KT6 .37 C1
Loxwood RH14 .212 F5
Pound Cres KT22 .94 D6
Pound Ct Ashstead KT21 .75 F1
Wood St V GU3 .108 B2
Pound Farm La GU12 .106 D1
Pound Field GU1 .109 D1
Pound Hill GU3 .108 B2
Pound Hill Cty Fst & Mid
Schs RH10 .202 C7
Pound Hill Par RH10 .202 C7
Pound Hill Pl RH10 .202 C6
Pound La Epsom KT19 .76 D8
Godalming GU7 .150 E4
Windlesham GU20 .48 C4
Wood St V GU3 .108 B2
Pound Pl GU4 .130 F3
Pound Place Cl GU4 .130 F3
Pound Rd Aldershot GU12 .105 C1
Banstead SM7 .78 A2
Chertsey KT16 .33 B2
Pound St SM5 .59 F5
Poundfield Gdns GU22 .90 C7
Poundfield La RH14 .212 B3
Povey Cross Rd RH6 .160 E1
Powder Mill La TW2, TW4 .16 A7
Powderham Ct GU21 .68 D1
Powell Cl Chessington KT9 .56 D5
Guildford GU2 .129 F7
Horley RH6 .160 E4
Wallington SM6 .60 E3
Powell Corderoy Prim Sch
RH4 .135 F6
Powell Ct CR0 .61 C6
Powell's Wlk W4 .7 F8
Powells Cl RH4 .136 C4
Powers Ct TW1 .17 D8
Pownall Gdns TW3 .5 B3
Pownall Rd TW3 .5 B3
Poyle 14 Trad Est SL3 .1 E4
Poyle Cty Fst Sch SL3 .1 F6
Poyle Gdns RG12 .27 D8
Poyle House GU4 .110 D2
Poyle New Cotts SL3 .1 F5
Poyle Rd Guildford GU1 .130 E7
Poyle SL3 .1 E5
Tongham GU10 .127 B7
Poyle Tech Ctr The SL3 .1 E5
Poynders Gdns SW12 .21 C8
Poynders Rd SW12, SW4 .21 D8
Poynes Rd RH6 .160 E5
Poynings Rd RH11 .200 E5
Prairie Cl KT15 .52 B7
Prairie Rd KT15 .52 B7
Pratts Cnr GU8 .193 A8
Pratts La KT12 .54 D6
Precinct The
Cranleigh GU6 .174 E4
East Molesey KT8 .36 B6
Egham TW20 .12 A3
Precincts The SM4 .40 A3
Prendergast House 7
SW4 .21 D8
Prentice Cl GU14 .85 B8
Prentice Ct 2 SW19 .19 F3
Prentis Rd SW16 .21 D4
Presburg Rd KT3 .38 E4
Presbury Ct GU21 .69 A1
Prescott RG12 .26 F2
Prescott Rd SL3 .1 E5
Presentation Mews SW2 .21 F7
Prestbury Cres SM7 .78 F3
Preston Cl TW2 .16 E5
Preston Ct KT12 .35 C1
Preston Dr KT19 .57 F4
Preston Gr KT21 .75 C2
Preston La KT20 .97 C7
Preston Pl TW10 .6 E2
Preston Rd Littleton TW17 .34 A4
South Norwood SE19 .22 B2
Wimbledon SW20 .18 F1
Prestwick Cl RH11 .200 D5
Prestwick La
Chiddingfold GU8 .190 C3
Grayswood GU8 .190 C3
Prestwood Cl RH11 .181 B1
Prestwood Gdns CR0 .42 C2
Prestwood La
RH11, RH12, RH6 .180 C3
Pretoria Rd Chertsey KT16 .32 F1
Streatham SW16 .21 C3
Pretty La CR5 .99 C6
Prey Heath Cl GU22 .89 C3
Prey Heath Rd GU22 .89 B3
Preymead Ind Est GU9 .126 B7
Price Cl SW17 .20 F5
Price Rd CR0 .61 B5
Price Way TW12 .15 E2
Prices La RH2 .139 B6
Prickley Wood BR2 .44 F1
Priddy's Yd 4 CR9 .61 C8
Prides Crossing SL5 .9 A1
Pridham Rd CR7 .42 D5
Priest Ave RG40 .25 F5
Priest Croft Cl RH11 .201 A6
Priest Hill Englefield Green
TW19, TW20 .11 C6
Limpsfield RH8 .123 B6
Priest Hill Sch Sports Ctr
KT17 .77 B8
Priest La GU24 .67 C5
Priestfield Rd SE23 .23 E5
Priestley Gdns GU22 .90 A7
Priestley Rd
Guildford GU2 .129 D8
Mitcham CR4 .41 A7
Priestley Way RH10 .182 A3
Priests Bridge SW14, SW15 .7 E4
Priestwood Ave RG42 .26 F8
Priestwood Court Rd
RG42 .27 A8
Priestwood Sq 1 RG42 .27 A8
Prim Sch of Our Lady
Immaculate KT6 .38 B1
Primrose Ave RH6 .161 B1
Primrose Cl Carshalton CR4 41 B1
Catford SE6 .24 C3
Crawley RH11 .201 B3
Primrose Copse RH12 .217 E7
Primrose Ct
New Malden KT4 .39 A2
11 Streatham SW12 .21 D8
Primrose Dr GU24 .68 A4
Primrose Gdns GU14 .84 E3
Primrose House 1 TW9 .6 F6
Primrose La CR0 .43 D1
Primrose Rd KT12 .54 C5
Primrose Ridge GU7 .150 B2
Primrose Way
Bramley GU5 .151 D5
Sandhurst GU47 .45 B1
Primrose Wlk
Bracknell RG12 .27 C4
Ewell KT17 .57 F3
Prince Albert Dr SL5 .28 D4
Prince Albert Sq RH1 .140 A4
Prince Andrew Way SL5 .28 D7
Prince Charles Cres GU14 85 C8
Prince Charles Way SM6 .60 B7
Prince Consort Dr SL5 .28 D5
Prince Consort's Dr
Old Windsor SL4 .10 A6
Winkfield SL4 .9 F4
Prince Dr GU47 .45 A1
Prince George's Ave
SW20 .39 C7
Prince Georges Rd SW19 .40 D8
Prince Of Wales' Rd SM1 .59 D8
Prince Of Wales Rd RH1 .141 A2
Prince of Wales Wlk 1
GU15 .65 C6
Prince Rd SE25 .42 E4
Prince Regent Rd TW3 .5 C4
Prince William Ct TW15 .13 F3
Prince's Ave
Farnborough GU11 .105 C5
Farncombe GU7 .150 C7
Prince's Cl TW11, TW12 .16 D4
Prince's Dr KT22 .74 E7
Prince's Rd Mortlake SW14 .7 D4
Redhill RH1 .139 F7
Teddington TW11, TW12 .16 D4
Weybridge KT13 .53 C5
Wimbledon SW19 .20 A2
Prince's St TW10, TW9 .6 E2
Princes Ave
Hamsey Green CR2 .81 B4
Tolworth KT6 .57 A8
Wallington SM5 .59 F2
Princes Cl Bagshot GU19 .47 E1
Hamsey Green CR2 .81 B4
Princes Ct New Malden KT3 .38 F6
Weybridge KT13 .53 B5
Princes Gdns GU3 .108 E8
Princes Mead GU14 .85 B4
Princes Mews TW3 .5 A3
Princes Rd Ashford TW15 .13 F3
Princes Rd *continued*
Egham TW20 .11 F2
Feltham TW13 .14 F5
Kingston u T KT2 .18 A1
Penge SE20 .23 D2
Richmond TW10 .6 F2
Richmond, Kew TW9 .6 F6
Princes St SM1 .59 D6
Princes Way
Aldershot GU11 .105 A2
Coney Hall BR4 .63 F7
Croydon CR0 .60 F5
Putney SW15, SW19 .19 E7
Princess Anne Rd RH12 .214 D6
Princess Ct
Aldershot GU14 .105 C8
9 Wimbledon SW19 .19 D1
Princess Gdns GU22 .70 B3
Princess House 1 RH1 .119 A2
Princess Margaret Rd
RH12 .214 D7
Princess Mary's Rd KT15 .52 C6
Princess Rd Crawley RH11 201 C6
Thornton Heath CR0 .42 C3
Woking GU22 .70 C3
Princess Sq RG12 .27 B7
Princess Way
Camberley GU15 .65 C5
Redhill RH1 .119 A2
Princethorpe Rd SE26 .23 D4
Princeton Mews 3 KT2 .38 A8
Pringle Gdns Purley CR8 .60 F1
Streatham SW16 .21 C4
Prins Willem-Alexander
Sch GU22 .70 C2
Prior Ave SM2, SM5 .59 E3
Prior Croft Cl GU15 .66 A4
Prior End GU15 .66 A5
Prior Heath Cty Inf Sch
GU15 .66 A5
Prior Rd GU15 .66 A5
Prior's La GU17 .64 A5
Prioress Rd SE27 .22 B5
Priors Cl GU14 .85 B8
Priors Croft GU22 .90 A7
Priors Ct Ash GU12 .105 E1
Woking GU21 .69 A1
Priors Field Sch GU7 .129 A1
Priors Hatch La GU7 .128 F1
Priors Lodge 4 TW10 .6 E1
Priors Mead KT23 .94 C2
Priors The KT21 .95 D8
Priors Wlk RH10 .201 F6
Priors Wood GU27 .207 F6
Priorsfield Rd GU7 .129 A1
Priorswood GU3 .128 F2
Priory Ave SM3 .58 D6
Priory C of E Mid Sch
SW19 .20 B3
Priory Cl Beckenham BR3 .43 E6
Dorking RH4 .136 A5
Hampton TW12 .35 F8
Horley RH6 .160 F4
3 Merton SW19 .40 B8
Sheerwater GU21 .70 D6
Sunbury TW16 .15 A1
Sunningdale SL5 .30 A2
Walton-on-T KT12 .54 A7
Priory Cres Cheam SM3 .58 D6
South Norwood SE19 .22 C1
Priory Ct Camberley GU15 .64 F5
Cheam SM3 .58 E6
Cheam SM1 .58 F5
Egham TW20 .12 C2
Hounslow TW3 .5 B4
Roehampton SW15 .7 F3
Priory Dr RH2 .139 A7
Priory Gdns Hampton TW12 .35 F8
Mortlake SW13 .7 F4
South Norwood SE25 .42 F5
Priory Gn TW18 .13 B3
Priory Hospl The SW15 .7 F3
Priory House Sch SE6 .24 B7
Priory La East Molesey KT8 .36 B5
Frensham GU10 .167 E8
Roehampton SW15 .7 F2
Priory Lodge BR4 .63 E7
Priory Mews TW18 .13 B3
Priory Pl KT12 .54 A7
Priory Rd Cheam SM3 .58 D6
Chessington KT9 .56 E7
Forest Row RH18 .206 D2
Hampton TW12 .16 A1
Isleworth TW3 .5 C2
Mitcham SW19 .20 D1
Reigate RH2 .139 A6
Richmond TW9 .7 A7
Sunningdale SL5 .30 A2
Thornton Heath CR0 .42 A2
Winkfield SL5 .28 B7
Priory Sch SE25 .42 F5
Priory Sch The SM7 .78 A4
Priory St GU14 .85 D4
Priory The Croydon CR0 .61 A7
Godstone RH9 .121 B3
21 Kingston u T KT6 .37 E4
Priory Way UB7 .2 E8
Priory Wlk RG12 .27 F5
Priscilla House 8 TW16 .14 F1
Probyn Rd SW2 .22 B6
Proctor Cl Crawley RH10 .202 C4
Mitcham CR4 .41 A8
Proctor Gdns KT23 .94 B2
Proctors Cl TW14 .15 A7
Proctors Rd RG40 .25 F6

Profumo Rd KT12 .54 D5
Progress Bsns Pk CR9 .60 F8
Progress Way CR0 .60 F8
Promenade Approach Rd W4 .7 E7
Promenade De Verdun CR8 .79 D8
Promenade The W4 .7 E6
Prospect Ave GU14 .85 B6
Prospect Cl Forest Hill SE26 23 B4
Hounslow TW5 .4 F6
Prospect Cotts RG42 .26 D8
Prospect Cres TW2 .5 C1
Prospect La TW20 .11 A3
Prospect Pl Crawley RH11 201 C6
Ewell KT17 .76 E6
Staines TW18 .12 F3
Wimbledon SW20 .19 B1
Prospect Rd Ash GU12 .106 A5
Farnborough GU14 .85 A5
Rowledge GU10 .145 E3
Thames Ditton KT6 .37 C3
Prossers KT20 .97 D6
Providence House GU19 .47 E3
Providence La UB3 .3 D7
Providence Pl Ewell KT17 .76 E7
Farnham GU9 .125 C2
Provincial Terr SE20 .23 D1
Prune Hill TW20 .11 E1
Prunus Cl GU24 .67 E6
Public Record Office TW9 .7 B7
Puckridge Hill Rd GU11 .104 E6
Puckshill GU21 .68 D2
Puckshott Way GU27 .208 D8
Puddenhole Cotts RH4 .116 A2
Pudding La RH6 .180 E7
Puffin Cl BR3, CR0 .43 D4
Puffin Rd RH11 .200 D5
Pulborough Rd SW18 .19 F8
Pulborough Way TW4 .4 C3
Pullman Ct SW2 .21 F7
Pullman La GU7 .150 C2
Pullmans Pl TW18 .13 A3
Pump Alley 8 TW8 .6 D7
Pump La SL5 .29 E8
Pump Pail N CR0, CR9 .61 C7
Pump Pail S CR0, CR9 .61 C7
Pumping Station Rd W4 .7 E8
Punch Copse Rd RH10 .201 F7
Punchbowl La RH4, RH5 .136 D6
Punnetts Ct RH11 .200 F2
Purbeck Ave KT3 .38 F3
Purbeck Cl RH1 .119 D7
Purbeck Ct 4 GU2 .108 E1
Purbeck Dr GU21 .69 F5
Purberry Gr KT17 .57 F1
Purberry Shot KT17 .57 F1
Purbrook Ct RG12 .27 E3
Purbrook House 2 SW15 .19 B7
Purcell House TW2 .5 D1
Purcell Rd Crawley RH11 .200 F3
Crowthorne RG45 .45 B7
Purcell's Cl KT21 .75 F1
Purdey Ct 3 KT4 .39 A1
Purley Bury Ave CR8 .80 C8
Purley Bury Cl CR8 .80 C8
Purley Cl RH10 .202 D3
Purley Ct CR8 .61 B1
Purley & District War Memorial Hospl CR8 .80 A8
Purley Downs Rd CR2 .80 E8
Purley Hill CR8 .80 B7
Purley Knoll CR8 .80 A8
Purley Oaks Prim Sch CR2 .61 D3
Purley Oaks Rd CR2 .61 D1
Purley Oaks Sta CR2 .61 D2
Purley Par 2 CR8 .80 A8
Purley Park Rd CR8 .61 B1
Purley Rd Purley CR8 .80 A8
South Croydon CR2 .61 D3
Purley Rise CR8 .79 F7
Purley Sta CR8 .80 A7
Purley Vale CR8 .80 B6
Purley View Terr CR2 .61 D3
Purley Way
Croydon CR0, CR9 .61 A4
Frimley GU16 .85 E8
Purley CR8 .80 A8
Thornton Heath CR0, CR9 .41 F1
Purmerend Cl GU14 .84 C5
Pursers Hollow GU5 .154 D8
Pursers La GU5 .154 D8
Purslane RG40 .25 D5
Purton Rd RH12 .217 B4
Putney Heath SW15 .19 B8
Putney Hill SW15 .19 D8
Puttenham Common Nature Trails GU3 .148 E8
Puttenham Heath Rd
Puttenham GU3 .128 E3
Wanborough GU3 .128 E3
Puttenham Hill GU3 .128 C5
Puttenham La GU3, GU8 .128 C1
Puttenham Rd GU10 .127 C4
Puttenham Sch CE (VA) GU3 .128 C4
Puttock Cl GU27 .207 D5
Pye Cl CR3 .100 D4
Pyecombe Ct 4 RH11 .200 F3
Pyegrove Chase RG12 .27 E2
Pyestock Cres GU14 .84 C4
Pylbrook Rd SM1 .59 B7
Pyle Hill GU22, GU4 .89 D3
Pymers Mead Dulwich SE21 22 D7
Pymers Mead *continued*
West Norwood SE21 .22 C7
Pyne Rd KT6 .38 A1
Pyrcroft Grange Prim Sch KT16 .32 E3
Pyrcroft La KT13 .53 B5
Pyrcroft Rd KT16 .32 E2
Pyrford Common Rd GU22 70 E2
Pyrford Cty Prim Sch GU22 .71 A3
Pyrford Heath GU22 .70 F3
Pyrford Rd
Pyrford GU22, KT14 .71 A4
West Byfleet GU22, KT14 .71 A4
Woking GU22, KT14 .71 A4
Pyrford Woods Cl GU22 .70 F4
Pyrford Woods Rd GU22 .70 F4
Pyrland Rd TW10 .6 F1
Pyrmont Gr SE27 .22 B5
Pyrmont Rd W4 .7 A8
Pytchley Cres SE19 .22 C2

Q

Quadrangle Lodge SW19 .20 A2
Quadrangle The GU2 .130 A8
Quadrant Ct RG12 .27 E6
Quadrant Rd Richmond TW9 .6 D3
Thornton Heath CR7 .42 B5
Quadrant The
Ash Vale GU12 .106 A4
Merton SW20 .39 E8
Richmond TW9 .6 E3
Sutton SM2 .59 C4
Quail Cl RH12 .217 D7
Quail Gdns CR0 .62 E1
Quakers Way GU3 .108 C5
Qualitas RG12 .26 F1
Quality St RH1 .119 B7
Quantock Cl
Crawley RH11 .201 B6
Harlington UB3 .3 D7
Quantock Dr KT4 .58 C8
Quarr Rd SM5 .40 E3
Quarry Bank GU18 .67 A8
Quarry Cl Horsham RH12 .217 F6
Oxted RH8 .122 E5
Quarry Hill GU7 .150 B3
Quarry Hill Pk RH2 .118 C4
Quarry Park Rd SM1 .58 F4
Quarry Rd Oxted RH8 .122 E5
Shackleford GU7 .150 A7
Woldingham RH9 .121 C7
Quarry Rise Cheam SM1 .58 F4
East Grinstead RH19 .186 A3
Quarry St GU1 .130 D7
Quarry The RH3 .116 D3
Quarter Mile Rd GU7 .150 E2
Quarterbrass Farm Rd RH12 .217 D7
Quartermaine Ave GU22 .89 F5
Quarters Rd GU14 .85 C2
Quay West TW11 .17 B3
Quebec Cl RH6 .162 A3
Quebec Gdns GU17 .64 D4
Queen Adelaide Ct SE20 .23 C2
Queen Adelaide Rd SE20 .23 C1
Queen Alexandra's Ct 5 SW19 .19 F3
Queen Anne Ave BR2 .44 F6
Queen Anne Dr KT10 .55 E3
Queen Anne's Cl SL4 .10 B5
Queen Anne's Gdns
Leatherhead KT22 .95 B6
Mitcham CR4 .40 F6
Queen Anne's Terr KT22 .95 B6
Queen Annes Cl TW2 .16 D5
Queen Annes Ct KT22 .95 B6
Queen Annes Gate GU9 .125 D7
Queen Eleanor's C of E Jun Sch GU2 .130 A8
Queen Eleanor's Rd GU2 129 F8
Queen Elizabeth Dr GU11 104 F2
Queen Elizabeth Gdns SM4 .40 A5
Queen Elizabeth Hospl SM7 .78 C1
Queen Elizabeth II Jubilee Sch The RH13 .217 F1
Queen Elizabeth Rd
Camberley GU15 .46 D1
Kingston u T KT2 .37 F7
Rudgwick RH12 .214 D7
Queen Elizabeth Way GU22 .90 A8
Queen Elizabeth's Dr CR0 63 D1
Queen Elizabeth's Gdns CR0 .63 D1
Queen Elizabeth's Training Coll KT22 .74 D2
Queen Elizabeth's Wlk SM6 .60 D6
Queen Mary Ave
Camberley GU15 .65 A5
West Barnes SM4, SW20 .39 D4
Queen Mary Cl
Tolworth KT9 .57 A8
Woking GU22 .70 C3
Queen Mary Rd
Charlton TW17 .34 C7
South Norwood SE19 .22 B2
Queen Mary's Ave SM5 .59 F3
Queen Mary's Dr KT15 .52 A1
Queen St Aldershot GU12 .105 D2
Chertsey KT16 .33 A1
Croydon CR0, CR9 .61 C6
Godalming GU7 .150 E4
Queen St *continued*
Gomshall GU5 .133 C4
Horsham RH13 .217 D1
Queen Victoria Cross Roads GU15 .65 A6
Queen Victoria Ct GU14 .85 B5
Queen Victoria Hospl The RH19 .185 F3
Queen Victoria Way GU24 .87 D8
Queen's Ave
Aldershot GU11 .105 B5
Farnborough GU11 .105 B5
Queen's C of E Jun Mix Sch The TW9 .7 A7
Queen's C of E Jun Sch The TW9 .7 A7
Queen's Cl
Farnborough GU14 .105 B8
North Ascot SL5 .28 E8
Wallington SM6 .60 B5
Queen's Ct
Beckenham BR3 .44 A8
Croydon CR2 .61 C5
Farnborough GU14 .105 C8
1 Kingston u T KT2 .18 A1
3 Richmond TW10 .6 F1
Staines TW18 .13 D2
Thornton Heath CR7 .42 A4
Queen's Dr
Farncombe GU7 .150 C7
Guildford GU2 .109 A4
Thames Ditton KT7 .37 A3
Queen's Gate Rd GU14 .105 B8
Queen's Gdns TW5 .4 E6
Queen's Hospl CR0 .42 C3
Queen's House TW11 .16 F2
Queen's Mead GU8 .191 B4
Queen's Mead Rd BR2 .44 F7
Queen's Park Rd CR3 .100 E4
Queen's Pl Ascot SL5 .29 A6
Morden SM4 .40 A5
Queen's Rd Ascot SL5 .29 D4
Beckenham BR3 .43 E7
East Grinstead RH19 .185 E1
Egham TW20 .11 F2
Feltham TW13, TW14 .15 B7
Guildford GU1 .109 D1
Hampton TW12 .16 B4
Horley RH6 .161 A3
Hounslow TW3 .5 B4
Kingston u T KT2 .18 A1
Knaphill GU21 .68 D1
Mitcham CR4 .40 D6
Mortlake SW14 .7 D4
New Malden KT3 .38 F4
Richmond TW10 .6 F1
Richmond, Richmond Park KT2, TW10 .18 A3
Teddington TW11 .16 F2
Thames Ditton KT7 .36 F4
Thornton Heath CR0 .42 C3
Wallington SM6 .60 B5
Wimbledon SW19 .20 A2
Queen's Rdbt GU11 .105 B7
Queen's Rise TW10 .6 F1
Queen's Terr TW7 .6 A3
Queen's Way GU24 .87 D8
Queendale Ct GU21 .68 F3
Queenhill Rd CR2 .62 B1
Queenhythe Rd GU4 .109 D7
Queens Acre SM2, SM3 .58 E3
Queens Ave Byfleet KT14 .71 D7
Feltham TW13 .15 C4
Queens Cl Bisley GU24 .68 A3
Walton on t H KT20 .97 A3
Queens Court Ride KT11 .73 A6
Queens Cres TW10 .6 F2
Queens Ct 3 Redhill RH1 .119 A2
Weybridge KT13 .53 E4
Queens Dr Oxshott KT22 .74 C8
Surbiton KT5 .38 A3
Queens Gate RH6 .182 A8
Queens Hill Rise SL5 .29 C6
Queens Keep
Camberley GU15 .65 D5
10 Twickenham TW1 .6 C1
Queens La GU9 .125 B7
Queens Park Gdns TW13 .14 F5
Queens Pine RG12 .27 E3
Queens Pl KT12, KT13 .53 E5
Queens Rd Aldershot GU11 104 F2
Belmont SM2 .78 A8
Bisley GU24 .67 F1
Camberley GU15 .65 B4
Farnborough GU14 .105 D8
Hale GU9 .125 C6
Hersham KT12 .54 A6
Morden SM4 .40 A5
Twickenham TW1 .17 A7
Weybridge KT13 .53 C5
Queens Reach KT8 .36 E5
Queens Sq RH10 .201 D6
Queens Way Croydon CR0 .60 F5
Feltham TW13 .15 C4
Queens Wlk TW15 .13 D4
Queensberry House 6 TW9 .6 D2
Queensbridge Pk TW7 .5 E2
Queensbury Ct CR7 .42 C7
Queensbury Pl GU17 .64 C3
Queensfield Ct SM3 .58 C6
Queensgate KT11 .73 D7
Queenshill Lodge SL5 .29 B6
Queensland Ave SW19 .40 B8
Queensmead GU14 .85 B3
Queensmead Ave KT17 .58 B1
Queensmere Cl SW19 .19 D6
Queensmere Rd SW19 .19 D6
Queensmere (Southlands Coll) SW19 .19 D6
Queensthorpe Rd SE26 .23 D4
Queensville Rd SW12, SW4 21 D8
Queensway Coney Hall BR4 .63 F6
Cranleigh GU6 .174 F2
Crawley RH10 .201 E6
East Grinstead RH19 .185 E1
Frimley GU16 .86 A7
Hersham KT12 .54 B5
Horsham RH13 .217 C1
Redhill RH1 .118 F2
Sunbury TW16 .35 B7
Queensway N KT12 .54 D6
Queensway S KT12 .54 C5
Queenswood Ave
Hampton TW12 .16 B2
Hounslow TW3, TW5 .4 F5
Thornton Heath CR7 .42 A4
Wallington CR0, SM6 .60 D6
Queenswood Ct 11 SE27 .22 D4
Queenswood Rd
Forest Hill SE23 .23 E5
Knaphill GU21 .88 D8
Quennel House 7 SW12 .21 C8
Quennell Cl KT21 .95 F8
Quennells Hill GU10 .145 E6
Quentin Way GU25 .31 B5
Quicks Rd SW19 .20 B1
Quiet Cl KT15 .52 A6
Quillot The KT12 .53 F5
Quince Cl SL5 .29 D5
Quince Dr GU24 .68 B4
Quincy Rd TW20 .12 A3
Quinneys GU14 .85 D1
Quintilis RG12 .26 F1
Quintin Ave SW20 .39 F8
Quintin Ct W4 .7 C7
Quintock House 2 TW9 .7 A6
Quinton Cl Beckenham BR3 .44 C6
Hackbridge SM6 .60 B6
Heston TW5 .4 B7
Quinton Rd KT7 .37 A1
Quinton St SW18 .20 C6
Quintrell Cl GU21 .69 B2

R

Rabbit La KT12 .54 B3
Rabies Heath Rd
Bletchingley RH1 .120 F2
Godstone RH1, RH9 .121 B1
Raby Rd KT3 .38 D5
Raccoon Way TW4 .4 C5
Racecourse Rd
Crawley RH6 .181 F8
Dormansland RH7 .165 A2
Lingfield RH7 .164 F3
Racecourse Way RH6 .181 F8
Rachel Ct SM2 .59 D3
Rackfield GU27 .207 D7
Rackham Cl RH11 .201 D4
Rackham Mews SW16 .21 C2
Racks Ct GU1 .130 D7
Rackstraw Rd GU47 .45 D2
Racquets Court Hill GU7 .150 C6
Rad La Peaslake GU5 .133 D1
Peaslake RH5 .133 E1
Radbourne Rd SW12 .21 D7
Radcliff Mews TW12 .16 C3
Radcliffe Cl GU16 .86 A7
Radcliffe Gdns SM5 .59 E3
Radcliffe Rd CR0 .61 F7
Radcliffe Way RG42 .26 E8
Radcot Point 2 SE23 .23 D5
Radford Cl GU9 .125 E5
Radford Rd RH10, RH6 .182 C4
Radius Pk TW6 .3 F3
Radlet Ave SE23 .23 B6
Radley Cl TW14 .14 F7
Radley Ct BR1 .24 C4
Radley Lodge 30 SW19 .19 D7
Radnor Cl CR4 .41 E5
Radnor Ct
6 Forest Hill SE23 .23 D5
Redhill RH1 .118 E1
Radnor Gdns TW1 .16 F6
Radnor La
Abinger Common RH5 .155 B7
Ewhurst RH5 .155 A2
Radnor Rd Bracknell RG12 .27 F6
Peaslake GU5, GU6 .154 E4
Twickenham TW1 .16 F6
Weybridge KT13 .53 A7
Radnor Wlk CR0 .43 E3
Radolphs KT20 .97 D5
Radstock Way RH1 .119 E7
Radstone Ct 1 GU22 .69 F1
Rae Rd GU14 .85 B1
Raebarn Ct 6 SW16 .21 E5
Raeburn Ave Surbiton KT3 .38 B3
Tolworth KT5, KT6 .38 B3
Raeburn Cl KT1 .17 D1
Raeburn Ct GU21 .89 A8
Raeburn Way GU47 .64 D6
RAF Staff Coll RG12 .27 D5
Rag Hill TN16 .103 E6
Rag Hill Cl TN16 .103 E6
Rag Hill Rd TN16 .103 E6
Raglan Cl Aldershot GU12 .105 C1
Frimley GU16 .86 A8
Hounslow TW4 .4 F2
Reigate RH2 .118 D3
Raglan Ct CR0, CR2 .61 B5
Raglan Prec The CR3 .100 E5
Raglan Rd Knaphill GU21 .68 E1
Reigate RH2 .118 C3
Raglans House RH2 .118 B4
Ragwort Ct 1 SE26 .23 B3
Raikes La RH5 .134 B2
Railey Rd RH10 .201 E7
Railshead Rd TW1, TW7 .6 B3
Railton Rd GU2 .109 B5
Railway App Chertsey KT16 .32 F1
East Grinstead RH19 .185 E1
10 Twickenham TW1 .17 A8
Wallington SM6 .60 B5
Railway Cotts CR8 .79 F6
Railway Rd TW11 .16 F4
Railway Side SW13, SW14 .7 E4
Railway Terr Egham TW18 .12 D3
Feltham TW13, TW14 .15 A7
Rainbow Ct GU21 .68 E3
Rainbow Ctr The KT17 .76 E7
Rake La Milford GU8 .171 A7
Witley GU8 .170 F7
Rakers Ridge RH12 .217 D5
Raleigh Ave SM6 .60 D6
Raleigh Ct Beckenham BR3 .44 B8
Crawley RH10 .182 A3
Dulwich SE19 .22 F3
Staines TW18 .13 A4
Wallington SM6 .60 B4
Raleigh Dr Esher KT10 .55 D5
Smallfield RH6 .162 A3
Tolworth KT5 .38 C1
Raleigh Gdns CR4 .40 F6
Raleigh House 1 KT7 .37 A2
Raleigh Rd
Feltham TW13, TW14 .14 F6
Penge SE20 .23 D1
Richmond TW9 .6 F4
Raleigh Sch The KT24 .92 C2
Raleigh Way Feltham TW13 .15 C3
Frimley GU16 .65 F3
Raleigh Wlk RH10 .201 E4
Ralliwood Rd KT21 .96 A8
Ralph Perring Ct BR3 .44 A5
Ralphs Ride RG12 .27 E6
Rama Cl SW16 .21 E1
Rambler Cl SW16 .21 C4
Ramblers Way 12 RH11 .201 B1
Rame Cl SW17 .21 A3
Ramillis Cl GU11 .105 E7
Ramin Ct GU1 .109 C4
Ramornie Cl KT12 .54 F6
Rams La GU8 .193 B3
Ramsay Rd GU20 .48 E5
Ramsbury Cl RG12 .26 E3
Ramsdale Rd SW17 .21 A3
Ramsdean House 1 SW15 19 B7
Ramsden Rd Balham SW12 .21 A8
Godalming GU7 .150 D3
Ramsey Cl Camberley GU15 .66 B8
Horley RH6 .160 F3
Horsham RH12 .217 D5
Ramsey Ct
18 Crawley RH11 .201 B1
Croydon CR9 .61 B8
Ramsey House SW19 .40 B8
Ramsey Pl CR3 .100 C5
Ramsey Rd CR7 .41 F3
Ramslade Rd RG12 .27 D5
Rances La RG40 .25 E5
Randal Cres RH2 .139 A7
Randall Schofield Ct RH10 .202 A7
Randalls Cotts KT11 .73 B7
Randalls Cres KT22 .95 A7
Randalls Park Ave KT22 .95 A7
Randalls Park Dr KT22 .95 A6
Randalls Rd KT22 .94 E7
Randalls Way KT22 .95 A7
Randell Cl GU17 .64 E1
Randisbourne Gdns SE6 .24 B5
Randle Rd TW10 .17 C4
Randlesdown Rd SE6 .24 B5
Randmore Ct 6 BR3 .24 A1
Randolph Cl
Kingston u T KT2 .18 C3
Knaphill GU21 .68 E2
Oxshott KT11 .74 A4
Randolph Dr GU14 .84 C3
Randolph Rd KT17 .76 F5
Ranelagh Cotts RH6 .162 B2
Ranelagh Cres SL5 .28 D8
Ranelagh Dr
Bracknell RG12 .27 C6
Isleworth TW1 .6 B2
Ranelagh Gdns W4 .7 C7
Ranelagh Pl KT3 .38 E4
Ranelagh Rd RH1 .118 E1
Ranelagh Sch RG12 .27 C6
Ranfurly Rd SM1 .59 A8
Range Ride GU15 .64 F7
Range The GU5 .152 A4
Range View GU47 .64 E8
Range Villas TW17 .33 E2
Range Way TW17 .34 A2
Rangefield Prim Sch BR1 .24 E3
Rangefield Rd Bromley BR1 24 F3
Catford BR1 .24 F3
Rankine Cl GU9 .126 A6
Ranmere St SW12 .21 B7
Ranmore Ave CR0 .61 F7
Ranmore Cl RH1 .119 A4
Ranmore Common Rd RH5 .114 D2
Ranmore Ct
Kingston u T KT6 .37 D4
Wimbledon SW20 .39 D8
Ranmore Pl KT13 .53 C5
Ranmore Rd Dorking RH4 .136 A8
East Ewell SM2 .58 D2
Wotton RH4, RH5 .114 E1

Rann House 1 SW14 7 D4
Rannoch Ct 9 KT6 37 E4
Ransford House 16 SE21 22 E4
Ransome Cl RH11 200 E3
Ranyard Cl KT9 56 F7
Rapallo Cl GU14 85 C4
Raphel Dr KT7 37 A2
Rapley Cl GU15 65 F8
Rapley Gn RG12 27 C3
Rapley's Field GU24 87 E4
Rapsley La GU21 68 B1
Rastell Ave SW12 21 D7
Ratcliffe Rd GU14 85 A8
Rathbone House
Crawley RH11 201 B1
8 Wimbledon SW19 19 D1
Rathfern Prim Sch SE23 23 F7
Rathfern Rd SE23, SE6 23 F7
Rathgar Cl RH1 140 A4
Rathlin Rd RH11 201 B3
Raven Cl RH12 217 E6
Raven La RH11 201 C8
Ravendale Rd TW16 34 F7
Ravendene Ct 3 RH10 201 D5
Ravenfield Rd SW17 20 F5
Ravens Cl Bromley BR2 44 F7
Knaphill GU21 68 C3
Redhill RH1 118 F2
Ravens Wold CR8 80 C4
Ravensbourne 3 TW1 6 C1
Ravensbourne Ave
Bromley BR2, BR3 44 E8
Catford BR2 24 D1
Stanwell TW19 13 E7
Ravensbourne Ct SE6 24 A8
Ravensbourne House BR1 24 D3
Ravensbourne Park
Cres SE6 23 F8
Ravensbourne Pk SE4, SE6 24 A8
Ravensbourne Rd
Forest Hill SE23 23 F7
Twickenham TW1 6 C1
Ravensbourne Sta BR3 24 D1
Ravensbury Ave SM4 40 C4
Ravensbury Ct CR4 40 D5
Ravensbury Gr CR4 40 D5
Ravensbury La CR4 40 D5
Ravensbury Rd SW18 20 B6
Ravensbury Terr SW18 20 B6
Ravenscar Lodge 11 SW19 19 D1
Ravenscar Rd Catford BR1 24 E4
Surbiton KT6 56 F8
Ravenscote Cty Jun Sch
GU16 66 A3
Ravenscourt TW16 34 F8
Ravenscroft Cl GU12 106 C3
Ravenscroft Ct RH12 217 C3
Ravenscroft Rd Penge BR3 43 D7
Weybridge KT13 72 C8
Ravensdale Gdns SE19 22 D1
Ravensdale Rd Ascot SL5 29 A4
Hounslow TW4 4 E4
Ravensfield TW20 11 C2
Ravensfield Gdns KT19 57 E6
Ravenshead Cl CR2 81 C8
Ravenside KT6 37 D4
Ravenslea Rd SW11, SW12 20 F8
Ravensmead Rd BR2 24 D1
Ravensroost SE19 42 D8
Ravenstone Jun & Inf Schs
SW12 21 A6
Ravenstone Rd GU15 66 D5
Ravenstone St SW12 21 A7
Ravensview Ct KT6 37 D4
Ravenswood Ave
Tolworth KT6 57 A8
West Wickham BR4 44 C1
Ravenswood Cl KT11 73 D4
Ravenswood Cres BR4 44 C1
Ravenswood Ct GU22 69 F1
Ravenswood Dr GU15 66 A5
Ravenswood Gdns TW7 5 E6
Ravenswood Rd
Balham SW12 21 B8
Croydon CR0, CR9 61 B7
Rawlins Cl CR2 62 F3
Rawlinson Rd GU15 64 F6
Rawnsley Ave CR4 40 E4
Raworth Cl RH10 202 C4
Ray Cl Chessington KT9 56 C4
Lingfield RH7 164 C5
Ray Cnr RH7 164 B6
Ray La Blindley Heath RH7 163 F7
Lingfield RH7 164 B6
Tandridge RH7 164 B6
Ray Rd KT8 36 B4
Raybell Ct TW7 5 F5
Rayford Ave SE12 24 F8
Rayleigh Ave TW11 16 E2
Rayleigh Ct 2 KT1 37 F7
Rayleigh Rd SW19 39 F8
Rayleigh Rise CR2 61 E4
Raymead Ave CR7 42 A4
Raymead Cl KT22 94 F5
Raymead Way KT22 94 F5
Raymer Wlk RH6 161 C4
Raymond Cl
Forest Hill SE26 23 C3
Poyle SL3 1 E6
Raymond Cres GU2 129 F8
Raymond Rd
Beckenham BR3 43 E5
Wimbledon SW19 19 E2
Raymond Way KT10 56 A4
Raynald House 15 SW16 21 E5
Rayners Cl SL3 1 C7
Raynes Park High Sch
KT3 39 B6
Raynes Park Sta SW20 39 C7
Raynesfield SW20 39 C6
Rays Rd BR4 44 C2
Raywood Cl UB7 3 C7
Read Rd KT21 75 D2
Readens The SM7 78 F3
Reading Arch Rd RH1 118 F1
Reading Rd
Blackwater GU17 64 B4
Farnborough GU14 85 D1
Sutton SM1 59 C5
Wokingham RG41 25 A7
Yateley GU17 64 B4
Readman Ct 9 SE20 43 B8
Reads Rest La KT20 98 A7
Reapers Cl RH12 217 D5
Reapers Way TW7 5 D2
Rebecca Ct BR3 44 A8
Recovery St SW17 20 E3
Recreation Cl GU14 64 F1
Recreation Rd Bromley BR2 44 F7
Forest Hill SE26 23 D4
Guildford GU1 109 D1
Rowledge GU10 145 E3
Recreation Way CR4, SW16 41 E6
Rectory Cl Ashstead KT21 95 F8
Bracknell RG12 27 C5
Byfleet KT14 71 E6
Ewhurst GU6 175 E5
Godalming GU7 150 F2
Guildford GU4 110 D3
Littleton TW17 34 A6
Long Ditton KT6 37 C1
Ockley RH5 177 C3
West Barnes SW20 39 C6
Wokingham RG40 25 C6
Rectory Ct Cranford TW5 4 C5
Feltham TW13 15 C4
Sanderstead CR2 80 F7
Wallington SM6 60 C6
Rectory Gdns BR3 44 A8
Rectory Gn BR3 43 F8
Rectory Gr
Croydon CR0, CR9 61 B8
Hampton TW12, TW13 15 F4
Rectory La Ashstead KT21 95 F8
Bracknell RG12 27 B5
Buckland RH3 116 F3
Byfleet KT14 71 E6
Charlwood RH6 180 D7
Crawley RH11 200 F8
Great Bookham KT23 113 F8
Long Ditton KT6 37 C1
Shere GU5 133 A4
Streatham SW17 21 A3
Titsey TN16 103 E4
Wallington SM6 60 C6
Windlesham GU20 48 C4
Woodmansterne CR5, SM7 78 F3
Rectory Orch SW19 19 E4
Rectory Pk CR2 80 F7
Rectory Rd Beckenham BR3 44 A8
Cranford TW5 4 C5
Farnborough GU14 85 D4
Lower Kingswood CR5 98 D2
Sutton SM1 59 B7
Wokingham RG40 25 C6
Rectory Row RG12 27 B5
Rectory Sch TW12 16 A3
Red Admiral St RH12 217 E5
Red Deer Cl RH13 218 B4
Red Gables Dr CR2 61 D1
Red House La
Elstead GU8 148 C2
Walton-on-T KT12 54 A8
Red House Rd CR0, CR9 41 D3
Red La Claygate KT10 56 A4
Headley Down GU35 187 B7
Limpsfield RH8 144 B7
South Holmwood RH5, RH3 136 F1
Red Lion Bsns Ctr KT6 56 F7
Red Lion La Chobham GU24 49 E2
Farnham GU9 125 B1
Red Lion Rd Chobham GU24 49 E2
Surbiton KT6 57 A8
Red Lion St TW10 6 D2
Red Lodge BR4 44 C2
Red Lodge Rd BR3, BR4 44 D2
Red Rd GU18, GU24, GU15 67 C7
Red River Ct RH12 217 B5
Redan Gdns GU12 105 C2
Redan Hill Est GU11 105 C2
Redan Rd GU12 105 C2
Redbarn Cl CR8 80 B8
Redberry Gr SE23, SE26 23 C5
Redcar House SE26 23 B2
Redcliffe Missionary
Training Coll W4 7 B7
Redclose Ave SM4 40 A4
Redclyffe Terr 2 SM2 59 A3
Redcote RH4 115 D1
Redcourt Pyrford GU22 70 E4
Woking GU22 70 D4
Redcrest Gdns GU15 65 F5
Redcroft Wlk GU6 174 E2
Redding Way GU21 68 C1
Reddington Cl CR2 61 D2
Redditch RG12 27 D2
Redditch Cl RH11 200 E2
Reddons Rd BR3 23 E1
Reddown Rd CR5 79 D2
Rede Ct KT13 53 B7
Redehall Prep Sch RH6 162 B2
Redehall Rd Burstow RH6 183 C8
Smallfield RH6 162 B2
Redesdale Gdns TW7 6 A7
Redfern Ave TW2, TW4 16 A8
Redfern Rd SE6 24 C8
Redford Ave
Horsham RH12 217 B4
Thornton Heath CR7 41 F5
Wallington, Clock House CR5 79 B4
Wallington, Roundshaw SM6 60 E4
Redford Cl TW13 14 F6
Redgarth Ct RH19 185 B3
Redgrave Cl SE25 42 F3
Redgrave Dr RH10 202 D5
Redgrove Ct GU12 105 F2
Redhall Ct CR3 100 D4
Redhearne Fields GU10 167 E2
Redhill Coll RH1 140 B8
Redhill Ct SW2 22 A6
Redhill Distribution Ctr
RH1 161 A8
Redhill Rd KT11 72 B5
Redhill Sta RH1 119 A2
Redhouse Rd TN16 103 C6
Redkiln Cl RH13 217 F4
Redkiln Way RH12, RH13 217 F3
Redknap House TW10 17 C5
Redlake La RG40 25 F2
Redland Gdns KT8 35 F5
Redlands Coulsdon CR5 79 E3
Teddington TW11 17 A2
Redlands CE Inf Sch The
RH4 136 B4
Redlands Cotts RH5 136 B1
Redlands Ct BR1 24 F1
Redlands Cty Jun Sch The
RH4 136 B4
Redlands La
Crondall GU10 124 B7
Dorking RH5 136 A1
Redlands The BR3 44 B7
Redlands Way SW2 21 F8
Redlane Cotts RH8 123 B2
Redleaves Ave TW15 14 B2
Redlees Cl TW7 6 A3
Redlin Ct RH1 118 F3
Redmayne GU15 66 C4
Redroofs Cl BR3 44 B8
Redruth House SM2 59 B3
Redshank Ct 5 RH11 200 D5
Redstart Cl CR0, CR9 63 D1
Redstone Hill RH1 119 A1
Redstone Hollow RH1 140 A8
Redstone Manor RH1 119 A1
Redstone Pk RH1 119 B1
Redstone Rd RH1 140 A8
Redvers Buller Rd GU11 105 D7
Redvers Ct CR6 81 C1
Redvers Rd Bracknell RG12 27 B4
Warlingham CR6 81 D1
Redway Cotts GU21 88 F8
Redway Dr TW2 16 C8
Redwing Ave GU7 150 E8
Redwing Cl Horsham RH13 217 F3
Selsdon CR2 81 D8
Redwing Gdns KT14 71 B7
Redwing Rise GU4 110 D3
Redwood TW20 32 E7
Redwood Cl Crawley RH10 201 E8
Kenley CR8 80 C5
Redwood Ct 10 KT6 37 D2
Redwood Dr Frimley GU15 66 D4
Sunningdale SL5 30 B3
Redwood Est TW5 4 B8
Redwood Gr GU4 131 C3
Redwood Manor GU27 208 C7
Redwood Mount RH2 118 A4
Redwood Wlk KT6 37 D1
Redwoods Addlestone KT15 52 A4
Roehampton SW15 19 A7
Reed Cl GU11 105 D5
Reed Pl GU21, KT14 70 E6
Reed Place Bsns Park
TW17 33 F1
Reed's Hill RG12 27 B4
Reed's Sch KT11 74 A7
Reedham Dr CR8 80 A6
Reedham Park Ave CR8 80 A3
Reedham Sta CR8 79 F6
Reedings RH11 200 D4
Reeds Rd The
Frensham GU10 146 E2
Tilford GU10 147 A3
Reedsfield Cl TW15 14 B5
Reedsfield Rd TW15 14 B4
Rees Gdns CR0 42 F3
Reeve Ct GU2 109 A5
Reeve Rd RH2 139 C5
Reeves Cnr CR0, CR9 61 B8
Reeves Rd GU12 105 C1
Reeves Way RG41 25 A4
Regal Cres SM6 60 B7
Regal Ct 1 Guildford GU1 109 D1
2 Mitcham CR4 40 F6
Regal Dr 10 RH19 205 F8
Regalfield Cl GU2 109 A5
Regan Cl GU2 109 B6
Regency Cl TW12 15 F3
Regency Ct 4 Penge SE19 23 A1
4 Surbiton KT5 37 F4
Sutton SM1 59 B6
Regency Dr KT14 70 F6
Regency Gdns KT12 35 D1
Regency Lodge KT13 53 E7
Regency Mews
Beckenham BR3 44 C8
Isleworth TW7 5 E2
Regency Wlk Croydon CR0 43 F3
8 Richmond TW10 6 E2
Regent Cl Cranford TW5 4 B6
New Haw KT15 52 D2
Regent Cres RH1 118 F3
Regent Ct Bagshot GU19 47 F2
Regent Ct *continued*
Guildford GU2 109 B3
Regent Lodge 9 SW2 21 F7
Regent Pk KT22 75 A1
Regent Pl Croydon CR0 42 F1
Wimbledon SW19 20 C3
Regent Rd KT5 38 A4
Regent St W4 7 A8
Regent Way GU16 66 A1
Regents Cl Crawley RH11 201 C2
South Croydon CR2 61 E4
Whyteleafe CR3 80 F1
Regents Ct
23 Beckenham BR3 24 A1
Bromley BR1 24 F1
Weybridge KT13 53 B4
Regents Pl
1 Kingston u T KT2 37 E8
Sandhurst GU47 64 C8
Regents Wlk SL5 29 C2
Regiment Cl GU14 84 C3
Regina Coeli RC Prim Sch
CR2 61 B3
Regina Rd SE25 43 A6
Reginald Ct BR3 44 C8
Regis Ct East Bedfont TW14 3 D1
Mitcham SW19 40 E8
Regnolruf Ct KT12 35 A2
Reid Ave CR3 100 D6
Reid Ct SW14 7 C5
Reidonhill Cotts GU21 68 B1
Reigate Ave SM3, SM4 40 B1
Reigate Cl RH10 182 D1
Reigate Coll RH2 118 B1
Reigate Day Hospl RH2 139 A7
Reigate Gram Sch RH1 118 C1
Reigate Heath Cotts RH2 117 E1
Reigate Hill RH2 118 B4
Reigate Hill Cl RH2 118 B4
Reigate Parish Church
Inf Sch RH2 118 C1
Reigate Priory Cty Prim
Sch RH2 118 A1
Reigate Rd Banstead KT17 77 C4
Betchworth RH3, RH4,
RH2, RH5 116 D2
Brockham RH3, RH4, RH2
, RH5 116 D2
Burgh Heath KT18 77 C4
Catford BR1 24 F5
Dorking RH4 115 E1
Ewell KT17 77 C4
Hookwood RH6 160 C4
Leatherhead KT22 95 D4
Reigate RH2 118 C1
Sidlow RH2, RH6 160 C4
Reigate Sch RH1 139 C6
Reigate Sch of Art &
Design RH2 118 D1
Reigate St Mary's Prep
Sch RH2 118 B1
Reigate Sta RH2 118 A2
Reigate Way SM6 60 E5
Reindorp Cl GU2 130 A8
Relko Ct KT19 76 D8
Relko Gdns SM1 59 D5
Rembrandt Ct KT19 57 F4
Rembrandt Way KT12 54 B8
Rendle Cl CR0, SE25 43 A4
Renfree Way TW17 34 A2
Renfrew Ct TW5 4 E5
Renfrew Rd Hounslow TW5 4 E5
Kingston u T KT2 18 C1
Renmans The KT21 75 F3
Renmuir St SW17 20 F2
Rennie Cl TW15 13 D5
Rennie Terr RH1 140 A8
Renown Cl CR0 42 B1
Renshaw House 11 SW27 22 B3
Replingham Rd SW18 20 A7
Repton Cl SM1, SM5 59 E5
Repton Ct BR3 44 B8
Restmor Way SM5, SM6 60 A8
Restormel Cl TW3 5 A2
Restwell Ave GU6 174 B6
Retreat Rd TW9 6 D2
Retreat The
Englefield Green TW20 11 E3
Mortlake SW14 7 E4
North Cheam KT4 58 B8
South Norwood CR7 42 D5
Surbiton KT5 37 F3
Revell Cl KT22 94 B5
Revell Dr KT22 94 B5
Revell Rd Cheam SM1 58 F4
Kingston u T KT1 38 B8
Revelstoke Ave GU14 85 B6
Revelstoke Rd SW18, SW19 20 A6
Revesby Cl GU24 67 D6
Revesby Rd SM5 40 E3
Rewley Rd SM4 40 B3
Rex Ave TW15 14 A3
Rex House TW13 15 E5
Reynard Cl RH12 218 B5
Reynard Dr SE19 22 F1
Reynolds Ave KT9 56 E3
Reynolds Cl
Carshalton CR4, SM5 40 F1
Mitcham CR4, SW19 40 D8
Reynolds Gn GU47 64 D6
Reynolds Pl Crawley RH11 201 C7
12 Richmond TW10 6 F1
Reynolds Rd
Crawley RH11 201 C7
New Malden KT3 38 D2
Reynolds Way CR0 61 E6
Rheingold Way SM6 60 E2
Rhine Banks GU14 84 D5
Rhodes Cl TW20 12 B3
Rhodes Ct TW20 12 C3
Rhodes Way RH10 201 F3
Rhodes-Moorhouse Ct
SM4 40 A3
Rhododendron Cl SL5 8 E1
Rhododendron Rd GU16 86 B8
Rhododendron Ride
SL4, TW20 10 F3
Rhododendron Wlk SL5 8 E1
Rhodrons Ave KT9 56 E5
Rialto Rd CR4 41 A7
Ribble Pl GU14 84 E7
Ribblesdale RH4 136 B5
Ribblesdale Rd SW16 21 B3
Ricardo Ct GU5 151 F5
Ricards Lodge High Sch
SW19 19 F3
Ricards Rd SW19 19 F3
Rice's Cnr GU4 131 A2
Rices Hill RH19 185 E1
Richard Atkins Prim Sch
SW2 21 E8
Richard Challoner Sch
KT3 38 D2
Richard Thornton House
SW19 40 A7
Richards Cl Ash GU12 106 A5
Harlington UB3 3 D8
Richards Ct BR3 43 D8
Richards Field KT19 57 D2
Richards Rd KT11 74 B5
Richardson Ct 17 RH11 201 B1
Richardson House TW7 5 F4
Richardson's Lawn Cotts
SL4 10 B5
Richbell Cl KT21 75 D1
Richens Cl TW3 5 D5
Richfield Ct BR3 43 F8
Richland Ave CR5 79 A5
Richlands Ave KT17 58 A6
Richmond Adult Coll TW9 6 D3
Richmond Athletic Gd TW9 6 D3
Richmond Ave
Feltham TW14 3 E1
Merton SW20 39 E8
Richmond Bridge TW1 6 D1
Richmond Bridge
Mansions 1 TW1 6 D1
Richmond Cl
Biggin Hill TN16 103 B8
Epsom KT18 76 E5
Farnborough GU14 84 D3
Fetcham KT23 94 C3
Frimley GU16 65 F1
Richmond Coll TW10 17 E8
Richmond Cres TW18 12 F3
Richmond Ct
12 Kingston u T KT2 18 A1
Mitcham CR4 40 D6
Wimbledon SW20 39 B7
Richmond Dr TW17 34 D3
Richmond Gn CR0 60 E7
Richmond Hill TW10 6 E1
Richmond Hill Ct 5 TW10 6 E1
Richmond House
12 Forest Hill SE26 23 A5
Sandhurst GU47 64 E7
Richmond House
(Annexe of Rectory Sch)
TW12 15 F3
Richmond Mansions 5
TW1 6 D1
Richmond Park Rd
Kingston u T KT2 17 E1
Mortlake SW14 7 D3
Richmond Rd Coulsdon CR5 79 B4
Farncombe GU7 150 E6
Horsham RH12 217 D4
Isleworth TW7 6 A4
Kingston u T KT2 17 E2
Sandhurst GU47 64 E8
Staines TW18 12 F3
Thornton Heath CR7 42 B5
Twickenham TW1 17 B8
Wallington CR0 60 E7
Wimbledon SW20 39 B8
Richmond Sq RH19 185 D2
Richmond Sta TW9 6 E3
Richmond Upon Thames
Coll TW2 16 E8
Richmond Way
East Grinstead RH19 205 F8
Fetcham KT23 94 C3
Richmondwood SL5 30 B1
Rickard Cl SW2 22 A7
Rickards Cl KT6 56 E8
Ricketts Hill Rd TN16 103 E7
Rickfield RH11 201 A5
Rickford Hill GU3 88 D1
Rickman Cl RG12 27 C3
Rickman Cres KT15 52 B7
Rickman Ct KT15 52 B7
Rickman Hill CR5 79 B2
Rickman Hill Rd CR5 79 B1
Rickman's La RH14 211 F2
Ricksons La KT24 112 B8
Rickwood RH6 161 B4
Rickyard GU2 108 D1
Riddens The RH12 214 A6
Riddings The CR3 100 F2
Riddlesdown Ave CR8 80 C7
Riddlesdown High Sch
CR2 80 E5
Riddlesdown Rd CR3, CR8 80 D5

Riddlesdown Sta CR8 80 C6
Ride La GU5 153 D7
Ride The RH14 212 C2
Ride Way GU5, GU6 154 C1
Riders Way RH9 121 C4
Rideway Cl GU15 65 B4
Ridge Cl Brockham RH3 137 B5
Woking GU22 89 B6
Ridge Ct CR6 81 A1
Ridge Gn RH1 140 E6
Ridge Green Cl RH1 140 E6
Ridge House 4 KT2 18 B1
Ridge Langley CR2 62 A2
Ridge Moor Cl GU26 188 E5
Ridge Mount Rd SL5 30 A1
Ridge Pk CR8, SM6 60 D1
Ridge Prim Sch SM3 39 E1
Ridge Rd Cheam SM3, SM4 39 F1
Mitcham CR4 21 B1
Ridge The Coulsdon CR5 79 E5
Epsom KT18, KT21 76 C1
Fetcham KT22 94 D3
Limpsfield CR3, CR6 102 D2
Surbiton KT5 38 A4
Twickenham TW2 16 D8
Wallington CR8 60 D1
Woking GU22 70 B2
Woldingham CR3 102 D2
Ridge Way Feltham TW13 15 E5
Thorpe GU25 31 E4
Ridge Way The CR2 61 E1
Ridgedale RH10 204 B8
Ridgegate Cl RH2 118 D3
Ridgehurst Dr RH12 216 F1
Ridgelands KT22 94 D3
Ridgemead Rd TW20 11 B5
Ridgemount Guildford GU2 130 B8
Oatlands Park KT13 53 E8
Ridgemount Ave
Coulsdon CR5 79 B2
Croydon CR0 62 D8
Ridgemount Cl SE20 23 B1
Ridgemount Est GU16 86 C7
Ridgemount Way RH1 139 D7
Ridges The GU3 130 C4
Ridgeside RH10 201 F6
Ridgeway
East Grinstead RH19 205 E7
Epsom KT19 76 C7
Pyrford GU22 71 A4
11 Richmond TW10 6 E1
Walton-on-T KT12 34 F1
Wimbledon SW19, SW20 19 D2
Woking GU21 69 D4
Ridgeway Cl
Cranleigh GU6 175 A3
Dorking RH4 136 A5
Lightwater GU18 67 A8
Oxshott KT22 74 C5
Woking GU21 69 D4
Ridgeway Ct RH1 118 F1
Ridgeway Dr RH4 136 A4
Ridgeway Gdns GU21 69 D4
Ridgeway Prim Sch CR2 61 E1
Ridgeway Rd Dorking RH4 136 A5
Hounslow TW7 5 E6
Redhill RH1 118 F1
Ridgeway Rd N TW7 5 E7
Ridgeway Sch The GU9 146 C7
Ridgeway The
Bracknell RG12 27 C6
Brookwood GU24 88 A7
Cranleigh GU6 174 F3
Croydon CR0 60 F7
Fetcham KT22 94 D3
Guildford GU1 131 A8
Horley RH6 161 A1
Horsham RH12 217 B4
Lightwater GU18 48 B1
Oxshott KT22 74 C5
Ridgewell Cl SE26 23 F4
Ridgewood Ctr (Hospl)
GU16 66 C3
Ridgley Rd GU8 191 B4
Ridgway Ct SW19 19 D2
Ridgway Gdns SW19 19 D1
Ridgway Hill Rd GU9 146 C8
Ridgway Pl SW19 19 E2
Ridgway Rd Farnham GU9 146 C8
Pyrford GU22 70 F4
Ridgway The SM2 59 D4
Riding Hill CR2 81 A6
Riding The Cranleigh GU6 174 E4
Sheerwater GU21 70 B5
Ridings The
Addlestone KT15 51 E4
Ashstead KT21 75 D2
Biggin Hill TN16 83 E2
Cobham KT11 74 A7
Crawley RH10 202 D7
East Horsley KT24 92 F2
Epsom KT18 76 F4
Ewell KT17 57 F2
Frimley GU16 66 B3
Kingswood KT20 97 F7
Redhill RH2 118 D3
Send Marsh GU23 91 A4
Sunbury TW16 35 A8
Surbiton KT5 38 A4
Ridlands Gr RH8 123 E5
Ridlands La RH8 123 E5
Ridlands Rise RH8 123 E4
Ridley Ct SW16 21 E2
Ridley Rd Bromley BR2 44 F6
Merton SW19 20 B1
Ridley Rd continued
Warlingham CR6 81 D1
Ridsdale Rd Penge SE20 43 B8
Woking GU21 69 B2
Riesco Dr CR0 62 C4
Rifle Way GU14 84 C3
Rigby Cl CR0, CR9 61 A7
Rigg House 2 SW4 21 E8
Riggindale Rd SW16 21 D4
Rikkyo Sch in England
The RH14 213 D8
Riley House 1 SW4 21 D8
Rill Wlk RH19 186 B1
Rillside RH10 202 A3
Rimbault Cl GU11 105 E7
Rinaldo Rd SW12 21 B8
Ring Rd N RH6 182 C8
Ring Rd S RH6 182 C7
Ring The RG12 27 C7
Ringley Ave RH6 161 A2
Ringley Oak RH12 217 F4
Ringley Park Ave RH2 139 D8
Ringley Park Rd RH2 118 C1
Ringley Rd RH12 217 E4
Ringmead Bracknell, Great
Hollands RG12 26 E4
Bracknell, Hanworth RG12 27 B2
Ringmore Dr GU4 110 C4
Ringmore Rd KT12 54 C7
Ringmore Rise SE23 23 B8
Ringstead Rd
Carshalton SM1 59 D5
Lewisham SE6 24 B8
Ringwold Cl BR3 23 E1
Ringwood RG12 26 F2
Ringwood Ave Redhill RH1 118 F4
Thornton Heath CR0, CR9 41 E2
Ringwood Cl Ascot SL5 29 B5
Crawley RH10 201 E4
Ringwood Gdns SW15 19 A7
Ringwood Lodge 1 RH1 119 A4
Ringwood Rd
Blackwater GU17 64 C6
Farnborough GU14 85 C7
Ringwood Way TW12 16 A4
Ripley Ave TW20 11 E2
Ripley By-Pass
Ockham GU23 91 C4
Ripley GU23 91 C4
Ripley C of E Inf Sch GU23 91 B6
Ripley Cl CR0 63 C4
Ripley Court Sch Rose La
GU23 91 C6
Ripley Ct CR4 40 D7
Ripley Gdns Mortlake SW14 7 D4
Sutton SM1 59 C6
Ripley House
13 Kingston u T KT2 18 B2
Mortlake SW14 7 E4
5 Penge SE26 23 B3
Ripley La Ripley GU23 91 F3
West Horsley KT24, GU23 112 A7
Ripley Rd
East Clandon GU4 111 D6
Hampton TW12 16 A1
Ripley GU23, GU4 111 D7
Riplington Ct SW15 19 B8
Ripon Cl Frimley GU15 66 D3
Guildford GU2 108 F3
Ripon Gdns KT9 56 D5
Ripon Rd GU14 84 A7
Ripplesmere RG12 27 D5
Ripplesmore Cl GU47 64 B8
Ripston Rd TW15 14 D3
Risborough Dr KT4 39 A2
Rise Rd SL5 29 F3
Rise The Crawley RH10 202 D6
Crowthorne RG45 45 A5
East Grinstead RH19 205 F8
East Horsley KT24 92 E1
Ewell KT17 57 F1
South Croydon CR2 62 C2
Tadworth KT20 97 C6
Wokingham RG41 25 A7
Ritchie Cl RH10 202 C2
Ritchie Rd CR0 43 B3
Ritherdon Rd SW17 21 B6
River Ave KT7 37 A2
River Bank KT7 36 F4
River Crane Way TW13 15 F6
River Ct Kingston u T KT6 37 D4
Sheerwater GU21 70 C5
River Gdns Carshalton SM5 60 A7
Feltham TW14 4 B2
River Gdns Bsns Ctr TW14 4 B3
River Grove Pk BR3 43 F8
River Hill KT11 73 B4
River House
Forest Hill SE26 23 B5
Mortlake SW13 7 E5
River Island Cl KT22 94 D7
River La Cobham KT11 73 E3
Farnham GU10, GU9 145 E7
Fetcham KT22 94 D6
Leatherhead KT22 94 E7
Richmond TW10 17 D7
Wrecclesham GU10, GU9 145 E7
River Mead Crawley RH11 181 A1
Horsham RH12 217 B1
River Meads Ave
TW13, TW2 16 B5
River Mount KT12 34 F2
River Mount Gdns GU2 130 C6
River Park Ave TW18 12 D4
River Rd TW18 32 F8
River Reach TW11 17 C3
River View KT15 52 C5
River View Gdns TW1 16 F6
River Way
Twickenham TW13, TW2 16 B6
West Ewell KT19 57 E5
River Wlk KT12 35 A3
Riverbank East Molesey KT8 36 E5
Staines TW18 12 F2
Riverbank Way TW8 6 C8
Riverdale Dorking RH4 115 C3
Wrecclesham GU10 145 E7
Riverdale Dr
Wandsworth SW18 20 B7
Woking GU22 89 F6
Riverdale Gdns TW1 6 C2
Riverdale Rd Feltham TW13 15 F4
Twickenham TW1 6 C1
Riverdene Ind Est KT12 54 D5
Riverfield Rd TW18 12 F2
Riverhead Dr SM2 59 B1
Riverholme Dr KT19 57 E2
Rivermead Byfleet KT14 71 F6
East Molesey KT8 36 C6
Kingston u T KT6 37 D4
Rivermead Cl
New Haw KT15 52 C3
Richmond TW11 17 B3
Rivermead House TW16 35 C6
Rivermead Rd GU15 65 B2
Rivernook Cl KT12 35 C4
Riverpark Gdns BR2 24 D1
Rivers Cl GU14 85 E1
Riversdale Prim Sch
SW18 20 A7
Riversdale Rd KT7 37 A3
Riversdell Cl KT16 32 F2
Riverside Catford SE6 23 F4
Dorking RH4 115 D1
Egham TW20 12 A5
Forest Row RH18 206 E3
Guildford GU1 109 D3
Horley RH6 161 A1
Horsham RH12 217 A2
Oatlands Park TW17 34 E2
Sunbury TW16 35 D7
Twickenham TW1 17 B7
Wraysbury TW19 11 C8
Riverside Ave
East Molesey KT8 36 D4
Lightwater GU18 67 C8
Riverside Bsns Ctr
Guildford GU1 109 C1
Wandsworth SW18 20 B7
Riverside Bsns Pk
Farnham GU9 125 D3
Merton SW19 40 C8
Riverside Cl
Brookwood GU24 87 F7
Farnborough GU14 84 F5
Hackbridge SM6 60 B7
Kingston u T KT1 37 D5
Staines TW18 32 F8
Riverside Ct Dorking RH4 115 D1
Farnham GU9 125 D3
Teddington TW11 17 C3
Riverside Dr Bramley GU5 152 A7
Chiswick W4 7 E6
Egham TW18 12 E3
Esher KT10 55 A6
Mitcham CR4 40 E4
Richmond TW10 17 B5
Staines TW18 32 F8
Riverside Gdns
Cobham KT11 73 A6
Old Woking GU22 90 B6
Riverside House SW19 40 C5
Riverside Ind Pk GU9 125 C3
Riverside L Ctr W4 7 E6
Riverside Pk GU9 125 D3
Riverside Pl TW19 2 D1
Riverside Rd Hersham KT12 54 E6
Staines TW18 12 F1
Stanwell TW19 2 E1
Wandsworth SW17, SW19 20 C5
Riverside The KT8 36 D6
Riverside Way GU15 65 A3
Riverside Wlk Isleworth TW7 5 E4
West Wickham BR4 44 B1
Riverstone Ct KT2 37 F8
Riverview TW17 34 D2
Riverview Cty Fst Sch
KT19 57 D6
Riverview Gr W4 7 B8
Riverview Pk SE6 24 A6
Riverview Rd Chiswick W4 7 B8
West Ewell KT19 57 D6
Riverway TW18 33 B8
Riverway Est GU3 151 C8
Riverwood Ct GU1 109 C3
Rivett-Drake Rd GU2 109 A5
Rivey Cl KT14 70 F5
Road House Est GU22 90 A7
Roakes Ave KT15 52 B8
Robert Cl KT12 54 B5
Robert Gerard House 7
SE27 22 D4
Robert May Cty Fst Sch
The RH10 201 F4
Robert St CR0, CR9 61 C7
Robert Way
Horsham RH12 217 F7
Mytchett GU16 85 F3
Roberts Cl Cheam SM3 58 D3
Stanwell TW19 2 C1
Roberts Ct SE20 43 C8
Roberts House 5 SE27 22 B5
Roberts Rd
Aldershot GU12 105 D1
Sandhurst GU15 65 A6
Roberts Way TW20 11 C1
Robertsbridge Rd SM5 40 D2
Robertson Ct 5 GU21 68 E1
Robertson House SW17 20 E3
Robertson Way GU12 105 F1
Robin Cl Addlestone KT15 52 D5
Ash Vale GU12 106 A6
Crawley RH11 201 C8
East Grinstead RH19 185 F2
Hampton TW12 15 E3
Robin Ct SM6 60 C4
Robin Gdns RH1 119 A3
Robin Gr TW8 6 C8
Robin Hill GU7 150 D7
Robin Hill Dr GU15 66 A3
Robin Hood Cl
Farnborough GU14 85 A7
Knaphill GU21 68 F1
Robin Hood Cres GU21 68 E2
Robin Hood Ct SM1 59 B5
Robin Hood Inf Sch SM1 59 A5
Robin Hood Jun Sch SM1 59 B5
Robin Hood La
Kingston u T SW15 18 E4
Sutton SM1 59 B5
Warnham RH12 216 F5
Woking GU4 89 F3
Robin Hood Prim Sch
SW15 18 E3
Robin Hood Rd
Knaphill GU21 68 E2
Knaphill GU21 68 F1
Robin Hood Rdbt SW15 18 E5
Robin Hood Way
(Kingston By Pass)
KT2, SW15, SW20 18 E3
Robin Hood Works GU21 68 E2
Robin La GU47 45 C1
Robin Way Guildford GU2 109 B5
Staines TW18 12 F5
Robin's Bow GU15 65 B4
Robin's Ct BR3 44 D7
Robinhood Cl CR4 41 C6
Robinhood La CR4 41 C6
Robins Ct TW10 6 E1
Robins Dale GU21 68 C2
Robinson Ct 4 TW9 6 F3
Robinson Rd
Crawley RH11 201 D5
Mitcham SW19 20 E2
Robinsway KT12 54 C6
Robinswood Ct RH12 217 F4
Robinwood Pl SW15 18 D4
Robson Rd SE21, SE27 22 C5
Roby Dr RG12 27 D2
Rochdale 7 SE19 22 E2
Roche Rd SW16 41 F8
Roche Wlk SM4, SM5 40 D3
Rochelle Ct BR3 24 B1
Rochester Ave TW13 14 F6
Rochester Cl SW16 21 E1
Rochester Ct SE25 43 A7
Rochester Gdns
Caterham CR3 100 E5
South Croydon CR0 61 E7
Rochester Par TW13 15 A5
Rochester Rd
Carshalton SM5 59 F6
Egham TW20 12 D2
Rochester Wlk RH2 139 B5
Rochford Way CR0 41 E3
Rock Ave 13 SW14 7 D4
Rock Gdns GU11 104 F1
Rock Hill SE19 22 F4
Rock La GU10 146 A5
Rockbourne Rd SE23 23 D7
Rockdale Dr GU26 188 D3
Rockery The GU14 84 E3
Rockfield Cl RH8 122 F4
Rockfield Rd RH8 122 F5
Rockfield Way 7 GU47 64 D8
Rockhampton Cl 4 SE27 22 A4
Rockhampton Rd
South Croydon CR2 61 E4
West Norwood SE27, SW16 22 A4
Rockingham Cl SW15 7 F3
Rockingham Ct 20 BR3 24 A1
Rockmount Jun Mix &
Inf Lower Schs SE19 22 D2
Rockmount Jun Mix &
Inf Upper Schs SE19 22 D2
Rockmount Rd SE19 22 D2
Rocks The RH19 206 D6
Rockshaw Rd
Caterham RH1 119 E8
Merstham RH1 119 E8
Rockwell Gdns SE19 22 E4
Rocky La RH1, RH2 119 A6
Rocombe Cres SE23 23 C8
Rodborough Sch GU8 170 F7
Rodd Est TW17 34 D4
Roden Gdns CR0, SE25 42 E3
Rodenhurst Rd SW4 21 C8
Rodgate La GU27 209 E5
Rodgers House 4 SW4 21 D8
Roding Cl GU6 173 F2
Rodmel Ct GU14 85 E1
Rodmill La SW2 21 E8
Rodney Cl New Malden KT3 38 E4
Thornton Heath CR0 42 B1
Walton-on-T KT12 35 C1
Rodney Gn 2 KT12 54 C8
Rodney Pl SW19 40 C8
Rodney Rd Mitcham CR4 40 E6
New Malden KT3 38 E4
Twickenham TW4 16 A8
Walton-on-T KT12 54 C8
Rodney Way
Guildford GU1 110 A2
Rodney Way continued
Poyle SL3 1 E6
Rodona Rd KT13 72 D8
Rodway Rd SW15 19 A8
Rodwell Ct Addlestone KT15 52 C6
Walton-on-T KT12 54 B7
Roe Way SM6 60 E4
Roebuck Cl Ashstead KT21 95 E7
Feltham TW13 15 B4
Horsham RH13 218 B4
Reigate RH2 118 A1
Roebuck Ct 2 KT3 38 E4
Roebuck Rd KT9 57 A5
Roedean Cres SW15 7 E2
Roedeer Copse GU27 207 E6
Roehampton CE Prim Sch
SW15 19 B8
Roehampton Club Golf
Course SW15 7 F2
Roehampton Gate SW15 7 E1
Roehampton Gate Cty
Prim Sch SW15 7 E1
Roehampton High St
SW15 19 A8
Roehampton La
Putney SW15, SW19 19 A8
Roehampton SW15, SW19 19 A8
Roehampton Vale SW15 18 F5
Roffes La CR3 100 D2
Roffey Cl Horley RH6 160 F3
Purley CR8 80 B3
Roffey Cnr RH12 218 B4
Roffey's Cl RH10 183 A4
Roffords GU21 69 B2
Roger Simmons Ct KT23 94 A3
Rogers Cl Caterham CR3 101 B5
Coulsdon CR5, CR8 80 B1
Rogers La CR6 81 F1
Rogers Mead RH9 121 B3
Rogers Rd SW17 20 E4
Rogosa Rd GU24 67 E6
Rojack Rd SE23 23 D7
Roke Cl Purley CR8 80 C5
Witley GU8 170 E5
Roke La GU8 170 F5
Roke Lane Cotts GU8 170 F5
Roke Lodge Rd CR8 80 B6
Roke Prim Sch Purley CR8 80 B6
Purley CR8 80 C5
Roke Rd CR8 80 C5
Rokeby Cl RG12 27 D8
Rokeby Ct GU21 68 F2
Rokeby House 9 SW12 21 B8
Rokeby Pl SW20 19 B1
Rokeby Sch KT2 18 C1
Rokell House BR3 24 B3
Rokers La GU8 149 D7
Roland Ct SE19 42 F8
Roland Way KT4 57 F8
Rollesby Rd KT19, KT9 57 A4
Rolleston Rd CR2 61 D3
Rollit Cres TW3 5 A2
Roma Read Cl SW15 19 B8
Roman Cl TW14 4 C2
Roman House RH2 138 F7
Roman Ind Est CR0 42 E2
Roman Rd RH4 136 B5
Roman Rise SE19 22 D2
Roman Way Croydon CR9 61 B8
Farnham GU9 125 E4
Thornton Heath CR9 61 B8
Winkfield RG42 27 F8
Romana Ct TW18 13 A4
Romanby Ct 1 RH1 139 F8
Romanfield Rd SW2 21 F8
Romanhurst Ave BR2 44 E5
Romanhurst Gdns
BR2, BR3 44 E5
Romans Bsns Pk GU9 125 D3
Romans Ind Pk GU9 125 D3
Romans Way GU22 71 A4
Romany Gdns SM3 40 A2
Romany Prospect SE19 22 D2
Romayne Cl GU14 85 A5
Romberg Rd SW17 21 A5
Romeo Hill RG42 27 F8
Romeyn Rd SW16 21 F5
Romley Ct GU9 125 D1
Rommany Ct SE27 22 D4
Rommany Rd SE27 22 D4
Romney Cl Ashford TW15 14 C3
Chessington KT9 56 E6
Romney House RG12 27 E5
Romney Rd KT3 38 D3
Romola Rd SE24, SW2 22 B7
Romsey Cl Aldershot GU11 126 C6
Blackwater GU17 64 C6
Romulus Ct 6 TW8 6 D7
Rona Cl RH11 201 B3
Ronald Cl BR3 43 F4
Ronald Ross Prim Sch
SW19 19 E8
Ronelean Rd KT6 56 F7
Ronneby Cl KT13 53 E7
Ronson Way KT22 95 A6
Ronver Rd SE12 24 F7
Rook La CR3 100 B3
Rook Way RH12 217 F6
Rookeries Cl TW13 15 C5
Rookery Cl KT22 94 E3
Rookery Dr RH4 135 A5
Rookery Hill Ashstead KT21 76 A1
Outwood RH1, RH6 162 B6
Rookery Rd TW18 13 B3
Rookery The RH4 135 A5
Rookery Way KT20 117 F8
Rookley Cl SM2 59 B2
Rooks Hill GU5 152 C2

Rooksmead Rd TW16 .....35 A7
Rookstone Rd SW17 ......20 F3
Rookwood Ave
Sandhurst GU47 ....45 E2
Wallington SM6 ....60 D6
West Barnes KT3 ....39 A5
Rookwood Cl RH1 ....119 B6
Rookwood Ct GU2 ......130 C6
Rookwood Pk RH12 .....216 F3
Roothill La RH3 ....137 A3
Roper House 13 SE19, SE21 22 E4
Roper Way CR4 ....41 A7
Ropers Wlk 13 SE24 ......22 A8
Rorkes Drift GU16 ....86 A4
Rosa Ave TW15 ....14 A4
Rosalind Franklin Cl GU2 129 E8
Rosamond St SE26 ....23 B5
Rosamund Cl CR2 ....61 D6
Rosamund Rd RH10 .....202 B3
Rosary Cl TW3, TW5 ....4 E5
Rosary Gdns TW15 ....14 B4
Rosary RC Inf Sch TW5 ....5 A8
Rosary RC Jun Sch TW5 ...5 A8
Rose Ave Mitcham CR4 .....40 F8
Morden SM4 ....40 C4
Rose Bank Cotts GU22 ....89 E5
Rose Bushes KT17 ....77 C3
Rose Cotts
Enton Green GU8 ....171 A2
Esher KT10 ....55 D5
Rose Ct 10 Wimbledon SW19 19 F3
Wokingham RG40 ....25 C6
Rose End KT4 ....39 D1
Rose Gdns
Farnborough GU14 ....84 E3
Feltham TW13 ....15 A6
Stanwell TW19 ....13 D8
Rose Hill Dorking RH4 ....136 B7
Sutton SM1, SM4 ....40 B1
Rose Hill Pk W SM1 ......59 C8
Rose La GU23 ....91 D5
Rose St RG40 ....25 C6
Rose View KT15 ....52 C5
Rose Wlk Purley CR8 ......79 D8
Surbiton KT5 ....38 B4
West Wickham BR4 ....63 D8
Rose Wood GU22 ....90 A8
Roseacre RH8 ....123 A1
Roseacre Cl TW17 ....34 A4
Roseacre Gdns GU4 .....131 F3
Rosebank Epsom KT18 .....76 C5
Penge SE20 ....23 B1
Rosebank Cl TW11 ....17 A2
Rosebay RG40 ....25 E8
Roseberry Rd KT18, KT21 ..96 E8
Rosebery Ave Epsom KT17 .76 E5
Kingston u T KT3 ....38 F6
South Norwood CR7 ....42 C7
Rosebery Cl SM4 ....39 D3
Rosebery Cres GU22 ......89 F7
Rosebery Gdns SM1 ......59 B6
Rosebery Rd
Cheam SM1, SM2 ....58 F4
Isleworth TW3, TW7 ....5 C2
Kingston u T KT1 ....38 B7
Rosebery Sch KT18 ....76 C5
Rosebery Sq KT1 ....38 B7
Rosebine Ave TW2 ....16 D8
Rosebriar Cl GU22 ....71 A3
Rosebriars Caterham CR3 .100 E7
Esher KT10 ....55 C5
Rosebury Dr GU24 ....68 A4
Rosecourt Rd CR0 ....41 F3
Rosecroft Cl TN16 ....83 F1
Rosecroft Gdns TW2 .....16 D7
Rosedale Aldershot GU12 .105 C2
Ashstead KT21 ....75 C1
Caterham CR3 ....100 E4
Rosedale Cl RH11 ....201 A4
Rosedale Gdns RG12 .....27 A4
Rosedale Rd
North Cheam KT17 ....58 A5
Richmond TW9 ....6 E3
Stoneleigh KT17 ....58 A5
Rosedene Ave Morden SM4 40 A4
Streatham SW16 ....21 F5
Thornton Heath CR0 ....41 E2
Rosedene La GU47 ....64 D7
Rosefield Cl SM5 ....59 E5
Rosefield Gdns KT16 .....51 D4
Rosefield Rd TW18 ....13 A4
Roseheath Rd TW4 ....4 F2
Rosehill Claygate KT10 .....56 A4
Hampton TW12 ....36 A8
Rosehill Ave
Carshalton SM1, SM5 ......40 C1
Woking GU21 ....69 C3
Rosehill Farm Meadow
SM7 ....78 B4
Rosehill Gdns SM1 ....59 C8
Rosehill Rd TN16 ....83 C2
Roseleigh Cl 3 TW1 ....6 D1
Rosemary Ave
Ash Vale GU12 ....106 A8
East Molesey KT8 ....36 A5
Hounslow TW4 ....4 D5
Rosemary Cl
Farnborough GU14 ....84 D4
Oxted RH8 ....123 A2
Rosemary Cotts SW19 ....19 C1
Rosemary Cres GU2 .....109 A5
Rosemary Ct
Haslemere GU27 ....208 C7
Horley RH6 ....160 E4
Rosemary Gdns
Blackwater GU17 ....64 D5
Chessington KT9 ....56 E6
Mortlake SW14 ....7 C4
Rosemary La Alfold GU6 ..212 E8
Blackwater GU17 ....64 D5
Charlwood RH6 ....180 E7
Horley RH6 ....161 B3
Mortlake SW14 ....7 C4
Rowledge GU10 ....145 E4
Thorpe TW20 ....32 B6
Rosemary Rd SW17 ......20 C5
Rosemead KT16 ....33 B2
Rosemead Ave
Feltham TW13 ....14 F6
Mitcham CR4, SW16 ....41 C7
Rosemead Cl RH1 ....139 D7
Rosemead Sch SE27 ......22 C6
Rosemont Rd
Kingston u T KT3 ....38 C6
Richmond TW10 ....6 E1
Rosemount 5 SM6 ....60 C4
Rosemount Ave KT14 .....71 A6
Rosemount Par KT14 .....71 A6
Rosemount Point 10 SE23 .23 D5
Rosendale Infs Sch SE21 ..22 C8
Rosendale Jun Sch SE21 ..22 C8
Rosendale Rd
Streatham SE21, SE24 ......22 C7
West Norwood SE21, SE24 ..22 C7
Roseneath Ct CR3 ....101 A2
Roseneath Dr GU8 ....191 B4
Rosery The CR0 ....43 D3
Roses Cotts RH4 ....136 A7
Rosethorn Cl SW12 ....21 D8
Rosetrees GU1 ....131 A8
Rosetta Ct SE19 ....22 E1
Roseville Ave TW3, TW4 ....5 A2
Rosevine Rd SW20 ....39 C8
Rosewarne Cl GU21 ......69 A1
Rosewell Cl SE20 ....23 B1
Rosewood Ct KT2 ....18 A1
Rosewood Dr TW17 ....33 F4
Rosewood Gr SM1 ....59 C8
Rosewood Way GU24 .....67 E6
Rosina Ct SW17 ....20 E3
Roskeen Ct SW19 ....19 C1
Roslan Ct RH6 ....161 B2
Roslyn Cl CR4 ....40 D7
Ross Cl RH10 ....201 F3
Ross Ct Croydon CR2 ......61 C4
4 Putney SW15 ....19 D8
Ross House TW2 ....16 B6
Ross Par SM6 ....60 B4
Ross Rd Cobham KT11 .....73 C6
South Norwood SE25 ......42 E6
Twickenham TW2 ....16 C7
Wallington SM6 ....60 C5
Rossal Ct SE20 ....23 B1
Rossdale SM1 ....59 E5
Rossendon Ct 1 SM6 .....60 C4
Rossett Cl RG12 ....27 B5
Rossetti Gdns CR5 ....79 F1
Rossignol Gdns SM5 .....60 A8
Rossindel Rd TW3 ....5 A2
Rossiter Lodge GU1 .....131 A8
Rossiter Rd SW12 ....21 B7
Rosslea GU20 ....48 A6
Rosslyn Ave Feltham TW14 ..4 A1
Mortlake SW13, SW14 ......7 F4
Rosslyn Cl Ashford TW16 ...14 E2
Coney Hall BR4 ....63 F7
Rosslyn House 8 TW9 .....6 F6
Rosslyn Pk KT13 ....53 D6
Rosslyn Rd TW1 ....6 C1
Rossmore Cl RH10 ....182 D2
Rossmore Gdns GU11 ...104 F1
Rosswood Gdns SM6 .....60 C4
Rostella Rd SW17 ....20 D4
Rostrevor Rd SW19 ....20 A3
Rothbury Gdns TW7 ....6 A7
Rothbury Wlk GU15 ......66 C4
Rother Cl GU47 ....64 C8
Rother Cres RH11 ....200 F5
Rother House 4 RH1 .....118 F2
Rother Rd GU14 ....84 E7
Rotherfield Ave RG41 .....25 A7
Rotherfield Rd SM5 ....60 A5
Rotherhill Ave SW16 .....21 D2
Rothermere Rd CR0 ......60 F5
Rothervale RH6 ....160 F5
Rotherwick Ct GU14 .....105 C8
Rotherwood Cl
SW19, SW20 ....39 E8
Rothes Rd RH4 ....136 B8
Rothesay Ave Merton SW20 39 E7
Mortlake SW14, TW10 ....7 B3
Rothesay Rd SE25 ....42 E5
Rothschild St SE27 ....22 C4
Rothwell House
Crowthorne RG45 ....45 C4
Heston TW5 ....5 A8
Rotunda Est The GU11 ...105 B2
Rougemont Ave SM4 .....40 A3
Rough Field RH19 ....185 D4
Rough Rd GU22 ....88 C5
Rough Rew RH4 ....136 B4
Rough Way RH12 ....217 F5
Roughets La RH1 ....120 E6
Roughlands GU22 ....70 E4
Rounce La GU24 ....67 D6
Round Gr CR0 ....43 D2
Round Hill SE23 ....23 C5
Round Oak Rd KT13 ......52 F6
Roundabout Cotts RH12 .214 C5
Roundacre SW19 ....19 D6
Roundals La GU8 ....191 E8
Roundell House 14
SE19, SE21 ....22 E4
Roundhay Cl SE23 ....23 D6
Roundhill GU22 ....90 B8
Roundhill Dr GU22 ....70 B1
Roundhill Way
Guildford GU2 ....108 F1
Oxshott KT11 ....74 B7
Roundshaw Ctr SM6 .....60 E3
Roundtable Rd BR1 ....24 F5
Roundthorn Way GU21 ....68 F3
Roundway Biggin Hill TN16 .83 D4
Egham TW20 ....12 C3
Frimley GU15 ....66 C6
Roundway Cl GU15 ....66 C6
Roundway Ct RH10 ......201 D8
Roundway The KT10 ......55 F4
Roundwood View SM7 ....77 D4
Roundwood Way SM7 ....77 D4
Roupell House 7 KT2 .....17 F1
Roupell Rd SW2 ....21 F7
Rouse Gdns SE21 ....22 E4
Routh Ct TW14 ....14 D7
Routh Rd SW18 ....20 E8
Row Hill KT15 ....51 F4
Row La GU5 ....153 E5
Row The RH7 ....164 D4
Row Town KT15 ....51 F3
Rowallan Ct SE6 ....24 F7
Rowan 2 RG12 ....27 F4
Rowan Ave TW20 ....12 C3
Rowan Chase GU10 .....146 A5
Rowan Cl Camberley GU15 ..65 F8
Crawley RH10 ....201 F6
Guildford GU1 ....109 C4
Horsham RH12 ....218 B5
Kingston u T KT3 ....38 E7
Mitcham SW16 ....41 C8
Reigate RH2 ....139 C7
Rowan Cres SW16 ....41 C8
Rowan Ct Forest Hill SE26 ..23 C4
11 Kingston u T KT2 ....18 A1
Wimbledon SW20 ....39 B7
Rowan Dr RG45 ....45 C6
Rowan Gdns CR0 ....61 F7
Rowan Gn KT13 ....53 D6
Rowan Gr CR5 ....99 B6
Rowan High Sch SW16 ...41 C7
Rowan Mead KT20 ....97 B8
Rowan Prep Sch KT10 ....55 F3
Rowan Rd Brentford TW8 ....6 B7
Mitcham SW16 ....41 C7
Rowan Way RH12 ....218 C5
Rowans Cl GU14 ....64 E1
Rowans The Ashford TW16 .14 F3
Grayshott GU26 ....188 D2
3 Woking GU22 ....69 E1
Rowanside Cl GU35 .....187 C4
Rowbarns Way KT24 .....112 F5
Rowbury GU7 ....151 A7
Rowcroft Cl GU12 ....106 A6
Rowden Rd Penge BR3 ....43 F8
West Ewell KT19 ....57 C6
Rowdown Cres CR0 ......63 E2
Rowdown Inf & Jun Schs
CR0 ....63 D1
Rowe La GU24 ....88 A3
Rowena House RH10 ....181 D1
Rowfant Bsns Ctr RH10 ..203 E6
Rowfant Cl RH10 ....202 E6
Rowfant Rd SW12, SW17 ..21 A6
Rowhill Ave GU11 ....125 F8
Rowhill Cres GU11 ......125 F8
Rowhill Nature Trail
GU9 ....125 D8
Rowhills GU9 ....125 E8
Rowhills Cl GU9 ....125 F7
Rowhook Hill RH12 ......215 F8
Rowhook Rd
Rowhook RH12 ....196 E1
Slinfold RH12 ....216 A8
Rowhurst Ave KT15 ....52 B4
Rowland Cl RH10 ....183 E5
Rowland Gr SE26 ....23 B5
Rowland Hill Almshouses
TW15 ....14 A3
Rowland Rd GU6 ....174 D3
Rowland Way
Littleton TW15 ....14 D1
Merton SW19 ....40 B8
Rowlands Rd RH12 ......218 A6
Rowledge CE (VC) Prim
Sch GU10 ....145 E3
Rowley Cl Bracknell RG12 ..27 E6
Pyrford GU22 ....71 B3
Rowley Ct CR3 ....100 C5
Rowlls Rd KT1 ....37 F6
Rowly Dr GU6 ....174 A6
Rowly Edge GU6 ....174 A6
Rowntree Rd TW2 ....16 E7
Rowplatt La RH19 ....184 E4
Roxborough Ave TW7 ......5 F7
Roxburgh Cl GU15 ....66 C4
Roxburgh Rd SE27 ....22 B3
Roxeth Ct TW15 ....14 A3
Roxford Cl TW17 ....34 E4
Roxton Gdns CR0 ....63 A5
Roy Gr TW12 ....16 B2
Royal Alexandra & Albert
Sch The RH2 ....118 E6
Royal Ascot Golf Club SL5 29 B7
Royal Ave KT4 ....57 E8
Royal Botanic Gardens
TW9 ....6 E6
Royal Cir SE27 ....22 B5
Royal Cl KT4 ....57 E8
Royal Ct 9 KT2 ....18 B1
Royal Dr KT18 ....97 B8
Royal Grammar Sch GU1 130 D8
Royal Holloway Univ of
London TW20 ....11 D2
Royal Horticultural
Society Cotts GU23, KT14 .71 E3
Royal Horticultural
Society's Garden GU23 ..71 E1
Royal Hosp SW19 ....19 E8
Royal Hospl TW9 ....6 E4
Royal Kent CE Prim Sch
The KT22 ....74 C5
Royal Logistic Corps Mus
GU16 ....86 D8
Royal Marsden Hospl
(Surrey Branch) The
SM2 ....59 C1
Royal Mews KT8 ....36 E6
Royal Mid-Surrey Golf
Club TW9 ....6 D4
Royal Military Acad GU15 .64 F6
Royal Military Acad Hospl
GU15 ....65 A8
Royal Military Sch of
Music (Kneller Hall) TW2 .5 D1
Royal Oak Ctr The CR2 ....61 C1
Royal Oak House RH10 ..204 B7
Royal Oak Rd GU21 ....69 D1
Royal Orchard Cl SW18 ...19 E8
Royal Rd TW11 ....16 D3
Royal Russell Sch
(Ballards) CR9 ....62 B5
Royal Sch for the Blind
KT22 ....95 C5
Royal Sch of Church
Music RH5 ....115 B4
Royal Sch The GU27 .....189 A2
Royal School SL4 ....10 C4
Royal Surrey County
Hospl GU2 ....108 E1
Royal Victoria Gdns SL5 ..29 A4
Royal Way The GU16 ......86 D7
Royal Wimbledon Golf
Course SW19 ....19 B2
Royal Wlk SM6 ....60 B7
Royale Cl GU11 ....126 C8
Royals The GU1 ....130 E8
Royce Rd RH10 ....182 A3
Roycroft Cl SW2 ....22 A7
Roydon Ct KT12 ....54 A6
Roydon Lodge KT15 ......52 D7
Roymount Ct TW2 ....16 E5
Royston Ave Byfleet KT14 ..71 E7
Carshalton SM1 ....59 D7
Wallington SM6 ....60 D6
Royston Cl Cranford TW5 ....4 B6
Crawley RH10 ....182 A2
Walton-on-T KT12 ....35 A1
Royston Ct
Hinchley Wood KT10 ....55 F8
3 Richmond TW9 ....6 F6
Tolworth KT6 ....57 A8
Royston Prim Sch SE20 ...43 D8
Royston Rd Byfleet KT14 ...71 E7
Penge BR3, SE20 ....43 D8
Richmond TW10 ....6 E2
Roystons The KT5 ....38 B4
Rozeldene GU26 ....188 E3
Rubens St SE6 ....23 F6
Rubus Cl GU24 ....67 E6
Ruckmans La RH5 ....197 B7
Rudd Hall Rise GU15 .....65 E4
Ruden Way KT17 ....77 B4
Rudge Rise KT15 ....51 F5
Rudgwick Cty Prim Sch
RH12 ....214 D7
Rudgwick Rd RH11 ......200 F7
Rudloe Rd SW12 ....21 C8
Rudolph Ct SE22 ....23 B8
Rudsworth Cl SL3 ....1 D7
Ruffetts Cl CR2 ....62 B3
Ruffetts The CR2 ....62 B3
Ruffetts Way KT20 ....77 E1
Rufus Bsns Ctr SW18 .....20 B6
Rufwood RH10 ....204 A8
Rugby Cl GU47 ....45 E1
Rugby La SM2 ....58 D2
Rugby Rd TW1, TW2, TW7 ...5 E1
Ruggles-Brise Rd TW15 ...13 D3
Ruislip St SW17 ....20 F4
Rumsey Cl TW12 ....15 F2
Runcorn Cl RH11 ....200 E2
Runes Cl CR4 ....40 E5
Runnemede Rd TW20 ....12 A4
Running Horse Yd 12 TW8 ..6 E8
Runnymeade Ctr The
KT15 ....52 B8
Runnymede SW19 ....40 D8
Runnymede Cl TW2 ......16 B8
Runnymede Cotts TW19 ..12 D7
Runnymede Cres SW16 ...41 E8
Runnymede Ct
Egham TW20 ....12 A4
Farnborough GU14 ....85 A7
1 Wallington SM6 ....60 B4
Runnymede Gdns TW2 ...16 B8
Runnymede Hospl The
KT16 ....51 D7
Runnymede Rd TW2 ....5 B1
Runnymede Rdbt TW20 ...12 B4
Runshooke Ct 10 RH11 ...201 A3
Runtley Wood La GU4 ....89 F2
Runwick La GU10 ....124 C1
Rupert Rd GU2 ....130 C8
Rural Life Centre GU10 ..146 F3
Rural Way Mitcham SW16 ..21 B1
Redhill RH1 ....119 A1
Ruscoe Dr GU22 ....70 A2
Ruscoe House 12 SW27 ...22 B3
Ruscombe Way TW14 ......14 F8
Rush Croft GU7 ....151 A8
Rush The SW20 ....39 F8
Rusham Park Ave TW20 ..12 A2
Rusham Rd Balham SW12 ..20 F8
Rusham Rd *continued*
Egham TW20 ....11 F2
Rushams Rd RH12 ....217 B3
Rushbury Ct 6 TW12 .....36 A8
Rushden Cl SE19 ....22 D1
Rushden Way GU9 ......125 D7
Rushdene Wlk TN16 ......83 D2
Rushen Wlk SM5 ....40 D1
Rushett Cl KT7 ....37 B1
Rushett Dr RH4 ....136 C4
Rushett La KT9 ....75 D7
Rushett Rd KT7 ....37 B2
Rushetts Pl RH11 ....181 C1
Rushetts Rd Crawley RH11 181 B1
Reigate RH2 ....139 C5
Rushey Cl KT3 ....38 D5
Rushey Gn SE6 ....24 B8
Rushey Green Prim Sch
SE6 ....24 B7
Rushfords RH7 ....164 E5
Rushmead TW10 ....17 B5
Rushmead Cl CR0 ....61 F6
Rushmere Ct KT4 ....58 A8
Rushmere House 2 SW15 .19 A7
Rushmere Pl
Englefield Green TW20 .....11 E3
Wimbledon SW19 ....19 D3
Rushmon Gdns KT12 .....54 B7
Rushmon Pl SM3 ....58 E4
Rushmoor Cl GU2 ....108 F5
Rushmoor Ct GU14 ......105 C8
Rushmoor Independant
Sch GU14 ....85 C1
Rushmoor Rd GU11 .....104 E4
Rusholme Gr SE19 ....22 E3
Rushton Ave RH9 ....142 D5
Rushworth Rd RH2 ......118 B2
Rushy House RG12 ....27 E5
Rushy Meadow La SM5 ...59 E7
Rushy Meadow Prim Sch
SM5 ....59 E7
Ruskin Ave Feltham TW14 ...3 F1
Richmond TW9 ....7 A7
Ruskin Cl RH10 ....182 C1
Ruskin Dr KT4 ....58 C8
Ruskin Par CR0 ....61 D5
Ruskin Rd Croydon CR0, CR9 61 B8
Isleworth TW7 ....5 F4
Staines TW18 ....12 F2
Wallington SM5 ....60 A5
Ruskin Way SW19 ....40 D8
Rusper Ct CR5 ....79 D3
Rusper Cty Prim Sch
RH12 ....199 C7
Rusper Rd Capel RH5 ....178 D2
Crawley RH11 ....200 E6
Faygate RH12 ....199 A1
Horsham RH12 ....217 F6
Lambs Green RH11 ....200 D7
Newdigate RH12, RH5 ....179 C4
Rusper RH11, RH12 ......200 D7
Ruspers Keep RH11 .....200 F7
Russ Hill RH5, RH6 ....180 C5
Russel Cl Beckenham BR3 ..44 C6
Bracknell RG12 ....27 D2
Russell Cl
Walton on t H KT20 ....97 A2
Woking GU21 ....69 C4
Russell Ct Blackwater GU17 64 D5
Bromley BR1 ....24 F1
Guildford GU1 ....109 C4
Hindhead GU26 ....188 F4
Leatherhead KT22 ....95 B5
Streatham SW16 ....21 F3
Surbiton KT6 ....37 E2
Wallington SM6 ....60 C5
Russell Dr TW19 ....2 D1
Russell Gdns
Harmondsworth UB7 ....3 A8
Richmond TW10 ....17 C6
Russell Green Cl CR8 .....61 A1
Russell Hill CR8 ....60 F1
Russell Hill Par 4 CR8 ....80 A8
Russell Hill Pl CR8 ....80 A8
Russell Hill Rd CR8 ......80 A8
Russell Kerr Cl W4 ....7 C7
Russell Par 3 CR8 ....80 A8
Russell Prim Sch The
TW10 ....17 D7
Russell Rd
Lower Halliford TW17 ......34 C2
Merton SW19 ....20 A1
Mitcham CR4 ....40 E6
Twickenham TW1, TW2 ......5 F1
Walton-on-T KT12 ....35 A3
Woking GU21 ....69 C4
Russell Sch The TW10 ....17 D6
Russell Way Crawley RH10 202 A5
Sutton SM1 ....59 B5
Russell Wlk 4 TW10 ......6 F1
Russells KT20 ....97 D5
Russells Cres RH6 ......161 A2
Russet Ave TW16, TW17 ...34 E6
Russet Cl Hersham KT12 ...54 E7
Horley RH6 ....161 C3
Stanwell TW19 ....1 F1
Tongham GU10 ....126 E7
Russet Dr CR0 ....43 E1
Russet Gdns GU15 ....65 D3
Russet Glade GU11 ......125 E8
Russet Ho TW3 ....4 F3
Russet Way RH5 ....136 D4
Russets KT20 ....97 C4
Russett Ct CR3 ....101 A2
Russetts Cl GU21 ....69 F4

Russington Rd TW17 34 D3
Russley Gn RG40 25 A1
Rusthall Cl CR0 43 C3
Rustic Ave SW16 21 B1
Rustington Wlk SM4 39 F2
Ruston Ave KT5 38 B2
Ruston Cl RH10 202 C3
Ruston Way SL5 28 E7
Rutford Rd SW16 21 E3
Ruth Cl GU14 84 C5
Ruthen Cl KT18 76 B5
Rutherford Cl SM2 59 D4
Rutherford Way RH10 182 A3
Rutherwick Cl RH6 160 F3
Rutherwick Rise CR5 79 E3
Rutherwyk Rd KT16 32 E2
Rutherwyke Cl KT17 58 A4
Rutland Cl Aldershot GU11 105 A3
Ashtead KT21 75 E2
Epsom KT19 57 D1
Mitcham SW19 20 E1
Mortlake SW14 7 C4
Redhill RH1 118 F2
Rutland Dr Morden SM4 40 A2
Richmond TW10 17 E7
Rutland Gate BR2 44 F5
Rutland Gdns CR0 61 E6
Rutland Lodge SE6 23 F6
Rutland Pk SE6 23 F6
Rutland Rd Mitcham SW19 20 E1
Twickenham TW2 16 D6
Rutland Terr GU11 105 A3
Rutland Wlk SE6 23 F6
Rutlish Rd SW19 40 A8
Rutlish Sch (Boys) SW20 39 F7
Rutson Rd KT14 71 F5
Rutter Gdns CR4, SW19 40 D5
Rutton Hill Rd GU8 189 E8
Ruxbury Ct TW15 13 E5
Ruxbury Rd KT16 32 D3
Ruxley Cl KT19 57 B5
Ruxley Cres KT10 56 B3
Ruxley Ct KT19 57 C5
Ruxley La KT19 57 C5
Ruxley Mews KT19 57 B5
Ruxley Ridge KT10 56 A3
Ryan Ct SW16 21 E1
Ryan Dr TW8 6 A8
Ryan Mount GU47 64 A8
Rycott Path SE22 23 A8
Rydal Cl Crawley RH11 200 D4
Farnborough GU14 84 D3
Frimley GU15 66 D5
Sanderstead CR8 80 D6
Rydal Dr BR4 63 E8
Rydal Gdns
Kingston u T SW15 18 E3
Twickenham TW2, TW3 5 B1
Rydal Pl GU18 67 B8
Rydal Rd SW16 21 D4
Rydal Way TW20 12 B1
Ryde Cl GU23 91 C6
Ryde Ct GU12 105 C1
Ryde Heron GU21 68 E2
Ryde Lands GU6 174 F4
Ryde Pl TW1 6 D1
Ryde The TW18 33 B8
Ryde Vale Rd SW12 21 C6
Ryde's Hill Cres GU2 108 F5
Ryde's Hill Rd GU2, GU3 108 F4
Rydens Ave KT12 54 C8
Rydens Cl KT12 54 C8
Rydens Gr KT12 54 D6
Rydens Pk KT12 54 D8
Rydens Rd KT12 54 C8
Rydens Sch KT12 54 C6
Rydens Way GU22 90 A7
Ryder House 5 SW19 40 B8
Ryders Way RH12 217 F7
Rydes Ave GU2 108 F4
Rydes Hill Prep Sch GU2 108 F3
Rydon Mews SW19 19 C1
Rydon's La CR3, CR5 100 C7
Rydon's Wood Cl
CR3, CR5 100 C7
Rye Ash RH10 202 A7
Rye Brook Rd KT22 75 A1
Rye Cl Farnborough GU14 84 E7
Guildford GU2 108 E3
Winkfield RG12 27 D8
Rye Ct BR3 43 F8
Rye Gr GU20, GU24 48 F2
Ryebridge Cl KT22 75 A1
Ryebrook Bsns Pk KT22 95 A7
Ryecotes Mead SE21 22 E7
Ryecroft Ave TW2 16 B7
Ryecroft Dr RH12 217 A3
Ryecroft Gdns GU17 64 E4
Ryecroft Rd SW16 22 A2
Ryedale Ct 8 TW12 36 A8
Ryefield Path 7 SW15 19 A7
Ryefield Rd SE19 22 C2
Ryehill Ct KT3 38 F2
Ryelands Crawley RH11 201 A5
Horley RH6 161 C4
Ryelands Cl CR3 100 E6
Ryelands Ct KT22 75 A1
Ryelands Inf Sch SE25 43 A6
Ryelands Pl KT13 53 E7
Ryemead La RG42, SL4 8 C5
Ryersh La RH5 178 C8
Ryfold Rd SW19 20 A5
Ryland Cl TW13 14 F4
Ryland House 11 SW16 21 C3
Rylandes Rd CR2 62 B1
Ryle Rd GU9 146 B8
Rylton House KT12 35 A1
Rymer Rd CR0 42 E2
Rythe Ct KT7 37 A2
Rythe House BR1 24 D3
Rythe Rd KT10 55 E5
Rythe The KT22 55 C1

S

Sabah Ct TW15 14 A4
Sable Cl TW4 4 C4
Sable Ct 3 KT3 38 E4
Sabre Ct GU11 104 E2
Sachel Court Rd
GU6, GU8 193 D3
Sackville Cl RH19 185 C3
Sackville Cotts RH1 120 D1
Sackville Ct 3 RH19 205 F8
Sackville Gdns RH19 185 C3
Sackville House 16 SW16 21 E5
Sackville La RH19 185 C3
Sackville Rd SM2 59 A3
Sackville Sch RH19 186 A1
Sacred Heart Catholic
Prim Sch KT3 39 A5
Sacred Heart Coll SL5 30 C3
Sacred Heart RC Prim Sch
TW11 17 B1
Saddleback Rd GU15 65 E8
Saddlebrook Pk TW16 14 E1
Saddler Row RH10 201 D3
Saddlers Cl GU1 110 D2
Saddlers Mews KT1 37 C8
Saddlers Scarp GU26 188 A4
Saddlers Way KT18 96 D8
Saddlewood GU15 65 C4
Sadler Cl CR4 40 F7
Sadlers Ride KT8 36 C7
Saffron Cl RH11 201 A3
Saffron Ct GU14 84 C4
Saffron Platt GU2 109 A5
Saffron Rd RG12 27 B5
Saffron Way KT6 37 D1
Sailors La GU8 169 A2
Sainfoin Rd SW17 21 A6
Sainsbury Ctr The KT16 33 A2
Sainsbury Rd SE19 22 E3
Saint Hill Manor RH19 205 C4
Saint Hill Rd RH19 205 C5
Saints Cl SE27 22 B4
SS Peter & Paul's RC
Prim Sch CR4 40 F5
St Agatha's Dr KT2 17 F2
St Agatha's Gr CR4, SM5 40 F1
St Agatha's RC Prim Sch
KT2 17 F2
St Agatha's RC Sch KT2 17 F1
St Agnes Rd RH19 185 E2
St Aidan's RC Prim Sch
CR5 79 C3
St Alban's Gdns TW11 17 A3
St Alban's Gr SM5 40 E2
St Alban's RC Prim Sch
KT8 36 C4
St Alban's Rd RH2 118 A3
St Alban's Rdbt GU14 105 C7
St Albans Ave
Feltham TW13 15 D3
Weybridge KT13 53 A7
St Albans Cl GU3 108 B2
St Albans House 2 SW16 22 A4
St Albans Rd Cheam SM1 58 F6
Kingston u T KT2 17 E2
St Amunds Cl SE6 24 A4
St Andrew's C of E Fst
& Mid Sch RH10 202 A4
St Andrew's CE Inf Sch
GU9 125 B2
St Andrew's Cl
2 Hounslow TW7 5 E6
Reigate RH2 139 B8
Upper Halliford TW17 34 D5
Wraysbury TW19 11 E8
St Andrew's Ct SW18 20 C6
St Andrew's High Sch CR0 61 B6
St Andrew's RC Sch KT22 95 D7
St Andrew's RC Sch The
Grange KT22 95 D7
St Andrew's Rd
Coulsdon CR5 79 B4
3 Croydon CR0, CR9 61 C6
Kingston u T KT6 37 D3
St Andrew's Sch GU21 69 D3
St Andrew's Sch Cobham
KT11 73 C6
St Andrew's Sq KT6 37 D3
St Andrew's & St Mark's
Sch KT6 37 D4
St Andrew's Way GU16 85 F7
St Andrew's Wlk KT11 73 B4
St Andrews Bracknell RG12 26 E3
Cranleigh GU6 174 B4
St Andrews Cl GU21 69 C2
St Andrews Ct Ascot SL5 29 C4
Chiswick W4 7 C6
St Andrews Gdns KT11 73 C6
St Andrews RC Prim Sch
SW16 21 E3
St Andrews Rd
Carshalton SM5 59 E7
Crawley RH11 200 D5
St Andrews Way RH8 123 F4
St Ann's Cl KT16 32 F3
St Ann's Heath Cty Mid
Sch GU25 31 E4
St Ann's Hill SW18 20 C8
St Ann's Hill Rd KT16 32 D3
St Ann's Rd KT16 32 F3
St Ann's Sch SM4 40 B4
St Anne's Way CR2 61 B4
St Anne's Ave TW19 13 D8
St Anne's Dr RH1 119 A2
St Anne's Prim Sch TW19 13 E8
St Anne's RC Prim Sch
Banstead SM7 78 A3
Chertsey KT16 33 A1
St Anne's Rd
Crawley RH10 182 C2
Godalming GU7 151 A5
St Annes Glade GU19 47 D3
St Annes Mount 7 RH1 119 A2
St Annes Rise RH1 119 A2
St Annes Way 5 RH1 119 A2
St Anns Rd SW13 7 F6
St Anselm's Ct SW16 21 E3
St Anselm's RC Prim Sch
SW17 21 A5
St Anthony's Ct
1 Balham SW12 21 A8
Upper Tooting SW17 21 A6
St Anthony's Hospl KT4 39 D1
St Anthony's Way TW14 3 F3
St Anthonys Cl
Bracknell RG42 27 A8
Upper Tooting SW17 20 E6
St Antony's RC Prim Sch
SE20 43 B8
St Arvans Cl CR0 61 E7
St Aubin Cl RH11 200 F2
St Aubyn's Ave
Hounslow TW3, TW4 5 A2
Wimbledon SW19 19 F3
St Aubyn's Ct SW19 19 E2
St Aubyn's Rd SE19 22 F2
St Augustine's Ave
Croydon CR2 61 C3
South Croydon CR2 61 C3
St Augustine's Cl GU12 105 D1
St Augustines Ct BR3 43 E7
St Augustines's RC Prim
Sch SE6 24 C3
St Austins GU26 188 D3
St Barnabas Cl BR3 44 C7
St Barnabas Ct RH10 202 C7
St Barnabas' Gdns KT8 36 A4
St Barnabas Rd
Mitcham CR4 21 A1
Sutton SM1 59 D5
St Bartholomew CE
Prim Sch GU27 208 C7
St Bartholomew's Cl
SE26 23 C4
St Bartholomew's
Ct GU1 130 F7
St Bartholomew's Prim
Sch SE26 23 C4
St Bede's C of E Mid Sch
GU23 90 D3
St Bede's RC Inf Sch
SW12 21 D7
St Bede's Sch RH2 118 E4
St Benedict's Cl
Aldershot GU11 105 A1
Upper Tooting SW17 21 A3
St Benet's Gr SM4, SM5 40 C2
St Benets Cl SW17 20 E6
St Bernadette RC Jun
Mix Sch SW12 21 C8
St Bernadette RC Prim
Sch GU14 85 A5
St Bernards CR0 61 E7
St Bernards Cl 8 SE27 22 D4
St Boniface Catholic
Prim Sch SW17 20 F3
St Brelades Cl RH4 136 A5
St Brelades Rd RH11 200 F2
St Catherine's Convent
Girls Prep & Senior Schs
TW1 17 A6
St Catherine's Cross
RH1 120 E2
St Catherine's Dr GU2 130 B5
St Catherine's Hill GU2 130 C5
St Catherine's Jun Sch
GU5 151 F7
St Catherine's Pk GU1 130 F7
St Catherine's RC Mid Sch
SW20 39 C4
St Catherine's Sch GU15 65 C4
St Catherine's Senior Sch
GU5 151 F6
St Catherines
Weybridge KT13 53 B7
Woking GU22 89 C8
St Catherines Bletchingley
Village Cty Prim Sch
RH1 120 E2
St Catherines Cl SW17 20 E6
St Catherines Ct TW13 15 A7
St Catherines Rd
Crawley RH10 182 D1
Frimley GU16 86 A8
St Cecilia's RC Prim Sch
SM3 58 D8
St Chad's RC Prim Sch
SE25 42 E4
St Chads Cl KT6 37 C2
St Charles Borromeo RC
Prim Sch KT13 53 A7
St Charles Pl KT13 53 A5
St Christopher's RH7 164 D4
St Christopher's Cl
Haslemere GU27 208 A6
Hounslow TW7 5 E6
St Christopher's Ct 3
KT12 54 C8
St Christopher's Gn
GU27 208 A6
St Christopher's Hospice
SE26 23 C3
St Christopher's Mews
SM6 60 C5
St Christopher's Rd 2
Farnborough GU14 85 A3
Haslemere GU27 208 A6
St Christopher's Sch BR3 44 C7
St Christopher's Sch
Trust Ltd KT18 76 E5
St Christophers Cl RH12 217 D4
St Christophers Day
Hospl RH12 217 D3
St Christophers Gdns
North Ascot SL5 28 D8
Thornton Heath CR7 42 A6
St Christophers Pl 1
GU14 85 A3
St Clair Cl Oxted RH8 122 D5
Reigate RH2 118 C1
St Clair Dr KT4 58 B6
St Clair's Rd CR0 61 E8
St Claire Cotts RH7 165 B1
St Clare Bsns Pk TW12 16 C2
St Clement Rd RH11 200 F2
St Clements Ct GU14 85 B7
St Clements RC Prim Sch
KT17 57 F2
St Cloud Rd SE27 22 D4
St Crispin's Sch RG40 25 E6
St Crispins Way KT16 51 C2
St Cross Rd Farnham GU9 125 C3
Frimley GU16 86 B7
St Cuthbert Mayne RC
Prim Sch GU6 174 E3
St Cuthbert's Cl TW20 11 D2
St Cuthbert's RC Prim Sch
TW20 11 C1
St Cyprian's St SW17 20 F4
St David's CR5 79 F2
St David's Cl
Farnborough GU14 84 F8
Heath End GU9 125 E7
Reigate RH2 118 C2
West Wickham BR3, BR4 44 B2
St David's Coll BR4 44 B2
St David's Jun Sch TW15 13 F5
St Davids Ct 4 GU12 105 B1
St Davids Dr TW20 11 C1
St Denis Rd SE27 22 D4
St Deny's Cl GU21 68 D1
St Dominic's Sch GU8 171 C1
St Dunstan's C of E Prim
Sch SM3 58 E3
St Dunstan's Coll SE6 24 A7
St Dunstan's Hill SM1, SM3 58 E5
St Dunstan's La BR3 44 C4
St Dunstan's RC Prim Sch
GU22 70 A2
St Dunstan's Rd
Cranford TW5 4 B5
Cranford TW5 4 C5
Feltham TW13 14 F5
South Norwood SE25 42 F5
St Ebba's Hospl KT19 57 C2
St Edith Cl KT18 76 C5
St Edmund Cl RH11 181 D1
St Edmund's Catholic
Prim Sch TW2 16 B8
St Edmund's La TW2 16 B8
St Edmund's RC Prim Sch
GU7 150 F2
St Edmunds Cl SW17 20 E6
St Edmunds Sch GU26 188 D3
St Edward's Cl RH19 185 C1
St Edwards Cl CR0 82 D8
St Elizabeth Dr KT18 76 C5
St Elizabeth's RC Prim
Sch TW10 6 F1
St Elphege's RC Prim
Sch SM6 60 E4
St Faith's Rd SE24 22 B7
St Fillans GU22 70 B3
St Fillans Rd SE6 24 C8
St Francis Gdns RH10 183 C4
St Francis of Assisi RC
Sch RH10 201 E4
St Francis RC Prim
Sch CR3 100 F6
St Francis RC Sch SL5 29 A3
St Francis Wlk RH11 200 E4
St George's Ave KT13 53 C4
St George's Bsns Ctr KT13 53 A2
St George's Cl
Farnham GU9 126 B6
Weybridge KT13 53 C5
St George's Coll KT15 52 D7
St George's Gdns
Epsom KT17 76 F5
Horsham RH13 217 E4
Tolworth KT6 57 B8
St George's Gr SW17 20 D5
St George's Hill Artisan
Golf Club KT13 53 C2
St George's Hill Golf
Course KT13 72 B8
St George's Hospl SW17 20 D3
St George's Ind Est KT2 17 D3
St George's La SL5 29 B5
St George's Lodge KT13 53 D5
St George's Rd
6 Aldershot GU11, GU12 105 B1
Beckenham BR3 44 B8
Camberley GU15 65 D6
St George's Rd *continued*
Farnham GU9 125 D1
Feltham TW13 15 D4
Isleworth TW1 6 B2
2 Kingston u T KT2 18 A1
Mitcham CR4 41 B6
Richmond TW9 6 F4
South Nutfield RH1 140 E1
Wallington SM6 60 B5
Weybridge KT13 53 D4
Wimbledon SW19 19 F2
St George's Rd E GU12 105 B1
St George's Sch SL5 29 B6
St George's Sq KT3 38 E6
St George's Wlk CR0, CR9 61 C7
St Georges Cl RH6 161 B3
St Georges Coll Jun Sch
KT15 52 D7
St Georges Cotts RH7 143 E4
St Georges Ct
Addlestone KT15 52 C6
Crawley RH10 201 D8
East Grinstead RH19 185 C3
Penge SE20 43 B8
St Georges Ind Est GU15 65 B3
St Georges Rd
Addlestone KT15 52 C6
Farnham GU10 126 B4
St Georges Yd 11 GU9 125 B2
St German's Rd SE23 23 E7
St Giles C of E Inf Sch
KT21 75 F1
St Giles' Sch CR2 61 B4
St Gothard Rd SE21, SE27 22 D4
St Gregory's RC Inf Sch
GU15 65 B6
St Helen's Cres SW16 41 F8
St Helen's Rd SW16 41 F8
St Helena Terr 23 TW9 6 D2
St Helens KT7 36 F2
St Helens Cres GU47 64 B8
St Helier Ave SM4 40 C3
St Helier Cl Crawley RH11 201 A2
Wokingham RG41 25 B3
St Helier Hospl SM5 40 C1
St Helier Sta SM4 40 A3
St Heliers Ave TW3, TW4 5 A2
St Hilary's Prep Sch GU7 150 D3
St Hilda's Ave TW15 13 E3
St Hilda's Cl
Crawley RH10 182 C1
Horley RH6 161 B3
Knaphill GU21 68 D2
St Hildas Cl SW17 20 E6
St Hugh of Lincoln RC
Primary Sch GU21 88 D8
St Hugh's Cl RH10 182 C1
St Hugh's Rd SE20 23 B1
St Hughes Cl SW17 20 E6
St Ignatius RC Fst & Mid
Sch TW16 35 A8
St Ives RH10 202 C7
St Ives Sch GU27 208 E8
St James Ave KT17 77 A8
St James' Ave GU9 125 D3
St James Ave SM1 59 A5
St James C of E Prim Sch
KT13 53 C7
St James CE Prim Sch
GU8 148 C3
St James Cl KT18 76 E5
St James' Cl KT3 38 F4
St James Cl GU21 69 A1
St James Ct Ashtead KT21 75 D2
Farnham GU9 125 C3
St James' Ct 7 KT1 37 E6
St James Ct CR0 42 B2
St James Mews KT13 53 B6
St James Rd SM5 59 E7
St James' Rd
Kingston u T KT6 37 D3
Mitcham CR4 21 A1
Purley CR8 80 C6
St James Rd SM1, SM2 59 A5
St James' Terr GU9 125 C3
St James The Great RC
(Aided) Sch CR7 42 B7
St James Wlk RH11 201 C2
St James's Ave
Beckenham BR3 43 E6
Hampton TW12 16 C3
St James's Cl SW17 20 F6
St James's Cotts 14 TW10 6 D2
St James's Dr
Balham SW12, SW17 20 F8
Upper Tooting SW17 20 F7
St James's Lodge 4 CR0 42 E1
St James's Pk CR0 42 C2
St James's Pl GU6 174 C3
St James's Rd Croydon CR0 42 D2
East Grinstead RH19 185 D1
Hampton TW12 16 B3
Kingston u T KT1 37 D7
Thornton Heath CR0 42 D2
St James's Sch TW2 16 E5
St James's Terr 3 SW12 21 A7
St Joan Cl RH11 181 D1
St John Baptist C of E
Prim Sch BR1 24 C4
St John Cl RH13 217 E1
St John Fisher RC Prim
Sch SW20 39 D4
St John Rigby RC Coll
BR4 63 D6
St John The Bapist Sch
GU22 90 A8
St John the Baptist C of E
Jun Sch KT1 17 D1

St John's RH5 136 C3
St John's Ave KT22 95 B6
St John's Beamont Prep Sch TW20 11 B6
St John's Beamont Sch TW19 11 B6
St John's C of E Fst Sch GU10 167 E1
St John's C of E Prim Sch SE20 23 C1
St John's CE Jun Sch CR3 101 B2
St John's CE Prim Sch KT1 37 E6
St John's CE (VA) Inf Sch CR3 101 B2
St John's Cl
East Grinstead RH19 185 E2
Guildford GU2 130 A8
Leatherhead KT22 95 C7
St John's Cotts 2 SE20 23 C1
St John's Court KT1 37 E5
St John's Cres RH12 216 E3
St John's Ct
Brookwood GU24 87 F7
Farnborough GU14 84 D5
Isleworth TW7 5 F5
St John's Cty Prim Sch GU21 68 E1
St John's Dr SW18 20 B7
St John's Gr Barnes SW13 7 F5
1 Richmond TW9 6 E3
St John's Hill CR8 80 A2
St John's Hill Rd GU21, GU22 89 B8
St John's Hospl TW1 17 A8
St John's Lye GU21 88 F8
St John's Lye (Festival Path) GU21 88 F8
St John's Meadow RH7 163 E8
St John's RC Sch RH12 217 A1
St John's Rd
Carshalton SM5 59 E7
Crawley RH11 201 C6
Croydon CR0, CR9 61 B7
East Grinstead RH19 185 E2
East Molesey KT8 36 D5
Farnborough GU14 84 E5
Farnham GU9 146 B8
Feltham TW13 15 F4
Guildford GU2 130 A8
Isleworth TW7 5 F5
Leatherhead KT22 95 C6
North Ascot SL5 8 F1
Penge SE20 23 C2
Redhill RH1 139 F7
Richmond TW9 6 E3
Sandhurst GU47 64 C7
Sutton SM1 59 B8
Teddington KT1 37 C7
Westcott RH4 135 C6
Wimbledon SW19 19 E2
Woking GU21 69 B2
St John's Rise GU21 89 B8
St John's Sch KT22 95 B6
St John's (Shirley) C of E Prim Sch CR0 62 D7
St John's St GU7 150 F6
St John's Terrace Rd RH1 139 F7
St Johns Ave KT17 77 A7
St Johns Ct Egham TW20 12 A3
South Godstone RH9 142 F5
Woking GU21 89 A8
St Johns Cty Prim Sch RH1 139 E7
St Johns Dr KT12 35 C1
St Johns Gr GU9 146 B8
St Johns Mews GU21 89 A8
St Johns Rd KT3 38 C6
St Johns St RG45 45 B4
St Johns Way KT16 33 A1
St Joseph's Convent Prep Sch KT8 36 C4
St Joseph's RC Coll SW16 22 B2
St Joseph's RC Inf Sch SE19 22 C2
St Joseph's RC Jun Sch SE19 22 C2
St Joseph's RC Prim Sch
Bracknell RG12 27 D7
Dorking RH4 136 A7
Epsom KT18 76 C5
Kingston u T KT1 37 F7
Redhill RH1 118 E2
St Joseph's RC Sch GU2 108 F3
St Joseph's Rd GU11, GU12 105 A1
St Joseph's Sch GU6 174 F6
St Josephs RC Prim Sch GU11 126 A8
St Jude's C of E Sch TW20 11 C2
St Jude's Cl TW20 11 C3
St Jude's Cotts TW20 11 C3
St Jude's Rd TW20 11 C3
St Julian's Cl SE27, SW16 22 A4
St Julian's Farm Rd SE27, SW16 22 B4
St Katharines Rd CR3 101 A2
St Kitts Terr SE19 22 E3
St Lawrence C of E Mid Sch KT8 36 D5
St Lawrence Ct GU24 68 E8
St Lawrence Cty Prim Sch KT24 113 D8
St Lawrence RC Sch TW13 15 B6
St Lawrence Way CR3 100 D4
St Lawrences Way RH2 118 A1
St Leonard's Gdns TW5 4 E6
St Leonard's Rd
Claygate KT10 55 F4
Croydon CR0, CR9 61 B7
Kingston u T KT6 37 D4
Thames Ditton KT7 37 A2
Windsor SL4 9 D8
St Leonard's Sq KT6 37 D4
St Leonard's Wlk SW16 21 F1
St Leonards C of E Prim Sch SW16 21 D3
St Leonards Ct SW14 7 C4
St Leonards Cty Inf Sch RH13 217 E2
St Leonards Dr RH10 202 A4
St Leonards Pk RH19 185 E1
St Leonards Rd
Burgh Heath KT18 97 C8
Horsham RH13 218 A1
Mortlake SW14 7 C4
St Louis Rd SE27 22 D4
St Luke's C of E Prim Sch
Kingston u T KT2 37 F8
Richmond TW9 7 A6
West Norwood SE27 22 C3
St Luke's Cl SE25 43 B3
St Luke's Hospl GU1 130 F7
St Luke's Rd CR3 80 F1
St Luke's Sq 9 GU1 130 F8
St Lukes Ct GU21 70 C5
St Margaret Clitherow RC Prim Sch RG12 26 F2
St Margaret's GU1 109 F1
St Margaret's Ave
Cheam SM3 58 E7
Dormans Park RH19 185 F6
St Margaret's CE Sch RH11 201 B7
St Margaret's Ct 9 TW1 6 B1
St Margaret's Dr TW1 6 B2
St Margaret's Gr TW1 6 A1
St Margaret's Rd
East Grinstead RH19 185 F3
Hooley CR5 99 B6
Isleworth TW1 6 B2
Twickenham TW1 6 B2
St Margaret's Sta TW1 6 B1
St Margarets Ave TW15 14 B3
St Margarets Bsns Ctr 11 TW1 6 B1
St Margarets Ct RH12 216 F7
St Margarets Dr KT18 76 C5
St Mark's C of E Prim Sch
Croydon SE25 43 A5
Farnborough GU14 105 D8
St Mark's Catholic Sch TW3 5 A4
St Mark's CE Prim Sch BR2 44 F6
St Mark's CE (VA) Prim Sch GU7 150 B3
St Mark's Fst Sch CR4 40 F7
St Mark's Hill KT6 37 E3
St Mark's La RH12 217 E6
St Mark's Pl SW19 19 F2
St Mark's Rd
Bracknell RG42 26 C8
Croydon SE25 43 A5
Teddington TW11 17 B1
St Marks Cl GU14 85 C1
St Marks Pl GU9 125 B7
St Marks Rd KT18, KT20 77 C1
St Martha's GU5 154 E8
St Martha's Ave GU22 89 F6
St Martha's Ct GU4 131 B3
St Martin's Ave KT18 76 E5
St Martin's C of E Inf Sch KT18 76 D4
St Martin's C of E Jun Sch KT18 76 D4
St Martin's C of E Prim Sch RH4 136 A8
St Martin's C of E Sch (Pixham) RH4 115 C1
St Martin's Cl KT17 76 E6
St Martin's Ct
Staines TW15 13 C3
West Norwood SE27 22 B6
St Martin's Way SW17 20 C5
St Martin's Wlk RH4 136 B8
St Martin-in-the-Fields High Sch SW2 22 A7
St Martins Cl KT24 112 E6
St Martins Ct KT24 112 E6
St Martins Dr KT12 54 C7
St Martins Mews RH4 136 B7
St Mary Ave SM6 60 B7
St Mary Magdalene C of E Sec Sch TW10 7 A2
St Mary's 4 KT13 53 D7
St Mary's Ave
Beckenham BR2 44 E6
Stanwell TW19 13 D8
Teddington TW11 16 F2
St Mary's C of E Inf Sch KT22 95 C5
St Mary's C of E Prim Sch
Chessington KT9 56 F4
Long Ditton KT7 37 B1
Winkfield RG42 8 B2
St Mary's C of E Sch TW19 13 E8
St Mary's CE (Aided) Sch RH19 185 D2
St Mary's CE controlled Inf Sch GU8 149 E6
St Mary's CE JunSch RH8 122 E7
St Mary's CE Prim Sch KT14 71 E6
St Mary's Church Sch TW1 17 A8
St Mary's Cl
Chessington KT9 56 F3
Ewell KT17 57 F2
Fetcham KT22 94 D4
Oxted RH8 122 E6
Stanwell TW19 13 D8
Sunbury TW16 35 A5
St Mary's Cottage Hospl TW12 35 F8
St Mary's Cres
Hounslow TW7 5 E7
Stanwell TW19 13 D8
St Mary's Ct
Kingston u T KT3 38 E6
Wallington SM6 60 C6
St Mary's Dr
Crawley RH10 202 B8
East Bedfont TW14 14 C8
St Mary's Gdns
Bagshot GU19 47 E3
Horsham RH12 217 C1
St Mary's Gn TN16 83 C1
St Mary's Gr
Biggin Hill TN16 83 C1
Chiswick W4 7 B8
Richmond TW10, TW9 6 F3
St Mary's High Sch CR0 42 C1
St Mary's Hill SL5 29 C4
St Mary's House RH12 217 C1
St Mary's Mt CR3 100 F3
St Mary's Pl GU9 125 C3
St Mary's RC Inf Sch CR0 42 D1
St Mary's RC Jun Sch
Carshalton SM5 59 F5
Croydon CR0 42 D1
St Mary's RC Prim Sch
Beckenham BR3 24 C1
Chiswick W4 7 E8
Isleworth TW7 6 A4
Merton SW19 20 A1
St Mary's RC Sch TW7 6 A4
St Mary's Rd Ascot SL5 29 B3
Ash Vale GU12 106 A5
Camberley GU15 65 C6
East Molesey KT8 36 D4
Kingston u T KT6 37 D3
Long Ditton KT6 37 C1
Oatlands Park KT13 53 D6
Reigate RH2 139 B8
South Croydon CR2 61 D2
South Norwood SE25 42 E6
Wimbledon SW19 19 F3
Woking GU21 69 C2
Worcester Park KT4 57 E8
St Mary's Roman Catholic Inf Sch SM5 59 F6
St Mary's Sch Ascot SL5 29 B2
Horsham RH12 217 C1
St Mary's & St Peter's Prim Sch TW11 16 F3
St Mary's Univ Coll TW1 16 F5
St Marys CE (VA) Prim Sch GU8 191 C4
St Marys Cl GU47 64 C8
St Marys La SL4 8 D5
St Marys Rd KT22 95 B4
St Marys Wlk RH1 120 D2
St Matthew's Ave KT6 37 F1
St Matthew's C of E Prim Sch RH1 118 F3
St Matthew's CE Fst Sch SW20 39 A8
St Matthew's CE Prim Sch KT6 37 E2
St Matthew's Ct TW15 14 A3
St Matthew's Rd RH1 118 F2
St Matthews (C of E) Sch KT11 73 B1
St Merryn Ct BR3 24 A1
St Michael's Ave GU3 108 C6
St Michael's C of E Prim Sch RG12 27 A4
St Michael's CE (VA) Fst Sch RH5 115 C8
St Michael's Cl KT12 54 C8
St Michael's Prim Sch
Forest Hill SE26 23 E4
Wandsworth SW18 19 F8
St Michael's RC Prim Sch TW15 14 A3
St Michael's Rd
Aldershot GU11, GU12 105 B1
Croydon CR0 42 C1
Farnborough GU14 85 B6
Sheerwater GU21 70 D5
Wallington SM6 60 C4
St Michael's & St Martin's RC Prim Sch TW4 4 F4
St Michaels C of E Inf Sch GU11 126 B8
St Michaels C of E Jun Sch GU11 126 C8
St Michaels Cl KT4 57 F8
St Michaels Cotts RG45 45 C8
St Michaels Ct 1 KT13 53 C5
St Michaels Rd
Ashford TW15 14 A3
Camberley GU15 65 B5
Caterham CR3 100 D5
East Grinstead RH19 185 E2
St Micheal's C of E Sch SL5 29 D4
St Mildred's Rd GU1 109 F2
St Mildreds Rd SE12, SE6 24 F8
St Monica's Rd KT20 97 F6
St Nazaire Cl TW20 12 C3
St Nicholas Ave KT23 94 B2
St Nicholas C of E Prim Sch Cranleigh GU6 174 D3
Shepperton TW17 34 B3
St Nicholas Ct RH10 202 C7
St Nicholas Ctr SM1 59 B5
St Nicholas Dr TW17 34 A2
St Nicholas Glebe SW17 21 A2
St Nicholas Hill KT22 95 B5
St Nicholas Rd Sutton SM1 59 B5
Thames Ditton KT7 36 F3
St Nicholas Sch
Croydon CR9 61 A6
Purley CR8 80 A6
St Nicholas Specl Sch RH1 119 D6
St Nicholas Way SM1 59 B5
St Nicolas Ave GU6 174 E3
St Nicolas CE Inf Sch GU2 130 C7
St Nicolas Cl GU6 174 E3
St Normans Way KT17 58 A1
St Olave's Cl TW18 12 F1
St Olave's Wlk SW16 41 D7
St Omer Rd GU1 131 A8
St Omer Ridge GU1 131 A8
St Osmund's RC Prim Sch SW13 7 F6
St Oswald's Rd SW16 42 B8
St Patrick's RC Prim Sch GU14 85 D4
St Paul's C of E Jun Sch KT2 18 A1
St Paul's C of E Jun Sch RG41 25 A6
St Paul's Catholic Sch TW16 35 A8
St Paul's CE Inf Sch GU10 127 A7
St Paul's CE Prim Sch
Addlestone KT15 52 A6
Chessington KT9 56 E6
St Paul's CE (VA) Prim Sch RH4 136 B6
St Paul's Cl
Addlestone KT15 52 A5
Ashford TW15 14 C3
Carshalton SM5 40 E1
Chessington KT9 56 D6
Hounslow TW3, TW4 4 E5
St Paul's Ct TW4 4 E4
St Paul's Gate RG41 25 A6
St Paul's RC Prim Sch KT7 36 E2
St Paul's Rd Brentford TW8 6 D8
Egham TW18 12 D2
South Norwood CR7 42 C6
St Paul's Rd E RH4, RH5 136 B7
St Paul's Rd W RH4 136 B6
St Pauls C of E Prim Sch TW8 6 D8
St Pauls' CE Fst Sch GU10 126 F6
St Pauls Cl GU10 126 F7
St Pauls Rd Richmond TW9 6 F4
Woking GU22 70 B2
St Peter & St Paul CE Inf Sch CR3 100 A2
St Peter's CE Jun Sch GU14 85 C4
St Peter's Cl
Old Woking GU22 90 C7
Staines TW18 12 F2
St Peter's Gdns
West Norwood SE27 22 A5
Wrecclesham GU10 145 F6
St Peter's Hospl KT16 51 D7
St Peter's Prim Sch CR2 61 E4
St Peter's RC (Aided) Sch RH19 185 C1
St Peter's RC Comp Sch GU1 110 C2
St Peter's RC Prim Sch KT22 95 C7
St Peter's Rd
Crawley RH11 201 C6
Croydon CR0, CR2 61 D6
East Molesey KT8 36 A5
Isleworth TW1 6 B2
Old Woking GU22 90 B7
St Peter's St CR0, CR2 61 D5
St Peter's Way
Addlestone KT15 51 F6
Addlestone KT15, KT16 51 F7
Chertsey KT15 52 B8
Frimley GU16 85 F7
St Peters CE Inf Sch RH8 122 A2
St Peters CE Prim Sch GU9 146 A7
St Peters Cl SW17 20 E6
St Peters Ct KT8 36 A5
St Peters Mead GU12 106 B2
St Peters Pk GU11, GU9 125 E8
St Peters Rd KT1 38 A7
St Peters Way UB3 3 D8
St Philip's Ave KT4 58 B8
St Philip's Rd KT6 37 D3
St Philips Sch KT9 56 D4
St Philomena's Sch SM5 59 E5
St Pier's La RH7, TN8 165 B5
St Pinnock Ave TW18 33 A8
St Polycarp's RC Prim Sch GU9 125 D1
St Richard's with St Andrew's CE Prim Sch TW10 17 B5
St Richards Ct TW10 17 B5
St Robert Southwell RC Sch RH12 218 A6
St Sampson Rd RH11 200 F2
St Saviour's Coll SE27 22 D4
St Saviour's Pl GU1 109 C1
St Saviour's Rd CR0 42 C3
St Stephen's C of E Jun Sch TW1 6 B1
St Stephen's CE Prim Sch RH9 142 F6
St Stephen's Cl GU27 207 F6
St Stephen's Cres CR7 42 A6
St Stephen's Gdns TW1 6 C1
St Stephen's Rd TW3, TW4 5 A2
St Stephens Ave KT21 75 E3
St Stephens Cl GU27 208 C7
St Stephens Ct RH9 142 E5
St Swithun's Cl RH19 185 F1
St Teresa's Prep Sch (Grove House) KT24 113 D7
St Teresa's RC Prim Sch SM4 40 D3
St Theresa Cl KT18 76 C5
St Theresa's RC Prim Sch RG40 25 D5
St Theresa's Rd TW14 3 F3
St Thomas' Cl KT6 37 F1
St Thomas Cl GU21 69 C2
St Thomas More RC Sch KT8 36 C4
St Thomas of Canterbury RC Mid Sch CR4 41 A6
St Thomas of Canterbury RC Sch GU1 110 B1
St Thomas' Rd W4 7 C8
St Thomas Wlk SL3 1 D7
St Thomas's Dr GU4 111 E4
St Thomas's Mews GU1 130 F7
St Vincent Cl
Crawley RH10 202 D5
West Norwood SE27 22 B3
St Vincent Rd
Twickenham TW2 5 C1
Walton-on-T KT12 54 B7
St Wilfrid's RC Sch RH11 201 B5
St William of York RC Prim Sch SE23 23 E7
St Winifred's RC Prim Sch SE12 24 F8
St Winifred's Rd
Biggin Hill TN16 83 F1
Teddington TW11 17 B2
St Winifreds CR8 80 C4
Salamanca Pk GU11 104 F3
Salamander Cl KT2 17 C3
Salamander Quay KT1 37 D8
Salbrook Rd RH1 140 A1
Salcombe Dr SM4 39 D1
Salcombe House SE23 23 C6
Salcombe Rd TW15 13 E5
Salcot Cres CR0 63 C1
Salcott Rd CR0 60 F6
Sale Garden Cotts RG40 25 C5
Salehurst Rd RH10 202 E6
Salem Pl CR0, CR9 61 C7
Salerno Cl GU11 105 A2
Sales Ct 7 GU11 105 A1
Salesian Catholic Comp Sch KT16 51 E8
Salesian Coll GU14 85 D1
Salesian Sch KT16 33 A1
Salesian View GU14 105 E8
Salford Rd SW12, SW2 21 D7
Salfords Cty Prim Sch RH1 140 A3
Salfords Sta RH1 140 B1
Salfords Way RH1 140 A1
Salisbury Ave SM1, SM2 58 F4
Salisbury Cl
Wokingham RG41 25 A2
Worcester Park KT4 57 F7
Salisbury Gdns SW19 19 E1
Salisbury Gr GU16 86 A3
Salisbury House SW19 19 D5
Salisbury Pl KT14 71 C8
Salisbury Rd Ash GU12 106 A3
Banstead SM7 78 B5
Blackwater GU17 64 C5
Crawley RH10 201 F2
Croydon CR0, SE25 43 A3
Farnborough GU14 85 C3
Feltham TW13 15 C7
Harlington TW6 3 C1
Hounslow TW4 4 C4
Kingston u T KT3 38 D6
Richmond TW9 6 E3
Tyler's Green RH9 121 C4
Wallington SM5 59 F4
Wimbledon SW19 19 E1
Woking GU22 89 E8
Worcester Park KT19, KT4 57 E7
Salisbury Terr GU16 86 A3
Salix Cl TW16 15 B1
Salliesfield TW2 5 D1
Salmons La CR3 100 F7
Salmons La W CR3 100 E7
Salmons Rd
Chessington KT9 56 E4
Effingham KT24 113 C6
Salt Box Rd
Guildford GU3, GU4 109 B6
Worplesdon GU3, GU4 109 B6
Salt La GU8 171 E5

Saltash Cl SM1 58 F6
Saltbox Hill TN16 83 B6
Saltdean Cl RH10 201 D3
Salter House 8 SW16 21 C4
Salter's Hill SE19, SE27 22 D3
Salterford Rd SW17 21 A2
Salterns Rd RH10 202 C3
Saltire Gdns 2 RG42 27 A8
Saltram Rd GU14 85 E2
Salvador SW17 20 F3
Salvation Pl KT22 95 A3
Salvington Rd RH11 200 F3
Salwey Cl RG12 27 B3
Samaritan Cl RH11 200 E4
Samarkand Cl GU15 66 B4
Sambrook Mews SE6 24 B7
Samos Rd SE20 43 B7
Samphire Cl RH11 201 A3
Sampleoak La
Chilworth GU4 131 E2
Wonersh GU4 131 E2
Sampson Bsns Pk GU15 65 B3
Sampson Ct TW17 34 C4
Sampson Pk RG42 26 D8
Sampson's Almshouses GU9 125 A1
Samuel Cody Sch The GU14 105 B7
Samuel Ct BR3 44 B6
Samuel Johnson Cl SW16 21 F4
San Carlos App GU11 105 C2
San Feliu Ct RH19 186 B2
Sanctuary Rd TW19, TW6 3 A1
Sanctuary The SM4 40 A3
Sand Hill GU14 85 B7
Sand Hill Ct GU14 85 B7
Sandal Rd KT3 38 E5
Sandalwood GU2 130 B8
Sandalwood Ave KT16 51 E7
Sandalwood Rd TW13 15 B5
Sandbourne Ave SW19 40 B7
Sandcross Cty Sch RH2 138 F6
Sandcross La RH2 139 A5
Sanders Cl TW12 16 C3
Sanders House SW16 21 E2
Sandersfield Rd SM7 78 B4
Sanderstead Cl SW12 21 C8
Sanderstead Court Ave CR2 81 A6
Sanderstead Ct CR2 81 A7
Sanderstead Hill CR2 80 F8
Sanderstead Hts CR2 81 A8
Sanderstead Rd CR2 61 D2
Sanderstead Sta CR2 61 D2
Sandes Pl KT22 75 A1
Sandfield Cty Prim Sch GU1 130 D8
Sandfield Gdns CR7 42 B6
Sandfield Pl CR7 42 C6
Sandfield Rd CR7 42 B6
Sandfield Terr GU1 130 D8
Sandfields GU23 90 D3
Sandford Ct GU11 104 F1
Sandford Down RG12 27 F4
Sandford Rd
Aldershot GU11 104 F1
Heath End GU9 125 B7
Sandgate House 14 BR3 24 A1
Sandgate La SW17, SW18 20 E7
Sandhawes Hill RH19 186 A4
Sandheath Rd GU26 188 C7
Sandhill La RH10 204 B7
Sandhills CR0, SM6 60 D6
Sandhills Ct GU25 31 E4
Sandhills La GU25, TW20 31 F4
Sandhills Meadow TW17 34 C2
Sandhills Rd RH2 139 A7
Sandhurst Ave KT5 38 B2
Sandhurst Cl CR2 61 E2
Sandhurst La GU17 64 B6
Sandhurst Prim Sch SE6 24 E7
Sandhurst Rd Catford SE6 24 D7
Crowthorne RG45 45 B3
Wokingham RG40 25 A1
Sandhurst Sch GU47 45 D1
Sandhurst Sta GU47 64 A8
Sandhurst Way CR2 61 E3
Sandiford House CR3 100 E3
Sandiford Rd SM3 58 F8
Sandiland Cres BR2 63 F8
Sandilands CR0 62 A7
Sandlands Gr KT20 97 A4
Sandlands Rd KT20 97 A3
Sandon Cl KT10 36 D1
Sandon House 5 SW2 21 E8
Sandown Ave KT10 55 C5
Sandown Cl
Blackwater GU17 64 D5
Cranford TW5 4 A6
Sandown Cres GU11 126 B7
Sandown Ct 2 SM2 59 B3
Sandown Dr Frimley GU16 65 E2
Wallington SM5 60 A2
Sandown Gate KT10 55 D7
Sandown House SE26 23 B2
Sandown Ind Pk KT10 55 A8
Sandown Lodge KT18 76 D5
Sandown Park KT10 55 C8
Sandown Rd Coulsdon CR5 79 A3
Croydon SE25 43 B4
Esher KT10 55 C6
Sandpiper Cl RH11 200 D4
Sandpiper Rd Cheam SM1 58 F5
Selsdon CR2 81 D8
Sandpit Hall Rd GU24 69 A7
Sandpit Heath GU3 108 D5
Sandpit Rd Catford BR1 24 E3
Redhill RH1 139 F8
Sandpits Rd
Richmond TW10 17 D6
South Croydon CR0 62 D6
Sandra Cl TW3 5 B2
Sandra House KT8 36 D4
Sandringham Ave SW20 39 E7
Sandringham Cl
East Grinstead RH19 206 A8
Farnborough GU14 105 B8
1 Putney SW19 19 D7
Pyrford GU22 71 A3
Sandringham Ct
Beckenham BR3 44 C8
Belmont SM2 59 A2
Sandringham Cty Inf Sch GU16 85 F7
Sandringham Dr TW15 13 D4
Sandringham Gdns TW5 4 A6
Sandringham Pk KT11 74 A7
Sandringham Rd
Crawley RH11 201 B2
North Cheam KT4 58 A7
Stanwell TW19, TW6 2 E2
Thornton Heath CR0 42 C4
Sandringham Way GU16 85 F8
Sandrock GU27 208 C6
Sandrock Hill Rd
Rowledge GU10 146 A5
Wrecclesham GU10 146 A5
Sandrock Pl CR0 62 D6
Sandrock Rd RH4 135 B5
Sandroyd Way KT11 74 A6
Sands Cl GU10 126 D2
Sands Rd Farnham GU10 126 D2
The Sands GU10 126 D2
Sandstone TW9 7 A7
Sandways 6 TW9 7 A6
Sandy Cl GU22 70 C2
Sandy Croft KT17 58 C1
Sandy Cross GU10 126 F4
Sandy Ct KT11 73 F6
Sandy Dr Cobham KT11 74 A8
East Bedfont TW14 14 E7
Sandy Hill Rd
Heath End GU9 125 B7
Wallington SM6 60 C2
Sandy Holt KT11 73 F6
Sandy La Albury GU5 132 D2
Artington GU2, GU3 130 B5
Belmont SM2 58 E2
Betchworth RH3 116 E1
Bletchingley RH1 120 C3
Bracknell RG12 27 C8
Camberley GU15 65 E6
Chobham GU24 49 E2
Cobham KT11, KT22 74 B7
Crawley Down RH10 204 A8
East Grinstead RH19 185 F1
Farnborough GU14 84 D7
Farncombe GU7 150 D6
Grayswood GU27 189 E1
Haslemere GU26, GU27 207 C7
Haslemere, Nutcombe GU26 188 F2
Kingswood KT20 98 A4
Limpsfield RH8 123 B7
Mitcham CR4 41 A8
Normandy GU3 107 D4
North Ascot SL5 28 C8
Nutfield RH1 119 E1
Oxted RH8 122 C6
Pyrford GU22 71 A3
Reigate RH2 138 B8
Richmond TW10 17 D6
Rushmoor GU10 168 B5
Sandhurst GU47 45 A2
Send GU23 90 C4
Shere GU5 133 A3
South Nutfield RH1 119 E1
Sunningdale SL5 30 A4
Teddington KT8, TW11 17 B1
Thorpe GU25 31 E5
Walton-on-T KT12 35 C3
Woking GU22 70 C2
Sandy La N SM6 60 D5
Sandy La S SM6 60 C3
Sandy Lane Jun Sch RG12 27 C8
Sandy Rd KT15 52 A4
Sandy Ride SL5 29 E5
Sandy Way Cobham KT11 74 A7
Croydon CR0 62 F7
Walton-on-T KT12 34 F1
Woking GU22 70 C2
Sandycombe Rd
East Bedfont TW14 15 A7
Richmond TW9 7 A5
Sandycoombe Rd TW1 6 C1
Sanger Ave KT9 56 F6
Sanger Dr GU23 90 C4
Sangers Cty Jun Sch RH6 160 F3
Sangers Dr RH6 160 F3
Sangley Rd Catford SE6 24 C7
South Norwood SE25 42 E5
Santina Cl GU9 125 D8
Sanway Cl KT14 71 E5
Sanway Rd KT14 71 E5
Sappho Ct GU21 68 E3
Sapte Cl GU6 175 A3
Saracen Cl CR0 42 D3
Sarah House SW15 7 F3
Sarah Way GU14 85 B4
Sardeson House 13 SW27 22 B3
Sarel Way RH6 161 B5
Sargent Cl RH10 201 F2
Sarjant Path SW19 19 D6
Sark Cl Crawley RH11 201 A2
Heston TW5 5 A7
Sarsby Dr TW19 12 A6
Sarsen Ave TW3 5 A5
Sarsfeld Rd SW12, SW17 20 F7
Sarum RG12 26 F1
Sarum Cres RG40 25 D7
Sarum Gn KT13 53 E7
Satellite Bsns Village The RH10 181 E2
Satis Ct KT17 76 F8
Saturn Cl RH11 200 E4
Saturn Croft RG42 8 B2
Saunders Cl RH10 202 B7
Saunders Copse GU22 89 B5
Saunders House 11 SW2 22 A7
Saunders La GU22 89 B5
Saundersfield House SM7 78 B5
Saunton Ave UB3 3 F7
Saunton Gdns 1 GU14 85 A6
Savernake Way RG12 27 F4
Savernake Wlk RH10 201 F3
Savile Cl New Malden KT3 38 E4
Thames Ditton KT7 37 A1
Savile Gdns CR0 61 F8
Savill Gardens The TW20 10 E2
Savill Gdns SW20 39 A6
Saville Cres TW15 14 D2
Saville Gdns GU15 66 B5
Saville Rd TW1 16 F7
Saville Row BR2 44 F1
Savin Lodge SM2 59 C3
Savona Cl 12 SW19 19 D1
Savona Ct SW20 39 D8
Savoy Gr GU17 64 D3
Sawkins Cl SW19 19 E6
Sawtry Cl SM5 40 E2
Sawyer House 15 SE21 22 E4
Sawyer's Hill TW10 17 F8
Saxby Rd SW2 21 E8
Saxby's La RH7 164 D5
Saxley RH6 161 C4
Saxon Ave TW13 15 F6
Saxon Bsns Ctr SW19 40 C8
Saxon Cl KT6 37 D3
Saxon Cres RH12 217 B4
Saxon Croft GU9 125 C1
Saxon Cty Jun Sch TW17 34 A4
Saxon Dr RG42 27 F8
Saxon House Feltham TW13 15 F6
Reigate RH2 138 F6
Saxon Rd Ashford TW15 14 D2
Bromley BR1 24 F1
Crawley RH10 202 E5
Thornton Heath CR0, SE25 42 D4
Walton-on-T KT12 54 D7
Saxon Way
Harmondsworth UB7 2 C8
Reigate RH2 117 F2
Saxonbury Ave TW16 35 B7
Saxonbury Cl CR4 40 D6
Saxonbury Gdns KT6 37 C1
Saxonfield Cl SW2 21 F8
Saxons KT20 97 D6
Sayer Ct 4 GU21 68 E1
Sayer's Wlk TW10 17 F8
Sayers Cl Fetcham KT22 94 C4
Frimley GU16 85 E7
Sayers The 5 RH19 185 C1
Sayes Court Farm Dr KT15 52 B5
Sayes Court Jun Sch KT15 52 B5
Sayes Ct KT15 52 C5
Scaitcliffe Sch TW20 11 A5
Scallows Cl RH10 202 A7
Scallows Rd RH10 202 A7
Scampton Rd TW6 2 F1
Scania Wlk RG42 8 B2
Scarborough Cl
Belmont SM2 77 F8
Biggin Hill TN16 83 C1
Scarborough Rd TW6 3 C1
Scarbrook Rd CR0, CR9 61 C7
Scarlet Oaks GU15 65 E3
Scarlet Rd SE6 24 E5
Scarlett Cl GU21 68 F1
Scarlett's Rd GU11 105 A3
Scarlette Manor Wlk 10 SE24 22 A8
Scarth Rd SW13 7 F4
Scawen Cl SM5 60 A6
Schaffer Ho RH10 202 C4
Schiller International Univ BR4 63 D6
Scholars Ct RH10 204 A8
Scholars Rd SW12 21 C7
Scholars Wlk GU2 130 B8
School Cl Bisley GU24 68 A4
Guildford GU1 109 D3
Horsham RH12 218 A6
School Cotts GU22 89 C5
School Hill
Crowthorne RG45 45 D4
Merstham RH1 119 C7
Sandhurst GU47 45 A1
Seale GU10 127 B4
Warnham RH12 216 F8
Wrecclesham GU10 145 F6
School House La TW11 17 C1
School Houses GU8 172 E4
School La Addlestone KT15 52 A6
Ashurst Wood RH19 206 E6
Bagshot GU19 47 E2
Chiddingfold GU8 191 C4
Crondall GU10 124 D8
East Clandon GU4 111 E4
Egham TW20 12 A3
Farnham GU10 146 D6
Fetcham KT22 94 D5
School La *continued*
Forest Row RH18 206 F2
Lower Halliford TW17 34 B2
Mickleham RH5 115 C8
Ockham GU23 92 B5
Pirbright GU24 87 E5
Puttenham GU3 128 C4
Shackleford GU8 149 E6
Surbiton KT6 38 A1
Teddington KT1 37 C8
Walton on t H KT20 97 A2
West Horsley KT24 112 B6
Westcott RH4 135 D6
Windlesham GU20 48 D4
School Pas 3 KT1 37 F7
School Rd Ascot SL5 29 D4
Ashford TW15 14 B2
Binstead GU10 145 E3
East Molesey KT8 36 D5
Grayshott GU26 188 B4
Hampton TW12 16 C2
Harmondsworth UB7 2 D8
Hascombe GU8 172 E4
Hounslow TW3 5 C4
Linchmere GU27 207 F5
Teddington KT1 37 C8
Windlesham GU20 48 B5
Wokingham RG40 25 D6
School Road Ave TW12 16 C2
School Wlk TW16 35 A6
Schroder Ct TW20 11 B3
Scillonian Rd GU2 130 B7
Scilly Isles KT10 55 E8
Scizdons Climb GU7 150 F4
Scoles Cres SW2 22 A7
Scoresdale SE19 42 E8
Scory Cl RH11 201 A3
Scotia Rd SW2 22 A8
Scotland Bridge Rd KT15 71 A8
Scotland Cl GU12 106 A5
Scotland Farm Rd GU12 106 A5
Scotland Hill
Sandhurst GU47 45 A1
Sandhurst GU47 64 A8
Scotland La GU27 208 C5
Scotlands Cl GU27 208 B5
Scotlands Dr GU27 208 C5
Scots Cl TW19 13 D7
Scotsdale Cl SM2 58 E3
Scotshall La CR6 82 C4
Scott Cl Guildford GU2 109 A3
Thornton Heath SW16 41 F8
West Ewell KT19 57 C5
Scott Farm Cl KT7 37 B1
Scott Gdns TW5 4 D7
Scott House TW10 17 C6
Scott Rd RH10 201 F3
Scott Terr RG12 27 E8
Scott Trimmer Way TW3 4 E5
Scott's Ave Ashford TW16 14 E1
Beckenham BR2 44 D7
Scott's Ct GU14 85 B7
Scott's Grove Cl GU24 68 D6
Scott's Grove Rd GU24 68 C6
Scott's Hill RH1, RH6 162 D5
Scott's La BR2, BR3 44 D7
Scott's Way TW16 14 E1
Scott-Broadwood CE Inf Sch The Capel RH5 178 D6
Ockley RH5 177 D4
Scotts Dr TW12 16 B1
Scotts Farm Rd KT19 57 C4
Scrooby St 3 SE6 24 B8
Scrutton Cl SW12 21 D8
Scylla Cres TW6&TW14 14 B8
Scylla Pl GU21 89 A8
Scylla Rd TW14, TW6 3 B1
Seabrook Dr BR4 63 E8
Seaford Rd Crawley RH11 201 A2
Stanwell TW19, TW6 2 D2
Wokingham RG40 25 D6
Seaforth Ave KT3 39 B5
Seaforth Gdns KT19 57 F5
Seaforth Lodge SW13 7 F5
Sealand Rd TW6 3 A1
Seale La GU10, GU3 126 E4
Seale Rd Elstead GU8 148 B7
The Sands GU8 148 B7
Seaman's Gn RH5 178 D8
Searchwood Rd CR6 81 B1
Searle Ct CR4 40 E8
Searle Hill RH2 139 A7
Searle Rd GU9 146 C8
Searle's View RH12 217 E5
Seath House 4 SE26 23 B3
Seaton Cl Putney SW15 19 B8
Twickenham TW2 5 D1
Seaton Dr TW15 13 E6
Seaton Rd Camberley GU15 65 B5
Mitcham CR4 40 E7
Twickenham TW2 5 C1
Sebastopol Rd 2 GU11 105 B2
Second Ave Mortlake SW14 7 E4
Walton-on-T KT12 35 B3
Woodham KT15 52 B2
Second Cl KT8 36 C5
Second Cross Rd TW2 16 E6
Seddon Ct RH11 201 B1
Seddon Rd SM4 40 D4
Sedgefield Cl RH10 202 E7
Sedgehill Rd SE6 24 B3
Sedgehill Sch SE6 24 B3
Sedgemoor GU14 85 B7
Sedgeway SE6 24 F7
Sedgewick Cl RH10 202 C6
Sedgewick House SW19 19 D6
Sedgewood Cl BR2 44 F2
Sedley Ct SE26 23 B6
Seebys Oak GU47 64 E6
Seeley Dr SE21 22 E4
Seely Rd SW17 21 A2
Seething Wells Halls Of Residence KT6 37 C3
Seething Wells La KT6 37 C3
Sefton Cl GU24 67 F6
Sefton Ct TW5 5 B6
Sefton Ho 16 GU11 105 A2
Sefton Lodge 2 TW1 6 C1
Sefton Rd Croydon CR0 43 A1
Epsom KT19 57 D1
Segal Cl SE23 23 E8
Segrave Cl KT13 53 A3
Segsbury Gr RG12 27 F5
Sekhon Terr TW13 16 A5
Selborne Ave GU11 126 C6
Selborne Cl GU17 64 C6
Selborne Gdns GU9 146 A7
Selborne Rd
Kingston u T KT3 38 E7
South Croydon CR0 61 F7
Selbourne Ave KT15 52 B2
Selbourne Cl
Crawley RH10 182 D2
Woodham KT15 52 B1
Selbourne Rd GU1 110 A4
Selbourne Sq RH9 121 C5
Selby Cl KT9 56 E3
Selby Ct TW2 16 D6
Selby Gn SM5 40 E2
Selby Rd Ashford TW15 14 C2
Carshalton SM5 40 E2
Penge SE20 43 A7
Selby Wlk 1 GU21 69 B1
Selbys RH7 164 E5
Selcroft Rd CR8 80 B7
Selham Cl RH11 201 A7
Selhurst Cl Putney SW19 19 D7
Woking GU21 69 F4
Selhurst New Ct SE25 42 E3
Selhurst New Rd SE25 42 E3
Selhurst Park SE25 42 E5
Selhurst Pl CR0, SE25 42 E3
Selhurst Rd
South Norwood CR0, SE25 42 E4
Thornton Heath CR0, SE25 42 E4
Selhurst Sta SE25 42 E4
Selkirk Rd Twickenham TW2 16 C7
Upper Tooting SW17 20 E4
Sellar's Hill GU7 150 D7
Sellincourt Inf Sch SW17 20 E2
Sellincourt Jun Sch SW17 20 E2
Sellincourt Rd SW17 20 E2
Sellindge Cl BR3 23 F1
Selsdon Ave CR2 61 D4
Selsdon Cl KT6 37 E4
Selsdon Cres CR2 62 C1
Selsdon High Sch CR2 62 D3
Selsdon Park Golf Course CR2 81 B7
Selsdon Park Rd
New Addington CR0, CR2 62 E2
Selsdon CR0, CR2 62 E2
South Croydon CR0, CR2 62 E2
Selsdon Prim Sch CR2 62 C2
Selsdon Rd Croydon CR2 61 D4
West Norwood SE27 22 B4
Woodham KT15 71 A8
Selsdon Road Ind Est CR2 61 D4
Selsey Ct 3 RH11 201 B2
Selsey Rd RH11 201 A2
Selsfield Rd
Turners Hill RH10, RH19 204 A2
West Hoathly RH19 204 B1
Seltops Cl GU6 174 F2
Selwood Cl TW19 2 C1
Selwood Gdns TW19 2 C1
Selwood Rd Cheam SM3 39 F1
Chessington KT9 56 D6
Croydon CR0 43 B1
Old Woking GU22 90 B7
Selworthy Rd SE23, SE6 23 F5
Selwyn Ave TW9 6 F4
Selwyn Cl Crawley RH10 182 C1
Hounslow TW4 4 E3
Selwyn Ct 7 TW10 6 F2
Selwyn Rd KT3 38 D4
Semaphore Rd GU1 130 E7
Semley Rd SW16 41 E7
Semper Cl GU21 68 E2
Send Barns La Send GU23 90 E2
Send Marsh GU23 90 E2
Send C of E Fst Sch GU23 90 E3
Send Cl GU23 90 C4
Send Hill GU23 90 C3
Send Marsh Rd Send GU23 90 E4
Send Marsh GU23 90 E4
Send Rd GU23 90 C4
Seneca Rd CR7 42 C5
Senga Rd CR4 41 A1
Senhouse Rd SM3 58 D7
Sequoia Pk RH11 201 D4
Serpentine Gn RH1 119 D6
Serrin Way RH12 217 E5
Service Rd Crawley, North Terminal RH6 181 F8
Crawley, South Terminal RH6 182 B7
Servite House
Beckenham BR3 43 F8
Dorking RH4 136 A5
Knaphill GU21 68 D2
Servius Ct 2 TW8 6 D7
Setley Way RG12 27 F6
Seven Acres SM5 59 E8
Seven Arches App KT13 53 A3
Seven Hills Cl KT12, KT13 53 E2

Seven Hills Rd KT12, KT13 .53 E3
Seven Hills Rd (South)
KT11 ....72 E6
Sevenoaks Cl SM2 ....59 B1
Severn Cl GU47 ....64 C8
Severn Cres SL3 ....1 B8
Severn Dr
Hinchley Wood KT10 ....56 A8
Walton-on-T KT12 ....54 D8
Severn Rd Crawley RH10 ..202 C5
Farnborough GU14 ....84 E6
Seward Rd BR3 ....43 D7
Sewell Ave RG41 ....25 A8
Sewer's Farm Rd RH5 ...155 F6
Sewill Cl RH6 ....180 F7
Seychelle Ct BR3 ....24 B1
Seymour Ave
Caterham CR3 ....100 C4
Ewell KT17 ....58 B2
West Barnes SM4 ....39 D2
Seymour Cl KT8 ....36 C4
Seymour Dr GU15 ....66 B7
Seymour Gdns
Feltham TW13 ....15 C4
Kingston u T KT5 ....37 F4
Twickenham TW1 ....17 B8
Seymour Mews KT17 .....58 A1
Seymour Pl Croydon SE25 ..43 B5
Woking GU23 ....89 B7
Seymour Rd Carshalton CR4 41 A2
Crawley RH11 ....201 B2
East Molesey KT8 ....36 C4
Godalming GU7 ....150 B3
Hampton TW12 ....16 C3
Headley Down GU35 ......187 C4
Teddington KT1 ....37 D8
Wallington SM5 ....60 A5
Wandsworth SW18 ....19 F8
Wimbledon SW19 ....19 D5
Seymour Terr SE20 ....43 B8
Seymour Villas SE20 ......43 A8
Seymour Way TW16 ......14 E1
Shabden Cotts CR5 ....98 F6
Shabden Park CR5 ....98 E5
Shabden Park Hospl CR5 .98 E5
Shackleford Rd
Old Woking GU22 ....90 A7
Shackleford GU8 ....149 E6
Shacklegate La TW11 .....16 E4
Shackleton Cl SE23 ....23 B6
Shackleton Ct
2 Dulwich SE21 ....22 D6
6 Stanwell TW19 ....2 E1
Shackleton Rd RH10 .....201 F3
Shackstead La GU7 .....150 D3
Shackster La GU7 ....150 C3
Shadbolt Cl KT4 ....57 F8
Shady Nook GU9 ....125 B6
Shadyhanger GU7 ....150 E6
Shaef Way TW11 ....17 A1
Shaftesbury Ave TW14 .....4 A1
Shaftesbury Cl RG12 ......27 D4
Shaftesbury Cres TW18 ...13 D1
Shaftesbury Ct
Farnborough GU14 ....105 C8
Wokingham RG40 ....25 D7
Shaftesbury House SE25 ..43 A3
Shaftesbury Mount GU17 .64 D3
Shaftesbury Rd
Beckenham BR3 ....43 F7
Bisley GU24 ....67 F3
Carshalton SM5 ....40 E2
Crawley RH10 ....202 D4
Richmond TW9 ....6 E4
Woking GU22 ....70 B2
Shaftesbury Way TW2 ....16 D5
Shafteswood Ct SW17 .....20 F5
Shagbrook RH2 ....117 C2
Shakespeare Ave TW14 ....4 A1
Shakespeare Gdns GU14 ..84 D5
Shakespeare Rd KT15 ....52 D6
Shakespeare Way
Feltham TW13 ....15 C4
Winkfield RG42 ....27 E8
Shalbourne Rise GU15 ....65 D5
Shalden House SW15 ....7 F1
Shalden Rd GU12 ....126 D8
Shaldon Dr SM4 ....39 E4
Shaldon Way KT12 ....54 C7
Shale Gn RH1 ....119 D6
Shalesbrook La RH18 ....206 F1
Shalford Cty Inf Sch GU4 130 E3
Shalford La GU4 ....130 E4
Shalford Mill GU4 ....130 E4
Shalford Rd GU1, GU4 ...130 D5
Shalford Sta GU4 ....130 E3
Shalston Villas KT5, KT6 ...37 F3
Shalstone Rd SW14, TW9 ...7 B4
Shambles The GU1 ....130 D7
Shamrock Cl Fetcham KT22 94 D6
Frimley GU16 ....85 D8
Shamrock House SE26 ....23 A4
Shamrock Rd CR0 ....41 F3
Shandys Cl RH12 ....217 A1
Shanklin Ct GU12 ....105 C1
Shannon Commercial Ctr
KT3 ....39 A5
Shannon Corner KT3 ......39 A5
Shannon Ct CR0 ....42 C1
Shannon Way BR3 ....24 B2
Shap Cres SM5 ....40 F1
Sharon Cl Crawley RH10 ..202 A4
Epsom KT19 ....76 C6
Great Bookham KT23 ....94 A3
Long Ditton KT6 ....37 C1
Sharonelle Ct RG40 ....25 B6
Sharpthorne Cl RH11 ....200 F6
Shaw Cl Ewell KT17 ....76 F8
Shaw Cl *continued*
Ottershaw KT16 ....51 C4
Sanderstead CR2 ....80 F7
Shaw Cres CR2 ....80 F7
Shaw Ct CR3 ....100 D6
Shaw Dr KT12 ....35 C2
Shaw Path BR1 ....24 F5
Shaw Pk RG45 ....45 B3
Shaw Rd Catford BR1 ......24 F5
Tatsfield TN16 ....103 C7
Shaw Way SM6 ....60 E3
Shawfield Cty Fst Sch
GU12 ....106 A3
Shawfield La GU12 ....105 F2
Shawfield Rd GU12 ....106 A3
Shawford Ct 9 SW15 ......19 A8
Shawford Rd KT19 ....57 D4
Shawley Cres KT18 ....77 D1
Shawley Cty Prim Sch
KT18 ....77 C1
Shawley Way KT18 ....77 C1
Shaws Rd RH10 ....201 F7
Shaxton Cres CR0 ....63 C2
Shearing Dr SM4 ....40 C2
Shears Ct TW16 ....14 E1
Shearwater Ct 6 RH11 ..200 D5
Shearwater Rd SM1 ....58 F5
Sheath La KT22 ....74 C6
Sheen Common Dr
SW14, TW10 ....7 A2
Sheen Court Rd TW10 ......7 A3
Sheen Gate Gdns SW14 ....7 C3
Sheen La SW14 ....7 C3
Sheen Mount Jun Mix &
Inf Sch SW14 ....7 B2
Sheen Pk TW10, TW9 ....6 E3
Sheen Rd TW10, TW9 ....6 F3
Sheen Way SM6 ....60 F5
Sheen Wood SW14 ....7 C2
Sheendale Rd TW9 ....6 F3
Sheenewood SE26 ....23 B4
Sheep Leas KT24 ....112 E2
Sheep Walk Mews SW19 ..19 E2
Sheep Wlk
Langley Vale KT18 ....96 D6
Reigate RH2 ....117 E4
Sheepbarn La CR6 ....82 F7
Sheepcote Cl TW5 ....4 A7
Sheepfold Rd GU2 ....108 F4
Sheephatch La GU10 .....147 C6
Sheephouse GU9 ....146 C8
Sheephouse Gn RH5 ....134 F3
Sheephouse La RH5 .....135 A2
Sheephouse Way KT3 .....38 E2
Sheeplands Ave GU1 ....110 C3
Sheeps Ditch Cl TW18 ....13 A1
Sheepwalk Littleton TW17 ..34 A3
Shepperton TW17 ....33 F3
Sheepwalk La GU5 ....113 A1
Sheerwater Ave KT15 .....70 F7
Sheerwater Bsns Ctr
GU21 ....70 C4
Sheerwater Cotts KT14 ...70 F6
Sheerwater Rd KT14, KT15 .70 F6
Sheet Street Rd
Old Windsor SL4 ....10 A7
Windsor SL4 ....10 A7
Sheet's Heath La GU24 ....88 A7
Sheffield Cl Crawley RH10 202 B4
Farnborough GU14 ....84 F4
Sheffield Rd TW14, TW6 ....3 C2
Sheffield Way TW14, TW6 ...3 D2
Shefford Cres RG40 ....25 D8
Shelburne House 9 SW16 21 C3
Sheldon Cl Crawley RH10 .202 D5
Penge SE20 ....43 B8
Reigate RH2 ....139 B8
Sheldon Ct 3 GU1 ....130 F8
Sheldon House TW11 .....17 A2
Sheldon St CR0, CR9 ......61 C7
Sheldrick Cl CR4 ....40 D7
Shelford 9 KT1 ....38 A7
Shelford Rise SE19 ....22 F1
Shelley Ave RG12 ....27 E7
Shelley Cl Coulsdon CR5 ....79 F2
Crawley RH10 ....202 C8
Shelley Cres TW5 ....4 D6
Shelley Ct Camberley GU15 .65 C5
9 Kingston u T KT2 ....17 D4
West Barnes KT3 ....39 A4
Shelley Dr RH12 ....216 C3
Shelley Rd
East Grinstead RH19 ....185 D1
Horsham RH12 ....217 B3
Shelley Way SW17 ....20 D2
Shellwood Dr RH5 ....136 C3
Shellwood Rd RH2, RH3 ..137 D1
Shelly Cl SM7 ....77 E4
Shelly Cty Prim Sch
RH12 ....216 E3
Shellys Ct RH13 ....218 A3
Shelson Ave TW13 ....14 F4
Shelton Ave CR6 ....81 C2
Shelton Cl Guildford GU2 .109 A6
Warlingham CR6 ....81 C2
Shelton Rd SW19 ....40 A8
Shelvers Gn KT20 ....97 C6
Shelvers Hill KT20 ....97 B6
Shelvers Spur KT20 ....97 C6
Shelvers Way KT20 ....97 D6
Shene Sec Sch SW14 ....7 E3
Shenley Rd TW5 ....4 E6
Shenstone House SW16 ..21 C3
Shenstone Pk SL5 ....29 E5
Shepherd Cl RH10 ....201 E3
Shepherd's Hill
Guildford GU2 ....109 A3
Haslemere GU27 ....208 C6
Shepherd's Hill *continued*
Merstham RH1 ....99 C1
Shepherd's Hill Bglws
GU27 ....208 C6
Shepherd's La GU2 ....108 F4
Shepherd's Way GU4 ....130 E4
Shepherds Chase GU19 ...47 E2
Shepherds Cl TW17 ....34 B3
Shepherds Hill RG12 ......27 C8
Shepherds La GU20 ....49 A6
Shepherds Way
Horsham RH12 ....218 A5
South Croydon CR2 ....62 D3
Tilford GU10 ....147 D4
Shepherds' Wlk
KT18, KT21 ....96 B7
Shepherds Wlk GU14 ......84 E7
Shepherdsgrove La RH19 186 F5
Shepley Cl SM5 ....60 A7
Shepley Ct SW16 ....21 C4
Shepley Dr SL5 ....30 D3
Shepley End SL5 ....30 D4
Sheppard Cl KT6 ....37 E5
Sheppard House 8 SW2 ..22 A7
Shepperton Bsns Park
TW17 ....34 C4
Shepperton Court Dr
TW17 ....34 B4
Shepperton Ct TW17 ......34 B3
Shepperton Rd
TW17, TW18 ....33 D5
Shepperton Sta TW17 .....34 C4
Shepperton Studios TW17 33 F6
Sheppey Cl RH11 ....201 C3
Sheraton Cl GU17 ....64 E4
Sheraton Dr KT19 ....76 C6
Sheraton The 22 KT6 ......37 E4
Sheraton Wlk 13 RH11 ...201 B1
Sherborne Cl
Burgh Heath KT18 ....77 C2
Poyle SL3 ....1 E6
Sherborne Cres SM5 ......40 E2
Sherborne Ct
Guildford GU2 ....130 C7
Penge SE20 ....43 C7
Sherborne Rd Cheam SM3 .40 A1
Chessington KT9 ....56 E5
East Bedfont TW14 ....14 D7
Farnborough GU14 ....85 D1
Sherbourne GU5 ....132 D5
Sherbourne Ct 2 TW12 ...36 A8
Sherbourne Dr SL5 ....30 D4
Sherbourne Gdns TW17 ...34 E2
Shere Ave KT17, SM2 ......58 C1
Shere CE Inf Sch GU5 ....133 A4
Shere Cl Chessington KT9 ..56 D5
Dorking RH5 ....136 C3
Shere Ct GU5 ....133 B2
Shere La GU5 ....133 A4
Shere Rd Albury GU4, GU5 .132 C6
Ewhurst GU6 ....175 D7
Shere GU5 ....133 B5
West Clandon GU4, KT24 ..111 B1
West Horsley KT24 ....112 C4
Sherfield Gdns SW15 ....7 F1
Sheridan Cl
Aldershot GU11 ....126 A8
East Grinstead RH19 ......185 C1
Sheridan Ct TW4 ....4 E2
Sheridan Dr RH2 ....118 B3
Sheridan Pl Hampton TW12 .36 C8
Mortlake SW13 ....7 F4
Sheridan Rd Frimley GU16 .85 D8
Merton SW19 ....39 F8
Richmond TW10 ....17 C5
Sheridan Way BR3 ....43 F8
Sheridans Rd KT23 ....94 C1
Sheringdale Prim Sch
SW18 ....19 F7
Sheringham Ave TW2 .....16 A7
Sheringham Rd SE20 ......43 C6
Sherland Rd TW1 ....16 F7
Shermanbury Ct RH12 ...217 D4
Sherringham Ave TW13 ...15 A5
Sherrydon GU6 ....174 F4
Sherwin Cres GU14 ....85 C7
Sherwood KT6 ....56 D8
Sherwood Ave SW16 ......41 D8
Sherwood Cl
Bracknell RG12 ....28 A7
Fetcham KT22 ....94 C4
Sherwood Cres RH2 ......139 B5
Sherwood Ct BR4 ....44 B1
Sherwood Park Rd
Mitcham CR4 ....41 D5
Sutton SM1 ....59 A5
Sherwood Park Sch SM6 .60 D7
Sherwood Prim Sch CR4 ..41 C5
Sherwood Rd Coulsdon CR5 79 C3
Croydon CR0, CR9 ....43 B1
Hampton TW12 ....16 C3
Knaphill GU21 ....68 E2
Merton SW19 ....19 F1
Sherwood Way BR4 ....63 C8
Sherwood Wlk RH10 .....201 F3
Shetland Cl Crawley RH10 .202 E7
Guildford GU4 ....110 B6
Shewens Rd KT13 ....53 D6
Shey Copse GU22 ....70 C2
Shield Dr TW8 ....6 A8
Shield Rd TW15 ....14 D4
Shifford Path SE23 ....23 D5
Shilburn Way GU21 ....69 A1
Shildon Cl GU15 ....66 D3
Shillinglee Park Golf
Course GU8 ....210 D6
Shillinglee Rd RH14 .....211 B4
Shimmings The GU1 .....110 A2
Shinners Cl SE25 ....43 A4
Shinwell Wlk 8 RH11 ....201 B1
Ship Alley GU14 ....85 C6
Ship Field Cl TN16 ....103 C6
Ship Hill TN16 ....103 D6
Ship La Farnborough GU14 ..85 C6
Mortlake SW14 ....7 C5
Ship St RH19 ....205 E8
Ship Yd KT13 ....53 B7
Shipka Rd SW12 ....21 B7
Shiplake Ct SW17 ....20 D4
Shiplake House RG12 .....27 F5
Shipley Bridge La RH10 .183 A3
Shipley Ct SE20 ....43 A7
Shipley Rd RH11 ....201 A6
Shipleybridge La
RH10, RH6 ....182 F4
Shipman Par SE23 ....23 E6
Shipman Rd SE23 ....23 D6
Shirburn Cl SE23 ....23 C8
Shire Cl GU19 ....47 E2
Shire Ct Aldershot GU11 ..104 E2
Ewell KT17 ....57 F3
Shire Horse Way TW7 ......5 F4
Shire Par RH10 ....202 D7
Shire Pl RH10 ....202 D7
Shires Cl KT21 ....95 D8
Shires House KT14 ....71 E6
Shires The TW10 ....17 E4
Shirley Ave Belmont SM2 ..58 F1
Carshalton SM1 ....59 E6
Coulsdon CR5, CR8 ....100 B8
Croydon CR0, CR9 ....43 C1
Redhill RH1 ....139 F4
Shirley Church Rd
Addington CR0 ....62 E7
Croydon CR0 ....62 E7
Shirley Cl Crawley RH11 ..200 E2
Isleworth TW3 ....5 C2
Shirley Cres BR3 ....43 E5
Shirley Ct Guildford GU1 ..130 D8
Thornton Heath SW16 ......41 F6
Shirley Dr TW3 ....5 C2
Shirley High Sch CR0 ......62 D7
Shirley Hills Rd CR0 ......62 D5
Shirley Hts SM6 ....60 C2
Shirley Hyrst KT13 ....53 D4
Shirley Lodge SE26 ....23 E4
Shirley Oaks Hospl CR0 ...43 C2
Shirley Oaks Rd CR0, CR9 .62 D8
Shirley Park Golf Course
CR0 ....62 C7
Shirley Park Rd CR0 ......43 C1
Shirley Pl GU21 ....68 C2
Shirley Rd
Croydon CR0, CR9 ....43 B1
Wallington SM6 ....60 C2
Shirley Way CR0 ....62 F7
Shoe La GU11 ....105 A6
Sholto Rd TW6 ....3 A2
Shop Cl TW10 ....17 D5
Shophouse La GU5 ......153 E7
Shord Hill CR8 ....80 D3
Shore Cl Feltham TW14 ....15 A8
Hampton TW12 ....15 E3
Shore Gr TW13 ....16 A6
Shore's Rd GU21 ....69 F5
Shoreham Cl CR0 ....43 C3
Shoreham Rd RH10 ......202 C3
Shoreham Rd (E) TW6 .....2 E2
Shoreham Rd (W) TW6 .....2 E2
Shorndean St SE6 ....24 C7
Short Cl RH11 ....201 D8
Short Dale Rd GU11 .....126 C6
Short Gallop RH10 ....202 D7
Short La Limpsfield RH8 ...123 B3
Stanwell TW15, TW19 ....13 F7
Short Rd Chiswick W4 ....7 E8
Stanwell TW19 ....2 E1
Short St GU11 ....105 A2
Short Way TW2 ....16 C8
Shortacres RH1 ....119 F2
Shortcroft Rd KT17 ....57 F3
Shortfield Rd GU10 ......146 C1
Shortheath Crest GU9 ...145 F6
Shortheath Rd
Farnham GU9, GU10 ......146 A7
Wrecclesham GU9, GU10 ..146 A7
Shortlands UB3 ....3 D8
Shortlands Gdns BR1, BR2 .44 E7
Shortlands Gr BR2 ....44 D6
Shortlands Rd
Beckenham BR2, BR3 ....44 E6
Kingston u T KT2 ....17 F1
Shortlands Sta BR2 ....44 E7
Shorts Rd SM5 ....59 E5
Shortsfield Cl RH12 ......217 C5
Shortwood Ave TW18 .....13 B5
Shortwood Cty Inf Sch
TW18 ....13 B5
Shotfield SM6 ....60 B4
Shott Cl SM1 ....59 C5
Shottermill RH12 ....218 A7
Shottermill Cty Fst Sch
GU27 ....207 F7
Shottermill Cty Jun Sch
GU27 ....207 F7
Shottermill Rd GU27 .....207 E5
Shottfield Ave SW14 ....7 E3
Shovelstrode La RH19 ...206 D8
Shrewsbury Ave SW14 .....7 D3
Shrewsbury Cl KT6 ....56 E8
Shrewsbury House Sch
KT6 ....56 D8
Shrewsbury Rd
Beckenham BR3 ....43 E6
Carshalton SM5 ....40 E2
Harlington TW14, TW6 ....3 D1
Shrewsbury Rd *continued*
Redhill RH1 ....118 E1
Shrewsbury Wlk 7 TW7 ....6 A4
Shrewton Rd SW17 ....20 F1
Shrivenham Cl 3 GU47 ...64 D8
Shroffold Rd BR1 ....24 E4
Shropshire Cl CR4 ....41 E5
Shrubbery Rd SW16 ....21 E4
Shrubbery The
Farnborough GU14 ....84 D3
2 Surbiton KT6 ....37 E1
Shrubbs Hill GU24 ....49 C2
Shrubbs Hill La SL5 ....30 C3
Shrubbs La GU10 ....145 F4
Shrubland Ct SM7 ....77 F3
Shrubland Gr KT4 ....58 C7
Shrubland Rd SM7 ....78 A3
Shrublands Ave CR0 ....63 A6
Shrublands Cl SE26 ....23 C5
Shrublands Dr GU18 ......67 B8
Shute End RG40, 41 ....25 B6
Sibthorp Rd CR4 ....40 F7
Sibton Rd SM5 ....40 E2
Sickle Mill GU27 ....207 F6
Sickle Rd GU27 ....208 A5
Sidbury Cl SL5 ....30 A4
Siddeley Dr TW4 ....4 E5
Siddons Rd
Croydon CR0, CR9 ....61 B7
Forest Hill SE23 ....23 E6
Sidings The
Aldershot GU11 ....105 C3
Rudgwick RH12 ....214 D7
Staines TW18 ....13 B4
Sidlaws Rd GU14 ....84 D6
Sidmouth Ave TW7 ....5 E5
Sidney Gdns TW8 ....6 D8
Sidney Rd Croydon SE25 ...43 A4
Penge BR3 ....43 E7
Staines TW18 ....13 A4
Twickenham TW1 ....6 B1
Walton-on-T KT12 ....35 B1
Signal Ct RH7 ....164 E5
Sigrist Sq 4 KT2 ....37 E8
Silbury Ave CR4 ....40 E8
Silbury House 9 SE26 ....23 A5
Silchester Ct CR7 ....42 A5
Silchester Dr RH11 ......201 B4
Silkham Rd RH8 ....122 E8
Silkin Wlk 8 RH11 ....201 B1
Silkmore La
West Horsley KT24 ....92 A2
West Horsley KT24 ....112 B7
Silo Cl GU7 ....150 F8
Silo Dr GU7 ....150 F8
Silo Rd GU7 ....150 F8
Silver Birch Cl KT15 ......70 E7
Silver Birches Way GU8 .148 E3
Silver Blades Ice Rink
SW16 ....21 D3
Silver Cl KT20 ....97 E3
Silver Dr GU16 ....66 C3
Silver Hill GU47 ....64 E8
Silver Jubilee Way TW4 .....4 B5
Silver La Purley CR8 ....79 E7
West Wickham BR4 ....63 D8
Silver Tree Cl KT12 ....54 A6
Silverdale SE23, SE26 ......23 C4
Silverdale Ave
Oxshott KT22 ....74 C5
Walton-on-T KT12, KT13 ....53 F7
Silverdale Cl
Brockham RH3 ....137 B5
Cheam SM1 ....58 F6
Silverdale Dr TW16 ....35 B7
Silverglade KT9 ....75 C7
Silverhall St TW7 ....6 A4
Silverlea Gdns RH6 ......161 C2
Silverleigh Rd CR7 ....42 A4
Silvermere Ct CR3 ....100 F3
Silvermere Rd 1 SE6 ......24 B8
Silversmiths Way GU21 ...69 C1
Silverstone Cl RH1 ......118 F3
Silverton Lodge SE19 .....22 E1
Silverwood Cl
Beckenham BR3 ....24 A1
New Addington CR0 ....63 A2
Silverwood Dr GU15 ......66 A7
Silwood RG12 ....26 E1
Silwood Cl SL5 ....29 D7
Silwood Park (Imperial
Coll) SL5 ....29 F6
Silwood Rd Ascot SL5 ......29 F5
Sunningdale SL5 ....29 F5
Sim's Cotts KT10 ....55 F4
Simkins Cl RG42 ....8 B2
Simmil Rd KT10 ....55 E5
Simmonds Cl RG42 ....26 E8
Simmonds Cotts GU7 ....150 B4
Simmondstone La
GU10 ....167 D2
Simmons Cl KT9 ....56 C4
Simmons Pl TW18 ....12 E3
Simms Cl SM5 ....59 E8
Simon Lodge 31 SW19 ....19 D7
Simone Dr CR8 ....80 C3
Simons Cl KT16 ....51 C4
Simons Wlk TW20 ....11 C1
Simplemarsh Ct KT15 .....52 B6
Simplemarsh Rd KT15 ....52 B6
Simpson Rd
Richmond TW10 ....17 C4
Twickenham TW4 ....4 F1
Simpson Way KT6 ....37 C3
Sinclair Cl RH10 ....202 C4

Sinclair Ct
22 Beckenham BR3 ... 24 A1
2 Croydon CR0 ... 61 F8
Sinclair Dr SM2 ... 59 B2
Sinclair House SW12 ... 21 D7
Sincots Rd RH1 ... 118 F1
Sine Cl GU14 ... 85 B8
Singlegate Prim Sch
SW19 ... 20 D1
Singleton Cl
Mitcham SW17, SW19 ... 20 F1
Thornton Heath CR0 ... 42 C2
Singleton Rd RH12 ... 216 D3
Sinhurst Rd GU15 ... 65 B4
Sion Ct TW1 ... 17 B7
Sion Rd TW1 ... 17 B7
Sipson Cl UB7 ... 3 A8
Sipson La UB7 ... 3 B8
Sipson Rd Harlington UB7 ... 3 A7
Harmondsworth UB7 ... 3 A7
Sipson Way UB7 ... 3 A7
Sir Cyril Black Way 2
SW19 ... 20 A1
Sir William Perkin's Ind
Sch for Girls KT16 ... 32 F1
Sirdar Rd CR4 ... 21 A2
Sirl Cotts SL5 ... 29 C5
Siskin Cl RH12 ... 217 E5
Sissinghurst Cl RH10 ... 202 D7
Sissinghurst Rd CR0 ... 43 A2
Sistova Rd SW12 ... 21 B7
Siward Rd SW17 ... 20 C5
Six Cross-Roads GU21 ... 70 A5
Sixth Cross Rd TW2 ... 16 C5
Skeena Hill SW18, SW19 ... 19 E8
Skelbrook St SW18 ... 20 C6
Skelmersdale Wlk RH11 ... 200 E2
Skerne Rd KT2 ... 37 D8
Skid Hill La Biggin Hill CR6 ... 82 F5
Fickleshole CR6 ... 82 F5
Skiff La RH14 ... 213 A1
Skiffington Cl SW2 ... 22 A7
Skimmington Cotts RH2 ... 138 D8
Skimpedhill La RG12 ... 27 B7
Skinners La Ashstead KT21 ... 75 D1
Chiddingfold GU8 ... 191 D5
Heston TW5 ... 5 B6
Skipton Way RH6 ... 161 B5
Sky Bsns Pk TW20 ... 32 C7
Skyes Dr TW18 ... 13 B3
Skylark View RH12 ... 217 D7
Skyport Dr UB7 ... 2 D7
Skyway 14 Trad Est SL3 ... 1 F4
Slade Ct KT16 ... 51 D4
Slade House TW4 ... 4 F1
Slade Rd Ottershaw KT16 ... 51 D4
Pirbright GU24 ... 87 D7
Slaidburn Gn RG12 ... 27 E2
Slattery Rd TW13 ... 15 C7
Slaugham Ct RH11 ... 200 F3
Sledmere Ct TW14 ... 14 E7
Sleets Rd RH12 ... 216 E3
Slim Cl GU11 ... 105 E7
Slim Rd GU15 ... 65 C7
Slines New Rd CR3, CR6 ... 101 E7
Slines Oak Rd CR3, CR6 ... 102 B6
Slinfold CE Sch RH12 ... 215 D4
Slinfold Park (Golf &
Country Park) RH12 ... 215 A2
Slinfold Wlk RH11 ... 201 A6
Slip Of Wood GU6 ... 174 F4
Slipshatch Rd RH2 ... 138 E5
Slipshoe St RH2 ... 118 A1
Sloane Hospl BR3 ... 44 D8
Sloane Wlk CR0 ... 43 F3
Slocock Hill GU21 ... 69 C2
Slough La Buckland RH3 ... 117 A3
Headley KT18 ... 96 C2
Sloughbrook Cl RH12 ... 217 F6
Slyfield Ct GU1 ... 109 E4
Slyfield Gn GU1 ... 109 E5
Slyfield Ind Est GU4 ... 109 E5
Small's La RH11 ... 201 C6
Smallberry Ave TW7 ... 5 F5
Smallfield Rd Horley RH6 ... 161 D3
Horne RH6 ... 162 E3
Smallmead RH6 ... 161 B3
Smalls Hill Rd
Charlwood RH2, RH6 ... 159 C6
Leigh RH2, RH6 ... 159 C6
Sidlow RH2, RH6 ... 159 C6
Smalls Mead RH11 ... 201 C6
Smallwood Jun & Inf
Schs SW17 ... 20 D4
Smallwood Rd SW17 ... 20 D4
Smart's Heath La GU22 ... 89 A4
Smart's Heath Rd GU22 ... 89 B5
Smeaton Cl KT9 ... 56 D4
Smeaton Rd SW18 ... 20 A8
Smith Cl RH10 ... 201 D3
Smith Ct GU21 ... 70 D6
Smith Rd RH2 ... 138 F6
Smith Sq RG12 ... 27 D7
Smith St KT5 ... 37 F3
Smith's Yd SW18 ... 20 C6
Smitham Bottom La
CR5, CR8 ... 79 D7
Smitham Cty Prim Sch
CR5 ... 79 D4
Smitham Downs Rd
CR5, CR8 ... 79 E6
Smitham Prim Sch CR5 ... 79 C3
Smitham Sta CR5 ... 79 E4
Smithbarn RH13 ... 218 A2
Smithbarn Cl RH6 ... 161 B4
Smithers Cotts RH12 ... 214 F7
Smithers House SE20 ... 23 D1
Smithers The RH3 ... 137 B7
Smithfield La GU35, GU10 ... 167 A1
Smithwood Ave GU6 ... 174 B7
Smithwood Cl SW19 ... 19 E6
Smithwood Common Rd
GU5, GU6 ... 174 B7
Smithy Cl KT20 ... 97 F1
Smithy La
Headley Down GU10 ... 166 E2
Lower Kingswood KT20 ... 97 F1
Smithy's Gn GU20 ... 48 D4
Smock Wlk CR0 ... 42 C3
Smoke La RH2 ... 139 B7
Smokejack Hill RH5 ... 196 D7
Smolletts RH19 ... 205 C8
Smoothfield TW3 ... 5 A3
Smugglers' La RH5 ... 197 E7
Smugglers' Way GU10 ... 126 E1
Snailslynch GU9 ... 125 D2
Snatts Hill RH8 ... 122 F6
Snelgate Cotts GU4 ... 111 D4
Snell Hatch RH11 ... 201 B6
Snellings Rd KT12 ... 54 C5
Snipe La GU27 ... 208 A1
Snow Hill Copthorne RH10 ... 183 F3
Domewood RH10 ... 183 F5
Snow Hill Bsns Ctr RH10 ... 184 A4
Snow House SE27 ... 22 B5
Snowdenham La GU5 ... 151 E5
Snowdenham Links Rd
GU5 ... 151 D6
Snowdon Rd
Farnborough GU14 ... 84 E7
Harlington TW6 ... 3 C1
Snowdown Cl SE20 ... 43 D8
Snowdrop Cl
Crawley RH11 ... 201 A2
2 Hampton TW12 ... 16 A2
Snowdrop Way GU24 ... 68 A2
Snowerhill Rd RH2, RH3 ... 137 F6
Snowhill La RH10 ... 183 F5
Snows Paddock GU20 ... 48 B7
Snows Ride GU20 ... 48 B6
Snowy Fielder Waye TW7 ... 6 B5
Snoxhall Field GU6 ... 174 D2
Soames Wlk KT3 ... 38 E8
Soane Cl RH11 ... 200 E4
Soho Mills SM6 ... 41 B1
Sol-y-vista GU7 ... 150 D6
Solartron Rd GU14 ... 85 B3
Sole Farm Ave KT23 ... 93 F2
Sole Farm Cl KT23 ... 93 F3
Sole Farm Rd KT23 ... 93 F2
Solecote KT23 ... 94 A2
Solent Rd TW6 ... 2 F1
Soloms Court Rd CR5, SM7 ... 78 E2
Solway Cl TW4 ... 4 E4
Somborne House SW15 ... 19 A8
Somerfield Cl KT20 ... 97 E8
Somergate RH12 ... 216 F2
Somers Cl RH2 ... 118 A2
Somers Pl 1 Reigate RH2 ... 118 A2
Streatham SW2 ... 21 F8
Somers Rd Reigate RH2 ... 118 A2
2 Streatham SW2 ... 21 F8
Somersbury
La GU6, RH12 ... 195 F7
Somersby Est SE20 ... 23 C1
Somerset Ave
Chessington KT9 ... 56 D6
Wimbledon SW20 ... 39 B7
Somerset Cl Epsom KT19 ... 57 E2
Hersham KT12 ... 54 B5
New Malden KT3 ... 38 E4
Somerset Ct 3 TW12 ... 36 A8
Somerset Gdns
Teddington TW11 ... 16 E3
Thornton Heath SW16 ... 41 F6
Somerset House SW19 ... 19 E5
Somerset Rd Brentford TW8 ... 6 C8
Farnborough GU14 ... 85 C1
Kingston u T KT1 ... 37 F7
Reigate RH1 ... 139 D7
Teddington TW11 ... 16 E3
Wimbledon SW19 ... 19 D5
Somerset Waye TW5 ... 4 E7
Somerswey GU4 ... 130 E1
Somerton Ave TW9 ... 7 B4
Somerton Cl CR8 ... 80 A3
Somertons Cl GU2 ... 109 A4
Somerville Ct SW16 ... 21 D2
Somerville Dr RH10 ... 182 C1
Somerville Rd
Cobham KT11 ... 74 A5
Penge BR3, SE20 ... 23 D1
Sondes Farm RH4 ... 135 F7
Sondes Place Dr RH4 ... 135 F7
Sondes Place Sch RH4 ... 135 F6
Sonia Gdns TW5 ... 5 A7
Sonnet Wlk TN16 ... 83 C1
Sonning Ct CR0 ... 62 A8
Sonning Gdns TW12 ... 15 E2
Sonning Rd CR0 ... 43 A3
Sonninge Cl GU47 ... 64 D8
Soper Dr CR3 ... 100 D4
Sopwith Ave KT9 ... 56 E5
Sopwith Cl Biggin Hill TN16 ... 83 D3
Richmond TW10 ... 17 F3
Sopwith Dr KT13, KT14 ... 71 E7
Sopwith Rd TW5 ... 4 C7
Sopwith Way KT2 ... 37 E8
Sorbie Cl KT13 ... 53 D4
Sorrel Bank CR0 ... 62 E2
Sorrel Cl Crawley RH11 ... 201 A2
Farnborough GU14 ... 84 C5
Wokingham RG40 ... 25 E8
Sorrel Dr GU18 ... 66 F7
Sorrel House TW3 ... 5 C6
Sorrel Rd RH12 ... 217 E5
Sorrento Rd SM1 ... 59 B7
South Albert Rd RH2 ... 117 F2
South Atlantic Dr GU11 ... 105 C3
South Ave Egham TW20 ... 12 C2
Heath End GU9 ... 125 D6
Richmond TW9 ... 7 A5
Wallington SM5 ... 60 A3
Whiteley Village KT12 ... 53 E1
South Bank KT6 ... 37 E3
South Bank Lodge 2 KT6 ... 37 E3
South Bank Terr KT6 ... 37 E3
South Bookham Cty Inf
Sch KT23 ... 114 C8
South Border The CR8 ... 79 E8
South Cl Crawley RH10 ... 201 F7
Morden SM4 ... 40 A3
Twickenham TW13 ... 16 A5
Woking GU21 ... 69 C3
Wokingham RG40 ... 25 D4
South Close Gn RH1, RH2 ... 119 B6
South Croxted Rd SE21 ... 22 D4
South Croydon Sta CR2 ... 61 D5
South Dr Banstead SM7 ... 78 E6
Beckenham BR3 ... 44 C4
Belmont SM2 ... 58 E2
Coulsdon CR5 ... 79 D4
Dorking RH5 ... 136 C7
Pirbright GU24 ... 87 C6
Wentworth GU25 ... 31 A2
Wokingham RG40 ... 25 C5
South Eden Park Rd
Beckenham BR3 ... 44 B4
West Wickham BR3 ... 44 B2
South End
Croydon CR0, CR9 ... 61 C6
Great Bookham KT23 ... 94 B1
South Farm La GU19 ... 48 A2
South Farnborough Cty
Jun Sch GU14 ... 85 D2
South Farnborough Inf
Sch GU14 ... 105 D8
South Farnham Cty Jun
Sch GU9 ... 125 D1
South Gate Ave TW13 ... 14 D4
South Gdns SW19 ... 20 D1
South Gr Chertsey KT16 ... 32 F3
Horsham RH13 ... 217 D1
South Hill Godalming GU7 ... 150 F4
Guildford GU1 ... 130 D7
South Hill Park RG12 ... 27 C2
South Hill Rd
Beckenham BR2 ... 44 E5
Bracknell RG12 ... 27 B3
South Holmes Rd RH13 ... 218 B4
South La Ash GU12 ... 106 B1
Kingston u T KT1 ... 37 D6
New Malden KT3 ... 38 D3
South La W KT3 ... 38 D5
South Lawn Ct GU7 ... 150 D6
South Lodge TW2 ... 5 C1
South Lodge Ave
CR4, CR7, SW16 ... 41 E5
South Lodge Rd KT12 ... 54 B2
South London Coll SE27 ... 22 B4
South Lynn Cres RG12 ... 27 B4
South Mead Redhill RH1 ... 118 F4
West Ewell KT19 ... 57 F3
South Mead Rd GU11 ... 126 B8
South Meadow RG45 ... 45 D3
South Merton Sta SW20 ... 39 F6
South Munstead La GU8 ... 172 B7
South Norwood Country
Park SE25 ... 43 C5
South Norwood High Sch
SE25 ... 43 B4
South Norwood Hill
SE19, SE25 ... 42 F7
South Norwood Prim Sch
SE25 ... 43 A5
South Oak Rd SW16 ... 21 F4
South Par RH6 ... 160 F4
South Park Cres SE6 ... 24 F7
South Park Ct 25 BR3 ... 24 A1
South Park Cty Inf Sch
RH2 ... 139 A6
South Park Gr KT3 ... 38 C5
South Park Hill Rd CR2 ... 61 D6
South Park La RH1 ... 142 A7
South Park Rd SW19 ... 20 B2
South Pier Rd RH6 ... 182 B7
South Pl Surbiton KT5 ... 37 F2
Wokingham RG40 ... 25 C6
South Rd Ash Vale GU12 ... 106 A4
Bisley GU24 ... 67 F3
Bracknell RG40, RG12 ... 26 E1
Crowthorne RG45 ... 45 E3
Englefield Green TW20 ... 11 D2
Feltham TW13 ... 15 D3
Forest Hill SE23 ... 23 D6
Guildford GU2 ... 109 B3
Hampton TW12 ... 15 F2
Merton SW19 ... 20 D2
Mitcham SW19 ... 20 D2
Reigate RH2 ... 139 B8
Twickenham TW2 ... 16 D5
Weybridge KT13 ... 53 B2
Weybridge KT13 ... 53 C5
Woking GU21 ... 69 C4
South Ridge KT13 ... 72 B8
South Rise SM5 ... 59 E2
South Side GU10 ... 126 F7
South St Dorking RH4 ... 136 A7
Epsom KT18 ... 76 D5
Farnborough GU14 ... 85 E1
Farnham GU9 ... 125 C2
South St *continued*
Godalming GU7 ... 150 D4
Horsham RH12 ... 217 C2
Isleworth TW7 ... 6 A4
Staines TW18 ... 12 F3
South Station App RH1 ... 140 F7
South Terr Dorking RH4 ... 136 B6
Surbiton KT6 ... 37 E3
South Vale SE19 ... 22 E2
South Vale Rd 4 KT6 ... 56 E8
South View
Copthorne RH10 ... 183 E3
Wimbledon SW19 ... 19 D2
South View Ct SE19 ... 22 C1
South View Rd KT21 ... 95 D8
South Way Croydon CR0 ... 62 E7
Sutton SM5 ... 59 D1
South West London Coll
Streatham SW16 ... 21 D5
Upper Tooting SW17 ... 20 E3
South Western Rd TW1 ... 6 B1
South Wimbledon Sta
SW19 ... 20 B1
South Wlk Aldershot GU12 ... 105 D2
Coney Hall BR4 ... 63 E7
Reigate RH2 ... 118 B1
South Worple Way SW14 ... 7 D4
Southall La TW5 ... 4 B8
Southam House KT15 ... 52 B5
Southampton Cl GU17 ... 64 C6
Southampton Gdns CR4 ... 41 E4
Southampton Rd TW19, TW6 ... 2 F1
Southampton St GU14 ... 105 B8
Southbank KT7 ... 37 B2
Southborough Cl KT6 ... 37 D1
Southborough Rd KT6 ... 37 E1
Southborough Sch KT6 ... 56 E7
Southbridge Pl CR0, CR9 ... 61 C6
Southbridge Rd CR0, CR9 ... 61 C6
Southbrook RH11 ... 201 C1
Southbrook Rd SW16 ... 41 E8
Southbury GU2 ... 130 C7
Southcote GU21 ... 69 D3
Southcote Ave
Feltham TW13 ... 15 A6
Tolworth KT5 ... 38 B2
Southcote Dr GU15 ... 66 A5
Southcote Rd
Croydon SE25 ... 43 B3
Merstham RH1 ... 119 C6
South Croydon CR2 ... 61 F1
Southcroft TW20 ... 11 B3
Southcroft Ave BR4 ... 63 C8
Southcroft Rd SW17 ... 21 A2
Southdean Gdns SW19 ... 19 F6
Southdown Cl RH12 ... 218 A5
Southdown Dr SW20 ... 19 D1
Southdown Rd
Hersham KT12 ... 54 E6
Wallington SM5 ... 60 A2
Wimbledon SW20 ... 39 D8
Woldingham CR3 ... 101 F5
Southend La Catford SE6 ... 24 B4
Forest Hill SE26, SE6 ... 23 F4
Southend Rd BR3 ... 44 A8
Southerland Cl KT13 ... 53 C6
Southern Ave
East Bedfont TW14 ... 15 A7
Salfords RH1 ... 140 A1
South Norwood SE25 ... 42 F6
Southern Bglws GU4 ... 131 B2
Southern Cotts TW19 ... 2 A2
Southern Ind Area RG12 ... 26 F6
Southern Perimeter Rd
East Bedfont TW6 ... 3 B1
Feltham TW14, TW6 ... 3 D2
Harlington TW14, TW6 ... 3 D2
Stanwell TW19, TW6 ... 2 D2
Southern Rd GU15 ... 65 C6
Southern Way
Farnborough GU14 ... 84 E3
Farnham GU9 ... 125 C1
Southerns La CR5 ... 98 C3
Southey Ct KT23 ... 94 B3
Southey Rd SW19 ... 20 A1
Southey St SE20 ... 23 D1
Southfield Gdns TW1, TW2 ... 16 F4
Southfield Pl KT13 ... 53 B3
Southfield Sta SW18 ... 19 F7
Southfields KT8 ... 36 E3
Southfields Ave TW15 ... 14 B2
Southfields Ct SM3 ... 59 A8
Southfields Rd CR3 ... 102 B3
Southfields Sch SW18 ... 20 A7
Southfields Special Sch
RG40 ... 25 D5
Southgate Ave
RH10, RH11 ... 201 E4
Southgate Cty Fst & Mid
Sch RH10 ... 201 D4
Southgate Dr RH10, RH11 ... 201 E4
Southgate Par RH10 ... 201 D4
Southgate Rd RH10, RH11 ... 201 D4
Southgate West Cty Fst
& Mid Schs RH11 ... 201 C4
Southholme Cl SE19 ... 42 E8
Southland Way TW7 ... 5 D2
Southlands
East Grinstead RH19 ... 205 E7
Horley RH6 ... 160 F3
Southlands Ave RH6 ... 161 A4
Southlands Cl Ash GU12 ... 106 A1
Coulsdon CR5 ... 79 F2
Wokingham RG40 ... 25 D5
Southlands Dr SW19 ... 19 D6
Southlands La RH8 ... 122 C1
Southlands Rd Ash GU12 ... 106 A1
Wokingham RG40 ... 25 D4
Southmead Jun & Inf Sch
SW19 ... 19 E7
Southmead Rd SW19 ... 19 E7
Southmont Rd KT10 ... 55 E7
Southridge Pl SW20 ... 19 D1
Southsea Rd KT1 ... 37 E5
Southside Comm SW19 ... 19 D2
Southview Cl SW17 ... 21 A3
Southview Cotts GU10 ... 146 D1
Southview Ct 14 GU22 ... 69 E1
Southview Gdns SM6 ... 60 C3
Southview Rd Catford BR1 ... 24 D4
Headley Down GU35 ... 187 B5
Woldingham CR3 ... 102 B3
Southviews CR2 ... 62 D2
Southville Cl
East Bedfont TW14 ... 14 E7
West Ewell KT19 ... 57 D2
Southville Cres TW14 ... 14 E7
Southville Jun & Inf Schs
TW14 ... 14 F7
Southville Rd
East Bedfont TW14 ... 14 E8
Thames Ditton KT7 ... 37 B2
Southwark Cl RH11 ... 201 B2
Southwater Cl BR3 ... 24 B1
Southway Camberley GU15 ... 65 B4
Guildford GU2 ... 108 F1
Wallington SM6 ... 60 C6
West Barnes SW20 ... 39 D5
Southway Ct GU2 ... 108 E1
Southways Pk RH10 ... 181 D3
Southwell Park Rd GU15 ... 65 C5
Southwell Rd CR0, CR7 ... 42 A3
Southwick GU19 ... 47 E1
Southwick Cl RH19 ... 185 D2
Southwick Ct RG12 ... 27 E3
Southwick House RH19 ... 185 D2
Southwold RG12 ... 26 E1
Southwood RG40 ... 25 D4
Southwood Ave
Coulsdon CR5 ... 79 C4
Kingston u T KT2, KT3 ... 38 C8
Knaphill GU21 ... 68 D1
Ottershaw KT16 ... 51 C3
Southwood Bsns Pk GU14 ... 84 D4
Southwood Chase GU6 ... 174 F1
Southwood Cl KT4 ... 39 D1
Southwood Cres
The GU14 ... 84 D3
Southwood Ct KT13 ... 53 B5
Southwood Cty Inf Sch
GU14 ... 84 D3
Southwood Dr KT5 ... 38 C1
Southwood Gdns KT10 ... 56 A7
Southwood Golf Course
GU14 ... 84 E3
Southwood La
Farnborough GU17 ... 84 A3
Farnborough,
Southwood GU14 ... 84 D3
Southwood Rd GU14 ... 84 E4
Sovereign Ct
East Molesey KT8 ... 35 F5
3 Richmond TW9 ... 6 F3
Sovereign Dr GU15 ... 66 B7
Sovereign House
Ashford TW15 ... 13 E4
Wimbledon SW19 ... 19 E2
Spa Cl SE19 ... 42 E8
Spa Dr KT18 ... 76 A5
Spa Hill CR7, SE19 ... 42 D8
Spa View 6 SW16 ... 21 F5
Space Waye TW14 ... 4 B2
Spalding Rd SW17 ... 21 B3
Sparks Cl TW12 ... 15 E2
Sparrow Cl TW12 ... 15 E2
Sparrow Farm Dr TW14 ... 15 D8
Sparrow Farm Inf Sch
TW14 ... 15 C8
Sparrow Farm Jun Sch
TW14 ... 15 C8
Sparrow Farm Rd
KT17, KT4 ... 58 B6
Sparrow Row GU24 ... 49 B4
Sparrowhawk Cl GU10 ... 124 D8
Sparrows Mead RH1 ... 119 A4
Sparvell Rd GU21 ... 88 B8
Sparvell Way GU15 ... 65 C6
Spats La GU35 ... 187 A8
Speaker's Ct 3 CR0 ... 42 D1
Speart La TW5 ... 4 E7
Speedbird Way UB7 ... 2 C7
Speedwell Cl GU4 ... 110 C4
Speedwell House 5 RH1 ... 119 A4
Speedwell Way RH12 ... 217 E5
Speer Rd KT7 ... 36 F3
Speirs Cl KT3 ... 38 F3
Speke Rd CR7 ... 42 D7
Speldhurst Cl BR2 ... 44 F4
Spelthorne Coll TW15 ... 13 F4
Spelthorne Cty Inf Sch
TW15 ... 14 E2
Spelthorne Gr TW16 ... 14 F1
Spelthorne La TW15, TW17 ... 34 C8
Spelthorne Mus TW18 ... 12 E3
Spelthorne Sports Club
TW15 ... 14 D1
Spence Ave KT14 ... 71 F5
Spencer Cl Frimley GU16 ... 85 E6
Langley Vale KT18 ... 96 E8
Sheerwater GU21 ... 70 D5
Spencer Ct
Leatherhead KT22 ... 95 C4
Wimbledon SW20 ... 39 B8
Spencer Gdns
Englefield Green TW20 ... 11 D3
Mortlake SW14 ... 7 C2

Spencer Hill SW19 . . . . . . .19 E1
Spencer Hill Rd SW19 . . . .19 E1
Spencer House
24 Putney SW19 . . . . .19 D7
Wimbledon SW19 . . . . .19 D5
Spencer Mews SE21 . . . . . .22 D7
Spencer Pl CR0 . . . . .42 D2
Spencer Rd Bracknell RG42 .26 F8
Bromley BR1 . . . . .24 F1
Carshalton CR4 . . . . .41 A2
Caterham CR3 . . . . .100 D6
Chiswick W4 . . . . .7 C7
Cobham KT11 . . . . .73 B4
East Molesey KT8 . . . . .36 C4
Hounslow TW3, TW5, TW7 . . . .5 C6
Mitcham CR4 . . . . .41 A6
South Croydon CR2 . . . . . . .61 E5
Twickenham TW2 . . . . .16 E6
Wimbledon SW20 . . . . .39 B8
Spencer Way RH1 . . . . . . .140 A4
Spencer's Rd RH12 . . . . . .217 B3
Spencers La RH6 . . . . .159 F2
Spencers Pl RH12 . . . . . . .217 B4
Spencers Rd RH11 . . . . . .201 D5
Spenser Ave KT13 . . . . .53 A2
Spenser Ct 5 TW10 . . . . . .17 D4
Spiceall GU3 . . . . .129 B3
Spicer Cl KT12 . . . . .35 C3
Spicers Field KT22 . . . . . . .74 E6
Spices Yd CR0 . . . . .61 C6
Spiers Way RH6 . . . . .161 B1
Spindle Way RH10 . . . . . . .201 F5
Spindlewood Gdns
CR0, CR2 . . . . .61 E6
Spindlewoods KT20 . . . . . .97 B4
Spinis RG12 . . . . .26 F1
Spinnaker Ct 2 KT1 . . . . . .37 D8
Spinner Gn RG12 . . . . .27 B4
Spinney Cl Cobham KT11 . . .74 A8
Crawley Down RH10 . . . . . .204 C8
Horsham RH12 . . . . .218 B6
New Malden KT3 . . . . .38 E4
Worcester Park KT4 . . . . .57 F8
Spinney Dr TW14 . . . . .14 C8
Spinney Gdns SE19 . . . . . . .22 F3
Spinney Hill KT15 . . . . .51 F5
Spinney La SL4 . . . . .9 B7
Spinney Oak KT16 . . . . .51 D4
Spinney The Ascot SL5 . . . . .29 E4
Burgh Heath KT18 . . . . .97 B8
Cheam SM3 . . . . .58 C6
Crawley RH11 . . . . .201 B4
Frimley GU15 . . . . .66 C6
Grayshott GU26 . . . . .188 A4
Great Bookham KT23 . . . . . . .94 B3
Haslemere GU27 . . . . .208 C8
Horley RH6 . . . . .161 A5
Oxshott KT22 . . . . .74 C7
Purley CR8 . . . . .80 B8
Ripley GU23 . . . . .111 C8
Streatham SW16 . . . . .21 D5
Sunbury TW16 . . . . .35 A8
Spinneycroft KT22 . . . . .74 D4
Spinning Wlk The GU5 . .133 A4
Spire Ct 10 TW10 . . . . .6 E1
Spital Heath RH4 . . . . . . .136 C8
Spoil La GU10 . . . . .126 F7
Spokane Cl GU11 . . . . .125 F8
Spook Hill RH5 . . . . .136 B3
Spooner House TW5 . . . . . . .5 A8
Spooner Wlk SM6 . . . . .60 D5
Spooners Rd RH12 . . . . . .218 A4
Sportsbank St SE6 . . . . . . .24 C8
Spout Hill CR0 . . . . .63 A5
Spout La TW19 . . . . .2 A3
Spout La N TW19 . . . . .2 B3
Spratts Alley KT16 . . . . . . .51 E4
Spratts La KT15 . . . . .51 E4
Spread Eagle Wlk 2 KT18 76 D6
Spreighton Rd KT8 . . . . . . .36 B5
Spring Ave TW20 . . . . .11 F2
Spring Bottom La RH1 . .120 C8
Spring Cnr TW13 . . . . .14 F5
Spring Copse
Copthorne RH10 . . . . .183 C3
East Grinstead RH19 . . . . . .185 D3
Spring Cotts KT6 . . . . .37 D4
Spring Ct Ewell KT17 . . . . . .57 F2
Guildford GU2 . . . . .109 A5
Spring Gdns Ascot SL5 . . . .29 B5
Biggin Hill TN16 . . . . .83 C1
Copthorne RH10 . . . . .183 C3
Dorking RH4 . . . . .136 A8
East Molesey KT8 . . . . .36 C5
Farnborough GU14 . . . . .85 A7
Frimley GU15 . . . . .66 A5
Wallington SM6 . . . . .60 C5
Spring Gr Brentford W4 . . . . .7 A8
Farncombe GU7 . . . . .150 E8
Fetcham KT22, KT23 . . . . . . .94 B4
Hampton TW12 . . . . .36 B8
Mitcham CR4 . . . . .41 A8
Spring Grove Cres
TW3, TW5 . . . . .5 C6
Spring Grove Jun & Inf
Sch TW7 . . . . .5 D5
Spring Grove Rd
Hounslow TW3, TW5, TW7 . . . .5 C6
Richmond TW10 . . . . .6 F2
Spring Hill SE26 . . . . .23 C4
Spring Hill Wildfowl
Park RH18 . . . . .206 A1
Spring House SW19 . . . . . .39 F8
Spring La
Croydon CR0, SE25 . . . . .43 B3
Hale GU9 . . . . .125 A7
Oxted RH8 . . . . .122 D4
Slinfold RH13 . . . . .215 C3
Spring La W GU9 . . . . . . .125 A6
Spring Meadow
Bracknell RG12 . . . . .27 D8
Forest Row RH18 . . . . .206 F1
Spring Park Ave CR0 . . . . . .62 D8
Spring Park Inf Sch CR0 . .63 A7
Spring Park Jun Sch CR0 .63 A7
Spring Park Rd CR0 . . . . . .62 D8
Spring Plat RH10 . . . . .202 C6
Spring Plat Ct RH10 . . . . .202 C6
Spring Rd TW13 . . . . .14 F5
Spring Rise TW20 . . . . .11 E2
Spring St KT17 . . . . .57 F2
Spring Terr TW10 . . . . .6 E2
Spring Way RH19 . . . . . . .186 A4
Spring Woods
Sandhurst GU47 . . . . .45 C1
Virginia Water GU25 . . . . . . .31 B5
Springbank Rd SE13 . . . . . .24 E8
Springbourne Ct BR3 . . . . .44 C8
Springclose La SM3 . . . . . .58 E4
Springcopse Rd RH2 . . . .139 C7
Springcross Ave GU17 . . . .64 D4
Springfarm Rd GU27 . . . .207 E5
Springfield
East Grinstead RH19 . . . . . .185 D4
Elstead GU8 . . . . .148 D3
Lightwater GU18 . . . . .67 D8
Oxted RH8 . . . . .122 D5
South Norwood SE25 . . . . . . .43 A6
Springfield Ave
Hampton TW12 . . . . .16 B2
Merton SW20 . . . . .39 F6
Springfield Cl GU21 . . . . . .68 E1
Springfield Cres RH12 . . .217 B2
Springfield Ct
Horsham RH12 . . . . .217 C2
9 Kingston u T KT1 . . . . .37 E6
Wallington SM6 . . . . .60 B5
Springfield Cty Prim Schs
TW16 . . . . .34 F7
Springfield Drive KT22 . . . .94 F8
Springfield Gdns BR4 . . . . .63 B8
Springfield Gr TW16 . . . . . .35 A8
Springfield Hospl SW17 . . .20 E5
Springfield La KT13 . . . . . .53 B6
Springfield Meadows
KT13 . . . . .53 B6
Springfield Park Rd
RH12 . . . . .217 B2
Springfield Pl KT3 . . . . .38 C5
Springfield Rd Ash GU12 .106 A5
Ashford TW15 . . . . .13 F3
Bracknell RG12 . . . . .26 C8
Brands Hill SL3 . . . . .1 B7
Crawley RH11 . . . . .201 D5
East Ewell KT17 . . . . .58 C1
Frimley GU15 . . . . .66 B5
Guildford GU1 . . . . .109 E1
Horsham RH12 . . . . .217 C2
Kingston u T KT1 . . . . .37 E6
Penge SE26 . . . . .23 B3
South Norwood CR7 . . . . . . .42 C8
6 Teddington TW11 . . . . . . .17 A3
Twickenham TW2 . . . . .16 A7
Wallington SM6 . . . . .60 B5
Westcott RH4 . . . . .135 C6
Wimbledon SW19 . . . . .20 A3
Springfield Rise SE26 . . . . .23 B5
Springfield Terr GU5 . . . . .151 F6
Springfield Way GU8 . . . . .148 E3
Springfields Cl KT16 . . . . . .33 B1
Springhaven GU8 . . . . .148 E3
Springhaven Cl GU1 . . . . . .110 A1
Springhill GU8 . . . . .148 E3
Springhill Ct RG12 . . . . .27 B5
Springholm Cl TN16 . . . . . .83 C1
Springhurst Cl CR0 . . . . . . .62 F6
Springlakes Est GU12 . . . .105 E3
Springmead Ct GU47 . . . . . .45 E1
Springpark Dr BR3 . . . . . . .44 C6
Springwell Cl SW16 . . . . . .21 F4
Springwell Ct TW5 . . . . .4 D5
Springwell Jun & Inf Schs
TW5 .4 E7
Springwell Rd
Beare Green RH5 . . . . .157 D3
Heston TW5 . . . . .4 D6
Streatham SW16 . . . . .22 A3
Springwood GU8 . . . . .150 A1
Springwood Ct CR2 . . . . . . .61 E6
Sprint Ind Est KT14 . . . . . . .71 D8
Spruce Dr GU18 . . . . .67 A7
Spruce Pk BR2 . . . . .44 F5
Spruce Rd TN16 . . . . .83 D3
Sprucedale Gdns
South Croydon CR0 . . . . .62 D6
Wallington CR8 . . . . .60 E2
Spur Rd Brentford TW7 . . . . . .6 B7
Feltham TW14 . . . . .4 B3
Spur The GU21 . . . . .68 B1
Spurfield KT8 . . . . .36 B6
Spurgeon Ave SE19 . . . . . . .42 D8
Spurgeon Cl RH11 . . . . . .201 C7
Spurgeon Rd SE19 . . . . .22 D1
Spurgeon's Coll SE25 . . . . .42 E7
Spurs Ct GU11 . . . . .104 E2
Spy La RH14 . . . . .213 A4
Square Dr GU27 . . . . .208 B1
Square The Bagshot GU19 . .47 E3
Bracknell RG12 . . . . .27 E5
Crawley RH10 . . . . .201 D6
Guildford GU2 . . . . .129 F7
Harmondsworth TW6 . . . . .2 B6
Lightwater GU18 . . . . .48 C1
Lingfield RH7 . . . . .164 C4
12 Richmond TW10 . . . . .6 D2
Rowledge GU10 . . . . .145 E3
Square The *continued*
Tatsfield TN16 . . . . .103 C7
Wallington SM5 . . . . .60 A5
Weybridge KT13 . . . . .53 C5
Wisley GU23, KT14 . . . . .71 E3
Squarey St SW17 . . . . .20 C5
Squire Ct 2 CR0 . . . . .42 E1
Squire's Bridge Rd TW17 .34 A5
Squire's Rd TW17 . . . . .34 A5
Squires Bridge Rd KT17 . . .33 F5
Squires Cl RH10 . . . . .204 A8
Squires Ct Chertsey KT16 . .33 B1
Wimbledon SW19 . . . . .20 A4
Squires Hill La GU10 . . . .147 C4
Squires Wlk TW15 . . . . . . .14 D1
Squirrel Cl Crawley RH11 .181 B1
Hounslow TW4 . . . . .4 C4
Sandhurst GU47 . . . . .64 B8
Squirrel Dr SL4 . . . . .9 B7
Squirrel La GU14 . . . . .85 A5
Squirrel Wood KT14 . . . . . .71 B7
Squirrel's Way KT18 . . . . . .76 D4
Squirrels Cl GU7 . . . . .129 D1
Squirrels Ct KT4 . . . . .57 F8
Squirrels Gn
Great Bookham KT23 . . . . . . .94 A4
12 Redhill RH1 . . . . .118 F2
Worcester Park KT4 . . . . .58 A8
Stable Cl RH10 . . . . .202 D3
Stable Croft GU19 . . . . .47 D2
Stable Ct CR3 . . . . .101 A5
Stable Mews Reigate RH2 .118 A1
West Norwood SE27 . . . . . . .22 C3
Stables The Cobham KT11 . .73 F5
Guildford GU1 . . . . .109 D4
Stace Way RH10 . . . . .202 E8
Stacey Ct RH1 . . . . .119 C6
Stacey's Farm Rd GU8 . .148 D4
Stacey's Mdw GU8 . . . . . .148 C4
Stack House RH8 . . . . . . .122 E5
Stackfield Rd RH11 . . . . . .200 E5
Staddon Ct BR3 . . . . .43 E5
Staff Coll GU15 . . . . .65 C7
Staff College Rd GU15 . . . .65 B6
Staff Rd GU12 . . . . .105 C2
Staffhurst Wood Rd RH8 144 C6
Stafford Cl Caterham CR3 .100 F4
Cheam SM3 . . . . .58 E4
Stafford Gdns CR0 . . . . .60 F5
Stafford Lake GU21 . . . . . . .68 A1
Stafford Pl TW10 . . . . .17 F8
Stafford Rd Caterham CR3 101 A6
Crawley RH11 . . . . .181 B1
Croydon CR0 . . . . .61 A6
Kingston u T KT3 . . . . .38 C6
Wallington CR0, SM6 . . . . . . .60 E4
Stafford Sq 2 KT13 . . . . . . .53 D6
Staffords Pl RH6 . . . . .161 B2
Stag Hill GU2 . . . . .130 A8
Stag La SW15 . . . . .18 F5
Stag Leys KT21 . . . . .95 E7
Stag Leys Cl SM7 . . . . .78 E4
Stagbury Ave CR5 . . . . .78 E1
Stagbury Cl CR5 . . . . .98 E8
Stagbury House CR5 . . . . . .98 E8
Stagelands RH11 . . . . .201 C8
Stagelands Ct RH11 . . . . .201 C8
Stags Way TW7 . . . . .5 F8
Stainash Cres TW18 . . . . . .13 B3
Stainash Par TW18 . . . . . . .13 B3
Stainbank Rd CR4 . . . . .41 B6
Staines Ave SM3 . . . . .58 D8
Staines By-Pass
TW15, TW18 . . . . .13 C3
Staines Central Trad Est
TW18 . . . . .12 E4
Staines La KT16 . . . . .33 A3
Staines Lane Cl KT16 . . . . .32 F4
Staines Prep Sch The
TW18 . . . . .13 A3
Staines Rd Chertsey KT16 . .33 A5
East Bedfont TW14 . . . . .14 D8
Feltham TW14, TW3, TW4 . . . .4 D2
Hounslow TW14, TW3, TW4 . . .4 D2
Laleham TW18 . . . . .33 B7
Staines TW18 . . . . .33 B7
Twickenham TW13, TW2 . . . .16 C6
Wraysbury TW19 . . . . .11 F7
Staines Rd E TW12, TW16 . .35 C8
Staines Rd W TW15 . . . . . .14 D1
Staines Sta TW18 . . . . .13 A3
Stainford Cl TW15 . . . . .14 D3
Stainton Rd SE13 . . . . .24 D8
Stainton Wlk GU21 . . . . . . .69 C1
Staiths Way KT20 . . . . .97 B7
Stake La GU14 . . . . .85 A4
Stakescorner Rd GU3 . . .130 A2
Stambourne Way
South Norwood SE19 . . . . . . .22 F1
West Wickham BR4 . . . . .63 C7
Stamford Ave GU16 . . . . . . .65 F1
Stamford Dr BR2 . . . . .44 F5
Stamford Green Prim Sch
KT19 . . . . .76 B7
Stamford Green Rd KT18 . .76 B6
Stamford Rd KT12 . . . . .54 D7
Stan Hill RH6 . . . . .180 D8
Stanborough Cl TW12 . . . . .15 F2
Stanborough Rd TW3, TW7 .5 D4
Stanbridge Cl RH11 . . . . .200 E6
Standard Rd TW4 . . . . .4 E4
Standen Cl RH19 . . . . .185 A4
Standen (National Trust)
RH19 . . . . .205 D4
Standen Pl RH12 . . . . .218 A7
Standen Rd SW18 . . . . .20 A8
Standinghall La RH10 . . . .203 A3
Standlake Point 1 SE23 . .23 D5
Standon La RH5 . . . . .176 F2
Stane Cl SW19 . . . . .20 B1
Stane St Ockley RH5 . . . . . .177 D4
Slinfold RH12, RH13 . . . . . .215 C4
Stane Way KT17 . . . . .58 A1
Stanedge Ct SW16 . . . . .21 E3
Stanford Cl TW12 . . . . .15 F2
Stanford Cotts GU24 . . . . . .87 E1
Stanford Mid Sch SW16 . .41 D8
Stanford Orch RH12 . . . . .216 F8
Stanford Pl RH7 . . . . .164 D3
Stanford Rd SW16 . . . . .41 E7
Stanford Way
Broadbridge Heath RH12 . .216 D3
Mitcham SW16 . . . . .41 D7
Stanfords The KT17 . . . . . . .76 F7
Stangate Mansions TW1 . .16 F5
Stanger Rd SE25 . . . . .43 A5
Stangrave Hall RH9 . . . . .121 B3
Stanhope Ave BR2 . . . . .44 F1
Stanhope Cotts RH7 . . . . .164 F3
Stanhope Gr BR3 . . . . .43 F5
Stanhope Heath TW19 . . . . .2 C1
Stanhope Rd
Camberley GU15 . . . . .64 F4
South Croydon CR0 . . . . .61 E7
Wallington SM5 . . . . .60 A3
Stanhope Way TW19 . . . . . . .2 C1
Stanhopes RH8 . . . . .123 B7
Stanier Cl RH10 . . . . .202 B5
Staniland Dr KT13 . . . . .52 F1
Stanley Ave
Beckenham BR2, BR3 . . . . . .44 C6
West Barnes KT3 . . . . .39 A4
Stanley Cl Coulsdon CR5 . . .79 F2
Crawley RH10 . . . . .201 E4
Stanley Cotts GU21 . . . . . . .68 D2
Stanley Ct Belmont SM2 . . . .59 B3
Wallington SM5 . . . . .60 A3
Stanley Ctr RH10 . . . . .181 F2
Stanley Cty Inf Sch TW2 . .16 E4
Stanley Cty Jun Sch TW2 .16 E4
Stanley Dr GU14 . . . . .84 C3
Stanley Gardens Rd TW11 .16 E3
Stanley Gdns
Hersham KT12 . . . . .54 C4
Mitcham CR4 . . . . .21 A2
Sanderstead CR2 . . . . .81 A7
Wallington SM6 . . . . .60 C4
Stanley Gr CR0, CR7 . . . . . . .42 A3
Stanley Hill GU24 . . . . .87 C5
Stanley Mansions SW17 . . .20 F6
Stanley Park High Sch
SM5 .60 A4
Stanley Park Inf Sch SM5 .59 F3
Stanley Park Jun Sch SM5 59 F3
Stanley Park Rd SM5, SM6 .60 A3
Stanley Rd Ashford TW15 . . .13 E3
Hounslow TW3 . . . . .5 C3
Mitcham CR4 . . . . .21 A1
Morden SM4 . . . . .40 A5
Mortlake SW14 . . . . .7 B3
Sutton SM2 . . . . .59 B3
Teddington TW11, TW2 . . . . .16 E3
Thornton Heath CR0, CR7 . . .42 A3
Twickenham TW2 . . . . .16 D5
Wallington SM5 . . . . .60 A3
Wimbledon SW19 . . . . .20 A2
Woking GU21 . . . . .69 F2
Wokingham RG40 . . . . .25 E6
Stanley Sq SM5 . . . . .59 F2
Stanley St CR3 . . . . .100 C5
Stanley Tech High Sch
SE25 .42 F6
Stanley Wlk RH13 . . . . . . .217 D2
Stanleycroft Cl TW7 . . . . . . .5 E6
Stanmore Cl SL5 . . . . .29 A5
Stanmore Gdns
Richmond TW9 . . . . .6 F4
Sutton SM1 . . . . .59 C7
Stanmore Rd TW9 . . . . .6 F4
Stanmore Terr BR3 . . . . . . .44 A7
Stannet Way SM6 . . . . .60 C6
Stansfield Rd TW4, TW5 . . . .4 B5
Stanstead Cl BR2 . . . . .44 F3
Stanstead Gr SE23 . . . . .23 F7
Stanstead Manor SM1 . . . .59 A4
Stanstead Rd
Caterham CR3, RH1 . . . . . . .100 E2
Forest Hill SE23, SE6 . . . . . .23 E7
Stansted Rd TW6 . . . . .2 F1
Stanthorpe Cl SW16 . . . . . .21 E3
Stanthorpe Rd SW16 . . . . . .21 E3
Stanton Ave TW11 . . . . .16 E2
Stanton Cl Cranleigh GU6 .174 A3
North Cheam KT4 . . . . .39 D1
West Ewell KT19 . . . . .57 B5
Stanton Rd Barnes SW13 . . . .7 F5
Thornton Heath CR0 . . . . . . .42 C2
Wimbledon SW20 . . . . .39 D8
Stanton Sq SE6 . . . . .23 F4
Stanton Way SE26, SE6 . . . .23 F4
Stanway Sch RH4 . . . . . . .115 B1
Stanwell Cl TW19 . . . . .2 D1
Stanwell Gdns TW19 . . . . . . .2 D1
Stanwell Moor Rd
Harmondsworth TW19,
TW6, UB7 . . . . .2 B4
Stanwell TW19 . . . . .2 B4
Stanwell New Rd
TW18, TW19 . . . . .13 B5
Stanwell Rd Ashford TW15 .13 E4
East Bedfont TW14,
TW19, TW6 . . . . .14 B8
Horton SL3, TW19 . . . . .1 C4
Stanworth Ct TW5 . . . . .5 A7
Stanyhurst SE23 . . . . .23 E7
Staple Hill GU24, KT16 . . . .49 E6
Staple La
East Clandon GU4 . . . . .111 E2
Shere GU4 . . . . .132 F8
Staplecross Ct 1 RH11 . . .201 A3
Staplefield Cl 3 SW2 . . . . . .21 E7
Stapleford Cl
Kingston u T KT1 . . . . .38 A6
Putney SW19 . . . . .19 E8
Staplehurst RG12 . . . . .26 E2
Staplehurst Cl RH2 . . . . . .139 C5
Staplehurst Rd
Reigate RH2 . . . . .139 C5
Sutton SM5 . . . . .59 E3
Stapleton Gdns CR0 . . . . . .61 A5
Stapleton Rd SW17 . . . . . . .21 A5
Star and Garter Hill TW10 17 E8
Star Hill Churt GU10 . . . . .167 D2
Woking GU22 . . . . .89 D8
Star Hill Dr GU10 . . . . . . .167 D2
Star La Aldershot GU12 . . .105 F2
Hooley CR5 . . . . .99 A6
Star Post Rd GU15 . . . . .65 F8
Star Rd TW7 . . . . .5 D5
Starborough Cotts RH7 . .185 F7
Starborough Rd TN8 . . . .165 E5
Starhurst Sch RH5 . . . . . .136 C5
Starling Wlk TW12 . . . . . . .15 E3
Starmead Dr RG40 . . . . .25 E5
Starrock La CR5 . . . . .99 A7
Starrock Rd CR5 . . . . .99 C8
Starwood Cl KT14 . . . . .71 C8
Staten Gdns TW1 . . . . .16 F7
Statham Ct RG42 . . . . .26 E8
Station App
Ash Vale GU12 . . . . .106 A7
Ashford TW15 . . . . .13 F4
Beckenham BR3 . . . . .44 A8
Beckenham, Lower
Sydenham SE6 . . . . .23 F3
Belmont SM2 . . . . .58 E3
Chipstead CR5 . . . . .78 F1
Coulsdon CR5 . . . . .79 D4
3 Croydon CR0 . . . . .61 D8
Dorking RH4 . . . . .115 C1
East Horsley KT24 . . . . .92 E1
Epsom KT17, KT19 . . . . .76 D6
Godalming GU7 . . . . .150 D4
Guildford GU1 . . . . .130 E8
Hampton TW12 . . . . .36 A8
Haslemere GU27 . . . . .208 B6
Hinchley Wood KT10 . . . . . . .55 F7
Horley RH6 . . . . .161 B2
4 Kingston u T KT1, KT2 . . . .38 A8
Leatherhead KT22 . . . . .95 A6
6 New Malden KT4 . . . . .39 A1
Oxted RH8 . . . . .122 E6
Purley CR8 . . . . .80 A8
Richmond TW9 . . . . .7 A6
Shalford GU4 . . . . .130 E3
Shepperton TW17 . . . . .34 C4
South Croydon CR2 . . . . .61 D2
Staines TW18 . . . . .13 A3
Streatham SW16 . . . . .21 D3
Sunbury TW16 . . . . .35 A8
1 Surbiton KT6 . . . . .37 E3
Sutton SM2 . . . . .59 B1
Tadworth KT20 . . . . .97 C4
Virginia Water GU25 . . . . . . .31 D5
West Byfleet KT14 . . . . .71 A7
Weybridge KT13 . . . . .53 A4
Whyteleafe CR3 . . . . .81 A1
Woking GU22 . . . . .69 F2
Worcester Park KT19 . . . . . . .58 A5
Station App E RH1 . . . . . .139 F7
Station App W RH1 . . . . . .139 F7
Station Approach Rd
Chiswick W4 . . . . .7 C7
Coulsdon CR5 . . . . .79 D4
Crawley RH6 . . . . .182 B7
Station Ave Caterham CR3 101 A3
Kingston u T KT3 . . . . .38 E6
Walton-on-T KT12 . . . . .54 A6
West Ewell KT19 . . . . .57 E2
Station Bldgs SW20 . . . . . .39 C7
Station Cl Hampton TW12 . .36 B8
Horsham RH13 . . . . .217 D2
Station Cres TW15 . . . . .13 E4
Station Est BR3 . . . . .43 D5
Station Estate Rd TW14 . . .15 B7
Station Flats SL5 . . . . .30 B2
Station Gdns W4 . . . . .7 C7
Station Hill Ascot SL5 . . . . .29 A5
Crawley RH10 . . . . .202 B7
Farnham GU9 . . . . .125 C2
Station Ind Est RG40 . . . . . .25 B6
Station La
Enton Green GU8 . . . . .171 A7
Milford GU8 . . . . .171 A7
Station Par Ashford TW15 . .13 F4
Chipstead CR5 . . . . .78 F1
East Horsley KT24 . . . . .92 E1
Feltham TW14 . . . . .15 B8
Richmond TW9 . . . . .7 A6
Sunningdale SL5 . . . . .30 A2
5 Upper Tooting SW12 . . . . .21 A7
Virginia Water GU25 . . . . . . .31 E4
Station Path TW18 . . . . . . .12 F4
Station Rd Addlestone KT15 52 D6
Aldershot GU11 . . . . .105 B2
Ashford TW15 . . . . .13 F4
Bagshot GU19 . . . . .47 E4
Barnes SW13 . . . . .7 F5
Belmont SM2 . . . . .59 A1
Betchworth RH3 . . . . .116 E3
Bracknell RG12 . . . . .27 B7

Station Rd *continued*
Bramley GU5 152 A7
Bromley BR2 44 E7
Carshalton SM5 59 F6
Chertsey KT16 33 A1
Chessington KT9 56 E5
Chobham GU24 69 B6
Claygate KT10 55 E5
Cranleigh RH12 195 C3
Crawley RH10, RH11 201 D5
Crawley Down RH10 204 B8
Croydon CR0 42 C1
Dorking RH4 136 A8
East Grinstead RH19 185 D1
Egham TW20 12 A3
Esher KT10 55 D8
Farnborough GU14 85 B4
Farncombe GU7 150 F7
Forest Row RH18 206 F3
Godalming GU7 150 D4
Gomshall GU5 133 D4
Hampton TW12 36 B8
Horley RH6 161 B3
Horsham RH13 217 D2
Hounslow TW3 5 B3
Hydestile GU8 171 D6
Kenley CR8 80 C5
Kingston u T KT2 38 A8
Leatherhead KT22 95 A6
Lingfield RH7 164 E4
Loxwood RH14 213 A3
Merstham RH1 119 C7
Merton SW19 40 C8
Penge SE20 23 C2
Redhill RH1 118 F2
Rudgwick RH12 214 D7
Shalford GU4 130 E3
Shepperton TW17 34 C4
South Godstone RH9 142 E5
South Norwood SE25 42 F5
Stoke D'Abernon KT11 73 E3
Sunbury TW16 15 A1
Sunningdale SL5 30 A4
Teddington TW11 17 A2
Teddington, Hampton Wick KT1 37 D8
Thames Ditton KT10 55 D8
Thames Ditton, Weston Green KT7 36 F2
Twickenham TW1 16 F8
Warnham RH12 217 B8
West Barnes KT3 39 B4
West Byfleet KT14 71 A7
West Wickham BR4 44 C1
Whyteleafe CR3 80 F1
Wokingham RG40 25 B6
Woldingham CR3 101 F5
Wraysbury TW19 1 A1
Station Rd E
Ash Vale GU12 106 A7
Oxted RH8 122 E6
Station Rd N
5 Egham TW20 11 F3
Merstham RH1 119 C7
Station Rd S RH1 119 C7
Station Rd W
Ash Vale GU12 105 F8
Oxted RH8 122 E6
Station Rise SE27 22 B6
Station Row GU4 130 E3
Station Terr RH4 136 A8
Station View GU12 106 A8
Station Way
Cheam SM2, SM3 58 E3
Crawley RH10, RH11 201 D5
Station Yd TW1 17 A8
Staunton Rd KT2 17 F1
Staveley Gdns W4 7 D6
Staveley Rd Ashford TW15 14 D2
Chiswick W4 7 D7
Staveley Way GU21 68 E2
Staverton Cl RG40 25 F6
Stavordale Rd SM4, SM5 40 C2
Stayne End GU25 31 A5
Stayton Rd SM1 59 A7
Steadfast Rd KT1 37 D8
Steam Farm La TW14 3 F3
Steel's La KT11, KT22 74 C5
Steele Rd TW7 6 A3
Steele's Rd GU11 105 B4
Steep Hill Chobham GU24 49 C3
South Croydon CR0 61 E6
Streatham SW16 21 D5
Steeple Cl SW19 19 E4
Steeple Heights Dr TN16 83 D2
Steepways GU26 188 B6
Steeres Hill RH12 199 C6
Steerforth Copse GU47 45 E2
Steerforth St SW18 20 C6
Steers La RH10 182 C4
Steers Mead CR4 40 F8
Steetley Ct SM2 59 C3
Steinman Ct TW7 5 F4
Stella Rd SW17 20 F2
Stembridge Rd SE20 43 B7
Stenning Ct KT22 95 B5
Stennings The RH19 185 C3
Stepgates KT16 33 B2
Stepgates Cl KT16 33 B2
Stepgates Prim Sch KT16 33 B2
Stephanie Chase Ct RG40 25 D7
Stephen Cl Crawley RH11 181 D1
Egham TW20 12 C2
Stephen Ct 18 SW19 19 D7
Stephen Gould Ho GU14 105 B8
Stephendale Rd GU9 125 D4
Stephenson Ct SM2 58 F3
Stephenson Dr RH19 205 F7
Stephenson Pl RH10 202 B6
Stephenson Rd TW4 16 A8
Stephenson Way RH10 202 B6
Stepney Cl RH10 202 C4
Sterling Ave TW17 34 E6
Sterling Bldgs RH12 217 C2
Sterling Pk RH10 182 B3
Sternhold Ave SW12, SW2 21 D6
Sterry Dr Thames Ditton KT7 36 E3
Worcester Park KT19 57 E6
Steucers La SE23 23 E7
Steve Biko La SE6 24 A4
Steve Biko Way TW3 5 A4
Stevenage Rd RH11 200 E3
Stevens Cl Beckenham BR3 24 A2
Epsom KT17 76 E6
Hampton TW12 15 F2
Stevens Ct BR3 24 A2
Stevens' La KT10 56 A4
Stevens Pl CR8 80 B6
Stewart KT20 97 D6
Stewart Ave TW17 34 A5
Stewart Cl Hampton TW12 15 E2
Woking GU21 68 F2
Stewart Fleming Prim Sch SE20 43 C6
Steyning Cl Crawley RH10 201 E8
Purley CR8 80 B3
Steyning Way TW4 4 C3
Sthrathbrook Rd SW16 21 F1
Stile Gdns GU27 207 F6
Stile House GU4 110 D2
Stile Path TW16 35 A6
Stirling Cl Banstead SM7 77 F2
Crawley RH10 202 C5
Farnborough GU14 85 A3
Frimley GU16 65 E2
Mitcham SW16 41 C8
Stirling Gr TW3 5 C5
Stirling House 13 RH1 118 F1
Stirling Rd Guildford GU2 108 E1
Stanwell TW19, TW6 2 F1
Twickenham TW2 16 B8
Stirling Way
East Grinstead RH19 186 B3
Horsham RH13 217 E3
Stirrup Way RH10 202 D7
Stites Hill Rd CR3, CR5 100 C7
Stoatley Hollow GU27 208 A8
Stoatley House 10 SW15 19 A7
Stoatley Rise GU27 208 A8
Stoats Nest Rd CR5 79 E5
Stoats Nest Village CR5 79 E4
Stock Hill TN16 83 D2
Stockbridge Dr GU11 126 C6
Stockbury Rd CR0 43 C3
Stockfield RH6 161 B4
Stockfield Rd
Claygate KT10 55 E5
Streatham SW16 21 F5
Stockhams Cl CR2 61 D1
Stocklund Sq GU6 174 D3
Stockport Rd SW16 41 D8
Stocks Cl RH6 161 B2
Stockton Rd RH2 139 A6
Stockwell Ctr RH10 202 A6
Stockwell Rd RH19 205 E6
Stockwell Works RH10 202 A6
Stockwood Rise GU15 65 F5
Stockwood Way GU9 125 F7
Stocton Cl GU1 109 C2
Stocton Rd GU1 109 D2
Stodart Rd SE20 43 C8
Stoford Cl SW19 19 E8
Stoke Brunswick Sch RH19 206 E7
Stoke Cl KT11 73 F3
Stoke Fields 8 GU1 109 D1
Stoke Gr GU1 109 D1
Stoke Hill Cty Prim Sch GU1 109 C4
Stoke Hills GU9 125 C3
Stoke Hosp (Almshouses) 6 GU1 109 D1
Stoke Mews GU1 130 D8
Stoke Park Ct 5 GU1 109 D1
Stoke Rd Guildford GU1 109 D1
Kingston u T KT2 18 C1
Stoke D'Abernon KT11 73 E3
Walton-on-T KT12 54 C7
Stoke Rd Cotts KT22 94 D6
Stokeford Cl 5 RG12 27 F4
Stokes Cl RH10 202 C4
Stokes Rd CR0 43 D3
Stokes Ridings KT20 97 D4
Stokesby Rd KT9 56 F4
Stokesheath Rd KT22 74 C8
Stompond La KT12 54 A8
Stoms Path SE6 24 A3
Stonards Brow GU5 152 D4
Stondon Pk SE23 23 E8
Stone Cres TW14 14 F8
Stone Hatch GU6 194 A3
Stone House Gdns CR3 100 E2
Stone Park Ave BR3 44 B5
Stone Pl KT4 58 A8
Stone Rd BR2 44 F4
Stone St Aldershot GU12 126 D8
Croydon CR0, CR9 61 A5
Stone's Rd KT17 76 E7
Stonebanks KT12 35 A2
Stonebridge Ct
Crawley RH11 201 C2
Horsham RH12 217 A2
Stonebridge Fields GU4 130 D2
Stonebridge Wharf GU4 130 D2
Stonecot Cl SM3, SM4 39 E1
Stonecot Hill SM4 39 E1
Stonecourt Cl RH6 161 C3
Stonecroft Way CR0 41 E2
Stonecrop Cl RH11 201 B3
Stonecrop Rd GU1, GU4 110 C3
Stonedene Cl GU35 187 B4
Stonefield Cl RH10, RH11 201 D5
Stonegate GU15 66 C6
Stonehaven BR3 44 B7
Stonehill Cl
Little Bookham KT23 94 A2
Mortlake SW14 7 D2
Stonehill Cres KT16 50 E4
Stonehill Pk GU35 187 C4
Stonehill Rd
Chobham GU24, KT16 50 D3
Headley Down GU35 187 C4
Lightwater GU18 48 A1
Mortlake SW14 7 D2
Ottershaw GU24, KT16 50 D3
Stonehill's Mansions 3 SW16 21 E6
Stonehills Ct SE21 22 E5
Stonehouse Rise GU16 65 E1
Stoneleigh Ave KT17, KT4 58 A7
Stoneleigh Broadway KT17 58 A5
Stoneleigh Cl RH19 185 F1
Stoneleigh Cres KT19 57 F5
Stoneleigh Ct GU16 65 F1
Stoneleigh Fst Grant Maintd Sch KT4 58 B6
Stoneleigh Lodge 12 TW9 6 F6
Stoneleigh Park Ave CR0 43 D3
Stoneleigh Park Rd KT19, KT4 58 A5
Stoneleigh Pk KT13 53 C4
Stoneleigh Rd
Carshalton SM5 40 E2
The Chart RH8 123 E5
Stoneleigh Sta KT19 58 A5
Stonepit Cl GU7 150 C4
Stoners Cl RH6 181 E7
Stones La RH4 135 C6
Stoneswood Rd RH8 123 B5
Stoneworth Ct SE25 43 A3
Stoney Bottom GU26 188 C3
Stoney Brook GU2 108 E2
Stoney Deep TW11 17 A4
Stoney La SE19 22 F2
Stoney Rd RG42 27 A8
Stoneybrook RH12 216 F1
Stoneycroft Cl SE12 24 F8
Stoneycroft Wlk 3 RH11 200 D5
Stoneyfield Rd CR5 79 F2
Stoneyland Ct 6 TW20 11 F3
Stoneylands Rd TW20 11 F3
Stonny Croft KT21 75 F2
Stony Hill KT10 54 F3
Stoop Ct KT14 71 B7
Stoop Memorial Ground TW2 16 E8
Stopham Rd RH10 202 C3
Stormont Way KT9 56 C5
Storr's La GU3 88 C3
Storrington Rd CR0 42 F1
Stoughton Ave SM3 58 E5
Stoughton Cl SW15 19 A7
Stoughton Grange Cty Jun Sch GU2 109 B4
Stoughton Inf Sch GU2 109 B4
Stoughton Rd GU1, GU2 109 B3
Stourhead Cl
Farnborough GU14 85 D4
6 Putney SW19 19 D8
Stourhead Gdns SW20 39 A6
Stourton Ave TW13 15 F4
Stovold's Way GU11 125 F8
Stovolds Hill GU6, GU8 193 D7
Stowell Ave CR0 63 D2
Stowford Coll SM2 59 C3
Strachan Pl SW19, SW20 19 C2
Strachey Ct 1 RH11 201 B1
Strafford Rd Hounslow TW3 4 F4
Twickenham TW1 17 A8
Straight Rd SL4, TW19 11 C8
Strand Cl Crawley RH10 202 D4
Langley Vale KT18 96 D8
Strand on the Green Inf Sch W4 7 A8
Strand on the Green Jun Sch W4 7 A8
Strand-on-the-Green W4 7 A8
Stranraer Way 1 TW6 2 E1
Stratfield RG12 26 E1
Stratfield House 12 GU11 105 A2
Stratford Ct
Farnborough GU14 85 C4
Farnham GU9 125 C1
New Malden KT3 38 D5
Stratford Rd
Harlington TW6 3 C2
Thornton Heath CR7 42 B6
Strathavon Cl GU6 174 B7
Strathcona Ave KT24 113 E7
Strathcona Gdns
Knaphill GU21 68 D1
Knaphill GU21 88 C8
Strathdale SW16 21 F3
Strathdon Dr SW17 20 D5
Strathearn Ave
Harlington UB3 3 F7
Twickenham TW2 16 C7
Strathearn Rd Sutton SM1 59 A5
Wimbledon SW19 20 A4
Strathmore Cl CR3 100 E6
Strathmore Rd
Crawley RH11 181 A1
Teddington TW11, TW2 16 E4
Thornton Heath CR0 42 D2
Wimbledon SW19 20 A5
Strathmore Sch TW10 17 D6
Strathville Rd SW18 20 B6
Strathyre Ave CR7, SW16 42 A6
Stratton Ave SM6 60 D2
Stratton Cl Heston TW5 5 A6
Merton SW19 40 A7
Walton-on-T KT12 35 C1
Stratton Ct 10 KT6 37 E4
Stratton Rd Merton SW19 40 A7
Sunbury TW16 34 F7
Stratton Wlk GU14 85 A7
Straw Cl CR3 100 C4
Strawberry Cl GU24 87 D7
Strawberry Fields GU24 68 A4
Strawberry Hill Cl TW1 16 F5
Strawberry Hill Golf Course TW2 16 E5
Strawberry Hill Rd TW1 16 F5
Strawberry Hill Sta TW2 16 F5
Strawberry La SM5 60 A7
Strawberry Rise GU24 68 A4
Strawberry Vale TW1 17 A5
Stream Cl KT14 71 E7
Stream Farm Cl GU10, GU9 146 D7
Stream Pk RH19 185 A3
Stream Valley Rd GU10 146 C6
Streatham Cl SW16 21 E6
Streatham Comm N SW16 21 F3
Streatham Comm S SW16 21 F2
Streatham Common Sta SW16 21 D1
Streatham Ct SW16 21 E5
Streatham High Rd SW16, SW2 21 E3
Streatham Hill SW2 21 E7
Streatham Hill & Clapham High Sch SW2 21 F7
Streatham Hill Sta SW2 21 E6
Streatham Pl SW2 21 E8
Streatham Rd CR4 41 A8
Streatham Sta SW16 21 D3
Streatham & Tooting Adult Inst SW16 21 F6
Streatham Vale SW16 21 D1
Streathbourne Rd SW17 21 A5
Streathem Wells Prim Sch SW2 22 A6
Streatleigh Par 4 SW16 21 E6
Street Hill RH10 202 E5
Street The Ashstead KT21 75 F1
Betchworth RH3 116 E1
Capel RH5 178 D6
Charlwood RH6 180 E7
Compton GU3 129 B2
Dockenfield GU10 166 E6
East Clandon GU4 111 E4
Effingham KT24 113 D8
Ewhurst GU6 175 E5
Fetcham KT22 94 D5
Frensham GU10 167 C7
Plaistow RH14 211 E2
Puttenham GU3 128 C4
Shackleford GU8 149 C8
Shalford GU4 130 E3
Slinfold RH13 215 D4
Thursley GU8 169 C4
Tongham GU10 126 F6
West Clandon GU4 111 B5
West Horsley KT24 112 B7
Wonersh GU5 152 A7
Wrecclesham GU10 145 F6
Streete Court Sch RH9 121 E5
Streeters Cl GU7 151 A6
Streeters La SM6 60 D7
Streetfield GU8 169 C4
Streetfield Rd RH13 215 E3
Streets Heath GU24 67 F7
Stretton Rd Croydon CR0 42 E2
Richmond TW10 17 C6
Strickland Cl RH11 200 E5
Strickland Row SW18 20 D8
Stringer's Ave GU4 109 D7
Stringhams Copse GU23 91 A3
Strode House 8 SW2 22 A7
Strode St TW20 12 A4
Strode's Coll TW20 11 F3
Strode's Cres TW18 13 C3
Strodes College La TW20 11 F3
Strood House 12 SE20 23 C1
Strood La Warnham RH12 216 C7
Winkfield SL5 9 C2
Stroud Cres SW15 19 A5
Stroud Green Gdns CR0 43 C2
Stroud Green Way CR0 43 C3
Stroud La GU5 153 A3
Stroud Rd Croydon SE25 43 A3
Wimbledon SW19 20 A5
Stroud Way TW15 14 B2
Stroude Rd Egham TW20 12 A1
Thorpe GU25, TW20 31 E6
Stroudes Cl KT4 38 F2
Stroudley Cl RH10 202 B5
Stroudwater Pk KT13 53 C4
Strudgate Cl RH10 202 B4
Strudwicks Field GU6 174 F4
Stuart Ave KT12 35 C1
Stuart Cl Crawley RH10 202 D5
Farnborough GU14 85 A5
Stuart Cres Croydon CR0 62 F7
Reigate RH2 139 A6
Stuart Ct Godalming GU7 150 E4
16 Redhill RH1 119 A2
Stuart Gr TW11 16 E3
Stuart House RG42 26 F8
Stuart Lodge
7 Epsom KT18 76 D6
South Norwood SE25 42 E7
Stuart Pl CR4 40 F8
Stuart Rd Reigate RH2 139 A6
Richmond TW10 17 B5
South Norwood CR7 42 C5
Warlingham CR3, CR6 101 C7
Wimbledon SW19 20 A5
Stuart Way
East Grinstead RH19 205 F7
Staines TW18 13 B2
Virginia Water GU25 31 A5
Stubbington House Sch SL5 29 B1
Stubbs Folly GU47 64 D7
Stubbs La KT20 118 A7
Stubbs Moor Rd GU14 84 F5
Stubbs Way SW19 40 D8
Stubfield RH12 217 A3
Stubpond La RH19, RH7 184 D7
Stubs Cl RH4 136 C5
Stubs Hill RH4, RH5 136 C4
Stubs Ind Site GU12 105 E5
Stucley Rd TW5, TW7 5 C7
Studios Rd TW17 33 F6
Studland Rd Byfleet KT14 71 F6
Kingston u T KT2 17 E2
Penge SE26 23 D3
Study Prep Sch The SW19 19 C3
Stumblets RH10 202 C7
Stumps Hill La BR3 24 A2
Sturdee Cl GU16 65 E1
Sturges Rd RG40 25 D5
Sturt Ave GU27 207 F5
Sturt Ct GU4 110 C3
Sturt Rd Frimley GU16 85 F5
Haslemere GU27 207 F5
Heath End GU9 125 B7
Sturt's La KT20 117 A8
Stychens Cl RH1 120 C2
Stychens La RH1 120 C2
Styles End KT23 114 B8
Styles Way BR3 44 C5
Styventon Pl KT16 32 F2
Succomb's Hill CR3, CR6 101 B7
Succombs Pl CR6 101 B8
Sudbrook Gdns TW10 17 E5
Sudbrook La TW10 17 E6
Sudbrook Pk (Richmond Golf Club) TW10 17 E6
Sudbury Gdns CR0 61 E6
Suffield Cl CR2 81 D7
Suffield La GU3, GU10, GU8 128 B2
Suffield Rd SE20 43 C7
Suffolk Cl Bagshot GU19 47 E2
Horley RH6 161 A2
Suffolk Ct 3 SW16 22 A4
Suffolk Dr GU4 110 B6
Suffolk House 4
Croydon CR0 61 D8
Penge SE20 43 C8
Suffolk Rd Barnes SW13 7 F7
South Norwood SE25 42 F5
Worcester Park KT4 57 F8
Sugden Rd KT7 37 B1
Sulina Rd SW2 21 E8
Sullington Hill RH11 201 D4
Sullington Mead RH12 216 E3
Sullivan Cl
East Molesey KT8 36 B6
Farnborough GU14 85 A4
Sullivan Ct 4 CR0 43 A1
Sullivan Dr RH11 200 E3
Sullivan House Kenley CR8 80 C5
Twickenham TW2 5 D1
Sullivan Rd GU15 65 A5
Sullivans Reach KT12 35 A2
Sultan St BR3 43 D7
Summer Ave KT8 36 E4
Summer Gdns
Frimley GU15 66 C5
Thames Ditton KT8 36 E4
Summer Rd
East Molesey KT8 36 D4
Thames Ditton KT7, KT8 36 F4
Summer Trees TW16 35 B8
Summer's Rd GU3, GU7 151 A8
Summerene Cl SW16 21 C1
Summerfield KT21 95 D8
Summerfield La
Long Ditton KT6 56 D8
Rowledge GU10 146 B2
Summerfield St SE12 24 F8
Summerfields Cl KT15 51 F5
Summerhayes Cl GU21 69 E5
Summerhays KT11 73 D6
Summerhill GU7 150 D6
Summerhill Way CR4 41 A8
Summerhouse Ave TW5 4 E6
Summerhouse Cl GU7 150 D4
Summerhouse Ct GU26 188 D3
Summerhouse La UB7 2 D8
Summerhouse Rd GU7 150 D3
Summerlands GU6 174 E4
Summerlay Cl KT20 97 E7
Summerleigh 3 KT13 53 D4
Summerley St SW18 20 B6
Summerly Ave RH2 118 A2
Summers Cl Belmont SM2 59 A3
Weybridge KT13 72 A8
Summers La GU7 150 A8
Summersbury Dr GU4 130 E1
Summersbury Hall GU4 130 E1
Summersby Cl GU7 150 F7

Summersell House SE27 22 D3
Summerstown SW17 20 C4
Summersvere Cl RH10 182 A1
Summerswood Cl CR8 80 D3
Summerville Gdns SM1 58 F4
Summerwood Rd TW1, TW7 5 F1
Summit Ave GU14 84 C3
Summit Ctr UB7 2 D7
Summit Pl KT13 53 A3
Summit The TW16 15 A1
Summit Way SE19 22 E1
Sumner Cl KT22 94 D3
Sumner Ct GU9 125 C3
Sumner Gdns CR0 42 A1
Sumner Pl KT15 52 A5
Sumner Rd Farnham GU9 125 C3
Thornton Heath CR0 42 B1
Sumner Rd S CR0 42 A1
Sun Alley 5 TW9 6 E3
Sun Brow GU27 208 A5
Sun Hill GU22 89 A6
Sun Inn Rd GU8 192 F5
Sun Life Trad Est TW14 4 A4
Sun Ray Est GU47 64 A8
Sunbury Ave SW14 7 D3
Sunbury Court Island TW16 35 D6
Sunbury Court Rd TW16 35 C7
Sunbury Cres TW13 14 F4
Sunbury Cross Centre 9 TW16 14 F1
Sunbury Ct TW16 35 D7
Sunbury Ct (Con Ctr) TW16 35 D7
Sunbury Int Bsns Ctr TW16 34 E8
Sunbury La KT12 35 A3
Sunbury Manor Sch TW16 34 F8
Sunbury Rd Cheam SM3 58 E7
Feltham TW13 14 F4
Sunbury Sta TW16 35 A8
Sunbury Way TW13 15 C3
Suncroft Pl SE26 23 C5
Sundale Ave CR2 62 C1
Sunderland Ct
Dulwich SE22 23 A8
11 Stanwell TW19 2 E1
Sunderland Mount SE23 23 D6
Sunderland Rd SE23 23 D6
Sundew Cl Crawley RH11 201 A2
Lightwater GU18 67 D8
Wokingham RG40 25 E7
Sundial Ave SE25 42 F6
Sundial Ct KT5 57 B8
Sundon Cres GU25 31 C4
Sundown Ave CR2 80 F8
Sundown Rd TW15 14 C3
Sundridge Rd
Croydon CR0, CR9 43 A1
Old Woking GU22 90 A7
Sunkist Way SM6 60 E2
Sunlight Cl SW19 20 C2
Sunmead Cl KT22 94 F5
Sunmead Rd TW16 35 A6
Sunna Gdns TW16 35 B7
Sunniholme Ct CR2 61 C5
Sunning Ave SL5 29 E2
Sunning House Ascot SL5 29 D5
Windlesham GU20 48 F8
Sunningdale Ave TW13 15 E6
Sunningdale Cl 2 KT6 56 E8
Sunningdale Ct
Crawley RH10 201 D4
13 Kingston u T KT2 18 A1
Sunningdale House CR4 40 D7
Sunningdale Park (Civil Service Coll) SL5 29 F4
Sunningdale Rd SM1 58 F6
Sunningdale Sch SL5 29 F3
Sunningdale Sta SL5 30 A2
Sunninghill Cl SL5 29 D5
Sunninghill Ct SL5 29 D5
Sunninghill Lodge SL5 29 C7
Sunninghill Rd Ascot SL5 29 D5
Windlesham GU20 48 A7
Winkfield SL4, SL5 9 E2
Sunningvale Ave TN16 83 D3
Sunningvale Cl TN16 83 D3
Sunny Ave RH10 204 A8
Sunny Bank Croydon SE25 43 A6
Epsom KT18 76 C3
Warlingham CR6 81 E2
Sunny Down GU8 170 E5
Sunny Hill GU8 170 E6
Sunny Hill Rd GU11 104 D2
Sunny Nook Gdns CR2 61 D4
Sunny Rise CR3 100 D3
Sunny View Cl GU12 105 C1
Sunnybank SL5 29 A5
Sunnybank Mews GU12 106 B3
Sunnybank Rd GU14 84 D6
Sunnybank Villas RH1 120 F3
Sunnycroft Rd
Croydon SE25 43 A6
Hounslow TW3 5 B5
Sunnydell La GU10, GU9 146 A6
Sunnydene Rd CR8 80 B6
Sunnydene St SE26 23 E4
Sunnydown Boys' Sch CR3 100 F6
Sunnyhill Cl RH10 204 A8
Sunnyhill Prim Sch SW16 21 F4
Sunnyhill Rd SW16 21 E4
Sunnyhurst Cl SM1 59 A7
Sunnymead Crawley RH11 201 D6
Crawley Down RH10 204 B8
Sunnymead Ave
CR4, SW16 41 D6
Sunnymede Ave
Sutton SM5 78 D8
West Ewell KT19 57 E3
Sunnyside Knaphill GU21 88 B8
Walton-on-T KT12 35 C4
Wimbledon SW19 19 E2
Sunnyside Pl SW19 19 E2
Sunnyside Rd
Headley Down GU35 187 C4
Teddington TW11 16 D4
Sunray Ave KT5 57 B8
Sunrise Cl TW13 15 F5
Sunset Gdns SE25 42 F7
Sunset Rd SW19 19 B3
Sunshine Way CR4 40 F7
Sunstone Gr RH1 119 E6
Sunvale Ave GU27 207 D6
Sunvale Cl GU27 207 D6
Surbiton Cres KT1, KT6 37 E5
Surbiton Ct KT6 37 D3
Surbiton Hall Cl KT1 37 E5
Surbiton High Sch KT1 37 E5
Surbiton High Sch Jun Sch for Girls KT1 37 E5
Surbiton Hill Pk KT5 38 A4
Surbiton Hill Rd KT6 37 E4
Surbiton Hospl KT6 37 E3
Surbiton Prep Sch KT6 37 E4
Surbiton Rd
Camberley GU15 47 A1
Kingston u T KT1 37 E5
Surbiton Sta KT6 37 E3
Surrey Ave GU15 65 A4
Surrey Bsns Pk KT17 76 E8
Surrey Gr SM1 59 D7
Surrey Heath Mus GU15 65 D6
Surrey Hills Ave KT20 116 C4
Surrey Hills Way KT20 116 C5
Surrey Inst of Art & Design KT17 76 E7
Surrey Inst of Art & Design The GU9 125 B2
Surrey Inst of Art & Tech KT18 76 D5
Surrey Lodge KT12 54 B5
Surrey Mews SE27 22 E4
Surrey Mount SE23 23 B7
Surrey Rd BR4 44 B1
Surrey Research Pk The GU2 129 D8
Surrey St CR0, CR9 61 C7
Surrey Tower 5 SE20 23 C1
Surrey Towers KT15 52 C5
Surridge Ct GU19 47 E2
Surridge Gdns SE19 22 D2
Sussex Ave TW7 5 E4
Sussex Cl Knaphill GU21 68 C1
New Malden KT3 38 E5
Reigate RH2 139 D8
4 Twickenham TW1 6 B1
Sussex Ct Addlestone KT15 52 C5
Barnes SW13 7 F5
Horsham RH13 217 E1
Knaphill GU21 68 C2
Sussex Gdns KT9 56 D4
Sussex Ho TW9 6 F5
Sussex Lodge RH12 217 C4
Sussex Manor Bsns Pk RH10 182 A2
Sussex Pl KT3 38 E5
Sussex Rd Croydon CR2 61 D4
Knaphill GU21 68 C1
Mitcham CR4 41 E4
New Malden KT3 38 E5
South Croydon CR2 61 D4
Wallington SM5 59 F4
West Wickham BR4 44 B1
Sutherland Ave
Biggin Hill TN16 83 E1
Guildford GU4 109 E7
Sunbury TW16 34 F7
Sutherland Chase SL5 28 E7
Sutherland Dr
Guildford GU1, GU4 110 A4
Mitcham SW19 40 D8
Sutherland Gdns
Mortlake SW14 7 E4
North Cheam KT4 39 B1
Sunbury TW16 34 F7
Sutherland Gr
Putney SW18, SW19 19 F8
Teddington TW11 16 E3
Sutherland House TW10 17 C6
Sutherland Rd Chiswick W4 7 E8
Thornton Heath CR0 42 A2
Sutton Arc SM1 59 B5
Sutton Ave GU21 88 E8
Sutton Cl BR3 44 B8
Sutton Common Rd
Cheam SM3 40 A1
Sutton SM1, SM3 59 B8
Sutton Common Sta SM1 59 B8
Sutton Court Rd
Chiswick W4 7 C8
Sutton SM1, SM2 59 C4
Sutton Courtenay House SW17 20 D4
Sutton Ct Chiswick W4 7 C8
East Molesey KT8 35 F4
Penge SE19 22 F1
Sutton SM2 59 C4
Sutton Dene TW3 5 B6
Sutton Gdns
Croydon CR0, SE25 42 F4
Merstham RH1 119 D6
Sutton Gr SM1 59 D5
Sutton Gram Sch For Boys SM1 59 C5
Sutton Green Rd GU4 89 F1
Sutton Hall TW5 5 A7
Sutton High Sch For Girls SM1 59 B4
Sutton Hospl SM2 59 B1
Sutton La
Abinger Common RH5 155 C8
Banstead SM2, SM7 78 B6
Brands Hill SL3 1 B8
Hounslow TW3, TW4, TW5 4 F5
Sutton La S W4 7 C8
Sutton Lodge GU1 109 E1
Sutton Park Rd SM1, SM2 59 B4
Sutton Pl Brands Hill SL3 1 B8
Peaslake RH5 154 F8
Sutton Rd Camberley GU15 47 A1
Heston TW5 5 A6
Sutton Sq TW5 4 F6
Sutton Sta SM2 59 C4
Sutton Way TW5 4 F6
Swaby Rd SW17, SW18 20 C6
Swaffield Prim Sch SW18 20 C8
Swaffield Rd SW18 20 C8
Swail House 8 KT18 76 D6
Swain Cl SW16, SW17 21 B2
Swain Rd CR7 42 C4
Swains Rd
CR4, SW17, SW19 20 F1
Swale House 2 RH1 119 A3
Swale Rd GU14 84 E6
Swaledale RG12 27 A4
Swaledale Cl RH11 201 C3
Swallands Rd SE6 24 A5
Swallow Cl Staines TW18 12 F4
Witley GU8 170 E7
Swallow Gdns SW16 21 D3
Swallow La RH5 136 B1
Swallow Pk KT6 56 F7
Swallow Rd RH11 201 C8
Swallow Rise GU21 68 C2
Swallowdale
New Addington CR2 62 D2
Selsdon CR2 62 D2
Swallowfield
Dormansland RH7 165 A2
Englefield Green TW20 11 B2
Swallows Ct SE20 23 D1
Swallowtail Rd RH12 217 E6
Swan Barn Rd GU27 208 D6
Swan Cl Croydon CR0 42 E2
Feltham TW13 15 E4
Swan Ct Guildford GU1 109 D3
Leatherhead KT22 95 B5
Swan Ctr SW17 20 C5
Swan House GU47 64 B7
Swan La Charlwood RH6 180 F7
Guildford GU1 130 D7
Sandhurst GU47 64 B7
Swan Mill Gdns RH4 115 D1
Swan Pl SW13 7 F5
Swan Rd TW13 15 E4
Swan Sq RH12 217 C2
Swan St TW7 6 B4
Swan Wlk Horsham RH12 217 C2
Oatlands Park TW17 34 E2
Swancote Gn RG12 27 B4
Swandrift TW18 12 F1
Swann Ct 6 TW7 6 A4
Swann Way RH12 216 E3
Swanns Meadow KT23 94 A1
Swans Ghyll RH18 206 E3
Swansea Rd TW14, TW6 3 D1
Swansmere Sch KT12 35 C1
Swanton Gdns SW19 19 D7
Swanwick Cl SW15 18 F8
Swanworth La RH5 115 B7
Swayne's La GU1 110 E1
Swaynesland Rd RH8 123 F1
Swaythling House SW15 7 F1
Swedish Sch SW13 7 F8
Sweeps Ditch Cl TW18 13 B1
Sweeps La TW20 11 F3
Sweet La GU5 154 E8
Sweetbriar RG45 45 A7
Sweetwater Cl GU5 152 D4
Sweetwater La
Enton Green GU8 171 B2
Shamley Green GU5 152 D4
Swievelands Rd TN16 83 C1
Swift Ct SM2 59 B3
Swift La Crawley RH11 201 C8
Windlesham GU19 47 F3
Swift Rd Feltham TW13 15 E4
Heath End GU9 125 C7
Swift's Cl GU10 126 B1
Swiftsden Way BR1 24 E2
Swinburne Cres CR0 43 C3
Swindon Rd Harlington TW6 3 C2
Horsham RH12 217 B4
Swinfield Cl TW13 15 E4
Swingate Rd GU9 146 D8
Swinley County Prim Sch SL5 29 A4
Swinley Forest Golf Club SL5 28 F2
Swinley Rd SL5 28 C4
Swiss Cl GU10 146 A4
Swissland Hill RH19, RH7 185 E7
Switchback La
Rowledge GU10 145 F4
Rowledge GU10 146 A3
Sycamore Ave RH12 218 C6
Sycamore Cl
Carshalton SM5 59 F6
Crawley RH11 181 C1
Feltham TW13 15 A5
Fetcham KT22 94 F5
Frimley GU16 65 E1
Sycamore Cl *continued*
Sandhurst GU47 64 B8
Sycamore Ct
Farncombe GU7 150 E8
Forest Hill SE26 23 C4
Hounslow TW4 4 E3
Ottershaw KT16 51 C5
Walton-on-T KT13 53 F7
10 West Norwood SW16 22 A3
Sycamore Dr
Ash Vale GU12 106 A7
East Grinstead RH19 186 A1
Frimley GU16 65 E1
Wrecclesham GU10 146 A6
Sycamore Gdns CR4 40 D7
Sycamore Gr
Kingston u T KT3 38 E6
Penge SE20 43 A8
Sycamore Lodge 7 TW16 14 F1
Sycamore Rd
Farnborough GU14 85 D2
Guildford GU1 109 D1
Wimbledon SW19, SW20 19 C2
Sycamore Rise
Banstead KT17, SM7 77 D5
Bracknell RG12 27 D6
Sycamore Way TW11 17 C2
Sycamore Wlk
Englefield Green TW20 11 B2
Reigate RH2 139 C6
Sycamores The
Blackwater GU17 64 B5
Farnborough GU14 85 D3
Sydenham Ave SE26 23 B3
Sydenham High Sch For Girls SE26 23 B4
Sydenham Hill SE21, SE22, SE23, SE26, SE19 23 B5
Sydenham Hill Sta SE21 22 F5
Sydenham House 10 KT6 37 D2
Sydenham Ind Est SE26 23 F3
Sydenham Park Mansions SE26 23 C5
Sydenham Park Rd SE23, SE26 23 C5
Sydenham Pk SE26 23 C5
Sydenham Rd Croydon CR0 42 D2
Forest Hill SE26, SE6 23 D3
Guildford GU1 130 E8
Thornton Heath CR0 42 D2
Sydenham Rise SE23 23 B6
Sydenham Sch SE26 23 B5
Sydenham Sec Sch SE26 23 B5
Sydenham Sta SE26 23 C4
Sydenham Station App SE26 23 C4
Sydmons Ct SE23 23 C8
Sydney Ave CR8 79 F7
Sydney Cl RG45 45 C7
Sydney Cotts KT10 55 F4
Sydney Cres TW15 14 B2
Sydney Pl GU1 130 F8
Sydney Rd
East Bedfont TW14 15 A7
Guildford GU1 130 F8
Merton SW20 39 D7
Richmond TW10, TW9 6 E3
Sutton SM1 59 A6
Teddington TW11 16 F3
Sydney Terr KT10 55 F4
Sydney Wood Forest Wlks GU6 193 C2
Sylva Ct 3 SW15 19 D8
Sylvan Cl Limpsfield RH8 123 B6
South Croydon CR2 62 B1
Woking GU22 70 B2
Sylvan Gdns KT6 37 D2
Sylvan Hill SE19 42 E8
Sylvan Rd Crawley RH10 202 A4
South Norwood SE19 42 F8
Sylvan Ridge GU47 45 A1
Sylvan Way Coney Hall BR4 63 E6
Redhill RH1 140 A8
Sylvanus RG12 26 F2
Sylvaways Cl GU6 175 A3
Sylverdale Rd
Croydon CR0, CR9 61 B7
Purley CR8 80 B6
Sylvia Cl GU24 68 A4
Syon Gate Way
Brentford TW8 6 B7
Hounslow TW7, TW8 6 A7
Syon Ho & Pk TW8 6 C6
Syon La Brentford TW7 5 F8
Brentford TW7, TW8 6 B7
Hounslow TW7 6 A7
Syon Lane Sta TW7 6 A7
Syon Park Cotts TW8 6 C6
Syon Park Gdns TW7 5 F7
Syon Pl GU14 85 D4
Sythwood GU21 69 B2
Sythwood Cty Prim Sch GU21 69 B3
Szabo Cres GU3 107 B1

T

Tabard House KT1 37 C8
Tabarin Way KT17 77 C3
Tabor Ct SM3 58 E4
Tabor Gdns SM2, SM3 58 F3
Tabor Gr SW19 19 F1
Tachbrook Rd TW14 14 F8
Tadlow KT1 38 A6
Tadmor Cl TW16 34 F5
Tadorne Rd KT20 97 C5
Tadworth Ave KT3 38 F4
Tadworth Cl KT20 97 D5
Tadworth Cty Prim Sch KT20 97 D5
Tadworth St KT20 97 C5
Tadworth Sta KT20 97 C5
Taffy's How CR4 40 E6
Tait Rd CR0, SE25 42 E2
Talavera Cty Inf Sch GU11 105 B3
Talavera Cty Jun Sch GU11 105 B3
Talbot Cl Mytchett GU16 86 A4
Reigate RH2 139 B8
Talbot La RH12 217 C1
Talbot Lodge KT10 55 A5
Talbot Pl GU19 47 E4
Talbot Rd Ashford TW15 13 E3
Farnham GU9 146 B8
Isleworth TW1, TW7 6 A3
Lingfield RH7 164 D4
South Norwood CR7 42 D5
Twickenham TW2 16 F7
Wallington SM5 60 A5
Talcott Path 12 SW2 22 A7
Taleworth Cl KT21 95 D7
Taleworth Pk KT21 95 D7
Taleworth Rd KT21 95 E7
Talgarth Dr GU14 85 D2
Taliesin Hts GU7 150 D6
Talisman Sq SE26 23 A4
Talisman Way KT17 77 C3
Tall Elms Cl BR2 44 F4
Tall Trees Poyle SL3 1 E6
Thornton Heath SW16 41 F6
Tallis Cl RH11 200 F3
Tally Rd RH8 123 E4
Talma Gdns TW2 16 E8
Talmage Cl SE23 23 C8
Talman Cl RH11 200 E5
Tamar Cl RH10 202 C5
Tamarind Cl GU2 109 A6
Tamarind Ct 3 TW20 11 F3
Tamarisk Rise RG40 25 C7
Tamerton Sq GU22 89 E8
Tamesa House TW17 34 A2
Tamesis Gdns KT4 57 E8
Tamian Ind Est TW4 4 C3
Tamian Way TW4 4 C3
Tamworth RG12 27 D2
Tamworth La CR4 41 B6
Tamworth Manor High Sch CR4 41 D6
Tamworth Pk CR4 41 B6
Tamworth Pl 3 CR0, CR9 61 C8
Tamworth Rd CR0, CR9 61 C8
Tanbridge House Sch RH12 216 F2
Tanbridge Pk RH12 217 B1
Tanbridge Pl RH12 217 B1
Tandem Ctr SW19 40 D8
Tandridge Ct
Caterham CR3 101 A5
Sutton SM2 59 B4
Tandridge Gdns CR2 81 A6
Tandridge Golf Course RH9 122 B4
Tandridge La
RH7, RH8, RH9 143 B4
Tandridge Rd CR6 101 D8
Tandridgehill La
Tandridge RH9 121 F6
Woldingham RH9 121 F6
Tanfield Ct RH12 217 B2
Tanfield Rd CR0, CR9 61 C6
Tangier Ct GU11 104 F2
Tangier Rd Guildford GU1 131 A8
Mortlake TW10 7 B4
Tangier Way KT20 77 E1
Tangier Wood KT20 77 E1
Tangle Oak RH19 184 E4
Tanglewood Cl
Longcross KT16 50 B7
South Croydon CR0 62 C7
Woking GU22 70 D3
Tanglewood Ride GU24 67 D7
Tanglewood Way TW13 15 B5
Tangley Dr RG41 25 B4
Tangley Gr SW15 18 F8
Tangley La GU3 108 F6
Tangley Park Rd TW12 15 F3
Tanglyn Ave TW17 34 B4
Tangmere Gr KT2 17 D3
Tangmere Rd RH11 200 F6
Tanhouse La RG41 25 A5
Tanhouse Rd RH8 122 E3
Tanhurst House 27 SW2 21 E8
Tanhurst La RH5 155 E2
Tank Rd GU15 64 F5
Tankerton Rd KT6 56 F8
Tankerton Terr CR0 41 F3
Tankerville Rd SW16 21 E1
Tanner House 1 SW19 40 C8
Tanner's Ct RH3 137 C5
Tanner's Hill RH3 137 B8
Tanners Cl KT12 35 B3
Tanners Dean KT22 95 D5
Tanners La GU27 208 C7
Tanners Meadow RH3 137 B5
Tanners Yd GU19 47 E3
Tannersfield GU4 130 E1
Tannery Cl
Beckenham BR3, CR0 43 D4
Slinfold RH13 215 D3
Tannery Cotts GU5 133 C4
Tannery La Send GU23 90 E5

Tannery La *continued*
Send Marsh GU23 ... 90 E5
Shalford GU5 ... 151 F8
Tannery The RH1 ... 118 F1
Tannsfeld Rd SE26 ... 23 D3
Tansy Cl GU4 ... 110 C3
Tantallon Rd SW12 ... 21 A7
Tanyard Ave RH19 ... 206 A8
Tanyard Cl Crawley RH10 . 202 C3
Horsham RH13 ... 217 E1
Tanyard Way RH6 ... 161 B4
Tapestry Cl SM2 ... 59 B3
Taplow Ct CR4 ... 40 E5
Tapner's Rd RH2 ... 137 F3
Tapping Cl 5 KT2 ... 18 A1
Tara Ct BR3 ... 44 B7
Tara Pk CR5 ... 98 F7
Taragon Ct GU2 ... 109 A5
Tarbat Ct 6 GU47 ... 64 D8
Target Cl TW14 ... 3 E1
Tarham Cl RH6 ... 160 E5
Tarleton Gdns SE23 ... 23 B7
Tarmac Way UB7 ... 2 B7
Tarn Cl GU14 ... 84 E2
Tarn Rd GU26 ... 188 E3
Tarnbrook Way RG12 ... 27 E2
Tarquin House SE26 ... 23 A4
Tarragon Cl GU14 ... 84 C4
Tarragon Dr GU2 ... 109 A5
Tarragon Gr SE26 ... 23 D2
Tarrington Cl SW16 ... 21 D5
Tartar Hill KT11 ... 73 B6
Tartar Rd KT11 ... 73 C6
Tasker Cl UB7 ... 3 C7
Tasman Ct TW16 ... 14 E1
Tatchbury House SW15 ... 7 F1
Tate Cl KT22 ... 95 C4
Tate Rd SM1 ... 59 A5
Tate's Way RH12 ... 214 D7
Tatham Ct RH11 ... 201 B1
Tatsfield Cty Prim Sch TN16 ... 103 D6
Tatsfield La TN16 ... 103 F6
Tattenham Cnr KT18 ... 77 A1
Tattenham Corner Rd KT18 ... 77 A1
Tattenham Corner Sta KT18 ... 77 B1
Tattenham Cres KT18 ... 77 B1
Tattenham Gr KT18 ... 97 B8
Tattenham Way KT18, KT20 77 E2
Tattersall Cl RG40 ... 25 E5
Taunton Ave
Caterham CR3 ... 100 F4
Hounslow TW3 ... 5 C5
Wimbledon SW20 ... 39 B7
Taunton Cl SM3 ... 40 A1
Taunton La CR5 ... 100 B8
Tavern Cl SM5 ... 40 E2
Tavistock Cl TW18 ... 13 D1
Tavistock Cres CR4 ... 41 E5
Tavistock Ct 1 CR0 ... 42 D1
Tavistock Gdns GU14 ... 85 B7
Tavistock Gr CR0 ... 42 D2
Tavistock Rd
Beckenham BR2 ... 44 F5
Carshalton SM5 ... 40 D1
Croydon CR0 ... 42 D1
Tavistock Wlk SM5 ... 40 D1
Tavy House 3 RH1 ... 118 F2
Tawfield RG12 ... 26 E2
Tawny Cl TW13 ... 15 A5
Tay Cl GU14 ... 84 E6
Tayben Ave TW2 ... 5 E1
Tayles Hill KT17 ... 57 F1
Taylor Ave TW9 ... 7 B5
Taylor Cl Hampton TW12 ... 16 C3
Hounslow TW3 ... 5 C6
Taylor Ct SE20 ... 43 C7
Taylor House 10 SW2 ... 22 A7
Taylor Rd Aldershot GU11 . 105 D7
Ashstead KT21 ... 75 D2
Mitcham CR4, SW19 ... 20 E1
Wallington SM6 ... 60 B5
Taylor Wlk RH11 ... 201 C6
Taylor's La SE26 ... 23 B4
Taylors Cres GU6 ... 174 F3
Taylors Ct TW13 ... 15 A6
Taymount Grange SE23 ... 23 C6
Taymount Rise SE23 ... 23 C6
Taynton Dr RH1 ... 119 D6
Teal Cl Horsham RH12 ... 217 C5
Selsdon CR2 ... 81 D8
Teal Ct Dorking RH4 ... 136 A8
Wallington SM6 ... 60 C5
Teal Pl SM1 ... 58 F5
Tealing Dr KT19 ... 57 D6
Teasel Cl Crawley RH11 ... 201 B3
Croydon CR0 ... 43 D1
Teazlewood Pk KT22 ... 75 A1
Tebbit Cl RG12 ... 27 D7
Tebbs House 14 SW2 ... 22 A8
Teck Cl TW7 ... 6 A5
Tedder Cl KT9 ... 56 C5
Tedder Rd CR2 ... 62 D2
Teddington Cl KT19 ... 57 D1
Teddington Memorial Hospl TW11 ... 16 E2
Teddington Park Rd TW11 16 F4
Teddington Pk TW11 ... 16 F3
Teddington Sch TW11 ... 17 C2
Teddington Sta TW11 ... 17 A2
Tedham La RH9 ... 163 B7
Tees Cl GU14 ... 84 E6
Teesdale RH11 ... 201 C3
Teesdale Ave TW7 ... 6 A6
Teesdale Gdns
Isleworth TW7 ... 6 A6
South Norwood SE25 ... 42 E7
Teevan Cl CR0 ... 43 A2
Teevan Rd CR0, CR9 ... 43 A2
Tegg's La GU22 ... 70 F3
Tekels Ave GU15 ... 65 D4
Tekels Ct GU15 ... 65 E4
Tekels Way GU15 ... 65 F3
Telconia Cl GU35 ... 187 C4
Telegraph La KT10 ... 55 F5
Telegraph Rd SW15 ... 19 C8
Telegraph Track SM5, SM6 . 60 A1
Telfei House 8 SE21 ... 22 E4
Telferscot Jun Mix & Inf Sch SW12 ... 21 D7
Telferscot Rd SW12 ... 21 D7
Telford Ave
Crowthorne RG45 ... 45 C8
Streatham SW12, SW2 ... 21 E7
Telford Avenue Mansions SW2 ... 21 E7
Telford Cl SE19 ... 22 F2
Telford Ct 2 GU1 ... 130 F8
Telford Dr KT12 ... 35 C2
Telford Parade Mansions SW2 ... 21 E7
Telford Pl RH10 ... 201 E5
Telford Rd TW4 ... 16 A8
Telham Ct 5 RH11 ... 200 F3
Tellisford KT10 ... 55 B6
Temperley Rd SW12 ... 21 A8
Tempest Rd TW20 ... 12 C2
Templar Cl GU47 ... 64 A8
Templar Ct CR0 ... 62 E2
Templar Pl TW12 ... 16 A1
Temple Ave CR0 ... 62 F7
Temple Bar Rd GU21 ... 88 F8
Temple Cl RH10 ... 202 D5
Temple Ct 9 TW10 ... 6 E2
Temple Field Cl KT15 ... 52 B4
Temple Gdns TW18 ... 32 F8
Temple La RH5 ... 178 F5
Temple Market KT13 ... 53 B6
Temple Rd Biggin Hill TN16 . 83 D2
Croydon CR0 ... 61 D6
Epsom KT19 ... 76 D7
Hounslow TW3 ... 5 C3
Richmond TW9 ... 6 F5
Temple Sheen SW14 ... 7 C2
Temple Sheen Rd SW14 ... 7 C3
Temple Way Bracknell RG42 26 E8
Carshalton SM1 ... 59 D7
Temple Wood Dr RH1 ... 118 F4
Temple's Cl GU10 ... 126 C1
Templecombe Mews GU22 ... 70 B3
Templecombe Way SM4 ... 39 E4
Templecroft TW15 ... 14 D2
Templedene BR2 ... 44 D7
Templedene Ave TW18 ... 13 C2
Templeman Cl CR8 ... 80 B3
Templemere KT13 ... 53 D7
Templeton Cl CR7, SE19 ... 42 D8
Templewood House RH1 . 118 F4
Ten Acre GU21 ... 69 A1
Ten Acre La TW20 ... 32 C7
Ten Acres KT22 ... 94 D3
Ten Acres Cl KT22 ... 94 D3
Tenbury Ct SW12 ... 21 D7
Tenby Dr SL5 ... 29 D4
Tenby Rd GU16 ... 86 A8
Tenchley's La
Limpsfield RH8 ... 123 D4
The Chart RH8 ... 123 E2
Tenham Ave SW2 ... 21 D6
Tenniel Cl GU2 ... 109 B3
Tennison Cl CR5 ... 100 B7
Tennison Rd Croydon SE25 . 42 F4
South Norwood SE25 ... 42 F4
Tennyson Ave
Twickenham TW1 ... 16 F7
West Barnes KT3 ... 39 B4
Tennyson Cl
Crawley RH10 ... 202 B8
Feltham TW14 ... 4 A1
Horsham RH12 ... 217 E6
Tennyson Ct 3 TW10 ... 17 D4
Tennyson Rd
Addlestone KT15 ... 52 E6
Ashford TW15 ... 13 E3
Hounslow TW3 ... 5 C5
Penge SE20 ... 23 D1
Wimbledon SW19 ... 20 C2
Tennyson Rise RH19 ... 205 C8
Tennyson's La
Haslemere GU27 ... 208 E4
Lurgashall GU27 ... 209 A2
Tennysons GU27 ... 208 E4
Tennysons Ridge GU27 ... 208 E5
Tensing Ct TW19 ... 13 E7
Tenterden Gdns CR0 ... 43 A2
Tenterden Rd CR0 ... 43 A2
Tern Rd RH11 ... 200 D5
Terra Cotta Rd RH9 ... 142 C5
Terrace Gdns SW13 ... 7 F5
Terrace La TW10 ... 6 E1
Terrace Rd KT12 ... 35 B3
Terrace The
Addlestone KT15 ... 52 E5
Ascot SL5 ... 29 D4
Barnes SW13, SW14 ... 7 E5
Camberley GU15 ... 65 A5
Crowthorne RG45 ... 45 D5
Mortlake SW13, SW14 ... 7 E5
Old Woking GU22 ... 90 A6
Wokingham RG40 ... 25 B6
Terrapin Ct SW17 ... 21 B5
Terrapin Rd SW17 ... 21 B5
Terrapins KT6 ... 37 D2
Terry House SW2 ... 22 A7
Terry Rd RH11 ... 201 B1
Testard Rd GU2 ... 130 C7
Testers Cl RH8 ... 123 B3
Teviot Cl GU2 ... 109 A4
Tewkesbury Ave SE23 ... 23 B8
Tewkesbury Cl KT14 ... 71 D8
Tewkesbury Rd SM5 ... 40 D1
Thackeray Cl Isleworth TW7 . 6 A5
Wimbledon SW19 ... 19 D1
Thackeray Manor SM1 ... 59 C5
Thackeray Lodge TW14 ... 3 D1
Thakeham Cl SE26 ... 23 B3
Thames Ave KT16 ... 33 A6
Thames Bank SW14 ... 7 C5
Thames Cl Chertsey KT16 ... 33 C2
East Molesey TW12 ... 36 B7
Farnborough GU14 ... 84 E6
Thames Ct KT8 ... 36 B7
Thames Ditton Cty Fst Sch KT7 ... 36 F3
Thames Ditton & Esher Golf Club KT10 ... 55 D8
Thames Ditton Hospl KT7 . 36 F2
Thames Ditton Island KT7 37 A4
Thames Ditton Jun Sch KT7 ... 36 F2
Thames Ditton Sta KT7 ... 36 F2
Thames Eyot 7 TW1 ... 17 A7
Thames Haven KT6 ... 37 D4
Thames Link House 6 TW9 6 E3
Thames Mead KT12 ... 35 A2
Thames Meadow
East Molesey KT8 ... 36 A6
Lower Halliford KT12, TW17 . 34 E1
Thames Rd Brentford W4 ... 7 B8
Chiswick W4 ... 7 B8
Thames Side
Kingston u T KT1 ... 37 D8
Laleham KT16, TW18 ... 33 C4
Staines TW18 ... 12 F2
Thames Ditton KT7 ... 37 B3
Thames St
East Molesey TW12 ... 36 B7
Kingston u T KT1, KT2 ... 37 D7
Staines TW18 ... 12 F3
Sunbury TW16 ... 35 B6
Walton-on-T KT12 ... 34 F2
Weybridge KT13 ... 53 B7
Thames View House TW12 ... 35 A3
Thames Village W4 ... 7 C6
Thamesfield Ct TW17 ... 34 C2
Thamesgate TW18 ... 33 B8
Thamesgate Cl TW10 ... 17 B4
Thameside TW11 ... 17 D1
Thamesmead Sch TW17 ... 34 D3
Thamespoint TW11 ... 17 D1
Thamesvale Cl TW3 ... 5 A5
Thanescroft Gdns CR0 ... 61 E7
Thanet House 1 SE27 ... 22 B5
Thanet Pl CR0 ... 61 C6
Tharp Rd SM6 ... 60 D5
Thatcher Cl RH10 ... 201 D3
Thatchers Cl Horley RH6 ... 161 B5
Horsham RH12 ... 217 E4
Thatchers La GU3 ... 108 E8
Thatchers Way TW7 ... 5 D2
Thaxted Pl 7 SW20 ... 19 D1
Thayers Farm Rd BR3 ... 43 E8
Theal Cl GU47 ... 64 D8
Thelma Gr TW11 ... 17 A2
Thelton Ave RH12 ... 216 D3
Theobald Rd CR0, CR9 ... 61 B8
Theobalds Way GU16 ... 66 C3
Thepps Cl RH1 ... 140 F6
Therapia La
Thornton Heath CR0 ... 41 E3
Wallington CR0, CR4 ... 41 D2
Wallington CR0 ... 41 E2
Theresa's Wlk CR2 ... 61 D2
Therfield Sch KT22 ... 95 A8
Thesiger Rd BR3, SE20 ... 23 D1
Thetford Ct SE21 ... 23 B6
Thetford Rd Ashford TW15 . 13 E5
New Malden KT3 ... 38 E4
Thetis Terr TW9 ... 7 A8
Theydon Cl RH10 ... 202 A4
Thibet Rd GU47 ... 64 C8
Thicket Cres SM1 ... 59 C6
Thicket Gr SE20 ... 23 A1
Thicket Rd
Penge SE19, SE20 ... 23 B1
Sutton SM1 ... 59 C6
Thickthorne La TW18 ... 13 C1
Third Cl KT8 ... 36 C5
Third Cross Rd TW2 ... 16 D6
Thirlmere Cl
Farnborough GU14 ... 84 E4
Thorpe Lea TW20 ... 12 B1
Thirlmere House TW1 ... 5 F2
Thirlmere Rd
Crawley RH11 ... 200 D4
Streatham SW16 ... 21 D4
Thirlmere Rise BR1 ... 24 F2
Thirlmere Wlk GU15 ... 66 D4
Thirsk Rd Mitcham CR4 ... 21 A1
South Norwood SE25 ... 42 D5
Thistle Way RH6 ... 162 C3
Thistlecroft Rd KT12 ... 54 C6
Thistledene
Thames Ditton KT7 ... 36 E3
West Byfleet KT14 ... 70 F6
Thistledown Vale RH14 ... 212 D3
Thistlewood Cres CR0 ... 82 D7
Thistleworth Cl TW7 ... 5 D7
Thistley La GU6 ... 174 E4
Thomas Ave CR3 ... 100 C6
Thomas Becket Jun Mix & Inf Sch SE25 ... 43 A3
Thomas Bennett Com Coll Crawley RH10 ... 201 D3
Crawley RH10 ... 201 E2
Thomas Dean Rd SE26 ... 23 F4
Thomas' La SE6 ... 24 A8
Thomas Moore House RH2 ... 118 C1
Thomas More RC High Sch CR8 ... 61 A1
Thomas Pooley Ct KT6 ... 37 E2
Thomas Rd GU11 ... 105 D7
Thomas Wall Cl SM1 ... 59 B5
Thompson Ave TW9 ... 7 A4
Thompson Ct 16 RH11 ... 201 B1
Thompson's La GU24 ... 49 D2
Thompsons Cl GU24 ... 87 D4
Thomson Cres CR0 ... 42 A1
Thorburn Chase GU47 ... 64 E6
Thorburn Way SW19 ... 40 D8
Thorkhill Gdns KT7 ... 37 B1
Thorkhill Rd KT7 ... 37 B2
Thorley Cl KT14 ... 71 A5
Thorley Gdns KT14 ... 71 A5
Thorn Bank GU2 ... 130 A7
Thorn Cl GU10 ... 145 F4
Thorn Rd GU10 ... 146 A5
Thornash Cl GU21 ... 69 C4
Thornash Rd GU21 ... 69 C4
Thornash Way GU21 ... 69 C4
Thornbank Cl TW19 ... 2 A2
Thornbury Ave TW7 ... 5 D7
Thornbury Cl RG45 ... 45 B5
Thornbury Ct Hounslow TW7 . 5 E7
Whyteleafe CR3 ... 100 F7
Thornbury Rd TW7 ... 5 D6
Thorncombe St GU5, GU8 151 E2
Thorncroft TW20 ... 11 C1
Thorncroft Cl CR5 ... 100 A8
Thorncroft Rd SM1 ... 59 B6
Thorndean St SW18 ... 20 C6
Thorndon Gdns KT19 ... 57 E6
Thorndown La GU20 ... 48 D3
Thorndyke Cl RH10 ... 202 D5
Thorne Cl Crowthorne RG45 45 A7
Littleton TW15 ... 14 C1
Thorne St SW13, SW14 ... 7 E4
Thorne's Cl BR3 ... 44 C6
Thorneloe Gdns CR0, CR9 . 61 B5
Thorneycroft Cl KT12 ... 35 C3
Thornfield Gn GU17 ... 64 F3
Thornfield Rd SM7 ... 78 A2
Thornhill RG12 ... 27 E5
Thornhill Ave KT6 ... 56 E8
Thornhill Cres GU11 ... 105 C3
Thornhill Rd
Aldershot GU11 ... 105 D4
Surbiton KT6 ... 56 F8
Thornton Heath CR0 ... 42 C2
Thornhill Way TW17 ... 34 A4
Thornlaw Rd SE27 ... 22 B4
Thornleas Pl KT24 ... 92 E1
Thornsbeach Rd SE6 ... 24 C6
Thornsett Pl SE20 ... 43 B7
Thornsett Rd Penge SE20 ... 43 B7
Wandsworth SW18 ... 20 B7
Thornsett Terr SE20 ... 43 B7
Thornton Ave
Streatham SW2 ... 21 D7
Thornton Heath CR0 ... 41 F3
Thornton Cl Guildford GU2 109 A4
Horley RH6 ... 160 E3
Thornton Cres CR5 ... 100 A8
Thornton Ct SW20 ... 39 D4
Thornton Dene BR3 ... 44 A7
Thornton Gdns SW12 ... 21 D7
Thornton Heath Sta CR7 ... 42 C5
Thornton Hill SW19 ... 19 E1
Thornton Pl RH6 ... 160 F3
Thornton Rd
Carshalton SM5 ... 40 D1
Mortlake SW14 ... 7 D4
Streatham SW12, SW2 ... 21 D7
Thornton Heath CR0, CR7, CR9 ... 41 F3
Wimbledon SW19 ... 19 D1
Thornton Rd E
Wimbledon SW19 ... 19 D2
Wimboldon SW19 ... 19 D2
Thornton Row CR7 ... 42 A4
Thornycroft Ct TW9 ... 6 F5
Thornyhurst Rd GU16 ... 86 A4
Thorold Cl CR0, CR2 ... 62 D1
Thorold House 6 SW2 ... 21 E8
Thorold Rd GU9 ... 125 C3
Thoroughfare The KT20 ... 97 A3
Thorpe By-Pass KT16, TW20 ... 32 B6
Thorpe C of E Fst Sch TW20 ... 32 B6
Thorpe Cl Forest Hill SE26 ... 23 D4
New Addington CR0 ... 82 C8
Wokingham RG41 ... 25 A3
Thorpe Ind Est TW20 ... 32 C8
Thorpe Ind Pk TW20 ... 32 C8
Thorpe Lea Prim Sch TW20 ... 12 D2
Thorpe Lea Rd
Egham TW20 ... 12 C2
Thorpe Lea TW20 ... 12 C2
Thorpe Park TW20 ... 32 E5
Thorpe Rd Chertsey KT16 ... 32 D4
Egham TW18, TW20 ... 12 D3
Kingston u T KT2 ... 17 E1
Thorpes Cl GU2 ... 109 A4
Thorpeside Cl TW18, TW20 . 32 E7
Thorpewood Ave SE23, SE26 ... 23 B6
Thorsden Cl GU22 ... 89 E8
Thorsden Ct 10 GU22 ... 69 E1
Thorsden Way 2 SE19 ... 22 E3
Thrale Almhouses SW16 ... 21 E3
Thrale Rd SW16 ... 21 C3
Three Acres RH12 ... 217 A1
Three Arch Rd RH1 ... 140 A5
Three Bridges Cty Fst Sch RH10 ... 202 A7
Three Bridges Cty Mid Sch RH10 ... 201 F6
Three Bridges Rd RH10 ... 202 A6
Three Bridges Sta RH10 . 202 B6
Three Gates GU1 ... 110 C3
Three Gates La GU27 ... 208 E8
Three Mile Rd GU6, RH5 . 155 A2
Three Pears Rd GU1 ... 110 E1
Three Stiles Rd GU9 ... 124 F3
Three Ways GU10 ... 166 D6
Threestile Rd RH12 ... 197 F1
Threshfield RG12 ... 27 A4
Thriffwood SE23, SE26 ... 23 D5
Thrift Vale GU4 ... 110 D4
Thrigby Rd KT9 ... 56 F4
Throat Handpost Cnr The RG40 ... 25 A1
Throwley Rd SM1 ... 59 B5
Throwley Way SM1 ... 59 B5
Thrupp Cl CR4 ... 41 B7
Thrupps Ave KT12 ... 54 D5
Thrupps La KT12 ... 54 D5
Thundery Hill GU10 ... 126 F4
Thurbans Rd GU9 ... 146 A7
Thurbarn Rd SE6 ... 24 B3
Thurbarns Hill RH5 ... 157 E1
Thurlby Rd SE27 ... 22 A4
Thurleigh Rd SW11, SW12 . 20 F8
Thurleston Ave SM4 ... 39 E4
Thurlestone Cl TW17 ... 34 C3
Thurlestone Par TW17 ... 34 C3
Thurlestone Rd SE27 ... 22 A4
Thurlow Hill SE21 ... 22 C6
Thurlow House 17 SW16 ... 21 E5
Thurlow Park Rd
Dulwich SE21, SE24 ... 22 C6
West Norwood SE21, SE24 ... 22 C6
Thurlow Park Sch SE27 ... 22 B6
Thurlow Towers SE27 ... 22 A5
Thurlow Wlk GU6 ... 174 E1
Thurlton Ct GU21 ... 69 E3
Thurnby Ct TW2 ... 16 E5
Thurne Way RH12 ... 214 D7
Thurnham Way KT20 ... 97 D7
Thursby Rd GU21 ... 69 A1
Thursley Cres CR0 ... 63 D3
Thursley Gdns SW19 ... 19 D6
Thursley House
3 Kingston u T KT2 ... 18 B1
13 Streatham SW2 ... 21 F8
Thursley Rd
Churt GU10, GU8 ... 168 C3
Thursley GU8, GU10 ... 169 B6
Thurso St SW17 ... 20 D4
Thurstan Rd SW20 ... 19 B1
Thurston House BR3 ... 24 B2
Thurza Ct TW7 ... 5 F5
Thyme Ct
Farnborough GU14 ... 84 C5
Guildford GU4 ... 110 B4
Tibbet's Cnr SW19 ... 19 D8
Tibbet's Ride SW19 ... 19 D8
Tibbets Cl SW19 ... 19 D7
Ticehurst Cl RH10 ... 202 E6
Ticehurst Rd SE23 ... 23 E6
Tichborne Cl GU17 ... 64 D5
Tichborne Pl GU12 ... 126 D8
Tichbourne Cl GU16 ... 65 F3
Tichmarsh KT19 ... 57 C1
Tidenham Gdns CR0 ... 61 E7
Tideswell Rd CR0 ... 63 A7
Tideway Cl TW10 ... 17 C4
Tideway Yd SW13 ... 7 E5
Tidwells Lea RG12 ... 27 E8
Tiepigs La
Coney Hall BR2, BR4 ... 44 F1
Hayes BR2, BR4 ... 44 F1
Tierney Ct 1 CR0 ... 61 F8
Tierney Rd SW2 ... 21 E7
Tierney Terr SW2 ... 21 E7
Tiffin Girls' Sch KT2 ... 17 E2
Tiffin Sch KT2 ... 37 F7
Tilburstow Cotts RH9 ... 121 C3
Tilburstow Hill Rd
Blindley Heath RH9 ... 142 D5
South Godstone RH9 ... 142 D5
Tile Barn Cl GU14 ... 85 A5
Tilehouse Rd GU4 ... 130 E5
Tilehurst La
Betchworth RH3, RH5 ... 136 F5
Dorking RH3, RH5 ... 136 F5
Tilehurst Rd Cheam SM3 ... 58 E5
Wandsworth SW17, SW18 ... 20 D7
Tiler's Way RH2 ... 139 C5
Tilford Ave CR0 ... 63 C2
Tilford Gdns SW19 ... 19 D7
Tilford House 11 SW2 ... 21 F8
Tilford Rd
Beacon Hill GU10, GU26 ... 188 E6
Farnham GU10, GU9 ... 146 F7
Hindhead GU10, GU26 ... 188 E6
Rushmoor GU10 ... 168 C4
Tilford GU10 ... 147 C4
Tilford St GU10 ... 147 D5
Tilgate Comm RH1 ... 120 C2

Tilgate Dr RH10, RH11 201 E2
Tilgate Forest Bsns Ctr RH11 201 D1
Tilgate Forest Golf Course RH10 202 A2
Tilgate Forest Recn Ctr RH10 201 D1
Tilgate Par RH10 201 E3
Tilgate Pk Ctry Pk RH11 201 F1
Tilgate Pl RH10 201 E3
Tilgate Way RH10 201 E3
Tilgates Cotts RH1 120 C3
Tilletts La RH12 216 E8
Tilley La KT18 96 C4
Tillingbourne Cty Jun Sch GU4 131 B2
Tillingbourne Rd GU4 130 E3
Tillingdown Hill CR3 101 A5
Tillingdown La
Caterham CR3 101 B2
Woldingham CR3 101 B3
Tillman House [8] SW2 21 F7
Tillotson Cl RH10 202 D5
Tilly's La TW18 12 F4
Tilney Ct KT6 37 D4
Tilson Gdns SW2, SW4 21 E8
Tilson House SW2 21 E8
Tilt Cl KT11 73 E3
Tilt Meadow KT11 73 E3
Tilt Rd KT11 73 D3
Tilthams Corner Rd GU7, GU7 151 C8
Tilthams Gn GU7 151 B8
Tiltview KT11 73 C4
Tiltwood Dr RH10 204 C8
Timber Bank GU16 86 A6
Timber Cl
Great Bookham KT23 114 C8
Pyrford GU22 70 F5
Timber Ct RH12 217 C3
Timber Hill KT21 95 E8
Timber Hill Rd CR3 101 A3
Timber La CR3 101 A3
Timber Pl [18] GU9 125 B2
Timbercroft KT19 57 E6
Timberham Farm Rd RH6 181 D8
Timberham Link RH6 181 E8
Timberham Way RH6 181 E8
Timberlands [14] RH11 201 B1
Timberling Gdns CR2 61 D1
Timbermill Ct GU27 207 F6
Timberslip Dr SM6 60 D2
Timbertop Rd TN16 83 C1
Times Sq SM1 59 B5
Timline Gn RG12 27 F7
Timperley Ct RH1 118 E3
Timperley Gdns RH1 118 E3
Timsbury Wlk [5] SW15 19 A7
Timsway TW18 12 F3
Tina Ct SW16 22 A5
Tindale Cl CR2 80 D8
Tinsey Cl TW20 12 B3
Tinsley Cl RH10 182 A1
Tinsley Gn RH10 182 B4
Tinsley La RH10 182 A1
Tinsley La N RH10 182 B3
Tinsley La S RH10 202 A8
Tintagel Cl KT17 76 F5
Tintagel Ct RH13 217 D1
Tintagel Dr GU16 65 F1
Tintagel Way GU22 70 A3
Tintells La KT24 112 B7
Tintern Cl SW19 20 C2
Tintern Rd Carshalton SM5 40 D1
Crawley RH11 201 A4
Tippits Mead RG42 26 D8
Tipton Dr CR0 61 E6
Tiree Path RH11 201 B3
Tirlemont Rd CR2 61 C3
Tirrell Rd CR0 42 C3
Tisbury Rd SW16 41 E7
Titchfield Rd SM5 40 D1
Titchfield Wlk SM5 40 D2
Titchwell Rd SW18 20 D7
Tite Hill TW20 11 D3
Tithe Barn Cl KT2 37 F8
Tithe Barn The GU4 111 D4
Tithe Cl Thorpe GU25 31 D3
Wentworth GU25 31 D3
Tithe La TW19 1 A1
Tithe Orch RH19 184 E4
Tithepit Shaw La CR2, CR6 81 B3
Titlarks Hill Rd SL5 30 B1
Titmus Dr RH10 201 F2
Titsey Cnr RH8 123 B7
Titsey Hill CR6, RH8 103 B4
Titsey Rd Limpsfield RH8 123 B8
Titsey RH8 103 B1
Tiverton Rd TW3 5 C5
Tiverton Way
Chessington KT9 56 D5
Frimley GU16 65 F1
Tivoli Rd Hounslow TW4 4 E3
West Norwood SE19, SE27 22 C3
Toad La GU17 64 E4
Tobias Sch of Art RH19 205 E6
Toby Way KT5, KT6 57 B8
Todds Cl RH6 160 E5
Toftwood Cl RH10 202 C5
Toll Bar Ct SM2 59 B2
Toll Gdns RG12 27 F6
Tolldene Cl GU21 68 E2
Tollers La CR5 99 F8
Tollgate GU1 110 D1
Tollgate Ave RH1 139 F4
Tollgate Ct RH1 139 F4
Tollgate Dr SE21 22 E6
Tollgate Hill RH11 201 C1
Tollgate Jun Mix & Inf Sch CR0 43 C3
Tollgate Rd RH4 136 B4
Tollhouse La SM6 60 C2
Tolson Ho [2] TW7 6 A4
Tolson Rd TW7 6 A4
Tolvaddon GU21 69 A2
Tolverne Rd SW20 39 C8
Tolworth Cl KT6 38 B1
Tolworth Girls' Sch KT6 56 F7
Tolworth Hospl KT6 57 A8
Tolworth Inf Sch KT6 37 F1
Tolworth Jun Sch KT6 37 F1
Tolworth Park Rd KT6 56 F8
Tolworth Rd KT6 56 E8
Tolworth Rise N KT5 38 B1
Tolworth Rise S KT5 38 B1
Tolworth Sta KT5 57 B8
Tolworth Underpass KT5, KT6 57 B8
Tomlin Cl KT19 76 D8
Tomlin Ct KT19 76 D8
Tomlins Ave GU16 65 F2
Tomlinscote Sch GU16 66 A1
Tomlinscote Way GU16 66 A2
Tompset's Bank RH18 206 F1
Tomtits La RH18 206 E1
Tonbridge Cl SM7 78 F5
Tonbridge Rd KT12, KT8 35 F5
Tonfield Rd SM3 39 F1
Tonge Cl BR3 44 A4
Tongham Meadows GU10 126 F7
Tongham Rd
Aldershot GU12 126 D8
Farnham GU10 126 C4
Tonstall Rd Epsom KT19 76 D8
Mitcham CR4 41 A7
Tooting Bec Gdns SW16 21 D4
Tooting Bec Rd
Streatham SW16 21 B4
Upper Tooting SW17 21 B4
Tooting Bec Sta SW17 21 A5
Tooting Broadway SW17 20 F3
Tooting Broadway Sta SW17 20 E3
Tooting Gr SW17 20 E3
Tooting High St SW17, SW19 20 E3
Tooting Mkt SW17 20 F4
Tooting Sta SW17 20 F2
Tootswood Rd BR2, BR3 44 E5
Top Pk BR3 44 E4
Topaz House KT4 38 D1
Topiary Sq TW9 6 F4
Topiary The Ashstead KT21 95 E7
Farnborough GU14 84 E3
Toplady Pl GU9 125 C7
Topsham Rd SW17 21 A4
Tor La KT13 72 D8
Tor Rd GU9 124 F2
Torcross Dr SE23 23 C6
Torin Ct TW20 11 C3
Torland Dr KT22 74 D6
Tormead Cl SM1 59 A4
Tormead Rd GU1 109 F1
Tormead Sch GU1 109 F1
Toronto Dr RH6 162 A3
Torr Rd SE20 23 D1
Torre Wlk SM5 40 E1
Torridge Rd Brands Hill SL3 1 B8
Thornton Heath CR7 42 B4
Torridon Cl GU21 69 B2
Torridon Inf Sch SE6 24 D6
Torridon Jun Sch SE6 24 D6
Torridon Rd SE13, SE6 24 D7
Torrington Cl KT10 55 E4
Torrington Ct SE26 23 A3
Torrington Rd KT10 55 E4
Torrington Sq CR0 42 D2
Torrington Way SM4 40 A3
Torwood La CR3 100 F8
Totford La GU10 127 E4
Totham Lodge SW20 39 B8
Totland Cl GU14 85 A6
Tottenham Rd GU7 150 E6
Tottenham Wlk GU47 45 D1
Totterdown St SW17 20 F3
Totton Rd CR7 42 A6
Toulouse Cl GU15 66 B7
Tournai Cl GU11 105 E7
Toutley Rd RG41 25 A8
Tovil Cl SE20 43 B7
Tower Cl
East Grinstead RH19 185 E2
Hindhead GU26 188 E4
Horley RH6 160 F3
Penge SE20 23 B1
Woking GU21 69 D2
Tower Cotts KT10 54 F1
Tower Ct RH19 185 E2
Tower Gdns KT10 56 A3
Tower Gr KT13 53 E8
Tower Hill Dorking RH4 136 B5
Farnborough GU14 85 A3
Tower Hill Cty Prim Sch GU14 84 F3
Tower Hill Rd RH4 136 B5
Tower Hill Rise GU5 133 C3
Tower Rd Crawley RH12 218 F8
Hindhead GU26 188 E4
Tadworth KT20 97 C4
Twickenham TW1, TW2 16 F5
Tower Rise TW9 6 E4
Tower View CR0 43 E2
Towerhill GU5 133 C3
Towers Dr RG45 45 B4
Towers Pl TW10 6 E2
Towers The Kenley CR8 80 C4
[1] Richmond TW9 6 F3
Towers Wlk KT13 53 B4
Towfield Ct TW13 15 F6
Towfield Rd TW13 15 F6
Town Barn Rd RH11 201 C7
Town End Cl
Caterham CR3 100 E5
Godalming GU7 150 E4
Town End St GU7 150 E4
Town Farm Cty Prim Sch TW19 13 D8
Town Farm Way TW19 13 D8
Town Field Way TW7 6 A5
Town Hill RH7 164 E4
Town La TW19 13 D7
Town Mead
Bletchingley RH1 120 D2
Crawley RH11 201 D7
Town Meadow TW8 6 D7
Town Quay TW18 33 C6
Town Sq Bracknell RG12 27 C7
Camberley GU15 65 C6
[3] Woking GU21 69 F2
Town Tree Rd TW15 14 A3
Townend CR3 100 E5
Townend Ct BR1 44 F8
Townfield Ct RH4 136 A6
Townfield Rd RH4 136 A6
Towngate KT11 73 E4
Townmead Rd TW9 7 B5
Townsend Cl RG12 27 E4
Townsend La GU22 90 B6
Townsend Rd TW15 13 E3
Townshend Rd TW9 6 F3
Townshend Terr TW9 6 F3
Townshott Cl KT23 94 A1
Townside Pl GU15 65 D6
Towpath Way CR0, SE25 42 F4
Towton Rd SE27 22 C6
Toynbee Rd
Merton SW19, SW20 39 E8
Wimbledon SW19, SW20 39 E8
Tracery The SM7 78 B4
Tracious Cl GU21 69 B3
Traemore Ct SW16 22 A5
Trafalgar Ave KT4, SM3, SM4 39 D1
Trafalgar Ct Cobham KT11 73 A6
Farnham GU9 125 C1
Hounslow TW3 4 F4
West Barnes KT3 39 B6
Trafalgar Cty Inf Sch RH12 217 B4
Trafalgar Dr KT12 54 B7
Trafalgar Inf Sch TW2 16 D6
Trafalgar Jun Sch TW2 16 D6
Trafalgar Rd
Horsham RH12 217 C4
Merton SW19 20 C1
Twickenham TW2 16 D6
Trafalgar Way
Camberley GU15 64 F4
Croydon CR0, CR9 61 A8
Trafford Rd Frimley GU16 85 D8
Thornton Heath CR7 41 F4
Traherne Lodge [3] TW11 16 F3
Tramway Path CR4 40 E5
Tranmere Ct SM2 59 C3
Tranmere Rd
Twickenham TW2 16 B8
Wandsworth SW17, SW18 20 C6
Tranquil Dale RH3 116 F3
Transport Ave TW8 6 B8
Transport & Road Research Laboratory RG45 45 C7
Trap La RH5 176 F2
Traps La KT2, KT3 38 E8
Trasher Mead RH4 136 C4
Travellers Way TW5 4 C5
Travis La GU47 64 C7
Treadcroft Dr RH12 217 E5
Treadwell Rd KT18 76 F4
Treaty Ctr TW3 5 B4
Trebor Ave GU9 146 D8
Tredenham Cl GU14 105 C8
Tredown Rd SE26 23 C3
Tredwell Rd SE27 22 B4
Tree Ave GU27 207 F8
Tree Cl TW10 17 D7
Tree Tops CR6 81 A1
Tree Tops Ave GU15 66 B8
Tree View Cl SE19 42 E8
Treebourne Rd TN16 83 C1
Treebys Ave GU4 109 D7
Treelands RH5 136 C4
Treemount Ct KT17 76 E6
Treen Ave SW13, SW14 7 F4
Trees Sch The GU22 90 B8
Treeside Dr GU9 125 E7
Treetops RH9 142 E6
Treetops Ct CR7 42 C4
Treeview RH11 201 C1
Treeview Ct [3] RH2 118 D1
Treeway RH2 118 B4
Trefoil Cl Horsham RH12 217 E5
Wokingham RG40 25 E7
Trefoil Cres RH11 201 A2
Trefusis Ct TW5 4 B6
Tregaron Gdns KT3 38 E5
Tregarth Pl GU21 68 F2
Tregarthen Pl KT22 95 C6
Treglos Ct KT13 53 E8
Tregolls Dr GU14 85 D3
Trehaven Par RH2 139 B6
Trehern Rd [12] SW14 7 D4
Treherne Ct SW17 21 A4
Trelawn Cl KT16 51 C3
Trelawne Dr GU6 174 E2
Trelawney Gr KT13 53 A4
Treloar Gdns SE19 22 D2
Tremaine Rd SE20 43 B7
Trematon Pl TW11 17 C1
Tremayne Wlk GU15 66 C4
Trenance GU21 69 A2
Trenchard Cl KT12 54 C5
Trenchard Ct SM4 40 A3
Trenear Cl RH13 217 E2
Trenham Dr CR6 81 C3
Trenholme Cl SE20 23 B1
Trenholme Ct CR3 101 A4
Trenholme Rd SE20 23 B1
Trenholme Terr SE20 23 B1
Trent Cl Crawley RH11 200 F4
Farnborough GU14 84 E6
Trent Rd SL3 1 B8
Trent Way KT4 58 C7
Trentham Cres GU22 90 A6
Trentham Rd RH1 140 A7
Trentham St SW18 20 A7
Trenton Cl GU16 66 A1
Treport St SW18 20 B8
Treryn Hts GU7 150 D6
Tresco Cl BR1 24 E2
Tresidder House [10] SW4 21 D8
Tresillian Way GU21 69 B2
Tresta Wlk GU21 69 A3
Trevanne Plat RH10 202 D7
Trevelayan Rd SW17 20 F2
Trevelyan RG12 26 E2
Trevelyan Ct KT3 38 F2
Trevelyan House [6] TW1 6 C1
Trevenna House [13] SE23 23 D5
Trevereux Hill RH8 123 F4
Treversh Ct BR1 44 F8
Treville St SW15 19 B8
Treviso Rd SE23 23 D6
Trevithick Cl TW14 14 F7
Trevor Cl Hayes BR2 44 F2
Isleworth TW7 5 F2
Trevor Rd SW19 19 E1
Trevose Ave KT14 70 F5
Trewenna Dr KT9 56 D5
Trewince Rd SW20 39 C8
Trewint St SW18 20 C6
Trewsbury Rd SE26 23 D3
Treyford Cl RH11 200 F6
Triangle The
Kingston u T KT3 38 C7
Woking GU21 69 C1
Trickett House SM2 59 B2
Trident Ind Est SL3 1 E4
Trig St RH5 178 F8
Trigg's Cl GU22 89 D8
Trigg's La GU21, GU22 89 D8
Trigo Ct KT19 76 D8
Trilby Rd SE23 23 D6
Trimmer Ct TW7 5 F4
Trimmer Wlk [11] TW8 6 E8
Trimmer's Almshouses GU9 125 A1
Trimmers Cl GU9 125 C7
Trimmers Field GU9 125 E1
Trimmers Wood GU26 188 E6
Trindles Rd RH1 140 F7
Tring Ct TW1 17 A4
Tringham Cl KT16 51 C5
Trinity GU47 45 E2
Trinity C of E Sch KT10 55 A7
Trinity Cl Crawley RH10 202 C8
Hounslow TW4 4 E3
South Croydon CR2 61 E2
Stanwell TW19 2 C1
Trinity Cotts TW9 6 F4
Trinity Cres
Sunningdale SL5 30 A4
Upper Tooting SW17 21 A6
Trinity Ct Croydon CR9 61 C8
Forest Hill SE23 23 C5
Thornton Heath SE25 42 E3
Twickenham TW2 16 E6
Trinity Fields GU9 125 A6
Trinity Hill GU9 125 A6
Trinity Mews SE20 43 B8
Trinity Par TW3 5 B4
Trinity Rd Knaphill GU21 68 B1
Richmond TW9 6 F4
Upper Tooting SW17, SW18 20 E7
Wandsworth SW17, SW18 20 E7
Wimbledon SW19 20 A2
Trinity Rise SE24, SW2 22 B8
Trinity Sch CR9 62 C8
Trinity St Mary's (C of E) Prim Sch SW12 21 A7
Tristram Rd BR1 24 F4
Tritton Ave CR0 60 E6
Tritton Rd SE21, SE27 22 D5
Trittons KT20 97 D6
Triumph Cl UB7 3 C6
Trodd's La GU1, GU4 110 E1
Trojan Way CR0 60 F7
Troon Cl RH11 200 D5
Troon Ct SL5 29 C4
Troston Ct TW18 12 F3
Trotsworth Ave GU25 31 E5
Trotsworth Ct GU25 31 D5
Trotters La GU24 69 B7
Trotton Cl RH10 202 C3
Trotwood Cl GU47 45 E2
Trout Rd GU27 207 E6
Troutbeck Wlk GU15 66 D3
Trowers Way RH1 119 B4
Trowlock Ave TW11 17 C2
Trowlock Way TW11 17 D2
Troy La TN8 144 F4
Troy Rd SE19 22 D2
Trumpeters Inn TW9 6 C2
Trumpetshill Rd RH2 138 B7
Trumps Green Cl GU25 31 E4
Trumps Green Cty Fst Sch GU25 31 D3
Trumps Mill La
Longcross GU25 31 F4
Thorpe GU25 31 F4
Trumpsgreen Ave GU25 31 D3
Trumpsgreen Rd GU25 31 D3
Trundle Mead RH12 217 C5
Trunk Rd GU14 84 C5
Trunley Heath Rd GU5 151 C8
Truslove Rd SE27 22 B3
Truss Hill Rd SL5 29 C4
Trust Wlk SE21 22 B7
Trys Hill KT16 51 A8
Trystings Cl KT10 56 A4
Tucker Rd KT16 51 D4
Tuckers Dr GU6 174 B3
Tuckey Gr GU23 90 F3
Tudor Ave Hampton TW12 16 A1
North Cheam KT4 58 B6
Tudor Circ GU7 150 E7
Tudor Cl Ashford TW15 13 E4
Banstead SM7 77 E4
Cheam SM3 58 E4
Chessington KT9 56 E5
Cobham KT11 73 F6
Coulsdon CR5 80 A1
Crawley RH10 202 D5
East Grinstead RH19 205 F8
Grayshott GU26 188 D2
Hampton TW12 16 C3
Hamsey Green CR2 81 B4
Little Bookham KT23 94 A3
Smallfield RH6 162 B3
Wallington SM6 60 C3
Woking GU22 70 A2
Wokingham RG40 25 F5
Tudor Ct Biggin Hill TN16 83 E2
Farncombe GU7 150 E5
Feltham TW13 15 C4
[12] Redhill RH1 119 A2
Stanwell TW19 2 E1
Teddington TW11 16 F2
Tudor Dr Kingston u T KT2 17 E3
Walton-on-T KT12 35 D1
West Barnes SM4 39 E3
Tudor Gdns
Mortlake SW13, SW14 7 E4
Twickenham TW1 16 F7
West Wickham BR4 63 C7
Tudor House
Bracknell RG12 27 B4
Horsham RH13 217 F3
Weybridge KT13 53 A4
Tudor La SL4 11 C8
Tudor Pl SW19 20 E1
Tudor Prim Sch SM4 39 D2
Tudor Rd Ashford TW15 14 D2
Beckenham BR3 44 C6
Croydon CR0, SE25 43 B4
Farncombe GU7 150 E7
Hampton TW12 16 A1
Isleworth TW3 5 D3
Kingston u T KT2 18 A1
Penge SE19 22 F1
Tudor Wlk
Leatherhead KT22 94 F7
[3] Weybridge KT13 53 B7
Tudors The BR3 44 B7
Tuesley Cnr GU7 150 D3
Tuesley La
Godalming GU7, GU8 150 D1
Milford GU7 171 C7
Tufton Gdns KT8 36 B7
Tugela Rd CR0 42 D3
Tugela St SE6 23 F6
Tuggles Plat RH12 216 E7
Tulip Cl Croydon CR0 43 D1
Hampton TW12 15 F2
Tulip Ct RH12 217 C4
Tull St CR4 40 F2
Tullett Rd RH10 202 B2
Tulse Cl BR3 44 C6
Tulse Hill SW2, SE24 22 A8
Tulse Hill Sta SE27 22 B6
Tulsemere Rd SE21, SE27 22 C6
Tulyar Cl KT20 97 B7
Tumber St KT18, KT22 96 C2
Tumblewood Rd SM7 77 E3
Tumbling Bay KT12 35 A3
Tummons Gdns SE25 42 E7
Tunbridge Ct [1] SE26 23 A5
Tunley Rd SW12, SW17 21 A6
Tunnel Link Rd TW6 3 A2
Tunnel Rd E TW6 3 B6
Tunnel Rd W TW6 3 B6
Tunnmeade RH11 200 E5
Tunsgate GU1 130 D7
Tunsgate Sq GU1 130 D7
Tunstall Ct [13] TW9 6 F6
Tunstall Rd CR0 42 E1
Tunstall Wlk [10] TW8 6 E8
Tunworth Cres SW15 7 F1
Tupwood Ct CR3 101 A2
Tupwood La CR3 101 A1
Tupwood Scrubbs Rd CR3, RH9 121 A8
Turf Hill Rd GU15 65 F8
Turfhouse La GU24 49 E2
Turkey Oak Cl SE19 42 E8

Turle Rd SW16 .41 E7
Turnberry RG12 .26 E2
Turner Ave Mitcham CR4 .40 F8
Twickenham TW2 .16 C5
Turner Cl Biggin Hill TN16 .83 C7
Guildford GU1 .109 F4
Turner Ct
East Grinstead RH19 .186 A3
Godalming GU7 .150 D4
Turner House RH5 .157 C4
Turner Lodge 10 SW19 .19 D7
Turner Pl GU47 .64 D6
Turner Rd KT3 .38 D2
Turner's Hill Rd RH19 .205 B6
Turners Cl TW18 .13 B3
Turners Hill CE (Controlled) Sch RH10 .204 A3
Turners Hill Rd
Copthorne RH10 .183 F2
Crawley RH10 .203 C5
Crawley Down RH10 .204 A7
Turners Hill RH10 .203 F5
Turners La KT12 .54 B3
Turners Mead GU8 .191 C3
Turners Meadow Way BR3 43 F8
Turners Way CR0, CR9 .61 A8
Turney Rd SE21 .22 D8
Turney Sch SE21 .22 C8
Turnham Cl GU2 .130 C5
Turnoak Ave GU22 .89 E7
Turnoak Cnr GU22 .89 E8
Turnoak La GU22 .89 E8
Turnpike La SM1 .59 C5
Turnpike Link CR0 .61 E8
Turnpike Pl RH11 .201 D8
Turnpike Rd RG42 .26 D7
Turnstone Cl CR0, CR2 .62 E1
Turnville Cl GU18 .48 A1
Turpin Rd TW14 .3 F1
Turpin Way SM6 .60 B3
Turpins Rise GU20 .48 B6
Turret Ct RH19 .185 C3
Turret House KT2 .17 E2
Turville Ct KT23 .94 B2
Tuscam Way GU15 .64 F4
Tushmore Ave RH10, RH11 .181 E1
Tushmore La RH10, RH11 .201 E8
Tushmore Rdbt RH11 .201 D8
Tussock Cl RH11 .201 A4
Tuxford Cl RH10 .202 C4
Tweed Cl GU14 .84 E6
Tweed La Brockham RH3 .137 B5
Rusper RH11 .180 F1
Tweed Rd SL3 .1 B8
Tweeddale Inf Sch SM5 .40 D2
Tweeddale Jun Sch SM5 .40 D2
Tweeddale Rd SM5 .40 D1
Tweedsmuir Cl GU14 .84 D3
Tweedy Rd BR1 .44 F8
Twelve Acre Cl KT23 .93 F3
Twelve Acre Cres GU14 .84 E5
Twickenham Bridge TW9 .6 C2
Twickenham Cl CR0 .60 F7
Twickenham Golf Course TW12 .16 B4
Twickenham Rd
Feltham TW13 .15 F5
Isleworth TW1, TW7 .6 A4
Richmond TW1, TW9 .6 C3
Teddington TW11 .17 A4
Twickenham Rugby Football Union Ground TW2 .5 E1
Twickenham Sta TW1 .17 A8
Twickenham Trad Ctr TW1 .5 F1
Twilley St SW18 .20 B8
Twining Ave TW2 .16 D5
Twinoaks KT11 .74 A6
Twitten La RH19 .184 E4
Two Oaks KT13 .53 B6
Two Rivers Sh Ctr TW18 .12 E4
Two Ways RH14 .213 A4
Twycross Rd
Farncombe GU7 .150 D7
Wokingham RG40 .25 E7
Twyford La GU10 .146 B6
Twyford Par KT6 .38 A1
Twyford Rd Carshalton SM5 40 D1
Wokingham RG40 .25 B8
Twyhurst Ct RH19 .185 D3
Twyne Cl RH11 .200 F4
Twyner Cl RH6 .161 D4
Twynersh Ave KT16 .32 F3
Tybenham Rd SW19 .40 A6
Tychbourne Dr GU4 .110 C4
Tydcombe Rd CR6 .101 D8
Tyers House 1 SW16 .21 C3
Tylden Way RH12 .217 F6
Tylecroft Rd SW16 .41 E7
Tylehost GU2 .109 A5
Tyler Gdns KT15 .52 C6
Tyler Rd RH10 .201 D3
Tylers Cl RH9 .121 B5
Tylers Path SM5 .59 F6
Tylney Ave SE19 .22 F3
Tymperley Ct RH13 .217 E3
Tynamara KT1 .37 D5
Tynan Cl TW14 .15 A7
Tyndalls Estate GU26 .188 F4
Tyne Cl Crawley RH10 .202 C5
Farnborough GU14 .84 E6
Tynedale Rd RH3 .137 B5
Tynemouth Rd CR4 .21 A1
Tynley Gr GU4 .109 D7
Tynwald House 14 SE26 .23 A5
Tyrell Ct SM5 .59 F6
Tyrolean Ct SM7 .78 B4
Tyrols Rd SE23 .23 D7
Tyrrell House BR3 .24 B3
Tyrrell Sq CR4 .40 E8
Tyrrell's Wood Golf Course KT22 .95 F2
Tyrwhitt Ave GU2 .109 B5
Tyson Rd SE23 .23 C8
Tythe The KT12 .35 B3
Tythebarn Cl GU4 .110 B6
Tythebarns La Ripley GU23 .91 B1
Send Marsh GU23 .91 B1
Tytherton RG12 .27 C7

U

Uckfield Rd CR4 .41 A8
Udney Park Rd TW11 .17 A2
Uffington Dr RG12 .27 E5
Uffington Rd SE27 .22 A4
Ujima Ct SW16 .21 E4
Ujima House SW16 .21 E4
Ullathorne Rd SW16 .21 C4
Ullswater RG12 .26 F2
Ullswater Ave GU14 .84 E3
Ullswater Cl Bromley BR1 .24 E1
Hale GU9 .125 A6
Kingston u T KT2, SW15 .18 D4
Lightwater GU18 .48 B1
Ullswater Cres
Coulsdon CR5 .79 E3
Kingston u T SW15 .18 D4
Ullswater Rd
Lightwater GU18 .48 B1
West Norwood SE27, SW16 .22 B6
Ulstan Cl CR3 .102 A4
Ulster Ct KT2 .17 D2
Ulverstone Rd SE27 .22 B6
Ulwyn Ave KT14 .71 E5
Underhill Cl GU7 .150 E3
Underhill La GU10 .146 B7
Underhill Park Rd RH2 .118 A4
Underhill Rd
Dulwich SE21, SE22 .23 B8
Newdigate RH5 .158 B1
Undershaw Rd BR1 .24 F5
Underwood Bracknell RG12 .26 E3
New Addington CR0 .63 C5
Underwood Ave GU12 .105 F1
Underwood Cl RH10 .204 B8
Underwood Ct CR3 .100 F2
Underwood Rd
Caterham CR3 .100 E2
Haslemere GU27 .207 F7
Undine St SW17 .20 F3
Unicorn Sch TW9 .6 F6
Union Cl GU47 .45 E2
Union Ct 2 TW10 .6 E2
Union Rd Farnham GU9 .125 C2
Frimley GU16 .86 D8
Thornton Heath CR0 .42 C2
Union St Aldershot GU11 .105 A2
Farnborough GU14 .85 B4
Kingston u T KT1 .37 D7
Pirbright GU24 .87 A6
Union Terr 7 GU11 .105 A2
Unity Cl New Addington CR0 .63 B2
West Norwood SE19, SE27 .22 C3
Univ of Greenwich The SW15 .19 A8
University Rd SW19 .20 D2
Unstead La GU5 .151 C7
Unstead Wood GU3 .130 C1
Unwin Ave TW14 .3 D2
Unwin Rd TW7 .5 E4
Upavon Gdns RG12 .27 F4
Upchurch Cl SE20 .23 B1
Updown Hill GU20 .48 D4
Upfield Horley RH6 .161 A1
South Croydon CR0, CR9 .62 B7
Upfield Cl RH6 .161 A1
Upfold Cl GU6 .174 B5
Upfold La GU6 .174 C5
Upfolds Gn GU4 .110 C5
Upgrove Manor Way 12 SE24 .22 A8
Upland Ct SE23 .23 C6
Upland Rd Camberley GU15 .65 D7
Croydon CR2 .61 D5
Dulwich SE21, SE22 .23 A8
Sutton SM2 .59 D3
Woldingham CR3 .102 B7
Upland Way KT18 .77 C1
Uplands
Ashstead KT21, KT22 .95 D7
Beckenham BR3 .44 A7
Warlingham CR6 .81 F1
Uplands Cl
Haslemere GU27 .208 D8
Mortlake SW14 .7 B2
Sandhurst GU47 .64 B8
Uplands Cty Prim Sch GU47 .64 B8
Uplands Dr KT22 .74 D5
Uplands Rd Farnham GU9 .125 E1
Kenley CR8 .80 C2
Uppark Gdns RH12 .217 F6
Upper Beulah Hill SE19 .42 E8
Upper Bourne La GU10 .146 B5
Upper Bourne Vale GU10 146 A5
Upper Bridge Rd RH1 .118 F1
Upper Brighton Rd KT6 .37 E2
Upper Broadmoor Rd RG45 .45 D5
Upper Butts TW8 .6 C8
Upper Charles St GU15 .65 C6
Upper Chobham Rd GU15 .66 B4
Upper Church La 11 GU9 .125 B2
Upper Cl RH18 .206 F2
Upper College Ride GU15 .65 E8
Upper Court Rd
Epsom KT19 .76 C8
Woldingham CR3 .102 A3
Upper Dr TN16 .83 C1
Upper Dunnymans 6 SM7 .77 F5
Upper Edgeborough Rd GU1 .130 F8
Upper Elmers End Rd BR3 43 E4
Upper Elms Rd GU11 .105 A1
Upper Fairfield Rd KT22 .95 B6
Upper Farm L Pk KT20 .115 F3
Upper Farm Rd KT8 .35 F5
Upper Forecourt RH6 .182 B7
Upper Gn E Mitcham CR4 .40 F6
Mitcham CR4 .41 A6
Upper Gn W CR4 .40 F7
Upper Gordon Rd GU15 .65 D5
Upper Gr SE25 .42 F5
Upper Grotto Rd TW1 .16 F6
Upper Guildown Rd GU2 130 C6
Upper Hale Rd GU9 .125 C6
Upper Halliford Rd
Upper Halliford TW17 .34 E5
Upper Halliford TW17 .34 E6
Upper Halliford Sta TW16 .34 E7
Upper Ham Rd KT2, TW10 .17 D4
Upper Harestone CR3 .121 A8
Upper High St KT17 .76 E6
Upper House La GU5 .152 F1
Upper Manor Rd
Farncombe GU7 .150 E6
Milford GU8 .149 F1
Upper Mount GU27 .189 F1
Upper Mulgrave Rd SM2 .58 E3
Upper Nursery SL5 .30 A4
Upper Old Park La GU9 .125 A5
Upper Park Rd
Camberley GU15 .65 E6
Kingston u T KT2 .18 A2
Upper Pillory Down SM5 .79 A7
Upper Pinewood Rd GU12 .106 D3
Upper Queen St GU7 .150 E4
Upper Rd SM6 .60 E5
Upper Richmond Rd SW15 .7 F3
Upper Richmond Rd W TW10, SW14, SW15 .7 C3
Upper Rose Hill RH4 .136 B6
Upper Sawleywood 3 SM7 .77 F5
Upper Selsdon Rd CR2 .62 A2
Upper Shirley Rd CR0, CR9 62 D7
Upper South View GU9 .125 C3
Upper Springfield GU8 .148 D3
Upper Sq Forest Row RH18 206 E3
Isleworth TW7 .6 A4
Upper St GU5 .133 A4
Upper St Michael's Rd GU11 .126 B8
Upper Stanford Rd GU24 .87 F1
Upper Sunbury Rd TW12 .36 A8
Upper Sutton La TW5 .5 A6
Upper Teddington Rd KT1, KT8 .37 C8
Upper Tooting Independent High Sch SW17 .20 F6
Upper Tooting Park Mansions 1 SW17 .21 A6
Upper Tooting Pk SW17 .20 F6
Upper Tooting Rd SW17 .20 F5
Upper Tulse Hill SW2 .21 F8
Upper Union St 1 GU11 .105 A2
Upper Union Terr 5 GU11 .105 A2
Upper Vann La GU8 .172 A1
Upper Vernon Rd SM1 .59 D5
Upper Verran Rd GU15 .65 D3
Upper Village Rd SL5 .29 D4
Upper Warlingham Sta CR6 .81 A1
Upper Way GU9 .146 B8
Upper West St RH2 .117 F1
Upper Weybourne La GU9 .125 E7
Upper Wlk GU25 .31 E5
Upper Woodcote Village CR8 .79 D7
Upperton Rd GU2 .130 C7
Upshire Gdns RG12 .27 F5
Upshott La GU22 .70 F2
Upton GU21 .69 B2
Upton Cl GU14 .85 D3
Upton Ct Penge SE20 .23 C1
4 Wimbledon SW19 .19 D1
Upton Dene SM2 .59 B3
Upton Rd Hounslow TW3 .5 A4
South Norwood CR7 .42 D7
Upwood Rd SW16 .41 E8
Urmston Dr SW19 .19 E7
Urquhart Ct BR3 .23 F1
Ursuline Convent Prep Sch SW19 .19 D1
Ursuline Convent Sch SW20 .39 D8
Usherwood Cl KT20 .116 C4
Uvedale Cl CR0 .82 D8
Uvedale Cres CR0 .82 E8
Uvedale Rd RH8 .122 F5
Uxbridge Rd
Feltham TW13 .15 D6
Hampton TW12, TW13 .16 B3
Kingston u T KT1, KT6 .37 D4

V

Vachery La GU6 .194 E7
Vaillant Rd KT13 .53 C6
Valan Leas BR2 .44 E6
Vale Cl Coulsdon CR5 .79 E5
Farnham GU10 .146 C4
Oatlands Park KT13 .53 D7
Twickenham TW1 .17 A5
Woking GU21 .69 E3
Vale Cres SW15 .18 E4
Vale Croft KT10 .55 F2
Vale Ct KT13 .53 D7
Vale Dr RH12 .217 B3
Vale Farm Rd GU21 .69 E2
Vale House GU21 .69 E2
Vale Lodge SE23 .23 C6
Vale Rd Ash Vale GU12 .106 A5
Camberley GU15 .65 A4
Claygate KT10 .55 F3
Mitcham CR4 .41 D5
Oatlands Park KT13 .53 D7
Sutton SM1 .59 B6
Worcester Park KT19, KT4 .57 F7
Vale Rd N KT6 .56 E8
Vale The Ashford TW16 .15 A2
Coulsdon CR5, CR8 .79 E5
Croydon CR0 .62 D8
Feltham TW14 .4 B1
Heston TW5 .4 E8
Vale Wood Dr GU10 .146 D4
Vale Wood La GU26 .188 C4
Valens House 1 SW2 .22 A7
Valentine Ct SE23 .23 D6
Valentyne Cl CR0 .82 E8
Valerie Ct SM2 .59 B3
Valeswood Rd BR1 .24 F3
Valewood Rd GU27 .208 C4
Valley Cres RG41 .25 A8
Valley Ct CR3 .101 A5
Valley End C of E Inf Sch GU24 .49 A4
Valley End Rd GU24 .49 B4
Valley Gardens The TW20 .30 E7
Valley Gdns SW19 .20 D1
Valley La GU10 .146 C7
Valley Mews TW1 .17 A6
Valley Pl KT6 .37 E3
Valley Prim Sch BR2 .44 F7
Valley Prospect 3 SE19 .22 E2
Valley Rd Beckenham BR2 .44 E7
Frimley GU16 .86 B8
Kenley CR3, CR8 .80 D4
Streatham SW16 .21 F4
Valley The GU2 .130 C5
Valley View Biggin Hill TN16 .83 D1
Godalming GU7 .150 D4
Valley View Gdns CR8 .80 E4
Valley Wlk CR0 .62 C8
Valleyfield Rd SW16 .21 F3
Vallis Way KT9 .56 D6
Valnay St SW17 .20 F3
Valornus RH1 .119 B5
Valroy Cl GU15 .65 D6
Van Dyck Ave KT3 .38 D2
Vanborough Ct SM2 .59 C4
Vanbrugh Cl RH11 .200 E3
Vanbrugh Dr KT12 .35 C3
Vancouver Cl KT19 .76 C8
Vancouver Ct RH6 .162 A3
Vancouver Dr RH11 .181 D1
Vancouver Rd
Forest Hill SE23 .23 E6
Richmond TW10 .17 C4
Vanderbilt Rd SW18 .20 C7
Vandyke RG12 .26 E3
Vandyke Cl Putney SW15 .19 D8
Redhill RH1 .118 F3
Vanfame Ct KT3 .38 F6
Vanguard Cl CR0 .42 B1
Vanguard House
7 Merton SW19 .20 C1
5 Stanwell TW19 .2 E1
Vanguard Way SM6 .60 E3
Vann Farm Rd RH5 .177 E4
Vann La Chiddingfold GU8 .191 E4
Hambledon GU8 .171 D1
Vann Lake RH5 .177 F4
Vann Lake Rd Ockley RH5 .177 F3
Ockley RH5 .178 A4
Vanners RH10 .201 E7
Vant Rd SW17 .20 F3
Vapery La GU24 .87 D6
Varley Way CR4 .40 D7
Varna Rd TW12 .36 B8
Varney Cl GU14 .84 E5
Varsity Dr TW1, TW7 .5 F1
Varsity Row SW14 .7 C5
Vaughan Almshouses TW15 .14 B3
Vaughan Rd KT7 .37 B2
Vaughan Way RH4 .136 A7
Vaux Cres KT12 .54 B4
Vauxhall Gdns CR2 .61 C4
Veals Mead CR4 .40 E8
Vectis Gdns SW17 .21 B2
Vectis Rd SW17 .21 B2
Vegal Cres TW20 .11 C3
Vellum Dr SM5 .60 A7
Venita Manor SE27 .22 A3
Venner Rd
Forest Hill SE20, SE26 .23 C3
Penge SE20, SE26 .23 C3
Ventnor Rd SM2 .59 B3
Ventnor Terr GU12 .105 C1
Venton Cl GU21 .69 B2
Verbania Way RH19 .186 B1
Verdant Ct 3 SE6 .24 E8
Verdant La SE6 .24 E7
Verdayne Ave CR0, CR9 .62 D8
Verdayne Gdns CR6 .81 C3
Vere Bank SW19 .19 F7
Vereker Dr TW16 .35 A6
Vermont Rd
South Norwood SE19 .22 E2
Sutton SM1 .59 B7
Verney House TW3 .5 C3
Vernon Ave SW20 .39 D7
Vernon Cl Horsham RH12 .218 A4
Ottershaw KT16 .51 D4
West Ewell KT19 .57 C4
Vernon Ct GU9 .125 A2
Vernon Dr Caterham CR3 .100 C5
North Ascot SL5 .28 E7
Vernon Rd Feltham TW13 .14 F6
Mortlake SW14 .7 D4
Sutton SM1 .59 D5
Vernon Way GU2 .108 F2
Vernon Wlk KT20 .97 D7
Verona Dr KT6 .56 E8
Veronica Gdns CR4, SW16 .41 C8
Veronica Rd SW17 .21 B6
Verralls GU22 .70 B2
Verran Rd Balham SW12 .21 B8
Camberley GU15 .65 D3
Versailles Rd SE20 .23 A1
Verulam Ave CR8 .79 C7
Veryan GU21 .69 A2
Vesey Cl GU14 .85 A5
Vestris Rd SE23 .23 D6
Vevers Rd RH2 .139 C6
Vevey St SE23, SE6 .23 F6
Vibart Gdns SW2 .21 F8
Viburnum Ct GU24 .67 E6
Vicarage Ave TW20 .12 B3
Vicarage Cl Farnham GU9 .146 D7
Kingswood KT20 .97 E3
Lingfield RH7 .164 D4
Little Bookham KT23 .94 A2
Vicarage Cres TW20 .12 B3
Vicarage Ct Beckenham BR3 43 E6
East Bedfont TW14 .14 C8
Egham TW20 .12 B2
8 Roehampton SW15 .19 A8
Vicarage Dr
Beckenham BR3 .44 A8
Mortlake SW14 .7 D2
Vicarage Farm Ct TW5 .4 F7
Vicarage Farm Rd
Heston TW3, TW4, TW5 .4 E6
Hounslow TW3, TW4, TW5 .4 E6
Vicarage Fields KT12 .35 C3
Vicarage Gate GU2 .130 A7
Vicarage Gdns Ascot SL5 .29 A4
Grayshott GU26 .188 C3
Mitcham CR4 .40 E6
Mortlake SW14 .7 D2
Vicarage Hill GU10, GU9 .146 D7
Vicarage House 1 KT1 .37 F7
Vicarage La Capel RH5 .178 D6
Farnham GU9 .125 B2
Farnham, Middle Bourne GU9 .146 D7
Haslemere GU27 .207 F6
Heath End GU9 .125 C7
Horley RH6 .160 F4
Laleham TW18 .33 C6
Leatherhead KT22 .95 B5
Send GU23 .90 D1
Wraysbury TW19 .11 F7
Vicarage Rd Ashford TW16 .14 F2
Bagshot GU19 .47 C3
Blackwater GU17 .64 E4
Chobham GU24 .68 E8
Crawley Down RH10 .204 A8
Croydon CR0, CR9 .61 A7
Egham TW20 .12 B3
Kingston u T KT1, KT2 .37 D7
Lingfield RH7 .164 D4
Mortlake SW14 .7 D2
Staines TW18 .12 E5
Sutton SM1 .59 B7
Teddington TW11 .17 A3
Teddington, Hampton Wick KT1, KT8 .37 C8
Twickenham TW2 .5 C1
Twickenham, Strawberry Hill TW2 .16 E6
Woking GU22 .89 F6
Vicarage Way SL3 .1 D7
Vicars Oak Rd SE19 .22 E2
Viceroy Ct 5 CR0 .42 D1
Viceroy Lodge 6 KT6 .37 E4
Vickers Ct 9 TW19 .2 E1
Vickers Dr N KT13 .52 E1
Vickers Dr S KT13 .71 E8
Vickers Rd GU12 .105 F5
Victor Ct RH10 .182 D1
Victor Rd Penge SE20 .23 D1
Teddington TW11 .16 E4
Victor Seymour Inf Sch SM5 .59 F6
Victoria Almshouses
4 Redhill RH1 .119 A4
1 Reigate RH2 .118 C1
Victoria Ave
Camberley GU15 .65 A5
East Molesey KT8 .36 B6
Hackbridge SM5, SM6 .60 A7
Hounslow TW3, TW4 .5 A2
Kingston u T KT6 .37 D3
South Croydon CR2 .61 C1
Victoria Cl
East Molesey KT8 .36 A6
Horley RH6 .161 A3

Victoria Cl *continued*
Oatlands Park KT13 53 D7
Victoria Cotts 7 TW9 7 A6
Victoria Cres Merton SW19 19 F1
West Norwood SE19 22 E2
Victoria Ct Bagshot GU19 47 E1
Guildford GU1 130 D8
Horsham RH13 217 D2
Penge SE26 23 C2
Shalford GU4 130 E3
Victoria Dr
Blackwater GU17 64 C4
Putney SW15, SW19 19 D7
Victoria Entertainments Ctr The GU21 69 E2
Victoria Gdns
Biggin Hill TN16 83 C4
Heston TW5 4 E6
Victoria Jun Sch The TW13 15 B7
Victoria La UB7 3 D8
Victoria Lodge SW19 19 C1
Victoria Mews SW18 20 C7
Victoria Pl 5 Esher KT10 55 B6
Ewell KT17 76 E7
16 Richmond TW10 6 D2
Victoria Rd
Addlestone KT15 52 D6
Aldershot GU11 105 A2
Ascot SL5 29 A4
Coulsdon CR5 79 D4
Cranleigh GU6 174 D3
Crawley RH11 201 C6
Farnborough GU14 85 B4
Farnham GU9 125 C2
Feltham TW13 15 B7
Godalming GU7 150 E4
Guildford GU1 109 E1
Horley RH6 161 B2
Kingston u T KT1 37 F7
Kingston u T, Seething Wells KT6 37 D3
Knaphill GU21 68 E1
Mitcham CR4, SW19 20 F1
Mortlake SW14 7 D4
Oatlands Park KT13 53 D7
Redhill RH1 140 A8
Sandhurst GU47 45 E1
Staines TW18 12 E5
Sutton SM1 59 D5
Teddington TW11 17 A2
Twickenham TW1 17 B8
Woking GU22 69 F2
Victoria St
Englefield Green TW20 11 C2
Horsham RH13 217 D2
Victoria Terr RH4 136 A7
Victoria Villas TW9 6 F3
Victoria Way
East Grinstead RH19 205 F7
Oatlands Park KT13 53 D7
Woking GU21, GU22 69 E2
Victors Dr TW12 15 E2
Victory Ave SM4 40 C4
Victory Bsns Ctr The TW7 5 F3
Victory Cotts KT24 113 E7
Victory Park Rd KT15 52 C6
Victory Pl SE19 22 E2
Victory Rd Chertsey KT16 33 A1
Horsham RH12 217 B3
Merton SW19 20 C1
Victory Road Mews 5 SW19 20 C1
Vidler Cl KT9 56 C4
Vienna Ct GU14 85 A6
View Cl TN16 83 C3
View Terr RH7 165 A1
Viewfield Rd SW18 19 F8
Viggory La GU21 69 C4
Vigilant Cl SE26 23 A4
Viking RG12 26 E4
Viking Ct TW12 36 B8
Village Cl 3 KT13 53 D7
Village Ct SL5 29 C4
Village Gate TW17 34 B4
Village Gdns KT17 57 F1
Village Green Ave TN16 83 E2
Village Green Way TN16 83 E2
Village Rd TW20 32 C6
Village Row SM2 59 A3
Village St RH5 158 B1
Village The SL4 10 B5
Village Way Ashford TW15 14 A4
Beckenham BR3 44 A6
Sanderstead CR2 81 A6
Villas The RH7 163 E8
Villiers Ave Kingston u T KT5 37 F5
Twickenham TW2 15 F7
Villiers Cl KT5 37 F5
Villiers Gr SM2 58 D2
Villiers Mead RG41 25 A6
Villiers Rd Hounslow TW7 5 E5
Kingston u T KT1 37 F6
Penge BR3 43 D7
Villiers The KT13 53 D4
Vinall Gdns RH12 216 D4
Vincam Cl TW2 16 A8
Vincent Ave Sutton SM5 78 D8
3 Tolworth KT5 38 B1
Vincent Cl Chertsey KT16 32 E2
Esher KT10 55 B7
Fetcham KT23 94 B4
Harmondsworth UB7 3 A8
Horsham RH13 217 F2
Vincent Dr Dorking RH4 136 A6
Upper Halliford TW17 34 E6
Vincent House KT3 38 F5
Vincent La RH4 136 A7
Vincent Rd Chertsey KT16 32 E2
Coulsdon CR5 79 C3
Croydon CR0 42 E2
Dorking RH4 136 A7
Hounslow TW7 5 D6
Hounslow, Hounslow West TW4 4 D4
Kingston u T KT1 38 A6
Stoke D'Abernon KT11 73 E3
Vincent Rise RG12 27 E6
Vincent Row TW12 16 C3
Vincent Sq TN16 83 C6
Vincent Wks RH4 136 A7
Vincents Cl CR5 98 F7
Vine Cl Farnborough GU11 105 A6
Rowledge GU10 146 A4
Stanwell TW19 2 A2
Surbiton KT5 37 F3
Sutton SM1 59 C7
Worplesdon GU3 88 D1
Vine Cotts GU6 174 B3
Vine Ct KT12 54 C4
Vine House Cl GU16 86 A3
Vine La GU10 146 A5
Vine Pl TW3 5 B3
Vine Rd Barnes SW13, SW15 7 F4
East Molesey KT8 36 C5
Mortlake SW13, SW15 7 F4
Vine St GU11 105 A1
Vine Way GU10 146 A5
Vineries Cl UB7 3 A8
Viners Cl KT12 35 C3
Viney Bank CR0 62 F2
Vineyard Cl Forest Hill SE6 24 A7
Kingston u T KT1 37 F6
Vineyard Hill Rd SW19 20 A4
Vineyard Path SW14 7 D4
Vineyard Rd TW13 15 A5
Vineyard Row KT1, KT8 37 C8
Vineyard Sch The TW10 6 E1
Vineyard The TW10 6 E2
Vineyards The TW13 15 A5
Vinter Ct TW17 34 A4
Viola Ave Feltham TW14 4 C1
Stanwell TW19 13 E7
Viola Croft RG42 27 F8
Violet Cl CR4 41 A1
Violet Gdns CR0 61 B5
Violet La CR0 61 B5
Violette Szabo House 4 SE27 22 D4
Virginia Ave GU25 31 C4
Virginia Beeches GU25 31 C6
Virginia Cl Ashstead KT21 75 D1
Kingston u T KT3 38 C5
Laleham TW18 33 C6
Weybridge KT13 53 C4
Virginia Ct GU25 31 D5
Virginia Dr GU25 31 C5
Virginia Gdns GU14 85 C2
Virginia Pl KT11 73 A5
Virginia Rd CR7 42 B8
Virginia Water SL5 30 E6
Virginia Water Prep Sch GU25 31 D5
Virginia Water Sta GU25 31 E4
Viscount Gdns KT14 71 E7
Viscount Ind Est SL3 1 E4
Viscount Rd TW19 13 E7
Viscount Way TW6 3 E3
Vivien Cl KT9 56 E3
Vivienne Cl Crawley RH11 181 D1
Twickenham TW1 6 D1
Vivienne House TW18 13 A3
Voewood Cl KT3 38 F3
Vogan Cl RH2 139 B6
Volta Way CR0, CR9 41 F1
Voltaire 14 TW9 6 F6
Voss Ct SW16 21 E2
Vowels Forest Wlk RH19 204 E3
Vowels La RH19 204 E2
Vulcan Bsns Ctr CR9 63 E2
Vulcan Cl Crawley RH11 201 C2
Sandhurst GU47 64 A7
Wallington SM6 60 F3
Vulcan Way
New Addington CR0, CR9 63 E1
Sandhurst GU47 64 B7

W

Waddington Ave CR5, CR8 100 B8
Waddington Cl
Coulsdon CR5 100 B8
Crawley RH11 201 A3
Waddington Way CR7, SE19 42 D8
Waddon Cl CR0, CR9 61 A7
Waddon Court Rd CR0, CR9 61 A7
Waddon Inf Sch CR9 61 A5
Waddon Marsh Way CR0, CR9 41 F1
Waddon New Rd CR0, CR9 61 B8
Waddon Park Ave CR0, CR9 61 A7
Waddon Rd CR0, CR9 61 B7
Waddon Sta CR0 61 A6
Waddon Way CR0, CR2, CR9 61 B4
Wade's La TW11 17 A3
Wadham GU47 45 F1
Wadham Cl Crawley RH10 182 C1
Shepperton TW17 34 C2
Wadhurst Cl SE20 43 B7
Wadlands Brook Rd RH19 185 D5
Wagbullock Rise RG12 27 C3
Wagg Cl RH19 186 A1
Waggon Cl GU2 108 E2
Waggoners Hollow GU19 47 E2
Waggoners Way GU26 188 A4
Waggoners Wells La GU26 188 A2
Wagtail Cl RH12 217 D7
Wagtail Gdns CR2 62 E1
Waights Ct KT2 37 E8
Wain End RH12 217 D5
Wainford Cl SW19 19 D7
Wainwright Gr TW7 5 D3
Wainwrights RH10 201 D3
Waite Davies Rd SE12 24 F8
Wakefield Cl KT14 71 E7
Wakefield Gdns SE19 22 E1
Wakefield House SE22 23 B7
Wakefield Rd 13 TW10 6 D2
Wakehams Green Dr RH10 182 D1
Wakehurst Dr RH10, RH11 201 D3
Wakehurst Mews RH12 216 F1
Wakehurst Path GU21 70 C5
Wakelin House SE23 23 E8
Wakeling House 8 SE27 22 B5
Wakely Cl TN16 83 C1
Walburton Rd CR8 79 C7
Walbury RG12 27 E5
Waldby Ct RH11 201 A3
Waldeck Gr SE27 22 B5
Waldeck Rd Brentford W4 7 A8
Mortlake SW14 7 C4
Waldeck Terr SW14 7 C4
Waldegrave Ct 1 TW11 16 F3
Waldegrave Gdns TW1 16 F5
Waldegrave Pk TW1 16 F4
Waldegrave Rd Penge SE19 22 F1
Teddington TW11 16 F4
Waldegrave Sch for Girls TW2 16 D5
Waldegrove CR0 61 F7
Waldemar Rd SW19 20 A3
Walden Cotts GU3 107 A3
Walden Gdns CR7, SW16 41 F5
Waldens Park Rd GU21 69 C3
Waldens Rd GU21 69 D2
Waldenshaw Rd SE23 23 C7
Waldo Pl SW19 20 E1
Waldorf Cl CR2 61 B2
Waldorf Hts GU17 64 D3
Waldram Cres SE23 23 C7
Waldram Park Rd SE23 23 D7
Waldram Pl 6 SE23 23 C7
Waldron Gdns BR2 44 D6
Waldron Hill RG12 27 F8
Waldron Rd SW17, SW18 20 C6
Waldronhyrst CR0, CR2 61 B6
Waldrons The Croydon CR0 61 C6
Oxted RH8 122 F4
Waldy Rise GU6 174 E4
Wales Ave SM5 59 E5
Walesbeech RH10 202 A5
Waleston Acres SM6 60 C4
Waley's La RH5 177 C1
Walford Rd RH5 136 C3
Walham Rise SW19 19 E2
Walk The Ashford TW16 14 F1
Tandridge RH8 122 A2
Walkden Hall (Hall of Residence) KT2 18 D4
Walker Cl
East Bedfont TW14 14 F8
Hampton TW12 15 F2
Walker Rd RH10 202 C4
Walker's Ridge GU15 65 E5
Walkerscroft Mead SE21 22 C7
Walkfield Dr KT18 77 B2
Walking Bottom GU5 154 C6
Wall Hill Rd RH18, RH19 206 E5
Wallace Cl Fairlands GU3 108 C4
Upper Halliford TW17 34 D5
Wallace Cres SM5 59 F5
Wallace Fields KT17 77 A6
Wallace Fields Cty Inf Sch KT17 77 A6
Wallace Fields Cty Jun Sch KT17 77 A7
Wallace Wlk KT15 52 C6
Wallage La RH10 203 D6
Wallbrook Bsns Ctr TW4 4 B4
Walled Garden The
Loxwood RH14 212 F7
Tadworth KT20 97 D5
Walled Gdn The
Betchworth RH3 137 D8
Sunbury TW16 35 B6
Waller La CR3 100 F4
Wallingford Cl RG12 27 E5
Wallington Ct 10 SM6 60 B4
Wallington High Sch for Boys SM6 60 B6
Wallington High Sch for Girls SM6 60 B2
Wallington Rd GU15 47 A1
Wallington Sq 4 SM6 60 C4
Wallington Sta SM6 60 B4
Wallis Ct RH10 181 D2
Wallis House RH19 185 E1
Wallis Mews KT22 95 A5
Wallis Way RH13 218 A4
Wallner Way RG40 25 E5
Wallop Sch KT13 53 B5
Wallorton Gdns SW14 7 D3
Walmer Cl
Crowthorne RG45 45 C5
Frimley GU16 86 A7
Walmer House 11 SE20 23 C1
Walmsley House 1 SW16 21 C4
Walnut Cl Aldershot GU11 126 A8
Carshalton SM5 59 F5
Epsom KT18 76 F4
Walnut Ct RH13 217 E1
Walnut Dr KT20 97 E3
Walnut Gr SM7 77 D5
Walnut House RH2 139 C7
Walnut La RH11 181 B1
Walnut Mews SM2 59 C3
Walnut Tree Ave CR4 40 E6
Walnut Tree Cl Barnes SW13 7 F6
Belmont SM7 77 E7
Guildford GU1 130 C8
Walnut Tree Gdns GU7 150 E7
Walnut Tree La KT14 71 D7
Walnut Tree Pk GU1 109 C1
Walnut Tree Rd
Brentford TW8 6 E8
Charlton TW17 34 C7
Heston TW5 4 F8
Walpole Ave Chipstead CR5 98 F8
Richmond TW9 6 F5
Walpole Cres 7 TW11 16 F3
Walpole Ct TW2 16 E6
Walpole Gdns TW2 16 E5
Walpole House 3 GU11 105 B2
Walpole Pl 6 TW11 16 F3
Walpole Rd
Croydon CR0, CR9 61 D8
Mitcham SW19 20 D2
Old Windsor SL4 11 B8
Surbiton KT6 37 E3
Teddington TW11 16 F3
Twickenham TW2 16 E6
Walsh CE Jun Sch GU12 106 A1
Walsh Cres CR0 82 E7
Walsh Memorial C of E Inf Sch GU12 105 F1
Walsham Rd TW14 15 B8
Walsingham Gdns KT19 57 F5
Walsingham Rd
Mitcham CR4 40 F4
New Addington CR0 63 C1
Walstead House 2 RH10 201 D5
Walter Cty Inf Sch RG41 25 A6
Walter St 2 KT2 37 E8
Walter's Mead KT21 75 E2
Walter's Rd SE25 42 E5
Waltham Ave GU2 109 B5
Waltham Cl GU47 45 D1
Waltham Rd
Carshalton SM5 40 E1
Caterham CR3 101 B5
Walton Ave Cheam SM3 58 F7
New Malden KT3 38 F5
Walton Bridge Rd KT12, TW17 34 E2
Walton Comm Hospl KT12 54 C8
Walton Ct GU21 70 A3
Walton Dr Horsham RH13 218 C4
North Ascot SL5 28 F8
Walton Gdns TW13 14 F4
Walton Gn CR0 63 C3
Walton Heath RH10 202 D8
Walton La
Lower Halliford TW17 34 D2
Oatlands Park KT12 34 E1
Weybridge KT12, KT13 53 C8
Walton Leigh Special Training Sch KT13 53 F6
Walton on the Hill Cty Prim Sch KT20 97 B3
Walton Park La KT12 54 D8
Walton Pk KT12 54 D8
Walton Rd Ashstead KT18 96 C6
East Molesey KT8, KT12 36 B5
Walton-on-T KT12&KT8 35 E4
Woking GU21 70 A3
Walton St KT20 97 B3
Walton Terr GU21 70 B4
Walton Way CR4 41 C5
Wanborough Dr SW15 19 B7
Wanborough Hill GU3 128 C6
Wanborough La GU6 175 A3
Wanborough Sta GU3 107 C1
Wandle Bank Merton SW19 20 D1
Wallington CR0 60 E7
Wandle Cl Ash GU12 106 A1
Crawley RH10 202 C5
Wandle Court Gdns CR0 60 E7
Wandle Ct Wallington CR0 60 E7
West Ewell KT19 57 C6
Wandle House Catford BR1 24 D3
5 Redhill RH1 118 F2
Wandsworth SW18 20 B8
Wandle Lodge CR0 60 E7
Wandle Prim Sch SW18 20 B7
Wandle Rd
Croydon CR0, CR9 61 C7
Hackbridge SM6 60 B8
Morden CR4, SM4, SW19 40 D4
Upper Tooting SW17 20 E6
Wallington CR0 60 E7
Wandle Side Croydon CR0 60 F7
Hackbridge SM6 60 B7
Wandle Tech Pk CR4 40 F2
Wandle Trad Est CR4 40 F2
Wandle Valley Sch SM5 40 E2
Wandle Way Mitcham CR4 40 F4
Wandsworth SW18 20 B7
Wandsdyke Cl GU16 85 F8
Wandsworth Common Sta SW12 20 F8
Wansford Gn 3 GU21 68 F2
Wanstraw Gr RG12 27 E2
Wantage Cl Bracknell RG12 27 E4
Wantage Cl *continued*
Crawley RH10 202 C3
Wantage Rd GU47 64 D8
Waplings The KT20 97 B3
Wapshott Rd TW18 12 E3
War Coppice Rd CR3 120 D7
War Memorial Homes W4 7 D7
War Memorial Hospl SM5 59 F4
Warbank Cl CR0 63 E1
Warbank Cres CR0 63 E1
Warbank La KT2 18 F1
Warblers Gn KT11 73 F5
Warbleton House 6 RH11 200 F3
Warboys App KT2 18 B2
Warboys Rd KT2 18 B2
Warburton Cl RH19 206 A8
Warburton Rd TW2 16 B7
Warbury La GU21 68 C3
Ward Cl RG40 25 D8
Ward La CR6 81 D2
Ward St GU1 130 D8
Wardle Cl GU19 47 E3
Wardley St SW18 20 B8
Wardrobe The 3 TW9 6 D2
Wards Stone Pk RG12 27 E2
Ware Ct SM1 58 F6
Wareham Cl TW3 5 B3
Wareham Rd RG12 27 F4
Warenne Hts RH1 139 D7
Warenne Rd KT22 94 C5
Warfield Rd Bracknell RG12 27 C8
East Bedfont TW14 14 E8
Hampton TW12 36 B8
Wargrove Dr GU47 64 D8
Warham Rd CR0, CR2 61 C5
Waring St SE27 22 C4
Warkworth Gdns TW7 6 A7
Warlingham Cty Sec Sch CR6 81 A3
Warlingham Park Sch CR6 82 A3
Warlingham Rd CR7 42 B5
Warltersville Way RH6 161 C1
Warminster Gdns SE25 43 A7
Warminster Rd SE25 43 A7
Warminster Sq SE25 43 A7
Warminster Way CR4 41 B7
Warner Ave SM3 58 E8
Warner Cl Crawley RH10 202 C2
Harlington UB3 3 D7
Warner Ct SM3 58 E8
Warner House BR3 24 B2
Warner Rd BR1 24 F1
Warners La GU5 132 E2
Warnford House SW15 7 E1
Warnham CE (Controlled) Sch RH12 216 F8
Warnham Court Rd SM5 59 F3
Warnham Ct Sch RH12 216 F7
Warnham House 9 SW2 21 F8
Warnham Nature Reserve RH12 217 B6
Warnham Rd
Broadbridge Heath RH12 216 D4
Crawley RH10 202 B4
Horsham RH12 217 B5
Warnham Sta RH12 217 C8
Warpole Pk KT13 53 A3
Warramill Rd GU7 151 A5
Warren Ave Belmont SM2 58 F1
Bromley BR1 24 E1
Mortlake SW14, TW10 7 B3
South Croydon CR2 62 D3
Warren Cl Esher KT10 55 B6
Felbridge RH19 184 E3
Sandhurst GU47 64 A8
West Norwood SE21 22 C8
Warren Cnr GU10 124 C7
Warren Ct
18 Beckenham BR3 24 A1
6 Croydon CR0 42 E1
Weybridge KT13 53 A5
Warren Cutting KT2 18 D1
Warren Down RG42 26 E8
Warren Dr Crawley RH11 201 A8
Kingswood KT20 98 A4
Warren Dr N KT5, KT6 38 B1
Warren Dr S KT5 38 C1
Warren Farm Mobile Home Pk GU23 91 B8
Warren Hill KT18 76 D3
Warren House Rd RG40 25 D8
Warren La Oxshott KT22 74 C7
Oxted RH8 123 A1
Woking GU22, GU23 71 B1
Warren Lodge KT20 97 E3
Warren Lodge Dr KT20 97 E3
Warren Mead SM7 77 C4
Warren Mead Cty Inf Sch SM7 77 D4
Warren Mead Cty Jun Sch SM7 77 D4
Warren Park Rd SM1, SM2 59 E4
Warren Pk Kingston u T KT2 18 C2
Warlingham CR6 81 D1
Warren Rd Ashford TW15 14 E1
Banstead KT17, SM7 77 D5
Croydon CR0 42 F1
Farncombe GU7 150 E7
Guildford GU1, GU4 131 A8
Kingston u T KT2 18 C2
Mitcham SW19 20 E2
Purley CR8 80 B8
Reigate RH2 118 B2

Warren Rd *continued*
Twickenham TW2 5 D1
Woodham KT15 52 A1
Warren Rise Frimley GU16 65 F3
Kingston u T KT3 38 D8
Warren Row SL5 28 D7
Warren The
Aldershot GU11 104 F1
Ashstead KT21 95 F7
East Horsley KT24 112 F5
Heath End GU9 125 E8
Heston TW5 4 F7
Kingswood KT20 97 E4
Oxshott KT22 74 D6
Sutton SM2, SM5 59 E2
Worcester Park KT19, KT4 57 D7
Warren Way KT13 53 C4
Warren Wood Cl BR2 63 F8
Warreners La KT13 53 D3
Warrenhyrst GU1 131 A8
Warrenne Rd RH3 137 C7
Warrington Cl RH11 200 E2
Warrington Mews GU11 125 E8
Warrington Rd
Croydon CR0, CR9 61 B7
21 Richmond TW10 6 D2
Warrington Spur SL4 11 B8
Warwick RG12 27 E3
Warwick Ave Staines TW18 13 C2
Thorpe Lea TW20 32 C8
Warwick Cl
Aldershot GU11 126 C8
Frimley GU15 66 B3
Hampton TW12 16 C1
South Holmwood RH5 157 B7
Warwick Ct Beckenham BR2 44 E7
Weybridge KT13 53 A5
Warwick Deeping KT16 51 C5
Warwick Gdns
Ashstead KT21 75 C2
Thames Ditton KT7 36 F4
Thornton Heath CR7 42 A5
Warwick Gr KT5 37 F2
Warwick House 6 KT2 37 E8
Warwick La GU21 89 A8
Warwick Lodge SM1 58 F6
Warwick Quadrant RH1 119 A2
Warwick Rd
Ash Vale GU12 106 A8
Ashford TW15 13 E3
Coulsdon CR5 79 D5
Hounslow TW4 4 B4
Kingston u T KT3 38 C6
Penge SE20 43 B6
Redhill RH1 118 F2
South Holmwood RH5 157 C7
Sutton SM1 59 C5
Teddington KT1 37 C8
Thames Ditton KT7 36 F4
Thornton Heath CR7 42 A6
Twickenham TW2 16 E7
Warwick Sch The RH1 119 A2
Warwick Villas TW20 32 C8
Warwick Wold Rd
Bletchingley RH1 120 A7
Caterham RH1 120 A7
Warwick's Bench Rd
GU1 130 E6
Warwicks Bench GU1 130 D6
Wasdale Cl GU47 45 D2
Washington Cl RH2 118 A3
Washington Ct SW17 20 F2
Washington Rd
Crawley RH11 200 E3
Kingston u T KT1 38 A7
North Cheam KT4 39 B1
Washpond La CR6 82 C1
Wasp Green La RH1 162 C8
Wassand Cl RH10 202 A6
Wastdale Rd SE23 23 D7
Watchetts Cty Jun Sch
GU15 65 B2
Watchetts Dr GU15 65 C2
Watchetts Lake Cl GU15 65 D3
Watchetts Rd GU15 65 B4
Watchmoor Pk GU15 65 A3
Watchmoor Rd GU15 65 A4
Watchmoor Trade Ctr
GU15 65 A3
Watcombe Cotts TW9 7 A8
Watcombe Rd SE25 43 B4
Water La
Abinger Common RH5 155 B8
Albury GU4, GU5 132 B5
Bisley GU24 87 E8
Cobham KT11 73 F5
Enton Green GU8 171 B4
Farnborough GU14 85 A7
Farnham GU9 125 F4
Kingston u T KT1 37 D8
Limpsfield RH8 123 A8
Lingfield TN8 165 D7
Little Bookham KT23, KT24 93 E1
Richmond TW10, TW9 6 D2
South Godstone RH9 142 D5
Twickenham TW1 17 A7
Wormley GU8 171 B4
Water Lea RH10 202 A5
Water Mill Way TW13 16 A6
Water Splash La SL5 29 E8
Water Tower Hill CR0, CR2 61 D6
Water View RH6 161 C3
Waterbank Rd SE6 24 C4
Watercress Way GU21 69 B2
Waterden Cl GU1 130 F8
Waterden Rd GU1 130 E8
Waterer Gdns KT20 77 E1
Waterer House SE6 24 C4
Waterer Rise SM6 60 D4
Waterers Rise GU21 68 D2
Waterfall Cl GU25 31 A6
Waterfall Cotts SW19 20 D2
Waterfall Rd SW19 20 D2
Waterfall Terr SW17 20 E2
Waterfield KT20 97 B7
Waterfield Cl RH13 217 E3
Waterfield Cty Fst Sch
RH11 200 E4
Waterfield Dr CR6 101 C8
Waterfield Gdns
Crawley RH11 200 E4
South Norwood SE25 42 E4
Waterfield Gn KT20 97 B7
Waterfields KT22 95 B8
Waterford Cl KT11 73 E8
Waterford Way RG40 25 C6
Watergardens The KT2 18 C2
Waterham Rd RG12 27 B3
Waterhouse Ct 5 TW11 16 F3
Waterhouse La
Bletchingley RH1 121 A3
Coulsdon CR8 100 C8
Kingswood KT20 97 E6
Waterhouse Mead GU47 64 D7
Waterlands La RH12 196 E1
Waterloo Cl
Camberley GU15 66 B7
East Bedfont TW14 14 F7
Waterloo Cres RG40 25 E4
Waterloo Pl TW9 7 A8
Waterloo Rd
Aldershot GU12 105 C1
Carshalton SM1 59 D5
Crowthorne RG45 45 B4
Epsom KT17, KT19 76 D6
Wokingham RG40 25 F5
Waterlow Rd RH2 139 D8
Watermans Bsns Pk The
TW18 12 E4
Watermans Ct 12 TW8 6 D8
Watermead
East Bedfont TW14 14 E7
Tadworth KT20 97 B6
Woking GU21 68 F3
Watermead La CR4 40 F2
Watermead Rd SE6 24 C4
Watermeads High Sch
SM4 40 D3
Watermen's Sq 1 SE20 23 C1
Watermill Cl TW10 17 C5
Watermill Way SW19 40 C8
Waterperry La GU24 49 F1
Waters Dr TW18 12 F4
Waters Rd Catford SE6 24 E5
Kingston u T KT1 38 B7
Waters Sq KT1 38 B6
Watersedge KT19 57 C6
Waterside Beckenham BR3 44 A8
East Grinstead RH19 186 B1
Horley RH6 161 A5
Waterside Cl
Crawley RH11 200 E4
Godalming GU7 151 A5
Surbiton KT6 56 E8
Waterside Dr KT12 35 B4
Waterside La GU7 150 C3
Waterside Mews GU1 109 C3
Waterside Rd GU1 109 D4
Waterside Trad Est KT15 52 E6
Waterside Way
Wimbledon SW17 20 C3
2 Woking GU21 69 B1
Waterslade RH1 118 E1
Watersmeet Cl GU4 110 A6
Watersplash Cl KT1 37 E6
Watersplash Rd TW17 34 A5
Waterway Rd Fetcham KT22 95 A5
Leatherhead KT22 95 A5
Watery La Chobham GU24 49 D1
Merton SW19, SW20 39 F7
Wates Way CR4 40 F3
Watford Cl GU1 109 F1
Wathen Rd RH4 136 B8
Watlings Cl CR0 43 E3
Watlington Gr SE26 23 E3
Watney Cotts SW14 7 C4
Watney Rd SW14 7 C4
Watneys Rd CR4 41 D4
Watson Ave SM3 58 E8
Watson Cl Crawley RH10 202 C3
Mitcham SW19 20 E1
Watson House 3 SW2 21 E8
Watson Rd RH4 135 C6
Watt's La Tadworth KT20 97 D5
Teddington TW11 17 A3
Watt's Mead KT20 97 D5
Wattenden Prim Sch CR8 80 B3
Wattendon Rd CR8 80 B3
Watts Cl KT20 97 D5
Watts Lea GU21 69 A4
Watts Rd Farnborough GU14 84 F5
Thames Ditton KT7 37 A2
Wavel Ct 7 SW16 21 E5
Wavel Pl SE19, SE26 22 F4
Wavell Sch The GU14 105 B7
Wavendene Ave TW20 12 C1
Waveney House 5 RH1 118 F1
Waveney Wlk RH10 202 B4
Waverleigh Rd GU6 174 E1
Waverley RG12 26 E4
Waverley Abbey GU9 147 B7
Waverley Abbey CE Jun
Sch GU10 147 D5
Waverley Ave Kenley CR8 80 E3
Sutton SM1 59 C8
Tolworth KT5 38 C3
Twickenham TW2, TW4 16 A7
Waverley Cl Farnham GU9 125 D2
Frimley GU15 65 F4
Waverley Ct
Horsham RH12 217 B2
1 Woking GU22 69 E1
Waverley Dr
Addlestone KT16 51 D7
Ash Vale GU12 106 A6
Camberley GU15 65 F5
Virginia Water GU25 31 A5
Waverley Gdns GU12 106 A6
Waverley La
Farnham GU10, GU9 147 C8
Farnham, Compton GU9 125 E1
Waverley Pl KT22 95 B5
Waverley Rd Bagshot GU19 47 E3
Croydon SE25 43 B6
Farnborough GU14 85 D3
Oxshott KT11, KT22 74 B5
Stoneleigh KT17, KT4 58 B5
Weybridge KT13 53 A5
Waverley Way SM2, SM5 59 E4
Waverton Rd SW18 20 C8
Wavertree Ct 5 SW2 21 E7
Wavertree Rd SW2 21 F7
Way The RH2 118 D2
Waye Ave TW5 4 A6
Wayland Cl RG12 27 F5
Waylands Mead BR3 44 B8
Waylett Pl SE27 22 B5
Wayman Rd GU14 84 E8
Wayneflete Tower Ave
KT10 55 A7
Waynflete Ave CR0, CR9 61 B7
Waynflete La GU9 124 F2
Waynflete St SW18 20 C6
Ways End GU15 65 E4
Wayside Capel RH5 178 D6
Crawley RH11 200 E4
Mortlake SW14 7 C2
New Addington CR0 63 B4
Wayside Ct Hounslow TW7 5 E5
Twickenham TW1 6 C1
Woking GU21 68 E3
WC Lee's Resthouses
GU20 48 D4
Weald CE Prim Sch The
RH5 157 D3
Weald Cl GU4 130 E3
Weald Day Hospl The
RH11 201 C6
Weald Dr RH10 202 A4
Weald The RH19 185 F4
Weald View Cotts RH5 156 D3
Weald Way Caterham CR3 120 E8
Reigate RH2 139 C5
Wealdon Ct 1 GU2 108 F1
Wealdstone Rd SM3 58 F8
Weare St Capel RH5 178 B4
Ockley RH5 177 F1
Weasdale Ct GU21 68 F3
Weatherall Cl KT15 52 B5
Weatherhill Cl RH6 161 F3
Weatherhill Cotts RH6 162 A4
Weatherhill Rd RH6 162 A3
Weatherill Ct SE25 43 B3
Weaver Cl RH11 200 E5
Weaver Wlk SE27 22 B4
Weavers Cl TW7 5 E3
Weavers Gdns GU9 145 F7
Weavers Yd GU9 125 B2
Webb Cl Bagshot GU19 47 E1
Crawley RH11 201 B1
Webb Ct RG40 25 E8
Webb House TW13 15 E5
Webb Rd GU8 170 C6
Webster Cl KT11, KT22 74 B5
Websters Cl GU22 89 B7
Weddell Rd RH10 201 F3
Wedgewood Ct BR2 44 F5
Wedgwood Way SE19 22 C1
Wedgwoods TN16 103 C6
Weeks House TW10 17 C4
Weighbridge Rd KT15 52 B2
Weighton Rd SE20 43 B7
Weihurst Ct SM1 59 E5
Weihurst Gdns SM1 59 D5
Weir Ave GU14 85 A3
Weir Cl GU14 85 A3
Weir House 8 SW12 21 C8
Weir Pl TW18 32 E8
Weir Rd Chertsey KT16 33 B2
Streatham SW12 21 C8
Walton-on-T KT12 35 A3
Wimbledon SW18, SW19 20 B5
Weir Wood Resr
(Nature Reserve) RH19 205 E2
Weirbrook RH10 202 A3
Welbeck RG12 26 E4
Welbeck Cl Ewell KT17 58 A3
Farnborough GU14 84 F3
New Malden KT3 38 F4
Welbeck Rd SM1, SM5 59 D8
Welbeck Wlk SM5 40 D1
Welcome Cotts CR3 102 A4
Welcome Terr CR3 80 F3
Welcomes Rd CR8 80 C3
Weldon Ct CR7 42 B4
Weldon Dr KT8 35 F5
Weldon Way RH1 119 D6
Welford Pl SW19 19 E4
Welham Rd SW16, SW17 21 B2
Welhouse Rd SM5 59 E8
Well Cl Camberley GU15 65 B4
Well Cl *continued*
Streatham SW16 21 F4
Woking GU21 69 C2
Well Farm Rd CR3, CR6 101 A8
Well House SM7 78 B4
Well La Haslemere GU27 208 D6
Mortlake SW14 7 C2
Woking GU21 69 C2
Well Path GU21 69 C2
Well Way KT18 76 A5
Welland Cl SL3 1 B8
Wellburn Cl GU47 64 B7
Weller Cl RH10 202 D5
Weller Dr GU15 65 C3
Wellesford Cl SM7 77 F2
Wellesley Cl
Ash Vale GU12 105 F7
Bagshot GU19 47 C3
Wellesley Court Rd 1
CR0, CR9 61 D8
Wellesley Cres TW2 16 E5
Wellesley Ct Cheam SM3 39 E1
Twickenham TW2 16 E5
Wellesley Garden GU9 125 C7
Wellesley Gate 3 GU12 105 B1
Wellesley Gr CR0, CR9 61 D8
Wellesley Rd
Aldershot GU11 104 E2
Croydon CR0 42 C1
Rushmoor GU10 168 C6
Sutton SM2 59 C4
Twickenham TW2 16 E5
Wellfield RH19 206 C7
Wellfield Gdns SM5 59 E2
Wellfield Rd SW16 21 F4
Wellhouse Rd
Beckenham BR3 44 A5
Betchworth RH3 137 D6
Wellington Ave
Aldershot GU11 104 F2
Hounslow TW3, TW4 5 A2
North Cheam KT4 58 C7
Virginia Water GU25 31 B4
Wentworth GU25 31 B4
Wellington Cl
Crawley RH10 182 E1
Sandhurst GU47 64 C8
Walton-on-T KT12 34 F1
Wellington Coll RG45 45 A3
Wellington Cotts KT24 112 E6
Wellington Cres KT3 38 C6
Wellington Ct
Stanwell TW19 13 E8
5 Surbiton KT6 37 E3
Teddington TW12 16 D3
Wellington Ctr The GU11 105 A2
Wellington Dr
Bracknell RG12 27 E4
Wallington CR8 60 F1
Wellington Gdns
Aldershot GU11 104 F1
Teddington TW12, TW2 16 D4
Wellington La GU9 125 D7
Wellington Pl
Cobham KT11 73 C7
Farncombe GU7 150 E7
Wellington Prim Sch TW3 4 F5
Wellington Rd
Ashford TW15 13 E3
Caterham CR3 100 C5
Crowthorne RG45 45 C4
Hatton TW14 3 E2
Horsham RH12, RH13 217 D2
Sandhurst GU47 64 C8
Teddington TW12, TW2 16 D4
Thornton Heath CR0 42 B2
Wimbledon SW19 20 A6
Wokingham RG40 25 B5
Wellington Rd N TW4 4 F4
Wellington Rd S TW4 4 F3
Wellington Rdbt GU11 104 E2
Wellington St 8 GU11 105 A2
Wellington Terr
6 Knaphill GU21 68 E1
Sandhurst GU47 64 C8
Wellington Town Rd
RH19 185 D2
Wellington Way
Byfleet KT13 52 F1
Horley RH6 160 F5
Weybridge KT13 52 F1
Wellingtonia House KT15 52 A5
Wellmeadow Rd SE13, SE6 24 E7
Wellow Wlk SM5 40 D1
Wells Cl
Great Bookham KT23 94 C3
Horsham RH12 216 F2
Wells Cotts GU9 146 A7
Wells La Ascot SL5 29 B5
Normandy GU3 107 C4
Wells Lea RH19 185 D3
Wells Meadow RH19 185 D3
Wells Park Ct SE26 23 B4
Wells Park Rd SE21, SE26 23 B4
Wells Pl RH1 119 B6
Wells Rd Crawley RH10 201 E2
Epsom KT18 76 B4
Guildford GU4 110 C4
Wells The GU27 208 C6
Wellside Gdns SW14 7 C2
Wellwood Cl
Coulsdon CR5, CR8 79 E5
Horsham RH13 218 B4
Wellwynds Rd GU6 174 E2
Welwyn Ave TW14 3 F1
Welwyn Cl RH11 200 E2
Wembley Rd TW12 36 A8
Wembury Pk RH7 163 E1
Wend The CR5 79 D5
Wendela Cl GU22 69 F1
Wendley Dr KT15 51 F1
Wendling Rd SM1, SM5 59 D8
Wendover Dr Frimley GU16 66 C3
New Malden KT3 38 F3
Wendover Pl TW18 12 D3
Wendover Rd TW18, TW20 12 D3
Wendron Cl 2 GU21 69 A1
Wendy Cres GU2 109 A3
Wenlock Cl RH11 201 A4
Wenlock Edge RH4 136 C5
Wensleydale RH11 201 C3
Wensleydale Dr GU15 66 D5
Wensleydale Gdns TW12 16 B1
Wensleydale Rd TW12 16 B1
Wentland Cl SE6 24 D6
Wentland Rd SE6 24 D6
Wentworth Ave SL5 28 C7
Wentworth Cl
Ash Vale GU12 106 A7
Ashford TW15 14 B4
Heath End GU9 125 F6
Long Ditton KT6 56 D8
Morden SM4 40 A2
Ripley GU23 91 B6
Wentworth Club GU25 31 A4
Wentworth Cres GU12 106 A6
Wentworth Ct
20 Kingston u T KT6 37 E4
Twickenham TW2 16 E5
Wentworth Dr
Crawley RH10 202 D7
Wentworth GU25 30 F5
Wentworth House KT15 52 B6
Wentworth Rd CR0 42 A2
Wentworth Way
Hamsey Green CR2 81 A4
North Ascot SL5 28 C7
Werndee Rd SE25 43 A5
Wesco Ct GU21 70 A3
Wescott Cty Inf Sch RG40 25 D6
Wescott Rd RG40 25 D6
Wesley Ave TW3 4 F5
Wesley Cl Crawley RH11 200 E3
Horley RH6 161 A5
Reigate RH2 138 F8
Wesley Dr TW20 12 A2
Wesley Pl SL4 9 B6
Wessels KT20 97 D6
Wessex Ave SW19 40 A6
Wessex Cl KT1, KT2 38 B8
Wessex Ct 4 TW19 2 E1
Wessex Pl GU9 125 C1
Wessex Rd TW19, TW6 2 E4
Wesson House 3 CR0 43 A1
West Ashtead Cty Prim
Sch KT21 95 E7
West Ave Crawley RH10 202 A8
Heath End GU9 125 D7
Redhill RH1 140 A3
Wallington CR0, SM6 60 E5
Whiteley Village KT12, KT13 53 E2
West Bank RH4 136 A6
West Barnes La
West Barnes KT3, SW20 39 B6
Wimbledon KT3, SW20 39 E4
West Byfleet Cty Inf Sch
KT14 71 B7
West Byfleet Cty Jun Sch
KT14 71 B7
West Cl Ashford TW15 13 E4
Heath End GU9 125 D7
West Cross Ctr TW8 6 B8
West Cross Way TW8 6 B8
West Croydon Sta CR9 42 C1
West Ct Guildford GU4 110 B5
Hounslow TW7 5 C7
West Down KT23 114 B8
West Dr Belmont SM2 58 E2
Burgh Heath KT20 77 D1
Streatham SW16, SW17 21 C4
Sutton SM5 59 D1
Wentworth GU25 30 E2
Woodham KT15 52 B2
West Dulwich Sta SE21 22 D7
West End Cty Inf Sch
GU11 104 F2
West End Gdns KT10 54 F5
West End Gr GU9 125 A2
West End La
Chiddingfold GU27 190 E1
Esher KT10 54 F4
Frensham GU10 146 B1
Harlington UB7 3 C7
West Ewell Cty Inf Sch
KT19 57 D5
West Ewell Cty Jun Sch
KT19 57 D5
West Farm Ave KT21 95 D8
West Farm Cl KT21 95 C8
West Farm Dr KT21 95 D8
West Flexford La GU3 128 E8
West Gdns Ewell KT17 57 F1
Mitcham SW19 20 E2
West Gr KT12 54 B6
West Green Cty Fst Sch
RH11 201 C7
West Green Dr RH11 201 C6
West Hall Rd TW9 7 B6
West Heath GU24 87 D4
West Heath Rd GU14 84 F4
West Hill Biggin Hill BR6 83 F7
Dormans Park RH19 185 E6
East Grinstead RH19 205 D8
Elstead GU8 148 C3
Epsom KT18, KT19 76 C6
Oxted RH8 122 D5

West Hill *continued*
Putney SW15 19 D8
South Croydon CR2 61 E2
Woking GU22 89 E8
West Hill Ave KT19 76 C7
West Hill Bank RH8 122 D5
West Hill Cl
Brookwood GU24 88 B7
Elstead GU8 148 C3
West Hill Rd
Wandsworth SW18 20 A8
Woking GU22 89 E8
West Hill Sch KT22 75 A1
West Hoathly Rd RH19 205 D4
West House Penge SE20 23 D1
9 Streatham SW12 21 C8
West House Cl SW19 19 E7
West La
East Grinstead RH19 205 D8
Wotton RH5 134 D4
West Leigh RH19 205 E7
West Mead KT19 57 E4
West Mead Sch RG40 25 E6
West Meads GU2 129 F8
West Middlesex Univ Hospl TW7 6 A5
West Mount GU2 130 C7
West Norwood Sta SE27 22 B5
West Oak BR3 44 D8
West Palace Gdns KT13 53 B7
West Par RH12 217 C4
West Park Ave TW9 7 B6
West Park Cl TW5 4 F8
West Park Hospl KT19 75 E7
West Park Rd
Domewood RH10 183 F5
Epsom KT19 75 F7
Horne RH7, RH10 184 B7
Richmond TW9 7 A6
West Pl SW19 19 C3
West Ramp TW6 3 A6
West Rd Bracknell RG40 26 D2
Camberley GU15 65 D5
Chessington KT9 75 C8
East Bedfont TW14 14 D8
Farnborough GU14 85 B8
Guildford GU1 130 E8
Kingston u T KT2, KT3 38 C8
Reigate RH2 139 B8
Weybridge KT13 53 B3
West Ring GU10 126 F7
West Sheen Vale TW9 6 F3
West Side Comm SW19 19 C3
West St Carshalton SM5 59 F6
Crawley RH11 201 D5
Croydon CR0, CR9 61 C6
Dorking RH4 136 A7
Dormansland RH7 165 A1
East Grinstead RH19 205 E8
Epsom KT18, KT19 76 C6
Ewell KT17 57 F1
Farnham GU9 125 A2
Haslemere GU27 208 C6
Horsham RH12 217 C2
Reigate RH2 117 F1
Sutton SM1 59 B5
Woking GU21 69 F2
West Street La SM5 59 F6
West Street Pl 1
CR0, CR9 61 C6
West Surrey Estates TW15 34 C8
West Sutton Sta SM1 59 A6
West Temple Sheen SW14 7 B2
West Thames Coll TW7 5 E6
West Thornton Prim Sch CR0 41 F3
West View TW14 14 C8
West View Ave CR3 80 F1
West View Gdns RH19 205 E8
West View Rd
Headley Down GU35 187 C4
Warlingham CR6 101 B8
West Way Crawley RH10 202 A7
Croydon CR0 62 E7
Heston TW5 4 F6
Shepperton TW17 34 D3
Slinfold RH13 215 D3
Sutton SM2, SM5 59 D1
West Wickham BR4 44 E3
West Way Gdns CR0 62 D8
West Wickham Sta BR3 44 C2
Westacres KT10 54 F3
Westbank Rd TW12 16 C2
Westborough Cty Prim Sch GU2 108 F2
Westbourne Ave SM3 58 E8
Westbourne Dr SE23 23 D6
Westbourne House
Heston TW5 5 A8
9 Twickenham TW1 17 B8
Westbourne Prim Sch SM1 59 A7
Westbourne Rd
Croydon CR0 42 F3
Feltham TW13 14 F5
Penge SE26 23 D2
Sandhurst GU47 64 E7
Staines TW18 13 B1
Westbrook RH18 206 E3
Westbrook Ave TW12 15 F1
Westbrook Gdns RG12 27 D8
Westbrook Hill GU8 148 C3
Westbrook Rd
Godalming GU7 150 C5
Heston TW5 4 F7
South Norwood CR7 42 D7
Staines TW18 12 F3
Westbury Ave KT10 55 F4
Westbury Cl
Crowthorne RG45 45 B6
Shepperton TW17 34 B3
Whyteleafe CR3 80 F1
Westbury Ct BR3 44 B8
Westbury Gdns GU9 125 E4
Westbury House Sch KT3 38 D4
Westbury Pl 2 TW8 6 D8
Westbury Rd
Beckenham BR3 43 E6
Feltham TW13 15 D6
New Malden KT3 38 D4
Penge SE20 43 D8
Thornton Heath CR0 42 D3
Westcar La KT12 54 B5
Westcombe Ave CR0 41 F2
Westcombe Cl RG12 27 E2
Westcoombe Ave SW20 38 F8
Westcote Rd SW16 21 C3
Westcott C of E Fst Sch RH4 135 D5
Westcott Cl CR0 63 B2
Westcott Rd RH4 135 F7
Westcott St RH4 135 B6
Westcott Way SM2 58 C1
Westcroft Gdns SM4, SW20 39 F5
Westcroft Rd SM5, SM6 60 A6
Westdene GU7 150 E3
Westdene Meadows GU6 174 A3
Westdene Way KT13 53 E7
Westdown Rd SE13, SE6 24 A8
Westende RG40 25 D6
Westende Cty Jun Sch RG40 25 D6
Westerdale Dr GU16 66 B3
Westerfolds Cl GU22 70 C2
Westerham 13 KT6 37 E4
Westerham Cl
Belmont SM2 59 A1
New Haw KT15 52 C4
Westerham Lodge 10 BR3 24 A1
Westerham Rd RH8, TN16 123 C6
Westerley Cres SE26, SE6 23 F3
Westermain KT15 52 C1
Western Apron Rd RH6 181 F8
Western Ave Chertsey KT16 33 A6
Thorpe TW20 32 B6
Western Cl KT16 33 A6
Western Ctr The RG12 26 F7
Western Dr TW17 34 D3
Western La SW12 21 A8
Western Perimeter Rd
TW19, TW6, UB7 2 B5
Western Perimeter Rd Rdbt
TW19 2 C2
Western Rd
Aldershot GU11 104 E1
Bracknell RG12 26 F7
Mitcham CR4, SW19 40 E7
Sutton SM1 59 A5
Westfield Ashstead KT21 75 F1
Peaslake RH5 154 E8
Reigate RH2 118 B4
Westfield Ave
Sanderstead CR2, CR8 80 E6
Woking GU22 89 E7
Westfield Cl SM1 58 F6
Westfield Comm GU22 89 E5
Westfield Ct
Kingston u T KT6 37 D4
New Haw KT15 52 D1
Westfield Dr KT23 94 B5
Westfield Gr GU22 89 F7
Westfield La GU10 145 E6
Westfield Par KT15 52 D1
Westfield Prim Sch GU22 89 E6
Westfield Rd
Beckenham BR3 43 F7
Camberley GU15 65 B2
Cheam SM1 58 F6
Crawley RH11 201 B6
Guildford GU1 109 E5
Kingston u T KT6 37 D4
Mitcham CR4 40 F7
Thornton Heath CR0, CR9 61 B8
Walton-on-T KT12 35 E2
Woking GU22 89 E5
Westfield Way GU22 89 F5
Westfields SW13 7 F4
Westfields Ave SW13, SW14 7 E4
Westfields Sch SW13 7 F4
Westgate Rd
Beckenham BR3 44 C8
Croydon SE25 43 B5
Westglade GU14 84 D4
Westhall Pk CR6 101 C8
Westhall Rd CR6 101 B8
Westhay Gdns SW14 7 B2
Westhumble St RH5 115 B4
Westland Cl TW19 2 E1
Westland Dr BR2, BR4 63 F8
Westlands RH13 217 E3
Westlands Ct
East Molesey KT8 36 E5
Epsom KT18 76 C4
Westlands Way RH8 122 D8
Westleas RH6 160 E5
Westlees Cl RH5 136 D4
Westleigh Ave CR5 79 B3
Westmacott Dr TW14 14 F7
Westmark Point 13 SW15 19 B7
Westmead
Farnborough GU14 85 B3
8 Farnham GU9 125 B2
Putney SW15 19 B8
Woking GU21 69 B2
Westmead Dr RH1 140 A1
Westmead Rd SM1 59 D6
Westminster Ave CR7 42 B7
Westminster Cl
East Bedfont TW14 15 A7
Teddington TW11 17 A3
Westminster Ct
Old Woking GU22 90 B6
South Norwood CR7 42 C7
Westminster Rd
Carshalton SM1, SM5 59 D8
Crawley RH10 202 C5
Westmoat Cl BR3 24 C1
Westmont Rd KT10 55 E8
Westmore Rd TN16 103 C7
Westmoreland Dr SM2 59 B2
Westmoreland Rd
Barnes SW13 7 F6
Beckenham BR2, BR3 44 F5
Westmoreland Terr SE20 23 B1
Westmorland Cl
Epsom KT19 57 E2
3 Twickenham TW1 6 B1
Westmorland Ct 12 KT6 37 D2
Westmorland Dr GU15 66 B3
Westmorland Sq CR4 41 E4
Westmorland Way CR4 41 E4
Weston Ave
Addlestone KT15 52 B6
East Molesey KT8 35 F5
Thames Ditton KT10, KT7 36 E2
Weston Cl Coulsdon CR5 99 F7
Farncombe GU7 150 E6
Weston Ct Farncombe GU7 150 E6
3 Kingston u T KT1 37 E6
Weston Fields GU5 132 C4
Weston Gdns Hounslow TW7 5 E6
Pyrford GU22 70 E3
Weston Gn KT7 36 E1
Weston Gr Bagshot GU19 47 F2
Bromley BR1 44 F8
Weston Green Prep Sch KT7 36 E1
Weston Green Rd KT7 36 E2
Weston Lea KT24 92 D2
Weston Park Cl KT7 36 E1
Weston Pk Kingston u T KT1 37 E7
Thames Ditton KT10, KT7 36 E1
Weston Rd Bromley BR1 24 F1
Ewell KT17 76 E8
Guildford GU2 109 A2
Thames Ditton KT7 36 E1
Weston Way GU22 70 E3
Westons Cl RH12 217 D7
Westover Cl SM2 59 B2
Westover Rd SW18 20 C8
Westow Hill SE19 22 F2
Westow St SE19 22 E2
Westpoint BR2 44 D6
Westview 5 GU22 69 F1
Westview Cl RH1 139 E6
Westville Rd KT7 37 A2
Westward Ho GU1 109 F3
Westwates Cl RG12 27 D8
Westway Caterham CR3 100 D5
Copthorne RH10 183 A3
Crawley RH6 182 B7
Guildford GU2 108 F3
West Barnes KT3, SW20 39 C5
Wormley GU8 190 F8
Westway Cl SW20 39 B6
Westway Ct CR3 100 D4
Westway Gdns RH1 119 A4
Westways KT19 57 F6
Westwell Rd SW16 21 E2
Westwell Road App SW16 21 E2
Westwick Gdns TW4, TW5 4 B5
Westwood Ave
South Norwood SE19 42 C8
Woodham KT15 70 F7
Westwood Cl KT10 55 C7
Westwood Ct
3 Forest Hill SE23 23 C7
Guildford GU2 108 F2
7 Wimbledon SW19 19 F3
Westwood Gdns SW13 7 F4
Westwood Hill SE19, SE26 23 B4
Westwood La
Flexford GU3 107 A2
Normandy GU3 107 A2
Wanborough GU3 128 B7
Westwood Park Cty Prim Sch GU2 108 E1
Westwood Pk SE23 23 B8
Westwood Rd
Coulsdon CR5 79 D1
Mortlake SW13, SW15 7 F4
Windlesham GU20 48 E6
Westwood Sch SE19 22 D1
Wetheral Ct SW17 20 D4
Wetherby Ct SE25 42 E7
Wetherby Gdns 2 GU14 85 C1
Wetherby House GU15 65 D7
Wetherby Way KT9 56 E3
Wettern Cl CR2 61 E1
Wetton Pl TW20 11 F3
Wexfenne Gdns GU22 71 B3
Wexford Rd SW12 20 F8
Wey Ave KT16 33 A6
Wey Cl Ash GU12 106 A1
Camberley GU15 65 B5
West Byfleet KT14 71 B6
Wey Ct Farncombe GU7 151 A6
New Haw KT15 52 D2
West Ewell KT19 57 C6
Wey Hill GU27 208 A6
Wey House Sch GU5 151 E8
Wey Manor Rd KT15 52 D2
Wey Rd Godalming GU7 151 A5
Weybridge KT13 52 F7
Wey Ret Pk KT14 71 E7
Wey View Ct GU1 130 C8
Weybank GU23 71 E3
Weybank Cl GU9 125 C3
Weybarton KT14 71 F6
Weybourne Cty Inf Sch GU9 125 E6
Weybourne Pl CR2 61 D1
Weybourne Rd GU11, GU9 125 E6
Weybourne St SW18 20 C6
Weybridge Bsns Pk KT15 52 E6
Weybridge Hospl KT13 53 A6
Weybridge House KT13 53 D5
Weybridge Pk KT13 53 B5
Weybridge Rd
Addlestone KT15, KT13 52 E6
Thornton Heath CR7 42 A5
Weybridge KT13, KT15 52 E6
Weybridge Sta KT13 53 A4
Weybrook Dr GU4 110 B6
Weycombe Rd GU27 208 C8
Weydon Hill Cl GU9 146 B8
Weydon Hill Rd GU9 146 C8
Weydon La Farnham GU9 146 A8
Wrecclesham GU9 145 F8
Weydon Mill La GU9 125 B1
Weydon Sch GU9 145 F7
Weydown Cl
Guildford GU2 109 A6
Putney SW19 19 E7
Weydown Ct GU27 208 B7
Weydown Ind Est GU27 208 B7
Weydown La GU2 109 A6
Weydown Rd GU27 208 B7
Weyfield Prim Sch GU1 109 D4
Weylands Pk KT13 53 D4
Weylea Ave GU1, GU4 110 A4
Weymead Cl KT16 33 C1
Weymede KT14 71 F7
Weymouth Ct Belmont SM2 59 A3
18 Streatham SW2 21 F8
Weyside GU9 125 C2
Weyside Cl KT14 71 F7
Weyside Gdns GU1 109 C3
Weyside Pk GU7 151 A5
Weyside Rd GU1 109 B3
Weysprings GU27 208 A6
Weyvern Pk GU3 130 B1
Weyview Cl GU1 109 C3
Weywood Cl GU9 125 F7
Weywood La GU9 125 E7
Whaley Rd RG40 25 D8
Wharf Bridge Rd TW7 6 B4
Wharf La Send GU23 90 C4
Twickenham TW1 17 A7
Wharf Rd Ash GU12 106 A4
Frimley GU16 86 A6
Guildford GU1 109 C1
Wraysbury TW19 11 D8
Wharf St GU7 150 E4
Wharf Way GU16 86 A6
Wharfedale Gdns
CR7, SW16 41 F6
Wharfenden Way GU16 85 F6
Wharncliffe Gdns SE25 42 E7
Wharncliffe Rd SE25 42 E7
Whateley Rd
Guildford GU2 109 B5
Penge SE20 23 D1
Whatley Ave SW20 39 E6
Whatley Gn RG12 27 B3
Whatman Rd SE23 23 D8
Whatmore Cl TW19 2 A1
Wheat Knoll CR8 80 C3
Wheatash Rd KT15 52 B8
Wheatfield Way
Horley RH6 161 C4
Kingston u T KT1 37 E7
Wheathill House SE20 43 B7
Wheathill Rd SE20 43 B6
Wheatlands TW5 5 A8
Wheatlands Rd SW17 21 A5
Wheatley RG12 26 E3
Wheatley House 3 SW15 19 A8
Wheatley Rd TW7 5 F4
Wheatley's Ait
Lower Halliford TW16 35 A4
Sunbury TW16 35 A4
Wheatsheaf Cl
Horsham RH12 217 E5
Ottershaw KT16 51 D4
Woking GU21 69 F3
Wheatsheaf La TW18 12 F1
Wheatstone Cl
Crawley RH10 182 B3
Mitcham SW19 40 E8
Wheeler Ave RH8 122 D6
Wheeler La GU8 170 E6
Wheeler Rd RH10 202 B4
Wheelers La
Brockham RH3 137 C7
Epsom KT18 76 C5
Smallfield RH6 162 B3
Wheelers Way RH19 184 E3
Wheelwrights La GU26 188 A4
Wheelwrights Pl SL3 1 C7
Whelan Way SM6 60 D7
Wherwell Lodge GU2 130 C7
Wherwell Rd GU2 130 C7
Whetstone Rd GU14 84 C4
Whimbrel Cl CR2, CR8 80 D8
Whinfell Cl SW16 21 D3
Whins Cl GU15 65 B4
Whins Dr GU15 65 B4
Whinshill Ct SL5 30 A1
Whipley Cl GU4 110 B6
Whistler Cl RH10 201 F3
Whistler Gr GU47 64 D6
Whistley Cl RG12 27 E6
Whitby Cl TN16 83 B1
Whitby Gdns SM1, SM5 59 D8
Whitby Rd SM1, SM5 59 D8
Whitchurch Cl GU11 126 D6
Whitchurch Ct SW17 20 D4
Whitchurch House SE6 24 C5
White Acres Rd GU16 85 F4
White Beam Way KT20 97 A6
White Bridge Cl TW14 3 F1
White Bushes RH1 140 A4
White City RG45 45 D5
White Cottage Cl GU9 125 D6
White Ct GU2 109 A4
White Hart Ct
Horsham RH12 217 C4
Ripley GU23 91 C6
White Hart Ind Est GU17 64 E4
White Hart La
Mortlake SW14 7 E4
Wood St V GU3 108 A2
White Hart Meadows
GU23 91 C6
White Hart Row KT16 33 A2
White Heron Mews TW11 16 F2
White Hill Kingswood CR5 98 D4
South Croydon CR2 61 D1
Windlesham GU20 48 B6
White Horse Dr KT18 76 C5
White Horse La GU23 91 C6
White House 3 SW4 21 D8
White House Ct BR3 44 C8
White House La GU4 109 D6
White House Prep Sch RG41 25 A3
White House Wlk GU9 125 D7
White Knights Rd KT13 53 C3
White Knobs Way CR3 101 A2
White La Ash GU10, GU12 127 C7
Guildford GU4 131 D7
Titsey RH8, TN16 103 B3
Tongham GU10, GU12 127 C7
White Lodge Ashstead KT21 95 E7
South Norwood SE19 22 B1
White Lodge Cl SM2 59 C3
White Lodge Gdns RH1 140 A1
White Lodge The Royal Ballet Sch TW10 18 D7
White Oak Dr BR3 44 D7
White Post La GU10 146 A4
White Rd GU15 64 F6
White Rose La
Farnham GU9, GU10 146 B7
Old Woking GU22 90 A8
Woking GU22 69 F1
White Way KT23 94 B1
Whitebeam Dr RH2 139 B6
Whitebeams Gdns GU14 84 C3
Whiteberry Rd RH5 156 B7
Whitebines GU9 125 D2
Whitecroft Cl BR3 44 D5
Whitecroft Way BR3 44 D5
Whitefield Ave CR8 80 B3
Whitefield House CR8 80 B3
Whitefoot La BR1, SE6 24 D5
Whitefoot Terr BR1 24 F5
Whitegate Way KT20 97 B7
Whitegates
Old Woking GU22 89 F7
Whyteleafe CR3 101 A8
Whitehall Cres KT9 56 D5
Whitehall Dr RH11 200 E6
Whitehall Farm La GU25 31 E6
Whitehall Gdns W4 7 B8
Whitehall La Egham TW20 11 F1
Horton TW19 1 A1
Reigate RH2 138 F6
Whitehall Park Rd W4 7 B8
Whitehall Pl SM5 60 B6
Whitehall Rd CR7 42 A4
Whitehead Cl SW18 20 C8
Whitehill Cl GU15 65 D7
Whitehill La
Bletchingley RH1 120 D6
Martyr's Green GU23 92 C4
Whitehill Pl GU25 31 E4
Whitehorse La SE25 42 E5
Whitehorse Manor Inf Sch CR7 42 D5
Whitehorse Manor Jun Sch CR7 42 D5
Whitehorse Rd
Horsham RH12 218 B6
South Norwood CR0, CR7, SE25 42 D3
Thornton Heath CR0, CR7, SE25 42 D3
Whitehouse Dr GU1 110 B1
Whitelands Coll, Roehampton Inst SW18 19 E8
Whitelands Dr SL5 28 D8
Whiteley House 9 SW4 21 D8
Whiteley House & Hospl KT12 53 F2
Whiteley Rd SE19 22 D3
Whiteleys House TW13 16 A5
Whiteleys Way TW13 16 A5
Whitelocke Cty Inf Sch RG40 25 D7
Whitely Hill RH10 202 F1
Whitemore Rd GU1 109 D5
Whiteoak House SE19 22 C1
Whiteoaks SM7 78 B6
Whitepost Hill RH1 118 E1
Whitepost House RH1 118 E1

Whites Dr BR2 44 F2
Whites Rd GU14 85 E1
Whitethorn Ave CR5 79 B4
Whitethorn Cl GU12 106 B1
Whitethorn Cotts GU6 174 B6
Whitethorn Gdns CR0 62 B8
Whiteways Ct TW18 13 B1
Whiteways End GU10 126 D4
Whitewood Cotts TN16 103 C7
Whitewood La RH9 163 B7
Whitfield Cl Guildford GU2 109 A4
 Haslemere GU27 189 C1
Whitfield Ct 3 SE21 22 E4
Whitfield Rd GU27 189 C1
Whitford Gdns CR4 40 F6
Whitgift Ave CR2 61 C5
Whitgift Ctr CR9 61 C8
Whitgift House CR2 61 C5
Whitgift Sch CR2 61 C5
Whitgift St CR0, CR9 61 C7
Whitgift Wlk RH10 201 D3
Whitland Rd SM5 40 D1
Whitlet Cl GU9 125 B1
Whitley Cl TW19 2 E1
Whitlock Dr SW19 19 E7
Whitmead Cl CR2 61 E4
Whitmead La GU10 147 E4
Whitmoor La GU4 89 D1
Whitmoor Rd GU19 47 F2
Whitmoor Vale Rd GU26 188 A5
Whitmore Cl GU47 45 D1
Whitmore Gn GU9 125 E6
Whitmore La SL5 30 A5
Whitmore Rd BR3 43 F6
Whitmore Vale
 Grayshott GU26 187 F6
 Headley Down GU26 187 F6
Whitmore Vale Rd
 Grayshott GU26 188 A4
 Headley Down GU10, GU26 187 E7
Whitmore Way RH6 160 E3
Whitmores Cl KT18 76 C4
Whitstable Cl BR3 43 F8
Whittaker Ave TW10, TW9 6 D2
Whittaker Ct KT21 75 D2
Whittaker Pl 24 TW10 6 D2
Whittaker Rd SM3 58 F7
Whittam House SE27 22 C3
Whittell Gdns SE26 23 C5
Whittingham Ct W4 7 E7
Whittington Coll RH19 185 A4
Whittington Ct SE20 43 B7
Whittington Rd RH10 201 E3
Whittle Cl GU47 45 A1
Whittle Cres GU14 84 F7
Whittle Rd TW5 4 C7
Whittle Rdbt GU14 84 C1
Whittle Way RH10 182 A3
Whittlebury Cl SM5 59 F3
Whitton Dene
 Isleworth TW2, TW3, TW7 5 D2
 Twickenham TW2, TW7 5 D1
Whitton Manor Rd TW7 5 C1
Whitton Rd Bracknell RG12 27 F6
 Hounslow TW3 5 B2
 Isleworth TW3 5 B2
 Twickenham TW1 17 A8
Whitton Sch TW2 16 B6
Whitton Sta TW2 16 C8
Whitton Waye TW2, TW3 5 A1
Whitworth Rd
 Crawley RH11 181 D2
 South Norwood SE25 42 F5
Whopshott Ave GU21 69 C3
Whopshott Cl GU21 69 C3
Whopshott Dr GU21 69 C3
Whynstones Rd SL5 29 A4
Whyte Ave GU12 126 D7
Whyteacre CR3 101 B7
Whytebeam View CR3 80 F1
Whytecliffe Rd N CR8 80 B8
Whytecliffe Rd S CR8 80 B8
Whytecroft TW5 4 D7
Whyteleafe Bsns Village
 CR3 80 F2
Whyteleafe Hill CR3 80 F1
Whyteleafe Rd
 Caterham CR3 100 F6
 Whyteleafe CR3 100 F6
Whyteleafe Sch CR3 80 F1
Whyteleafe South Sta
 CR3 101 A8
Whyteleafe Sta CR3 80 F2
Wick House 1 KT1 37 D8
Wick La TW20 10 F3
Wick Rd
 Englefield Green TW20 11 B1
 Teddington TW11 17 C1
Wickers Oake SE19 22 F4
Wicket Hill GU10, GU9 146 A6
Wicket The CR0 63 A5
Wickets The TW15 13 E4
Wickham Ave
 Cheam KT4, SM3 58 C5
 Croydon CR0 43 E1
Wickham Chase BR4 44 E2
Wickham Cl Horley RH6 160 F4
 New Malden KT3 38 F4
Wickham Court Rd BR4 63 C8
Wickham Cres BR4 63 C8
Wickham La TW20 12 A1
Wickham Rd
 Beckenham BR3 44 B6
 Camberley GU15 65 E8
 Croydon CR0, CR9 62 E8
Wickham Vale RG12 26 E3
Wickham Way BR3 44 C4
Wickhurst Gdns RH12 216 E3
Wickhurst La RH12 216 E3
Wickland Ct RH10 201 D3
Wicklow Ct SE26 23 C3
Wide Way CR4, SW16 41 D6
Widgeon Way RH12 217 C5
Widmer Ct TW5 4 E5
Wiggie La RH1 119 A3
Wigley Rd TW13 15 D7
Wigmore La RH5 157 C1
Wigmore Rd SM5 40 E1
Wigmore Wlk SM5 59 D8
Wilberforce Ct KT18 76 D5
Wilberforce Way
 Bracknell RG12 27 D4
 Wimbledon SW19 19 D2
Wilbury Ave SM2 58 F1
Wilbury Rd GU21 69 D2
Wilcot Cl GU24 68 A3
Wilcot Gdns GU24 68 A3
Wilcox Gdns TW17 33 F6
Wilcox Rd Sutton SM1 59 B6
 Teddington TW11 16 D4
Wild Acres KT14 71 C8
Wildacre Cl RH14 212 D3
Wildbank Ct 2 GU22 69 F1
Wildcroft Dr Dorking RH5 136 D4
 Wokingham RG40 25 A1
Wildcroft Manor SW15 19 C8
Wildcroft Rd SW15 19 C8
Wildcroft Wood GU8 170 D6
Wilde Pl SW18 20 D8
Wilde Theatre RG12 27 C2
Wilderness Ct GU2 129 F7
Wilderness Rd
 Frimley GU16 65 E2
 Guildford GU2 129 F7
 Oxted RH8 122 E5
Wilderness Rise RH19 186 A6
Wilderness The
 East Molesey KT8 36 C4
 Hampton TW12 16 B4
Wilders Cl Frimley GU16 65 E3
 Woking GU21 69 C1
Wilderwick Rd RH19, RH7 186 A5
Wildfell Rd SE6 24 B8
Wildfield Cl GU3 108 B2
Wildgoose Dr RH12 216 F3
Wildridings Cty Prim Sch
 RG12 27 A5
Wildridings Rd RG12 27 A5
Wildridings Sq RG12 27 A5
Wildwood Cl
 East Horsley KT24 92 F2
 Lewisham SE12 24 F8
 Pyrford GU22 70 F4
Wildwood Ct CR8 80 D4
Wildwood La GU6 194 C5
Wilford Rd CR0 42 C2
Wilfred Owen Cl SW19 20 C2
Wilfred St GU21 69 D1
Wilhelmina Ave CR5 99 C8
Wilkes Rd 3 TW8 6 E8
Wilkins Cl CR4 40 E8
Wilkinson Ct
 4 Crawley RH11 201 B1
 Upper Tooting SW17 20 D4
Wilkinson House TW7 5 F4
Wilks Gdns CR0 43 E1
Will Miles Ct 6 SW19 20 C1
Willats Cl KT16 33 A3
Willcocks Cl KT9 56 E7
Willems Ave GU11 104 F2
Willems Rdbt GU11 104 F2
Willerton Lodge 1 KT13 53 D4
Willett Pl CR7 42 A4
Willett Rd CR7 42 A4
Willetts RH4 136 C4
Willey Broom La CR3 100 A2
Willey Farm La CR3 100 C1
Willey La CR3 100 D2
William Booth Rd SE20 43 A8
William Brown Ct SE27 22 B6
William Byrd Sch UB7 3 D8
William Cobbett Cty Jun
 Sch GU9 125 E6
William Evelyn Ct RH5 134 F4
William Farthing Cl 17
 GU11 105 A2
William Harvey House 1
 SW19 19 E7
William Lilly House KT12 54 C5
William Morris Mid Sch
 CR4 41 D6
William Morris Way
 RH11 201 C1
William Rd Caterham CR3 100 D5
 Guildford GU1 109 C1
 Merton SW19 19 E1
 Sutton SM1 59 C5
William Russell Ct 3
 GU21 68 E1
William Sim Wood RG42 8 B2
William St SM5 59 F7
William Wood House
 SE26 23 C5
Williams Cl
 Addlestone KT15 52 B5
 Ewhurst GU6 175 E5
Williams House 14 SW2 22 A7
Williams La Morden SM4 40 C4
 Mortlake SW14 7 C5
Williams Terr CR0 61 A4
Williams Way RH10 202 B5
Williamson Cl GU27 189 F1
Willingham Way KT1 38 A7
Willington Cl GU15 65 B6
Willington Prep Sch SW19 19 F3
Willis Ave SM2 59 E4
Willis Cl KT18 76 B5
Willis Rd CR0 42 C2
Willlows The CR0 62 E8
Willmore End SW19 40 B7
Willoughby Ave CR0 60 F6
Willoughby Rd
 Bracknell RG12 26 F6
 Kingston u T KT2 37 F8
 Twickenham TW1 6 D2
Willoughbys The SW15 7 E3
Willow Ave SW13 7 F5
Willow Bank GU22 89 F6
Willow Brean RH6 160 E5
Willow Cl
 Beare Green RH5 157 C4
 Brentford TW8 6 C8
 Catford SE6 24 F7
 Colnbrook SL3 1 C7
 Crawley RH10 201 E8
 East Grinstead RH19 185 D3
 Mytchett GU16 85 E4
 Woodham KT15 70 F8
Willow Cnr RH6 180 F7
Willow Cotts
 Carshalton CR4 40 F2
 Richmond TW9 7 A8
Willow Cres GU14 85 B7
Willow Ct Ash Vale GU12 106 A7
 Frimley GU16 65 D1
 Horley RH6 161 B6
 3 Streatham SW16 21 F5
 Thornton Heath CR7 42 D4
 Wokingham RG41 25 B6
Willow Ctr The CR4 40 F3
Willow Dr Bracknell RG12 27 C8
 Flexford GU3 107 C1
 Send Marsh GU23 91 A3
Willow End KT6 37 E1
Willow Gdns TW5 5 A6
Willow Glade RH2 139 B6
Willow Gn GU24 68 A6
Willow House TW14 4 B2
Willow La Blackwater GU17 64 D4
 Guildford GU1 110 A2
 Mitcham CR4 40 F3
Willow Lodge 6 TW16 14 F1
Willow Manor SM1 58 F6
Willow Mead Dorking RH4 136 A8
 8 East Grinstead RH19 205 F8
 Witley GU8 170 E5
Willow Mount CR0 61 E7
Willow Pk GU12 105 F2
Willow Rd Farncombe GU7 150 F8
 Horsham RH12 218 B5
 Kingston u T KT3 38 C5
 Poyle SL3 1 E5
 Reigate RH1 139 C6
 Wallington SM6 60 B3
Willow Ridge RH10 204 A3
Willow Tree Cl SW18 20 B7
Willow Vale KT23 94 B4
Willow View SW19 40 D8
Willow Way
 Aldershot GU12 126 E8
 Forest Hill SE26 23 C5
 Godstone RH9 121 B3
 Guildford GU1 109 B5
 Heath End GU9 125 D6
 Sunbury TW16 35 A5
 Twickenham TW2 16 B6
 West Byfleet KT14 71 C8
 West Ewell KT19 57 D4
 Woking GU22 89 E7
Willow Wlk Box Hill KT20 116 B5
 Cheam SM1, SM3 58 F7
 Chertsey KT16 33 B2
 Englefield Green TW20 11 C3
 Redhill RH1 140 B7
Willow Wood Cres SE25 42 E3
Willowbank Gdns KT20 97 B5
Willowbrook Rd TW19 13 E6
Willowdene Cl TW2 16 C8
Willowfield 4 RH11 201 D5
Willowhayne Dr KT12 35 B2
Willowhayne Gdns KT4 58 C6
Willowherb Cl RG40 25 E7
Willowmead TW18 33 B8
Willowmead Cl GU21 69 A3
Willowmere KT10 55 C6
Willows Ave SM4 40 B4
Willows End GU47 64 B8
Willows Path KT18 76 B5
Willows The
 Beckenham BR3 44 A8
 1 Bracknell RG12 27 F5
 Byfleet KT14 71 E6
 Chiddingfold GU8 191 A4
 Claygate KT10 55 E4
 Farnham GU10 126 C4
 Guildford, Bushy Hill GU4 110 D3
 Guildford, Pitch Place GU2 108 F6
 Horsham RH12 217 D5
 Lightwater GU18 48 C1
 2 Redhill RH1 139 F8
 Weybridge KT13 53 A7
Willowtree Way SW16 42 A8
Wills Cres TW3 5 B1
Willson Rd TW20 11 B3
Wilmar Gdns BR4 44 B1
Wilmer Cl TW10 17 F3
Wilmer Cres KT2, TW10 17 F3
Wilmerhatch La
 KT18, KT21 76 B2
Wilmington Ave W4 7 D7
Wilmington Cl RH11 201 C1
Wilmington Ct SW16 21 E1
Wilmot Rd Purley CR8 80 A7
 Wallington SM5 59 F5
Wilmot Way Banstead SM7 78 A5
 Frimley GU15 65 F3
Wilmot's La RH1, RH6 162 E5
Wilmots Cl RH2 118 C2
Wilna Rd SW18 20 C8
Wilson Ave CR4, SW19 40 E8
Wilson Cl Crawley RH10 202 D3
 Croydon CR0 61 D5
Wilson Dr KT16 51 B5
Wilson Hospl CR4 40 F5
Wilson Rd Aldershot GU12 105 D1
 Chessington KT9 56 F4
 Farnborough GU14 84 F3
Wilson Way GU21 69 D3
Wilson's Sch SM6 60 E4
Wilsons KT20 97 D6
Wilsons Rd GU35 187 B5
Wilton Cl UB7 2 D8
Wilton Cres SW19 39 F8
Wilton Ct
 Farnborough GU14 85 D3
 4 Richmond TW10 6 E2
Wilton Gdns
 East Molesey KT8 36 A6
 Walton-on-T KT12 35 D1
Wilton Gr Merton SW19 39 F8
 New Malden KT3 38 F3
Wilton Par TW13 15 B6
Wilton Pl Beckenham BR3 44 C6
 New Haw KT15 52 D2
Wilton Rd Camberley GU15 65 B3
 Hounslow TW4 4 D4
 Mitcham SW19 20 E1
 Redhill RH1 139 F8
Wilton Wlk TW13 15 B7
Wiltshire Ave RG45 45 B5
Wiltshire Dr RG40 25 D7
Wiltshire Gdns TW2 16 C7
Wiltshire Rd
 Thornton Heath CR7 42 A6
 Wokingham RG40 25 C7
Wilverley Cres KT3 38 E3
Wilwood Rd RG42 26 E8
Wimbart Rd SW2 21 F8
Wimbledon Bridge SW19 19 F2
Wimbledon Chase Mid
 Sch SW20 39 E8
Wimbledon Chase Sta
 SW20 39 E7
Wimbledon Cl
 Camberley GU15 46 F1
 2 Wimbledon SW20 19 D1
Wimbledon Coll SW19 19 D1
Wimbledon Common
 Prep Sch SW19 19 D1
Wimbledon High Sch
 SW19 19 E2
Wimbledon Hill Rd SW19 19 F2
Wimbledon House Sch
 SW19 40 A8
Wimbledon Lawn Tennis
 Mus SW19 19 E5
Wimbledon Park Ct SW19 19 F7
Wimbledon Park Prim Sch
 SW19 20 B6
Wimbledon Park Rd
 Putney SW18, SW19 19 F7
 Wandsworth SW18, SW19 19 F7
Wimbledon Park Side
 SW19 19 D7
Wimbledon Park Sta
 SW19 20 A5
Wimbledon Rd
 Camberley GU15 46 F1
 Wandsworth SW17 20 C4
Wimbledon Sch of Art
 SW19 39 E8
Wimbledon Sch of Art
 Annexe SW19 20 A1
Wimbledon Sta SW19 19 F2
Wimbledon Stadium
 SW17 20 C4
Wimbledon Stadium
 Bsns Ctr SW17 20 B5
Wimblehurst Ct RH12 217 C4
Wimblehurst Rd RH12 217 C4
Wimboldon Windmill
 Mus SW19 19 C5
Wimborne Ave RH1 140 A4
Wimborne Cl Epsom KT17 76 E6
 North Cheam KT4 39 C1
Wimborne House
 Croydon CR0 43 C4
 Upper Tooting SW12 21 C5
Wimborne Way BR3 43 E5
Wimbourne Ct
 Mitcham SW19 20 D1
 South Croydon CR2 61 E4
Wimland Hill RH12 199 D2
Wimland Rd
 Faygate RH12 199 D1
 Rusper RH12 199 C4
Wimlands La RH12 199 E3
Wimpole Cl 1 KT1 38 A7
Wimshurst Cl CR0 41 E1
Wincanton Rd SW18 19 F8
Winchcombe Rd SM5 40 E1
Winchelsey Rise CR2 61 F4
Winchendon Rd
 TW11, TW12 16 D4
Winchester Ave TW5 4 F8
Winchester Cl
 Beckenham BR2 44 F6
 Esher KT10 55 A7
 Kingston u T KT2 18 B1
Winchester Cl *continued*
 Poyle SL3 1 E6
Winchester Pk BR2 44 F6
Winchester Rd Ash GU12 106 A3
 Beckenham BR2 44 F6
 Crawley RH10 201 E2
 Feltham TW13 15 F5
 Harlington UB3 3 E7
 Rushmoor GU10 168 B7
 Twickenham TW1 6 B1
 Walton-on-T KT12 35 A1
Winchester St GU14 105 C8
Winchester Way GU17 64 C6
Winchet Wlk CR0 43 C3
Winchfield House SW15 7 F1
Winchfield Rd SE26 23 E3
Winchilsea Cres KT8 36 C7
Winchstone Cl TW17 33 F5
Windborough Rd SM5 60 A3
Windermere Ave
 SM4, SW19 40 B6
Windermere Cl
 East Bedfont TW14 14 F7
 Farnborough GU14 84 E3
 Stanwell TW19 13 D6
 Thorpe Lea TW20 12 B1
Windermere Ct
 Barnes SW13 7 F8
 Purley CR8 80 B4
Windermere House TW1 5 F2
Windermere Rd
 Coulsdon CR5 79 E4
 Croydon CR0 42 F1
 Kingston u T SW15 18 E3
 Lightwater GU18 48 B1
 Mitcham SW16 41 D7
 West Wickham BR4 63 E8
Windermere Way
 Hale GU9 125 A6
 Redhill RH2 118 E2
Windermere Wlk GU15 66 D5
Windfield KT22 95 B5
Windfield Cl SE26 23 D4
Windgates GU4 110 C4
Windham Ave CR0 63 D1
Windham Rd TW9 6 F4
Winding Wood Dr GU15 66 B3
Windings The CR2 80 F8
Windle Cl GU20 48 D4
Windlebrook Gn 3 RG42 27 A8
Windlemere Golf Ctr
 GU24 67 E8
Windlesham Ct GU20 48 C6
Windlesham Gr SW19 19 D7
Windlesham House CR4 40 D7
Windlesham Rd
 Bracknell RG42 26 F8
 Chobham GU24 49 C3
 West End GU24 67 F7
Windlesham Village Cty
 Inf Sch GU20 48 B6
Windley Cl SE23 23 C6
Windmill Ave KT17 76 F8
Windmill Bridge
 House CR0 42 E1
Windmill Bsns Village
 TW16 34 E8
Windmill Cl Caterham CR3 100 C6
 Charlton TW16 14 E1
 Ewell KT17 76 F7
 Horley RH6 161 B3
 Horsham RH13 218 A4
 Long Ditton KT6 37 C2
Windmill Ct RH10 201 D8
Windmill Dr
 Headley Down GU35 187 B6
 Leatherhead KT22 95 C4
 Redhill RH2 118 E3
Windmill End KT17 76 F7
Windmill Field GU20 48 D4
Windmill Gr CR0 42 C3
Windmill La
 Ashurst Wood RH19 206 C7
 East Grinstead RH19 185 D3
 Ewell KT17 76 F7
 Thames Ditton KT7 37 B2
Windmill Lodge TW16 34 E8
Windmill Rd
 Aldershot GU12 105 C1
 Bracknell RG42 27 A8
 Brentford TW8 6 D8
 Charlton TW16 34 E8
 Hampton TW12 16 C3
 Mitcham CR4 41 C5
 Roehampton SW19 19 B5
 Thornton Heath CR0 42 C2
Windmill Rd W TW16 34 E8
Windmill Rise KT2 18 B1
Windmill Terr TW17 34 E2
Windmill Trad Est TW16 34 E8
Windmill Way RH2 118 D3
Windrush Cl Bramley GU5 151 F6
 Chiswick W4 7 C7
 Crawley RH11 200 F4
Windrush House 3 RH1 118 F2
Windrush Hts GU47 64 B8
Windrush La SE23 23 D5
Winds Ridge GU23 90 C2
Windsor Ave Cheam SM3 58 E7
 East Molesey KT8 36 A6
 Merton SW19 40 C8
 New Malden KT3 38 C4
Windsor Cl Crawley RH11 201 C2
 Guildford GU2 129 F7
 West Norwood SE27 22 C4
Windsor Cres GU9 125 B6
Windsor Ct Ashford TW16 15 A1
 Chobham GU24 49 E2

Windsor Ct continued
Horsham RH13 217 F3
South Norwood SE19 42 E8
Windsor Dr TW15 13 D4
Windsor Gdns Ash GU12 105 F1
Wallington CR0 60 E7
Windsor Gr SE27 22 C4
Windsor Great Pk SL4 10 D4
Windsor House RH2 139 B4
Windsor Mews Catford SE6 24 C7
Forest Hill SE23 23 E7
Windsor Park Rd UB3 3 F7
Windsor Pk SW19 40 C8
Windsor Pl Chertsey KT16 33 A3
East Grinstead RH19 206 A8
Windsor Rd Ashford TW16 15 A2
Chobham GU24 49 D3
Cranford TW4, TW5 4 C5
Englefield Green TW19, TW20 11 E6
Farnborough GU14 85 D1
Kingston u T KT2 17 E1
North Ascot SL5 29 A8
Richmond TW9 6 F5
South Norwood CR7 42 B7
Teddington TW11 16 D3
Worcester Park KT4 58 A8
Windsor Ride Bracknell SL5 28 C4
Sandhurst GU15 65 A8
Windsor St KT16 33 A3
Windsor Way
Aldershot GU11 105 B2
Frimley GU16 85 F8
Woking GU22 70 C3
Windsor Wlk
Walton-on-T KT12 35 D1
Weybridge KT13 53 B5
Windways GU8 192 F7
Windy Ridge Cl SW19 19 D3
Windy Wood GU7 150 C3
Windycroft Cl CR5, CR8 79 D6
Windyridge RH11 201 A5
Winern Glebe KT14 71 D6
Winery La KT1 37 F6
Winfield Ct RH5 158 B1
Winfield Gr RH5 158 B1
Winfrith Rd SW18 20 C7
Wingate Cres CR0 41 E3
Wingate Ct GU11 104 F2
Wingfield Cl KT15 52 B1
Wingfield Gdns GU16 66 D3
Wingfield Rd KT2 18 A2
Wingham House 3 SE26 23 B3
Wingrove Rd SE6 24 E6
Wings Cl Hale GU9 125 B6
Sutton SM1 59 A6
Wings Rd GU9 125 B6
Winifred Rd Coulsdon CR5 79 B4
Hampton TW12 16 A4
Merton SW19 40 A8
Winkfield Cl RG41 25 B3
Winkfield La SL4 8 D7
Winkfield Plain SL4 9 B8
Winkfield Rd Ascot SL5 29 B7
Windsor SL4 9 C8
Winkfield Row RG42 8 B3
Winkfield St SL4 8 C6
Winkworth Arboretum GU8 172 C7
Winkworth Pl
Banstead SM7 78 A5
Farnham GU9 125 C3
Winkworth Rd SM7 78 A5
Winlaton Rd BR1, SE6 24 D4
Winner Way RH6 181 D6
Winnington Way GU21 69 C1
Winscombe RG12 26 E4
Winsford Rd SE6 23 F5
Winslade Way SE6 24 B8
Winslow Way
Feltham TW13 15 E5
Walton-on-T KT12 54 C7
Winstanley Cl KT11 73 B5
Winstanley Wlk KT11 73 B5
Winston Churchill Sch The GU21 68 F1
Winston Cl GU16 85 F6
Winston Dr KT11 73 E3
Winston Way GU22 90 B7
Winston Wlk GU10 146 C6
Winter Box Wlk TW10 6 F2
Winterbourne RH12 217 F7
Winterbourne Ct RG12 27 D7
Winterbourne Gr KT13 53 C4
Winterbourne Inf Sch CR7 42 A5
Winterbourne Jun Boys' Sch CR7 42 A5
Winterbourne Jun Girls' Sch CR7 42 A5
Winterbourne Rd
Forest Hill SE23, SE6 23 F7
Thornton Heath CR7 42 A5
Winterbourne Wlk GU16 85 F8
Winterdown Gdns KT10 54 F4
Winterdown Rd KT10 54 F4
Winterfold RH10 202 A3
Winterfold Cl SW19 19 E6
Winterhill Way GU4 110 B5
Winters Rd KT7 37 B2
Wintersells Ind Est KT14 52 D1
Wintersells Rd KT13, KT14 52 E1
Winterstoke Rd SE23, SE6 23 F7
Winterton Ct RH13 217 D2
Winton Ct 15 KT6 37 D2
Winton House CR8 80 A3
Winton House Sch CR0 61 F8
Winton Rd Aldershot GU11 105 A1
Farnham GU9 125 D4
Winton Way SW16 22 A3
Wire Mill La RH7 184 F8
Wirrall House 15 SE26 23 A5
Wisbeach Rd CR0 42 D4
Wisborough Ct RH11 200 F3
Wisborough Rd CR2 61 F2
Wisdom Ct 5 TW7 6 A4
Wiseman Ct 12 SE19 22 E3
Wiseton Rd SW17 20 F7
Wishanger La GU10 167 B2
Wishbone Way GU21 68 F3
Wishford Ct KT21 75 F1
Wishmoor Cl GU15 65 E8
Wishmoor Rd GU15 65 E8
Wishmore Cross Sch GU24 49 F1
Wisley Gdns GU14 84 D2
Wisley La GU23, KT14 71 E3
Wispers Sch GU27 189 C1
Wiston Ct RH11 200 F3
Witham Rd Hounslow TW7 5 D6
Penge BR3, SE20 43 C6
Wither Dale RH6 160 E4
Witherby Cl CR0, CR2 61 E6
Withers Cl KT9 56 C4
Witherslack Cl GU35 187 C4
Withey Brook RH6 160 D1
Withey Meadows RH6 160 D1
Witheygate Ave TW18 13 B2
Withies La GU3 129 C2
Withies The Knaphill GU21 68 E2
Leatherhead KT22 95 B6
Withy Cl GU18 48 C1
Withybed Cnr KT20 97 B4
Withypitts RH10 204 A3
Withypitts E RH10 204 A3
Witley CE Inf Sch GU8 170 F4
Witley Commons Visitor Ctr GU8 170 C6
Witley Cres CR0 63 C4
Witley House 5 SW2 21 F8
Witley & Milford Commons NR GU8 170 B6
Witley Point 8 SW15 19 B7
Witley Sta GU8 190 F8
Witney Path SE23 23 D5
Witten House KT3 38 D1
Wittenham Rd RG12 27 F8
Wittering Cl KT2 17 D3
Wittersham Rd BR1 24 F3
Wittmead Rd GU16 85 F4
Wivenhoe Ct TW4 4 F3
Wiverton Rd SE20, SE26 23 C3
Wix Hill KT24 112 B4
Woburn Ave
Farnborough GU14 85 D3
Purley CR8 80 A8
Woburn Cl Frimley GU16 66 A1
Merton SW19 20 C2
Woburn Ct Croydon CR0 42 C1
Richmond TW9 6 F4
Woburn Hill KT15 52 D7
Woburn Hill Pk KT15 52 D8
Woburn Rd Carshalton SM5 40 E1
Crawley RH11 201 A4
Croydon CR0 42 C1
Wodeland Ave GU2 130 B7
Woffington Cl KT1, KT8 37 C8
Woking Bsns Pk GU21 70 B4
Woking Cl SW15 7 F3
Woking Coll GU22 90 A7
Woking Comm Hospl GU22 69 F1
Woking High Sch GU21 69 D4
Woking Nuffield Hospl The GU21 69 E5
Woking Rd GU1, GU4 109 D5
Woking Sta GU22 69 F2
Wokingham Hospl RG41 25 A6
Wokingham Rd RG42 26 F8
Wokingham Sta RG40 25 B6
Wokingham Theatre RG40 25 B8
Wold Cl RH11 200 F4
Wold The CR3 102 A5
Woldhurstlea Cl RH11 201 A4
Woldingham Rd CR3, CR6 101 C7
Woldingham Sch CR3 101 E2
Woldingham Sta CR3 101 D5
Wolf's Cnr RH8 123 A5
Wolf's Hill RH8 123 A4
Wolf's Rd RH8 123 B5
Wolfe Rd GU12 105 C1
Wolfington Rd SE27 22 B4
Wolfs Wood RH8 123 A3
Wolseley Ave SW18, SW19 20 A6
Wolseley Gdns W4 7 B8
Wolseley Rd
3 Aldershot GU11 105 A1
Carshalton CR4 41 A2
Farncombe GU7 150 F6
Wolsey Cl Isleworth TW3 5 C3
Kingston u T KT2 38 B8
Wimbledon SW20 19 B1
Worcester Park KT19, KT4 58 A6
Wolsey Cres
New Addington CR0 63 C2
West Barnes SM4 39 F2
Wolsey Ct BR1 24 F1
Wolsey Dr Kingston u T KT2 17 E2
Walton-on-T KT12 35 D1
Wolsey Gr 2 KT10 55 B6
Wolsey House 2 TW12 16 B2
Wolsey Inf & Jun Schs CR0 63 D3
Wolsey Pl Sh Ctr GU22 69 E2
Wolsey Rd Ashford TW15 13 F4
Ashford, Felthamhill TW16 14 F2
East Molesey KT8 36 D5
Wolsey Rd continued
Esher KT10 55 B6
Hampton TW12 16 C2
Wolsey Way KT9 57 A5
Wolsey Wlk 4 GU21 69 F2
Wolstonbury Cl RH11 201 C4
Wolvens La
Coldharbour RH5 156 E5
Westcott RH4, RH5 135 B2
Wolverton Ave KT2 38 A8
Wolverton Cl RH6 160 F1
Wolverton Gdns RH6 160 F2
Wolves Hill RH5 178 C4
Wonersh Ct GU5 152 B7
Wonersh & Shamley Green CE Inf Sch GU5 152 D5
Wonersh Way SM2 58 D2
Wonford Cl King T KT2, KT3 38 E8
Walton on t H KT20 97 A1
Wonham La RH3, RH2 137 F8
Wonham Way
Gomshall GU5 133 D3
Peaslake GU5 133 D1
Wontford Rd CR8 80 B4
Wontner Rd SW12, SW17 20 F6
Wood Cl RH1 161 A8
Wood Ct GU2 109 B2
Wood End RH12 218 C5
Wood End Cl GU22 70 F3
Wood End The SM6 60 B2
Wood La Banstead KT20 77 F2
Bracknell RG42 26 E8
Caterham CR3 100 D3
Farnborough GU14 85 A3
Hounslow TW7 5 F7
Knaphill GU21 68 D1
Seale GU10 127 B5
Weybridge KT13 53 C2
Wood Lodge La BR4 63 C7
Wood Rd
Beacon Hill GU26 188 D6
Biggin Hill TN16 83 C1
Camberley GU15 65 B1
Farncombe GU7 150 F7
Heath End GU9 125 C7
Littleton TW17 34 A5
Wood Riding GU22 70 E4
Wood Rise GU3 108 E3
Wood St Ash Vale GU12 106 A6
Carshalton CR4 41 A2
East Grinstead RH19 185 D1
Kingston u T KT2 37 E8
Merstham RH1 119 C7
Wood Street Cty Inf Sch GU3 108 C3
Wood Vale SE22 23 B8
Woodall House TW7 5 F4
Woodbank Rd BR1 24 F5
Woodbarn The GU9 125 C1
Woodbastwick Rd SE26 23 E3
Woodberry Cl
Ashford TW16 15 A2
Chiddingfold GU8 191 A5
Woodbine Cl
Sandhurst GU47 64 C7
Twickenham TW2 16 D6
Woodbine Cotts GU4 130 E2
Woodbine Gr SE20 23 B1
Woodbine La KT4 58 C7
Woodbines Ave KT1 37 D6
Woodbourne GU9 125 E7
Woodbourne Ave SW16 21 D5
Woodbourne Cl SW16 21 E5
Woodbourne Dr KT10 55 F4
Woodbourne Gdns SM6 60 B3
Woodbridge Ave KT22 75 A1
Woodbridge Ct RH12 218 A5
Woodbridge Dr GU15 65 D7
Woodbridge Gr KT22 75 A1
Woodbridge Hill GU2 109 B2
Woodbridge Hill Gdns GU2 109 A2
Woodbridge Meadows GU1 109 C2
Woodbridge Park Est GU1 109 C2
Woodbridge Rd
Blackwater GU17 64 B5
Guildford GU1, GU2 109 C2
Woodbrook Sch BR3 43 F8
Woodbury Ave RH19 186 B1
Woodbury Cl
Biggin Hill TN16 83 F1
East Grinstead RH19 206 B8
South Croydon CR0 61 F8
Woodbury Dr SM2 59 C1
Woodbury House SE26 23 B5
Woodbury St SW17 20 E3
Woodby Dr SL5 29 F2
Woodcock Dr GU24 49 C3
Woodcock Hill RH19, RH7 184 F6
Woodcock La GU24 49 B3
Woodcombe Cres SE23 23 C7
Woodcot Gdns GU14 84 D4
Woodcote Artington GU2 130 B5
Cranleigh GU6 174 B4
Farncombe GU7 150 D6
Horley RH6 161 C4
Woodcote Ave
Thornton Heath CR7 42 B5
Wallington SM6 60 B2
Woodcote Cl Epsom KT18 76 D5
Kingston u T KT2 17 F3
Woodcote Dr CR8 60 D1
Woodcote End KT18 76 D4
Woodcote Gn SM6 60 C2
Woodcote Green Rd KT18 76 C4
Woodcote Grove Rd CR5 79 D5
Woodcote Hall
Epsom KT18 76 D5
Wallington SM6 60 B2
Woodcote High Sch CR5 79 D6
Woodcote House KT18 76 D4
Woodcote House Ct KT18 76 D4
Woodcote House (Sch) GU20 48 B5
Woodcote Hurst KT18 76 C3
Woodcote Inf Sch CR5 79 D5
Woodcote Jun Sch CR5 79 D5
Woodcote La CR8 79 D7
Woodcote Mews SM6 60 B4
Woodcote Park Ave CR5, CR8 79 C7
Woodcote Park Golf Club CR5 79 B5
Woodcote Park Golf Course KT18 76 D2
Woodcote Park Rd KT18 76 C4
Woodcote Pl
North Ascot SL5 28 F8
1 West Norwood SE27 22 B3
Woodcote Rd Epsom KT18 76 D5
Epsom KT18 76 D5
Forest Row RH18 206 F2
Wallington CR8, SM6 60 C2
Woodcote Side KT18 76 B4
Woodcote Valley Rd CR5, CR8 79 E7
Woodcott House 1 SW15 19 A8
Woodcott Terr GU12 126 D8
Woodcourt RH11 201 C1
Woodcrest Rd CR8 79 E6
Woodcrest Wlk RH2 118 E3
Woodcroft Rd
Crawley RH11 200 D4
Thornton Heath CR0, CR7 42 B3
Woodcut Rd GU10 145 F6
Woodend
Farnborough GU14 85 D3
Leatherhead KT22 95 C2
South Norwood SE19 22 C2
Sutton SM1 59 C8
Thames Ditton KT10 55 C8
Woodend Cl
Crawley RH10 202 A8
North Ascot SL5 28 E8
Woking GU21 89 A8
Woodend Dr SL5 29 B4
Woodend Pk KT11 73 D4
Woodend Rd GU16 86 C7
Woodenhill RG12 26 E1
Woodenhill Cty Prim Sch RG12 26 E2
Wooderson Cl SE25 42 E5
Woodfield KT21 75 D2
Woodfield Ave
Streatham SW16 21 D5
Wallington SM5 60 A3
Woodfield Cl
Ashstead KT21 75 D2
Coulsdon CR5 99 C8
Crawley RH10 201 E7
Redhill RH1 118 E3
South Norwood SE19 22 C1
Woodfield Gdns KT3 38 F4
Woodfield Gr SW16 21 D5
Woodfield Hill CR5 99 B8
Woodfield House
11 Forest Hill SE23 23 D5
New Malden KT3 38 F4
Woodfield La KT21 75 E2
Woodfield Rd
Ashstead KT21 75 D2
Cranford TW4, TW5 4 B5
Crawley RH10 201 F7
Hinchley Wood KT10, KT7 55 F8
Rudgwick RH12 214 D7
Woodfield Sch RH1 119 E6
Woodfield Way RH1 118 E3
Woodfields Ct SM1 59 C7
Woodfields The CR2 80 F8
Woodford Gn RG12 27 F5
Woodgate Ave KT9 56 D5
Woodgate Dr SW16 21 D1
Woodgates Cl RH13 217 F3
Woodgavil SM7 77 F3
Woodger Cl GU1, GU4 110 C3
Woodgrange Ct BR2 44 F1
Woodhall Ave SE21 22 F5
Woodhall Dr SE21 22 F5
Woodhall La SL5 48 E8
Woodham La
New Haw KT15 52 B1
Sheerwater GU21, KT15 70 D7
Woodham KT15 52 B1
Woodham Park Rd KT15 51 F1
Woodham Park Way KT15 70 F8
Woodham Rd Catford SE6 24 C5
Woking GU21 69 F4
Woodham Rise GU21 70 A4
Woodham Waye GU21 70 B5
Woodhatch Rd
Redhill RH1, RH2 139 E5
Reigate RH1, RH2 139 E5
Woodhatch Spinney CR5 79 E3
Woodhaw TW20 12 B4
Woodhayes RH6 161 B4
Woodhayes Rd SW19, SW20 19 C2
Woodhill GU23 90 D2
Woodhill La GU5 152 F4
Woodhouse La RH5 155 A8
Woodhouse St RG42 26 E8
Woodhurst La RH8 122 E4
Woodhurst Pk RH8 122 E5
Woodhyrst Gdns CR8 80 B4
Wooding Gr 15 RH11 201 B1
Woodland Ave GU6 174 F3
Woodland Cl
East Horsley KT24 112 F8
Horsham RH13 218 B4
West Ewell KT19 57 E4
West Norwood SE19 22 E2
Woodland Ct Cheam SM1 59 A4
Ewell KT17 76 F7
Oxted RH8 122 E7
Woodland Dr
Crawley Down RH10 204 B8
East Horsley KT24 112 F8
Farnham GU10 146 B6
Ockley RH5 178 A5
Woodland Gdns
Isleworth TW7 5 E4
Selsdon CR2 81 C8
Woodland Gr KT13 53 D6
Woodland Hill SE19 22 E2
Woodland Rd
Thornton Heath CR7 42 A5
West Norwood SE19 22 F2
Woodland Rise RH8 122 E5
Woodland View GU7 129 E1
Woodland Way
Caterham CR3 120 E8
Croydon CR0, CR9 43 E1
Horsham RH13 218 B4
Kingswood KT20 97 E4
Merton SM4 39 F5
Mitcham CR4 21 A1
Purley CR8 80 A6
Tolworth KT5 57 B8
West Wickham BR4 63 C7
Weybridge KT13 53 D5
Woodlands Beckenham BR3 24 B1
Chertsey KT15 52 E7
Crawley RH10 202 D8
Horley RH6 161 C4
Send Marsh GU23 90 F2
West Barnes SW20 39 D5
Woodlands Ave
Heath End GU9 125 F7
Kingston u T KT3 38 D8
Redhill RH1 139 F8
West Byfleet KT14, KT15 70 F7
Worcester Park KT4 58 A8
Woodlands Cl Ascot SL5 28 F3
Ash GU12 106 A5
Claygate KT10 55 F3
Cranleigh GU6 174 F2
Crawley Down RH10 204 B7
Farnborough GU17 64 E1
Ottershaw KT16 51 B1
Woodlands Ct Bromley BR1 44 F8
Dulwich SE22 23 B8
Sandhurst GU47 45 F1
7 Woking GU21 69 A1
Woking GU22 89 E8
Woodlands Dr
South Godstone RH9 142 E6
Sunbury TW16 35 C7
Woodlands Gr
Coulsdon CR5 79 B2
Isleworth TW7 5 E5
Woodlands House GU21 70 C5
Woodlands La
Haslemere GU27 207 F7
Stoke D'Abernon KT11 74 B2
Windlesham GU20, GU24 48 E3
Woodlands Par TW15 14 C2
Woodlands Pk
Addlestone KT15 51 F5
Box Hill KT20 116 B4
Guildford GU1 110 B2
Sheerwater GU21 70 C5
Woodlands Rd
Ashstead KT11, KT22 74 D1
Camberley GU15 65 B5
East Grinstead RH19 186 A4
Effingham KT23, KT24 113 F6
Epsom KT18 76 A4
Farnborough GU14 84 D6
Guildford GU1 109 D5
Hambledon GU8 171 D1
Isleworth TW7 5 E5
Leatherhead KT11, KT22 74 D1
Mortlake SW13 7 F4
Pyrford KT14 70 F5
Redhill RH1 139 F7
Surbiton KT6 37 D2
Virginia Water GU25 31 C5
Woodlands Rd E GU25 31 C5
Woodlands Rd W GU25 31 C5
Woodlands Ride SL5 29 A3
Woodlands Sch KT22 95 C5
Woodlands St SE13 24 D8
Woodlands The
Isleworth TW7 5 F5
Lewisham SE13 24 D8
Mitcham CR4 41 A6
Smallfield RH6 162 B3
South Norwood SE19 22 C1
Thames Ditton KT10 55 C8
Wallington SM6 60 B2
Woodlands Way
Ashstead KT21 76 B2
Box Hill KT20 116 C5
Woodlands Wlk GU17 64 E1
Woodlawn Cres TW2 16 B6
Woodlawn Dr TW13 15 D6
Woodlawn Gr GU21 69 F4
Woodlea Cty Prim Sch CR3 101 F5

Woodlea Dr BR2 44 E4
Woodlee Cl GU25 31 C7
Woodleigh 1 KT5 37 F4
Woodleigh Gdns SW16 21 E5
Woodley Cl SW17 20 F1
Woodley House GU7 150 E8
Woodley La SM1, SM5 59 E7
Woodlodge Ashstead KT21 75 E2
4 Wimbledon SW19 19 F3
Woodman Rd CR5 79 D4
Woodmancote Ct RH12 217 D5
Woodmancote Gdns KT14 71 A6
Woodmancott Cl RG12 27 F3
Woodmancourt GU7 150 C8
Woodmans Hill RH11 201 C2
Woodmansterne Cty Prim Sch SM7 78 F5
Woodmansterne La
Banstead SM7 78 D4
Wallington SM5, SM6 79 A7
Woodmansterne SM7 78 D4
Woodmansterne Prim Sch SW16 41 D8
Woodmansterne Rd
Coulsdon CR5 79 C4
Streatham SW16 41 D8
Sutton SM5, SM2 59 E2
Woodmansterne St SM7 78 E4
Woodmansterne Sta CR5 79 B3
Woodmere RG12 27 E5
Woodmere Ave CR0 43 D2
Woodmere Cl CR0 43 D2
Woodmere Gdns CR0 43 D2
Woodmere Way BR3 44 D4
Woodnook Rd SW16 21 B3
Woodpecker Cl
Cobham KT11 73 E7
Crondall GU10 124 D8
Woodpecker La RH5 158 C2
Woodpecker Mount CR0 62 F2
Woodpecker Way GU22 89 D3
Woodpeckers
Bracknell RG12 27 B5
Witley GU8 170 E7
Woodplace Cl CR5 79 C1
Woodplace La
Coulsdon CR5 99 C7
Hooley CR5 99 C7
Woodridge Cl RG12 27 C6
Woodrough Copse GU5 152 A5
Woodrow Dr RG40 25 F6
Woodroyd Ave RH6 160 F2
Woodroyd Gdns RH6 160 F1
Woodruff Ave GU1 110 B4
Woods Hill Cl RH19 206 D6
Woods Hill La RH19 206 D6
Woodshore Cl GU25 31 B3
Woodside Blackwater GU17 64 C3
1 Farnborough GU14 85 B7
Fetcham KT22 94 B5
Horsham RH13 218 B4
Hydestile GU8 171 E5
Lower Kingswood KT20 117 F7
Sandhurst GU15 64 F7
Walton-on-T KT12 35 A1
West Horsley KT24 92 C1
Wimbledon SW19 19 F3
Woodside Ave
Croydon SE25 43 B4
Hersham KT12 54 B6
Thames Ditton KT10 36 E2
Woodside Cl
Caterham CR3 100 E3
Chiddingfold GU8 191 B4
Knaphill GU21 68 D2
Tolworth KT5 38 C2
Woodside Cotts GU8 148 C3
Woodside Court Rd CR0, CR9 43 A2
Woodside Cres RH6 162 A3
Woodside Gn CR0, SE25 43 A3
Woodside House SW19 19 F2
Woodside Jun & Inf Sch CR0 43 A2
Woodside La SL4, SL5 9 C3
Woodside Park Est GU7 150 F4
Woodside Pk SE25 43 B3
Woodside Rd
Beare Green RH5 157 D3
Chiddingfold GU8 191 B5
Cobham KT11 74 A6
Crawley RH10 201 F8
Croydon SE25 43 B3
Farnborough GU11 104 F7
Guildford GU2 108 F2
Heath End GU9 125 E7
Kingston u T KT2 17 E1
Kingston u T KT3 38 E7
Purley CR8 79 E6
Sutton SM1 59 C7
Woodside Way
Croydon CR0 43 C3
Redhill RH1 140 A3
Redhill RH1 140 A8
Streatham CR4 41 C8
Virginia Water GU25 31 B6
Woodsome Lodge KT13 53 C4
Woodspring Rd SW19 19 E6
Woodstock
East Grinstead RH19 185 C2
West Clandon GU4 111 B7
Wokingham RG40 25 C6
Woodstock Ave
Cheam SM3, SM4 39 F2
Isleworth TW7 6 A2
Woodstock Cl
Cranleigh GU6 174 F1
Horsham RH12 217 D5
Woking GU21 69 E3
Woodstock Ct KT17 76 D7
Woodstock Gdns BR3 24 B1
Woodstock Gr GU7 150 E7
Woodstock La N KT6 56 C8
Woodstock La S KT10, KT6 56 C6
Woodstock Rd
Coulsdon CR5 79 B3
Croydon CR0, CR9 61 D7
Wallington SM5, SM6 60 A5
Woodstock Rise SM3 39 F2
Woodstock Way CR4 41 C7
Woodstocks GU14 85 D6
Woodstone Ave KT17, KT4 58 A5
Woodsway KT22 74 E5
Woodsyre SE19, SE26 22 F4
Woodthorpe Rd
Ashford TW15 13 D4
Staines TW15 13 D4
Woodvale Ave SE25 42 F7
Woodvale Ct SE25 42 F6
Woodvale Wlk SE27 22 C3
Woodview KT9 75 C8
Woodview Cl
Hamsey Green CR2 81 B5
Kingston u T SW15 18 D4
Woodview Ct KT13 53 C5
Woodville Cl
Blackwater GU17 64 B5
Teddington TW11 17 A4
Woodville Gdns KT6 37 D2
Woodville Pl CR3 100 C5
Woodville Rd
Leatherhead KT22 95 B7
Merton SM4 40 A5
Richmond TW10 17 C5
South Norwood CR7 42 D6
Woodville Sch The KT22 95 B7
Woodward Cl KT10 55 F4
Woodwarde Rd SE22 22 F8
Woodwards RH11 201 C1
Woodway Camberley GU15 65 B5
Guildford GU1 110 B2
Woodyard La SE21 22 E8
Woodyers Cl GU5 152 B7
Wool Rd SW20 19 B2
Woolborough Cl RH10 201 E7
Woolborough La
Crawley RH10 181 F1
Crawley, Three Bridges RH10 202 A8
South Nutfield RH1 161 F8
Woolborough Rd RH10 201 E7
Woolford Cl RG42 8 C1
Woolfords La GU8 169 B7
Woolhampton Way RG12 27 D4
Woolhams CR3 101 A1
Woollards Rd GU12 106 B4
Woolmead Rd GU9 125 C3
Woolmead The GU9 125 C3
Woolmer Hill Rd GU26, GU27 207 D7
Woolmer Hill Sch GU27 207 D7
Woolmer View GU26 188 D3
Woolsack Way GU7 150 F4
Woolstone Rd SE23, SE6 23 E6
Woosehill La RG41 25 A5
Wootton Cl KT18 76 F3
Wootton Grange GU22 89 E8
Worbeck Rd SE20 43 C7
Worcester Cl Croydon CR0 63 A8
Farnborough GU14 85 B7
Mitcham CR4 41 A7
Worcester Ct Ashford TW15 14 B3
Walton-on-T KT12 35 C1
Worcester Park KT4 57 E7
Worcester Dr TW15 14 B3
Worcester Gdns KT4 57 E7
Worcester Park Rd KT4 57 D7
Worcester Park Sta KT4 39 A1
Worcester Rd Belmont SM2 59 B3
Crawley RH10 201 E2
Guildford GU2 108 F3
Reigate RH2 118 A2
Sutton SM2 59 B3
11 Wimbledon SW19 19 F3
Wordsworth RG12 26 F4
Wordsworth Ave CR8 80 D4
Wordsworth Cl RH10 202 B8
Wordsworth Dr KT4, SM3 58 C6
Wordsworth Mead RH1 119 B3
Wordsworth Pl RH12 217 E7
Wordsworth Rd
Addlestone KT15 52 D6
Hampton TW12, TW13 15 F4
Penge SE20 23 D1
Wallington SM6 60 D4
Wordsworth Rise 6 RH19 185 C1
Works Rd KT15 52 B2
Worlds End Hill RG12 27 F3
Wormley La GU8 171 B1
Worple Ave Isleworth TW7 6 A2
Staines TW18 13 B2
Wimbledon SW19 19 D1
Worple Ct SW19 19 E2
Worple Prim Sch TW7 6 A3
Worple Rd Epsom KT18 76 D4
Epsom KT18 76 E5
Isleworth TW7 6 A3
Leatherhead KT22 95 B4
Staines TW18 13 B1
Wimbledon SW19, SW20 39 D8
Worple Road Mews SW19 19 F2
Worple St SW14 7 D4
Worple Way TW10 6 E3
Worplesdon Cty Prim Sch GU3 108 D4
Worplesdon Golf Course GU22 88 D4
Worplesdon Hill Heath House Rd GU22 88 D5
Worplesdon Rd GU2 109 A4
Worplesdon Sta GU22 89 B3
Worslade Rd SW17 20 D4
Worsley Bridge Jun Sch BR3 24 A1
Worsley Bridge Rd
Beckenham BR3, SE6 24 A2
Catford SE6 23 F3
Worsley House SE23 23 B6
Worsley Rd GU16 85 F7
Worsted Gn RH1 119 D6
Worsted La RH19 206 B8
Worth Abbey & Sch RH10 203 B1
Worth Park Ave RH10 202 C7
Worth Rd RH10 202 C6
Worth Way RH10 202 E5
Worthfield Cl KT19 57 D3
Worthing Rd Heston TW5 4 F8
Horsham RH12 217 B1
Worthington Cl CR4 41 B6
Worthington House 16 SW2 22 A8
Worthington Rd KT6 37 F1
Wortley Rd CR0 42 A2
Worton Ct TW7 5 E3
Worton Gdns TW7 5 D5
Worton Hall Est TW7 5 E3
Worton Rd TW7 5 E4
Worton Way TW3, TW7 5 D5
Wotton Dr RH5 134 E3
Wotton Way SM2 58 C1
Wrabness Way TW18 33 B8
Wray Cl RH19 206 D6
Wray Common Cty Prim Sch RH2 118 D2
Wray Common Rd RH2 118 D2
Wray House 11 SW2 21 E7
Wray La RH2 118 D4
Wray Mill House RH2 118 E3
Wray Mill Pk RH2 118 E3
Wray Park Rd RH2 118 C2
Wray Rd SM2 58 F2
Wrayfield Ave RH2 118 C2
Wrayfield Rd SM3 58 D7
Wraylands Dr RH2 118 D3
Wraymead Pl RH2 118 B2
Wraymill Ct 4 RH2 118 D1
Wraysbury Cl TW4 4 E2
Wraysbury Rd
Staines TW18 12 C5
Wraysbury TW19 12 C5
Wraysbury Sta TW19 1 A1
Wrecclesham Hill GU10 145 E5
Wrecclesham Rd
Farnham GU10, GU9 145 F8
Wrecclesham GU10, GU9 145 F8
Wrekin The GU14 85 E1
Wren Cl Horsham RH12 217 D7
Selsdon CR2 62 D2
Wren Cres KT15 52 D5
Wren Ct Ash GU12 106 B3
Crawley RH10 201 E3
South Croydon CR0 61 D6
Wren House 4 TW12 16 B2
Wren Way GU14 84 F7
Wren's Hill KT22 74 C4
Wrens Ave TW15 14 C4
Wrenthorpe Rd BR1 24 E4
Wright Cl RH10 202 C2
Wright Gdns TW17 34 A4
Wright Rd TW5 4 C7
Wright's Row SM5 60 B6
Wrighton Ct SM1 58 F4
Wrights Rd SE25 42 E6
Wriotsley Way KT15 52 A4
Wrotham Hill GU8 192 E3
Wrotham House BR3 23 F1
Wroxham RG12 26 F4
Wroxham Wlk RH10 202 B4
Wrythe Gn SM5 59 F7
Wrythe Green Rd SM5 59 F7
Wrythe La SM1, SM5, SM4 59 E7
Wyatt Cl TW13 15 D7
Wyatt Park Mansions 1 SW2 21 E6
Wyatt Park Rd SW2 21 F6
Wyatt Rd TW18 13 A3
Wyatt's Almshouses GU7 151 A6
Wyatt's Cl GU7 151 A6
Wych Elm Rise GU1 130 E6
Wych Hill GU22 89 C8
Wych Hill La GU22 89 E8
Wych Hill Pk GU22 89 D8
Wych Hill Rise GU22 89 D8
Wych Hill Way GU22 89 D8
Wyche Gr CR2 61 D2
Wychelm Rd GU18 67 C8
Wychwood RH14 212 D3
Wychwood Ave
Bracknell RG12 27 F5
South Norwood CR7 42 C6
Wychwood Cl
Aldershot GU12 105 F2
Ashford TW16 15 A2
Wychwood Pl GU15 66 B8
Wychwood Way SE19 22 D2
Wycliffe Bldgs GU2 130 C7
Wycliffe Ct RH11 200 E3
Wycliffe Rd Merton SW19 20 B2
Wimbledon SW19 20 B2
Wydell Cl SM4 39 D3
Wydenhurst Rd CR0, CR9 43 B2
Wye Cl TW15 14 B4
Wyecliffe Gdns RH1 119 C5
Wyeth's Mews KT17 76 F6
Wyeth's Rd KT17 76 F6
Wyke Ave GU12 106 E3
Wyke Bglws GU12 106 D3
Wyke Cl TW7 5 F8
Wyke Cty Prim Sch The GU3 106 F4
Wyke Green Golf Course TW7 5 F8
Wyke La GU12 106 D2
Wyke Rd SW20 39 C7
Wykeham Cl UB7 3 A8
Wykeham House
Farnborough GU14 105 C8
Merton SW19 40 A8
Wykeham Rd
Farnham GU9 125 C3
Guildford GU1 110 D2
Wylam RG12 26 F4
Wyleu St SE23 23 E8
Wymering Ct GU14 85 D3
Wynash Gdns SM5 59 E5
Wynbourne Ct SE20 43 B7
Wyncote Way CR2 62 D2
Wyndham Ave KT11 73 A6
Wyndham Cl SM2 59 A3
Wyndham Cres
Cranleigh GU6 174 A3
Twickenham TW4 5 A1
Wyndham Rd
Kingston u T KT2 17 F1
Woking GU21 69 B1
Wyndham St GU12 105 C1
Wyndhams GU22 70 B3
Wynell Rd SE23 23 D5
Wynfields GU16 85 F3
Wynlea Cl RH10 204 A8
Wynne Ct 4 TW7 6 A4
Wynnstow Pk RH8 122 F4
Wynsham Way GU20 48 B6
Wynton Gdns SE25 42 F4
Wynton Gr KT12 54 A7
Wyphurst Rd GU6 174 E4
Wyresdale RG12 27 F2
Wysemead RH6 161 C4
Wythegate TW18 12 F1
Wyvern Cl Ash Vale GU12 105 F5
Bracknell RG12 27 A5
Wyvern Est The KT3 39 A5
Wyvern Pl KT15 52 B6
Wyvern Rd CR8 61 B1

Y

Yaffle Rd KT13 53 C1
Yale Cl Hounslow TW4 4 F2
Sandhurst GU47 45 F2
Yarborough Rd SW19 40 D8
Yarbridge Cl SM2 59 B1
Yard Mead TW20 12 A5
Yardley RG12 26 F4
Yardley Cl RH2 118 B3
Yardley Ct SM3 58 C6
Yarm Cl KT22 95 C4
Yarm Court Rd KT22 95 C4
Yarm Way KT22 95 D4
Yarmouth Cl RH10 202 A4
Yarnold Cl RG40 25 F7
Yarrow Cl RH12 217 E5
Yateley Ct CR8 80 C5
Yatesbury Cl GU9 145 F7
Yattendon Jun Sch RH6 161 A4
Yattendon Rd RH6 161 B3
Yaverland Dr GU19 47 D2
Ye Market CR0 61 D5
Yeats Cl RH1 139 C6
Yeend Cl KT8 36 A5
Yehudi Menuhin Sch KT11 94 A8
Yellowcress Dr GU24 68 A3
Yelverton Ct KT23 94 A1
Yelverton Lodge TW1 17 C8
Yenston Cl SM4 40 A3
Yeoman Cl SE27 22 B5
Yeoman Ct TW5 4 F7
Yeoman Way RH1 140 B4
Yeomanry Cl KT17 76 F7
Yeomans Cl
Ash GU10, GU12 126 F8
Farnborough GU14 85 A3
Yeomans Mews TW7 5 D2
Yeomans Way GU15 65 E5
Yeoveney Cl TW19 12 D6
Yeovil Cl GU14 85 D1
Yeovil Rd Farnborough GU14 85 E1
Sandhurst GU47 45 E1
Yeovilton Pl KT2 17 C3
Yetminster Rd GU14 85 D1
Yew La RH19 185 B3
Yew Pl KT13 53 F7
Yew Tree Bottom Rd KT17, KT18 77 C2
Yew Tree Cl Chipstead CR5 98 F8
Farnborough GU14 84 C3
Horley RH6 161 A4
New Malden KT4 38 E1
Yew Tree Cotts KT10 55 D8
Yew Tree Ct SM2 59 C3
Yew Tree Dr
Caterham CR3 100 F2
Guildford GU1 109 C6
Yew Tree Gdns KT18 76 C4
Yew Tree House KT4 38 E1
Yew Tree La RH2 118 B4
Yew Tree Rd
Charlwood RH6 180 E7
Dorking RH4 115 A1
Witley GU8 170 D6
Yew Tree Wlk
Effingham KT24 113 D8
Frimley GU16 65 F1
Hounslow TW4 4 F2
South Croydon CR8 61 C1
Yew Trees TW17 33 F5
Yewbank Cl CR8 80 D4
Yewdale Cl BR1 24 E2
Yewens GU8 191 B5
Yewlands Cl SM7 78 C4
Yewlands Wlk RH11 200 D4
Yews The TW15 14 B4
Yewtree Rd BR3 43 F6
Yewtrees TW20 32 C6
Yockley Cl GU15 66 D3
Yolland Cl GU9 125 C7
York Ave
East Grinstead RH19 206 A8
Mortlake SW14 7 C2
York Cl Byfleet KT14 71 E7
Horsham RH13 217 F3
Morden SM4 40 B5
York Cres GU11 104 F1
York Ct Beckenham BR3 44 D8
Kingston u T KT2 17 D2
Wallington SM6 60 C4
York Gdns KT12 54 D8
York Hill SE27, SW16 22 B5
York House Bracknell RG42 26 F8
Forest Hill SE26 23 C3
4 Kingston u T KT2 17 F1
Richmond TW9 7 A6
South Norwood SE25 42 E5
York Rd Aldershot GU11 104 F1
Ash GU12 106 A3
Belmont SM1, SM2 59 A3
Biggin Hill TN16 103 B8
Byfleet KT14 71 E7
Camberley GU15 65 D7
Crawley RH10 201 E2
Farnborough GU14 85 C1
Farnham GU9 125 C1
Guildford GU1 130 D8
Hounslow TW3 5 B4
Kingston u T KT2 17 F1
3 Richmond TW10 6 F2
Selsdon CR2 62 D1
Teddington TW11 16 E4
Thornton Heath CR0 42 A2
Weybridge KT13 53 C6
Wimbledon SW19 20 C2
Woking GU22 69 E1
York St Carshalton CR4 41 A2
Twickenham TW1 17 A7
York Town Ind Est GU15 65 A5
York Way Chessington KT9 56 E3
Feltham TW13 15 F5
Sandhurst GU47 64 B8
Yorke Gate Rd CR3 100 D5
Yorke Gdns RH2 118 A2
Yorke Rd RH2 118 A2
Yorkshire Rd CR4 41 E5
Yorktown Rd
Sandhurst GU47 64 C7
Sandhurst GU47 64 E7
Youlden Cl GU15 66 A5
Youlden Dr GU15 66 B6
Young St Fetcham KT22 94 F3
Leatherhead KT22 95 A3
Youngman RH7 165 B4
Youngs Dr GU12 105 F2
Youngstroat La GU24 50 E1
Yukon Rd SW12 21 B8

Z

Zealand Ave UB7 2 E7
Zennor Rd SW12 21 C7
Zermatt Rd CR7 42 C5
Zig Zag Rd Kenley CR8 80 C3
Mickleham KT20, RH4, RH5 115 D4
Zinnia Dr GU24 68 A3
Zion Pl CR7 42 D5
Zion Rd CR7, SE25 42 D5
Zodiac Ct CR0 42 B1

The Street Atlases are available from all good bookshops or by mail order direct from the publisher. Orders can be made in the following ways. **By phone** Ring our special Credit Card Hotline on **01933 443863** during office hours (9am to 5pm) or leave a message on the answering machine, quoting your full credit card number plus expiry date and your full name and address. **By post or fax** Fill out the order form below (you may photocopy it) and post it to: **Philip's Direct, 27 Sanders Road, Wellingborough, Northants NN8 4NL** or fax it to: **01933 443849.** Before placing an order by post, by fax or on the answering machine, please telephone to check availability and prices.

STREET ATLASES
ORDER FORM

COLOUR LOCAL ATLASES

PAPERBACK	Quantity @ £3.50 each	£ Total
CANNOCK, LICHFIELD, RUGELEY	☐ 0 540 07625 2	➤ ☐
DERBY AND BELPER	☐ 0 540 07608 2	➤ ☐
NORTHWICH, WINSFORD, MIDDLEWICH	☐ 0 540 07589 2	➤ ☐
PEAK DISTRICT TOWNS	☐ 0 540 07609 0	➤ ☐
STAFFORD, STONE, UTTOXETER	☐ 0 540 07626 0	➤ ☐
WARRINGTON, WIDNES, RUNCORN	☐ 0 540 07588 4	➤ ☐

COLOUR REGIONAL ATLASES

	HARDBACK	SPIRAL	POCKET	
	Quantity @ £10.99 each	Quantity @ £8.99 each	Quantity @ £4.99 each	£ Total
MERSEYSIDE	☐ 0 540 06480 7	☐ 0 540 06481 5	☐ 0 540 06482 3	➤ ☐
	Quantity @ £12.99 each	Quantity @ £8.99 each	Quantity @ £5.99 each	£ Total
BERKSHIRE	☐ 0 540 06170 0	☐ 0 540 06172 7	☐ 0 540 06173 5	➤ ☐
	Quantity @ £12.99 each	Quantity @ £9.99 each	Quantity @ £4.99 each	£ Total
DURHAM	☐ 0 540 06365 7	☐ 0 540 06366 5	☐ 0 540 06367 3	➤ ☐
	Quantity @ £12.99 each	Quantity @ £9.99 each	Quantity @ £5.50 each	£ Total
GREATER MANCHESTER	☐ 0 540 06485 8	☐ 0 540 06486 6	☐ 0 540 06487 4	➤ ☐
TYNE AND WEAR	☐ 0 540 06370 3	☐ 0 540 06371 1	☐ 0 540 06372 X	➤ ☐
	Quantity @ £12.99 each	Quantity @ £9.99 each	Quantity @ £5.99 each	£ Total
BIRMINGHAM & WEST MIDLANDS	☐ 0 540 07603 1	☐ 0 540 07604 X	☐ 0 540 07605 8	➤ ☐
BUCKINGHAMSHIRE	☐ 0 540 07466 7	☐ 0 540 07467 5	☐ 0 540 07468 3	➤ ☐
CHESHIRE	☐ 0 540 07507 8	☐ 0 540 07508 6	☐ 0 540 07509 4	➤ ☐
DERBYSHIRE	☐ 0 540 07531 0	☐ 0 540 07532 9	☐ 0 540 07533 7	➤ ☐
EDINBURGH & East Central Scotland	☐ 0 540 07653 8	☐ 0 540 07654 6	☐ 0 540 07656 2	➤ ☐
NORTH ESSEX	☐ 0 540 07289 3	☐ 0 540 07290 7	☐ 0 540 07292 3	➤ ☐
SOUTH ESSEX	☐ 0 540 07294 X	☐ 0 540 07295 8	☐ 0 540 07297 4	➤ ☐
GLASGOW & West Central Scotland	☐ 0 540 07648 1	☐ 0 540 07649 X	☐ 0 540 07651 1	➤ ☐
NORTH HAMPSHIRE	☐ 0 540 07471 3	☐ 0 540 07472 1	☐ 0 540 07473 X	➤ ☐

STREET ATLASES ORDER FORM

Ordnance Survey
STREET ATLAS
South Essex
BEST BUY AUTO EXPRESS
Unique comprehensive coverage
SOUTHEND-ON-SEA
Plus Chingford, Dagenham, Ilford, Romford
PHILIP'S

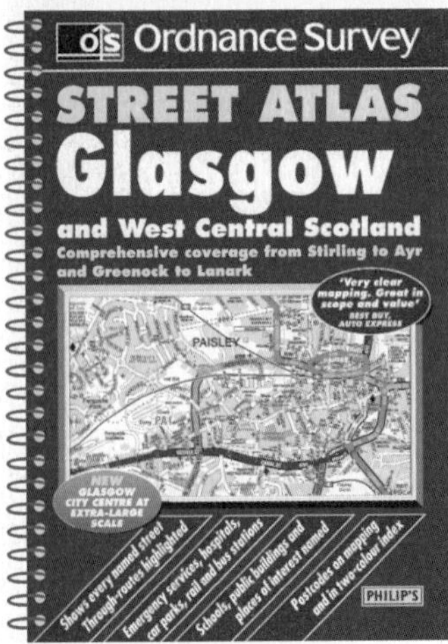

COLOUR REGIONAL ATLASES

	HARDBACK	SPIRAL	POCKET	
	Quantity @ £12.99 each	Quantity @ £9.99 each	Quantity @ £5.99 each	£ Total
SOUTH HAMPSHIRE	☐ 0 540 07476 4	☐ 0 540 07477 2	☐ 0 540 07478 0	➤ ☐
HERTFORDSHIRE	☐ 0 540 06174 3	☐ 0 540 06175 1	☐ 0 540 06176 X	➤ ☐
EAST KENT	☐ 0 540 07483 7	☐ 0 540 07276 1	☐ 0 540 07287 7	➤ ☐
WEST KENT	☐ 0 540 07366 0	☐ 0 540 07367 9	☐ 0 540 07369 5	➤ ☐
NORTHAMPTONSHIRE	☐ 0 540 07745 3	☐ 0 540 07746 1	☐ 0 540 07748 8	➤ ☐
OXFORDSHIRE	☐ 0 540 07512 4	☐ 0 540 07513 2	☐ 0 540 07514 0	➤ ☐
SURREY	☐ 0 540 07794 1	☐ 0 540 07795 X	☐ 0 540 07796 8	➤ ☐
EAST SUSSEX	☐ 0 540 07306 7	☐ 0 540 07307 5	☐ 0 540 07312 1	➤ ☐
WEST SUSSEX	☐ 0 540 07319 9	☐ 0 540 07323 7	☐ 0 540 07327 X	➤ ☐
WARWICKSHIRE	☐ 0 540 07560 4	☐ 0 540 07561 2	☐ 0 540 07562 0	➤ ☐
SOUTH YORKSHIRE	—	☐ 0 540 07667 8	☐ 0 540 07669 4	➤ ☐
WEST YORKSHIRE	☐ 0 540 07671 6	☐ 0 540 07672 4	☐ 0 540 07674 0	➤ ☐
	Quantity @ £14.99 each	Quantity @ £9.99 each	Quantity @ £5.99 each	£ Total
LANCASHIRE	☐ 0 540 06440 8	☐ 0 540 06441 6	☐ 0 540 06443 2	➤ ☐
NOTTINGHAMSHIRE	☐ 0 540 07541 8	☐ 0 540 07542 6	☐ 0 540 07543 4	➤ ☐
STAFFORDSHIRE	☐ 0 540 07549 3	☐ 0 540 07550 7	☐ 0 540 07551 5	➤ ☐

BLACK AND WHITE REGIONAL ATLASES

	HARDBACK	SOFTBACK	POCKET	
	Quantity @ £11.99 each	Quantity @ £8.99 each	Quantity @ £3.99 each	£ Total
BRISTOL AND AVON	☐ 0 540 06140 9	☐ 0 540 06141 7	☐ 0 540 06142 5	➤ ☐
	Quantity @ £12.99 each	Quantity @ £9.99 each	Quantity @ £4.99 each	£ Total
CARDIFF, SWANSEA & GLAMORGAN	☐ 0 540 06186 7	☐ 0 540 06187 5	☐ 0 540 06207 3	➤ ☐

Name...

Address...

....

....

....

....Postcode...................

◆ **Add £2 postage and packing per order**

◆ All available titles will normally be dispatched within 5 working days of receipt of order but please allow up to 28 days for delivery

☐ Please tick this box if you do not wish your name to be used by other carefully selected organisations that may wish to send you information about other products and services

Registered Office: 2-4 Heron Quays, London E14 4JP
Registered in England number: 3597451

Total price of order £☐

(including postage and packing at £2 per order)

I enclose a cheque/postal order, for £☐

made payable to *Octopus Publishing Group Ltd*,

or please debit my ☐ Mastercard ☐ American Express ☐ Visa account by £☐

Account no ☐☐☐☐ ☐☐☐☐ ☐☐☐☐ ☐☐☐☐

Expiry date ☐☐ ☐☐

Signature...

Post to: Philip's Direct, 27 Sanders Road, Wellingborough, Northants NN8 4NL